HARDY HERBACEOUS PERENNIALS

Leo Jelitto and Wilhelm Schacht

HARDY HERBACEOUS PERENNIALS

Volume II, L–Z

Third Edition
revised by
Wilhelm Schacht and Alfred Fessler

In collaboration with
Lothar Denkewitz, Fritz Encke, Carl Feldmaier,
Fritz Köhlein, Fritz Kummert, Bruno Müller,
Hermann Müssel, Hans Simon

Translated by Michael E. Epp

John Philip Baumgardt, Technical Editor

TIMBER PRESS
Portland, Oregon

© 1950/51, 1985 as *Die Freiland-Schmuckstauden*
by Eugen Ulmer GmbH & Co., Stuttgart

Translation © 1990 by Timber Press, Inc.
All rights reserved.

Reprinted 1995

ISBN 0-88192-159-9 (2 volumes)

Printed in Hong Kong

TIMBER PRESS, INC.
The Haseltine Building
133 S.W. Second Avenue, Suite 450
Portland, Oregon 97204, U.S.A.

Library of Congress Cataloging-inPublication Data

Jelitto, Leo.
    [Freiland-Schmuckstauden.   English]
    Hardy herbaceous perennials / Leo Jelitto and Wilhelm Schacht ;
translated by Michael E. Epp ; John Philip Baumgardt, technical editor. —
3rd ed. / revised by Wilhelm Schacht and Alfred Fessler in collaboration
with Lothar Denkewitz . . . [et al.]
      p.   cm.
    Translation of : Die Freiland-Schmuckstauden.
    ISBN 0-88192-159-9
    1. Perennials—Dictionaries.   I. Schacht, Wilhelm, 1903–   .   II. Epp,
Michael E.   III. Baumgardt, John Philip.   IV. Fessler, Alfred.   V. Title.
SB434.J4513   1990
635.9'32'03—dc20   89-5171
                                          CIP

Contents

Volume II

Lactuca alpina

Lactuca L.
Compositae

Fifty to 90 species of mostly annual, some perennial, tall herbs containing milky sap, most in the North Temperate Zone. Stems usually solitary, branched, with lobed leaves. Flower heads numerous. Sepals in several rows. Flowers blue, occasionally whitish blue or purple-blue, pink, white or yellow.

Naturalizing perennials for collectors, botanic gardens and parks. Grow best in neutral to acidic, moist, humus soil in semi-shade with other herbaceous plants of similar cultural requirements. Valued for its attractive foliage and the flowers. Good companion plants are *Adenostyles*, *Aconitum*, *Actaea*, *Geum rivale*, *Prenanthes* and various wild ferns. Propagate by seed and division.

L. alpina (L.) A. Gray. (*Mulgedium alpinum* (L.) Less., *Cicerbita alpina* (L.) Wallr). Mountain Sow Thistle. Arctic and alpine Europe. In subalpine meadows, wooded ravines and thickets on moist, fertile, loose, gravelly soil. 0.6–0.2m high. Stems racemosely branched on the upper half, and densely covered with reddish glandular pubescence. Leaves blue-green beneath, basal leaves pinnately cleft with a large terminal lobe, upper leaves stem-clasping, decurrent. Flower stalks densely red-brown, glandular pubescent. Sepals dull green. Flower heads blue-violet, 2cm wide, in a racemose-panicled inflorescence. Flowers from after midsummer. z4

L. bourgaei (Boiss.) Irish & N. Taylor. (*Mulgedium bourgaei* Boiss., *Cicerbita bourgaei* (Boiss.) Recurved. Asia Minor, Caucasus, in tall grass meadows. Very stout, leafy stems, 1.5–2m high, the basal leaves petioled and roughly pubescent as are the panicled, 70cm-long and 16cm-wide inflorescences. Flowers violet; midsummer. z5

L. plumieri (L.) Gren. et Godr. (*Mulgedium plumieri* (L.) DC., *Cicerbita plumieri* (L.) Kirsch). Pyrenees, W. Alps to the Vosges Mts. (France), Black Forest (W. Germany), SW. Bulgaria. Found in subalpine tall grass meadows, on moist, fertile, mostly lime-free, coarse, gravelly soil. Similar to *C. alpina*, but in all parts smaller, only 0.6–1.3m high, glabrous. Leaves coarsely pinnately partite, dentate, basal leaves petioled, apical ones deeply cordate, stem-clasping, terminal leaves simple. Sepals turning violet. Flowers blue; after midsummer. z5 (E.)

Lagenophora Cass.
Compositae

About 25 species in Australia, New Zealand, S. Asia and S. America. Perennials, normally rhizomatous, with basal and at least 2 stem leaves. Flower heads small, solitary, flower stalk naked to very leafy. Ray florets white or purple, disc florets yellow. Achenes sticky. Flowers from June to August. Grow in well-drained soil in full sun. Suitable for combining with other plants of the Southern Hemisphere. Often short-lived, but comes readily from seed without becoming a nuisance. Propagate by seed.

L. pinnatifida Hook.f. New Zealand, North and South Island. Found at the edge of open forests and in grasslands. Stems 5–15cm high, simple or branched. Basal leaves in rosettes, leaves to 60 × 25mm, obovate-oblong to oblong, tapering toward the base, pubescent on both sides. Leaf margins normally deeply dentate or pinnately lobed. Stem leaves similar, few. Flowers *Bellis*-like, 10–15mm wide. z7 (K.)

Lagotis Gaertn.
Scrophulariaceae

20 species of perennials from N. and Central Asia, south to the Caucasus, Himalayas and W. China. Closely related to *Veronica*, with the following species occasionally found in cultivation. A procumbent, unpretentious perennial, spreading by stolons and forming a loose groundcover. Thrives on any average garden soil in full sun and is easily propagated by seed or separation of the rooted runners. Recommended only for collectors; for the rockery.

L. stolonifera (K. Koch) Maxim. Caucasus. Stems 10–15cm high. Leaves in open, basal rosettes, lanceolate, glossy green. Flowers small, pale violet, in short, erect spikes. Blooms from May to June. z6 (E.)

Lamiastrum Heist. ex Fabr.
(*Galeobdolon* Adans.)
Labiatae
Yellow Archangel, Golden Nettle

Only 1 species.

L. galeobdolon (L.) Ehrend. et Polatsch. (*Lamium galeobdolon* L., *Lamium luteum* (Huds.) Krock., *Galeobdolon luteum* Huds.), Golden Archangel, Golden Nettle. Europe, W. Asia. To 20cm high. Erect shoots with large, yellow, labiate flowers, a pubescent exterior, May to June. The nettlelike leaves are bright green, somewhat mottled. Wide, spreading growth habit with long, rank stolons. Of the many subspecies, only the evergreen cultivars are garden worthy. The most popular selection is 'Florentinum', with distinct, silvery-white-speckled foliage, turning somewhat reddish in winter. Primarily used for a large area groundcover in shaded or semi-shaded understory situations. Competes well with weeds but is also invasive, overrunning other desirable perennials and low woody plants. 'Silberteppich' (Silver Carpet) (Pagels), a conspicuous, slow-growing cultivar with intense silvery, green-veined leaves; somewhat demanding. 'Variegatum', is similar to 'Type Ronsdorf', with smaller, rounded, mottled leaves and only moderately vigorous growth rate, more suitable for small gardens. z4 (M.)

Lamium L.
Labiatae
Dead Nettle

About 40 species in Europe and W. Asia. Annuals and perennials, with 4-angled, stems, opposite, crenate, nettlelike leaves and labiate flowers with a distinct, hoodlike upper lip; mostly spring bloomers. Only a few species are garden worthy. *L. maculatum* and the former *L. galeobdolon*, now *Lamiastrum galeob-*

Lagotis stolonifera

dolon (which see), are very meritorious groundcover perennials for semi-shade to shady sites. All species are easily cultivated in any garden soil so long as it is not too cold or poorly drained. All propagate very easily by division and cuttings.

L. album L., White Dead Nettle. Found nearly throughout Europe, W. Asia to Himalayas, Japan. 20–40cm high. The white labiate flowers are grouped 6–16 in false whorls in the leaf axils; May to June. Will naturalize even on poorly drained, high clay, but fertile soil; relatively maintenance-free and therefore well suited to parks and public areas. Grows well in semi-shade. z4

L. galeobdolon see **Lamiastrum galeobdolon**

L. luteum see **Lamiastrum galeobdolon**

L. maculatum L., Spotted Dead Nettle. Europe, north to N. Germany and N. Central Russia, Asia Minor, N. Iran. Short-branched stoloniferous species about 20cm high with reddish purple flowers from May to July. Leaves dark green, occasionally silvery mottled. Suitable for covering small areas in semi-shade in a light to medium heavy soil. Will not tolerate dense shade, particularly in wet soil. Particularly colorful foliage and flowering cultivars include:

'Album', strong silvery leaves, flowers white; 'Argenteum', leaves white speckled, reddish flowers; 'Aureum', leaves yellow with narrow white midstripes, slow and compact grower;

'Beacon Silver' ('Silbergroschen'), leaves almost entirely silver with a narrow green margin, flowers purple-lilac; 'Chequers', leaves dark green with a broad silvery middle stripe, conspicuously marked, flowers violet-pink, floriferous, an improved 'Argenteum'; 'Roseum', with pure pink flowers, slow-growing; 'White Nancy', leaves entirely silver, similar to 'Beacon Silver', flowers white, vigorous grower. z4

L. orvala L. N. Italy and W. Austria to W. Yugoslavia and S. Hungary. Leaves broadly ovate, glossy dark green. Flowers brownish red; May to June. Forms a stout bushy plant 40–60cm high; best suited for naturalizing in sunny to semi-shaded sites on a woodland margin. This species deserves more

in its permanent garden spot as a seedling. Good companions include the low to medium-sized plants of the S. Dolomite Mts. Propagate by seed.

L. siler L. (*Siler montanum* Crantz). Found in the mountains of S. and S. Central Europe in rock crevices and screes, on gravelly slopes and dry mountain meadows among dwarf shrubs. Usually on calcareous, gravelly soil in the Alps to 2400m. A vigorous, glabrous, blue-green bushy plant from 0.3–1, occasionally

Leaves mostly pinnate with paired leaflets. Flowers usually axillary, papilionaceous, solitary or on long-stemmed racemes in spring and midsummer. The low-growing species are good spring bloomers for the rock garden, open shrubberies and open shady sites. The climbers are suitable for covering a trellis, fence or other support. Propagate by seed and division. Only the showiest sorts are listed here; other worthwhile species are not available in the trade.

Lamiastrum galeobdolon 'Florentinum'

Lamium orvala

attention. Increase by seed, but seeds must be protected from mouse damage. z6 (H.& M.)

Lamyra see **Ptilostemon**

Laserpitium L.
Umbelliferae

Thirty five species of mostly large herbs in Europe, on the Canary Islands and from the Mediterranean region to SW. Asia. Useful for dry, rocky sites in the wild or large rock garden where it makes a good specimen plant between large stones or in crevices. Requires a dry, well-drained loam, strongly calcareous soil. Very difficult to transplant having a carrot-like root, hence should be planted

1.8m high, with scented roots. The large leaves are 3–4 times pinnatisect, the umbels are 25–40 rayed, to 25cm across at anthesis, flowers white or pink. Blooms from June to August. Used as a medicinal plant in the 13th and 14th centuries. (E.)

Lasiagrostis

L. splendens see **Spodiopogon sibiricus**

Lathyrus L.
Leguminosae
Vetchling, Wild Pea

More than 100 species from Europe to the Mediterranean region. Annuals and perennial low bushy or scandent plants with tendrils (climbing to 2m high).

L. gmelinii Fritsch (*L. luteus* (L.) Peterm. non Moench, *Orobus luteus* L.). Central and S. Ural Mts. and the mountains of Central Asia. Bushy to barely scandent stems 30–50cm high. Average leaves with 3–6 pairs of broadly lanceolate leaflets. Flowers nodding, 4–12 in racemes, yellow to orange-yellow, brown striped; May to July. Similar is *L. gmelinii* var. *aureus*, flowers orange or buff-yellow. z4

L. grandiflorus Sibth. et Sm. S. Balkan region, S. Italy, Sicily. Climbing to 2m high. Stems 4-angled, not winged. Leaves paired with tendrils. Pedicels 1–3 flowered. Flowers 3cm across, banner petal rose, keel purple; June to August. A very attractive collector's plant. z6

L. laevigatus (Waldst. et Kit.) Gren. Central Europe to N. Spain, N. Balkan region and W. Russia. Stems 20–70cm high, usually unbranched; leaves 3–6 paired pinnate; leaflets bluish green beneath. Flower racemes 3–17 flowered, corolla yellow; May to July. Plants in culture are usually:

L. laevigatus ssp. **transsylvanicus**, 60cm high, upright clump form, with buff-colored flowers from May to June. A good choice for warm, dry slopes combined with *Anthericum liliago* and *Lilium bulbiferum* ssp. *croceum*. z5

L. vernus (L.) Bernh. (*Orobus vernus* L.). Spring Vetchling. Europe to W. Siberia, Caucasus, N. Asia Minor. A low, dense, bushy species without stolons, 20–30cm high. Flowers rose-violet at first, later fading greenish-blue, 5–15 in racemes; April to May. Very persistent, valuable spring bloomer for shady sites under trees and shrubs. Some attractive forms include 'Albiflorus', white-flowering, 'Alboroseus', with bicolored white and pink flowers and 'Roseus', a pink-flowered cultivar. z4 (H.& M.)

of course, as a low hedge to enclose the herb or vegetable garden. Above all, requires dry, loamy humus, somewhat alkaline soil in full sun.

For edging and small hedges, plants must be sheared lightly. More severe pruning might be necessary on frost-damaged plants. Propagation of the species is by seed, the cultivars by cuttings in April, May and August; older plants may be layered easily. Self-seeds in large, undisturbed areas.

Good companion plants are *Achillea*

Laserpitium siler

Lathyrus vernus

Lavandula angustifolia

L. latifolius L. Central and S. Europe, Mediterranean region to N. France, naturalized in Germany, Belgium, England, and N. America. Climbing to 2m high, without support sprawls widely. Flowers 3–8 in racemes; carmine pink; June to August; resembles in form and size the scented, annual Sweet Peas, but is not fragrant. The following forms are especially attractive: 'Rose Queen', mallow pink, and 'White Pearl', a dazzling white; also a long-lasting cut flower. z5

L. luteus see **L. gmelinii**

L. niger (L.) Bernh. (*Orobus niger* L.). Europe, Caucasus, Syria, N. Africa. Found in open forests. Stems 40–60cm high, mostly branched. Leaves with 4–6 pairs of leaflets. Flowers nodding, 3–6 in racemes, soft purple; June to July. Only for the collector. z6

Lavandula L.
Labiatae
Lavender

Perhaps 28 species of aromatic biennial herbs, sub- and small shrubs from the Atlantic islands of Europe and the Mediterranean region, from Somalia to India. Leaves entire or finely laciniate. Flowers in whorls of 2–10, in loose or compact spikes with small bracts. Calyx tubular, 13–15 veined, 5-lobed. Corolla blue, violet, purple, occasionally white. Corolla tube longer than the calyx. Upper lip 2-lobed, lower lip 3-lobed. Lavender has a place in every garden for its fine fragrance and attractive blue flowers. Excellent plant for edging, low hedges, or groundcover use, for example, among roses. Also desirable as a specimen or small group in the rock garden, terrace bed, dry stone wall and,

clypeolata, *Echinops humilis* and *E. ritro*, *Eryngium* species and some grasses, as *Festuca cinerea*, *F. ovina*, *F. vallesiaca* 'Glaucantha' and *Helictotrichon semper-virens*.

L. angustifolia Mill. (*L. officinalis* Chaix, *L. spica* L.p.p., *L. vera* DC.), Lavender. Mediterranean regions. Grows on dry, warm slopes, rocky south-facing cliffs, dry stone walls, mostly on limestone. Small, evergreen subshrub, aromatic, gray-green to silvery gray or more in its native habitat. With 2–4cm long, lanceolate, oblong or linear, entire leaves, white-tomentose when young with revoluted margins. The long-stemmed spikes are 2–8cm long with 6–10 lavender-blue flowers in each whorl. Blooms in late spring or early summer, also reblooms on occasion. Some cultivars are: 'Alba', white-flowered; 'Dwarf Blue', low with dark blue flowers;

'Grappenhall', (= 'Gigantea') plant 60–90cm high, vigorous, spikes very long, flowers lavender-blue; 'Hidcote Blue', plant 30cm high, flowers deep violet-blue; 'Hidcote Giant', plant 50–80cm high, vigorous, flowers violet; 'Jean Davis', flowers white, sometimes tinged pink; 'Munstead', plant 40–50cm high, wide-growing, flowers lavender-blue; 'Rosea', flowers pink; 'Twickel', low-growing, flowers dark purple in large spikes. z5–6 (E.)

Other ornamental *Lavandula* species are too tender for year-round outdoor planting but are valuable as potted plants on the terrace or in the herb garden; they must overwinter in the deep coldframe or cool greenhouse.

Lavatera L.
Malvaceae
Tree Mallow

Twenty to 25 species of a bushy, erect annual or perennial herbs and shrubs with large, simple, lobed leaves and mallow-like flowers in the leaf axils. Only 2 herbaceous species are noteworthy.

L. olbia L. S. France to Portugal. Plant to 2m high. Stems woody at the base, branched, rough hispid. Leaves 5-lobed, the upper ones 3-lobed, soft, gray-tomentose. Flowers 7–8cm wide, purple-pink; June to October. Attractive, but not completely winter hardy; may be cut down and deeply mulched each autumn. Requires a protected site. 'Rosea' is a more colorful form. Propagation is by cuttings from basal shoots in spring and fall. z8(6–7)

L. thuringiaca L. Central and SE. Europe to Italy and Russia. Stems to 1.5m high; wide bushy habit, very leafy with 5-lobed, dull green mallow-type leaves. Flowers 4–5cm wide, light pink; July to September. A very vigorous perennial for an open forest margin or open garden site. Propagation is easy by seed. z5 (H.& S.)

Leibnitzia Cass.
Compositae

Five species in Asia. Perennials with scaly stems and many basal, mostly pinnately lobed leaves. Flower heads dimorphic, the spring flower heads with ray florets and bisexual disc, the summer and fall flower heads with only cleistogamous disc florets. Sometimes only the latter are fertile and produce achenes. Flowers from May to June (spring flowers) and again from August to September (fall flowers). Grow in any soil, in a sunny to semishady site. Also for the rock garden. Propagate by seed.

L. anandria (L.) Nakai (*Tussilago anandria* L., *T. lyrata* Willd., *Gerbera anandria* (L.) Schultz-Bip., *Percidium tomentosum* Thunb.). Japan, Sakhalin, S. Kurile Islands, Manchuria, Siberia, China, Taiwan. Rhizomes short; leafless scapes 10–20cm high, unbranched, spider-web-like hairy, loose scaly. Rosette leaves broadly oblanceolate, 5–16mm long and 13–45cm wide, pinnately cleft or lobed, occasionally (by reduction of the basal lobes) cordate or triangular-cordate, underside exceptionally white tomentose. Flower heads to 2.5cm wide, ray florets white, underside red-purple. The fall flowers to 60cm high, not particularly conspicuous. z3

L. kuntzeana (A. Br. et Aschers.) Pobedim. From the Himalaya Mts. and *L. nivea* (Wall.) Pobedim, from India are not found commonly in cultivation, though are grown in a few American botanic gardens. (K.)

Leontice L.
(see also *Gymnospermium*)
Berberidaceae

About 10 species in N. Africa, SE. Europe, Asia Minor to Central Asia. Glabrous perennials with large, tuberous rhizomes. Leaves 2–3 parted, not all are basal. Flowers in terminal and axillary leafy racemes. Perianth segments 6 (–8), conspicuous, yellow, are petaloid. Nectary glands 6, very small. Stamens 6. Fruits 1–4 seeded, irregularly dehiscing. Seeds without an aril. Flowers in April and May. This interesting plant from the Asian steppes thrives best in a correspondingly open, sunny, dry natural garden on a gravelly loam soil with good drainage. Propagation is only by seed, a slow process. Seedlings should be kept in deep containers the first growing season and grown relatively dry.

L. albertii see **Gymnospermium albertii**

L. altaica see **Gymnospermium altaicum**

L. armeniaca Boivin (*L. minor* Boiss.). Iraq, Syria, Transjordan, Iran, Afghanistan, Uzbekistan, Transcaucasia. Similar to *L. ewersmannii*, but more dwarf, only 5–10cm high. z5

L. chrysogonum see **Bongardia chrysogonum**

L. ewersmannii Bunge. Syrian Desert, W. Iran, W. Pakistan, Transcaspian region. Similar to *L. leontopetalum*, but with elliptic to lanceolate leaflets. z6

L. incerta Pall. Central Asia. 10–16cm high. Leaves ternate or twice-ternate with 5cm-long, ovate or elliptic, slightly fleshy leaflets. Flowers yellow. Fruits inflated. z5

L. leontopetalum L. SE. Europe, N. Africa, SW. Asia. Found in fields, steppes and on arid land. Stems 30–50cm high, erect, branched; leaves to 20cm long, basal leaves with long petioles, upper leaves sessile, bi- to triternate. Leaflets broadly ovate, undivided. Racemes normally numerous, in the axils of the upper leaves, pedicellate, with conspicuous bracts, the lower being compound or lobed. Racemes 15–40 flowered. Flowers golden yellow, 15mm across. Fruits 25–40mm, ovate. Tubers to just larger than a man's fist. z6 (K.)

L. minor see **L. armeniaca**

L. odessana see **Gymnospermum altaicum**

L. smirnowii see **Gymnospermium smirnowii**

Leontopodium (Pers.) R. Br.
Compositae
Edelweiss

About 40 species in the mountains of Europe and Asia. Low to medium-sized perennials with oblong, mostly pubescent leaves, basal or alternate, and erect or ascending stems. Flower heads small, several within a cluster of white-woolly, bractlike leaves.

Flowers from June to August. Grow in infertile, calcareous, gritty soil in full sun where drainage is good. Suitable for the rock garden, trough or small perennial bed among rocks or gravel. Also a good container plant (*L. alpinum* clones, *L. souliei*) and cut flowers. Propagation is by seed (although not very productive), best by division in early spring or after flowering. While many leontopodiums are quite cold hardy, most are intolerant of summer heat and humidity.

L. alpinum Cass. ssp. **alpinum**, Alpine Edelweiss. Pyrenees, Alps, Jura, Carpathian and N. Balkan Mts. Grows on ridges, cliffs, steep grassy slopes and screes, on limestone or chalk, from 1700–3400m. Stems 5–20cm high; densely white-tomentose perennial with oblong, basal and stem leaves. Quite variable in height and the pubescence of the upper leaves; not entirely due to cultural conditions. Very compact cultivars (remaining small in fertile soil) with pure white, starlike flower head clusters are often found in seedling beds and should be selected for propagation by division. 'Mignon' is a well-known form 8–10cm high, a dense cushion form, with pure white inflorescences. Easily cultivated in any well-drained soil in full

Leontice leontopetalum

sun. Taxonomists list an astonishing array of natural varieties, largely based on geographic origin but distinguishable by leaf, stem and flower head characteristics in cultivation. These are for botanic gardens and alpine garden specialists. z4

L. alpinum var. **campestre** see **L. leontopodioides**

L. alpinum ssp. **nivale** (Ten.) Tutin (*L. nivale* (Ten.) Huet ex Hand.-Mazz.), Snow Edelweiss. Abruzzi (Italy), Yugoslavia, SW. Bulgaria. Usually found

over a marble substrate, to 2450m. Similar to the above subspecies, but more compact, to only 5cm high. Leaves broadly lanceolate, rounded to spatulate, densely gray-tomentose. Flower head cluster densely white-shaggy. Somewhat sensitive to winter wetness, slow-creeping and therefore best cultivated by seed. For best seed source, look for compact plants with round leaves at least 10–15m away from other Edelweiss plants. z5

L. alpinum var. **sibiricum** see **L. leontopodioides**

L. alpinum var. **stracheyi** see **L. stracheyi**

L. calocephalum (Franch.) Beauverd. Tibet, SW. China. Rootstock slow-creeping. Stem stout, to more than 40cm high, strongly upright, gray-white pubescent, leafy. Flower heads yellowish white; June to July. z5

L. forrestianum Hand.-Mazz. Tibet, SW. China. Cushion form, young lateral stems rooting. Stems erect, 8–10cm high, angular, very leafy, foliage gray-white pubescent. Bractlike leaves numerous, doubled and much overlapping, gray

pubescent. Flower heads light purple. z5

L. himalayanum DC. (*L. calocephalum* Diels non (Franch.) Beauverd). Himalayas. Stems to 25cm high. Stem leaves lanceolate, upper leaves broader, silver-tomentose, bract-like leaves silver-woolly forming stem 5.5–7cm wide. z5

L. japonicum Miq. (*Gnaphalium sieboldianum* Franch. et Sav.). Japan, China. Grows grasslike, with leaves glossy green above, densely woolly tomentose beneath with small inflorescences. The compact var. **shiroumense** Nakai et Kitamura is more attractive than var. **japonicum**, which reaches 40cm high. Not a showy species; grown mostly as a collector's plant. z5

L. kurilense Takeda. Kurile Islands. Stems 5–10cm high. Attractive with its silvery new growth, flowers in late May. Propagates well by division. z5

L. leontopodioides (Willd.) Beauverd (*L. alpinum* var. *campestre* Beauverd, *L. alpinum* var. *sibiricum* (Cass.) O. Fedtsch., *L. ochroleucum* Beauverd). Altai Mts. to Himalaya Mts. A vigorous perennial, to 40cm high. Stems very slender. Leaves broadly ligulate to spatulate, both sides ash gray woolly. Bract-like leaves shorter than the stem leaves, but usually wider, oval to linear-lanceolate, yellowish tomentose. Flower heads numerous, inflorescence leaves with black-brown tips. z5

L. × lindavicum Süend. (*L. himalayanum* × *L. japonicum*), particularly long-flowering hybrid. z5

L. nivale see **L. alpinum** ssp. **nivale**

L. ochroleucum see **L. leontopodiodes**

L. palibinianum Beauverd (*L. sibiricum* DC., *Gnaphalium leontopodioides* Rchb.). Mongolia, Siberia. Vigorous perennial to 45cm high. Leaves lanceolate, to 20cm long, both sides white-gray tomentose. Bractlike leaves as large as the upper stem leaves, ovate to oval-linear, densely white tomentose, greenish beneath, in a starshaped cluster, 7cm long. Very vigorous species. z4

L. sibiricum see **L. palibinianum**

L. souliei Beauverd. Sichuan, Yunnan. Stems 10–25cm high, plants tight cushion-forming with many underground runners. Leaves linear to linear-ligulate, white tomentose, occasionally also greenish. Flower head clusters 3–

4cm wide, very abundant. A vigorous, important species which is easily increased by division. Also good for pot culture. Needs damp soil in summer, otherwise needs protection from excess moisture. z5

L. stracheyi (Hook. f.) C. B. Clarke (*L. alpinum* var. *stracheyi* Hook. f.). SW. China. Upright plant, to 50cm high. z5

Some Japanese species, which are more readily available than the Central Asian species, are to be highly recommended, i.e., *L. fauriei* (Beauverd) Hand.-Mazz., *L.*

and subshrubs, often with dentate to pinnately lobed or divided lyreform (pandurate) leaves, strongly aromatic when crushed. Flowers small, mostly yellowish or white, in racemes. Flowers from early spring to early summer. Grow in a well-drained soil in full sun. Ornamental species are suitable for the rock and trough garden; many species are weeds. Propagate by seed or cuttings.

L. nanum S. Wats., Dwarf Cress. USA: Nevada, the Great Basin region. Found on dry, volcanic soil. A cushion to mat-form composed of many 8mm rosettes.

Leptarrhena (D. Don) R. Br.
Saxifragaceae

A monotypic genus.

L. pyrolifolia (D. Don) R. Br. Kamchatka, Aleutian Islands, Alaska, W. Canada, Washington. Rhizomes creeping above-ground, with short, mostly prostrate, very leafy stems. Basal leaves 4–5cm long, oval-spatulate, dark green, leathery. Flowering stems 15–20cm high, with few smaller leaves and dense panicles of small, white flowers; July. Poor bloomer

Lavatera olbia

Leontopodium alpinum **ssp.** *alpinum*

fauriei var. *angustifolium* Hara et Kitam., *L. hayachinense* (Takeda) Hara et Kitam. and *L. shinanense* Kitam.

Lit.: Handel-Mazzetti: *Monographie der Gattung Leontopodium*. In Beih. Bot. Centralblatt 44, II, p.1–178, 1927. (K.)

Lepachys see Ratibida

Lepidium L.
Cruciferae
Pepper Grass, Upland Cress

About 150 species in all parts of the world, some species nearly cosmopolitan. Annuals, long-lived perennials

Leaves oval-spatulate, 3-lobed, 2–5mm long. Leaf margin ciliate, blades short pubescent. Flowers yellowish green, 3–4mm, clustered 1–5. A nice, nearly unknown cushion plant. Needs protection from excessive winter wetness. z5

L. nebrodense Guss. S. Italy. Stems 10–20cm high. Leaves acutely ovate, glabrous. Flowers white. Fruits winged, single seeded. z9(8) (K.)

Leptandra

L. virginica see **Veronicastrum virginicum**

in many gardens and suitable largely as an evergreen groundcover for collectors. Grow in lime-free humus in the bog or somewhat moist rock garden, in full sun to semi-shade. Propagate by seed and division. z5 (Sch.)

Leptosyne

L. gigantea see **Coreopsis gigantea**

Leucanthemopsis

L. alpina see **Chrysanthemum alpinum**

Leucanthemum

L. coronopifolium see **Chrysanthemum atratum**

L. hosmariense see **Chrysanthemum mariesii**

Leptarrhena pyrolifolia

Leucorinum Nutt.
Liliaceae
Star-lily, Sand-lily

L. montanum Nutt. Star-lily. W. USA, Nebraska and S. Dakota to California and Oregon. Deep growing rhizome with fleshy roots. Leaves all basal, strap-shaped 10–18cm long, less than ½cm wide, spreading. Scape naked, very short. Flowers funnel-shaped, perianth 6-lobed, white, fragrant, 3–12cm long, usually in clusters at ground level, in spring. An alkaline soil rock garden plant. z4

Leucojum L.
Amaryllidaceae
Snowflake

Nine species of bulbous plants with a few basal, very narrow, or flat strap-shaped leaves. Scape hollow. Flowers solitary or few in umbels, usually pendulous, tubular-campanulate, white or pink with green or yellow tips, perianth segments separate, equal, unlike Snowdrops (*Galanthus*) which look similar at a distance. Indigenous to Central Europe and the Mediterranean region.

Leucojum aestivum

L. aestivum L. Summer Snowflake, Giant Snowflake. Central and E. Europe in moist meadows. Bulbs ovate, to 4cm in diameter. Leaves narrow strap-shaped, 30–45cm long, 1.5cm wide, dark green. Scapes only slightly longer. Flowers 3–7, pendulous, on 5–10cm long pedicels, smaller than *L. vernum*, white with green tips; the cultivar 'Gravetye' has larger flowers in the clusters; May to June. Needs a moist to wet soil. Will tolerate standing water with *Caltha* and *Primula rosea*, where winters are not too severe. Plant bulbs in the fall in groups of 5 and leave undisturbed. Most effective after established for several years. Bulbs should be planted 10–20cm deep. Propagate by seed sown when ripe and by division of older clumps in early fall. Good for cutting. z4

L. autumnale L. Portugal, Morocco. Leaves thread-like, appearing soon after the flowers. Scapes to 15–29cm high, slender, flowers 1–3, nodding, white, tinged red, in fall. Not winter hardy far north or where summers are cool and damp, therefore recommended for the alpine house or milder climates in a protected site. Will grow further north (z5) where summers are hot and dry so bulbs harden properly. Needs some sun.

L. hiemelis see **L. nicaeense**

L. nicaeense Ardoina (*L. hiemelis* of auth. not DC.) Mediterranean Region. Leaves blackish-green, lax, 2–4 produced in the fall, to 25cm long but very narrow. Flowers usually solitary, white marked green, to 1.25cm long in very early to early spring. z7(6)

L. roseum Martin. Mountains of Corsica. Foliage slender, 5–12cm high. Flowers on very slender scapes, solitary, pink to red, September to October. Not very winter hardy in the temperate zone, though hardier where summers are hot and dry. z7(6)

L. vernum L., Spring Snowflake. Central and S. Europe. Found in shady, moist meadows and streamsides in heavy soil which floods in spring. Bulbs globose, to 3cm in diameter. Leaves strap-shaped, 15–30cm long, glossy bright green. Scapes hollow, flattened, to 30cm high. Flowers usually solitary, occasionally in pairs, bell-shaped, to 3cm long, white with a green or yellow spot at the end of the 6 uniform segments, March to April. Leaves die back in June and should not be mown off before then if planted in turf. Grow in moist, loamy woodland soil in semi-shade to full (summer) shade. Effective planted with *Primula elatior*, *P. japonica* and similar perennials as well as with ferns, rhododendrons and other moisture-loving shrubs. Plant the bulbs in 3's or 5's 30–60cm apart and 6–10cm deep. A preventive insecticide dip treatment for bulb flies is advisable, especially when planting into sandy soil. A good plant for naturalizing in a moist, humus-rich park setting or a moist woodland clearing. Self-seeds under favorable conditions. In the garden mulch the bulbs with leafmold in the fall. Seedlings produce many desirable variants which are sometimes offered as cultivars. However, the observant gardener may make selections from seedlings for vegetative propagation. 'Carpaticum' is like the species, but with a clear yellow spot at the tips of the perianth segments. 'Vagneri' has especially wide leaves and distinctly larger flowers, usually 2 per stem. Quite vigorous in a suitable site, to 40cm. Propagate by seed sown when harvested, and division. Transplanting during the vegetative period or even while flowering is often more successful than fall planting. z5 (D.)

Leuzea DC.
Compositae

Four to 6 species in S. Europe and N. Africa. Genus very closely related to *Centaurea*. Characterized by the solitary, terminal flower heads subtended by a globose involucre of imbricated bracts with orbicular papery appendages. Flowers all tubular, bisexual. Achenes glabrous, pappus plumose in several rows.

L. conifera (L.) DC. Mediterranean region from Portugal to Sicily. Stems 30–50cm high, white woolly pubescent, leafy to just below the flower heads. Leaves petioled, woolly pubescent beneath, dark green above, ovate-lanceolate, smaller and entire above, deeply pinnately lobed low on the stems. Immature flower heads large, rounded-ovate. Conspicuous and attractive for its scaly, yellowish brown, glossy bracts. Flower heads pale purple, midsummer, later in cool climates. An interesting collector's plant for a warm, dry site in the informal or wildflower garden. z8(7)

L. rhapontica (L.) Holub (*Centaurea*

rhapontica L., *Rhaponticum scariosum* Lam.). Found mostly in the S. Alps. Stems 1–1.8m high. Rootstock very stout, cylindrical. Basal leaves long-petioled, to 60cm long, partly pinnatisect, oblong-ovate in outline, acuminate, dull green above, underside gray-white; stem leaves simple, somewhat undulate and dentate. Stems of younger plants usually simple, 1 or few branched; older plants branched above the middle. Budding flower heads nearly the size of a chicken egg and very decorative, with closely overlapping, dry-membranous, silver-gray glossy scales; flowers lilac-

Leuzea rhapontica

pink; July to mid-August. Plants are also attractive in seed with yellowish, umbrella-shaped plumes rising out of the buds. A good, persistent specimen plant for large informal gardens and parks. Combines well with Mugo Pines. z5 (Sch.)

Levisticum Hill
Umbelliferae
Lovage

Three species of tall herbs from SW. Asia. Lovage is an old medicinal plant, still commonly found in modern gardens. An attractive and stately plant, for every garden, even in the perennial border. Grow in any well dug and fertile, moist garden soil in full sun to semi-shade. Propagate by division and seed. Seeds remain viable for only a short time and should be sown soon after harvest. Also spreads by self-seeding.

L. officinale W.D.J. Koch, Lovage. Iran, cultivated and naturalized in many parts of Europe and the USA, but usually dies out after some time in colder areas. Stout herb, 1–2m high with stems strongly channeled at the base and with large, dark green, glossy, bi- to tripinnatisect, serrate leaves. Scented like celery. Flowers small, greenish yellow, in 12–20 rayed umbels subtended by numerous membranous, narrow, deflexed bracts. Blooms from midsummer. z4 (E.)

Levisticum officinale

Lewisia Pursh
Portulacaceae
Bitter Root

About 15–20 species in W. North America. Fleshy herbs with thick, starchy roots or corms. Leaves basal in rosettes, flat or round, evergreen or deciduous (dying off completely in summer), stem leaves few, dying as seeds mature. Flowers small to large, usually in floriferous panicles or solitary.

Three groups are distinguished:

1. Rediviva group (**R**). Three species. Deciduous. Leaves rounded in basal rosettes. Flowers large, appearing when the leaves begin to senesce.

2. Pygmaea group (**P**). Nine species. Deciduous. Leaves flat in basal rosettes or on the stem. Flowers mostly small, except for *L. brachycalyx*.

3. Cotyledon group (**C**). Seven

species. Evergreen, only *L. congdonii* is deciduous. Leaves flat in basal rosettes. Inflorescences many flowered (except *L. tweedyi*), flowers usually small.

Flower mid-spring to early summer, many species and hybrids flower intermittently until fall. Cultivate the Rediviva and Pygmaea groups in a very gravelly, lime-free with humus added soil, somewhat protected in winter, with full sun. The evergreen species need a lime-free, very well-drained soil and a collar of gravel around the crown of the plant. All species are easily grown in an alpine house, or it is a charming collector's plant in trough gardens, containers, rock beds and dry stone walls (except *L. cotyledon*) together with other small perennials and dwarf woody plants. Propagate by seed sown quickly after ripening or by cuttings. Many species can be increased by leaf cuttings.

L. alba see **L. rediviva**

L. aridorum see **L. pygmaea**

L. aurantiaca see **L. tweedyi**

L. bernardina see **L. nevadensis**

L. brachycalyx Engelm. ex Gray (*L. brachycarpa* S. Watson). **(P)**. W. USA: S. California, Arizona, Utah, New Mexico. Grows in moist, summer-dry mountain meadows. Corm large, sometimes multi-stemmed. Leaves spatulate or oblanceolate, 10cm long and 12mm wide, green with a bluish cast. Flowers to 4cm, white, very rarely light pink, solitary, scapes to 5cm, usually with 2 bracts next to the calyx. May to June. To grow in very moist areas dig plants in summer and keep dry. Self-sterile. z5

L. brachycarpa see **L. brachycalyx**

L. cantelowii Howell **(C)**. W. USA: California, on the wet cliffs of the Sierra Nevada Mts. In summer, a dry, mossy covering on the rocks. Leaves in rosettes, evergreen, to 10cm long, scabrous-toothed, widened toward the tip. Stems to 48cm; flowers in panicles 10–12mm, pale pink with rosy veins. May to July. May be cultivated in the landscape with some protection. z7

L. columbiana (Howell) Robins. **(C)**. W. North America: British Columbia, Washington and Oregon. Requires a sunny to semi-shaded site, often found with shrubby penstemons, at 1500–2700m. Leaves evergreen, flat, linear-

spatulate, 2–10cm long and to 8mm wide. Flowers whitish-pink or pure white in 10–30cm high panicles, only 8–15mm long. May to July. Two subspecies are *L. columbiana* ssp. *rupicola* (Englisch) Ferris and *L. columbiana* ssp. *wallowensis* (Hitchcock) Hohn, dwarfer habit. Relatively trouble free in culture. Best planted in groups on a north exposure. Self-seeding. 'Rosea' is a sterile hybrid which sometimes develops many plantlets in the inflorescence, with white, pink-veined flowers. z6

Lewisia nevadensis

L. columbiana ssp. **congdonii** see **L. congdonii**

L. congdonii (Rydb.) Howell (*L. columbiana* ssp. *congdonii* Ferris). **(C)**. W. USA: California, on the canyon walls of the Sierra Nevada. Similar to *L. cantelowii*, but usually deciduous. Leaves linear-lanceolate, entire, inflorescences to 40cm high. May to June. Suitable for the landscape if protected from excessive summer moisture, best grown in the alpine house. z7(6)

L. cotyledon (S. Wats.) Robins. **(C)**. W. USA: NW. California, SW. Oregon. Found on gravelly sites, in foothills and the mountains. Leaves evergreen, quite variable in form, in starfish-like rosettes. Multiple-crowned with age, forming clumps to 40cm wide. Leaves to 15cm long and 30mm wide. Flowers 2–3.5cm wide, in many-flowered to 40cm-high panicles, white, pink, yellow, salmon,

orange. May to June. Reblooms until August. z6

The following subspecies are defined: *L. cotyledon* ssp. *cotyledon*, a mountain plant with entire leaves; *L. cotyledon* ssp. *howellii* (S. Wats.) Hohn, from lower elevations with crispate leaves and usually white, pink striped or pure pink flowers, and *L. coytledon* ssp. *heckneri* (Morton) Hohn, also from the lowlands, with toothed leaves and usually white, pink-striped flowers. The species and subspecies have been hybridized with various other Lewisias giving rise to the so-called *Lewisia cotyledon* Hybrids of the trade. Grow these in a semi-shaded dry stone wall or rock bed (with gravel collar), on a slope (to prevent water from standing in the rosettes). Propagate by seed or cuttings. 'George Henley', magenta red, and various other hybrids selections are good cultivars.

L. disepala Rydb. (*L. rediviva* var. *yosemitana* Brandeg.) **(R)**. W. USA: California, in the mountains bordering the Yosemite Valley, in coarse granite gravel. Similar to *L. rediviva*, but with leaves somewhat thickened at the ends, flowers with 2 sepals. Not generally cultivated, probably more temperamental than *L. rediviva*.

L. exarticulata see **L. pygmaea**

L. Hybrids. Generally referred to here are the *L. cotyledon* hybrids mentioned under under *L. cotyledon*. Important garden hybrids include:

L. × *brachyheck* hort. (*L. brachycalyx* × *L. cotyledon*). Intermediate in form between the perfect species, usually pink flowered, reblooming until fall. Easily propagated by rosette cuttings.

'Pinkie' (*L. pygmaea* ssp. *longipetala* × *L. cotyledon*). Enormously abundant and persistent flowers, pink with a yellowish tint.

'Trevosia' (*L. columbiana* × *L. cotyledon*). Rosettes similar to *L. columbiana*, flowers 12–15mm, lilac-copper-brown, on 25–30cm high stalks.

Many other hybrids have been developed but are not widely distributed.

L. kelloggii Brandeg. (*L. yosemitana* Jeps.) **(P)**. W. USA: California, Idaho, in a very gravelly substrate. Leaves spatulate, 1.5–4cm long. Flowers white to light pink, nearly sessile, to 2cm wide. May to June. Grow like *L. rediviva*. z5

L. leana Robins. **(C)**. W. USA: California, Oregon. Often included with *L. cotyledon*. Leaves evergreen, narrow-linear, glaucous, to 6cm long, in crowded rosettes. Flowers in crowded, to 25cm-high panicles, 12mm wide, magenta, sometimes pure violet, occasionally white or pink. May to July. Needs a very well-drained site, best with 80% coarse gravel, otherwise like *L. cotyledon*. z6

L. maguirei A. H. Holmgr. **(R)**. W. USA: Nevada. Found in loam pockets in limestone. Similar to *L. rediviva*, but 3-flowered. Not wide-spread in cultivation. z6

L. megarhiza (Hemsley) Mac Bryde (*Calandrinia megarhiza* Hemsley, *Oreobroma mexicana* Rydberg) **(P)**. W. USA: Washington, California, Colorado. Grows on spring-moist, other times dry, grassy sites. Corms yellowish brown. Leaves deciduous, linear, often widening toward the tips, occasionally turning brownish. Flowers nearly sessile or short-pedicelled, white to light pink. May to June. The white forms grow easily without protection in the rock garden. Seeds itself under favorable conditions. z5

L. minima see **L. pygmaea**

L. nevadensis (A. Gray) B. L. Robinson (*L. bernardina* A. Davidson.) **(P)**. W. USA, California north to Washington east to Rocky Mts., in spring wet, stony, grassy areas. Deciduous, yellow-brown root fleshy, tuberlike. Leaves linear, to 6cm long. Flowering scape shorter than the leaves with 2 bracts near the middle. Flowers solitary, petals white to bright pink, to 1.5cm long. The white sorts are easy to grow without winter protection. Often self-seeds. z5(4)

L. oppositifolia (S. Wats.) Robins. **(P)**. W. USA: N. California and S. Oregon. Grows on rocky slopes, moist in spring, dry in summer. Rootstock carrotlike, occasionally branched. Leaves to 10cm long, hoodlike at the tips. Flowers with 10 crowded petals, pure white, occasionally light pink ('Dwarf Form'), 2.5cm wide. May to June. z6

L. pygmaea (A. Gray) Robins. (*L. minima* A. Nels., *L. exarticulata* St. John, *L. aridorum* Clay). **(P)**. W. North America: Canada, USA. Found between 2400 and 3700m, in very well-drained, gravelly soil. Root fleshy, carrot-shaped, occasionally branched. Leaves to 12cm long and 5mm wide, in rosettes. Inflorescences shorter than the leaves, 1–3 flowered. Flowers with 6–8 white, pink or deep rose-red petals, 2cm wide, floriferous. May to June. z4

Includes *L. pygmaea* ssp. *glandulosa* (Rydb.) Ferris with stalked glands on the sepals and *L. pygmaea* ssp. *longipetala* (Piper) Ferris, with glandular teeth on the petals. Not too difficult to cultivate, given light winter protection.

L. rediviva Pursh (*L. alba* Kellog). **(R)**. Bitter Root. W. North America: Canada, USA. Root fleshy, thick, often branched, shaped like a radish or stubby carrot, usually cinnamon-brown with a very bitter cortex. Leaves fleshy, rounded in cross section, 2–4mm thick, to 6cm long, in dense rosettes, often turning bluish,

Lewisia tweedyi

often senescing at anthesis. Flowers solitary, pedicels usually longer than the petals, with 12–18 petals, rose-red or white, to 7cm wide. May to June. For the alpine house, or the rock garden with moisture protection (summer and winter), or plant in a vertical crevice. Propagation is easy by seed. Plants grow without a dormant period for the first 2 or 3 years. American Indians used the starchy root of this species as it does not become bitter until summer. z4

L. redivivia var. **yosemitana** see **L. disepala**

L. serrata Heckard et Stebbins **(C)**. W. USA: California, in the canyon walls of the American River. Found on shaded, mossy rocks, from 900–1300m. Similar to *L. cantelowii*, but with serrated leaves, stem leaves 3 (rarely 6–12). Petals 6mm (7–8mm) long with 3–5 (–7) deep pink veins. z6

L. sierrae Ferris **(P)**. W. USA: Sierra Nevada, on gravelly, grassy slopes between 2400 and 4050m. Rootstock spindle-shaped. Leaves narrow-linear, to 4cm long, in rosettes. Flowers 10–12mm wide, grouped 1–3, white, pink veined or pink. May to June. Requires a very well-drained site. Buds may be damaged by a late frost. z6

L. stebbinsii Gankid et Hildreth **(P)**. W. USA: California, Cape Mendocino, on very gravelly sites. Similar to *L. oppositifolia*, but with procumbent flower stalks, flowers very typically bicolored, dark pink with white centers. z7

L. triphylla (Wats.) Robins **(P)**. W. USA: California, Washington, Colorado, between 1500 and 3200m in coarse granite gravel. Tubers about pea pod size. Leaves not basal, rather 2–3 in whorls. Flowers 8–10mm across, in simple or compound racemes, white or pink. Very small and inconspicuous, quickly senescing. May to June. z5

L. tweedyi (A. Gray) Robins. (*L. aurantiaca* A. Nils.) **(C)**. W. North America: Washington, British Columbia, on granite screes and grassy slopes. Roots large, thick and fleshy, orange-brown. Leaves to 18cm long and 6cm wide, in loose rosettes; these leaves die toward fall and are replaced by shorter, thicker overwintering leaves. Flowers in 3's, 5cm across, light salmon-pink, pink or white. April to June. Self-sterile. Sow seeds quickly with capsules placed into a well-drained substrate in the alpine house or coldframe in full sun to semi-shade. Or grow in a vertical crevice in a dry wall or rock garden. Needs deep rooting media. Should not be kept too dry in winter or the flower buds will die off. Rosette cuttings taken from May to September will readily root and are taken primarily from the pink and white forms, which come less true from seed. z4

L. yosemitana see **L. kelloggii**

Lit.: Kummert, F.: Lewisien-Pflanzen fuer Tröge, Alpinum und Gewächshaus. Gartenpraxis (1977), pp. 284–286, 345–348, 390–393, 444–445. Elliott, R. C.: *The Genus Lewisia*. Alpine Garden Soc. Lye End Link, Woking, Surrey, England 1968. A monograph in the Kew Series by Brian Mathew is in press. (K.)

Liatris Gaertn. ex Schreb.
Compositae
Gay Feather, Blazing-star, Button-snakeroot

About 40 species in E. North America, mostly in prairies and stony forest glades. Perennials, with more or less grasslike tufted leaves and spiked or spicate-racemose inflorescences, flowering from top to bottom. Flowers all tubular, bisexual, 5–40 in small to large heads, set very close or spaced along stem. Blooms from midsummer to fall,

purple or, rarely, white; the "purple" of *Liatris* actually is rosy-purple. *Liatris* grows in any garden soil, but some species may be damaged by excessive winter wetness. The tuberous rootstock is a favorite of mice. The most important species for the garden is *L. spicata* and its varieties which also produce good cut flowers. Various other species also make attractive flowering plants for the perennial border, especially when combined with other American prairie species such as *Penstemon hirsutus*, *P. digitalis* and other penstemons, *Coreopsis verticillata*, *Echinacea purpurea*, *Solidago caesia* and

grasses such as *Panicum virgatum* and *Chrysopogon nutans*. A bee-attracting plant. Propagate by seed, cultivars by division.

Classification of *Liatris* is notably unsatisfactory. Though several technical monographs purport to sort out all of the species, none completely account for all of the specimens in herbariums and in the field. The below listed species are among the better defined sorts.

L. aspera Michx. Cormlike rootstock. Stems stiffly upright, stout, to 1.8m high, often less, solitary on young plants to

Liatris spicata

several on older ones, harshly bristly or hairy, rarely glabrous. Lower leaves narrow-linear to lanceolate, to 45cm long, stem leaves progressivly shorter and narrower, becoming sessile. Flower heads about 2.5cm across, 25–40 flowers in each head. Flower heads distinctly separated on the stems, to 150 heads on a stem. Flowers purple, rarely white. z5(4)

L. cylindracea (Michx.) Kuntze. E. North America. Rootstock corm-like. Stems 1 to several, 30–60cm high. Basal leaves long, grasslike, rough, 3–5 veined, upper leaves linear, rough; flower heads bright purple, to 2.5cm across, well spaced along the stems. September. z4

L. elegans (L.) Willd. USA: Virginia to Florida. Stems 1 or 2, 60–120cm high, from a corm-like rootstock. Leaves linear, 4–8cm wide, distinctly punctate. Flower heads rosy-purple, in a 20–30cm long, dense, inflorescence; July to September. z7(6)–9

L. pycnostachya Michx. Central USA: Indiana and Kentucky to Minnesota, S. Dakota, Texas and Louisiana. Stiffly upright, coarse stems 0.8–1.5m high. Leaves linear, densely clustered, 30cm long. Flower heads bright purple, in dense spikes to 45cm long, bracts acutely ovate; July to September. Excellent on dry soil. For cut flowers, plants are best left to grow for 2 years after seeds are sown in the spring. z3

L. scariosa (L.) Willd. Canada, USA: S. Pennsylvania to N. Georgia. Stems 0.4–1.5m high; distinguished from the other species in the rather large, open, nearly racemose inflorescences with flower heads nearly 5cm across in purplish tones. Also characteristic are the harsh 3cm-wide, lanceolate leaves. 'Alba' is a white-flowering form; 'Magnifica' has particularly large flower heads. Requires a well-drained, dry soil. z6–7

L. spicata (L.) Willd. E. and S. USA: New York to Michigan, south to Florida and Louisiana. Stems 0.6–1.5m high. Leaves linear, to 10mm wide, slightly punctate. Flower heads rosy purple to whitish in rather dense spikes; June to October. Frequently grows on moist sites and ditch banks rather than dry spots. Longer lived and more easily cultivated in gardens than some other species. z4
One unauthorized subspecies is *L. callilepis*, cultivated as 'Callilepis', with long, bright carmine-purple spikes. The form 'Kobold' is only 40–50cm high, violet-lilac; seedlings are often easily recognizable as descendants of *L. spicata*

var. *montana*, 25–30cm high. Some cultivars are specifically bred for cut flowers and seed, propagated with stem lengths of about 90cm, for example, 'Floristan Violet, 'Floristan White' and 'Picador', deep purple.

L. squarrosa (L.) Hill. E. and Central USA. Stiff stems 60–90cm high, usually in clumps. Similar to *L. cylindracea*; tips of the bracts are divergent (not appressed); flowers bright purple. z5 (H.& M.)

American gardeners with access to seed from botanical gardens and wildflower seed specialists should seek out additional *Liatris* species such as *L. graminifolia*, *L. ligulistylis*, *L. novae-angliae*, and *L. punctata*, as well the natural varieties of all species and the several hybrids which occur where species grow together.

Libertia K. Spreng.
Iridaceae

About 20 species of fibrous-rooted perennials from S. America, Australia and New Zealand. Leaves linear, crowded in a tuft 30–50cm high. Stems 50–90cm long, flowers clustered along the stems in sheathing bracts, mostly bracts. Three or four species available for z8–9 gardens in sun, in deep, fertile, average to moist soil.

Ligularia Cass.
Compositae
Golden Ray, Leopard Plant

A genus of about 80–150 species of coarse, showy herbaceous perennials mostly from E. Asia. Distinguished from the closely related genus *Senecio* by the following substantial characteristics: leaf petioles sheathlike, clasping the stem, bracts with wide, overlapping membranous margins; pappus in multiple rows; *Senecio* lacks the stem-clasping leaf petiole, the margins of the bracts are just touching, the pappus is only a single row. Ligularias are mostly tall and decorative, with yellow to orange flower heads, in midsummer. Leaves are alternate, basal in some species. In the wild, they are sometimes found in tall grass meadows, sometimes along mountain streams. All are large and coarse, with beautiful foliage and showy inflorescences; for specimen use or massing in semi-shade and moist sites on the forest margin or in association with water.
Good companion species are the midseason *Aconitum* species, *Eupatorium*

species, *Veronica longifolia*, and *Veronicastrum virginicum*. Require moist, humus to peaty or loamy soil. Plants will wilt in the sunshine and fail to fully develop on infertile, dry soil. Slug damage is a problem. Propagation of the cultivars is only by division, the species usually by seed; cross pollination of species growing close together sometimes occurs.

L. clivorum see **L. dentata**

L. dentata (A. Gray) Hara (*L. clivorum* Maxim.). Japan, China. 1–1.5m high. Leaves large, rounded to cordate, crenate along the margin, long petioled and quite ornamental as a dense foliage clump on a suitable site. Flowers 8–10cm, in flat cymes, 6–12cm wide, borne well above the foliage, orange-yellow; August to September.
Some particularly attractive cultivars include: 'Desdemona' (Hesse 1940), 1m high, stems, petioles, and undersides of leaves glossy purple, flowers reddish orange, the best dark-leaved form; 'Moorblut' (Moor's Blood), 80cm high, leaves deep reddish brown, later fading, flowers light orange; 'Orange Queen', 1.5m high, leaves green, flowers very large, bright gold-orange; 'Othello' (around 1915), 1m high, leaves dark brownish, flowers orange; 'Sommergold' (Bornimer Perennials 1973), 80cm, compact foliage clump, green, bright yellow flower heads in dense inflorescences. All the dark-leaved forms are injured by strong sunlight. z4

L. × hessei (Hesse) Bergm. (*L. dentata × L. wilsoniana*). Originated by Herm. A. Hesse (W. Germany) in 1934. To 2m high with large, oblong-cordate leaves and to 1.9m-high, panicled inflorescences of flower heads 8cm wide; flowers from early August, a few days before *L. dentata*. Similar to, but more vigorous than, the English cultivar 'Gregynog Gold' (1950) (*L. dentata × L. veitchiana*), 1.8m high, with very large, cordate leaves and bright orange-yellow flower heads in large, conical inflorescences in August. z5

L. hodgsonii Hook. f. Japan. Stems 80cm high. Much like *L. dentata* but smaller overall. Basal leaves long petioled, reniform, scabrous toothed. Flower heads wide, in a thyrse at the end of the shoot. Leaves and petioles often purple-brown toned, the flowers orange. z5

L. intermedia see **L. stenocephala**

L. japonica Less. ex. DC. (*Senecio*

palmatifidus (Sieb. et Zucc.) Juel). Japan, Korea, China, Taiwan. Stems branching, to 2m high. Basal leaves long petioled, reniform to cordate in outline, very deeply divided into 3 lobes which are also lobed and serrated. Flower heads about 10cm across, 2–8 or more, in loose-panicled racemes, orange-yellow; June to July, the earliest flowering species. z5

L. kämpferi see **L. tussilaginea**

L. macrophylla (Ledeb.) DC. (*Senecio ledebourii* Schultz Bip.). Altai Mts., Caucasus. Unbranched stems 1.4–1.8m

above, lighter beneath. Stems to 1.8cm high, often purple, with smaller leaves to just beneath the very slender, dense, spicate-panicled inflorescence. Flower heads small, with 3 disc flowers and 2 ray flowers, clear yellow; July to August. Conspicuous and attractive particularly in association with water and with a dark background. The species is closely related to *L. stenocephala* and will easily cross-pollinate, but intermediate forms are produced of quite variable garden worth. 'The Rocket', about 1.9m high, is a strong-growing cultivar. z4

Koidz. (*L. intermedia* hort.). Japan, N. China, Taiwan. Stems 1.2m high, dark purple to red-brown. Basal leaves to 35cm long, cordate or reniform-sagittate, abruptly acuminate, sharply triangular-toothed. Flower heads to 4cm in diameter with 1–3 ray florets in a crowded, slender, cylindrical, racemose inflorescence. June to July. z5

Similar are the many cultivars and hybrids of *L. przewalskii*, with normally deeper lobed or sinuate leaves. 'Globosa', with rounded-reniform leaves and flower heads with 4–7 ray florets in short conical racemes, is a hybrid of

Ligularia dentata 'Othello'

Ligularia przewalskii

Ligularia veitchiana

high. Basal leaves large, to 60cm long, elliptic to ovate, distinctly toothed, tapering to a winged petiole, bluish green. Flower heads small, with few ray florets, in long, dense, panicled spikes, yellow; July to August. z4

L. × palmatiloba hort. Hesse (*L. dentata* × *L. japonica*). To 1.8m high. Basal leaves large, rounded, deeply lobed; flowers large, in erect, loose racemes; July to August. An imposing, conspicuous plant. Like *L. japonica* most effective in front of a dark background. (*L. × yoshizoeana* (Makino) Kitam in Ohwi, *Flora of Japan*.) z5

L. przewalskii (Maxim.) Diels (*Senecio przewalskii* Maxim.). Kansu, N. China. 1.2–1.8m high. Basal leaves deeply palmately lobed, lobes irregularly lobed or toothed, acuminate, blade dark green

L. sibirica (L.) Cass. S. France, Central and E. Europe, south to Austria, Bulgaria, S. Ural Mts., Siberia to Japan, China. Stems 1–1.5m high. Basal leaves long petioled, cordate to sagittate, sharp and deeply toothed. Flower heads to 4cm across, with long, yellow ray florets in racemose inflorescences; July to August. z3

L. sibirica var. **speciosa** (Schrad. ex Link) DC. (*L. speciosa* (Schrad. ex Link) Fisch. et Mey.). Japan, Korea, Sakhalin, Manchuria, E. Siberia, China. Stems 1–2m high. Flower heads 4–5cm across, otherwise similar to the type. Both require a garden site corresponding to their moist to wet habitat. z3

L. speciosa see **L. sibirica** var. **speciosa**

L. stenocephala (Maxim.) Matsum. et

uncertain origin.

L. tangutica (Maxim.) Mattf. (*Senecio tanguticus* Maxim.). N. China. 1–1.5m high. Rootstock vigorously creeping. Leaves coarsely pinnatisect. Inflorescences broadly pyramidal, flowers opening from top to bottom; the small, numerous florets are yellow; September to October. The feathery, gray-white seed clusters remain decorative deep into the winter. This vigorous, somewhat invasive species is recommended only for larger parks and gardens. z5

L. tussilaginea (Burm f.) Mak. (*L. kämpferi* Siebold & Zucc.; *Senecio kämpferae* (Siebold & Zucc.) Benth.) China, Japan, Korea, Taiwan. Stems to 60cm high, scape-like with few bracts but no leaves. Leaves all basal, evergreen, leathery, reniform to 15cm long, 30cm wide, irregularly toothed. Inflorescence a loose corymb of pale yellow heads 3–7cm wide. Suitable only for mild climates. z8(7)

Cultivars include: 'Argentea', leaves mottled dark green, gray green and ivory; 'Aureo-maculata', Leopard Plant, leaves randomly marked with round yellow spots of various sizes; 'Crispata', Parsley Ligularia, with leaf margins ruffled. All are grown as house plants where not hardy.

L. veitchiana (Hemsl.) Greenm. (*Senecio veitchianus* Hemsl.). W. China. Introduced by the Veitch Nursery (England). Stems to 2.4m high. Basal leaves broadly triangular-cordate, deeply sinuate, distinctly toothed. Leaf petiole 40–60cm long, channeled above, solid (not hollow). Inflorescence a pyramidal raceme to 90cm long, with many yellow flower heads to 7cm across, each with 12–14 ray florets; July to August. z5

L. wilsoniana (Hemsl.) Greenm. Giant-groundsel. (*Senecio wilsonianus* Hemsl.). Central China. Stems 1.5–2m high. Basal leaves similar to the above species, cordate to reniform, but petioles 20–25cm long, hollow, round. Flower racemes crowded, columnar; flower heads with 6–8 golden yellow ray florets each; August to September. The woolly-looking fruiting heads with brownish involucre are decorative in the fall. z5

Both of the latter species prefer a cool, moist site for best development.

L. × yoshizoeana see **L. × palmatiloba**

Some recent introductions:
'Weihenstephan'. Found in the Weihenstephan Test Garden (W. Germany), 1972, as a chance seedling questionably of *L. stenocephala* 'Globosa'. Stem 1.6m high, with large, 40cm-long, 10–12cm wide inflorescences. Flower heads 6–7cm across with 5 ray florets (30mm long and about 10mm wide), nearly twice as long and wide as those of the supposed parent cultivar, bright yellow in dense racemes; July to August. Similar to the parent cultivar in foliage and general appearance, but considerably more stately with a conspicuous flower color.
'Zepter' (Scepter) (K. Partsch 1975). A chance seedling (*L. przewalskii* × *L. veitchiana*) of exceptionally stately habit, to over 2m high. Leaves cordate-reniform, irregularly coarse toothed. Flower heads densely arranged in racemes to 1m long. (H.& M.)

Lilium L.
Liliaceae
Lily

Lilies are among the most interesting and attractive of all perennial flowering plants. The many species and cultivars range through the entire color spectrum, excepting pure blue. Flower forms range from simple trumpet shapes to the truly bizarre. Sizes covered in this work vary from dwarf gnomes to 3m giants. Eighty to 90 species exist, with many varieties, numerous hybrids and countless cultivars. The native range stretches across the entire Northern Temperate Zone to subtropical regions. Many well-known lily species of modern garden culture come from E. Asia, W., N. and Central China and Japan; some species are indigenous to Europe from the Pyrenees to the Caucasus region, others range from Canada to Florida west to California in N. America. While there are 10 European and perhaps 22 N. American species, the Asiatic species number over 50.

Most species for temperate gardens originate from a band between 30–50 degrees latitude. All require a very well-drained, deeply dug medium-heavy soil. Some require humus. A few species (*L. regale*, *L. lancifolium*) thrive even in fertile, sandy, somewhat alkaline soil. Most, however, grow only in neutral or slightly acidic soil; many are intolerant of limestone and become chlorotic and eventually die in alkaline soils. More or less lime-tolerant species include:

The Aurelian Hybrids, *L. bulbiferum*, *callosum*, *candidum*, *carniolicum*, *cernuum*, *chalcedonicum*, *concolor*, *davidii*, *hansonii*, Hansonii Hybrids, *henryi*, *leucanthum* var. *centifolium*, *longiflorum*, *martagon*, *pardalinum*, *pomponium*, *regale*, *szovitsianum*, *testaceum*.

Almost all of the American species and their hybrids require acid soil, as do the Japanese species, especially *L. auratum*, *L. speciosum* and their hybrids and cultivars. Nearly all lilies grow best in a wind-protected site with bright sunshine or minimal shade (for example, in front of or between evergreens such as *Rhododendron*). The best lily climates are areas with high atmospheric moisture where summers are not too hot, such as coastal regions. The best planting time is October to November, but March to April is also suitable. When planting modern, hybridized lily bulbs, set them to a depth twice their height. Mulch the bed with leafmold or well-rotted manure (particularly in fall). Plants should also be fertilized regularly during the

growing season. Many species are damaged by late frost and slugs on the new growth. Propagate by seed, division, bulb scales and bulbils, and offset bulbs. It should be noted, however, that the American Lilies, Oriental Lilies and those of the Section Candidum are slow to germinate. They should be sown in fall, or receive a warm-cold-warm stratification treatment. In the garden, there is hardly a site where some lilies would not be suitable. Whether for the landscape, perennial border or cut flowers, lilies are highly prized by professionals and amateur gardeners alike and are widely promoted through garden societies.

There are several classifications of lilies. That used here divides the genus into 4 subgenera:
1. Cardiocrinum
2. Lilium
3. Notholirion
4. Lophophorum
Only the first two subgenera will be covered in this work as the others are not sufficiently hardy for temperate gardens.

1. Subgenus Cardiocrinum
Three species, all distinguished by their large, heartshaped, long-petioled leaves.

Cardiocrinum giganteum (Wall.) Mak. (*Lilium giganteum* Wall.)., Giant Lily. Himalaya Mts. Leafy flower stem 2–3m high, nearly as thick as a man's arm at the base, alternately leaved. Leaves 30–40cm long, broadly cordate. Flowers trumpet-shaped, 15–20cm long, white with faint reddish-purple stripes on the interior, 10–20 flowered; July to August. Bulb 15–18cm in diameter, dark green with few large scales, dies after flowering, but surrounding offset bulbs maintain the planting. Suitable for a rich, high humus, continuously moist soil, in full to semi-shade. Plant bulbs with a loose mulch so the tips are just above the soil. Winter protection by deeper mulching is necessary. Coarse peat mixed with leafmold or shredded leaves is an ideal year-round mulch. Propagation is relatively easy with seed, but bulbs flower only after 4 or 5 years. z6 (See photo, page 377).

C. giganteum var. **yunnanense** Leicht. W. and Central China. Distinguished from the species by its lower height (1.5–2m) and the metallic bronze-colored new growth. z6

Two other species, *C. cathayanum* and *C. cordatum*, are similar but tender; for z8 gardens where summers are cool and misty.

2. Subgenus Lilium The Subgenus Lilium was once divided into 4 Sections based exclusively on the flower form and the arrangement of the petals, by the Austrian botanist Endlicher. This division ignored many taxonomically important properties. In 1949 H.F. Comber presented a new system of classification with 7 Sections taking into account the range, seed germination, leaf arrangement, bulb form, bulb scales, flower form, flower arrangement and many other distinguishing characteristics. This new system accounts for the historical development of the species and is generally accepted as the best method of classification to date. The 7 sections include the most closely related Lilies as follows:

1. Martagon Section (**MA**)
2. American Section (**AM**)
3. Candidum Section (**CA**)
4. Oriental Section (**OR**)
5. Asiatic Section (**AS**)
6. Trumpet Section (**TR**) (**LO**)
7. Dauricum Section (**DA**)

This division of the genus generally supercedes the system of classification set forth by Dr. Lighty, which was less comprehensive than that of Harold Comber.

Martagon Section (MA). This Section includes Asiatic and European lilies of the typical Turk's Cap shape, with distinctly reflexed petals and widely exserted pistils and anthers and includes: *L. carniolicum, L. distichum, L. hansonii, L. martagon, L. medeoloides, L. tsingtauense.*

American Section (AM). This Section includes the lilies of N. America, which are further divided into 4 subsections based on their historical development and genetics. It is presumed that in prehistoric times the lilies were distributed across the Land Bridge linking Asia and North America (now the Bering Straits between Asia and N. America) and after separation, developed independently of their Asian counterparts.

a) *L. bolanderi, L. columbianum, L. humboldtii, L. kelloggii, L. rubescens, L. washingtonianum*

b) *L. harrisianum, L. maritimum, L. nevadense, L. occidentale, L. pardalinum, L. parryi, L. parvum, L. vollmeri*

c) *L. canadense, L. grayi, L. iridollae, L. michauxii, L. michiganense, L. superbum*

d) *L. catesbaei, L. philadelphicum*

Candidum Section (CA). These species are mostly from Europe and the Caucasus. *L. candidum, L. carniolicum, L. chalcedonicum, L. kesselringianum, L. monadelphum, L. pomponium, L. pyrenaicum, L. rhodopeum, L. polyphyllum.*

Oriental Section (OR). This Section includes the majority of the lilies from Japan with wide-open reflexed or trumpet forms. Including: *L. alexandrae, L. auratum, L. brownii, L. japonicum, L. nobilissimum, L. rubellum* and *L. speciosum.*

Asiatic Section (AS). This is the most species-rich Section, stretching from Europe across Asia to China. Includes the following species with flowers of various shapes: *L. amabile, L. bulbiferum, L. callosum, L. cernuum, L. concolor, L. duchartrei, L. lancifolium, L. lankongense, L. leichtlinii, L. maculatum, L. nanum, L. nepalense, L. pensylvanicum, L. pumilum, L. wardii, L. wilsonii* as well as many other rare species, not found in culture.

Trumpet-Lily Section (TR/LO). This Section is divided into:

a) China Trumpets (**TR**) and the
b) S. Asian Trumpets (**LO**)

The China trumpets include: *L. leucanthum, L. regale, L. sargentiae, L. sulphureum,* all indigenous to China. *L. henryi,* a Turk's Cap, has also been included in this Section due to its botanical relationship. The S. Asian trumpets include: *L. formosanum, L. longiflorum, L. neilgherense, L. philippinense, L. wallichianum.*

Dauricum Section (DA). *L. dauricum* is the only lily of this Section, often considered to be like *L. bulbiferum,* one of the Asiatic Section.

L. alexandrae Wallace. (**OR**) Found in Japan, only on the Ryukyu Island, Ukeshima. With large, white, horizontal trumpetshaped flowers on leafy stems to 60cm high. Not winter hardy, used only for hybridizing. In the British and American literature as *L. nobilissimum* (Mak.) Mak. z9

L. amabile Palib. (**AS**) Korea, Dagelet Island. Bulbs white, globose. Stem 0.4–1m high, leaves oblong-lanceolate, inflorescences racemose with 1–6 nodding Turk's Cap-shaped flowers. Flowers glossy orange-red with black spots, unpleasantly scented. Blooms in midsummer. Thrives on a sandy loam soil. Not generally offered in the trade. Propagate by fresh seed which is quick to germinate. z6

L. amabile var. **luteum** hort. (**AS**) glossy yellow.

L. auratum Lindl. (**OR**). Gold-banded Lily. Indigenous to Japan on the main island of Honshu. Grows on east-facing mountain slopes, among low grasses, bamboos and rhododendrons from sea level to 1500m, on loose, rich volcanic soil (even on thatch roofs). Bulbs 7.5–10cm in diameter, flat-globose, yellowish. Stems stout, dark green. Leaves narrow to broadly lanceolate, short petioled, to 22cm long. Flowers outward-facing, large, fragrant, flattened bowshaped, the sepals somewhat reflexed, flowers to 25cm across, waxy white with gold midstripes, carmine red spots and papillae on each petal. Plants in nature produce up to 6 flowers, twice as many in culture, in late summer. This lily grows best in a moist, mild maritime climate.

The following cultivars are particularly attractive: 'Platyphyllum' with wide petals, and more intense colors; 'Rubrovittatum', is somewhat later flowering, with yellow midstripes and crimson strips running to the petal tips, distinctly red-spotted; 'Rubrum', with crimson red middle stripes; 'Virginale', pure white with a gold band and yellow spots. Several other cultivars are listed.

Bulbs of *L. auratum* were once exported from Japan for forcing and naturalizing in gardens. They have been replaced, however, by the modern hybrids from the USA and Holland. z5

L. bolanderi S. Wats. (**AM**). Thimble Lily. S. Oregon and California. Leafy stems 30–90cm high; to 9 trumpet-shaped flowers in a raceme, brick to wine red. Grows in rocky or gravelly loam, from 900–1800m; an area with rain only in spring. Difficult in areas with summer rainfall. z8(6)

L. brownii F.E. Br. ex Spae (**TR**). Introduced into England from Canton, China. Bulb yellowish white. Stems 0.9–1.3m, with outward-facing, spreading trumpet flowers, pure creamy white inside, purple-pink running to chocolate brown outside. Blooms in July. z7(6)

L. brownii var. **australe** (**TR**). S. China. Smaller bulbs, not winter hardy.

L. brownii var. **colchesteri** (hort) = var. *viridulum* (**TR**). Central China Mts, to 1500m. Bulbs large, creamy white. Stems 1–2m high. Leaves oblong-lanceolate, trumpet flowers to 15cm long, very pale yellow to white, outside stained rose-purple shaded with green; blooms in late summer. Difficult to maintain in the garden. Bulbs are grown as a food in China. Seed propagated. z6

L. bulbiferum L. (**AS**), Orange Lily, Fire Lily. Occurs nearly throughout Europe. Described in herbals as long ago as the 16th century. Two forms go by the name Fire Lily in Europe, the typical *L. bulbiferum* which produce bulbils in the leaf axils, and ssp. *croceum* which does not. z5

L. bulbiferum ssp. **bulbiferum** Deutschl. **(AS)**. This form is rare; N. Bavaria, Thuringia, Erz Mts. Bulbs white. Stems 0.6–1.2m high, with many narrow-lanceolate leaves, and with green bulbils in the upper leaf axils in summer. Flowers in terminal umbels with up to 20 erect, orange-red cupshaped flowers with red petal tips, lightly spotted red. Subspecies *croceum* is easier to cultivate and bring into flower. z5

L. bulbiferum var. **chaixii (AS)** is a dwarf form from the French Maritime Alps and Corsica.

L. bulbiferum ssp. **croceum** (Chaix) Bak. **(AS)**. Major range in the Alps; in the N. Alps, Austria, Carinthia, Tirol, Switzerland, E. France, N. and Central Italy, Corsica. Grows among rocks, in screes, in fields, on loam soil, and thrives on loess and loam soil. Large cup-shaped flowers of fiery yellow-orange with brown-spotted interior; transplants poorly, will not tolerate root disturbance. Flowers in June. z5

L. bulbiferum var. **giganteum (AS)**. Stems 1.5–1.8m high, reputed to occur on Mt. Vesuvius and the crater region of the Cigliano Mts. (N. Italy). z8

L. callosum Sieb.et Zucc. **(AS)**. The mostly widely distributed lily in E. Asia, occurring in China, Manchuria, Japan, Taiwan and S. Korea. Not an important ornamental for gardens. Stems 30–90cm high, with small, brick red flowers of Martagon shape. Several cultivars are listed including: 'Flaviflorum', flowers yellow; and 'Luteum', flowers pale lemon yellow. Propagate by seed. Suitable for the rock garden. z7(5)

L. canadense L. **(AM)**, Canadian Lily, Wild Yellow Lily, Meadow Lily. Its range in N. America reaches above the 50th parallel to 35 degrees latitude southward. Widely distributed in E. North America. In moist meadows; grows in ditches and on forest margins. Fleshy, sparsely scaled, rhizomous rootstock with new, few scaled small bulbils at the tip each year, from which arise 0.6–1.5m high stems with whorled leaves. The long, gracefully arched peduncles carry up to 20 flowers in an umbellate inflorescence. Blooms late spring to early summer. Flowers nodding, flaired trumpet-shaped segments, scarcely reflexed. Flowers mostly yellowish with dark spots, although varieties are listed with flowers brick red, orange shades, and pure yellow. Not very easy to cultivate, requires an acidic, moist, well-drained soil such as a sand-peat-loam mix with a gravelly substrate. It is worth the trouble for this is one of the most elegant lilies. Also cultivar 'Coccinea', flowers brick red with yellow-spotted throat; and var. *editorum* Fern., from drier areas, leaves elliptic. Propagate by seed, although slow to germinate. z3–7

L. candidum L. **(CA)**, Madonna Lily. E. Mediterranean region, Lebanon, Israel, Turkey, Greece. Brought to Europe first by the Romans, later reintroduced by the Crusaders. Cultivated long ago as a medicinal plant. A symbol of purity and virginity. In fall, a small cluster of linear-lanceolate, wavy margined leaves develop and overwinter, followed in spring by a 0.8–1.5m high leafy stem. Stem leaves smaller and appressed to the stem, flowers 5–20 in erect racemes, flowers 10–15cm long, pure white, broadly funnelform, fragrant. The stem and leaves die back after flowering and the bulb remains dormant until leaves grow again in September. A light, open cover of brushwood is advisable for the overwintering clump of foliage. Bulbs yellowish white; should be planted in late August. Cover the tip of the bulb with only 3cm of soil. The Madonna Lily is a highly prized garden plant, growing in medium-heavy limed loam in a sunny, protected site. In lighter soil plants may require irrigation so soil never dries deeply. Plants may be damaged by various insects, mildew or *Botrytis*, and should be treated accordingly. Propagate by division or bulb scales. Seed is not produced. Blooms in June. z6

L. candidum var. **salonikae (CA)**. A seed-producing wild form from Greece. Petals are narrower, leaves smaller and acute. The 'Cascade Strain' introduced soon after World War II from the Oregon Bulb Farms is a selection of *L. candidum* and, being virus-free unlike the general population of *L. candidum*, is particularly vigorous. Unfortunately the true strain has disappeared. z6

L. carniolicum Bernh. ex W. D. J. Koch **(MA)**. Balkan region, Carniola (Yugoslavia), The Balkan States including Greece. Stem to 90cm high. Leaves alternate, lanceolate, 7.5cm long or shorter, ascending, veins hairy beneath. Flowers 1–6 in a terminal raceme, sepals and petals strongly reflexed, red or orange. Quite variable in form, divided into the folowing 4 varieties:

L. carniolicum var. **albanicum**, leaves smooth, glabrous; flowers yellow. z6

L. carniolicum var. **bosniacum**, leaves smooth, glabrous; flowers orange or red. z6

L. carniolicum var. **carniolicum**, leaf venation and undersides flowers orange or red. z6

L. carniolicum var. **jankae**, bulb yellow. Flower stem 30–90cm, with many scattered, pubescent, lanceolate leaves. The yellow flowers are Turk's Cap form, blooming from late May to June. Occurs in mountain pockets of loam and gravel soil among rocks and dwarf shrubs from 600–1300m. Not generally found in the trade. Propagate by seed which is slow to germinate. Suitable for the alpine garden. z6

L. carolinianum see **L. catesbaei** and **L. michauxii**

L. catesbaei Walt. (*L. carolinianum* Bosc et Lamb.) Leopard Lily, Pine Lily. E. North America, N. Carolina to Louisiana. Rootstock stoloniferous, stout, with scattered scales and terminal bulbs. Stems to 60cm tall. Basal leaves overwinter, linear; stem leaves linear to almost lanceolate, alternate, to 7.5cm long. Flowers terminal, solitary, upright, cup-shaped, to 12cm long, red yellowing toward the base, brown-spotted. And var. **longii** Fern., Virginia to Alabama. Basal leaves absent, stem leaves broader, perianth segments without recurved tips. z7(6)

L. cernuum Kom. **(AS)**. Korea, Manchuria, Ussuri region. A delicate Lily, stems 30–90cm high, with narrow, grasslike leaves; 1–6 flowers, nodding strongly reflexed Turk's Cap form, lilac colored, short-lived, always propagate from seed. Used in breeding work for pink, pastel and white hybrid lilies. Blooms in July. z5

L. chalcedonicum L. **(MA)**. Scarlet Turk's Cap Lily. This lily was introduced from Greece long ago. Stems 0.6–1.2m high, with crowded lanceolate or oblanceolate leaves to 12cm long which become smaller toward the top of the stem, and appressed; 1–10 flowers in a raceme, Martagon form, fleshy, vermilion-red. July to August. A beautiful lily, for warm, calcareous, loamy soil. Very susceptible to *Botrytis*. *L. heldreichii* Freyn, also indigenous to Greece, is usually considered a variety of *L. chalcedonicum*. Cultivar 'Maculatum', flowers spotted with purple. Blooms in July. z8

L. columbianum Henson ex Bak. Columbia Lily, Oregon Lily. USA; N. California to British Columbia and Idaho. Stems to 1.5m high, with whorled lanceolate to oblanceolate leaves to 10cm long. Flowers nodding, few to many in a terminal raceme, segments strongly reflexed, to 5cm long, yellow, golden or red, often maroon spotted. 'Ingramil', stouter, flowers larger, numerous, deep orange.

L. concolor Salisb. **(AS)**. Central China, Hubei, Hunan, Yunnan. Grows on limestone, in loamy humus, among grass and

unicolor Cotton., stems to 1m, flowers small, paler, with purplish or reddish spots, hardier; and var. **willmottiae** Raffill., stems to 2.2cm high and purple-spotted, flowers to 40, on drooping pedicels to 15cm long, bright orange. z5

Cultivar 'Maxwill' is a selection from Dr. F. L. Skinner (Canada, 1928), chosen for its strict and vigorous habit. Form, arrangement and color resemble that of *L. davidii*. All these Davidii forms are frequently used in hybridizing to increase vigor in the progeny. z5

L. distichum Nakai ex Kamis. NE.

3000m, on volcanic soil and grassy meadows with bamboo. Stems to 2m high, often less, purple-brown; leaves dark green, linear to 20cm long, many, alternate, with prominent veins beneath. White flowers 1–several, trumpet shaped, fragrant. This lily is easy to grow from seed, but flowers well only in the greenhouse, not winter hardy in temperate gardens where summers are cool and wet. z7(6)

L. formosanum var. **pricei** Stocker is an alpine form from 3000m. Only 30–40cm high with 1–2 long, white flowers, some-

Lilium auratum

Lilium canadense

Lilium candidum

shrubby plants. A small lily with erect stems to 90cm high with stiff, white hairs, and nearly linear-leaves to 10cm long; 1–10 star-shaped upright flowers. Comes in many shades of lemon yellow, red, orange-red or scarlet red. The small, stellate flowers are prized for use in flower arranging. Several varieties and cultivars are listed by specialists. Grown from seed. Blooms in June. z6

L. dauricum see **L. pensylvanicum**

L. davidii Duchartre ex Elwes **(AS)**. China, Sichuan, Yunnan, at elevations of 1500–3000m. The bulbs are grown for food in its native range. Rigid, stiffly upright stem to 1.8m high, with alternate close-spaced, narrow-lanceolate leaves spreading obliquely upward or horizontal. The 6–20, often to 40, nodding orange-red flowers are Turk's Cap form with black or brown spots. Easily grown from seed, a very good, long-lasting lily for the rock garden or perennial bed. And variety **macranthum** Raffill. with stems to 2.1m high, flowers 1–2 on a pedicel, orange; var.

Manchuria and Korea. Stems 30–95cm tall, hollow, ribbed, at least near the ground. Leaves oblong-lanceolate to oblanceolate-ovate, to 15cm long; a single whorl near the base, alternate and scattered above. Flowers 3–8 in a raceme; reflexed, nodding, orange-red spotted brown, in midsummer. A woodland species for cool, damp, high humus soils; not easy to grow and apparently unsuitable for hybridizing. z6

L. duchartrei Franch. **(AS)**, Marble Turk's Cap Lily. China, Sichuan, Kansu, on mountain meadows in moist damp or swampy sites from 2400–3500m. Bulbs white, stems 0.45–1.5m, often stoloniferous; 2–12 marble white, nodding flowers with wine red speckles, Turk's Cap form, on outward ascending pedicels. Flowers fragrant. Rare in cultivation, requires a cool, moist shaded soil into which the stoloniferous stem can spread. Blooms in July. z5

L. formosanum (Bak.) Wallace **(LO)**. Occurs only on Taiwan from sea level to

what reddish on the exterior; hardier and suitable for the rock garden. Blooms in September. z7

L. grayi Wats. Orange-bell Lily, Roan Lily. E. USA, Virginia, North Carolina and Tennessee. Stoloniferous. Stems to 1.3m, often less, with 3–6 whorls of 4–8 leaves. Leaves variable, 1– rarely 8, flaired-trumpet-shape, slightly nodding or outward facing, to 5cm long, reddish-orange spotted purplish-brown. Demanding, like most North American species, but worth the trouble. z7(6)

L. hansonii Leichtl. ex D.D.T. Moore **(MA)**, Gold or Japanese Turk's Cap Lily. Japan, Korea, and adjacent Siberia. Stems 1–1.2m high. Leaves wide, dark green, in whorls. Flowers nodding, strongly reflexed and fragrant, segments waxy thick, orange-yellow, brown-spotted; flowers in a loose 4–10 flowered raceme; midsummer. Bulbs pink-white, firm, acute-conical. Grow in semi-shaded, high-humus soil; hardy and floriferous, emerges early and therefore is susceptible to frost damage.

Cross-pollinates readily with *L. martagon* (*L. hansonii* hybrids). *L. hansonii* is often grown for a cut flower. z6

L. harrisianum Beane et Vollmer **(AM)** (*L. pardalinum* var. *giganteum* Stearn et Woodc.). This lily, grown in America as 'Sunset Lily' or 'Red Giant', tolerates moist sites. Vigorous, it multiplies quickly. Stems 1.2–2m high, with several leaf whorls. Large flowers are Martagon form, brilliant carmine red with orange, and with brown spots; midsummer. The rhizomatous roots are very stout, best divided after 3–4 years. An imposing lily,

stem. Easily propagated by the numerous bulbils along the stem and bulblets. A persistent and untiring garden lily, requiring a deep planting in a fertile, slightly alkaline garden soil. Also thrives on gravelly soil. Effective as specimens or in groups. 'Citrinum' is a mutation with lemon yellow, brown spotted, flowers.

'Improved' is a selection with stiffly erect stems. *L. henryi* is often crossed with the Trumpet Lilies and also with *L. speciosum*. z5

L. humboldtii Roeal. & Leichtl. ex

Japan, only in S. Honshu, from sea level to 1050m with bamboos and rhododendrons. The Japanese name is "Sasa Juri" (Bamboo Lily). Stem to 1m high; leaves alternate, lanceolate to oblong, to 15cm long, hard, dark green. Raceme 1–5 flowered. Flowers are flaired trumpets of pure pink. This lily is somewhat rare in cultivation, disease susceptible and demanding, but very beautiful and used primarily only for breeding. Blooms from May to August. z7

L. kelleyanum Lemm. (*L. nevadense* Eastw.; *L. nevadense* var. *shastense* Eastw.;

Lilium harrisianum

Lilium japonicum

Lilium 'Schützenlisl', Asiatic hybrid

well suited to moist soil in semi-shade with rhododendrons and ferns. Note that no native source is cited; the final classification of this lily is in doubt, possibly it is a hybrid of *L. humboldtii* and *L. pardalinum*. z5

L. heldreichii see **L. chalcedonicum**

L. henryi Bak. Central China (Hupeh, Kweichow). This lily, with moderate-sized, orange Turk's Cap flowers is difficult to classify, possibly related more closely to the Trumpet and Oriental Lilies than to the Asiatic Lilies. Bulbs usually larger than a man's fist, with large, elliptic scales and strong, deeply penetrating, dark purple roots. Stems flexible 1.4–2.4m long, usually slightly arched (this lily grows in rocky cliffs where the stem curves up from the wall). Leaves broad-lanceolate, dark green. Flower pedicels curve outward. The nodding Turk's Cap flowers are clear orange with many brown speckles and papillae, and green nectaries. Flowers abundantly after midsummer. Poor seed producer. Produces prop roots on the

Duchartre. Humboldt Lily. USA: Central California Sierra Mts. Stems to 2m, stout, often rough-hairy. Leaves in whorls, oblanceolate, to 12.5cm long, margins pubescent. Flowers few to 15 in pyramidal raceme, nodding, to 8cm long, segments strongly reflexed, orange-yellow spotted purplish. Var. *bloomerenum* perianth segments red-margined, very dark-spotted; var. *ocellatum*, flower segments with maroon spots ringed with red. A rare and demanding species. z8(7)

L. iridollae M. Henry. Pot-of-Gold Lily. USA: NW. Florida and S. Alabama, in acid bogs. Stems to 1.5m high. Leaves mostly whorled, to 8cm long, oblanceolate to obovate, hairs on margins and veins beneath. Flowers 1 to rarely 8, nodding, perianth segments strongly reflexed, to 10cm long, golden-yellow spotted brown. Slightly fragrant. A rare subtropical lily of difficult culture. The shoot tip overwinters above-ground. z8(7)

L. japonicum Thunb. Japanese Lily. **(OR)**

L. pardalinum Kellogg var. *shastense* (Eastw.) Stoker; *L. shastense* (Eastw.) Beane.) USA: Central and N. California. Rhizomatous with scattered scales and 1-year bulbs at the tips. Stems 60–200cm high. Leaves mostly in whorls, oblong-lanceolate, to 15cm long. Loose raceme with 1–25 fragrant flowers with strongly reflexed segments, to 3.5cm long, yellow with orange tips, spotted maroon. A difficult lily to grow out of habitat. z8(7)

L. kelloggii Purdy. USA: NW. California. Stems to 1.3m high. Leaves whorled, lanceolate to oblanceolate to 10cm long. Open raceme with rarely 1–20 fragrant flowers, sometimes few flowers in a false umbel. Flowers nodding, to 5cm long, cream-colored to pink, aging dull purple. A rare and demanding lily in cultivation. z8(7)

L. kesselringianum Mishchenko **(CA)**. Caucasus, east of the Black Sea, from Russia to Turkey. Similar to *L. monadelphum*. Bulbs large. Stem sturdy, to 60cm high. Leaves many, alternate, lanceolate, to 12.5cm long. Inflorescence with 8–10 flowers, creamy-white to straw yellow, inside finely cinnamon-spotted; segments to 11cm long, tips recurved. For planting in loamy, high humus soil. Blooms in late spring. z6

L. lancifolium Thunb. **(AS)** (*L. tigrinum* Ker-Gawl.), Tiger Lily. Japan, Korea, E. China, Manchuria. This triploid Tiger Lily originated from a diploid form. Bulbs, grown for consumption in China and Japan, are white, thick-fleshy scaled and wide. Purplish scabrous stems 1–2m high, with alternate, linear to lanceolate, evenly distributed leaves to 18cm long. Black bulbils produced in the leaf axils. Raceme of 1–25 flowers to 13cm wide, strongly reflexed orange-vermilion spotted purple-black. Blooms after midsummer. Does not set seed, but the bulbils provide a ready means of vegetative propagation.

L. lancifolium 'Diploid' has the normal chromosome count (2n = 24), is self-sterile and crosses with carotenoid producing lilies. This and the handsome yellow-flowering *L. lancifolium* var. *flaviflorum* Makino are both used primarily for breeding. Cultivar 'Florepleno', with double flowers. z5

L. lancifolium var. **fortunei** Bak., a horticultural variety (not botanical) is somewhat less vigorous, with salmon-red flowers; stems and flower buds are woolly pubescent. This lily takes readily to garden culture. Plant 5–10 bulbs together for best effect. After 3–4 years they should be transplanted into fresh soil. z5

Cultivar 'Giganteum' is listed as an improper form.

The triploid form, 'Splendens', is generally available, flowers larger, more of them, brilliant red with bold spots.

Cultivar 'Supurtum', flowers bright orange spotted black.

L. lankongense Franch. **(AS)**. NW. Yunnan. Grows at about 3000m. Bulbs white, stoloniferous. Stems 0.6–1.2m high, leaves alternate, oblong to oblong-lanceolate, to 10cm long, many. Flowers to 15 in a raceme, nodding, fragrant, Turk's Cap form to 6.5cm long, white tinged soft rose-purple, spotted purple. Blooms after midsummer. Plant in a light, moist and acid soil, culture similar to that of *L. duchartrei*. Rare in cultivation. z5

L. leichtlinii Hook. f. **(AS)**. Japan. Stoloniferous. Stems to 1.3m high. Leaves many, alternate, linear-lanceolate to 15cm long. Strongly reflexed flowers, 1–5, nodding, to 7.5cm long, lemon-yellow, spotted purplish-brown. Not found in cultivation in Europe, rare in N. America. z7(6)

L. leichtlinii var. **maximowiczii** (Regel) Bak. Japan, Korea, Manchuria. Stems 0.6–2m high with many linear-lanceolate leaves. Inflorescence irregular, with 12 nodding flowers, Turk's Cap form, red-orange, copiously brown-spotted. The flower buds are usually floccose, a characteristic also present in its hybrids. This lily is often used in breeding work. July to August. z5

L. leucanthum (Bak.) Bak. (*L. formosanum* French. not Lem.) Chinese White Lily. Central China. Stems to 120cm high. Lanceolate leaves alternate, many, to 10cm long. Fragrant trumpet-shaped flowers outward-facing, slightly drooping, to 15cm long, white, with yellowish throat inside and greenish flush outside. A tolerably easy garden lily for the rhodendron border (partial shade, deep, moist, high humus soil) but not as satisfactory as the following variety. z6(5)

L. leucanthum Bak. var. **centifolium** (Stapf) Stearn **(TR)** (*L. centifolium* Stapf). From S. Kansu, NW. China. Stems to more than 2m high, very leafy, leaves dark green, to 20cm long. Raceme with 10–20, white trumpet-shaped flowers to 18cm long, fragrant, greenish-purple outside. Bulbs with red-brown scales. This lily is winter hardy given excellent drainage and a winter mulch. Early- to midsummer. This variety is much used for hybridizing because the pyramidal inflorescence is very attractive. z5(4)

L. leucanthum var. **chloraster** Wils. Shorter, to 1m, the white trumpetshaped flowers are greenish outside.

L. longiflorum Thunb. **(LO)**, The Easter Lily, White Trumpet Lily. Japan (Ryukyu Island). Grows on humus rich coral cliffs near the sea. Many million bulbs once were shipped into the USA each year for forcing; today, cultivars dominate the market. Bulbs whitish yellow, 5–7cm wide. Stems 30–90cm high with broadly lanceolate, bright green leaves, closely spaced, to 18cm long. Several pure white, elongated trumpetshaped flowers to 18cm long face outward. This lily will grow in the open landscape, flowering about midsummer, but grows better under glass away from moderate maritime regions. It is the most popular lily for forcing. The clones 'Croft', 'Creole' and 'Estate' have been partially surpassed and replaced by 'Arai', 'White Queen' and 'Nellie White'. Bulbs are used for forcing mostly in the USA and Japan. Several botanical varieties with subtle distinguishing characteristics are listed. In 1980, stems of *L. longiflorum*, mostly cultivars and varieties, totaling 30 million buds were sold in Holland. z6(5)

L. maculatum Thunb. **(AS)** Hokkaido, Japan; growing from sea level to 1000m. Stems 0.3–1m with 3–12 large flowers in umbels. Mostly orange-red with numerous dark speckles. Thrives on a slightly acidic soil. The various clones of *L. maculatum* commonly found in the trade are often wrongly listed as *L. elegans*. These are actually hybrids, crossed or selected by Japanese gardeners about 200 years ago and introduced by Siebold into Holland. These were the only colored lilies in the trade for many years. Blooms from late May to early August. z5

L. maritimum Kellogg. Coast Lily. Coastal N. California. Stems to 1.25m tall, sometimes taller. Leaves alternate (very rarely whorled), linear to narrowly oblanceolate, to 12cm long. Racemose inflorescence of 1–12 flowers, flowers horizontal, wide-flaired trumpets to 8cm long, dark red spotted purple. A very rare, demanding species. z8(7)

L. medioloides A. Gray. Wheel Lily. China, S. Korea, Japan. Stem to 75cm tall. Leaves lanceolate to oblanceolate, to 11cm long, mostly in showy whorls (hence, the name Wheel Lily) a few alternate below the umbellate inflorescence. Flowers 1–10, strongly reflexed, nodding, to 5cm long, apricot to scarlet, spotted black. z6(5)

L. martagon L. **(MA)**, Martagon Lily, Turk's Cap Lily. Central and S. Europe, in Russia to Siberia; mostly in deciduous woodlands on limestone. Stems purplish, 0.5–1m high, leaves mostly whorled, mostly oblanceolate, to 16cm long, rarely hairy. Inflorescences racemose, with 5–30 flowers, segments strongly recurved, nodding, pale wine red to soft purple, brown-spotted (rarely white flowered), unpleasantly scented. June to July. Bulbs yellow, small, somewhat pointed. Many cultivars of this lily are local in Europe. The following cultivars are particularly desirable for garden culture: 'Album', pure white, with green stems, vigorous, attractive with a dark background; 'Albiflorum', white with carmine red spots, rare; 'Cattaniae' (*L. dalmaticum* Vis.), usually very floriferous, dark wine red with conspicuous white hairs on petals, good choice for a light wall. Grow in a sunny to semi-shaded site, in a high humus, limy soil. Propagate by seed (slow to germinate) and bulb scales. z4

L. michauxii Poir. **(AM)** (*L. carolinianum* Michx. non Bosc). SE. North America. Carolina Lily. Stoloniferous bulb, stems 30–120cm high, green. Leaves broadly lanceolate to obovate, in whorls, to 12cm long. Turk's Cap flowers, 1–5, fragrant, glossy orange-red with yellowish white throats and purple brown spots. Not entirely winter hardy; for a lime-free peaty-sandy soil. Slow to germinate from seed. Not generally found in the trade. Blooms about midsummer. z7(6)

L. michiganense Farw. **(AM)**. E. North America. Stoloniferous. Resembles *L. canadense*, but segment more reflexed. Stems 0.6–1.5m high, with lanceolate leaves to 12cm long in whorls. Leaves minutely spiculate below and along the margins. Solitary or to 8 flowers, pendulous, Turk's Cap form, red-orange, red-brown speckled toward the base, May-July depending on latitude. Thrives in an acid, deep, moist loamy soil, mostly in open sites in full sun to partial shade. A slow-germinating species, but develops quickly from scales potted in peat and sand. Not generally found in the trade. Several regional varieties of this lily are poorly defined. z4

L. monadelphum M. B. **(CA)**. Caucasian Lily. N. Caucasus to the Kuban River; on mountain slopes to 2100m, in beech forests. Stems 0.6–1.2m high, with 5–20 very fragrant, pendulous, open trumpet-shaped pure yellow flowers, with light rose-lilac spots inside. Stamen filaments fused into a tube or separate. Bulbs are rather large, acute-ovate, requires humus-rich, well-drained soil. Bloom May to June. Should be transplanted only in the fall. Combines well with the very similar *L. kesselringianum* and *L. szovitsianum*, also from the Caucasus. These three lilies are very effective when planted together on the edge of a woodland or shrub border. z5

L. myriophyllum see **L. sulphureum**

L. nanum Klotzsch et Garcke **(AS)**. Himalayan region from Bashahr through Nepal, Sikkim to NW. Yunnan. An alpine lily growing from 2700–4500m. Stems 15–40cm high with alternate, linear leaves to 15cm long. Flowers campanulate, solitary, nodding, to 3.5cm long, pale lilac, rose, purple or cream yellow, purple-spotted. Long classified in the genus *Nomocharis*, this small lily requires fast drained, high humus, constantly moist acidic soil, where summers are cool and misty and winters are mild. z6(5)

L. neilgherrense Wight **(LO)**. Found in the Nilgiri, Pulney, and Cardamon Hills of S. India from 1830–2600m. Stem to 1m. Leaves glabrous, alternate, lanceolate to 12.5cm long. Flowers 1 or 2, 18–20cm long, species. Pure white, trumpet-shaped, borne horizontally, fragrant, in late summer. Suitable for glass house culture. z9

L. nepalense D. Don **(TR)**. Himalayas, Nepal, Bhutan and Kuamon; 2000–3300m high. Bulbs flat with white-pink scales, stems run horizontally 30–60cm in the soil, then grow upright to 1.2m high. Leaves alternate, to 14cm long, broadly lanceolate to oblanceolate. Flowers 1–5, in racemes, open trumpet-shaped, nodding, segments reflexed, pale lemon colored or pea green, throat dark purple. An exotic-looking flower. The variety *robustum*, offered in the trade, is hardier than the wild form, with larger flowers of better texture. This lily, in its habitat, is dormant and covered with snow for 6 months after October, and emerges with the snow melt in May. It will grow outdoors and overwinter if kept dry, but is best kept in a container in a cool, dry place over winter, then set into the garden and watered in May. Blooms in July. z5

L. nevadense see **L. kelleyanum**

L. nobilissimum T. Makino **(OR)**. Only on Ryukyu Island, Japan; on steep cliffs. Stem to 60cm high. Leaves alternate, lanceolate, to 15cm long. Flowers in an umbel, upright-facing, fragrant, pure white, trumpet-shaped to 15cm long. Used for breeding, with progeny retaining the upright flower characteristic. Blooms from June to July. z7

L. occidentale Purdy. Western Lily, Eureka Lily. USA, N. California and S. Oregon; coastal, in wet places. Rhizomotous, with scattered scales. Stems to 2m high. Leaves whorled but alternate above the middle of the stem, narrow-oblanceolate, to 13cm long. Flowers 1–5 in a raceme, nodding, segments to 6cm long, flairing, recurved, bright orange with maroon spots, and green centers.

L. pardalinum Kellogg **(AM)**, Leopard Lily, Panther Lily. USA: S. Oregon to S. California. Vigorous, branching rhizomatous bulbs with brittle scales, stem 1–2.3m high. Leaves linear to lanceolate, to 18.5cm long, in whorls below, alternate above. Flowers solitary or several in a raceme, nodding, to 10cm wide, with strongly reflexed segments, in a glossy orange-red with carmine red tips and red-brown, orange-bordered spots. July. Thrives in sandy, high humus soil and develops, in time, a stout clump. Must be repeatedly divided. Cultivar 'Californicum', with smaller leaves, larger flowers. Cultivar 'Giganteum', Sunset Lily, yellow, tipped bright red, spotted brown (probably a hybrid, *L. pardalinum* × *L. humboldtii*). Cultivar 'Johnsonii', flowers mostly red. z7

L. pardalinum var. **giganteum** see **L. harrisianum**

L. pardalinum var. **shastense** see **L. kelleyanum**

L. parryi S. Wats. **(AM)**. Lemon Lily. USA: S. California, S. Arizona; from 1800–3000m. Stems erect, 0.6–1.8m, lower leaves whorled, upper leaves alternate, all lanceolate to linear-oblanceolate, to 15cm long. Racemes with 1–15 slightly reflexed horizontal, fragrant trumpets to 10cm long, lemon-yellow, sometimes maroon-spotted. Blooms in midsummer. This lily is one of the prettiest of the American lilies, but also one of the most difficult to grow. It requires a non-limestone soil, and is under ice and snow for nearly half the year in its native habitat. Requires very fast drainage and protection from fall and winter rains. Best planted in a container with a mix of peat, humus, gravel (not limestone) and charcoal. Store cool and dry over winter, water abundantly during the growing season. Seeds are slow to germinate. Rarely found in the trade. z7(5–6)

L. parvum Kellogg. Alpine Lily, Sierra Lily. S. Oregon and California Mts. Rootstock of thick stolons with scattered scales and bulbous tips. Stems to 150cm tall. Leaves mostly whorled, rarely alternate above, linear to lanceolate, to 12.5cm long. Racemose inflorescence; flowers few to many, widely flaired trumpets to 3.5cm long, ascending to erect, bright orange to red spotted purplish brown. Grows along mountain streams and in wet meadows. And forma *crocatum* Stearn. N. California, flowers clear orange-yellow with tiny maroon spots. z7

L. pensylvanicum Ker-Gawl. Candlestick Lily. **(AS)** (*L. dauricum* Ker-Gawl.). NE. Asia, Altai Mts., Mongolia, Amur River region, N. Korea, Sakhalin, Japan. This is a hardy lily, which thrives in moist, lime-free soil. Bulbs white with narrow scales. Stem horizontal, stolon-like below ground, 30–100cm high, linear to oblanceolate alternate leaves to 15cm long. Flowers 1–6 in an umbel or raceme, erect shallow trumpets, orange-red spotted purple-black. Also a yellow-flowered form, var. *luteum* Wallace. This lily was used in hybridizing in Japan over 200 years ago. The misleading name was given in a mistaken belief that this species was of NE. USA origin. The *L. elegans* Hybrids are a result of a cross with *L. maculatum*. Also, more recently used as a parent for the Stenographer

tains to be a continuation of the Andes, hence the name. Seed is slow germinating. Not generally found in the trade. Blooms in June. z5

L. philippinense Bak. **(LO)** From Luzon Island, Philippines, at 1500–2000m. Not entirely winter hardy, but will produce flowering plants within 18 months from seed in the greenhouse. Stem to 90cm high, green. Leaves alternate, many nearly linear, to 15cm long. Flowers 1–2, pure white, slender trumpets, to 2.5cm long, horizontal, fragrant. Blooms after midsummer. Suitable for pot and cut

purple, unpleasantly scented. June. A lily for infertile soil mixed with limestone gravel in the alpine garden. z7(6)

L. pumilum Del. **(AS)** Coral Lily. (*L. tenuifolium* Fisch.). N. Korea, Manchuria, Mongolia, E. Siberia, N. China. Bulb small, white, conical. Stem wiry, to 45cm high with many grasslike, linear leaves to 10cm long. Raceme with 1–20 fragrant, nodding Turk's Cap flowers, glossy sealing-wax red, 5cm wide; in late spring. Requires full sun and well-drained, gritty or sandy, calcareous soil. Not long-lived, but easily propagated by

Lilium martagon 'Album'

Lilium wardii

Lilium 'Sonnentiger', Asiatic hybrid

and Fighter Hybrids of Isabella Preston and the Midcentury Hybrids of Jan de Graaf. Blooms in early June. z4

L. philadelphicum L. **(AM)**, Wood Lily, Orange-cup Lily. NE. North America, in open fields. Bulbs form on short stolons. Stems 45–90cm, with 1–5 erect, open bellshaped flowers, bright orange-scarlet to orange in the center. The segments narrow abruptly to a clawlike base. The flower color can range from pale lemon yellow through all the orange and red shades to dark blood red, with and without spotting, though the variation is much less in nature, suggesting some hybridization in garden stocks. Plant in well-drained, sandy loam with compost or leafmold and peat incorporated. Protect from winter wetness. Var. **andinum** Nutt. Ker-Gawl. (*L. umbellatum* Pursh, not hort.) Western Orange-cup Lily. W. Quebec to British Columbia south to Kentucky, Nebraska and New Mexico. Smaller leaves mostly alternate, not whorled. Perianth segments with smaller claws. Nuttall considered the Rocky Moun-

flower culture. z9

L. pitkinense Beane & Vollmer. Sonoma County, California, restricted to the Pitkin Marsh. Bulbs with short stolons. Stems to 1.9m tall; leaves yellow-green, to 14cm long, linear, whorled or alternate; inflorescence an umbel; flowers 1 to several, perianth segments to 5.5cm long, strongly reflexed past the middle, scarlet-vermillion with a yellow zone toward the throat, spotted black. A rare and demanding species which is valuable in breeding programs, as indicated below under American Hybrids Class.

L. pomponium L. **(MA)**. Lesser Turk's Cap Lily, Turban Lily. France and Italy, Maritime Alps between Nice and Ventimiglia. Grows on limestone, in grass and hazelnut thickets in full sun. Bulbs cream-white, pointed, 4–5cm in diameter. Stems 40–50cm high, sometimes higher, with many, alternate, narrow-linear leaves to 12.5cm long. Raceme with 1–10 nodding Turk's Cap flowers, brilliant red, spotted dark

the abundantly set seed. A popular cut flower for arranging. z3

L. pyrenaicum Gouan **(MA)**. Yellow Turk's Cap Lily. N. Spain, Pyrenees, SW. France; forest margins in the mountains and on meadows from 500–1500m. Bulbs broadly rounded, yellowish. Stems 0.3–1.2m. Leaves many, alternate, linear-lanceolate to 12.5cm long. Raceme with 1–12 nodding flowers 3.5cm across, sulfur yellow with purple-black spots, strongly reflexed segments. Unpleasant scent. May to June. Requires a heavy loam with humus and limestone gravel; in full sun to semi-shade. A lily for the alpine garden. Naturalized in England. Cultivars 'Aureum', flowers deeper yellow; 'Rubrum', flowers red-orange with maroon spots. z6

L. regale Wils. **(TR)**, Regal Lily, Royal Lily, King's Lily. China, in the Min River Valley, north of Chengtu. This beautiful lily was an important discovery made by E. H. Wilson in China in 1903. The flowers grow on long, wiry stems out of the rocky walls of the valley from

1500m–5500m in the mountains, flowering in June with thousands of fragrant, white trumpets. Bulbs round, about 10cm with lanceolate scales, turning dark purple when exposed to sunlight. Stems wiry, 0.8–1.2m high. Leaves linear, many, single-veined, to 12.5cm long. Rotate umbel with 1–8, often more, horizontal trumpet-shaped, fragrant, glossy white flowers with chrome yellow throats and pink-purple outer ribs. Anthers and pollen chrome yellow, stigma green. Blooms in early summer. Sets abundant seed by self-pollination. Plant in full sun, in well-drained, fertile, high humus soil. Early new growth may be damaged by a late frost if not covered. Plant this species for a quick garden full of lilies. Also much used for breeding. Cultivar 'Album', flowers pure white. z5

L. rubellum Bak. **(TR)**. Honshu Island, Japan. The Japanese name is "Otome-Yuri," Maiden Lily. Bulb oblong, white. Stems 30–50cm high, with many, alternate, broadly lanceolate to narrowly oblong leaves to 10cm long. Flowers 1–9, horizontal, campanulate trumpets, soft pink, fragrant, in an umbel. Easiest in container culture in a light soil mix with sphagnum moss and plenty of moisture. Used for breeding work in the development of early-blooming hybrids. May. z7

L. rubescens S. Wats. Chaparrel Lily, Redwood Lily. S. Oregon to Central California, in Coastal Mts. Stems to 1.8m tall. Leaves in whorls, oblanceolate to 10cm long. Inflorescence racemose with 1–several flowers, trumpet-shaped, ascending to upright-facing, to 5cm long, fragrant, white or pale lilac, spotted purple, flowers age to rose-purple.

L. sargentiae Wils. **(TR)**. This lily was also discovered by E.H. Wilson in 1903 in W. China, in the Tung River Valley, and in the drainage system of the Jansekiang River in Sichuan from 1100–1500m. Grows on rocks and sloping clay soil in grass and scrub. Bulbs round, 15cm wide, with red-purple, wide scales. The purple, stiff stems are 1.2–1.5m high, with many dark green, lanceolate leaves to 20cm long and with bulbils in the leaf axils. Umbel with 1–8 horizontal flowers, pure white with a yellow throat, to 12cm wide, fragrant, purple-red or brownish outer ribs. Blooms in midsummer. Seeds germinate quickly. More demanding than *L. regale*, requiring good drainage and a warm site in high humus soil. Often used in hybridizing. Not generally cultivated. z7(6)

L. speciosum Thunb. **(OR)**. Showy Lily, Japanese Lily. Next to the Goldband Lily (*L. auratum*), this is the most attractive lily from Japan. Grows on both of the southern islands, Shikoko and Kyushu. Bulbs round, yellowish to purple-brown. Stems wiry, 0.9–2m high with alternate, broadly lanceolate to oblong leaves, to 18cm long. Flowers in a leafy panicle, 1–many, nodding or outward-facing, with reflexed segments, white suffused rose inside, with undulate margins, carmine spots and papillae in the center, fragrant. The late summer flowering period often keeps this species from reaching its

Lilium martagon

fullest potential in cool climates. Container culture is possible with moist humus-peaty media, also suitable for forcing under glass, especially the pure white forms. Some cultivars and varieties include:

'Album', 'Album-Novum', both pure white; var. *gloriosoides*, from China and

Taiwan, leaves narrower, segments spotted white scarlet-red; 'Krëtzeri', white flowers with central green stripe; 'Magnificum', stems reddish, flowers large, suffused crimson with pink spots; 'Melpomene', flowers deep carmine, segments with white margins; 'Punctatum', white flowers flushed pink, spotted red; 'Roseum', stems green, flowers carmine; 'Rubrum', stems purple, with flower segments carmine, red-spotted flowers; 'Uchida', selected for its vigor and strong pink color. All are good for forcing. z5

L. sulphureum Bak. **(TR)** (*L. myriophyllum* Franch.). China, Yunnan, Shan States (E. Burma) and Upper Burma. Grows at 1200–1500m. Bulb red-purple, to 10cm in diameter, stem 1–1.8m high, erect, with numerous, alternate, linear-lanceolate leaves to 20cm long, and with bulbils in the axils of the upper leaves.

Flowers 1–15 in a raceme or sub-umbel, horizontal trumpets 15–20cm long, throat deep yellow turning ivory, exterior wine-red more or less turning pink, fragrant. Sets seed poorly. Very temperamental species. Not generally cultivated, but used in hybridizing. Late summer. z7

L. superbum L. **(AM)**. N. America, mostly in the USA along the east coast to Alabama. Grows in a rich humus on moist slopes and in acid soil meadows and marshes. Rootstock of stout stolons with few scales, terminating in round, acuminate, whitish bulbs. Stems purple, to 3m high in cultivation. Lower leaves lanceolate in whorls, upper leaves alternate. Pyramidal inflorescence with few to 40 long pedicelled, large, nodding, Turk's Cap flowers, orange-yellow with carmine-red tips, brown speckled throat, green. Flower colors vary from yellow to red. Thrives in a deep, lime-free, moist soil. Should be planted 15–20cm deep on a gravelly substrate in full sun to light shade. Good for filling in, as feature plants, among dwarf shrubs. Rather scarce in cultivation. Blooms early- to midsummer. z5–9

L. szovitsianum Fisch. ex Avé-Lall. **(CA)**. In southern Transcaucasian forests, woodland clearings, mountain slopes of the subalpine zone (Kura River region), and the south bank of the Black Sea. Grows between 600 and 1500m elevation. Bulb large; stems 1–1.15m high, with alternate, oblong-lanceolate leaves usually with 8, but 1–20 flowers in garden culture. Flowers light yellow, nearly Turk's Cap form, but only half reflexed. Should be transplanted in fall to a loamy soil and mulched heavily. Cultivated like the closely related *L. monadelphum*. z5

L. taliense Franch. W. China, Tali Mts. Bulbs globose, of many scales. Stems often grow horizontally underground for some distance before emerging to grow upright to 1.5m. Leaves many to scattered, alternate, linear-lanceolate, to 12cm long. Flowers in a raceme, 1–5 or rarely more, Turk's Cap form, white to cream with many purple spots, fragrant. Much used in hybridizing. z6

L. tenuifolium see **L. pumilum**

L. tigrinum see **L. lancifolium**

L. tsingtauense Gilg **(MA)**. Korea, Tsingtao (China). Stems 40–90cm high, leaves in whorls, the uppermost alternate, oblong-lanceolate to 7.5cm long,

glabrous; leaf blade may be lightly marbled possibly indicating a virus infection. Inflorescence subumbellate with 1–6 flowers, which are erect with spreading segments, sessile cupform, glossy orange-red with reddish spots, not totally symmetrical in radial arrangement. June. This lily is used for breeding, particularly with the *Martagon-Hansonii* Hybrids. Appears quite vigorous, seed slow to germinate. z6

L. umbellatum. Botanically *L. philadelphicum* var. *andinum* but in horticulture generally *L.* × *hollandicum* (= *L. maculatum* × *L. bulliferum* or *L. bulbiferum* var. *croceum*.)

L. volmeri Eastw. NW. California and SW. Oregon, on boggy ground. Rootstock of sturdy stolons with few scales and with bulbous tips. Stems to 1m.; leaves alternate or rarely whorled, linear-lanceolate, to 15cm long. Flowers 1–3, rarely several, in a raceme, nodding, Turk's Cap form with perianth segments strongly reflexed, to 7.5cm long, yellow to reddish-orange, in midsummer. A rare and demanding lily. z7(6)

L. wallichianum Schult. et Schult. f. **(LO)**. Grows on the south side of the E. Himalaya Mts., Nepal, Bhutan, Sikkim. Stems grow horizontally below ground before emerging to reach 1.8m high. Leaves many, alternate, linear-lanceolate to 25cm long. One or rarely several slender, horizontal trumpet flowers, cream-white inside, greenish white outside, fragrant. Not reliably winter hardy, better suited for greenhouse culture. z7(6)

L. wardii F.C. Stern **(AS)**. SE. Tibet in the Tsangpo Valley (reaches to the Brahmaputra Valley). Grows at 1500–3000m in thickets and coniferous forests on steep slopes and dry sites. Found in 1924 by the English plant collector Frank Kingdon Ward for whom it was named. Bulbs small, round. The stem migrates slightly in the soil before emerging to 1.5m high with many scattered, dark green, lanceolate leaves. The racemose inflorescences bear up to 40 Turk's Cap flowers, deep pink with carmine spots, fragrant. For a well-drained, lime-free soil, in loam and leafmold. Scarce in culture. July to August. z5

L. washingtonianum Kellogg **(AM)**. Washington Lily. California, Sierra Nevada, Mount Shasta, Cascade Mts. Bulbous rhizome (or stoloniferous rootstock with bulbous tips), stems to 1.2m or taller, with broadly lanceolate leaves

to 15cm long. Blooms in June to July with 2–20 horizontal trumpet flowers with slightly reflexed petals, pure white with a purple-spotted throat, gradually turning to purple-lilac, fragrant. Not easily cultivated, tolerates neither cold, drought, nor excessive wetness. Slow to germinate. And *L. washingtonianum* var. *minor*, smaller than the type, from the base of Mt. Shasta. *L. washingtonianum* var. *purpurascens* with smaller white to wine red flowers which fade to purple-lilac. The bulbs deteriorate quickly when stored in open air. z7

L. wigginsii Beane & Vollmer. N. California. Stoloniferous, the thick stolons with scattered scales and terminal bulbs. Stems to 90cm tall; leaves alternate or whorled in the middle of the stem, to 13cm long. Flowers horizontal to nodding, perianth segments flairing, strongly reflexed from the middle, to 7cm long, bright yellow, spotted or finely dotted purple. z7

L. wilsonii Leichtl. **(AS)** (*L. maculatum* Thunb.). Possibly from Japan. Validity of this lily as a natural species may be debatable; often included as a variety of *L. maculatum*. Bulbs white, globose; stems 90cm high with lanceolate, variably arranged leaves. Flowers in an umbel, large, cup-shaped and erect, 12cm in diameter, reddish orange with golden yellow midstripes and large dark brown spots, in midsummer or later. Plant 10–15cm deep in light loam soil, in full sun or partial shade. Cv. 'Flavum' is a primula yellow-flowering form. Both are used in hybridizing for their vigor. z5

Lily hybrids

The classification of lily hybrids in England and America is substantially dependent on the parent species and divided into 8 groups:

    I. Asiatic Hybrids
   II. Turk's Cap (Martagon) Hybrids
 III. Candidum Hybrids
 IV. American Hybrids
  V. Longiflorum Hybrids
 VI. Trumpet Hybrids
VII. Oriental (Japanese) Hybrids
VIII. Other hybrids of various origin

I. Asiatic Hybrids

This group includes all the hybrid lilies from the Asiatic species section, plus *L. bulbiferum* and *L. dauricum*. It is further subdivided into 3 classes according to flower arrangement:

1a) flowers erect, early blooming
1b) horizontal (outward) facing flowers
1c) nodding flowers

The table beginning below lists the best hybrids in the trade as well as some of the better old cultivars. It should be understood that many of the old lilies for forcing have undergone substantial improvement. Heights given are the average for plants under favorable cultural conditions. The flowering times correspond to USDA hardiness zone 6. The information regarding a plant's origin comes from the breeder, the literature, and particularly the International Lily Register of the RHS, 1982 and its subsequent supplements so far produced annually since then.

Abbreviations:
OBF = Oregon Bulb Farms, USA
Vl d H = Vletter de Haan, Holland
Laan = Laan Brothers, Holland
St + P = Stone and Payne, USA
Wadekamper = Julius Wadekamper, USA
Use—O = Outdoor, G = Greenhouse, C = Container

All cultivars are clones; strains not designated.

Asiatic Hybrids

Name	Class	Height in meters	Flowering Period	Description	Use	Breeder and Year of intro. Distributor
'Achilles'	1a	1.0	late	yellow with darker spots	O G	C. North 1970 Lingarden Holland
'Agnes Bernauer' Tigrinum Hybrid	1b	1.2	midseason	orange-red with a reddish sheen, dark brown spots, with bulbils	O	Feldmaier 1977
'Algoma'	1b	1.0	midseason	golden yellow, lightly spotted, long flower pedicels	O	Byam 1968 Wadekamper
'Amber Gold'	1c	1.2	midseason	butter yellow Turk's Cap flowers with brown spots	O G	deGraaff 1963 OBF
'Armada'	1a	1.2	early	dark blood red, shallow flared, bowl shaped flowers, black spotted	O G	deGraaff 1966 Holland
'Avalon'	1a	1.0	midseason	pure white, very spotted, floriferous, sturdy	O G	OBF 1978
'Bellona'	1a	0.7	early to midseason	yellow-orange bowl shaped flowers, lightly spotted	O G	Laan 1975 Holland
'Bianca'	1a	0.8	midseason	pure white, with few spots, floriferous	O G	deJong Holland
'Bittersweet' 'Fuga'	1c	1.2	midseason	glossy orange-red, large Turk's Cap flowers	O G	OBF Holland
'Black Butterfly'	1c	1.2	early to midseason	panicles of dark scarlet red flowers with a blackish sheen	O	Simonet 1966 Wadekamper
'Brauner Bär'	1b	1.5	midseason to late	a subdued orange bowl shaped flower with reddish veins, brown-spotted with axillary bulbils	O	Feldmaier 1972 Wadekamper
Bronzino Fiesta Hybrid	1c	1.0	midseason	bronze toned in reddish and orange, Turk's Cap flowers	O	deGraaff 1959 Holland
'Burgundy' Fiesta Hybrid	1c	1.2	midseason	panicles with wine red Turk's Cap flowers	O G	deGraaff 1959 Holland
'Charisma'	1a	0.3	early	orange bowl flowers with yellow, not spotted	O G	OBF 1976

Name	Class	Height in meters	Flowering Period	Description	Use	Breeder and Year of intro. Distributor
'Chinook'	1a	0.9	midseason	ocher yellow, open bowl flowers, sturdy	O G	OBF 1972
'Chiquita'	1a	0.9	midseason	canary yellow, inside green-yellow, dark spotted, sturdy	O	Wadekamper 1976
'Cinnabar' Midcentury Hybrid	1a	0.8	early	bright red cup flowers, center darker spotted	O G C	OBF 1950
Citronella Fiesta Hybrid	1c	1.0	midseason	lemon yellow selection, Turk's Cap shape	O G	OBF 1958 P. Groot Holland
'Concorde'	1a	0.8	midseason	lemon yellow, brown-spotted	O G	Vl d H 1976 Holland
'Connecticut Beauty' ('Medaillon')	1a	1.0	midseason	large bright yellow flowers, tips white, lightly speckled	O G	St + P 1958 Holland
'Connecticut King'	1a	0.7	midseason	cadmium yellow, center golden yellow, not spotted, very vigorous	O G	St + P 1967 OBF Holland
'Connecticut Lemonglow'	1b	0.8	midseason	lemon yellow without spots, vigorous	O G	St + P 1965 Wadekamper Holland
'Connecticut Yankee'	1c	1.2	midseason	large flowers, salmon orange, not spotted	O G	St + P 1958 Wadekamper
'Corsage'	1b	1.0	midseason	soft pink with cream and yellow, small flowers, produces no pollen	O G	deGraaff 1958 OBF Wadekamper
'Czardas'	1a	1.0	midseason	bowl shaped brown-red flowers, center light yellow-orange, with secondary and tertiary flowers	O	Hoerster 1978 Wadekamper
'Dayspring'	1a	0.7	midseason	lemon yellow cup flowers, the centers turning gold, sparsely spotted	O G	OBF 1977 Holland
'Diana'	1a	0.8	midseason	dark yellow, sparsely spotted	O G	deJong Holland
'Diskus'	1a	0.9	midseason	flat Saturn red bowl shape, sparsely brown-spotted	O G	Feldmaier 1978
'Destiny'	1a	0.8	early	golden yellow, brown-spotted, tips recurved	O	deGraaff 1949 OBF Holland
'Earlybird' Preston Hybrid	1b	0.7	early	apricot orange, center with spots, early bloomer	O	Porter 1956 Wadekamper
'Earl of Rochester'	1a	0.9	midseason	floriferous, erect bowl shaped flowers, yellow, very vigorous	O	Tesca 1972 Wadekamper
'Embarrassment' Scottiae Hybrid	Ib 1c	1.0	midseason	pink, floriferous panicles	O G	Simonet 1975 Wadekamper
'Enchantment' Midcentury Hybrid	1a	0.9	midseason	nasturtium orange-red, flared bowl shaped flowers, the best for forcing	O G C	deGraff 1944 Holland

Name	Class	Height in meters	Flowering Period	Description	Use	Breeder and Year of intro. Distributor
'Esther'	1a	1.2	midseason	orange-red with a nasturtium blush, dark brown spots	O G	I. Boon 1980 Holland
Fiesta Hybrid	1c	0.8 to 1.0	midseason	various colors of yellow, orange, bronze, and red with Turk's Cap flowers	O G	deGraaff 1946 Holland
'Firebrand' ('Prominenz')	1a	0.7	early	bright red bowl shaped flowers, dark, glossy foliage	O G C	OBF 1977
'Firecracker'	1a	1.0	midseason	dark cherry red with purple spots, white nectaries, very vigorous	O	OBF 1974 Holland
'Fireking'	1b	0.9	early	good orange-red bowl shaped flower, tips recurved	O G	Holland 1946
Golden Chalice Hybrid	1a	0.5 to 0.9	early	attractive bowl shaped flowers in various shades of gold-orange, low	O G C	deGraaff 1947 Holland
'Golden Melody' ('Gold Lode')	1a	1.0	midseason	pure yellow bowl shaped flowers with some gold, spotted in the center	O G	Windus Wadekamper Holland
'Grand Prix'	1a	0.8	midseason	orange-red with pale brown veins, dark brown spots in the throat	O G	Bischoff-Tulleken 1980 Holland
Harlequin Hybrid	1c	1.0	midseason	pastel colors ivory, yellow, pink, soft lilac, terra cotta, Turk's Cap shape	O G	deGraaff 1950 OBF Holland
'Harmony' Midcentury Hybrid	1a	0.8	early	orange with reddish throat, with broad segments, brown-spotted	O G C	deGraaff 1950 OBF Holland
'Harvest'	1a	0.6	early	lemon yellow–orange, broad segments, brown-spotted	O G C	OBF 1978 Holland
'Hawaiian Punch'	1b	0.6	midseason	lavender-pink with dark spots	O	Koehler 1968 Wadekamper
'Herkules'	1a	1.2	late	golden yellow bowl shaped flower with golden colored center brown-spotted, large-flowered, vigorous	O G	deJong 1979 Holland
'Herold'	1a	1.0	midseason to late	persimmon orange bowl shaped flowers shading to orange	O G	Feldmaier 1977
L. × hollandicum 'Erect'	1a	0.5 to 0.8	early to midseason	glossy red bowl shaped flowers shading to orange	O	Krelage Holland
L. × hollandicum 'Golden Fleece'	1a	0.5 to 0.8	early to midseason	golden yellow, tips reddish	O	Holland
L. × hollandicum 'Invincible'	1a	0.5 to 0.8	early to midseason	stylish bowl shaped flowers, deep orange, tips reddish	O	

Name	Class	Height in meters	Flowering Period	Description	Use	Breeder and Year of intro. Distributor

L. × hollandicum, other old forms are rarely available

   From *L. × maculatum × L. bulbiferum croceum*

Name	Class	Height in meters	Flowering Period	Description	Use	Breeder and Year of intro. Distributor
'Hornback's Gold'	1c	1.2	midseason	mimosa yellow, large flowers, very spotted	O G	OBF 1972
'Joan Evans' Midcentury Hybrid	1a	1.0	early to midseason	orange with a reddish throat, red-brown spots	O G	deGraaff 1950 OBF
'John Dix'	1b	1.0	early	pure orange, with small spots, segments recurved	O G	van der Zweet 1958 Holland
'Juliana'	1a	0.8	midseason	cream colored to white, slightly spotted, vigorous	O G	OBF 1977 Holland
'Katinka'	1b	1.0	midseason	flowers soft salmon pink with cream white tips, brown spotted, vigorous	O	Mattas 1964 Wadekamper
'Ladykiller'	1a	0.7	midseason	flowers persimmon orange, spots blood red	O	Laan 1974 Holland
'Levant'	1c	1.2	midseason	pyramidal raceme, with secondary and tertiary flowers chrome yellow, reddish-spotted	O G	Laan Holland
L. × maculatum (*L. × elegans*) 'Alice Wilson'	1a	0.4 to 0.5	early	flower bowl shaped, lemon yellow, red-spotted	O	Holland?
L. × maculatum (*L. × elegans*) 'Batemaniae'	1a	0.8 to 1.0	early to midseason	flower bowl shaped, apricot colored, not spotted	O	Holland?
L. × maculatum (*L. × elegans*) 'Mahogany'	1a	0.5 to 0.6	early to midseason	flower bowl shaped with broad segments, bright crimson to mahogany red	O	Holland

L. × maculatum, other old forms are seldom available

   From *L. dauricum × L. maculatum*

Name	Class	Height in meters	Flowering Period	Description	Use	Breeder and Year of intro. Distributor
'Manuella'	1a	0.8	midseason	bright red, throat primula yellow	O G	Laan 1975
'Matchless'	1a	1.0	midseason	dark orange, not spotted, tall stemmed, wide leaves	O G	OBF 1979
'Maxwill'	1c	1.2	midseason	Saturn red, dark-spotted, Turk's Cap shape	O	Skinner 1932
Milk and Honey	1a	0.9	early	soft sulfur yellow with dark orange center, nectary channel green, not spotted	O	St + P 1967
'Ming Yellow'	1b	0.9	midseason	bright yellow with reddish spots, greenish center, floriferous	O G	OBF 1976 Wadekamper
'Mont Blanc'	1a	0.6	midseason	pure white, center lightly spotted	O G	Vl d H 1978 Holland
'Moulin Rouge'	1b	1.0	midseason	orange-red with light orange, black-brown spots	O G	Vl d H 1978 Holland

Name	Class	Height in meters	Flowering Period	Description	Use	Breeder and Year of intro. Distributor
'Nutmegger'	1c	1.2	midseason to late	canary yellow, dark brown spots, segments recurved, vigorous	O	St + P 1964 Wadekamper
'Obrist'	1a	1.4	midseason	flat bowl shaped flowers, burnt orange, sparsely brown-spotted, very vigorous	O	Feldmaier 1978
'Panamint'	1c	0.8	midseason	cream colored with pink, Turk's Cap shape	O	deGraaff 1964 Wadekamper
'Paprika'	1b	0.7	early	bright crimson bowl shaped flowers, black-brown spotted	O G C	deGraaff 1958 Holland
'Parfait'	1a 1b	0.6	midseason	large flowered, dark apricot, center golden yellow, sparsely spotted	O G C	OBF 1976 Holland
Pastel Hybrid	1a 1b	0.8	early	pastel color, flared bowl shaped flowers, white, cream-pink, yellow, small flowers	O G	OBF 1976 Holland
'Peachblush'	1a 1b	0.8	midseason	large flowered, flat bowl shaped flower, salmon-apricot, few spots, very good cut flower	O G	OBF 1972 Holland
'Picasso'	1a	0.9	midseason	dark orange with red-brown markings in the center	O G	OBF 1978 Holland
'Pink Champagne'	1b	1.0	midseason	yellowish with pink blush, flower segment tips pink, reflexed, very vigorous	O	Porter Wadekamper
'Pink Tiger'	1b	0.8	midseason to late	pink-lilac, brown-red spotted	O	Laan 1976 Holland
'Pirate'	1a	1.0	early to midseason	nasturtium red flared bowl shape, tips orange, vigorous	O G	deGraaff 1966 Holland
'Prawn Tiger'	1c	1.5	midseason to late	lobster red, with few spots, large flowered, very tall	O	St + P 1974 Wadekamper
'Primrose Green'	1a	1.2	midseason	light primula yellow with a green center, light brown spots	O G	St + P 1976 Wadekamper
'Prince Charming'	1a	1.0	midseason	lilac pink with a white center, few spots	O	deGraaff 1964 Wadekamper
'Prosperity'	1b	0.8	early to midseason	canary yellow, center dark-spotted	O G	deGraaff OBF 1955
Rainbow Hybrid	1a	0.6	early	flared bowl shaped flowers in yellow, orange, and red	O G C	deGraaff 1948 OBF
'Red Bess'	1c	1.2	midseason	currant red, nectary channel white, with few spots	O	St + P 1969 Wadekamper
'Redbird'	1a	1.0	early	flared bowl shaped flowers, glossy red with dark red, black spotted	O	E. F. Palmer 1957 OBF

Name	Class	Height in meters	Flowering Period	Description	Use	Breeder and Year of intro. Distributor
'Red Carpet'	1a	0.3	early	scarlet bowl shaped flowers, not spotted	O G	Porter 1960 Wadekamper
'Red Fox'	1c	1.0	midseason	racemes of dark to brown-red Turk's Cap flowers, dark brown spotted	O	Laan 1963
'Red Knight'	1c	1.0	midseason	floriferous racemes with waxy red Turk's Cap flowers, spotted	O	Wright 1957 Wadekamper
'Red Lion'	1a	1.0	midseason	scarlet, bowl shaped flowers, with few spots, floriferous	O G	Laan 1978 Holland
'Red Night'	1b	0.8	midseason	dark black-red bowl shaped flowers; with axillary bulbils	O G C	Laan Holland
'Red Tiger'	1b	1.2	midseason	blood red, reflexed flowers with few spots, vigorous	O St + P	Warner 1964 Wadekamper
'Red Velvet'	1b	1.2	early	dark red flowers, somewhat reflexed, sparsely spotted	O	St + P 1964 Wadekamper
'Rosabelle'	1a	0.8	late	deep pink flared bowl shaped flowers with brown-red spots	O	Porter 1956 Wadekamper
'Rosita'	1a	0.8	early	purple-red, dark-spotted, early	O G	deJong 1979 Holland
'Roter Cardinal'	1a	0.7	midseason	dark red, with a splash of brown-red, spotted	O G	Laan 1974 Holland
'Roter Prinz'	1b	1.5	early to midseason	racemes with brick red, flared, bowl shaped flowers, brown-spotted, black nectaries	O G	Feldmaier 1955
'Sahara'	1a	0.6	midseason	yellow-orange with lemon yellow	O G	Bischoff-Tulleken 1940 Holland
'Sally'	1c	1.2	midseason	red-orange, tips yellow-orange, brown spotted	O	Lighty 1965 Wadekamper
'Sandra'	1a	1.0	midseason	orange-red, centers black spotted, large flowered	O G	deJong 1979 Holland
'Scarlet Emperor'	1a	0.6	early	scarlet red bowl shaped flowers, with small spots, very leafy stems	O G	OBF 1976
'Schellenbaum'	1b	1.8	midseason	racemes to 2m high, to 40 flowers, capsicum red, orange centers, brown-red papilla and spots, triploid, very vigorous	O	Feldmaier 1955 Wadekamper
'Schützenlisl'	1b	1.2	midseason to late	umbels with up to 12 bowl shaped flowers, persimmon orange, brown spotted	O	Feldmaier 1966 Wadekamper

Name	Class	Height in meters	Flowering Period	Description	Use	Breeder and Year of intro. Distributor
'Showboat'	1a	1.0	early to midseason	chestnut brown, flared, bowl shaped flowers with white nectary spot	O G	OBF 1975
'Silvia'	1a	0.7	early	marigold orange, cup shaped flowers, center spotted	O G	deJong 1978
'Sonja'	1a	0.7	midseason	lemon yellow, brown spotted	O G	deJong 1978 Holland
'Sonnentiger'	1a	1.0	midseason	umbels of wide bowl shaped, golden yellow flowers, centers saffron yellow, brown spotted	O G	Feldmaier 1960 Wadekamper
Southern Belles	1c	1.0	midseason	a new *L. lankongense* × Asiatic Lily cross, soft pink Turk's Cap flowers, clear pink outside	O G	Columbia-Platte-Marshall 1980 Wadekamper
'Sterling Star'	1a	1.0	midseason	white to light cream-colored, flared bowl shaped flowers, center reddish-spotted	O G	OBF 1973 Holland
'Sun Ray'	1a	0.7	midseason	cadmium yellow, centers golden yellow, nectary channel greenish, slightly spotted	O G C	St + P 1965 Wadekamper
'Sunrise'	1b	0.5	midseason	white flared bowl shaped flowers, shaded pink	O G C	OBF 1974
Sutter's Gold	1c	1.2	midseason	racemes of chrome yellow, nodding, wide flared flowers, dark brown spotted	O	deGraaff 1964 Wadekamper
'Suzanna'	1a	0.9	midseason	canary yellow bowl shape, center spotted, vigorous	O G	deJong 1978
'Tabasco'	1a	0.5	midseason	red-brown bowl shaped flowers	O G	deGraaff 1958
'Talisman'	1c	1.2	midseason	Saturn red Turk's Cap flowers in elongate racemes	O	deGraaff 1949
'Tamara'	1a	0.5	early	pink, center amber yellow, blood red spotted	O G	deJong 1978
'Tetra Mountaineer'	1a	0.9	early	dark red bowl shaped flowers, dark-spotted, tetraploid	O	Emsweller 1960 Feldmaier
'Trues Herz'	1a	1.0	midseason to late	umbels with nasturtium-orange bowl shaped flowers, spotted center	O	Feldmaier 1968 Wadekamper
'Twilight'	1b	0.9	midseason	deep pink flared flowers, segments recurved, lightly spotted	O G C	OBF 1976 Holland
'Uncle Sam'	1a	0.9	midseason	glossy canary yellow, large flowered, black spotted	O G	deGraaff 1964 Holland

Name	Class	Height in meters	Flowering Period	Description	Use	Breeder and Year of intro. Distributor
'Vanguard'	1a 1b	1.2	midseason	orange-yellow with conspicuous red-brown spots	O G	OBF Wadekamper
'Vonnie'	Ib 1c	1.0	midseason	bronze-yellow, segments recurved, throat and nectary channel green	O	Kroell 1976 Wadekamper
'White Tiger'	1b	0.6	midseason	small white flowers with purple spots	O	St + P 1968 Wadekamper
'Yellow Blaze'	1a	1.0	late	canary yellow bowl shaped flowers with darker spots	O	St + P 1965 Wadekamper
'Zigeunerliebe'	1b	0.9	midseason	bright red with a scarlet blush, center salmon red spotted	O G	deJong 1979

II. Martagon Hybrids

Includes hybrids involving *L. martagon*, *L. hansonii*, *L. tsingtauense* and *L. medeoloides*.

Some significant hybrids with vigorous habit and light yellow to orange, thick, fleshy flowers are: *L. × dalhansonii* Powell (C. Bader-Powell 1980), from *L. dalmaticum* (*L. martagon cattaniae*) × *L. hansonii* and the Marhan Hybrids (Tubergen 1886) from *L. martagon* var. *album* × *L. hansonii*. *L. × dalhansonii* produces floriferous, pyramidal inflorescences of glossy reddish brown flowers with orange centers.

The modern Paisley Hybrids (Jan de Graaff) with stems to 1.2m high, bear flowers of light yellow, orange and salmon to wine red.

J.S. Dijt (Texel, Holland), has introduced some new Marhan Hybrids, the best of which is called 'Jacques S. Dijt' (cream-yellow with red spots).

In recent years, hybrids between *L. tsingtauense* and the Marhan Hybrids have been made by Ed Robinson (Wanesa, Canada), Joachim Petruske (Berlin, Germany) and Otto Beutnagel (Braunschweig, W. Germany). These plants are very vigorous and quite promising, but not yet generally available. The cross between *L. martagon* and *L. medeoloides* has not yet produced a noteworthy hybrid.

III. Candidum Hybrids

L. × testaceum Lindl. is generally recognized as the first hybrid. Found as a chance seedling in 1836 by F.A. Haage (Erfurt, E. Germany) in a shipment of Dutch Lily bulbs and determined to be a cross of *L. candidum* with *L. chalcedonicum*. Cultivate like *L. candicum*. 'June Fragrance' (*L. candidum × L. monadelphum*) is a hybrid from Robinson with *L. candidum* characteristics in soft yellow. This lily is significant in that it hybridizes with the various Asiatic hybrids resulting in strong-colored hybrids of the *L. candidum* type. These are very promising plants being developed by Wilbert G. Ronald and Oregon Bulb Farms.

IV. American Hybrids

Some American species cross readily with each other, especially within geographically related species. Many hybrids have resulted from crosses between; *L. harrisianum*, *L. pardalinum*, *L. humboldtii*, *L. parryi*, *L. kelloggii*, *L. bolanderi*, *L. nevadense*, *L. pitkinense* and others. These plants require sandy humus to peaty soil in a moist, maritime climate. One of the more popular of the American crosses in the Bellingham Hybrids strain, developed by David Griffith of Bellingham, Washington, in 1924. Of the 10 clones, 'Shuksan' and the Jan de Graaff introductions 'Afterglow' and 'Buttercup' are most widely grown in the trade. These lilies grow to about 1.5m high with racemose inflorescences. Flowers are Martagon form, mostly yellow, lemon and orange with carmine petal tips and usually brown spots. Some recent cultivars from the Oregon Bulb Farms include 'Robin' (strong red), 'Bunting' (soft pink) and 'Nightingale' (deep magenta red) with stout flower stalks. Should be planted in a fertile, moist, sandy, lime-free, acidic humus soil. Highly recommended as floriferous, easily propagated lilies for semi-shade. Suitable for planting among rhododendrons and dwarf shrubs.

Some recent crosses with *L. kelloggii*, by Dr. Fritz Ewald, of Leiferde, W. Germany, have proven particularly well suited to the European climate.

V. Longiflorum Hybrids

Included here are all the hybrids involving *L. longiflorum*, *L. formosanum*, *L. neilgherense* and *L. wallichianum*. All have beautiful, long, trumpet-shaped flowers. Some promising hybrids for the future are being developed by the Japanese breeders, Hiroshi Myodo and Yoshito Asano at the Hokkaido University, Sapporo. These are crosses between *L. longiflorum* and various other lilies, including the Asiatic Hybrids, produced by embryo culture. The results of this work may one day be colorful Longiflorum Hybrids for the open landscape.

VI. Trumpet Hybrids

A large number of very vigorous garden lilies has resulted from crosses between the various trumpet-flowered lilies and these and their progeny with *L. henryi*. These have been somewhat neglected, however, in the USA in recent years and the availability of strains and cultivars in this class has shrunk. Possibly their powerful scent, which may be a liability for cut flowers in a room, accounts for this lack of interest but if these lilies are kept in the garden the scent is a bonus, not a problem. The first cross was by Professor F. Scheubel (Germany) in 1913 when he pollinated *L. sulphureum* with *L. regale* pollen. The resulting hybrid was *L. × sulphurgale*, now cultivated in England. In 1916 a spontaneous cross occurred between *L. regale* and *L. sargentiae* in the Farquhar Nursery, Roslindale, Massachusetts. It was named *L. × imperiale* and appears to be intermediate between the parents, but with wide flaring flowers. Prof. J.W. Crow of Ontario crossed *L.* × *sulphurgale* with *L.* × *imperiale*. These Crow Hybrids were later named *L.* × *gloriosum* and are quite vigorous with mostly ivory white flowers with greenish throats; they are nearly forgotten in cultivation today. The current market is dominated by named cultivars of Trumpet and Aurelian Hybrids. The Aurelian Hybrids were developed by E. Debras from Orleans, France. They are a result of the cross *L. sargentiae* × *L. henryi*. The large, white- to orange-colored hybrids were named for their place of origin, *L.* × *aurelianense*. The

in a vase, 1.5–2m (OBF)

Carrara, strain, pure white trumpet lily of good structure (OBF)

Copper King, strain, very vigorous, with large, orange- to apricot-colored, wide open trumpets, exterior with copper- to chestnut-colored ribs, 1.2–1.5m (OBF)

'Gold Eagle', a newcomer with very wide, reflexed petals, 1.5–1.8m high, August (Strahm, Rex)

Golden Splendor, strain, with large trumpet-shaped, rich golden yellow flowers, exterior with reddish ribs, 1–1.5m (OBF)

Golden Sunburst, strain, deep golden

form with a yellow throat, bears up to 20 flowers, 1–1.5m high (OBF)

Shellrose Hybrids, shellrose to amethyst pink trumpets, 1.2–1.5m (Rex)

'Thunderbolt', clone, with golden yellow stellate flowers, resembling its parent *L. henryi* (OBF)

'White Henryi', clone, with wide flaired, cream-colored flowers; the interior is orange spotted; an elegant lily, 1.5m, August (Woodruff)

All of these trumpet lilies and Aurelian Hybrids grow between 1–1.8m high and flower variously from early to late July. They need an average, fertile,

Cardiocrinum giganteum. See page 359.

Lilium hansonii

Lilium pumilum

following Trumpet and Aurelian Hybrids, just a sample of the current listing, may be found in the trade as various strains, mostly propagated by seed, though the cultivars are cloned by scales or tissue culture. Their origins are noted by the following abbreviations:
OBF = Oregon Bulb Farms; Sandy, Oregon
Rex = Rex Bulb Farms; Port Townsend, Washington
Woodriff = Leslie Woodriff; McKinleyville, California

Black Dragon, strain, with large, exceptionally abundant trumpet flowers, pure white inside, purple-brown outside. A very attractive lily for displaying

yellow, like 'Golden Splendor, but with wide-open trumpets, 1–1.5m (OBF)

'Honey Dew', clone, long, yellow-green trumpets with greenish reverse, has a classical, attractive pyramidal inflorescence, 1.2–1.5m (OBF)

Jade Emperor, strain, with long white trumpets, shaded greenish in the throat, and brownish purple outside, 1.2–1.8m (Rex)

Marble Temple Hybrids, large trumpets, white inside, outside cream or ivory to gold, shaded pink to purple-red, 1.2–1.8m (Rex)

Pink Perfection, strain, with fuchsia red trumpets of exceptional beauty, 1.5–2m (OBF)

Sentinel, strain, also a white trumpet

humus-rich, well-drained garden soil to thrive. The bulbs may be bedded over sand when planted. Protect new shoots from a late frost by mulch if necessary. They are suitable for a dominant position in the perennial bed. Avoid underplanting them with low, cushion-form plants as these will harbor slugs which feed on the young lily shoots. They are best planted in groups of 3–5. Their height and beautiful inflorescences make the trumpet lilies quite conspicuous in the garden. The white trumpet lilies are particularly effective against a dark background. All the red and pink forms should be given only partial sun, since the red flowers will fade and turn gray in bright sunshine.

These plants can reach a height of 2m and therefore should be protected from strong winds. Because of their tall stems, the bulbs must be planted sufficiently deep, 10–15cm. Every garden planting should include a sample of these trumpet or Aurelian Hybrid lilies. Their beauty, size and fragrance in early to midsummer are a yearly experience not to be missed.

Lily societies and breeders generally recognize subdivisions within the Trumpet Lilies and Aurelian Hybrids Class:

mate with neutral to acidic soil; otherwise, they may be grown in the proper soil in containers with the cans set out or into the ground each growing season. The potting media should be a lime-free peat and loam mix. The bulbs should also be bedded in sand. Set the containers in a sunny, but windless site as buds develop.

The first breeders to be successful in this group were Australians. Among them are Roy M. Wallace, B. Hayler, G. Chandler, E. Genat and Dr.R.M. Withers, as well as Dr.J.S. Yeates from New Zealand. American breeders of the

strong red middle band; Jamboree Strain, crimson red, white-bordered flowers, reflexed; Everest Strain, pure white, recurved; 'Allegra', clone, pure white with a green center. All these hybrids are vigorous, reaching heights of 1.2m with bowl-shaped to reflexed flowers from 18–24cm across. 'Black Beauty; a sterile diploid clone, is an introduction by Leslie Woodriff. It is a rather undemanding cross between *L. henryi* and *L. speciosum* var. *punctatum* which thrives in the open landscape. Plants have attractive, dark green leaves with abundant flowers in August.

Lilium regale

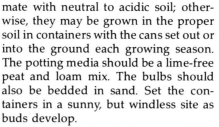

Lilium 'Enchantment', Asiatic hybrid

Lilium 'Milk and Honey', Strain Asiatic hybrid

(a) Trumpet types
(b) Bowl-shaped types
(c) Pendant types
(d) Sunburst types

VII. Oriental (Japanese) Hybrids

L. auratum, L. japonicum, L. rubellum, L. speciosum and more recently *L. alexandrae* and *L. nobilissimum* are the parents of these hybrids, primarily native to Japan. These species and their hybrids are very sensitive to continental climates and alkaline soil. They are better suited for garden culture in a moist, maritime cli-

Oriental Hybrids include G.L. Slate, Dr.S.L. Emsweller, Norma Pfeiffer, Jan de Graaff, Edgar L. Kline and Leslie Woodriff.

Some of the notable Oriental Hybrids are:

From the Oregon Bulb Farms, Oregon: Imperial Crimson Strain, crimson red with a white border; Imperial Silver Strain, white with red spots; Imperial Gold Strain, white with wide, golden mid-stripes, dark red spotted; Imperial Pink Strain, wide bowl-shaped flowers, red to soft pink; Magic Pink Strain, soft pink with dark red speckles; Pink Glory Strain, salmon pink; Red Band Strain, white with a

Flowers are crimson maroon with much reflexed perianth segments and green, starlike throat markings. Even more attractive is the fertile tetraploid form of 'Black Beauty' with flowers twice as large in the same color. This form was recently developed by LeVern Freimann, Bellingham, Washington (USA), but is not yet generally available. (F.)

The Oriental Hybrids (Japanese or Far Eastern) Class often is subdivided as follows:
(a) Trumpet-shaped flowers
(b) Bowl-shaped flowers
(c) Flat-faced flowers
(d) Recurved flowers

Limnanthemum

L. nymphoides see Nymphoides peltata

Limonium Mill.
Plumbaginaceae
Sea Lavender, Marsh-rosemary, Statice

About 150 species of annual or perennial herbs or subshrubs, often woody at the base. Distributed throughout the world in coastal regions, plains and deserts, especially in the Mediterranean region and Central Asia. These was once included, with *Armeria*, in the now abandoned genus *Statice*. Closely related to *Armeria*, but the flowers are in large, panicled inflorescences or spikes. Leaves usually in basal rosettes, simple or pinnatisect. Flowers nearly or entirely sessile. Calyx tube-shaped, often colored, dry membranous, corolla of 5 petals united only at the base. Stamens 5, inserted at the base of the corolla, stigma thread-like. The species of the first group are only conditionally winter hardy and often freeze out in the open landscape, especially during cold, wet winters and so are best grown in an alpine house. In suitable climates, plants should be situated in a rock bed in full sun and very well-drained sandy loam soil. Division of older plants is possible, but not very productive; propagation is therefore usually by seed. Young plants of both groups should be raised in containers so that they may be moved into the garden with a soil ball. The species of the second group are best used for naturalizing, also effective planted at the base of a stone wall. Their wildflower characteristics, however, may make these plants unsuitable for the formal perennial border. All require deep, well-drained, sandy loam and full sun. They produce attractive, long lasting bouquets of cut flowers for dry arranging. The species of this group also are primarily propagated by seed since division is difficult and unproductive. *L. latifolium* may also be propagated by root cuttings. Good companions in the wild garden include *Anaphalis, Achillea, Armeria, Aster linosyris, Eryngium, Inula ensifolia, Nepeta, Oenothera, Santolina* and various grasses.

1. Low, conditionally winter-hardy species

L. **bellidifolium** (Gouan) Dumort. Found on the coasts of the Mediterranean and Black seas, S. Russia, England. Grows in salty marshes along the seacoast and in otherwise salty soil in the USSR. Leaves 1.5–5.5cm long and 3–6mm wide, acute, spatulate, usually wilted or totally lacking at anthesis. Unlike the closely related *L. vulgare*, the 10–30cm high stems are zig-zag flexuose, but not branched. Calyx papery, white. Corolla 4–5mm wide, light violet. Blooms from August to October. Sensitive to frost damage. z8

L. **cosyrense** (Guss.) O. Kuntze. Malta, Pantelleria, Sicily. Found on rocky slopes. Leaves 2–3cm long and 2–3mm wide, obtuse, with revolute margins, in rosettes. Stems somewhat woody, basal, 1–3cm long. Inflorescences to 25cm high, forked, branched, spikelets only single flowered. Calyx about 4mm wide. Blooms from July to August. Scarcely winter hardy, best suited for the alpine house in a gravelly bed or container. z9

L. **gougetianum** (Girard) O. Kuntze. Balearic Islands, Algeria. Grows on saline meadows. Leaves in dense basal rosettes, glabrous, somewhat rough, 1.5–3cm long and 3–9mm wide, obovate to obtuse. Flower scape 10–25cm long, forked from the ground up, with short branchlets. Spikelets 2-flowered. Calyx limb whitish above, underside reddish. Corolla lavender-violet. Flowering from July to August. Best overwintered in an alpine house, but also short-lived. z8

L. **minutum** (L.) Fourr. SE. France. Found on limestone along the coast. Cushionlike tufted perennial with a woody rhizome. Leaves 8–10mm long and 2–3mm wide, spatulate, with revoluted margins, bullate. Flower scapes 2–12cm, branched from the ground up and zig-zagged, usually with many flowerless branchlets. Spikelets 1–4 flowered. Calyx white. Corolla rosy to violet. Blooms from July to August. The smallest of the species described here. Lime-loving plant for the alpine house, difficult to cultivate. z8

2. Taller, mostly winter-hardy species

L. **ferulaceum** (L.) O. Kuntze. W. Mediterranean region. Leaves in a crowded basal rosette. Flower scape to 80cm high with delicate panicles. Flower clusters one-sided with tiny white flowers, later turning lilac. Blooms from July to Fall. Grows best in well-drained loam with a pH of 6.5–7.0. For the first winter mulch the plants with a layer (5cm-thick) of leafmold or straw. Fresh-cut material stays green for up to 2 weeks. Cut material also dries well. Distributed since 1981 as the cultivar 'Karel de Groot'. z7

L. **globulariifolium** see L. **ramosissimum**

L. **gmelinii** (Willd.) O. Kuntze. E. Central and SE. Europe, Siberia. Found on the steppes on alkaline soils. Scapes 20–60cm high, glabrous. Leaves in a basal rosette, 7–11cm long and 2–3cm wide, occasionally larger, spatulate, pinnately veined. Spikelets 1–2 flowered. Calyx limb small, dark purple-blue. Corolla about 5mm wide, pink. Blooms from July to August. z5

L. **latifolium** (Sm.) O. Kuntze., Sea Lavender, Statice. Rumania, Bulgaria to SE. Russia. Grows on the steppes and open grasslands. Scapes 50–80cm high, mostly stellate-pubescent. Leaves 25–60cm long and 8–15cm wide, spatulate to elliptic, sparsely pubescent, pinnately veined. Stems loosely branched, with large, *Gypsophila*-like inflorescences. Calyx whitish, with 5 short, rounded lobes. Corolla about 6mm wide, light violet. Blooms from May to July. 'Violetta' has dark blue flowers. z5

L. **ramosissimum** (Poir.) Maire (*L. globulariifolium* (Desf.) O. Kuntze). Mediterranean region in salt marshes. Quite a variable species, with a woody rootstock. Leaves in basal rosettes 3–10cm long and 0.7–2cm wide, obovate to nearly spatulate, 3-veined, covered with bluish, chalklike spots. Inflorescences to 50cm, but usually not over 20cm high, sparsely branched. Spikelets 1-sided, 2–5 flowered. Corolla 5–7mm wide, light pink. Blooms from June to September. For the alpine house. z8

L. **speciosum** see Goniolimon speciosum

L. **tataricum** see Goniolimon tartaricum

L. **vulgare** Mill. Atlantic coast of Europe, the Baltic Sea, eastward to Ruegen Island and SW. Sweden, Mediterranean region, on saline flats along the sea coast, on moist, salty, sand or sandy clay. Leaves mostly erect in loose basal rosettes, 10–15cm long and 1.5–4cm wide, oblanceolate to spatulate, short-prickly-tipped, tapering at the base to the sheathing widened petiole. Inflorescences 20–40cm high, forming a more or less flattened panicle. Spikelets 2-flowered. Corolla 6–9mm wide, blue-violet. Blooms from July to September. Only for botanic gardens and collectors of coastal flora. Requires a wet clay-loam soil. z6 (E.)

Linaria Mill.
Scrophulariaceae
Toadflax

Depending upon the interpretation, between 75 and 150 species of annual and biennial, as well as perennial herbs in the nontropical zones of the Northern Hemisphere, especially in the Mediterranean region. Similar to *Antirrhinum* but the corolla has a long or short spur at the base and the capsule is 4–10 valved instead of opening by pores. The lower leaves and those of the nonflowering lateral shoots are usually opposite or 3–4 in whorls, the others nearly always alternate. Flowers yellow, white, violet, purple or variegated, in terminal spikes or racemes.

Also see **Cymbalaria**

L. alpina is a charming, often only annual, loose carpetforming alpine plant for the rock garden or trough, in deep, fertile garden soil. Plants are lime-loving, but will also thrive on lime-poor, gravelly-loam soil. Requires a site in full sun, preferably between rocks where it can self-seed but not spread out of bounds. The taller species are suitable for a collector of unusual plants for the perennial border, or sunny dry slopes in the wild garden. They require well-drained sandy loam and full sun, but may not be entirely winter hardy or not very long-lived. Easily perpetuated by seed, division and late summer cuttings. Difficult to transplant, so young plants must be grown in containers for setting out with a soil ball. Resist the temptation to plant the beautiful *L. vulgaris* as it will quickly become a persistent weed. The taller species combine well on a dry slope with *Anaphalis margaritacea, Anthericum liliago, Anthyllis, Filipendula vulgaris, Jasione perennis, Origanum vulgare* and *Salvia pratensis.*

L. aequitriloba see **Cymbalaria aequitriloba**

L. alpina (L.) Mill. Mountains of Central and S. Europe, from the Jura and Carpathians to Central Spain, Central Italy and Central Greece. A gravelly meadow plant of the subalpine and alpine levels to the snow line. Found on moderately moist, usually calcareous, gravelly humus. Short-lived perennial, often grown as an annual, blue-green, carpet-forming plant with procumbent or ascending, 5–25cm long stems, the linear leaves usually in whorls of 4. Flowers usually in crowded racemes of 3–15, corolla violet, with yellow-orange markings on the lower lip, occasionally a pretty whitish or pink. Blooms from June to September. z4

L. anticaria Boiss. et Reut. From S. Spain, where it grows on shaded limestone cliffs. Another rarely offered species of similar habit to *L. alpina.* Recommended only for alpine gardeners. z7

L. cymbalaria see **Cymbalaria muralis**

L. dalmatica see **L. genistifolia** ssp. **dalmatica**

L. genistifolia ssp. **dalmatica** (L.) Maire et Petitm. (*L. dalmatica* (L.) Mill., *L. macedonica* Griseb.). Balkan region, Rumania, S. Italy, Mediterranean region, occasionally naturalized in Central Europe. Grows in dry grassy sites on sunny, shrubby slopes. Also found among weedy growth on rubble and fallow fields. Stems 30–100cm high, erect, with leafy stems, branched mostly above the middle. Leaves ovate to lanceolate, divergent, stiff, corolla yellow, 20–50mm long, with 4–25mm long spurs. Blooms in midsummer. z5

L. glareosa see **Chaenarrhinum glareosum**

L. hepaticifolia see **Cymbalaria hepaticifolia**

L. macedonica see **L. genistifolia** ssp. **dalmatica**

L. origanifolia see **Chaenarrhium origanifolia**

L. pallida see **Cymbalaria pallida**

L. pilosa see **Cymbalaria pilosa**

Linaria purpurea

L. purpurea (L.) Mill. Central and S. Italy, Sicily. Found on dry slopes. Stems 60–80cm high, blue-green, bushy, noninvasive perennial with stems branched on the upper half. Leaves linear, usually in whorls, the uppermost leaves alternate. Flowers in slender, long, crowded racemes. Corolla 9–12mm long, purple-violet, spurs about 5mm long, curved. Flowers from July to October. Cultivar 'Canon Went' has light pink flowers. z6

L. triornithophora (L.) Willd. Three Birds Flying. NW. and W. Central Spain,

N. and Central Portugal. Grows in hedges and brushy thickets. Stems 50–130cm high, light blue-green, erect or spreading perennials with simple or branched stems. Leaves lanceolate to ovate-lanceolate, in whorls of 3, occasionally 4–5. Inflorescences to 10cm long, loose, with 3–15 flowers, usually in whorls of 3. Corolla 35–55mm long, pale lilac, dark lilac striped, with yellow palate. Spurs 16–25mm long. Blooms from July to September. One of the prettiest species, but usually not winter hardy. However, seed can be sown each year in March, potted until May, and then

Linaria alpina

set into the border or a dry slope. Plants will bloom from July on, just 4 months after seeding. z7(6) (E.)

L. villosa see **Chaenarrhinum villosum**

L. vulgaris Mill. Butter-and-eggs, Common Toadflax, Wild-snapdragon. Europe and E. Asia, naturalized in North America. Stems 30–90cm high from a vigorously spreading stoloniferous rootstock. Stems simple to sparsely branched, leaves glaucous, linear flowers in terminal racemes, to 3cm long,

yellow with orange markings on the lower lip, spar about equal to the corolla. Suitable only for naturalizing on rough ground as its invasive behavior is almost unmanageable in the garden. z4

Lindelofia Lehm.
Boraginaceae

About 4 species of annual and perennial herbs from Central Asia, Afghanistan and the Himalayas. Differs from the closely related genus, *Cynoglossum*, in its

longer, 1–1.5cm long, flower tubes and the exserted stamens of equal length.

L. longiflora (Benth.) Baill. (*L. spectabilis* Lehm.). W. Himalaya Mts. between 3000 and 5000m. Pubescent, 30–50cm high perennial herbs with lanceolate to oblong-lanceolate, 7–25cm long, basal leaves, stem leaves cordate, sessile. The bright blue flowers have a long tube with 5 lobes, and are sessile in terminal, racemose scorpioid cymes. Blooms from May to June. Rare, but attractive perennials, conditionally hardy and some-

times short-lived, sensitive to winter wetness. Plants in the garden may be protected by cloches. It is advisable to keep some young plants dry and frost free in the cold frame. Not suitable for the perennial border, rather for the large rock garden on a dry, gravelly, loamy slope in sun or semi-shade. Propagate by seed or careful division. Seedlings flower in the second year after seeding. z7(6) (E.)

L. spectabilis see **L. longiflora**

Linnaea L.
Caprifoliaceae
Twinflower

One species from the cooler regions of the Northern Hemisphere. An attractive, dwarf ground cover for collectors and botanic gardens. Requires a lime-free, moist humus-rich soil and only nonalkaline water. Twinflower should not be considered unless all of these conditions can be met. The best substrate is pure peat, therefore it is a good groundcover for the bog garden where it makes a tight mat, or in the rhododendron bed; otherwise, useful for the heather garden. Generally thrives in light semi-shade, but tolerates full sun where summers are cool. The occasionally offered var. *americana* (J. Forbes) Rehd. is more vigorous than the species. Propagate by division and separation of rooted stem sections. Stems root upon contact with the ground. Good companion species are *Betula nana*, *Empetrum nigrum*, *Vaccinium myrtillus*, *V. uliginosum* and *V. vitis-idaea*, and also its native companion of North American forests, *Cornus canadensis*.

L. borealis L., Twinflower. N. and N. Central Europe, arctic and boreal N. America, N. Asia, Alps, Sudetes, Carpathian, Ural and Caucasus Mts. Grows in mossy coniferous forests, heaths and on the mossy tundra, on moist, infertile, acidic, rough humus soil. A variable species. Creeps with 0.3–10cm (to 4m in its habitat), wiry, long woody shoots. Usually has 8–15cm high secondary shoots on the second-year growth. Leaves evergreen, 5–15mm long and 4–10mm wide, broadly ovate to rounded, crenate on the basal half. The short lateral shoots bear the delicate, campanulate, slightly pendulous flowers, mostly paired, occasionally in 4's on long peduncles. Corolla 7–10mm long, pink or white, interior pubescent and red striped, occasionally with yellow speckles. Fruit a nutlet enveloped by 2 bracts. Blooms from June to August. z1–7 (E.)

Linosyris

L. vulgaris see Aster linosyris

Lindelofia longiflora

Linum L.
Linaceae
Flax

About 200 species in the temperate and subtropical climates of both hemispheres. Annuals, perennials and subshrubs or shrubs with sessile, entire, occasionally glaucous blue leaves. Stipules of some species modified to paired glands at the base of the leaves. Flowers 5 parted, somewhat symmetrical, petals distinct or rarely united at the base, blue, yellow, red, pink or white. Flowers only short-lived, but new ones open daily. Many species are heterostylous. Capsules with 5 or 10 locules, each locule containing a flat, brown or black seed. Flowers from mid-spring to late summer. Grow on a sunny or semi-shaded site in well-drained, not

too heavy soil. Some species are suitable for the rock garden, xerophytic bed or perennial border. Propagate by seed or cuttings of nonflowering shoots from May to August. Good potted plant. Often short-lived, so young plants should be maintained and the mother plant rejuvenated. Needs a loose, brushy cover as protection from the winter sun.

L. alpinum see L. perenne ssp. alpinum

L. anglicum see L. perenne ssp. anglicum

L. arboreum L. Crete, Greece, SW.

Linnaea borealis

Anatolia, Rhodes. A dense, bushy 20 to rarely 50cm high shrublet with many sterile shoots. Flowers golden yellow, in compact, many-flowered cymes. Hardy only on favorable sites, best grown on limestone or in the alpine house. z8

L. aretioides Boiss. Turkey: on the mountain peaks Boz Dag and Baba Dag. High mountain plant with a compact cushion form and singular, golden yellow flowers. Plants were brought into cultivation by English expeditions. Only for the alpine house. z8

L. austriacum L. Central and S. Europe, Mediterranean region, W. Asia to the Caucasus Mts. Similar to L. perenne ssp. perenne, but the fruit stalks droop and flowers azure blue. The cultivar 'Loreyi' is nearly decumbent and the lilac flowers have dark stripes. The subspecies

collinum, rare in cultivation, is smaller overall. z5

L. boissieri see L. elegans

L. boreale see L. perenne ssp. alpinum

L. caespitosum Sibth. et Sm. Crete, i.e. climbing into the Samaria Gorge. Similar to L. arboreum, but dwarf (to only 15cm high). Only for an alpine house. z8

L. campanulatum L. Mediterranean Europe. Suffruticose glabrous perennial; stems 5–25cm high; leaves spatu-

Linum flavum, behind Linum perenne

late to lanceolate with transparent margins. Cymes 3–5 flowered, corolla glowing yellow with orange veins, an appendage of each petal extends downward simulating a perianth tube. Grown in cool moist clusters, plants produce numerous sterile shoots. A dwarf form is described in S. France. z8(7)

L. campanulatum L. W. Mediterranean region. 5–25cm high, charming dwarf form from SE. France. With numerous, nonflowering rosettes. Inflorescences 3–5 flowered. Petals 25–35mm long, bright yellow, with a long, drawn out claw, making the flowers appear tube form. z7

L. capitatum Kit. ex Schult. Central and S. Italy, Balkan region and Asia Minor. Similar to L. flavum, but cymes with 5–10 flowers. Stems 40cm high, with numerous sterile rosettes. A very attractive species. z6

L. densiflorum Davis. Turkey, Iraq. Intermediate between *L. viscosum* and *L. hypericifolium*, with very large, pink flowers. Grow like *L. viscosum*. z6

L. elegans Sprun. ex Boiss. (*L. iberidifolium* Auch. ex Planch.). Albania, Greece, Yugoslavia, Asia Minor. Shoots very woody at the base, with many sterile rosettes. Stems 10–15cm high, cyme with 1–5 golden yellow flowers. *L. boissieri* Aschers. et Sint. ex Boiss, from W. Asia Minor, is similar but usually only single flowered.

The very attractive Gemmell's Hybrid was developed in England in about 1940 from the cross *L. campanulatum* × *L. elegans*. The plant is only 10cm high, with very glaucous blue foliage and golden yellow flowers. The Waterperry strain comes from a back cross on *L. elegans*; it is quite rare. z6

L. flavum L. Golden Flax. Central and SE. Europe, north to Central Russia. Stems 30–60cm high, the woody base of the stems without or with a few sterile rosettes. Leaves oblong-spatulate, the upper leaves more lanceolate. Flowers 2cm across, clear yellow, in 10–50 flowered cymes. 'Compactum' is only 25–30cm high. z5

L. hirsutum L. From Austria and Czechoslovakia eastward to Russia and Turkey. Stems 45–70cm high, erect; leaves 10–45mm long and to 10mm wide; all parts except corolla and fruit hairy. Flowers in cymes, pure blue to light violet-blue with white or yellowish eye, 35mm wide. Found in nature on rocky, sunny slopes, in mountain meadows and under brushy growth. Very attractive. z5

L. hirsutum var. **olympicum** see **L. olympican**

L. hypericifolium K.B. Presl. Caucasus. Similar to *L. viscosum*, but more robust and vigorous, with stems to 80cm high. Flowers pink with darker venation, to 4.5cm wide. Young blooming plants are more or less upright while older plants are more vaselike. Unfortunately little used, but hardy and attractive. z5

L. iberidifolium see **L. elegans**

L. julicum see **L. perenne** ssp. **alpinum**

L. kotschyanum see **L. olympicum**

L. leucanthum Boiss. et Sprun. SE. Greece. Similar to *L. elegans* but the leaves are more or less densely covered with short, stiff hairs and white flowers. Only for the alpine house, and not particularly attractive. z9

L. narbonense L. W. and Central Mediterranean region. The best of the blue-flowered garden species. Stems to 50cm or more high. Glaucous leaves lanceolate, sharply acuminate. Flowers sky blue with a white eye, 3cm wide, in flat, compound cymes, usually long-lived, fading, only in the afternoon. The cultivars 'Six Hills' and Heavenly Blue' are particularly attractive, bold forms, both propagated only by cuttings; seeds listed under these names, taken from the cultivars, produce varying progeny. z7(6)

L. olympicum Boiss. (*L. hirsutum* var. *olympicum* Boiss., *L. kotschyanum* Hayek). Turkey, on various mountain massifs. Similar to *L. hirsutum*, but cymes only 1–7 flowered and to 15cm high. Introduced into cultivation by recent English collection expeditions. Attractive plants, better situated in protected sites or in an alpine house. z8

L. perenne L. Flax, Perennial Flax. Quite variable species, between 10–60cm high, slender. Stems glabrous, procumbent, ascending or erect in a vase-shaped cluster, from a more or less woody base. Leaves glaucous, linear mostly toward the upper part of the stem. Flowers in branched panicles, 2–2.5cm across. All subspecies of *L. perenne* flower on sunny days only until late morning, but they bloom for several weeks. Classification of the subspecies not yet completed. Three subspecies are found in cultivation as well as cultivars 'Alba' with white flowers, and 'Caerulea' with clear, sky blue flowers.

L. perenne ssp. **alpinum** (Jacq.) Ockendon (*L. alpinum* Jacq., *L. julicum* Hayek, *L. boreale* Juz.). Pyrenees, Alps, Apennines, Rhodope and N. Ural Mts. Especially valuable low grower. Shoots procumbent to ascending, 15–30cm long. Flowers light aquamarine to dark blue (*L. julicum*). z4

L. perenne ssp. **anglicum** (Miller) Ockendon (*L. anglicum* Miller). England. Procumbent to ascending, flower color medium blue. z6

L. perenne ssp. **perenne**. Central and E. Europe. Strongly erect, to 60cm high. Flowers light aquamarine blue, frequently also white. z5

L. spathulatum Hal. Mountains of N. Greece and S. Albania, on limestone. Similar to *L. hirsutum*, but with a more woody base, stems to 25cm, more sparsely flowered. Commonly found on the Thessalian Olympic Mts. between *L. hirsutum* and *L. olympicum*. Attractive in the rock garden. z7

L. salsoloides see **L. suffruticosum** ssp. **salsoloides**

L. suffruticosum L. ssp. **salsoloides** (Lam.) Rouy (*L. salsoloides* Lam.). Central Spain, W. Alps, north to Central France. 5–25cm high. Stems obliquely ascending, with many sterile shoots forming a dense mat beneath. Flowers 2.5–3cm wide, white veined, purple, violet or pink on the claw. Very floriferous. 'Nanum' is a form identical to the species, collected from the wild, about 10cm high. z5

L. tenuifolium L. Central and S. Europe, reaching to Belgium and the Ukraine. Stems glabrous, to 45cm high, with few sterile shoots. Glabrous leaves linear, needlelike. Flowers 2cm wide, blush colored to dark pink, always distinctly veined. Not always long-lived, but perpetuates itself by self-seeding without becoming weedy. z5

L. usitatissimum L. Flax. An annual, or short-lived perennial species to 1.3m high. In cultivation since man's earliest history for its fibers used in cordage and weaving into linen thread, and later also for its seeds as a source of linseed oil, a mucilage, and for stock feed. This species is widely naturalized over North America. z4(3)

L. viscosum L. South and S. Central Europe, along forest roadsides, in open, dry, pine forests, and in woodland glades. Stems to 60cm high. Hairy leaves 4–9mm wide, glandular on the margin, stems also hairy. Flowers in corymbs, 3cm wide, light pink with violet veins. Grow in partial shade to full sun on very well drained, gritty or stony soil. z6 (K.)

Lippia L.
Verbenaceae
Lemon Verbena

About 100 species, primarily from the warmer regions of America, but the species listed here is pandemic. Herbs or shrubs, most now transferred by botanists to the genus *Aloysia* and *Phyla*, with opposite or whorled leaves. Flowers small, in spikes or heads on slender, axillary stalks. Calyces small, 2–4 parted, flower tube cylindrical, the corolla mostly bilabiate. Nutlets paired.

L. canescens see **L. nodiflora** var. **rosea**

L. nodiflora Michx. var. **rosea** (D. Don) Munz (*L. canescens* Knuth, *L. repens* hort. non Spreng., *Phyla nodiflora* (L.) Greene var. *rosea* (D. Don) Moldenke). Pink Fogfruit, Capweed, Matgrass. S. America. Stems 5–10cm high, vigorously creeping tender perennial ground cover. Freezes back if not under favorable conditions, but is relatively root hardy. Recovers its mat form by early July in W. Europe from the many small rhizome pieces. Shoots slender, leaves small, lanceolate to obovate, entire or dentate, 1–2cm long. Flowers light pink, in heads similar to garden verbena. A sun-loving plant, suitable for the xerophytic bed or as a ground cover under *Lavender*. This species, and its North American counterpart *Lippia lanceolata*, Fogfruit, occasionally useful in wet ditches and at water's edge, and listed under the genus *Phyla* in recent English and American publications. z6 (K.)

L. repens see **L. nodiflora** var. **rosea**

Liriope Lour.
(See also *Ophiopogon*)
Liliaceae
Lilyturf

A genus of about 5 species of evergreen perennial plants with basal, sessile, grasslike, linear leaves in tufts from an underground rootstock. The small-pedicelled, flowers are borne at a 45 degree angle to the stout scape, forming a dense spike or raceme. Perianth segments 6, not united, stamens 6, anthers pointed. The ovary is superior, 6- locular; fruit is a black drupe, with 1 or 2 seeds. While in the 1950s only one species with several varieties was recognized, today these are considered to be separate species. Many horticultural selections as well as the species are grown in the gardens of the S. USA.

Despite many desirable properties, the liriopes are not universal groundcovers. All grow best on acid soil, preferring light and porous to heavy. The evergreen foliage is sensitive to sun scald in winter and sunburn in summer but these problems are overcome by planting in partial to full shade. If given the proper conditions, Lilyturf can be a tough and long-lived perennial ground cover.

Much confusion exists between *Liriope* and the almost identical *Ophiopogon*, which see; whereas the ovary of

Liriope muscari 'Majestic'

Liriope is superior, that of *Ophiopogon* is inferior or partially so. From a gardener's viewpoint, other differences are important: *Liriope* forms dense clumps, bears flowers above the foliage and is relatively hardy; *Ophiopogon* is stoloniferous and as such more valuable as a grass substitute, bears flowers on shorter scapes, and is less hardy. The two are much confused in the trade. Most liriopes eventually produce tubers below the root cluster.

L. exiliflora (L.H. Bailey) Hume. China, Japan. Rhizomatous perennial, occasionally with short stolons. Leaves to 40cm long, 12mm wide with 6 parallel veins. The pale violet flowers are in 16cm-long racemes, in clusters of 5, carried well over the foliage. Reputed to be in the trade in the S. USA. The form 'Ariaka Janshige' (known as 'Silvery Sunproof' in England), with white-striped, drooping leaves, probably belongs here. z7

L. gigantea Hume. China. The largest of the rhizomatous strains and widely distributed across the S. USA is probably a variety or cultivar of *L. muscari*. z7(6)

L. graminifolia (L.) Bak. China, Vietnam. Carpetforming perennial with underground rhizomes. Leaves with 4–5 parallel veins, flowers pale violet, in 3-flowered clusters. This variable species has the form 'Minor' with even narrower leaves. Both are suitable groundcovers for filling in between clumpform plants, like ferns. Plants sold under this name commonly are *Liriope spicata* var. *densiflora*, a dwarf variety or cultivar of *L. muscari* or an *Ophiopogon* species. *L. graminifolia* does not seem to be grown or marketed in Europe or the USA. z8

Liriope graminifolia

L. graminifolia var. **densiflora** see **L. muscari**

L. muscari (Decne.) L. H. Bailey (*L. graminifolia* var. *densiflora* Bak., *L. muscari* var. *densiflora* hort.) China. The most important ornamental species of the cultivated liriopes. The leaves, opposite, arising in tufts from the rootstock, are 25–45cm long and to 2cm wide, but often narrower. Obtuse tipped with 10 longitudinal stripes on the underside. The scape is 15–30cm long, greenish violet, stiff and furrowed. The peduncles are darker and occasionally branched toward the apex. Racemes are to 2cm wide and 8–12cm long, just to well above the foliage. The individual flower clusters have 4–7 densely crowded buds or flowers. The perianth inserts directly (without a tube) on the pedicel. Often with 4 or more berry-like fruits per stem, black, glossy and 5–8mm thick. The species has given rise to many cultivars from chance seedlings. Flower color varies from dark and light violet to pure white. The evergreen foliage is narrow to wide, usually straight, but also twisted, light to dark green and on some forms, variably yellow striped. Selections from seed constantly produce improvements. The forms with flowers held high above the foliage are particularly meritorious. It seems that most of the cultivars to date are inclined, with age, to produce flowers further down within the foliage. *L. muscari* is very useful as a companion to the smaller woody evergreens such as *Skimmia, Sarcococca, Ilex, Taxus* and *Viburnum*. Effective when combined with the evergreen ferns, *Asarum* species and *Waldsteinia*. The late summer to fall flowers can heighten the effect of the fall foliage of small deciduous plants. This also holds true for the small-growing fall bloomers. *Liriope muscari* is an excellent choice for small inner-city gardens against a protecting, heat-trapping wall which enhances the flowers above the decorative, evergreen foliage. z6

While trade lists include more than 50 named strains of this species, only a few are common to all lists and clearly definable as cultivars. These include: 'Grandiflora', flower spikes tall, large, showy lavender-pink; 'Majestic', leaves narrower, flower spikes often fasciated cockscomb-fashion, flowers lavender; 'Munroe White', flowers pure white on green scapes, plant only in shade; and 'Variegata', leaves emerging with longitudinal yellow stripes which may fade with age in some strains, or become stronger in others; the flower color generally is dark lavender; best in full sun. Many other names appear in various catalogues. z5

L. muscari var. **densiflora** see **L. muscari**

L. platyphylla Wang et Tang. China. A clump form, like *L. muscari*, but with a taller flower scape and long, loose flower racemes. Little-known species in America. Sometimes taken for the wild form of *L. muscari* or perhaps only an oriental cultivar of *L. muscari* or *L. spicata*. z7

L. spicata Lour. Creeping Liriope. (*Ophiopogon spicatus* Lodd.). China, Vietnam. Of all the liriopes, this species probably was the first to be grown in the West. A winter-hardy groundcover, but may be deciduous in colder climates. Quickly forms a dense stand with underground rhizomes. The leaves are up to 25 to rarely 40cm long, over-arching, grass-like, the midvein is raised on the dorsal side of the leaf with about 9 parallel veins, the leaf margin is cuticular denticulate. The scape is to 2mm wide and tinged violet-brown, with short racemes with 3–6 flowers in a cluster.

The flowers are pale violet to white with a 1mm-long perianth tube. The fruit is black, glossy and 9mm thick. z5 (S.)

L. spicata var. **densiflora** see **L. graminifolia**

Lithodora Griseb.
Boraginaceae

A genus of 7 species of dwarf, hairy shrubs with alternate, simple, entire

Lithodora diffusa

leaves and small blue flowers in a terminal, racemose, scorpioid cyme (cincinnus) on leafy stems. Propagation is by semi ripe cuttings from nonflowering shoots. Requires some winter protection.

L. diffusa (Lag.) Johnst. (*Lithospermum diffusum* Lag., *L. prostratum* Loisel.). SW. Europe. Stems to 15cm high, dwarf shrub with procumbent branches, small lanceolate leaves and bright gentian blue flowers from May to June. 'Grace Ward' is large flowered, sky blue; 'Heavenly Blue' is light gentian blue, particularly attractive and the most widely grown cultivar. This species requires a lime-free, humus-rich acidic soil in a protected, but sunny site. Where suitably protected, provides a good, early summer-blooming groundcover around *Erica* and *Calluna*. Winter protection is necessary. Several selections have been

made since its introduction including 'Cambridge Blue' and 'Barker's Form'. Also var. *alba* with white flowers is sometimes offered but rather less striking than the blue flowered forms. z8(7)

L. oleifolia (Lapeyr.) Griseb. (*Lithospermum oleifolium* Lapeyr.). Endemic to a limited area in the E. Pyrenees. Subshrub-like, dense, 10–15cm high, with short, underground runners, gradually building large colonies. Shoots white pubescent, leaves sessile, elliptic, gray above, white-pubescent below, clustered at the tips of nonflowering shoots. Flowers 3–7 in terminal cymes, first pink, later light blue, from May to July. Very attractive, lime-tolerant and sun-loving, densely bushy plant from rocky meadows. z8 (H.& S.)

Lithophragma Nutt.
Saxifragaceae
Woodland Star

About 9–10 species in W. North America. Perennials with slender, tuber-producing rootstocks. Leaves mostly basal, rounded to reniform in outline, mostly 3–5 lobed or parted. Simple, slender, *Tiarella*-like inflorescences. Flowers in simple, terminal racemes, sepals 5 around the partly inferior ovary; petals 5, white or pink, clawed, entire to dentate or parted, often uneven; anthers 10; pistil perigynous (half-inferior) of 3 carpels and with 3 styles. Blooms in May and June. Grows best in moist, humus soil in semi-shade. Useful together with other shade-loving perennials at the edge of a woodland. Propagate by seed or division.

L. affine A. Gray (*Tallima affinis* (A. Gray) A. Gray) California and S. Oregon. Sturdy plant, pubescent to hairy, rarely nearly glabrous. Inflorescence to 60cm high. Basal leaves orbicular to kidney-shaped, 3-lobed, long-petioled. Petals white, shallowly 3-lobed.

L. glabrum Nutt. (*L. bulbiferum* Rydb.) British Columbia to California east to Rocky Mts. Plant delicate, to 30cm high, nearly glabrous to sparsely pubescent. Basal leaves short-petioled, 3-parted orbicular; stem leaves small, 3-parted, often with axillary bulbils. Flowers pink, rarely white, 2–5 in a raceme, sometimes replaced by bulbils.

L. parviflora (Hook.) Nutt. (*Tellima parviflora* Hook.). W. North America, British Columbia to California, E. to Rocky Mts. Stems 25–50cm high, glandular-pubescent. Basal leaves orbicular, 1–3cm wide, somewhat white-haired, with 3–5 cuneate divisions which are further shallowly 3-cleft. Stem leaves 2–3, alternate. Petals white or light pink, 5–10cm long, deeply 3–5 parted in linear-oblong lobes. An attractive plant for collectors. *Tiarella unifoliata* Hook., which can be distinguished from *T. cordifolia* by the 3–5 stem leaves and a branched inflorescence, is often cultivated under this name. z6 (K.)

L. tenallum Nutt. W. North American Mts. Slender inflorescence to 30cm high. Leaves pale green, sparsely pubescent; basal leaves orbicular, entire, 3–5 lobed or 3–5 (or more) cleft; stem leaves very deeply 3-lobed appearing pinnatifid. Flowers pink, rarely white, petals deeply 5-lobed.

Lithospermum
(see also *Buglossoides* and *Lithodora*)
Boraginaceae
Gromwell, Puccoon

About 44 species of hairy, deciduous perennials or subshrubs on all continents except Australia, many weedy or of no garden merit. Roots commonly with orange, red, or purple-staining juice once used as dyestuff. Leaves alternate, simple, sessile, mostly cauline, rarely basal. Flowers yellow, orange or white in simple or branched scorpioid cymes; calyx and corolla 5-lobed, sometimes hairy, sometimes with appendages; stamens 5, always included; 2-carpelled ovary deeply 4-lobed. Fruit of 4 glossy, hard nutlets.

L. canescens (Michx.) Lehm. (*Batschia canescens* Michx.) Puccoon, Indian-paint. Central North America east to Georgia, a prairie and woodland margin species. Plant of 1 to several sparsely branched or unbranched leafy stems from woody crown with a very deep, ropy root. Grows 20–45cm high, hoary pubescent stems and leaves. Leaves oblong to linear. Flower 1.5cm long in nearly flat cymes, bright orange to yellow-orange, corolla lobes entire, tube glabrous within. Blooms in early spring. Roots with a staining red dye. For the rock garden or naturalizing on well-drained, stony soil. Propagate by seed or summer cuttings; grow in pots until bedded because established plants cannot be moved. A yellow-flowered var. *pallida* is listed but is not in the trade. z4(3)

L. distichum Ort. A tender Central American species.

L. incisum Lehm. (*L. angustifolium* Michx.; *L. linearifolium* J. Goldie, *L. mandenensis* K. Spreng.) Yellow Puccoon. Ontario and British Columbia south to Indiana, Arkansas, Texas, Arizona and adjacent Mexico. Herbaceous perennial 30–60cm tall; stems 1 or few, simple or rarely branched, from woody crown with a massive, deep-growing unbranched root. Leaves linear, hairy. Flowers on short cymes in head-like clusters; flowers of 2 kinds, the early larger, to 3cm long, bright yellow and showy, the corolla lobes fimbriate; later flowers much smaller, paler. Begins to flower in early spring. Suitable for prairie and steppe natural gardens; attractive but not as showy as *L. canescens*. z4(3)

L. multiflorum Torr. Wyoming south to Arizona and W. Texas and adjacent Mexico. Branching herbaceous perennial with simple, linear to linear-lanceolate, hairy leaves. Cymes terminal on all branches. Flowers many, 1.75cm long, yellow or orange, the corolla lobes rounded, throat glabrous within, heterostylic. A semi-xerophytic species for high in the sunny rock garden or to be naturalized on rocky, alkaline slopes. z4(3)

L. purpureo-caeruleum see **Buglossoides purpurocaerulea**

Llogdia Salisb. ex Rchb.
Liliaceae
Alp Lily

About 12 species, few in cultivation, of alpine perennials from Europe, Asia and W. North America. Bulbs tunicate from a creeping rhizome. Leaves basal and cauline, grasslike. Flowers white, solitary or in a terminal raceme. Perianth of 6 separate segments each with a basal gland; 6 stamens with basally attached anthers, fruit a capsule with many 3-angled seeds in 2 rows in each of 3 cells.

L. serotina (L.) Salisb. ex Rchb. Mts. of Europe, Asia and North America, Alaska to Oregon, Montana south to New Mexico. Basal leaves from bulb, several in a tuft to 10cm long; grass-like stems to 15cm high with few leaves. Flowers usually solitary, rarely few, yellowish-white, less than 1cm long. Suitable for the alpine rock garden; intolerant of warm climates. z5(4)

Lobelia L.
Campanulaceae
Cardinal Flower, et al

In this large genus of mostly temperate and warm zone plants, with some highly specialized, high mountain giant species in the Southern Hemisphere which are impossible to cultivate out of habit, only a few are moderately winter hardy. Suitable for planting in the perennial border, streamsides and on pond banks. Grow in any fertile, moist garden soil in an open, sunny to partially shady site. Propagate by division, seed, and cuttings of rarer selections.

L. cardinalis L., Cardinal Flower. Eastern and Gulf States of the USA, found in wet meadows and on riverbanks. Stems mostly glabrous, often reddish, 60–120cm high. Leaves alternate, oblong-ovate, acuminate, green, to 10cm long. Stems mostly unbranched, erect with bracted spike-like racemes. Flowers bright red, pink, or white; July to September. Requires good winter protection in cool climates. Grows best with ample moisture. Competes poorly with other herbaceous material. A valuable plant for its beautiful red flowers in mid- to late summer. Combines well with *Hemerocallis, Tradescantia* Andersoniana Hybrids, *Primula florindae, Veronica virginica, Molinia caerulea* 'Variegata', and late lilies in yellow colors. Botanists list several forms of the species, grassy-leafed, etc. Cultivars 'Alba', white-flowered, and 'Rosea', pink-flowered, are listed, and specialists propagate (vegetatively) unusual colors, mauve, bi-colors, etc. See also *L. siphilitica* for hybrids. z3

L. fulgens Willd. Mexico. To 1.2m high. Similar to *L. cardinalis*, but with dark reddish stems and sometimes foliage. The leaves are linear to lanceolate, raceme one-sided. The dark-leaved, scarlet-red-flowering form 'Queen Victoria', possibly a hybrid (*L. fulgens* × *L.* ?) or a cultivar or hybrid of *L. cardinalis*, is particularly attractive; very effective plants for the summer border. Perennial only under cover in mild winters; best overwintered in a frost-free cold frame. z9

L. × gerardii Chabanne ex Nicolas (*L. cardinalis?* × *L. siphilitica*). 'Vedrariensis', a horticulture term of no botanical significance, is probably from this cross. Stems 60–80cm high. Leaves broadly lanceolate, dark green, turning reddish. Flowers purple-violet. Uses and culture like that of *L. fulgens*; considerably hardier.

The pure pink 'Rosenkavalier' (Rose Cavalier) comes nearly 100% true from seed and was originated from the form 'Blauzauber' (Blue Magic). These also require some winter protection. z8(7)

L. sessilifolia Lamb. Japan, Kuril Islands, Sachalin, Taiwan, Korea, Manchuria, E. Siberia. Stems 40–60cm high, slender, unbranched, stiffly erect, leafy. Leaves lanceolate, dentate, sessile. Flowers in the leaf axils, violet; June to July. Thrives

forms resulting in the *L. × speciosa* Sweet group of tetraploids. These plants are very winter-hardy lobelias in reds, pinks and purple shades. Bowden recommends they be planted in full sun and in loam soil with ample moisture and fertility. Protective straw mulch is advisable in winter temperatures of -22 degrees F. (-30 degrees C.). z3 (H.& Mü.)

L. tupa L. Chile. A particularly splendid species with stems to 2m. Leaves pale green felted, lanceolate to 30cm. Flowers brick red in terminal spikes 30–70cm.

corniculatus 'Pleniflorus' is better for garden culture since the species can easily become weedy by self-seeding. Suitable as a persistent bloomer in the rock garden, also for dry slopes. Grow in full sun, in loose, well-limed garden soil. Although lime-loving, tolerates neutral soil. Propagate the species by seed, the cultivars by division. Young plants are best grown in pots because of their long taproots. Good companion species include the drought tolerant: *Alyssum* species, *Antennaria*, *Anthericum*, *Armeria*, *Dianthus deltoides*, *D. gratianopolitanus*, *D.*

Lithodora oleifolia

Lobelia fulgens

in a moist site on lime-free soil, winter hardy. z5

L. siphilitica L. Great Lobelia, Blue Cardinal Flower. E. North America. Stems 40–80cm high, erect, very leafy. Leaves oval-lanceolate, 5–10cm long, somewhat pubescent, light green, irregularly toothed. Flowers bright blue or white, 2.5–3.5cm long, in dense racemes, 10–15cm long; pedicels with leaf-like bracts, calyx lobes with basal auricles. July to October. Hardy and undemanding. Where *L. siphilitica* and *L. cadinalis* grow together naturally in the Central E. USA, spontaneous hybrids of these 2 species sometimes occur. Natural and cultivar forms of *L. siphilitica* include 'Alba' with white flowers and 'Nana', a dwarf form to 30cm or less. This is a valuable species for hybridizing. z5

L. × speciosa Sweet. Wray Bowden of Ontario, Canada, crossed a particularly hardy selection of *L. cardinalis* from S. Ontario with *L. siphilitica* and *L. fulgens*

Protect wild stems in winter where temperatures of less than -10 degrees C. Best grown against a sunny wall. z8

Lomaria

L. alpina see **Blechnum penna-marina**

Lotus L.
Leguminosae

About 100 species of perennial, occasionally annual herbs or subshrubs in W. North America, parts of Asia and Africa, the Canary Islands, Europe and especially the Mediterranean region. Usually with 5-part pinnate, but also trifoliate and odd-pinnate leaves, and axillary umbels or single flowers. Flowers medium-sized, yellow, red, occasionally white, papilionaceous, keel beaked, stamens 9 united plus 1 separate. Pods longer than the calyx. The double form *L.*

plumarius, *Jasione perennis*, *Origanum vulgare*, *Salvia pratensis*, *Satureja montana*, *Thymus serpyllum*, *Veronica spicata* ssp. *incana*.

L. corniculatus L. Birds-foot Trefoil. Europe, N. and E. Africa, W. Asia, Himalayas, Tibet, E. Asia. Grows in meadows, semidry grassy sites, roadsides, primarily on calcareous, fertile, loose loam soils, but also on all other nonacidic soils. Found in the Alps to 2300m. Stems 5–10cm high; a small perennial without stolons, but with many 10–40cm long, procumbent-ascending stems. Leaves with 3 leaflets; the stipules resemble leaflets. Long-peduncled umbels 3–6 flowered. Flowers short-pedicelled, yellow, banner often tinged reddish. 'Pleniflorus' with double flowers. Blooms from May to October. Also, var. *arvensis* (Schkuhr) Ser. ex DC. Broadleaf Bird's-foot Trefoil, with cuneate-obovate leaflets and var. *tenuifolium* L., Narrow Bird's-foot Trefoil, stems prostrate with linear or linear-oblanceolate leaflets. z4–5, intolerant of heat in warmer climates. (E.)

Two W. North American species are of some value in the sunny wildflower garden: **L. crassifolius** (Benth.) Green. Stems to 1.3m high; leaves with 3–7 pairs of leaflets; peduncle pinnate-bracted with 8–15 flowers with greenish-yellow corolla, the keel marked purple. And **L. pinnatus** Hook. Stems to 50cm high; leaves with 2–4 pairs of glabrous, obovate leaflets; peduncle without bracts, with 3–7 flowers, yellow with white wings.

L. annua L. (*L. biennis* Moench). SE. Europe, Italy. Relatively short flowering period in early to mid-spring, but effective planted under *Ribes sanguineum*, together with narcissus. After the silicles ripen, only the silver-white replum remain. Used as a dried flower, cut while green. Annual or biennial species which regularly self-seeds in culture. Also var. *alba* with white flowers; var. *atrococcinea* with wine red flowers; var. *corcyrensis* from Corfu (tender) with blue flowers; 'Munstead Purple', flowers rich purple, and var. *variegata*, leaves with irregular

shrubs with deep, branched roots possessing nodules of nitrogen-fixing bacteria. Leaves rounded in outline, palmately compound, leaflets entire. Papilionaceous flowers, standards erect with reflexed margins; stamens 10, united, showy, in erect terminal spikes or racemes in spring to early summer. Of the perennial species, only a few are of garden significance, the most importance of which is *L. polyphyllus* and its hybrids. All lupines require deep, well-drained, lime-free soil.

Lotus corniculatus

Lunaria rediviva

L. siliquosus see **Tetragonolobus maritimus**

Lunaria L.
Cruciferae
Honesty, Money Plant, Moonwort

Two or 3 species. Erect, branching herbs with large, deltoid, toothed, petioled leaves and purple or white flowers in loose terminal racemes. Flowers with 4 sepals, falling early, petals 4, long-clawed, stamens 6, 2 shorter than the other 4. Fruit a large silicle, flat, broadly elliptic or oblong, the valves falling early leaving the silvery translucent-horny replum (septum). Naturalizes well in a semi-shaded forest margin, where the soil is sufficiently moist and cool.

creamy-white margins, comes true from seed. Naturalized in NE. USA. z5

L. rediviva L. Europe, W. Siberia. Stems 80–100cm high, bushy. Leaves dark green, rounded to triangular-cordate. Flowers pale purple in loose racemes; spring to early summer. Silicle broadly elliptic-lanceolate with silvery white replum. Valuable, persistently naturalizing perennial, thriving in semi-shade and any soil. Propagate by seed and division. z4(3) (H.& M.)

Lupinus L.
Leguminosae
Lupine

A genus with 200–300 species, many from W. North America. These are stately annuals, perennials and sub-

L. argentus Pursh. Alberta and the Dakotas south to New Mexico, also California and Oregon. Stems 15–60cm high, plants silvery-pubescent. Leaves mostly cauline, few or no basal leaves; 6–9 leaflets, narrow-lanceolate to oblanceolate, about 2.5cm long. Flowers white, rose, blue or violet, with a white spot on the glabrous standard. And var. *depressus* (Rydb.) C.L. Hitchc., a subalpine species to 26cm high with flowers in very crowded racemes.

L. latifolius var. **subalpinus** (Piper and B.L. Robinson) C.P. Sm. Alaska to Washington, in Mtn. meadows. Plants very dwarf, 10–25cm tall, stems and foliage white to villous. Flowers blue to purple, to 1cm long, in stout racemes. The species *L. latifolius* J. Agardh and its other varieties, growing to 1.3m high and with flower racemes to 45cm long, are good wildgarden candidates.

L. lyallii A. Gray. Washington to California. Plant silky-pubescent overall, to only 10cm high in flower. Leaflets 5–6, less than 1cm long, acute-tipped. Flower racemes head-like; flowers dark blue or bicolor with a paler center, about 1cm long. A maritime mountain plant difficult to grow out of habitat but a choice rock garden plant.

L. nootkatensis J. Donn. Coastal Washington to Aleutian Islands. Somewhat hairy plant to 1m high. Leaflets 5–9, 7cm long, obtuse. Flowers blue, marked purple, also white to yellow, about 1.75cm long, showy. This attractive species has proven to be sufficiently adaptable to become naturalized on the NE. coast from Newfoundland to New England.

L. ornatus Dougl. W. North America. 30–40cm high, bushy subshrub. Leaves 4–7 parted, silky-pubescent. Flowers small, pink with blue; May to October. A conspicuous species for its silver-glossy, 3–5cm leaves. Requires full sun, dryness and a very protected site in the rockery.

Propagation is by seed. z7

L. plattensis S. Wats. Wyoming, Colorado and Kansas. Stems to 60cm high; stems and leaves mostly hairy; leaflets thick, sometimes nearly glaucous, to 7cm long. Flowers pale blue, standards with a darker spot. Not an unattractive species for the dry, more or less alkaline prairie or steppe garden, and important as the most "inland" of the perennial lupines, and a possible source of hardiness for plant breeders.

Lupinus Russell Hybrids

L. polyphyllus Lindl. W. North America. To 1.2m high. Leaves mostly 13–15 parted, leaflets lanceolate, glabrous above, softly pubescent beneath. Flower racemes to 50cm long, lilac-blue, pink on 'Roseus' or white on 'Albus'; June to July. A wildflower for the large garden. Propagation is by seed. z7

In addition to the above mentioned species, a few others, selected from the long list of mostly beautiful but demanding species, may be of interest to gardeners, wildflower enthusiasts, rock garden specialists, and plant breeders.

Hybrid Lupines

Many colorful lupines were developed during the middle of the 20th century by crossing *L. perennis* L. with the woody,

Lupinus polyphyllus hybrids

yellow-flowering *L. arboreus* Sims. and by further selection. These selections were developed to their fullest potential especially by the English breeder, George Russell. Vegetatively propagated clones of the Russell Hybrids are exceptionally colorful, very large-flowered, and with dense, tight, stout, long-persisting inflorescences. Colors range from pure white through all the pink, red, yellow, orange, brownish and blue tones to a rich blue-black. Some are monochrome, others multicolored. Unfortunately, due to the relative difficulty of vegetative propagation, these clones have virtually disappeared from the trade in favor of selections which come true from seed. Most seed-propagated forms have good growth habit and are floriferous, although the character of the old Russell Lupines is not fully realized.

As some of the most colorful perennials, these plants are suitable for specimen use as well as for massing, especially in mixed colors. Good companion species include the larger poppies, white Meadow Rue and the large irises, in appropriate colors. They are also valued as a cut flower.

In general the cultivars are winter hardy, the most tender are the yellow-flowered forms; all, however, do poorly in mid-continental climates. Blooming period is from May to June. Plants with spent flowers may sometimes be encouraged to rebloom by cutting them back to force new shoots. Grow in nearly any, not too fertile, lime-free soil. On calcareous soils the foliage will be chlorotic and the plants short-lived. Plants are also short-lived on heavy, periodically wet soils. Excessively light sandy soils, too, pose problems with overwintering, particularly with fall-planted material. Propagation is commonly by seed; the older, superior cultivars, however, can be maintained only by cuttings. The seed-propagated Russell Hybrids are usually from 0.8–1m high, but include the shorter race 'Minarette', 60cm plants in all the colors of the typical Russell Hybrids. z5 (H.& M.)

Luronium Raf.
Alismataceae

Similar to *Alisma*, but with floating, leafy stems; stoloniferous, rooting at the nodes, also occasionally creeping onto the banks, 10–60cm long. Only 1 species:

L. natans (L.) Raf. (*Alisma natans* L., *Elisma natans* Buchenau). Central Europe, to S. Sweden, Central Russia, N. Spain. Submerged leaves mostly awlshaped to linear, single veined; floating leaves oval or oblong, 5–10cm, translucent-punc-

Luronium natans

tate, 3-veined. Inflorescences with leaf-like bracts, flowers arranged in singly to 3 or 5, long-pedicelled, with 3 bracteoles, white, June. One of the most attractive aquatic plants; thrives in soft water. Also suitable for cold-water aquariums, the submerged leaves persist year round. Propagated by the runners, abundantly produced in summer. If possible, plant in a mixture of peat, loam and unwashed sand. z4 (D.)

Luzula DC.
Juncaceae
Wood Rush

Grasslike perennials, about 80 Eurasian species in cold and temperate regions; with flat, hairy leaves and flowers in spikes, umbels or heads. Flowers with 3 scale-like sepals, 3 scale-like petals, 6 stamens and a 1-celled ovary. The seed capsules are 3-seeded, the seeds have a basal appendage at most. Useful, particularly in selections from the wild, for understory woodland plantings as well as in thin, open grassy sites, on rocky

plains and heaths. Most species are impartial to soils. Species found in woodlands will tolerate root competition and shade. Propagation is possible by seed. Clones selected for garden uses must be vegetatively propagated by division.

L. albida see **L. luzuloides**

L. luzuloides (Lam.) Dandy et Wilm. (*L. nemorosa* E. Mey, *L. albida* (Hoffm.) DC.) Central and S. Europe, naturalized in N. Europe. A loose, tufted perennial with short stolons, leaves to 6mm wide, dull

Luzula nivea

green, hairy. Flower heads loosely arranged, erect, later becoming pendulous, flowers with a white or brownish copper-toned perianth. Good understory plant for mature, species-poor woodlands. z6

L. maxima see **L. sylvatica**

L. nemorosa see **L. luzuloides**

L. nivea (L.) DC. NE. Spain, Central France to Slovenia (Yugoslavia) and Central Italy. An open, tufted perennial, leaves evergreen, distinctly hairy on the margin, 4mm wide, to 25cm high. Inflorescences about 40cm high, 6–20 flowers clustered densely together, perianth white, segments uneven and acuminate, June to August. This species from open mountain forests requires moist, loamy humus. Should be cultivated on a rocky forest margin or the edge of the alpine garden with small shrubs, i.e., *Rhododendron*. The inflorescences are suitable as cut flowers. z6

L. pilosa (L.) Willd. Europe. A loose tuft, occasionally with short stolons, 20–35cm high, leaves to 10mm wide, flat and white-hairy. Flowers solitary, brownish, in umbellate inflorescences, April to May. Greens very early in spring, a good clump "grass" for a wooded site. Flowers early and will cover a small area understory. z6

L. purpureosplendens Seub. Azores. Resembling *L.sylvatica*, but a more compact clump "grass" with purple-brown perianth segments. Tender, but worthy of further trial in a protected site. z8

L. sylvatica (Huds.) Gaud. (*L. maxima* DC.). S., W. and Central Europe. Very loose, short, ascending tufts in stoloniferous mats. Leaves to 20mm wide, sparsely hairy, 20–30cm high, stiff, glossy dark green, semi-evergreen. Flowers grouped 3–4, clustered in dense, brown inflorescences, April to June. Prefers a humid atmosphere. Evergreen when situated out of the morning sun in winter. Most of the selections have more persistent foliage.

'Farnfreund' (Fern Friend) is decorative and compact and therefore a good choice to use among ferns.

'Hohe Tatra' (High Tatras) has wide, bright green, distinctly hairy leaves in erect, cylindrical tufts.

'Marginata' has a yellowish, later white, narrow leaf margin. The clumps are tighter than those of the species.

'Tauernpass' has wide, bright green leaves in flat rosettes, more resistant to winter browning than the species. Becomes compact in time, forming a wide cushion.

Best suited for tree understory planting. Thrives in a somewhat moist, humus soil. Tolerates deep shade and root competition. Pure stands, however, can be harmful by tying up water otherwise available to the trees. (S.)

Lychnis L.
Caryophyllaceae
Catchfly, Campion

About 35 species of erect, bushy herbs from the North Temperate and Arctic zones. Some species are biennial, not persisting in some sites and soils. Annual species are often used for hybridizing, but to date no-one has produced perennial hybrids. Leaves opposite, without stipules. Inflorescence cymose; flowers usually bisexual; calyx tube-shaped or inflated, 5-toothed; 5 petals with coronal scales where blade and claw join, white, scarlet, or pink to purple; 10 stamens; ovary 1-celled or with 5 cells toward the base, usually 5 styles; fruit a 5-toothed capsule enclosed by the calyx.

Useful as border plants in sunny sites and any fertile garden soil, although *L. flos-cuculi* is best on swampy soils and pond banks. Propagate by seed; all species set abundant seeds; propagation of the cultivars and hybrids is by

Lychnis chalcedonica

division or by basal cuttings in early spring.

L. alba see **Silene pratensis**

L. alpina L. (*Viscaria alpina* (L.) G. Don). N. Europe, Alps, Apennines, Pyrenees. NE. North America. Stems to 12cm high, not sticky. Leaves lanceolate, basal ones clustered in rosettes. Flowers purple-red or rarely white, to 1cm across, 6–20 in capitate clusters; May to June. A mat-forming plant for the rock garden, a sunny site, in lime-free soil; only for collectors. Propagate by seed. Also 'Alba' with white flowers; and 'Rosea' with rose-pink flowers. z5

L. Arkwrightii Hybrids (*L. chalcedonica* × *L. haageana*) intermediate between the parents in appearance but with fleshier rootstock. Flowers large, to 3.5cm across

in 5–10 flowered capitate heads, bright orange-red; July. Dies back after flowering. The dark-leaved form 'Vesuvius' with very large, orange-scarlet colored flowers is particularly conspicuous. z5

L. atropurpurea see **L. viscaria** ssp. **atropurpurea**

L. chalcedonica L. Maltese Cross. Central, SW. and SE. Russia. Stems 0.6–1m high, hispid. Leaves oblong-ovate, rough-haired. Flowers fiery red in capitate heads from 5–10cm across on leafy, stiff, hispid stems; June to August. A very popular and well-known garden plant; the forms 'Alba' with white flowers and the deep red, double flowering 'Plena' are less valuable. Other cultivars are 'Grandiflora' with very large flowers; 'Rosea' with rose-pink flowers; and 'Salmonea' with salmon-rose flowers. z4

L. cognata see **L. fulgens**

L. coronaria (L.) Desr. (*Agrostemma coronaria* L.). Mullein Pink, Rose Campion. SE. Europe, Asia Minor to Turkestan, Himalayas. Entire plant white-woolly. Stems 60–90cm high, erect, forked branching above the middle. Leaves oblong-ovate, to 10cm long, lower leaves petioled, upper sessile. Flowers long pedicelled, solitary or few in a terminal head, 2–3cm across, bright purplish-red, also flesh colored or white ('Alba'); midsummer. Usually biennial or short lived, 2 or 3 year plants, but perpetuated by self-seeding. z4

L. dioica see **Silene dioica**

L. diurna see **Silene dioica**

L. flos-cuculi L. Cuckoo Flower, Ragged-robin. Europe, in open meadows; naturalized Quebec to Pennsylvania. Branched, sparsely scabrous-pubescent stems 30–50cm high. Lower leaves petioled, upper sessile, clasping, nar-

Lychnis viscaria **ssp.** *atropurpurea*

rower. Inflorescence panicled. Flowers rose-pink or white; petals 4-cleft; May to June. Only important for collectors; also the double cultivars 'Alboplena', white, and 'Roseoplena', pink. z6

L. flos-jovis (L.) Desr. (*Agrostemma flosjovis* L.). Joe's Flower. Central and W. Alps. Stems 60–90cm high, upright, little branched. Leaves of basal rosette lanceolate to spatulate, acute, stem leaves clasping, entire plant densely white-tomentose. Inflorescence 4–10 flowered, capitate. Flowers purplish, red or white, 2–3.5cm across; May to July. z5

L. fulgens Fisch. ex Sims (*L. cognata* Maxim.) E. Asia, Japan. Rhizomatous perennial. Stems to 90cm tall, sparsely white-hairy; leaves sessile, ovate-lanceolate, to 5cm long. Calyx to 2cm long; petals deeply 2-lobed, to 2cm long, toothed, dark red. Midsummer. z6

L. haageana Lem. (*L. fulgens* × *L. coronaria* var. *sieboldii*; *L.* × *haageana* Regel). Stems

30–40cm high, stems and leaves hairy. Flowers large, to 5cm across, fiery red, orange-red, scarlet or crimson, petals toothed. Blooms summer-long. Somewhat slow growing and not reliably winter hardy, therefore not too widely planted. Also, 'Grandiflora', flowers larger, red; 'Hybrida', flowers red; and 'Salmonea', flowers salmon-rose. z6(7)

L. lagascae see **Petrocoptis glaucifolia**

L. pyrenaica see **Petrocoptis pyrenaica**

L. sartorii Boiss. Greece. Similar to *L. vulgaris*, but the calyx is scarcely 6mm long and obconical. Flowers purple-red; May to June. Grows well in dry soil in full sun. In America and England this species is sometimes considered to be identical to *L. viscaria* ssp. *atropurpurea*; more study is needed here. z7

L. vespertina see **Silene pratensis**

L. viscaria l. (*Viscaria vulgaris* Bernh., *V. viscosa* Aschers.). Continental Europe, W. Siberia, Transcaucasus. Stems glabrous to hairy above, sticky beneath the enlarged nodes, to 50cm high. Leaves

Lysichiton camtschatcensis

mostly basal, petioled, glabrous, oblong-lanceolate; stem leaves narrower. Flowers rose-colored, dark purple, purple-pink or white, 3–6 racemose-panicled, nearly whorled; May to June. This plant is useful for a dry, sterile site with lime-free subsoil. Best planted in a heather garden among low woody plants. The double-flowering cultivars are good for cutting; 'Albiflora', white; 'Fontaine', vigorous, large, double, light carmine red; 'Plena', 40cm, flowers carmine pink, double; 'Splendens', large-flowered, bright red; 'Thurnae', dark carmine. z4

L. viscaria ssp. **atropurpurea** (Griseb.) Chater (*L. atropurpurea* (Griseb.) Nym. *Viscaria atropurpurea* Griseb., *V. sartorii* Boiss.). Balkan region, Rumania. Found in moist mountain meadows. Leaves nearly all basal and linear-lanceolate, tapered at the base. Flowers dark purple-red; May. A better form of this subspecies is 'Kugelblitz' (Ball of Lightning) (Pötschke/Walther 1971); only 20cm high, flowers carmine-red, crowded over a tight leafy cushion.

L. × walkeri Dickson (*L. coronaria × L. walkeri* Boom et Ruys, *L. × media* hort., *L. coronaria × L. flos-jovis*). A garden hybrid. Intermediate between the (debatable) parents. Silvery-hairy stems. Flowers many, in tighter heads; color variable. The most important attributes are larger flowers (sterile), better flower color, and more tenacious plants. Propagate by division. Available in the light carmine-pink cultivar 'Abbotswood Rose'. z6 (M.)

Several other *Lychnis* species appear in botanical and horticultural lists but are not presently in the trade.

Lycoris Herb.
Amaryllidaceae

Eleven or more species in China, Japan, and SE. Asia. Bulbs with a papery tunic and short neck. Leaves basal, in a tuft, strap-shaped, dying away before flowering begins. Flowers on a solid naked scape in an umbel; perianth segments separated or basally united, red, pink, white or yellow, to 7.5cm long; stamens 5; ovary inferior. The listed species should be planted in full sun in a sheltered site with well-drained, fertile soil. Winter mulch is advisable. Most species, not included here, are hardy only in warmer climates.

L. incarnata Comes ex. Spreng. Central China. Flowers salmon pink to bright rose with dark middle lines on the segments, about 30–40cm high, in September. Recommended for collectors; plant in a protected site. Not as vigorous as *L. squamigera.* z8

L. radiata (L'Hér.) Herb. (*Amaryllis radiata* L'Hér.) Japan, China. Red Spider-lily. Leaves linear, 0.5–0.75cm wide and to 18cm long, dark green with paler midrib, appearing in October and holding until late spring. Scape 30–45cm high with 3–9 flowers; perianth segments vivid red, 4–5cm long, reflexed,

Lycoris squamigera

with very wavy margins, slightly irregular; stamens exserted. Flowers in September. Widely naturalized in S. USA. Also cv. 'Alba' with white flowers. z6(5), where summers are hot.

L. sprengeri Comes ex Bak. Japan. Has purple-pink flowers with an unusual blue tinge. Less vigorous, smaller and shorter than the following, closely related species. z7

L. squamigera Maxim. Magic Lily, Naked Lady, Resurrection-Lily. Japan. Bulbs large, rounded with long necks; strap-shaped glaucous leaves 30–40cm long, to 3cm wide, in spring. Foliage dries off by late June, flowers appear in late summer. Flowers 3–8 in an umbel on a 60cm-high scape, pink, fragrant, 10–12cm long. For protected, sunny sites in milder climates, or where summers are hot. Needs abundant water in spring. Attractive situated near water and on the south side of a wall. Performs poorly in climates with cool summers. Flowers reliably before *Amaryllis belladonna* under favorable conditions. Develops a large clump in just a few years. Leaves die away, leaving a bare spot in June, then the very attractive *Nerine*-like flowers appear in August. Requires good winter protection. Propagation is by offset bulbs and seed. Worthy of wider garden use. z5(4) (Mü.)

Lygodium Swartz.
Schizaeaceae
Climbing Fern

Forty species of mostly tropical or subtropical ferns with highly modified fronds; the rachis, of indeterminate growth, stem-like, twining, with scattered, lacy pinnules.

L. palmatum (Bernh.) Swartz. Hartford Fern, Climbing Fern. E. USA: Massachusetts south to Florida, west to Tennessee. Fronds twining or climbing, 30–100cm or more high bearing stalked and variously lobed, to very compound, pinnules alternately in pairs. Pinnules cordate-palmate, 3.25–5cm long, fertile pinnules 3–4 pinnatifid, ultimate lobes linear. Sporangia large, ovoid. This unusual fern thrives in moist, acid soil in thickets, marshes, and open, damp woods. A charming addition to tree trunks in the water garden or marsh. z6

Lymanthiemum

L. nymphoides see **Nymophoides peltata**

Lysichiton Schott
Araceae
Skunk-cabbage

Two species of robust, stemless swampland perennials. The large, conspicuous, conch-like spathes appear in spring before the large leaves, which

L. camstschatcense (L.) Schott. Kamchatka, Japan, E. Siberia. Similar to the previous species, slower growing, leaves shorter, blunter, glaucous-green, spathe white, broader, blooming in mid-spring to early summer. Requires a lime-free, moist to wet soil, occasionally flooding. z6(5) (D.)

Lysimachia L.
Primulaceae
Loosestrife

L. ciliata L. (*Steironema ciliatum* (L.) Baudo.) N. America, naturalized in Europe. Herbaceous, stems to 5m high with leaves opposite, ovate to ovate-lanceolate, to 15cm long, petioles conspicuously ciliate. Flowers axillary, solitary to 2.5cm across from upper nodes, in midsummer. Especially attractive naturalized in the partially shady wild garden; may become invasive in the formal garden. z5(4)

L. clethroides, Duby. Gooseneck Loosestrife. Japan, Korea, China. Herbs to 70cm high. Stems erect, slightly

Lysimachia clethroides

Lysimachia nummularia

Lythrum salicaria

fully develop in summer from the stout rhizomes. Indigenous to E. Asia and N. America, in deep, moist topsoil. Useful for watercourses and pond banks, for specimen planting or small groups. Propagate by seed or division, which may be difficult in ornamental plantings. Seedlings are easily grown on loamy humus in a swampy bed.

L. americanus Hult. et St. John (*L. japonicus* Schott). Yellow Skunk-cabbage. California to Alaska, east to Idaho and Montana. Underground rootstock thick. Leaves in rosettes, outspread, to 1m long, 30cm wide, petiole 15cm long, blade narrowing toward the winged petiole, rounded-acuminate at the apex, dark green. Peduncle to 30cm, spathe (flower sheath) oblong-lanceolate, 20–25cm long, 8–12cm wide, bright yellow; spadix, bearing male and female flowers, 10–15cm long, early to mid-spring. For deep, moist to wet soil; tolerates occasional flooding. z4

About 165 species of creeping or erect annuals, perennials, or rarely shrubby species, often glandular-punctate. Leaves opposite, whorled or alternate, entire. Flowers solitary or in umbels, spikes, racemes or panicles, yellow or white, rarely pink or purple. Distributed in the temperate or subtropical zones of the Northern Hemisphere. The yellow species are more common in Europe, the white more in E. Asia. Good plants for naturalizing or in the informal garden. All species grow best in a wet site but adapt to most garden soils. Some species, though handsome, are invasive-weedy. Propagation is by division, seed and some by cuttings.

L. barystachys Bunge. E. Asia. A perennial to 60cm high. Stems erect, slightly pubescent. leaves alternate, oblong-lanceolate, hairy on both sides, entire, sessile, underside somewhat bluish. Flowers small, in nodding, dense racemes, white, July to August. z5

pubescent or glabrous. Leaves alternate, lanceolate, tapered toward the base, lightly pubescent, very attractive in new growth. Flowers in dense, 25–30cm long, widely arching spikes, about 1cm across, pure white, July to September. The best of the white-blooming species. Requires protection in a harsh winter. z4

The above 2 species merit wider garden use. Plants prefer a moist, cool soil, particularly when in full sun, but are also tolerant of relatively dry soil.

L. ephemerum L. Pyrenees. A perennial to 1m high with gray-green, stem-clasping leaves. Flowers in terminal racemes, with long bracts, milk white, June to September. Attractive for naturalizing, but needs protection in cold winters. z7

L. lanceolata Walt. (*Steironema lanceolatum* (Walt.) A. Gray.) E. North America. Herbaceous perennial, stems to 90cm high, 4-angled above the middle; leaves opposite, lower leaves elliptic to ovate, upper leaves lanceolate to linear. Flowers yellow, to 2cm wide, long-petioled in upper leaf axils, solitary or becoming panicled; in midsummer. Especially suitable for wet ground in half-shade. z5(4)

L. nemorum L. SW. and Central Europe. A procumbent herb. Stems ascending 10–30cm, leaves decussate. Flowers solitary on wiry pedicels, yellow, May to July. A decorative shade-loving plant, in a humus-rich, not too dry soil. z6

L. nummularia L. Money Plant. Creeping Jenny, Creeping Charlie. Europe, Central Russia, naturalized in North America, on stream banks and in moist meadows. Stems prostrate, creeping to 50cm wide, sparsely branched, rooting at the nodes. Leaves opposite, flat, rounded, entire, short-petioled, bright green, slightly red glandular-punctate. Flowers axillary, solitary, on long pedicels, bright yellow, red-glandular-punctate inside, 1.5cm wide, spring to midsummer, intermittant to frost. The gold-leaved form 'Aurea' is interesting and contrasts with green foliage. Both forms are good herbaceous groundcovers in shade to semi-shade, though the species is invasive. Also suitable for the banks of ponds where plants will spread right into the water or quickly cover a concrete wall. Propagation is easy by division or better yet from cuttings. Each stem section roots readily. z4

L. punctata L. Garden Lysimachia. S. and Central Europe and Asia Minor, naturalized in North America, on moist sites. Perennials with underground runners, 0.6–1m high. Stems sparsely branched, angular, pubescent. Leaves in whorls of 3–4, ovate-lanceolate, pubescent. Flowers several in the leaf axils, lemon to golden yellow, July to August. A valuable lasting bloomer; indestructable and apt to become a persistant weed, but a vigorous perennial for understory planting. z5

L. thyrsiflora L. (*Naumbergia thyrsiflora* (L.) Rchb.) Tufted Lysimachia. Grows throughout the North Temperate Zone, on pond banks, in swamps and moors. Stems 30–50cm high; from creeping rhizomes. Stems hollow, angular, unbranched, occasionally reddish green. Leaves opposite, narrow-lanceolate, stem-clasping, slightly woolly-pubescent beneath. Flowers small, in the leaf axils in dense racemes, yellow, May to July. A spreading collector's plant for swampy beds, in a muck, acid soil. z4

L. vulgaris L. Garden Lysimachia. Temperate Eurasia, naturalized in North America. Found in ditches, in thickets along riverbanks and islands. A 1.2m-high perennial with vigorously spreading underground runners. Leaves whorled, lanceolate-ovate, slightly woolly-pubescent. Flowers in terminal leafy panicles, golden yellow with reddish centers, June to August. An invasive wildflower for a moist site. Propagation is by seed and division. z5 (D.)

Lythrum L.
Lythraceae
Loosestrife

About 30 species of annual and perennial herbs, rarely subshrubs, with 4-angled or winged, branched, often woody, stems. Leaves mostly opposite or alternate above the middle of branches, lanceolate, sessile. Flowers solitary and axillary, or in axillary clusters, or the uppermost flowers erect, forming slender false spikes, pink to purple-red, or white, July to September. Wide spread in the North Temperate Zone and some in the South. Found on low moorlands, in ditches, moist meadows and wet thickets. Used as a persistent bloomer in the perennial border but especially for naturalizing near ponds and streams. Good companions include *Tradescantia*, *Iris pseudacorus*, *Acorus*, *Trollius*, *Iris sibirica* and *Brunnera*. Easily naturalizes by self-seeding, though named cultivars are far superior to seedlings. The flowers are sought out by butterflies, therefore best situated in clear view or near a walkway. Thrives on moist to wet soils, but also suitable for average garden soil where it remains smaller. Seed propagation will result in a seedling mix of colors. Clonal propagation is by cuttings; the woody rootstock is not easily divided. Cuttings are stuck under glass from April to May. Three species are generally cultivated.

L. alatum Pursh. N. America: Ontario to British Columbia south to Georgia and Texas, mostly in swales on prairies or on moist to wet soils. Subshrub-like, 50–120cm high with angular, partly winged stems. Leaves lanceolate, sessile, lower leaves opposite or in 3's, upper frequently alternate. Flowers solitary, axillary, with bracts, purple, June to August. Keep moist, and in a sunny site. Rarely found in culture in Europe, commonly brought in from the wild in North America. This species has been hybridized with *L. virgatum*. z3–7

L. salicaria L., Purple Loosestrife. North Temperate Zone and S. Australia. Often escapes and naturalizes in moist lowlands, ditches and swampy ground. Rootstock firm, woody. Stems firm, nearly shrublike, 4-angled, branched near base, stems and leaves more or less downy. Leaves mostly alternate or opposite toward the base of the plant, sessile, narrow-lanceolate, rounded or cordate at the base, with distinctly raised venation on the underside. Flowers small, axillary, in 15–25cm long, false spikes, purple-red, June to August. Spent flower stalks are attractive in dried flower arrangements. z4

L. virgatum L. E. Europe and W. Asia, naturalized in NE. USA, on swampy meadows and moist ditches. A perennial to 1.2m high, stems 4-angled, glabrous. Leaves opposite, sessile, narrow-linear, acuminate, tapered toward the base. Flowers grouped 1–3 in loose, often branched, leafy spikes, purple-red, June to August.

The following cultivars come from *L. virgatum*: 'Rose Queen', delicate pink-red panicles, 60cm; 'The Rocket', bright pink, 80cm. z4 (D.)

A variable species, producing a wide range of seedling forms. Over the years, numerous *Lythrum* cultivars have arisen which cannot be attributed to a particular species, though American authors tend to assign them to *L. virgatum* while European authors refer them to *L. salicaria*. Quite possibly some are hybrids involving 2 or more species. Among the most notable cultivars are:

'Brightness', pink, 90cm; 'Dropmore Purple', 90–120cm, purple; 'Feuerkerze' (Fire Candle), bright pink red, 1.2–1.5m; 'Happy', dark pink, 45cm; 'Lady Sackville', bright pink-red, 1.3m; 'Morden's Pink', known to be an *L. virgatum* mutant, pink-colored, 70–80cm; 'Morden's Gleam', this and the following cv. from 'Morden's Pink' × *L. alatum*, to 1.5m, deep rose-pink; 'Morden's Rose', 90–120cm, rose-red; 'Rakete', a strong red, 80cm; 'Robert', bright red, 80cm; 'Superbum', pink-red, 1m; 'The Beacon', dark red, 70–80cm. z4

Macleaya R. Br.
Papaveraceae
Plume Poppy

Two species of tall, upright-growing, more or less glaucous herbaceous perennials from E. Asia with brownish-yellow milky sap, gray-green leaves and small flowers each with 2 early-falling, obtuse-lanceolate sepals and no petals, in erect, open, showy panicles. Used as a specimen plant for its decorative foliage. Also suitable for hiding an unsightly object or blocking an undesirable view. Does well against a wall or among densely rooted woody plants. Spreads rapidly on a light, warm soil by underground stolons. New growth may be damaged by a late frost. Propagate by division and root cuttings. Plants in this genus differ from the closely related *Bocconia* species (all are woody) in having palmately lobed leaves and membranous fruits which dehisce from the apex downward. Many garden books

Macleaya microcarpa

list *M. cordata* under both *Bocconia* and *Macleaya* as if it were 2 different plants.

M. cordata (Willd.) R. Br. (*M. cordata* 'Alba'). Plume Poppy, Tree Celandine. China, Japan. 2–3m high. Herbaceous stems stout, glaucous blue-gray. Leaves large, to 20cm wide, rounded-cordate, palmately lobed, the margins sinuate, blue-green, undersides white and more or less densely short-pubescent. Flowers with white sepals and 24–30 stamens in very large, to 30cm long, loose panicles; midsummer. Seed capsules are quite large, about 2cm long and 5mm wide, flat, gray-brown. With fewer root sprouts than *M. microcarpa* and therefore less invasive. z4

M. cordata var. **yedoensis** (André) Fedde, with large, gray-blue leaves, whitish beneath, and less incised; brown flower panicles. z4

M. × kewensis Turrill. Herbaceous stems to 1.5m high; sepals cream-colored, to brownish; sterile or seldom producing seed. Possibly a hybrid between the two species. Origin unknown. The distribution or availability of plants in cultivation is also not known. z4

M. microcarpa (Maxim.) Fedde. N. Shansi, Kansu. Herbaceous stems 2–2.5m high. Similar in vegetative appearance to *M. cordata*. The leaves rounded, attractively lobed, gray-green above, gray-white beneath. Flowers very numerous, small, leather to copper

Maianthemum bifolium

colored with only 8–12 stamens; midsummer. Needs more room because of its suckering habit. Long cultivated as *M. cordata*. The form 'Kelway's Coral Plume' (Kelway before 1930) is worthy of note. Inflorescences coppery pink, the foliage also more intensely cinnamon colored· less vigorous habit. z5 (M.)

Macrochloa

M. arenaria see **Stipa gigantea**

Maianthemum Wiggers
Liliaceae
False Lily-of-the-Valley

Three similar Northern Hemisphere species, distinguished largely by geographical region and specific botanical characteristics. Low, perennial herbs

with creeping rhizomes with slender roots. Leaves 2–3, simple. Flowers white in terminal racemes; perianth segments 4, separate, spreading, stamens 4; ovary 2-loculed; fruit a 1–2 seeded berry.

M. biflorum var. **kamtschaticum** see **M. kamtschaticum**

M. bifolium (L.) F. W. Schmidt (*Convallaria bifolia* L.). Europe, Siberia, E. Asia. Stem 8–20cm high, white-hairy above, glabrous below; rhizomes thin, creeping. Flowers white, in small racemes, borne just above the 2 deltoid-ovate, cordate leaves; May to June. This attractive, small woodland plant occurs mostly in species-poor deciduous and coniferous stands. Best used in the garden as a similar understory groundcover in woodsy, high humus soil. Propagate by division or seed. z3

M. canadense Desf. (*Unifolium canadense* (Desf.) Greene). Two-leaved Solomon's Seal, Wild Lily-of-the-Valley. Newfoundland to the NW. Territories, south to North Carolina, Tennessee, Indiana and South Dakota. Stem 5–20cm high; glabrous; erect, often flexuose, with 1–3 leaves. Leaves ovate to ovate-oblong, 3–10cm long, glabrous, with a narrow V-shaped sinus, almost sessile. Flower racemes 2.5–5cm long; flowers fragrant. Apparently only one clone is in cultivation in Europe, with leaves ciliate above, hairy below = var. *intereus* Fern. Quite vigorous plants, deserving additional garden use. z1–7 (M.)

M. dilatatum see **M. kamtschaticum**

M. kamtschaticum (Cham.) Nakai. (*M. biflorum* var. *kamtschaticum* (Chem.) Trauv. & C. A. Mey.; *M. dilitatum* (A. Wood) A. Nels. & Mac'or.). Alaska to Idaho and Central California, E. Asia. Stems to 35cm high, glabrous. Leaves ovate, to 20cm long and 10cm wide, cordate with a deep sinus, petioles to 15cm long. Flowers on 5cm long pedicels, in racemes to about 5cm long. A beautiful, bold ground cover plant for a woodland setting in a cool rainforest climate. Combines well with ferns, primulas and ericaceous shrubs. z5(4)–7

Malva L.
Malvaceae
Mallow

About 30 species in Europe, N. Africa and Asia. Annual to biennial herbs or bushy, branched, midsummer-flowering perennials. Only a few suitable garden culture. These are attractive, persistent bloomers for the natural garden in combination with shrubs. Plants will survive in any garden-type soil in full sun. Propagate by seed.

M. alcea L., Hollyhock Mallow. Europe, naturalized in E. USA. Stems 0.8–1m high, with stellate pubescence, well-branched, bushy habit. Leaves rounded-cordate, 5-lobed, divided nearly to the base. Flowers with 3 ovate involucral bracts, calyx with 5 lobes, corolla with 5 separate petals, stamens many, united into a hollow tube, 5–6cm across, attrac-

Malva alcea

tive, clear pink; June to September. Mericarps glabrous. Thrives on a sunny, dry slope or sunny spot on a woodland edge. Self-seeds, under favorable conditions. 'Fastigiata' (*M. alcea* var. *fastigiata* Cav.), 80cm high, grows more stiffly upright, often flowers until frost, deep pink. z5

M. moschata L., Musk Mallow. Europe. North Africa. Stems 60–90cm high, branched, erect, rough-pubescent with spreading, simple hairs, as are the leaves. Lower leaves orbicular, palmately 5–7 lobed, the upper, palmate leaves 3, 5, or 7 lobed, segments sometimes deeply sinuate or lobed. Flowers with 3 linear-lanceolate involucral bracts, light pink, fragrant; June to September. This species also thrives in a sunny bed or shrub border with a lime-free soil The white-flowering form, 'Alba' is attractive and

comes true from seed, as is 'Rosea' with rose-mauve flowers. z6(5) (M.)

Malvestrum

M. coccineum see **Sphaeralcea coccinea**

Manfreda

M. virginica see **Agave virginica**

Marrubium L.
Labiatae
Horehound

White-woolly, bitter-aromatic perennials and subshrubs with 4-angled, basal branching stems; rugose, opposite, crenate or dissected leaves, and only moderately decorative, whorled flowers. Of the 30 primarily Mediterranean species, only a few should be considered for cultivation by collectors. They are rock garden plants for barren, dry sites. Will not tolerate long periods of wet soil. Propagated mainly by cuttings, but also by division.

M. libanoticum Boiss. Lebanon. White-tomentose, rounded leaves, with inconspicuous, pink flowers. Stems 15–25cm high. Needs very good drainage and winter protection. Blooms June to July. z8

M. sericeum see **M. supinum**

M. supinum L. (*M. sericeum* Boiss.). Central and S. Spain, NW. Africa. A cushionform perennial, 15–20cm high, soft woolly-tomentose. Leaves oval-rounded. Flowers small, pink-lilac; June to July. z8

M. velutinum Sibth. et Sm. N. and Central Greece. Stems 20–30cm high, many procumbent, cushionforming. Leaves nearly orbicular, yellowish-tomentose. Flowers small, yellow. June to July. z8 (H.& Kö.)

M. vulgare L. Common Horehound. Central and W. Asia, Mediterranean Counties, and the Canary Islands. Stems to 45cm high, pubescent. Leaves white-pubescent, broadly orbiculate-ovate, crenate to 5cm long, petioled. Flowers crowded in verticillasters, small, whitish. Not ornamental but essential in traditional herb gardens. Widely naturalized in N. America. z4

Marsilea L.
Marsileaceae
Pepperwort, Water Clover

About 65 species of aquatic or marsh ferns in tropical and temperate regions. Fronds with a long stalk terminating in 4 flat-spread pinnae giving a clover-like appearance. Propagation by division. Many species are tender.

M. quadrifolia L. Pepperwort. An aquatic fern distributed from Spain to Japan, naturalized in E. North America.

Marrubium supinum

Rhizomes thin, creeping, with 10–40cm long-stalked, clover-like, 4-part glabrous fronds. The fruiting structures (sporocarps) podlike, 2–3, containing sporangia with megaspores and microspores, at the base of the frond stalk. Pepperwort has submergent forms in deeper water. Produces megaspores (origin of female gametophyte) and microspores (precursors of pollen grains). Megaspores visible as a whitish yellow mucilaginous clouding of the water, microspores invisible. Only for collectors. Grow on swampy sites in water to 10cm deep. z4

M. mucronata A. Br. Temperate N. America, Rocky Mts. eastward, including S. Canada, the USA and adjacent Northern Mexico, shallow ponds, pools, and wet banks. Fronds very like the above species, but pubescent, pinnae more angular, and usually with a single sporocarp.

Pilularia globulifera L., the Pill Fern, 1 of 6 species in this genus, all similar, is a relative of the Pepperwort in the Marsileaceae Family. This fern, with its grasslike, undivided fronds is not especially ornamental and of interest only to botanic gardens. Grow like *Marsilea*. Pill Ferns are nearly extinct and should not be removed from their natural habitats. (D.)

drained, loamy garden soil and are easily propagated by seed and division. They are attractive groundcovers for planting between bulbs of wild *Crocus, Iris reticulata, Muscari, Scilla mischtschenkoana* (*S. tubergeniana*).

M. caucasica (Willd.) Poir. (*Tripleurospermum caucasicum* (Willd.) Hayek). Mountains of Bulgaria, Albania, the Caucasus, Asia Minor, found on alpine meadows. Carpetforming, as are the following species. Stems procumbent, only the flowering shoots are erect. Entire plant nearly glabrous. Leaves

somewhat rough on the dorsal side, pappus white. Blooms from May to July. This species tolerates mowing to give a lawn effect, and plants survive limited foot traffic. z7(6) (E.)

Matteuccia Tod.
Polypodiaceae
Ostrich Fern

Three species from the temperate zone. Vigorous, large ferns with a stout, scaly, ball or dome-shaped rootstock, often

Marsilea quadrifolia

Matricaria oreades

Matteuccia orientalis

Matricaria L.
Compositae
Wild, or False Camomile

About 40 species of annual, biennial or perennial, fragrant or odorless herbs in Europe, the Mediterranean region, W. Asia, S. Africa and North America with 1–3 pinnatisect, alternate leaves and white or yellow flower heads, solitary and terminal, or in corymbs, rayed or discoid. The genus is very closely related to *Chrysanthemum*.

Of the 3 species mentioned below, which botanists now classify as *Tripleurospermum*, *M. oreades* is the most valuable and noteworthy as a garden ornamental; the others are inconsistent in growth habit and frequently die out in winter. These are attractive, dense, semi-evergreen carpet-forming perennials for large areas in the alpine garden, rock garden or for covering sunny, dry slopes. The chrysanthemum-like flower heads are long persistent over the green carpet of leaves. They thrive in any loose, well-

twice pinnatisect. Flower heads terminal, solitary, chrysanthemum-like, 3–5cm wide. Fruits smooth, with a brownish pappus. Blooms from May to July. z7(6)

M. oreades Boiss. (*Chrysanthemum oreades* (Boiss.) Wehrh., *Tripleurospermum oreades* (Boiss.) Rech.f.). Mountains of Asia Minor and Syria. Similar to the above species but more distinctly pubescent, with more finely divided leaves and only 2–3cm wide flower heads on 10–20cm long stems. Fruits warty gray on the dorsal side, pappus white. Blooms from April to July. The most drought resistant species. z6

M. tchihatchewii (Boiss.) Voss. Turfing Daisy. (*Tripleurospermum tchihatchewii* (Boiss.) Bornm.). Coastal region of Asia Minor, on dry hills. Somewhat taller than the previous 2 species, adpressed pubescent, with creeping, rooting, ascending stems. Basal leaves nearly palmately compound. Flower heads to 3cm wide on 15–30cm long stems. Fruits

growing above the soil. Individual plants with a vase-like or funnel-shaped cluster of sterile fronds; fertile fronds central, clustered, stiffly upright, more or less club-shaped. Suitable for shaded sites on moist to wet humus-rich soil. Impressive as a specimen plant.

M. orientalis (Hook.) Trev. (*Struthiopteris orientalis* Hook.)., Japanese Ostrich Fern. China, Japan, India, Himalaya Mts., in moist, shaded forests. Rhizome thick, blackish, largely above-ground, not stoloniferous. Fronds to 1m long, elongate-lanceolate not attenuate toward the base, long-stalked, outward-arching in an irregular clump or forming a flattened, irregular funnel. Frond blade to 45cm wide, simple-pinnate, dark green, firm, deciduous. Spore-bearing fronds appear in June, 50cm long, with pinnae contracted inward, dark brown. The Japanese Ostrich Fern is a charming, tropical-looking fern for specimen use. Grows best in cool, wet, very rich humus soil. Can be quite vigorous under favorable conditions. Deteriorates during drought and must then be watered. Winter protection is advisable. Propagation is by spores which ripen from October to January. z7

M. pensylvanica (Willd.) Raymond (*M. struthiopteris* var. *pensylvanica* (Willd.) C.V. Morton), American Ostrich Fern. Indigenous to N. America, on flood plains along rivers in alluvial soils and in swampy woodlands. Can grow 2–3m high under favorable conditions. Sterile fronds with rachis steel blue from emergence until mature, pinnae contracted from the middle outward but not to the

Similar to *M. pensylvanica*, but paler green. Frond stalks brown below the pinnae. Pinnae present down to the rachis base, free stalk 10cm long at most. Lowest pinnae small, whitish-green. Rhizomes erect, reaching to 15cm out of the soil on old plants. Sterile fronds 0.8–1m long. Fertile fronds appear from July to August, olive green at first, later light brown, stiffly erect in the center of the foliage vase, 40cm high.

A vigorous fern for a humus woodland site or in full sun beside a pond or stream. Covers large areas through vigorous stolons; can be inva-

pubescent, long, entire, sinuate or pinnatifid; flowers purple, lilac or white, sepals 4, petals 4, stigma deeply 2-lobed, usually fragrant, in racemes; spring to summer.

M. fruticulosa (L.) Maire (*M. varia* (Sibth. et. Sm.) DC., *M. tristis* R. Br.). S. Europe, Mediterranean region. Stems 10–15cm high; basal axis branched, creeping underground. Leaves narrow, entire, gray-pubescent. Flowers dull purple; reddish violet on *M. fruticulosa* var. *vallesiaca* Conti, appearing in April and May in few-flowered racemes. A col-

Matteuccia struthiopteris

Matthiola fruticulosa

base as with *M. struthiopteris*. Fronds dark green, simple-pinnate, deeply pinnatisect, forming a tall funnel. Fertile fronds appear from June to July, to 60cm; the narrow, round, spore-bearing pinnae are black-green at first, later dark brown. Spreads slowly through limited production of underground stolons which are produced more freely in warmer climates.

For a moist site with very fertile, high humus soil; i.e., near a pond or stream. Old specimens dominate their section of the garden by sheer size. Under favorable conditions, this is the largest of all the garden ferns except *Osmunda regalis*. Propagation is by spores, stolons and stolon cuttings. Spores ripen from October to January. z4

M. struthiopteris (L.) Tod. (*Struthiopteris germanica* Willd.), European Ostrich Fern. Europe including Scandinavia and Russia, E. Asia, China, along streams and rivers in the alpine valleys, always on deep, alluvial soils, but not in standing water.

sive. Turns brown prematurely on a dry site in full sun; then the fronds must be cut back, plants fertilized and well watered. There are various strains which vary in height, from 0.6–1m, and leaf form, pinnae smooth to lightly undulate. Propagation is by spores, stolons or stolon cuttings. Spores ripen from November to January. Fertile fronds of all three Ostrich Ferns are useful in dry flower arranging. A good fall foliage color. z4 (D.)

M. struthiopteris var. **pensylvanica** see **M. pensylvanica**

Matthiola R. Br.corr. Spreng.
Cruciferae
Stocks

About 30–50 species, mostly annual and biennial, but a few perennials or subshrubs indigenous mostly to the Mediterranean basin. Leaves gray-

lector's plant for a sunny rock bed. Propagate by seed and division. z7 (M.)

Mazus Lour.
Scrophulariaceae

About 20–30 species of small, more or less deciduous mat-forming, perennial herbs from E. and SE. Asia, Indomalaysia, Australia and New Zealand. Stems creeping or procumbent, mostly rooting at the nodes. Basal leaves rosetted or opposite, stem leaves alternate, leaves toothed or incised. Flowers short-pedicelled, bilabiate, in terminal, 1-sided racemes. The upper lip 2-lobed, the much larger lower lip 3-lobed, with 2 conspicuous crests. Usually only for collectors and botanic gardens. Attractive, small groundcovers, but unfortunately not reliably winter hardy. For a sunny or semi-shaded place in the rock garden, spreading to form a dense mat in humus-rich, lime-free soil. Should be covered with conifer branches for winter protection, but still freezes out in some years. Hence, a stock of replacement plants should be maintained in pots in a cold frame or greenhouse. Propagation is by division. Good companions are New Zealand plants such as: *Hebe armstrongii*, *H. cupressoides*, *H. pinguifolia*, *Coprosma petriei*, *Carex buchananii*, *Epilobium inornatum*, and various *Raoulia* species.

M. miquelii Mak. (*M. stolonifera* (Maxim.) Mak.). Japan, on moist sites, especially in the vicinity of rice paddies.

grouped 1–6 on 3–5cm high, thin stems, white, occasionally blue, with yellow throats. Blooms from May to June. z8(7)

M. radicans (Hook.f.) Cheesem. New Zealand. In habitats similar to those described for the previous species. Creeping stems, rooting at the nodes, form a dense, flat carpet. Leaves 2–5cm long including the petiole, closely attached to the stem, obovate to narrowly obovate, obtuse, mostly entire or coarsely toothed, and softly pubescent, often with brown markings, lying on the ground. Flower stems 1–3

Includes about 45 annual, biennial and perennial species, mostly in S. Central Asia; only one species endemic to Europe. Most species are high alpine plants growing in the Himalaya Mts. from 3000–4000m. Species with silky-pubescent leaf rosettes are generally monocarps, dying after the seeds ripen, blooming after 2–4 years. These very attractive, stately, foliage and flowering plants (to 2m) include *M. discigera* Prain, light blue or purple; *M. horridula* Hook.f.et Thoms. (*M. rudis* Prain) steel blue, leaves small, blue green with yellow bristles; *M. integrifolia* (Maxim.)

Mazus pumilio

Meehania urticifolia

Stoloniferous, with 7–15cm long stems and narrow, 4–7cm long and 1–1.5cm wide, green, spatulate leaves with winged petioles. Flowers light purple, occasionally white, 1.5–2cm long. Blooms from April to May. Plants offered under this name in commerce usually are another species. z8(7)

M. pumilio R. Br. New Zealand, Australia, Tasmania, from the lowlands to lower mountainous regions on the edges of swamps, and on moors and moist meadows. Plants 5–10cm high, with short, underground stems. Leaves dark green, obovate, to 7.5cm long, entire or coarsely dentate. Flowers

flowered, erect. Flowers white, with a yellow or pale-violet throat, or largely lilac. Dealers offer both white- and lilac-flowering strains. Blooms from May to July. z6(5) (E.)

M. stolonifera see **M. miquelii**

Meconopsis Vig.
Papaveraceae
Asiatic Poppy, Blue Poppy, Himalayan Poppy, Welsh Poppy

Genus closely related to *Papaver*, differing in the distinctly defined style.

Franch., large flowered, yellow, low; *M. napaulensis* DC. (*M. wallichii* Hook.), blue, purple and red shades; *M. paniculata* D. Don, yellow; *M. regia* G. Taylor, yellow, leaves with golden, silky-shaggy pubescent; *M. superba* Prain, white.

All *Meconopsis* need wind protection, and a cool, moist summer climate. They grow best in light shade and well-drained, fertile, humus-rich, acid soil, with an occasional dousing of water during the growing season; require dryness in winter. Easily grown from seed sown in spring under glass. Seedlings should be kept constantly moist and shaded, potted up for the cold frame and set into the garden in late July with a soil ball. The removal of spent flower heads from young perennial plants to prevent seed setting and encourage root growth is critical. Valuable in large rock gardens and natural gardens.

Perennial, persistent and relatively easily cultivated species are:

M. betonicifolia Franch. (*M. baileyi* Prain). Blue Poppy. Tibet, W. China, Upper Burma at 3000–4000m. Blooms 0.9–1.2m high. Rootstock short, covered with brown bristles. Stems with scattered leaves, glabrous or brownish-pubescent, like the leaves. Leaves long-

tivated, less attractive species, perpetuates by self-seeding. 'Aurantiaca' flowers orange-yellow, 'Plena' is double. z6

M. grandis Prain. Nepal, Sikkim, Tibet, at 3000–4000m. Stiffly upright, 0.8–1m high, perennial with a taproot. Entire plant brownish-pubescent. Stems erect, with few leaves. Basal leaves 30cm long, elliptic, entire or crenate, reddish brown pubescent. Flowers solitary, bowl-shaped, to 12cm wide, bright violet-blue on scapes or in axils of upper leaves; May to June. A beautiful species, requiring a

tions place them beyond the scope of a general garden book.

Lit.: Taylor, G: *An Account of the Genus Meconopsis.* London 1934. (Sch. & S.)

Meehania Britt.
Labiatae
Meehan's Mint,
Japanese Dead Nettle

Of this genus, only the following 2 species appear in cultivation. Propagate

Meconopsis napaulensis

Meconopsis regia

petioled, oval, crenate. Flowers gently nodding, mostly 4-petalled, on long pedicels, borne in the uppermost leaf axils, sky blue, anthers golden yellow; June to July. A beautiful species on favorable sites, i.e. among *Rhododendron*. Very long-lived, but only in climates with cool, cloudy, misty summers and mild, drier winters. z7(6)

M. cambrica (L.) Vig. W. Europe, including Britain. Flowers borne 30–40cm high; plant with dense, bushy habit. Leaves palmately lobed, grassy light green, bluish beneath, with upright hairs. Flowers long-pedicelled. 3–5cm wide, yellow; June to October. Easily cul-

cool site and lime-free soil. The most spectacular selection is 'G.S. 600' but this is rarely available and can only be propagated from cuttings. z5

M. × sheldonii G. Taylor (*M. betonicifolia* × *M. grandis*), a garden hybrid to 1m high. Flowers large, rich blue, available in cultivars, June. Similar to *M. betonicifolia* in habit, very attractive, only vegetatively propagated. z6

M. villosa see **Cathcartia villosa**

Numerous additional *Meconopsis* species, hybrids, and cultivars are listed, but their stringent environmental limita-

by division of the rhizomes or cuttings.

M. cordata (Nutt.) Britt. (*Cedronella cordata* (Nutt.) Benth.) Meehan's Mint, Creeping Mint. E. North America, Pennsylvania and Illinois to North Carolina and Tennessee, in rich woods. Delicate herb; flowering stems ascending 7.5–20cm high with very slender basal stolons; leafy, leaves cordate, crenate, blades to 5cm long, nearly as broad, slender petiole equals blade length. Flowers in terminal spikes, corolla 2.5–3.5cm long, bright lavender or lilac, in May and June. Attractive ground cover in a woodland with moist, humus-rich, fertile soil. z4

M. urticifolia (Miq.) Mak. (*Dracocephalum urticifolium* Miq., *Dedronella urticifolia* (Miq.) Maxim., *Glechoma urticifolia* (Miq.) Mak.). Throughout the mountain forests of Honshu (Japan). Very similar to *Lamiastrum galeobdolon* in habit and woodland habitat, similarly, produces low, rooting runners following development of the erect flower stems. Flowers appear in late May, about 3cm long, and somewhat resembling *Melittis*, but violet-blue with white. This attractive, very winter-hardy perennial enriches the assortment of plants for understory planting; being deciduous, it is well adapted to tolerating leaf drop in deciduous woodlands. Unfortunately, very susceptible to slug damage. z5 (S.)

Megasea see Bergenia

Melandrium see Silene

Melanthium L.
Liliaceae

Four species closely related to *Veratrum* and vaguely similar in habit, from E. North America, but rhizomatous. Stems leafy, leaves linear to ovate or oblanceolate; flowers greenish or white, both bisexual and 1-sexed flowers present in the large, terminal panicle; perianth segments 6, clawed, separate and spreading, stamens 6, ovary 3-celled. Only *M. virginicum* is occasionally offered for sale and is recommended for collectors and botanic gardens; requires a moister site than *Veratrum*, while *M. hybridum* requires a drier situation. These grow in a sunny or semi-shaded site and loamy humus soil or a mixture of loam and peat. Propagation by division is hardly possible; seeds must be sown right after ripening, but usually do not germinate until spring. Plants bloom only after 4–5 years. Uses and companions are the same as for *Veratrum*.

M. hybridum Walt. (*M. latifolium* Desr.). Bunchflower. USA: Connecticut to Pennsylvania south to Georgia, in dry woodlands and headlands. Stems 0.6–1.2m high. Leaves oblanceolate, 5.5cm wide. Panicles terminal, 30cm and longer, with divergent or ascending branches. Flowers greenish white, later becoming darker, fragrant, with crispate suborbicular segments. Blooms in late summer. Sometimes found in botanic gardens. z5–8

M. latifolium see **M. hybridum**

M. virginicum L. USA: New York to Florida, Minnesota to Texas, in moist meadows, damp woodland margins, and marshy ditches on the prairie. Stems to 1.5m high. Leaves chaneled, to 30cm long and to 2cm wide. Panicles terminal, 15–35cm long. Flowers cream-colored to greenish yellow, later turning green to amber. Perianth segments oblong to ovate, not undulate. Blooms in midsummer. Adapts to average garden soils. z4–7 (E.)

Melanthium virginicum

Melica ciliata

Melica L.
Gramineae
Melic, Melic Grass

Medium-high grasses with 2–several-flowered spikes in usually one sided panicles. Of the 60 species only a few are considered for garden use, some are invasive. Propagation is easy by division and seed.

M. altissima L. Siberian Melic. Central Czechoslovakia to N. Bulgaria and Central Russia. Inflorescences to 1m high. Leaves to 20cm long, forming a dense, sap-green clump. Flower panicles

15cm long, silver-gray, purple-brown on the form 'Atropurpurea'; May to June, suitable for naturalizing in a partially shaded garden. z4

M. ciliata L. Silky-spike Melic. Europe, N. Africa, Caucasus, on sunny mountain slopes and on rocks, usually limestone. Inflorescences 30–70cm high; clump-forming, foliage gray-green, leaves usually furled, flat or folded; spike-like panicles cylindrical, silky, pale yellow when ripe; May to June. For natural prairie plant beds or rock gardens. z6

Iran. *Melissa* species with inconspicuous flowers, not particularly ornamental, but they are valuable herbs in the kitchen garden for their lemon scent and essential to the traditional herb garden. Collectors of scented plants may wish to include them in their ornamental gardens. Thrives in a sunny or semi-shaded site in any normal garden soil. May be left undisturbed for many years, even decades. Propagate by seed, division and cuttings. Spreads in the garden by self-seeding and by sterile, prostrate, basal shoots with adventitious roots.

rate, lightly pubescent, distinctly veined. Flowers clustered in the leaf axils, large, white with a pink or lilac lower lip, or also entirely white, May to June. An attractive wildflower for a shaded site in gardens and parks. Grows in calcareous, loamy soil. Propagate by division, seed and cuttings.

One of the more variable wild herbaceous plants for flower color. Since the species is not stoloniferous and the seeds ripen at various times, making collection tedious, this plant is seldom found in the trade. A trouble-free garden plant

Melissa officinalis

Melittis melissophyllum

M. nutans L., Nodding Pearl, Melic Grass. Europe, Caucasus, in deciduous forests on slightly acidic soil. Inflorescences 30–60cm high, grows as a loose ground cover; stoloniferous. Leaves furled, grass green; panicles narrow, occasionally longer than 10cm; spikelets oblong-ovate, glumes purple-brown with a white membranous margin. Best when grown in semi-shade and loose, fertile soil. z6

M. transsilvanica Schur. E. Central and E. Europe. Distinguished from *M. ciliata* by the midrib on a flat leaf, shorter panicle, and glumes strongly unequal. z6 (S.)

Melissa L.
Labiatae
Balm, Lemon Balm

Three species of persistent, aromatic herbs from Europe to Central Asia and

M. officinalis L., Balm, Lemon Balm. S. Europe, Mediterranean region, W. and Central Asia. Grows naturally among shrubs, hedgerows, in fences and on stone walls. Stems 50–80cm high, lemon-scented plants with short stolons. Leaves ovate, coarsely serrate. Flowers in 6 to many-flowered, loose, more or less one-sided false whorls, whitish or yellow. Blooms from June to August. An old medicinal herb, used since antiquity for attracting bees. Brought to Spain by Arabian merchants and probably taken by monks into Central Europe. 'Variegata' is a white-variegated form. z5(4) (E.)

Melittis L.
Labiatae

M. melissophyllum L. Europe, in open woodlands. Stems 40–50cm high. Habit like that of Dead Nettle, erect. Stems 4-angled. Leaves large, ovate, coarsely ser-

for open woodland margins together with: *Aster divaricatus, Lamium orvala, Dictamnus, Stachys macrantha* 'Grandiflora', *Omphalodes cappadocica, Pulmonaria, Geranium, Amsonia, Rosa willmottiae.* z6(5) (Mü.)

Mentha L.
Labiatae
Mint

Twenty-five species of aromatic, erect or decumbent, persistent herbs in the North Temperate Zone, S. Africa and Australia. Stems mostly 4-angled, leaves opposite, rarely alternate, sessile or petioled. Flowers clustered in whorls, usually in terminal spikes. Calyx campanulate or tubeform, 10–13 veined, mostly 5-toothed. Corolla lavender, pink or white, tube within the calyx, 4 lobes protruding, upper lobe reflexed, larger. Stamens epipetalous, 4, in pairs, ovary with 4 loci. Variable genus with many intermediate forms and hybrids. Peppermint, with its various varieties and cultivars, is suitable for the herb or kitchen garden. Only the following species is recommended for the rock garden for its fragrance and mat-forming habit. Grows well in a semi-shaded, evenly moist site to fill in between large and smaller herbs. Not reliably winter hardy, but a few shoots usually resprout in spring and quickly recover the ground. Also spreads by self-seeding. Winter protection with conifer branches is advisable. To assure overwintering,

M. × piperita L. Peppermint var. **citrata** Bergamot Mint.

M. pulegium L. Pennyroyal var. **gibraltarica**, Gibralter Mint, White-woolly Mint.

M. spicata L. Spearmint. cv. 'Crispa' or 'Crispii' or 'Crispata', Curly-leaf Spearmint.

M. suaveolens J.F. Ehrh., Apple Mint cv. 'Variegata' Pineapple Mint.

area. Very attractive combined with *Iris kaempferi, Myosotis palustris* and *Mimulus,* and also among tall swamp iris and cattails.

Requires lime-free peaty bog soil. Propagate by division, May to June, or rhizome cuttings, taken June to August and grown on wet containers under glass or in a bog bed. The flowers are supposed to have medicinal qualities, for breaking a fever and stomach disorders. z4 (D.)

Menyanthes trifoliata

Mercurialis perennis

Merendera pyrenaica

some plants should be potted and kept free from frost. Propagate by division. Suitable for a low ground cover around small bulbous plants, but also for planting in spaces between stepping stones, and for the alpine house.

M. requienii Benth., Corsican Mint, Menthella. Corsica, Sardinia, Monte Christo; naturalized in parts of W. Europe, in moist and shaded sites. Flat, matforming plants with filamentous, glabrescent, procumbent stems, rooting at the nodes. With 1–4mm wide round leaves and tiny, inconspicuous flowers in few-flowered whorls, light violet. Blooms in summer. z7(6) (E.)

Several mints belong in the traditional herb garden, grown for their scent and some for foliage variegations or texture. All are vaguely similar with leafy, upright stems and rhizomatous rootstocks. They grow in full sun to partial shade in deeply dug, fertile moist loam. Among the most common are:

Menyanthes L.
Menyanthaceae
Bogbean, Buckbean,
Marsh Trefoil

Only one species.

M. trifoliata L. Circumboreal, in bogs and soggy moors, in shallow water, margins or ponds and streams. Plant to 30cm high, entirely glabrous. Rhizome creeping, segmented, abundant roots. Leaves alternate, petioles to 25cm long, with 3 sessile leaflets, leaflets lanceolate, rounded at the tip, entire, glossy dark green. Scape leafless, rising above the leaves. Inflorescence an erect, terminal raceme with 10–15 flowers. Flowers funnelform, 5-cleft, fleshy with 5 epipetalous stamens, white to purplish, a white beard, May to June. A very attractive swamp plant for bank planting and flat sites in all types of water gardens. A harmless spreader, easily kept within bounds, but capable of covering a large

Mercurialis L.
Euphorbiaceae

Eight species of low, annual or perennial dioecious herbs from the Mediterranean region and from Eurasia to Thailand. Plants with opposite, simple leaves; lack a milky sap. Staminate flowers in dense helicoid cymes in the axils of bracts. Pistillate flowers in clusters in the axils of upper stem leaves or in racemes.

Of no real ornamental value but perhaps suitable for greening up shady sites in large parks, especially beneath tall shrubs and deciduous trees. Quickly spreads in such situations by underground runners and may become weedlike. Thrives only on a loose, loamy soil with leafmold. The deeper the shade, the more intense the blue-black color of the leaves. Propagate by division and stolon cuttings. In partial shade these plants combine well with *Arum, Asarum, Circaea lutetiana, Dryopteris filix-mas,*

Galium odoratum, Hedera, Maianthemum, Melica uniflora, Oxalis acetosella, Sanicula and *Leucojum*. Forms a groundcover monoculture in deepest shade.

M. perennis L. Found nearly throughout Europe, N. Africa and W. Asia. Grows in the Alps to 1800m; colonizing on moderately moist to wet, gravelly humus soil in shady, mixed deciduous forest. Plant 15–30cm high, with blackish-green, pubescent, oblong-ovate leaves. Flowers inconspicuous, April to May. Not recommended for private gardens. z5 (E.)

Merendera Ram.
Liliaceae

Genus of 9 or more species growing from Spain through Iran to Afghanistan. Related to *Colchicum*, but the 6 perianth segments completely free to the base, and abruptly constricted toward the base. Unlike *Bulbocodium*, the 3 styles are completely free. Small herbs with tuberous bulbs about 3–5cm high at flowering, mostly blooming in early spring, but some in autumn. Leaves narrow, usually appearing with or immediately after the star-shaped flowers. An excellent plant for collectors, especially for pot culture since plants may be short-lived in the garden. Suitable for planting among small perennials in the rock garden in sunny sites. Requires moisture in spring, dryness in summer. Propagated by seed.

M. pyrenaica (Pourr.) P. Fourn. (*M. bulbocodium* Ram., *M. montana*) Lange. Pyrenees, Spain and Portugal. A fall bloomer, August to September. Leaves appearing during anthesis or just after. Tuberous bulbs globose-ovate with a black-brown tunic, *Colchicum*-like. Flowers solitary or paired, pinkish-lilac, with linear, obtuse segments. z6

M. sobolifera Fisch et. Mey. Central and E. Balkan Peninsula, Asia Minor, Iran. A spring bloomer, March to April. The 3 narrow-lanceolate, furrowed leaves appear with the pale, rosy-lilac flowers and are no longer than these. The tuberous bulbs produce horizontal runners with new bulbs at the tips. z6 (S.)

Mertensia Roth
Boraginaceae
Bluebells

About 40 species in E. Europe, Asia and N. America. Dwarf, carpet-forming or erect, medium-high, bushy perennials with alternate, lanceolate or broad, entire, usually bluish green leaves with pellucid dots. The tubular-funnelform to campanulate, nodding, variably blue flowers are mostly sessile in pendulous, terminal racemose, scorpioid or panicled cymes; spring to summer. The calyx is 5-

Mertensia virginica

lobed, corolla 5-lobed with (rarely without) crests in the throat, stamens 5, ovary 2-lobed. These are mountain and woodland plants. The low species are suitable rock garden plants, single specimens or in groups, best in full sun in moist, humus soil. The taller species are better suited for naturalizing with woody plants in full sun to dappled shade. Propagate by division, cuttings and seed. Alpine and rock gardeners grow a great many Mertensias; the species listed below include the more readily available ones.

M. alpina (Torr.)G. Don. (*M. tweedyi* Rydb.) USA: Rocky Mts. generally above tree-line. Glabrous herb, grows as a small clump, to 20cm high. Leaves spatulate to lanceolate, hairy above, glabrous beneath. Flowers showy, dark blue, 12.5cm long, with prominent crests. An alpine garden plant.

M. ciliata (James) G. Don. W. North America (Rocky Mountains). Stems 0.6–

1m or more high, upright, pale gray-green. Leaves oval-lanceolate, glabrous beneath, margins ciliate. Flowers pink at first, later bright blue, with crests campanulate; May to July. z4

M. echioides Benth. Himalaya Mts. Soft, hairy plant 20–30cm high, mat-forming. Leaves short-petioled, oblong-spatulate. Flowers dark blue in dense, terminal cymes, throat of the corolla tube without crests; May to July. Very satisfactory, dense ground cover rock bed plant; requires fertile, loamy soil. z6

M. lanceolata (Pursh) DC. N. America: Rocky Mts. and westward. Stems slender, erect, unbranched, 15–30cm high. Leaves lanceolate or spatulate, sparsely floccose, ciliate, glabrous beneath. Flowers in loose racemes; corolla campanulate, short 5-lobed, light blue; buds pink; May. z4

M. paniculata (Ait.) G. Don. E. North America: mostly in Canada, E. Asia. Stems 60cm high, erect, green, softly pubescent. Leaves ovate to broadly-lanceolate, rough-hairy above and below. Flowers purple-blue, pinkish while opening, sometimes white, with crests, in loose racemes; in midsummer. Also var. *borealis* (Macbr.) L. O. Williams. Leaves completely glabrous or only pubescent beneath. z4

M. primuloides C. B. Clarke. Himalaya Mts. Dwarf plant 10–15cm high; rootstocks somewhat creeping. Stems very leafy, particularly below the middle. Leaves petioled, elliptic, narrowing at both ends, hairy overall. Flowers erect in few-flowered, nearly flat, crowded racemes; flower corolla flat, about 1.2cm wide, indigo blue with white or yellow centers, fading to yellowish; corolla tube with crests; May to June. Unfortunately, rarely cultivated. Requires lime-free, sandy loam. For a semi-shaded rock garden site. z5

M. pterocarpa Tatew. et Ohwi. Japan, S. Kurile Islands. Bushy plant 15–20cm high. Leaves blue-gray, oval, acuminate, with conspicuous veins. Flowers sky blue, in panicled racemes; May to

nodding clusters, buds pink, opening to rich sky blue or rarely pink or white; April to May. A wonderful species, but unfortunately dies back soon after flowering. Needs a semi-shaded to shaded site and moist, woodland-type soil. Also, cv. 'Rubra', flowers pink, and 'Alba', flowers white. All are beautiful naturalized with various ferns, *Dicentra spectabilis*, *Endymion* and *Scilla* species, and similar early-blooming woodland ornamentals. z5–8 (M.)

all loamy humus-rich soils in cultivation, in sun or semi-shade. Propagation is possible by division, but not very productive. Best results are from freshly harvested seed. Companion plants include *Alchemilla xanthochlora* (*A. vulgaris*), *Crepis aurea*, *Eryngium alpinum*, *Gentiana lutea*, *Genista pilosa*, *Hieracium villosum*, *Chrysanthemum vulgare*, *Phyteuma orbiculare*, *Polygonum bistorta*, *Ranunculus aconitifolius*. z5 (E.)

Meum athamanticum

Michauxia campanuloides

Micromeria croatica

August. Attractive, broad bush-like rock garden plants. z7

M. pulmonarioides see **M. virginica**

M. sibirica (L.) G. Don. E. Siberia. Stems 0.5–1m high, unbranched, erect, light green, entirely glabrous. Basal leaves petioled, rounded-cordate, stem leaves sessile, ovate, acuminate. Flowers variable, purple-blue to white, pendulous, in a forked raceme; spring to summer. z4(3)

M. tweedyi see **M. alpina**

M. virginica (L.) Pers. (*M. pulmonarioides* Roth). Bluebells, Virginia Bluebells, Virginia Cowslip. USA: New York to S. Carolina, Tennessee, Alabama, west to Kansas. Stems 40–60cm high; rootstock black-brown, fleshy, spindle-shaped. Leaves elliptic to ovate, blackish purple to green, emerging with a metallic shine, later paler blue-green to lettuce green, glabrous. Flowers 2–3cm long in

Meum Mill.
Umbelliferae

Only one species.

M. athamanticum Jacq. Bald-money. Mountains of W. and Central Europe, to S. Italy and Bulgaria; mostly on infertile fields, mountain slopes and roadsides. In the mountain foothills on moist, lime-free, moderately acid, sandy loam to humus-rich loam. Also found on limestone in the E. Alps to 2500m. Entire plant spicy scented, 15–50cm high, root crown with a brown fibrous crest. Leaves mostly basal, glabrous, grass green, finely divided to nearly hairlike segments. Umbels 6–15 rayed, bracts fewer, usually absent, petals white, very occasionally reddish or slightly yellowish white. Blooms from May to June.

One of the very attractive foliage plants among the medium-sized perennials for grouping in the natural garden and rock garden. Although only found in nature on lime-free soil, tolerates nearly

Michauxia L'Hérit.
Campanulaceae

This genus has been reclassified as *Mindium* Adams by some botanists. 6–7 species in W. Asia. Biennial, erect, tough herbs with alternate, irregularly toothed and lobed leaves. Flowers in spikes, racemes, or panicles, large white or tinted rose or lavender. Calyx lobes (6)–7–10, petals lobes (6)–7–10, narrow, outspread or recurved, nearly distinct, stamens separate, (6)–7–10. Capsules capped by the wilted corolla. Blooms from July to September. Grow in well-drained, gravelly soil in full sun, best in the rockery or even xerophytic garden. A collector's plant, and never truly perennial; propagated by seed sown where plants are to bloom.

M. campanuloides L'Hérit. Asia Minor, in limestone crevices. Stems stout, to 1.5m high, unbranched. Basal and stem leaves to 20cm long. Flowers white to rose- or lavender shaded on the outside, with up to 5cm-long, narrow lobes. Flower form resembles that of *Lilium martagon*. Needs protection in winter from excessive moisture. Plants die back somewhat in June, and may flower (then die) only after 3 or 4 years old. z7(6) (K.)

Micromeria Benth.
Labiatae

Probably 70–100 cosmopolitan species of perennial herbs and low shrubs; few with ornamental value. Differs from the closely related genus *Satureja* in the anthers more or less included under the upper lip. Calyx usually 13-veined. Small herbs or dwarf shrubs, recommended only for collectors in the alpine garden, rock garden or rock bed. They require a dry site in full sun, best when grown on gravel or in a rock crevice in a sterile, gravelly soil. May freely self-seed, especially *M. croatica*. Propagated by seed and cuttings. Light winter protection is advisable.

M. cristata (Hampe) Griseb. N. and Central Balkan Mountains. Stems 5–10cm high, erect, simple, short and densely pubescent. Leaves opposite, small, overlapped, with revolute margins. False whorls with 2–10, usually 6 flowers. Corolla 4–6mm long, purple. Blooms from June to July. z5

M. croatica (Pers.) Schott (*Satureja croatica* (Pers.) Briq.). Yugoslavia, in the mountains on cliffs and rocky sites. Caespitose subshrub 10–25cm high with a creeping rootstock. Stems upright, slender, brown. Leaves oval, entire, finely pubescent. 2–12 flowers in false whorls. Corolla with short upper lip, slightly notched at the tip, lower lip 3-lobed, lateral lobes largest, scoop-shaped, pink. Calyx pubescent, 15-veined, segments stiffly ciliate. Blooms from June to July. z7

M. microphylla (D'Urv.) Benth. S. Italy, Sicily, Crete and Kárpathos, on rocky sites. A small, 10–30cm high shrub with more or less wiry, procumbent or ascending, often branched stems. Leaves 3–6mm long, 2–4mm wide, deltoid-ovate to elliptic, nearly sessile. False whorls 1–6 flowered. Corolla 5–8mm long, purple. Blooms from June to July. z7

M. pygmaea see **Satureja montana** ssp. **illyrica**

M. thymifolia (Scop.) Fritsch (*M. rupestris* (Wulf.) Benth., *Satureja thymi-*

folia Scop.). W. Balkan region to Hungary and reaching to N. Italy, on rocks and gravelly sites. Herbaceous to subshrub-like, 20–50cm high, erect, stems much branched, glabrous or somewhat pubescent. Leaves with petioles, 5–20mm long, 3–12mm wide, elliptic to ovate, sparsely crenate or nearly entire, underside punctate. False whorls dense, 10–30 flowered, short-stalked, the lower flowers shorter than the leaves. Calyx 3mm long, glabrous. Corolla 5–9mm long, white with violet spots on the lobes. Blooms from July to October. z6 (E.)

Mimulus cupreus

Milium L.
Gramineae
Millet Grass

Genus with only 6 species of annual and perennial grasses in North America and Eurasia. Leaf blades flat. Panicles open. One species with an ornamental cultivar.

M. effusum L. Loose clump-form, leaves glabrous, 20 to rarely 30cm long and 1.5cm wide. Flower panicles to 1.8m high, often less, panicle branches outspread during anthesis in early summer, later drooping. *Milium* is a demanding grass for a shaded, woodland site, rarely cultivated. More common is *M. effusum* 'Aureum', found in collectors' gardens. This cultivar has gold-green leaves and stems with yellow panicles. Cultivar 'Aureum' is slower growing than the species and is very

effective in deep shade. Comes true by self-seeding when not cross-pollinated with the species. To guarantee bright color, selected plants may be increased by division. z6 (S.)

Milla

M. biflora see **Bessera elegans**

M. uniflora see **Ipheion uniflorum**

Mimulus L.
Scrophulariaceae
Monkey Flower

About 120–150 species of low, annual or perennial herbs, occasionally also shrubs native to South Africa, Asia, Australia, South America, and especially numerous in North America. The perennial species are shallow-rooted with ascending, fleshy stems. Leaves opposite, undivided, entire or dentate, occasionally incised. Flowers axillary, solitary, or the upper flowers occasionally racemose, pedicelled, often relatively large. Corolla 2-lipped to nearly regular, with an open or closed, long or shorter tube; upper lip 2-lobed, erect and laterally recurved, or outspread; lower lip 3-lobed outspread; blue, red, purple, yellow and occasionally white. The stigmas are sensitive to the touch, closing together upon contact.

Most species are long lived and require winter protection. The natural species are suitable for rock and naturalized gardens in shady, wet sites. The large-flowered cultivars of *M. luteus* are best handled as annuals. Particularly effective for interplanting among *Rhododendron* and similar shade-loving plants. *Mimulus*, with its colorful, abundant flowers, is very worth growing in most shaded gardens. Propagation is by division, seed and cuttings. Seed should be sown in March, in warmth. Young seedlings should be grown on in small pots, then set into the garden in May, or after the last frost date. Early flowering (tulip-time) can be achieved by seeding in fall and overwintering in a moderately cool greenhouse. Cuttings taken in April should be placed under glass; rooting takes place in 12–15 days.

M. aurantiacus Curt. (*M. glutinosus* J.C. Wendl.). Bush Monkey Flower. Oregon and California. Shrubby, sticky, glandular-pubescent, 0.5–1.5m high. Leaves narrow oblong to 5cm long, flowers 3.5–5cm long, brownish orange to salmon, May to August. Suitable as a floriferous greenhouse plant, placed into the garden in summer in a moist site. Sow seed in February and March, or take from summer cuttings. Grow in humus-rich, fertile soil. z8

M. cardinalis Dougl. ex Benth. Scarlet Monkey Flower. North America: Oregon to Northern Mexico, east to Utah, Nevada and Arizona. Herbaceous perennial often grown as an annual, 50–70cm or more high. Stems branched, lax or erect, sticky-pubescent. Leaves obovate-lanceolate, upper leaves to 11cm long, connate at the base, dentate and distinctly veined, nearly rugose. Flowers long-pedicelled, axillary, upper lip erect, recurved, lower lip reflexed, corolla limb distinctly oblique, scarlet red. Stamens exserted, May to September.

Some good cultivars include 'Aurantiacus' ('Orange Perfection'), fiery orange-red; 'Grandiflorus', dark red; 'Roseus' ('Rose Queen'), pink-red with dark spots, very large-flowered; 'Roseus Superbus', dark pink-red, large. z7

M. cupreus Dombr. Chile. Short-lived perennial to annual, 6–20cm high, rapid growing. Stems procumbent, ascending, branching from the ground up and leafy to the top. Procumbent stem sections node-rooting. Leaves small, dentate, usually with only 3 primary veins. Flowers 1–6, axillary, 2–6cm long, copper-red fading to golden yellow.

One of the most attractive of all rock garden plants. Flowers from July to September.

Cultivars of *M. cupreus*:
'Bees' Dazzler', brilliant crimson-red
'Brilliant', deep purple-crimson
'Burnetii', yellow with large red spots
'Duplex', a form with an enlarged, colorful calyx, creating a hose-in-hose effect.
'Fireflame', bright flame-red.
'Leopard', yellow, spotted red-brown, very large.
'Nanus', a dwarf form with glossy dark green leaves. Flowers bright orange to gold-yellow with a red punctate throat. Especially well suited for edging.
'Roter Kaiser' (Red Emperor), 20cm high, crimson to scarlet red. A widely distributed cultivar. Not generally winter hardy, but perpetuates by self-seeding.
'Whitecroft Scarlet', vermilion, similar to 'Roter Kaiser' z8

M. glutinosus see **M. aurantiacus**

M. guttatus Fisch. ex DC. (*M. luteus* auct. non L., *M. langsdorffii* Donn ex Greene). Common Monkey Flower. N. America: Alaska to Mexico, naturalized in Central Europe. Stoloniferous short-lived perennial, dense mat-forming. Stems erect, 15 to rarely 60cm high. Leaves ovate to oblong-lanceolate, dentate, to 15cm long. Flowers several in a raceme, corolla to 6cm long, bearded on the upper lip, yellow, throat often red-spotted. For moist stream banks. Quickly forms a dense, weed-smothering mat. Covered with golden yellow flowers the entire summer. Self-seeding can be troublesome. Propagation is by seed and division. z6–8

M. langsdorffii see **M. guttatus**

M. lewisii Pursh. W. Canada (British Columbia) to California and Utah. Perennial, 30–60cm high, viscid-floccose, leaves sessile, narrowly lanceolate, finely dentate. Flowers on long stalks. Corolla to 5cm long, petals rounded, all outspread, red, pink to white, June to August. Garden uses and propagation like the previous species. Needs winter protection. z6–8

M. luteus L. Chile. Glabrous perennial, 20 to rarely 40cm high. Stems decumbent or prostrate, often rooting at the nodes. Leaves 2.5cm long, oblong-oval, rounded to nearly cordate, toothed. The uppermost leaves sessile, often stem-clasping, tips dentate, the lower leaves occasionally with a deep sinus,

bright green. Flowers in racemes or in terminal clusters of 1–6, large, 1.5–6cm long, corolla limb 2–6cm, throat open or closed by the swelling of the lower lip, bright golden yellow with a few small, dark red or purple patches on the lower lip, June to September, overwintering plants from May to July. For naturalizing in the wild garden; tolerates occasional flooding. Can become a troublesome weed, especially in cool wet sites. Some confusion exists about the natural range of this S. Andes species; at least 1 reputable reference places it in W. North America.

M. luteus has many cultivars, some from crosses with *M. cardinalis* and *M. cupreus*. Apparently *M. luteus* and *M. cupreus* or *M. guttatus* hybrids are listed in the trade as *M. tigrinus* but a better name is *M. × hybridus*. The origins are often unclear with plants being classified by their dominant characteristics. Current lists of these beautiful but confusing cultivars are extensive.
'Rivularis', 25–40cm high, yellow. Lower lip with a large, dark brown patch.
'Tigrinus Grandiflorus', 20–30cm, very large-flowered. Corolla bright-striped and -spotted. Most widely distributed cultivar in the trade.
'Variegatus', light purple-red with violet dorsal sides and a white throat. Lower lip brown-speckled.

The cultivars are not very cold hardy and should be treated as annuals in temperate gardens. Uses and cultivation as for *M. cardinalis*. z8

M. moschatus Dougl. ex Lindl. Musk Plant, Musk Flower. British Columbia and Montana to California and Utah, also in NE. USA, naturalized in various regions of Europe. Sticky-hairy, spreading, creeping rhizomes, and with creeping, rooting stems, to 30cm long, mat-forming, usually only 5–10cm high. Leaves to 5cm long, ovate or oblong-ovate, yellowish green, softly pubescent, glutinous. Flowers about 2cm across, pale yellow with few small brown dots. The entire plant is musk scented and once was cultivated primarily for this reason. Modern plants have lost much of the scent.

Grow in well-drained, moist soil; cover loosely with conifer branches for overwintering. Self-seeding. Seeds germinate quickly when planted out in March to April. Seeds remain viable for up to 4 years. z7

M. primuloides Benth. Mountains of N. America: Washington to California. Tufted downy perennial, 10–15cm high, matforming with wiry stolons, long-lived. Leaves clustered in rosettes, obovate to oblanceolate, softly pubescent at first, later glabrous. Flowers solitary, on threadlike scapes, to 10cm high, with a funnelform tube and bilabiate limb, corolla gold-yellow, July to September. Very floriferous and recommended for the rock garden. Hardy, given a light covering with conifer branches, but suffers from summer heat. Propagate by division in summer or seed in spring. z7

Minuartia sedoides

M. ringens L. Allegheny Monkey Flower. N. America: Nova Scotia to Manitoba and North Dakota to Virginia, Texas, and Colorado. Perennial, 40–80cm high with a persistent rootstock. Stems 4-angled, branched. Leaves elliptic, oblong, or oblong-lanceolate, acuminate, to 10cm long, serrate, stem-clasping at the base. Flowers 3cm long with a narrow throat, blue to blue-violet, also pink or white, 2-lipped, anthers exserted. June to August. Grow in a cool, moist soil in light shade. Performs poorly in excessive wetness or standing water, deteriorates in excessive heat. z4–8 (D.)

M. tigrinus see **M. luteus** cultivars

Mindium see Michauxia

Minuartia L.
Caryophyllaceae
Sandwort

About 60 species in the temperate and colder zones of the Northern Hemisphere. Mostly cushion-form or mat-forming small perennial herbs with very narrow, subulate (awl-shaped) or filamentous leaves and small, white or greenish, singular or cymose flowers. Very like *Arenaria* but differing in the leaves which are only 1–2mm wide and in the 3–4 toothed, dehiscent capsules. Flowers from May to July. Grow in any well-drained garden soil on a sunny site. Useful for the dry stone wall, rock garden or trough. Propagate by seed, division and cuttings.

M. aretioides see **M. cherlerioides**

Minuartia verna

M. cherlerioides (Hoppe) Becherer (*M. aretioides* Sch. et Thell.). E. Alps, in limestone crevices. Plants with creeping rootstock, much branched, dense cushion-form, 2–5cm high, leaves 2–3mm long. Flowers 4-part. Demanding and inconspicuous collector's plant. z5

M. graminifolia (Ard.) Jáv. (*Alsine rosanii* Guss.). Italy, Sicily, Yugoslavia, Albania, Rumania. Shaggy carpet-form, a flat grass-green cushion. Stems erect, 4–7cm high. Leaves linear-lanceolate, lower in a rosette. Umbels on 3–8cm high stalks, 2–7 flowered, flowers white. July to August. Not exceptional for flowers but an attractive cushion plant. z6

M. juniperina (L.) Maire et Petitm. (*Alsine juniperina* (L.) Wahlenb.). Greece, SW. Asia. Loose, dark green carpet 10–15cm high. Stems procumbent to ascending. Leaves awlshaped, acute-prickly. Inflorescences nearly umbellate. Flowers small, white. July to August. z7

M. laricifolia (L.) Schinz et Thell. (*Alsine laricifolia* (L.) Crantz, *Arenaria laricifolia* L.). Mountains of S. and Central Europe, from Spain to the Carpathian Mts. Plant 10–15cm high, dense, dark green, a matlike groundcover. Leaves subulate-filamentous. Flowers to 1cm wide in open racemes, white. June to August. Floriferous, vigorous, valuable rock garden plant, attractive with dwarf cam-panulate flowers. z5

M. recurva (All.) Schinz et Thell. (*Alsine recurva* (All.) Wahlenb.). Mountains of S. and S. Central Europe. Dense, 10–15cm high, carpetforming, woody at the base. Leaves mostly involuted, sickleshaped. Flower stems glandular-floccose, 1-, 3- or 5-flowered. Flowers white, July to August. z6

M. sedoides (L.) Hiern. (*Cherleria sedoides* L.). Alps, in poor, open rocky turf at alpine elevations, usually on lime-free sites. Dense, hard, matforming. Flowers solitary, pale greenish, May to June. An undemanding trough garden plant for the collector. z5

M. stellata (E.D. Clarke) Maire et Petitm. (*Alsine stellata* (E.D. Clarke) Hal.). Mountains of Greece and S. Albania. A dense, cushion forming plant. Leaves glabrous, short-triangular-lanceolate, acute. Inflorescences 1–2 flowered. Flowers white. July to August. z7

M. verna (L.) Hiern. Quite variable and widely disseminated aggregate species. Includes *M. verna* ssp. *verna*. Found in lime-starved grassy sites in the Central Alps. Carpetforming, to 15cm high, not woody at the base. Stems 4- to many-flowered. Flowers white, May to June. *M. verna* ssp. *hercynica* (Willk.) Schwarz is a cushionforming subspecies, found on mine tailings. Closely related to the glabrous, dense carpetforming, 1–3 flowered *M. gerardii* (Willd.) Hayek, a high alpine-arctic species. z1 (K.)

Miscanthus Anderss.
Gramineae
Eulalia

Genus of 17 species of tall, erect grasses with narrow leaves and spreading, terminal flower panicles. Distributed from the Himalayas to N. China and Japan. Many of the species from the W. Chinese mountains have yet to be introduced to Western gardens. Without a garden trial it is doubtful that they would be hardier than the tender *M. nepalensis* (Trin.) Hack. The species in cultivation are ornamental, tall garden grasses. They fill an important niche in the framework of the perennial garden with long-lasting ornamental effect, better than many other grasses. Also suitable for an open woodland margin, at water's edge, near buildings, steps and walls or for flower arranging.

Propagation is by division in spring. Seed propagation is only for the purpose of selection and for increasing newly introduced species. Seeds of many species are produced in the greenhouse only if the outdoor growing season is not long and warm. Young propagules should be raised in containers to ensure success when placing in the garden. The best planting time is in April. In cooler climates, young plants should be protected in winter.

M. floridulus (Labill.) Warb. (*M. japonicus* Anderss., *Saccharum floridulum* Labill. *Erianthus floridulus* Schult., *M. sinensis* Thunb. 'Giganteus' hort). Giant Chinese Silver Grass. Anhwei, Kiangsu, N. China and Japan. A clumpforming perennial with short, thick, ascending rhizomes. Culms stiffly erect, 2 to rarely 4m high, leaves linear, furrowed, to 3cm wide, arching, to 90cm long. Inflorescences conical to oval, to more than

30cm long, spikelet-bearing rachis to ⅔ the length of the spike. Spikelets in pairs, 3–3.5mm long. Flowers do not develop in climates with cool or short summers. This giant grass is decorative even without flowers for its erect, wide-leaved clumps. Grow in sites corresponding to its native habitat as at the foot of hills and other low, moist sites. When planted on the edge of an open, deciduous woodland, an understory of autumn color is achieved. Also suitable for blocking undesirable views or for separating flowering perennials in the border. In China, the young shoots are

harvested for livestock fodder, the ripe leaves and stalks are used in paper production or for building materials. A medicinal tea is produced from the roots. Transplant Giant Chinese Silver Grass late in spring. Propagation by division may be difficult with the hard rhizomes of large stock plants; frequent division of older plants makes the job easier. z6

M. japonicus see **M. floridulus**

M. oligostachyus Stapf. Japan. A loose, clumpforming grass with short stolons. Leaves elliptic-lanceolate, about 17mm

Miscanthus sacchariflorus

wide; culms relatively short, to 30cm-long, often dark-colored. Inflorescences silvery, 10–15cm long, 0.8–1.2m high. Mountain meadow plant, intolerant of drought. Effective in combination with autumn-flowering plants and worthy of further trial in garden culture. z7

M. polydactylos see **M. sinensis**

M. saccharifer see **M. sacchariflorus**

M. sacchariflorus (Maxim.) Hack. (*M. saccharifer* Benth., *Imperata sacchariflora* Maxim.). Silver Banner Grass, Amur

Banner Grass grows in moist mountain meadows and along streams. Suitable also for open woodland margins in the garden where its growth is somewhat checked. If plants grow too dry flowering will be poor. In warmer climates, this species may become a troublesome spreader, the rhizomes reaching widely, and self-sown seedlings may appear in surrounding areas. z5

M. sinensis (Thunb.) Anderss. (*Eulalia japonica* Trin. *M. polydactylos* Voss.). Eulalia-grass, Chinese Silver Grass. S. to N. China and Japan. Clumpforming

Miscanthus sinensis 'Condensatus'

leaves with wide yellow or whitish crosswise bands. Young plants should be given winter protection in cool climates where propagation is often difficult. Quite hardy where summers are warm and are of the most widely grown cultivars in Britain. z5

'Strictus' (Porcupine Grass), often is confused with the above cultivar, but the leaves are stiffer, more channeled and not over-arching. Especially distinguished by its improved hardiness and better vigor. z5(4)

'Variegatus' leaves are longitudinally striped white; of erect habit. Very effective in combination with brightly colored perennials such as *Kniphofia*, *Zauschneria* or *Salvia azurea* or with woody evergreens. z5

'Silberpfeil' (Silver Arrow) is distinguished from the above forms by its wider leaves. Originated from 'Condensatus', but not fountaining so widely. Leaves white-variegated and even more effective than 'Variegatus'.

M. sinensis var. **purpurascens** (Anderss.) Matsun. This variety is regarded as a cultivar in America and England. Panicles with fine purple-colored, pubescent glumes. The reddish autumn foliage is disappointingly short-lived. This form and most cultivars of the species flower so late that the inflorescences fail to fully develop in cool climate gardens, but bloom freely where summers are warm. The best garden qualities have been selected over the years and, more recently hybridized, resulting in the introduction of the following cultivars:

'Silberfeder' (Silver Feather), represents the best qualities of the species, more than 2m high, flowering dependably in late summer. Clumps to 2m wide are very decorative with the long, overarching leaf blades. The inflorescences are decorative in early winter; later the sturdy clump of dry culms and foliage are ornamental. This cultivar is very undemanding, but deteriorates on wet soil.

Recent selections from Ernst Pagels include the promising forms 'Graziella', 'Juli' (July), 'Malepartus', 'Rotsilber' (Red-Silver) and others.

'Gracillimus' (Maiden Grass), develops into a very dense, erect clump with stiffly arched, narrow, channeled leaves with silvery midribs. The leaf blades furl in spirals when dried, making them decorative for dry arrangements. Grows to over 3m high in warmer climates, but normally to 2m. Seldom flowers in cooler climates. Suitable as a fine-textured and stiffly upright foliage

Silver Grass. NW. China to Central China, Korea and Japan. Creeping perennial grass with stout, long, rhizomes. Stems stiffly erect, 0.6–2m high, leaves linear, 10–12mm wide. Inflorescences conical, to 20cm long, rachis less than half as long as the spike. Spikelets in pairs, one shorter, one longer, 5–6mm long, each 2-flowered, one flower fertile. 'Robustus' (Giant Silver Banner Grass) is particularly noteworthy, blooms in climates with shorter summers. The inflorescences turn reddish silver in September, becoming increasingly feathery as they ripen and remaining effective long into the winter. Also displays a good, red-brown autumn foliage. Earlier blooming strains are not so effective. In its habitat, the Silver

grass usually with stiffly erect to outward-growing stems and silvery, furrowed leaves. The inflorescences are silvery feathered, the rachis is half as long as the spike. Spikelets 4.5–6mm long. This species has varying ultimate heights, leaf cross-sections, lengths and widths. z5(4)

The following cultivars are distinguished:

'Condensatus', dense clumpform habit, the stems somewhat spreading and the wide blades nodding. The newly emerging flower panicles are distinctly wavy and glossy brown-violet, in late summer to fall.

'Zebrinus' (Zebra Grass) develops large, dense clumps with over-arching, mostly basal, flat, broad strap-shaped, plant, effective in formal applications. Plants grown from seed are more inclined to have reddish fall foliage. Very similar, but much dwarfer in habit, are newly introduced plants from the higher elevations of Yakushima Island. All flower in cooler regions. Dwarf cultivars, to 1m or less, commonly are planted z5 southward in America. Well suited to the cooler, wetter parts of the British Isles. z5 (S.)

M. repens L. N. America: Nova Scotia to Minnesota, south to Florida and Texas; E. Mexico. Found in woodlands, often creeping at the base of trees, especially around conifers. A matforming plant with trailing, rooting stems and opposite, rounded-ovate, 6–18mm long, dark green, often finely white-veined leaves. Flowers always paired, terminal, white, fragrant, petals bearded inside, heterostylous. The resulting paired drupes are scarlet red, occasionally white in forma *leucocarpa* Bissell, and contain 8 seeds. They are edible, but nearly tasteless,

Columbia to California, also Alberta, Montana and Idaho. Small, rounded, bright green leaves, evergreen. Height about 25cm, with small greenish yellow flowers. z6(5)

M. caulescens Nutt. N. America: British Columbia to Montana, N. California. Foliage 10–15cm high; entire plant rough-pubescent. Scapes usually with 3 leaves, leaves cordate, irregularly serrate. Flowers pale yellow in few-flowered, one-sided racemes which bloom from the top downward; May. z5

Mitella diphylla

Moehringia muscosa

Mitchella L.
Rubiaceae
Partridge Berry, Teaberry

Two species of evergreen, creeping perennials from North America, Japan and S. Korea. Forms very flat mats; winter hardy, but often demanding, small perennials. For shady and semishady sites in the rockery, peat or bog garden, or in association with conifers. Grow in moist, acidic, humus rich soil. Since plants are often short-lived in culture, they are best grown in a shady spot in an alpine house or in pots in an alpine case. Must also be watered with nonalkaline water. Under suitable conditions, plants will thrive for many years. Propagation is by division, also by seed, although the process is quite tedious. Therefore, it is best to remove rooted stems and pot them.

adorning the plants until late winter. Blooms from April to July. z3–8 (E.)

Mitella L.
Saxifragaceae
Miterwort, Bishop's Cap

Small, groundcover perennials, primarily from North America. Related to *Tiarella* and, like it, a shade plant for moderately moist soil. Leaves mostly basal, cordate, long petioled. Flowers in slender, simple racemes, small and not very effective. Plants quickly cover the ground by spreading rhizomes, stolons, or both. Wind and winter protection (conifer branches or dried leaves) is essential. Propagate by division and seed.

M. breweri A. Gray. Mts. British

M. diphylla L. N. America: Quebec to Minnesota, North Carolina, Missouri. Scapes 20–45cm high, with 2 sessile stem leaves. Basal leaves broadly cordate, 3–5 lobed. Flowers small, whitish; April to May. z3–7

M. nuda L. N. America. A little grown species, typically with rounded, reniform leaves. Few-flowered stems with greenish flowers. z4

M. pentandra Hook. N. America: S. Colorado, E. California, along the Rocky Mts. and into Alaska. Scapes 20–30cm high, with only basal, rounded-reniform leaves and small, yellowish feathery flowers in May to June. z3–6

M. trifida Grah. USA. Scapes 10–30cm high. Leaves ternate. Flowers small, in dense, one-sided racemes. z6 (H.& Kö.)

Moehringia L.
Caryophyllaceae

Twenty-one species closely related to *Arenaria*. Tender annual or perennial herbs with small, linear to obovate leaves and white flowers. American horticulturists include these in *Arenaria*, but Europeans maintain the genus as a distinct entity.

M. muscosa L. Mountains of S. and Central Europe to 50 degrees North lati-

soil should be calcareous, loose, a humus-rich loam. In a shady site with even moisture; plants bloom from May to September. Propagation is by seed and division. Good companions include small ferns such as *Asplenium rutamuraria*, *A. trichomanes*, *A. viride*, *Cystopteris fragilis*, *Currania robertiana*, *Phyllitis scolopendrium*, *Polypodium vulgare*; also *Alchemilla conjuncta*, *Aster bellidiastrum*, *Campanula cochleariifolia*. z5 (E.)

tions include both foliage and flower stalk heights. The foliage turns a golden yellow in autumn, especially under favorable conditions and in selected forms. Cultivars are propagated by division of early spring growth. Grow in humus-rich garden loam. All Moor Grasses are noninvasive and combine well in perennial borders of many species. Suitable as cut flowers when green or in autumn color.

M. altissima see **M. caerulea** ssp. **arundinacea**

Molinia caerulea ssp. *caerulea* 'Variegata'

tude. Grows in alpine and subalpine regions, with moist limestone scree vegetation, or in shaded, moist cliffs, rock crevices and walls with seeping water on a gravelly, limestone humus rich soil. Often on rotten logs. Stems 5–20cm long, loose, mosslike, bright green, carpetforming. Leaves narrow-linear to threadlike, semiterete, 2.5–3cm long. Flower pedicels terminal, 1–3cm long, 2–6 flowered. Flowers 4-part, cruciform, white. Blooms from May to September. *M. muscosa* is a low, carpetforming perennial for semi-shaded, moist sites among stones in the alpine garden and rock garden or rock crevices and walls. The

Molinia Schrank
Gramineae
Moor Grass

About 3 species of clump grasses from seasonally wet, boggy heaths and open woodlands on infertile, high-humus soils. The dense, tufted habit of *M. caerulea*, the only cultivated species, makes Moor Grass suitable for specimen planting, and also for combining with other perennials. The typical, very long, erect flower stems, without nodes, above the short tufts of foliage are very decorative. Therefore the following descrip-

Molopospermum peloponnesiacum

M. caerulea (L.) Moench, Purple Moor Grass. Europe, a native and ornamental species representing the genus. For garden use, the two subspecies are better ornamentals.

M. caerulea ssp. **arundinacea** (Schrank) H. Paul (*M. altissima* Link, *M. caerulea* var. *litoralis* Asch. et Graebn.), Tall Purple Moor Grass. Flower panicles to 2.5m high, plants stout, leaves to 12mm wide, blades stiff, panicle branches long and semierect. This subspecies occurs on periodically wet, low humus soils. The following selections are particularly meritorious:

'Karl Foerster' is an old, stately, diffuse-growing clone of good color. 0.5/2m (foliage/flower)

'Windspiel' (Wind Play) is more vigorous, very densely tufted and upright, coloring light yellow early in autumn. 0.6m/2.5m.

'Transparent' is a graceful plant well suited to informal garden settings. 0.5m/1.8m. z5

M. caerulea ssp. **caerulea** is the widely indigenous species type on infertile, humus soil locations. Reaches 90cm high, panicle branches are short, erect and relatively tight. With the cultivars of the taller-growing *M. caerulea* ssp. *arundinacea*, this subspecies can also be massed in beds with other perennials. Particularly effective in fall with its bright russet foliage. This subspecies also has produced cultivars with increased garden merit for special situations.

'Strahlenquelle' (Radiant Fountain), well-spaced, numerous flowering culms

leaved herbaceous plants, to 2m high. Flowers are borne in large, white umbels; aromatic. Leaves to 1m wide, palmately compound, individual leaflets lanceolate, glossy and deeply pinnatisect. Fruits 12mm long, yellow with brown ribs. Native habitat gravelly soil to scree sites, well suited to cultivation in the large rockery for its architectural effect. Good specimen plant. Young plants are cultivated from fresh seed. z6 (S.)

M. doerfleri Wettst. NE. Albania. A rhizomatous, herbaceous perennial 30–40cm high. Leaves oblong-lanceolate. Flowers bright blue in terminal, clustered racemes. June to July. z6(7)

M. graminifolia see **M. suffruticosa**

M. × intermedia (Froeb.) Ingram (*M. petraea × M. suffruticosa*). Stems 20cm high. Leaves nearly linear, blue-green. Flowers bright blue in helicoid cymes. July to August. A commendable rock garden plant. And cultivar 'Fröbelii', flowers azure-blue. z7

Moltkia petraea

Monarda fistulosa 'Morgenröte'

radiate from a loose clump of foliage. The flower stems persist until the first snowfall; 40–80cm.

'Moorhexe' (Moor-witch) is more upright and can therefore be planted closer to neighboring plants; 40–70cm.

'Variegata' is a yellowish-white variegated cultivar with attractive new growth, well suited for edging in the formal garden or planting with brightly colored perennials; 30–50cm high. z5 (S.)

Molopospermum W. D. J. Koch
Umbelliferae

M. cicutarium see **M. peloponnesiacum**

M. peloponnesiacum (L.) W. D. J. Koch (*M. cicutarium* DC.). S. Alps and Pyrenees. Vigorous, stately and large-

Moltkia Lehm.
Boraginaceae

About 6–8 species in S. Europe and Asia. Subshrubs and small perennials with rough-haired, lanceolate leaves and usually blue flowers in helicoid cymes, in midsummer. These grow in well-drained limestone soil, often in rock crevices, in full sun. Suitable for the rock garden, troughs, dry stone walls, etc. Propagation is by seed and cuttings. Young plants should always be handled in pots since they develop root balls.

M. coerulea (Willd.) Lehm. Asia Minor. Subshrub, 30–40cm high, with stiff, rather stout branches, gray-pubescent. Leaves oblong-spatulate, tapered to the base. Stem leaves lanceolate, sessile. Flowers blue, in forked inflorescences. June to July. Best grown in the alpine house. z8

M. petraea (Tratt.) Griseb. Mountains of Central Yugoslavia to Central Greece, on limestone, a 1.5m-wide subshrub in its habitat. Stems 20–45cm high in cultivation, entire plant silky pubescent. Leaves dark green, linear-oblong to oblanceolate. Flowers deep violet-blue with blue anthers in small, curling, branched inflorescences (helicoid cymes); with a prolonged blooming period, spring to midsummer. z6

M. suffruticosa (L.) Brand. (*M. graminifolia* (Viv.) Nym.). Italian Alps. A dense carpetforming subshrub, 30–45cm high. Leaves linear, grasslike, white-tomentose beneath. Flowers azure blue to deep blue in terminal, branched helicoid cymes. June to August. Not reliably hardy, best grown in the alpine house. z8(7) (K.)

Monarda L.
Labiatae
Bergamot

About 12 species of annual herbs and tall, bushy, aromatic perennials with upright, mostly 4-angled stems and opposite, entire or toothed leaves. Flowers mostly in terminal whorls or heads, pink, red, violet or white, some with colorful bracts, in summer. Very satisfactory perennials, garden sorts much hybridized. Useful as attractive, long-flowering border perennials, also

Moneses uniflora

for cut flowers. Suitable also for underplanting in open woods or in shady beds. Tolerate any garden soil, and drought, especially *M. fistulosa*. Propagate by division or cuttings in spring.

M. bradburiana Becker. (*M. russelliana* Nutt. ex Sims.) USA: Indiana and Louisiana, to Kansas and E. Texas. Grows in dry, open woods. Stems 30–60cm high, rarely branched. Leaves sessile, ovate to lanceolate, entire to remotely serrate, glaucous. Flowers small, pinkish to white with purple spots, in large terminal verticillasters; bracts green to reddish; spring to early summer. The most recent classification in America places this as *M. russelliana* again. z5(4)

M. didyma L. USA: New England, south to Georgia and Tennessee, in rich, moist woods. Stems 0.80–1.5m high, sharply 4-angled. Leaves opposite, ovate, acute, scabrous-toothed, dark green, undersides softly pubescent. Flowers scarlet red, in whorled verticillasters, sur-

rounded by reddish bracts; June to September; pleasantly balm scented. Grown as an ornamental and for use as an herbal tea. Parent of many garden cultivars, some few hybrids with *M. fistulosa*.

'Adam', 1m, cherry red, summer; 'Blaustrumpf' (Blue Stockings) (Kayser & Seibert 1955), 1.4m, dark lilac, often midsummer; 'Cambridge Scarlet', 1m, dark scarlet, summer; 'Coccinea', 1m scarlet, summer; 'Croftway Pink', 1.3m, light pink, July to August; 'Donnerwolke' (Thundercloud) (Marx 1973) 1m, purple-red, summer; 'Granite Pink', dwarf, to 20cm, pink, midsummer;

Montia sibirica

'Mahogany', 90cm, dark red-brown, summer; 'Morgenroete' (Morning Red) (Marx 1975) 1m, salmon red, early summer; 'Präriebrand' (Prairie Fire) (Kayser & Siebert 1955), 1.2m, deep salmon red, summer; 'Prärienacht' (Prairie Night) (Kayser & Seibert 1955), 1.5m, purple-lilac, August to September; 'Rosea', 80cm, rose-pink, midsummer; 'Salmon Queen', 90cm, salmon-pink, midsummer; 'Salmonea', 90cm, salmon, late summer; 'Schneewittchen' (Snow White) (Foerster 1956), 1m, white; 'Sunset', 1m dark red, midsummer; 'Violacea', possibly the same as 'Violet Queen', 1m or less, dark violet, late summer. z4 (H.& M.)

M. russelliana see **M. bradburiana**

M. fistulosa L. E. North America. A prairie and woodland margin species, on dry sites. Stems 0.8–1.2m high, with 4-angled, rounded edges, often hollow. Flower whorls few-flowered to many; flowers lilac rarely whitish, or pinkish;

bracts sometimes similarly colored; July to September, sometimes later than *M. didyma*. Generally, a species for the wildflower garden; sometimes used in hybridizing a good bee plant.

Moneses Salisb. ex S.F. Gray
Pyrolaceae

Only one species in the boreal region of the Northern Hemisphere, a glabrous perennial with slender rhizomes and a basal cluster of simple leaves. Intermediate between *Chimaphila* and *Pyrola*. Similar to *Pyrola* in the opposite leaves and solitary flowers.

M. uniflora (L.) A. Gray (*Pyrola uniflora* L.). One-flowered Shineleaf, One-flowered Pyrola. A delicate wildflower, 10–12cm high, with creeping rhizomes. Leaves glabrous, orbicular to ovate, in 2s or 3s, petioled, persistent. Flower scape with 1 or 2 leaves, slender, terminating in a large, white or pink, nodding flower in summer. Calyx 5-lobed; petals 5; stamens 10. A collector's plant with very specific cultural requirements in a shady, moist site, best in decaying organic matter or coarse humus; mycorrhizal. Propagate by careful division in spring. z2 (K.)

Montbretia

M. crocata see **Tritonia crocata**

M. pottsii see **Crocosmia pottsii**

Montia L.
Portulacaceae
Miner's Lettuce

Fifteen to 50 species, depending on taxonomic grouping, in N. and S. America, in temperate Eurasia, in the mountains of tropical Africa and Australia. Annual or perennial herbs with petiolate, rather fleshy, bright green leaves. Stem leaves frequently several, alternate, or only 2, opposite and sessile. Flowers small, whitish or whitish pink, in

shade. Suitable for shady areas of the rock garden. Generally thrives in humus-rich soil. Unwanted seedling plants are easily weeded out. The long flowering period and bright green foliage make this an ideal shade-loving plant which combines well and is never a problem. Propagate by seed. z3 (E.)

flowers about 5cm across. *M. spathulata* is well suited for warm, walled garden beds where it may form stately colonies. In cooler, open sites, winter protection will be necessary. Next to seed, division is a possible method of propagation. z8 (S.)

Morina L.
Dipsacaceae

Ten to 17 species of attractive herbs with thistlelike leaves from the E. Mediter-

Moraea spathulata

Morina persica

Morisia monanthos

axillary or terminal racemes. Fruit a 3-valved capsule.

M. parvifolia see **Claytonia parvifolia**

M. sibirica (L.) Howell (*Claytonia sibirica* L.). Siberian Purslane. N. America: Alaska to California, eastward to Montana and Utah, naturalized in the British Isles, on moist, shady sites on the high plains and middle mountain elevations. Short-lived, 6–30cm high, mostly monocarpic plants with semievergreen, fleshy, small, long-petioled basal leaves and 2 opposite, short-petioled stem leaves or leaves sessile with axillary bulbils. Flowers white or pink, in many-flowered, terminal, somewhat procumbent racemes. Blooms from April to July.

Only this species is generally found in cultivation. It is short-lived, but self-seeds abundantly and will therefore naturalize in shaded and semi-shaded park and garden sites. Grows vigorously, greening up all but the deepest, dark

Moraea Mill. corr. L.
Iridaceae

About 100 species of tender tropical and South African tunicate-cormaceous or rhizomatous herbs with grass- to iris-like foliage and flowers of very brief duration.

M. spathacea see **M. spathulata**

M. spathulata (L.f.) Klatt (*M. spathacea* (Thunb.) Ker-Gawl., *Iris spathulata* L.f., *I. spathacea* Thunb.). Cape, Orange Free State and Natal Provinces of S. Africa. The only more or less winter-hardy perennial of this species-rich genus; related to *Iris*. From a short rhizome, a .5–1.2m long solitary leaf arises in summer, folded at the base, gray-green and long-persistent. The following May, a flower scape arises from the base of the leaf to 50cm high with attractively marked, bright yellow, Dutch iris-like, fragrant

ranean region to the Himalayas and SW. China. Flowers in dense false whorls in the axils of the upper stem leaves, with leaflike, spring-toothed bracts. Calyx 2-lipped in a bristly-toothed involucel; corolla 5-lobed, tending to be 2-lipped, with a long tube, yellow, white, pink, red, or purple; stamens 2 or 4. The hardiest, most vigorous and most commonly cultivated species is *M. longifolia*. This species, like the others, has attractive foliage and flowers. Well suited to dry plant beds along walls or in the rock garden where it can be left undisturbed for many years. It is lime loving, but also thrives, particularly *M. longifolia*, in a lime-free substrate. All require full sun and a well-drained, sandy humus loam soil. Deteriorates on wet soils or with standing moisture. Propagate by seed. Seedlings grow quickly to flowering plants, but should be shifted to pots and then to the garden with a root ball. Division is not advisable, but large, thick root cuttings may be taken. The best use of all the *Morina* species is as free standing plants between rocks and low, heat-loving rock garden plants. Tall plants are *not* good companions. Other than the species covered here, the *Morina* are of doubtful hardiness (i.e. *M. bulleyana* Forrest et Diels) and despite their beauty, should be restricted to warm climate botanical collections.

M. kokanica Regel. Turkestan. Stems round, 20–90cm high, leaves mostly basal, ascending, lanceolate, long-acuminate, with ciliate-bristly hairs on the margins. Flowers tubular, rosy-pink to lilac. Differs considerably from *M. longifolia* in habit. Blooms June to July. An interesting, high mountain, clump-forming plant, sometimes sensitive in lowland gardens. Plants cultivated as *M. kokanica* often are *M. longifolia.* z6

M. longifolia Wall. Nepal, between 3000 and 4700m. Ridged stems 0.6–1m high; with whorled drooping, pinnately cleft, linear-lanceolate, prickly toothed, thistlelike leaves 15–20cm long and 2–3cm wide. Flowers white, later crimson, fragrant, in dense, stacked whorls at upper nodes. Blooms from June to August. z6

M. persica L. S. and E. Balkan region, Iran, Asia Minor. Very similar to the above species, but generally smaller and more bizarre, with narrow-lanceolate, distichous, prickly leaves. Flowers dark pink, in widely spaced whorls. Blooms from July to August. More sensitive to wet soil than the above species. z6 (E.)

Morisia J. Gay
Cruciferae

One species on Sardinia and Corsica. Small, stemless, rosetted perennials with 5–7cm long, saw-tooth incised leaves and short-pedicelled, 1.5cm wide, solitary yellow flowers in the leaf axils. Fruits occasionally produced; the pedicel elongates and curves, pushing the 2-jointed silique into the soil. Flowers in mid-spring. Grow in infertile, sandy soil in full sun, preferably protected, though the species is more or less hardy in mild climates. Useful for a sheltered site in the rock garden, trough garden or alpine house. Propagate by root cuttings.

M. hypogaea see **M. monanthos**

M. monanthos (Viv.) Aschers. (*M. hypogaea* J. Gay). Closely related to the Moroccan-Algerian *Raffenaldia primu-*

loides Godr. (*Cossonia africana* Durieu). A sun-loving, loose rosette plant with large, yellow, summer flowers on 10cm-high pedicels. Only for the alpine house. z8 (K.)

Muehlenbeckia Meissn.
Polygonaceae

About 20 species of more or less woody, prostrate or climbing plants from sub-tropical S. Pacific regions, mostly too tender for gardens but some are grown indoors or in very mild climates.

Muehlenbeckia axillaris

M. axillaris (Hook.f.) Walp. Wire Plant. New Zealand, Tasmania and Australia. Deciduous, dense, creeping, mat-forming shrubby plant. Shoots wiry-thin and dark, leaves alternate, nearly circular, brownish green. Flowers inconspicuous, yellowish green, of one sex or perfect, fruits glassy with dark seeds. Develops persistent mats with short, underground stolons. Grow in a sunny site with not too dry soil. From this variable plant comes a cultivar 'Compacta' which is smaller in all respects. Propagation is by division or cuttings. Young plants should be container grown and moved only with a root ball. z7 (S.)

Muhlenbergia Schreb.
Gramineae

Most muhlenbergias are late-flowering, wiry-stemmed, slender-leaved grasses

classified as pernicious and invasive weeds in the US. The below listed species grows throughout most of the US. (excepting the gulf states and arid Rocky Mts. areas) in most woodlands where it is an insignificant part of the forest floor.

M. alpestris see **Spodiopogon sibiricus**

M. mexicana (L.) Trin. N. America. Long in cultivation but little disseminated. A loose, clumping grass, rhizomatous with 20cm-long, narrow, 1cm-wide leaves and to 1m-tall flower stems. Panicles narrow, purple-toned. The panicle branches are densely covered with spikelets. The species is best suited for a warm site with plentiful moisture. z3–8 (S.)

Mulgedium see **Lactuca**

Muscari Mill.
Liliaceae
Grape Hyacinth

Small, spring-flowering bulbous plants with a few, basal, linear, somewhat fleshy leaves and densely crowded, terminal racemes of small, usually blue flowers on naked scapes. The flowers at the apex are often sterile. About 40–50 species, primarily from the Mediterranean region. At present computer "taxonomists" are fragmenting the genus (*Hyacinthella, Brimeura*, etc.), which see, but horticulturists tend to stay with the traditional classification, and geneticists will have the final say based on DNA relationships. Easily cultivated and increased by self-seeding and offset bulblets in a sunny to semi-shaded site on a well-drained soil. The thin-skinned, naked bulbs must not be stored in the open air for long; best transplanted in September. They are not attacked by mice. Best planted in masses with other spring-flowering bulbs or naturalized in an open woodland setting. The low, abundantly flowering species are also good for edging, for cut flowers or for forcing as potted plants. Propagate by

species, quite rare; 'Blue Spike', very floriferous sport with many clusters of double, soft blue flowers; very persistent, 12–15cm high. The cultivar 'Fairway Seeding' is rarely available. At least 1 white-flowering cultivar is listed. *M. szovitsianum* Bak. is a degenerative species from the N. Caucasus region. It is smaller, paler in flower color, and the flowers are less constricted at the mouth. Its validity as a separate species is somewhat questionable. z4

M. atlanticum see **M. neglectum**

M. botryoides 'Heavenly Blue' see **M. armeniacum**

M. botryoides var. **heldreichii** (Boiss.) D. Stuart (*M. heldreichii* Boiss.). Greece. Leaves broadly linear, dark green, furrowed, longer than the flower stalk. With 12 or more, ovate, rather large, dark blue flowers and recurved, triangular, white teeth. The entire raceme appears ovate. Similar to *M. botryoides*, but with substantially larger flowers. Often flowers in March. z4

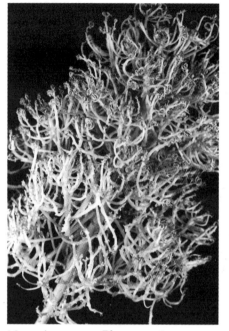

Muscari comosum 'Plumosum'

Muscari tubergenianum

Myosotidium hortensia

division of the bulb clusters in late summer, or sow freshly gathered seed. Plants grown from seed bloom after 3 or 4 years. Grape Hyacinths listed here include the more commonly available and attractive species.

M. armeniacum Leichtl. ex Bak. (*M. botryoides* 'Heavenly Blue', *M. polyanthum* Boiss.). Macedonia, Rumania, Asia Minor, Caucasus. Closely related to *M. botryoides*, but the leaves of *M. armeniacum* are rosetted, emerging in the fall, and the scapes are shorter. The short flower racemes are on stout scapes, 20–25cm high. Flowers cobalt blue with small white teeth. The blue color is, however, variable. Fragrant. Flowers from April to early May. A good species for forcing. Easily cultivated, one of the easiest species. Several cultivars exist in the trade: 'Cantab' with sky blue flowers and shorter stalks; 'Heavenly Blue', not substantially different from the species; 'Early Giant', flowers earlier than the

M. aucheri Boiss. Asia Minor, in high mountain meadows near the snow line. Small, to 15cm tall, attractive plants with short, medium blue racemes and paler, sterile flowers at the apex; the perianth has a white, toothed margin. This species produces only 2, thickish leaves. z5

M. azurea see **Hyacinthella azurea**

M. botryoides (L.) Mill. emend. DC. Central Europe to Asia Minor and Transcaucasia. Scapes 15–30cm high. z4

M. botryoides var. **botryoides**. Leaves erect, narrowly channeled, about as long as the flower scape. Flowers globose to urceolate, sky blue with white marginal teeth, unscented; racemes rather short, globose-ovate, the apical flowers are sterile; April to May. The white-flowering form 'Album' is attractive; 'Caeruleum' has beautiful blue flowers and 'Carneum' has flesh-colored flowers. z4

M. comosum (L.) Mill. France, Central Europe, S. Russia, Mediterranean region, W. Asia. Tassel Grape Hyacinth. Leaves broadly linear, channeled, erect. Scape 30–50cm high, inflorescences cylindric, loose; the upper infertile flowers are blue, the lower flowers yellowish green; May to June. All representatives of this species are botrytis-prone in warm, humid weather. The bulbs of the species are sold as the table vegetable Cipollino in Italy. 'Monstrosum' pyramidal racemes on slender, violet-spotted scapes; 'Plumosum', broadly cylindrical racemes of only infertile flowers, appearing entirely violet-blue; June; good for cut flowers. z5

M. heldreichii see **M. botryoides** var. **heldreichii**

M. latifolium Armitage, J. Kirk et Playne ex J. Kirk. W. Asia Minor. Scape 30–40cm high. Bulbs usually with 1, rarely 2, 2cm-wide leaves. Racemes oblong, loose, 10–

many flowered. Infertile apical flowers sessile, tubular, violet-blue; lower flowers oblong-ovate, blackish-violet. z5

M. macrocarpum Sweet (*M. moschatum* f. *flavum* Bak.). Greece. Scape 20cm high. Leaves 5–7, linear-lanceolate to strap-shaped, to 40cm long. Racemes loose; flowers yellow with brownish-purple lobes, fragrant; April to May. z7

M. moschatum f. **flavum** see **M. macrocarpum**

M. neglectum (Guss ex Ten. (*M. racemosum* (L.) DC., (*M. atlanticum* Boiss. et Reut.). France, SW. and Central Europe, W. Asia, N. Africa. Scape 15–30cm high. Leaves many, narrowly linear, limply recurved. Inflorescences densely cylindrical, dark blue, white-pruinose, plum-scented; April. z7(6)

M. paradoxum C. Koch. Asia Minor. Scape 30cm high. Leaves 3–4, to 2cm wide, to 45cm long. Racemes wide; flowers black-blue, interior greenish-spotted; May to June. z5

M. pinardii (Boiss.) Boiss. Asia Minor. Closely related to *M. comosum*, but leaves narrower and much shorter. Scapes to 75cm high, often less. Sterile flowers pale violet, fertile flowers tubular-clavate, yellowish with brownish tips. Blooms in May. z5

M. polyanthum see **M. armeniacum**

M. pycnanthemum see **Bellevalia pycnantha**

M. racemosum see **M. neglectum**

M. szovitisianum see **M. armeniacum**

M. tubergenianum Th. Hoog. N. Iran. Leaves 2–3, shorter than the inflorescences, narrowly lanceolate, stems 15–30cm long with dense, 5–7cm long racemes; flowers light blue with white limbs, upper sterile flowers lighter blue. An attractive, vigorous species. z6

In addition, Alpine Garden and Rock Garden Society seed lists sometimes include *M. alpinum*, a small plant with greenish flowers; *M. altanticum*, plant with 3–5 linear, nearly round leaves and white-toothed blue, fragrant flowers; *M. conicum*, with 6 linear leaves and white-toothed violet flowers; *M. elegans*, with very short linear leaves and violet-blue flowers on a red scape, *M. polyanthum*, with channeled, linear leaves, deep blue flowers, and its white cv. 'Album'; and *M.*

racemosum, the Musk or Nutmeg Hyacinth, with 5 or 6 strap-shaped leaves and musk-scented purplish flowers aging yellow or brown with cvs. 'Majus' and 'Minus'.

Some *Muscari* species are found in the trade with uncertain botanical status. These are probably of hybrid origin. 'Argaei Album', has small inflorescences with pure white flowers. Very valuable for its late, rather long-persisting flowers. Spreads very little, good for trough planting. 'Massayanum', a rare form from Asia Minor. flower tips tinted pink; 15cm high; May.

Newly introduced into cultivation are *M. colchicum* from the Caucasus region, flowers blue with white teeth, to 20cm high; and *M. woronei* 'Alba', white, fading to soft pink, 15cm high or more; April to May. Attractive flowers for small bouquets. (H.& Kö.)

Myosotidium Hook.
Boraginaceae

Only 1 species on New Zealand's Chatham Islands. Distinguished from the closely related genus *Myosotis* by its winged nutlets. A unique and attractive, albeit tender and demanding herbaceous perennial, cultivated only in a frost-free alpine house or a well-ventilated temperate greenhouse. Its culture and maintenance is only rarely successful. Try growing it in a somewhat moist, sandy loam, or better, in pure seaweed compost with good subsurface drainage. Also, requires constantly high humidity and cool summer temperatures. Division is hardly possible, therefore propagated by seed obtained from collectors or New Zealand. In its habitat, *Myosotidium* is nearly extinct, but it grows in many gardens along the west coasts of Ireland and England.

M. hortensia (Decne.) Baill. New Zealand: Chatham Island; on sandy beaches and rocky sites along the coast. Rootstock thick, cylindrical; stems 30–60cm tall; basal leaves long-petioled, 30 × 12cm, cordate, fleshy, distinctly veined, glabrous, undulate along the margin; stem leaves smaller, broadly ovate and sessile. The 1cm-wide, Forget-me-not-like, light blue flowers are sessile in dense, terminal cymes, 15cm wide. Blooming in July and August. Introduced to England in 1858. z9 (E.)

Myosotis L.
Boraginaceae
Forget-me-not

About 50 species of hairy annual, biennial or perennial herbs. Leaves alternate, simple, entire; basal leaves with petioles, stem leaves sessile. Flowers solitary or in racemose to spicate scorpioid cymes, blue, pink and white; March to August. Calyx 5-lobed; corolla 5-lobed, salverform with scales in the throat; stamens 5; fruit 5, separating, smooth nutlets.

Myosotis sylvatica 'Indigo Compacta

A horticulturally important genus, with very popular species for cut flowers, forcing and garden ornamentals. Unfortunately many are only biennial, with the exception of the summer-blooming, perennial swamp Forget-me-not (*M. palustris*), which is very popular as a low bog-garden plant and well suited for cut flowers. Most cultivated species are indigenous to a range from Europe to Siberia. There are, however, species from N. America, S. Africa, New Zealand and Australia, as well as Eurasia, with little horticultural merit and excluded here.

The tall species are useful as cut flowers grown along streams together with *Primula rosea*, *Caltha*, *Trollius* and other perennials; the biennial species as spring-blooming bed and border plants. The low species are best suited to the alpine garden in a moist to wet site near a stream or fountain. Impartial to soil type. Propagate by division, cuttings and seed.

M. alpestris F.W. Schmidt (*M. rupicola* Sm., *M. sylvatica* Ehr. ex Hoffm. ssp. *alpestris* (F.W. Schmidt) Gams), Alpine Forget-me-not. Mountains of Europe, Asia and N. America, distributed in many local races. A dense, bushy growing perennial, 10cm high, densely pubescent. Leaves oblong-linear, somewhat acuminate. Flowers on very short pedicels in dense, short, scorpioid cymes. Corolla tube whitish, corolla flat, sky blue with small, yellow center; often fragrant, May to August. In the trade, *M. sylvatica* is commonly grown under this name. z4

M. caespititia see **M. rehsteineri**

M. caespitosa see **M. rehsteineri**

M. palustris see **M. scorpiodes**

M. palustris ssp. **caespititia** see **M. rehsteineri**

M. rupicola see **M. alpestris**

M. scorpioides L. (*M. palustris* (L.) L.) Swamp Forget-me-not. Europe to Siberia, widely distributed on moist meadows and watery sites. A quite variable perennial, 10–40cm high, with stolon-like rhizomes. Stems angular, pubescent. Leaves oblong-lanceolate, bright green and somewhat glossy. Flowers in cymose, later loose racemes, sky blue with white throat scales and yellow centers; May to August.

The handsomest and most important garden species. The species and its selected cultivars not only produce summer-long cut flowers, but they also combine well in the water garden with moisture-loving *Primula* spp., *Caltha*, *Leucojum vernum* and particularly *L. aestivum*, *Trollius* and all the moisture-loving *Iris*. Also tolerates shallowly flooded soil.

The following cultivars are listed: 'Alba', white-flowered; 'Graf Waldersee' (Count Waldersee), deep blue, early; 'Meernixe' (Sea Nymph), light blue; 'Perle von Ronneberg' (Pearl of Ronneburg), dark blue; 'Semperflorens', dwarf plant, long and abundant flowering; 'Thüringen' (Thuringia), large-flowered, dark blue. Unfortunately, these cultivars are rarely offered in the trade today. All must be propagated vegetatively, progeny from self-seeding are often untrue from cross-pollination. z5

M. rehsteineri Wartm. (*M. caespitosa* K.F. Schultz ssp. *rehsteineri* (Wartm.) Nym., *M. caespititia* (DC.) Kerner, *M. palustris* ssp. *caespititia* (DC.) E. Baumann).

Central Europe, on the banks of several lakes. A persistent dwarf perennial, 3–5cm high, of grasslike habit. Leaves oblong, obtuse, appressed-pubescent. Inflorescences usually leafy at the base. Flowers small, sky blue, April to May. An attractive dwarf species, but not easily cultivated. Likes full sun and a moist to wet sandy, peaty, loam. Very effective with *Mimulus cupreus* in the alpine garden or along a gravelly stream. Winter protection with conifer branches is advisable, or overwinter in a cool, temperate greenhouse. Seed sets

Myrrhis odorata

sparsely, propagation is, therefore, generally by division. z7(6)

M. sylvatica Ehrh. ex Hoffm. (*M. alpestris* hort. non. F.W. Schmidt), Woodland Forget-me-not. The popular garden Forget-me-not with many cultivars grown as biennials. z5 (D.)

Myriophyllum L.
Haloragaceae
Water Milfoil

Forty to 45 species, nearly cosmopolitan, except in the Arctic and rarely in Africa. Mostly perennial, aquatic or wet ground plants with finely divided, whorled or opposite underwater leaves, emerged leaves entire or serrate. Rooting stems often spread widely. Flowers usually inconspicuous, in the leaf axils, extending above the water. Calyx lobes and petals usually 4, stamens 4 or 8. Underwater plants, especially for ponds. The dense, feathery foliage provides a good spawning habitat for fish. Not too desirable in ornamental ponds, since plants can quickly cover the water's surface. Propagate by cuttings.

M. alterniflorum DC. Atlantic Europe, E. North America. Very succulent, nearly always submerged aquatic plant. For a nonalkaline pond, in water not over 20 degrees C. (68 degrees F.). z6

M. aquaticum (Vell.) Verde. (*M. brasiliense* Cambess., *M. proserpinacoides* Gill. ex Hook. et Arn.). Parrot's Feather. Argentina, Chile to S. USA. Submerged at first, later stem tips also grow above water for a few inches. Dioecious, often with only the female plants in cultivation. Underwater leaves dense, yellowish to bright green, occasionally reddish. Leaves above water are nearly pectinate-pinnate (pinnatifid), tougher, bluish green. Very attractive, non-winter-hardy species, only for the warmest regions or heated pools. Overwinter by root cuttings in shallow pots in the greenhouse. z8

M. brasiliense see **M. aquaticum**

M. hippuroides Nutt. ex Torr. & A. Gray. Western Milfoil, Red Water Milfoil. USA: S. Washington to Central California. Stems to 60cm long; leaves 4–6 in whorls, submerged leaves pinnately dissected, emerged leaves linear to lanceolate, mostly entire. Flowers axillary on emerged shoots. z7

M. spicatum L., Spiked Milfoil. Nearly cosmopolitan with the exception of Central and S. America, Australia and Central Africa. Node-rooting stems to 3m long, underwater. Leaves whorled in 4s, occasionally 3 or 5, 3.5cm long. Pink flowers reaching far above the water on red stalks. June to September. z6

M. proserpinacoides see **M. aquaticum**

M. verticillatum L. Myriad Leaf. Europe, Asia, Algeria, Canada. Usually submersed, with one-meter-long stems. Leaves 4.5cm, finely pinnatifid, in 5, occasionally 4 or 6 part whorls. Flowers borne 25cm above the water in whorled spikes, unpretentious, reddish, June to September. Overwinters as winter buds, which fall to the pond bottom to remain frost-free. Young plants grown from winter buds gathered in February may be raised in aquariums at room temperature. z4 (D.)

Myrrhis Mill. emend. Scop.
Umbelliferae
Myrrh

One species, a perennial deciduous herb grown for its sweetly scented foliage.

M. odorata (L.) Scop. Mountains of Europe. Ribbed stems to 1.5m high, softly pubescent, anise-scented; with 2 to 3-part pinnate, large, pale green irregularly serrate leaves. Flowers small, white, in flat, compound umbels, in mid-summer. Fruits glossy blackish-brown, strongly ribbed, to 25mm long. Aromatic-scented wild herbs, attractive planted next to *Pinus mugo*. Grow from seed, actually fruits, collected and sown immediately upon ripening. z5 (S.)

Narcissus L.
Amaryllidaceae
Daffodil

Popular and widely planted spring flowers with papery-tunicate bulbs, linear leaves and usually solitary, sometimes corymbose flowers subtended by a 1-valved membranous spathe. Flowers white or yellow on the wild species, usually nodding, often fragrant. Perianth regular, with 6 segments, salverform, with a long and tubular or short and cup-like corona separate from the stamen filaments, ovary inferior. Only *M. poeticus*, and its cultivars have red or red-margined coronas. These latter are important in breeding programs, producing not only orange to red-, but also pink-crowned progeny. About 26 species exist, primarily in the W. Medterranean region with some species reaching to Central Europe and N. Africa. *N. tazetta* and its cultivars range from the Mediterranean to E. Asia and are naturalized in S. North America as is *N. pseudonarcissus*. Most species bloom in the winter or early to late spring.

Most of the W. European species are dwarf and have special niches in the garden; some fit best in rock gardens. The N. African species are generally not hardy enough for temperate zone gardens. Garden Narcissus are, however, one of the most popular and indispensable spring flowers. In Great Britain and Ireland, they are absolutely the most important spring flowers, bar none.

Culture of the narcissus: Garden Narcissus have no narrowly defined soil requirements. An optimal site is a deep loam topsoil, rather moist but well-drained, no standing water. Summer dryness is beneficial, but not nearly as important as for tulips. Some growers advise setting the bulbs on a layer of sand, others claim that the sand holds water, imperiling the bulb. A side dressing of humus is helpful; most bulbs are sensitive to fresh manure. The most important fertilizers are calcium and phosphorus, particularly bone meal,

incorporated at planting time. The best planting time is early September, and no later than late October, because narcissus have a brief summer dormant period, shorter than that of tulips; progeny of *N. poeticus* have the shortest natural rest period.

In gardens, clumps should be divided every 4–5 years and replanted at 12–15cm deep; this deters reduction of flowers. The leaves of narcissus turn yellow from early to mid-June. Cutting them back earlier than this (or tying them up) will weaken the bulbs. Narcissus also may persist for years as a vigorous groundcover, somewhat like *Sedum spurium* 'Album Superbum'. They are also suitable for planting in turf which is not mowed until mid-June. During the vegetative period plants require as much light as possible, performing poorly in the full shade of evergreens or early-leafing deciduous plants. The ease with which narcissus spring back after being driven down by a spring thunderstorm or late frost is surprising.

They are indispensable plants in the perennial border, particularly with *Hemerocallis*. Also well suited to planting with rhododendron and azaleas, provided they receive sufficient light. Daffodils can be combined with tulips (especially *Tulipa praestans* 'Fuesilier'), which require more summer dryness than many species if they are to last for a several years. Blue-flowering companion plants mix well with certain cultivars of Narcissus: i.e. *Chionodoxa*, *Scilla*, *Hyacinthus* 'Borah', *Muscari*, *Anemone blanda* and *A. apennina*, *Omphalodes cappadocica*, the blue *Pulmonaria* spp., *Brunnera* and *Primula denticulata*.

Diseases and pests: Unlike tulips and lilies, narcissus are not eaten by mice. Also, unlike tulips, they are resistant to many diseases associated with wet summers. Viruses, however, can be a problem, being spread by aphids and nematodes, and viruses are far more destructive in warm climates. A virus-infected bulb ought to be destroyed. Viruses spread to daffodils from other bulbous species; botrytis fungus may originate from tulips or peonies. Pokeweed, *Phytolacca americana* and other *Phytolacca* species are virus reservoirs and should be eliminated from all garden areas. The Greater Bulb Fly and Lesser Bulb Fly may be a problem. The Greater Bulb Fly is active from May to late June. The larvae enter at the base of the bulb and feed on the inside of the bulb. The Greater Bulb Fly lays 1 egg in each bulb. The Lesser Bulb Fly is active from May to October with a second generation being active from early July to fall. It lays from 5–30 eggs, and the larvae enter through wounds. The most effective treatment is a systemic insecticide drench. The Lesser Bulb Fly also affects iris, hyacinth and potatoes.

Garden Narcissus

Hybridization began around the middle of the 19th century in Great Britain and Ireland and these countries have led in daffodil breeding ever since. In addition, narcissus are hybridized in the USA, Tasmania, S. Australia, New Zealand and Holland; in Holland several

perianth, the second is the corona): W = white, whitish, G = green, Y = yellow, O = orange, R = red, P = pink.

A few of the most common daffodils are included in the following list:

Class 1: Trumpet Narcissus

Single-flowered, trumpet (corona) as long or longer than a perianth segment; (primarily early-blooming cultivars).
1a = 1Y-Y golden yellow:
   'King Alfred', an old cultivar from 1899, has dominated over the years; now often virus-infected, and superseded by superior cultivars such as 'Golden

'W.P. Milner', yellow-white dwarf cultivar from 1884, very early; 'Colleen Bawn', a rare dwarf cultivar from 1889 with nodding, white "Easter bells," from *N. alpestris* (*N. pseudonarcissus* ssp. *alpestris*).

1d = 1Y-W reversed bicolor:
   'Spellbinder', very early, colors not very contrasting, but a vigorous, lemon yellow cultivar; 'Honeybird' and 'Lunar Sea', early, perianth a cool sulfur yellow, elegant.

Myriophyllum brasiliense

Narcissus 'Scarlet Elegance'

naturalizing forms are propagated in large numbers. Through the years, more than 10,000 cultivars have been registered with the Royal Horticultural Society in London, England.

It has become necessary, therefore, to undertake a thorough classification of the cultivars. In 1950 a system was devised comprising 11 Classes (Divisions) which is largely applicable today. However, it certainly is not completely inclusive; i.e., category 2b refers to a large narcissus blossom with white perianth and colored corona, but does not indicate whether the corona is yellow, orange, red or pink. Therefore, since 1977 a system has been used that retains the notation of the classes, but also includes the color of the perianth and corona (crown) with the following abbreviations (the first letter is for the

Harvest', 'Golden Perfection', 'Kingscourt', and 'Unsurpassable'.
   'Arctic Gold', early; 'Viking', middle early; 'Aurum', middle early;
rich golden light yellow:
   'Mulatto', one of the earliest forms, persistent;
trumpets orange: 1 Y-O
   'Red Curtain', middle early

1b = 1W-Y white perianth, yellow trumpets:
   'Preamble', early; 'Newcastle', middle early; 'Ballygarvey', midseason, strong contrast; 'Little Beauty', miniature form, very early, from *N. minor* var. *conspicuus;*
white perianth and pink trumpets: 1 W-P
   'Rima', middle late

1c = 1W-W, white trumpets
   'Cantatrice', early; 'Empress of Ireland', early; 'Panache', middle early

Class 2: Large-crowned Narcissus

Single-flowered, corona longer than ⅓ of a perianth segment, but shorter than the entire segment. Originated as a cross of *N. pseudonarcissus* × *N. poeticus* (*N.* × *incomparabilis* 1768). Nearly half of all registered Narcissus belong in this class.

2a = yellow perianth, colored corona golden yellow: 2 Y-Y
   'Carlton', early, an old cultivar with a medium-long corona, medium yellow; 'Golden Aura', late, golden, firm flower or good texture; 'Ormeau', middle early, golden, nearly trumpet cultivar; 'Yellow Sun', early, quite showy, but also well suited for naturalizing
light yellow: 'Euphony', middle late with orange-colored to red corona.

The above cultivars are exceptionally popular in Europe with innumerable, cultivars of superior texture.

The following have intensely colored coronas:
2 Y-O and 2 Y-R

'Ceylon', middle early, flowers more upright, looking at the observer; 'Sun Chariot', middle early; 'Falstaff', unusually early, brighter contrast; 'Vulcan', early, warm golden yellow; 'Moneymore', middle late; 'Tawny Lad', midseason, perianth nearly orange-yellow; 'Gypsy', midseason, perianth orange-gold; 'Ambergate', perianth more apricot-orange, a novel, conspicuous cultivar.

Breeders are constantly looking for cultivars are more orange than red; cultivars with upright-facing flowers are especially desirable. 2 W-O and 2 W-R

'Kilworth', late, an important cultivar, very commonly used in breeding work; 'Avenger', late; 'Cool Waters', very late, with a nearly red corona, similar to 'Ulster Knight', middle late; 'Kentucky Cardinal', middle late, nearly red corona.

Pink crowns: 2 W-P

'Passionale', midseason, soft-colored, perfect form; 'Roseworthy', small cultivar, middle late, elegant; 'Rising Dawn', corona with a pink rim, middle late; form, light perianth, vigorous; 'Daydream', middle late, low, good contrast, firm texture; 'Impresario', middle early, nearly trumpet form; 'Cloud Nine', middle late, a charming cultivar with the flowers of *N. jonquilla*.

Class 3: Small-cupped cultivars

Single-flowered, corona shorter than ⅓ of a perianth segment; this group is much smaller than the large-crowned group and contains more late-flowering forms (similar to *N. poeticus*).

3a = yellow perianth, colored corona orange-red corona: 3 Y-R

Narcissus 'Roseworthy'

Narcissus 'Stainless'

Narcissus 'Stratosphere'

cultivars which help in developing a red perianth. Cultivars are also sought to help in the development of a light yellow perianth with a pink corona.

2b = Large-crowned with a white perianth and colored corona
with yellow corona: 2 W-Y

'Brunswick', early, especially vigorous, persistent old cultivar; 'Green Island', middle late, greenish yellow, much used in breeding; 'Greeting', middle late, small-crowned, perianth lightly recurved; 'Woodgreen', extremely early, nearly trumpet form, good contrast.

The so-called "foul weather cultivars" from Holland have disc-like crowns and are, to some, less attractive in form; the most popular is 'Duke of Windsor'.
orange-red crowns: the coronas of many

'Accent', midseason, deep pink; 'Cool Flame', middle late, the red in the corona comes from pink rather than orange; a novelty. The modest colors of some cultivars can be effectively combined with other perennials, such as the violet to purple flowers of *Primula* 'Gruss aus Königslutter' (Greetings from Königslutter).

2c = 2W-W large-crowned, white:

'Stainless', late, smaller corona; 'Woodvale', middle late, nearly trumpet cultivar, rather sulfur-white, especially elegant.

2d = reversed bicolor, perianth yellow, corona white: 2 Y-W

'Binkie', middle late, sulfur yellow perianth, smaller corona, the first of these cultivars, very large and vigorous; 'Charter', early and long, nearly trumpet

'Birma' (earlier classified under 2a), middle early, old cultivar; 'Altruist', perianth light copper orange, 3 O-R, fades in strong sunshine, middle late.

3b = white perianth, colored corona, yellow corona: 3 W-Y

'Aircastle', middle late; 'Delightful', late, low; 'Grace Note', very late, low, charming, starry effect from the slightly inward folded perianth segments, unique.
red corona: 3 W-R

'Limerick', late, snow white perianth, deep red corona, a valuable cultivar of this color, also grown for exhibition; 'Snow Gem', midseason, like *N. poeticus*.
pink corona: 3 W-P

'Audubon', midseason, deep pink limb.

3c = white, small-crowned: 3 W-W

'Frigid', extremely late, flowering in

May with *Rhododendron repens* hybrids, green eyed; 'Cool Crystal', late, tall, slightly reflexed; 'Jade', the latest narcissus, green eyed.

Class 4: Double Narciccus
Included here are the double mutations of wild species and hybrids. Many collectors consider double narcissus to be grotesque in appearance. 'Yellow Cheerfulness' is suitable for forcing after February; this is a pale yellow cultivar, a predecessor of the Poetaz group with double coronas.

Narcissus rupicola ssp. *rupicola*

Narcissus 'Vulcan'

Class 5: Hybrids with *N. triandrus*
Distinctly showing the influence of the wild species. Most are multi-flowered. Not subdivided, according to the most recent classification. As established in 1950:

5a = Corona not less than ⅔ the length of a perianth segment
white:
'Thalia', midseason, 2–3 flowered, elegant, small; 'Tresamble', midseason, 3-flowered, somewhat more vigorous.
light yellow:

'Liberty Bells', middle late, 2–3 flowered; 'Harmony Bells', middle late, 2–3 flowers, very floriferous.

5b = Corona shorter than ⅔ of a perianth segment
white:
'Arish Mell', middle late, 2–4 flowered, perianth recurved; 'Petrel', late, to 7 flowers per stem, with the flowers of *N. jonquilla*.
white perianth, yellow corona:
'Lapwing', midseason, perianth reflexed, occasionally 2-flowered; 'Tuesday's Child', midseason, usually 3-flowered.
yellow miniature cultivars:
'Hawera' (*N. jonquilla* × *N. triandrus* var. *concolor*), late, lemon yellow, 2–4 flowers, wonderfully formed, very slow-growing.
yellow perianth, orange-red corona:
'Puppet', midseason, elegant, 1–2 flowered, long-flowering.

Class 6: Hybrids with *N. cyclamineus*
Perianth reflexed; most cultivars flower very early to early, flowers long-lasting; usually single-flowered. The cultivars of this group are somewhere between widely popular and highly prized; the earliest, large-flowered class. After the revised classification, only the color codes were added to the 1950 system.

6a = Coronas not shorter than ⅔ of a perianth segment
yellow:
'February Gold', the most common cultivar, persistent; 'Peeping Tom' and 'Bartley', taller, trumpet becomes erect during anthesis; 'Baby Doll', low, very vigorous; 'March Sunshine', early, wild-like; 'Little Witch', smaller than the above cultivars, somewhat later; 'Prefix', especially early, deep golden'; 'Bushtit', middle early, strong flowers, elegant; 'Charity May', early, light yellow; 'Tête-à-Tête', very early, popular, small cultivar usually with 2 flowers per stem, originated from a very interesting and difficult cross with *N. tazetta* ('Soleil d'Or'); also good for forcing.
'Jumblie', early, miniature cultivar, 2–3 flowered, corona orange-yellow to orange-red, yellow perianth.
'Satellite', extremely early, not always consistent in color.
'Jetfire', early, more intensely colored, floriferous, vigorous.
white perianth, yellow corona:
'Ibis', very early, starry flowers, less reflexed; 'Jack Snipe', early, miniature corona fading to white.
completely white:
'Jenny', one of the most graceful

narcissus, not quite so early.
white perianth, lilac-pink corona:
  'Lilac Charm', midseason.

6b = Corona shorter than ⅔ of a perianth segment:
  'Beryl', middle early, from a cross with *N. poeticus*: perianth yellow at first, then cream white, corona orange at first, then yellow, one of the best cultivars for naturalizing, tolerates semi-shade better than many narcissus; 'Foundling', midseason, white perianth, deep pink crowns.

Class 7: Hybrids with *N. jonquilla* (and other closely related species).
Included here are the intensely fragrant, primarily multiflowered late forms, from medium size to miniature. Various forms have a tendency to produce leaves in winter. Many are generally considered to be healthy, vigorous and undemanding. The classification of 1950 distinguishes:

7a = Corona not shorter than ⅔ of a perianth segment
yellow:
  'Sweetness', middle late, the most popular, important garden cultivar, gold-yellow, only 1-flowered, excellent fragrance, very long-persisting.
reversed bicolor:
  'Canary', late, 1–2 flowered, starry-flowers, lemon yellow with a white "halo", corona white; 'Step Forward', middle late, 2–3 flowered, corona white, wide perianth.

7b = Corona shorter than ⅔ of a perianth segment
yellow:
  'Trevithian', middle late, lemon yellow, very fragrant, 2–3 flowered, medium size, widely planted.
  'Oregon Gold', middle late, golden yellow, multiflowered, exceedingly floriferous, 1–3 flowered.
  'Stratosphere', midseason, somewhat taller, corona more orange-yellow, 1–3 flowered.
  'Tittle-Tattle', beginning only in May, one of the latest yellow narcissi, light yellow, 2–3 flowered, tall, twice as large as *N. × gracilis*, firmer flowers; also suitable for showing at garden shows.
  'Chit Chat' (= *N. juncifolius × N. jonquilla*), late, golden yellow miniature cultivar, 2–3 flowered, vigorous.
orange-red coronas:
  'Bunting', middle late, 2-flowered, perianth golden, long-flowered; 'Skylon', midseason, small, round flowers, red corona, 2-flowered, for the rock garden, effective combined with blue *Aubretia* spp.

white:
  'Eland', late, 2–3 flowered, light lemon yellow, fading to white; 'Dainty Miss', midseason, small, snow white (from *N. watieri*).
pink coronas:
  'Bell Song', middle late, 3-flowered, floriferous, ivory colored perianth
reversed bicolor:
  'Pipit', midseason, 2–3 flowered, lemon yellow perianth, light, corona turning white, very floriferous, vigorous, graceful, valuable.

Narcissus bulbocodium

Class 8: Tazetta Narcissus, Cluster Daffodils
The true Tazettas are not reliably winter hardy north of USDA z8, emerging to bloom in winter. The earliest are mostly used for forcing:
  'Paperwhite' (*N. papyraceus* = *N. tazetta* L. ssp. *papyraceus* (Ker-Gawl.) Bak.), 10–12 flowered, white, scented nearly as strongly as 'Soleil d'Or' (from *N. tazeta* L. ssp. *cupularis* (Salisb.) Bak.) 12-flowered, golden yellow perianth, orange-colored crowns.
(*N. canaliculatus*: Class 10)
A cross with *N. poeticus* resulted in the following forms, once known as the "Poetaz" Narcissus:
  'Cragford', white, orange-red crowns, often forced for Christmas, not commonly recommended for garden plantings though suitable in e. US.
  'Geranium' (and 'Orange Wonder') middle late to late, white perianth, orange corona, many flowered, very

fragrant, very vigorous, at least in zone 5, problem-free and persistent.
  'Silver Chimes' is from a cross with *N. triandrus* 'Loiseleurii', many flowered, white perianth, cream white corona, very fragrant, elegant.
  A new, promising race has been developed in Oregon from a cross with *N. jonquilla*: 'Hoopoe', perianth a fresh, light yellow, corona orange, many flowered, very floriferous, very fragrant.

Class 9: Poeticus Narcissus, Poet's Narcissus
Only crosses from varieties of *N. poeticus*, therefore only a few, mostly late to very late cultivars.
  'Actaea', middle late but much earlier than related cultivars, very widely planted and reliable, purest white, coronas green, yellow with a red rim, very fragrant. 'Cantabile', late, greenish coronas, red-rimmed.

Class 10: Species, Wild Forms and their Hybrids

N. alpestris ssp. **alpestris** see **N. pseudo-narcissus**

N. asturiensis (Jord.) Pugsley (*N. minimus* (Bak.) hort.). Mountains of N. Spain; flowering in winter to February, tiniest, earliest yellow trumpet type, 8–12cm, leaves 10cm long, narrow, furrowed. Hardly propagates vegetatively;

requires a hot, dry site to eventually seed itself. z6

N. bulbocodium L. (*Corbularia bulbocodium* Haw. (L.) Hoop Petticoat Daffodil. West central Mediterranean region, 10–20cm high, leaves thin, nearly cylindrical, but furrowed. Flowers more or less erect, not nodding, with a broadly funnelform corona (paracorolla), and small, lanceolate, reduced lobes. Propagation is vegetative by division, not always floriferous. Naturalized in the rock garden at Wisley near London, England. Quite variable, young genus or

Narcissus 'Frigid'

species, still being taxonomically classified.

N. bulbocodium ssp. **monophyllus** see **N. cantabricus** ssp. **monophyllus**

N. bulbocodium ssp. **obesus** (*Corbularia bulbocodium* ssp. *obesus* (Salisb.) Maire.) Native to Spain and Portugal. Leaves erect, corona longer, wider and less membranous than the perianth lobes, not as narrow at the base as the other varieties, the latest to flower, late April to May. Thrives on various soil types, from alkaline to acid. z5–6

N. bulbocodium ssp. **vulgaris**. (*Corbularia bulbocodium* ssp. *citrina* (Bak.) Wehrh.) 15–20cm high, leaves more lax, flowers lemon yellow, mid April. One of the largest-flowered forms, rarely offered in the trade. z6

N. bulbocodium ssp. **romieuxii** (*Corbularia bulbocodium* ssp. *romieuxii* Br. -Bl. et Maire.) From N. Africa and not hardy; better suited to alpine house. Creamy sulfur yellow, large flowered, 15–20cm high, flowering at Christmas time or

soon after, or late November; a jewel of a plant. z7–9

N. canaliculatus Gussone, a wild form from S. France, stemming from *N. tazetta* L. ssp. *lacticolor* Bak. Miniature Tazetta, 20cm high, with 6–8 flowers per stalk, April; starry white perianth, golden yellow corona, sweetly fragrant; short, narrow leaves, propagates well, but not always very floriferous, reasonably winter hardy. z5

N. cantabricus DC. ssp. **monophyllus** Bak. (*Narcissus bulbocodium* var. *monophyllus* (Bak.), *Corbularia monophylla* Dur.) White flowers, gradually becoming transparent. Very fragrant, long-lasting flowers in winter. Mostly one leaf per bulb.

N. cantabricus ssp. *cantabricus* is much like *N.c. monophyllus* but with 3–8 leaves per bulb and therefore somewhat more vigorous in cultivation. These grow wild in the shade of shrubs in S. Spain, Morocco and Algeria where soil is quite

arid in summer; keep potted plants dry and in the shade in summer. More susceptible to frost damage than *N. bulbocodium* and *N.b.* ssp. *romieuxii*. Not easily cultivated, craved by collectors. English breeders have hybridized both of the North African forms and others. 'Nylon' is a good cultivar for the alpine house. It is a white, vigorous form, floriferous after November and more floriferous than *N. cantabricus* var. *monophyllus*. The English have also crossed the narcissus species in this group with *Narcissus triandrus*.

Narcissus cyclamineus hybrid 'Peeping Tom'

N. cernuus see **N. pseudonarcissus** ssp. **moschatus**

N. cyclamineus DC., Cyclamen Narcissus. Spain to Portugal, naturalized in parts of England. Scapes 12–15cm high, leaves narrowly linear, keeled, flowers golden yellow, nodding; corona slender, tubular, perianth segments reflexed, like *Cyclamen*; February to March. In cultivation, prefers a moist, slightly acid, humus site, in light semi-shade. Propagated by seed in mild climates. Good companions are *Scilla mischtschenkoana*, (*S. tubergeniana*), *Primula* Juliae Hybrids. z6

N. × gracilis Sabine (*N. jonquilla × N. poeticus*). S. France. Stems 30cm high, nearly round, 3-flowered, flowers sulfur yellow, fragrant, after mid-May. A very late narcissus. z5

N. × johnstonii (Bak.) Pugsley **'Queen of Spain'** (*N. pseudonarcissus × N. triandrus* var. *cernuus*). N. Spain. 25cm high, single-flowered, medium-sized, light

Belgium. Perianth paler than the corona, very early in March, 20cm, for naturalizing. z5

N. minimus see **N. asturiensis**

N. obvallaris see **N. pseudonarcissus** ssp. **obvallaris**

N. minor L. var. **conspicuus** Haw. (carried in the trade as *N. nanus*). Spain, Portugal. Scape to 20cm, corona light yellow, perianth lighter, March, with the garden crocus. Multiplies so quickly that it must be frequently divided, otherwise

late, beginning in June. Stems 40cm high, flowers purest white, corona green at the base, then yellow, with a red rim W-GYR, very fragrant, flowering in May in the garden, very vigorous form naturalizing in moist sites, suitable for semi-shade. z5

N. pseudonarcissus L., Daffodil, Trumpet Narcissus. SW. Europe to Belgium, Switzerland, Germany, N. Italy. The original, long trumpet, yellow daffodil with strap-shaped, often more or less glaucous leaves. In various forms, March to April; for naturalizing. z5

Narcissus cyclamineus **hybrid 'Jack Snipe'**

Narcissus poeticus

Narcissus triandrus

yellow, April. Persistent and reliable, but very difficult to propagate vegetatively, rarely offered in the trade. z7

N. jonquilla L., Jonquil. Spain to Dalmatia and N. Africa. Scapes 20–30cm high, leaves terete or nearly so, reedlike, bright green, emerges in winter; stems round, 2–6 flowered, flower gold-yellow, with a cupshaped corona, strongly orange-scented, April to May. Very heat loving, requires well-drained soil, not always reliably hardy without winter protection. Propagates well vegetatively, must be frequently divided. z6

N. juncifolius Lag. SW. Europe. Leaves semiterete, grass green. Stems 2 to many-flowered, 20–25cm high; flowers gold-yellow, smaller than those of *N. jonquilla*, fragrant. Vigorous in loam soil, charming species. z6

N. lobularis: actually a synonym for *N. minor* var. *conspicuus*; plants erroneously listed in the trade as *lobularis* usually are a form of *N. pseudonarcissus* from S.

produces many leaves and few flowers. z6

N. moschatus see **N. pseudonarcissus** ssp. **moschatus**

N. nanus see **N. minor** var. **conspicuus**

N. × odorus L. (*N. pseudonarcissus × N. jonquilla*) 'Rugulosus' (hort.). Tall and larger flowered than *N. jonquilla*, light yellow, very fragrant, earlier (with *Scilla sibirica*). 'Orange Queen', entire flower yellow-orange. z5

N. poeticus L., Poet's Narcissus. Distributed from Spain to Greece in geographical varieties. Found from moist lowland meadows at sea level to the high mountains. Coronas red margined or entirely red. Very important for breeding. Widely disseminated in the trade is:

N. poeticus L. var. **recurvus** (Haw.) Fernd. 'Pheasant's Eye'. Switzerland, on mountain meadows where it blooms

N. pseudonarcissus L. ssp. **alpestris** (Pugsl.) Fernd. (*N. alpestris* Pugsl.). Pyrenees. Leaves bluish, 10–15cm, flowers nodding, pure white, nearly unscented, perianth twisted; for a moist, peaty soil, in a lightly shaded site (includes the cultivar 'Colleen Bawn'). z5

N. pseudonarcissus L. ssp. **moschatus** (L.) Bak. (*N. moschatus* L., *N. cernuus*). Pyrenees. Stems 25–30cm; flowers nodding, greenish soft yellow at first, later milk white, mildly fragrant; thrives in moist, humus soil, but must be frequently divided for best bloom. z5

N. pseudonarcissus L. ssp. **obvallaris** (Salisb.) Fernd. (*N. obvallaris* Salisb.), Tenby Daffodil. Original habitat unknown, naturalized in Great Britain. Scape 25cm high, pure golden yellow flowers of good form, very garden worthy, March to April, also for naturalizing in a well-drained soil. z5

N. rupicola Dafour. Spain to Portugal. 10–14cm; similar to *N. juncifolius*, but with 3-angled terete leaves and solitary, small, bright yellow flowers in April and May. Fragrant. z7

N. triandrus L. Angel's Tears. Spain, Portugal. Scape 15–30cm high, leaves slender, nearly round, ridged; flowers nodding, stems 3–6 flowered; corona cupshaped, perianth segments reflexed, April. Includes many forms, i.e. var. **albus** Baker, white, var. **concolor** Baker, shorter than *albus*, lemon yellow, var. **loiseleurii** Rouy with 2–3 large, pure

Class 12
This category was left open in the revision of 1977 to accommodate future cultivars that do not fit into the other 11 classes.

Nardus L.
Gramineae

N. stricta L. Europe, N. Asia, Greenland. A dense, clump grass, 10–40cm high with stiff, bristly, gray-green leaves and one-sided spikes. Typically found in a meadow or pasture on a poor, acid soil.

intolerant perennials and dwarf woody shrubs; typically found in Europe with *Erica tetralix*. Propagate by seed or division.

N. americanum Ker.-Gawl. Yellow Asphodel. USA. New Jersey, Delaware south to South Carolina, in swamps. Leaves linear to 20cm long and 3mm wide; scape to 45cm tall; flowers in a simple, terminal raceme; flowers 7mm long on pedicels 7mm long; perianth segments 6, separate; stamens 6, filaments white woolly. z7(6)

Nardus stricta

Nelumbo nucifera

white flowers; found only on the Glenan Island off the west coast of France; more sensitive to frost. This species requires well-drained, not too dry soil, and a protected site. z7(6)

N. watieri Maire. High Atlas Mts., Morocco. Stems 10cm high; similar in habit to *N. rupicola*, but with snow white flowers; gray leaves; April to May. Thrives in sandy soil and requires a completely dry resting period in summer. Very attractive, but sensitive to frost; best grown as a pot plant in the alpine house. z9

Class 11: Narcissi with split coronas
Flat coronas, incised at least ⅓ of their length; this class of Dutch hybrids is regarded as grotesque by many gardening purists and collectors.

Good companion for such flowering plants as; *Gentiana purpurea*, *Arnica montana* and *Potentilla erecta*. Also suitable for marshy, peaty sites. Propagates easily by division or seed, intolerant of lime. z2 (S.)

Narthecium Huds.
Liliaceae
Bog Asphodel, Yellow Grass

Four to 6 species in the Northern Temperate Zone. Persistent perennials with a creeping rhizomatous rootstock. Stems slender, erect, unbranched. Basal leaves linear, grasslike, stem leaves few or none, reduced. Flowers greenish yellow together in dense terminal racemes; mid- to late summer. Grow in fertile, moist, heath or peaty soil in full sun. Suitable for the bog or heather garden, together with other lime-

N. asiaticum Maxim. Japan, on wet ground. Similar to the above but larger over-all. Leaves larger and slightly wider; scapes to 60cm tall; racemes to 12cm long, flowers to 1.25cm long on pedicels to 1.5cm long. z7(6)

N. californicum Bak. USA, SW. Oregon to Central California in marshes. Leaves to 30cm long, .75cm wide; scape to 50cm high; flowers 1cm long on pedicels to 1.5cm long in racemes to 15cm long. Perianth segments wider than other species and anthers red, other species yellow. z7(6)

N. ossifragum (L.) Huds. W. and NW. Europe, NW. Germany. Scape 10–30cm high, resembles *Tofieldia*, but with 6–8mm long perianth segments, greenish outside, yellow inside, stamen filaments woolly pubescent. z6 (D.)

Naumbergia

N. thyrsiflora see **Lysimachia thyrsiflora**

Nelumbo Adans.
(*Nelumbium* Juss.)
Nymphaeaceae
Lotus

Two species of aquatic plants which grow only in quiet water with horizontal creeping rhizomes. The leaves are green to blue-green, peltate, orbicular

Narthecium ossifragum

concave, borne on long petioles above the water; the large, solitary bowl-shaped, fragrant flowers and the seed structures stand above the leaves. Sepals 4–5; petals several to many, stamens many; the receptacle enlarges as flowers fade, becoming an almost woolly flat-topped structure in which the 1-ovuled, stony fruits are embedded. These fruit containers are favored for dried arrangements. *Lotus*, with *Acanthus*, has served as a fine arts pattern since man's earliest history.

Indigenous to temperate N. America and Asia. Both species require a warm climate, a wind sheltered site in full sun, in shallow water. In cool climates a sunny wall will reflect heat into the pool. For most success, select a 60–80cm deep pool, fill it to within 20–40cm with loamy, organic soil mixed with well-rotted manure. The organic matter in shallow water will heat up more easily in the sun.

In cool climates, in the fall drain the water in 2 or 3 stages then mulch heavily for winter with composted leafmold to protect from freezing. In the USA, from z5 southward, leave the lotus pond undisturbed. Propagation is by seed or division. Seed is best obtained from natural stands which, in cool climates, may require hand-pollination. Specialists now offer an exciting array of cultivars of these superb species.

Sow seed (actually, fruit) in a warm greenhouse in late February to March. With a triangle file cut a small notch through the bony fruits, and place them individually in small pots set 5cm under water; keep at 30–35 degrees C. (86–95 F.). Germination should follow in 8–10 days. By repeated shifting to larger pots and deeper water (also gradual exposure to more air and sunshine) the young plants will become acclimated for eventual planting in a warm (heated?) pool in late April or May.

For division, pot individual rhizome pieces in late March with the budded tip slanting upward in the pot. Cover with a thin layer of fine, washed gravel. Acclimate as with seedlings. With older plants, the soil may need to be renovated every 3 years; an annual topdressing of well composted barnyard manure, during the dormant season, is beneficial. New plantings should be handled like the rhizome divisions where summers are chilly, unless a heated pool is provided. Success is dependant upon the weather; plants perform best and flower only in sunny, warm summers.

N. lutea (Willd.) Pers. (*Nelumbium luteum* Willd., *N. pentapetala* (Walt.) Fern.), American Lotus, Yanquapin. N. America from the 43rd parallel, southward to Columbia, S. America. Petioles 1m or more, light green, slightly prickly. Leaves 45–60cm, bluish-green, with a yellow spot at the petiole junction and entire margins. Flowers 20–28cm across, fragrant, pale to bright yellow, July to August. z4–9

N. nelumbo see **N. nucifera**

N. nucifera Gaertn. (*N. nelumbo* (L.) Duce, *N. speciosum* Willd.), Indian Lotus. From the Caspian Sea to Japan, south to NE. Australia. Leaf petiole rough, especially the lower half, 1.5–2m high, with a milky sap. Leaves 30–60cm across, blue-green, covered with a waxy layer, with sinuate margins. Flowers 18–35cm, white to pink, April to August. z5–10 (D.)

From this quite variable, but more demanding species, have come a number of cultivars for temperate gardens; 'Alba Striata', 'Flavescens', 'Pekinensis Rubra', 'Pygmea', 'Siroman' ('Alba Plena') are older cultivars. z6–10

All lotus are easily grown in heated pools under glass, where they can attain their maximum potential.

For a review of all lotus species and the many oriental cultivars, with exceptionally fine illustrations, see Gugi Sakamoto *Lotus*, published in Japan in 1872 by Kodansha.

N. speciosum see **N. nucifera**

Nepeta L.
Labiatae
Catmint, Catnip

A genus of 150–250 species, from temperate Eurasia and Africa of which only a few are ornamental. Mostly low to medium high, usually aromatic herbs with usually blue, terminal or axillary flowers. Calyx tubular, 5-toothed; corolla tube dilated, limb 2-lipped, upper lip 2-lobed-upright, lower lip 3-lobed. Stems mostly 4-angled. Leaves opposite, usually petioled, green to gray, dentate. Cultivate in any soil, particularly in sunny, dry sites. Suitable primarily for herb gardens, wild and rock gardens. Propagate by seed, division and cuttage.

N. cataria L. Catnip. Eurasia but widely naturalized elsewhere. Gray pubescent, 4-angled stems to 90cm high; leaves to 7.5cm long, cordate, ovate to lanceolate, acuminate, crenate, viscid-hairy, pungent-scented when bruised. Flowers white to pinkish with purple spots in verticillasters in summer and fall. Plants often with short, evergreen winter leafy shoots. Scarcely an ornamental but for herb gardens and kitchen gardens. z4

N. × faassenii Bergm. ex Stearn (*N. mussinii* × *N. nepetella*; *N. mussinii* hort.), Blue Catmint. 25–30cm high, small, bushy. Leaves short petioled, oval, crenate, gray-green. Flowers lavender blue, in axillary verticillasters; persistent bloomers, May to September; flowers continuously after a shearing in July to August. Very valuable large edging plant or among roses, and with *Potentilla fruticosa* on a sunny, dry site; any garden soil is suitable. Attracts bees. The cultivar 'Six Hills Giant' is nearly twice as large as the type; 'Superba' is more upright growing, flowers somewhat darker; both, however, are less effective than *N. × faassenii* in the quantity of flowers and general appearance. Propagation of particular selections is by cuttings and division. z5–9

N. grandiflora M.B. Caucasus. Stems 60–90cm high, glabrous to pubescent. Leaves to 5cm long, oblong-cordate, green. Flowers to 2cm long, blue-violet in false spikes; May to June. Usually wrongly labeled in cultivation. z5

N. mussinii Spreng. ex Henckel, Mauve Catmint. Caucasus, Caspian region, N. Iran. Stems decumbent, pubescent, about 25cm high. Leaves cordate,

Nerine Herb.
Amaryllidaceae

At least 20 species of S. African Amyrillids, mostly tender, with tunicate bulbs and strap-shaped leaves, all basal. Naked scapes emerge in the fall with a terminal umbel, subtended by 2 spathe valves; flowers trumpet-shaped, perianth segments 6, equal, free or barely united basally, ovary inferior. Leaves emerge after flowers fade and must not be frost damaged over winter, which limits planting in gardens north of z8.

of 3–8 (or more) trumpet flowers, segments to 4cm long, margins undulate to crispid; scarlet. Strap-shaped leaves emerge after flowering, growing to 30cm long, about 1.5cm wide. Cultivar 'Maxima', flowers crimson-red; var. *corusca* (Ker-Gawl.) Bak. Leaves broader with cross-bars, flowers large, salmon-red; var. *rosea* (Herb.) Bak. Leaves darker, rose-red. z8

In recent years, British breeders, especially, have introduced a fine array of hybrid and cultivar nerines, some with improved hardiness, most with exceptionally beautiful flowers which are a

Nepeta × faassenii

Nerine bowdenii

crenate, on widely sprawling stems. Flowers in terminal and sub-terminal false spikes, whorled, lavender blue; the form 'Grandiflora' is particularly attractive, better than N. × *faassenii*; June to July, reblooming after a shearing in August. Only rarely found in cultivation. z4

N. nervosa Royle ex Benth. Kashmir. Stems 30–50cm high, plant open bush-like, erect. Leaves lanceolate, distinctly veined, gray-green, the basal leaves short-petioled, upper leaves sessile. Flowers light blue (or yellowish), in dense, cylindrical spikes to 12.5cm long; July to September. Attractive, and should be more widely planted. z5 (H.& M.)

N. bowdenii W. Wats. S. Africa. The most common species of the genus hardy enough for temperate landscapes, given winter protection. A bulbous plant with shiny, strap-shaped leaves which emerge in late winter or early spring, die back in summer. The beautiful pink flowers appear in umbels on 35–60cm-high scapes in the fall. For warm, south-facing walls with the concurrently blooming, blue *Crocus speciosus*. Propagation is by separation of the offset bulblets or by cutting the bulbs so that a piece of the base remains with each segment; the segments are then handled like lily bulb scales. A summer dormancy period is essential, after which bulbs may be transplanted. 'Fenwick' is a selection for the landscape. z7 (S.)

N. sarniensis (L.) Herb. Guernsey Lily. Scape to 45cm high with terminal umbel

great addition to southern gardens and to northern greenhouses.

Nierembergia Ruiz et Pav.
Solanaceae

Thirty to 35 species of annual and perennial herbs and subshrubs from Mexico to subtropical S. America. Closely related to *Petunia*, but differing in the non-glandular glabrous to rarely pubescent leaves and stems. Stems decumbent to erect, diffusely branched; leaves alternate, simple, entire. Flowers axillary, solitary or in cymes; calyx tubular to ball-shaped, deeply 5-lobed; corolla salver-form to cup-shaped, 5-lobed, white, blue or violet, stamens epipetalous, diadelphous with one staminodium; pistil 2-lobed.

N. gracilis Hook. Paraguay, Argentina. Short-lived perennial or annual. Branches to 45cm high, slender, downy-pubescent; leaves linear to spatulate, 1 to rarely 6cm long; flowers axillary on pedicels to 1cm long, corolla white with blue or violet shading and yellow throat, about 2.5cm wide. z7

N. hippomanica Miers. Argentina, naturalized in subtropical USA. Stems 15–30cm high, pubescent; leaves linear-spatulate to 1.5cm long; flowers axillary on pedicels to .25cm long, corolla bluish, about 2cm wide. More commonly cul-

or on short pedicels, fragrant, pure white or creamy white, occasionally turning pink or bluish, with yellow throats. Blooming from June to September. Suitable for a somewhat moist, lime-free site in the rock garden border where it can spread undisturbed. Forms an extensive mat over time, covered with large, attractive flowers. Where soil is moist enough, it will tolerate full sun, otherwise better suited to semi-shade. Even given a loose, protective layer of brushwood in the winter, plants will occasionally freeze out north of zone 7. It is therefore advisable to keep a few young plants

Nomocharis Franch.
Liliaceae

Genus closely related to *Lilium* and *Fritillaria* with few scaled, more or less oblong bulbs, leafy stems and usually saucer-shaped or flat, nodding flowers (spotted on many species) in June and July. About 10–14 species in Himalaya Mts., Tibet and W. China. All are high alpine plants, found between 2700 and 4500m on meadows or forest margins in monsoon regions. They require high humidity, very well-drained, loamy

Nierembergia rivularis

Nuphar lutea

tivated is var. *violacea* Millán. Argentina. Stems to 20cm high; leaves linear or linear-lanceolate; corolla bright violet, to 3.75cm across. z7

N. repens Ruiz et Pav. (*N. rivularis* Miers), Whitecup Cupflower. Argentina, Chile, Uruguay. Commonly found on river banks. Decumbent stems to 5–10cm high, creeping and rooting at the nodes, a dense ground cover perennial with long-petioled, oval or oblong-spatulate, 25 long, 6–12mm wide, glabrous leaves. Flowers solitary, sessile

frost free over winter for replacements. Propagation is by separation and potting of rooted stems, best done with the new spring growth. Also increase by division and seed in early March in the greenhouse. Seedlings and rooted cuttings should be quickly shifted to small pots, once or twice pruned and set into the garden in May where they will bloom in the first summer. z7 (E.)

humus, completely lime-free, and moist, but not wet. Success in the garden is only possible under these conditions, which generally indicates a maritime climate.

Beautiful, but very difficult plants for the collector in a semi-shaded, cool and bright rock garden or among rhododendrons. Grow from seed sown in spring, in the greenhouse; seedlings are best shifted to deep pots and set out into the garden the following year, then left undisturbed. Bulbs produce flowers after 3 or 4 years. Protect from slug damage. Worthy of trial are:

N. aperta (Franch.) W.W. Sm. et W.E. Evans. W. China. Stems 40–90cm high. Leaves alternate, elliptic to lanceolate, slender acuminate. Inflorescence 1–6 flowered, flowers 10cm wide, rose to purple with deep carmine red spots. z6

N. farreri (Cox) Harrow. NE. Burma. Closely related to *N. pardanthina* of which it is often considered a variety. Very attractive. Leaves whorled, narrower than those of *N. pardanthina*. The inner segments are mostly entire, not fimbriate. Flower stems 90cm or more high. Flowers pink with a maroon eye and

Nomocharis pardanthina

with reddish purple spots. z6

N. mairei Levl. W. China. Stem 40–100cm high. Leaves lanceolate to ovate-lanceolate, acuminate, often whorled, 2–3 flowered, flowers white, occasionally shaded purple, purple-pink spotted, inner segments fimbriate, resembling flowers of *Odontoglossum crispum*, anthers purple. z5

N. pardanthina Franch. Yunnan. Stems 30–50cm high, rarely higher, leaves to 5cm long, lanceolate, whorled. Flowers to 8cm across, nodding, almost flat, light to dark pink, inner segments dark carmine spotted especially the lower third, and toothed or fringed. z7(6)

N. saluensis Balf. Burma, W. Sichuan, NW. Yunnan, SE. Tibet. Flower stem 60–90cm high, usually with 6 saucer-shaped open flowers, 8–9cm wide, light pink or pale yellow, the upper flowers are erect, the outer ones borne horizontally. Flowers are purple spotted, the inner segments have a reddish purple zone at the base. Similar to *N. aperta*, but lacking the fringe. Also comes in forms with brighter-colored flowers. z6 (Sch. & Kö.)

Nitholaena

N. marantae see **Cheilanthes marantae**

Nothoscordum Kunth
Liliaceae
False Garlic

North American perennials, about 20 species, related to *Allium*, but the bulb lacks garlic scent and the corolla segments are barely united basally. A collector's plant, usually cultivated only

Nothoscordum inodorum

in warmer climates; the bulbs should be planted 20cm deep and covered well in winter; requires a well-drained soil. Propagated by offset bulbs and seed.

N. bivalve Brith. (*N. striatum* Jacq.) USA, Virginia, Ohio and Nebraska south to the Gulf, on stony outcrops and dry prairies. Scapes 30 to very rarely 40cm high. Bulbs white, small, globose. Leaves linear to almost terete, striped, shorter than the flower scape. Inflorescences umbellate, to 10-flowered, 2–3cm across, with white or yellowish flowers to 1.25cm long. Early spring to early summer, often reblooms in the fall. May to July. z5 (H.& Mü.)

N. inodorum (Ait.) Nichols. (*N. fragrans* (Vent.) Kunth), False Garlic, Vanilla Onion. Subtropical America(?). Scape to 60cm high. Leaves gray-green, linear to 30cm long and 1cm wide, arching, flower umbels erect, to 10-flowered; flowers 3cm across, strongly vanilla scented, white, with rose-colored stripes. Over the months, new flower stalks will appear; hardly effective from a distance. Very vigorous and easily propagated in warmer climates. z7(6)

Nuphar Sm.
Nymphaeaceae
Spatterdock, Yellow Pond Lily, Cow Lily

Genus of 7–25 species, somewhat difficult to classify and therefore not finally established. Water-lilylike aquatic plants with vigorous, creeping rhizomes. Leaves large, entire cordate, usually floating, also often submerged in spring, lobed, rarely standing erect, covering the surface in still water. Flowers yellow or purplish, usually raised a few inches above the water, sepals 5–12, petaloid, very concave, giving a globose appearance, petals numerous, inconspicuous, stamens numerous, pistil ovate or flask-shaped with a 10–24 rayed stigmatic disc. Flowers from May to August. In the temperate zone of the Northern Hemisphere in standing or slowly flowing water, 50cm–3m deep, with a mud bottom. Not as ornamental as *Nymphaea*. Grow in any pond soil in full sun or light shade. Naturalized in a pond, the lush foliage will cover a large area. In a flowing current and in the first year, plants develop only underwater leaves. The strong rhizomes are propagated by division.

N. advena (Ait.)., American Spatterdock. E. and Central USA: Vermont to Texas. Leaves floating and often raised above the water, glossy green, to 30cm long and 23cm wide, leaves out of the water are leathery firm and thick; rarely with underwater leaves. Flowers 4–6cm wide, golden yellow with red markings, stamens sulfur yellow, May to August. Very vigorous species. z4–8

N. japonicum DC., Japanese Cow Lily. Japan. Leaves leathery oblong to narrowly ovate, nearly sagittate, floating, to 20cm long. Underwater leaves thin, narrow cordate, undulate and folded. Flowers borne high above the water, 4–6cm across, golden yellow, partly red, pistil flask-shaped, stigmatic surface with about 11 rays, July to August.
   A similar species is *N. sagittifolium* Pursh from S. North America with very long (to 40cm) leaves and relatively small flowers. z6

N. luteum (L.) Sm., Yellow Cow Lily. E. North America, Europe, N. Asia. Widely distributed. Rhizomes about arm thick, often 1m long, light yellow, covered with leaf scars, in water to 3m deep. Underwater leaves in rosettes in spring or, in flowing currents, resembling a large plant of leaf lettuce. Floating leaves with 3-angled petioles, cordate, glossy above, leathery and thick, bright green, to 40cm long and 30cm wide. Flowers only slightly above the water, egg yolk yellow, fragrant, to 6cm wide; stigmatic disc 15–20 rayed, June to September. Suitable for sunny and shaded sites, also gently flowing water. Usually only develops underwater leaves in the first year, floating leaves produced in the second year. z4

N. pumila (Timm) DC. (*N. minimum* Spenner), Lesser Spatterdock. Central and E. Europe, W. Siberia, in swamps. Leaves small, oval, deeply cordate, to 13cm long, rising to 25cm out of the water, undersides finely silky-pubescent. Flowers nearly starlike with narrow sepals, 2–3cm wide, yellow, June to August. Resembles a small form of *N. luteum* and is an attractive addition to the small water garden. z4 (D.)

Nymphaea L.
Nympaeaceae
Water Lily

Thirty-five or more species of popular and beautiful aquatic plants. Rhizomes horizontal or erect, occasionally tuberous, slowly spreading in a muck soil base, very high in starch content. Leaves simple, often more or less orbicular with a deep sinus, entire, lobed or dentate, floating on the water surface, occasionally reaching above water, speckled or monochrome, glossy green, undersides often a different color. Flowers impressively large, 10–20cm across, floating on or borne above the water, sepals 4, exterior green, interior colorful, petals and stamens numerous; sometimes day-sometimes night-blooming, white, pink, red, yellow and blue. Fruit, a fleshy berry ripening and disintegrating underwater. Most species are native to all the tropical or subtropical regions of the world. Only a few occur in the temperate zone. The tropical Water Lilies have larger leaves and larger, more colorful flowers than the hardy species; they may bloom by day or by night. The few winter hardy species are less valuable horticulturally than the hybrids which are often achieved by crosses with the less hardy, but beautiful species of warmer climates. Water Lilies are certainly the most beautiful of aquatic plants, suitable for any body of water from lakes to tubs.

For best performance they require a fertile, organic garden loam, with well-rotted manure thoroughly incorporated, preferably a year before planting. In large streams and ponds they are best planted in the ground. However, in smaller pools or when adding to a completed water garden, plants may be planted in wooden crates, baskets, or specially designed perforated containers, then sunk in place. Rhizomes are potted slanting upwards in the soil with the tips slightly exposed. To prevent containers floating, add weight such as coarse gravel topdressing or fasten bricks or stones to the container. A minimum summer temperature of 15–25 degrees C. (59–77 degrees F.) is essential for free flowering. Shaded, too deep, or too small ponds are unsuitable.

Water depth recommendations are specific for the various cultivars and species. The optimum depth can vary from 2m for the cultivar 'Gladstoniana' to 5–10cm for *N. tetragona*. It is, therefore, important to select plants which perform well at available water depth. In pools, containers can be adjusted by placing them on piers (stacks of concrete blocks) to arrive at optimal depth for the individual plant. Planting generally is done from late April to June, when the water becomes warm. Container plants can also be set out in fall or even during the open winter months. However, the warmer the water, the faster the plants establish themselves. Water Lilies for temperate gardens, especially the tender species and cultivars, must tolerate a water depth of more than 40cm and remain frost free, and many tropical species must be brought indoors as cold water damages them. This, of course, would vary considerably with local conditions, but all reasonably hardy species for deeper water would usually have no problem. Where plants grow in shallow pools which may freeze to the bottom, drain the water in the fall, then cover the plants with at least 30cm of leafmold to prevent freezing, if possible. Provided plants in containers have not rooted into the surrounding soil, the containers may be removed and overwintered in a cool, moist, frost-free location (i.e. a cellar). This is a standard technique for tropical Water Lilies. Botanical Gardens often overwinter these in small, gently heated tanks of water so growth begins more quickly the following year.

All Water Lilies require full sun for optimum development, best flower set, and to achieve their greatest potential. They are also less susceptible to pests and diseases when in full sun. Water Lilies make excellent cut flowers for a vase, but they are difficult to keep fully open. One trick is to apply drops of nail polish, or better, wax, to the base of each petal to prevent closing. It is possible to lay the freshly cut flowers in the open sun for 20–30 minutes; the blooms will then last for 4 or 5 days. Best of all is to use a special Water Lily syringe to pump the spongy stems so full of water that droplets ooze from the blossom. Water plant specialists supply these.

The following species were some of those used in the development of cultivated Water Lily hybrids and cultivars. While the list is not inclusive, the species commonly available from commercial sources all are represented.

N. alba L., White Water Lily. Europe, Mediterranean region, Asia Minor. Rhizomes yellowish white, to 3–8cm thick with age, horizontal, sparsely branched. Leaves oval, leathery, new growth reddish, otherwise green on both sides, smooth. Flowers 12cm across, fragrant, white, May to August. Flowers open in the morning. Preferred water depth 0.3–1.8m. Including the following cultivars: 'Candidissima', robust, flowers large, white, petals broad; possibly a hybrid with the next sp.; 'Rosea' soft carmine pink; 'Rubra' exterior pink, interior pink-red. z5

N. candida J. S. et K. B. Presl. N. and Central Europe, Siberia, Scandinavia. Closely related to *N. alba*. Distinguished by the smaller, more starry flowers, the stigma disc visible when open. The line of attachment of sepals to the receptacle is sharply angled, not rounded. June to August. For standing, relatively cool water and swampy soil. z4

N. × daubenyana hort. (*N. caerulea* × *N. micrantha*). A natural hybrid or an early cultivar (and sold as such) from an African and an Egyptian species. Flowers 5–18cm across, 20cm above the water, blue. Flowers open in the morning. For heated streams or warm climates, best under glass or overwintered in a greenhouse. Leaves with adventitious buds (viviparous). z8

N. flava see **N. mexicana**

N. mexicana Zucc. (*N. flava* Leitn). Yellow Water Lily. Mexico, Florida, Texas. Presumably, all or most all of the yellow-and copper-colored forms stem from this species, determined by the similar morphological characteristics, such as: rhizome erect with runners, leaves orbicular, green blotched brown above, crimson-brown with blackish dots beneath, 10–20cm across. Flowers 6–13cm across, standing above the water, yellow, opening on dry days.

Thriving only under optimal conditions; not hardy outdoors. Of no garden merit outside the tropics. z9(8)

N. odorata Ait., Fragrant Water Lily, White Pond Lily. N. America from Newfoundland to Mexico and Guyana, in quiet back waters and swampy sites with open water. Rhizomes horizontal, rhizome buds with small reniform bracts. Leaves orbicular, sinus lobes nearly touching, attenuated to small tips (odorata tips), glossy green, undersides reddish. Flowers 10–15cm across, floating, often held obliquely, white, fragrant,

rounded-cordate, dark green, blackish speckled or marbled while young, undersides pale green to reddish. Flowers 2.5–5cm, squarish, white, fragrant, June to fall.

An elegant water lily for the smallest streams, rock garden pools, troughs and pots. The smallest species in cultivation, much used in hybridizing. Propagates by self-seeding. Water only 5–15cm deep. z2–9

N. tuberosa Paine. Magnolia Water Lily, Tuberous Water Lily. N. and Central USA. Rhizomes horizontal, creeping,

mercial stocks. The French breeder Marliac developed most of the currently grown hardy cultivars in the late 19th century. He began with the vigorous species *N. alba*, *N. candida*, *N. tuberosa* and *N. odorata*. Later he also used *N. mexicana*. These vigorous-growing cultivars were distributed under the collective name "Marliacea", as 'Marliacea Chromatella'. Most of his hybrids of the small species *N. tetragona* crossed with a larger species or cultivar) were named "Laydekeri". These cultivars were at least partly of tropical parentage. Much information is lacking about the

Nymphaea alba

Nymphaea hybrid 'Gladstoniana'

flowering over 3–4 days, June to September. z3

var. **gigantea** Tricker. Florida to Guyana. Larger overall, more vigorous; leaves bright red beneath; flowers not as fragrant.

var. **rosea** Pursh. Cape Cod Pink Water Lily. Cape Cod, Massachusetts. Medium-sized, deep pink-flowered.

N. pygaea see **N. tetragona**

N. tetragona Georgi, Dwarf Water Lily. Often listed as *N. pygmaea* in the trade. Finland, Russia, Siberia, China, Japan, N. East Indies, N. America, between 43 and 61 degrees N. latitude. Rhizomes short, 1–3cm thick, partly covered with 1 to 3cm thick, woolly, black hairs. Leaves 4–10cm long, 3.5–7cm wide, oval or

with many short tuberous branches, easily removed. Leaves orbicular, sinus lobe ends close together, undulate-margined, new growth red, later green on both sides. Petiole with brown-red longitudinal lines. Flowers often above the water, 10–22.5cm across, clear white, nearly or entirely lacking in fragrance, June to August. Vigorous, requiring much room to grow.

Particularly attractive, large-flowered cultivars from *N. tuberosa* are 'Pöstlingberg', 'Richardsonii' and 'Rosea' (see the list) z3–9

Nymphaea Hybrids and Cultivars
The many hybrids are better ornamentals than the species. Most cultivars sold are not very young since they are usually propagated from a single seedling (i.e. from a single rhizome) requiring many years to build up com-

parentage and methods by which Marliac developed these cultivars; or even if he indeed was able to obtain seed from his hybrids, since most of the modern cultivars are sterile. After Marliac, the British especially, but also the Swiss and Germans began breeding Water Lilies. Tropical Water Lily hybridizing reached a high point during the first half of the present century with the work of the late George Pring at the Missouri Botanical Garden in St. Louis, which resulted in many outstanding cultivars with huge day or night flowers in intense colors; rose, reds, fuschia, violet, purples, yellow, and whites in various shapes. Many of these are notable for their elegant foliage.

The following cultivar descriptions include notes on parentage and the water depth which produces best growth and flowering. Most are hardy from zones 3–10 given the appropriate winter preparation and aftercare. This list includes many of the currently available Water Lily cultivars but specialists offer additional sorts, especially among the tropicals.

'Atropurpurea', flowers to 20cm across, dark crimson, leaves reddish, dark-spotted, later green, margin lightly undulate (*N. tuberosa* characteristics), identical to 'Granat', 30–50cm water depth. One of the darkest cultivars.

'Attraction', clear red flowers 12–15cm across, petals acute, paler toward the tips. Anthers gold-yellow. Leaves circular, green, lobe tips diverging (*N. odorata?*), 40–80cm water.

'Cardinal', flowers large, 20cm wide, center dark red, paler toward the outside, entire flower fading before closing. Anthers light yellow, tinged coppery. Leaves dark green, reddish margined. 40–80cm.

'Charles de Meurville', flowers 20cm across, center wine red, petal tips lighter, spotted, undersides reddish, lobe tips diverging from the base. Water depth 40–60cm.

'Conqueror', flowers 18cm wide, dark wine red, outer petals lighter. Anthers golden yellow. Leaves large, round, dark green. 40–80cm.

'Ellisiana', flowers medium sized, fiery red at first, later darkening; floriferous. Anthers orange. Leaves dark green, red beneath. Water depth 20–40cm deep.

'Escarboucle' (Marliac: *N. tuberosa* parentage). Flowers 15–18cm wide, ruby red, anthers orange, fragrant. Leaves together, dark green, margin undulate. Vigorous, suitable only for larger pools. Water depth 60–90cm, to 2m deep.

'Gloriosa', flowers 16–18cm wide, bowl-shaped, interior currant red, exterior mottled. Stamens orange-yellow, oblong buds. Leaves round, dark green, reddish (authenticity of plants in cultivation is doubtful). Water depth 40–90cm.

'Granat' see 'Atropurpurea'

'Graziella' (Marliac: *N. alba* 'Rubra' × *N. mexicana*). Flowers 8cm wide, orange-red, fading with time, stamens orange. Leaves small, green, chestnut brown

Nymphaea hybrid 'James Brydon'

Nymphaea hybrid 'Moorei'

whitish. Leaves oblong, conspicuously grass green. Leaf tips diverging. Long and freely flowered. Opening until late. 60–90cm deep.

'Chrysantha', flowers 8cm wide, apricot colored, later vermilion. Leaves 15cm wide, reddish to red at first, very speckled. Water depth 20–30cm.

'Colonel A.J. Welch', flowers medium sized, starry, 20–30cm above the water, canary yellow, appearing first in July. Leaves speckled at first, vigorous. Develops rooted plantlets on the fruit structure. 50–90cm deep.

'Colossea' (Marliac: *N. alba* × *N. odorata* 'Rosea'). Flowers large, bowl-shaped, soft flesh colored to white, fragrant. Leaves large, round, dark green, vigorous. Water depth 50–80cm.

'Comanche', flowers 12cm across, starry, borne a few centimeters above the water, yellowish, later darker. Anthers coppery yellow. Leaves light green, large, light green, margin lightly undulate. Very attractive cultivar, but difficult to propagate since the rhizome grows slowly. Water depth 40–80cm.

'Formosa', flowers 16cm wide, starry, on the water surface, peach-pink, carmine in the center. Water depth 40–80cm.

'Froebelii' (Froebel, Zürich: presumably a seedling of *N. alba* 'Rubra'). Flowers 10cm wide, always only half open, just a few centimeters above the water, carmine red, anthers also red. Leaves reddish, later grass green. Also flowers in cool water. Water depth 20–40cm deep.

'Gladstoniana' (*N. tuberosa* 'Gladstoniana', *N. tuberosa* 'Pöstlingberg'), (Richardson: *N. alba* × *N. odorata*, then crossed with *N. tuberosa*). Flowers over 20cm wide, saucer-shaped, pure white. Stamens golden yellow. Leaves luxurious, to 50cm across, lobes tightly marbled, undersides brown-red. Water depth 20–30cm.

'Helvola', strain of *N. tetragona* (*N. pygmaea* var. *alba*) × a yellow cultivar, presumably 'Marliacea Chromatella'. Flowers elegant, sulfur yellow. Leaves olive green, brown-speckled. Water depth 10–20cm. Propagated only by seed.

'Hermine' (identical to 'Albatros'). flowers large, tulip-like, pure white, very early. Leaves grass green, lobes overlapping. Vigorous and undemanding. Water depth 50–80cm.

'Indiana', flowers 10cm wide, globose, orange-copper, stamens orange. Leaves 17cm wide, distinctly spotted. Water depth 20–30cm.

'James Brydon', Dreer: *N. alba* 'Rubra' × *tetragona*. Flowers 14cm wide, globose, cherry red. Stamens orange-yellow. Leaves orbicular, distinctly reddish-spotted when young. Vigorous, undemanding and reliable bloomer. Water depth 30–70cm.

'Laydekeri Fulgens', flowers 10cm wide, few petals, wine red, with somewhat lighter petals intermixed, slightly over the water. Stamens fiery red. Leaves reddish at first, then dark green, reddish-spotted on both sides. 20–50cm.

'Laydekeri Lilacea', flowers similar to the above cultivar, lilac-pink, carmine-dotted, lightly mottled, darker in the center. 20–30cm.

'Laydekeri Purpurata', flowers carmine, lighter outside, nearly white, red-spotted. 20–30cm. The Laydekeri cultivars are among the most useful of the older dwarf Water Lily cultivars.

'Luciana' (possibly identical to *N. tuberosa* 'Rosea'?). Flowers 12cm across, sepals curved widely downward, uniformly soft pink, stamens yellow. Leaves green, slightly reddish, sinus clearly spread. Water depth 30–40cm.

'Mme Wilfron Gonnére', flowers 16cm wide, globose, the purest pink, fully double with light yellow stamens. Leaves grass green, orbicular, sinus scarcely open (*N. tuberosa* influence). Water depth 40–60cm.

'Marliacea Albida', flowers 15cm wide, perfectly formed, pure white, stamens light yellow. Leaves uniformly grass green, red veined. Water depth 40–80cm.

'Marliacea Carnea', flowers to 18cm wide, flesh pink, nearly white. Leaves red when young, later grass green, red margined. Flowers and leaves stand above a still water surface. Water depth 50–80cm.

'Marliacea Chromatella' (Marliac: *N. alba* (also *N. tuberosa*) × *N. mexicana*). Flowers 16–18cm wide, bright yellow. Stamens yellow. Leaves distinctly mottled. Water depth 60–90cm. One of the most widely distributed, but thrives only in warmer climates, otherwise flowers poorly. Can freeze out in shallow water. Vigor regressing in recent years, at least in European stocks.

'Marliacea Rosea', flowers similar to 'Marliacea Carnea', somewhat darker. Flowers are long open. A gratifying and reliable form. Water depth 0.6–1m deep. Parentage of all the white and pink Marliacea forms is presumably *N. alba* × *N. odorata* 'Rosea'.

'Masaniello', flowers 15cm across, saucer-shaped, deep pink, darker in the center, carmine-spotted. Stamens light yellow. Leaves to 25cm wide, dark green, reddish margined, scarcely opening. Flowers and leaves reaching slightly above the surface in shallow water. Water depth 50–80cm.

'Maurice Laydeker', flowers 10cm across, orange to cherry red, lighter toward the tips. Stamens dark golden yellow. Leaves 15cm wide, conspicuously dark green, undersides reddish. Water depth 20–30cm.

'Moorei', flowers 14cm wide, well formed, dark chrome yellow, standing above the water, fragrant. Stamens light yellow. Leaves 20cm wide, dark green, slightly mottled, lobes slightly divergent. Water depth 40–80cm.

'Newton', flowers 12–15cm wide, segments narrow, starry, pink, borne high above the water, sepals very reflexed,

Nymphaea hybrid 'Marliacea Rosea'

resembling the tropical Water Lilies. Water depth 40–80cm.

'Odalisque' (*N. tuberosa* 'Rosea'). Flowers 12cm wide, flesh-colored pink, calyx bronze to olive, reflexed to the pedicel when open. Petals loosely divergent. Leaves 25cm wide, grass green, undersides reddish, lobes nearly overlapping, petioles red striped. Water depth 0.6–1m deep.

'Paul Hariot', flowers 12–14cm wide, soft yellow, copper-red shaded. Stamens yellow, turning darker. Flowers fragrant.

Leaves red spotted on both sides. Water depth 20–50cm.

'Pöstlingberg' see 'Gladstoniana'

'Princess Elizabeth', flowers 12cm wide, very full, calyx recurved; light peach-pink, borne a few centimeters above the water. Anthers golden yellow. Leaves grass green, undersides reddish. 30–50cm.

'Pygmaea Rubis'. A strain similar to 'Helvola', only this one is from a cross of *N. tetragona* × red hybrids. Since the rhizome of this form is not very easily divided, it must be propagated by seed and is therefore variable, not a true cul-

tivar. These are dwarf red Water Lilies for the smallest gardens sites. Water depth 10–20cm deep.

'René Gérard', flowers 15–18cm wide, semidouble, dark carmine, lightly mottled at the tips, long open. Leaves grass green, lobe tips widely divergent. One of the most floriferous, gratifying forms. Water depth 40–80cm.

'Richardsonii' (*N. tuberosa* 'Richardsonii'). Flowers 16–18cm across, saucer-shaped, pure white, fragrant. leaves glossy green, smooth. Floriferous. Water depth 40–90cm.

'Rose Arey'. Flowers elegant, uniformly salmon pink. Stamens gold-yellow. Floriferous. Water depth 40–80cm.

'Rosennymphe' (N. odorata 'Rosennymphe'). Flowers 12–14cm wide, starry, flat funnelform, light pink, fading, floriferous. Leaves cordate, reddish at first, then green. Water depth 30–70cm.

'Sioux' (Marliac: N. alba 'Rubra' × N. mexicana). Flowers 10–15cm across, from yellow through copper-pink to reddish. Leaves conspicuously spotted and blotched. For warm, sunny sites. Should be planted only where summers are warm. Water depth 20–50cm.

'Sulphurea' (N. odorata 'Sulphurea'). Flowers 14–16cm wide, stellate, sulfur yellow, situated above the water. Stamens golden yellow. Leaves spotted. Vigorous, but flowers in cool water poorly. Water depth 40–90cm deep; grows best in the deeper end of the range.

'Sunrise', flowers to 20cm wide, starry, held above the water, opening early in the morning, sulfur yellow. Leaves and flower stalks pubescent, undersides reddish. Water depth 40–80cm.

'W.B. Shaw', flowers 10cm wide, cupform, soft pink. Stamens gold-yellow. Very fragrant (N. odorata progeny). Leaves 20cm wide, orbicular, not spotted. Water depth 20–40cm.

'William Falconer', flowers 14–16cm wide, a good double cultivar, ruby red, stamens golden yellow. Leaves 20cm wide, green, very dark spotted. Water depth 30–50cm.

The propagation of the Water Lily hybrids and cultivars is by rhizome division. The species can also be grown from seed which must be kept underwater since it looses viability quickly upon drying. Expose the clear, water-filled jars with seeds to light at 10–12 degrees C. (50–54 F.) in March or April. Most seeds will germinate within 3 weeks; the rest will remain dormant until the following year. Remove seedlings as soon as they are big enough to handle and plant them in a shallow container of loamy soil. Sink the planted containers in shallow water in the greenhouse tank, in full sun. Water depth at the second transplanting later in summer should be 5–6cm. Overwinter young plants frost free and moist; best in the shallow tank or packed in wet live sphagnum moss in a cool place. The following year, floating leaves and possibly flowers will develop.

To propagate the cultivars, divide the rhizomes of older plants in late April to May. Carefully remove decayed portions of the rhizomes and treat the wounds with an appropriate fungicide. Better growth and fewer disease problems will result if the propagules are grown under glass in slightly warmed water. The established plants can then be moved to a shallow water bed in summer. Winter protection of young plants is an absolute necessity; rhizomes must not be frosted. Infestations by Waterlily Aphid or Waterlily Leaf Cutters may be controlled by spraying with a strong pyrethrum preparation. Be careful not to use a chemical that would be harmful to fish if present. Fish are also effective in controlling the Waterlily Leaf Cutter by feeding on the larvae. (D.)

Nymphoides J. Hill
Menyanthaceae (or Gentianaceae)
Floating-heart

About 20 species of floating aquatic or creeping swamp plants, most perennial, occasionally annual. Leaves elliptic, ovate or orbicular, with a deep sinus at the point of petiole attachment, margins smooth, sinuate or crenate, green above, undersides often dark. Submerged stems bear alternate or opposite leaves with a sheathlike petiole base. Flowers pedicelled in dense axillary umbels, corolla deeply 5-cleft, yellow or white, stamens epipetalous. Distributed throughout the world in tropical and temperate climates. Only one species is commonly grown in European gardens but more are seen in the Western Hemisphere.

N. aquatica (Watt.) O. Kuntze. Fairy Water-lily. USA: New Jersey south to Florida and west to Texas. Submersed stems with clusters of short, tuberous roots at the flowering nodes, hence "Banana Plant". Floating leaves nearly orbicular to kidney-shaped, to 15cm wide, lower surface and petioles usually with purple glandular hairs. Corolla white, 2cm across; flowers in summer. z7(6)

N. cordata (Elliott) Fern. E. North America. Submersed stems with clusters of slender, elongate tuberous roots at the flowering nodes. Leaves broadly ovate with a deep sinus, to 6cm long, glandular-hairy beneath. Corolla white or cream-colored. Summer. z5

N. peltata (S.G. Gmel). E. Ktze. (Limnanthemum nymphoides (L.) Hoffmgg. et Link), Yellow Floating Heart, Water-fringe. S. and Central Europe, temperate Asia (to China and Japan), naturalized in the U.S. An aquatic perennial for standing or slowly flowing water. Rooting runners slender; rapidly creeping in the bottom muck. Stems floating to the water surface. Leaves cordate to orbicular, 8–15cm wide, margins sinuate, dark green, occasionally brownish mottled. Flower pedicels to 10cm long, several in the leaf axils, (no axillary roots), corollas 5-lobed, 3cm wide, yellow, July to September. z6

Two tropical species are widely grown in frost free, warm portions of the U.S. and often are placed in sunny pools as "annuals" where winters are cold; they also are seen in indoor pools: N. humboldtiana (H.B.K.) O. Kunze. Flowers white with yellow centers, to 2cm across, corolla lobes somewhat fringed, and N. indica (Thwaites) O. Kunze. Water Snowflake. Flowers about 1cm across, corolla lobes deeply fimbriate, snowflake-like. Charming, aquatic plants with floating leaves resembling Water Lilies for 20–50cm of water. Despite their delicate appearance, plants of hardy species are capable of quickly taking over small ponds. May be contained by planting in pots or by repeated division. Suitable companions for bank planting are such vigorous species as Butomus, Acorus, Iris.

Propagation is easy by division of the stems with rooted nodes or by runners of N. peltata. The propagules are either stuck directly in the bottom muck or preferably potted. A good water depth for initial development is 10–20cm. Propagation from seed is less productive since seed is sparsely set. Seeds are sown, however, immediately after ripening in pots underwater. Germination normally takes place early the following spring. (D.)

Oenothera L.
Onagraceae
Evening Primrose, Sundrops

About 80 species, nearly all indigenous to N. America. Upright or procumbent, floriferous annuals, biennials and perennials with axillary, usually yellow or white, rarely pink, flowers. The Evening Primroses are night-bloomers with flowers fading in strong morning sun; the Sundrops and Suncups bloom in daylight. Only a few species, however, are winter hardy in north temperate gardens where summers are cool. The taller species are useful as persistent bloomers for massing in a sunny border, the lower species belong in the rock garden. Propagation of the species is by seed and division, the cultivars by cuttings and division.

O. × arendsii St. et Schn. (hort.). Garden hybrid of *O. rosea × O. speciosa*, with all the best properties of both parents. Good pink flowers, persistent plants, but hard to find in the trade. z6(5)

O. caespitosa Nutt. (*O. marginata* hort.). USA: N. Rocky Mts. and adjacent plains. Biennial to perennial, stemless, loose rosettes. Leaves narrowly lanceolate, glabrous and dentate. Flowers to 8cm wide, white, fading to pink, night bloomer; June to July. Very attractive for the rock garden, unfortunately, short-lived when grown under less than optimum conditions. Propagate by seed, raise seedlings in containers. And *O. caespitosa* ssp. **marginata** (Nutt. ex Hook. & Arn.) Munz. Washington and California south to Rocky Mts. Densely villous-hairy overall; leaves pinnatifid. And ssp. **montana** (Nutt.) Munz. Rocky Mts. Completely stemless, leaves hairy only on veins and margins. z4

O. fruticosa L. Sundrops. E. USA. Stems erect, 30–60cm high, often reddish, somewhat pubescent, rarely branched toward the upper portion. Leaves oblanceolate below, 2.5–7.5cm long, upper leaves ovate to lanceolate, partially dentate. Flowers yellow in terminal racemes; June to August. This species often is confused in the trade and literature with *O. tetragona* and its varieties. The cultivar 'Yellow River' has large, canary yellow flowers. z4

O. fruticosa var. **linearis** Wats. (*O. linearis* Michx.) USA: E. coastal states and lower Mississippi states. Leaves narrower; flowers smaller, bright yellow. Recently very large-flowered cultivars, certainly hybrids, have been introduced: 'Golden Moonlight' (Marx 1980), with large, bright yellow flowers and 'Silvery Moon' (Marx 1980), with large, bright, light yellow flowers, both 70–80cm high. z5

O. fruticosa var. **youngii** see **O. tetragona**

O. linearis see **O. fruiticosa** var. **linearis**

O. macrocarpa see **O. missouriensis**

O. marginata see **O. caespitosa**

O. missouriensis Sims. (*O. macrocarpa* Nutt.), Missouri Primrose, Ozark Sundrops. S. USA: Missouri and Kansas to

Texas. Rootstock stout, deep; habit procumbent, 10–20cm high. Leaves lanceolate, silvery green, leathery. Flowers to 10cm wide, light yellow, night bloomer; May to September. Large, winged seed capsules. A valuable, lasting bloomer for the large rock garden, as a wall and ground cover perennial in a sunny site. Propagate by seed and cuttings. z5

O. perennis L. (*O. pumila* L.). Sundrops. E. North America. Stems 20–50cm high, upright. Often biennial. Leaves linear-lanceolate, lowest leaves wider. Flowers yellow, 2cm wide, in loose, leafy

Oenothera missouriensis

racemes; June to August. Day bloomer for the perennial border; may become invasive in warm climates. z5

O. pumila see **O. perennis**

O. rosea L'Hérit ex Ait. S. USA. to South America. Stems 15–50cm high, slender, scarcely branched. Leaves scattered, oblong-ovate, to 2.5cm long. Flowers rose to purplish-red. Very similar to *O. speciosa*. Rarely grown in cultivation. z7(6)

O. speciosa Nutt. White Evening Primrose. Central USA: Missouri and Kansas to Texas; Mexico. Stems 30–50cm high. Running, branched, slender, rhizomes. Stems upright, unbranched or with few branches. Leaves lanceolate to obovate,

lowest leaves oblanceolate, occasionally pinnately lobed. Flowers white, fading to pink, or sometimes pink, very fragrant, night and day blooming; June to September. Sometimes overly vigorous, and with an untidy habit, hardy. Used as a lasting bloomer in a natural setting in a warm, sunny site together with *Yucca*, *Liatris*, and other prairie species. Propagate by division and root cuttings. z5

O. tetragona Roth. (*O. fruticosa* var. *youngii* L. H. Bailey)., Common Sundrops. NE. USA: New York to Illinois, south to Georgia, Tennessee. Stems 30–50cm high, with basal rosettes. Stem leaves lanceolate-linear. Stems with hair tufts, blue-green. Flowers light yellow. A persistent bloomer; June to August. z5

And var. **fraseri** (Pursh) Munz. S. Appalachian Mts. Glabrous overall, leaves broader, glaucous beneath, flowers larger, z6. Var. **riparia** (Nutt.) Munz. North and South Carolina. Flowers smaller, differences in the capsule shape and hairs. z7(6). In horticulture, *O. tetragona* and *O. fruticosa* often are confused. *O. tetragona* generally is less hairy on stems and leaves, capsules are oblong to oblong-ellipsoid, but not clavate, and have some glandular hairs; *O. fruticosa* is strigose to hairy overall; the capsule is slender, tending toward being club-shaped because the basal portion is sterile, the capsule is without glandular hairs.

A very attractive cultivar is 'Fyrver-keri' (Fireworks), yellow, red buds, floriferous. Rarely true to name. 'Sonnenwende' (Summer Solstice) introduced by Marx, 1983, with dark foliage, is a substantial improvement. 'Hohes Licht' (Bright Light) introduced by Baltin, 1961, bright pure yellow, 60cm high, a worthwhile form of the species. z5 (H.& M.)

The late Claude A. Barr, homesteader in SW. South Dakota, introduced several superb oenotheras from his general area which are scarcely known outside North

Omphalodes Mill.
Boraginaceae
Navelwort

Annual plants and small perennials with white or blue, Forget-me-not like flowers and long-petioled, ovate to oblong, minutely hairy leaves. About 25 species, most native to the Mediterranean region and Asia, which grow in moist soil in sun or semi-shade. Flowers in loose racemes; calyx 5-lobed; corolla 5-lobed with a short tube and scales in the throat; 5 stamens; the compound

O. lusitanica see **O. nitida**

O. nitida Hoffmgg. et Link (*O. lusitanica* auct. non (L.) Pourr. ex Lange). Spain, Portugal. A clump, 20–60cm high, of oblong leaves, glassy-smooth above, pubescent beneath. Flowers sky blue in long, loose racemes; April to May. Requires a cool, shaded site. z7

O. verna Moench., Creeping Forget-me-not. S. Europe. Stoloniferous. Leaves ovate, petioled, bright green. Flowers in loose racemes, sky blue with white centers or pure white on 'Alba'; March to

Nymphoides peltata

Omphalodes verna

Omphalogramma vincaeflora

America excepting to some rock garden enthusiasts. In general, these species grow in a harsh climate with very cold winter, hot, dry summer, wind much of the time, and more or less alkaline soil. They deservedly are described by Barr as jewels of the prairie. Some are:

O. caespitosa, described above.

O. lavanduliflora Torr. & A. Gray. Great Plains. A dense, clumped, perennial 15–20cm high with a deep-growing woody rootstock. Leaves linear to obovate, gray-hairy. Flowers with a long tube, to 5cm long and rhombic petals to 2.5cm long, yellow. This is an evening-flowering species found in the Rocky Mts. area. z5(4)

O. serrulata Nutt. Long-lived perennial with several gray-pubescent stems growing as a loose clump 15–30cm high. Leaves entire to serrate, 2.5–5cm long, lanceolate to oblanceolate. Flowers open in the evening, flowers yellow. And ssp. **drummondii** (Torr. & A. Gray) Munz. W. Texas. Taller growing, leaves with sharper teeth, flowers somewhat larger.

ovary maturing into 4 nutlets. Propagation of the species is by division or seed. Cultivation of young plants should be in pots.

O. cappadocica DC. (*O. cornifolia* hort. *O. loykae* Somm. et Lev.), Navelwort. W. Caucasus, Asia Minor. Plant 10–15cm high, habit bushy, with short, creeping rhizomes. Leaves oval-lanceolate, acuminate, long petioled, matte green. Flowers long pediceled in loose racemes, clear blue with white centers; April to May. Attractive rock garden plants for sun to semi-shade. Susceptible to frost damage in open sites. z6

O. cornifolia see **O. cappadocica**

O. loykae see **O. cappadocica**

O. luciliae Boiss. Greece, Asia Minor. Plant 10–15cm high; a tufted rock garden ornamental. Gray-green leaves about 3cm-long, ovate, smooth. Flowers light blue; April to May. Attractive collector's plant for the alpine garden. Requires a well-drained, gravelly soil which is never excessively dry. Thrives in a bright situation, but not in full sun, best in a rock crevice. z6

May. 'Grandiflora' is a particularly large-flowered clone. This species is the most valuable for garden culture, suitable for understory planting. Requires a moist site, at least in spring, tolerates many garden soil types and naturalizes under favorable conditions. Somewhat invasive, overgrowing smaller neighboring plants. Propagation of the cultivars is only by division. z6 (S.)

Omphalogramma Franch.
Primulaceae

About 13 species from E. Himalayas and W. China. Related to *Primula*, but differing in the bractless pedicels, winged seeds and solitary, homostylous flowers with a two sided symmetrical, generally 6-part, corolla. Blooms in spring with the new growth, leaves basal, simple, with amber-colored glands beneath. Flowers large, funnelform with a flattened limb, usually violet to purple-blue. Flowers from April to May. Grow in heavy, lime-free soil. Requires high humidity and not-too-high summer temperatures. Also requires a long period of winter dormancy (dryness); snow-covered in its habitat for 6–7 months. These collectors' plants grow in British gardens and in the Pacific Northwest, USA. Propagate by seed, division and leaf cuttings. In cultivation at present are:

O. elwesianum (King ex G. Watt) Franch. Himalaya Mts. Sturdy rhizome with rosette of oblanceolate leaves to 10cm long; bractless scape to 12.5cm high; flowers purple, to 2.5cm across, with yellow throat. z7

Onobrychis viciifolia

O. minus Hand. Mazz. China to Burma. Rosetted leaves, hairy, broadly ovate with wavy margins; scape 5–20cm high; flowers dark indigo purple to plum purple. z8(7)

O. souliei Franch. W. China. Leaves ovate, entire, with hairs on veins and margins; flowers large, blue-violet, corolla lobes hairy on reverse side. z7

O. vincaeflora (Franch.) Franch. Yunnan, China. Woody crown small or lacking. Leaves in basal rosette, to 9cm long, oblong to oblong-ovate, glandular-haired on both surfaces. Naked scapes to 20cm high. Flowers violet, darker throated, to 2cm across or wider in some selections. Reputed to be the most easily grown species; also quite variable. z7

Rock Garden Society seed lists sometimes include *O. delavayi, O. elegans, O. ferreri,* and others, all more or less similar.

Onobrychis Mill.
Leguminosae

About 120 species of annual and perennial herbs or prickly shrubs in Europe and the Mediterranean region to Central Asia. Leaves alternate, odd pinnate; papilionaceous flowers in axillary racemes or spikes; calyx campanulate, with 5 even teeth; corolla white, pink or purple, occasionally yellow. Stamens 10, 9 united and 1 free. Fruit indehiscent, more or less rounded and compressed. *O. viciifolia* Scop. is a widely used plant

Oncolea sensibilis, **fall foliage**

for livestock fodder in Europe and Asia, however, it is unsuitable for the garden.

O. montana DC. Spain, Italy, Alps, Jura Mts., Balkan Mts., Asia Minor and the Caucasus Mts., at subalpine and alpine elevations, in dry alpine meadows on calcareous soil. Entire plant sparsely pubescent, stems procumbent, ascending terminally, 10–50cm long. Leaflets 5–8 paired plus 1, elliptic or ovate to oblong. Corolla 10–14mm long, pink, usually darker-veined. Fruits flattened-orbicular, pubescent, with 4–8 teeth on the margin. Blooms from July to August. *O. montana* is an attractively blooming, low perennial for larger rock gardens. Requires dry, limestone-gravelly-loam soil, best between large rocks in full sun. Sow seed directly in the desired spot, or plant 2–3 seeds in a small pot so they may be moved with a ball of soil. z5 (E.)

Onoclea L.
Onocleaceae
Sensitive Fern, Pearl Fern

Genus with a single species occurring in the North Temperate Zone in both hemispheres, and growing in humus-rich and moist woodland soil in bright shade or partial sun.

O. sensibilis L. Sterile fronds, oval-triangular, long stipes, once pinnate, pinnae deeply lobed, light green, to

Ononis natrix

90cm high, dying back at the first frost (*sensibilis*). Fertile fronds 20–50 long, stiff, erect, with spore-bearing pinnae contracted and aligned like strings of beads, persisting overwinter. Rhizomes vigorously creeping, quickly branching.

Because of its vigor this fern often becomes invasive, even weedy, under ideal garden conditions. Best suited for large gardens among *Rhododendron* and other shrubs. Plants also grow in still water, along pond banks and streamsides in full sun. Fertile fronds are useful for dried flower arranging. Propagation is by spores, rhizome divisions or rhizome cuttings. *O. sensibilis* occasionally produces red stiped progeny in large sporeling populations. These are used like the species; propagation is by division or rhizome cuttings. z4 (D.)

Ononis L.
Leguminosae
Rest-harrow

About 75 species of annual, biennial and perennial herbs, subshrubs and small shrubs on the Canary Islands and the Mediterranean region from Europe to Central Asia. Mostly glandular-pubescent. Leaves usually ternate, occasionally simple, very rarely odd-pinnate. Flowers papilionaceous, axillary, in spikes or racemes, pink-red, yellow, whitish or bicolored. Calyx campanulate, deeply 5-parted. Banner petal nearly rounded. Stamens 9 connate plus 1 free. Ovaries stalked, oblong or oval. Except for *O. natrix* and *O. spinosa*, all species mentioned here are borderline hardy and should be mulched in cold climate winters with conifer branches; even so, plants often freeze out in winter. All species except *O. spinosa* are attractive plants for the collector, suitable for the alpine garden or rockery. Requires full sun and a warm, dry protected site as in a scree or between rocks. Also requires a well-drained and gravelly loam soil. *O. rotundifolia* is lime-loving.

O. repens and O. spinosa will cover a dry, infertile, sandy slope in a large park situation. When massed in a suitable site, the flowering effect can be very decorative. Seeds of these are best sown directly into the desired garden site.

Propagation of other species is also by seed, sown in pots to avoid severing the large taproot when transplanting to the garden. Subshrub and shrub species may also be propagated by spring cuttings. Good companions plants include *Achillea millefolium* 'Cerise Queen', *Alyssum saxatile*, *Anaphalis*, *Antennaria*, *Anthyllis montana* and *A. vulneraria*, *Centaurea pulcherrima*, *Lavandula*, *Linum perenne*, *Nepeta*, *Satureja montana*, *Thymus* and *Veronica spicata* ssp. *incana*.

O. cenisia L. (*O. cristata* Mill). SW. Alps, Central Apennines, E. Pyrenees, mountains of E. Spain and N. Africa, on dry, rocky sites. Procumbent, mat-forming, 5–30cm high somewhat suffruticose perennial with short-pubescent, glandular stems. Leaves ternate, leaflets 5–10mm long, oblong or oblanceolate, leathery. Inflorescences on long, jointed peduncles, 1–6 flowered. Corolla 10–14mm long, rose. Flowers from June to August. Winter protection is advisable. z7

O. natrix L. S. and W. Europe, north to N. France, occasionally on the Balkan Peninsula, N. Africa, on dry, grassy, rocky slopes and in olive groves on warm limestone soil. Well-branched, small subshrubs with erect or ascending, 20–50cm high, densely glandular-pubescent stems. Leaves mostly ternate. Leaflets ovate to linear. Flowers in loose, bracted panicles. Corolla 6–20mm long, yellow with a usually red-striped banner petal. Blooms from May to July. Lime-loving. Requires winter protection. z7

O. rotundifolia L. SE. Spain to E. Austria and Central Italy, in the mountains on rocky slopes and in open forests, on limestone. Subshrub 20–40cm high, with rough-haired, glandular stems. Leaves ternate, leaflets 25mm long, elliptic to orbicular, coarsely toothed, somewhat glandular. The middle leaflet is larger and long stalked, the lateral leaflets sessile. Inflorescence of 2–3 flowers in the axils of the upper leaves on peduncles to 7cm long. Corolla 16–20mm long, pink or whitish, banner petal red striped. Blooms from May to August. Requires limestone soil and winter protection. z7

O. spinosa L. W., Central and S. Europe, N. Africa, W. and Central Asia, in dry grassy meadows and pastures, on dry slopes, on warm and summer-dry limestone loam. Quite a variable species. Woody at the base; 20–60cm high perennial with more or less procumbent, never rooting stems with lateral branches, usually terminated in unbranched spines. Leaves usually ternate, leaflets quite variable in form. Flowers in the leaf axils, solitary, occasionally paired. Corolla 6–20mm long, pink or purple colored, much longer than the calyx. Blooms from June to September. *O. repens* L. is similar, but stoloniferous and thornless, and used just like *O. spinosa*. z7 (E.)

Onopordum L.
Compositae
Cotton-, Scotch Thistle

A genus of over 25 biennial, occasionally triennial species. Decorative, tall, thistlelike herbs with broad-winged, spined stems. Leaves large, sinuately toothed with stiff spines, usually white-tomentose-pubescent. Flower heads purple, violet or white, thistle-like. Suitable as a specimen plant in the sunny wildflower garden. All species require full sun and well-drained soil. Grow from seed.

O. bracteatum Boiss. et Heldr. S. Balkan region, Aegean Sea and Asia Minor. Stems to more than 2m high, with white pubescent, yellow-spined leaves; erect, coarsely branched stems and purple flower heads. The most striking species. z6

O. tauricum Willd. (*O. viscosum* Hornem. ex Spreng., *O. virens* DC.). SE. Europe. Stems to more than 1m high, with deeply lobed and toothed, glabrous leaves, silver-white beneath. Flower-heads purple with distinctly glandular-sticky bracts. Both species seed themselves under favorable conditions. z7 (H.& Kö.)

Onopordum bracteatum

O. virens see **O. tauricum**

O. viscosum see **O. tauricum**

Several other somewhat ornamental, biennial species are listed.

Onosma L.
Boraginaceae
Golden-drop

About 125–130 species, primarily in the E. Mediterranean region to Central Asia. Rough-haired small annual, perennial or subshrub. Basal leaves oblong, simple, sessile, often gray, stem leaves alternate. Flowers nodding, usually yellow, white, pink or bicolored, tubular, usually in racemose-helicoid cymes. Bloom from May to June. Grow in a sunny well-drained and dry site in the rock or trough garden. The densely pubescent species require protection from winter wetness. Useful as attractive collector's plants, but very sensitive to moisture on the leaves. Lime loving. Be cautious when handling these plants as the hairs of some species may cause a skin inflamation on susceptible persons. Propagation is by seed or cuttings.

O. alboroseum Fisch. et Mey. Asia Minor. A persistent, procumbent, well-branched, somewhat woody plant with non-flowering leafy rosettes. Rosetted leaves narrowly ovate or nearly lanceo-

Onosma alborosea

late, 30–90mm long and 6–20mm wide, with stellate hairs. Inflorescences to 20cm high with 2–3 terminal helicoid cymes, elongating to 40cm at fruiting. Corolla 22–26mm long, white at first, then turning pale pink to red from the tip, later turning blue. z7

O. inexspectatum Teppner. Turkey: Amanos Mts. Similar to *O. alboroseum*, but with the leaves usually 3–6mm wide, inflorescences strongly upright, to 30cm high, corollas 18–21mm long, glabrous, white at first, later entirely or distally pale pink to red. Less persistent than *O. alboroseum*, but with better color. z7

O. sanguinolentum Vatke. Turkey, Iraq.

Similar to *O. alboroseum*, but the fruits are substantially larger (8–12mm long). Very attractive species with bright pink flowers and somewhat less glaucous-blue leaves that are very distinctly stellate pubescent. z6

O. sieheanum Hayek is not found in cultivation.

O. sorgerae Teppner. Turkey: E. Central Anatolia. Similar to *O. alboroseum*, but the leaves only 20–70mm long and 2–5mm wide, corolla 21–24mm long, flowers light pink at first, later turning red.

Choice, beautiful perennial species deserving of much wider use. z6

O. stellulatum Waldst. et Kit. W. Yugoslavia. 20–40mm high. Leaves narrow, margin involuted. Flowers gold-yellow, in several helicoid cymes at the end of the strongly upright stems. Easily cultivated species. z7

O. tauricum Pall. ex Willd. SE. Europe. Similar to the previous species, but with flowers sessile and larger, to 40mm. z6

Many other species exist in culture in botanic and collectors' gardens. Since the nomenclature is still quite confused, these species are not described here.

Literature for the horticulturally useful *O. alboroseum* related species: Teppner, H.: Die *Onosma alboroseum*-Gruppe (Boraginaceae). Phyton (Austria) Vol. 20, Fasc. 1–2, 135 to 157, 1980. (K.)

Ophiopogon Ker-Gawl.
Liliaceae
Lilyturf, Mondo Grass

The ophiopogons are very similar to the species of the genus *Liriope* into which they have often been included. Aside from the many properties in common with *Liriope*, *Ophiopogon* differs in the subinferior ovaries and blue, glossy fruit. The flowers are white or pale, usually violet on *Liriope*. The species comes from Asia and has long been cultivated there. Like *Liriope*, it thrives in loamy, well-drained, slightly acidic humus soil, and a climate not too cold in winter.

O. jaburan (Sieb.) Lodd. Jaburan Lilyturf, White Lilyturf. Japan. Primarily a temperate greenhouse plant in Europe but a valuable garden plant where summers are warmer, USA z6–10. Plants tufted, with cord-like, non-tuberous roots and long-reaching subsurface stolons terminating in plantlets. Leaves strap-shaped, leathery, lax and often somewhat curled or twisted, to 60cm but often less, to 10cm wide. Flowers white, to 1cm long, clustered in short racemes on naked scapes in late summer. Several more or less white-variegated cultivars are listed which may be indistinguishable: 'Argenteo-vittaus', 'Javanensis', 'Variegatus', and 'Vittatus'. Here probably belongs the almost white-leaved plant listed in horticulture as 'Liriope White Dragon'. Also 'Aureovariegatus', leaves yellow-striped; and 'Caeruleus', with violet flowers.

O. japonicus (L.f.) Ker-Gawl., Dwarf Lilyturf, Mondo Grass. Japan and Korea. A good temperate garden species, quickly covering the ground by slender stolons. Somewhat clumpy at first, eventually a dense, grasslike, blackish-green groundcover. Leaves to 25cm long and 3mm wide; there are forms or similar species with shorter ('Intermedius') and very short leaves ('Minor'). 'Minor' forms a particularly dense, low groundcover with its curling or drooping leaves. The foliage is most attractive in a warm, protected site, but not in full sun. z7

O. planiscapus Nakai. Japan, on warm hilly areas at woodland margins. Needs a protected site in cooler climates. This species is most commonly grown in the cultivar 'Arabicus' ('Nigrescens', 'Ebony Knight' of the trade), with almost black foliage, and pink flowers followed by abundant black fruits. Propagation by seed will also yield green plants; selection is necessary if not propagated by division. z6(5) (S.)

Ophrys L. emend.R. Br.
Orchidaceae

Thirty to 50 species depending upon interpretation of the genus, mostly in the

Ophiopogon japonicus

Mediterranean region. Terrestrial orchids growing on limestone soil, with small rounded tubers, basal leaf rosette often formed in fall, basal leaves deteriorate during anthesis. Flowers in loose, 1–10 (or more) flowered racemes from April to June. Interestingly, the flowers are designed to attract male hymenoptera (bees, wasps, etc.) by their form, fragrance and pubescence; pollination takes place when these insects attempt to copulate with the flowers.

Only for the experienced gardener as cultivation is quite difficult. Grow either in pots in the alpine house (the Mediterranean species are usually easier), or in a prepared site in the wildflower garden. Preferred substrate is a moderately light, limestone-gravelly, not-too-fertile humus with excellent drainage. *Ophrys* will not tolerate standing water. Propagation is also very difficult. Seed sown directly into the garden site is sometimes successful. Substantially better results are obtained by tuber division during anthesis. The procedure is as follows: the old and current year's tuber growth will be brittle while in bloom. Remove the new tuber growth by cutting or breaking it off, then pot the

mother plant and the piece of tuber separately. Remove the flowers and keep the pot evenly moist (never let dry out) to retard the senescing of the leaves. Sometimes a second, although smaller, tuber will develop which can then be removed and potted. The key to success with *Ophrys* propagation is keeping the leaves green as long as possible. Many individual plants of *O. sphegodes* will form tubercles in wet years which may then be carefully removed when the plant clump goes dormant. Some of the Mediterranean species are reasonably hardy in a favorable site when given a

Ophrys sphegodes

light cover of leafmold. For specific comparisons of the species, the reader is referred to one of the many orchid books or floras. (K.)

Opuntia Mill.
Cactaceae
Prickly-pear, Cholla

A genus of about 300 hardy to tender species of cacti from the Western Hemisphere, mostly in North America. Only the Prickly-pears and their low-growing relatives are considered here. Procumbent in habit, forming dense, 20cm-high colonies, with prickly green pads, not leaves but highly modified stems, and silky-glossy, yellow or reddish, bee-attracting flowers. All species require very dry sites in full sun and a sandy to medium-heavy, well-drained soil.

Many species are more sensitive to excess moisture than to cold. Winter protection, when necessary, is best accomplished by a light cover of spruce branches. Because of their unique appearance, best suited for rock or suc-

culent gardens among *Yucca*, *Sedum* and various grasses. Propagation is by separation of the joints, which will easily root if laid flat on the soil. Most are unsuitable for the damp oceanic climate of W. Europe, perhaps with the exception of *O. fragilis*, *O. compressa*, and *O. polyacantha*.

O. camanchica see **O. phaeacantha**

O. compressa *O. humifusa* (Raf.) Raf. (*O. vulgaris* Mill non. dub., *Cactus opuntia* L., *O. rafinesquei* Englem., (Salisb.) Macbr.). USA: Massachusetts to Ontario and

Opuntia phaeacantha

Montana, south to South Carolina, Georgia, Alabama, Missouri and Oklahoma. Creeping, joints large, dark green, orbicular to obovate, 7.5–12.5cm long. Spines sometimes absent, when present 2.5cm long, solitary, rigid and with 1–2 smaller lateral spines. Glochidia reddish brown; flowers sulfur yellow, to 8cm wide with reddish centers. Fully hardy on sandy soil and widely distributed in cultivation. A. variety known under the synonym *O. humifusa* var. *austrina*, with fleshy, tuberous roots, is naturalized in South Tirol (Italy-Austria) and often grown as *O. compressa*; see *O. macrorhiza*, below. Gloshidia hellowish green, flowers yellow.

O. compressa var. **macrorhiza** see **O. macrorhiza**

O. erinacea Engelm. et Bigel. USA: California, Nevada, Utah, Arizona, New Mexico. Also belonging here are the forms distributed as *O. hystricina*. z7(6)

O. erinacea var. **hystricina**, Porcupine Cactus. Develops procumbent, wide-spreading clumps with erect, 6–10cm wide joints, becoming more rounded with age. With numerous, pale brown to white, 6–10cm long spines (good identification characteristic) Glochidia (barbed thorns) yellow, flowers 7cm wide, orange or pink. Fruit about 3cm long, ovate to oblong, prickly tipped. Rather hardy and also somewhat moisture tolerant. z5

O. erinacea var. **ursina** (*O. hystricina* var. *ursina*). Grizzly Bear Cactus. SE. California to Arizona. Very attractive, to 15cm-long shoots with a dense, long white bristle covering; bristles to 20cm long. Flowers usually yellow, but also with pink- and orange-flowering cultivars. Will not tolerate long periods of temperatures below –10 degrees C. (14 degrees F.). Best suited for dry spots against a warm wall. z8

O. erinacea var. **utahensis** (Engelm.) SE. California to W. Nebraska. Smaller, joints 5–10cm long, obovate; spines 1–8, deflexed, often lacking from the lower areoles. The hardiest variety. Often listed in horticulture as *O. rhodantha, O. xanthostemma*, which see, below.

O. fragilis (Nutt.) Haw. N. America: Manitoba to British Columbia, south to Texas and Arizona. Joints sub-globose to flattened, to 5cm long, quite brittle. Glochidia tufted, white at first, then yellowish, with 1–4 awlshaped spines, one of which is 2cm long and brown, the others short and white. Flowers yellow. z3–7

O. grandiflora see **O. macrorhiza**

O. humifusa var. **austrina** see **O. macrorhiza**

O. hystricina see **O. erinacea**

O. hystricina var. **ursina** see **O. erinacea** var. **ursina**

O. juniperina Britt. et Rose. New Mexico. Procumbent, slightly ascending, forming wide-spreading colonies, with 12cm-long, ovate joints, broad-rounded above. Spines only in the uppermost areoles, glochidia usually with a main spine and few lateral spines. Flowers light yellow. 3cm-long, reddish, nonprickly fruits. Very hardy species. z5

O. lindheimeri Engelm. SW. Louisiana, SE. Texas, NE. Mexico. Quite a variable species, sometimes grows almost treelike in its native habitat. Green joints to 25cm-long, often more or less glaucous, orbicular to ovate, with widely spaced areoles, 1–6 spines, 3–4cm long.

Several varieties are listed. There are cultivars with yellow and dark red flowers. Sensitive to wetness, hardy to about −15 degrees C. (5 degrees F.). z7

O. mackensii see **O. macrorhiza**

O. macrorhiza Engelm. (*O. compressa* var. *macrorhiza* (Engelm) L. Bens., *O. grandiflora* Engelm., *O. mackensii* Rose, *O. tortispina* Engelm Bigelow.). USA: California, Idaho, Louisiana, Kansas to Texas. Mostly tuberous-rooted. Very procumbent, forming colonies to 1m wide. More or less rounded joints, 16cm long, 1cm

Opuntia rhodantha

thick with a bluish green, matte surface. Rather large areoles. Glochidia numerous, yellow-green to brownish. Spines sometimes absent, otherwise in 4s, unequal, to 2.5cm long. Usually with yellow flowers, turning orange or occasionally yellow with a red center. Good winter hardiness. z5

O. missouriensis see **O. polyacantha**

O. phaeacantha Engelm. (*O. camanchica* Engelm. et Bigel.). New Mexico, Arizona, Texas. Joints oblong-rounded, 10–15cm long. Glochidia yellow to brown, spines 1–6cm long, usually directed downward, brown or whitish gray. Flowers yellow, with orange centers. Quite variable species with many difficult to distinguish forms. z6

O. phaeacantha var. **camanchica** (Engelm. et Bigel.) Borg (*O. camanchica* Engelm. et Bigel.). Oklahoma to New

Mexico. Low, quite prostrate, round to ovate matte green joints, to 17cm long and wide. 1–3 or more compressed spines, to 6cm long, brown, lighter and whitish at the tip. Flowers yellow to orange. Very hardy and somewhat tolerant of wetness. With many cultivars, all with garden merit. z6

O. polyacantha Haw. (*O. missouriensis* DC.). N. America: North Dakota to Alberta and Washington, south to Texas and Arizona. Joints somewhat ascending, nearly round, scarcely 10cm wide. Glochidia yellow, spines 10–12, to 4cm long, brown and divergent, usually directed downward. Flowers yellow, exterior reddish. Hardy, also tolerant of wetness. With many varieties and cultivars worth growing. z3–8

O. rafinesquei see **O. humifusa**

O. rhodantha K. Schum. USA: SE. California to W. Nebraska. Joints obovate, somewhat knobby, gray-green. Glochidia reddish brown; the 2–4, about 3cm-long spines are surrounded by secondary spines. Flowers and stamen filaments carmine red, 8cm wide. Unusually attractive, garden-worthy species with many cultivars and garden selections. Sometimes listed as *O. erinacea* var. *utahensis* (Engelm.) L. Bens. z5

O. tortispina see **O. macrorhiza**

O. vulgaris see **O. compressa**

O. xanthostemma K. Schum. Colorado, Utah, Nebraska. Similar to *O. rhodantha*, but primarily differing in the yellow stamen filaments. There are numerous cultivars with pale rose to carmine red flowers. Also sometimes listed as *O. erinacea* var. *utahensis* (Engelm.) L. Bens. z5

In addition to the opuntias, there are many other cacti that are winter hardy or relatively so. Growing conditions depend upon microclimate, rainfall, drainage, fertility, and similar environmental factors. For these reasons it is

Orchis sancta

nearly impossible to recommend cacti based solely on hardiness. The following species are, however, worthy trying: *Escobaria vivipara* (Nutt.) Buxb. (*Coryphantha vivipara* (Nutt.) Engelm.), *Maihuenia poeppigii* (Otto) Web., *Corypantha missouriensis* var. *robustior* (Engelm.) L. Bens. (*Neobesseya missouriensis* (Sweet) Britt. et Rose, *N. wissmannii* (Hildm.) Britt. et Rose, *Pediocactus knowltonii* L. Bens., *P. simpsonii* (Engelm.) Britt. et Rose. (Kö.)

Orchis see Dactylorhiza

Oreobroma

O. mexicana see **Lewisia megarhiza**

Orchis L.
Orchidaceae
Orchis, Shin Plasters

About 50 species in Eurasia, N. Africa and Alaska. Perennial, 10–80cm high. Tubers usually 2, also 3, rounded to ovate, unsegmented. Bracts thin, membranous. Flowers either hoodlike or with both sepals outspread to reflexed. Lip quite variably formed. Flowers with spurs. Blooms from April to June. Garden cultivation is similar to *Ophrys* (which see) but generally easier. The European species, *O. militaris* and *O. morio* are self-seeding; the culture of *O. laxiflora*, *O. mascula*, *O. pallens*, *O. palustris*, *O. purpurea*, *O. simia*, *O. tridentata* and *O. ustulata* is possible under favorable conditions in zone 7. Plants may be increased by division of the tubers. The species *O. papilionacea*, *O. pauciflora*, *O. provincialis* and *O. sancta* require winter

Origanum amanum

cover or cultivation in the alpine house. In America the eastern woodland species *O. spectabilis* L., indigenous from the Atlantic Coast to the Western Ozarks, is available from wildflower nurseries and grows fairly readily in moist, humus-rich acidic soils in the shady wildflower garden. z4 (K.)

Oreopteris

O. limbosperma see **Thelypteris limbosperma**

Origanum L.
Labiatae
Wild Marjoram, Winter Sweet, Oregano

Fifteen to 20 species of annual, biennial or perennial, commonly aromatic herbs and low shrubs from the Mediterranean region of Europe to Central Asia. Stems mostly 4-angled. Leaves opposite, simple. Flowers in few- to many-flowered false whorls with large or medium-sized, colored or leaflike bracts. Terminal spikes solitary or in racemes, panicles, cymes or corymbs. Calyx bell-shaped or tube-shaped, nearly equally 5-toothed or obliquely truncate with active upper lip and toothed lower lip, or entire but deeply split on 1 side; corolla 2-lipped, upper lip entire or emarginate, lower lip 3-lobed; stamens diadelphous. Attractive, low, late-flowering perennials or small shrubs for the herb garden, the rock garden, or trough as well as for the alpine house. All species require excellent drainage and a well-drained, gravelly loam soil. It is important that the soil remain dry through the winter dormant period so no water should be given in the alpine house from early November to mid-March. Tender species suitable for pot culture, to be overwintered in a frost-free cold frame or alpine house. Propagate by seed; many species also by division as well as by spring and summer cuttings.

The winter-hardy species *O. laevigatum* and *O. vulgare* thrive on a dry slope with other low, extremely drought tolerant perennials. *O. amanum* belongs in a sunny rock crevice, but must be protected from winter wetness by covering with a raised pane of glass or polyethylene cloche.

Winter-hardy species

A 10cm high, underground-creeping, sometimes aromatic, attractive, bushy perennial with slender, wiry, 10–15cm long stems. Leaves cordate, small, gray-green, ciliate on the margin. Flowers in umbellate panicles, with purple-red bracts. Corolla with 4cm long, narrow, rust-colored tube. Flowers from July to August. If given dry winter conditions will grow better in the garden than in the alpine house. z6

O. laevigatum Boiss. Asia Minor, Syria, in the mountains on rocky sites and slopes. Nearly unscented, 20–50cm high perennial when flowering. Nonflowering shoots short, pubescent; leaves pubescent only on the midrib, triangular-ovate, 8–12mm long, gray-green. Flowers numerous, in rather loose racemes in a long panicle. Bracts elliptic, shorter than the purple, 4mm-long calyx. Blooms from August to September. z6

O. vulgare L., Pot Marjoram. Europe, Siberia, Himalayas, Asia Minor, Iran, on dry, gravelly slopes, in infertile meadows and in open woodlands, on alkaline to acidic soils. Variable species. Entire plant aromatic, 20–60cm high, stoloniferous. Stems erect, branched, softly pubescent, like the petioled, acutely ovate leaves. Bracts often brown-red. Flowers in 1–3 flowered false whorls, grouped into panicles and umbellate inflorescences. Corolla small, purple- to flesh-colored, occasionally whitish. Blooms from July to October.

The cultivar 'Aureum' with its conspicuous gold-yellow leaves and 15cm-high bushy habit, is at least as worth growing as the species; also, the 15–20cm high form 'Compactum' is attractive. Both are well suited for planting on large open sites, such as a dry slope or bank. z4

Species sensitive to frost and winter wetness, best suited for the alpine house

O. dictamnus L. (*Amaracus dictamnus* (L.) Benth.). Dittany of Crete. Crete (Greece), on rocky, dry sites in the mountains. White-woolly, low, 20cm-high subshrub with branches densely leafy, especially at the base. Leaves 13–25mm long, 12–25mm wide, broadly ovate to circular, entire, white woolly, the basal leaves short-petioled. Inflorescences are hopslike, nodding heads. Bracts 7–10mm long, conspicuous, purple, longer than the calyx. Corolla pink, the corolla tube twice as long as the calyx tube. Blooms from July to August.

A tender species which occasionally freezes out in an unheated alpine house. It is therefore advisable to maintain a few potted replacement plants in a frost-free location. z9(8)

O. × hybridum Mill. (probably *O. dictamnus × O. sipyleum*). Decumbent subshrubs 30–40cm high, aromatic, with short-petioled, 2.5cm-long gray-pubescent leaves. Flower heads similar to those of *O. dictamnus*, bluish-purple colored. Blooms from July to October. Overwinters in the garden given protection from winter wetness. Very attractive, and valuable for its late flowering period. z7

O. pulchellum (Boiss.) O. Kuntze (*Amaracus pulchellus* (Boiss.) Briq.). Asia Minor. Similar to *O. dictamnus*, but with smaller, 2cm-long, less pubescent leaves, distinctly toothed calyx, and pink flowers. Blooming from July to August. z8

O. scabrum Boiss. et Heldr. Mountains of S. Greece, on dry, gravelly slopes. Perennial to 40cm-high, with erect glabrous stems branched above the middle. Leaves 11–30mm long and 11–20mm wide, ovate to nearly orbicular, cordate, glabrous or nearly so, with stiff-haired margins, sessile. Inflorescences nodding, with conspicuous, glabrous, purple bracts. Corolla pink. z9

O. scabrum ssp. **pulchrum** (Boiss. et Heldr.) P. H. Davis (*Amaracus pulcher* (Boiss. et Heldr.) Briq.). More commonly cultivated, similar to the species, with smooth leaf margins. Blooms from July to August. z9 (E.)

Ornithogalum L.
Liliaceae
Star-of-Bethlehem

Bulbous plants with narrow, basal leaves and white flowers in terminal, erect racemes or flat corymbs, often umbellate. Only a few of the nearly 100, primarily Mediterranean species, are considered to be hardy in temperate zone gardens. They are undemanding plants which thrive in most garden soils. Suitable for rock and wild gardens, some valuable for cutting. Usually grown from seed, also propagated by offset bulblets.

O. balansae Boiss. NE. Turkey (Anatolia) and adjacent USSR, in alpine meadows near the snow line to 2500m. With 2–3 glossy green, linear leaves, 4–8cm long, 1cm wide; flowers 1–5, large (2.5cm

wide) pure white with green exteriors, 10cm high; March to April. The earliest, very garden-worthy species. A suitable companion with *Hepatica*, *Dentaria glandulosa*, *Cyclamen coum*, *Daphne mezereum*.

O. magnum Kraschen. et Schischk. Ciscaucasia. Spikes to 80cm high; stately species with beautiful white flowers in racemes from May to June. Effective with early *Paeonia* hybrids. z7

O. narbonense L. Widely distributed in the Mediterranean countries, N. Africa, W. Asia, particularly Turkey and Iran.

Ornithogalum umbellatum

Scape 30–50cm high, above a tuft of narrow gray-green leaves. Racemes of many pure white flowers, with only a narrow, green stripe on the outside. Flowers 1–2cm wide. For sunny sites and well-drained soil. Early June, differing primarily from the earlier-flowering *O. pyramidale* in the flowering time. z7

O. nutans L. SE. Europe, naturalized in parts of Central Europe and the E. USA. Scape 20–40cm high. Leaves broadly lanceolate, gray-green, somewhat channeled, still green and attractive at anthesis. Flowers large, campanulate, erect at first, later nodding, interior white, exterior with a greenish stripe, in loose, few to 12-flowered, nearly one-sided racemes; April to May. Good plant for naturalizing under trees. z6

O. pyramidale L. S. Europe, Asia Minor. Scape 40–80cm high. Leaves gray-green, fleshy, about 1cm wide, channeled. Stems stiffly upright. Flowers white, with green midstripes on the reverse, in dense, pyramidal (at first), few to 50-flowered racemes; perianth segments furl as flowers fade; June to July. Useful as a cut flower. Effective companion for *Triteleia* × *tubergenii* or *T. laxa* 'Queen Fabiola'. z6

O. pyrenaicum L. Star-of-Bethlehem, Prussian Asparagus. W. and S. Europe to Asia Minor. Scape to 1m high. Leaves linear-lanceolate, dying back before flowering finishes. Flowers whitish to yellow-green, spent flowers remain open, in 30–50 flowered racemes; June to July. z6

Orobranche amethystea

O. thyrsoides Jacq., Chincherinchee. Tender species from S. Africa, long cultivated for cut flowers. The flowers are long lasting and color well. Bulbs must be lifted and stored frost free over winter. z10

O. umbellatum L., Star-of-Bethlehem. S. and Central Europe, widely naturalized in E. USA. Scape 10–20cm high; bulbs clustered with many offset bulblets. Leaves linear, deeply channeled, bright, glossy green with conspicuous white middle stripes. Flowers stellate, white, with a green middle stripe on the dorsal side in a many-flowered, flat corymb, only opening from 11:00 AM to 3:00 PM; throughout spring. An attractive but invasive species, dies back soon after flowering. Poisonous to livestock. z5 (H.& Mü.)

Orobanche L.
Orobanchaceae

About 100 species of Broom-rapes or Cancer-root in the Northern Hemisphere. Parasitic plants with rather fleshy stems lacking chlorophyll, yellow, brown, violet or whitish colored. Stems leafless but with alternate scales. Flowers complete, with a persistent calyx. Corolla tubeform, bilabiate, the upper lip usually 2-lobed, the lower one 3-lobed. Anthers 4, in 2 pairs. Seeds many, minute. Flowers from June to August.

Orontium aquaticum

Culture of this exceptional collector's plant is possible on the roots of a suitable host; one that is not too vigorous (danger of suppression) or too weak (danger of starvation). Most species are annual. Of the perennial species those that can be brought into flower are: *O. alba* Steph. ex Willd. (*O. epithymum* DC.) on *Thymus*; *O. gracilis* Sm. on *Lotus corniculatus* 'Plenus'; *O. hederae* Duby on *Hedera helix*, even in pots on 'Conglomerata'; and *O. uniflora* L. on *Sedum spathulifolium*.

It is often difficult to obtain seed, but is sometimes obtainable from botanic gardens. The dust-like seeds tolerate dry storage. They are scattered on the soil surface at the base of potted host plant in spring, or may be applied directly on the roots. Both plants are later transplanted to the garden. Seeds may also be sown directly onto roots in the garden but with considerably less success. Other interesting and attractive species include *O. amethystea* Thuill. on *Eryngium campestre*

or *O. teucrii* Holandre on *Teucrium montanum*. Seed of the perennial genus *Boschniakia* C. A. Mey is occasionally available from botanic gardens in N. America; but garden trials with *Boschniakia hookeri* Walp. on *Gaultheria shallon* and *B. strobilacea* Gray on *Arctostaphylos* and *Arbutus* species have thus far been unsuccessful in Europe.

Orobus see Lathyrus

Orontium L.
Araceae
Golden Club, Water Dock

Only 1 species.

O. aquaticum L., Golden Club. Atlantic E. North America. A swamp and aquatic plant with thick rhizomes. Leaves basal, elevated or floating depending upon the water depth, oblong-oval, short-acuminate, gray-green, silvery beneath, 25cm long, 5–12cm wide. Spadix gold-yellow, narrow-cylindrical, on long, apically thickened, white peduncles. Spathe quickly abscises. April to June.

Interesting swamp or water plants for small and large ponds or pools in gardens and parks. Grows best in 30cm of water in loamy humus, fertile soil and full sun. Often self-seeds. Fruit clusters ripen lying on the water. Because of its tropical appearance, *Orontium* can be effectively combined with *Azolla mexicana*, *Eichhornia*, *Pistia* and *Cyperus papyrus* in large tubs or small pools on a sunny terrace.

Overwintering in the garden is possible if frost does not reach the rhizome. Plants should be appropriately protected. Propagation is by division in May to June or seed just after ripening in June to July. z8 (D.)

Orostachys Fisch. ex Berger
Crassulaceae

About 10 species of N. Asian succulent herbs closely related to *Sedum*, usually overwintering as a compact winter bud of hard callose leaves. This develops into a succulent leafy rosette from which a terminal flowering spike, rarely thyrse, is produced. Flowers with 5 sepals, 5 nearly distinct petals and 10 stamens. When the spike dies away so does rosette, leaving winter buds for next season.

O. iwarenge Hara. A collector's plant from Japan. The large, gray-green, rosettes, slender-stoloniferous, are killed back by frost, but the small, few-leaved rosettes will overwinter. z6

O. spinosa (L.) Sweet (*Umbilicus spinosus* (L.) DC.). Siberia, Mongolia, Altai Mts., W. Tibet. Dense, glabrous, and floriferous rosetted plant. Leaves gray-green, linear to spatulate, with long, horn-textured white tips. Inflorescences 30cm high, cylindrical, flowers yellow, stellate, appearing only on plants several years old, June to July. An interesting plant for the rock garden or tufa rock planters; in a somewhat shaded site. Propagate by the many secondary rosettes and by seed. z4

In recent years, several other species have been introduced into garden culture. An as yet undetermined species is grown under the name *Orostachys* 'Spec. Mongolei'. (H. & Kö.)

Orthilia Raf.
(*Ramischia* Opiz ex Garcke,
Pyrola L. in England
and the USA.)
Pyrolaceae

One species from the Northern Hemisphere. Distinguished from *Pyrola* by some Continental authors by the one-sided racemes, anthers unappendaged, pollen grains solitary. Flowers from June to July. Cultivated, used and propagated like *Pyrola*.

O. secunda (L.) House (*Pyrola secunda* L.). Scape 5–15, occasionally to 25cm high. Leaves ovate-acuminate (resembling pear leaves). Flowers greenish white in one-sided, nodding (at first) racemes. z6 (K.)

Oryzopsis Michx.
Gramineae
Rice Grass, Mountain Rice

O. miliacea (L.) Benth. et Hook.f. ex Aschers. et Graebn. (*Piptatherum miliaceum* Coss.). Smilo Grass. S. Europe,

Osmunda regalis

naturalized in E. USA. and California. A hot climate clump grass with very loose panicles on 1.5m high stout culms. The inflorescences are very similar to those of *Deschampsia*, but the number of panicle branches per node is higher, up to 20, the spikelets are 1-, not 2-flowered. Indigenous to hot, summer-dry, rocky plains. Under these conditions, plants will bloom from May to October with graceful, airy, nodding panicles and are reasonably hardy. The loose panicles are suitable for cutting. Propagate by division in spring and by seed. z6 (S.)

Osmunda L.
Osmundaceae
Royal Fern, Cinnamon Fern, Interrupted Fern

Ten to 14 species of large, somewhat coarse ferns from the temperate zone and the tropics, 3 of which are generally hardy. Plants with a thick, much branched or budded rhizome with fibrous, blackish roots which penetrate deep into the ground. Fronds are pinnatifid to bipinnate; spore-bearing pinnae are conspicuously different in form. The unrolling fronds called croziers or fiddle heads are covered with a dense tomentum of brownish or white hairs. The genus *Osmunda* includes the oldest ferns from an evolutionary standpoint. In addition, many individual plants of the Royal Fern are quite old; specimens in the swampy forests of the Caucasus region have been estimated at over 1,000 years old. Also noteworthy is the size of many cultivated examples of Royal Fern (*O. regalis*), with fertile fronds reaching 1.5m, sterile fronds to 2m high in clumps to 3m wide.

These are ferns which, once established, grow larger and more luxuriant with the passing years. All osmundas thrive in high humus, or peaty moist soil in a semi-shaded site, and require wet soil in full sun. Most effective among trees or tall perennials.

Propagation is seldom by division, usually by spores in Europe; in America, division and tissue culture are the more common methods. Sow spores immediately after ripening. Spores ripen early, often in late May.

O. cinnamomea L., Cinnamon Fern. N. America, W. Indies, S. America and E. Asia, in moist, open woodlands. Sterile fronds in a vase-shaped cluster, to 1.5m high, emerging croziers brown-woolly-pubescent, later glabrous, frond 1-pinnate, deeply lobed, dark green, barely glossy, with tufts of red-brown hair at the base of the pinnae. Fertile fronds somewhat shorter, developing in the center of the plant before the sterile fronds emerge, without green pinnae, turning cinnamon brown, condensed and erect after the spores ripen. Young vegetative croziers are edible. z4

Suitable for cool, moist garden sites, especially attractive near pools, alone or among low shade-loving perennials or other ferns. Propagate by spores, harvested and sown immediately after

wide, leathery, firm, with fine-toothed margins. Stipe 60cm long. Fertile pinnae toward the apex of the fronds forming a terminal panicle. These apical pinnae are much reduced, erect, with clustered sporangia on the the margins, turning golden brown after ripening. Fall color an intense yellow to yellow-brown.

One of the most vigorous and, for the bright spore-bearing panicles, one of the showiest of garden ferns. Plants reach giant proportions in moist to wet soil, to 2m high, 3m wide. Well suited for specimen planting on large ponds or beside streams in park settings. Propa-

9) lobes. Capsule 5–9 locular, opening at the apex by lateral slits, twice as many as calyx lobes. Flowers in June and July. Cultivated only in warm regions. Very susceptible to damp soil damage, therefore usually elevated and provided with a well-drained substrate. New growth susceptible to late frost damage. Best suited for collectors and planted in the wild alpine garden, large rockery or dry stone wall. Best propagated by seed. Capsules may have to be removed in September and artificially dried to avoid decay in fall rains. Plants take 3–5 years to flower. The first year only the seed

Orostachys spinosus

Osmunda cinnamomea

Ostrowskia magnifica

the fronds turn from green to brown. Young plants should be raised in a high-humidity environment. Spores ripen from late May to June. z3–10

O. claytoniana L., Interrupted Fern. N. America and E. Asia from Japan and the Himalaya Mts. to Siberia, in moist woodlands, but also on dry sites. Plants very similar to the Cinnamon Fern in height, generally somewhat shorter, and appearance, but fronds soft-textured and broader-lobed, pinnae without axillary hair tufts. Sporangia-bearing fronds erect in the center of the plant; 3–4 fertile pinnae lacking chlorophyll and reduced to spore-bearing structures in the middle of these fronds. The spore-bearing pinnae abscise soon after ripening, the others persist. The outer fronds form a vase-like funnel. Garden use and propagation like that of *O. cinnamomea.* z2–8

O. regalis L., Royal Fern. Northern and Southern Temperate Zones, nearly cosmopolitan, in open woodlands, in moist depressions and on slopes, scattered or in colonies. Sterile fronds to 2m long, bipinnate, bright green to yellow green, pinnae oval, 4cm long, 1–2cm

gate by spores. Spores ripen in early June. z3–8

Cultivar 'Cristata', Cockscomb Royal Fern. With flat-spreading, somewhat contorted, forked terminal fertile pinnae often partially vegetative, producing spores on only about 1/6 of the pinnae surface. A collector's cultivar, vigorous but not especially attractive. Remains green long into fall, fall color not effective. Propagates true from spores.

Cultivar 'Purpurascens', Purple Royal Fern. Like the species in general appearance, but with red stipe and rachis, the color especially intense on the new growth. Fronds darker green, fertile fronds more intensely golden brown. Fall color also more intense. More attractive than the species; used similarly in the garden. Plants come true from spores. (D.)

Ostrowskia Regel
Campanulaceae
Giant Bellflower

One species in Turkestan, from around 2000m elevation. Perennial with a tuberous rootstock. Calyx lobes 5–9, corolla campanulate, usually with 7 (5–

leaves (cotyledons) are produced. Non-flowering plants usually die back in early June. Raise seedlings individually in pots from fresh seed and plant while young where they are to bloom as they transplant poorly.

O. magnifica Regel. Giant Bellflower. Clump-forming perennial, 1–1.2m high, with a tuberous rootstock. Stems thick, unbranched, glabrous, leafy. Leaves 4–5 in whorls, 10–15cm long, ovate, dentate, short-petioled, glabrous. Uppermost stem leaves alternate. Flowers long-pediceled, light blue, silky glossy, to 15cm in diameter, in few-flowered, terminal racemes. Culture similar to that of *Iris hoogiana* and *I. stolonifera*. Beautiful, but very heat-loving collector's plant. z7(6) (K.)

Ourisia Comm ex Juss.
Scrophulariaceae

About 25 species, of which 12 are from S. America, 1 from Tasmania and the others from New Zealand. Stems prostrate, decumbent or erect. Perennials with mostly basal, rounded leaves and funnelform to tubular, red, pink or white flowers in scapose racemes, corymbs or superimposed whorls, or sometimes solitary-axillary, often on stiffly upright scapes. Flowers from May to September. Grow in high humus, lime-free soil in a semi-shaded to shaded, mild and humid site. Protection must be provided from excessive winter wetness. Small species may be damaged by any competing growth of liverworts. Suitable for an intensively cultivated peat bed or trough. An excellent plant for collectors. Propagate by seed or division.

O. caespitosa Hook.f. New Zealand.

pubescent leaves clustered at the ends of stems growing 10–30cm long, from 1–2cm thick, creeping rhizomes. Flowers smaller than *O. macrocarpa*, white with yellow throats, in several tiered whorls; July. z7

O. microphylla Poeppig et Endl. Chile. Cushion habit, scarcely 5cm high, with 1.5–2mm long leaves. Flowers 1–3 at the branch tips, 1cm wide and long, light pink with a white throat. A beautiful plant for the alpine house, little used in the north temperate garden. Older plants will die back somewhat from

Oxalis L.
Oxalidaceae
Wood Sorrel

About 850 species, from all continents, most from S. Africa and S. and Central America. Perennials and subshrubs, leaves clover-like, 3- to many leaflets, basal or alternate on long (partly underground) stems. Plants often rhizomatous, tuberous or bulbous. Flowers in many colors except blue, in 1- to several flowered scapose cymes. Sepals 5, petals 5, stamens 10 in 2 series, the outer 5

Ourisia macrocarpa

Oxalis adenophylla

Well-branched, creeping and rooting, matform perennial. Leaves to 10 × 5mm, with 3 divisions on either side. Inflorescences 4–10cm high. Flowers white with yellow throat, paired on var. *caespitosa*, solitary on the dwarf var. *gracilis* Hook.f., May to June. z7

O. coccinea Pers. Chile. Stems 20–25cm high. Leaves cordate, irregularly crenate. Flowers 3cm long, scarlet red, nodding, in small, terminal racemes. May to September. z7

O. macrocarpa Hook. New Zealand. Similar to *O. macrophylla*, but leaves always leathery glabrous, orbicular to oblong, to 20cm long, crenate, on stout stems 20–60cm long. Flowers in superimposed whorls, white with yellow throat, to 2.5cm wide. z7

O. macrophylla Hook. New Zealand. A vigorous, variable perennial with

senescence. Grown from seed and cuttings. z8

O. sessilifolia Hook. New Zealand. A creeping and rooting perennial with overlapping leaves, very hairy on the upper surface. Flowers white with yellow throat markings, on 10cm-high pedicels. z7

In addition to the above described species, other species and garden hybrids are grown in British gardens. The most common of the hyrids is 'Loch Ewe' (*O. coccinea* × *O. macrophylla*), originated in Inverewe Gardens (Scotland), mat-forming, 30cm high, with flowers borne in clusters, flowers pink; and 'Snowflake' (*O. macrocarpa* × *O. caespitosa* var. *gracilis*), originated by Jack Drake, with a compact mat form and 12cm-high inflorescences with relatively large, white, yellow-eyed flowers. (K.)

shorter. Capsules 5-locular, as capsules open seeds disperse explosively by the rupturing of the somewhat elastic capsule segments.

Garden species bloom variously from early spring to summer. Wild, woodland species are cultivated in a humus-rich, acid soil in semi- and full shade. The alpine species require a well-drained, gravelly, (preferably) acid substrate and protection from winter wetness. Suitable for groundcovers in shaded sites. Recommended for collectors in the rockery or trough garden; some for pot culture in the alpine house. Propagate by seed sown immediately upon ripening, and division.

O. acetosella L., Wood Sorrel. Europe to Siberia, Caucasus, Central Asia to Japan, in moist deciduous woodland, also in young spruce forests. Scapes 5–15cm high; rhizome scaly, creeping underground. Leaves ternate, cloverlike, bright green. Flowers solitary, white with purple to rose veins. April to May. A charming, but often invasive, groundcover for semishady, moist, humus soil sites. Good understory plant. Similar to the W. American *O. oregana* Nutt. (larger in all respects) and the E. American *O. montana* Schlecht. (with only minimal differences). z3

O. adenophylla Gill. Chile, W. Argentina. Scapes 8–10cm high. Rootstock tuberous with fibrous scales. Leaves gray-green, round in outline, with many (9–22) leaflets, leaves

Oxalis acetosella

forming a dense clump. Leaves of the garden strain are pure blue-green; red zonal variants are also found in nature. Flowers 2.5cm wide in 1–3 flowered umbels, light to dark pink. Very persistent and hardy. z5

O. corniculata L. S. Europe, W. Asia, naturalized throughout the world, the most common rhizomatous, stemmed species with yellow flowers, leaves green, with 3 leaflets. An invasive, weedy species; the purple-leaved var. *atropurpurea* Planch. may have garden merit if used with caution. z5

O. depressa Lodd. (*O. inops* Jacq.) S. Africa. The most winter-hardy of the South African species. Bulbous and with few rhizomes. Leaves ternate, bluegreen, leaflets rounded or nearly triangular. Flowers large, solitary, 3cm in diameter, pink, white and yellow in the throat. June to September. Frost damaged only in extreme winters in temper-

ate zone gardens. Occasionally shows a vigorous spreading tendency. z5

O. enneaphylla Cav. Falkland Islands, Patagonia. Similar to *O. adenophylla*. Flowers solitary white, pink ('Rosea') or dark pink ('Rubra'). More demanding than *O. adenophylla*. z6

O. inops see **O. depressa**

O. laciniata Cav. Patagonia. An attractive alpine species. Rhizome 7mm thick, white scaly with orange spots. Leaves 7–12 parted, leaflets undulate, gray-blue. Flowers 2cm wide, light smoky gray-blue to deep violet and ruby red, with sap stains. May to July. As yet rare in the trade, hardy given protection, or for pot culture or the alpine house. 'Ione Hekker' (*O. enneaphylla* × *O. laciniata*) with large flowers also rarely offered. z8

O. magellanica G. Forst. S. South America, S. Australia, New Zealand. A rhizomatous, dense carpet species, often too vigorous, 2–5cm high. Flowers solitary, 1cm across, white to cream-colored, borne above the foliage mat. Blooms from May to July, and sporadically until October. Not suitable for planting near slower-growing neighbors, but attractive with *Hebe* or *Carmichaelia*. Very similar to *O. lactea* Hook. from New Zealand. z6

O. violacea Zucc. Violet Wood Sorrel. E. North America. With brown, scaly bulbs usually clustered. Ternate leaves in a dense basal cluster, leaflets often with r-shaped maroon markings. Flowers lavender, pink, rarely white, in 3–10 flowered umbels borne above the foliage on 10cm scapes. Requires gravelly, acid soil for optimum development but will grow on humus topsoil. z5 (K.)

Oxyria Hill
Polygonaceae
Mountain Sorrel

Two species of low, perennial herbs; not very conspicuous, but attractive small alpine plants for collectors and botanic gardens in the alpine garden or rock garden. Indigenous to alpine and arctic regions of Europe, Asia and North America. In cultivation is:

O. digyna (L.) Hill. Arctic Europe, Asia and N. America, higher alpine regions of the Pyrenees, Alps, Asia Minor, Caucasus, Central and E. Asia, the Rocky Mts., Cascades and Sierra Nevada, on screes on a low-lime, moist substrate, in

the mountains from about 1700–2800m. Plants 10–60cm high with long-petioled, orbicular to reniform, light green, nearly all basal, leaves. Stems turning red. Branched terminal panicles, leafless, flowers small, greenish; sepals 4, apetalous, stamens 6. Fruit a lentil-shaped, broadly winged red achene. Blooms from July to August.

O. digyna thrives only in a nonalkaline soil, and can be troublesome as it self-seeds into neighboring cushion-form plants. The plant will not succeed on a calcareous soil. Grows best on moist,

Oxyria digyna

gravelly, humus-loam soil between rocks or in a scree, in full sun to semi-shade. Propagate by seed and division. z1 (E.)

Oxytropis DC.
Leguminosae
Locoweed

About 300 species in the cooler regions and mountains of Asia, N. America and Europe. Very closely related to the genus *Astragalus*, largely distinguished by the beaked keel petal. Low to medium-high, deep-rooted perennials with odd pinnate leaves, the leaflets oblique basally, with flowers in spikes or racemes. Flowers papilionaceous, stamens 9 united, 1 free. Many of these species accumulate selenium from the soil and become poisonous to grazing animals, hence the name Locoweed.

Bloom from May to July. Grow in deep, gravelly, very well-drained soil in full sun. Suitable for the collector's rock garden or trough garden. Difficult or impossible to transplant. All gray-haired species are very sensitive to excessive winter wetness. Propagation is by seed. Seedlings have a strong tap root and must be put quickly into containers.

O. albiflora see **O. sericea**

O. besseyi Blank. Locoweed. N. America: Montana. A low, cushion forming plant. Leaves densely silver-haired, with 11–25 lanceolate leaflets. Flowering stems 10–15cm high. Ra-

Oxytropis pilosa

cemes 3–5cm long. Calyx somewhat inflated, densely silver-haired. Flowers red to blue-violet, 2cm long. An interesting selenium accumulating plant. Very sensitive to wetness, but more attractive than *O. halleri*. z4

O. campestris (L.) DC. N. Europe, N. Asia, Pyrenees, Alps, Carpathians, N. North America. Stems 10–30cm high. Leaves to 15cm long, gray-green, pubescent, with 11–25 linear-oblong to oblong-lanceolate leaflets to 2.5cm long. Flowering racemes long-peduncled, white to yellow to purple. June to July. Grows in neutral to slightly acidic soil. Botanical varieties are described. z3–7

O. halleri Bunge ex W.D.J. Koch (*O. sericea* (Lam.) Simonkai non Nutt., *O. prenja* G. Beck). Pyrenees, Alps,

Carpathians, Scotland, E. Albania and W. Macedonia, on a lime-free soil. A rosetted plant with a long taproot. Entire plant densely covered with whitish, silky hairs. Leaves with 17–37 elliptic-acute leaflets. Flowering stems 5–12cm high, 5–15 flowered. Flowers red-violet. June to July. Very susceptible to wetness, requires a sunny, dry site and a gravelly soil. This is not the *O. sericea* of the Central US. Mts.; see *O. sericea*, below. z5

O. jacquinii Bunge (*O. montana* auct. non L.). Alps, French Jura Mts. Stems 10–15cm high. Leaflets to 19 pairs, nearly glabrous. Inflorescences clustered, 5–15 flowered, violet. June to July. Undemanding. z5

O. lambertii Pursh. Purple Locoweed. North America, Saskatchewan and Montana to Missouri, Texas and Arkansas, on the short-grass prairies. Caespitose perennial with massive, deep, woody roots. Leaves to 20cm long, upright-growing, with 15 or more linear to oblong-acute leaflets, mostly silky gray-pubescent, hairs dichotomous. Scapes longer than the leaves, racemes 10–25 flowered, to 15cm long, flowers large, mostly purple but also rosy-purple or white. z4(3)

O. lazica Boiss. Asia Minor. Similar to *O. halleri*, but with less pubescent leaves, flowering scape stiffly erect, flowers

redder and with a short banner petal. May to June. Very attractive and substantially more vigorous. z5

O. megalantha H. Boiss. Japan. Similar to *O. halleri*, but less silky-pubescent, the pubescence reddish. Leaves with many more leaflets. Scapes 30cm high or higher, racemes to 7.5cm long. Flowers more violet-blue. Little disseminated. z6

O. montana see **O. jacquinii**

O. multiceps Nutt. USA: Wyoming, N. Colorado and NW. Nebraska Mts. and high plains on stony, neutral to alkaline soil. The smallest species of *Oxytropis* and one of the most beautiful. Roots woody and deep-growing. Plant a 2.5–7.5cm high and wide bun of silver-pubescent leaves to 2.5cm long, leaflets slender, acute. Flowers 1–4 on limber scapes barely above the foliage, purple-tinted pink, large. A superb and difficult rock garden plant recently introduced to American gardeners by the late Claude Barr, and unknown in Europe. z3–5

O. prenja see **O. halleri**

O. sericea Nutt. ex Torr. & A. Gray. (*O. albiflora* (A. Nels) K. Schum., not Bung.) USA: Montana to New Mexico, high plains and mountains on stony soil. Silky, pubescent, leaves to 30cm long, upright, leaflets to 3.5cm long, ovate to lanceolate; racemes stand above the foliage clump, few to 27 flowered, to 21cm long, white or yellowish, keel dotted purple, or entirely lilac to purple. The *O. sericea* of (Lem.) Simonk. is *O. halleri*. z4(3)

O. todomoshiriensis Miyabe et Miyake. Sachalin. Similar to *O. halleri*, but less silky-pubescent. Flowers blue-violet with sap stains. Very attractive, but needs some protection. z7(6) (K.)

Gardeners interested in *Oxytropis* species and varieties for the rock garden should refer to that genus in Claude A. Barr's *Jewels of the Plains*, U. of Minnesota Press, 1983.

Pachistima see Paxistima

Pachysandra Michx.
Buxaceae
Spurge

Genus of about 5 species in E. Asia and E. North America. Only the following species are, thus far, important in ornamental horticulture. Monoecious perennials and subshrubs with simple leaves mostly crowded at stem ends. Flowers in erect axillary or terminal spikes, male flowers above with 4 sepals, apetalous and 4 stamens, female flowers below with 4 or more sepals and a usually 3-lobed pistil. Sepals may be petal-like, showy, but plants are grown mostly as an evergreen ground cover.

P. procumbens Michx. Allegheny Spurge. E. North America. Stems 20–30cm high, with deciduous (evergreen in warmer climates), clearly veined, brownish-mottled, large, soft-pubescent ovate to sub-orbicular toothed leaves, which turn a good bronze in fall. The procumbent shoots produce pinkish, fragrant, flower spikes at the base of the clustered leaves in very early spring. Plants colonize to form a dense, wide clump; non-stoloniferous, and thrive in rich, moist woodland soil in deciduous shade. Propagate by cuttings in early summer. z7(6)

P. terminalis Sieb. et Zucc. Japanese Spurge. A perennial ground cover from the deciduous woodlands of Japan. Plants stoloniferous, about 20cm high. Unbranched, upright stems bear terminally clustered, leathery, evergreen, coarsely toothed, narrowly rhombic leaves. Flowers are creamy white, in terminal spikes, relatively insignificant. The species is a valuable groundcover on a moderately moist soil in semi-shade, suitable for covering large areas. On non-acid soils *Pachysandra* will have yellowish foliage and a poor growth rate. Propagation is by division, cuttings of the rhizomes or the erect branches, best taken when partially hardened in July and August. When planting bare root, place rhizomes flat and barely cover them. Avoid setting potted plants too deep.
 Variegata' with white-bordered, somewhat pale green leaves, is not so vigorous.
 'Green Carpet' is substantially shorter-growing and less vigorous than the species, smaller leaved, and therefore suitable for filling limited spaces. z5(4) (S.)

Paederota L.
Scrophulariaceae

Two species of perennial herbs in the E. Alps and the SE. mountain ranges to Herzegovina (Yugoslavia). Opposite, simple leaves and a terminal, spikelike bracted raceme. Flowers yellow or blue.

Calyx with 5 somewhat uneven lobes; corolla with a long cylindrical tube and bilabiate limb, limb usually shorter than the tube; upper lip usually entire, lower lip 3-lobed. Differs from *Veronica*, with which it is often included, in the elongated corolla tube. Attractive small perennials but only recommended for experienced gardeners. Suitable for the alpine garden, rock garden and an east-facing dry stone wall. From the Dolomites, both species are lime loving and require very well-drained but moist, loamy humus soil, thoroughly mixed with dolomite (or limestone) gravel.

Pachysandra terminalis

Propagate by seed, careful division, and cuttings. Both species flower rather poorly in deep garden soils, performing much better at higher elevations in an alpine situation, especially *P. lutea.*

P. bonarota (L.) L. (*Veronica bonarota* L.). E. Alps, in crevices of more or less vertical, often shadowy rock walls and cliffs at the subalpine and alpine elevations to 2500m; always on dolomitic limestone. Plant 8–15cm high, with many, downy to woolly stems. Lower leaves broadly ovate to rhombic or nearly orbicular, the uppermost leaves ovate to oblong-lanceolate. Flowers in a dense, terminal, 2–4cm long, spikate raceme. Corolla 10–13mm in diameter, violet-blue, rarely pink. Blooms from June to August. z5

P. lutea Scop. (*Veronica lutea* (Scop.) Wettst.). SE. Alps, mountains of W. Yugoslavia. Found in habitats similar to those of the previous species. Similar to the above, but generally less pubescent and the stems 10–20cm long. Leaves somewhat larger, most narrowly ovate to lanceolate, with at least 10 teeth on either side. Corolla yellow. Blooms from June to August. z5 (E.)

Paeonia L.
Ranunculaceae (or Paeoniaceae)
Peony

About 33 species of extraordinarily attractive herbaceous perennials or open-growing shrubs. Most are quite ornamental. Nearly all peonies have a woody crown and tuberous root. Some are low-growing, about 50cm high, and some are large species to 1.5m and more. The woody shrub or tree peonies (Suffruticosa Group) will not be considered here. The large leaves usually are 2 or 3 part irregularly compound, but finely laciniate on a few species (Fernleaf Peonies). The flowers are relatively large, bowl-shaped. Peonies bloom in spring and early summer. Unlike many other tall, early flowering perennials, the foliage of peonies remains decorative until fall. The most important group (*Paeonia* Lactiflora Hybrids and cultivars) flower from spring to very early summer. The habitat of *Paeonia* ranges from Europe to E. Asia. Peonies are excellent garden plants, very long-lived, thriving undisturbed for many years even under less than favorable conditions. The planting site should be well prepared as plants improve when left undisturbed for decades. They may be combined with many other garden perennials for their complimentary summer foliage. The more vigorous species are, however, best given room to spread as individual specimens. Effective when used with spring-flowering woody plants such as Japanese Flowering Quince (*Chaenomeles*), *Kerria japonica* (the single-flowering form with single-flowered peonies and the double-flowered form with double-flowered peonies), *Kolkwitzia amabilis* and lilacs. Peonies may also be grouped, bedded in the lawn. Highly prized as cut flowers from the cut flower bed. For garden care, see the section on the Chinese Peonies. Cultivars are propagated by division. Of course, the species may also be propagated in this manner, but division is often difficult with large clumps. If soil seems wet, let the lifted clumps air dry somewhat to facilitate removal of the soil before division. Or hose off the clumps to expose the extensive root system and crown where the eyes (buds) are found. Then divide the crown with a sturdy

covered with about 5 cm of soil, less if soil is heavy. Plants are stunted if planted too deeply and require some years to achieve normal flowering. Planting on the shallow side is, therefore, preferable to planting too deeply since plants will usually settle somewhat. While peonies are fully winter hardy, requiring no winter protection, newly planted divisions should be protected against frost heaving. Heaving can be a real problem with a late fall planting, in which case the plants should be covered with loose mulch, such as a layer of conifer branches.

tion may be hastened by scarifying the hard seed coat with a file or lightly cracking it with a rubber mallet.

Culture: peonies are slow-growing perennials, requiring several years after planting to reach their performance potential. Consequently, cultural mistakes such as planting too deeply will take a long time to show up and correct. All peonies have fleshy roots and develop best on heavy, fertile soil. This is especially true for the Chinese Peonies. They thrive in a medium-heavy, loamy humus soil which holds a little moisture even in dry periods. The subsoil must be

Paederota bonarota

Paeonia tenuifolia

knife into segments with at least 2–5 strong eyes and a good, undamaged tuberous root or two. Each undamaged eye should produce a vigorous shoot the following year, often with flower buds which should be removed to retain nourishment for the new root system. Root sections without eyes are generally worthless, since they will sprout late, if at all, though a few species and cultivars do regenerate from root division. Herbaceous peony clumps usually are lifted and divided in late summer; spring divisions usually take an extra year or two to become established.

The divisions will often fail to "take" due to planting too shallowly or deeply. The base of the eye (bud) should be

The species as well as many hybrids are also propagated by seed. Peonies have relatively large, thick-coated seeds amounting to only 2–5 seeds per gram. Peony seeds usually require 2 periods of cold stratification with a warm period in between, though many germinate with only a warm, then a cold stratification. They will usually germinate in the seed bed the second spring after sowing, therefore stratification of the seed is advisable, but requires close observation so that the seeds are sown as soon as they begin to germinate. With unstratified seed, beds should not be allowed to dry out during the summer between cold seasons as most seeds will produce roots (no shoots) in the first spring. Germina-

well drained; standing water, even in winter, is harmful. A moderately acid soil with a pH of 5 or 6 is suitable, but a circumneutral pH is optimal. In consideration of peonys' permanence, it is advisable to dig the bed to a depth of 2 spade lengths.

The best time for transplanting is early fall. New root growth is active from late summer into early winter. For cut flower production, plants are spaced at 90 × 50 cm or 90 × 40 cm. This spacing provides a continuous row with the plants supporting each other and not requiring staking. The flowers are cut while in bud.

How long can peonies be left in a given site, undisturbed? This depends on the fertility of the soil. In any case, they should be transplanted when it seems that they have surpassed their peak, producing only a few, small flowers. Also, the effective period depends upon the cultivar; rapidly growing cultivars may last 10–15 years on a favorable site, while the slower-growing cultivars will last longer. A peony field should be managed so that a new crop of peonies does not follow a previous crop on the same ground. A soil change or new site is highly advisable for a new planting. When transplanting older plants, divide them. Peonies respond to regular fertilizing, especially while developing in the years following planting, but in carefully measured amounts. Overfertilizing is worse than underfertilizing, especially on the slower-growing cultivars. It is a good practice to prepare the bed by incorporating composted manure 1 year prior to planting to help build the humus content of the soil. It is harmful, however to incorporate fresh manure during or after planting. Old, well-rotted, preferably cow, manure can be shallowly incorporated around older plants; keep composted manures several inches from the crown of the plant to avoid possible decay. In field situations, old manure may be spread between the rows in fall and then lightly incorporated in the following spring.

If using chemical fertilizers, proceed with extreme caution. Well-balanced premixed fertilizers not too high in nitrogen are suitable, but a better fertilizer mix is as follows:

1 part: commercial fertilizer, such as 10-6-4

1 part: superphosphate

2 parts: sulfate of potash

Apply this mix at the rate of 2 kilograms per 100 square meters, 60% just before the new growth in spring, and 40% right after blooming in summer. Bone meal or a similar low nitrogen, organic fertililzer may be incorporated into the soil in the fall.

Peonies require an open site in full sun for optimum growth. They tolerate some summer drought quite well; supplemental watering is seldom necessary. Water may be necessary if the dry period comes just before the flowering. In general, peonies are not troubled by pests and disease, although, if predisposed, they may be attacked by any of many potential problems. One of most common diseases is Botrytis blight (*Botrytis paeoniae*). The bud scales, flower stalk, leaves and leaf petioles become covered with an ash gray fungal coating, then blacken. The stems will fall over in a

short time. The cause is often cultural, such as an application of excessive nitrogen. To prevent excess damage to the stem, treat with a fungicide as soon as fungus appears. The application should be repeated every 5–10 days, particularly in rainy weather.

Peonies may also be attacked by several leaf spot fungi, including *Septoria paeoniae* West.; the symptoms are round, light brown, to 0.5cm spots with a purple, indistinctly bordered ring. The stem may also be covered with small, brown-red spots. Some other leaf spot fungi are *Cladosporium paeoniae* Pass.,

Paeonia peregrina hybrid

Cercospora paeoniae, Alternaria sp., and others. The best control is, of course, prevention by sanitation, starting with cleaning up all leaf and stem residue in the fall. In addition the appropriate fungicides may be applied periodically in the spring.

Other diseases occasionally found on peonies include Downy Mildew, Root Rot, Stem Rot and Verticillium Wilt. Most of these diseases can be prevented by clean cultural practices. For control measures, consult the appropriate, current literature.

Peonies are also affected by several virus diseases. Among these are Leaf Curl, Ringspot, Le Moine Disease and Crown Elongation. Plants infected with viruses should be destroyed, with a new location found for further peony plantings.

Among the insects attacking peonies are Japanese Beetles, Rose Leaf Beetle, Rose Chafer, Flower Thrips, Scales and both root and foliar Nematodes. Refer to

current literature for control methods and chemicals for these and other pests. While it may seem that peonies have many problems, it should be noted that problems rarely occur in a well-kept garden and in general are rarely serious.

Only a few *Paeonia* species and groups have been hybridized. The others are either difficult to cross or are of little horticultural importance. The most commonly encountered garden groups are listed here in the order of their approximate flowering time:

1. Wittmanniana Group

2. Officinalis Group
3. Anomala Group
4. Chinese Group (*Paeonia lactiflora* hybrids)

While the last-named group includes most of the garden cultivars, it flowers later than the others.

Species covered in this work:

1. The Wittmanniana Group

This group includes 3 species, all with light yellow flowers, limited to the S. Caucasus Mts. and neighboring regions. They are particularly valuable for early flowers.

P. macrophylla (Alboff) Lomak. (*P. wittmanniana* var. *macrophylla* (Albow) N. Bush ex Grossh.). Caucasus. With large, pallid leaves, 24cm long, 15cm wide, scented somewhat like boxwood. Buds yellow, opening to nearly white. Early spring. Ripe seeds are blue-black. Rarely offered in the trade. z5

P. mlokosewitschii Lomak. Found by the forester E. D. Mlokosiewicz near Lagodechi, a small town in the SE. Central Caucasus region. Stems to 70cm high. Leaves biternate, bluish green, venation and margin occasionally red. Petals usually 8, rounded, somewhat more yellow than those of *P. wittmanniana*, anthers yellow; mid-spring. Plants and seed offered in the trade under this name often are mislabeled. z5

P. tomentosa see **P. wittmanniana**

P. wittmanniana Hartwiss ex Lindl. (*P. tomentosa* Stapf). NW. Caucasus. Stems to 90cm high. The lower leaves are biternate, the upper leaves are once ternate; the leaflets are broad oval, acuminate. The flowers usually have 7 petals, yellow in bud, opening whitish yellow and fading nearly to white; the stamen filaments are red, the anthers orange-yellow; the flower stems always carry solitary flowers, the carpels are tomentose; May to June. z5

P. wittmanniana var. **macrophylla** see **P. macrophylla**

P. wittmanniana var. **nudicarpa** Schipcz. W. Caucasus. Flowers 9–11cm wide, cream-yellow, carpels glabrous. Grows best in light, rather dry, well-drained soil.

Around the turn of the century, Georg Arends (Wuppertal-Ronsdorf, Germany) and Lemoine (Nancy, France) crossed *P. wittmanniana* var. *nudicarpa* with *P. officinalis* ssp. *humilis* and *P. lactiflora*; the following cultivars resulted:

'Alpha', 'Avant Garde', 'Le Printemps', 'Mai Fleuri', 'Maikönigin' (May Queen), 'Messagerre'.

Because of their short flowering

Paeonia hybrid 'Chalice'

period, the cultivars of *P. wittmanniana* var. **nudicarpa** are of little garden merit, more suitable for collectors. 'Mai Fleuri' (*P. wittmanniana* var. *nudicarpa* × *P. lactiflora*), is a hybrid by Lemoine (1905) with light flesh pink flowers with a soft orange blush.

2. The Officinalis Group

This group includes the species variously hybridized to yield the most common garden peonies. The flowering period of this group overlaps that of the Anomala Group. The species of the Officinalis Group are indigenous to the Mediterranean basin and the neighboring countries.

P. cambessedesii (Willk.) Willk. Balearic Islands. Stems 40–50cm high. Stems and leaves glabrous, leathery, leaves biternate, dark green above with purplish veins, undersides deep purple. Flowers 6–10cm wide, deep pink; mid- to late spring. Unfortunately not very hardy, requiring good winter protection. z7

P. corallina see **P. mascula**

P. coriacea Boiss. S. Spain, Morocco. Stems 50–60cm high, reddish, entire plant glabrous. The leathery leaves are matte dark green above, gray-green beneath; the lower leaves biternate; leaflets oval, entire. Flowers bright carmine red, 7–15cm wide, stamens red, carpels 2–3, seeds dark purple-red; late spring. Requires a warm, protected site and a winter covering, emerges early and is then susceptible to damage by a late frost. z7

P. daurica Andr. (*P. triternata* Pall.). Yugoslavia, Rumania, Russia, Asia Minor. Stems glabrous, 40–60cm high, green or reddish. Lower leaves biternate, leathery, glabrous; leaflets with an undulate, somewhat upturned margin, sometimes pubescent, oblong-oval to orbicular. Flowers to 12cm wide, rose-red, stamens yellow, carpels 2–3, densely

tomentose; mid- to late spring. z5

P. decora see **P. peregrina**

P. humilis see **P. officinalis** ssp. **humilis**

P. lobata see **P. peregrina**

P. mascula (L.) Mill. (*P. corallina* Retz.). S. Europe, north to N. Central France and Austria, N. Africa, Caucasus. Carrotlike tuberous roots. Stems 70–90cm high. Leaves short petioled, usually with 9 lobes, leaflets broad, entire, pubescent-tomentose beneath. Flowers 9–14cm wide, purple, occasionally white; stamen filaments red, anthers yellow, carpels 3–5, densely pubescent; April to May. Cultivated since the Middle Ages in cloisters and convents. Very attractive, hardy and undemanding species. Unfortunately has short-lived flowers. z5

P. obovata Maxim. China, in mountain meadows. Tuberous roots cylindrical, elongated. Stems 40–60cm high; leaves biternate; leaflets membranous, softly pubescent beneath. Flowers rose to white; purple-red; stamen filaments white or pink, anthers yellow, carpels 2–3, stigmas recurved or coiled; late spring.

Only the white form 'Alba' and *P. obovata* var. **willmottiae** (Stapf) F. C. Stern, with densely pubescent leaf undersides and white flowers, somewhat difficult to cultivate, are found in culture. z5

P. officinalis L. was recently subdivided into the ssp. *officinalis* and ssp. *humilis* (Retz.) Cull. et Heyw.

P. officinalis ssp. **humilis** (Retz.) Cull. et Heyw. (*P. humilis* Retz., *P. peregrina* var. *humilis* (Retz.) Huth). SW. Europe. Stems to 50cm high, glabrous or pubescent. Lower leaves leathery, biternate; leaflets 30 or more, with numerous oblong to elliptic lobes, glabrous above, densely tomentose beneath, flowers red, anthers yellow, carpels 2–3, nearly glabrous; May to June. Very similar to *P. officinalis* ssp. *officinalis*, but with smaller sized leaf lobes, only 4–6cm and 1–2cm wide, those of *P. officinalis* ssp. *officinalis* 8–11cm long by 1.5–2.5cm. z5

P. officinalis ssp. **officinalis**. France to Hungary and Albania. Tubers oblong with long necks. Stems to 60cm high; leaves biternate, terminal leaflets deeply incised, glabrous above, underside somewhat whitish-pubescent. Flowers 9–13cm wide, red; stamen filaments red, anthers yellow, carpels 2–3, white-tomentose; seeds dark blue, glossy; mid- to late spring. z5

Some cultivars of the Officinalis Group are the common garden peonies:

'Alba Plena' double, only slightly pink at first, then white, rare, often confused with the more attractive 'Mutabilis'.

'Anemonaeflora Rosea', flowers simple, bright pink, only 30cm high. Tolerates light semi-shade.

'Carnea Plena' see 'Rosea Plena'

'China Rose', bright salmon pink, single flowers. To 1m high.

'Crimson Globe', single, bright carmine red flowers with a pleasant scent, about 60cm high.

'J.C. Weguelin', single, large-flowered, carmine red flowers, about 80cm high.

'Lobata', single flowers with salmon staminoides.

'Mollis', flowers single, deep dark pink; flowers rather early, about 50cm high.

'Mutabilis Plena', double, growth habit spreading, flowers flatter, light pink at first, later fading to nearly white, about 80cm high.

'Nemesis', bright vermilion carmine, petals finely cut.

'Purpurea Plena' see 'Rubra Plena'

'Rosea Plena', globose flower, bright pink, later lighter, 80cm high.

'Rosea Superba Plena', double, pure pink, brighter.

'Rubra Plena', globose flower, dark red, 80cm high.

P. peregrina Mill. (*P. decora* G. Anders., *P. lobata* Desf.). Italy, Balkan region, S. Rumania. Stems to 90cm high. Leaves glossy green above, biternate; leaflets crenate on the margin; with a finely pubescent line in the channels of the primary veins; somewhat resembles *P.*

Paeonia hybrid 'Burma Ruby'

anomala, but differing in the upright flowers. Flowers 7–11cm wide, deep carmine red, occasionally white ('Alba'); 2–3 carpels, pubescent; seeds dark red, glossy; late spring. The cultivars 'Otto Froebel', single-flowered, orange-salmon; 'Fire King' and 'Sunshine' are not substantially different from the species. Alexander Steffen has worked with *P. peregrina* and obtained various attractive selections. z6

P. peregrina var. **humilis** see **P. officinalis** ssp. **humilis**

P. triternata see **P. daurica**

3. The Anomala Group

Not important ornamentals in the garden. Other than a few cultivars of *P. tenuifolia*, such as 'Rosea' and 'Plena', and the species itself, the species of this group are rarely found in cultivation.

P. anomala L. E. Russia, Central Asia. Stem to 90cm high; with biternate leaves. Leaf form is intermediate between *P. officinalis* and *P. tenuifolia*. Flower diameter to 10cm, pink to purple-lilac, but somewhat variable in depth of color; flowers usually solitary on the stems and nodding, which makes these species less suitable for garden culture than *P. tenuifolia*, with flowers borne erect. z5

P. anomala var. **intermedia** (C.A. Mey.) Fedtsch. Kola Peninsula to W. Siberia and the Altai Mts. With narrower leaf lobes and smaller, light carmine flowers, and with tomentose carpels; very late. More commonly cultivated than the species. z5

P. emodi Wall. ex Royle. The Anomala type from the W. Himalayans, growing between 1500 and 3000m elevation between Kumaun (India) and Kashmir. With white, nodding flowers from 7–10cm wide, normally several on a stem. Carpels 1–2, tomentose. Leaf tips 2–4cm wide; late-flowering. Winter hardy only in very protected sites with a good winter covering. z8

P. tenuifolia L. SE. Europe, Asia Minor, Caucasus, in dry meadows. Roots tuberous, thick. Stems to 50cm high, unbranched. Leaves ternate, finely incised (fernlike), segment tips undivided, 1–2mm wide, decurrent. Flowers brick- to purple-red, petals 8–10, stamen filaments red, anthers yellow; carpels 2–3, brown-red shaggy pubescent; stigma red, coiled. Seeds dark brown, usually glossy; early to mid-spring. Cultivars include 'Latifolia', with the coarsest leaf divisions, carmine-red; 'Plena', a very old cultivar with dark red, double flowers, blooms after the single 'Rosea', which has soft pink flowers. 'Alba' is very rare. z5

P. veitchii Lynch. Was introduced into England in 1907 from W. China (Sichuan) by E.H. Wilson. Stems to 70cm high. Leaves glossy light green with about 15 lobes. Flowers reddish purple, 10cm diameter, nodding with several on a stalk; mid-spring. z6

P. veitchii var. **woodwardii** (Stapf et Cox) F.C. Stern. Small, only 30cm-high, pink variety from NW. China (Kansu) flowering for about 2 weeks. Species and variety require loamy soil and are choice plants for the collector. z6

Paeonia officinalis

4. The Chinese Paeonia Group

Over the last 100 years, this group has been the most important of all the peony groups for gardens. Hundreds of cultivars are listed, with new introductions every year.

P. albiflora see **P. lactiflora**

P. chinensis see **P. lactiflora**

P. lactiflora Pall. (*P. albiflora* Pall., *P. sinensis* or *P. chinensis* hort.). Garden Peony, Chinese Peony. E. Siberia, Manchuria, Korea, China, Tibet. Stems to 1m high;

Paeonia hybrid 'Maimorgen'

tuberous roots are long, thick and rubbery; brown. Leaves usually bi- to rarely 1-ternate. Leaflets short-stalked, borne laterally; lobes running together at the base, very finely denticulate, lanceolate to elliptic, red veined. Sepals large, foliaceous, petals 8 or more, large, white or pink, carpels 3–5, recurved-divergent with coiled or recurved stigmas, stamens golden yellow; June. z5

P. lactiflora var. trichocarpa (Bge.) F.C. Stern. Single flowers, carpels strongly pubescent.
This species was described in 1788 by Pallas as *P. albiflora* from the Amur region, after he had already named the plant *P. lactiflora* in 1776. Most garden cultivars are certainly not descended from the wild species, but rather from the Chinese garden types introduced into W. Europe in the early 19th century.

Several flower types can be distinguished among the Chinese Peonies:
  a) Single Peonies, with 8 petals in a single row.
  b) Japanese Peonies:
    aa) single flowers with one row of petals (stamens widened)
    bb) semi-double flowers (petals in multiple rows, stamens widened)
  c) Anemone-flowered Peonies. Petals in single or multiple rows; stamens modified and somewhat petaloid, more or less narrow with incised tips; petaloid stamens, however, not widening petal-like.
  d) Double Peonies. In the double-flowered cultivars, the stamens are fully petaloid. The carpels may appear unmodified, or in every stage from slightly to fully petaloid. In this case, the flower has a "cap" formed from the inner petals which is often variably colored.

This cap character is not constant. This flower type normally occurs only on fully developed plants in highly fertile sites. The actual petals (guard petals) are occasionally distinctly larger than the petaloid and are somewhat cupped.

The various cultivar forms can be further subdivided, since there are many intermediate flower forms between the above-mentioned flower types. The following flower categories have been developed in the USA:
  1. Single — single row of petals, many stamens
  2. Japanese — with wider, more conspicuous stamens
  3. Anemone — petals in one or more rows, stamens narrow-petaloid
  4. Semidouble — many stamens broad-petaloid

Chinese Peonies (*Paeonia*-Lactiflora-Cultivars)

Cultivar	Flower Color	Flowering Time (June)	Height (cm)
Double:			
'Avalanche'	White	middle-early	90
'Inspecteur Lavergne'	red	late	80
'La Perle'	soft pink	late	80
'Sarah Bernhardt' (C)	light pink	late	100
'Bunker Hill'	cherry red	middle	80
'Claire Dubois'	soft pink	late	90
'Felix Crousse'	carmine red	late	80
'Karl Rosenfield'	purple-red	middle	80
'Lady Alexandra Duff'	soft pink	middle	70
'Mme. de Verneville'	white	early	80
'Noemie Demay'	soft pink	early	80
'Reine Hortense'	soft salmon pink	middle-early	70
'Solange'	creamy white	late	80
'Solfatare'	yellowish white	early-middle	80
'Triomphe de l'Exposition de Lille'	silvery pink	late	70
'Wiesbaden'	light pink	early	70
'Duchesse de Nemours' (C)	white	early	70
'Festiva Maxima' (C)	white	early	80
'M. Jules Elie' (C)	rose-pink	early	80
'Adolphe Rousseau' (C)	dark red	early	100
'Le Cygne'	creamy-white	early	80
'M. Martin Cahuzac'	dark velvety red	middle	70
'Primevère'	white, yellowish	early	80
Simple:			
'Angelika Kauffmann'	white (trace of lilac)	middle	80
'Hogarth'	purple-red	early	100
'Holbein'	pink	middle	90
'King of England'	carmine red	middle	80
'Clairette'	white	early	80
'Murillo'	soft pink	middle	90
'Petite Renée'	silvery pink	early	90
'Rembrandt'	red	middle	80
'Schwindt'	carmine pink	early	90
'Surugu'	deep red, yellow center	early	90
'Torpilleur'	purple-red	early	90
'Watteau'	creamy-white	early	80

(C) = Especially good for cut flowers

5. Crown — stamens and carpels petaloid

6. Bomb — some stamens modified to narrow petals giving the flower center a pom-pom look.

7. Semi-rose — carpels fully petaloid, occasional anther-stamens show.

8. Double — stamens and carpels full petaloid, indistinguishable from normal petals

In addition to the cultivars listed in the table, the following also are noteworthy:

'Adolphe Rousseau', double, dark

Paeonia lactiflora 'Mons. Jules Elie'

red, early blooming, 80cm.

'Albert Crousse', light pink, double, dark red, late, 80cm.

'Alexander Steffen', single, dark pink, lightly crispate flowers, early, 1.2m.

'Alice Harding', creamy-white, double, middle early, 80cm; with unstable chromosome number and thus sometimes crossing with Tree Peonies.

'Antwerpen', carmine pink, single, large yellow anthers, 80cm.

'Balliol', single, dark red, 1m.

'Bandmaster', wine red, large single flowers, vigorous, late.

'Better Times', a strong carmine red, flat form, double, with visible yellow stamen filaments, middle late.

'Bowl of Beauty', *Fuschia* pink, single, early, 80cm.

'Burma Ruby', bright red, very early, 80cm, cup-shaped.

'Chalice', huge, cream-colored flowers, early, 1.2m.

'Chocolate Soldier', black-red, double with conspicuously visible yellow stamen filaments.

'Claire de Lune', yellow cup with somewhat darker petaloid center, fragrant, early.

'Couronne d'Or', ivory-white, double, late, 1m.

'Dresdener Pink', rose-pink, double, very sturdy, very late.

'Dürer', pure white, single, 80cm.

'Etienne Mechin', cherry red, double, early, 1m.

'Eugenie Verdier', soft salmon pink, double, late, 1m.

'Florence Nicholts', soft flesh-colored to white, double, middle late.

'F. Koppius', carmine red-violet, flat double, low.

'Fokker', carmine red-violet, flat double, low.

'Gertrud Allen', ivory-white cup form with banded, lemon yellow stamen filaments petaloid, and pink carpels, middle early.

'Gay Paree', cherry red, cup-shaped with flat, cream-colored petaloid centers, middle late, 70cm.

'General Betrand', red, double, middle late.

'Gene Wild', soft pink, loosely double, opening white with red stripes, midseason.

'Germaine Bigot', pink-red, double, low, late.

'Granat' (Garnet), bright garnet red, single, gold-yellow anthers.

'Guider', pink-red, double, low, late.

'Heimburg', cherry red, double, midseason, 1m.

'Highlight', dark, warm red, double, low.

'Hoffnung, pink-red, semidouble, very early, 80cm.

'Jean Claude Allard', cream-white, fragrant, large-flowered, late, 1m.

'John Howard Wigell', strong pink-red, double, midseason to late.

'Kansas', carmine red, double, fine form, midseason.

'Lady Anna', silky pink-red, double, large-flowered, midseason.

'La France', soft pink, carmine centers, 80cm.

'La Tulipe', soft flesh pink, double, midseason to late, good cut flower.

'Laura Dessert', cream-white, double, middle early, 1m.

'L'Etincelante', bright pink, single, middle early, 1m.

'Lottie Dawson Rea', soft pink, double, silvery at first; cut flower.

'Louis Barthelot', cream-white, double, very late, 1m.

'Lovell Thomas', dark carmine, semidouble, middle late.

'Ludovica', carmine salmon-pink, semidouble, with conspicuous gold-yellow stamen filaments, very early.

'Mme. Claude Tani', pure white, double, large-flowered, 1m.

'Mme. Ducel', lilac-pink with a silvery cast, double, early, 1m.

'Mme. Durufle', pure white, double, early, 1m.

'Mme. Eduard Doriat', pure white, late, 1m.

'Mme. Emile Debatène', salmon pink, double, rose type, middle late.

'Mme. Julie Berthier', purple-red, double, 1m.

'Mandaleen', silvery salmon pink, double, early to midseason.

'Marie Lemoine', ivory-white, double, late, 80cm.

'Marie Crousse', soft flesh-colored cups with cream-white petaloid centers, floriferous, midseason.

'Marxburg', dark amaranthine red, double, middle early, 1m.

'Margarete Klose', dark pink, double, early, 1m.

Pancratium illyricum

'Marquis C. Lagergren', cherry red with a violet cast, midseason.

'Miss Eckardt', pure pink, double, late, tall.

'Mlle. Lionie Calot', pink salmon double with a yellowish center, late, for cut flowers.

'Mobuchi', bright red, single, 1m.

'Modeste Guerin', carmine pink, rose-scented, early.

'Nick Shaylor', double, pink, yellowish- and salmon-toned, late.

'Philoméle', fresh pink cups with chamois-colored petaloid centers, fragrant, midseason.

'Pierra Dessert', dark red, double with visible stamen filaments, tall, sturdy.

'Pottsi Plena', amaranthine red, double, very early, 80cm.

'Red Charm', warm red, densely double bomb form, very early and low, long-persistent.

'Red Ensign', blood red, double with visible stamen filaments, floriferous, late.

'Reine des Français', lilac-pink cups with cream-colored petaloid centers, early to midseason, fragrant.

'Robert W. Auten', blackish-red, semidouble with yellow stamen filaments, early.

'Shirley Temple', soft pink, large flowered, double, middle late, 1m.

'Sister Margaret', ivory white double, particularly attractive form, late.

'Somo Ganoko', dark carmine, single, low, fragrant, middle late.

'The Mighty Mo', velvety dark red, double with visible stamen filaments, early.

'Thoma', lilac-pink, single, early.

'Tokio', rose-pink, single, 1m.

'Toro No Maki', attractive lilac-pink, single with yellow anthers.

'Ville de Nancy', wine red, double, low, midseason.

Panicum virgatum

'Walter Faxon', soft pink double, darker in the center, midseason.

'Wilbur Wright', chestnut brown, single, 1m.

This cultivar listing contains yellow- and lilac-hued flowers, colors that were once available only in the tree and shrub peonies.

Despite the flood of new cultivars, a large portion of the most valuable forms are old cultivars, some more than 100 years in cultivation. The fact that the first flowers on seedlings are generally not representative of the final flower form is important in hybridizing work. It takes several years before the flower form of a given seedling can be finally established. The enormous number of cultivars, particularly from the USA, can only be touched upon. There is, currently, much more breeding being done with peonies which should result in many more cultivars, possibly between heretofore uncrossed species. This

should further widen the scope of the available flower types and possibly require revision of the classification system.

Lit.: Stern, F.C.: *A Study of the Genus Paeonia.* London 1946. (L.J. & Kö.)

Pancratium L.
Amaryllidaceae
Sea Daffodil

Small genus with about 12 species ranging from India to Africa and the Mediterranean region to the Canary Islands. Summer-flowering plants with large bulbs and strap- to sword-shaped leaves in 2 opposing rows. The flat flower scape bears a terminal umbel of white flowers subtended by 1 or more bracts. The outer perianth segments are narrow and recurved, the inner ones connate; stamens united basally into a corona. Only 1 species is worth a trial in temperate gardens.

P. illyricum L. From the islands of the W. Mediterranean region. Leaves strap-shaped. Perianth segments (as opposed to those of *P. maritimum*) more that twice as long as the corona, flowers only 6–9cm wide, May. For warm bed near a wall, with good drainage and a loose covering of leaves and conifer branches in winter. Grow from seed sown in the greenhouse. z8 (S.)

Panicum L.
Gramineae
Switch-, Panic Grass

About 600 species of annual and perennial panicled grasses, many from warmer zones, which require some winter protection, at least for rough, exposed sites. Species from the prairies of North America are very hardy. The perennial species are quite decorative and develop well in warm sites and fertile soil. Well suited for separating flowering species or filling gaps in the

Papaver orientale 'Catharina'

perennial border, or for specimen use, as well as planting on a woodland margin. The loose panicles are good for cutting, very decorative in a vase. Propagation of selected clones is by division in spring with the onset of new growth; the species are also grown from seed.

P. clandestinum L., Deer Tongue Grass. N. America. Very wide-leaved, 1.2m-high clump grass, unfortunately not very sturdy, sometimes damaged by heavy wind or beating rain. Flowers brown, from July to August. z5

P. maximum Jacq., Guinea Grass. Ethiopea, naturalized on the limestone cliffs of Sicily and z8–9 USA. A vigorous, 2.5m-high clump grass with hairy nodes. Panicles to 50cm long, showy. Requires a warm, fertile soil for best development, winter protection is advisable. z7

P. virgatum L., Red Switch Grass. Central and E. North America, north to Nova Scotia and Ontario, a major tall grass prairie species. The most important perennial species for gardens, to 1.6m high. The panicle branchlets are long and the wide, loose panicles are very attractive cut flowers. Unfortunately, old species plants are often not very sturdy in cool summer areas, the flower stalks become weak, breaking over the weight of the flower panicles. The following cultivars are free of this problem:

'Hänse Herms' is a color improvement of the older 'Rehbraun' (Deer-, Red-brown). Grows to only 80cm high, and the red-brown late summer color comes early and strong. There are many possibilities for combining with late summer- and fall-blooming perennials.

classified variously which accounts for the number difference. Primarily from the Old World, especially Central and S. Europe as well as temperate Asia, only a few indigenous to W. North America. Low-growing to medium-high, with milky sap (latex) -producing plants with lobed or compound leaves and nodding flower buds. The perennial poppies, especially the species *P. nudicaule* and *P. orientale*, are exceptionally valuable for the brilliant color they provide to the garden, also prized for cut flowers. *P. nudicaule* is an especially important cut flower that can be somewhat forced in a

Plants may be damaged by feeding mice. The low-growing species will usually die out after 2–3 years, but often are replaced by self-seeding.

P. alpinum see **P. burseri, P. kerneri, P. rhaeticum** and **P. sendtneri**

P. anomalum Fedde. Central China. Resembles the widely used *P. nudicaule*, but more vigorous, 30–40cm high. Leaves all basal, about 10cm long, bipinnatisect, bluish, nearly glabrous. Flowers yellow and white, 3–4cm across, capsules globose, fully glabrous; late

Papaver alpinum ssp. *kerneri*

Papaver orientale 'Feuerriese'

'Rehbraun' is a 1.2m-high cultivar for use in a sunny, open site. For optimal development, the soil should not be too dry, although plants are drought tolerant.

'Rubrum' appears to be less attractive and is probably a form of 'Strictum', a 1.6m-high cultivar, recognized by the short panicle branchlets. The cultivars are better garden plants than the species and valuable for their drought tolerance. The attractive, light brown fall color is a bonus for garden use. z5 (S.)

Papaver L.
Papaveraceae
Poppy

Fifty to 100 variable and form-rich species of annual and perennial herbs,

cold frame or near a warm wall. The flowers must be cut in the bud stage as soon as they show color.

The taller species are suitable for the sunny border in well-drained, deep topsoil; the low-growing species are better suited for the rock garden and the alpine garden. *P. alpinum* requires a more gravelly, limestone soil; all need a sunny site.

Propagation usually is by seed; the tall species, *P. orientale*, may also be propagated by root cuttings after blooming or in winter. Poppies generally transplant poorly; therefore, they are best raised in containers. *P. orientale* and *P. bracteatum* die back after flowering and may then be moved bare root, or also in spring just before new growth emerges. Transplanting sets back the plants to recover from root damage; they usually flower the second year.

spring. z6

P. atlanticum (Ball.) Coss. Morocco. About 40cm high, with nearly woody, thick rhizomes. Leaves not basal, silky-hairy, pinnatisect, lanceolate. Flowers dark orange-red, 5–7cm wide; early summer. z6

P. bracteatum Lindl. Caucasus, Iraq. To 1m high, similar to *P. orientale* and usually listed as such or a variety thereof, flowers somewhat earlier. Flowers subtended by bracts, blood red, not scarlet red, with large black spots on the base. Capsule oblong-globose; early summer. z5

P. burseri Crantz (*P. alpinum* L. ssp. *alpinum* sensu Markgr. non L.), Alpine Poppy. N. Alps, N. Carpathians, between 1900 and 2500m, usually on limestone.

With multipinnately partite, narrow-lobed, basal, blue-green leaves, and a leafless, single-flowered stem to 15cm high, capsule oblong; summer. Flowers white with yellowish undertones. z4

P. kerneri Hayek (*P. alpinum* ssp. *kerneri* (Hayek) Fedde). SE. Alps, Central Yugoslavia, Siebengebirge. Related closely to *P. burseri*, and quite similar. Flowers golden yellow, also orange-yellow, somewhat larger than those of *P. burseri*. Capsule broadly top-shaped. z5

P. nudicaule L., Iceland Poppy. Arctic

unusually large flowered with stout, long scapes, grown especially for cutting flowers. All cultivars are cultivated only as biennials and usually die out during the winter after flowering. z4

P. orientale L., Turkish Poppy. Orient. Plants very hairy overall 1–1.5m high with deep-growing, brittle, pencil-thick or thicker roots and pinnately lobed or dissected leaves, single-flowered stems with white, bicolor, pink-, lavender-, scarlet-, blood-, vermilion- or brick-red flowers with a black patch at the base of each petal; early summer. Plants go

'Catharina' (Zeppelin 1970), 80cm, good salmon pink, very large-flowered.
'Derwisch' (Dervish) (Zeppelin 1976), 70cm, salmon-red with small black basal patches, late and long persistent.
'Feuerriese' (Fire-giant) (Foerster), 80cm, brick red, stiff scapes.
'Karine' (Zeppelin 1976), 60cm, pure light pink with red basal spots, only moderately large, open bowl-shape; very undemanding.
'Marcus Perry' (Perry 1942), 50cm, orange-scarlet.
'Mary Finan' (Finan), 80cm, scarlet-

Papaver nudicaule

Papaver alpinum ssp. *sendtneri*

and subarctic regions of Asia and N. America, south to the Colorado Rocky Mts. Scape to 40cm high. Leaves rosetted, basal, velvety, petiolate, pinnatisect, somewhat bluish green, not as finely divided as *P. alpinum*. Scape wiry, leafless, single-flowered. Flowers of the typical species yellow, fragrant; April to fall. The species is quite variable, with several botanical varieties. z1

P. nudicaule var. **croceum** Ledeb. Central Asia. Leaves less divided, more pubescent; flowers orange. May be a parent of the old 'Miniatum' cultivars, such as 'Album', pure white; 'Golden Wonder', large-flowered, gold-yellow, 40cm; 'Kardinal', cardinal red, 40cm. Only the several-colored cultivars are commonly found in modern cultivation; 'Matador' (Benary), 50cm, large-flowered, scarlet, in color combinations, and 'Gartenzwerg' (Garden Dwarf) (Benary), 20–30cm, large flowers on firm, straight scapes, in many colors; excellent for rock gardens and terrace beds, also for cutting; 'San Remo',

dormant after flowering. Divide or transplant only in midsummer to early fall. Overwinters with young leaves. Propagate by root cuttings from summer to winter; pot these quickly after rooting. Often crossed with *P. bracteatum*, giving rise to many valuable cultivars.

Many cultivars came into the trade in the early decades of this century, unfortunately, few of these are still grown today. Several new cultivars have been introduced by American breeders. Most of these are larger flowered and stronger stemmed, with flowers of more substance in fresh colors.

The following cultivars are a sample of currently cultivated Oriental Poppies:
'Aladin' (Zeppelin 1981), 80cm, bright red, very large-flowered.
'Ali Baba' (Zeppelin 1976), 80cm, firetruck red with small black basal spots, large-flowered, slightly undulate margins.
'Beauty of Livermere', 1m tall, deep red, very early; direct progeny from *P. bracteatum*, comes true from seed.

red, petals very fringed.
'Rosenpokal' (Rose Cup) (Foerster 1952), 1m, salmon pink, very pleasant color, floriferous and vigorous.
'Sindbad' (Zeppelin 1975), 1.1m, bright red, early.
'Sturmfackel' (Battletorch) (Goos & Koenemann), 50cm, fiery red, firm scapes.

P. pilosum Sibth. et Sm. Bithynian Olympus Mts. 0.8–1m. Flower stems branched, leafy, densely hairy. Leaves oblong, crenate-margined. Flowers in corymbose panicles, tile red; early summer. z6

P. pyrenaicum see **P. rhaeticum** and **P. sendtneri**

P. radicatum Rottb. NW. Europe, N. Asia, N. America. Scapes 10–20cm high, small, rosetted-bushy, entire plant densely pubescent. Leaves pinnately lobed or divided, with obtuse segments. Flowers sulfur yellow; late spring. Requires a lime-free gravel soil. z3

P. rhaeticum Leresche (*P. alpinum* ssp. *rhaeticum* (Leresche) Nym., *P. pyrenaicum* ssp. *rhaeticum* (Leresche) Fedde). E. Pyrenees, SW. and E. Alps. Plants tuft-like, nearly stemless, to rarely 20cm high. Leaves 1-pinnate, greenish, softly pubescent. Flowers golden yellow, fading to orange-yellow; spring. Requires a lime-free soil. z4

P. sendtneri Kerner ex Hayek (*P. alpinum* ssp. *sendtneri* (Kerner ex Hayek) Schinz et Keller, *P. pyrenaicum* ssp. *sendtneri* (Kerner ex Hayek) Fedde). Central and E. Alps, on limestone. Resembles the previous species; flowers white, inside greenish yellow at the base; spring. z4 (L.J. & M.)

Paradisea Mazzuc.
Liliaceae
Paradise-, St. Bruno's Lily

Two species in Europe (the report of a Tibetan species is erroneous and refers to an invalid synonym of *Notholirion thompsonianum*). Similar to the genus *Anthericum*, but scape bracted, with racemose inflorescences, flowers campanulate, corolla lobes appearing to form a tube at first then diverging, with a claw, style and anthers curved, the anthers attached dorsally. Glabrous perennials with short rhizomes with clustered, fleshy roots, and linear basal leaves. Perianth segments 6, separate, stamens 6, anthers versatile. Fruit a 3-sided capsule. Flowers in late spring or early summer. Grow in well-drained, fertile soil in a sunny site. The fleshy roots are sensitive to wetness. Suitable for borders, rock gardens and cut flowers. Propagate by seed.

Paradisea liliastrum

P. liliastrum (L.) Bertol. Pyrenees, Alps, Jura Mts. and N. and Central Apennines, in mountain meadows. Scape 30–50cm high. Leaves 12–25cm long, flat. Racemes loose, one-sided, with 4–10 (occasionally 20) somewhat fragrant flowers. Petals 30–50mm long, pure white. Capsule 1.5cm-long, elliptic-triangular, with many, black, triangular seeds. 'Major' (apparently little different from the species), 'Gigantea' (supposedly infertile), 'Flore Pleno' and × *Antherisia arethusae* Wehrh. (a bigeneric hybrid with *Anthericum liliago*), are no longer in the trade and probably no longer in culture. (K.)

P. lusitanica (Coutinho) Samp. Mountains of N. Portugal and W. Central Spain. Similar to *P. liliastrum*, but the petals only 20–25mm long, racemes not one-sided. More vigorous in habit, but emerges earlier and is somewhat more sensitive to winter wetness. Very ornamental species. z7 (K.)

Papaver orientale 'Rosenpokal'

Pardanthus

P. chinensis see **Belamcanda chinensis**

Paris L.
Liliaceae

Twenty species in Europe and temperate Asia. Perennial herbs with 4 or more subterminal, net-veined leaves in false whorls and solitary, terminal, 4-merous flowers. Grown mostly by collectors and botanic gardens. A unique plant, not

Paris quadrifolia

easily cultivated but suitable for naturalizing in open deciduous or mixed woodlands in moist, humus-rich soil. Unusual in that occasionally the above ground plant parts may not appear for an entire year although the rhizome persists underground. Plants live with a mycorrhizal root fungus in a loose humus woodland soil. Propagate by careful division of the rhizome or by seed, preferably in soil from the collection site to supply mycorrhizal innoculum. Seedlings take several years to mature. Differs from *Trillium* in its 4-merous flowers.

P. quadrifolia L. Europe, N. Mediterranean region, Asia Minor, Siberia, Altai Mts., in mixed woodlands, occasionally coniferous forests, with wetland vegetation in moist to wet, heavy humus loam with a leafmold cover. Grows to nearly 2000m elevation in the Alps. Stem upright, 10–40cm high, terminating in a whorl of 4 (rarely more or fewer) sessile, elliptical to ovate, net-veined leaves. Flower pediceled, solitary, sepals 4 (rarely more or fewer) petals 4 (rarely more or fewer), greenish yellow, inconspicuous, emerging from the center of the foliage whorl. Blue-black berries follow later. Flowers and berries are poisonous. Blooms in early summer. z5 (E.)

Parnassia L.
Saxifragaceae
Grass-of-Parnassus

Fifteen to 44 species, depending on taxonomic classification, from the cooler regions of the Northern Hemisphere. Suitable plants for streamsides and pool banks in moist soil, tolerates semi-shade; mostly for the collector. Basal leaves in a tuft, long petioled, blade often more or less cordate, entire; scape with 1 sessile leaf and a solitary terminal flower; calyx with short tube and 5 lobes, petals 5,

Parnassia palustris

often with green veins, stamens 5, ovary superior, stigmas 4. Species distinctions often based on the presence, number, and form of staminoides inserted among the stamens. Propagate by division and seed. All require moist soil preferably in a semi-shaded woodland site.

P. fimbriata Koenig. North America, Alaska south to Colorado and California, somewhat larger than *P. palustris*, Plant to 30cm high; leaf blades reniform or broadly cordate; the white petals are fringed on the sides. Very serviceable plant. z3

P. foliosa Hook. f. et Thoms. Japan, N. India and China. Plant to 30cm high. Stems sharply 4-angled, of varied length, stem leaf sessile, broadly cordate, lobed. Petals fringed at the base. z5

P. nubicola Wall. Himalaya Mts. Plants 15–30cm high. Leaves long petioled, elliptic, matte green, 5–10cm long. Stems nearly winged. Flowers white, usually with 3 staminodes; late summer. Less temperamental in culture than the following species. z4

P. palustris L. Europe, North America, Asia, on flat moors, lowland meadows, and moist and dry pastures. Plant 10–20cm high; with long-petioled, cordate, basal leaves, and white, attractive, solitary flowers with elaborate staminoides; July to September. Several botanical varieties are listed, all worth growing. z5

P. parviflora DC. North America, S. Canada south to Idaho, Montana and Minnesota. Resembles *P. palustris*, but the flowers are somewhat smaller, petals greenish or purple veined. z3 (L.J. & Kö.)

In addition, worth growing, especially in gardens within the species' natural range, are *P. asarifolia* Venten., SE. and S. Central US.; *P. glauca* Raf., NE. and N. Central US. south to Virginia; *P. grandiflora* DC., S. US. west to Mississippi Valley. All are more or less similar in overall appearance, valuable for summer flowers in the water garden.

rooted pieces of stem in the fall and keep them in a bright, frost-free place until spring when they are replanted into the garden. Also suitable for a large alpine house, but only if kept at or above freezing. Propagation is best by division or by seeding if fertile seed can be obtained.

P. communis Buch.-Ham. ex D. Don. Mountains of cooler tropical Asia (in the Himalaya Mts. between 1300 and 4300m) and E. Africa (Mozambique). Plant 5–10cm high, perennial, quickly covering large areas with wide-creeping

soil; slow growing, but persistent. Propagate by division and cuttings.

P. argentea Lam. Mediterranean region. Plants procumbent, rarely to 30cm high, matted. Leaves lanceolate to elliptic, prickly tipped, to 6mm long, silvery gray-green. Flowers in dense clusters under the leaves, silvery bracts large; June to September. z7

P. capitata (L.) Lam. Pyrenees. Caespitose, to 15cm high. Leaves narrowly oblong-lanceolate, acute, pubescent, gray-green. April to June. z5

Parochetus communis

Paronychia kapela ssp. *serpyllifolia*

Parochetus Buch.-Ham. ex D. Don.
Leguminosae
Blue-oxalis, Shamrock-pea

One species in cooler tropical Asia and E. Africa. With alternate trifoliate leaves. Differs from the closely related genus *Trifolium* in that the corolla abscises after blooming.

Flowers axillary, papilionaceous with 10 stamens, 9 connate and 1 distinct.

A good plant for collectors and botanic gardens with its large, gentian blue flowers. Plant with slender, trailing stems in a dense carpet, but unfortunately not reliably winter hardy. Suitable for the edges of the rock garden or rock bed where, if planted in spring, it will cover large areas by summer with its cloverlike foliage. Thrives in a sunny or semi-shaded, somewhat moist site on a well-drained, humus-loam soil. The safest overwintering method is to pot up

stems, rooting at the nodes. Leaves ternate, cloverlike, green, leaflets brownish only at the base. Flowers solitary, 12–18mm wide, gentian blue, sometimes hidden by the foliage. Blooms from early summer through fall. z8(7) (E.)

Paronychia Mill.
Caryophyllaceae
Whitlow-wort

Forty to 45 species of herbaceous annuals and perennials, often difficult to distinguish, in the temperate and warmer regions of the world. Tufted or carpet-forming plants distinguished from *Herniaria* in the dehiscent fruit capsules and the large, membranous, glossy stipules. Flowers minute, often hidden; plants grown mostly for their foliage. Useful as a ground cover over slopes and rocks or for separating low perennials. Grow in a sunny site in a well drained

P. kapela (Hacq.) Kerner. Mediterranean region., on rocks. Plant matted, 5–10cm high. Leaves bluish green, crowded, ciliate, 4mm long, 2mm wide; to 2cm wide; flower clusters both above the foliage, bracts silvery. May to June. z7

Several natural varieties, useful in the rock garden, are described, including:

P. kapela ssp. **serpyllifolia** (Chaix) Graebn. Spain, Maritime Alps, Apennines. Procumbent, matted. Leaves dark green, rounded, densely appressed, crowded, in 2 ranks, red-brown fall color; blooms June to July. z7 (L.J.)

North American paronychias are not in the trade but are grown by some New World rock garden enthusiasts; most are green-leaved rather than silvery (as the Mediterranean spp.), including: **P. argyrocoma**, (Michx.) Nutt. Allegheny Nailwort, Silverling. E. US. Mts., Maine to Georgia. Tufted, 20–30cm high, silky-hairy; flower bracts awned. **P. sessili-folia** Nutt. Rocky Mts., Canada to New Mexico. Caespitose mats to 20cm wide, 2–12cm high, foliage yellow-green, leaves very crowded; bracts brownish-amber, awned. **P. virginica** K. Spreng. Midsouth west to Oklahoma and Texas. Tufted, bushy, to 42cm high, glabrous; leaves large, to 3cm long, subulate, flowers in branching terminal cymes. All z6 or hardier.

Passiflora caerulea

Parthenium L.
Compositae

Sixteen species of aromatic annuals, perennials and shrubs in North America and the W. Indies: too coarse to be ornamental but important in prairie restorations and habitat restorations; refer to American taxonomic textbooks.

Parrya

P. menziesii see **Phoenicaulis cheiranthoides**

Passiflora L.
Passifloraceae
Passion-flower

About 400–500 species of climbing, mostly woody plants with axillary tendrils, mostly from the Americas, some from Asia and one in Madagascar. Climbing plants often with attractive and colorful flowers in the leaf axils. Leaves alternate, entire or lobed, blade often attractively marked silver or brownish, margins entire; flowers solitary or few in racemes, of regular but complex struc-

Patrinia triloba

ture and subtended by green bracts; 5 sepals and 5 petals all united basally to form an elaborate corona with several rings of fringed or tube-like structures, and with a central membrane (operculum) within the corona; stamens 5–10, filaments united only basally, inserting on the elongate column bearing the pistil with 3 massive stigma lobes. Three species are winter hardy in moderately cold areas with a winter cover of conifer branches and leaves sufficiently thick so frost does not penetrate the soil. Suitable for climbing on lattice work and fences, and especially for a warm sunny house wall. The woody shoots of *P. caerulea* will freeze back nearly to soil level, but will bud in spring low on the stem. *P. incarnata* and *P. lutea* are herbaceous perennials dying completely back to the ground in winter. All thrive in any good, fertile garden soil and will respond

favorably to an additional fertilizing in spring and early summer. Propagate by herbaceous cuttings in a hothouse or by seed.

P. caerulea L., Blue Passion-flower. Southern Brazil, Paraguay, Argentina, naturalized in many parts of the tropics and subtropics. A semiwoody climber, stem angled or channeled; leaves broadly cordate, deeply 5–9 lobed; flowers 7–9cm wide, white or pinkish flowers with 4 rings of corona filaments, filaments purple at the base, white in the middle, and blue-tipped; styles purple. Flowers from summer to fall. Cultivars are listed, including the all white-flowered 'Constance Elliott'. z7

P. incarnata L. Maypop, Wild Passion-flower. USA: Maryland to Missouri and Oklahoma, south to Florida and Texas; Bermuda Islands. Grows on dry soil, easily becoming weedy. Stoloniferous; cylindrical climbing stems to 10m high, herbaceous; leaves deeply 3 lobed, 8–15cm long, sometimes sparsely short-haired above. Flowers 3–8cm wide, flat, solitary, in the leaf axils; lavender, purple, pink, or white corona with 2-rings of twisted filaments, each banded purplish at the base, white in the middle, purplish or pink at the tip, as long as the petals. Blooms from June to September. Plant populations vary greatly in the wild; some with rich purple flowers are found in W. Arkansas and E. Oklahoma while completely white-flowered variants occur in SW. Missouri. z6(5) (E.)

P. lutea L. Yellow Passionflower. USA: Pennsylvania and Florida west to E. Kansas and E. Texas, in open deciduous woodlands on acid soil. Herbaceous stems 2–3m long, very slender, cylindrical, glaucous; leaves 3-lobed, wider than long, often beautifully marked with a silvery pattern; pedicels without bracts, flowers 1–1.75cm across, mostly greenish-yellow but minute petals whitish and corona sometimes pinkish at the base; fruits very small, blue-black. z5

Patrinia Juss.
Valerianaceae

Fifteen to 20 species of rhizomatous or stoloniferous, often erect-growing perennials, from Central Asia and the Himalaya Mts. to E. Asia. Similar to *Valeriana*. Stems from 0.2–1m high with more or less undivided basal leaves and opposite, simple or bipinnate stem leaves. The paniclelike cymes are branched; flowers yellow, occasionally white; calyx 5-toothed, corolla 5-lobed, sometimes with 1 spur, with 4 stamens, ovary inferior with 3-locules. Taller species for the perennial border, low-growing sorts for the sunny rock garden; all of modest ornamental value. *P. gibbosa* and the more commonly offered *P. triloba* thrive well in semi-shaded areas of the rock garden or rock bed; i.e. on the north side of a large rock. *P. scabiosifolia*, unfortunately rarely offered, requires a sunny, dry site in the wildflower garden. All species thrive on loamy humus soil and are easily propagated by division in spring, or by seed.

P. gibbosa Maxim. Mountains of Japan. With 50–70cm high stems and broadly ovate to ovate-elliptic, 7–15cm long, pinnatisect, serrate, long-petioled leaves. Flowers in cymes to 10cm across, yellow, 4–5mm wide, with a 1mm-long spur at the base of the corolla tube. Blooms early to midsummer. z5

P. palmata see *P. triloba*

P. scabiosifolia Fisch. Japan, Kuril Islands, Sachalin, Ryukyu Island, Taiwan, Korea, China, Manchuria, E. Siberia, in sunny, grassy areas on hills and mountains. Stems 0.6–1m high, with sessile or short-petioled, pinnately cleft, coarsely toothed leaves. Basal leaves ovate or oblong, deeply toothed, pubescent. Flowers yellow, 3–4mm wide, not spurred at the base of the tube, in many-flowered cymes. Blooms early to midsummer. z7–6

P. triloba Miq. (*P. palmata* Maxim.). Mountains of Japan. Stems nearly simple (unbranched), reddish, 20–60cm high. Leaves mostly basal, petioled, 3–5-palmately lobed to parted, serrate to irregularly toothed. Corolla yellow, fragrant, 7–8mm wide, tube with a 2.5–3mm long spur at the base. Blooms early to midsummer. The species, nearly unavailable in the trade today, is valuable in the rock garden, flowering well after most other plants are finished. z5 (E.)

Several other species appear in horticultural literature but not in the trade.

Paxistima Raf.
(*Pachistima* auct.)
Celastraceae

Two species of small evergreen shrubs with opposite, simple, leathery leaves set closely on slender twiggy branches. Flowers nearly insignificant, reddish-brown, solitary or in axillary cymes; complete, 4-merous. Fruit a capsule.

P. canbyi A. Gray. Cliff-green, Mountain-lover. E. North USA., Virginia, W. Virginia. A small, stoloniferous evergreen, woody shrub with decumbent to ascending branches, and with very narrow, dense-growing leaves and numerous, small, reddish flowers in mid-spring. The persistent dwarf shrub gradually grows to 30cm high, spreading indefinitely, and is reasonably adaptable. Tolerates not only shady and sunny sites, but both acidic and barely alkaline soils, but not intense summer heat or drought. After 2 years in the garden *Paxistima* forms a small, dense colony with its short stolons. Recommended for the foreground for its neat appearance year-round with little care. A good plant for placing among more tender species to help provide winter protection, as among shrub roses. Propagation is best by cuttings; division or stooling of older plants is also possible. For container culture, provide at least a 9cm-wide pot. z5 (S.)

The other species, *P. myrsinites*, Oregon Boxwood is woodier, not a perennial-like species.

Pedicularis L.
Scrophulariaceae
Lowsewort, Wood Betony

More than 350 species, all but 1 in the Northern Hemisphere and most in the New World. Attractive annuals, biennials and perennials, but not in the trade (although rock garden specialists are beginning to grow them), and not included in this text by the original author, possibly because many (most?) are parasitic and therefore difficult in the average garden. For species lists and descriptions refer to encyclopedia works, especially North American but also British Ed.

Pelargonium L'Hérit. ex Ait.
Geraniaceae

About 280 species of herbs and shrubs, most from S. Africa. Related to *Geranium* and *Erodium*, but differing in the twice-forked umbellate inflorescences and other morphological characteristics.

The following species is reasonably winter hardy, but more suitable for the alpine house or for pot culture in an alpine case where it can be kept in a dry atmosphere. Only the experienced gardener need bother with cultivation of this unique and attractive plant. Plants in the garden require a sunny, warm wall or rock crevice in a southern exposure, best under an overhanging rock ledge. Protecting from winter wetness by covering with a cloche is essential. In cooler winters also cover lightly with conifer branches. However, cold damage is less likely than damage from winter wet. Grow in well-drained loam mixed with tufa stone grit. Propagate by cuttings and seed.

P. endlicherianum Fenzl. S. Asia Minor, Armenia, N. Syria, on limestone rocky sites in the mountains. Stems short, thick, fleshy, rarely branched above, mostly crenate, basal leaves, petioled, rounded, covered with whitish appressed hairs. Flowering scapes 5–15cm or more long. Flowers deep pink, dark carmine veined in 4–10 flowered umbels. The 2 upper petals are conspicuously large. Blooms from June to July. z7 (E.)

Pellaea Link
Polypodieceae
Cliff Brake

About 80 small, xerophytic fern species growing on cliff walls. Primarily from the dry zones of S. America, S. Africa, New Zealand, north to Canada. Only 1 species common in garden cultivation, but in the W. USA. gardeners collect and grow 4–5 additional more or less hardy species, and in mild USA. areas several more subtropical species are found in gardens.

Pelargonium endlicherianum

P. atropurpurea (L.) Link., Cliff Brake. North America, on stone ledges and cliffsides. Stipe purple, glossy, 10–25cm long. Rachis similarly colored, floccose. Fronds hastate or oval-lanceolate 1–2-bipinnate. Pinnae widely separated, opposite, entire, often auricled at the base, glabrous above and gray-green, somewhat pruinose, 4–5cm long, 6mm wide. Sorus lines broad. Attractive, lime-loving small gray-green fern. Only for warm, dry, sunny sites in the garden, also for the alpine house where it easily spreads by spores. Spores ripen nearly year round indoors. z4 (D.)

Peltandra Raf.
Araceae
Arrow Arum

Three species, all from North America. Swamp plants to 90cm high, with stout, slow-creeping rhizomes and hastate leaves. Flowers unisexual, with no perianth, the staminate flowers toward the top of the slendered club-shaped spadix which is not exserted beyond the spathe. Spring to early summer. Fruits 1–3 seeded, leathery berries.

Suitable for bogs and swamps, shallow pools and slow-moving streams, but should be easily accessible so that winter protection can be provided. Rare and considered to be demanding in cultivation in Europe, but easily grown in warm summer regions of the US. Propagate by division of the rhizomes and by removal of the secondary shoots in spring, or plant seeds in moist loam under glass.

P. alba see **P. sagittifolia**

P. sagittifolia (Michx.) Morong (*P. alba* Raf.). White Arrow Arum. USA: N. Carolina southward, in swampy lowlands. Rootstock fleshy rhizomatous. Leaves sagittate. Spathe white, but not widening *Calla*-like at the apex, May to June. Fruit single seeded, red. More tender than the following species, which occurs further north. z8(7)

Pellaea atropurpurea

P. undulata see **P. virginica**

P. virginica (L.) Schott et Endl. (*P. undulata* Raf.). Arrowleaf, Tuckahoe. USA., Main to Florida west to Missouri and Texas. Fibrous, tough rhizome. Leaf petiole long, lower ⅓ sheathlike, leaves large, glossy sagittate-acuminate. Spathe slender, green, May to June. Fruits green, 1–3 seeded. z5–9 (D.)

Peltiphyllum Engl.
Saxifragaceae

A monospecific genus.

P. peltatum (Torr. ex Benth.) Engl. (*Saxifraga peltata* Torr. ex Benth.) (*Darmera peltata* (Torr. ex Benth.) Voss) Umbrella Plant. SW. Oregon to Mts. of N. California. A groundcovering perennial with flower stems 1–2m high. Rhizomes horizontal, fleshy, covered with wide, rounded scales. Leaves long-petioled, to 90cm, blades peltate, 30cm, occasionally to 60cm in diameter, with conspicuous venation, deeply 10–15 lobed, coarse-serrate, dark green, with an attractive coppery fall color. Flowers appear before the leaves, the stem leafless, rough-haired. Inflorescence a many-flowered cyme, pink, April to May.

Unpretentious but very bold, easily cultivated perennial for moist or normal garden sites. For specimen use or grouped with ornamental grasses (*Miscanthus* and *Spartina*), *Iris sibirica* or also with similar, large perennials like *Rheum* and *Heracleum*. Cultivated beside ponds and streams in full sun to semishade. Best protected from a late frost. Propagate by division in spring, or seed. Very decorative, somewhat sensitive to frost damage on the flowers, otherwise hardy. z5 (D)

Pennisetum japonicum

Peltiphyllum peltatum

Peltoboykinia

P. tellimoides see **Boykinia tellimoides**

Pennisetum L.C. Rich.
Gramineae
Fountain Grass

About 80 annual and perennial grasses from tropical regions. Some are not winter hardy and are treated as garden annuals. The cylindrical, loose, feathery inflorescence of this genus resembles

Penstemon newberryi

soft bottle-brush. The spikelets or clusters of spikelets are surrounded by bristly modified bracts and insert closely on the main axis. In cultivation, thrives in a warm, light and sufficiently moist site. Propagation is usually by division, although seed is better for *P. orientale*.

P. alopecuroides (L.) Spreng. (*P. compressum* R. Br., *P. japonicum* Trin., *P. purpurascens* (Thunb.) O. Kuntze non H.B.K.). Chinese Pennisetum. Unfortunately, the botanists have lumped together this widely distributed and variable species from E. Asia and Australia. Plants under the name *P. japonicum* Trin. seem to be less hardy and shorter lived. The long, cylindrical inflorescences with a white tuft at the

top, above upright foliage tufts, are produced only in climates with long, warm summers. This stately, 1m-high species is, therefore, highly prized in warmer climates.

Plants introduced as *P. compressum* R. Br., Australian Fountain Grass, are hardier, more persistent and flower in shorter, cooler summers. This strain should, therefore, be listed as *P. compressum* in the catalogues of nurseries in the cooler climates. The fluffy, brownish, often somewhat rosy-panicled spikes are up to 25cm long and appear in early September. They are very effective on the 80cm-high clumps until winter. The compact, bushy plants are good companions to fall-blooming perennials. In close competition with other plants, pennisetums will require additional water and fertilizer. For vigorous flower production, divide dense clumps and move them to a freshly prepared soil every few years. The panicles are especially attractive in the morning dew. Also suitable for cut flowers. 'Hameln' is the best cultivar to date. Comes into bloom weeks earlier with attractively harmonious panicles and foliage, somewhat lower than the species at 60cm. Vegetative propagation is preferable for both the cultivars and the species. z6

P. compressum see **P. alopecuroides**

P. flaccidum see **P. incomptum**

P. incomptum Nees (*P. flaccidum* Griseb.). NE. China to the Himalaya Mts. Dense, stoloniferous grass to 1.5m high. The narrow, spiked inflorescences appear after July, red-violet toned at first, then straw colored. This grass is for large, open areas on a woodland margin, slopes or open spaces where it can form large colonies. The panicles are suitable for cutting. z6

P. japonicum see **P. alopecuroides**

P. latifolium Spreng. (*Gymnothrix latifolia* Schult.). Uruguay Pennisetum. S. America. To 2.5m-high grass with short rhizomes and stout culms; inflorescences terminal and axillary. Nodes are densely pubescent; the long metallic-glossy leaves to 6cm wide. Each culm branch bears an inflorescence with many bristly spikelets, with some awns twice as long as others. A decorative, large grass requiring winter protection. Best to overwinter small plants in a temperate greenhouse for replacements. z8

P. orientale L.C. Rich. Central Asia to the Caucasus and NW. India. To 40cm high clump grass with many, gently nodding, cylindrical inflorescence appearing as early as June. Rosy pale violet at first, turning light brown and expanding after flowering. The very long flowering period (June to October) is quite unusual among perennial ornamental grasses. Worthy, therefore, of much further use, even though often mislabeled as nonhardy, or even annuals. This grass needs a warm site and ample moisture, making it a suitable companion for other heat-loving perennials of various flowering times. The young stems are good for cutting. Propagate by seed; self-seeds under favorable conditions. z7 (S.)

P. purpurascens see **P. alopecuroides**

P. ruppelii see **P. setaceum**

P. setaceum (Forssk.) Chiov. (*P. ruppelii* Steud.) Fountain Grass. Africa. Clumping perennial grass with overarching slender leaves. Bottle-brush type inflorescence borne on an unbranched culm to 1.2m high, just above the fountain of foliage, nodding, pinkish to purple, becoming plumose with maturity. More important are the several cultivars: 'Atrosanguineum', foliage and inflorescences purple; 'Cupreum', foli-

age reddish, inflorescences bright copper-colored; 'Rubrum', foliage and inflorescences rose-colored. While these may appear on seed lists, it is best to grow a large seedling population, then select and maintain by division the brightest individuals. These are the most important display bedding grasses in America. z7

Penstemon Mitch.
Scrophulariaceae
Beard-tongue

About 250 species, North American (1 Asian), of perennial or woody, upright, bushy or procumbent plants with opposite or occasionally whorled leaves, or the upper leaves alternate. Flowers attractive, in terminal panicles or racemes, or rarely solitary, scarlet, purple, blue, white or yellow, in many shades. This genus contains some of the most beautiful summer-blooming perennials. The flowering time varies according to species from April to September. Penstemons are suitable for cut flowers, planting among other large perennials in the border, and for the wild garden; the many low-growing species are suitable for the rock garden and dry wall plantings. The majority thrive in light, humus-rich neutral to midly acidic garden soils, though some plains and Rocky Mtn. species occur on alkaline soils, in a warm, sunny to semi-shaded site. Winter hardiness is somewhat doubtful for many species. This is not necessarily due to a lack of cold hardiness, since many species are native to cold, mountainous regions, but because plants in nature are covered by snow in winter and therefore are protected from winter sun, wind and wetness. In most cases, it is best to treat the penstemons as short-lived perennials with replacement plants propagated by cuttings in summer, especially the cultivars. Overwinter these young plants frost free but cold. Propagation by seed usually is easy. The seeds of *P. barbatus* and Penstemon Barbatus Hybrids run about 1000 per gram. The best time for sowing is from December to March. Penstemon specialists often sow seed in open seed beds in autumn, lifting seedlings as they appear in the next 1–3 years. The alpine species may suffer from crown rot fungi, especially with insufficient drainage, or where summers are hot and humid.

P. acaulis L.O. Williams. USA: Wyoming and Utah. Low, tufted perennial to 5cm high, with underground stems and

linear leaves to 1.5cm long, and with large blue flowers, solitary on very short pedicels. Worth searching out the true species for the rock garden; the validity of material in the trade is doubtful. z4

P. acuminatus Dougl. USA: Washington to Texas. Stems 15–60cm high. Leaves glaucous, glabrous, leathery, with a cartilaginous margin, obovate or oblong. Racemose panicles are leafy, with several-flowered branchlets; flowers 12–18mm wide, pale blue or lilac to violet; midsummer. Needs protection in wet or snowless winters. z5

P. alpinus Torr. (*P. glaber* Pursh var. *alpinus* (Torr.) A. Gray). USA: in the higher Rocky Mountains. Stems 20–75cm high, similar to *P. glaber*, but sometimes pubescent. Stem leaves narrow to broadly lanceolate. Racemose panicles short and few flowered; flowers blue to bluish-purple; spring-flowering. z3

P. arizonicus see **P. whippleanus**

P. auriberbis Penn. USA: Colorado. Bushy perennial, about 20cm high. Leaves linear or linear-lanceolate, about 4–4.5cm long. Lilac to purplish-blue flowers in loose clusters. Cover in wet winters. z4

P. barbatus (Cav.) Roth (*P. barbatus* var. *torreyi* A. Gr., *Chelone barbata* Cav., *Ch. glabra* hort.). North America: Utah to Mexico. To 1.5m high; with a creeping rootstock. Leaves glabrous, sometimes glaucous, lanceolate to linear-lanceolate. Flower panicles slender-pyramidal; flowers to 2.5cm long, 2-lipped, the lower lip often yellow-bearded, scarlet, also white, pink and violet; several cultivars and a subspecies are listed; flowers midsummer to early fall.

Hybrids with *P. virgatus* and other species are known as the *Penstemon* Barbatus Hybrids, available in attractive, mixed colors. A low cultivar, 'Praecox Nanus', is about 50cm high, and has slender flower panicles with pink, red or violet wide-open flowers. Needs winter protection. z6(5)

P. barrettiae A. Gray. Oregon. Much-branched bushy perennial, 20–25cm high; leaves ovate to elliptic-ovate, blue glaucous, glabrous, leathery, serrate, to 7cm long with lilac to rose-purple flowers. Generally resembles *P. rupicola*, but *P. barrettiae* is more erect. z6

P. caespitosus Nutt. ex A. Gray. USA: Colorado, Wyoming, Utah. Matted perennial with prostrate, creeping and rooting stems; to 10cm high. Leaves linear to very narrow-lanceolate, sessile, entire, usually pubescent, sometimes glabrous. Flowers light blue with purplish throat, in short, terminal racemes, also occasionally solitary; June to July. Very attractive, mat forming species. Light winter protection is required. At least 3 subspecies are listed. z4

P. campanulatus (Cav.) Willd. (*P. pulchellus* Lindley). Mexico, Guatemala. Stems glabrous, 30–60cm high. Leaves linear to linear-lanceolate, sharply serrate, sessile or stem-clasping. Inflorescences loose, mostly 2-flowered, rose-purple or violet, rarely white; 'Richardsonii' reddish-violet to wine purple, floriferous. The species is far too large for the rock garden. A strain in the trade known as *P. pulchellus* and *P. pulchellus* var., forms low mats of excellent form with brilliant flowers. Not too hardy, but undemanding. Needs some protection. z8

P. cardwellii T.J. Howell. USA: Washington, Oregon. Loose cushion form, 15–25cm high. One of the most attractive, lower growing *Penstemon* species. Attractive, glabrous elliptic, serrate leaves. Relatively large, lilac-pink flowers. One cultivar is listed, 'Roseus', with rose-pink flowers. z6

P. cobaea Nutt. USA: Nebraska to Arkansas, Oklahoma and Texas. Sturdy pubescent perennial to 80cm high; leaves oblong to ovate, to 6.5cm long, dentate, the upper leaves clasping. Corolla large, to 5cm long, 2cm wide, scarcely 2-lipped, white, flesh-pink to pale violet, always with purple bee lines in the throat; late spring. And var. **purpureus**, with very large, rich purple flowers found only on a few limestone glades adjacent the White River in S. Missouri, N. Arkansas. It is on the endangered species list. z5(4)

P. coloradoensis see **P. linarioides** ssp. **coloradoensis**

P. confertus Dougl. W. North America: Alberta and Montana to British Columbia and Oregon. Stem to 60cm high, glabrous. Leaves broadly lanceolate, entire, sessile, the basal leaves tapered to a petiole. Inflorescence with 2–5 whorled, crowded flower clusters; flowers small, corolla to 1.5cm long, yellow to yellowish-white; midsummer. The lavender flowered cultivar 'Violaceus' is listed. z4

P. crandallii A. Nels. USA: Colorado.

Species rare in cultivation. Tufted perennial about 12cm high, stems procumbent or erect; leaves linear-oblanceolate, to 12mm long, glabrous. Flowers dark blue, corolla with lines in the throat; flowers rarely pale blue. Several subspecies and varieties are listed. z4

P. cristatus see **P. eriantherus**

P. cyananthus Hook. (*P. glaber* Pursh var. *cyananthus* Hook.) A. Gray). USA: Utah, Idaho, Wyoming. Superficially similar to *P. glaber*, but leaves glaucous, thicker, larger on taller stems (to 90cm), flowers smaller of similar blue color. Requires complete protection from winter wet. z4

P. davidsonii Greene (*P. menziesii* Hook var. *davidsonii* (Greene) Piper). North America: British Columbia to Oregon. Matted subshrub 10–15cm high, evergreen. Stems creeping underground and rooting. Leaves to 3cm long, pubescent, rounded, entire, bluish green. Flowers lilac-purple, to 3.5cm long. Intolerant of lime; midsummer. A hybrid with *P. eriantherus* (*P. cristatus*) is grown in the trade under the name 'Six Hills'. Requires some protection in winter. Also cultivar 'Albus', with white flowers, and 2 subspecies. z6

P. diffusus see **P. serrulatus**

P. digitalis Nutt. (*P. laevigatus* var. *digitalis* (Nutt.) A. Gray). North America: Maine, Quebec to South Dakota, south to Virginia and Texas. A tall, to 1.7m high, vigorous, glabrous perennial, stems usually turning reddish, leaves oblanceolate to 18cm long, flowers white to very rarely light pink; spring to early summer. z5(4)

A shorter cultivar, about 30cm high, is carried in the trade as *P. digitatus* 'Nanus'. This cultivar is semievergreen with porcelain white flowers; April to June. Requires a winter cover. z6(5)

P. eriantherus Pursh. (*P. eriantherus* ssp. *saliens* (Rydb.) Penn., *P. cristatus* Nutt., *P. saliens* Rydb.). North America: North Dakota and Nebraska west to British Columbia and Washington. Small, sometimes suffruticose perennial; about 30cm-high subshrub, pubescent, evergreen, with large, rosy-purple flowers. Requires a cover in winter. z4

P. fruticosus ssp. **scouleri** see **P. scouleri**

P. gairdneri Hook. Oregon. Rarely cultivated species. Tufted, gray-pubescent perennial about 30cm high; leaves alternate, recurved, linear to 3.5cm long.

Corolla lavender-purple with blue limb. And ssp. **oreganus** (A. Gray) Keck. Leaves more or less opposite; corolla pale lavender-blue to almost white. z6

P. gentianoides see **P. hartwegii**

P. glaber Pursh. USA: North Dakota, Wyoming, Nebraska. Glabrous perennial 30–60cm high. Leaves bluish-green, upper leaves oval-lanceolate, lower leaves oblong-lanceolate, entire, glabrous. Flowers blue or violet-purple; spring. z3 (intolerant of heat and humidity).

P. glaber var. **alpinus** see **P. alpinus**

P. glaber var. **cyananthus** see **P. cynanthus**

P. glaucus R. Grah. (*P. speciosus* Dougl.). USA: Rocky Mountains. Stems to 60cm high, bluish-green, glabrous. Leaves narrow-lanceolate, to 15cm long, upper leaves wider, entire, sessile. Racemes many-flowered, to 30cm long; flowers short-pediceled, blue to rose-violet, throat usually pinkish-white; spring. This "species" often encountered in horticulture, is not valid according to some authorities who refer some of the plants to *P. gracilis*, others to *P. whippelanus*. More taxonomic study seems indicated. z4

P. gracilis Nutt. North America: British Columbia to Ontario, south to Wisconsin and New Mexico. Stems 20–60cm high. Stem leaves linear-lanceolate, often acute, subentire to finely serrate; basal leaves oblanceolate to elliptic. Racemose panicles sticky-pubescent; flowers lilac to dingy white; summer. z5

P. hallii A. Gray. USA: Colorado. Bushy little upright plant to 20cm high. Bluish-green, leaves thickish, linear, entire. Racemes short, spike-like, violet to blue-violet; late spring. Cover in winter. z4

P. hartwegii Benth. (*P. gentianoides* Lindl.). Mexico, in the cooler regions. Often somewhat woody at the base, stems to 1.25m high. Leaves lanceolate to ovate-lanceolate, glabrous, glossy, entire, the upper leaves wider, stem-clasping. Inflorescences nearly leafless, long and loose; flowers to 5cm long, scarlet red or dark purple-red, usually in 3-flowered sprays; late spring to summer. Only for very warm sites with good winter protection. A number of good cultivars are in the trade. A cultivar with exceptionally large, scarlet red flowers is grown under the names

'Schönholzeri', *P. hybrida* 'Schönholzeri' or *P. hybrida* 'Paul Schönholzer', 'Firebird' in England and the USA. Other similar cultivars are 'Friedhelm Hahn', wine red; 'Ruby' deep, clear ruby-red; 'Southgate Gem', bright red, large-flowered. z7(6)

P. heterophyllus Lindl. USA: California, in arid areas. Shrub or suffruticose plant 60cm high. Leaves to 5cm long, bluish green, lanceolate to linear, somewhat tapered at the base, entire. Flowers purple to rarely azure blue; summer. 'Blue Gem', a dwarf cultivar, rock garden plant. A newer cultivar is 'Züriblau' (not Zürichblau), 50cm high, with bright blue flowers. Several subspecies also are listed, including ssp. **purdyi** (Munz. & I.M. Johnst.) Keck, a matted, procumbent shrub with blue to pale purple-blue flowers, apparently synonymous with cultivar 'California Blue Bedder'. Winter protection is necessary. z8

P. hirsutus (L.) Willd. (*P. pubescens* Soland.). North America: Quebec, Ontario to Wisconsin, southward to Virginia, Kentucky and Tennessee, on dry sites. Stems 50–90cm high, erect, glandular-pubescent. Leaves to 11cm long, oblong to lanceolate; basal leaves ovate, regularly serrate, inflorescences leafless, very open; flowers usually nodding, attached at right angles, long-pediceled, sordid violet to purplish, throat densely bearded; spring to summer. Grows on very well drained soil and in full sun. Cultivars include 'Caeruleus', flowers bluish; 'Pur-pureus', flowers clear purple; 'Pyg-maeus', 15cm high, free flowering, violet; 'Roseus', flowers pinkish; and 'Rosinus', flowers rose-pink. z5

P. humilis Nutt. ex A. Gray. USA: California to Idaho, Wyoming and W. Colorado. A true caespitose plant to 30cm high; leaves oblong to lanceolate below, linear lanceolate above, entire, dwarf; with pubescent petioles. The flowers are deep blue to blue-violet, rarely almost white. Cover in winter. z4

P. Hybrids. Under this collective name are included all the hybrids of uncertain origin. 'Blue Spring' is a relatively recent cross, about 30cm high, flower color is a pure light blue; May to June. Winter protection is advisable. 'Lena Sheba', also 30cm high, white flowers, very attractive. The hybrid 'Garnet' grows to 75cm high, has wine red flowers and apparently is allied to *P. campanulata*. 'Hidcote Pink' is a similar pink-flowered cultivar. 'Weald Beacon' is of unknown

parentage; resembling *P. roezlii* in form, but the flowers are more bluish. 'Amethyst' is a hybrid with the habit of *P. scouleri*, with tubular, amethyst blue flowers. Requires some winter protection in colder climates. Many complex hybrid populations, strains and cultivars trace their origin to the breeding work of the late Dr. Glenn Viehmeyer at the University of Nebraska North Platte Experiment Station; refer to Viehmeyer's work in the Journal of the American Penstemon Society and in Research Station Publications. z6

P. laevigatus (L.) Ait. USA: Pennsylvania, south to Florida and Mississippi. Stems to 1m high, nearly glabrous. Leaves to 15cm long, oblong or lanceolate, upper leaves stem-clasping, regularly serrate. Inflorescences loose, many flowered, glandular pubescent, branched; flowers purplish. Spring. May need a light covering in winter. z6

P. laevigatus var. **digitalis** see **P. digitalis.**

P. laetus ssp. **P. roezlii** see **P. roezlii**

Penstemon menziesii

P. lentus Penn. USA: Mtns. of Colorado and Arizona. Small-growing, glaucous, glabrous perennial to 30cm high. Leaves leathery, entire, lower leaves elliptic, stem leaves clasping, ovate to ovate-lanceolate; flowers purple-blue, or, in ssp. **albiflorus** Keck., white. For the gravelly rock garden bed in sun. z5(4)

P. linarioides A. Gray. Also distributed as *P. coloradoensis* A. Nels = *P. linarioides* ssp. *coloradoensis*. USA: W. New Mexico and SE. Arizona. Grows on xerophytic sites. Subshrub 15–45cm high, stems wiry, gray hairy, scaly, or glabrous. Leaves to 2.5cm long, linear, entire. Inflorescences racemose or panicled; pedicels short; flowers lilac to purple; summer. A good rock garden plant. Definitely requires a winter cover to protect from winter wet. And ssp. **coloradoensis** (A. Nels.)Keck (*P. coloradoensis* A. Nels.) with staminode bearded only at the base. z6

P. linearifolius see **P. lyallii**

P. lyallii (A. Gray) A. Gray (*P. linearifolius* J. Coult. et E.. Fisher). USA: N. Idaho and W. Montana. Handsome, small, suffruticose perennial rarely to 90cm high; leaves entire to serrate, linear to lanceolate, to 11cm long. Inflorescence with clusters of large, lavender to purple-violet flowers. z4

P. menziesii Hook. W. North America, south to Washington. Stems 15–20cm high; leaves broadly ovate or obovate, glabrous. Inflorescences racemose, glandular-pubescent, purple flowers, 2–5cm long; summer. Intolerant of lime. Probably this species, still apparently listed in horticultural literature, is the same as *P. davidsonii* ssp. *davidsonii*. A small-leaved form with lavender flowers is in the trade under the name 'Microphyllus'. Only 8–10cm high, very compact. Needs some winter protection. z4

P. menziesii var. **davidsonii** see **P. davidsonii**

P. menziesii var. **newberryi** see **P. newberryi**

P. micranthus see **P. procerus**

P. newberryi A. Gray (*P. menziesii* Hook. var. *newberryi* (A. Gray) A. Gray). Mountain Pride. California and adjacent Nevada. Woody-based creeping or nearly prostrate, matted perennial to 30cm high; glabrous. Leaves elliptic to ovate, leafless, serrate, to 3.5cm long.

Flowers rose- or purple-pink; summer. Attractive, but needs winter protection, intolerant of summer heat and humidity. And ssp. **barryi** (Eastw.)Keck. Flowers larger. z7(6)

P. newberryi var. **rupicola** see **P. rupicola**

P. ovatus Dougl. North America: British Columbia, Washington and Oregon. Stems to 90cm high, glabrous to pubescent. Leaves thin, light green, basal leaves lanceolate to ovate, stem leaves deltoid-ovate. Flowers ultramarine to pinkish-purple; late spring. z5

P. pinifolius Greene. W. North America, SW. New Mexico, SE. Arizona and adjacent Mexico. Shrubby, much branched, glabrous to pubescent perennial to 60cm high. Leaves small, needlelike, evergreen. Flowers slender tubular form, brilliant scarlet, in erect racemes; summer. A very attractive rock garden plant. z6

P. procerus Dougl. ex R. C. Grah. (*P. micranthus* Nutt.). North America: Rocky Mts., Alaska and Yukon to S. Colorado. Glabrous, branchy perennial 20–45cm high. Leaves entire, thin; basal leaves lanceolate to oblanceolate, stem leaves oblong to lanceolate, to 7.5cm long. Flowers lilac-blue to purple-blue. Summer. *P. procerus* ssp. **tolmiei** (Hook) Keck. with more compact habit, leaves crowded basally. z3

P. pubescens see **P. hirsutus**

P. pulchellus see **P. campanulatus**

P. roezlii Regel. California, Oregon, Nevada. Grows on dry sites. Hirsute shrub to 30–70cm high. Leaves sometimes glabrous, entire, basal leaves oblanceolate, upper stem leaves linear-lanceolate o linear. Racemose panicles glandular; flowers dark blue to violet. Late spring to summer. A rock garden plant. Classification of this species and the cultivars are in dispute. The native plant is referred to *P. laetus* A. Gray ssp. *roezlii* in the USA. Needs winter protection. Intolerant of summer heat and humidity. z7(6)

P. rupicola (Piper) Howell (*P. newberryi* A. Gray var. *rupicola* Piper). USA: Washington, Oregon, N. California. One of the best penstemons for the rock garden. Low, spreading, suffruticose mat, 10cm high, leaves elliptic to orbicular, thick, gray-green, toothed, to 2cm long; and with deep rose-colored flowers in clusters. Late spring to early

summer. 'Albus' is a white-flowered cultivar and 'Roseus' is an older pink-flowered selection. Cultivar 'Pink Dragon' flowers somewhat later, early to midsummer, light salmon pink flowers, plant somewhat more compact; also distributed as 'Pink Cultivar'. Requires a light winter cover. z6

P. saliens see **P. eriantherus**

P. scouleri Lindl. (*P. fruticosus* (Pursh) Greene). North America: British Columbia to Idaho. Stems to 25cm high. Leaves linear-lanceolate, acute, serrate, somewhat semievergreen, suffruticose. Flowers racemose, lavender-blue, rarely purplish; June. Lime intolerant. Needs light winter protection. This species has yielded a large number of cultivars with various flower colors. 'Albus', very attractive, summer-blooming white; 'Six Hills'; fuschia-pink flowers on about 15cm-high pedicels in spring; 'Red Cultivar', light rosy-purple flowers, 25cm high, late spring or early summer; 'Purple Gem' only 5–10cm high with violet-purple flowers, late spring to early summer. *P. scouleri* is now considered by botanists to be a *P. fruticosus* ssp. *scouleri*. z6

P. secundiflorus Benth. USA: Wyoming to Central New Mexico. Glabrous, mostly glaucous perennial. 30–60cm high. Basal leaves oblanceolate, to 7.5cm long; stem leaves lanceolate, clasping. Racemose panicles long, many flowered; flowers lilac to pinkish-lilac; early summer. Massing and border plant. And ssp. **lavandulus** Penn., flowers lavender-pink to lavender-blue, smaller. z4

P. serrulatus Menz. ex Sm. (*P. diffusus* Dougl.). North America: SW. Alaska to NW. Oregon. Mostly glabrous subshrub 40–60cm high. Leaves elliptic, ovate or lanceolate, nearly entire to deeply toothed; flowers blue to purple; late spring to early summer. z6

P. teucrioides Greene. USA: Colorado. Plant with a stout woody crown and ascending to erect gray-pubescent stems to 10cm high. Leaves almost needlelike, to 2.25cm long, mucronate; with beautiful blue flowers. Requires winter protection. z4

P. tolmiei see **P. procerus** ssp. **tolmiei**

P. tubiflorus Nutt. E. USA, in scattered population. Glabrous perennial to 90cm high. Stems often reddish. Leaves ovate lanceolate, entirely or finely toothed, to 10cm long. Flowers in short pediceled whorls around the upper ⅛ to ¼ of the stem, crowded, snowy white. z5(4)

P. whippleanus A. Gray (*P. arizonicus* A. Heller). USA: SW. Montana to Arizona and New Mexico. Stems several in a clump, erect, 20–60cm high, lowest branches often flat-spreading. Leaves elliptic to ovate or lanceolate, deep green, entire or toothed. Flowers with glandular calyx, purple or lavender, in a loose, somewhat one-sided inflorescence. Early summer. Needs a winter cover. z4

This is indeed a genus of many beautiful plants, fewer than half of those grown by specialists in the USA are included here, and too few of which are utilized in gardens. Hardier cultivars are needed, however, as most species, with their broadleafed evergreen or semi-evergreen foliage suffer winter sunscald, as do some of the species with needlelike foliage. (L.J. & Kö.)

Pentaglottis Tausch
Boraginaceae

Only one species. Hairy herbaceous perennial with conspicuously veined ovate leaves and blue flowers in scorpioid cymes. Calyx 5-lobed, corolla 5-lobed with scales in the throat, stamens 5.

P. sempervirens (L.) Tausch ex L.H. Bailey (*Anchusa sempervirens* L.). SW. France, Spain, Central Portugal. Broad, ovate basal leaves, petioled; stem leaves sessile. Flowering stems 0.3–1m high, erect, well branched. Short cymose inflorescences with 5–15 deep blue flowers on each branchlet. Spring-flowering. For the wildflower or naturalized garden on moist, and partially shaded sites. Grow from seed. (Kö.)

Percidium

P. tomentosum see **Leibnitzia anandria**

Perezia Lag.
Compositae

About 70–80 species in the Americas, from California southward. Erect and branched or stemless, occasionally somewhat woody herbs. Leaves basal or alternate, often sessile, entire, toothed, pinnatisect or deeply incised. Flower heads rather large, solitary on leafless scapes or also smaller, in clustered or loose terminal panicles or cymes. Flowers all 2-lipped, perfect, rose, purple, blue or white. Flower in early summer. Grow in well-drained, not too moist soil in full sun or partial shade. Requires protection from excessive winter wetness. Suitable for the rock garden and trough, also the alpine house. Propagate by cuttings and division.

P. recurvata Less. Chile. Dense, mattted habit. Leaves in rosettes, dark green, 3cm long, linear, toothed on the margin and

Petasites paradoxus

pubescent. Flowers solitary on 8cm-high stalks, light blue. z6–7

Perovskia Kar
Labiatae

Perhaps 7 S. Asian perennial species in Iran, Afghanistan and NW. India. Roots deep, woody. Stems more or less woody below, 4-angled. Leaves opposite, cut or dissected. Flowers bilabiate, small, in 2–many-flowered false whorls in terminal racemes or panicles. Calyx tubular, 2-lipped; corolla tube longer than the calyx, limb 5-lobed; stamens 2, staminoides 2; ovary 4-celled. Hardy, hot-climate plants for the large rock garden or for bedding.

P. abrotanoides Kar. Turkestan to NE. Iran. Stems to 90cm high. Upper leaves ovate, 2-pinnatifid, to 5cm long. Inflorescence an almost cylindrical panicle, flowers mid-blue, in summer. z5

Petasites hybridus, **staminate flowers**

P. artemesioides Boiss. SE. Iran to N. Pakistan. Stems to 90cm high. Upper leaves ovate, to 3cm long, pinnately cut. Inflorescence a narrow panicle with purple-blue flowers in summer. z5

P. atriplicifolia Benth. W. Pakistan. Stems to 1m high, upper leaves ovate-oblong to 3.5cm long, entire or barely toothed. Inflorescence a spreading panicle, flowers lavender-blue, in summer. z5

These hardy, summer-flowering plants, blooming in midsummer are light and airy-looking but perform well only where summers are quite warm.

Persicaria

P. amphibia see **Polygonum amphibium**

Petalostemon
Leguminosae

About 40–50 herbaceous perennial species, often with a wide vase-shaped habit from a small woody crown; all are indigenous to North American prairies and plains. Leaves alternate, glandular-dotted, crowded, odd-pinnate, the leaflets very slender, often gray or gray-green. Flowers in dense terminal heads or short spikes. Corolla with 4 petals united basally, the standard free. Suitable for the sunny wildflower garden or the rock garden.

P. candidum (Willd.) Michx. (*P. oligophyllum* (Torr.) Rydb.) White Prairie Clover. North America; S. Central Canada to Mississippi, Arizona and Colorado. Stems to 75cm high, often less. Leaflets 7–9, linear to oblong, flowers white or whitish in dense, elongated terminal spikes. The least showy of the species listed. z4(3)

P. oligophyllum see **P. candidum**

P. mollis see **P. purpureum**

P. purpureum (Ventan.) Rydb. (*P. mollis* Rydb.). Purple Prairie Clover. North America: Saskatchewan to Indiana, Texas and New Mexico. Fountain-like habit, numerous, rarely branched stems 30–90cm high. Leaflets 3–5, linear, to 2cm long. Flowers in dense terminal spikes, violet to rosy-purple. Very showy rock garden and border perennial. z4

P. villosum Nutt. Silky Prairie Clover. North America: Michigan to Saskatchewan and Texas. Stems to 60cm high, often less, ascending or decumbent; stems and leaves densely soft-hairy, hairs silky white. Leaflets 13–19, elliptic to oblanceolate, to 1cm long. Flowers in a dense terminal spike, rose-purple, or in var. *album*, white. Flor gravelly, very well drained soil in full sun. z4

Petasites Mill.
Compositae
Butterbur, Sweet Coltisfoot

About 15 species. Herbaceous plants with horizontally creeping or crown-like, persistent rootstocks, often vigorous-growing in Europe, N. Asia and North America. Leaves usually appear after the flowers, basal, large, long petioled, more or less cordate. Flower heads radiate, of two sorts, fertile heads of many, mostly female, flowers with or without ligules, sterile heads with many perfect (2-sexed) disc flowers and with or without a few female but sterile ray flowers; in terminal racemes or thyrselike panicles and 15–60cm high scape, scape with many bracts. Flowers purple, pink, white, occasionally yellow. Plants require ample room to spread without invading less vigorous neighboring plants. Propagate by division.

P. albus (L.) Gaertn. White Butterbur. In mountainous regions throughout Europe to the Altai Mts. Perennials to

Petasites albus

30cm high, rhizomatous, creeping. Leaves appear after the flowers, blades distinctly rounded, angular-lobed, toothed, entirely white-woolly at first, later tomentose only on the undersides, 15–40cm wide, petioles laterally compressed. Flower scapes rounded, with many lanceolate bracts. Inflorescences corymbose, flowers whitish, 15–30cm high; scape elongates to 80cm after flowering. Late winter to early spring. An attractive early bloomer; sun or semishade, along small streams in the rock garden, good companion for *Leucojum, Primula rosea, Eranthus* and moisture-loving ferns. z5

P. fragrans (Vill.) K.B. Presl. "Winter Heliotrope" of English gardeners. From the Mediterranean region, cultivated in W. and S. Europe, and generally naturalized. Perennials 20–30cm high. Leaves rounded-cordate, matte green, undersides soft-pubescent, appearing with or usually shortly after the flowers. Flower heads densely clustered in corymbs, pink-white, powerfully vanilla-scented; mid-winter to early spring. Only for warm, protected sites, not entirely winter hardy. Cut flowers are long lasting in a vase and fill a room with fragrance. Propagate by separation of the rhizomes. z7(6)

P. hybridus (L.) Ph. Gaertn., B. Mey. et Scherb. (*P. officinalis* Moench). Found throughout Europe, N. and W. Asia, naturalized in N. America. Often forms large colonies on stream banks, swampy sites, low woodlands, and similar permanently moist sites. Perennial, 15–20cm high at anthesis, fully developed leaves to 1m high. Rhizome about thumb size, widely creeping. Leaves appear after the flowers, furled at first, then cordate to rounded, 60cm wide, matte green, gray-tomentose beneath, later glabrous.

Staminate flower heads (plants dioecious) bright purple, wilting down immediately after blooming; pistillate flower heads duller-colored, to pale brownish, scape stretching after blooming, then to 80cm high. Only the staminate plants should be cultivated. Suitable for naturalizing large areas of moist stream banks and lowlands. In small gardens, plants may be contained by planting in sunken tubs. Very attractive. Propagation is by division. To quickly establish a colony of plants, lay pencil-sized rhizome pieces horizontally about 5cm deep. z4

P. japonicus (Sieb. et Zucc.) Maxim. E. Asia, Japan, Sachalin. Long-cultivated, vigorous perennials with widely creeping rhizomes, even more invasive than *P. hybridus*. Leaves to 1m high, 80cm wide, orbicular with a deep sinus, dentate, glabrous on both sides. Leaf petiole channeled, winged. Flower scapes covered closely with wide, obtuse-linear bracts below the densely clustered flower heads, flowers milk white, like small "bridal bouquets". Scape later elongates into an oblong fruiting corymb. Blooms late winter to early spring. Grow like *P. hybridus*. Quite vigorous. The even more vigorous cultivar 'Giganteus' (leaves more than 1m wide, margin undulate, flowers fragrant) is often cultivated. The species is cultivated in Japan for its edible rhizomes. z5

P. niveus see **P. paradoxus**

P. officinales see **P. hybridus**

P. paradoxus (Retz.) Baumg. (*P. niveus* (Vill.) Baumg.). Pyrenees, Alps. Usually found in colonies in gravelly streamside locations, in ravines and open woodlands, only on limestone. Leaves acutely cordate, dark green, white-tomentose beneath. Flower scapes 30cm high, pale green, white-tomentose with reddish bracts. Flowers in dense, short racemes, rose to reddish-white. For moist, cool sites in the large rock garden. z5

P. spurius (Retz.) Rchb. (*P. tomentosus* DC.) N. Europe to S. Russia, on sand dunes with a moist substrate. Perennials to 30cm high. Rhizomes creeping

Pyrenees, on dry, sunny limestone cliffs, crevices, and screes from 1700–3400m. Very low, or flat, dense, to 30cm-wide cushion, with crowded, rosetted, cuneate, 3–5 cleft, bristly ciliate leaves, 4–6mm long. Flowers borne tightly over the cushion in few-flowered corymbs, fragrant, lilac or pink, occasionally white. Spring-flowering. The white-flowering cultivar 'Albiflora' is more easily cultivated than the species.

Only recommended for alpine plant collectors. Best suited for an east-facing rock crevice or scree with abundant limestone. Tolerates dry to moist soil.

petals imbricate before anthesis and seed with densely tomentose hilum.

Small, decorative plants for the rockery, alpine garden or trough garden of collectors and botanic gardens. Plants require a sunny, completely winter-dry location (protected from midday sun), an east-facing crevice or limestone scree. All species are lime loving, often short-lived in deep garden soils, but easily grown from seed for replacements. Good companions are other small rock plants such as the dwarf, lime-loving *Dianthus*, *Draba*, and small *Saxifraga* species.

Petrocallis pyrenaica

Petrophyton caespitosum

widely. Leaves appear after the flowers, conspicuously 5-angled, wider than long, coarsely serrate. Flower scapes ridged, white-woolly tomentose, covered with long sheathlike bracts. Flower heads sordid white to pale yellow, late winter to early spring. For sandy soil, best grouped with other dune plants. Propagate by division. z4 (D.)

P. tomentosus see **P. spurius**

Petrocallis R. Br.
Cruciferae

Two species of perennial, high alpine plants from the Alps, Pyrenees and N. Iraq. Differs from the closely related genus *Draba* in the simple, unbranched hairs on palmately lobed leaves.

P. pyrenaica (L.) R. Br. Tatra Mts., Alps,

Attractive in the shadow of a large rock. Also suitable for planting for a trough garden with other rock and scree plants or potted for the alpine house. Propagation is best done in late August to early September by rooting the lower, lateral shoots in sand; also grows from seed. good companions include *Androsace lactea*, *Callianthemum anemonoides*, *Draba aizoides*, *D. tomentosa*, *Carex firma*, *Kernera saxatilis*, *Moehringia muscosa*, *Papaver sendtneri*, *Primula wulfeniana*. z4 (E.)

Petrocoptis A. Br. ex Endl.
Caryophyllaceae

Seven species of low, suffruticose rock plants with basal leaf rosettes, found exclusively in the limestone outcroppings of the Pyrenees and other Spanish mountains. Differs from the closely related genus *Lychnis* in the

P. glaucifolia (Lag.) Boiss. (*P. lagascae* Willk.) Willk., *Lychnis lagascae* (Willk.) Hook.). Mountains of N. Spain, on limestone. Flowering stems to 10cm high, without leaf rosettes but branched widely at the base. Lower stem leaves 1–2cm long, ovate-lanceolate or lanceolate, rather thick, blue-green. Flowers long-pediceled, about 12mm wide, purple-pink. Blooms from June to August. z7

P. lagascae see **P. glaucifolia**

P. pyrenaica (Bergeret) A. Br. (*Lychnis pyrenaica* Bergeret). W. Pyrenees, on limestone. Similar to the previous species, but lower growing in loose mats. Flower stems from leafy rosettes, leaves usually green and thin. Flowers somewhat smaller, white or pale purple-pink. Blooms from June to July. z7 (E.)

Petrophyton (Nutt. ex Torr. et A. Gray) Rydb. (also **Petrophytum**)
Rosaceae
Rock-spiraea

Four species of evergreen, low-growing matted, dwarf shrubs in W. North America. Branches very short with oblanceolate or spatulate leaves clustered at the ends, and white or greenish white complete flowers in usually racemose inflorescences. Sepals and

P. cinerascens (Pip.) Rydb. USA: Washington, found on basalt. Similar to the above species, but the leaves 3-veined beneath, sparsely gray-pubescent to glabrous, 10–25mm long. Peduncle 5–15cm long. Raceme often branched at the base. Flowers white. Calyx lobes acute. Stamens 20–25. Blooms from July to August. Slower growing and more demanding than the other species. z5

P. hendersonii (W. Canby) Rydb. (*Spiraea hendersonii* (W. Canby) Pip.). USA: Washington, Olympic Mts., on

entire, bifid, irregularly toothed, or 4-lobed; stamens 10; pistil with 1-celled ovary and 2 styles. Propagate by seed, double forms by division and cuttings. Most species are not reliably hardy.

P. saxifraga (L.) Link (*Tunica saxifraga* (L.) Scop.). Tunic Flower, Coat Flower. S. Europe, Asia Minor, Iran. Stems numerous, suffruticose, to 30cm high, in a loose cushion; leaves linear-lanceolate, somewhat bristle-haired, serrate. Ascending flowering stems with small, usually light pink, shallowly cupped flowers in loose clusters; June to

Petrorhagia saxifraga 'Rosette'

Peucedanum ostruthium

petals 5, stamens 20, more or less, pistils 3–5.

A rock shrub for the collector and botanic garden, for a sunny site in a loose, limestone soil among stones and in crevices in the sun. Performs better in pot culture in the alpine house in cooler climates. Propagate by seed and division.

P. caespitosum (Nutt. ex Torr. et A. Gray) Rydb. (*Spiraea caespitosa* Nutt. ex Torr. et A. Gray). USA: NE. Oregon to California, eastward to Idaho, Montana, South Dakota, New Mexico and Texas, from the foothills to alpine regions, usually in rock crevices. Low, densely matted shrub. Leaves densely silky-pubescent, 5–12mm long, single-veined on the underside. Peduncles 2.4–10cm high, with 2.5–3.5cm long, dense spikes. Flowers very small, white, with 20 stamens. Blooms from July to August. z3–8

steep rock walls. Similar to the previous species, leaves 3-veined beneath, only sparsely silky-pubescent or glabrous, with pink-tinged margins, occasionally bronze-colored. Peduncles 1–5cm long, with simple racemes. Flowers pale greenish-yellow. Calyx lobes obtuse. Stamens 35–40. Blooms from July to August. Does well in pot culture. z5 (E.)

Petrorhagia (Ser.) Link
Caryophyllaceae

About 30 species in of perennial herbs in S. Europe and E. Asia, but only the following species is garden worthy. Suitable for a dry, sunny place in the rock or heather garden in sandy, well-drained soil. Leaves opposite, awl-shaped to oblong; flowers in a compound cyme, in clusters, heads or solitary; calyx 5-toothed; corolla of 5 separate petals,

September. Cultivars include: 'Alba', white; 'Alba Plena', white, double, only 20cm high; 'Pleniflora', rose-pink, double; 'Rosette', dark pink, double, stronger growing. z6 (Mü.)

Peucedanum L.
Umbelliferae

Genus of stately perennials, with umbellate inflorescences of various kinds. The following species are suitable for filling out wildflower or natural gardens. These seem to be unknown in North America.

P. cervaria (L.) Lapeyr. Central and S. Europe. Flowering stems to 1m-high, species of dry woodlands, thickets and infertile meadows. Leaves tough, gray-green beneath, 2–3-pinnate. Inflorescence yellow-green. Suitable for very dry sites. z6

P. ostruthium (L.) W.D.J. Koch. Alps. Bright green perennial with wide, ternate leaves and large umbels of white flowers. Once used for medicine and as a spice. Requires a moist and fertile soil. z5

P. verticillare (L.) K. Koch ex DC. (*Tommasinia altissima* (Mill.) Thell.). SE. Europe, Central Italy. A stately, mostly 2.5m-high, glabrous perennial, lightly bluish-pruinose; emerging spring growth is pink. Leaves, to 50cm long, bipinnate, alternate toward the lower part of the stem. Stems to 5cm thick, somewhat channeled at the base.

pinnate leaves, leaves to 15cm long with 4–8 pairs of leaflets. Panicled cymes with pink-lavender, pale blue, mauve-colored or white flowers during the entire summer. Grow from seed in a sunny site. Requires winter protection. z8

P. sericea (R. C. Graham) A. Gray. USA: Central Washington to NE. California and Nevada. A sun and drought tolerant, short-lived, small, suffruticose, silver-silky perennial for the collector, growing to about 45cm high. Requires gravelly, lime-free soil and is best grown in an alpine house. With dense clusters of

Phalaris L.
Gramineae
Canary, Ribbon Grass

About 15 species of annual or perennial grasses from North America, Europe and North Africa. Leafy, the blades flat. Panicles mostly narrow or spike-like. Most perennial species are aggressively rhizomatous, so even the attractively variegated cultivars have to be considered weedy.

P. arundinacea L., Reed Canary Grass.

Phacelia sericea

Phalaris arundinacea 'Picta'

Inflorescences appear in June with whorled rays, yellow-green. A suitable, finer-textured replacement for *Heracleum*, which sometimes is not grown because of its skin rash potential. Propagate by seed sown immediately after harvest; often self-seeding. z7 (S.)

Phacelia Juss.
Hydrophyllaceae
Scorpion Weed, California Bluebell, Fiddleneck

The genus *Phacelia* includes about 200 species primarily from W. North America, and mostly annuals. Valuable bee-attracting plants.

P. platycarpa (Cav.) K. Spreng. North America: Mts. of Mexico. Prostrate to ascending stems from a basal plant rosette of silvery, linear to oblong

silvery-pubescent, deeply divided to lobed leaves with 10–45cm long flower stems in summer. Inflorescence is a crowded panicle of short cymes of lavender, blue or purple-blue flowers. Several geographic subspecies are listed. z6 (Sch. & Kö.)

In addition, other perennial phacelias are sometimes grown locally in the USA., including *P. hastata*, to 40cm high, leaves entire, silvery, flowers many, white to lavender; *P. lyallii*, to 18cm high, leaves pubescent, lanceolate, deeply lobed, flowers dark blue to purple; *P. racimosa*, hispid perennial to 1.25m high, sprawling, leaves pinnately divided, the lobes further cut or divided, flowers blue or whitish in short, dense cymes. All have garden potential but are not in the trade.

Eurasian and North American species. Narrow-panicled grass with condensed, rounded spikelets; to 2m high, very stoloniferous. The species resembles a reed, but with 4–6mm long leaf blades. Like the reeds, *Phalaris* thrives on periodically wet sites or along rapidly flowing streams with periodic flooding. Suitable as a pioneer plant for erosion control, will also grow under trees in shade; as in nature, tolerates dryness in the garden. In extreme drought, the leaves may become brown, but will regrow after a hard shearing. Several variegated cultivars (most very similar or identical), are found in cultivation, primarily for cutting. Easily propagated by division.

'Luteo-Picta' with yellow longitudinally striped foliage, somewhat less conspicuous than the 'Picta' ('Elegantissima', 'Tricolor'), often called Ribbon Grass or Gardener's Garters, with alternately white and green longitudinally striped blades, half strong green and half strong white. The young shoots are often pink tinted. Both cultivars are quite vigorous, leaves low, culms to 1m high. 'Feesey's Form' is a sport of 'Picta' with a greater number of white and pale green stripes. The rhizomes remain much shorter and the plants are then more clumped. For small gardens, this is a substantially better cultivar.

'Dwarf's Garters' is another dwarf sport of 'Picta', remaining only 30cm high and less vigorous. z4–9 (S.)

Pharium

P. elegans see Bessera elegans

Phegopteris see (Gymnocarpium) and Thelypteris

Phlomis L.
Labiatae
Jerusalem Sage

A genus of about 100 perennials and small shrubs from the Mediterranean region and W. Asia. The labiate flowers are clustered in several nodal whorls (verticillasters), one above the other toward the stem ends. The bold, usually woolly or tomentose leaves are opposite. Most species are suitable for sunny and warm sites as well as the woodland margin. Pleasing summer bloomers, with attractive yellow, purple, or white flowers. The dried stems and fruit clusters are long-lasting. The non-flowering rosettes of some species form a dense groundcover. The shrublike species are worth trying in warm beds near a protecting wall. Propagation is by division or seed, the subshrub species also by cuttings.

P. fruticosa L. Jerusalem Sage. Mediterranean region, east of Sardinia. The hardiest of the shrub-like species; to 1.3m high; leaves elliptic to lanceolate-ovate, to 9cm long and white woolly pubescent. Flowers 3cm or more long in more or less 20-flowered whorls at the shoot tips, bright yellow. The similar sp. P. chrysophylla Boiss., is more site specific in cultivation. z7(6)

P. herba-venti L. Mediterranean region and SE. Europe. Little-grown perennial, 45–60cm high, with violet to rose flowers in 10–14 flowered whorls in June to July.

Calyx, leaves, and the slender stems are pubescent. z7

P. russeliana (Sims) Benth. (P. samia sensu Boiss.). Asia Minor: SW. and S. Anatolia. Shrubby. Basal leaves ovate to lanceolate, cordate to sagittate at the base, petioled, glandular stellate pubescent, as is the entire plant. Non-flowering basal shoots form a dense groundcover. Flowering stems appear in June and grow to 1m high, with yellow flowers to 20, in verticillasters; the fruits remain decorative until winter. This species is used on banks and in large

Phlomis russeliana

rock gardens. Propagate by seed; easier than division. z7

P. samia L. Asia Minor and Greece to S. Yugoslavia. Basal leaves ovate to lanceolate, whitish-pubescent, cordate to sagittate at the base, petioled. Entire plant glandular stellate pubescent. Nonflowering shoots form a dense groundcover. Flowering stems appear in June and grow to 1m high, with purple flowers to 20 in verticillasters; fruit clusters remain decorative until winter. This species is also planted on sunny banks and in large rock gardens. Propagate by seed; easier than division. z7

P. tuberosa L. Central and SE. Europe. Leaves oval-lanceolate to cordate, somewhat woolly, with a crenate margin. The

roots bear a few small tubers. Stems to 1.8m high with several verticillasters of 14–40 pink to purple flowers, white bearded in the throat. The species is quite variable, especially in Russia; the many varieties often listed as separate species. (P. glandulifera seems to differ only in its glandular pubescence). Especially well suited for open, sunny sites and warm, summer-dry woodland margins together with Geranium sanguineum and Aster linosyris. z6

P. viscosa Poir. A shrubby species which may be only a variety of P. russeliana, from SW. Asia, occasionally is cultivated in the gardens of the Mediterranean region. z8 (S.)

Phlox L.
Polemoniaceae

This genus contains about 60 species distributed throughout N. America and 1 in Siberia. Very distinctive in appearance, with low, flat-growing, diffuse, or tall, erect species. Most are perennial; only a few annual. Basal leaves opposite, upper leaves sometimes alternate, simple, entire. Flowers borne on a terminal cyme or panicle, or are solitary, white, pink, rose, red, violet or blue. The low species are spring and summer bloomers, the taller species are largely midsummer bloomers. Many are popular, easily grown garden plants with attractive and colorful flowers. In addition to the natural variability of the species, there are many intermediate hybrids, genetically wide-ranging and much hybridized, as well as numerous cultivars. These have long been some of the most important garden plants with many uses. The low and shorter-growing species are for the rock garden, terrace walls or edging; the taller species are for the perennial border, the woodland margin or the cut flower bed. Good companions for the taller phlox include grasses such as *Panicum virgatum* 'Strictum' and *Hystrix patula*.

Since the flowering times of various species stretch nearly uninterrupted from spring to fall, it is possible to create a special phlox garden. Attention must be paid to companion species since phlox species have quite different cultural requirements. The tall-growing species require moist, fertile garden soil generously supplied with peat, compost, or well-rotted cow manure, in a sunny to semi-shaded site. Heavy loam or light sandy soil must be improved with generous amounts of fertile organic matter. Mature plants of *Phlox paniculata* require a spring topdressing of mineral, chloride-free fertilizer (50–70 grams/sq. meter) or organic fertilizer (100–140 grams/sq. meter). This produces vigorous plants with large panicles and discourages attack by nematodes. Propagation is primarily vegetative by division or cuttings in spring, division of *Phlox subulata* (in late summer), and by rootstock (crown) cuttings of *P. paniculata*, to prevent carryover of nematodes. Early fall is the best time to handle root or rootstock cuttings. Seed not commonly used

Phlox douglasii hybrid 'Red Admiral'

except for true species or for breeding work, though in recent years seed-propagated ornamental strains of *P. paniculata* have been marketed; sow in early fall. Seeds have a hard coat and lie dormant through the winter. Difficulty in growing phlox often is associated with soil and climatic conditions. Their native habitats, with relatively mild winters and annual rainfall of around 1m, make understandable the failure of many cultivars in areas with dry summers. Most species thrive in a moist mountainous or maritime climate. Plants massed in moist, semi-shaded woodland sites often do better than those used as specimens in open, sunny sites. Supplementary soaking of the roots and spring fertilizing is also beneficial in preventing many disease and insect problems. In the garden watch for symptoms of Bulb or Stem Nematode infestation; distorted, swollen, brittle stems and abnormal leaves. Destroy infected plants and sterilize the soil. These nematodes are not transmitted by root cuttings. *P. paniculata* cultivars are susceptible to mildew, controlled by frequent spraying with an appropriate fungicide; they also deteriorate from a physiogenic disease apparently associated with old, hard-crowned plants, and sometimes become infected with yellows and mosaic viruses.

Where Powdery Mildew is merely a cosmetic problem, spray with an appropriate fungicide at 10–14 day intervals regularly throughout the season. Leaf spot fungi, such as *Septoria*, *Cercospora*, and others, may be controlled by adding a compatible sulfur compound to the mildew fungicide.

Phlox douglasii hybrid 'Iceberg'

For practical garden plantings the species are grouped according to height.

1. Low-growing Species

Usually flowering from April to June and to 40cm high or less, mostly drought tolerant.

P. adsurgens Torr. W. North America: N. California to S. Oregon, usually in open conifer stands. Stems decumbent to creeping, flowering stems erect to 30cm. Leaves elliptic, glossy evergreen, thin. Flowers 2.5cm wide, bright purple, lilac or salmon-pink sometimes with darker stripes and a white eye, May to June. Requires a peaty soil, light shade and protection from the winter sun. Similar to *P.* × *procumbens*. z6

P. amoena hort. see **P.** × **procumbens**

P. amoena Sims non hort. SE. USA: N. Carolina to N. Florida. Stems erect, to 30cm high. Leaves narrow-lanceolate, pubescent. Flowers crowded in a terminal cluster subtended by a leafy involucre, magenta red, purple, pink, rarely lavender or white; April to May. Rare in cultivation. z7

P. bifida Beck. (*P. stellaria* A. Gray), Sand Phlox. E. North America, on rocky slopes and sandy hills. Flower stems 10–20cm high. Leafy stems procumbent to ascending, rough-pubescent. Leaves linear, acute (subulate), to 6cm long, ciliate. Inflorescences loose, 6–9(–12) flowered. Flowers lavender or rarely white, with deeply incised petals. April to May. Attractive, but demanding and quickly senescing. European literature suggests that this species is involved in some of the *P. subulata* cultivars, but not so. See *P. subulata* and *P. nivalis*.

Phlox missoulensis

P. borealis Wherry. W. North America: Alaska, Canada. Flowering stems 10–12cm high. Vegetative stems decumbent or ascending. Leaves 15–25mm long and 3mm wide. Flowers lilac, lavender, pink or white, round, 2cm across, 1–3 in a cluster. May to June. Not too difficult to cultivate. z2

P. brittonii Small (*P. subulata* var. *brittonii* (Small) Wherry). USA: Virginia, N. Carolina. Stems 4–6cm high, very leafy. Flowers somewhat smaller than those of *P. subulata*, lavender-blue or white; 'Rosea', pale pink. This plant now is considered to be a subspecies of *P. subulata*. May to June. z7

P. bryoides Nutt. W. USA: Pacific NW. Mts. to N. Rocky Mts. and Nebraska. Dense cushion plant 2–5cm high. Leaves 1–2mm long, dark green, densely silver-gray pubescent, cobwebby. Flowers solitary, 7–9mm wide, pure white or lavender. May to June. Very demanding, difficult to propagate species for sunny, dry sites. z3

P. caespitosa Nutt. W. North America, on rocks and in dry conifer stands. Densely caespitose (cushion) plant to 12cm high. Stems procumbent with crowded foliage. Leaves subulate (awlshaped), stiff, prickly, to 13cm long. Flowers solitary, sessile, white to pale lilac. May.

Quite variable and crosses with the *P. douglasii* cultivars. Not in the trade but interesting are the several geographical subspecies varying in height from 3.25cm to 25cm high. z5

P. canadensis see **P. divaricata**

P. decussata. Name of no botanical standing though common in hort. literature. = *P. paniculata*, but also sometimes misapplied to *P. maculata* and *P. carolina*.

P. diffusa Benth. W. North America: Oregon to S. California. Loose or dense mat or cushion plant to 15cm high and wide. Leaves linear or linear-subulate, 10–15mm long, somewhat prickly. Flowers usually solitary, 15mm wide, pink, lilac, sometimes white. Not too difficult to cultivate. The subspecies *scleranthifolia* grows more inland, to Utah and South Dakota, with rigid, harsh-pointed leaves. z7

P. divaricata L. (*P. canadensis* Sweet)., Wild Sweet William. E. North America, in open woodlands. To 35cm high, sterile, procumbent leafy shoots persist throughout the winter. The upper stem leaves somewhat sticky from glandular-tipped hairs. Flower umbels on un-branched stems, blue-violet to lavender, or white in var. *alba*, also lilac or light purple, though individuals of these colors may be natural hybrids with *P. pilosa*. The following subspecies can be distinguished:

P. divaricata ssp. **divaricata**, wide leaved with deeply incised petals, and ssp. **laphamii**, from the western edge of the range covered with rounded, entire petals and rich, blue-lavender flowers, or white in forma *candida*. April to June. Thrives in any fertile, moist, woodsy garden soil, in sun, but best in light shade. 'Chattahoochee' is either a cultivar of *P. divaricata* ssp. **laphamii** or a natural hybrid with *P. pilosa* found by Mrs. J. Norman Henry. Flowers deep violet with intense, purple eyes. Slow growing and difficult to propagate, but very attractive. z4

P. douglasii Hook. USA: Washington and Oregon to W. Montana. Resembles *P. caespitosa*, but occurs on limestone in its habitat. Various clones are found in cultivation, but whether they trace back to this species or another (such as *P. subulata*) will be determined ultimately by genetic mapping. Flowers 1–3 in a cluster, usually soft pink with darker eyes, or lavender or white often with more than 5 lobes. The *P. douglasii*

hybrids originated by crossing this species with *P. subulata* and surely with other species, such as *P. caespitosa*.

The many cultivars include: 'Apollo', good violet-pink; 'Boothman's Variety', violet-pink with a dark eye; 'Crackerjack', bright carmine red, a dense mat, floriferous, the best cultivar; 'Georg Arends' ('Hybrida'), violet-pink with a dark eye; 'Iceberg', pure white with a light violet blush; 'Lilakönigin', whitish violet, very vigorous habit; 'Red Admiral', carmine red, round flowers; 'Rose Cushion', dull pink, very compact, very floriferous; 'Violet Queen', deep

Phlox nana

violet, very compact, occasionally chlorotic; 'Waterloo', black-violet-red, loose habit. Botanists list several subspecies and varieties of *P. douglasii*. z5

P. hoodii Rich. W. USA: California. Dense, tufted mat habit to 5cm high. Leaves subulate, to 10 × 1mm, very woolly-pubescent. Flowers borne singly, mostly white, sometimes light violet, demanding, cultivate like *P. bryoides*. z7 Several very similar botanical subspecies are listed, including:

P. hoodii ssp. **viscidula** Wherry. NW. USA, on dry slopes. Stem base hard, woody. Shoots procumbent to erect, leaves lanceolate, 25 × 4mm. Flowers to 18mm wide, terminal-cymose, light mallow colored. Inflorescence with both gland-tipped and glandless hairs. May to June. z6

P. missoulensis Wherry. USA: Montana to Nevada and Glorcola, on gravelly, south-facing slopes. Dense cushion

perennial, 5–10cm high. Leaves linear to linear-lanceolate, to 15mm long; flowers solitary, white, bluish- or rose-blushed. April to May. Very attractive, but difficult to propagate. z4

P. nana Nutt. S. USA: New Mexico to W. Texas, SE. Arizona and N. Mexico. Procumbent stems to 30cm high in a tuft from a woody rootstock. Leaves to 30mm long, narrow-elliptic to lanceolate, gray-pubescent. Flowers 4cm wide, purple to lilac, light pink, white, or yellow, few in terminal corymbs. Drought-tolerant species, best grown under cover in areas with wet winters. For garden cultivation only in climates with hot, dry summers. Propagation is difficult, cuttings root poorly, root cuttings and seed are possibilities. Similar to *P. mesoleuca* var. *ensifolia* Brand (*P. nana* var. *ensifolia*), but the nodes are clustered at the shoot tips, leaves straight, not recurved. The N. Mexican (horticultural) species, *P. lutea* Pringle and *P. purpurea* (Brand) Maslin, have recently been introduced with yellow and rose-colored flowers respectively. There are also hybrids between these species with flowers orange and other colors. These are not yet well tested in culture. Colorful, but very delicate plants for collector. Blooms very long, from May to July. z7

P. nivalis Lodd ex Sweet. Trailing Phlox. USA: Virginia to Florida and Alabama. Glandular pubescent plant, stems decumbent or trailing, flowering stems ascending to 15cm high. Leaves subulate to linear-acute, to 12mm long. Stigmas never reaching out of the tube.

Flowers about 12.5mm across; corolla wide, lobes entire or shallowly notched, often light colored pink, purple, scarlet, white. The longest anthers are deep in the corolla tube, unlike those of *P. subulata*. Usually on acid soil, thrives in a semi-shaded site. Cultivars include 'Azurea' with pale blue flowers; 'Camla' with salmon-pink flowers; 'Sylvestris' with rose-pink, small flowers. z6(5)

P. pilosa L. Prairie Phlox. E. USA. Stems pubescent to 40cm high, often shorter. Distinguished from *P. divaricata* by the absence of procumbent, semiever-

crowded, purple to magenta-red. April to May.

'Rosea', dark pink; 'Folio-variegata', leaves yellowish-white variegated; 'Millstream', dark pink with a white zone and red star. Tolerates semi-shade and grows best in slightly acid soil. z4

P. reptans see **P. stolonifera**

P. setacea see **P. subulata**

P. speciosa Pursh. W. USA: Washington and Oregon, east to Montana, on dry slopes. Suffruticose to woody plant 20–

with lustrous foliage, flowers heliotrope colored; 'Pink Ridge', light pink. Thrives in a semi-shaded site, as at the edge of a shade bed. Propagates easily by stolon cuttings. Intolerant of lime. z4 (deteriorates in hot, humid summer weather)

P. subulata L. (*P. setacea* L.), Moss Pine, Moss Phlox, Creeping Phlox. E. USA. Spreading, matted, carpeting plants to 10cm high, on dry sites or sandy slopes, also in the light shade of shrubs. Variable in its native habitat with 2 subspecies distinguished:

Phlox subulata hybrid 'Scarlet Flame'

Phlox paniculata hybrid 'Herbstglut'

green, sterile winter shoots and the linear or lanceolate leaf shape (also oblong or ovate in varieties). Also differs in the pubescent corolla tube exterior, the entire corolla lobes, and the bright magenta, pink, purple or red-eyed white flower color. Variable in scent, but mostly sweet, like the scented *Dianthus* or jasmine. April to May. Also subspecies **fulgide** (Wherry) Wherry. Flowers white, hairs without glands; and subsp. **ozarkana** (Wherry) Wherry. Mostly glandular-pubescent, upper leaves often ovate-cordate, mostly magenta. z5

P. × procumbens Lehm. (*P. amoena* hort. non Sims, *P. stolonifera* × *P. subulata*). An old garden hybrid, described at the beginning of the 19th century. Stems erect, to 25cm high. Sterile winter shoots curving down to the ground, occasionally rooting. Leaves elliptic or oblanceolate, pubescent. Flowers in a flat panicle,

40cm high with erect to ascending branches arising from a very woody base. Leaves linear to lanceolate, occasionally ovate-acuminate, 15–40mm long. Flowers in terminal corymbs, pink, to 25mm across, corolla lobes incised. Attractive, xerophytic species; grows best with moisture only in the spring, before and during flowering. For a well-drained rockery. Propagate easily by tip cuttings. z4

P. stellaria see **P. bifida**

P. stolonifera Sims (*P. reptans* Michx.) E. USA: Pennsylvania to Georgia; an Appalachian species. Plant to 25cm high, stoloniferous, quickly forming a large cushion. Leaves spatulate, evergreen. Flowering stems stiffly erect. Flowers in pubescent terminal cymes, violet, blue, or pinkish; also white in cultivation. Spring. Some good cultivars are: 'Ariane', bright pure white; 'Blue Ridge',

P. subulata ssp. **brittonii** (Small) Wherry. (*P. brittonii* Small). Britton's Phlox. USA: Appalachian Mts. and Potomac Valley. Flowers lavender-white to rarely whitish, corolla lobes deeply notched, otherwise resembling the species, with exerted stamens, and matted habit.

P. subulata var. **subulata**. Anthers exserted from the corolla tube, unlike those of *P. nivalis* which are deeply included, stigmas reaching to the corolla limb, grows on any good garden soil but best on a gravelly and sunny site; flower color variable, purple, red, pink, lilac, white, occasionally lavender and pale violet, often with a conspicuous eye. The wild types are rarely found in cultivation today. Rather, a large number of cultivars, some with influence from other species are grown and should be referred to as *P. subulata* cultivars.

Some popular cultivars are listed here, with small flowers (10mm), medium flowers (10–15mm) and large flowers (over 15mm diameter):

'Alexander's Surprise', salmon pink, large flowered.

'Atropurpurea', soft red, medium flowers, surpassed by the newer forms, but very vigorous.

'Avalanche', pure white, large flowered, strong growing.

'Betty', deep pink, large flowered, long flowering.

'Camla' (*P. camlaensis*) see **P. nivalis**.

'Daisy Hill', bright pink, medium always easily cultivated.

'Samson', salmon-pink with red eye, large flowered.

'Scarlet Flame", bright carmine red, large flowered, not always reliably hardy.

'Schneewittchen' (Snow White), pure white, small flowered, compact.

'Silberlicht' (Silvery Light), pure white, small to medium flowered, compact. Similar to 'Bijou', which is pale pink.

'Sensation', bright salmon-pink with a darker eye, medium flowered.

'Snow Queen' ('Maischnee') tionally strong growing.

2. Tall-growing Species

Flowering from early summer to fall, 0.5–1m high. These require constantly moist soil.

P. Arendsii Hybrids (*P.* × *arendsii* hort.). Hybrids between *P. divaricata* and *P. paniculata* cultivars, introduced to the trade by Georg Arends from 1912 to 1927. Clearly combining the characteristics of both species, they flower after the spring-blooming phlox and precede

Phlox paniculata hybrid 'Kirmesländler'

Phlox paniculata hybrid 'Pax'

flowered, forming large cushions.

'Gartenstadt Schnee' (Lahoda), pure white, medium flowered, very vigorous, with unusually pale foliage color.

'G.F. Wilson', slate blue, medium flowered, tall and strong growing.

'Leuchstern' (Bright Star) (Arends), dark pink, medium flowered; tight cushion.

'Moerheimii' (Ruys), dark pink, medium-flowered, vigorous.

'Oakington Blue Eyes', darker than 'G.F. Wilson', medium flowered, vigorously creeping.

'Pink Seedling' (Drake), salmon pink, similar to 'Snow Queen' in habit.

'Red Wings', scarlet red, large-flowered, strong-growing, not exceptionally hardy.

'Ronsdorfer Schöne' (Ronsdorf Beauty) (Arends), bright salmon pink, medium flowered.

'Rotraud', dark pink-red with a darker eye, medium flowered, compact, not (Arends), pure white, round flowered, dense cushion, but sometimes demanding.

'Temiskaming', rich purple-red, exceptionally bright, medium flowered, dark leaves, very vigorous, unfortunately not always easily propagated.

'Veseli' very compact seedling from Czechoslovakia with pure white flowers of 5–6mm wide.

'Violet Seedling', heliotrope with dark eye, medium flowered, slender and strong growing.

'Vivid', clear light pink, small flowered, very compact but best in the rock garden on acidic, gravelly soil, very attractive cultivar, possibly a hybrid with *P. nivalis*. Many cultivars have approached this form in color, but not quite matched it.

'White Delight', pure white, medium to large flowered, strong growing.

'Wiener Neustädter Zwerg' (Lahoda), pale lavender, medium flowered, excep- the *P. paniculata* cultivars; June to August. A hard shearing after flowering will encourage reblooming in the fall. Very few cultivars are found with brighter flower colors than the following more recent introductions:

'Anja' (Arends 1966) 40–60cm, bright purple-red; 'Hilda', 40–60cm, white with pink centers; 'Susanne', 40–60cm, white background with large, red centers, becoming lighter toward the edges.

P. carolina L. (*P. suffruticosa* Vent.). Thick-leaf Phlox, Carolina Phlox. E. USA: North Carolina to NW. Florida, west to Missouri and Mississippi, in open woodlands and occasionally in slightly acidic meadows. Closely related to *P. ovata* L., but distinguished by the scarcely elongating sterile shoots, numerous nodes on the stems, shorter calyx, mostly smaller flowers. The leaves are distinctive in form and size; the basal leaves are always linear, the apical leaves broadly ovate or elliptic and larger than those of *P. ovata*, glabrous or lightly pubescent. Flowers monochromatic, bright purple, occasionally pink or, in cultivation, white; May to September.

The Carolina Phlox is a good grower with a long flowering period, extending from early summer to fall. The following cultivars are recommended: 'Gloriosa', 75cm, salmon-pink; 'Magnificence', 70cm, carmine-pink, large flowered; 'Miss Lingard', before 1933, 70–80cm pure white; 'Nettie Stuart', 60cm, white; 'Perfection', 70cm, white with red centers; 'Snowdon', 60cm, pure white. z5

pubescent. The type species is of the Piedmont region; plants growing further inland are var. *interior*. z4

P. maculata L., Meadow Phlox. Sweet William. E. USA: Connecticut to North Carolina west to Iowa and Missouri, mostly in moist meadows and alluvial lowlands along rivers. Stems frequently with purple spots but these may be lacking on individual plants. Rootstock slender, horizontal, lacking procumbent sterile shoots. Flowering stems with many nodes. Smooth, linear to lanceolate or ovate leaves to 12.5cm long with

'Schneelawine' (Avalanche) (Arends 1918), 1m, pure white; all flowering from June to August. z5

P. ovata L. Mountain Phlox. E. USA: Pennsylvania to Indiana and Alabama, on moderately acidic humus in the upland oak forests, occasionally in moist, grassy and rocky sites. Flowering stems to 90cm high, sterile basal shoots short, but conspicuous, not stoloniferous. Flowering shoots with only a few nodes. The leaves are nearly glabrous, lower leaves long-petioled, upper leaves sessile. Some strains have rather dull magenta-colored flowers, others bright purple, pink or white. *P. ovata* var. **pulchra** is native to Walker County, Alabama (now listed by Wherry as a separate species, *P. pulchra* Wherry), with broader inflorescences and relatively large flowers, mostly soft pink, or whitish. The lower leaves are short-petioled. z5

P. paniculata L. (*P. decussata* hort.), Perennial Phlox, Summer Phlox (in cultivation, Garden Phlox). E. USA: New York to Georgia west to Missouri and Arkansas, many along the Ohio River. In the wild found in thinly wooded, alluvial lowland where the soil is fertile with a nearly neutral pH. Distinguished from all the other species by thin leaves with raised, reticulate veins and with minutely ciliate-toothed margins. Anthers cream colored or white and not bright yellow as most other species. Leaves subopposite, elliptic, lanceolate, or oblong-ovate, glabrous or occasionally pubescent. Corolla tube nearly always pubescent, commonly an unpleasant magenta-pink but also purple, lilac, scarlet, salmon and white. June to August. Also, subspecies **ozarkana** (Wherry) Wherry. Missouri to E. Oklahoma south to N. Louisiana. Upper leaves mostly ovate-cordate, plant glandular-pubescent. *P. paniculata* was introduced into cultivation by Sherard in 1732. John Bertram sent plants to Collinson in 1743, and Miller first illustrated them in 1760.

Phlox paniculata hybrids

P. decussata see **P. paniculata**

P. glaberrima L. Smooth Phlox. E. USA: Virginia to South Carolina, west to Wisconsin and Arkansas. Primarily on moist lowlands or occasionally in open woodlands, generally in infertile, acidic soil. Botanically between *P. carolina* and *P. maculata*, differing from the former by the numerous nodes, narrower leaves and shorter calyx. The stems of *P. maculata* have more nodes, and the inflorescence is long, and conical instead of shallow-crowned, panicled cymes. *P. glaberrima* has moderately large purple to pink flowers, occasionally white. Despite the name, plants are sometimes lightly

branching veins. Inflorescences long, cylindrical or rarely narrowly conical panicled cymes. Flowers with a short calyx; both characteristics easily recognizable. Flowers purple with a violet tube, or pink or white; fragrant; June to September.

The so-called Maculata Hybrids, originated from a cross with *P. carolina*, are the result of an effort by G. Arends to create an early-blooming race of phlox. Once very common, but today little known, are the cultivars: 'Alpha' (Arends 1918), 1.5m, bright lilac-pink with darker centers, large-flowered; 'Rosalinde' (Arends 1918), 1m, carmine-pink, darker than the previous cultivar;

P. suffruticosa see **P. carolina**

Breeding of Garden Phlox

Modern cultivars can be considered largely true descendants of *P. paniculata*. Few show any sign of influence of other species; these few cultivars are hybrids between *P. paniculata* and *P. maculata* or perhaps, *P. carolina*. For this reason, the group should be referred to as Paniculata Cultivars and the terms *P. decussata* hort., *P.* × *hortorum* (Bergm.) should be dropped. This group includes some of the most vigorous and colorful flowering plants in the perennial border and similar situations, even in small gardens. Their use should not, however, be indiscriminate. Many cultivars are so bright and dominant in color that they are difficult to combine well. The popular bright red and salmon colors are best combined with white and light blues, but also with the fall asters and the neutral green tall grasses. The strong yellows of many summer and fall perennials contrast well with the lilac to purple cultivars of phlox. Annual *Penstemon* hybrids are also good companions for Garden Phlox. Systematic breeding work on the large perennial phlox began with thousands of seedlings being produced by Lierval in France about 1839. The Belgian and English breeders soon followed, achieving a wider selection of colors and lower growth habit.

In Germany, W. Pfitzer was the first phlox breeder, with his first cultivar appearing in 1867. Many valuable cultivars came along from the turn of the century to the 1920s. Albert Schöllhammer (Germany) spent more than half a century on the improvement of Garden Phlox. Other German breeders include Goos & Koenemann, Georg Arends and Karl Foerster. In Holland, B. Ruys of Dedemsvaart brought many good cultivars into the trade. Among the most popular are 'Mia Ruys', 'Spitfire', 'Wilhelm Kesselring' and 'Starfire'. In France, before 1913, the Lemoine Nursery, Nancy, introduced 'Jules Sandeau', which is still widely grown in modern gardens. The most successful British *Phlox* breeder was Captain B. Symons-Jeune, whose introductions came into the trade through the Bakers Nursery, Coolsall.

The modern assortment includes not only a wide range of colors, but also variable flowering periods from late June to September. Many cultivars rebloom periodically; some tend toward elongating inflorescences. After the fourth revision of the following recommended list since 1954, it seems the older cultivars are increasingly valuable:

'Aida' (Pfitzer 1933), 1m, violet-red, mid-early.

'B. Symons-Jeune', rose-pink, crimson eye, midseason, 1.2m high.

'Balmoral', rosy-lavender, midseason, 60–70cm high.

'Blue Boy,' bluish-mauve, midseason, 1m high.

'Bornimer Nachsommer' (Foerster 1951), 1.2m, salmon-pink, late.

'Bright Eyes', clear, soft pink, ruby-red eye, midseason, 60cm high.

'Caroline van den Berg', imperial purple shading to mauve, late midseason, 90cm high.

'Dodo Hanbury Forbes', pure pink, rose-red eye, large, midseason, 90cm high.

'Dorffreude' (Foerster 1939), 1.2m, lilac-pink, late.

'Duchess of York', bright salmon-pink, late, 85cm high.

'Fairest One', clear shell pink, no markings, large, early midseason, 90cm high.

'Fairy's Petticoat', light pink, ruby-red eye, midseason, 90–100cm high.

'Frau A. von Mauthner' = 'Spitfire' (Ruys 1927), 90cm, salmon red, midseason.

'Frauenlob' (Foerster 1949), 1.2m, salmon-pink, early.

'Gaity', cherry red, large, midseason, 80–100cm high.

'Hampton Court', amethyst-blue, midseason to late, 90cm high.

'Kirchenfürst' (Foerster 1956), 1m, dark carmine, midseason.

'Kirmesländler' (Foerster 1938), 1.2m, white with a red eye, late.

'Landhochzeit' (Country Wedding) (Foerster 1949), 1.2m, light pink, midseason.

'Leo Schlageter', brilliant scarlet-crimson with very dark eye, midseason, 90cm high.

'Look Again' (Symons Jeune), 80cm, light blood red, midseason.

'Mia Ruys', pure white, very large, midseason, 60cm high.

'Mrs. R. P. Struthers, scarlet-red, midseason, 70cm high.

'Mt. Fujiyama', pure white, exceptionally fine, midseason, 75cm high.

'Nymphenburg' (Buchner 1954), 1.4m, white, late.

'Orange' (Schöllhammer 1955), 80cm, bright orange-red, late.

'Orange Perfection', closest to true orange, midseason, 90cm high.

'Pax' (Schöllhammer 1955), 1m, white, late.

'Prime Minister', pure white, red eye, late midseason, 90cm high.

'Progress', light blue, deep purple eye, very large flowers, midseason, 90cm high.

'Rosa Pastell' (Pink Pastel) (Foerster 1958), 1m, pink, midseason.

'Rotball' (Red Ball) (Linden 1972), 80cm, bright purple carmine, midseason.

'Schaumkrone' (White Caps) (Bornimer Perennials 1975), 1m, pure white, red eye, late.

'Schneeferner' (Snow Caps) (Foerster 1958), 1m, white, midseason.

'Sir John Falstaff', deep salmon-pink, purple eye, midseason, 1m high.

'Sommerfreude' (Summer Joy) (Schöllhammer 1954), 90cm, warm pink, midseason.

'Spätrot' (Late Red) (Foerster 1934), 1m salmon red, late.

'Starfire' crimson-red, leaves dark green, midseason, 90cm high.

'Sternhimmel' (Starry Sky) (Schöllhammer 1950), 1m, light violet, midseason.

'Tenor', soft ruby-red, midseason, 60cm high.

'The King', very deep purple, large, midseason, 60–75cm high.

'Toits de Paris', lavender-blue, faint white eye, midsesaon, 90cm high.

'Violetta Gloriosa' (Foerster 1956), 1.3m, light violet, midseason.

'Wilhelm Kesselring' (Ruys 1923), 80cm, red-violet with white centers, early.

'White Admiral', pure white, sturdy, late, 70–90cm high.

'Windsor', carmine-rose, red eye, midseason, 90cm high.

'Württembergia' = 'Jules Sandeau' (Pfitzer 1919), 80cm, bright pink, early.

Lit: Hitchcock/Cronquist: *Flora of the Pacific Northwest.* Foster, H.L.: *The Genus Phlox.* Alpine Garden Society Bulletin 38 (1970) pp.66–90. Maslin, T.P.: *Phlox nata* Nuttall. Alpine Garden Society Bulletin 46 (1978) pp.163–167. Maslin, T.P.: *The Rediscovery of Phlox lutea* and *Phlox purpurea.* Bulletin of the American Rock Garden Society 37 (1979) pp.62–69. Wherry, Edgart.: *The Genus Phlox.* Morris Arboretum Monographs, III. Philadelphia, Pa.

Garden Phlox cultivars do not move freely across international borders because of the possibility of introducing nematodes, particularly, the Golden Nematode. A few cultivars are, therefore, in international distribution but by and large, each country has its own recommended cultivar list. English gardeners may consult the R.H.S. Dictionary of Gardening Supplement, also trial garden results from Wisley published in the Journal of the R.H.S. American gardeners must rely, alas, on descriptions in mail order catalouges.

Phoenicaulis Nutt.
Cruciferae

Two species of small, perennial herbs from Pacific North America. Rare, small herbs for the experienced collector, requiring a sunny, dry site with sandy, humus-rich loam in the rock garden. Easily damaged by winter wet; best grown as a potted plant in the alpine house. Propagate by seed. Some of the *Artemisia* and *Draba* species are good companions.

A small, tufted perennial with a simple or branched pubescent crown. Leaves basal, rosetted. Flowers showy, in a raceme; sepals 4, petals 4, pinkish, purple, rarely white, long-clawed. Fruit a silique.

P. cheiranthoides Nutt. (*Parrya menziesii* (Hook.) Greene). USA: Washington and N. California, Idaho and Nevada among artemisias in the desert and in ponderosa pine forests, on dry, well-drained, sandy soil. Leaves in rosettes, gray-pubescent, 3–10cm long, oblanceolate, entire, larger than the bractlike leaves of the 15–20cm high, racemose inflorescence. Corolla pink to reddish purple. Silique 2–8cm long and 2–6mm wide, often more or less sickleshaped. Blooms from April to June. z5 (E)

Phragmites Adans.
Gramineae
Reed

P. australis (Cav.) Trin. ex Steud. (*P. communis* Trin.). Reed Cosmopolitan Grass. Found in wet sites and flood plains of the temperate zones, somewhat in the tropics. A pioneer species, establishing large expanses of soil in shallow water by the quickly and widely spreading rhizomes. Plants reach more than 3m

Phuopsis stylosa 'Purpurea' (= 'Rubra')

high in flower after August. The flower panicles are to 50cm long and purple tinged. The foliage is bluish-green, leaf blades long-acuminate to 50cm long, the leaf sheaths tightly enclose the stem and cover the nodes, ligules reduced to a ring of hairs. The leaf blades abscise in the fall, but the stems persist overwinter. The species is important for reclaiming flooded land, stream bank erosion control and streamside wildlife habitat. Also assists in clearing up polluted streams. Reeds are quite invasive; companion plants must be situated on the edge of the site in conditions less conducive to reed growth. To control reeds, mow or clip back the young plants repeatedly to discourage growth.

Because of their extraordinary vigor, reeds are difficult to use in the garden. In small pools, plants must be confined to tubs. Propagation is usually by division of the rhizome. For quick colonizing, young shoots may be stuck as cuttings, just under the surface of the soil, in shallow water, in spring. Seed propagation is used only for the species, and occasionally when seeding lowlands for reclamation. For gardening purposes,

Phragmites australis

the following cultivars are more ornamental, differing primarily in habit, also in leaf color.

Cultivar 'Pseudodonax' is not recognized as a botanically distinct variety. Plants may reach 10m high under favorable conditions. Spreads less vigorously than the species. A valuable cultivar if a waterside screen is desired. Resembles *Arundo*, but tolerates much more wind and is fully winter hardy. 'Humilis' is a stiff-leaved dwarf cultivar with compact inflorescences. Plants often to only 12cm high. 'Aurea' is a golden yellow variety found in nature. The British have a cultivar by this name with golden yellow inflorescences. 'Striatopictus', longitudinally striped yellowish-white, of slower growth. Not very effective. 'Variegatus' is a choice, small-growing form with bright gold-yellow, longitudinally striped leaves. The color fades somewhat when plants are in flower; recommended for small garden pools and streams. The botanical subspecies, segregated by details of inflorescence structure, habit, and other subtle characteristics, include: ssp. *australis*, to 3.5m high, and ssp. *altissimus*, to nearly 6m high, a Mediterranean basin plant.

Phuopsis (Griseb.) Hook.f.
Rubiaceae

One species, closely related to *Asperula*. Strong-growing, weak-stemmed perennial, forming large mats in time. Suitable for planting in open, sunny, somewhat dry sites on the fringe of a large rock garden or on a dry slope. A poor choice for small gardens, since it is somewhat invasive. Entire plant is fragrant, somewhat vanilla scented, especially after a rain; the flowers are spicy sweet scented. Large plantings may be livened up with various species of spring-flowering bulbs. In very cold, snowless winters plants may freeze out. Propagation is by removal of young plants, formed abundantly on the procumbent shoots; also by division and seed.

P. stylosa (Trin.) Jacks. (*Crucianella stylosa* Trin.). Caucasus, E. Asia Minor, NW. Iran. Superficially similar to Sweet Woodruff (*Asperula odorata*) with 10–30cm long, procumbent, 4-angled, leafy stems. Leaves sessile, lanceolate, slender pointed, spiny-ciliate, 6–9 in whorls. Terminal inflorescences hemispherical, involucrate. Flowers pink, purple-pink on the form 'Purpurea', fragrant. Calyx tube-shaped, corolla tubular-funnel-shaped, 5-lobed; styles widely exserted from the corolla tube. Blooming from June to August. z7 (E.)

Phygelius E. Mey.ex Benth
Scrophulariaceae
Cape Fuschia

Two species of upright-growing sub-shrubby plants with more or less herbaceous branches and with opposite, petioled, crenate leaves. Flowers long-tubular, nodding, in terminal panicles, bright scarlet or salmon. Useful for planting with sun-loving plants such as *Perovskia*, and *Gladiolus* 'Citronella' on southern exposures, in borders and among massed plants. Quite effective in

Phygelius capensis

front of a white wall. They thrive in most well-drained garden-type soils. Problem free and undemanding in warmer climates. Must be protected from cold and winter wet in colder climates. Propagate by seed, division and cuttings in spring. Pollinated by birds in its native habitat.

P. aequalis Harv. S. Africa. Stems about 90cm high, with tubular, one-sided (unlike *P. capensis*), nodding or drooping flowers; coral pinkish-red to salmon-red with a yellow throat, chocolate brown anthers, not quite as spreading as those of *P. capensis*, floriferous from summer to fall. Exceptionally charming, though little cultivated. z7

P. capensis E. Mey. S. Africa. Grows to 1.2m high in warm regions. With 4-angled stems, broadly ovate leaves and tubular, glossy orange-red, to 5cm-long flowers with yellow throats, drooping in loose panicles. July to fall. 'Coccineus', is even more brightly colored, vermilion red. z7 (Mü)

Lit. A. J. Coombes *Phygelius* in the wild and in cultivation. *The Plantsman* 9(4):233–246.

Phyla see Lippia

Phyllitis Hill
Polypodiaceae
Hart's-tongue Fern,
Deer-tongue Fern

About 8 species distributed through nearly all climatic zones. Small- to medium-sized ferns with simple, entire fronds, mostly short-stiped, semievergreen to evergreen, in a vase-shaped cluster from an upright rootstalk.

Phyllitis scolopendrium

P. scolopendrium (L.) Newm. (*Asplenium scolopendrium* L., *Scolopendrium vulgare* Sm., *S. officinarum* SW.), Hart's-tongue Fern. Found in stony mountain woodlands, in ravines and moist cliffsides in Europe, Asia Minor, on the Atlantic Islands, in Japan, N. Africa and E. North America. Usually grows on limestone.

Rhizome short, upright; fronds oblong-lanceolate, simple, 30–60cm long, often shorter, 4–8cm wide, clustered; solitary plants are regularly funnel-form. Fronds often undulate, cordate, tip acute or obtuse, glossy dark green, leathery, persistent. Sori linear, yellow-green at first, later clustered in thick, brown rows. With its many forms one of the most important garden ferns. For shady sites in the rock garden among rhododendrons and other humus-loving woody plants. A good companion for many small- and medium-sized shade-loving perennials. Grows best in humus woodland soil, also in any average, always moist, even slightly acid, garden soil when topdressed in fall with leafmold or other organic humus. The fall mulch should not be removed in spring, nor should the old fern leaves, at least until the new ones have been fully developed. Propagation is by spores or frond stipe cuttings. Spores ripen from July to October.

The Hart's-tongue Fern has many cultivars, the best of which are:

'Angustifolia', (Narrow Hart's-tongue Fern). Fronds to 50cm long, but only 3–4cm wide.

'Capitata', (Tasselled Hart's-tongue Fern). Frond to 30cm long, terminating in a cristate structure, resembling a tassel.

'Crispa', (Wavy-frond Hart's-tongue Fern). Often confused with 'Undulata'. Fronds to 40cm long, bright green, evenly and distinctly undulate, sterile. Certainly the most attractive cultivar.

'Cristata', (Cockscomb Hart's-tongue Fern). Frond tips pectinate-parted.

'Digitata Cristata', (Palmate Cockscomb Hart's-tongue Fern). Fronds forked branched distally, segment tips cut comb-like.

'Kaye's Lacerata', (Kaye's Shredded Hart's-tongue Fern). Frond margins unevenly deep divided and shredded, tips comb-like.

'Marginata', (Bimarginate Hart's-tongue Fern). Named by Prof. R. Maatsch. Fronds to 45cm, margins more or less incised, fronds entirely or partially with distinctly membranous lamella (forming a double margin).

'Marginata Angustissima', (Dwarf Bimarginate Hart's-tongue Fern). Like 'Marginata', but substantially smaller, 8–15cm high with thick lamella, distinctly incised, appearing fimbricate. Occurs among sporelings of 'Marginata'. Suitable for trough gardens and small rockeries.

'Ramosa', (Twin Hart's-tongue Fern). Many forms produce sporelings with fronds parted at the base to form 2 blades.

'Ramosa Cristata', (Twin Cockscomb Hart's-tongue Fern). Fronds split at the base, frond tips lobed or pectinate.

'Ramosa Cristata Nana', (Dwarf Cockscomb Hart's-tongue Fern). Only 6–10cm high miniature form of the previous cultivar. May be used like the dwarf form of 'Marginata'.

'Undulata', (Wavy Hart's-tongue Fern). Somewhat less undulate than 'Crispa', but fertile and dark green.

These cultivars usually come true from spores, but new forms frequently occur. These and other cultivars only come entirely true when propagated vegetatively. z5 (D.)

Phyllostachys Sieb. et Zucc.
Gramineae
Golden Bamboo

This genus of tall, evergreen woody grasses belongs to a subfamily of the Bambusoideae, important for its hardiness. *Phyllostachys* includes about 50 species, all indigenous to China. Long-recognized ornamental and utility plants, now distributed throughout the world, some species only introduced to Western gardens relatively recently. The hardiest species are often naturalized in

Phyllostachys aurea

parks and gardens. *Phyllostachys* species are distinguished from some other bamboo genera, especially *Sinarundinaria*, by their need for warm temperatures during the vegetation period.

The growth habit depends upon the characteristics of the rhizomes. The length of rhizomes is partly dependent upon the species and partly upon the age of the plant and site conditions. Plants easily become overly vigorous and quite invasive. For this reason the *Phyllostachys* are not as widely useful as the clumpforming *Sinarundinaria*.

Where climatic conditions allow, *Phyllostachys* spp. will bring unique ornamental properties to the garden which are lacking in other genera. Many characteristics of growth and development are typical throughout the genus. The plants may emerge any time from April to August, depending somewhat upon species, even more on soil temperature, and reach their annual height within 6 weeks. The planting may, however, take 5–15 years to become established and attain its ultimate height. Until established, new canes are increasingly tall annually. Short lateral branches, 2 at each node in most *Phyllostachys* species, develop as the cane is growing taller. These are produced

from beneath the nodal sheaths which dry and fall as the cane matures producing the typical flattening on one or both sides of the stem. These flat sides alternate from node to node, corresponding to the alternating, distichous arrangement of the branches. Leaves, emerging at the nodes from stem sheaths, vary considerably among the species, and also according to position on the stem. Stem sheathes becomes larger on the upper part of the stem. Precise identification of species is possible during the vegetation period only by the characteristics of the stem sheaths

Phyllostachys nigra

and the characteristics of ciliate hair clusters on the blade base. Species may also be identified, at least tentatively, by close examination of the hidden leaf bases, comparing them with other species for the relatively short time of new growth emergence, which varies with each species. All of these identifying methods are important since the bamboos flowers rarely and when they do, the entire clump dies. Interestingly, a given species of bamboo flowers simultaneously world-wide and dies, almost totally, depleting that species for several years. It is very difficult to say how large a *Phyllostachys* planting will grow on a given site and microclimate. Only experience and similar growing conditions provide a basis for estimating the behavior of bamboo. This uncertainty about performance is especially true for the relatively unknown species.

The same may be said for rhizome vigor and spreading habit. In cool summer climates, rhizomes of *Phyllostachys* are seldom as invasive as those of *Pleioblastus chino-pumilus* (*Sasa pumila*) or *Sasaella ramosa* (*Sasa vagans*), but the opposite is true where summers are hot. New shoots of *Phyllostachys* are, in any case, brittle enough to be broken off as they appear in an unwanted place. The final judgment on the garden merit of *Phyllostachys* species will only come with many more years of experience with the various species in culture. A study is needed to evaluate all the available bamboo in a given area under similar conditions.

The various species have widely varying cultural preferences, depending upon their native habitats. Bamboos in general, being naturally evergreen, are sometimes placed in a semi-shaded site. This practice, however, is not recommended for *Phyllostachys* which thrive in a warm site in full sun. Protection from wind, especially during periods of temperature extremes, summer and winter, is important if foliage is to remain green.

It helps, when planning a bamboo planting, to refer to conditions in the species' native habitat. Also, select species with a reasonable degree of winter hardiness, at least such that plants will survive if cut back for the winter. The plants are best left unsheared to help protect the below-ground rhizomes. Most *Phyllostachys* species will suffer leaf damage at −17 degrees C. (about 0 degrees F.). Even if the entire plant is damaged above ground, however, it will survive provided periods of deep cold are infrequent, and summers are long and warm, with optimal water and fertilizer available. Hardiness may be considerably improved by choosing a microclimate near a warm wall or other protected site. To help protect the rhizome and root system, a mulch layer of the plant's own leaves is best (also for its high silica content). Additional mulch of leafmold, composted wood chips, or bark may be added for additional protection. *Phyllostachys*, like other bamboos, require large amounts of fertilizer, preferably with nitrogen ratings twice to three times as high as that of the phosphorus and potassium. Most typical lawn grass fertilizers, with 3:1:1 or 4:1:1 N:P:K ratios, are right for bamboos. Many organic fertilizers have such analyses, but in low concentrations. In mineral fertilizers, the soil-acidifying types are preferable.

Recent studies have shown that all bamboos are strengthened by the addition of silicon (silica). All of the most impressive bamboos stands and specimens in Europe grow on a siliceous soil.

The simplest source of silica is from the plant's own foliage; or a compost of *Equisetum* (Horsetail) or siliceous clay (bentonite).

The best time for transplanting bamboos is brief, after the ground warms up, but before new growth is active. Greater success is possible with potted plants than with plants moved bare root or with a root ball.

Propagation is only possible by division. Even this may be difficult, with some difficult species, being divided only in a temperate greenhouse in late winter. The following species descriptions include those time-tested as well as several species introduced only in the last few decades and not yet widely available. The ultimate heights given represent the heights commonly found in cultivation (first figure) and the heights given in the literature for plants under ideal conditions (second figure).

P. aurea A. (Carr.) C. Riv., Golden Bamboo. China. Long-cultivated and widely distributed species. Somewhat clump form in culture with only short rhizomes recognizable by the stem swelling beneath the nodes and the condensing of the nodes at the stem base. Occasionally several internodes are compressed, usually near the shoot base. The stiffly erect habit of the species and the dense, gold-green foliage make this an effective wind and visual barrier. Tolerates −20 degrees C. (−4 degrees F.), 4–10m high. z6

P. aureosulcata McClure. Chekiang (China). Yellow-green Bamboo, Stake Bamboo. Widely cultivated, probably the hardiest of the known species. New growth appears early, April or May. Grows strongly upright, although the young shoots, being succulent, often cause a bow at the base. New canes are conspicuously rough, and the flat side is golden yellow colored. The foliage is dark green, loose and translucent. Plants tolerate −20 degrees C. (−4 degrees F.) and probably colder minimums. 5–10m. z6

P. bissettii McClure, Sichuan. The far inland habitat, near Chengdu, suggests that this uncommon species will be more winter hardy. In fact, very low temperatures have been tolerated by specimens planted in Michigan. Canes are crowded, the foliage is dense, and the lateral branches rebranch. Quite garden worthy as specimen plants, but also suitable as a windbreak for more tender plants. 3–7m. z5

P. flexuosa A. et C. Riv. Zig-Zag Bamboo.

China, so widely distributed that its exact place of origin is not certain. Long cultivated in Europe, quite hardy. Its name comes from growth habit; the growing cane changes direction of growth somewhat at each branching node. Young canes, especially, tend to nod; becoming stiffer and coloring blackish with age. Tolerates −20 degrees C. (−4 degrees F.), 3–10m high. z6

P. glauca McClure. Kiangsi. Sometimes found listed as *P. violescens*. This plant is not identical to *P. bambusoides* 'Violescens'. *P. glauca* is one of the tallest *Phyllostachys* species in cultivation. The canes are dark green, densely crowded, the leaves are stiff and firm, unlike the other species. Tolerates −17 degrees C. (1 degree F.), 5–15m high. z7

P. nigra (Lodd. ex Lindl.) Munro. Black Bamboo. The various clones of this variable species are best considered as cultivars. Long cultivated for ornament and utility in Japan and China. It is unclear which clone is the typical species, certainly not the form generally distributed as *P. nigra*. Several strains may qualify, but in this work the most likely, with all the typical characteristics of the species, is the cultivar 'Nigra'. The common characteristics of all the cultivars are the broad, spreading colony habit, the gracefully nodding shoots and the attractive, dense foliage. The shoots are green at first on all forms.

'Boryana', with brown speckles on green canes, reasonably hardy and garden worthy for its strictly erect habit. Tolerates −20 degrees C. (−4 degrees F.), 4–15m high.

'Fulva', very fine brown-spotted canes by the first fall on young canes, the mottling concentrated mostly below the nodes. The internodes, therefore, appear as if highlighted with spray paint. Later, the green base color turns yellow giving the stems a gold-brown effect. Thereafter, the color intensifies, old stems turning black. The mature leaves of 'Fulva' have a very fine black-brown margin, often only on one side. A very decorative, tall and hardy form of *P. nigra*. 4–12m high, to −20 degrees C. (−4 degrees F.).

'Henonis', one of the most attractive bamboos. The only form of the group to keep the green stems even on older plants. Often referred to as the "Flying Bamboo" in its native habitat because of the nodding of the branch tips from the weight of the densely clustered uppermost leaves. Also tolerates −20 degrees C. (−4 degrees F.) and more; 5–16m high.

'Nigra', stems turning entirely black

after the first summer. Especially conspicuous, unique for the species, is the white pulverulent ring under each node. Unfortunately, the true 'Black Bamboo' is not as hardy as the various cultivars and therefore is better suited to warmer sites and tub planting. Tolerates −15 degrees C. (5 degrees F.), 4–8m high.

'Punctata', more common in culture, more vigorous and hardier than 'Nigra', but stems color more slowly, are spotted, and often not completely black. 5–10m. z7(6)

P. propinqua McClure. Kwangsi.

Despite its southern origin in Peking, this is a reasonably hardy species. Ornamental plants with crowded branches on nodding cane tips. 3–7m. z8(7)

P. violescens see **P. glauca**

P. viridiglaucescens (Carr.) A. et R. Riv. China. A poorly defined species, commonly cultivated in Europe; although only relatively recently mentioned in Chinese literature. Plants with long rhizomes forming a small grove rather than a clump. Stems often rise obliquely from the ground, especially on young

plants. Often confused with *P. bambusoides*, which is however, less vigorous and invasive, with thicker, pale green new shoots. The species tolerates less than −20 degrees C. (−4 degrees F.). Suitable as an open-growing evergreen on a woodland margin or foreground for a wall or slope. 6–10m. z7(6)

P. viridis (Young) McClure. China. An important utility plant in its habitat and in many E. Asiatic countries. A clone or the form 'Robert Young' is usually cultivated. This cultivar is highly recom-

Physalis alkekengi **var.** *franchetii*

mended for warm sites for its gold-yellow stems with scattered green stripes and attractive gold-green, airy foliage. Also does not grow as rapidly as the other species. Tolerates to −20 degrees C. (−4 degrees F.), 6–15m high (6–25m for *P. viridis*). z7 (S.)

Hundreds of bamboos in several genera, including *Phyllostachys*, have been introduced into the S. USA. by the U.S.D.A. Plant Introduction Division. Refer to various U.S.D.A. publications on bamboos, to Experimental Station Publications from universities in southern

fruits are decorative, globose, orange-colored berries surrounded by an orange-scarlet, inflated, papery, persistent calyx. Popular for cutting for dried arrangment material. The single ornamental species thrives in moist, somewhat alkaline soil and a sunny site. This plant can be quite vigorous under favorable conditions. Should be situated where it can naturalize or be contained by vertical partitions inserted into the ground to stop the spread of long, slender, fast-growing rhizomes. Propagate by division, stolon cuttings, or seed. About 800 seeds per gram. Germina-

otherwise similar to the previous variety. Leaves larger, calyx to 7cm long. The cultivar 'Zwerg' (Dwarf), is only 20cm high and suitable for pot culture and the rock garden, although rarely available. Catalogs list 'Gigantea' and 'Monstrosa' with large celices, 'Pygmaea', presumably the same as 'Zwerg; dwarfer overall. z5 (Kö.)

P. bunyardii see **P. alkekengi** var. **franchetii**

P. franchetii see **P. alkekengi** var. **franchetii**

Physoplexis comosa

Physostegia virginiana

states, also California. Gardeners should refer also to *Phyllostachys* in *Hortus Third*, MacMillan Publishing Co., but the hardiness zone numbers tend to be too high.

Physalis L.
Solanaceae
Ground Cherry, Chinese Lantern

About 80 species of annuals and perennials; only 1 species is of interest as an ornamental though several produce edible fruit. Upright, bushy habit. Leaves alternate, entire or undulate-margined or pinnatisect, ovate. The pediceled, small, whitish flowers are inconspicuous, borne in the leaf axils. The

tion is irregular over a long period of time, the first seeds germinating in about 50 days. A cold temperature treatment is beneficial.

P. alkekengi L. Chinese-lantern Plant, Japanese Lantern is cultivated in 2 varieties:

P. alkekengi var. **alkekengi**. Indigenous from SE. Europe to W. Asia. Stems 30–60cm high. Inconspicuous yellowish-white flowers with yellow anthers. The following variety is larger and more ornamental. z5

P. alkekengi var. **franchetii** (Mast.) Mak. (*P. franchetii* Mast., *P. bunyardii* hort., *P. franchetii* var. *bunyardii* (hort.) Mak.). Japan, Korea, N. China. About 1m high,

Physoplexis (Endl.) Schur
Campanulaceae

One species from the S. Dolomite Mts. Like *Phyteuma*, and almost universally included with it; the flowers in heads on stems to 15cm high, flowers flaskshaped, petal tips joined laterally, or rarely entirely connate; filaments linear.

P. comosa (L.) Schur (*Phyteuma comosum* L.), Devil's Claw. Rock plant found in crevices in the Dolomite Mts. Plants 10–15cm high, alternate leaved, with a milky latex sap. Flowers many, in headlike inflorescences. Individual flowers flask-shaped, bright lilac at the base, blackish toward the tips, occasionally pure white or violet-red colored. Flowers from May to June in culture, July to August in nature. Not easy to grow; either plant young seedlings in rock crevices (in an intensively cultivated rockery) or grow them in pots. Shade is preferable, in a half peat/half limestone, broken brick and sand mix. Useful mainly only as a collector's plant. Propagate by seed. z6 (K.)

Physostegia Benth.
Labiatae
False Dragonhead, Obedient Plant

About 15 species of medium-height, glabrous to puberulous annuals or perennials, some with creeping rhizomes and 4-angled stems; leaves opposite, often toothed and long, axillary and terminal flower spikes. The flowers are unique in that they are mobile, as if hinged; blooming from midsummer to fall. Indigenous to E. North America, most on moist, sunny central or southern prairies. Suitable for large herbaceous borders, also grown for cut flowers. Undemanding plants for any average garden soil as long as the site is not too hot and dry. Easily propagated by division and cuttings, very prolific and may become weedy and invasive.

P. virginiana (L.) Benth. (*Dracocephalum virginicum* L.). E. North America: New Brunswick to Minnesota, south to the Carolinas and Missouri. Glabrous stems to 1.2m high. Leaves to 12.5cm long, whorled, lanceolate, sharp serrate, smaller and narrower near the top. Flowers in spike-like panicles, bright lilac-pink; July to September. Cultivars include:
'Alba', flowers white, early.
'Bouquet Rose', 70cm high, flowers bright violet-rose, early.
'Gigantea', to 2m high, flowers glowing lilac-pink.
'Schneekrone' (Snow Crown) is a pure white cultivar.
'Summer Snow', 60cm high, flower spikes snow white, midseason.
'Summerspire', 1m high, flowers showy dark pink, midseason.
'Variegata' to 65cm high, leaves bordered and sometimes mottled milk-white, flowers magenta-pink.
'Vivid', a dwarf cultivar 60cm high, with purple-pink flowers, late, may be potted or transplanted at any time except when in full bloom. z4–8 (L.J.& M.)

Phyteuma L.
Campanulaceae
Horned Rampion

About 40–50 species from Europe and W. Asia. Perennials of low or tall habit with mostly carrot-like taproots, rosetted basal leaves and alternate stem leaves. Flowers in terminal heads or elongated spikes. Flowers 5-merous, corolla blue, purplish or white, petals narrow to linear, separate almost to the base but often connate at the tip, later often spreading; style long-exerted, stigmas 2–

Phyteuma nigrum

3. The low and medium-sized species are best in the rock garden, but not in full sun. The taller species thrive in a wooded site, in a well-drained, not too dry soil. Propagate by seed. Because of the taproot, young plants should be raised in containers. The hardiest species are listed:

P. canescens see **Asyneuma canescens**

P. coeruleum R. Schulz. Similar to *P. spicatum*, but flowers pure blue. Its natural range is between the northern *P. nigrum* and the southern *P. spicatum*. z6

P. comosum see **Physoplexis comosa**

P. confusum Kerner. Alps. A dwarf alpine species with dark blue flower heads. z5

P. globulariaefolium Sternb. et Hoppe. Alps. The dwarfest species with few-flowered heads of bright violet-blue, occasionally white flowers. Plants to 5cm high, leaves spatulate, relatively wide at the tip. Demanding and short-lived. z5

P. hemisphaericum L. S. Central Europe, east to E. Austria. Stems to 30cm high. Basal leaves few, entire linear, grasslike. Flower heads 1–2cm wide, lavender-blue, occasionally white. June to July. Collector's plant, lime-intolerant, demanding. z5

P. michelii All. S. Alps (France, Italy). Stems 30–50cm high. Leaves ovate to ovate-cordate. Flowers crowded in ovate spikes, bluish-lilac. May to June. z6

P. nigrum F. W. Schmidt. Belgium to E. Austria. Stems 20–25cm high. Basal leaves long petioled, glabrous, cordate-oval, rarely nearly orbicular. Inflorescences in oval, later cylindrical spikes. Flowers black-violet. June to July. Widely distributed European woodland plant growing longer-stemmed in deep shade. z6

P. orbiculare L. S. England and Lithuania, south to S. Spain and Albania. Stems 10–45cm high, leaves usually cordate-ovate. Basal leaves petioled, stem leaves sessile. Flowers in round heads, blue or blue-violet, occasionally white. May to June. z6

P. scheuchzeri All. Europe: S. Alps and N. Apennines. Stems to 45cm high. Basal leaves ovate to ovate-lanceolate, 5–12.5cm long, crenate or dentate, long petioled. Flower heads globose, to about 2.5cm across, flowers deep blue. Thrives on calcareous soil. Long-lived and attractive. June to July. z6

P. sieberi Spreng. Europe: SE. Alps. Stems to 20cm, similar to the above species but with more ovate than lanceolate leaves. June to July. Generally somewhat more demanding in cultivation. z6

P. spicatum L. Spiked Rampion. Europe. Limited to south of the range of *P. coeruleum*. Stems to 80cm high. Basal leaves long petioled, deeply cordate, ovate, glabrous. Flowers in cylindrical spikes, 5–7.5cm long, yellowish-white, tips greenish. Blooms from May to June, woodland plant. z6 (K.)

Phytolacca L.
Phytolaccaceae
Pokeweed, Pokeberry

Twenty-five species of perennial herbs with massive, fleshy, roots; shrubs and tree-like perennials primarily from the tropics and subtropics. Herbaceous stems often brightly colored. Leaves often large, alternate, simple. Flowers in racemes or panicles, small, sepals 5, petals 0, stamens 6–33 and carpels 5–16. Fruits usually juicy, berrylike, dark red to blackish. Only the following species can be recommended for gardens with reservations. Stately foliage plants with inconspicuous flowers but decorative stems and blackish-purple berries. The

fruit juice was once used for coloring red wine, candies and rough. While fruit juice and emerging shoots are more or less edible, mature stems and leaves, seeds, and especially the massive root are extremely poisonous. Thrives in any loamy humus garden soil, in sun or semi-shade. Propagate by seed, best sown in March in a warm greenhouse or by division in spring. Suitable for specimen planting or massing. A good companion for non-winter-hardy *Solanum* and other tender foliage plants. Plant pathologists have determined that *P. americana* is a major reservoir for many of the most

Phytolacca americana

damaging plant viruses including mosaics, yellows', ring-spot and several others. These are transmitted especially to Liliaceae, Amaryllidaceae, and Golaneceae, but many dissimilar genera as well. Leaf-hoppers, aphids and other piercing-sucking insects serve as vectors.

P. americana L. (*P. decandra* L.), Pokeweed. North America: from the New England states, Quebec, New York and Ontario, south to Florida and Texas; Mexico; also naturalized in S. Europe and N. Africa. For open sites in fertile soil, suitable for woodland clearings and open fields. Stems 1–4m high, with large, fleshy, poisonous roots (and seeds), with stems turning reddish. The young shoots are edible and a substitute for asparagus, but caution is needed not to include pieces of the poisonous root. Entire plant is unpleasantly scented. Leaves oblong to oval-lanceolate, to 30cm-long.

Simple racemes somewhat drooping,

15cm and longer. Flowers hermaphroditic, white or pinkish, with usually 10 stamens and 10 connate carpels. Fruit a purple berry, turning black, with a claret-colored, staining juice. Blooms from June to September. Similar to *P. acinosa* Roxb. (*P. esculenta* Van Houtte) from China, with hermaphroditic flowers usually with 8 stamens and 8 separate carpels. Also similar to *P. clavigera* W.W. Sm. from Yunnan with 12 stamens, ovary with 8 locules, purple-pink sepals and inky black fruits. Both species with erect inflorescences and green stems, smaller than *P. americana*. z4–9 (E.)

P. decanda see **P. americana**

Pimpinella L.
Umbelliferae
Anise

One hundred forty or more species of annual, biennial and perennial herbs, none of great ornamental importance, from Eurasia and Africa, one species in Pacific North America and a few in South America. Basal leaves usually entire or 3-cleft, occasionally 1–3-pinnate, the middle stem leaves usually bipinnate. Calyx very small. Corolla white or yellow, occasionally pink or purple, lobes not or only slightly emarginate.

Rarely used umbellate flowering herbs for meadow plantings, especially in parks and grassy slopes. *P. saxifraga* thrives in a dry, sunny site while *P. major* grows best in semi-shade and moist soil. Propagation is by fresh seed. Both species are suitable for grouping with other meadow plants of similar requirements.

P. major (L.) Huds. Europe, Asia Minor, Caucasus, in meadows, hedgerows and woodland margins, in thickets and open woodlands from the plains to the mountains on moist, fertile, loamy humus soils. Quite a variable species, 0.4–1m high, with sharply angular-channeled, leafy, usually glabrous stems and 1-pinnate leaves. Umbels 10–15 rayed.

Pinguicula alpina

Corolla white, occasionally pink, on var. **rubra** (Hoppe) Fiori et Beguinot from the higher mountains of Central Europe. Blooms from June to September. z5

P. saxifraga L. Europe, W. and Central Asia, Siberia, in dry fields and woodlands, on gravelly slopes on calcareous, sandy loam from the plains to the subalpine, rarely alpine, elevations. Quite variable but generally similar to the previous species. Stems cylindrical, 30–60cm high, fine-channeled or slightly angular, nearly leafless toward the top, glabrous or slightly pubescent at the base. Leaves 1- or multipinnate. Umbels 5–16 rayed, small. Corolla white, occasionally pink or red. Blooms from July to September. An old medicinal plant, cultivated since 1560. z4 (E.)

Pinellia Ten.
Araceae

Three of the 6 E. Asian tuberous species are cultivated in Europe as semi-shade-loving perennials. Leaves and flowers borne together, plants much like *Arisaema* but with a single ovacle in the ovary, and male and female flowers separated on the spadix by a membrane; staminate flowers with 2 stamens. Grown from seed. These are not particularly attractive plants and are grown only for botanical interest. This genus is not in

Plagiorhegma dubium

the trade in North America.

P. integrifolia Ten. E. China, Japan. Tuber small, flattened. Leaves 1–3, 7.5–22.5cm high, blade entire, ovate, acute. Spadix exerted beyond the spathe tube. Curious, but scarcely ornamental.

P. ternata (Thunb.) Breit. (*P. tuberifera* Ten., *Arum ternatum* Thunb.). Japan, Korea, China. Tubers small, flattened with several small tubercles at the stem base. Plant 10–20cm high when in flower. Spathe greenish, often purple-tinged, narrow-cylindrical, 5cm long with a slightly nodding tip. Leaves with 3 leaflets. Blooms from May to June in its native habitat, often into late summer in cultivation. Can be troublesome, spreading by tubercles. z6

P. tripartita Schott. Japan. Similar to the previous species with ternate leaves, but leaflets substantially wider, petioles longer. Spathe pale green, 7cm long, with a waxy consistency. June to September. z6 (Kö.)

P. tuberifera see **P. ternata**

Pinguicula L.
Lentibulariaceae
Butterwort, Bog-violet

About 40–50 species, most from the temperate zones. Interesting insectivorous plants; small, low perennials with fleshy, entire, involuted leaves in a flat rosette. The upper leaf surface with small, glutinous glands for trapping insects. Flowers solitary on a leafless scape, calyx 4–5 lobed; corolla 5-lobed,

Plantago nivalis

2-lipped, lobes spreading, corolla with a basal spur, stamens 2. Seedlings with a single cotyledon. The species listed here, with the exception of *P. hirtiflora*, overwinter in nature by special overwintering buds.

Flowers from May to June. Butterworts grow in moist, peaty soil in full sun or preferably semi-shade, usually among live sphagnum moss plants. An excellent collector's plant for a permanently boggy site in the alpine garden; also suitable for large pots in the alpine house. Propagate by single leaves laid on clean sand in a humid terrarium, by separation of the winter buds (formed at the base of the dying leaves in fall) or seed. Not easy to grow from seed in the open but terrarium-grown plants often produce seedlings; if several species grow in proximity, hybrids are almost sure to be among the seedlings.

P. alpina L. Arctic and subarctic Europe, mountains of Scandinavia, islands of the Baltic Sea, mountains and highlands of Central Europe, Pyrenees. Leaves elliptic, slightly pilose above. Scape 8–12cm high. Flowers to 21mm, white with yellow spots in the throat. z3

P. grandiflora Lam. SW. Ireland, mountains of SW. Europe, from the Cordillera Cantabrica to the Jura Mts. Leaves pale green, fleshy, oval or oblong. Scape 15cm high. Flowers relatively large, to 3.5cm, violet. Very attractive and long-lived species. z7

P. hirtiflora Ten. S. and W. parts of the Balkan Peninsula, Central and S. Italy. Scape 8–14cm high. Flowers to 32mm, pink to light blue, with yellow in the throat. Very attractive, overwinters as a rosette. z7(6)

P. leptoceras Reichenb. Alps, Apuane Alps, Apennine Mts. Scape 10–14cm. Flowers to 3cm, blue. Slender and long spurred. z5

P. longifolia Ramond ex DC. Mountains of S. Europe. 7–15cm high. Flowers to 46mm, lilac or light blue. z6

P. vulgaris L., Common Butterwort. N., W. and Central Europe, east to the Ukraine, Central Asia, N. North America, Greenland. Scape to 15cm high. Flowers 16–20mm, blue-violet, short spurred. z3 (K.)

Piptatherum see Oryzopsis

Plantago L.
Plantaginaceae
Plantain

About 265 cosmopolitan species of annual or perennial herbs, occasionally subshrubs; some are common lawn weeds. Flowers very small, in spikes or heads, inconspicuous, subtended by a membranous bract; sepals 4; corolla 4-lobed; stamens 4, long exerted, pistil with superior ovary 2-celled. Some species are familiar as persistent weeds (Plantain). Only a few species are worthy of cultivation, but primarily for collectors and botanic gardens. All are propagated by seed or division.

P. argentea Chaix. S. and S. Central Europe from the E. Pyrenees to N. Greece and Rumania, on dry limestone soils. Leaves in a flat rosette, rosettes may be clustered, 10–30 long, 1.5cm wide, linear-lanceolate, entire, showy silvery-tomentose with appressed hairs, underside usually silky pubescent. Scape striped. Spike whitish, ovate, 0.5–2cm

long. Blooms from May to June. For large rock gardens in sunny, warm, dry sites between rocks in sandy loam. Winter protection is advisable. z7

P. major L. Europe, Asia and N. Africa, naturalized in North America. The species is a persistent weed, not for cultivation, the red-leaved form 'Purpurea' ('Rubrifolia', 'Atropurpurea') is only slightly ornamental. In England, however, usually in old gardens, a cultivar called 'Rosularis' ("Rose Plantain"), is to be seen, which is recommended as a curiosity for the collector. The flowers of

Platanthera bifolia **and** P. chlorantha **to the left of** *Dactylorhiza maculata*

this cultivar are replaced by roselike, 8cm-wide rosettes of small green leaves. Grows well in sandy or loam soil. z5

P. nivalis Boiss. S. Spain: Sierra Nevada, on flat peaks between 2000 and 3000m; covered with snow from October to early summer; on screes and in rock crevices. Leaves, even the `youngest, densely

silvery-pubescent, in appressed rosettes, 5–10cm wide. Greenish flowers in terminal, 1cm-long globose heads on 2.5–5cm high scapes. Blooms mid- to late summer. Certainly the most attractive species, for planting in the alpine garden or rockery in a scree or rock crevice. Will not tolerate winter wet, therefore best kept in an alpine house where it will spread by self-seeding. Thrives only where water and soil are lime- free. Requires abundant moisture in summer, but should not be watered from December to early March. Grows in gravelly (not limestone) loam soil. Suitable for pot culture in an alpine house. Good companion plants, also found in its native habitat, include *Chaenarrhinum glareosum*, *Linaria nevadensis* and *L. glacialis*, *Artemisia granatensis*, *Galium pyrenaicum*. z6

P. subulata L. S. France, on Ischia Island in S. Italy, Sardinia and Sicily, always found near the sea. Single rosettes are grouped into a dense, hard cushion. Leaves stiff, linear, only 1–2mm wide, densely crowded, dark green. Inflorescences shorter than or as long as the leaves. z7

P. subulata ssp. **insularis** (Gren. et Godr.) Nym. Corsica, Sardinia, Sicily, at higher elevations. Similar to the species, but somewhat smaller and more winter hardy. Blooms from June to July. More interesting than attractive, resembling *Armeria juniperifolia* (*A. caespitosa*). Most effective in a scree or rock crevice in loamy soil. For collectors. z6 (E.)

Platanthera L.C. Rich.
(*Habenaria* Willd.)
Orchidaceae
Fringed Orchid, Rein Orchid

About 80 species, primarily from Asia and N. America, reaching to the tropics. Long known as *Habenaria*, the change to *Platanthera* has been accepted only minimally and the botanical community now is trending back to *Habenaria*. Tuberous terrestrial orchids with 2 ovate, more or less basal leaves, and a leafy or bracted scape. Inflorescence a cylindrical terminal raceme with several to many flowers, usually not crowded. Lip undivided, ligulate, cut or deep-fringed. Flowers spurred. Blooms from spring to midsummer. For cultivation, landscape uses, and propagation, see **Orchis**. In the USA., especially in the southeast where numerous species are native, botanical gardens, spurred by the necessity of salvaging dwindling orchid populations from land under development, have learned to manage these orchids in cultivation. Seed reproduction of temperate zone terrestrial orchids, unlike tropical epiphytes, has long stymied scientists, but recent successes in the laboratory have been promising.

P. bifolia (L.) L.C. Rich. Lesser Butterfly Orchid. Europe, Asia, N. Africa, in woodlands, heaths and bogs, from the plains to the higher mountains. Stems to 50cm high. Flowers pure white with a slender spur, sweetly fragrant. Similar is *P. chlorantha* (Cust.) Rchb., with greenish flowers, softer pollen sacs. z5–10 (K.)

American gardeners can look for the showier *Platanthera* (always listed as *Habeneria*) species in wildflower specialists catalogues; among the handsomest are: *P. ciliaris*, Yellow Fringed Orchid; *P. cristata*, Golden Fringed Orchid; *P. dilatata*, Tall White Bog Orchid; *P. lacera*, Green Fringed Orchid; *P. peramoena*, Purple-spire. Numerous other species can be grown locally in many parts of the USA.

Platycodon A.DC.
Campanulaceae
Balloon Flower

One quite variable species. Medium height, erect bellflower plant with a carrotlike, fleshy root and bluish-green, usually opposite or whorled leaves. Flowers very attractive, terminal in few-flowered corymbs or solitary, broadly

Platycodon grandiflorus

bell-shaped with abruptly pointed lobes; blue or white, midsummer. Used for open perennial beds or rock gardens in full sun to semi-shade. Requires fertile, well-drained soil. Propagate by seed.

P. grandiflorus (Jacq.) A. DC. (*Campanula grandiflora* Jacq., *Wahlenbergia grandiflora* (Jacq.) Schrad.). Japan, N. China, Manchuria, Ussuri River region. Stem glabrous, branched above, to 70cm high. Leaves whorled below, alternate above, lanceolate to oval-lanceolate, toothed; flowers broadly campanulate, to 8cm wide, deep blue; var. *mariesii*, is 40cm high, very floriferous; cultivars of var. *mariesii* include: 'Album', white; and 'Roseum', flowers rose-lilac. Among cultivars of the species are: 'Album', flower white, usually with some blue venation; 'Alpinus' and 'Apoyama', dwarf-growing; 'Autumnalis', late flowering; 'Azureus', flowers paler blue; 'Caeruleus', flowers darker blue; 'Japonicus', corolla 10-lobed; 'Micranthus', flowers small; 'Nanus', plants dwarf; 'Perlmutterschale' (Mother of Pearl), 60cm high, with large, beautiful, mother-of-pearl pink flowers, rock garden plant; 'Plenum', semidouble, light blue; 'Pumilus', plants dwarf; 'Semiduplex' and 'Semiplenus', flowers partly doubled. z4 (L.J.& M.)

Pleioblastus Nakai
(*Arundinaria* Michx.)
Gramineae
Bush Bamboo, Cane

A genus separated by some horticulturists from *Arundinaria*, also with round stems but without persistent stem sheaths. Unlike *Sasa*, *Sasaella* and *Pseudosasa*, *Pleioblastus* species have many lateral branches per node. The species are long and abundantly rhizomatous, forming dense and extensive colonies, especially the low-growing sorts. Well suited, therefore, for bank stabilizing on sunny slopes, or woodland understory as in its native habitat. The small species respond well, with dense, bright new growth, to a hard shearing every few years. Propagate easily by division; young plants should be grown in containers. The taxonomic trend is to refer all *Pleioblastus* species to *Arundinaria*.

P. chino (Franch. ex. Sav.) Mak. N. and Central Japan. A variable and cultivar-rich species, often under erroneous names. The cultivars differ in the leaf width and color. Canes usually over 2m high. A good bank cover for a difficult site.

'Albovariegata', has white to cream yellow stripe on leaves, making it a good specimen, or tub plant.

'Argentea' (*Arundinaria pumila* 'Argentea') is regularly and distinctly white-variegated on dark green leaves, good winter hardiness.

'Elegantissima', notable for very narrow leaves, white stripes on a pale green background, and thin, flexuose shoots.

All the variegated forms are less vigorous, and best in a warm, semi-shaded site where the leaves persist longer. In warm, dry climates, protect plants from the midsummer sun.

'Pumilus' is a small bamboo, often offered as *Sasa pumila* or *Arundinaria pumila* in the trade. Very similar to the species, growing to 2m high, after remaining lower for many years; tolerates a hard shearing very well. z6

P. fortunei (Van Houtte) Nakai. Honshu to Kiushu (Japan). Leaves more or less uniformly white-striped, often somewhat cream yellow-tinged on new growth, yellow on the autumn-falling leaves. A tendency toward evergreen foliage is enhanced by a warm, protected site on fertile soil (out of direct midday sun). Only invasive to small neighboring plants. z6

P. gramineus (Bean) Nakai. Ryukyu Islands. Closely related to *P. linearis*, distinguished by the glabrous sheaths and somewhat twisted leaf blades. z7

P. hindsii (Munroe) Nakai. From S. China, also narrow-leaved, like *P. linearis*, distinguished by the leathery, stiffly erect leaves. z7

P. kongosanensis see **P. viridistriatus**

P. linearis (Hackel) Nakai. Ryukyu Islands. Conspicuous for its very narrow leaves. Plants grow to more than 3m high with gracefully nodding branches due to the weight of leaves clustered at the cane

tips. The rhizomes are short, hence forming a dense clump. z7

P. pygmaeus (Miquel) Nakai. Japan. Only known in culture, very rich in varieties. All cultivars are notable for their dense, non-spreading habit. Cane branches grow upward with leaves clustered at the tips.

The variety **P. pygmaeus** var. **distichus** (Mitford) Nakai is often considered the same as the species. Also, *Sasaella ramosa* is often confused with this species and offered as *Sasa* or *Arundinaria pygmaea*. z6

Pleione limprichtii

P. shibuyanus Mak. ex Nakai. Honshu to Kiushu. Only important for its widely distributed variety often labeled as *P. fortunei* (which see).

P. simonii (Carriere) Nakai. Honshu to Kiushu. This species from the Medakea Section (with those species of the Caespitosa Section, *P. gramineus*, *P. hindsii* and *P. linearis*) is distinguished from other *Pleioblastus* species by its taller, less stoloniferous habit. *P. simonii* may grow to 4m high in a warm site. Distinguished from other tall-growing bamboos by the clustered branching at the cane tips and the radiating, narrow leaves. z6

P. simonii var. **heterophyllus** Nakai. A very noteworthy plant, with up to 5 different leaf forms on one cane, leaves both wide and narrow, white, yellow or

striped; unlike the consistently white-striped, narrow-leaved 'Variegatus'. z6

P. viridistriatus (Sieb.) Mak. Honshu. Includes the plant distributed in the trade as *P. kongosanensis*. *P. viridistriatus* has long been cultivated as *Arundinaria auricoma*. Grows to 2m high; the softly pubescent, 3cm-wide leaves are irregularly and variably gold-green striped. Generally considered the most attractive yellow-variegated bamboo, and because of its hardiness, is found in many cold climate gardens. Leaf and stem damage will occur in severe winters, but damaged plants cut back to the ground in spring, like non-woody ornamental grasses, quickly make new growth. New growth from sheared plants of *P. viridistriatus* have unusually large and colorful leaves. z5 (S.)

Pleione D. Don
Orchidaceae
Tibetan Orchid

About 10–15 species of pseudobulbous terrestrial orchids, some of which are reasonably winter hardy. Closely related to the genus *Coelogyne*, differing in the annual, corm-like pseudobulbs and short-lived roots. Flowers from fall to late spring in warm regions; the hardy sorts flower April to May. For a better understanding of cultural requirements, a note on morphological development is in order.

Active growth begins in autumn, winter or spring (depending on species), 1–3 flowering shoots, rarely non-flowering leafy buds, appear laterally from the pseudobulb. The flowers appear singly or paired, 8cm wide, with a basally furled, fimbriate lip. The plicate leaves appear after (on the fall bloomers) or with the flowers and new roots emerge from the junction of leaf base and pseudobulb; the roots on the old pseudobulb then die out over the course of the year.

The new roots must then penetrate the soil to reestablish contact with nutrients. An application of soluble fertilizer at this stage of vigorous root growth is beneficial. While the new psuedobulbs are forming, older ones are senescing, totally abscising on some species; on others they turn glossy brown and persist until late fall before abscising. The roots die away and the leaves drop during the late summer and autumn, putting the plant into a dormant period which lasts until growth resumes in autumn, winter or spring (depending on the species).

Two groups can be clearly distinguished for cultural purposes. The first, the fall bloomers, being tender, will not be covered here. The second group includes the spring-blooming species. These are all single-leaved, requiring a soil mixture of sphagnum peat, bog peat, sand, dry cow manure and, for a contemporary touch, styrofoam pellets. Plants need cool, frost free winters −20 degrees C. (−4 degrees F.). They should be transplanted in winter and deeply mulched with fresh sphagnum moss. The flowering period is from March to May. Suitable for pot culture in the alpine house, P. limprichtii also for garden culture. All pleiones are intolerant of summer heat and drought. Propagate by removing the corm-like offset pseudobulblets, formed at the end of the pseudobulb; or by seed (like tropical orchids).

P. bulbocodioides (Franch.) Rolfe (*P. yunnanensis* hort. non (Rolfe) Rolfe). Yunnan. Pseudobulbs flat, distinctly one-sided, main shoot arises from the bulging side. Pseudobulbs mainly underground. Flowers tall or stemmed, pink with a scarlet-red lip. Rare, demanding species. z7

P. × confusa see **P. forrestii**

P. formosana Hayata. Pseudobulbs flask- or top-shaped, to 4.5cm long. Flowers to 10cm wide, blooming with the leaves. Grown mostly are cultivars: 'Blush of Dawn', light pink petals and a whitish lip with yellowish speckles; 'Polar Sun', pseudobulbs more top-shaped, flowers smaller, pure white. Also available in white and pink cultivars with mustard-colored to light brown dots. *P. pricei* is now considered to be a variety of *P. formosana*. Pseudobulbs of *P. formosana* dark brown, smaller. Flower color duller, lips always mustard-spotted. Some valuable forms are: 'Oriental Grace', 'Oriental Jewel', 'Oriental Splendour', the softest and smallest, and 'Serenity'.

Pleione forrestii

These four clones are very similar; the best is undoubtedly 'Oriental Grace'.

The transition forms between *P. formosana* and *P. pricei* have light brown, very large pseudobulbs; the flowers are usually pink with yellow-brown spots. Found in 1958 in a shipment of plants to England (Rawinsky).

Species and cultivars of the Taiwan group produce abundant offsets. The pseudobulbs should never freeze. z9

P. forrestii Schlecht. Yunnan. Pseudobulbs resemble those of *P. limprichtii*, larger under favorable conditions. Flowers pale yellow, lip red-spotted. Rare and difficult in cultivation, introduced in 1979. *P. forrestii* of garden culture is actually *P. × confusa* Cribb et C.Z. Tang (*P. forrestii × P. albiflora* Cribb et C.Z. Tang). Somewhat less demanding, but still very delicate. z8

P. hookeriana (Lindl.) B. S. Williams. India, Bhutan, Thailand, Laos. Pseudobulbs ovate, purple-red to greenish. Buds short and broad. Single leaved. Flowers small, white, occasionally with a pink blush, lip with a central mustard yellow patch and brownish-purple tip stripes. May to June. Treat more like the fall bloomers in cultivation. z8

P. limprichtii Schlecht. Sichuan. Pseudobulbs dark green, oval-acuminate to spherical-acuminate, 2–2.5cm tall. Flowers solitary, but well-developed pseudobulbs produce 2 or 3 flowers. Flowers short-stemmed, 7cm wide, lilac-pink. Lips lighter lilac-pink, brownish-pink-mottled. Produce offsets freely. Has withstood −20 degrees C. (−4 degrees F.). 'Pale Form', with smaller and lighter flowers. z7

P. pogonioides see **P. speciosa**

P. pricei see **P. formosana**

P. speciosa Ames et Schlecht. (*P. pogonioides* hort. non (Rolfe) Rolfe). Hubei. Similar to the above species, with dark red-spotted lip, conspicuous for the contrast between the petals and the lip. z8

P. yunnanensis see **P. bulbocodioides**

Hybrids have only recently become significant in *Pleione*: The Versailles Hybrids (*P. formosana × P. limprichtii*) are intermediate between the species.

Shantung Hybrids (*P. confusa × P. formosana* 'Blush of Dawn') are in the trade as various cultivars, including 'Apricot Brandy' and 'Muriel Harberd', both with peach-colored flowers. Other hybrids exist, some with pure yellow flowers resembling *P. forrestii*. As yet quite rare and very expensive forms.

Lit.: Cribb/Tang/Butterfield: *The Genus Pleione*. Curtis Bot. Magazine Vol. CLXXXIV, Part III, New Series tt. 860–871, 1983. (K.)

Plumbago

P. larpentae see **Ceratostigma plumbaginoides**

Poa L.
Gramineae
Bluegrass, Meadow Grass

A large genus of perennial or annual panicled grasses, spikelets to 10-flowered, laterally compressed. Most are forage and turfgrasses. Several species, very distinctive in appearance and use, are cultivated from this widely distributed genus. All ornamental species are generally propagated by division.

P. abbreviata R. Br. in Parry. Greenland and Arctic Russia, on dry, gravelly soil. A stoloniferous, dwarf, mat-forming grass. The wiry, stiff leaves are only 2cm high. Flowers appear only sparsely. An excellent dwarf grass for the alpine collector, combining well with all alpine plants. Also suitable for trough gardens under dwarf conifers. z2(1)

P. alpina L. var. **vivipara** L. Europe, in the mountains, also in the northern lowlands. A desirable fodder grass for mountain pastures, growing on moist, fertile soil. It is a typical mountain grass for the alpine gardener. Flowers seldom set seed, but rather form small plantlets in the panicles which root upon removal and planting. A dwarf clone should be selected for the alpine garden. z5

P. badensis Haenke. A dense clump grass distributed throughout Central and SE. Europe in dry sites. The leaves are blue-green with a whitish cuticular margin, densely clustered. An attractive, compact specimen plant worthy of more wide-spread use. z6

P. caesia see **P. glauca**

P. chaixii Vill. Central and S. Europe, in mountain forests, but often naturalized as escapees from cultivation. A clump grass with 10mm-wide leaves (unlike the other *Poa* listed here), bright green with conspicuous closed (canoe-end) tips. Flower panicles appear in June, to 25cm long, and borne on 1m-high culms. The species is suitable for the woodland margin and tolerates infertile, seasonally moist soil. z6

P. colensoi Hook. New Zealand. This loose, tufted, evergreen grass has wiry, more or less furled, beautiful blue blades; to 20cm high in leaf. The broadly ovate panicles are 5cm long, bluish at first, later brown, borne well above the foliage. An as yet not well-known species with great garden merit. Holds its color better than many other species, summer and winter. The species is deep rooted and drought tolerant, requires light, porous soil in a sunny site. z7(6)

P. glauca Vahl (*P. caesia* Sm.) N. Europe and the mountains of Europe and SW. Asia. Cushiony clump grass with 10cm-high, stiff foliage overtopped by bluish, stiffly erect culms, 20–35cm high. Thrives in dry, rocky conditions. Suitable for rock and trough gardens. Will grow on any well-drained, deep garden soil. z6

P. labillardieri Steud. Australia, Tasmania, New Zealand. A dense, tufted, evergreen grass, 60cm high in leaf, 1m high with the flower stems. Leaves blue-green, only 4mm-wide, furling, thereby appearing slender-wiry. Panicled inflorescences in summer, to 20cm-long and to 7cm-wide. This little-known species could replace *Helictotrichon sempervirens* in humid maritime climates where the latter may suffer from Rust fungi. Grows in well-drained, warm, rocky sites in full sun, corresponding to its habitat on exposed mountainsides. Because of its wide range, a suitable strain should be selected for a given climate. z7

P. nemoralis L. Circumpolar, densely tufted, shallow rooting grass from sparse woodland sites. This species is well suited for low maintenance, natural areas under trees; and tolerant of mowing. Establish from divisions or seed. z3(2) (S.)

Podophyllum L.
Berberidaceae
May Apple

A genus with 2–8 species, depending on taxonomic treatment, many species or varieties from China, others from the Himalaya Mts., Taiwan, and one species in E. North America. A unique, shade-loving plant with stout, tough horizontal rhizomes; decorative, peltate or palmately lobed radical leaves and solitary, nodding or upright, anemone-like flowers of firm texture; with conspicuously large, fleshy fruits in summer or fall. Suitable for a moist, humus soil as a very decorative shade plant. Needs ample space for the rhizomes to spread. Attractive among rhododendrons or on the margin of a shaded shrubbery. Good perennial companions are the anemones, *Mertensia virginica*, *Epimedium*, and various ferns. Also effective among evergreen foliage or rising from a primula carpet (*P. vulgaris* or *P.* × *polyantha*). Propagate by division in late summer or spring and by stratified seeds. Seeds germinate slowly and irregularly even after stratification.

P. diphyllum see **Jeffersonia diphylla**

P. emodi see **P. hexandrum**

P. hexandrum Royle (*P. emodi* Wall. ex Hook.f. et Thoms.). Himalaya Mts., in open forests. Leaves 50–80cm high, with bronze-red new growth and white or pale pink, unscented, upright, solitary flowers; May. The fruits reach the size of a hen's egg, bright coral-red. The cultivar 'Majus' with red-marbled young leaves also is larger in all respects. Intolerant of drought or very hot summers. z6

P. peltatum L., May Apple. N. America: Quebec to Minnesota, south to Florida and Texas. Leaves 30–60cm high. Leaves green, 5–9-deep-lobed. Flowers solitary, nodding, creamy-white to pale pink or rose, fragrant, spring; fruits yellowish, rarely red, also scented; midsummer to autumn. A vigorous, spreading perennial. And, rare in nature, scarce in cultivation, forma *biltmoreana*, with orange fruits; and *P. deamii*, with pink to rose-colored flowers and maroon-red fruits. z4–9

P. pleianthum Hance. China, Taiwan. Leaves 30–90cm high, palmate, distinctly marbled. Flowers pink, several in the leaf axils; May. Fruits red. Requires winter cover in an exposed site. z7

P. versipelle Hance. W. China. Plant to 80cm high, often shorter. Leaves usually paired, pale green, resembling those of the previous species. Flowers borne between the leaves, several in clusters (4–5), pendulous, deep crimson; May. Fruits red. Winter protection is advisable. z7

Polemonium L.
Polemoniaceae
Jacob's Ladder

About 20–25 species. Pinnate-leaved, low or medium high, annuals, perennials, or rhizomatous perennials. Flowers clustered in axillary or terminal cymes, or solitary, saucer-shaped to campanulate, spring to summer. Taller species grow well in average but never dry garden loam in full sun or semi-shade. The dwarf, alpine species need a well-drained, gravelly substrate and full sun. The tall species are suitable for the perennial border or the wildflower garden; the low species are for the rock or trough garden. Propagate by seed, also by cuttings or division.

P. boreale Adams (*P. humile* Willd. ex R.et S.). Circumboreal. Plants to 30cm high, usually shorter. Leaves mostly basal, with 13–23 elliptic to suborbicular leaflets. Inflorescence capitate. Flowers to 25mm wide, light blue to purplish. Rare in cultivation. Demanding. z4(3)

P. brandegei Greene. USA: Colorado, in Rocky Mts. Tufted, upright-growing alpine species, 15–20cm high; leaves mostly basal, glandular. Flowers in loose racemes, pale yellow to straw-colored. Closely related to *P. viscosum* ssp. *mellitum*. z4

P. caeruleum L. Jacob's Ladder, Greek Valerian. Europe, Asia, America, in the mountains. Stems to 45cm high. Leaves with 19–27 leaflets, occasionally bipinnate; leaflets oblong-lanceolate, entire. Inflorescences loose, cymose, flowers clustered, 10–25mm wide, sky blue, or rarely white, in spring or early summer. Numerous subspecies, varieties and cultivars are listed, few of special interest to gardeners except 'Album', with white flowers, and the following variety. z4

P. caeruleum var. **himalayanum** Bak. (*P. himalaicum* hort.). Flowers very large, lilac-blue and darker, calyx densely glandular. 'Album', white; 'Gracile', lower-growing, more compact, blue; 'Variegatum' with white-variegated leaves. April to June. Produces abundant seed under favorable conditions. z5

P. carneum A. Gray. USA: Oregon, California. Stems 15–40cm high from a horizontal rhizome. Leaves coarsely pinnate, with 13–21 leaflets. Inflorescence a cymose-panicle. Flowers flat campanulate, flesh colored, fading purple-blue, yellowish in bud, sometimes remaining yellow in var. **luteum** (*P. luteum* Howell). Also cultivar 'Album', with white flowers. Very attractive species which flowers summer-long, often short-lived. z7(6)

P. confertum see **P. viscosum**

Podophyllum hexandrum 'Majus'

P. elegans Greene. W. North America: Cascade Mts., Oregon, Washington and British Columbia. Dwarf, caespitose perennial to 12cm high. Basal leaves tufted; leaflets many, crowded, ovate to orbicular, densely glandular-pubescent. Inflorescence a head-like cyme. Flowers campanulate, light blue with yellow throat. A high alpine plant, not easily cultivated, but attractive. z5

P. filicinum see **P. foliosissimum**

P. foliosissimum A. Gray (*P. filicinum* Greene). USA: Rocky Mts. Rhizome

Polemonium carneum

short-creeping, woody. Stem to 80cm high. Leaves mostly cauline with 11–25 narrow leaflets, fernlike in appearance. Inflorescence a cymose panicle. Flowers 10–15mm across, light blue, whitish or violet. The fernlike leaves are very attractive. z4

P. grandiflorum Benth. North America: Mountains of N. Mexico. Downy, branching stem to 40cm high; plant very leafy; leaves with 15–23 oval or oblanceolate leaflets. Flowers solitary or 2–3 flowered clusters on branch ends; to 35mm wide, lilac or light blue or rarely yellow (*P. luteum* Greene). Fails on alkaline soils. Rarely cultivated but attractive. z8(7)

P. haydenii see **P. pulcherrimum**

P. himalaicum see **P. caeruleum** var. **himalayanum**

P. humile see **P. boreale**

P. luteum see **P. carneum** var. **luteum, P. grandiflora, P. pauciflorum**

P. mellitum see **P. pauciflorum**

P. pauciflorum S. Wats. North America: Texas, Arizona and Mexico, a mountain species. Perennial, but often short-lived in cultivation. Downy stems to 60cm high, often shorter. Leaves mostly cauline, with 11–25 elliptic or lanceolate leaflets, very glandular. Inflorescences on stem branches, flowers solitary or few at the branch tips, long, almost tubular, to 40mm long, pale yellow with a red blush. A beautiful species. Often mislabeled as *P. luteum* or *P. mellitum*. z7(6)

P. pectinatum Greene. W. USA: Washington. Stems to 70cm high. Leaves

Polemonium viscosum

with 11–21 narrow leaflets. Inflorescence cymose. Flowers to 20mm wide, white- or cream-colored. Rarely found in cultivation, usually short-lived, similar to *P. pauciflorum*. z7(6)

P. pulcherrimum Hook. (*P. haydenii* A. Nels.). Alaska, W. Canada, W. USA, in the mountains. Stems clustered and branched, 5–25cm high. Leaves with 11–23 oval leaflets. Inflorescences cymose. Flowers campanulate, to 8mm wide, light blue, tube yellowish. Usually easy to cultivate. z5(4)

P. reptans L. E. USA, in moist woodlands and meadows. Stems clustered, to 60cm high. Rhizome creeping, occasionally producing offshoots. Leaves with 7–19 ovate leaflets. Inflorescence loosely cymose. Flowers campanulate, 15–20mm wide, light blue: spring to early

summer. 'Album' with white flowers; 'Blue Pearl', with glossy blue flowers; 'Königsee', (rarely available), with very dark blue flowers. Thrives in semi-shade to shade, in humus-rich, moist soil. Often damaged by slugs. z4

P. × richardsonii hort. Possibly a hybrid of *P. caeruleum* × *P. reptans*. The key in Davidson's Monograph identifies this plant as *P. reptans*, and *Hortus Third* identifies it as *P. boreale*. Stems to 50cm high; rootstock somewhat creeping. Flowers large, sky blue. 'Album', white; 'Pallidum' (Arends) dark blue. Valuable

Polygala chamaebuxus 'Grandiflora'

for its floriferous reblooming from June to July after the first flowers appear in May. z6

P. viscosum Nutt. (*P. confertum* A. Gray). W. North America: Rocky Mts., Cascade Mts. and the Coastal Mts. (Wallowas). Stems to 30cm high. The endemic forms are quite variable (in all respects) from one site to another, but consistent within groups from the long periods of isolation. Leaves all basal, leaflets distichous, but 3–5 parted, therefore appearing to be whorled, densely glandular and terpentine-scented. Inflorescences densely capitate to oblong. Very attractive, lime-intolerant species for a dry rockery or alpine garden. Similarly cultivated are both subspecies: *P. viscosum* ssp. **mellitum** (A. Gray) J. F. Davidson (*P. mellitum* A. Nels.), with yellow flowers, and *P. viscosum* ssp. **viscosum** (ssp.

genuinum Wherry) with pure blue to violet flowers. z5

Lit.: Davidson, J. F.: *The Genus Polemonium* (Tournef.) L. University of California Publications, Vol.23, No.5, pp. 209–282, 1950. (K.)

Polygala L.
Polygalaceae
Milkwort

Five hundred to 600 species of annual or perennial herbs, subshrubs or shrubs

the entire winter in their native habitat. In the garden plant them in well-drained, alkaline or neutral, gravelly loam in a sunny, protected site among large and small rocks. Both species perform much better in the alpine house where they will thrive untouched for many years. Cover plants from November to early March with conifer branches. After uncovering, plants will flower in April. Propagated by seed sown right after ripening, or by cuttings taken in August and September. Cutting propagation is most successful under glass with bottom heat. Careful removal of outer (often

spotted on top, fragrant. Blooms from March to June, sporadic throughout the summer and especially in fall. Quite variable in flower color, the S. Alpine form 'Grandiflora' (*P. grandiflora* Gaud.) has pink-red wings. In E. USA. this species is grown in a shady cleft between stones in gravelly acidic leafmold, with winter protection. z6

P. grandiflora see **P. chamaebuxus**

P. vayredae Costa. E. Pyrenees, in similar habitats to the closely related, previous species. Differs, however, in the lower

Polygonatum odoratum

and trees, distributed worldwide, except in New Zealand, Polynesia and the Arctic region. Leaves simple, entire, alternate, opposite or whorled. Flowers in racemes or spikes, terminal, axillary, occasionally in racemose heads or panicles. Sepals 5, very irregular, the inner 2 largest, wing-like, and colored like the petals. Petals 3–5, often united, the lower petal with a split basal tube and often with an appendage (crest), the 2 outer (lateral) separate, or united with the hooded lower petal; 2 linear petals usually reduced or absent. Only 2 species are commonly grown in Europe, in the alpine garden or rock garden of the experienced collector, because polygalas are difficult to cultivate in the garden, short-lived and flower poorly. These 2 species are covered with snow through

already rooting) shoots of established plants is another option.

P. chamaebuxus L. Alps and W. Central Europe, south to S. Italy and W. Yugoslavia, on sunny, very well drained, infertile mineral or humus soil, usually on limestone, but also on granite, gneiss, and porphyry, found from the plains to lower alpine elevations (2400m) among mugo pine, dwarf rhododendrons, coniferous woodlands, on mats and gravelly slopes, mostly in the mountains. Dwarf shrub 5–20cm high with creeping or ascending branches. Leaves leathery, similar to those of Boxwood, oval to linear-lanceolate, 15–30mm long and 5–10mm wide. Flowers solitary or paired in the leaf axils, rather large, yellow or whitish, frequently red-

habit, not exceeding 15cm, and linear-lanceolate to linear leaves, and the pinkish-purple flowers with a yellow navicular petal. Blooms from April to May. Produces long, underground stolons, giving rise to small, widely scattered, eventually floriferous clumps. Very demanding in cultivation. Appears to be a delicacy for mice, with shoots nipped back to the ground in some years. z7 (E.)

American gardeners grow a few additional *Polygala* species. Rock gardeners, through z5, grow the evergreen swiss alpine **P. calcarea** F. W. Schultz, Lime Polygala, a low, bushy plant to 20cm high or shorter, with masses of blue flowers in spring. This plant needs gravelly, alkaline soil, never too dry, in full sun.

White- and rose-pink-flowered cultivars sometimes are available.

In the E. USA. about 15 species are indigenous; only a few are both perennial and ornamental. The most common is **P. pauciflora**, Willd., Fringed Polygala, Bird-on-the Wing, growing from Quebec to the mountains of Georgia in open moist woods on light soil. Stoloniferous perennial; upright stems 10–18cm high with several ovate leaves and a terminal cluster of 1–5 flowers. Flowers to 2.5cm long, rose-pink (var. *alba* with white flowers) in late spring or early summer. Not easy to grow, but worthwile.

Polygonatum Mill.
Liliaceae
Solomon's-seal

About 30 species with thick, fleshy, often white rhizomes covered with large, round scars from past stems, and much jointed. Stems erect or nodding, with parallel-veined leaves and one-sided, pendulous, cylindrical, white, cream-colored or greenish flowers in the leaf axils; May to June. Indigenous to the temperate regions of the Northern Hemisphere; usually in woodlands. Suitable for shady and wildflower gardens. A very decorative shade-loving perennial for a moist, shaded but bright site together with ferns, *Rodgersia*, and *Podophyllum*. Propagate by division; seed propagation is tedious, seeds must lie dormant over the winter and seedlings are slow growing. Occasionally damaged by slugs and sawflies.

P. biflorum (Watt.)Elliott. (*P. canaliculatum* (Muhlenb.) Pursh.) Small Solomon's-seal. North America: Connecticut to Ontario and Nebraska, south to Florida and Texas. Stems to 1m high, rarely higher, arching; leaves alternate, sessile, elliptic-lanceolate, to 12cm long, glabrous, glaucous beneath. Flowers greenish white, 1–3 on axillary peduncles. Fruits to 75m across, blue-black, in early fall. A preferred garden species proportioned to smaller gardens. And forma **racemosum** (McGivney) Fern. USA: S. Michigan and N. Indiana. Flowers borne on short axillary branches. A curiosity. z3

P. canaliculatum see **P. biflora**

P. commutatum (Schult.f.) A. Dietr. (*P. giganteum* A. Dietr.). Great Solomon's-seal. North America: N. Hampshire to Manitoba, south to Georgia and Mexico. Stems arching 0.6–2m high; leaves alter-

nate, ovate to ovate-lanceolate, 15cm long, 10cm wide. Flowers greenish, large, 15–20mm long, 3–8 on a peduncle, perianth not narrowed at the tip; May to June. A valuable species for large shady gardens and parks but too coarse for smaller gardens. Rarely true in cultivation in Europe, often represented by *P. × hybridum*; American wildflower specialists supply correctly identified plants. z2–6

P. falcatum A. Gray. Japan, Korea. Stems erect, 10–15cm high, with distichous, oval leaves. Flowers greenish white, solitary, pendulous, below the leaf axils; May. z6

P. giganteum see **P. commutatum**

P. hookeri Bak. Asia: W. Sichuan, Tibet, Sikkim. Stems erect, 5–7cm high. Leaves alternate, 1–1.5cm long, oval. Flowers about 1cm long, solitary, erect at the leaf axils, lilac or purple; May. Interesting plant for the rock garden. Requires humus-rich soil and a shady, cool site. z7(6)

P. × hybridum Brugger (*P. multiflorum × P. odoratum*). A diverse hybrid group of variable ornamental value, often listed under the name *P. multiflorum*. 'Weihenstephan', originally cultivated as *P. japonicum* and later erroneously included with *P. macranthum*, is a particularly stately, vigorous form. Plants reach 60–90cm high, leaves broadly lanceolate. Flowers large, in groups of 4, pendulous, about 22mm long, cream-white, mid- to late May. A sterile type, very vigorous, forms large colonies. For bright, shaded warm sites. z6

P. latifolium (Jacq.) Desf. Eurasia: Austria, Italy, Balkan region, Russia and the Caucasus. Reaches a height of 1m and more. With alternate, oblong leaves 7–15cm long, puberulous beneath. Flowers 1–5, long-peduncled, not very conspicuous; May to June. Usually a shorter form is found in culture, growing to about 30cm high. Quite vigorous, rapidly spreading species. z5

P. multiflorum (L.) All. Europe, Mediterranean region, Asia Minor, Himalaya Mts., Siberia; in deciduous woodlands. Stems round, to 60cm high, nodding. Leaves spreading more or less on flat plane, ovate to elliptic, 5–15cm long. Flowers grouped 3–5, long-peduncled, pendulous, white, greenish at the apex; May to June. Fruits blue-black. Several cultivars are listed in Europe, more or less resembling the species, but including 'Flore Pleno', with double

flowers; and 'Striatum' with foliage variegated in stripes. z4–8

P. odoratum (Mill.) Druce (*P. officinale* All.), Solomon's Seal. Europe, Mediterranean region, Siberia to Dahuria, at the sunny edges of oak thickets and in open coniferous forests, on loose, gravelly loam, loess and sandy soil. Stems angular, arching, to 45cm high. Leaves stem-clasping, distichous, alternate, ovate to elliptic-oblong, glabrous, somewhat ascending. Flowers solitary or paired, white, green-spotted in the throat; May to June. And var. **thunbergii** (C. Morris & Decne.) Hara. Japan. Plant shorter, stems to 110cm high, leaves to 15cm long. The recently introduced cultivar of this variety 'Varietgatum' is one of the handsomest polygonatums; like the variety but leaves boldly blotched and striped ivory-white. New shoots emerge in spring, mostly watermelon-red and ivory with traces of green, and the bright color holds until stems are almost fully grown. Fruits blue-black. z4

P. officinale see **P. odoratum**

P. roseum (Ledeb.) Kunth. Altai Mts., Dzungaria (W. China). Stems channeled, to 90cm high. Leaves linear-lanceolate, 7.5–12cm long, sub-peltiolate; basal leaves alternate, upper leaves opposite, rarely whorled. Flowers paired, small, on short peduncles pink or rose-colored; May to June. Fruits red. A choice but almost unknown species. z5

P. verticillatum (L.) All. Europe, Asia Minor, Caucasus, Afghanistan, Ural Mts., in mountain forests. Stems angular, erect, to 70cm high. Leaves whorled, 4, rarely 5 at a node. Flowers 1–3 on a peduncle; white with green lobes; May to June. Fruits red at first, later sometimes blue-black. Not very important in horticulture; short-lived if not grown in a cool, moist, humid situation. z5 (L.J.& M.)

Polygonum L.
Polygonaceae
Fleece Vine, Smartweed, Knotweed

About 150 species distributed throughout the entire world. Plants with very distinctive habits, some cushionlike rock plants, some floating aquatic plants, some to over 2m tall specimen annuals or perennials with attractive spicate or panicled inflorescences, at least one a high twining perennial to woody climber; many are too vigorous and weedy. For landscape use refer to the individual species. All of the tall, noninvasive species are suitable for the herbaceous border and as specimens in beds, at watersides, and elsewhere. The more vigorous, invasive species are often found thriving in a neglected garden and, therefore, may be suitable for some low-maintenance applications. Most species, with few exceptions (which are pointed out in the descriptions), have no particular cultural requirements. Propagation is by division in spring or by seed. In this treat-

Polygonum polystachyum

ment 3 species have been transferred to a new, and probably botanically unacceptable genus, *Reynoutria*.

Species covered here:

For a better overview, the species will be divided into 3 groups.

1. Tall, upright-growing plants 0.5–3m.

P. alpinum All. Europe: Alps, Asia Mts. Asia. Stems grow to 60–90cm high. Leaves oblong to lanceolate. Flowers white to rosy-white in loose, cylindrical,

Polygonum bistorta 'Superbum'

panicled false racemes; May to July. Slow growing, for the large rock garden in a semi-shaded site. *P. sericeum* Pall is of better garden merit. z5

P. amplexicaule D. Don (*P. multiflorum* hort.). Mountain Fleece. A very attractive species from the Himalaya Mts. Stems 60–100cm high, somewhat woody at the base. Leaves stem-clasping, ovate to lanceolate. Flowers rather large, in long-peduncled spikes, bright red; white on 'Album', bright rose-red on 'Atropurpureum'. 'Speciosum', claret-colored, is also very ornamental, known as 'Firetail' in England. Flowers August to October. Attractive plants for the border and open sites. Effective as a background for the medium-high asters. Ideal with *Aster × frikartii*. z5

P. bistorta L. (*Bistorta major* S.F. Gray). Snakeweed, Bistort. Eurasia. Stems hairy, 45–60cm high with hairy basal and stem leaves, leaves oblong-ovate, 7.5–15cm long, blunt, wavy, glaucous beneath, tending toward winged petioles. Flowers white or pink in a 5cm

long, solitary, terminal, dense cylindrical spike. The cultivar 'Superbum' grows to 60cm or slightly higher, flowers pink, larger, in larger spikes, clumps gradually spread. A smaller cultivar, flowers pinkish, remains in a tight clump. All bistorts grow best on moist soil, but are intolerant of hot summers and wind. Best combined with other moisture-loving plants like *Trollius*, *Iris sibirica*, *Iris versicolor*, *Iris pseudocorus*, *Carex pendula*. z4

P. campanulatum Hook. f. Asia: Himalaya Mts., W. China. Stems slender, in

Polygonum amphibium

nodding panicles 60–80cm high, stoloniferous, at the base procumbent, ascending. Leaves petioled, elliptic, lanceolate or ovate, 7.5–15cm long. Flowers campanulate, pink or white. z8(7)

P. campanulatum var. **lichiangense** (W.W. Sm.) Steward (*P. lichiangense* W.W. Sm.). China. More widely cultivated than the species. Very valuable fall bloomer, midsummer to late fall. Requires somewhat moist soil and light shade. A good companion for *Aconitum carmichaelii* or *Aconitum × arendsii*. z5

P. cuspidatum see **Reynoutria japonica**

P. cuspidatum var. **compactum** see **Reynoutria japonica** var. **compacta**

P. filiforme Thunb. Japan. Stems 50–150cm high, light brown, hollow, leaves large, ovate to oval, acuminate, green with 2 red-brown blotches. Flowers red, in a wiry, erect, axillary spike; July to August. Thrives in semi-shade and is notable for understory planting. The cultivar 'Variegatum', leaves marbled and blotched ivory and green is also available. z6

P. lichiangense see **P. campanulatum** var. **lichiangense**

P. multiflorum see P. amplexicaule

P. polystachyum Wall. ex Meissn. Asia. Himalaya Mts. to Siberia; naturalized in Central and NW. Europe. Woody-based, stems to 1.5m high, branches grooved; rootstock enlarges but does not run. Leaves mostly short-petioled, oval-lanceolate, alternate-acute, 10–22.5cm long. Flowers white or pink, fragrant, in terminal panicles; September to October. Good for cut flowers, but can also become invasive. Only suitable for large gardens, tolerates semi-shade. z6(5)

P. reynoutria see Reynoutria japonica

P. sachalinense see Reynoutria sachalinensis

P. sericeum Pall. (P. alpinum hort.). Siberia. Stems 1–1.25m high. Leaves oval-lanceolate. Flowers in panicled spikes, white; May to June. Noninvasive, but somewhat demanding. z5

P. weyrichii Fr. Schmidt. Sachalin, S. Kurile Islands. Stems rough hairy below, hairy above, to 1m or more high. Leaves gray-tomentose, ovate, short-petioled. Inflorescence a terminal racemose spike, greenish-white or white; September. Tolerates light shade, noninvasive, quite ornamental species. Requires a moist site. Attractive among woody plants with good fall colors, or conifers. Tolerates root competition. Good companions include Miscanthus sinensis 'Strictus' or Vernonia crinita. z5

2. Low-growing, creeping or mattted species.

P. affine D. Don (P. brunonis Wall.). Nepal. Tufted, low-growing foliage below flower spikes to 30cm high. A delightful green leafy carpet bronzing in winter, with bright rose-pink flower spikes. Leaves mostly radical lanceolate, rarely to 10cm long. Vigorous grower; very attractive plants for the rock garden or alpine garden. 'Darjeeling Red' is more compact, 25cm high, with rose-red flowers; 'Superbum' grows to 25cm, especially floriferous, pink. Another good cultivar with coral pink flower spikes is 'Donald Lowndes' ('Lowndes Variety'). Considered too invasive for the rock garden, often used among shrubs. Good companions include Anemone japonica (especially 'Honorine Jobert') or Campanula macrantha and C. trachelium. Tall grasses are also effective companions. August to October. z3

P. brunonis see P. affine

P. macrophyllum D. Don (P. sphaerostachyum Meissn.). Himalaya Mts., China. Flower spikes about 30cm high. Without stolons. Basal leaves from a stout woody crown, rosetted, long-petioled, to 24cm long. Stem leaves broadly lanceolate, dark green. Flowers in dense, cylindrical spikes, pink to carmine-red; July to September. A very satisfactory species for the rock garden. A plant circulated recently in Europe as P. milettii is either a cultivar of P. macrophyllum or a valid species from W. China. With narrow leaves and spikes about 50cm high of deep carmine-red color, the flowers are long persistent. Requires fertile, moist garden soil. z5

P. milettii see P. macrophyllum

P. sphaerostachyum see P. macrophyllum

P. tenuicaule Biss. et Moore. Japan. Plants 5–10cm high with spreading rhizomes. Leaves glabrous, broadly oval-lanceolate, soft green above, purple beneath. Flower spikes erect, white. A very attractive species for the rock garden; requires moist, acidic, humus soil and semi-shade. Blooms from April to June. z6

P. vacciniifolium Meissn. Himalaya Mts. Procumbent, with creeping habit, spikes 20–30cm high; leaves elliptic-acute, glossy green. Flowers bright pink; August to October. Only for warm, protected areas, and also requires protection from winter wet. z7(6)

P. viviparum L. (Bistorta vivipara (L.) S.F. Gray. Serpent-grass, Alpine Bistort. Mountains of the North Temperate and Arctic Zones. Flowering stems to 30cm. Rootstock slender with fiber tufts. Leaves mostly basal, with revolute margins, narrow oblong to linear. Inflorescence a slender raceme, flowers white or pink, basal flowers modified into purple budlike bulbils. June to August. Tolerates drier soil than most species but not prolonged drought. A collector's plant. z4

3. Aquatic species

P. amphibium L. (Persicaria amphibia (L.) S.F. Gray). Willow-grass. North Temperate Zone. Semi-aquatic plants with a creeping, woody rootstock; stems to 1m long with floating, oblong-lanceolate leaves. Flowering spikes cylindrical; flowers pink, crowded. June to July. Only suitable for large ponds and lakes. z5(4) (L.J. & Kö.)

Polypodium L.
Polypodiaceae
Polypody

A much revised genus divided by some taxonomist into 20 or more separate genera, thus Polypodium includes 300–1100 species, depending on species' grouping. Mostly pantropical, only a few are suitable for temperate gardens. Rhizome creeping, mostly on thin humus layers over rocks; or epiphytic, especially if tropical. Old fronds abscise completely from the rhizome.

P. glycerrhiza D.C. Eat. (P. vulgare var. occidentale Hooke). Licorice Fern. W. North America: Alaska to Central California, coastal. Rhizome stout, branching. Fronds deciduous, oblong-deltoid to narrow-ovate, to 45cm long and 17.5cm wide, deeply pinnatifid, the lobes linear-attenuate, serrate. Sori nearer the midrib than the margin. z7(6)

P. hesperium Maxon. (P. vulgare var. columbianum Gilb.). Western Polypody. W. North America: Alaska south to California and inland to South Dakota. Rhizomes more slender than the above species and tougher. Fronds deciduous, firm-textured, to 25cm long and 5cm wide, pinnatifid almost to the rachis, lobes oblong to elliptic, rounded, entire or crenate. Sori midway between midrib and margins. A fern of pine forests; more tolerant of dryness than most polypodies. z5(4)

P. incanum see P. polypodioides

P. interjectum Shivas (P. vulgare L. ssp. prionodes Rothm.). Wall Polypody, European Polypody, Greater Polypody. Occurs sporadically throughout Europe and W. Asia. Grows in mts. Fronds evergreen, ovate-lanceolate, to 60cm long, 15cm wide, once-pinnate, rarely pinnatifid, pinnae sub-alternate, narrowly acuminate and blunt, barely serrate, basal two pinnae slightly ascending. Sori oval, without indusia, borne halfway between midrib and margin. In the US., this fern is classified as a variety of P. vulgare. Europeans list several subspecies and varieties, and cultivars.

Reaches its fullest potential only under favorable conditions. Best massed under deep-rooted woody plants, among large rocks, in wide crevices and north-facing slopes and terraces, rhizomes planted horizontally in woodsy, humus soil, and never allowed to dry completely. The fine-pinnate cultivars (Feathery Polypody Ferns), previously known as *P. interjectum*, are particularly attractive. Var. **cambricum** ('Plumosum'). Found in Wales, U.K., in 1743. Fronds to 50cm long, 15–20cm wide, ovate-lanceolate, bipinnnate, bright green above, bluish beneath. Pinnae further pinnately partite, widely spaced, obliquely overlapping. Sterile.

'Cornubiense'. Found in Cornwall in 1867. Fronds oblong-triangular, to 50cm long, 20cm wide, firm, dark green, bipinnate. Pinnae further bipinnately partite, distinctly serrate. Occasionally produces nonpinnate leaves, which

Swartz). Resurrection Fern. Tropical and warm-temperate North Central and S. America. Many epiphytic on deciduous tree limbs in wet places. Rhizomes creeping. Fronds in tufts or scattered, evergreen, leathery, to 18cm long, 5cm wide, pinnatifid or pinnatisect, pinnae oblong, entire, gray-scaly below. z7(6) And var. **michauxianum** Weatherby. Delaware to Illinois south to Florida and E. Texas, and Tropical Americas. Differing from the species mostly in the shape of the scales on frond undersides and rhizomes. These ferns respond to

epiphytic. Grows in deep to semi-shade. Fronds glabrous, once pinnate, 20–30cm long, only 5cm long on infertile soil, to 60cm long if growing near water; 2–16cm wide, lanceolate, pinnae acute to rounded. Sori naked, orbicular, yellow, in 2 rows paralleling the midvein, pinna indented above at the point of origin of the sori underneath.

Rhizome creeping, sweet to the taste; stipes erect, fronds somewhat nodding, dark green above, lighter beneath, evergreen. New growth appears earlier than that of *P. interjectum*, old petioles abscise

Polypodium vulgare 'Ramosum'   *Polystichum setiferum* 'Proliferum'

should be removed at the rhizome. Fertile.

'Hadwinii' ('Cambricum Hadwinii'). A small cultivar with once-pinnate leaves, pinnae acuminate and serrate.

'Omnilacerum'. Slender version of 'Cambricum', fertile.

'Pulcherrimum' ('Cambricum Pulcherrimum'). Similar to 'Cambricum', but with rounded pinnae, finer-textured, fertile.

'Semilacerum' ('Hibernicum'). Resembles 'Cambricum' at the basal part of the fronds but the upper portion is once-pinnate, feʀtile.

Propagate the species by spores and division. The Feathery Polypody Ferns are difficult to grow from spores since cultivars vary in spore viablility; progeny often revert to the species and the finely cut leaves are a recessive genetic trait. Propagate, therefore, by division; young plantlets are slow to develop. z5

P. polypodioides (L.) D. Watt (*P. incanum*

drought by in-rolling their fronds from the tips; with a return of moist conditions fronds unroll to normal extension. Interesting and attractive for a special habitat, as horizontal, mossy tree limbs extending over water. Difficult to establish. z7(6)

P. virginianum L. Rock Polypody, American Wall Fern. E. North America: on cliffs and rocks in cool, moist places. Much like the Eurasian *P. vulgare* but rhizomes not sweet to the taste and fronds somewhat different. Fronds evergreen, to 90cm long, 12.5cm wide, pinnatifid, the pinnae somewhat attenuate. Stipe not bent. Sori nearly to pinnae margins among glandular hairs. Handsome fern intolerant of any dryness or wind; will colonize on rocks around a spring or on streambanks. z5

P. vulgare L. Found throughout Europe, in the old dunes along the coast, on the mossy floor of the mountain forests and in the thin humus layer of rock walls, also

with emergence of the new. Suitable for moist, shady garden sites, tolerates root competition. Does especially well on mossy boulders, thin peaty soils, on old stone walls, tree stumps and wide rock crevices, but always in shade. Increases itself by spores in moist, mossy sites. Requires nonalkaline, high humus soil. Two cultivars have the same cultural requirments, but better suited for foreground plantings where their unusual habit can be seen.

'Bifido Multifidum', Forked Polypody. (Syn. 'Bifido Grandiceps'.) Fronds to 45cm long, relatively narrow, pinnae wide, and flat forked at the tips, frond tips branched tassel-like, fronds often long branched from the middle, sterile.

'Ramosum', Twin Polypody. More compact than the species, fronds pinnatisect below, the pinnae mostly 2-forked, pinnae more dissected above, the segment tips acute, fronds to 20cm wide. Propagate the species by spores and division, the cultivars only by division. z4 (D.)

P. vulgare ssp. **prionodes** see **P. inter-jectum**

P. vulgare var. **occidentale** see **P. glycer-rhiza**

P. vulgare var. **columbianum** see **P. hesperium**

Polystichum Roth
Polypodiaceae
Christmas Fern, Holly Fern, Shield Fern

About 120–250 species, nearly cosmopolitan in the mountain forests of the temperate zone and tropics. Rhizome short, erect (crown, in horticulture). Frond stipe short, covered with chaffy scales, fronds usually leathery, often evergreen, 1- to 2-pinnate (very rarely 3-pinnate), narrow, relatively long-lanceolate. Pinnae often serrate or dentate, the teeth awned. Sori on the small veins on frond undersides; indusia peltate. The genus *Polystichum* includes a large number of very decorative, ever-green garden ferns, useful for livening up a semi-shaded site with other perennials, especially in winter. Provides both shelter and a frame for many spring and early spring flowering perennials such as *Eranthis* and *Leucojum.* The Holly Ferns thrive in acidic to neutral, moist, humus soil in shade to semi-shade, especially the evergreen forms. Some will tolerate full exposure on a north-facing slope.

P. acrostichoides (Michx.) Schott, Christmas Fern. E. North America to Canada, on acidic humus-rich, rocky slopes. Fronds 40–60cm long, 10cm wide, 1-pinnate, outermost fronds sterile, more divergent to nearly horizontal, the inner fronds erect, spore bearing on the upper pinnae. Sterile pinnae are wider and longer than the fertile ones, which are smaller, crowded, with many sori. Fronds leathery, dull, dark green, evergreen. Often used for cut greenery at Christmas. A valuable, evergreen fern, combines well with *Cyclamen, Trillium* and the pastel-colored primulas and most spring-flowering woodland wildflowers. In exposed plantings these require wind protection. Winter hardy. Requires a lime-free humus soil. Propagate by spores. Spores ripen from June to September. Cultivars with ornamental fronds are listed. z6(5)

P. aculeatum (L.) Roth (*P. lobatum* (Huds.) Chev.). Hardy Shield Fern, Hedge Fern. (See also *P. setiferum.*)

Mountain woodlands of the temperate zone and the tropics of both hemispheres, except North America, on gravelly slopes and screes to timberline. Rhizome short, often just a single crown. Fronds to 80cm long, 20cm wide, pinnate-pinnatifid to 2-pinnate, lanceolate, tapered toward the base, with short, brown-scaly stipe, leathery, glossy green, persisting until late into the following spring. Pinnae oblong-lanceolate, acuminate, alternate or opposite toward the base. The basal pinnules are larger, pinnules with ser-

Polystichum polyblepharum

rate, awned margins. Sori large with a tough indusium, in 2 rows along the midrib of the pinnules. Fronds elegantly outward-arching, forming a vase to 1.2m-wide, one-sided on a slope. Besides this widely cultivated species, there is also an erect variety with narrow fronds not affected as much by snow load in winter, as well as other botanical varieties and horticultural cultivars. One of the most important landscape ferns, especially for the evergreen garden. For planting in a humus garden soil among rhododendrons and other evergreens. Also combines well with *Carex morrowii, Luzula sylvatica, Helleborus niger* and various primulas, also with *Colchicum* and the autumn-flowering crocuses as well as all the early-flowering bulbs.

Propagation is by spores. Spores often ripen from early July to September. Two cultivars are available but difficult to find.

'Cristatum'. About half the size of the species, fronds irregularly bipinnate,

apical pinnae occasionally forked, pinnules distinctly serrate and prickly tipped. A unique fern for the shaded rock garden. Propagation from spores, largely consistent.

'Pulcherrimum Bevis'. Found in Dorset, England in 1876. Fronds more slender, pinnae and pinnules more decorative than those of the species. Sterile. Propagation only by division, therefore quite rare. z5

P. aculeatum var. **japonicum** see **P. polybepharum**

P. andersonii Hopkins. Anderson's Holly Fern. NW. USA: in cool, moist forests and on shaded slopes, Alaska to Oregon, Idaho and Montana. Rhizomes and stipes with brown chaffy scales, the midrib and the underside of the pinnules also slightly scaly.

Stipe and fronds upright, fronds narrow, lanceolate, to 80cm long, 13cm wide, 2-pinnate. Pinnae alternate, narrow-cuneate, pinnules distinctly serrate, basal ones enlarged. Sori large, between the veins and the margin. Cultivated like *P. aculeatum.* Propagation is by spores or the scattered gemma at the frond tips. z5(4)

P. angulare see **P. setiferum**

P. braunii (Spenn.) Fée. Braun's Holly Fern, Shield Fern. Temperate Europe, Caucasus, Japan, NE. America. Relatively wide distribution, but occurs sporadically. Grows in shady mountain forests, near water courses. Fronds to

80cm long, 20cm wide. Stipe 15cm long, brownish-green, pale green; rachis densely covered with pale brown chaffy scales and hairs, nearly white on the new growth. Fronds erect, in a vase-shaped cluster, arching outward, nodding at first, 2- to 3-pinnate, dull-glazed, white pubescent beneath, soft textured, evergreen. Pinnae nearly at right angles, short petioled, basal pinnules scarcely enlarged. Sori large, on the upper portion of the frond.

Must be protected from late frost in the garden, preferably grown in a cool site to discourage early growth. New growth and plant habit are unique, deserving of a special place in the garden. Propagate by spores. Spores ripen from July to August. z5

P. falcatum see **Cyrtomium fortunei**

P. japonicum see **P. polyblepharum**

P. laserpitiifolium see **Dryopteris standishii**

P. lobatum see **P. aculeatum**

P. lonchitis (L.) Roth. A mountain fern from Europe, N. and Central Asia, the Himalaya Mts. and N. America; in Europe on screes or among mugo pines and dwarf rhododendrons. Fronds 40–60cm long, but usually only 30cm, narrow, lanceolate, stiff, glossy dark green, 1-pinnate. Pinnae sickle-shaped curving upward, crowded, prickly tipped. Sori only on the uppermost pinnae. Evergreen. Thrives in the shade of large stones. Naturalizes itself by spores under favorable conditions. Persists for many years, colonizing and creating a bright spot in the shaded rock garden. Propagate by spores, which ripen from July to September. z4

P. mohrioides (Bory) Presl., Falkland Island Holly Fern. The Americas: Washington through California to Chile in the Andes Mts. and on the subarctic islands, on rocky slopes over 2000m high. Grows into a multiple-crowned clump. Fronds 30cm long, only 7cm wide, leathery, dark green, evergreen, densely glandular with chaffy scales and hairs. Fronds 2-pinnate, pinnules oval, without pointed tips. For shaded rock gardens. Still rare in culture. Propagate by spores and division. z5

P. munitum K.B. Presl. Giant Holly Fern, Western Sword Fern. W. USA.: Alaska to California, in Idaho and Montana, in fertile, moist woodlands and on shady slopes. Discovered by Adalbert von Chamisso in 1816. Usually grows as a multiple-crowned, broad, dense clump. Fronds 65–90cm long (stipes 15cm of that length), almost uniformly 12–15cm wide, tip lanceolate, 1-pinnate, lightly pubescent beneath. Pinnae crowded, to 12mm wide, curved sickle-shaped (falcate), tips acuminate, distinctly auricled at the base, awn-toothed. Leaves matte, leathery, dark, evergreen. Sori in a single row near the margin. A very attractive fern for a protected, high humus site among rhododendrons and evergreen grasses. Requires a thick mulch in winter; crowns may otherwise freeze out, particularly young plants. Fronds are suitable for cut greens. Propagate by spores which ripen in September, also by division. z6(5)

P. polyblepharum K.B. Presl (*P. aculeatum* Roth var. *japonicum* Christ, *P. japonicum* Diels), Bear's Paw, Japanese Holly Fern. E. Asia: Japan, China, Korea, in moist forests. Fronds clustered in a funnel, arched outward, 50–70cm long, 15–20cm wide. Stipes 15–20cm long, densely covered with glossy brown scales. Fronds pubescent, 2-pinnate, the basal pair of pinnae bent toward the frond tip; conspicuously glossy dark green. Pinnules auricled, broadly oval, serrate, prickly tipped. Sori small, in 2 rows, only on the first fronds. Evergreen and suitable for cutting. A very attractive fern, grown like *P. aculeatum*. Unfurling fronds look somewhat like a bear's paw (hence the common name). Some strains emerge early and therefore need protection from a late frost. New fronds develop all season long. Plants should be well mulched in winter. Propagate by spores which ripen from July to August. z5

P. rigens Tagawa, Stiff Bear's Paw Fern. Japan. Fronds stiff, few, in funnel-shaped clumps, 30–50cm long, 15–20cm wide, with long stipe, scarcely nodding at the tip, dark green, dull-glazed. Blade oblong-ovate, 2-pinnatisect. Pinnules very bristle-toothed. A somewhat demanding, conspicuous, evergreen fern for a protected and shaded rock garden site or the edge of a rhododendron bed. Propagate by spores which ripen from July to September, Gametophyte apogamous. z7(6)

P. setiferum (Forssk.) Woynar (*P. angulare* (Kit. ex Willd.) Presl, *P. aculeatum* (Sw.) Schott non (L.) Roth, *Aspidium angulare* Kit.), Hedge Fern, English Hedge Fern. Indigenous to the tropics and to mild regions of the temperate zone. Grows on moist to wet mineral soil in a mixed woodland and in the moun-tain valleys. Fronds to 1m high, several in an arching, vase-shaped 1.2m wide cluster, 15–20cm wide, stipe from 15–25cm long, densely covered with brown chaffy scales at the base. Fronds narrow-lanceolate, 2-pinnate, dull green, tender, only evergreen in milder climates. Sori small, light brown, in 2 rows, between the midrib and the margin.

A very attractive fern of soft green color and elegantly drooping fronds which combine well with many medium-sized shade-loving perennials. Suitable companions include the astilbes, Fall Anemones and *Cimicifuga*,

Polystichum setiferum 'Proliferum Dahlem'

and also lilies such as *L. hansonii*, *L. martagon* and the many lily cultivars suitable for massing. Requires a generous leafmold mulch in winter.

Propagate by spores, which ripen from July to August. This fern is available in many cultivars and in several varieties, especially in England, including some of the most beautiful garden ferns. The most important ones are listed here. A collector desiring to learn about the other cultivars should consult the appropriate literature or a specialist nursery catalogue. Since the fronds of these ferns are mostly 3-pinnate, they sometimes are referred to as Filigree Ferns.

'Multilobum', Dissected Filigree Fern. Rarely 40cm high, with pinnae divided and redivided to very slender lobes. Propagation is by division and spores.

'Proliferum', Narrow Filigree Fern. The most popular Filigree Fern with 3-pinnate, dark green fronds, bearing many with gemmae in the pinnae axils. Plants to 1m wide, 40cm high. Evergreen. Fronds good for cut-flower arranging. Very vigorous, suitable for many garden sites, including those with partial sun, but needs protection from the winter sun. Propagation is by gemmae.

'Proliferum Dahlem'. A sporeling of *P. setiferum*, found by R. Maatsh about 1940 and later named for the Dahlem Botanic Garden (Germany). Resembles *P. aculeatum*, but not glossy, and produces gemmae on the basal portion of the fronds. One of the most attractive ferns. Vigorous, forming a broad, flattened funnel to 1.4m wide. Fronds to 1.1m long, soft green, but bright green when young, evergreen. Fronds 3-pinnate. For specimen use in semi-shade or in small groups together with grasses and perennials of the shade garden. Thrives in average garden soil, reaches its fullest potential in fertile soil. Mature fronds are suitable for cutting. Plants come true only from gemmaceous buds.

'Proliferum Herrenhausen'. Flat and broad-growing 'Proliferum' type, also found and named by R. Maatsch. Fronds with short stipe, 50–70cm long, to 30cm wide at the base. Fronds 2- to 3-pinnate, dark green, evergreen. Suitable for cutting. Plant in small groups in front of rhododendrons or use to edge a shaded pathway. Propagation is by gemmaceous buds.

'Proliferum Iveryanum', Crested Filigree Fern. Narrow, to 60cm-long fronds, with bright green pinnae, all repeatedly dissected to comb-like lobes which are somewhat twisted, intertwined. A conspicuous fern for specimen use among low shady perennials or beside a large boulder. Evergreen. Propagation is by gemmaceous buds (borne on the rachis). Somewhat variable from spores.

'Proliferum Plumosum Densum', Downy Filigree Fern. Named by Karl Foerster, this is the finest textured, most elegant shield fern. The fronds are multipinnate, pinnules overlapping. The flat-spreading fronds resemble moss. Old plants develop a thick, 20cm-high crown from the old frond bases. Evergreen. Suitable for specimen or small group planting in semi-shade with other shade-loving perennials. Also effective as a contrast to the lower growing, large-leaved rhododendrons of the Yakushimanum group. Propagated only by gemmaceous buds. Fronds are excellent for cutting.

'Proliferum Wollastonii', Wollaston's Filigree Fern. Resembles 'Proliferum', but the fronds of at least some of the plants have somewhat coarser pinnules. The validity of this cultivar has been questioned of late. Garden uses the same as for 'Proliferum'. Propagate by spores, choice specimens by gemmaceous buds. z7

P. standishii see **Dryopteris standishii**

P. tripteron (Kunze) K.B. Presl, Cross Fern (Jumonji-Shida in Japanese). Common in Japan, also found on the Kurile Islands, in Korea, China and Siberia, in woodlands. Quite different from the other *Polystichum* species in habit. Fronds with a long stipe, 1-pinnate above, basal 2 pinnae spreading horizontally, 2-pinnate, pinnae and pinnules short-stalked, pinnately cleft, bristle-toothed. Propagate by spores which ripen in early June. z7(6)

P. tsus-simense (Hook.) J. Sm., Narrow Holly Fern (Hime-Kana-Warabi in Japanese). Very similar to *P. rigens*, but more elegant, fronds only 30cm long, 8–9cm wide, matte dark green. A graceful fern for the alpine house or for a very protected site in the rock garden or trough. Should be covered with conifer branches to protect from the winter sun and drying winds. Propagate by spores. Spores ripen from July to September. z8(7) (D.)

P. varium see **Dryopteris varia**

Pontederia L.
Pontederiaceae
Pickerelweed

Five species of colonizing, aquatic perennials in North and South America in water 30cm deep or less. Stems submerged, floating, creeping (rhizomatous) or ascending. Leaves elliptic-oval or sagittate. Flowers in crowded false spikes, corolla with 6 perianth segments, more or less 2-lipped, the upper and lower lips 3-lobed, blue, June to October. Decorative swamp plants for garden streams and small pools. Most effective as a specimen planting. Suitable companion plants are *Scirpus lacustris* 'Albescens' and *S. tabernaemontani* 'Zebrinus', best cultivated in 20–30cm deep water. Rhizomes of pontederias must be protected from freezing in winter. If not under water they should be heavily mulched in winter. Propagation is by division from May to June or stolon cuttings from June to August; also from seed. z5

P. cordata L. North America: Nova Scotia to Ontario and Minnesota south to Florida and Texas. A bog plant, 0.6–1m high. Rhizome thick, creeping in the bottom muck. Leaves long petioled, cordate, thick, glossy green, with parallel veins. Flowers in 10cm-long spikes, bright blue, upper lobe with 2 yellow spots, young flowers covered with white, matted hairs, flowers profusely throughout the entire summer. The hardiest species, but still requiring some winter protection. And f. **angustifolia** (Pursh) Sohns-Laub. Leaves narrow-lanceolate, cordate, flowers smaller and brighter blue. z4–9

Pontederia cordata

P. lanceolata Nutt. Tropical and subtropical America. Similar to *P. cordata*, but not as hardy. z7 (D.)

Potamogeton L.
Potamogetonaceae
Pondweed

About 100 species of water plants with slender rhizomes and stems, some persistent, some overwintering by special dormant buds. With submerged and, in some species, floating leaves. Leaves alternate, or opposite, thin, sometimes translucent, with netted venation, slender (thread-like) or broad. Flowers small, in spikes above the water surface, green or brownish-red, June to August.

Pondweeds occurs throughout the world. They serve to oxygenate the water and provide cover for spawning fish. Dense colonies can, however, be troublesome in flowing water such as in streams and canals as well as in cold water lakes. Plants are attractive naturalized in large park or garden streams or lakes, for wildlife habitat. Not well suited for aquariums as plants are short-lived under these conditions. Require fresh, cool water.

Potamogeton natans

P. americanus see **P. nodusus**

P. crispus L. Europe, naturalized in E. USA. and California. Stems 4-angled. Leaves linear-oblong to lanceolate-obtuse, to 12mm wide, 10cm long, very undulate. Flowers from June to August. Forms winter buds. A vigorous, submerged or floating plant for 50–60cm deep water. z6

P. filiformis Pers. North America, Eurasia, Upper Egypt, Australia. Stems thread-like, to 40cm long; all stems and leaves submerged; blades linear to 20cm long, with a single vein. Leaf sheath tubular. Spikes small, flowers in discontinuous whorls. An excellent choice for small, cold water ponds with breeding ornamental fish. z4

P. gramineus L. Circumboreal. Stems to 1m long, willowy. Submersed leaves sessile, linear or linear-lanceolate to oblanceolate near the surface, thin,

margins fine-toothed; floating leaves petioled, elliptic, to 8cm long. Flower spikes dense, cylindrical. Both attractive and good fish cover. z3

P. lucens L. Europe, W. Asia. Stems 2–4m long, sometimes much longer, leaves all submersed, short-petioled, glossy green, oblong-lanceolate, margin finely serrate, 8–14cm long, to 4.5cm wide. Flowers from June to August in 6cm-long spikes. Rhizomes overwinter in mud. Grows at 2m water depth. z5

Potentilla × tonguei

P. natans L. Europe. Vigorously spreading plant with floating leaves, ovate to oblong, 10cm long and 4cm wide, submersed leaves much narrower. Flowers in spikes, 8cm long, July to August. The most garden-worthy species for 0.2–1m deep water. z6

P. nodosus Poir. (*P. americanus* Cham. & Schlecht.) North America. Stems to 5mm thick. All leaves petioled; submersed leaves linear to elliptic-lanceolate; floating leaves lanceolate-oblong to elliptic. Flowers crowded on spikes on thick 15cm long peduncles.

P. pectinatus L. N. and E. USA. to South America, Eurasia, Africa. Floating species, densely covering the water. Stems leaf-like, long, well-branched. Leaves thread-like to 2.5mm wide, gradually acuminate. Flower spikes flexuous, flowers in spaced whorls, to 5cm long, on flexuous peduncles. June to August. Provides excellent cover for breeding fish, but may overwhelm a pond. Produces overwintering buds. Thrives in a water depth 0.5–1.5m, tolerates a slight current, in lakes with

alkaline water, or estuaries with brackish, even saline water. z6 (D.)

Potentilla L.
Rosaceae
Cinquefoil

A very extensive genus with more than 500 species, primarily in the North Temperate Zone; also in the Arctic and high alpine regions, a few in the Southern Hemisphere. The Cinquefoils

Potentilla atrosanguinea 'Gibson Scarlet'

are quite variable with a number of natural hybrids making classification somewhat difficult. The perennial species have either erect, creeping or stoloniferous habits. The leaves are compound, palmate or pinnate. The flowers are usually yellow, occasionally red or white, solitary or in cymes or cymose-panicled inflorescences. The Potentillas exhibit an extensive habitat range in nature and therefore tolerate a wide range of garden conditions. Some species thrive on infertile fields and rocky plains, preferring, therefore, a similar garden site. Only the truly alpine species are suitable for the alpine garden; other low-growing species are often too vigorous. All species grow best in full sun; the small species also thrive in well-drained, infertile soils. The most common methods of propagation are by division and cuttings of selected plants. Seed propagation is possible for the species. Some easily self-seed.

P. alba L., White Cinquefoil. Central and E. Europe, south to N. Italy and Macedonia. Crown non-stoloniferous, thick and multistemmed with procumbent branches, to 25cm high. Leaves glabrous, silver-green above, white-silky beneath, 5-part palmate. Abundant white flowers about 2cm across, from April to June. The species requires a warm site, and sandy-gravelly or fertile mineral loam soil. In the wild often on the south-facing edge of a lime-free woodland or thicket. Correspondingly used in cultivation. z5

P. ambigua Cambess. (*P. cuneata* Wall., *P. cuneifolia* Bertol.), Himalaya Mts. Low, tufted subshrub with short, underground shoots, sometimes matted. Leaves ternate, leaflets 5–10mm long, obovate with 3 teeth at the tips, dark green, bluish beneath. Flowers yellow, solitary, 2.5cm across, on short peduncles; summer. Grows into persistent mats on gravelly, but not too dry, sites in full sun. Sometimes in the trade as *P. cuneata*. z5

P. × anglica Laicharding (*P. procumbens* Sibth.). W. and Central Europe. A naturally-occurring hybrid, *P. erecta* × *P. reptans*. Differs from commonly produced hybrids in its higher fertility. Flowers 4–5 petaled, on procumbent stems from a persistent rosette of 3–5 part leaves. These stems will later become stolons, with roots at the nodes. Non-flowering basal runners are also produced, with rooting rosettes. Rapidly forms a dense, leafy carpet. A good groundcover among clumps of large perennials. Only the best clones should be selected for the garden. Division is simple. z5

P. argentea L., Silver Cinquefoil, Hoary Cinquefoil. N. Europe, Alps, naturalized in E. North America. The most important species in a group of many similar, related species. Basal rosette leaves 3–9 part palmate, leaflets 12.5–25mm long, obovate-cuneate, dark green, white-tomentose beneath; rosette leaves senesce with development of the taller, branched, leafy stem, to 30cm high. Flowers small, golden yellow. For infertile sites with sandy, gravelly, lime-free soil. Some varieties of *P. argentea* have been found which closely resemble *P. calabra* Ten. z6

P. argyrophylla Wall. ex Lehm. Himalaya Mts. Leaves and stems white-hairy, basal palmate leaves with 3–5 leaflets, elliptic ovate to ovate, toothed. Branched stems to 40cm high with 3cm-wide, golden

yellow flowers in panicled cymes, June to August. Suitable for establishing open mats over large sites. Cultivars of this species are listed. z6

P. atrosanguinea Lodd. ex D. Don. Himalayas. Leaves silvery pubescent, to 5-parted, otherwise similar to the previous species, but more abundantly branched. Black-red flowers on ascending stems in June and July. 'Gibson Scarlet' differs from the species with green foliage. The bright scarlet red flowers are borne on long, procumbent stems, but are capable of climbing up into taller neighboring plants. Very valuable cultivar for its flower color; must be vegetatively propagated. 'Russeliana' is a reputed hybrid, *P. atrosanguinea* × *P. nepalensis* Hook, with 3cm-wide, deep red, but fading flowers. 'Splendens' flowers earlier than the species, blood red. z5

P. aurea L. S. and Central Europe, in the mountains. This is included in a group of species which are often polyploid, and which yield apomictically propagated hybrids. Many beautiful cultivars thus have been developed. The plants are low-growing, often suffruticose; stems 10–15cm high, in tufts. Basal leaves long petioled, palmate, leaflets 5, oblong, toothed; stem leaves short-petioled, smaller. Flowers bright yellow, petals with darker base, 2cm wide; from June to July. Occurs on spring-wet, summer-dry mountain sites in a humus loam soil. z5

P. aurea ssp. **aurea**, with 5-part leaves and occurs over the same range except for the S. and E. Balkan Peninsula. 'Goldklumpen' (Gold Nuggets) is a relatively new, unusual floriferous cultivar.

'Rahboneana', with semidouble, gold-yellow flowers in June. z5

P. aurea ssp. **chrysocraspeda** (Lehm.) Nym. (*P. ternata* K. Koch), with ternate leaves, flowers earlier and more attractively than the species, ranging over the S. and E. Carpathian Mts. 'Aurantiaca' is a cultivar introduced by Arends. Never exceeds 10cm high, with soft orange-colored flowers, abundantly produced. z5

P. calabra Ten. (*P. argentea calabra* Ser.). Italy, Sicily and the W. Balkan Peninsula. Much like the closely allied species *P. argentea*, but leaves silvery-gray hairy on the upper as well as the lower side of the leaflets. z6

P. caulescens L. Alps and mountains of S. Europe from Spain to Yugoslavia, in limestone crevices in the Dolomites.

Leaves palmate, with 5–7 leaflets; oblong-ovate to elliptic, pubescent, silky-ciliate on the margin. The stems grow to 25cm high, corymbose, with 3–7 white, rarely pink, flowers. z5

P. cinerea Chaix ex Vill. (*P. tommasiniana* F.W. Schultz). Central, S. and E. Europe. Rootstock stout. Plants tufted. Leaves palmate, with 3–5 leaflets, densely stellate-pubescent and silvery gray. The procumbent stems root easily, so dense mats of plants develop. The yellow flowers are borne on 10cm-high stems. The species occurs in dry sites and is suitable for sunny rock terraces. z5

P. crantzii (Crantz) Beck ex Fritsch. N. Europe and the mountains of Central and S. Europe. A widely distributed, variety-rich species. Stems several, arching and ascending, from a rosette of mostly 5-part leaves; leaflets obovate-cuneate, to 2cm long, with 2–5 teeth on each side, green, undersides very hairy. The species grows more in tufts than the similar, mat forming *P. aurea*. Golden yellow flowers in a loose cyme, few to 12, petals often have an orange-colored basal patch. In its habitat, plants tolerate cold, windy sites together with *Carex firma*. Occurs on limestone, in crevices, screes and sparse turf. Suitable for trough planting and rockeries.

'Goldrausch' (Gold Rush) is an unusually attractive cultivar from the S. Alps. Propagation is by cuttings in late summer; young plants are raised in pots. z5

P. cuneata see **P. ambigua**

P. cuneifolia see **P. ambigua**

P. erecta (L.) Raeusch. (*P. tormentilla* Stokes, *Tormentilla erecta* L.). Tormentil. An upright perennial with a fibrous rootstock and quickly senescing basal rosette of leaves. One or several slender, tough, erect or ascending stems from the rosette, to 45cm high, with scattered leaves, with a spreading terminal corymb; flowers many, to 12.5mm across. Conspicuous in the genus with its 3–4-part leaves. Notable as a medicinal plant. Lime-intolerant. z5

P. fragiformis see **P. megalantha**

P. megalantha Takeda (*P. fragiformis* Willd.). Asia, Altai Mts. to Alaska. A compact-growing, noncreeping, tufted species 15–20cm high, Leaves long petioled, large, to 7.5cm across, gray-tomentose; leaflets 3, broad, deeply crenate, green with few hairs above, gray-green, long-hairy below. Flowers 3cm-wide, golden yellow, appearing after June on long peduncles. With many garden uses, tolerates semi-shade. z5(4)

P. nepalensis Hook. W. Himalaya Mts. Basal leaves 5-, upper leaves 3-parted, leaflets obovate-oblong to oblanceolate, 2.5–7cm long, coarsely dentate, with spreading hairs, green on both sides. Stem reddish, 45–60cm high, with open branched, forking panicles. Long-pediceled, 2.5cm flowers are purple-veined, salmon pink; from June to September.

'Miss Willmot' ('Willmottiae'), dwarf, cherry-red, a natural variety, coming true from seed.

'Roxana' flowers coppery-pink with a cherry-red eye. z5

Like the cultivars of *Potentilla atrosanguinea* and *P. argyrophylla*, *P. nepalensis* can be planted with wildflowers or garden perennials, but requires increased attention and fertility.

P. neumanniana Rchb. (*P. tabernaemontani* Aschers., *P. verna* auct. non L.). N. W. and Central Europe. Basal leaves palmate, with 5–7 leaflets, grass green, with 2–9 teeth on each side, with stiff, appressed hairs. Stems at the base, woody procumbent, rooting at the nodes to form large mats. Flowers in loose cymes to 10cm high with up to 12 small, yellow flowers, to 12.5mm across. The main flowering period is in April; reblooms sporadically until August. The species is usually found in lowlands on rocky sites and in dry grasslands. Well suited to planting on shallow soils and in containers. Very form-rich species. This species appears in American and British literature as *P. tabernaemontani*. 'Nana' grows to only 5cm high. z5

P. nitida L., Dolomite Cinquefoil. SE. Alps. Forms dense mats with procumbent shoots. Leaves silvery, silky-hairy, mostly ternate; leaflets about 12.5mm long, oblanceolate to narrow-obovate, toothed or entire. Flowers very short-peduncled, mostly solitary and pink to rose-colored, rarely white. The species flowers freely only in its native habitat, and therefore floriferous cultivars or varieties such as 'Rubra' and 'Albiflora' are more commonly found in cultivation; numerous cultivars are listed by perennials specialists. The species requires an infertile soil or limestone crevice in full sun. Propagation is by cuttings, with young plants grown in containers; the species by seed. z5

P. poetarum see **P. speciosa** var. **minor**

P. procumbens see **P. anglica**

P. pyrenaica Ram. ex DC. Pyrenees, N. and Central Spain. Similar to *P. aurea* but stems to 30cm high, curved at the base, then upright, and leaflets not silvery-hairy margined. Leaves 5-part, glabrous above, silky pubescent beneath. Inflorescence a few-flowered raceme with golden yellow flowers to 2.5cm across, from June to July, thereby extending the blooming period for the low-growing golden yellow species. z6

P. recta L. Europe, Caucasus, Siberia, naturalized in E. North America and weedy-invasive in some areas. Basal leaves 5–7 parted, gray-green. Stems erect, to more than 50cm high, branched above, and with both short, stiff, and long, softer hairs. Basal and lower leaves palmate with 5–7 oblong to oblanceolate, serrate, green leaflets 2.5–10cm long. Large, pale yellow flowers many, in flat umbellate cymes. June to August. Undemanding also as pioneer plants for fertile, but lime-free soil. z4

'Macrantha', with large, butter-yellow flowers. Var. *sulphurea*, with paler yellow to cream-colored flowers.

'Warrenii' with canary yellow flowers.

P. rupestris L., Rock Cinquefoil, Prairie Tea. W. and Central Europe, Balkan Peninsula, N. Italy and S. Sweden, NW. North America south to California. Plant pubescent. Leaves pinnate, leaflets 5–9, dentate. Flowering stems 45cm high, flowers several in an open, forked cyme, white, to 2.5cm across; June to July. The species is found on the edge of dense thickets, rock outcroppings and stone walls. Treated as a wildflower. z5

P. rupestris var. **pygmaea** Duby, to 20cm high, most suitable for rocky flat sites in the rock garden. z5

P. speciosa Willd. W. and S. Balkan Peninsula, Crete. Leaves ternate, leaflets obovate, crenate-dentate, less than 2.5cm long, white woolly, as is the entire plant. The flower stems 5–28cm high with few to many, small, white flowers. The species requires a warm and dry site on limestone. z7(6)

P. speciosa var. **minor** Lehm. (*P. poetarum* Boiss.). Only 6cm high and smaller in all respects, highly prized for the alpine garden. z7(6)

P. tabernaemontani see **P. neumanniana**

P. ternata see **P. aurea** ssp. **chrysocraspeda**

P. tommasiniana see **P. cinerea**

P. × tonguei Baxt. (*P. aurea* or *P. anglica* × *P. nepalensis*). Leaves with 5 (rarely 3) obovate leaflets, dark green; stems procumbent, not rooting as *P. anglica*, flowers uniquely apricot colored with a carmine-red eye, July to August. For the foreground, as in a paved terrace bed or a trough garden. The epithet *P. × tonguei* is unaccepted by botanists as is the horticulture alternative name *P. tormentilla-formosa*. Most recent information indicates the true parentage to be *P. anglica* Laich × *P. nepalensis* Hook. which should clear the way for assigning a proper name to this important ornamental. z5

P. tormentilla see **P. erecta**

P. verna see **P. neumanniana**

Hybrids occur in this genus. Where their origins are known, the parent species can be ascertained. But, the multiple crosses and the seedling races are lumped under *Potentilla* Hybrids. They are mostly medium-sized perennials with brightly colored flowers, effective in the perennial border to liven up the midsummer weeks. Also suitable for cut flowers. Many of these strains, unfortunately, are very short-lived. The following list includes many plants now uncommon in the trade, all propagated vegetatively. Breeding work is needed to eliminate their short-lived duration for the future.

'Etna', semidouble, deep velvety red with yellow margin.

'Feuerball' (Fireball), double, fiery blood-red.

'Master Floris', single yellow with red center.

'Monsieur Rouillard', double, deep blood-red with yellow margins.

'Mrs. John Harkness', double, dark red with yellow center.

'Perfecta Plena', double, scarlet red with yellow center.

'Vase d'Or', double, yellow.

'Volcan', double, clear red with darker center.

'Wm. Rollisson', semidouble, deep orange with a yellow center.

'Yellow Queen', double, pure yellow. (J.& S.)

Poterium

P. sanguisorba see **Sanguisorba minor**

Pratia Gaudich.
Campanulaceae (or Lobeliaceae)

About 25 species of tender to barely frost tolerant perennials in tropical Asia, Australia, New Zealand and S. America. Mostly creeping or procumbent herbs with rooting shoots and sessile, alternate, somewhat fleshy, rounded, leaves. *Lobelia*-like flowers borne single in leaf axils, and fleshy, globose berry-like fruits. Blooms June to August. Cultivate in moist, peaty or boggy substrate in full

P. begoniifolia see **P. nummularia**

P. macrodon Hook.f. New Zealand. Stems creeping. Leaves glabrous, distinctly toothed, nearly succulent. Corolla tubes to 12mm long, white or pale yellow. Fruits purplish-red, rounded (not oblong like those of *P. angulata*), fruit stalks short. z7

P. nummularia (Lam.) A. Brown & Asche. (*P. begoniifolla* (Wallach ex Roxb.) Lindl.) Tropical and sub-tropical Asia. Slender-stemmed, somewhat pilose plant forming loose or tight mats.

Prenanthes L.
Compositae
Rattlesnake Root

Thirty to 40 species of perennials with milky latex in N. America, Europe, the Canary Islands, tropical Africa and temperate and tropical Asia. Roots tuberous. Stems erect, leafy. Flower heads in racemes or panicles, nodding. Flowers all ligulate, white or purple. The only species considered here, *P. purpurea*, is rarely grown outside of botanic gardens. A shade-loving plant suitable

Pratia angulata

Pratia pedunculata

sun or semi-shade. Require protection in winter or a place in the alpine house in colder climates. Very susceptible to slug damage. Suitable for the bog garden, rock garden or pot-grown in the alpine house. Propagate by separation of rooted shoots or seed.

P. angulata (G. Forst.) Hook.f. New Zealand. Shoots creeping. Leaves broadly oval to rounded, to 14mm long, normally with 2–3 teeth on either side, quite variable. Flowers white with purple venation, 7–20mm long. Peduncles elongate as the purple fruits ripen. z7

Leaves orbicular, to almost 2cm across, serrate-dentate. Flowers about as long as the leaves, lilac to rose or sometimes yellowish-green, lower lip marked purple. Fruits purplish, to 12mm across.

P. pedunculata Denth. Australia. With above- and below-ground stolons, rapidly forming a dense, small-leaved, gray-green mat. Flowers soft light blue or whitish, small and *Lobelia*-like, densely covering the matted plant. Garden-worthy, vigorous perennial for a protected site near a building. This species is also distributed as *Isotoma fluviatilis*. z7 (K.)

Prenanthes purpurea

for planting with *Adenostyles* and other lime-intolerant woodland species and various ferns. Thrives in a woodland, on moist humus-rich soil. Propagate by division and seed.

P. purpurea L. From Central France, Central and S. Germany, S. Poland to S. Europe, S. Russia and the Caucasus region, in deciduous and mixed mountain forests in clearings, on a moist, fertile, humus, usually nonalkaline, neutral to moderately acidic loam. Deciduous perennial with knobby, clumped rootstock. Stems slender, 0.3–1.5cm high, very leafy, glabrous. Basal leaves petioled, apical leaves stem-clasping, sessile, undersides bluish, oblong-spatulate, widely sinuate-toothed to entire. Flower heads numerous, long-pediceled, few-flowered, nodding at first, in loose, floriferous panicles. Corolla rosy-violet, occasionally white. Blooms in midsummer. z5 (E.)

Primula L.
Primulaceae
Primrose

About 400–550 species in Europe, Asia and N. America; a few species occur in Arabia, Africa, Java and S. America. Perennial, rarely annual or biennial, herbs or near subshrubs with leaves in basal rosettes. Leaves simple or parted, petioled or sessile. Flowers are nearly always heterostylous (with styles of various lengths), sessile on a leafless scape, umbellate or capitate, in superimposed whorls, racemes or spiked inflorescences, or solitary in the leaf axils. Many are prominent ornamental plants for pot culture and the landscape. The landscape primulas are undoubtedly some of the most important flowering perennials for spring and early summer. Modern breeding tends toward producing strains and cultivars with parentage involving 2 or more species. The genus *Primula* has been divided into Sections by W.W. Smith and G. Forrest, following earlier work. The Sections have since been revised individually in several papers. In the following alphabetical list of Sections, the source of the revision is noted as follows:

x) Transactions Botanical Society of Edinburgh (Royal Botanic Garden, Edinburgh)

xx) Transactions Royal Society of Edinburgh (Oliver & Boyd. Tweedale Court, Edinburgh)

xxx) Journal Linn. Soc. of London, No. LII, No. 334 (Burlington House, London)

The following species descriptions will be arranged according to Sections since species within those groups are more or less of similar cultivation requirements, garden use and propagation.

The genus is botanically subdivided into 7 Subgenera by some taxonomists: Aleuritia, Auganthus, Auriculastrum, Carolinella, Craibia, Primula and Sphondylia. For garden practice, however, the further subdivision into Sections is more serviceable. Species of the following Sections are covered:

Aleuritia (Farinosa) xx)
Amethystina x)
Auriculastrum (Auricula) xx)
Bullatae xx)
Capitatae x)
Cortusoides x)
Cuneifolia xx)
Craibia (Petiolaris) xx)
Crystallophlomis (Nivales xx)
Denticulata xx)
Grandis xx)
Julia x)
Megaseifolia x)
Minutissimae x)
Muscarioides x)
Parryi xx)
Primula (Vernales) x)
Proliferae (Candelabra) x)
Reinii xx)
Rotundifolia (Cordifolia x)
Sikkimensis x)
Soldanelloideae xxx)
Sphondylia (Verticillata or Floribundae) xx)

Species covered and mentioned in this work:

abchasica see *vulgaris* ssp. *sibthorpii* p. 534
acaulis see *vulgaris* p. 534
— var. *iberica* see *vulgaris* ssp. *sibthorpii* p. 534
— var. *rubra* see *vulgaris* ssp. *sibthorpii* p. 534
agleniana p. 529
algida p. 518
allionii p. 521
alpicola p. 538
— var. *alba* p. 538
— var. *luna* p. 538
— var. *violacea* p. 538
amoena p. 532
angustidens see *wilsonii* p. 536
angustifolia see Section Parryi p. 532
anisodora p. 535
× *anisodoxa* p. 536
apennina p. 522
× *arctotis* see × *pubescens* pp. 525–526
atrodentata p. 530
aurantiaca p. 535
aureata p. 528
auricula hort. see × *pubescens* pp. 525–526
auricula L. p. 522
— ssp. *bauhinii* p. 522
— ssp. *ciliata* p. 522

— var. *albocincta* see *auricula* ssp. *bauhinii* p. 522
— var. *nuda* see *auricula* ssp. *bauhinii* p. 522
— var. *monacensis* see *auricula* ssp. *bauhinii* p. 522
auriculata p. 518
balbisii see *auricula* ssp. *ciliata* p. 522
bayernii p. 529
beesiana p. 535
— var. *leucantha* p. 535
bellidifolia p. 531
× *berninae* p. 522
bhutanica p. 528
× *biflora* see × *floerkeana* p. 523
× *bilekii* see × *forsteri* p. 523
boveana p. 540
× *bowlesii* p. 522
bracteosa p. 528
× *briscoei* p. 536
× *bullesiana* p. 536
Bullesiana Hybrids see × *bullesiana* p. 536
bulleyana p. 535
burmanica p. 535
cadinensis see *daonensis* p. 522
calderiana p. 528
canescens see *veris* ssp. *canescens* p. 534
capitata p. 527
— ssp. *craibeana* p. 527
— ssp. *crispata* p. 527
— ssp. *lacteocapitata* p. 527
— ssp. *mooreana* p. 527
— ssp. *sphaerocephala* p. 527
capitellata p. 518
carniolica p. 522
carpatica see *elatior* ssp. *elatior* pp. 532–533
× *caruelii* p. 522
caveana p. 537
cawdoriana p. 539
chionantha p. 529
chumbiensis p. 538
chungensis p. 535
× *chunglenta* p. 536
clarkei p. 518
clusiana p. 522
cockburniana p. 535
columnae see *veris* ssp. *columnae* p. 534
concholoba p. 531
conspersa p. 518
cortusoides hort. see *saxatilis* p. 528
cortusoides L. p. 527
cottia see *villosa* p. 526
× *crucis* p. 522
cuneifolia p. 528
cusickiana p. 532
daonensis p. 522
darialica p. 518
— ssp. *farinifolia* p. 518
decipiens p. 518
denticulata p. 530
— var. *cashmiriana* p. 530
deorum p. 522
dickieana p. 520
× *discolor* p. 522
eburnea p. 539

Primula macrophylla

Section Aleuritia (Farinosa), Mealy Primulas

Includes about 90 species; the most extensive Section. The species are all non-pubescent, many are yellow- or white-farinose (mealy). Petioles usually shorter than the leaf blades, blade very occasionally rounded or lobed. Farinose exudate, when present, is especially conspicuous on the leaf undersides. Leaves indented dimple-fashion, occasionally attenuated, tips spur-like. Flowers mostly on scapes, pediceled, lilac, mallow-colored or red-violet, occasionally pink, yellow or white.

Capsules usually cylindrical, occasionally globose. Perennials, but often short-lived in cultivation and better treated as biennials. Most species are indigenous to Asia, the rest are from Europe and N. America with a few from S. America. Grow in moist, well-drained humus-rich soil in full sun or semi-shade. Need protection from deep cold. Many species will lift themselves above soil level in winter because of their shallow roots. These need to be reset in early spring. Suitable for peat and bog gardens, shady rock gardens and along streams. Propagate by seed.

P. algida Adams. W. Asia. Scapes to 15cm high, resembles a vigorous *P. farinosa*, but with very short-pediceled flowers, rose-violet, May. z5

P. auriculata Lam. Turkey, Iran, Caucasus, in mountain meadows. Scapes to 35cm high. Leaves not farinose, elliptic-lanceolate, to 20cm long and 3cm wide. Flowers pink, violet or lilac, in many-flowered, somewhat farinose umbels, to 2cm wide. April to May. z5

P. capitellata Boiss. Iran, in mountain meadows. Closely related to the previous species, but with farinose leaves. z5

P. clarkei G. Watt. Kashmir. A dwarf form of a pink primula, only 5cm high. Leaves rounded-reniform, long-stalked, not in rosettes. Flowers solitary or 2–6 in an umbel, light pink with a yellow, white-bordered eye. Very sensitive to late frost. April. z7(6)

P. conspersa Balf.f. et Purd. Kansu, in moist, alpine meadows at 2700–3000m. Scape to 10–50cm high, from branching, rosetted rhizomes of somewhat untidy habit. Leaves leathery, white-farinose beneath. Stems white-mealy, with 1–3 whorls, each with to 12 lilac to rose flowers, 15mm wide, with an orange eye. May. Produces basal, overwintering buds. Best in a moist bed. z5

P. darialica Rupr. NE. Caucasus, in moist rock crevices at alpine elevations. Closely related to *P. frondosa*, but somewhat more tender and less floriferous. Scapes to 10cm high; leaves narrow-obovate, oblong or spatulate. Leaves often to 7.5cm long, yellow-mealy beneath. Flowers rose to cherry-red, corolla lobes notched, to 13mm wide, in 2–5 flowered umbels. Grow like *P. frondosa*. z6

P. darialica ssp. **farinifolia** Rupr. is a subspecies with leaf undersides white-farinose; scapes longer. May. z6

P. decipiens Duby non Stein. Falkland Islands, Cape Horn. Rosettes 6–8cm wide. Leaves narrowly-lanceolate, dentate, somewhat reflexed along the midrib, underside very white-farinose, resembling leaves of the Chrystallophlomis Section. Scapes 8–14cm long, flowers very short-pediceled, white or pale pink, only 7–9mm wide, with a yellow eye. April to May. Grow in a peat bed with ample drainage. Not easily cultivated; short-lived. z6

P. egaliksensis Wormsk. Greenland, NE. North America, N. Rocky Mts., Alaska. Similar to *P. nutans*, of subarctic S. America. Rosetted leaves to 5cm long, obtuse, mostly entire, tapering to a short, winged petiole. Scape 2.5–15cm high with 1–9 flowers in an umbel on erect pedicels to 2cm long; corolla limb to 8mm across, tube to 1cm long. White, purple, or violet. Occasionally offered as seed, difficult to grow. z2

P. elliptica Royle. Kashmir. Similar to *P. rosea*, but flowers purple, not pink, leaves elliptic, long-petioled. Seed is available from India, germination is very poor. z6

P. farinosa L. Bird's-eye Primrose. N. Europe, Pyrenees, Alps, Carpathians, N. Asia, mountains of W., Central and E. Asia. Leaves obovate, 2–8cm long, 1–2cm wide, undersides white-farinose; denticulate. Scape 10–20cm high. Umbels many-flowered, flowers pink with yellow throat, occasionally white. April to May. *P. farinosa* thrives in a moist, peaty site, easily damaged by soggy soil

Candelabra hybrids

in winter. Shallow-rooted and susceptible to frost heaving. Short-lived. Use in large masses. Propagation is easy by seed, seedlings must be protected from aphids. z4

P. fauriae Franch. Japan. Similar to *P. farinosa*, but more dwarf and yellow-farinose. z5

P. frondosa Janka. Central Bulgaria, Stara Planina (in the Schipka Pass), on small, shaded rock walls, near the melting snow. Similar to *P. farinosa*, but substantially more vigorous and persistent. Flowers with acuminate-tipped

calyx teeth. Corolla 10–15mm across, pink-lilac or reddish purple; sometimes homostylous. Grow like *P. farinosa*, but a substantially better garden species; the best Mealy Primula, in fact. May. z5

P. gemmifera Batal. Kansu, E. Tibet, Sichuan. Perennial, but not long-lived. Forms basal overwintering buds, tolerates hard winters better than mild ones. Leaves spatulate, not mealy, finely glandular-pubescent. Scape somewhat white-mealy, 10cm high on the typical ssp. **gemmifera**, to 35cm high on the ssp. **zambalensis** W.W. Sm. et Fletcher from Yunnan. Flowers in 1 or 2 whorls, 15mm across, violet or silvery-lilac with a yellow eye. April to May. Grow in humus rich, gravelly but never dry soil, among dwarf shrubs. z5

P. glabra Klatt. Nepal, Sikkim, Bhutan, S. Tibet, between 4000 and 5000m on rocks and grassy slopes. Rosette compact. Leaves 12–30mm long, sparsely toothed. Scapes 2–10cm high. Flowers pale pink, darker toward the center, with an orange eye. April to May. Difficult to grow and short-lived. Rarely offered in the trade. z4

P. halleri J.F. Gmel. (*P. longiflora* Jacq.). Alps, Carpathians and the Balkan Mts. Particularly conspicuous for the 2–3cm long corolla tube; always homostylous. Leaves 2–8cm long and to 3cm wide, oblong-obovate or elliptic or oblanceolate, nearly entire or very small-toothed, with mealy glands above, underside densely yellow-farinose. Scape to 20cm high, with umbels of 2–12 flowers. Flowers pink-lilac. Grow like *P. farinosa*; easier but often only biennial. z5

P. inayatii Duthie. Kashmir. Leaves narrow-lanceolate, prostrate, 10cm long at anthesis, to 25cm long as fruit ripens, green above, underside yellow- or white-farinose. Scape to 20cm high, umbel to 12-flowered. Flowers 10mm wide, pale lilac with a yellow eye. March to April. Very difficult, flowers too early for cool climates (January to March in its habitat). Seeds are available in India. z6

P. incana M.E. Jones. N. America: Rocky Mts. Leaves to 5cm long, distinctly silvery-mealy or white mealy below. Scape to 15cm high. Flowers pink, lilac-pink or white. Grow like *P. farinosa*. Seeds are regularly offered in the trade. z4

P. involucrata Wall. W. Himalaya, Sikkim, Bhutan, SE. Tibet, Sichuan, between 4000 and 5000m on boggy peat

and moist, gravelly sites. Leaves to 8cm long, elliptic-ovate, cordate, oblong or rounded, entire or indistinctly crenulate. Scape to 25cm high. Umbels 4–10 flowered. Flowers white to purple with a yellow throat. May to June. A vigorous and satisfying species. z5

P. laurentiana Fern. Bird's-eye Primula. Labrador, Quebec, Nova Scotia, Maine. Similar to *P. farinosa*, but taller, with longer bracts, more farinose calyx and substantially larger fruit capsules. Seeds are regularly offered. z2

Primula darialica

P. longiflora see **P. halleri**

P. luteola Rupr. E. Caucasus, on moist meadows and boggy sites. Leaves long, not mealy, lanceolate-elliptic, gradually tapered to the petiole. Scape to 20cm high, umbel many-flowered, rather crowded. Flowers sulphur yellow. May to June. Requires abundant moisture, thrives in sun or semi-shade. Needs somewhat less moisture than *P. rosea*, with which it is closely related. Not easily cultivated in every garden. z5

P. mistassinica Michx. Bird's-eye Primrose. Labrador, Newfoundland, eastern provinces of Canada, NE. USA. Similar to *P. farinosa*, but forming leafy stolons. Flowers pink to pale blue. Seeds are regularly offered in the trade. z2

P. modesta Bisset et Moore. Japan. Similar to *P. farinosa*, but only 10–12cm high, flowers rosy purple or white. z6

P. modesta ssp. **yuparensis** (Takeda) W.W. Sm. et Forrest has longer corolla tubes, resembling a dwarf *P. halleri*. Available in pink or white, vigorous specimens have 2 whorls of flowers. z6

P. nutans Georgi (*P. sibirica* Jacq.). China, Yunnan, Sichuan. Similar to *P. egaliksensis*, but larger and more vigorous, occasionally with short stolons. Leaves elliptic to oblong-oval, to 7cm long and 1.8cm wide. Scape to 25cm high. Umbel to 12-flowered. Flowers small, usually 6–8mm across, white or lavender to violet. May. Difficult to grow; best in semi-shade in a sandy to gravelly peat soil. z4

P. rosea Royle. W. Himalayas, Kashmir, Afghanistan. One of the prettiest primulas. The crimson-rose flowers appear before rosetted leaves develop fully, on a stout scape, in many-flowered umbels. Leaves oblong-ovate, crenate or dentate. Grow in any moist soil, in full sun or semi-shade. Blooms from March to April. Flowers are susceptible to late frost damage. The cultivars include:

'Gigas' ('Wassemés Giant'), large-flowered, tall-stalked; 'Grandiflora', similar to the species, large-flowered; 'Micia Visser de Geer' ('Delight'), large, deep pink flowers, somewhat later.

Propagate by seed, either as soon as ripe or from seed stored at 3–5 degrees C. (37–41 degrees. F.). Division is possible, but not commonly practiced except for cultivars. Grows in any moist garden soil. Susceptible to damage from Red Spider Mites during dry weather. Plants can be forced into flower after January in pot culture. Some beautiful hybrids have resulted from crosses with *P. clarkei* and *P. warshenewskiana*, but these are quite rare in the trade.

P. scotica Hook. N. Scotland. Grows on moist slopes near the sea. Homostylous. Rarely taller than 6cm, often with several scapes from one rosette, each with rarely more than 6 flowers. Flowers 8mm wide, typically deep purple with a yellow throat, occasionally also pure white. Stigma interestingly 5-parted. April to May, reblooming in July. May be short-lived in the landscape, best grown under cover to prevent heaving of the over-wintering crowns. Otherwise grow like *P. farinosa*. z4

P. sibirica see **P. nutans** Georgi

P. wardii see **P. yargongensis**

P. warshenewskiana Fedtschenko. Afghanistan. Resembles *P. rosea*, but only 3cm high, umbels usually only 4-flowered, quickly forming dense mats by underground stolons in a gravelly, peaty substrate. Flowers pale pink. Also ssp. **rhodantha** Balf.f. et W.W. Smith, flowers deeper pink, more stellate, unusually attractive and persistent. Propagation is by division. z5

P. yargongensis Petitm. (*P. wardii* Balf.f.). Yunnan, Sichuan, SE. Tibet, Bhutan, on swampy meadows and along streams at 3000–4500m. Similar to *P. involucrata*, but the flowers always pale mauve to pink or purple, usually with a white eye, tubular-bell-shaped. April to May. An

Primula modesta and *P. modesta* 'Alba'

easily cultivated species. Propagate by seed, abundantly set. z6

Section Amethystina

8 species in E. Himalayas, SE. Tibet, SW. China and Burma. Plants with short, slender to stout rootstocks. Leaves stiff to fleshy, normally with a cuticulate, indistinctly toothed margin, glabrous, not mealy. With the exception of *P. dickieana*, the flowers are always campanulate. These are very difficult to grow since they originate in high alpine meadows and are accustomed to a long snow-covered winter. All require a very

well-drained humus substrate, and high humidity in summer, with protection from moisture in winter. Excellent collector's plants. Propagate by seed and division.

P. dickieana Watt. Sikkim, Bhutan, SE. Tibet, N. Burma, NW. Yunnan. Leaves 2–7cm long and 0.3–1cm wide. The winged petioles are shorter at first, then equally long as the elliptic-obovate to oblanceolate blade. Scape 8–20cm high with 1–6 flowers. Corolla yellow, white, mauve, violet or purple, usually with a yellow eye, about 2cm long and 3cm wide. z6

Primula flaccida

P. kingii Watt. Himalaya Mts., Sikkim, Bhutan, SE. Tibet, Assam. Leaves 2–6cm long, 0.5–1cm wide, elliptic-lanceolate, margin cartilaginous, entire or sparsely small toothed. Scape 1–20cm high with 2–10 flowers. Corolla campanulate, claret-colored to deep violet, 1.8cm long and 1.5cm wide. Very attractive species. z6

Section Auriculastrum (Auricula)

Twenty-one species, exclusively in Europe. Forms the Subgenus Auriculastrum with the Sections Cuneifolia and Parryi. Distinguished from other primulas (except those of the Subgenus Sphondylia and the Sections Cuneifolia and Parryi) by the involuted leaves in the bud stage.

Low perennials, occasionally hanging from rock crevices by long woody shoots. Leaves fleshy or leathery, but never bullate-rugose. Leaf margins entire, sometimes cartilaginous, or distinctly toothed. The sepals are short and wider than long or long and linear, but never pouchlike at the base. The cylindrical or oval calyx is never angular and normally short, the surface of the green part is glabrous or glandular pubescent. Plants mealy-farinose primarily on the upper part of the scape and on the flowers, sparsely on the leaves, more on the upper leaf surface than beneath. Flowers naturally pink to violet, often with a white eye (but very rarely occurring in white forms) or yellow. Flowers of cultivars of many colors including green. Always heterostylous.

Outline of the Subsections
(revised by Widmer and Wehrhahn)
1. Flowers yellow
          Euauricula (Auricula, Luteae)
— Flowers pink, red or violet (occasionally white)   2
2. Leaves entire with a cartilaginous margin
          Arthritica (Cartilagineomarginatae)
— Leaves dentate, without the cartilaginous margin when entire   3
3. Plants very to sparsely mealy-farinose (particularly in the corolla throat), leaves glabrous or glandular (*P. latifolia*)
                              Brevibracteatae
— Plants not mealy (farinose)   4
4. Leaves densely glandular or hairy 5
— Leaves covered with tiny glands, appearing glabrous   6
5. Glands red, brown or black (or so colored when dried)
          Erythrodrosum (Rufiglandulae)
— Glands colorless   Rhopsidium
6. Flowers pink to rose-red (rarely white), solitary or paired
                              Chamaecallis
— Flowers violet to lavender-rose (rarely white), in many-flowered umbels
                              Cyanopsis

The following descriptions have the Subsections noted in parenthesis. Growing requirements vary with each species or hybrid. But they may be generally divided into 3 groups:

a) Problem-free culture in containers or garden sites, any standard garden soil, well-drained and out of bright sun. Including: *P. auricula, P. marginata, P. hirsuta, P. clusiana, P. × pubescens, P. × sendtneri, P. × elisabethae.*

b) Somewhat more demanding in cultivation. For plastic containers or clay pots, require a peaty soil in shade. Substrate should be loosened by incorporating sand and perlite. For intensively cultivated rockeries and trough gardens. Including: *P. carniolica, P. latifolia, P. pedemontana, P. villosa, P. wulfeniana, P. integrifolia, P. minima, P. ×*

heerii, P. × forsteri, P. × intermedia, P. × vochinensis.

c) Most fastidious species for the alpine case or alpine house in the same substrate as the above group. Including *P. allionii, P. kitaibeliana, P. tyrolensis* and hybrids of these. The collector may choose to protect individual plants with cloches, glass, plastic caps, or other covers.

Propagation. The most common method is by seed. Many species (i.e., those of the Subsection Erythrodrosum) never come true from open garden seed and must be isolated or hand-pollinated.

Seed should be sown from October to November (seed of *P. palinuri* and *P. allionii* are just ripening at that time); germination occurs the following spring. Seeds require a light frost before germinating; cover only with a thin layer of sand. Division is done after flowering, when the new white roots form just over the old roots. This method of propagation is good for cultivars of *P. × forsteri, P. × vochinensis* and *P. villosa × allionii.* Dwarf forms and smaller cultivars are also increased by cuttings. Although more tedious than division, removal of old stems is very effective for invigorating older plants.

Pests and Diseases. Many common garden pests attack primulas. Among these are aphids, beetles, black vine weevil, slugs, spider mites and nematodes. With the exception of the nematodes, all of these insect pests can be routinely controlled with the appropriate insecticides. Diseases of primula are those relatively common among garden plants. They include the rust fungi, root rot, leaf spots (bacterial and fungal) and Botrytis as well as Mosaic Virus and Aster Yellows (virus). For control measures, consult current plant pathology literature.

Primula rosea with *Caltha palustris* var. *alba* (white) and *C. palustris* (yellow)

P. allionii Loisel. (Rhopsidium). Maritime Alps, between 700 and 1900m, on steep (not always shaded), limestone outcroppings. In its native habitat, it often has long stems covered with old leaves, and forms large cushions. Leaves to 4.5 × 1cm, oblanceolate to spatulate or rounded to oblong, occasionally toothed or with undulate margins, very glandular. Scape very short, nestled in the rosette, not visible, to 7-flowered. Flowers 12–40mm wide, pink to rose-purple, with a white eye, or occasionally white. March to April. Requires protection from winter wetness. Propagate by division, cuttings or seed. Many cultivars are available in England. z7

P. apennina Widmer (Erythrodrosum). N. Apennines: Monte Orsaro, grows in sandstone crevices. Similar to *P. pedemontana*, but somewhat smaller. Leaves to 6.5 × 2cm. Upper leaf surface not glabrous, the marginate gland hairs 0.25mm, less dark. Scape 3–8cm high. Umbel 1–8 flowered, flowers rose or violet, to 1.5cm across. Rarely cultivated. More difficult to cultivate than *P. pedemontana*. z7

P. auricula L. (Euauricula). Alps, Carpathians, Apennines, in limestone rock crevices or on moist alpine grasslands. Leaves to 15 × 6cm, fleshy, rounded-obovate, obovate or oblong-lanceolate, entire, dentate or denticulate, with a distinctly cartilaginous margin, white-mealy or sometimes entirely glabrous; tapering to a winged petiole. Scape to 15cm high, to rarely 35-flowered. Flowers mostly fragrant, yellow, 1.2–1.8cm wide, lobes parted to the middle, with a mealy throat. Quite variable, with the following subspecies: z5

P. auricula ssp. **bauhinii** (Beck) Luedi. With more or less farinose, rather short (0.1mm-long) marginate glands and strongly scented. Includes var. **albocincta** Widm. with a densely mealy margin; var. **nuda** Widm. leaves not farinose, only the calyx mealy; var. **monacensis** Widm. with relatively narrow leaves, unusually tall plants, to 35cm, and sulfur yellow flowers, from the moors of SE. West Germany. z6

P. auricula ssp. **ciliata** (Moretti) Luedi (*P. balbisii* Lehm.) with bright green, non-farinose leaves, margins with 0.3mm-long glands; flowers nearly always odorless. Transition forms are labeled var. **obristii** (Stein) Beck. The var. **serratifolia** comes from the Carpathian Mts., leaves very distinctly and deeply toothed. Grow in a limestone, gravelly humus-rich loam, not too sunny, in rock crevices or flat sites. Propagate by seed. z5

P. balbisii see **P. auricula** ssp. **ciliata**

P. × berninae Kern. (*P. hirsuta* × *P. latifolia*). Switzerland: Engadine Valley; Italy: Bergamasque Alps. Found among the parents, fertile. Flowers large, violet to blue-mauve, in one-sided umbels; scapes 7.5cm high. Includes the form 'Windrush', with bright pink flowers flushed mauve. z6

P. × biflora see **× floerkeana**

P. × bilekii see **× foersteri**

P. × bowlesii Farrer (*P. latifolia* × *P. pedemontana*). France: Mont Cenis. Intermediate between the parents; upper leaf surfaces and pedicels densely glandular, umbels one-sided, few flowered, lavender to pinkish purple. Found among the parents, very rare. z6

P. cadinensis see **P. daonensis**

P. carniolica Jacq. (Brevibracteatae). Yugoslavia, foothills of the Julian Alps especially in Idrija, on limestone, in shady, mossy, wooded ravines, occasionally on moist cliffs. Rootstock with

Primula auricula

several crowns. Leaves to 15 × 4.5cm, obovate to oblong-lanceolate, gradually or abruptly tapered into a long petiole, light green, glossy, nonfarinose, with slightly undulate margins. Scape to 25cm high, to 8-flowered. Flowers pink to violet, conspicuously white-mealy in the throat, 14–25mm wide. April to May. Somewhat difficult to grow; for a moist shady site. Propagate by seed. z6

P. × caruelii Porta (*P. glaucescens* × *P. spectabilis*). Italy: Bergamasque Alps. Found among the parents, recognized by the marginate, pitted glands; flowers rose to pinkish lavender. Very rare. z6

P. clusiana Tausch (Arthritica). NE. Dolomitic Alps, from E. Bavaria to Vienna, south to Steiermark, on infertile, short grass meadows, gravelly, rocky sites and snowy basins, between 600 and 2200m. Multistemmed. Leaves in dense rosettes, to 9 × 3cm, ovate to elliptic or oblong, tapering to a short, broad-winged leaf petiole, leathery, entire, dark green and glossy above, gray-green beneath. Leaf margin narrow, white-

cartilaginous, densely covered with long glands. Scape to 1cm high, 2–6 flowered. Corolla rose to lilac, with a white eye. April to May. Easily cultivated, needs abundant water and some nitrogen fertilizer.

P. cottia see **P. villosa**

P. × crucis Bowles ex Farrer (*P. latifolia* × *P. marginata*). France: Maritime Alps. A beautiful hybrid, somewhat inclined toward *P. latifolia*, very rare. z7

P. daonensis Leyb. (*P. cadinensis* Porta, *P. oenensis* Thomas ex Gremli, Erythrodrosum). Switzerland, Rhaetian Alps, on rocky grasslands from 1600–2800m. Distinguished from the other species of this subsection by the relatively narrow leaves, 7 × 2cm, with dense, very short hairs 0.15–0.25mm long, very short flower pedicels, 1–9mm, and tall scape, 1.5–9cm wide. Flowers pink to violet-pink, with a white eye. Calyx tightly appressed to the fruit structure. Cultivation is similar to that of *P. hirsuta*, but somewhat more difficult. z5

P. deorum Velen. (Cyanopsis). Bulgaria: Rila Mts., between 1900 and 2500m on moist, grassy, seasonally flooded sites directly below the snow fields or on the edge of melt water streams, over a siliceous substrate. Rootstock thick and strong. Leaves to 10cm long and 1.5cm wide, narrow-lanceolate to spatulate-lanceolate, entire, glabrous, somewhat leathery and sticky. Scape to 15cm high, to 10-flowered, one-sided. Flowers somewhat pendulous, dark purple-violet to rose-violet. May. Difficult to cultivate, requiring a very moist, peaty, somewhat sandy bed, in full sun to semi-shade. z5

P. × discolor Leybold (*P. auricula* × *P. daonensis*). Italy: southern Adamello Mts. Similar to *P. × pubescens*, but more compact. An attractive and rare wild hybrid. z6

P. × elisabethae Sündermann (*P. marginata* × *P. villosa*). Sündermann's original plant is lost from cultivation, but the back crosses are easily cultivated; similar to *P. × wockei*. Flowers to 3cm across, primrose-yellow with densely farinose eye, solitary or paired on a 15cm high stout scape. z6

P. × escheri Bruegger (*P. auricula* × *P. integrifolia*). E. Switzerland. Very rare, infertile wild hybrid, similar to the more vigorous *P. integrifolia*, but more red-violet with a yellow eye. z5

P. × facchinii Schott (*P. minima × P. spectabilis*). Italy: S. Adamello Mts. Intermediate between the parents, very attractive, with bright flower colors. Not difficult to grow. z6

P. × floerkeana Schrad. (*P. × biflora* Huter, *P. × salisburgensis* Floerke, *P. glutinosa × P. minima*). Widely distributed natural hybrid, incredibly variable. Flowers rose-colored, 3–4 on a 7.5cm high scape. Often a very poor bloomer in culture. z5

P. × forsteri Stein (*P. × steinii* Obrist ex Stein, *P. × kellereri* Widm., *P. × bilekii* Suendermann, *P. hirsuta × P. minima*). N. Tirol, S. Tirol. Quite variable, usually more inclined toward *P. minima* in nature, but with seedling progeny ranging from one extreme to the other. Leaves moderately glandular. Umbels usually few-flowered, flower color deep rose-red with a white eye.

Several distinctly different clones are grown under the names: *P. × bilekii*, round, compact Minima-type rosettes and 1–2 flowered scapes, flowers dark red with a white eye; *P. × forsteri* has more cuneate leaves and huge, to 35mm-wide, rose-red, white-eyed flowers, including 'Dianne' from J. Drake, which resembles *P. × bilekii*, but taller. The prettiest natural hybrid, next to *P. × pubescens*, worthy of much wider cultivation. Propagation is easy, by division or cuttings. z5

P. glaucescens Moretti (Arthritica). Italy: Bergamasque Alps. Similar to *P. clusiana*, but the leaves are substantially glossier with a wider and toothed cartilaginous margin. Sepals to 30mm long, the longest of this Subsection. Flowers purple to pale lavender, rarely pink. z6

P. glaucescens ssp. **longobarda** (Porta). Widmer found this plant in the eastern part of the species range. Smaller habit, small-flowered, calyx less deeply incised, calyx teeth obtuse. More easily cultivated than *P. clusiana*, flowers well. May. z6

P. glutinosa Wulf. (Cyanopsis). E. Alps, Bosnia, between 1800 and 3100m on north-facing slopes, in moist clay and rubble, always over a siliceous substrate. Leaves to 6cm long and 1cm wide, oblanceolate to narrow oblong, somewhat cartilaginous margin, serrate on the apical half, steeply erect, very sticky. Several one-sided scapes 6–9cm high, to 8-flowered. Flowers blue-violet, pure blue, mallow-colored, occasionally white, rarely dark purple, very sweet scented, somewhat overpowering. May.

Unusually difficult to cultivate, needs a moraine bed with constantly flowing, cold subsurface water, like *Ranunculus glacialis*. z4

P. × heerii Brügger (*P. hirsuta × P. integrifolia*). W. Austria, E. Switzerland. One of the prettiest hybrid primulas. Very vigorous and floriferous, usually dark violet or dark red, umbels many-flowered. Propagation is best from cuttings since the rootstock is very short. Rarely, if ever, sets seed in cultivation. z5

P. hirsuta All. (*P. rubra* J.F. Gmel., *P. vis-*

Primula marginata

cosa Vill. non All., Erythrodrosum). Alps, Central Pyrenees. A typical rock plant on a siliceous substrate, between 2300 and 3600m, down to 400m at Lake Maggiore. Leaves to 15 × 4cm, broadly obovate or rhomboid, abruptly tapered to a petiole, densely covered with glandular hairs, and very sticky. Scape shorter than the leaves, to 30-flowered. Scape 2–16mm high, flowers rose or red, with or without a white eye, occasionally pure white. Recognizable in fruit by the long, outspread calyx lobes. April to May. Grows in gravelly humus soil in semi-shade, best in rock crevices. Intolerant of excessive moisture after flowering.

'Ethel Barker' from *P. allionii × P. hirsuta* is very compact and attractive. The English and American literature now list this species as *P. rubra*. z5

P. × hortensis see **P. × pubescens**

P. integrifolia L. (Rhopsidium). Central Alps, E. and Central Pyrenees, between 1500 and 3050m, in snowy valleys, only on siliceous soils. A tiny plant. Leaves to 4 × 1cm, elliptic or oblong to spatulate, always entire, rather thin and soft, densely covered with 0.7mm-long hairs. Scape 1–3 flowered, 3–5cm high. Flowers light pink with a white eye, occasionally white, darker in the Pyrenees. Grow in a moist, cool, but not too shady site, preferably in a peat bed. Rarely floriferous. z5

P. × intermedia Portenschlag (*P. clusiana × P. minima*). E. Alps, i.e. snowy peaks around Vienna, Austria. Very attractive hybrid, thriving in garden culture, but not always floriferous. Quite variable, ranging in appearance from one parent to the other. Easily increased by division. Sometimes produces seed. Not to be confused with the Asiatic "*P. intermedia*" of the R.H.S. *Dictionary of Gardening*. z5

P. × **juribella** Sündermann (*P. minima* × *P. tyrolensis*). Italy, in the vicinity of Passo di Rolle. A beautiful natural hybrid, very rare. Dense mat-forming hybrid, compact, floriferous. Leaves elliptic with tiny, irregular teeth. Scape to 2.5cm high with 1 or 2 rosy purple flowers. Infertile. z6

P. kitaibeliana Schott (Rhopsidium). Yugoslavia, Dinaric Alps, Velebit, Kapela, south to Hercegovina, between 350 and 1700m, on limestone, in low turf or humus in rock crevices. Similar to a tender *P. clusiana*, leaves entire or sparsely toothed, oblong, ovate or elliptic. Flowers to 35mm-wide, rose, lilac, occasionally white. The strong terpentine scent of young leaves is characteristic. Cultivation is quite difficult, best grown in the alpine house. Propagate by division, cuttings or seed. z7

P. × **kolbiana** Widmer (*P. daonensis* × *P. latifolia*). Italy: southern Bergamasque Alps. Resembles *P.* × *berninae*, but smaller and rarer in nature. z6

P. latifolia Lapeyr. (*P. viscosa* All., *P. hirsuta* Vill. non All., Brevibracteatae). SW. and Central Alps, E. Pyrenees. Always in lime-free rock, occasionally on screes at alpine elevations from 1800–3050m. Rootstock to 20cm long. Leaves to 18 × 5cm, oval to obovate-oblong or lanceolate-cuneate, with stout, uneven teeth toward the end, or occasionally lacking teeth. Densely covered with sticky, colorless hairs, yellowish green, slender, often undulate. Scape to 18cm high, one sided, with many flowers. Flowers nodding, violet or rosy violet, occasionally white, to 15mm wide. This species often is listed as *P. viscosa* in American and English literature. z5

P. latifolia var. **cynoglossifolia** Widmer, from the Maritime Alps, with untoothed leaves; vigorous, satisfactory species for the garden. Requires a lime-free soil, shady site and only moderate soil moisture. z7

P. × **lempergii** F. Buxb. (*P. auricula* × *P. clusiana*). Collected by Eng. Martin and taken to F. Lemperg in Germany. Long since vanished from cultivation.

P. × **loiseleurii** Sündermann (*P. allionii* × *P. auricula*). According to Wocke, intermediate between the parents. The original hybrid is no longer cultivated, but certainly the parents have been recrossed. z6

P. marginata Curt. (Brevibracteatae).

Maritime and Cottian Alps. Always found on limestone. Rootstock woody, to 20cm long. Young leaves and margins of the older leaves farinose. Leaves to 10 × 4cm, oblong or obovate, obtuse, regularly deep-toothed, tapering to a short petiole. Scape 12–15cm high, to 20-flowered. Pedicels and calyx farinose, the latter often turning reddish. Flowers light blue to lilac, occasionally white, 18–28mm wide, often with a white throat. March to April. z7(6)

Includes many cultivars: 'Linda Pope', wide leaves with distinct white margin, flowers large, round, attractive violet-

Primula hirsuta

blue, white-mealy; 'Clear's Variety' and 'Drake's Form', both blue with attractive leaves; 'Beatrice Lascaris' and 'Highland Twilight' are dwarf cultivars, the former flowers blue, the latter lilac-pink; 'Prichard's Variety' has small, campanulate, violet flowers; 'Crenata' is small-flowered, with attractive foliage; 'Coerulea' is nearly pure blue.
Hybrids with other primulas are: *P.* × *wockei* Arends, from *P.* × *pubescens* × *P. marginata*, leaves finely dentate, greener, flowers light violet-blue; 'Marven', from *P. marginata* × *P.* × *venusta*, deep rose-violet, white-mealy, small-flowered. Especially interesting for the collector

are the hybrids between *P. marginata* and *P. allionii*, including 'Beatrice Wooster', pink, very floriferous; 'Helen Gianella', pink-lilac, small-flowered, borne in the exact center of the plant; 'Joan Hughes', compact, rose-violet, very floriferous; 'Margaret', pink, very large, flat flowers; 'Rose Fairy', similar to 'Beatrice Wooster', but not so vigorous. Cultivars of the species are more persistent, attractive and easy to cultivate; the last named hybrids with *P. allionii* should be limited to the alpine house. Propagation is by cuttings, division and seed. Leggy plants should be heavily mulched or staked for

Primula × *pubescens* (seedling)

support. *P. marginata* is the most attractive and satisfactory early spring primula for the alpine garden and rock garden, pots or trough. z6

P. minima L. (Chamaecallis). E. Alps to the Sudetic Mts., Central Carpathians and Balkans, between 1200 and 1300m, on limestone or siliceous substrata, but growing in a surface layer of humus if on limestone. Mat-forming. Leaves to 3 × 0.8cm, cuneate or triangular, apex truncate or with 3–9 teeth, smooth and glossy. Scape usually only 0.5cm high, occasionally taller, 1–2 flowered. Corolla rose to pink, always with a white eye, or occasionally pure white. Cultivation not difficult, but often not free flowering. Requires a peaty, gravelly soil, abundant moisture and fertilizer. Best in semi-shade in hot summers, otherwise sun. Young plants from cuttings and division usually flower better. z5

P. × **muretiana** Moritzi (*P. integrifolia* × *P. latifolia*). E. Switzerland, W. Austria. Very conspicuous in nature for the dark flower color, intermediate between the parents. Rather difficult and poor-flowering in deep garden soils. z5

P. × obovata Huter (*P. auricula* × *P. tyrolensis*). Italy: Belluno, in the vicinity of the Rolle Pass. Very rare natural hybrid. Flowers similar to *P. × escheri*. z6

P. oenensis see **P. daonensis**

P. palinuri Petagna (Euauricula). SW. Italy, in the foothills of Palinuri, in cliffs adjacent to the sea. Thick basal stem, to 3cm. Leaves to 20 × 6.5cm, light green, very glandular, only cartilaginous-tipped. Flower umbels surrounded by leaflike bracts. Flowers fragrant, nodding, in up to 40-flowered umbels, corolla tubular to funnel-shaped, 12–15mm wide, yellow, interior very farinose. Closely related to *P. auricula*, but differing in the vigorous habit (to 40cm high × 40cm wide), strongly *P. obconica*-scented leaves, and the thick shoots. Usually cultivated in the alpine house, but hardier than generally believed. Has tolerated −27 degrees C. (−16 degrees F.), given a covering of conifer branches. Suitable for dry, open, sunny garden sites in a stone wall or rockery. Propagation is by cuttings or seed. z5

P. pedemontana Thomas ex Gaud. (Erythrodrosum). SW. Alps, Cantabrian region, on siliceous substrata. Resembles *P. hirsuta* and *P. villosa*. Flower scapes longer (rarely to twice as long) as the 2–8cm long leaves. Leaf margins densely glandular downy, glands 0.1–0.25mm long, reddish-brown or -black. Leaf surface densely downy when young, later sparse fuzzy or typically glossy. Flower color bright purple with a white eye, occasionally entirely white. The Subspecies **iberica** Losa et P. Monts. from the Cantabrian Cordillera is scarcely different. April to May. An attractive species, grown like *P. hirsuta*. z6

P. × pubescens Jacq. (*P. × rhaetica* Gaud., *P. × arctotis* Kerner, *P. auricula* hort. non L., the large-flowered cultivars of *P. × hortensis* Wettst., *'P. auricula* × *P. hirsuta*). In Great Britain, where primrose breeding and growing developed very early, the epithet *P. × pubescens* has at times been applied to the progeny of *P. auricula* × *P. viscosa* and also *P. auricula* × *P. villosa*. In referring to older literature, watch for these now unaccepted hybrid names. Also, in British and American literature, the *P. × pubescens* parent *P. hirsuta* often is listed as *P. rubra*. The

colorful garden Auriculas, time-tested in culture since 1582 in Europe, and divided into many groups, races and cultivars. The Auricula Primulas were at their height of garden popularity at the end of the 18th and early 19th centuries with collections containing over 100 forms. Today, the Auriculas are divided into 4 major groups:

1. Common Garden Auriculas: flowers of a single color, usually with a mat-white eye; these are the most frequently cultivated.

2. Belgian Auriculas: flowers of 1 or 2 main colors, becoming darker toward

Primula sielboldii, behind *Astilboides tabularis*

the eye, lighter toward the margin, usually with a yellow- or olive-colored eye; the plants are usually not mealy.

3. English Auriculas: flowers with a white eye which radiates toward the corolla margin through the ground color of the lobes, giving a striped appearance. Often bordered by a third color on the margin; the plants are white-farinose.

4. Double-flowering Auriculas: colored like the other groups, rarely available in modern culture.

Auriculas are bred and grown extensively today mostly in Great Britain where the English Auricula group is further divided into 3 main sub-groups;

Alpine Auriculas, Border Auriculas and Show Auriculas. The so-called Alpine Auriculas are quite worthy of more extensive cultivation, but for garden use they are almost too sensitive to hot, dry, continental summers. Cultivars that are still available in the trade include:

'Alba', compact-growing, white; 'Alice Rushton', very large-flowered, purple with a large white eye; 'Blairside Yellow', mass bloomer with bright yellow flowers; 'Blue Wave', violet-blue flowers with undulate margins and a yellow eye; 'Broadwell Gold', deep yellow flowers with crinkled margins; 'Celtic King', large-flowered, pure yellow with a mealy white eye; 'Christine', vigorous habit, well-formed pink flowers; 'Faldonside', an old cultivar with carmine red flowers; 'Kingscote', a good growth habit, carmine red flowers, late bloomer; 'Mary', a good double form, yellowish white flowers; 'Mrs. J.H. Wilson', mass bloomer with white-eyed, violet flowers; 'Nigel', good double cultivar, lilac flowers; 'Old Red Dusty Miller', wine red sport of 'Old Yellow Dusty Miller', mealy yellow flowers with a strong fragrance; 'Rufus', very vigorous; flowers bright rust with large yellow eye; 'The General', terracotta flowers; 'Zambia', a good double cultivar, black-red flowers.

All these cultivars belong to groups 1, 2 and 4. Under favorable conditions, all will need dividing every 2 or 3 years. The Show Auriculas are only raised in containers, annually transplanted. The easiest to grow is perhaps 'Neat and Tidy'. Very recently, several very choice cultivars of Garden Auriculas have appeared in nursery and seed catalogues, indicating, perhaps, a resurgence of interest in these "Georgian" hybrids. z5

P. × pumila Kerner (*P. daonensis × P. minima*. Italy: S. Adamello Mts. Similar to *P. × forsteri*, but smaller and substantially rarer in nature. z6

P. rubra see **P. hirsuta**

P. salisburgensis see **P. × floerkeana**

P. × salomonii Sündermann (*P. auricula × P. marginata*). Sündermann's original plants are no longer in culture.

P. × sendtneri Widmer (*P. auricula × P. pedemontana*). Developed by Keller in Munich, W. Germany. Back crosses have been more impressive, the first generation is intermediate, the leaves are distinctly typical of *P. pedemontana*. The F(2) generation has many salmon orange progeny. Very attractive. z5

P. × seriana Widmer (*P. daonensis × P. hirsuta*). Italy, Bergamasque Alps, Val Seriana. Intermediate between the parent species, very difficult to identify. Very rare in culture. z6

P. spectabilis Tratt. (Arthritica). Italian Alps eastward to Monte Baldo. Rosettes funnelform only in the center, leaves more widely spread than the other species of this Subsection, densely covered with translucent glandular spots, to 9 × 4cm. Scape 2.5–12cm tall, to 7-flowered. Flowers rose-red to strong red, 20–35mm large. Somewhat more difficult to grow than *P. clusiana* and *P. glaucescens*. z6

P. × steinii see **P. × forsteri**

P. × sturii see **P. × truncata**

P. × truncata Lehm. (*P. minima × P. villosa; P. × sturii* Schott). Austria, in the silicaceous mountains of Steiermark and Carinthia. Similar to *P. × forsteri*, but with longer glands. Very rare. z5

P. tyrolensis Schott (Rhopsidium). Italy, SE. South Tirolian Dolomites, between 1000 and 2300m, in somewhat shaded limestone crevices or on balds in gravelly turf. Small cushion clump from a stout rhizome. Leaves rounded with distinct teeth, to 2.5 × 1.2cm. Scape 0.5–2cm long, with 1–3 flowers. Flowers in nature rose, occasionally somewhat lilac-blushed, almost always lilac-pink in culture, with a white eye. April to May. More difficult than the otherwise very similar *P. allionii*. Propagate by cuttings or seed. z5

P. × venusta hort. (*P. auricula × P. carniolica*). Yugoslavia, Krain. Very attractive natural hybrid, but very much overcollected and quite rare today. Hybrids

Primula denticulata

from home-made crosses of the parent species are highly recommended. z6

P. × venzoides Venzo (*P. tyrolensis × P. wulfeniana*). Italy; in the eastern part of the range of *P. tyrolensis*. Intermediate, very rare in cultivation. z6

P. villosa Wulf. Jacq. (*P. cottia* Widmer). (Erythrodrosum). E. Alps, very scattered in the SW. Alps and the Pyrenees Mts., on rock outcrops and gravelly slopes; lime-intolerant. Leaves to 15 × 3.5cm, wide to narrowly obovate, dentate or entire toward the tip, very sticky from the 1mm-long glands. Scape to 15cm, to 7-flowered. Flowers rose to lilac with a white eye. April to May. The Subspecies **commutata** (Schott) Widmer, from the Steiermark region at 400m, is not significantly distinguished botanically, but for garden use, ssp. *commutata* is interesting for its unusually vigorous growth habit. Grow like *P. auricula*. z5

P. × vochinensis Gusmus (*P. minima × P. wulfeniana*). Yugoslavia and Austria; Karawanken and Julian Alps. Often forming large mats. Flowers readily and abundantly in the garden, flower color nearly always rich red from the influence of *P. wulfeniana*. Should be more widely cultivated. z6

P. × widmeriana Sündermann (*P. auricula × P. latifolia*). The original plant from Sündermann is unfortunately lost; garden crosses of the parent species are recommended.

P. wulfeniana Schott (Arthritica). Austria; SE. Alps, S. Carpathian Mts. (ssp. **baumgarteniana** Degen et Moess.) Alpine grasslands and gravelly slopes. Leaves to 4 × 1.2cm, oblanceolate or obovate, firm, margins especially strong-cartilaginous. Scape to 7cm, 1–3 flowered. Flowers rose to purplish-red. April to May. Not always easy to grow. Subspecies *baumgarteniana* is not substantially different, but occurs in woodlands on limestone. z5

Section Bullatae

Seven species in SW. Sichuan, NW. Yunnan and the neighboring E. and SE. regions of Tibet. Somewhat woody, evergreen perennials with bullate leaves. The plants are widely spreading, rhizomatous. Rhizomes covered with old leaf scars. Leaves leathery, rugose, simple, sometimes farinose, exudate often glandular-sticky. Flowers in many-flowered umbels, usually yellow or rust-colored. Only one species is commonly found in cultivation:

P. forrestii Balf.f. Yunnan. Found in dry, somewhat shaded rock crevices. Rhizome long, woody, covered with old leaf scars and remnants. Plants vigorous, 30–40cm high, nearly subshrub-like, densely covered with glandular hairs. Leaves long-petioled, blades to 20 × 5cm, ovate-elliptic or elliptic-oblong, crenate, very bullate-rugose, undersides white- or yellow-mealy when young. Scape to 50cm high but often less, 25-flowered. Flowers pale to bright yellow, orange-eyed. Grow in a very well-drained, winter-dry site. Substrate should be a sandy loam incorporating limestone chips. Best in semi-shade. Propagate by seed, usually abundantly set. z6

Section Capitatae

Two species, but only the following is in cultivation. Entire plant usually extremely farinose. Flowers nodding, in dense, round heads capitulae. Attractive, summer-flowering primulas. Best grown in a loose, well-drained humus soil, in semi-shade. The roots lack vigor and therefore often frost heave in snowless winters. When plants are planted closely together they root down more deeply and are less subject to damage by frost heaving. Mulch plants or cover with evergreen boughs in winter. Propagate by seed. Grow seedlings annually to provide replacements for winter losses.

P. capitata Hook. Himalaya, Tibet and SW. China, in coniferous forests on moist loam and on boggy river banks from 4000–5000m. Leaves narrow oblong or oblanceolate, obtuse or acute, finely denticulate and rugose. Scapes 15–30cm high, slender, elegant, with ball-shaped, densely flowered umbels, flowers blue to dark violet; the outer flowers develop first, drooping downward, while the inner form a globose to circular crest; calyx and scape silvery white-farinose. z5 The subspecies are:

P. capitata ssp. **craibeana** (Balf.f et W.W.

Sm.) W.W. Sm. et Forrest; leaves very narrow, undersides densely yellow-farinose, not mealy above, inflorescences globose, not disc-like. z5

P. capitata ssp. **crispata** (Balf.f. et W.W. Sm.) W.W. Sm. et Forrest; is not farinose. With more disc-shaped flower heads; resembles a half-headed *P. capitata*. z5

P. capitata ssp. **lacteocapitata** (Balf.f. et W.W. Sm.) W.W. Sm. et Forrest; leaf undersides pale yellow-farinose and leaf base red. z5

P. capitata ssp. **mooreana** (Balf.f. et W.W. Sm.) W.W. Sm. et Forrest; leaf green above, pure white farinose and reticulate below, base green; flower head flattened. z5

P. capitata ssp. **sphaerocephala** (Balf.f. et Forrest) W.W. Sm. et Forrest; also lacks mealy exudate; the flower heads are globose. Blooms from July to November. An attractive cultivar, 'Early Lilac', blooms in June. z5

Section Cortusoides

Twenty-three species, all Asiatic except the type species, *P. cortusoides*, from Siberia to E. Europe. The other species are distributed from Japan and Korea through Siberia, Central Asia to the N. and W. Provinces of China, Tibet and the E. Himalayas. Plants not farinose. Leaves distinctly petioled, distinctly lobed, covered with segmented hairs. Bracts never pouchlike. Flowers funnelform, never sessile. Capsule enclosed in the calyx. Not difficult in the garden, grow best in loose humus soil; tolerate sun and semi-shade, naturalize well. Suitable for the wild garden, among rhododendrons, and for woodland margins. The nomenclature is somewhat confused. Propagate by seed; cultivars of *P. sieboldii* by division and eventually rhizome cuttings.

P. cortusoides hort. see **P. saxatilis**

P. cortusoides L. Forests of the Urals and Altai Mts. Cultivated since 1794 and commercial stock still is not true. Most plants cultivated under this name are actually *P. saxatilis*. Entire plant somewhat woolly-floccose. Scape 15–30cm high, much longer than the leaves, with many-flowered umbels. Flowers pink. April to May. *P. cortusoides* is distinguished from *P. saxatilis* by the shorter flower pedicels, umbels therefore appear denser and more compact. z5

P. geraniifolia Hook.f. Tibet, Sikkim, Nepal, Bhutan, Yunnan; in woodlands and rock shadows from 2900 to 4100m. Leaves long-petioled, margin incised and undulate. Scape 10–30cm high, 3–12 flowered. Flowers pale to deep purple. Foliage similar to *Cortusa* or *Geranium*. April to May. z5

P. heucherifolia Franch. W. Sichuan; on grassy sites, in the shade of large rocks, also in woodlands between 2000 and 3200m. Leaves long-petioled, 6–15cm long and 3–6cm wide, rounded, cordate at the base, 7–11 part lobed. Scape 15–30cm high, 3–10 flowered. Flowers mauve to deep purple, to 2.5cm wide. April to May. z5

P. jesoana Miq. Central Japan. Leaves upright to 30cm long, blade rounded, cordate at the base, 7–9 lobed, lobes further lobed and coarsely toothed. Scape to 60cm high with 1–4 whorls of 4–6 flowers. Flowers rose to rose-purple with yellow eye, occasionally white, to 2cm wide. April to May. Hairy plants are var. **pubescens** Takeda et Hara, and glabrous ones are var. **glabra** Takeda et Hara. z6

P. kisoana Miq. SW. Japan. Leaves 5–15cm long, blade rounded, deeply cordate at the base, flat-lobed, lobes undulately toothed. Scape 5–20cm high with 2–6 flowers. Flowers rose-colored, 3cm wide. Very attractive, but rare. May. z6

P. lichiangensis see **P. polyneura**

P. mollis Nutt.ex Hook. Himalaya Mts., W. China; shady sites in thickets and along streams, between 2300 and 3300m. Leaves rounded with cordate base, crenate-lobed. Scape to 60cm, with 2–6 whorls of 4–9 flowers. Flowers crimson to soft rose with a yellow or green-yellow eye, 2cm wide. May to June. Only winter hardy under favorable conditions, best reserved for the alpine house or temperate greenhouse. z7

P. patens see **P. sieboldii**

P. polyneura Franch. (*P. veitchii* Duthie, *P. lichiangensis* (Forr.) Forr., *P. saxatilis* var. *pubescens* Pax et K. Hoffm.). Yunnan, Sichuan, SE. Tibet, Kansu; from 2300–4300m. Entire plant soft-downy or glabrous. Leaves to 16cm long, rounded to broadly triangular, 7–11 lobed; petioles 2–6cm long, sparsely or densely rough-haired, or glabrous. Scape to 30cm high, with usually 2, occasionally 3, 2–12 flowered whorls. Flowers quite variable, pale rose, bright rose-red, crimson, or purple, with greenish yellow to orange eye. May to June. z5

P. saxatilis Kom. (*P. cortusoides* hort. non L.). Amur region, Manchuria; in humus-rich rock crevices. Flowers rose-lilac. Generally comparable to *P. cortusoides*. April to May. Easily naturalized without becoming troublesome. Very good for pot culture; pot in late summer, over-winter in a cold frame. Force after January at 6–8 degrees C. (42–46 degrees F.); plants will flower in a few weeks. z4

P. saxatilis var. **pubescens** see **P. polyneura**

P. sieboldii E. Morr. (*P. patens* Turcz.). Japan, Korea, Manchuria, E. Siberia; on swampy meadowlands. Quite variable. The entire plant is downy. Leaves to 20cm-long and to 7cm-wide, blade ovate to oblong-ovate, cordate at the base, rounded at the tip, margin regularly lobed, lobes irregularly toothed. Scape to 30cm high with up to 15 flowers. Pedicels 5–40mm long. Variably colored: pink, red, lilac, pure white, often with greenish dots, corolla lobes entire, distinctly fringed or notched. Flowers variable in size, 2–4cm. The wild form from the E. Asian continent, sometimes listed as *P. patens*, is substantially more gray pubescent, and small-flowered. The Japanese forms and cultivars are choice garden ornamentals, also good for cut flowers. Since the rhizome grows obliquely upward, the species thrives on annual mulching. Leaves die back right after flowering (May to June). Propagate by division and seed. Seedlings of Japanese forms are quite variable. The prettiest species of the Section. z5

P. veitchii see **P. polyneura**

Section Cuneifolia

Three to five species in Asia and N. America. Closely related to the Section Auriculastrum. Small, mostly high-alpine or arctic species of very difficult culture. Includes **P. cuneifolia** Ledeb. from the alpine regions of Japan and the E. Asian continent, to the Aleutian Islands and Alaska. Leaves obovate or obovate-cuneate, toothed below or rarely the whole margin toothed, to 7.5cm long. Scape to 30cm high with 1–9 flowers in a terminal umbel. Flowers rose-red or crimson with yellow eye. The subspecies are ssp. *hakusanensis* (Franch.) W.W. Smith et Forr. and ssp. *saxifragifolia* (Lehm.) W.W. Smith et Forr.; from the Sierra Nevada in N. America comes **P. suffrutescens** A. Gray,

flowers rose or red. Other subspecies are listed.

Section Craibia (Petiolaris)

About 60 species, the second largest Section. Plants are farinose. Flowers generally petiolate, occasionally sessile and then with pouchlike bracts. Capsules globose, not opening with valves, and toothed, rather disintegrating when ripe. Himalaya Mts. to W. China. Very distinctive species, either dying back or forming overwintering buds in fall covered by scalelike, densely farinose primary leaves. Flowers pink to deep purple, occasionally yellow or white.

Most are very difficult to grow; the easiest are *P. edgeworthii* and *P. petiolaris*. They need dryness in winter (protect by conifer boughs or cloches), moderate moisture in spring and early summer. Best situation is in semi-shade; many species also tolerate full shade. Plants deteriorate with alternate freezing and thawing in winter. Container culture is possible; overwinter in an alpine house, under a bench; in summer move to a shaded coldframe. These thrive in a well-drained and humus-rich substrate. Propagate by seed (sow immediately after ripening of the capsules), division and leaf cuttings.

P. aureata Fletcher. Nepal, Sikkim. Rosettes distinctly white-mealy. Leaves broadly cuneate to oval-oblong, irregularly toothed, 4–20cm long and 2cm wide. Scape very short, with a 10 flowered umbel. Flowers cream colored, tinged yellow toward the center, to 3.75cm across. With 2 forms in culture. April to May. z6

P. bhutanica Fletcher. Himalaya Mts., Assam, Bhutan and S. Tibet; on moist, mossy banks under rhododendrons between 3000 and 4400m. Leaves spatulate to oblong-spatulate, to 20cm long, irregularly toothed, smaller at anthesis and clustered in regular rosettes. Scape short, to 7.5cm high at flowering, elongating to 20cm in fruit, with few to 10-flowered umbels. Flowers nearly sessile, calyx bell-shaped, the lobes 3-toothed, 2.5cm wide, light violet-blue with a yellow eye. Forms winter buds after August. Flowers in April. z5

P. bracteosa Craib. Himalaya Mts., Bhutan, Assam, Sikkim. Leaves quite variable, spatulate to obovate-spatulate, to 18cm long and 6cm wide, rounded at the tip, margin dentate, petiolate or scarcely so. Scape short at first, later

elongating, umbel many-flowered, the pedicels slender, farinose. Flowers pink-lilac with yellow eye to 2.5cm wide. April. After blooming the scape bends downward and forms plantlets. z6

P. calderiana Balf.f. et Copper. Sikkim, Nepal, SE. Tibet. Leaves lanceolate to narrow-obovate or spatulate, irregularly toothed margin, to 30cm long and 7cm wide. Scape 5–25cm high, 5– rarely 25-flowered. Flowers 2.5cm across, intense purple or maroon, darker toward the middle, with a yellow eye. May. Grow from seed, not necessarily collected right after ripening. Plants are disagreeably scented when bruised. z6

P. edgeworthii Pax. (*P. winteri* W. Watson). NW. Himalaya Mts., from 2000–5000m. Entire plant, with the exception of the corolla, gold-yellow farinose. Summer leaves obovate-spatulate, tapering to a short winged petiole, irregularly toothed. Summer leaves ovate with cordate or truncate base, long petioled. Scape to 5cm high, umbel many flowered. Flowers light lavender-blue or mauve with a yellow eye (eye with a broad white border). Flowers 3cm wide, March to April. Grow in well-drained, high-humus soil in semi-shade. Thrives during moist, cool summers and dry winters; very sensitive to standing water at any time of year. Various forms are known, some with semidouble flowers. The white-flowered 'Alba' has been listed for many years. z4

P. gracilipes Craib. Nepal, Sikkim, Bhutan, S. Tibet. Leaves 4–15cm long and 1–5cm wide, oval-oblong to spatulate or rarely oval-oblong to elliptic, margin irregularly toothed, without farina. Scape undeveloped or very short. Umbel many-flowered. Pedicels 1–6cm long. Flowers light mauve-pink with orange-yellow eye surrounded by a white ring, to 3cm wide. April. Very attractive and somewhat easier to cultivate than the other Craibia Primulas. z5

P. griffithii (Watt) Pax. Bhutan, SE. Tibet. Flowers deep violet-blue with a white-ringed golden eye, to 2.5cm across. Scape 20cm high, farinose umbel of to 15 flowers. Leaves slender ovate, to 60cm long. Plants in the trade seldom are the true species. Similar in appearance, but easier to grow are the *P. griffithii* Hybrids, originating from a cross with *P. strumosa*. Available in many colors from purple to yellow. z6

P. petiolaris Wall. Nepal, Bhutan. Leaves in a loose rosette, 3–5cm long and 1–

1.5cm wide, spatulate to oval-oblong-spatulate, outer leaves spiny-toothed, inner leaves toothed. Scape scarcely developed, the umbel of many pedicels, 2–5cm long, appear to be sessile. Flowers dark magenta-pink, with white eye, without a mealy coating in the bud stage. Very similar to the closely related *P. gracilipes*. Seldom true in the trade. z5

P. scapigera Craib. Sikkim, Nepal. Leaves 5–15cm long and 1–4cm wide, oval-oblong-spatulate to obovate, coarsely and irregularly toothed, often lobed. Scape about 4cm high from

broad-winged petiole, irregularly small-lobed, the lobes toothed. Scape short at first, later as long as the leaves, with a 3–20-flowered umbel. Flowers lavender-blue or purple-blue to bright blue, or intensely indigo-violet, occasionally white ('Alba'), always with a white-ringed yellow eye. Unlike the closely related *P. bhutanica*, leaf midribs of this species are pale green, not red. April. Intolerant of summer heat. z5

P. strumosa Balf.f. et Cooper. Nepal, Bhutan, SE. Tibet. Leaves 10–23cm long and to 6cm wide, oblanceolate to

Section Crystallophlomis (Nivalis)

About 50 species, nearly exclusively in Asia. Leaves fleshy, glabrous, mostly farinose. Bracts not pouchlike. Flowers pediceled, in 1–3 whorls, white, red, purple, violet, pink or yellow.

Some species are easily grown, but most are more difficult. These often deteriorate from root rot in excessive winter moisture if not protected. Grow in well-drained, humus-rich, not too moist soil in semi-shade. Propagate by seed. Seedlings are very sensitive to excess moisture and damping-off. Best handled as biennials and displayed in a peat bed.

P. agleniana Balf.f. et Forr. Tibet, Yunnan, SE. Tibet, Upper Burma; on rather rocky soil between 3500 and 3900m. Leaves 20–30cm long, lanceolate, acuminate, toothed or laciniate-toothed, underside farinose, the blade tapering to a winged petiole of equal length. Scape farinose, 3–8-flowered, 25–40cm high. Pedicels nodding, later erect. Flowers primrose yellow with an orange throat, the exterior mealy, to 4cm wide, fragrant. June to July. A desirable species rarely found in cultivation and quite demanding, rarely persisting in the garden. z6

P. bayernii Rupr. Caucasus. Seed of this very temperamental and little-known species is occasionally collected in the wild and made available. Leaves are conspicuously toothed, white-farinose. Flowers violet. z6

P. chionantha Balf.f. et Forr. Yunnan; in open alpine meadows, along streams, among tall weeds. To 50cm high. Leaves broadly oblanceolate, 20–25cm long, nearly entire, underside yellow-mealy. Flowers snow white, fragrant, in 2–4 dense whorls, pediceled, to 3cm wide. May to June. Possibly a white form of *P. sinopurpurea*, but unlike it, and other Crystallophlomis species, relatively simple to grow in moist, peaty, well-drained soil. Sets abundant seed. z6

P. macrophylla Don (*P. purpurea* Royle). Himalaya Mts. Leaves 10–15cm long and to 3cm wide, lanceolate or oblanceolate, tapered or obtuse, underside white-farinose, margin entire or fine-toothed. Scape 7–25cm high, umbel 5–25 flowered. Flowers purple, violet or lilac, usually with a very dark eye. May. Quite demanding. The easiest form to grow is H 78 (Huggins), flowers lilac-purple with rust colored eye. z6

Primula sinopurpurea and *P. chionantha* (white)

anthesis, later elongated, umbel with slender pedicels to 5cm long. Flowers purplish-pink with a yellow eye and white ring, to 3cm wide. Similar to *P. edgeworthii* but lacks any trace of farina. April to May. z5

P. sonchifolia Franch. W. Yunnan, Sichuan on the border region between Burma and SE. Tibet; from 3500–4500m, forming loose mats at the snow line. Rhizomes modified into a bulb-like overwintering organ. Covered with imbricate scale-like leaves, 10–15cm long. Leaves appear with the flowers, short at first, later to 30cm long and 12cm wide, oblong to obovate, tapered to a

obovate, irregularly dentate, tapering to a short, winged petioled, mostly not farinose. Scape 20–35cm high, with 15-flowered umbel. Flowers yellow with an orange-yellow eye, 2cm wide. The true species is only grown in a few English and Scottish gardens. A hybrid with *P. griffithii*, however, is distributed in the trade. z5

P. winteri see **P. edgeworthii**

P. maximowiczii Regel. N. China. Similar to *P. sinopurpurea*, but slower growing. Leaves narrow-elliptic with rounded apex, crenulate, to 25cm long, tapering to a winged petiole. Scape sturdy, to 30cm high, with 1–4 umbels of tubular flowers with reflexed lobes. Usually dark purple or maroon, zygomorphic. Rarely found in cultivation. z5

P. melanops W.W. Sm. et Ward. W. China. Somewhat smaller than *P. sinopurpurea*. Leaves to 25cm long, linear-lanceolate or lanceolate, tapering to a winged petiole, leaves white-mealy on the underside. Scape 20cm high with 1–2 umbels of 6–12 flowers. Flowers fragrant, Tyrian purple with a black eye. June. z5

P. nivalis Pallas. Central Asia: Altai, Siberia, Ala Tau Mts. Leaves oblong-elliptic, rounded at the apex, with a short winged petiole, with or without farina beneath. Scape 10–40cm high, stout, with 25-flowered umbel; flowers purple, to 2.5cm across, the corolla cup-shaped, short lobes lanceolate. Very demanding, continental species. Seed occasionally is available in seed exchanges. z4

P. obliqua W.W. Sm. Sikkim, Nepal, SE. Tibet. Leaves to 20 × 5cm, lanceolate to obovate, with winged petiole, underside yellow-farinose, margin serrated. Scape stout, farinose, to 45cm high. Umbel few (usually 5) flowered, pedicels densely farinose. Flowers light yellow or white, then often with a pink blush, to 3cm wide, upper petals reflexed. The base of the plant is enclosed in mealy, reddish scale-like leaves to 5cm long. June to July. Seeds and plants are somewhat difficult to grow. z6

P. obtusifolia Royle. W. Himalaya Mts. Leaves elliptic to obovate-oblong, to 20cm long, with rounded apex and tapering to a winged petiole, sparingly white farinose beneath. Scape 7–45cm high, with a 2–6-flowered umbel or 2–3 whorls with 10–12 flowers. Corolla 2.5cm across, the lobes usually obovate, entire, purple or bluish-purple with white or yellow eye. Rarely cultivated species. z6

P. purpurea see **P. macrophylla**

P. sinoplantaginea Balf.f. et Forr. Yunnan, Sichuan. Rhizome with reddish scales and old leaf bases below fresh leafy rosettes. Leaves leathery, narrowly lanceolate with recurved margins, blunt-tipped, dark green above, underside yellow-farinose. Scape stout, farinose, 15cm high. Umbel globe-shaped with 5–12 flowers. Flowers fragrant, violet-purple or deep purple, to 2cm across, with gray eye. Calyx purple. April to July. z5

P. sinopurpurea Balf.f. Yunnan to Tibet; on a loose humus in snowy corries. Entire plant, except the corolla, with light greenish yellow farina. Leaves to 20cm long, oblanceolate, apex rounded or acute, evenly fine-serrate. Scape 30–50cm high; umbel 6–12 flowered, the pedicels nodding. Flowers to 3cm across, lavender-pink to rose-violet with paler eye, somewhat oblique. May to June. A strong-growing species, not too difficult to cultivate. The easiest next to *P. chionantha*. z5

P. stuartii Wall. Nepal, NW. Himalaya Mts. Leaves lanceolate, sharply serrate, tips round or acute to 35cm long and 4cm wide, underside yellow-farinose. Scape 20–30cm high, farinose above. Umbellate or with 2 whorls of 6–12 flowers on somewhat nodding pedicels. Flowers gold-yellow, to 2.5cm across. June. Seeds obtainable from India. z6

P. tschuktschorum Kjellmann. Seeds of this almost unknown and undescribed species are often offered from Alaska. Very demanding and with a short history in cultivation. z5

Section Denticulata

Five species in Asia. Bracts lanceolate, not pouchlike. Inflorescence a dense, many-flowered globose umbel, with sessile or short-pediceled, more or less upwardly directed flowers. *P. denticulata* is easily grown in any moist, humus-rich soil; the other species are more demanding. Useful for the rock and bog garden in full sun to partial shade. Propagate by seed, division and root cuttings taken during or shortly after flowering.

P. atrodentata W.W. Smith. E. Himalaya Mts. Similar to *P. denticulata*; leaves spatulate to long obovate, finely toothed past the middle, hairy above, densely white-farinose below. Scape 7.5–10cm high. Umbel small, sub-globose. Flowers to 2cm across, pale lavender with white eye, or darker. Somewhat more delicate than *P. denticulata*. Thrives only in a cool site. z6

P. denticulata Sm. Afghanistan, eastward through the Himalayas to W. China. A popular spring primula. Leaves appear with the flowers and ultimately growing to 30cm long and 7.5cm wide but shorter at anthesis; spatulate to obtuse-oval-lanceolate narrowing to a short, broadly winged petiole, denticulate. Scape 5–30cm high. Dense umbel almost globose. Yellow-eyed flowers light to dark lilac, or white, pink or rose. March to April. The form 'Cashmiriana' (*P. denticulata* var. **cashmirlana** (Munro) Hook.f.) has large purple flowers which unfortunately often appear in fall only to be spoiled by a frost. Many selections have been made from *P. denticulata*. They are propagated either by seed (sown quickly after ripening) or root cuttings. The cuttings should be made early, while plants are in flower, and may provide flowers the following spring under ideal conditions. Especially desirable are strong red, violet-pink and white tones. Among those commonly offered are 'Bressingham Beauty', 'Inshriach Carmine' and 'Robinson's Red. z5

P. erosa Wall. Kashmir. Similar to *P. denticulata*, but with smaller, very farinose leaves. Flower heads smaller, elegant, pink-lilac. Early flowering, appearing just after *P. rosea* and therefore susceptible to late frost damage. Quite persistent blooms. z6

Section Grandis

Only one species, distinctly different from all the other species of the genus.

P. grandis Trautv. Caucasus; in alpine and subalpine meadows at 2000–3200m. 50–70cm high. Leaves large, broad ovate, cordate, 10–25cm long, crenate, with no farina. Scape stout, 30–72cm high, glabrous, with a many-flowered, crested-globose umbel. Flowers small, to 1cm across, long-pediceled, nodding, light yellow. May to June. Requires heavy soil and a moist, semi-shaded site. Only of value for the collector in the shade garden with *Rhododendron ponticum*, *Daphne pontica*, *Symphytum caucasicum*, *Trachystemon orientalis* and other shade plants of the Caucasus region. z4

Section Julia

Only one species, closely related to the Section Primula.

P. juliae Kusn. E. Caucasus; on moist, rocky, grassy slopes. Very easy to grow, quickly spreading species. Mat-forming, with rooting shoots. Leaves glossy, cordate, coarsely dentate, rounded-reniform to rounded ovate, 10cm long including the winged petiole. Flowers basal, rich violet, some lighter, some darker. Rose-colored and white cultivars are listed. Sets seed poorly. Requires a shaded site with a somewhat heavy, moist humus soil. When the flowers decline after 3 or 4 years, plants should be transplanted, or regularly topdress with a fertile compost. z5

Juliae Hybrids

P. × *pruhoniciana* hort. (*P.* × *helenae* hort., *P.* × *juliana* hort.), originated from a cross between *P. juliae* and *P. vulgaris*. *P. juliae* crossed with the Elatior Hybrids is *P.* × *margotae* hort., both are collectively considered the *P.* Juliae Hybrids. They are separated here since the former resembles *P. vulgaris*, and the latter *P. elatior*.

P. × **pruhoniciana** hort. Very valuable early spring primulas with crowded, rounded, glossy, sometimes brownish-tinged leaves and abundant, rich red, violet, pink and white flowers. Many cultivars are available in the trade. All flower from March to April. Some of the best are:
  'Betty Greene', velvety carmine.
  'Blaukissen' (Blue Cushion), light violet-blue.
  'Blütenkissen' (Flower Cushion), bright red with a salmon cast.
  'Blue Ribaud', bluish-violet.
  'Dr. van Vleuthen', light red.
  'Duburg', very attractive blue form, early flowering.
  'E.R. Janes', bright rose, very conspicuous.
  'Flensburg', with light yellow new leaves in spring, flowers purple carmine.
  'Frühlingsbote' (Spring Messenger), dark red, large flowered.
  'Frühlingsfeuer' (Spring Fire), glowing purple-red.
  'Frühlingsglut' (Spring Embers), glowing orange-red.
  'Frühlingszauber' (Spring Magic), lilac-rose.
  'Garden Delight', purple with orange.
  'Garteninspektor O. Sander', red-violet.
  'Garteninspektor Bartens', rosy purple.
  'Grönekan's Glory', lilac-pink, very floriferous.
  'Hortensia', light pink.
  'Juwel' (Jewel), rosy magenta, paler than 'Wanda'.
  'Krähenwinkel' (Rustic), very large, pink-carmine colored flowers.
  'Lizzy Green', fiery red.
  'Mme. Ferguson', bright rose-purple, large flowered.
  'Oberschlesien' (Upper Silesia), purple-violet with a yellow eye.
  'Ostergruss' (Easter Greeting), rich blue-purple.
  'Perle von Bottrop', bright purple-red with a yellow eye.
  'Primavera', soft peony purple with a yellow center.
  'Purple Flame', purple carmine.
  'Purple Splendour', purple with orange-yellow eyes.
  'Purpurkissen' (Purple Cushion), purple-violet.
  'Rubin', velvety carmine-red.
  'Samtkissen' (Velvet Cushion), dark red.
  'Schneekissen' (Snow Cushion), pure white.
  'Schneetreiben' (Snow Blossom), soft cream white, large flowered.
  'Schneewittchen' (Snow White), white, small flowered.
  'Springtime', rose-violet.
  'Vorfrühling' (Early Spring), pink-lilac, an early and double flowering form.
  'Wanda', crimson-purple with a yellow eye.
  'Wanda Hose-in-Hose', a calycanthemic (sepals petaloid) sport of 'Wanda'.

P. × **margotae** C. Schn. is distinguised by its umbellate flowers on a short scape. This group includes substantially fewer cultivars, blooming from April to May: 'Dorothy', yellow; 'Garryarde Guinevere', bronze-colored leaves and pink flowers; 'Gartenglück' (Garden Treasure), carmine-red with yellow center; 'Helge', light yellow; 'Lebensfreude' (Joy of Life), salmon pink and light violet; 'Marianne', bright purple-red; 'Schlesierkind' (Silesian Offspring), bright violet-red; 'Wisley Crimson', bronze-colored leaves and dark purple flowers. z5

Section Megaseifolia

Two species. Plants persistent but not very cold hardy, non-farinose, covered with segmented hairs. Leaves long-petioled, not lobed. Inflorescence a simple umbel. Capsule opening with uneven teeth.

P. megaseifolia Boiss. Pontus Mts. on the coast of the Black Sea, in the mountain forests. Leaves large, oval rounded to cordate, entire or denticulate, pubescent beneath, resembling small *P. obconica* leaves. Scape stout, 7–12cm high. Flowers bright lilac-red. April to May. Grow in loamy humus soil in a warm site, not too moist and semi-shaded. Needs protection from winter wetness. Not entirely winter hardy, good plant for the alpine house. Propagate by seed or division. z7

Section Minutissimae

About 22 species from the Himalayas, Tibet and W. China. Inflorescences very much reduced, mostly single-flowered. Often stoloniferous and matforming. Very similar to the Section Aleuritia, but differing in not having pouch-like bracts. Very difficult to cultivate. For cool, well-drained, sandy-humus, gravelly substrate in full sun or light semi-shade. A collector's plant. Propagate by seed and division.

P. reptans Hook.f. NW. Himalaya. Scarcely 2cm high in flower, matforming. Rhizomes with scattered leaves that are very small, almost palmate to spatulate, cordate, concave, crenate. Flowers large, solitary or paired, on short scapes, deep violet with a white eye. Attractive alpine species, but difficult to grow in lowland gardens. z4

Section Muscarioides

About 17 species from the E. Himalayas, Tibet and W. China. Closely related to the Section Capitatae, but with spike-like or cylindrical inflorescences. Cultivation is somewhat difficult; perennial, but best treated as biennials. Sow seeds every year to assure replacement plants. Thrives with abundant moisture during the growing season, but requires dryness in winter and a raised bed in semi-shade. The preferred soil is a mix of old topsoil, peat and a sharp river sand. Provide winter protection with evergreen boughs. The new growth appears very late in spring, in May. Propagation is relatively easy by seed. Avoid sowing seed too densely.

P. bellidifolia King ex Hook. Sikkim, SE. Tibet, Bhutan; grows between 4000 and 5300m. Leaves 4–15cm long and 1–2.5cm wide, oblanceolate to spatulate, margin obscurely toothed, resembling *Bellis* leaves. Scape 10–35cm high, 7–15 flowered. Flowers light violet-blue to mauve-blue with a farinose eye. June. z5

P. concholoba Stapf et Sealy. Found along the border of Assam and Tibet at 4000m on steep, grassy slopes and rocks among *Juniperus* and *Rhododendron*. Leaves to 8 × 2cm, oblanceolate-oblong tapering to a winged petiole, pubescent on both sides. Scape 7–20cm high, with a compact, globose to conical, 10–20 flowered inflorescence. Flowers bright violet, exterior distinctly farinose. June. z5

P. giraldiana see **P. muscarioides**

P. hyacinthina W.W. Sm. SE. Tibet. Leaves oblanceolate to oblong, blunt, denticulate, often farinose beneath. Scape 20–45cm high, farinose. Umbel many-flowered. Flowers violet, fragrant, tubular, pendant, to 13mm across. Occasionally offered as seed from India. June. z6

P. littoniana see **P. vialii**

P. muscarioides Hemsl. (*P. tsarongensis* Balf.f.et Forr., *P. giraldiana* Balf.f. non Pax). W. China; at 3000–4000m, on moist meadows. Leaves nearly fleshy, light green, obtuse-obovate to spatulate, 10–20cm long, rounded, tapered to the very short, winged petiole, crenate, dentate, finely ciliate. Scape to 40cm high, farinose above. Inflorescence many flowered, a conical umbel or a 2.5–3.5cm long spike. Flowers pendulous, small, tubular, rich purplish-blue, fragrant. June to July. Includes the subspecies *conica* Balf.f. et Forr. z5

P. tsarongensis see **P. muscarioides**

P. vialii Delav. ex Franch. (*P. littoniana* Forr.). NW. Yunnan, SW. Sichuan; at 3100–3900m, in moist meadows, but also in evergreen woods and in dry, rocky meadows. Leaves broadly lanceolate to oblong to 30 × 7cm, irregularly dentate, hairy on both sides, tapering to a winged petiole. Scape to 60cm high, farinose toward the top. Inflorescence a spike to 18cm long. Calyx broadly campanulate, bright scarlet, later pink. Flowers tubular, to 13mm across, lavender-blue, fragrant. June to July. Requires semi-shade and moist, humus soil in the garden. A striking, gaudy, unprimrose-like primula of great ornamental value. Not for regions with hot summers. z7(6)

Section Parryi

Six species, all from N. America, earlier classified with *Crystallophlomis*, but differing in the involuted leaves. Flowers red-violet to pink, always in simple umbels. Grow in a well-drained, high humus soil in full sun or light shade. Collector's plants for a peat bed or rock garden. Propagate by seed or by removal of plantlets formed on the heaved roots upon exposure to sunlight. In addition to the following species, *P. angustifolia* Torr. and *P. ellisiae* Pollard et Cockerell are rarely offered.

P. cusickiana A. Gray. NE. Oregon. Leaves rather fleshy, 2–5cm long including the petiole, oblanceolate to oblong-spatulate, rounded or blunt, margin dentate. Scape 4–6cm high, 1–5 flowered. Flowers with no eye, deep violet, occasionally white, with a violet scent. Active growth lasts only for 3–6 weeks in the spring. Seeds are occasionally offered; a very difficult and demanding species, March to April. z5

P. parryi A. Gray. USA: Central Rocky Mts., at about 4400m. Leaves to 25cm long, narrowly obovate to lanceolate

Primula juliae

tapering to a sheathing base, finely toothed or entire, minutely downy beneath, clustered in stout rosettes. Scape 15–40cm. Umbel many-flowered, pedicels 2.5–7.5cm long. Flowers to 2.5cm across, bright purple to magenta with yellow- or orange-colored throat and eye. May. Found at the higher alpine elevations. Best grown in a peat bed, moist but well-drained. Floriferous in autumn. Intolerant of summer heat. z4(3)

P. rusbyi Greene. New Mexico, Arizona. Leaves narrow spatulate, 7.5–12cm long, acute-tipped, leathery, crenulate to dentate, narrowing to a short, winged petiole. Scape 12–15cm high. Umbel one-sided, with 4–14, bright, rosy-purple, yellow eyed flowers to 2cm across. May. Requires a warm site and protection from excessive winter wetness. z7(6)

Section Primula (Vernales)

Includes four species of very important garden primulas, indigenous to Europe, Asia Minor, the Ural Mtn. region, the Caucasus Mts., Armenia, Iran, eastward to the Altai Mts. and Algeria. Perennial, nonfarinose. Leaves decurrent, not lobed. Flowers funnelform, corolla lobes outspread. Nearly all species have long been cultivated and interbred. These are relatively easy to cultivate. Propagate by division and seed.

P. abchasica see **P. vulgaris** ssp. **sibthorpii**

P. acaulis see **P. vulgaris**

P. acaulis var. **iberica** see **P. vulgaris** ssp. **sibthorpii**

P. acaulis var. **rubra** see **P. vulgaris** ssp. **sibthorpii**

P. amoena M.B. (*P. elatior* var. *amoena* Duby). Caucasus, reaching to Armenia and Lazistan (NE. Turkey); at 1000 to nearly 4000m, often found near melting snow on a humus mat between rhododendrons and vacciniums. Resembles *P. elatior*, but differs in the narrower leaves with gray-tomentose undersides, and the purple flowers. Leaf blade spatulate-oblong to elliptic or oblong, 2.5–7cm long, tip rounded, margin irregularly crenate, petiole to 7.5cm long. Scape 15–18cm high. Flowers 6–10 in one-sided umbels, violet-blue or lavender-blue, with some rose tinge, or occasionally white, eye yellow, to 2.5cm across. Scarce in culture and usually found in the purple-violet forms, but rarely true to type. Cultivated in semi-shade, in a cool, moist humus-rich soil. In many gardens, *P. vulgaris* var. *sibthorpii* often mistakenly is labeled as this species. April. z5

P. canescens see **P. veris** ssp. **canescens**

P. carpatica see **P. elatior** ssp. **elatior**

P. columnae see **P. veris** ssp. **columnae**

P. elatior (L.) Hill. Oxlip. Europe to Asia, Asia Minor and N. Iran. To 30cm high. Flowers sulfur yellow, not fragrant, umbellate. A variable species. z5

P. elatior ssp. **carpatica** see **P. eliator** ssp. **elatior**

P. elatior ssp. **elatior** (inkl. ssp. *carpatica* (Griseb. et Schenk) W.W. Sm. et Forr., *P. carpatica* (Griseb. et Schenk) Fuss, *P.*

poloninensis (Domin) Fedorov). Leaves rounded to ovate, abruptly tapered to the petiole, crenate to dentate, undersides slightly pubescent, very wrinkled. One-sided umbel many-flowered. Calyx inflated, about 10mm wide, pubescent, lobes triangular. Corolla 20–25mm across, limb flat, light yellow. Found throughout the range of the species in S., W. and Central Europe, northward to Denmark, east to the Ukraine, occasionally found in Siberia, W. and Central Asia. z4

P. elatior ssp. **intricata** (Gren. et Godr.) Lüdi (*P. intricata* Gren. et. Godr., *P. pallasii* Lehm. ssp. *intricata* (Gren et Godr.) H.-Harrison. Leaves ovate-elliptic, gradually tapered to the winged petiole, entire when young, later slightly crenate, slightly wrinkled, pubescent above and beneath. Scape short. Umbel few-flowered. Calyx tubular, to 15mm, pubescent, lobes triangular. Corolla to 20mm wide, limb flat, light yellow. Found in the mountains of S. and S. Central Europe, in moist meadows. z5

P. elatior ssp. **leucophylla** (Pax) H.-Harrison ex W.W. Sm. et Fletcher (*P. leucophylla* Pax). Leaves oval-oblong or elliptic, gradually tapered to the petiole, slightly crenate or entire, undersides gray-pubescent, blade very wrinkled. Scape pubescent. Calyx to 11mm, hairy, lobes short, lanceolate, E. Carpathians. z5

P. elatior ssp. **lofthousei** (H.-Harrison) W.W. Sm. et Fletcher. Leaves ovate-oblong, gradually tapered to the petiole, slightly crenate, very wrinkled, pubescent on both sides. Umbels many-flowered. Corolla to 18mm wide, cup-shaped, yellow. S. Spain (Sierra Nevada). z7(6)

P. elatior ssp. **pallasii** (Lehm.) W.W. Sm. et Forr. Leaves obovate to elliptic, gradually tapered to the petiole, dentate, scarcely wrinkled and glabrous. Umbel 3–6 flowered. Calyx tube narrow with reflexed lobes. Corolla 20–25mm wide, limb flat, light yellow. Central Ural Mts., Caucasus to Armenia, Iran, Altai Mts. z6(5)

P. elatior ssp. **pseudoelatior** (Kusn.) W.W. Sm. et Forr. Leaves ovate rounded, cordate, abruptly narrowed, underside lighter and softly pubescent. Calyx tubular, lobes very long, broad-lanceolate. Caucasus. z5

All these subspecies are important only for their botanical interest. Several others are listed. They will naturalize under favorable conditions. The species and subspecies bloom from April to June.

P. elatior var. **amoena** see **P. amoena**

P. Elatior Hybrids have been improved by hybridizing (*P. Polyantha Hybrids, P. × polyantha* hort.), found in all colors in cultivation. These are exceptionally floriferous, pure in color and usually have large individual flowers. Some races are bred for the long scapes and

Primula vialii

prized for cut flowers. These cultivars are found in the trade as *P. elatior* 'Grandiflora', 'Gigantea', 'Colossea-hybrids', 'Pacific' hybrids, etc.

Some double cultivars include 'Curiosity', yellow-brown; 'Golden-traum' (Golden Dream), deep gold-yellow; 'Olga Menden', bright red; and 'Schön Rottraut' (Lovely Red Darling), bright dark red. Seed and plants are available from Great Britain with calycanthemic flowers (with the otherwise green calyx colored like the corolla). The Gold Laced and Silver Laced strains, dark red-brown to nearly black flowers with golden yellow or whitish-yellow margins, also available from England, are particularly appealing.

Generally, these plants are vigorous and persistent in semi-shade. All thrive in moist, never dry, loamy humus soil. The true species and subspecies are suitable for naturalizing in parks and large gardens. Propagation is by seed, the double and calycanthemic forms by division.

P. heterochroma see **P. vulgaris** ssp. **heterochroma**

P. inflata see **P. veris** ssp. **canescens**

P. intricata see **P. elatior** ssp. **intricata**

P. leucophylla see **P. elatior** ssp. **leucophylla**

P. macrocalyx see **P. veris** ssp. **macrocalyx**

P. officinallis see **P. veris**

P. pallasii see **P. elatior** ssp. **intricata**

P. pannonica see **P. veris** ssp. **canescens**

P. sibthorpii see **P. vulgaris** ssp. **sibthorpii**

P. suaveolens see **P. veris** ssp. **columnae**

P. uralensis see **P. veris** ssp. **macrocalyx**

P. veris L. (*P. officinalis* (L.) Hill). Cowslip. Europe, Siberia, W. and Central Asia from sea level to 2000m; in sunny meadows, in open thickets and especially on sunny slopes. Grows on drier sites than *P. elatior* and is further distinguised from this species by the smaller, egg-yolk-yellow flowers with 5 orange-colored patches in the throat. Leaves ovate to ovate-lanceolate, to rarely 15cm long including the winged petiole which narrows abruptly, white-pubescent beneath, irregularly crenate-toothed and crimped. Scape 7.5–20cm high, downy. Umbel mostly many-flowered and 1-sided, April to May. *P. veris* is sweetly scented, *P. elatior* is not. A form-rich species. z5

P. veris ssp. **canescens** (Opiz) Hayek ex Lüdi (*P. canescens* Opiz, *P. pannonica* Kerner, *P. inflata* Duby). Central Europe to S. France and N. Spain. Leaf blade gray-pubescent beneath, gradually tapered to the winged petiole. Calyx open-campanulate to 2cm long. Corolla to 20mm wide, somewhat concave. z5

P. veris ssp. **columnae** (Ten.) Lüdi (*P. columnae* Ten., *P. suaveolens* Bertol.). Mountains of S. Europe. Leaf blade oval to oblong, cordate, densely white-haired beneath. Corolla to 22mm, nearly flat. z5

P. veris ssp. **macrocalyx** (Bunge) Luedi (*P. macrocalyx* Bunge, *P. uralensis* Fisch.). SE. Russia, Crimea, Turkestan, Dzungaria, N. Iran, Caucasus, Ural Mts. Leaf blade tapered to a long, winged leaf petiole, slightly pubescent or glabrous beneath. Calyx to 20mm wide, funnel-form. Corolla orange-yellow, to 29mm across. z5

P. veris ssp. **veris**. Europe, Siberia, W. and Central Asia. Leaf blade usually abruptly tapered, slightly hairy to glabrous, petiole winged. Corolla to 20mm wide, somewhat concave. z5

Many valuable hybrids have originated from *P. veris*, but these always are difficult to distinguish from the *P. Elatior* Hybrids. The species (and hybrids) thrive in sunny, grassy sites in wild gardens and parks where plants spread easily by self-seeding. When grown in turf, the grass should not be mown too early as this removes the unripened seed heads. For naturalizing, simply cast seed in the desired site any time from fall to winter.

P. vulgaris Huds. (*P. acaulis* (L.) Hill). English Primrose. W. and S. Europe with a range reaching from S. Sweden and Central Norway, Denmark, N. Germany, England and France over the Mediterranean region to Asia Minor, Armenia and Iran; also extends to Algeria and N. Africa. Its native habitat is open woodland, semi-shaded meadows and thickets, occasionally in sunny meadows. The vegetative period begins in the autumn and often results in plants overwintering with half-developed flower buds. Leaves obovate to oblanceolate, gradually tapering to the petiole, margin irregularly crenate-serrate, surfaces wrinkled, downy beneath. Scape very short or obsolete; pedicels 5–12.5cm long. Flowers several (to 25), apparently basal, arising from the center of the leaf rosette, unscented, pale sulfur yellow, broadly open to 3cm across, throat with darker spots. September to May. Unlike the other three species in this section, the seeds are scattered by ants from the slender and procumbent fruit pedicels. *P. amoena, P. elatior* and *P. veris* are spread by the wind. *P. vulgaris* includes the following subspecies, especially important in breeding programs:

P. vulgaris ssp. **balearica** (Willk.) W. W. Sm. et Forr. Mountains of Mallorca. Petiole longer than the blade, narrowly winged; leaf underside glabrous. Flowers white, very fragrant. z6

P. vulgaris ssp. **heterochroma** (Stapf) W. W. Sm. et Forr. (*P. heterochroma* Stapf). N. Iran, Caspian Sea. Leaf broad-obovate abruptly contracted to the red petiole, a distinguishing character. Spider-web-like tomentum on the leaf undersides. The many flower colors including: white, pink, purple, violet and lemon yellow. z6

P. vulgaris ssp. **ingwerseniana** H.-Harrison. Thessalian Olympus Mts.: Enipev Valley (Greece). Equivalent to a white *P. vulgaris* ssp. *sibthorpii*. Similar plants are also found in the Taygetus Mts.

P. vulgaris ssp. **sibthorpii** (Hoffmgg.) W. W. Sm. et Forr (*P. sibthorpii* Hoffmgg. *P. acaulis* var. *rubra* Sibth. et Sm., *P. vulgaris* var. *rubra* (Sibth. et Sm.) Luedi, *P. acaulis* var. *iberica* Hoffm., *P. abchasica* Sosn.). E. Balkan region, Crimea, Asia Minor, Armenia, Caucasus, N. Iran. Long cultivated, especially in naturally occurring variants. Pure progeny are rarely found in cultivation. Flowers early, in February and March. Distinguished from the other subspecies by its preferred habitat in open deciduous woodlands where the other subspecies might not thrive. Leaf blade cuneate, abruptly tapered to the petiole, underside somewhat hairy. Flowers mostly red, purple or pink. Here belongs the pale pink double cultivar 'Lilacina Plena'. It is regrettable that this subspecies is not more widely grown in gardens. Does poorly in sunny sites, requires a semi-shaded, somewhat mossy site in an open, deciduous thicket. Spreads by self-seeding under favorable conditions. Undoubtedly used mainly for breeding, with many cultivars available in various solid colors. This is a parent of many red, pink and purple Garden Primroses, usually *P. veris* is the other. z5

P. vulgaris ssp. **vulgaris**. Found nearly throughout the range of the species. Leaf blade gradually tapers to a short, winged petiole, underside with hairy venation. Flowers pale yellow with 5 yellow-green or orange speckles in the throat, fragrant. Occasionally white-flowered variants come from N. Austria, Slovenia (Yugoslavia) and Lake Garda (Italy). z5

The double cultivars are especially prized. Examples are 'Atrosanguinea Plena', dark red; 'Arthur Dumoulin' ('Platypetala Plena'), violet-purple; 'Cloth of Gold' ('Lutea Plena'), lemon yellow; 'Croussei Plena', pink-purple; and the above mentioned 'Lilacina Plena', pale pink; 'Alba Plena', pure white, and 'Rosea Plena', pink. Seed of these double forms come 30–50% true and are more vigorous than the older garden forms. It is important when propagating *P. vulgaris* by division to carefully remove all remnants of the old stem since it will produce a negative influence on the growth of young propagules. The Jack-in-the-Green strains produce foliate sepals; the leafy cluster enclosing the corolla are interesting, although not for every gardener. Comes true from seed in all colors. Another abnormality, developed into a strain called Hose-in-Hose, features one corolla within another.

P. vulgaris var. **rubra** see **P. vulgaris** ssp. **sibthorpii**

Section Proliferae (Candelabra)

About 30 species, mostly in the mountains of SW. China, Burma, Sikkim, Assam and Bhutan, and the mountains of Japan, Sumatra and Java. A quite unique Section with flowers arranged in tiered whorls. Leaves large, deciduous or evergreen with notched or toothed margins, blades tapered to a furrowed petiole. Partly farinose, sometimes only on the calyx or also on the stems and leaves. Some species also produce farina on the flowers. All species, excepting *P. cockburniana*, which tends to be biennial in less than ideal conditions, are persistent perennials. Seed capsules are round, except those of *P. poissonii*, which are oblong. *P. aurantiaca* forms plantlets in the upper flower whorls. These are not too difficult provided they are grown in damp loamy humus, fertile soil, in semishade. In heavy soils mix peat through the topsoil; rework subsoil to a gravelly, well-drained consistency. Suitable for massing in the shady garden. Propagation is easy by seed. Many species such as *P. anisodora*, *P. burmanica* and *P. helodoxa* come true. The other species easily hybridize, so that commercial lines of *P. beesiana* and *P. bulleyana* are no longer pure species. Plants should be frequently divided in arid climates. The best time for division is early summer, when the divided plants will be more vigorous and healthy. If division is postponed until late summer, the roots may fail to become sufficiently established for overwintering. Plants will self-seed under favorable conditions. The purest progeny come from *P. japonica*.

P. angustidens see **P. wilsonii**

P. anisodora Balf.f. et Forr. NW. Yunnan, Sichuan. Leaves aromatic, 18–25cm long, evergreen, obovate, tip obtuse, both sides glabrous, denticulate. Scape stout, to 60cm high, with 3–5 superimposed whorls of 8–10 flowers with nodding pedicels. Flowers tubular, funnel-shaped, rather small, deep brownish-purple with a blue pruinose yellow throat, in 3–5 whorls. Non-farinose. June to July. Roots particularly strong scented. In the garden this primrose appears almost black. z6

P. aurantiaca W.W. Smith et Forr. Yunnan. Leaves deciduous, very thin, glabrous, oblanceolate to obovate with blunt tip, to 20cm long, finely toothed, blade tapering to a winged petiole. Scape 25–30cm high, red-tinged with 2–6 superimposed whorls of 6–12 flowers. The upper whorls occasionally form plantlets. Calyx dark red. Corolla flat, orange-yellow to orange-red, to 3cm wide, red in bud. Plants not farinose. July. z6

P. beesiana Forr. NW. Yunnan, SW. Sichuan. Leaves very large, ovate-lanceolate, blunt-tipped, to 50cm long, finely serrate, deciduous. Scape stout, to 60cm high. Flowers in 2–8 whorls; corolla flat, rose-lilac to rose-carmine, eye yellow or orange, pedicels and calyx pruinose. June to July. Includes var. **leucantha** (Balf.f. et Forr.) Fletcher, pure white. *P. beesiana* is very much crossbred in cultivation and should be reintroduced from the wild. z6

P. bulleyana Forr. NW. Yunnan, SW. Sichuan. Leaves large, ovate to ovate-lanceolate, tip rounded, to 40cm long, coarse and irregularly toothed, deciduous, midrib red. Scape stout, to 60cm high, with 5–7 many-flowered whorls, corolla orange-yellow to usually deep orange, flat, 2.5cm wide. Plant not farinose, or sometimes pedicels farinose. June to July. z6

P. burmanica Balf.f. et Ward. Upper Burma, Yunnan. Leaves oblanceolate, obtuse, to 30cm long, coarsely serrate, tapering to a winged petiole, deciduous. Scape stout, to 60cm high with 3–6 superimposed whorls of 10–18 flowers. Corolla reddish-purple with orange-yellow eye, flat, 2cm wide. Pedicels and calyx farinose. June to July. z6

P. chungensis Balf.f. et Ward. Yunnan, Sichuan, Bhutan, Burma, Assam. Leaves oblong-obovate, elliptic or oblong, tip rounded, to 35cm long, coarsely serrate, glabrous, deciduous. Scape to 70cm high, with with 2–5 whorls of 10 flowers. Corolla pale orange with red blush, flat, to 2cm across. Stems and calyx not farinose, or calyx sometimes mealy. June to July. z6

P. cockburniana Hemsl. SW. Sichuan. Leaves scarcely petioled, oblong to oblong-ovate, tips rounded, to 20cm long, obscurely lobed and finely toothed, deciduous. Scape slender, with 1–3 whorls of 3–8 flowers. Corolla flat, to 2.5cm wide, fiery copper-orange. Calyx farinose. May to June. A biennial or perennial under ideal conditions. z5

P. glycocosma see **P. wilsonii**

P. helodoxa Balf.f. Burma, Yunnan. Leaves oblanceolate, oblong-ovate, rarely lanceolate, tapering to a long, winged petiole, 20–40cm long, finely dentate, glabrous, evergreen. Scape stout, to 90cm high, with 2–6 superimposed umbels of 12–20 flowers. Corolla shallow-campanulate, to 2.5cm, golden yellow. Golden yellow or cream-colored farina on calyx and pedicel. June to July. Conspicuous for the broad, white

midrib on the leaves. This show Candelabra Primrose requires amply moist, peaty soil throughout the growing season. z6

P. ianthina Balf.f. et Cave. Sikkim. Leaves to 25cm long, oblong-lanceolate with blunt tips and fine-toothed margins, tapering to a winged and sheathing petiole, evergreen, yellow-farinose. Scape 45–50cm high, with 2–4 superimposed whorls of to 12 flowers. Corolla violet to violet-pink. Rarely cultivated; seed is sometimes available from India. z6

P. imperialis Junghuhn. Java. Not winter hardy; leaves very large, evergreen. Related to *P. prolifera*. Flowers golden yellow, to yellow-orange. z8

P. japonica A. Gray. Japan. Leaves to 30cm long, obovate-oblong or broad-spatulate, blunt tipped and irregularly lobed and fine-toothed, tapering to a winged petiole. Scape stout, 45–75cm high, with 1–6 tiered whorls of numerous flowers. Corolla to 3.5cm wide, flat, purple-red, pink or white, occasionally striped. Farinose only on the inside of the calyx. Numerous cultivars of this easy to grow primrose are listed, mostly color selections. May to June. z5

P. miyabeana Ito et Kawakami. Taiwan. Leaves oblanceolate, blunt-tipped or acute, denticulate, tapering to a very broad-winged, sheathing petiole, deciduous. Scape 50–60cm high with 2–4 superimposed whorls of 6–10 flowers. Corolla purple with golden yellow farinose throat. Related to *P. japonica* and *P. burmanica*. z7

P. poissonii Franch. Yunnan, Sichuan. Leaves glaucous, stiff and leathery, oblong-ovate, blunt-tipped, denticulate, 20–30cm long, evergreen. Scape 70–150cm high with 2–6 superimposed whorls of 3–12 flowers. Corolla shallow-campanulate to flat, 3cm wide, deep crimson-purple with yellow eye. July to August. The latest flowering species. z6

P. polonensis Ward. Assam. A primrose with pendulous, yellow flowers for the temperate greenhouse. z8

P. prolifera Wallich. Yunnan. Leaves oblong to spatulate, to 30cm × 7.5cm, evergreen, remotely fine-toothed. Scape 60–80cm high with a terminal umbel, or 2–3 tiered, many-flowered whorls. Corolla shallow-campanulate, to 3cm wide, gold-yellow. Calyx and pedicels farinose. May to June. The earliest flowering species and possibly a better garden plant than *P. helodoxa*. z6

P. pulverulenta Duthie. W. Sichuan. Leaves oblanceolate to obovate or ovate, blunt, deciduous, to 30cm long, coarsely toothed, underside rugose, tapering to a winged petiole. Scape 80–90cm high, slender, farinose, with several to many superimposed, many-flowered whorls, Corolla deep red with a darker eye or pink (Bartley Strain), flat, to 3cm wide. Pedicels and calyx very mealy. This species, much used in breeding pro-

Primula Elatior Hybrid

grams, is one parent of many superb hybrids. June to August. z6

P. serratifolia Franch. Yunnan, SE. Tibet, Burma. Leaves oblong, obovate-oblong or obovate, blunt-tipped, strongly and irregularly toothed, to 20cm long. Scape 45–50cm high with an umbel or 2 superimposed whorls of 5–10 flowers. Rare, candelabra-flowered species. Corolla 2.5–3cm across, bright yellow with radiating intense orange rays, or pale yellow with a pink cast (var. **roseotincta** Forr.) or pale yellow (var. **unicolor** Forr.). z6

P. smithiana Craib. Sikkim. Leaves oblanceolate, blunt-tipped, to 20cm long, glabrous scabrous-toothed, deciduous. Scape 60cm high, with 1–4 superimposed whorls of 10–15 flowers. Corolla flat, to 2.5cm across, pale yellow with a mealy throat, in 2–4 whorls. Stems and calyx, rarely also the leaves, yellow-farinose. May to June. z6

P. wilsonii Dunn (*P. angustidens* (Franch.) Pax, *P. glycocosma* (Petitm.). Yunnan, Sichuan. To 80cm high. Leaves oblanceolate, rounded, 20, rarely to 30cm long, evergreen, leathery, irregularly fine-toothed, narrowing to a winged petiole. Scape to 80cm high, with 3–6 superimposed whorls of several flowers. Corolla violet-purple, becoming somewhat lighter with age, shallow-campanulate, with a yellow throat, very fragrant. The plant is generally not farinose, not glabrous. June to July. z6

Primula elatior

Hybrids

The Section Proliferae has a large number of hybrids due to the ease with which the species cross. The most common are listed below, some coming true from seed:

P. × anisodoxa hort. (*P. anisodora × P. helodoxa*), creamy-beige to pale terracotta colored.

P. × briscoei hort. (*P. japonica × P. bulleyana*), soft red.

P. × bullesiana Bees (*P. Bullesiana Hybrids, P. bulleyana × P. beesiana*). Flowers yellow, orange, red, pink, violet and lilac ('Ashtore', 'Moerheim Hybrids', 'Ipswich Hybrids').

P. × chunglenta hort. (*P. chungensis × P. pulverulenta*).

P. × silva-taroucana hort. (*P. pulverulenta × P. cockburniana*), also includes the 'Lisadell Hybrids'.

Many more hybrid complexes involve 3, 4, or more species, such as the attractive 'Inshriach Hybrids' from Jack Drake. Particularly noteworthy is 'Aileen Aroon' (*P. pulverulenta × P. cockburniana*) from Richardson (1931). By doubling the chromosome number, this hybrid remains entirely consistent from seed. This hybrid line seems to have disappeared, however, from modern garden culture.

Especially good forms are cloned. Among the prettiest is 'Ravenglass Vermilion' dark orange-red with reddish foliage; also 'Red Hugh', a *P.* Cockburniana Hybrid with orange-scarlet colored flowers and a low growth habit; and 'Edina', light salmon-colored.

Section Reinii

Five species indigenous to Japan. Leaves rounded, petioled. Calyx small, fruit capsules cylindrical, the calyx lobes widely expanded. These species resemble the Cortusoides Primulas, but are more closely related botanically to the species of the Section Sinensis. Growing these demanding alpine primroses is difficult.

They require protection from excessive winter wetness to prevent rotting of the winter buds. Propagation is by seed. Three species from Japan are occasionally offered:

P. reinii Franch. et Savatier, with 1–3 (–3.5)cm wide pink flowers; *P. takedana* Tatewaki with 1–3 white flowers in the umbel; and *P. tosaensis* Yatabe, which resembles *P. reinii*, flowering pale purple with a longer corolla tube.

P. reinii Franch. Japan; in woodlands. Leaves long-petiolate, orbicular to

Primula vulgaris ssp. *vulgaris*

reniform, 10–15cm across, base deeply cordate to nearly one-third the blade depth, the lobes overlapping. Scape scarcely longer than the leaves, 2–6 flowered in a loose umbel. Flowers pale violet, the corolla starry, with deeply bifid lobes. Entire vegetative plant with dense, long, many-celled hairs, especially petioles and leaf upper surfaces.

P. tosaensis Yatabe. Japan; a woodland understory plant. Leaves petiolate, orbicular to broadly ovate, to 5cm wide, base cordate, membranous, pubescent below and ciliate, slightly lobed and dentate; the petiole scarcely equals the blade depth, pubescent. Scape exceeds leaf height, pubescent below, glabrous above with an umbel of 2–4 flowers or 2 superimposed umbels. Corolla limb about 3cm across, pale purple. z7(6)

Section Rotundifolia (Cordifolia)

Nine species from Himalaya and Tibet. Leaves long-petioled with a rounded blade with cordate base. The capsules are similar to those of the Crystallo-

phlomis Primulas. Culture of these demanding alpine species is similar to that for the species of the Section Crystallophlomis. Seeds from India are occasionally offered in the trade. The difficulty is in maintaining the species for a long time since they only set seed under favorable conditions.

P. caveana W.W. Sm. E. Nepal, Sikkim, Bhutan, SE. Tibet; usually between 4600 and 4900m; its native habitat in the Kharta Valley in Tibet at 6100m is the highest elevation for any primula. Leaves 2–15cm long, oval-oblong to

Primula pulverulenta

obovate, occasionally rounded, dentate, underside densely white-farinose, tapering to a broad, winged petiole. Scape 2–2cm long, 1–9-flowered, slightly farinose. Flowers pale purple, occasionally pinkish-purple, with a yellow eye, 20mm wide. April. Very attractive, dwarf species, best grown in the alpine house. z6(5)

P. gambeliana Watt. Nepal, Sikkim, Bhutan, SE. Tibet; at about 4500m. Leaf blade 2–7.5cm long and 0.5–6cm wide, ovate to rounded, deeply cordate at the base, dentate; the slender petiole to 30cm long. Scape 3–25cm high, umbel

1–8-flowered, pedicels short. Flowers purplish-pink or violet with a yellow throat, to 25mm wide. May. z5

P. rotundifolia Wall. Nepal, Sikkim; 4000–5000m. Leaves 5–20cm long including the stout petiole, blade 2–12cm and wide, cordate-reniform to cordate-orbicular, dentate. Scape 10–30cm high; umbel 2–16-flowered. Flowers pale purplish-pink with a yellow eye, to 20mm wide. z5

Section Sikkimensis

About 11–13 species in Nepal, Sikkim, Bhutan, Tibet, Yunnan, Sichuan and NW. Burma. Flowers nodding, funnel-form or nearly tubular with a flat limb, in umbels. Only the very vigorous species, particularly *P. florindae*, and well-fertilized plants form a second umbel. Nearly all species are very fragrant. Leaves are either round or cordate with distinct petioles or oblong-lanceolate, tapered to the petiole. Farina is general among this primroses.

Grow these mostly perennial species is in a sunny or semi-shaded, moist site.

Improve heavy soils with peat. The dwarf species require careful handling and may be lost when planted next to vigorous companion plants. Propagation is easy by seed and division.

P. alpicola Stapf (*P. microdonta* var. *alpicola* W.W. Sm.). SE. Tibet. Leaves elliptic to oblong-elliptic, 5–15cm long, rounded at tip and base, or base obscurely cordate, petioled winged, glabrous but rugose above, dentate to crenulate. Scape 15–50cm high, farinose above, with 1 or 2 umbels. Flowers broad funnel-shaped, limb spreading, in 15–25

P. firmipes Balf.f. et Forrest. SW. Tibet, Assam, NW. Burma. Leaf blades ovate to suborbicular, 3–8cm long, deeply serrated or toothed, with cordate base; petiole winged, with sheathing base, 20cm long. Scape 10–40cm high, yellow farinose above. Umbel of 2 to rarely 15 flowers. Flowers light yellow, funnelform, flat-limbed on slender pedicels 1–3cm long. Calyx and flowers farinose. June to July. z6

P. florindae Ward. SE. Tibet. Leaves broad ovate-cordate, apex rounded, blade 5–20cm long, dentate, dark green

a violet blush, umbels 2–10 flowered. This is a very soft-textured species. June to July. z6

P. microdonta var. **alpicola** see **P. alpicola**

P. microdonta var. **alpicola** f. **micromeris** see **P. sikkimensis** var. **pudibunda**

P. prionotes see **P. waltonii**

P. reticulata Wall. Nepal, Sikkim, W. Bhutan, S. Tibet. Leaf blade oblong to broad-ovate, base cordate, toothed, 5–10cm long; petiole to 30cm long. Scape

Primula cawdoriana

Primula sikkimensis

flowered umbels, light yellow. The flower color is quite variable, var. **alba** W.W. Sm. is white; var. **luna** (Stapf) W.W. Sm. et Fletcher is pale lemon yellow and var. **violacea** (Stapf) W.W. Sm. is violet. Calyx and flower corolla distinctly farinose. June to July. z6

P. chumbiensis W.W. Sm. S. Tibet. Leaves with petiole 7–10cm long, blade elliptic to oblong, 4–6cm long, with rounded tip and cuneate bsae, finely toothed, dark green with a red blush when young. Scape 12–30cm high. Umbel with 2–7 flowers, the pedicels 1–3.5cm long. Flowers pale sulphur yelow, occasionally red-blushed, funnelform lobes ovate, entire or notched. Calyx farinose. June to July. z6

and glossy, petiole stout, winged, often reddish, 5–22cm long. Scape stout, 70–90cm high. Umbel farinose, with 40–80 flowers. Flowers funnel-shaped, pendant, clear sulphur yellow with ample creamy farina inside. Hybrids appear in various shades of red or amber. June to August. z6

P. ioessa W.W. Sm. SE. Tibet. Leaves narrow-oblong-ovate to oblanceolate, irregularly and sharply toothed, 7–20cm long, half the length being the petiole. Scape slightly farinose 10–30cm high. Umbel yellow-farinose, pedicels 1–7cm long. Flowers funnel-shaped, light pink-violet, pink-lilac to mauve, 1cm across. Flowers of the var. **subpinnatifida** (W.W. Sm.) W.W. Sm. et Fletcher are white with

20–40cm high. Umbel farinose, pedicels erect or nodding, 1–5cm long, with 10–25 flowers. Flowers funnel-shaped, white or yellow. June to July. z6

P. secundiflora Franch. (*P. vittata* Bur. et Franch.). Yunnan, Sichuan, Tibet. Leaves oblong to oblanceolate, acuminate or blunt, finely crenate to serrate, very tough, underside often yellow-farinose when young, to 30cm long. Scape 30–60cm high, farinose above, with 1 or sometimes 2 umbels of 10–20 flowers on 2.5–5cm long pedicels. Flowers reddish-purple to purple or deep rose-red, funnel-shaped, pendant. Calyx often dark red, with 5 mealy lines. May to June. The earliest-flowering species of the Section. z6

P. sikkimensis Hook. (*P. microdonta* Fr. ex Petitm.). Nepal, Bhutan, Tibet, Sikkim, Sichuan, Yunnan and NW. Burma. Leaves elliptic to oblong or oblanceolate, apex acute or rounded, serrate or dentate, glossy and wrinkled, narrowing rather abruptly to the petiole, which may be one-fifth to one-half of the total leaf length of 30–45cm. Scape 40–90cm high. Terminal umbel with 10–30 flowers on 5–10cm long, upward-arching pedicels. Flowers shallow funnel-shaped with flat limb to 3.25cm across, yellow, rarely creamy white. Hybrids are often bicolored, as in Jack

Primula reidii

Drake's cultivar 'Crimson and Gold'. The scape and the calyx are farinose. Var. **pudibunda** (W.W. Sm.) W.W. Sm. & Fletcher (*P. microdonta* var. *alpicola* f. *micromeris* W.W. Sm. & Ward, is a high alpine plant not found in Yunnan or Burma. Similar to the type but with much smaller flowers. June to July. z6

P. vittata see **P. secundiflora**

P. waltonii Watt (*P. prionotes* Balf.f. et Watt). SE. Tibet, Bhutan. Leaf blade oblanceolate to elliptic-oblong, sharply toothed to crenate, apex rounded, base cuneate, petiole winged, half the length of the 30cm long leaf. Scape 20–70cm high. Terminal umbel few to many-flowered with 1–6cm long pedicels.

Flowers soft violet-pink, dark violet or deep wine-purple, nodding, funnel-shaped with flat limb to 22mm across. Scape and calyx somewhat farinose. June to July. The true species is probably no longer found in cultivation; many *P. waltonii* Hybrids result from crosses with yellow-flowering species. z6

Section Soldanelloideae

Twenty-two, mostly high alpine species with a range centered on the Himalaya Mts. Distinguished from the species of the Section Muscarioides by their campanulate flowers with nonreflexed lobes. Attractive, often fragrant species. Usually these are difficult to grow since in nature plants are covered with snow for 4–6 months of the year. Best grown in a mix of 2/3 stone chips and 1/3 humus loam soil. Many species, such as *P. flaccida* and *P. reidii*, set seed abundantly in cultivation, from which they may be propagated. All these species require dryness in winter.

P. cawdoriana Ward. SE. Tibet. Leaves obovate to oblanceolate or spatulate, to 4 × 1.5cm, blade tapering to a broad petiole, coarse and irregularly toothed, appressed to the ground. Scape 6–15cm; umbel 3–6-flowered. Flowers funnel-shaped, the narrow lobes deeply 2–3

cleft, pale violet to pale mauve, reverse white or greenish white, to 3cm long. May to June. z6

P. eburnea Balf.f. et Cooper. Bhutan, SE. Tibet. Leaves elliptic, oblong-ovate or ovate, blunt tipped, to 10 × 3.5cm, scabrous-toothed or lobed, glandular, with a winged petiole. Scape 10–20cm high, more or less farinose; umbel 6–12-flowered. Flowers flaired-funnel-shaped, ivory white, 1.5cm long, 1cm wide. May to June. z6

P. flaccida see **P. nutans**

P. nutans Delavay ex Franch. (*P. flaccida* Balakr.). W. China. Leaves narrowly elliptic to broadly oblanceolate, to 20 × 5cm, apex obtuse, denticulate, soft hairy, blade narrowing to a winged petiole. Scape 20–40cm high, farinose above. Inflorescence a dense umbel or 2–5cm long compact spike of 5–25 flowers. Flowers lavender-blue to violet, farinose, funnel-shaped, nodding. June to July. Relatively easy to grow and sets abundant seed. Cultivated in loose, lime-free soil with good drainage. z6

P. reidii Duthie. NW. Himalaya Mts.; in wet screes. Leaves oval-oblong or oblanceolate, to 20 × 3cm, blunt-tipped, crenate or somewhat lobed, tapering to a winged petiole. Scape slender, mealy, 6–15cm high. Umbels, 3–10 somewhat nodding flowers. Flowers ivory white, with glistening farina, to 22mm long, campanulate, fragrant. Includes the var. **williamsii**, larger, with campanulate flowers varying from lilac-blue to white, more vigorous and more attractive. Hybrids are produced between the species and this variety. Very good seed producer. June. z6

P. sapphirina Hook f. et Thoms. Sikkim, Bhutan, SE. Tibet. One of the tiniest primulas. Leaves oblanceolate to ovate, to 2.2 × 1cm. Scape 5cm high. Inflorescence a loose umbel of 1–4 small, semipendulous flowers; violet-purple to blue. Often only biennial. June. z6

P. sherriffiae W.W. Sm. SE. Bhutan; at 1700m, only hardy in the alpine house. Leaves oblanceolate to elliptic, to 17 × 5cm, almost entire, apex rounded, soft-hairy. Scape 4–10cm; umbel 2–7 flowered. Flowers, borne horizontally, 3cm wide, pale violet with white margins, farina flecked, corolla tube 5cm-long. June. Quite rare. z8

P. wattii King ex. Watt. E. Himalaya Mts. Similar to *P. nutans*, but lower-growing and with few, twice as large flowers. Leaves oblong to oblanceolate, to 10cm long, coarsely toothed, apex blunt, both sides with long hairs. Scape 10–18cm high, glabrous. Umbel compact-rounded, with 5–10 flowers. Flowers campanulate, bright violet with a white eye, lobes almost fringed, to 13cm wide. April and May. z6

The following species are also occasionally found in culture: *P. buryana* Balf.f., *P. sandemanniana* W.W. Sm., *P. uniflora* Klatt, *P. wigramiana* W.W. Sm. and *P. wollastonii* Balf.f.

P. edelbergii Schwarz. Afghanistan. Leaves lettuce green, flowers golden yellow. This very rare species is only hardy under suitable conditions, and apparently is not presently in cultivation. z7 (K.)

P. verticillata ssp. **boveana** see **P. boveana**

shaded site. Some species for the rock and heather garden. At least some prunellas, however, become pernicious and hard to eradicate weeds under optimal conditions; try them with caution. Propagate by cuttings from September to November, stuck directly into the bed; also by division after flowering, and by seed.

P. grandiflora (L.) Scholler. A number of cultivars come from this species. The species type is a meadow plant, indigenous to Europe, sparsely naturalized elsewhere. Important for its

Prunella grandiflora

Pseudosasa japonica

Pteridium aquilinum

Section Sphondylia (Verticillata or Floribundae)

Includes 5–8 species, depending on the interpretation, all resembling the tender greenhouse hybrid *P. × kewensis*. Flowers in superimposed whorls, leaves creased at the midrib and involuted. Grow these in well-drained, humus loam in the alpine house. Attractive collector's plants. All propagate easily by seed.

P. boveana Dcne. (*P. verticillata* Forsk. ssp. *boveana* (Dcne.) S.W. Sm. et Forest). Yemen, Sinai. Leaves lanceolate to ovate-lanceolate, apex acute to 12cm long and 4cm wide, densely farinose below, irregularly small-toothed. Scape to 25cm high with 2–4 superimposed, many-flowered whorls, flowers surrounded by leafy bracts, 8mm wide, pale yellow. Has tolerated –13 degrees C. (8 degrees F.) in the alpine house. This often is listed as *P. verticillata* ssp. *boveana*. z6

Prunella L.
Labiatae
Self-heal, Heal-all

About 7–12 species of low herbaceous perennials with creeping rootstock. Stems mostly 4-angled. Leaves opposite, entire or deeply toothed or pinnatifid. Flowers in crowded spikes of 6-flowered whorls with broad, overlapping bracts. Calyx tubular-campanulate; corolla tubular-bell-shaped, 2-lipped, upper lip erect, lower lip spreading, purple, bluish or white. In flower from early summer to autumn. The native habitat of most garden species is Europe, SW. and Central Asia. Undemanding ground cover plants, attractive and long-blooming; suitable for naturalized gardens and meadows. Grow equally well in moist, semi-shaded sites and in full sun in moist soil. Good bee attracting plants. Suitable for planting among and in front of woody plants in a warm, semi-

dense, matted growth habit. The species flowers violet purple. Cultivar 'Alba' flowers whitish; 'Rosea' pink; 'Rotkäppchen' (Red Cap), (Klose) carmine-red; 'Loveliness' pale lilac; 'Loveliness White', white; 'Loveliness Pink' pink. z5

P. grandiflora ssp. **pyrenaica** (Gren. et Godr.) A.et O. Bolos, from SW. Europe, is larger flowered with hastate leaves. June to July. z6

P. incisa see **P. vulgaris**

P. vulgaris L. (*P. incisa* Link) Europe, Mediterranean region to Central Asia. Good purple-violet flower heads. Leaves incised. Includes a rare white and a pink form. Does not attain the beauty of the previous species, but is useful for warm, dry sites, the species is naturalized world wide in temperate regions, often a troublesome weed. May to September. z6

P. × webbiana Paul, possibly *P. grandiflora × P. hastifolia* or a cross between 2 *P. grandiflora* subspecies. More vigorous than the previous species, with large, violet-purple flowers. June to September. A good colonizer for the natural garden. And 'Rosea' with pink flowers. z5 (L.J.& Kö.)

Pseudolysimachion

P. longifolium see **Veronica longifolia**

P. spicatum see **Veronica spicata**

leaf litter makes this a good species for streamsides. Foliage and occasionally the canes will suffer in severe winters, but the plants are generally hardy. z6 (S.)

Psilostemon

P. orientalis see **Trachystemon orientalis**

P. aquilinum (L.) Kuhn Bracken. Twelve geographic varieties, widely varying (especially in height), have been defined. A very conspicuous fern in semi-shaded woodland margins, often forming large colonies in clearings. The ultimate height depends upon the soil fertility; 60–80cm in sandy soils, to 2m in moist, sour humus, somewhat climbing to 4m high and more in damp, open deciduous forests. Rhizome very vigorous, 20–50cm deep. Petiole to 1cm thick, yellowish-green, the vascular bundles in cross-section somewhat reminiscent of a 2-headed eagle. Fronds

Pteridophyllum racemosum

Pterocephalus perennis

Ptilostemon afer

Pseudomuscari

P. azureum see **Hyacinathella azurea**

Pseudosasa Mak. ex Nakai
Gramineae

P. japonica (Sieb. et Zucc. ex Steud.) Mak. Hardy Bamboo, Metake. Honshu to Kiushu (Japan) and S. Korea. Long cultivated; sometimes labeled as *Arundinaria japonica*. This woody plant, sometimes used as a background for perennial plantings, grows to 4m high in protected sites. The broad, dark green leaves are more or less clustered at the branch tips. The emerging canes are strictly erect, but eventually the tops nod with increasing branching. While this species is less decorative than many bamboos, its density and shade tolerance make it a good plant for screening, hedges and tub planting. The minimal

Pteridium Gled. ex Scop.
Polypodiaceae
Brake, Bracken Fern

A monotypic genus, this fern is somewhat variable, and cosmopolitan in the temperate and tropical zones of the world.

The 3–4 pinnate triangular fronds of this fern, with stiff upright stipes, rise from strong-running, invasive, and very persistent underground rhizomes. Spores are borne in sori with double indusia in marginal rows on the underside of the pinnules. Bracken foliage poisons livestock and the spring croziers, once much eaten by humans, now are known to contain cancer-causing chemicals. Scarcely suitable for most gardens due to its invasive character, bracken might have some value as an erosion deterring ground cover in unused, woodland or moorland areas.

0.2–4m long, triangular, 3–4 pinnate, the lowest segments long-stalked, tough, light green, more or less distinctly pubescent. The sori are on the pinnae margins, but only developed under favorable conditions. Golden yellow autumn color.

Two attractive forms have been found in English woodlands: 'Crispum', fronds leathery, undulate; and 'Cristatum', pinnae forked. Suitable only for large parks or wild gardens. Plants should be contained by underground barriers or stone walls to prevent invasion of neighboring plants. May be used as a specimen plant if planted in a container. Rhizomes quite vigorous; young plants should be raised in containers. Propagation is often by division of the rhizome, but this is a tedious process; best grown from spores when available. The dried fronds, non-toxic, are suitable for use as livestock bedding and winter mulches and covers. The ashes of burnt Bracken Ferns are sometimes used in the manufacture of soap and glass for their silicic acid and potassium content. Despite its poisonous properties, a malt beer is brewed in Siberia from the rhizomes. z4 (D.)

Pteridophyllum Sieb. et. Zucc.
Papaveraceae

One species in Japan.

P. racemosum Sieb. et Zucc. Glabrous, stemless perennial with pinnatisect, *Blechnum*-like leaves. Flowers campanulate and small in erect, 25cm-high, loose branched racemes, white, resembling *Leucojum autumnale*. Sepals 2, falling early; petals 4, equal and free; stamens 4; pistil 2-carpelled developing into a 2-valved silique with few seeds. Flowers from June to August. Grow in light shade in moist humus-rich, sandy, peaty, well-drained soil. Susceptible to damage from a late frost. A very attractive plant for a well-tended shade bed. Desirable novelty for the shaded rock garden. Propagate by seed or division. z7(6) (K.)

Pterocephalus Adans.
Dipsacaceae

Twenty-five species of annual or perennial herbs and shrubs, distributed from the Mediterranean region and tropical Africa to Central Asia, the Himalaya Mts., and W. China; distinguished from the closely related genus *Scabiosa* by the 12–24 bristles on the calyx; *Scabiosa* has only 5 bristles.

P. hookeri (C. B. Clark) Airy-Shaw & M.L. Green. Bhutan, Sichuan, Yunnan. Tufted perennial. Leaves all basal, entire but the lowest pinnatisect, oblanceolate, to 20cm long. Flower heads more than 6cm across, solitary, on scapes to 30cm high, pink to pale violet with purple anthers. A rarely available and poorly defined beautiful species; very rare in cultivation. z7(6)

P. parnassi Spreng. (*Scabiosa perennis* ssp. *parnassii* (Spreng.), *P. perennis* Coult. ssp. *perennis* (Vierh.)). S. and E. Greece; among rocks in the mountains. Procumbent, mat-forming, 5–10cm high perennial with very leafy stems, woody at the base, and opposite, small, simple, spatulate, undulate-crenate, silky-tomentose, pubescent leaves. Flower heads solitary, about 3cm wide, flat. Flowers dark pink, calyx with 16 or more feathery bristles. A pretty summer bloomer for the rock or trough garden or south-facing dry stone wall. Thrives only in full sun in a calcareous, infertile, but deep, well-drained soil in rock crevices. Stems creep across the stones, hidden by the dense foliage. Winter protection is advisable, for wetness more than for cold. Plants require wetness protection the entire year. Propagate by seed and late summer cuttings. Blooms from July to August. z6 (E.)

P. perennis ssp. **perennis** see **P. parnassi**

P. pyrethrifolius Boiss.et Hoh. Kurdistan. Similar to *P. parnassi* but the leaves mostly ovate to lyrate in outline, the blade pinnatisect, feathery. Flower heads to 5.5cm wide, pinkish-lavender, in midsummer. Another rare species.

Other worthwhile but almost species include *P. bretschneideri* and *P. pinardii*, as well as varieties of *P. parnassi*.

Ptilostemon Cass.
(*Lamyra* (Cass.) Cass. and *Chamaepeuce* DC.)
Compositae
Ivory-thistle

About 10 species in Europe and Asia Minor. Thornless, dwarf shrubs or prickly herbs. Leaves alternate, entire or pinnate, usually prickly. Flower head scales prickly. Flowers purple, occasionally white. Flowers from July to August. Grow in a sunny, dry site in the rock or wild garden together with *Yucca* or hardy *Opuntia* species. Lime-loving. Propagate by seed. The potted, sturdy young seedlings may be planted in a suitable garden site. Usually only biennial but self sown seedlings often germinate near the parent plants.

P. afer (Jacq.) Greuter (*Cirsium afrum* (Jacq.) Fischer, *C. diacanthum* hort. non DC., *Chamaepeuce afra* (Jacq.) DC.), Ivory-thistle; on wastelands and fallow fields in the Balkans and Asia Minor. Leaves glossy green above, undersides white-tomentose, narrow, white-prickly, forming a 20–30cm wide, bizarre rosette. Flower heads several on 50–70cm high stems, lilac-purple. Similar and occasionally cultivated are *P. chamaepeuce* (L.) Less. (*Cirsium chamaepeuce* (L.) Ten.), Greece and the Aegaean region; and *P. casabonae* (L.) W. Greuter (*Chamaepeuce casabonae* (L.) DC.), W. Mediterranean region. z5 (K.)

Ptilotrichum C.A. Mey.
Cruciferae

About 10 species in Europe and N. Africa. Perennial herbs or small shrubs, resembling the closely related *Alyssum* in which these are sometimes included; occasionally thorny and always with white, pink or red flowers. Leaves with stellate or scalelike hairs. These bloom mostly from spring to early summer. Grow in very well-drained gritty soil in full sun. Useful for the rock garden or dry stone wall. Propagate by seed or cuttings. Young plants should be raised in pots since they do not hold a root ball very well.

P. pyrenaicum (Lapeyr.) Boiss. (*Alyssum pyrenaicum* Lapeyr.). E. Pyrenees Mts. Found on limestone outcroppings. Small, procumbent shrubs with obovate-lanceolate, densely silvery, alternate leaves. Flowers in dense corymbs, white. z6

P. reverchonii Degen et Hevier. SE. Spain: Sierra de Cazorla and the surrounding mountains. Resembles *P. pyrenaicum*, but has broadly spatulate leaves. z6

P. spinosum (L.) Boiss. (*Alyssum spinosum* L.). E. and S. Spain, S. France, Algeria, Morocco. Rounded, strongly branched shrublet, to 50cm high in its habitat, seldom over 30cm high in cultivation. Prickly from the spiny shoots. Leaves of the nonflowering rosettes obovate-spatulate, those of the flowering shoots linear-lanceolate, all silvery-scaly. Flowers in dense corymbs, white, pink or dark rose-red ('Purpureum'). Very attractive, satisfactory and persistent plants, with an excellent honey scent. z6 (K.)

Other species sometimes encountered in rock gardens, especially in the United Kingdom, include: *P. cappadocicum*, from Armenia and Cappocia, tufted perennial to 7.5cm high with tiny leaves and white corymbose flowers; *P. halimifolium*, Italy, Spain, sub-shrub 20–30cm high, leaves silvery, flowers white (z7); and the more tender yet *P. leypeyrousianum*, *P. longicaule*, *P. purpureum*, all from Spain, and *P. rupestre* from Greece, all suitable only in mild climates but beautiful, with silvery foliage and white or pinkish flowers.

Pulmonaria L.
Boraginaceae
Lungwort

About 12 species of hairy herbaceous to evergreen perennials in Europe and Asia. These are not always easy to distinguish; the basal leaves in summer are important for identification. Low, rough-haired, glandular perennials, with creeping rootstock. Leaves simple, large, green or spotted; basal leaves rosetted, long-petioled, stem leaves few, smaller. Flowers narrow to flairing, funnel-form,

P. montana see **P. rubra**

P. officinalis L., Common Lungwort, Jerusalem-Cowslip. Holland and S. Sweden, south to N. Italy, Bulgaria. To 25cm high, plant for moist, peaty soil. Found in mixed deciduous forests, on fertile, usually calcareous soil. Leaves rough-haired, often cordate at the base, not tapered to the petiole, usually white-spotted, running together, or occasionally not spotted. Var. **immaculata** Opiz. Flowers pink at first, then purplish-blue, rarely blue or reddish. March to April. Self-seeds. Also available is the white

lapping spots. Flowers of the species bright rose red, fading bluish; April. Includes the cultivars: 'Argentifolia' with particularly good foliage; 'Bowles Red', flowers remaining reddish, leaves coarse; 'Janet Fisk', lavender-pink, leaves with most silver-white markings of all cvs.; 'Pink Dawn' 20–25cm high with pink flowers and attractive, white-spotted foliage; 'Margery Fish', similar to 'Mrs. Moon', but more attractive and contrasting; 'Mrs. Moon', buds large, pink, then flowers gentian blue, leaves moderately spotted; 'Sissinghurst White', low-growing, flowers pearly

Ptilotrichum spinosum

Pulmonaria saccharata

red, violet, blue, occasionally white, in terminal forked helicoid cymes. Valuable, early-blooming, semi-shade to shade plants for moderately dry to moist sites among woody plants. Propagation is by division from April to June, or seed of the species. Often self-seeds under suitable conditions.

P. angustifolia L. Cowslip Lungwort. NE., E. and Central Europe, Caucasus. To 30cm high. Leaves lanceolate, unspotted. Flowers carmine-red at first, later cobalt to azure blue. 'Alba' white, and 'Azurea' light gentian blue. April to May. Suitable for forcing. Newer cultivars include: 'Munstead Blue', 30cm high, vigorous, also with pale blue flowers. The very similar 'Mawson's Variety' is generally less available. Johnson's Blue', flowers gentian blue, grows only to 20cm high. z4

cultivar, 'Alba'. Leaves once used medicinally. z6

P. picta see **P. saccharata**

P. rubra Schott. (*P. montana* Lej.). Carpathian and Balkan Mts. Stems to 45cm high. Leaves pale green, not spotted, abruptly tapered to the petiole, soft-hairy. Flowers brick red to salmon-red. Flowers very abundantly from March to April. Not as compact-growing as the other species. 'Redstart' is a charming cultivar; 'Albocorolla', white-flowered. z5

P. saccharata Mill. Bethlehem Sage. (*P. picta* Rouy). SE. France, N. and Central Apennines. Variously 15–45cm high, resembles *P. officinalis*, but the outermost basal leaves are somewhat tapered to the petiole, always with large, white, over-

white, foliage with many small white spots. z4

P. stiriaca Kerner. E. Alps. Stems to 30cm high. Leaves with rounded, white blotches. Stem leaves sessile, not decurrent. Flowers azure blue; April to May. Very attractive foliage and flowering perennial. z5 (L.J.& Kö.)

Several additional species appear in geographical or shady wildflower gardens in botanical gardens but they are scarcely ornamental and are not in the trade.

Pulsatilla Mill.
Ranunculaceae
Pasque Flower

About 12–30 species in the temperate to arctic regions of the Northern Hemisphere; some authorities refer these to the genus *Anemme*, a growing trend. Rhizomatous, persistent herbs, leaves, stems and calyx often with long and dense silver hairs, at least when young. Leaves basal, petioled, palmate, ternate or pinnately compound, occasionally simple. Flower stem erect, naked except for the involucre, single-flowered. The involucral leaves resemble the basal leaves or are palmately divided, with narrow-linear lobes. Flowers erect or nodding, cup-shaped to flat-spreading. Sepals 5–12, abscising, petaloid. Ovaries many. Styles feathery, elongating to 5cm as a wing for the ripe fruits (this is the feature separating *Anemone* and *Pusatilla*). Flowers from March to July. Culture varies among the species. Many species, as in the group including *P. alpina* and *P. vernalis*, are very demanding, some are very lime intolerant, for special beds or sites in the rockery, only for collectors. Others, such as *P. vulgaris* and *P. pratensis*, are easily grown in any good, somewhat limy garden soil in a sunny location. Propagation is by seed; some forms of *P. vulgaris* also by root cuttings.

P. alba Reichb. In the highest elevations of the Central European mountains: the Vosges, Harz Mts. and Riesengebirge (Higher Sudetes); also the Carpathians and E. Alps, always over a siliceous substrate. Similar to *P. alpina*, but smaller, sepals nearly always bluish on the outside. Terminal segment of the leaves incised to the midrib. June. Somewhat demanding, for the peat bed. The taxonomic status of this and related pulsatillas is not clear. Wehrhan equates *P. alba* to *P. myrrhidifolia* and apparently to *P. alpicola*, and possibly to certain present subspecies of *P. alpina*—see **P. alpina** ssp. **apiifolia**, below. These closely related forms may be varieties of a single unstable species. z5

P. albana (Stev.) Bercht. et J. S. Presl. Caucasus, Iran. Quite variable. Stems 10–15cm high, hairy. Leaves bipinnately partite, light to medium green, usually gray-green-hairy. Flowers small, pendulous to horizontal or nearly upright, pale lilac, violet, bluish white, yellowish white, or pure yellow. May. Long-lived, but not for strong, direct sun. The following forms are particularly attrac-

tive: var. **andina** Rupr., endemic to the Dagestan region with wide, yellow, obliquely upright flowers; ssp. **armena** (Boiss.) A. et S., Armenia, Cappadocia, flowers deep violet; var. **georgica** (Rupr.) A. et S., E. Caucasus region, flowers bright purple; and var. **violacea** (Rupr.) A. et S. with whitish blue flowers. z5

P. alpina (L.) Delarbre. Alps, Apennines, Corsica, Pyrenees and the Spanish mountains. Stems more or less hairy, 15–35cm high. Leaves 2-ternate, more or less hairy. Flowers solitary, white within, tinged violet to reddish outside, erect or somewhat nodding. June. Not easy to grow, best in a sandy-peat mix in a sunny location. With 2 subspecies:

P. alpina ssp. **alpina**. Dolomitic Alps. Pure white, the outer perianth occasionally bluish, easier to cultivate. z5

P. alpina ssp. **apiifolia** (Scop.) Nyman (ssp. *sulphurea* (L.) Hegi), siliceous Alps. Sulphur yellow, occasionally bluish, very difficult to grow. A recent classification lists this as *P. alpina* var. *sulphurea*. The smaller ssp. *austriaca* A.et S. is possibly a form of *P. alba*. z5

P. alpina ssp. **sulphurea** see **P. alpina** ssp. **apiifolia**

P. aurea (Sommier et Levier) Juz. Caucasus. Found on alpine and sub-alpine meadows. Often grows in *Rhododendron* thickets. Resembles *P. alpina*, but slender and more tender with bright golden yellow flowers. A demanding plant. z6

P. bungeana C.A. Mey. Altai and Alashan Mts. (China). Similar to *P. albana*, but the flowers are a unique blend, yellowish and bluish. Long cultivated, very easy and persistent. z5

P. cernua (Thunb.) Bercht. et J.S. Presl. Japan, Korea, Manchuria. Similar to *P. pratensis*, but usually red-flowered. May. Occasionally offered in seed exchanges. z5

P. chinensis (Bunge) Regel. E. Asia. Stems 25cm, to 50cm at fruiting. Leaves large, biternate. Flowers small, nodding, pale whitish violet. Particularly conspicuous for the 10cm-wide, hairy fruit heads, the most attractive of the genus. May. z6

P. dahurica (Fisch.) Spreng. E. Asia. Similar to *P. cernua*. Occasionally available through seed exchanges. z6

P. flavescens (Zucc.) Juz. Ural to Central Asia. A beautiful species. Closely related to *P. patens*, but flowers sulphur yellow, occasionally bluish outside, 8cm-wide. April. Sets seed poorly and therefore rare. z5

P. grandis Wender. Bavaria, Austria and Moravia (Central Czechoslovakia) to the Dnieper River (USSR). Similar to *P. vulgaris*, but distinguished by the feathery leaves with 40–50, 3–7mm wide lobes, substantially larger flowers, to 9cm across, and the conspicuous, silvery or gold-brown-hairy flower buds. April.

Pulsatilla alpina (Anemone alpina)

Very attractive and better suited for the rock garden than *P. vulgaris*. 'Budapest Variety' is grown in English gardens. z5

P. halleri (All.) Willd. Stems slender, hairy, to 30cm high. Leaves appearing just after the flowers, spreading bipinnate, similar to those of *P. patens*, silky-hairy. Flowers upright, shaggy-hairy outside, like the stalks, violet, occasionally pink. April to May. Occurs in several subspecies:

P. halleri ssp. **halleri** SW. and Central Alps. Leaves with fewer than 50 segments and primarily 5-parted. z5

P. halleri ssp. **rhodopaea** K. Krause. Yugoslavia, S. Bulgaria, N. Greece. Basal leaves densely hairy, with 50–100 segments, primary segments petiolulate. z6

P. halleri ssp. **slavica** (G. Reuss). Zamels. W. Carpathians. Similar to ssp. *halleri*, but the leaves are primarily 3-parted. z5

P. halleri ssp. **styriaca** (G.A. Pritzel) Zamels. SE. Austria. Similar to ssp. *halleri*, but with larger leaves. z5

P. halleri ssp. **taurica** (Juz.) K. Krause. Crimea. Similar to ssp. *rhodopaea*, but the primary segments of the leaves are sessile. z5

P. montana (Hoppe) Rchb. SW. Switzerland to E. Rumania and Bulgaria. Similar to *P. pratensis*, but the basal leaves have divisions. Flowers bluish to dark violet, wide funnel-form. April to May. z6

P. nuttaliana ssp. **nuttaliana**, ssp. **multi-fida** see **P. patens**

After flowering the stem elongates to 30–60cm tall topped by a shaggy drumstick of winged fruits. Flowers whitish or bluish outside, 3–6cm across. An alpine-arctic species scarcely adaptable to lowland cultivation, especially where summers are hot or where snow cover is lacking in winter. z3–4

P. patens (L.) Mill. E. and E. Central Europe, west to Sweden, E. Germany, and N. America from S. Central Canada to Illinois, Missouri, Oklahoma and Texas to the Pacific Northwest and

Basal leaves and bracts much divided with 150 segments, appearing with the flowers. Flowers always nodding, campanulate, dark purple, reddish, pale violet, greenish yellow, occasionally white, very occasionally scarlet red. May. Flowers of these plants are quite variable in color. The dark purple forms are considered ssp. **nigricans** (Störck) Zamels, the sordid yellow of these plants are quite variable in color. The dark purple forms are pale grayish-violet and included in ssp. **pratensis**. In Austria, besides campanulate flower forms, flat

Pulsatilla vernalis

P. occidentalis (Watson) Freyn. N. America. Similar to *P. alpina* ssp. *alpina*, but found on sandstone or granite, basal leaves finely divided. More demanding than *P. alpina*. z5

P. occidentalis Wats. North America: all alpine, sub-alpine species in the Rocky Mts. of Montana north to Alaska and in the N. Pacific Coastal mountains; in gravelly and stony mountain meadows, blooming at the edge of melting snow. Flowers bloom almost sessile on a massive woody caudex surrounded by 3-ternate leaves, the divisions cleft into numerous linear lobes; basal leaves petiolate, stem leaves subtending, each solitary blossom sessile, all shaggy-hairy.

Pulsatilla grandis

through the Yukon to Alaska. Stems 7–15cm high, to 45cm high in fruit. Leaves appearing after the flowers, palmately lobed, lobes 2 or 3-partite, the segments linear-lanceolate. New growth very white-shaggy-pubescent, later more or less glabrous. Flowers upright to obliquely ascending, blue-violet, occasionally white. March to April. In fruit, this plant is uncommonly showy. Uncommon in cultivation, grown like *Adonis vernalis*. Similar to, and by many botanists including, *P. nuttalliana* ssp. *nuttalliana* (DC.) Bercht. et J.S. Presl., "Prairie Crocus" from N. America and ssp. *multifida* (Pritzel) Aichele et Schegler from Asia. z5

P. pratensis (L.) Mill. Central and E. Europe, west to SE. Sweden, W. Denmark and N. Yugoslavia; on sunny, dry heaths and mountain slopes. Stem 7.5–30cm high, elongating later to 45cm.

forms are found resembling those of *P. montana* (f. *patula*). Long-lived and attractive species. z5

P. rubra (Lam.) Delarbre. Central and S. France, Central and E. Spain. Similar to *P. montana*, but the basal leaves divided with about 20 segments; flowers dark red-brown to purple or blackish red, occasionally dark violet. April to May. Rarely grown, but the seeds of wild plants are easily obtainable. Certainly, this is the mother plant of all the red-flowering *P. vulgaris* hybrids. z6

P. turczaninowii Krylow et Sergiewskaja. E. Asia. Similar to *P. bungeana*, but taller with violet flowers. z6

P. vernalis (L.) Mill. Scandinavia to S. Spain, N. Italy, Bulgaria, Siberia; on dry alpine meadows, lowlands, heaths. Flower stems 10–15cm high, later elongating to 30cm. Basal leaves are short-petioled, evergreen, once pinnate with 3–5 toothed lobes. Flowers to 6cm wide, nodding at first, then erect; interior white, outside red, pink, violet or blue, very occasionally white, with long, usually golden-brown hairs. White, dwarf forms can be found in the Central Alps among the normal forms. March to April. Very sensitive to calcareous soils, grows best in a sunny peat bed with sand and conifer needles incorporated into the soil. Easily grown from seed, short-lived but easily replaced. z5

smaller, more numerous, blooming later than most scillas, and flowers more campanulate, not as flat and stellate as those of *Chionodoxa*. Unlike its relatives, *Puschkinia* flowers have a small, daffodil-like perianth tube (corona), the surest and easiest taxonomic character. Bulbs globose. Puschkinias are good spring blooming ornamentals for the perennial rock garden, open woodlands, in shrub borders or in turf which is mowed only two or three times a year, though the flower color is not bright. These are indestructible plants, appearing every

hyacinthoides Baker., *P. sicula*, *Scilla sicula*, *Adamsia sicula*). Lebanon; in thickets, among rocks, on mountain meadows to elevations above 3000m. Leaves broadly lanceolate, stem-clasping at the base. Scape to 15m high. Flowers small, 1–2.5cm across, flat-campanulate with a short, sharp-toothed corona, in crowded, few to 20-flowered racemes, the segments bluish-white with a blue middle stripe. March

The pure white form, distributed as *Puschkinia scilloides* 'Alba' is quite a good garden plant, alone or combined with

Puschkinia scilloides **var.** *libanotica*

Pygmaea pulvinaris

P. vulgaris Mill. England and W. France, north to Sweden, east to the Ukraine; on sunny, dry, calcareous moors. To 25cm high, leaves pinnatisect, appearing with or after the flowers, feathery, with more than 100 segments. Flowers dark to pale violet, occasionally white or pink. March to April. The various cultivars are attractive, i.e. 'Mrs. van der Elst', salmon pink; 'Röde Klokke', deep red; 'Weisser Schwan' (White Swan), white; etc. z5 (K.)

Puschkinia Adams
Liliaceae
Striped Squill

Small bulbous plants similar and closely related to *Scilla*, also *Chionodoxa*. Puschkinia stamen filaments, unlike those of *Chionodoxa*, are connate. Nectaries united at the base, then lobed; distinguishes *Puschkinia* from *Scilla mischtschenkoana* (*S. tubergeniana*) which has similar colors. *Puschkinia* flowers are

year; plant in fall. Propagate by bulbils in August and also by seed. Multiplies freely by self-seeding.

According to the British authorities (Martyn Rix, Brian Matthew and Patrick M. Synge), the separation of *P. scilloides*, *P. scilloides* var. *libanotica* and *P. hyacinthoides* is incorrect and all three forms should be considered *P. scilloides* Adams. According to this possibly debatable interpretation, the plant is a widely variable species ranging from the Caucasus, S. Turkey, N. Iraq, Iran to Lebanon and bound together by transition forms. The form from Lebanon is considered the best garden ornamentals. According to other classifications, the latter plants should be:

P. hyacinthoides see **P. scilloides** var. **libanotica**

P. libanotica see **P. scilloides** var. **libanotica**

P. scilloides Adams var. **libanotica** (Zucc.) Boiss. (*P. libanotica* Zucc., *P.*

Chionodoxa sardensis, *Scilla bifolia*, *Tulipa pulchella*, and *Primula* Juliae Hybrids. The pale bluish selections combine well with *Helleborus* hybrids, *Leucojum vernum*, *Narcissus cyclamineus* hybrids, *Cornus officinalis*, *Rhododendron* × *praecox* and *Acer rubrum* cultivars. z5 (Mü.)

P. sicula see **P. scilloides** var. **libanotica**

Pycnanthemum Michx.
Labiatae
American Mountain Mint

Related to *Origanum*, a North American genus with 21 species of little garden merit. Plants upright-growing, stems freely branched, mostly 4-angled. Leaves opposite, entire, nearly sessile, aromatic, pungent-scented. Flowers in dense terminal or axillary heads or cymose clusters, small and pubescent, blooming in late summer to fall. Calyx tubular, 5-toothed; corolla 2-lipped, the upper lip entire, lower 3-lobed, sordid-whitish or pinkish, 3–5mm long, stamens 2 pairs. Grow in any garden soil in full sun to semi-shade. Only a few are recommended for collectors for their late flowers. All species become invasive weeds in sunny regions with warm summers.

P. flexuosum (Walt.) B.S.P. (*Koellia flexuosa* (Walt.) MacM.). E. North America. Stems 60–100cm high or more, slender. Leaves narrowly lanceolate, 5cm long. Flowers pale mauve-pink to whitish, calyx teeth awl-like acuminate. z5

P. virginianum (L.) Pers. (*Koellia virginiana* (L.) MacM.). E. North America. Stems 90–110cm high. Stems stiffly upright, very much branched above the middle, finely pubescent to hirsute. Leaves lanceolate, aromatic. Flowers sordid white, calyx teeth ovate-triangular; July to September. z5 (K.)

Pygmaea Hook.f.
Scrophulariaceae

About 8 species in New Zealand, Tasmania and Australia. Small, dense, cushion-forming perennials or dwarf shrubs with tiny, opposite, sessile leaves with ciliate margins, glaucous or pubescent. Flowers solitary, borne in the upper leaf axils, 5-parted, similar to many *Hebe* flowers, pure white. Blooms from May to June. Grow in well-drained, but humus-rich substrate. Needs protection from excessive winter wetness, but is not suitable for the alpine house. Good plant for trough gardens or the high-maintenance rockery. Propagation is by cuttings, also from rarely available seed.

P. pulvinaris Hook.f. (*Veronica pulvinaris* (Hook.f.) Benth. et Hook.f.). New Zealand: South Island. Perennial, dense cushion-form, to 4cm high and 10cm wide. Stems 3–5mm thick. Leaves crowded-imbricate, to 4 × 1mm, obtuse to subacute, sparsely coarse-haired on the margins. Corolla white, sparsely hirsute, to 8mm long. *P. thomsonii* Buchan is similar, but somewhat more difficult to grow. This genus is sometimes known as *Chionohebe*. z8(7), only where summers are cool and misty. (K.)

Pyrethrum

P. cinerariifoliuim see **Chrysanthemum cineariifolium**

P. corymbosum see **Chrysanthemum corymbosum**

P. densum see **Chrysanthemum densum**

Pyrrocoma

P. lyalli see **Haplopappus lyalli**

Pyrola L.
(see also *Orthilia*)
Pyrolaceae
Shineleaf, Wintergreen

About 12–20 species in Eurasia and N. America. Low perennials, usually less than 30cm-high. Rootstock scaly, often stoloniferous, leaves evergreen or semievergreen, usually petiolate, mostly rounded or oval, basal or caudex, scape erect, with bracts. Flowers in terminal racemes, greenish, white yellowish, pink or pale purple; sepals 5, petals 5, stamens 10, fruit a 5-celled globose capsule with minute seeds. Flowers from June to July. Most pyrolas are rather difficult to grow. Except for *P. rotundifolia* and *P. asarifolia*, all require a mycohrrizal root fungus. Suitable for shade gardens with peat beds. Propagation is by division, but also by seed, germinated in soil collected around the mother plant.

P. asarifolia Michx. Pink Wintergreen. North America, New Brunswick to British Columbia, southward into the northern states and along mountain ranges, on moist soils, in the shade, often in coniferous forests. Leaves reniform to rounded, shiny dark green above, often brown beneath, blade about 5cm deep, petiole of equal length. Scape to 35cm; flowers many, spirally arranged, pale pink, to 15mm wide. June to July. And var. **purpurea** (Bunge) Fern. Asia, North America. Leaf blades obovate to nearly round, flowers rose-pink to reddish-purple. Late summer. A very satisfactory species for the cool-summer garden, forming dense, stoloniferous mats. z4

P. chlorantha SW., **P. media** Sw. and **P. minor** L. are generally too demanding for garden culture, but will thrive under favorable conditions. *P. media* may be contained for about 7 years in a sunny, peat bed among *Cassiope*. z6

P. rotundifolia L. Wild Lily-of-the-Valley. Eurasia, North America. Leaf blades nearly round, to 5cm long, glossy, thick-leathery, petiole slender, longer than the blade. Scape to 35cm high, flowers spirally arranged, white, fragrant, in racemes of 5–20-flowers, corolla segments thick. June to July. Strong stolons. And var. **americana** (Sweet) Fern. Slightly larger overall. z5

P. uniflora see **Moneses uniflora**

P. urceolata see **Galax urceolata** (K.)

Raffenaldia

R. primuloides see **Morisia monanthos**

Ramischia see Orthilia

Ramonda L.C. Rich.
Gesneriaceae
Rosette-mullein

A small S. European genus of about 3 species (dating back to the Tertiary Period) of an otherwise tropical plant family. Evergreen rosetted perennial with elliptic, tough, rugose, crenate-margined leaves, hirsute brown beneath. Flowers solitary or few in irregular umbels on ascending scapes. Ramondas are some of the most interesting and attractive rock garden plants. They thrive in a wind-protected site in shade or shadow, preferably in a fertile-humus-filled crevice of a vertical wall. Most effective with small ferns. Spreads by self-seeding, especially on moss-covered tufa rock. Exceptionally tenacious plants, surviving severe summer droughts, very long-lived. The evergreen rosettes are effective without the flowers. Propagate by seed and division of old clumps, also by leaf cuttings.

R. heldreichii see **Jankaea heldreichii**

R. myconi (L.) Rchb. (*R. pyrenaica* Pers.). Pyrenees, Montserrat (Spain); only on limestone. Rosettes to 20cm wide. Leaves matte dark green, ovate to elliptic, short-petioled, upper surface sparsely pubescent, underside densely tomentose. Scape reddish, to 12.5cm high, 1–7 flowered. Corolla 5-parted, pale bluish violet to mauve, pinkish, or white, anthers light yellow; May to June, always later than both the Balkan species. Listed also are 'Carnea' and 'Rosea', soft pink and 'Alba' white-flowering. z6

R. nathaliae Panc. et Petr. Central Macedonia, Albania and N. Greece; on limestone and sandstone or granite.

Rosettes to 15cm-wide. Leaves glossy green, short-petioled, broadly ovate, crenate. Scapes 1–3 flowered. Corolla usually 4-lobed, lavender-blue with an orange-yellow eye, anthers yellow. May, 3 weeks before *R. myconi*. Perhaps the most valuable garden species. z6

R. pyrenaica see **R. myconi**

R. × regis-ferdinandii Kellerer (*R. myconi × R. nathaliae*). Rosettes to 25cm wide. Leaves glossy dark green. Scape to 5-flowered. Corolla 5-parted, violet-blue, orange-eyed, flowers before *R.*

Pyrola rotundifolia

myconi. Very attractive, vigorous, but rare garden hybrid. Propagate only by leaf cuttings. z6

R. serbica Panc. Albania to NE. Bulgaria and NW. Greece; only on limestone. Leaves narrowly spathulate, margins somewhat incurved, growing upward, deeply irregular-toothed, longer-petioled than the other species. Corolla 5-parted, somewhat campanulate, pale lilac, with a yellow eye. Anthers dark violet-blue. Rarely true in cultivation. z6 (Sch. & S.)

Ranunculus L.
Ranunculaceae
Buttercup, Crowfoot

A very large genus of about 250 annual and perennial herbs of world-wide distribution, but most in the North Temperate Zone in temperate or cold regions. Many are invasive weeds, a few

are choice garden ornamentals. The perennial species have short rhizomes, fibrous roots, or sometimes are tuberous. Leaves mostly lobed, palmate or much divided, rarely occasionally simple and entire. Flowers solitary or in loose cymes, with 5 early-falling sepals, 5 yellow or white (sometimes red) petals, many stamens and numerous simple pistils which mature to become a head of small nutlets The most important garden species is doubtlessly *R. asiaticus* L. from W. Asia. Unfortunately, this species is not very winter hardy and is best suited for the cold frame or moder-

ate greenhouse. In the garden the tuberous roots must be well mulched in winter. After flowering, when foliage has matured and dried, the plants are dug and kept dry through the summer. Often cultivated in warmer climates. Makes a good cut flower, particularly the glossy, semi- or double, so-called Persian and Turkish Ranunculus in red, yellow, white and sometimes green flowers. The winter-hardy species come from various habitats, their cultural requirements and companion plants are correspondingly varied. Many alpine and high-alpine species do well in screes. They require

Ramonda myconi

mostly fertile, loamy soils and abundant water, at least during their growing period. The meadow species are vigorous perennials of various heights, requiring ample water during spring growth. A summer dormant period is very important for the many species that survive extreme summer dryness in their native habitats. Some other species are woodland margin plants or aquatic plants. Propagation of most species is by division, especially for desirable selections. Seed should be sown immediately after ripening. Botanists separate the genus into several sections based on phylogenetic affinities; as plants in some sections share similar habitats, a study of these is helpful to the serious gardener interested in growing *Ranunculus* species.

R. aconitifolius L. White Bachelor's Buttons. Central Europe to Central Spain, Central Italy and Yugoslavia. Herbaceous perennial with tuberous roots. Leaves long-petioled, 3–7 lobed, sometimes 3-lobed and deeply notched. The stem is well branched, leafy, to 60cm high; pedicels 1–3 times as long as the bracts, with appressed stiff hairs; buds reddish, flowers white, to 2cm-wide. This species occurs near springs and moist sites in an open woodland, and on stream banks and on moist mountain meadows. Ssp. *platanifolius* is similar, but larger, to 90cm high, leaves less divided, pedicels glabrous. 'Luteus Plenus', flowers double, yellow; 'Pleniflorus' or more frequently, 'Flore-pleno', Fair Maids of France, flowers double, white, but not commonly offered in the trade. The large-flowered cultivar 'Grandiflorus' seems to have disappeared from cultivation. z6

R. acris L. Common Buttercup, Tall Buttercup. Europe and N. Asia, naturalized nearly throughout the world from meadow seed mixes. Leaves generally hairy, 3–7 partite, the segments of lower leaves deeply cut and lobed. Lower leaves petiolate, upper leaves sessile. Plants low to 1m high. The species includes numerous forms; several subspecies can be distinguished by their fleshy roots, pubescence, shape of the achenes and by their native range. Cultivar 'Flore-pleno', sometimes called 'Multiplex' is densely double, golden-yellow flowered, grown as a long-blooming bedding perennial or cut flower with stiff stems. Perhaps also a less invasive plant for use in a flowering meadow situation. z5

R. aduncus see **R. montanus**

R. alpestris L. Pyrenees, Alps, Carpathians and Apennines. 5–15cm high. Leaves small, long-petioled, rounded, 3–5 lobed, glossy green. Stems mostly with 1 flower and 1 leaf. Flowers to 2cm wide, white; April. Requires a shaded site in the rock garden, in moist, fertile, limestone soil; a plant for collectors. z5

R. amplexicaulis L. Pyrenees. Roots slender, somewhat fleshy, in a tuft. Stems 10–30cm high. Leaves gray-green, glabrous, stem-clasping, elliptic-lanceolate, entire. Stems branched, 3–6 flowered. Flowers 2.5cm across, white;

Ranunculus aconitifolius 'Pleniflorus'

May to June. A very attractive species for the rock garden. Requires a deep, loamy peat soil and ample moisture. z6

R. aquatilis L. (*Batrachium aquatile* (L.) Dumort.). Water Buttercup. Nearly cosmopolitan aquatic plant in still and flowing water. Stems submerged, to over 1m long. Underwater leaves 1–3 multifid, the segments almost filamentous; floating leaves rounded to reniform, 3–5 cleft with obtuse crenate lobes. Flowers long-pediceled, borne above the water, white with a yellow spot in the throat; May to August. Suitable for garden pools and streams. A highly variable species sometimes split into several species. Other aquatic species are occasionally cultivated, such as *R. fluitans* Lam., with only submerged, finely divided leaves; best in flowing water. z5

R. × arendsii hort. (*R. amplexicaulis* × *R.*

graminifolius). An attractive garden hybrid with pale yellow flowers which fade to nearly white, on 15cm high stems. May to June. Similar to *R. gramineus* in habit, but the leaves are gray-green, broadly lanceolate. Rock garden plants for moderately dry sites. Propagation is by division. z5

R. asiaticus L. Persian Buttercup. Asia Minor, possibly SE. Europe. This is the parent of the florists' Ranunculus which comes in many colors and white, mostly doubled; see introductory note regarding their cultivation. Roots tuberous.

Ranunculus aquatilis

Stems with sharp, appressed hairs, 15–40cm high, simple or sparingly branched. Leaves 2–3 ternate, the segments toothed or deeply cleft. The wild form bears large, 5 petaled, bright red flowers with reflexed sepals. Cultivated forms are white, shades of yellow, orange, red and rose, usually very double, to 4cm across. z8 A tender Crete var. **albiflorus** is taller, above 45cm, much branched, downy, with to 7 flowers in a cyme, the flowers to 10cm across, white with a greenish flush at the base of the petals. z9

R. bilobus see **R. crenatus**

R. bulbosus L. Europe, Asia, North Africa. Leaves ternate, plants hairy; stem 20–50cm high, flowers golden-yellow, to 30mm wide. Quite a variable species, with differing forms mostly from S. Europe. The rootstock is a bulb-like tuber. After fruits mature, tops die back over the dry late summer months. Grows best on lime-free, fertile loam soil. Suitable for greening periodically dry sites. Propagation is by seed and division. This species has naturalized along the E. US. coast and is moving inland where it becomes weedy in some areas. Also in New Zealand. Cultivar 'Pleniflorus' is a decorative perennial for similar sites in the garden. Propagation is by division in the late summer dormant period. z5

R. calandrinioides Oliv. Morocco; Atlas Mts.; between 1300 and 2800m. Rootstock thick, cylindrical with a fibrous coat of old leaf bases; roots fleshy. Stems erect, branched, 10 to rarely 15cm high. Leaves long-petioled, broadly lanceolate with an undulate, entire margin, glaucous gray-green. Flowers 1–3 in terminal clusters, 5–7cm wide, bowl-shaped, white, usualy pink-tinged on the outside of newly opening flowers; March to April. A wonderful, heat-loving species for a sunny, protected rock garden; needs ample moisture in spring and is tolerant of dryness when dormant in summer. Best cultivated in an alpine house in harsh climates. Should be potted in deep pots with fertile, loamy soil; flowers in February under glass. z7

R. crenatus Waldst. et Kit. SE. Alps, Carpathian and Balkan Mts. Leaves nearly orbicular-cordate, rounded-crenate, dull, dark green. Stems 8–10cm high. Flowers to 2.5cm wide, white; April. Needs a cool, sheltered site in the rock garden, and gravelly loam soil; more satisfactory in cultivation and more decorative than *R. alpestris*. z7(6)

The lime-loving **R. bilobus** Bertol. from N. Italy, is very similar. z7

R. delphinifolius see **R. flabellaris**

R. eschscholtzii Schlect. USA.; Alaska to California and New Mexico, in high mountain meadows. Fibrous rooted from a stubby, hard rootstock. Plant scapose; leaves basal, orbicular, deeply 3-lobed, the middle lobe further 3-lobed to entire, sinuses and segments rounded. Flowers usually solitary on 12–45cm high scape, to 28cm across, bright yellow. Var. **eximius** (Greene) L. Bens. Montana, Idaho and Utah, basal leaves with middle lobe entire, segments acute-tipped.

R. ficaria L. (*Ficaria verna* Huds.). Figwort, Lesser Celandine, Pilewort. Europe and SW. Asia. Tuberous roots with fleshy, fibrous rootlets. Stems ascending to 15cm, often procumbent.

Leaves broadly ovate with a cordate base, glabrous. Flowers terminal, yellow, with 3 sepals and 8–12 petals. Quite variable over its range, including flower size and color. In addition to the single, yellow-flowering species, white, pale yellow and orange, single and double cultivars are grown. Needs fertile, high humus soil and ample moisture, especially in spring. Forms a bright green, leafy carpet in early spring with starry, glossy golden yellow flowers. Plants have already died back by late May. Naturalize in the shaded wildflower garden with the appropriate soil. The

Ranunculus ficaria

cultivars are less vigorous and do well in small gardens under shrubs, planted with *Galanthus*, *Scilla*, *Leucojum* and cultivars of *Anemone nemorosa*. Cultivar 'Albus' has white flowers. 'Aurantiaca' is particularly valuable, with distinctly brown-marbled, cordate leaves and very glossy, orange-yellow flowers. 'Grandiflorus' is larger in all respects and comes from the Mediterranean region, and is presumably identical to ssp. *ficariiformis*. 'Plena' is an attractive, evenly double, yellow cultivar; there is also another, more greenish-yellow double cultivar. z5

R. flabellaris Raf. (*R. delphinifolius* Torr.) Yellow Water Buttercup. North America, Maine to British Columbia southward to North Carolina, Louisiana, Utah and California. An aquatic species growing submerged or floating. Stems stout, glabrous, hollow. Submerged leaves

widely spaced, ternately compound and redivided to many limp, thread-like segments; above water leaves thick with many broader, stiffer segments. Peduncle with 1–7 flowers; sepals 5, petals 5, bright yellow; flowers 12–30mm across. An attractive water plant for ponds and quiet backwater of streams but may require control under optimum growing conditions. z4

R. flammula L. Lesser Spearwort. Europe, temperate Asia. A poisonous bog plant. Rootstock short, with or without stolons. Stems 20–50cm high, ascending or procumbent, sometimes floating in water, forked-branched. Basal leaves petiolate, ovate-cordate; stem leaves sessile, lanceolate, entire. Flowers to 2cm wide, yellow; June to October. Notable for collectors of bog plants; requires a swampy soil or shallow water; effective with *Myosotis palustris*. And var. *repens*, plants quite prostrate. British horticulturists favor *R. lingua* over this species for the bog garden. z5

R. geraniifolius see **R. montanus**

R. glacialis L. Greenland, Europe; on mountain moraines. Roots stout, long. Stems 7.5–15cm high. Lowest leaves palmately 3-partite or deeply 3-lobed, the segments further 3-cleft, obtuse, glabrous or rarely hairy. Flowers 1–3 in a cluster, to 28cm across, white or tinged pink or purplish. This is strictly a moraine plant which grows in stony loam over running cold water; for the experienced alpine gardener in a cool climate. z4

R. gouanii Willd. (*R. montanus* Willd. var. *dentatus* Baumg.). Pyrenees. A vigorous relative of *R. montanus*, stems to 25cm-high, with more deeply incised, velvety pubescent leaves, and 5cm-wide, yellow flowers. z6

R. gramineus L. Mediterranean region. Rootstock short and thick, fibrous above, with fleshy, clustered roots. Stems 20–40cm high, erect, sparsely branched, smooth. Leaves linear-lanceolate, glaucous, entire. Flowers lemon-yellow, to 2.5cm across, May to June. Dies back soon after flowering; the new growth appears again in fall. Easy to grow, recommended for rock gardens; attractive when combined with *Linum narbonense*. And cultivar 'Flore-pleno' with double flowers; var. *phoenicifolius*, with lanceolate leaves. z7

R. illyricus L. Central and SE. Europe, Asia. Rootstock tuberous with short, thick roots, somewhat stoloniferous. Stems upright, 30–40cm high, with few branches. Basal leaves long-petioled, ternate with entire linear-lanceolate lobes or lobes further segmented. Flowers 2–3cm wide, glossy golden-yellow; May to June. Entire plant silver-silky-woolly. For sunny, dry sites in the rock or heather garden; thrives in sandy soil. z6(5)

R. japonicus Thunb. Japan. As yet, a little-known species, creeping and rooting at the nodes with ternate, further segmented, 1cm-wide leaves. Flowers

glabrous. Leaves short-petioled, lanceolate, acute-tipped, entire, grey-green, glabrous. Flowers to 4cm wide, glossy, golden-yellow; June to August. Always decorative bog plant for pond banks and large streams with shallow banks; grows and flowers best in water no deeper than 5–30cm. z4

R. lyallii Hook.f. New Zealand. The largest-flowered species of the genus with 12cm-wide, Poppylike white flowers in panicles above the foliage. Unfortunately, thrives only in damp climates with cool summers and mild

September.

'Molten Gold' is a valuable, low, large-flowered cultivar for the garden.

A group of closely related species, including *R. gouanii* Willd. (which see), **R. aduncus** Gren. et Godr. (*R. villarsii* DC.) and **R. sartorianus** Boiss. et Heldr. are found in the mountains of S., Central and E. Europe. They are occasionally brought into cultivation for their attractive flowers. These thrive on seeping, moist (at least in spring), fertile, loamy soils and require a corresponding garden site. These plants make particularly good companions for the stemless

Ranunculus montanus

Ranunculus thora

12mm wide borne above the 1cm-high leafy mat on 5cm-high pedicels, with glossy, golden-yellow, rounded nectaries. An interesting species for the alpine garden or trough garden. z6(5)

R. lanuginosus L. S. and Central Europe, Caucasus Mts.; in humus-rich woodlands, especially on limestone. The entire plant is shaggy-pubescent. Rootstock short, fibrous. Basal leaves 5-cleft with wide lobes. Stems erect, 60–80cm high, much branched, many-flowered. Flowers to 4cm wide, rich yellow; May to June. An attractive woodland plant, for naturalizing in parks and wild gardens; thrives in moist, humus-rich soil, in light shade. The double-flowering cultivar 'Pleniflorus' produces attractive cut flowers. z5

R. lingua L. Greater Spearwort. Europe, Siberia. Rootstock with stolons to 80cm long. Stems hollow, strictly erect, well-branched toward the top, 0.8–1.5m high,

winters. Generally considered to be short-lived and difficult in cultivation. z7

R. millefoliatus Vahl. Balkan Peninsula, Mediterranean Region. Rootstock short, tuberous-thickened. Stem 20–30cm high, erect, sparingly branched. Basal leaves prone, rounded, crispate, 2- to 3-pinnate and redivided cleft, lobes linear, glabrous. Flowering stems almost leafless to scape-like, hairy, mostly 1-flowered. Flowers yellow, to 2.7cm across. May. Dies back after flowering. For the rock garden. And cultivar 'Grandiflorus', with much larger flowers. z6

R. montanus Willd. Alps, Jura Mts. This plant is listed in the British literature as *P. graniifolius*. Rootstock short, cylindrical. Stems 1-flowered, appressed-hairy, 10–20cm high. Basal leaves petioled, orbicular 3–5 cleft, with cuneate, obtuse-margined lobes, smooth. Flowers 2.5cm across, golden-yellow, glossy; May to

gentians in the rock garden. z6(5)

R. montanus var. **dentatus** see **R. gouanii**

R. parnassifolius L. Pyrenees, Alps, to Austrian Mts., mostly on limestone. Leaves cordate to ovate, simple, entire, bluish green, reddish woolly-pubescent margins. Stems erect, 4–10cm high, 1–6 flowered. Flowers white, exterior often reddish. Handsome but difficult to grow alpine species; requires moist, gravelly loam. Only for experienced collectors. z5

R. platanifolius L. Europe; in open tall grassy meadows and open brush in the mountains; in the lowlands in deciduous woodlands, always on moist, fertile soil. Resembles *R. aconitifolius*, and is considered to be a subspecies of it by some taxonomists, but larger over-all. Leaves 5–7 lobed, the middle lobe not separated basally. Peduncles 4–5 times as long as the bracts. Flowers pure white, to 4cm wide on plants to 1.2m high. Plants die back on seasonally moist, summer-dry soils. z5

R. psilostachys Griseb. Balkan Peninsula. 30–40cm high. Rootstock a cluster of fleshy roots; short, with slender, above ground stolons. Stems erect, branched toward the top, with leaf-like bracts at the nodes, pubescent, 1–14 flowered. Leaves basal, long-petioled, ternate, with long, silky hairs on both sides, but very hairy beneath. Flowers upright, 4.5–5.5cm across, glossy yellow, sepals reflexed; May to June. Dies back after flowering. Requires a sunny site; attractive, easy to

Ranzania japonica

grow rock garden plant. z6

R. sartorianus see **R. montanus**

R. seguieri Vill. W. and E. Alps, Apennines; only on limestone. Leaves 3–5 part palmate with scabrous, acuminate lobes, fleshy, glabrous. Stems 1–3 flowered, 5–10cm high. Flowers white, to 2.5cm wide; April to May. Similar in appearance to *R. glacialis*. Very attractive, high alpine plant, but only for experienced collectors. Requires moist, gravelly loam soil, or better, a moraine. z5

R. thora L. Pyrenees, Alps, Carpathians, Dalmatia, only on limestone. Roots tuberous. Stems sparsely branched, slender. 10–15cm high. Basal leaves die away early; the lowest stem leaves are erect, large, nearly orbicular to reniform, crenate toward the apex, bluish green. Flowers 1–2cm across, 1–3 per stem, yellow. Very poisonous alpine plant, only for collectors; for a slightly shaded spot in the alpine garden. z5

R. traunfellneri Hoppe. SE. Alps. Very similar to *R. alpestris*, and sometimes listed as a variety of it, but with 3-partite

or lobed leaves, the middle lobe 3-parted, the lateral lobes 2-parted. An attractive species, thriving on moist, gravelly limestone soil. z6 (Sch. & S.)

Ranzania T. Ito
Berberidaceae

Monotypic genus, named for Ono Ranzan, the "Japanese Linnaeus". Found on N. Hondo, in deciduous forests at 700–1000m with *Caulophyllum* and *Cimicifuga*. Flowers from March to April.

Raoulia australis

Grows in loose, high humus soil in light shade. Propagate by division and seed from the abundantly produced white, fleshy berries; the seedlings will flower after four years.

R. japonica T. Ito. Stems simple, herbaceous, sensitive to a late frost, with two opposite, ternate leaves at the top, 15–20cm high in flower, later growing to 50cm high. Flowers with 6 petal-like sepals, 6 petals smaller than the sepals, and 6 stamens surrounding a simple pistil, 3cm wide, nodding, lilac, in terminal, loose, 1–6 flowered clusters. Very attractive and rare, related to *Epimedium*. The flowers appear with the new growth, before the leaves, and densely cover the ground on rapidly growing stems. z7 or 8 (K.)

Raoulia Hook.f. ex Raoul
Compositae

Twenty-five species of perennial herbs or subshrubs, most from New Zealand, a few in New Guinea, Australia and Tasmania. Most very low-growing, either dense cushion-forming or creeping and procumbent, often forming soft-like mats, tightly appressed to the soil or a stone. Leaves alternate, often crowded-imbricate, gray- or white-tomentose or glabrous. Flower heads solitary, small, with disc flowers only sessile or nearly

so. All flowers hermaphrodite or the outermost pistillate; corolla toothed, anthers caudate. Pappus bristles not feathery.

Charming, low, often ground- or rock-hugging perennial for the rock garden, trough or alpine house. Especially for collectors and botanic gardens. Sensitive to wetness and cold winters; always pot up some plants in late summer for overwintering in a cold frame or alpine house. For the landscape in suitable climates, in full sun, creeping among rocks. These require well-drained, sandy, humus-loam soil. In snowless regions, provide an airy winter blanket of conifer branches covered with polyethylene to exclude rain. Many species are best grown in the alpine house. Propagation is possible by seed, but easiest by division. Good companion plants are other New Zealand species such as *Hebe cupressoides* and *H. pinguifolia*, *Carex buchananii*, *Epilobium inornatum* and the Japanese *Mazus radicans*. Also effective in combination with silver-leaved dwarf perennials.

R. australis Hook.f. ex Raoul (*R. lutescens* Beauverd). New Zealand; on barren ground and in dry stream beds from the plains to 1600m. Forms dense, flat, silver-white mats. Stems flat-spreading, very branched, creeping, rooting. Leaves crowded, imbricate, erect or reflexed, no longer than about 2mm, single-veined, glabrous beneath, densely silver-white tomentose above. Flower heads inconspicuous, 4–5mm across. Bracts with yellow tips. Blooms from July to August. Certainly the most attractive and most conspicuous species. z7

R. glabra Hook.f. New Zealand; grassy, open sites from the lowlands to 1300m. Stems flat-spreading, loosely branched, rooting, forming mats to 30cm wide. Branchlets ascending. Leaves 3–5mm wide, yellowish green, loosely imbricate or rather widely spaced, ovate-oblong or linear-oblong, 3-veined, flat, glabrous or sparsely silver-pubescent. Flower heads 7–9mm across, with 30–50 disc florets. Inner bracts with yellowish or white, radiating tips. Blooms in July. z7

R. lutescens see **R. australia**

R. subsericea Hook.f. New Zealand; on grassy, open sites, in the mountains from about 300–1350m. Stems flat spreading, freely branched, rooting, forming dense mats. Leaves loosely to densely imbricate, narrowly oblong, 3–6mm wide, 3-veined, light green, undersides sparsely silver or golden tomentose. Flower heads to 10mm wide. Disc florets fewer than those of *R. glabra*. Bracts with white, radiating tips. Blooms from April to May. z7

R. tenuicaulis Hook.f. New Zealand; usually in gravelly or sandy dry stream beds, from sea level to 1600m. Creeping, with very slender stems which root, sparsely to much branched. Branchlets ascending. Leaves loosely imbricate, to 5 × 2mm, nearly lanceolate, single-veined, sparsely white-tomentose at the tip. Flower heads to 6mm across, with 10–20 disc florets. Inner bracts with dark tips. Blooms from July to August. z7 (E.)

Other, similar species suitable for a region of cool summers and mild winters include *R. eximia*, *R. grandiflora*, *R. haastii*, *R. mammilaris* and *R. tenuicaulis*; all are similar in habit, flat, dwarf matting plants, and all are or have been grown by specialists in the Pacific Northwest and in the U.K.

Ratibida Raf.
(*Lepachys* Raf.)
Compositae
Prairie Coneflower, Green Coneflower, Mexican Hat

Five or more biennial and perennial herbs in North America, mostly on the prairies, plains, and in the SW. USA where they have become useful garden ornamentals. Rootstock is a hard crown, becoming woody with age, with wiry roots spreading widely and penetrating deeply in some species. Stems grow strongly erect, branching above the middle, the branches also ascending. Leaves are alternate pinnatifid, 3-lobed or rarely simple. Flower heads terminal, solitary, with a single row of involucral bracts, high-domed to mostly columner, slender for its height; disc flowers usually leaf-green, opening to rust-brown; ray flowers long and showy, drooping, lemon yellow, or zoned basally bright rust brown to mahogany-purple, or dark throughout except for yellow tips. Full sun plants. Grow in well-drained, fertile garden loam, natural to sub-alkaline. These bloom from early summer to early fall.

R. columnaris see **R. columnifera**; in recent years a spate of name changing has occurred. *R. columnifera* is the legitimate epithet.

R. columnifera (Nutt.) Woot. & Standl. (*R. columnaris* (Pursh.) D. Don; *Lepachys columnaris* (Pursh) Torr. & A. Gray; *L. columnifera* (Nutt.) Macbr.; *Rudbeckia columnaris* Pursh; *Rudbeckia columnifera* Nutt.) Prairie Coneflower, Long-head Coneflower, Mexican Hat. North America: SW. Canada to Northern Mexico, eastward to Minnesota and Texas but naturalized much further eastward. Perennial, rarely biennial, herbaceous perennial; rootstock a small, hard crown. Stems green, leafy below, branching and sparsely leafy above the middle. Leaves gray-green with stiff appressed hairs, leaves pinnately lobed or rarely dissected, the segments mainly linear to narrowly oblong, usually entire or nearly so, occasionally 2–3 cleft. Flower heads on long peduncles; the disc cylindrical or column-like, 15–40mm high, 2–4 times as long as thick; ray florets as long as or shorter than the disc. z4(3) Two forms are listed:

f. **columnifera**, ray flower ligules entirely yellow; and f. **pulcherrima** (DC.) Fern., ray flower ligules partly or completely purple-brown or purple. The latter form grows much shorter (to 30cm) in the SW. US where it is known as Mexican Hat due to the flower head resemblance to a sombrero; it is a favorite garden perennial.

R. pinnata (Vent.) Barnh. (*Rudbeckia pinnata* Vent.). Gray-head Coneflower, Green Coneflower, Drooping Coneflower. North America: Ontario, New York and Minnesota and South Dakota south to Nebraska, Oklahoma, Arkansas and Georgia; naturalized beyond this natural range. Taller species than the above, 50–150cm high, with larger leaves and flowers. The rootstock is a hard crown. One or few stems grow strongly upright with few to several branches above the middle. Most leaves are below the middle. Leaves pinnatifid, the segments lanceolate and toothed on lower and middle leaves, somewhat glaucous and sparsely appressed hairy. Flower heads on long peduncles, the disc globe-shaped, ovoid or a short ellipsoid, greenish-grey before disc florets open; disc florets bright rust-colored; ray floret ligules 3–5cm long, bright, clear yellow, drooping. This is a beautiful, summer-long flowering, full sun plant. z4(3)

R. tagetes (James) Barnh. (*Lepachys tagetes* (James) A. Gray; *Rudbeckia tagetes* James). North America: Kansas and Colorado south to New Mexico. Low, bushy-branching herbaceous perennial with a stout, long taproot. Stems branch widely from the base, to 45cm high, often shorter. Leaves many, pinnate with 3–7 segments, linear, entire, rather rough-hairy. Flower heads terminal. Disc globe-shaped or oblong, 8–12cm long, nearly as thick; ray flower ligules yellow, rarely purple, 6–10mm long, or lacking. A plains species from low rainfall and alkaline soil regions; grown only as a curiosity or in the hot, sunny wildflower garden. z4(3)

The first two species of *Ratibida* belong in every sunny herbaceous border and sunny wildflower garden. They also are suitable for cutting.

Rehmannia Libosch. ex Fisch. et Mey
Gesneriaceae (or Scrophulariaceae)

Eight species of persistent herbs native to China with affinities for 2 plant families; at present, the family assignment remains moot. Root fibrous, tufted from a small crown-like unelongated stem. Leaves large, unevenly serrate, in a basal rosette and alternate on the erect flowering stem, to 90cm high, viscid-hairy. Flowers large, foxglove-like, in a terminal, leafy raceme. Calyx ovoid-campanulate, 5-toothed; corolla hairy, with a long, inflated tube and oblique limb, somewhat 2-lipped; stamens 4, epipetalous, ovary 1–2 celled, stigma 2-lobed. Most species are non-winter-hardy herbs of great beauty. In addition to *R. glutinosa*, only *R. elata* is cultivated, but the other species merit attention. Best handled as a biennial overwintered in a cool greenhouse or frost-free cold frame. Plants may then be set out in spring from pots into the perennial border. Plants may be removed after flowering since the rate of over-wintering success is poor. Sow seeds in late winter in the greenhouse; transplant once, then set into a loamy humus bed. Pot up in fall and overwinter frost-free. It takes 12–14 months to produce plants from seed. The most winter-hardy is *R. glutinosa*. Gardeners in frost-free areas or with a cool greenhouse should seek out additional species.

R. angulata Hemsl. C. China. Softly pubescent, erect perennial. Stems 15–50cm, leaves in large basal rosettes, sessile or short stalked on flowering stems, lobed and irregularly toothed. Bracteoles present, small, leaf-like. Corolla 5.5–6cm, magenta with yellow throat, lobes rounded. Blooms June–September. See also following species. z8

R. elata N.E. Br. (*R. angulata* hort. non (D. Oliv.) Hemsl.). China. Perennial with branched stems to about 1.5m-high. Leaves to 25cm long and to 10cm wide, with 2–6 entire, or sometimes toothed, very hairy lobes on either side. Flowers in leafy racemes. Corolla 7–10cm long, bright rose-purple. Throat yellow, red-spotted. Blooms in May and June. Only seed of the better types should be collected for propagation. z8(7)

R. glutinosa (Gaertn.) Libosch. N. China. Perennial with somewhat fleshy stolons. Entire plant sticky-hairy, stems and underside of leaves frequently reddish. Leaves obovate, unlobed, 3–7cm long, coarsely toothed, distinctly veined. Flowering stems 30–60cm high. Flowers solitary, axillary. Calyx campanulate, with reflexed lobes. Corolla yellowish, rarely purplish with a lavender-purple, darker-veined throat, exterior pubescent. Blooms in May and June.

The barely winter-hardy *R. glutinosa* is worthwhile for the landscape or alpine house. Requires loamy humus, well-drained, and should be covered with conifer needles and boughs in winter.

Rehmannia elata

Propagate by seed and by stolon cuttings. z7(6) (E.)

Reineckea Kunth
Liliaceae

A monotypic, barely hardy genus; plants in foliage greatly resemble *Liriope*.

R. carnea (Andr.) Kunth (*Sansevieria sessiliflora, S. carnea* Andr.). China and Japan. Leaves broadly linear, 10–30cm high, upright-arching, in tufts of 6–12 on prostrate, sparsely leafy rhizomes. The flesh-pink, flowered spikes are borne on bracted scapes which are shorter than the leaves, as the later-appearing berries. Flowers very small; perianth segments 6, tube-like; stamens 6, epipetalous; fruit a red berry. This evergreen perennial forms large stands in a warm, protected site. Suitable for underplanting woody evergreens and the large evergreen ferns. Hardiness is apparently not so much related to winter minimum temperatures as to sufficient summer heat and late summer dryness to harden off the plants. Should be considered for planting near walls and buildings. z7(6) (S.)

Reynoutria Houtt.
Polygonaceae

Relatively recently split from *Polygonum*, but retained in that genus by many taxonomists. All species have small flowers in axillary panicles, white, pink or red. All are vigorous. Blooms from August to October. Propagated by division.

R. japonica Houtt. (*Polygonum cuspidatum* Sieb. et Zucc., *P. reynoutria* Mak.). E. Asia. Roots widely creeping,

Reineckea carnea

vigorously rooting. Stems hollow, to 2m high. Leaves large, broadly ovate. Inflorescences pendulous, axillary, spicate, cream white; July to August. Suitable only for large gardens, as the dense clump increases annually with unbelievable speed and vigor. z5

R. japonica var. **compacta** (Hook.f.) Buchheim (*Polygonum cuspidatum* var. *compactum* (Hook.f.) L.H. Bailey). Japan. A shorter form of the above. Stems 40–60cm high, spreading widely. Brownish-red tinged leaves. Flower panicles and fruits decorative, red. August to September. Thrives in a moist, sunny site in the rock garden if walled into contain the rhizomes, also a fast-spreading groundcover perennial for large areas, but top vigorous and is usually invasive. z5

R. sachalinensis (Fr. Schmidt) Nakai (*Polygonum sachalinense* Fr. Schmidt). Japan, Sachalin, S. Kuril Islands. Stems to 3m high. Similar to *P. cuspidatum*, but with striped stems and even more vigorous habit; September to October. Can be very attractive for its fall color, but requires much room to grow and should be planted with caution as plants are difficult to eradicate. z5 (L.J. & Kö.)

Rhazya Decne.
Apocynaceae

One species in Greece and NW. Anatolia and one species from Arabia to NW. India. Erect, latex-producing herbs with woody bases, alternate leaves and terminal, corymbose or thyrsoid inflorescences. Rare plants, found only in botanic gardens in geographical collections or wild gardens, but attractive plants for collectors. Plant in a sunny, warm site in well-drained, somewhat moist, sandy loam soil. Propagate by

Reynoutria japonica

division and seed.

R. orientalis (Decne.) A.DC. Thracian region (Greece/Turkey), NW. Anatolia; on moist sites near the sea. Rhizomes about pencil thick, hard, light brown. Stems clustered, few to many, unbranched, to 50cm high. Leaves about 4 × 2cm, mostly lanceolate, thin, glabrous above, ciliate along the margin and the midrib. Flowers in terminal, loose corymbs. Corolla funnel-shaped with limb of 5 flat, acute segments, about 1cm wide, bright blue to dark violet; tube 1–1.5cm long; stamens epipetalous; fruit a follicle. Blooms from June to August. z6 (E.)

Rhaponticum

R. scariosum see **Leuzea rhapontica**

Rheum L.
Polygonaceae
Rhubarb

A genus of about 20 species. Some very decorative perennials with thick, fleshy or woody rootstocks of crowded rhizomes, and very large leaves in a basal clump. Depending upon the species, these are sinuate, palmately incised or toothed and 3–8 veined at the base. Flowers are clustered in panicles on a tall stem. The 6-part calyx (no petals) encloses the 6–9 stamens, and a triangular ovary with usually 3 styles. *Rheum officinale* Baill., common Rhubarb, is indigenous to W. China and was introduced to the Western world centuries ago. All the rheums require very deeply dug fertile soil and full sun. Effective as specimens, near water or at the base of a large rock garden. These are among the most imposing perennials for their stout, usually reddish shoots in spring and the flowers from May to June. Unfortunately most species die back somewhat after flowering and are then unattractive. Propagate by division and seed.

R. acuminatum Hook.f. et Thoms. Sikkim Rhubarb. Sikkim. 0.6–1m high. Rootstock slender, orange. Leaves broadly cordate, with a deep sinus at the base, lanceolate, acuminate. Stems sparsely branched, furrowed, wine red. Flower panicles erect, lurid purple, blood-red, or brownish red. May to June. z6

R. alexandrae Batal. Tibet, W. China. Stems 1m high. One of the most conspicuous species for the hand-sized, light yellow bracts imbricately covering the inflorescence. Leaves relatively small, glossy light green, yellowish-white-veined, oblong-ovate, entire; May to June. Grows best in shaded site with ample moisture. Very decorative, also for small gardens. z5

R. australe D. Don (*R. emodi* Wall.). Himalaya Mts. Leaves very large, rounded to cordate, obtuse, 5–7 veined, undulate, somewhat rough and lightly copper-toned above, underside and margin softly pubescent. Stems fastigiate-branched, 2–3m high, yellowish green, brown-striped. Inflorescence slender, ascending, with leafy bracts. Flowers small, amaranth-red, as is the 3-winged fruit. June to July. z6

R. emodi see **R. australe**

R. kialense Franch. China. Unlike the other species, this is a dwarf; stems 30–50cm high with rose-red inflorescences and hand-sized, brownish green leaves. An attractive species for the rock garden. May to June. z6

R. palmatum L., Chinese Rhubarb. NW. China, NE. Tibet. Leaves nearly round, deeply palmately lobed, segments acute, 3–5 ribbed, undersides reddish and floccose. Stems 2–2.5m high, panicle much branched with erect, softly pubescent peduncles. Flowers cream yellow. Fruits rust brown. z5

R. palmatum var. **dissectum** see **R. palmatum** var. **tanguticum**

R. palmatum var. **tanguticum** Maxim. (*R. palmatum* var. *dissectum* Stapf). Leaves of new growth reddish, later dark green. Stems 2m high, with red flowers and fruits; considered by the author to be the most attractive and satisfactory of the tall ornamental rhubarbs. June. z5

R. rhabarbarum L. (*R. undulatum* L.). E. Siberia to N. China, Manchuria. 1.5m high. Leaves roundish-cordate to oblong-cordate, to more than 50cm high, gray-green with undulate margin. Flower stems branched, flowers crowded, small, yellowish white. The parent species of the common garden rhubarb; May. Not a good ornamental, but suitable for the herb garden. z5

R. ribes L. Lebanon, Iran. Leaves very undulate, rounded to cordate, wider than long, dentate, 5-veined, gray-green above, underside light green. Stems 1–

able in North America and difficult to find in Europe.

Rhexia L.
Melastomataceae
Meadow Beauty, Deer Grass

About 10 species. Low, erect, mostly bristly, glandular, herbaceous or suffruticose perennials. Only a few species are more or less hardy in temperate gardens.

winter mulch for protection. For sunny, moist sites in peaty, sandy soil. In colder climates the tuberous rootstock must be overwintered in a frost-free area; set out again in early spring.

Propagate by division in spring or seed. Seed may be sown in the cold frame or bed, with young plants being grown in containers for 1 or 2 years, until sufficiently sturdy to be planted into the garden. z6(5) (D.)

Similar but taller growing with somewhat larger rose-purple or white flowers is **R. mariana** L., Atlantic Coast and

Rheum palmatum var. *tanguticum*

1.5m high, leafy on the lower half. Flowers greenish; stamen filaments bright red. Fruits narrowly winged, blood red. May to June. z6 (Sch. & Kö.)

R. undulatum see R. rhabarbarum

Such a list of several species incorrectly seems to indicate that ornamental rheums are general in distribution. As a matter of fact, they are virtually unavail-

R. virginica L., Meadow Beauty. E. and Central N. America; in bogs, or sandy, moist meadows. Tuberous perennial. Stems 4-angled, 30–50cm high, reddish-striped, branched on the upper half. Leaves sessile, oval-lanceolate, pubescent above or on the margin, underside glabrous. Flowers 2.5cm wide, with 4 petals, solitary or in terminal, paniculate cymes, rose-pink to purplish, July to August. The hardiest species, requiring

Oklahoma south to Texas; rarely in the trade but seed sometimes is listed in plant society exchanges. z7(6)

Rhinopetalum

R. bucharicum see **Fritillaria bucharica**

Rhodiola L.
Crassulaceae

Opinions regarding total number of species in this genus vary widely. About 7 species are cultivated. This genus was split from the genus *Sedum*, but the species still frequently are retained in *Sedum* by many botanists and are found under *Sedum* in books and catalogs. All rhodiolas have a stout, branched, underground rootstock giving rise in spring to mostly unbranched, stiff stems, more or less densely covered with leaves. Stems

Rhodiola rosea

bear crowded, hemispherical terminal inflorescences with greenish-white, yellow or rosy flowers. These surpass the genus *Sedum* in decorative merit. For collectors to some extent, for the large rock garden and other alpine plantings. Bloom from May to July. Plant in a sunny site; most garden soils are suitable.

R. crassipes (Hook. f. et Thoms.) Boriss. (*Sedum crassipes* Hook.f. et Thoms., *Sedum asiaticum* hort.). W. Himalaya Mts., W. China, Tibet. Rootstock with many stolons. Stems 30–35cm high with crowded, obtuse and dentate, oblanceolate leaves. Bracts on the inflorescence. Flowers pale yellow to white. June. Often not true in cultivation. z5

R. heterodonta (Hook.f. et Thoms.) Boriss. (*Sedum heterodontum* Hook.f. et Thoms.). W. Himalaya Mts., Tibet, Afghanistan. Rootstock fleshy, multiple-stemmed. Stems 30–40cm high, unbranched, developing into a formal, hemispherical bush. Leaves alternate, small, triangular-oval, irregularly coarse-toothed. Flowers in dense, small, terminal heads, dull greenish yellow or pinkish. Interesting collector's plant, particularly conspicuous in spring with its bright reddish, globose stem buds. z5

R. hobsonii (Prain ex Hamet) Fu (*Sedum praegerianum* W.W. Sm.). Tibet. With short, thick rootstock. The lower leaves oblong-linear to oblong-rhombic. The basally branched flowering stems bear pink flowers. June to July. Rare in cultivation. z5

R. kirilowii (Regel) Regel ex Maxim. (*Sedum kirilowii* Regel). NW. China, Mongolia, Himalaya Mts. Rootstock thick, branched. Stems stiffly erect, 20–30cm high, unbranched; leaves usually crowded, petioled, lanceolate, irregularly scabrous-toothed, thin, green. Inflorescence of densely crowded, small flowers, hemispherical, greenish yellow; May. z5

R. kirilowii var. **rubrum** Praeg. Leaves sparsely toothed; flowers brownish-red; one of the most interesting *Rhodiola* species. Unfortunately plants die back right after flowering, leaving a void in the planting. May to June. z5

R. rhodantha (A. Gray) Jacobs. (*Sedum rhodanthum* A. Gray). USA: Montana to Arizona, Rocky Mts. Rootstock carrot-like, fleshy, few-stemmed. Stems 20–30cm high, erect, stiff, unbranched, very leafy. Leaves opposite, sessile, linear-lanceolate, usually entire or dentate only at the apex. Flowers funnelform, in short, erect racemes, rose-red; June. A uniquely attractive species, but does not thrive in lowland gardens; apparently intolerant of lime. z4

R. rosea L. (*Sedum roseum* (L.) Scop.). A circumpolar, variable species usually found over sandstone or granite rocks in the mountains. Rootstock thick, fleshy, multiple-stemmed, scented like roses, particularly when dried. Stems erect, 20–30cm high, unbranched, with many crowded leaves. Leaves alternate, sessile, oval to narrowly lanceolate, serrate, gray-green. Flowers in dense, hemispherical cymes, yellowish; May to June. Only for collectors, requires a semidry site among stones. z1

R. semenowii (Regel et Herd.) Boriss. (*Sedum semenowii* (Regel et Herd.) Mast.). Turkestan. Rootstock carrotlike. Stems 30–50cm high, erect, unbranched, very leafy. Leaves alternate, almost linear, acute, entire. Flowers funnelform in densely cylindrical racemes, greenish-white; June to July. A plant for collectors. z7(6) (Sch. & Kö.)

Rhodohypoxis Nel
Hypoxidaceae

Two or three species in S. Africa, once classified as *Hypoxis*. Interesting small perennials from moist mountain slopes with hazelnut-sized, tuberous rootstocks and tufts of basal, narrow-lanceolate, almost grasslike, 7cm-long, channeled leaves with silky-pubescence and ciliate margins. Flowers flat-spreading, star-like with 6 separate perianth segments (unlike *Hypoxis*) about 3cm wide, solitary on wiry, short pedicels. Flowers from June to August. Grow in lime-free, well-drained soil in a sunny rock garden, in pots in the cold frame, or in the alpine house. Not reliably winter hardy. Requires abundant moisture in summer, but dryness in winter; therefore, the plants should be removed in fall and stored dry for the winter, or covered to protect from winter wetness. Attractive and valuable plants with a long flowering period, for collectors and botanic gardens. Propagation is best by division in early spring as new growth begins, or by the fine, silver-gray seeds. Seeds sown in March will produce flowering plants the following year.

R. baurii (Bak.) Nel. Mountains of S. Africa (Basutoland, Natal). Basal leaves to 5cm high, 5 or 6 in a tuft. Flowers of the species rose, to 2.5cm across; garden seedlings in various colors (light magenta red, pink, white, very occasionally dark red) in the trade. z6

Rhodohypoxis baurii

R. baurii var. **platypetala** (Bak.) Nel. Flowers white with a pink base. Commonly grown cultivars include: 'Alba', pure white, small-flowered, unusually bright; 'Dawn', pale pink, large-flowered; 'Fred Broome', a strong pink; 'Great Scott', bright, dark carmine; 'Perle', pure white, large-flowered. Tetraploid forms are available from Japan. z6 (K.)

Rindera Pall.
Boraginaceae

About 25 species of perennial herbs from the Mediterranean region, W. and Central Asia. A genus closely related to *Cynoglossum*, but differing in the calyx

being lobed to the base, mostly included style, and nutlets lacking barbs. Only a few *Rindera* species are occasionally found in botanic gardens or European wildflower gardens. They are relatively short-lived perennials for droughty sites, recommended only for experienced gardeners or collectors. Grow in a sheltered, sunny, dry site in the rock garden; plants often fail to survive cold, wet winters. The low-growing *R. graeca* and *R. caespitosa* are better suited for the alpine house where they will bloom for weeks. Easily propagated by seed.

R. caespitosa (DC.) Gürke. Asia Minor; on dry, rocky, wasteland. Dense, bushy plants 5–20cm high, with yellow or gray hairs. Basal leaves linear-lanceolate, long-petioled, 2.5–7cm long, single-veined. Stems simple, very leafy. Inflorescences corymbose. Flowers pink or bluish, narrowly cylindrical, about 1cm long. Flowers from May to August. z7(6)

R. graeca (A.DC.) Boiss. et Heldr. Greece; on rocks in the mountains. Similar to the above, but with silver-white, scaly pubescence and with purple flowers on 7.5–20cm high. Flowers from April to July. z8(7)

R. umbellata (Waldst. et Kit.) Bunge. E. Yugoslavia to SW. Ukraine; on dry, open

sites. One or few stems, 25–70cm high, sparsely hairy. Basal leaves linear-lanceolate to oblong-elliptic. Stem leaves smaller, sessile, lanceolate. Inflorescence an umbellate raceme, with many reddish yellow or dark brownish-red tubular flowers. Blooms from May to July. Propagate annually by seed with the young plants overwintered in a cold frame. z7 (F.)

Rodgersia A. Gray
Saxifragaceae

Four to six species depending on the interpretation. Strongly growing perennials, related to *Astilbe*. Conspicuous for their thick, flat-creeping, black-brown rhizomes, and especially for the large, tough, dark green, long-petioled, peltate, palmate or pinnately partite basal leaves and the floriferous, panicled, white inflorescences in summer.

Rodgersias are prominent bog, waterside, and water garden ornamentals, very effective when healthy and vigorous. The rich green (or bronze-toned in full sun), umbrella-shaped leaves create a dense, 1m-high wall of foliage. The mostly yellowish-white inflorescences are very effective in early summer. Best naturalized along a woodland margin, with rhododendrons, large ferns, Japanese Primulas and other vigorous shade-loving, moist soil perennials. They are very beautiful at the waterside. For best results select a wind-protected site in a very fertile, humus-rich soil with ample moisture, quite damp if in full sun. Plants will not, however, tolerate standing water. Be sure to allow a generous space for the slow but steadily spreading growth habit. Propagate by division and seed.

R. aesculifolia Batal. Central China. Leaves rounded in outline, 0.7–1.8m high, to 50cm across, mostly 7-parted, the leaflets overlapping at the base. Leaves very like those of the Horse Chestnut tree. Stems and leaf veins brown-shaggy-pubescent. Inflorescence 0.7–1m high, pyramidal, loosely branched; flowers small, long-petioled, white; June to July. z5–6

R. henrici see **R. pinnata**

R. japonica see **R. podophylla**

R. pinnata Franch. China (Yunnan). Especially showy planted on the banks of water courses. Leaves 0.9–1.2m high, dark green, glossy, with 6–9 leaflets, palmate, usually with the middle three leaflets clustered, longer petioluled, offset from the other leaflets, usually overlapping at the base. Inflorescence a much branched panicle, to 1m high; stem reddish, sparsely pubescent. Flowers pinkish on the typical form, but generally variable; yellowish-white on the form 'Alba'; 'Rubra', flowers deep red. June to July. The taller-growing form 'Superba', with pale pink flowers and dark red seed capsules in a 50cm-long inflorescence, is currently considered a separate species, *R. henrici*. z6

R. podophylla A. Gray (*R. japonica* A.

Rodgersia aesculifolia

Gray ex Regel). Japan, Korea. Leaves to over 50cm across, 0.9–1.2m high, glossier than those of the other species, usually palmate with 5 leaflets, deep margins and sharply jagged-serrate, bronze-colored when young, then brown-hairy. Inflorescences reaching about 2m with attractively nodding panicles, yellowish-white; the best species for flower. June to July. Seedling variability has given rise to these selections: 'Pagode' (Pagoda) (Pagels 1972), flowers white, later greening, in large, attractive inflorescences; 'Rotlaub' (Red Leaf) (Pagels 1976) broad-growing, with green leaves and creamy white flowers. z5–6

R. purdomii hort. (introduced by Purdom from China in 1922). Young leaves and petioles reddish brown; mature leaves to 75cm wide, palmate, 6–7 parted, similar to *R. pinnata*, but the

leaflets are narrower, longer-stalked and regularly palmate-parted to the base, but not overlapping. A beautiful perennial with inflorescences more than 1m-high, open, pure white. June to July. Seed capsules only half as large as those of *R. pinnata*. Only the most colorful clones such as 'Irish Bronze' should be selected for further propagation. z6

R. sambucifolia Hemsl. China (Yunnan, Sichuan). Leaves 60–90cm high; easily recognizable by the outstretched, 3–5 paired oblong-lanceolate, nonglossy leaflets. Inflorescences to 1m high, densely paniculate, white. June to July. 'Rothaut' (Red Skin) (Goetz 1970) is a valuable, dark-leaved cultivar with brown-red new growth and a vigorous habit. z6

R. tabularis see **Astilboides tabularis**. This species is retained in *Rodgersia* by many American and British botanists and horticulturists as leaf form, alone, seems insufficient for the erection of a separate genus. (L.J.& M.)

Rohdea Roth
Liliaceae

Two or three ill-defined species of *Aspidistra*-like perennials; only one is commonly in cultivation.

R. japonica (Thunb.) Roth. Japan. Rhizome stout, short. Leaves 9–12cm high, rarely higher, basal, leathery and evergreen, oblanceolate. Flowers in a dense, axillary cluster at ground level, fleshy, greenish white. The species develops vigorous, evergreen leafy clumps. A good understory plant for dryish areas under established trees, in mild climates. Cultivar 'Marginata', with a thin, not very conspicuous white-striped margin on the leaves. Division of the thick rhizomes is somewhat difficult. Seed propagation is best if seed is available. Seed set is seldom observed, perhaps because only the clones are normally found in cultivation. z7 (S.)

Romanzoffia Cham.
Hydrophyllaceae

Four species of low, fairly tender perennials from the mountainous regions of W. North America and the Aleutian Islands. Resemble *Saxifraga granulata* in habit with long-petioled, usually basal, rounded-reniform, lobed leaves and sparsely flowered, terminal, racemelike cymes of white flowers. Calyx 5-lobed,

almost separated; corolla bell-shaped or campanulate-funnel-shaped, 5-lobed; stamens 5, included, stigma undivided, fruit a capsule. Rare herbs of difficult culture for experienced collectors and botanical gardens. They require a cool, moist, lime-free, high humus soil in semi-shade to shade; plant between stones in the rock garden. Not long lived in cultivation outside North Temperate rain forest habitat. For longevity, plants should be restricted to pot culture in the alpine house under light shade. Plants often go through a dormant period after flowering during which they lose most of the leaves, making new leaves with the onset of cooler fall weather. Propagation is by separation of the tuberous rhizomes, division or seed.

R. sitchensis Bong. Alaska to California; on wet rocks and outcroppings in the mountains, occasionally above the tree line. Rootstock somewhat bulbous but without tubers. Leaves rounded, lobed. Stems 5–20cm high. Flowers white, funnel-shaped, on pedicels to 2.5cm long. Pedicels longer than the calyx after the fruits ripen. Blooms in May and June. z5

R. unalaschkensis Cham. E. Aleutian Islands, habitat similar to that of the above species. Similar to the above, but slightly smaller, to 15cm high. Pedicels short, much shorter than the calyx at fruit ripening. Blooms from May to June. Even rarer than these species is the 30cm-high *R. suksdorfii* Greene. z7(6) (E.)

Romneya Harv.
Papaveraceae
Matilija Poppy, California Tree Poppy

One, or questionably two, species in California and NW. Mexico. Attractive perennial to subshrubby plants. Woody rootstock sparsely branched, brownish yellow, deep. Stems pale gray-green, smooth, to 1.5m-high. Leaves alternate, blue-green, pinnately partite or 3-part lobed. Flowers poppy-like, 10–15cm wide, silky-glossy, and silver-white. Sepals 3, falling as petals expand; petals 6 in 2 ranks; many. Stamens yellow.

This beautiful plant is, unfortunately, only winter-hardy in mild climates or under cover. Best grown in front of a south wall in deep, well-drained soil. Quite heat and drought tolerant. Exceptionally difficult to transplant. The best planting time is spring; move from containers. Propagation by seed is tedious, requiring several years from seedlings to flowering plants. The seed is only viable for a short time, therefore must be sown right after ripening. Propagated best by pencil-thick root cuttings stuck individually in 3-inch deep pots and kept in a propagation frame until new growth appears. Keep the soil moderately moist.

R. coulteri Harv. Rarely or only sparsely stoloniferous. Stems much branched above the middle, to 2.4m high on mature plants. Leaves papery, irregularly pinnate. Flowers very fragrant, 10–12cm

Romulea Maratti
Iridaceae

An extensive and little cultivated genus of about 75 species. All are crocus-like plants with small corms, but the flowers are distinctly stemmed, unlike crocus, and the stems often are branched. The leaves of *Romulea* lack the keel so apparent on crocus foliage. Those species from E. and S. Africa are not suitable for North Temperate Zone gardens. Species from S. Europe and Asia Minor will overwinter under favor-

frame cultivation: *R. atranda, R. aurea, R. columnae, R. ramiflora, R. requienii, R. rosea, R. saldankensis, R. tinaresii.* (Kö.)

Roscoea Sm.
Zingiberaceae

About 15 species in China. Interesting, orchid-like perennials with fleshy, clustered roots and sheathing lanceolate leaves which form a flaired funnel through which the scape emerges. Flowers in a terminal spike; calyx tube

Rodgersia sambucifolia

Rohdea japonica

wide, with crepe-like, delicate petals. Stamens yellowish orange. Sepals round-tipped, nearly glabrous. Blooms from August to September. z7

R. coulteri var. **trichocalyx** (Eastw.) Jeps. (*R. trichocalyx* Eastw.). Differs in its generally more vigorous habit. Always stoloniferous. Stems stout, only branched toward the base, leafy above. Leaves coarser, tougher and more gray-green. Flowers larger, nonfragrant. Sepals acute, with appressed hairs. Blooms from July to September. z7

R. trichocalyx see **R. coulteri** var. **trichocalyx**

R. × vandedenii hort. (*R. coulteri × R. coulteri* var. *trichocalyx*). Intermediate between the parents. 'White Cloud' is a selection from the USA. z7 (E.)

able conditions. *Romulea* has the disadvantage of opening its flowers only in sunlight. Growing in the moderate greenhouse is generally problem-free. The following species is the hardiest, not reliably hardy in cold winter climates. z7

R. bulbocodium (L.) Sebast. et Mauri. Mediterranean region. Leaves limp, 2–several, 10–25cm long, nearly thread-like or rounded, emerging before the flowers. Scape 5–12cm long, wiry, with succulent green valves. Pale to bright lilac, yellow-throated, March to April. Requires a sunny, warm, protected site with additional winter covering, and well-drained, loose, sandy soil. Flower perianth of 6 segments about 2.5cm long, broadly funnel-shaped; stamens 3, anthers appressed to the slender style; stigma with 3 strongly horizontal lobes.

Other species for greenhouse or garden

long, split, the 2 lobes petal-like, subtending the corolla lobes; corolla long-tubular, inflated above, with 3 lobes, the dorsal lobe erect, incurved, the lateral lobes smaller, spreading or recurved. Early summer to fall. Grow in a fertile peat loam or woodland humus in full sun or dappled semi-shade, in a not too dry site in the wildflower or rock garden. Plant the rootstock at least 10cm deep in spring. Mulch plants heavily in the fall to successfully overwinter and eventually develop vigorous, multiple-stemmed clumps. Some species will self-seed under favorable conditions. The new growth normally appears very late, often in late May. Highly desirable plants for collectors. Propagate by seed and division.

R. alpina Royle. Himalaya Mts.; Kashmir, Nepal. Leaves usually 3, oblong-lanceolate, to lanceolate, 10–20cm long, emerging fully as flowers fade. Scape 10–20cm high. Flowers exceed the leaves, purple, tube white; July to August. Not showy, but choice, especially in the small rock garden. z6(5)

R. × beesiana hort. is reputed to be a hybrid between *R. purpurea* and *R. humeana* but as these both are purple-flowered and the flowers of this plant are yellow, purple-striped, possibly it is related to *R. cautleoides* var. *beesii*. z6

R. cautleoides Gagnep. W. China (Yunnan, Sichuan). Leaves usually

Romneya coulteri

sessile, to 15cm long, 2.5cm wide, lanceolate to oblong-lanceolate, gray-green or green. Scape 40–60cm high. The 4cm-wide, pale yellow flowers appear with the new foliage in June. The earliest species, very attractive, of slender habit. Somewhat variable in flower color, bloom period and ultimate height. 'Grandiflora' is particularly attractive, a good yellow cultivar, and not quite so tall. z6

R. humeana Balf.f. et W.W. Sm. W. China, W. Yunnan. Rootstock spindle-shaped. Leaves 4–6, usually matured at flowering, broadly lanceolate, glabrous, 10–20cm long, sessile. Scape 20–30cm high. Flowers 4–8, 7cm across, lilac-purple; July. A beautiful species. z7

R. purpurea Sm. (*R. sikkimensis* hort.). E. Himalaya Mts., Sikkim. Leaves 5–6, sessile, narrow-lanceolate, long-slender-pointed, emerging from 2 sheaths. Scape 20–30cm high. Flowers purple; August to September. The most vigorous and hardiest, but not the most attractive species. z5

R. purpurea Sm. var. **procera** (Lindl.) Wall. Himalaya Mts. Scapes taller, 30–40cm high. Flowers much larger than the species, lilac, white-striped; July to August. Very attractive, large and late-flowering species. z6 (Sch.& S.)

R. sikkimensis see **R. purpurea**

Romulea bulbocodium

Rosularia (DC.) Stapf
Crassulaceae

About 25 species from Asia Minor to Central Asia; only a few are cultivated. This genus of succulents was once included in *Umbilicus*, some species in *Cotyledon*. Rapidly growing, evergreen leafy rosettes, resembling *Sempervivum*. Rootstock tuberous. Leaves rosetted, sessile, flat and broad. Flowering stems mostly emerge laterally, the inflorescence more or less panicled. Flowers tubular with flaired limb, calyx and corolla 5 or 6 part, stamens 10–12; pistil erect. Not particularly decorative, but interesting for the collector of succulents. Requires dry pockets in the rock garden or trough, in full sun to light shade. Some species are very sensitive to wetness and are best kept in the alpine house with other succulents. Propagation is easy by division.

R. aizoon (Fenzl) Berger (*Umbilicus aizoon* Fenzl, *Cotyledon aizoon* (Fenzl) Schönl). Anatolia. Dense rosettes with

1cm-long, tongue-shaped, softly ciliate leaves, sparsely flowered. Flowers yellow. July. z6

R. chrysantha see **R. pallida**

R. pallida (Schott et Kotschy) Stapf (*R. chrysantha* (Boiss et Heldr.) Takht., *Umbilicus chrysanthus* Boiss. et Heldr.). Anatolia. Rosettes crowded into a spreading mat. Leaves 1.2–1.8cm long, spatulate, densely gray-hairy. Flowering stems to 20cm high; flowers large, cream-white, in loose cymes; June to July. z6

R. persica. Plants cultivated under this name are actually a vigorous form of *Sempervirens calcareum*. Found in English catalogs as 'Grigg's Surprise'.

R. platyphylla (Schrenk) Bgr. Central E. Turkey. Plants offered in the trade are usually a local form from the Mural Dag mountain. Rosettes of smooth to hairy-glandular, fleshy leaves; short lateral spikes of white flowers. Requires some winter protection. z7

R. radiciflora (Steud.) A. Borris. Turkey. Somewhat variable. The rosette leaves are pubescent and the small yellow flowers appear on lateral stems which are pubescent. The rosettes exhibit a summer dormancy period unique to this species. z6 (Sch.& Kö.)

Other *Rosularia* species occasionally encountered are: *R. glabra, R. globulariae-folia, R. sempervivum, R. serrata* and *R. turkestanica*, etc.; as these occur in areas of persistent armed conflict, they seem to be disappearing from occidental collections.

Rubia L.
Rubiaceae

R. tinctorum L. Madder. S. Europe and Asia Minor. A popular and ancient dye plant resembling Bedstrew (*Galium*) with whorled, lanceolate leaves and sprawling, rough stems, over 2m-long. Inconspicuous, yellowish flowers in summer and black berries in fall. Suitable for covering herb garden walls with summer greenery, but not particularly decorative. Easily grown from seed, also propagated by division. The brick-red dye, alizarin, now synthesized, was once prepared from Madder roots. z6(5) (Sch.)

Rubus L.
Rosaceae
Raspberry, Blackberry

A few suffruticose perennials are of interest in this primarily shrubby genus of 250 species. The genus is cosmopolitan, especially distributed throughout the North Temperate Zone, but also found in the tropics and subtropics. *R. chamaemorus* requires a lime-free acid soil, best cultivated between a layer of live sphagnum moss and peat soil. *R. arcticus* is somewhat more easily

N. America, reaching south to Newfoundland, Manitoba and Alberta; on rocky tundra, in thickets and forests. It spreads underground vigorously, and is 10–20cm high with simple, 3-lobed or ternate leaves. Flowers are solitary or several at the shoot tips, appearing the entire summer. The pink flowers are followed by a raspberrylike fruit, which is quite decorative in the fall. Probably some New World material is the very similar species *R. stellatus* Sm. z1

R. calycinoides Hayata (*R. fockeanus* hort.). Taiwan, at 2300-3600m. 3 to 5cm

Europe and into NW. Czechoslovakia, in N. America south to Maine, Manitoba and British Columbia. Found in bogs in sphagnum peat and on moist heaths. Creeping underground; leafy stems erect, 8–20cm high. Leaves simple, cordate-ovate, 5-lobed. Flowers terminal, solitary, white. Fruits orange to red, edible. Flowers in summer. Difficult to cultivate. z1

R. fockeanus see **R. calycinoides**

R. illecebrosus Focke. Strawberry-raspberry. Japan; in thickets and on

Rosularia pallida

Roscoea humeana

cultivated, growing as a more or less dense ground cover under suitable conditions. Requires acidic humus soil mixed with lime-free gravel. Combines well with *Empetrum, Vaccinium myrtillus* and *V. vitis-idaea*, in full sun to semishade. An entirely different species, *R. illecebrosus*, takes readily to any shaded, deep garden soil. Its vigorously spreading underground stolons may be troublesome, but it is generally trouble-free when planted among woody plants. All three species are easily propagated by division, also by cuttings.

R. arcticus L. Crimson Bramble, Arctic Bramble. N. Europe, Arctic N. Asia and

high. Stems, more or less woody, procumbent, creeping and rooting. Leaves short-petioled, 3–4cm, rounded-cordate, shallowly 3-lobed, rugose, evergreen, glossy dark green above, gray-tomentose beneath. Flowers white, solitary or paired at the shoot tips, fruits scarlet red, 1.5cm wide; flowers and fruits rarely. Attractive and interesting ground cover in a somewhat shaded rock garden site; requires winter protection. Especially handsome creeping up and over a large fissured boulder. Propagation is easy by division and cuttings. z7

R. chamaemorus L. Cloudberry, Salmonberry. Circumpolar, scattered in S.

wasteland. Subshrub or perennial with long, underground, creeping rhizomes. Canes 20–60cm high, erect-prickly. Leaves pinnate. Flowers white, to 4cm in diameter, in terminal, few-or many-flowered corymbs. Fruits nearly round or broadly elliptic, scarlet-red, edible, but insipid, showy. Flowers from July to September. z5

Rudbeckia L.
Compositae
Coneflower

A N. American genus of 25–30 species, named by Linnaeus in honor of his teacher, Olaf Rudbeck. Many species annual or grown as annuals, some perennial. The perennial species are medium-high to tall plants with strong, low-branching upright stems and usually yellow flower heads in summer and fall. Flower heads large with a high-domed, conical, usually black-brown disc.

All the perennial rudbeckias are effective summer border plants, producing fine cut flowers. The most common is the prairie coneflower and its cultivar

'Goldsturm', surpassing many similar rudbeckias in its beauty. The tall growing *R. laciniata* is particularly suitable for the large perennial border, but is also effective as a specimen or grouped with other midsummer-blooming perennials. It is especially attractive near water. All species thrive in any good garden soil, given sufficient moisture during anthesis. Propagation is by division or cuttings with root pieces attached, and by seed scattered in spring.

R. californica A. Gray. California Coneflower. USA: California, in the

Rubus illecebrosus

Sierra Nevada Mts. Fibrous roots below a small crown. Stems to 1.5m high, branching above. Leaves simple, sparsely hairy, lower leaves petioled, broadly lanceolate to oblanceolate, toothed; upper leaves sessile, clasping, entire. Flower heads large, to 10cm across, disc conic-columnary, flowers greenish-yellow, ray flowers bright yellow, spreading. z6 And var. **glauca** S.F. Blake, N. California, S. Oregon, in open forests. Leaves glaucous, glabrous.

R. columnaris see **Ratibida columnifera**

R. columnifera see **Ratibida columnifera**

R. deamii see **R. fulgida** var. **deamii**

R. fulgida Ait. A variable species from the E. USA, varietal differences usually

foliar. Rootstock rhizomatous. Stems 0.4–1m high. Leaves simple, more or less hairy, lower leaves long-petioled, lanceolate to ovate, entire, toothed or crenate, upper leaves stem-clasping, 3-veined; disc short-conic, flowered brown-purple ray flowers orange-yellow, spreading. z4 Var. *fulgida*, New Jersey to Illinois south to N. Alabama with 2–3cm long ray florets. Basal leaves narrowly lanceolate to oblanceolate.

R. fulgida var. **deamii** (S.F. Blake) Perdue (*R. deamii* S.F. Blake). Indiana. 0.8–1m high. Lower leaves long-petioled, broadly elliptic to ovate, acuminate, coarsely crenate or serrate, short-haired, stem leaves with small, well-spaced teeth. Stems branched, rough-haired. Very floriferous and desirable; drought tolerant.

R. fulgida var. **speciosa** (Wender.) Perdue (*R. speciosa* Wender., *R. newmanii* Loud.). New Jersey to Missouri, south to Georgia and Alabama. Basal leaves many, entire or obscurely crenate; stem leaves coarsely serrate or lacerate. A very popular border and cut flower plant but surpassed today by the related cultivar 'Goldsturm' but this variety is more persistent, with longer-lasting flowers. z4

R. fulgida var. **sullivantii** (Boynton et Beadle) Cronq. (*R. sullivantii* (Boynton et Beadle). Connecticut to West Virginia

west to Michigan and Missouri. Lower leaves wider and less pubescent, dark green, dull-glazed, coarsely dentate; stem leaves successively smaller, the uppermost bract-like. Ray flower ligules longer than those of the other varieties, 2.5–5m long, golden-yellow. Two attractive cultivars of this variety, 'Goldsturm' and 'Oraile', with 12cm-wide, rich golden-yellow flower heads, are generally cultivated; prominent border perennials.

R. grandiflora (Sweet) DC. USA: Missouri and Oklahoma to Louisiana and Texas. Rhizomatous rootstock. Stems to 90cm high. Lower leaves long petioled, ovate-acute; upper leaves sessile, smaller. Heads 1 or few on a long peduncle; disc conic, florets brown-purple; ray flowers yellow, drooping, 3.5–7cm long. Very showy. z6(5)

R. hirta L. Black-eyed Susan. E. USA, naturalized in most of North America. Annual to short-lived perennials. Roots fibrous. Stems to 90cm high, branched. Leaves simple, lower leaves petioled, upper leaves sessile, hairy. Disc domed, florets brown-purple; ray flowers spreading, yellow, to 3.5cm long. Summer-flowering. z4 Var. **hirta**, Appalachian Mts., Maine to Georgia west to Illinois. Leaves coarsely toothed, upper leaves ovate, var. **pulcherrima**, middle western states. Leaves entire or fine-serrate, upper leaves oblanceolate to linear. Ray flowers often banded maroon, or multiple. The parent of the tetraploid Gloriosa Daisies.

R. laciniata L. N. America: Quebec to Florida, west to Montana and New Mexico. Rootstock a woody crown with stolons. Stems to over 2m high or more. Basal leaves pinnate, leaflets deeply lobed; stem leaves 3-lobed, glaucous green, rarely glabrous. Stems branch only toward the top. Flower heads pale yellow, ray florets slightly drooping; conical disc greenish yellow. July to September. The wild form, usually found on moist sites, is rarely cultivated. More commonly cultivated is the double cultivar 'Golden Glow' (= 'Hortensia'), found by a J. L. Childs and listed by Bailey as early as 1894. The plant was distributed worldwide within a few decades because of its ease of cultivation and rhizome propagation. It is different in habit, invasive and aphid-prone, and often replaced today with the lower cultivars such as: 'Goldquelle' (Golden Fountain) (Benary/Walther 1963), lemon yellow, double, 70cm high; 'Gold-kugel' (Golden Globe) (Pötschke/

Walther 1963), golden yellow double form, 1.6m high, somewhat poorly received because of its stiff habit, slow growth and susceptibility to slug damage. An older single-flowered cultivar, 'Soleil d'Or', with broad, showy rays, has all but vanished. *R. laciniata* var. **humilis** L. H. Gray (*R. laevigata* Pursh), only 30–60cm high, from the mountains of Virginia, Kentucky to Georgia and Tennessee, is as yet rarely cultivated. z4

R. laevigata see **R. laciniata** var. **humilis**

R. maxima Nutt. N. America: Missouri south to Louisiana and Texas; mostly in pine forests. Stems 2 (to 3)m high. Leaves simple, glabrous glaucous, gray-green, ovate to elliptic, entire, the upper leaves sessile, partly stem-clasping. Flower heads large, ray flower ligules drooping, 5cm long, yellow; disc conical-cylindrical, blackish; August to September. An attractive but coarse, wild perennial for a moist, bright situation among woody plants. z6

R. newmanii see **R. fulgida** var. **speciosa**

R. nitida Nutt. N. America: Georgia to Florida and Texas, on moist sites. Not in cultivation; plants listed under this name in horticulture are selections of *R. laciniata*. Stems to 1m high; similar to *R. laciniata*, but the leathery, light green, glossy leaves are not incised, but entire, dentate. Flower heads large, golden-yellow; ray flowers drooping, disc green, conical. Frost tender; z9(8)
The 2m-high cultivar 'Herbstsonne'

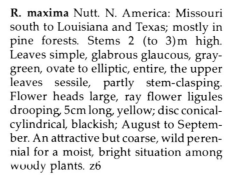

Rudbeckia nitida

(Autumn Sun) is bright yellow, single, probably a cross with *R. laciniata* or an *R. laciniata* cultivar 'Juligold' (July Gold) (Weihenstephan, before 1960). A chance seedling and perhaps a natural hybrid. Golden yellow, single, 1.8–2m high, July to August. Valued for its early flowering period. z7

R. purpurea see **Echinacea purpurea**

R. pallida see **Echinacea pallida**

R. pinnata see **Ratibida pinnata**

R. speciosa see **R. fulgida** var. **speciosa**

R. sullivantii see **R. fulgida** var **sullivantii** (Sch.& M.)

Rudbeckia fulgida **var.** *deamii*

R. tagetes see **Ratibida tagetes**

Several additional *Rudbeckia* species grow wild in North America but are not presently in cultivation, though they attract attention when flowering in prairie and plains preserves.

Ruellia L.
Acanthaceae

About 250 species of perennial herbs or shrubs, most in tropical America, Africa or Asia, a few in temperate regions of N. America. Stems of hardy herbaceous species simple or sparingly branched. Leaves opposite, sessile or petioled, mostly simple, entire. Flowers usually large and conspicuous, solitary or in axillary cymes or terminal panicles. Fruit a capsule with 4–20 seeds which are thrown free when the capsule breaks open. Many tender species are attractive flowering plants for the greenhouse. Only *R. strepens* and a few other as yet unintroduced North American species are reasonably winter hardy. *R. strepens* is normally found only in botanic gardens, but is also recommended for collectors. Requires protection from winter wetness, sometimes freezes out nonetheless. Collect the abundantly set seed for possible replacement plants. Sow seeds in March in the greenhouse and set plants into the garden in May. Young plants will flower in the first summer, growing best under an open canopy of woody plants in dryish, sandy, humus soil. Cuttings are possible in a heated bed.

R. strepens L. USA: New Jersey to Kansas, south to South Carolina and Texas; bordering dry, open woodlands and in open meadows. Stems to 90cm high. A pubescent to furry perennial with petioled, to 15cm-long, ovate to oval-lanceolate leaves. Flowers sessile, several in axillary clusters. Corolla to 5cm long, light blue or violet. Flowers from August to September. Due to the nature of the woody rhizome, this plant can become a hard to eradicate pest in a warm climate. Hardy North American ruellias include *R. cardiniensis*, and var. *dentata*; *R. lumilis* with several varieties; *R. pedunculosa*, and *R. purshiana*. None are of exceptional ornamental merit. z6 (E.)

Rumex L.
Polygonaceae
Dock, Sorrel

More than 100 perennial species distributed throughout the temperate world but only a few are suitable for ornamental plantings. Only *R. alpinus* is suitable for the natural garden. Grows easily from seed.

R. alpinus L. Monk's Rhubarb, Mountain Rhubarb. Grows in the high mountains of Central and S. Europe to the

Rupicapnos africana

Caucasus region and Armenia. A typical plant of alpine and tall grass meadows; quite effective in the alpine garden in front of Mugo Pines, but only suitable for large sites. Stout-rooted perennial. Stems to 1m high with few leaves and a terminal panicle. Basal leaves large, ovate-cordate. Flowers many, white, in a showy inflorescence. Young leaves of culinary value. Blooms from July to August. z5

R. flexuosus Soland. ex Hook. f. New Zealand. Stems slender, flexuous, procumbent-ascending, 20–45cm high. Leaves linear to lanceolate, undulate. Entire plant copper-colored. Conspicuous for its unusual habit and unique coloration. Suitable for exotic garden effects with *Carex buchananii*, *Acaena*, *Yucca*, *Opuntia*, etc. Self-seeds without becoming invasive. Should be considered only for collectors. Some winter protection is advisable. June to July. z7(6)

R. hydrolapathum Huds. Giant Water Dock. Central and S. Europe, on stream and pond banks. Clumps with oblong-lanceolate leaves to 60cm long. Stems to 2m high, with very large, reddish-brown, terminal inflorescence. A good waterside plant for the large garden, with an effective, bronze-red fall color. z6 (Sch.)

Rupicapnos Pomel
Fumariaceae

About 32 quite variable, evergreen species of nearly stemless herbaceous perennials in the mountains of Spain

Ruta graveolens

and N. Africa. Similar to *Fumaria* or *Corydalis*, with bluish gray pinnate leaves with pinnatisect leaflets, and floriferous, subcorymbose racemes. Flowers with 2 sepals, 4 petals, the lower petal separate, the uppermost petal spurred. An excellent inhabitant of rock crevices.

Blooms from May to October. Plant in rock crevices, best in calcareous soil. Grows only in warmer climates unless well sheltered. Best for pot culture in an alpine house. An attractive collector's plant, conspicuous for its long flowering period. Propagates only by seed. Abundantly self-seeding. z8

R. africana Pomel. S. Spain, N. Africa. Quite a variable species. Leaves basal, pinnate, bluish-pruinose and somewhat fleshy, segments ovate, oblong or linear. Racemes in the leaf axils, short, capitate at first, later pedicels elongate, with fruits and flowers. Flowers about 13mm long, quite variable in color; rose-purple with dark purple tips, pink or deep rose, or white, mostly with darker markings. z8 (K.)

Ruta L.
Rutaceae
Rue

About 40 species of pungent or aromatic perennials and subshrubs ranging from

Rumex alpinus

the Canary Islands and the Mediterranean region to SW. Asia. Leaves alternate, 2–3 part pinnatisect, glandular punctate. Inflorescence a terminal corymb or panicle. Flowers yellowish, with 4 sepals, 4 petals, hoodlike, usually dentate or fimbricate, with 8 or 10 stamens.

Usually poisonous medicinal and herb plants of old country gardens, but little used today, though some are suitable for today's gardens. Many people suffer severe reactions when plants of this genus come in direct contact with the skin. In addition to the herb garden, also for dry slopes in the wild garden. Undemanding plants which grow in most garden soils, given a dry, sunny site. Plants may be cut back to old wood in spring. Propagate by seed and cuttings. Particularly attractive when combined with *Alyssum argenteum*, *Anthyllis vulneraria*, *Carlina*, *Iris pumila*, *Sedum album*, *Thymus serpyllum*, *Petror-*

hagia saxifraga, and taller plants such as *Anthericum liliago* and *Asphodelus* as well as grasses such as *Stipa*.

R. patavina see **Haplophyllum patavinum**

R. suaveolens see **Haplophyllum patavinum**

R. graveolens L., Common Rue, Herb-of-Grace (for its medicinal use as an aborting agent). Balkan Peninsula and Crimea, possibly indigenous elsewhere in the Mediterranean region, naturalized

Sagittaria sagittifolia

in many areas; occurs naturally on dry, warm, rocky slopes, on screes and rocky plains. Stems 30–90cm high, woody at the base; aromatic perennial or subshrub with blue-green, 2- to 3-pinnate leaves and loose cymose inflorescence with yellow flowers 20mm across. Bloom from May to July. Modern cultivars include: 'Jackman's Blue', more compact, 45–60cm high, with showy, bluish, glaucous foliage; 'Variegata', leaves irregularly splotched creamy yellow. And var. **divaricata** (Ten.) Willk., leaves yellow green with linear-lanceolate segments. Ancient medicinal

plant, popular in the Middle Ages, still used today to a limited degree in veterinary medicine; poisonous, causing a rash and itching upon contact with susceptible persons. Several other *Ruta* species grow in z8(7) gardens including: *R. chalepensis*, *R. divaricata*, and *R. suaveolens*. z5 (E.)

Rydbergia

R. grandiflora see **Hymenoxys grandiflora**

Saccharum

S. floridulum see **Miscanthus floridus**

Sagina L.
Caryophyllaceae
Pearlwort

Twenty to twenty-five species of mat-forming annuals and perennials, many weedy, from cool temperate and Arctic regions of the Northern Hemisphere southward in the mountains to Mexico and Chile, and Central Africa mountains. Leaves minute, awl-shaped or filiform, flowers tiny, white, pediceled, in few flowered umbels; sepals and petals 5 or 4, stamens 4, 5, 8 or 10, carpels 5 or 4 unlike the very similar *Minuartia*. Garden species are moss-like, suitable for pavement crevices, on banks and in the rock garden. All are intolerant of summer heat or drought.

S. boydii (Aut.incog.) Scotland. A dense, flat, dark, evergreen cushion. Stems prostrate, rooting. Leaves awl-shaped, to 18cm long, strongly recurved, mucro-

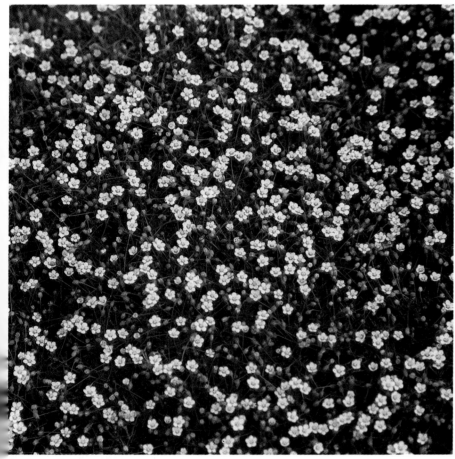

Sagina subulata

nate, glabrous. Flowers insignificant. This rare Scottish native is difficult to grow and therefore a popular challenge among alpine garden specialists. z5

S. × normaniana Lagerh. A naturally occurring hybrid, *S. procumbens* × *S. subulata*, found in Europe where the parent species grow together; usually the seed is not viable. Plant a mat of rosettes with leaves to 2.5cm long. The flowers are solitary or paired, on pedicels to 3.25cm high. Rather more open habit than *S. subulata*. z6(5)

S. subulata (Sw.) K.B. Presl. SW. and

Central Europe to Sweden and Norway. A well-branched cushion plant, forming a dense carpet, with awl-shaped, dark evergreen leaves and white flowers; June to August. A unique, mosslike groundcover for the rock garden. The most horticulturally important species of the genus; the short, rich green mats are good fillers between stepping stones and on terrace walls. The golden yellow form 'Aurea' is less common. Both perform best on a somewhat sandy, but not too dry soil. Propagate quickly and easily by division; the green form is also grown from seed. z4 (Sch. & M.)

Other Pearlworts occasionally encountered in collectors' rock gardens include *S. glabra*, *S. linnaea*, *S. pilifera* and the unreliably persistent *S. procumbens*.

Sagittaria L.
Alismataceae
Arrowhead

More than 20 species of sometimes tuberous, herbaceous, stoloniferous, monoecious plants, mostly perennial, in bogs or shallow water. Leaves thick and long-petioled, basal, elliptic-lanceolate or sagittate, submerged leaves straplike, often translucently striped or punctate. Flower stems erect, flowers mostly in whorls of 3, in spikes or panicles, terminal flowers often staminate, the lower ones pistillate or hermaphroditic; sepals 3, green, petals 3, white, stamens 4 to many, simple pistils many, spirally arranged on the receptacle. Indigenous to tropical and temperate zones of the world, particularly in America.

Very decorative aquatic plants for water to 40cm deep. Best combined with other plants, such as *Butomus* and various ornamental *Typha* species which complement, but do not detract from the effect of the *Sagittaria*. These grow in most riparian soils. Propagation is easiest by stolons, which often are so abundant their spread must be limited. Seed is often self-sown or can be sown right after ripening into pots kept in shallow trays of standing water; germinate readily. When transplanting the seedlings, the crowns of the plants must be kept in water. Many hardy arrowheads overwinter by more or less large tubers, considered a delicacy in China.

S. chinensis see **S. latifolia**

S. gracilis see **S. latifolia**

S. graminea Michx., Grassleaved Arrowhead. N. America: from Newfoundland to South Dakota, south to Florida and Texas. An elegant species. Underwater leaves 30cm long, oblong, straplike, about 1.5–2cm wide. Surface leaves linear, lanceolate, elliptic, or broadly ovate, long-petioled, thin-membranous. Flowers similar to *S. sagittifolia*. Overwinters as an ovate, brown tuber. Not hardy in shallow water. Several botanical varieties are listed. z4–10

S. hastata see **S. latifolia**

S. latifolia Willd. (*S. gracilis* Pursh, *S. hastata* Pursh, *S. simplex* Pursh, *S. sagittifolia* auct.non L., *S. chinensis* Pursh), Duck Potato, Wapato, Broadleaved Arrowhead. N. America. Species with numerous varieties and cultivars. Scapes 30–120cm high. Forms stolons and tubers. Petioles long, 3- to several-angled in cross-section. Leaf blades quite variable in form and size, mostly broadly sagittate, occasionally lanceolate, but sometimes also narrow and straplike. In deep water the leaves are narrow and acute, in shallower water or swampy sites, broad and obtuse. Flowers 3–4cm wide, petals rounded, white, stamens yellow, June to August. Overwintering tuber pinkish to bluish. Northern strains are recommended for cool climate gardens; these require 20cm of water depth. The cultivar 'Flore Pleno', with very double white flowers, is scarcely more beautiful than the single-flowered species. z5–10

S. sagittifolia L., Arrowhead, Swamp Potato, Swan Potato. Indigenous to Europe and Asia. Rootstock tuberous, plants also stoloniferous. Leaves basal, the submerged leaves linear in springtime or in deep water, 10–80cm

Salvia lavandulifolia

long, to 2cm wide. Emerged leaves of similar length, erect, to 40cm high, long-petioled, hastate to sagittate; leaf form variable. Slender-leaved forms with linear basal lobes as well as broad-leaved specimens are found. The deep-water leaves are narrow and acute, in shallow, swampy sites, wider and more obtuse. Flower scapes 0.2–1m high, reaching about ⅓ above the leaves, triangular in cross-section. Flowers in loose, whorled spikes, 3-part, pistillate, 11–15mm across; the staminate flowers 20–25mm across, white with a purplish spot at the base of each petal. Anthers brownish-violet, June to August. Winter tubers green-blue marked, walnut-sized. 'Flore Pleno', double flowering, white, petals brown-red on the base. 'Leucopetala', petals pure white. 'Leucopetala Plena', double, pure white. z5–10 (D.)

S. simplex see **S. latifolia**

Numerous wild or escaped species of *Sagittaria* appear in water gardens, apparently transported by waterfowl. Species so encountered include: *S. cuneata, S. engelmanniana, S. longiloba* and *S. subulata*, all reasonably hardy. Less hardy sorts may appear over summer following the spring northward waterfowl migration but these freeze out with the coming of winter.

Salvia nemorosa 'Mainacht'

Salvia L.
Labiatae
Sage

A large genus comprising about 800 species of annual, perennial, and woody, mostly aromatic plants. Most are perennial and suffruticose with opposite, reticulately veined, variably formed leaves. Leaves often clustered into false rosettes on the perennial species. Flowers usually attractive, in densely whorled or interrupted false racemes or

false spikes in summer. Indigenous to the temperate and warm zones nearly throughout the world. Their primary ranges are Central America (mostly woody to subshrubby, non-winter-hardy species) and SW. Asia. Most of the following species of sage are from the wild, best suited for the natural or rock garden. Nearly all grow best in full sun and a limy soil; often collectors' plants, only *S. × superba* has general garden merit as an undemanding border perennial. Propagate by seed, cuttings and division.

S. argentea L. (*S. candidissima* Guss.), Silver Sage. S. Europe, eastward to Bulgaria, N. Africa. Leaves to 15cm long, oval, entire, densely shaggy, silvery-silky-pubescent, forming a large, showy, silvery-white rosette. Inflorescences broadly pyramidal, 50–80cm high; flowers white with a yellow, rarely pinkish, lip; June to July. A beautiful foliage plant, especially attractive in the morning dew; usually lives only 2–3 years, often dying out after flowering unless the inflorescence is not quickly removed. Very effective with drought tolerant dwarf woody plants and sub-shrubs such as lavender, *Perovskia, Salvia officinalis* and *Santolina* as well as other heat-loving perennials such as *Echinops ritro, Nepeta* × *faassenii* and *Salvia* × *superba*. Easily grown from seed, self-seeds on favorable sites. This salvia requires fast drainage and loose, gravelly soil. z5

S. azurea Blue Sage. USA: central Canadian Border southward to Kentucky, Arkansas and Texas. A narrowly upright perennial from a basal cluster of leaves; stems branched mostly above (responds to being cut back in early summer), .5–2m high, glabrous to glabrescent. Lower leaves lanceolate, 5–8cm long, serrate, petioled; upper leaves smaller, narrow to linear. Inflorescence a false spike on each stem or branch, corolla tube 2cm long, lower lip large, azure blue, rarely white. Var. **grandiflora** Benth. (*S. pitcheri* Torr. ex Benth.) range approximately that of the species. Flowers much larger; showy light blue perennials for full sun in fertile, well-drained loam. z4

S. bulleyana see **S. flava**

S. candelabrum Boiss. S. Spain. Stems 50–60cm high, woody at the base; 4-angled, red brown below, green above, sparsely branched. Leaves petioled, oval, caudate-sinuate and coarsely crenate. Flowers violet-blue with broad white midstripes on the lips, calyx reddish brown; July to August. z7

S. candidissima see **S. argentea**

S. elegans Vahl. (*S. rutilans* Carriére). Pineapple Sage. Mexico. Suffruticose perennial to shrub-like in mild, hot climates, to 1.5m high, an almost globose, dense, dark green plant. Stems with branches at every node and with sub-surface runners spreading widely below. Leaves ovate-lanceolate, 5–10cm long, petiolate, serrate, pubescent to hairy, intensely pineapple-scented when bruised. Flowers in long, false spikes, terminal on all stems and branches; flowers arranged in whorls, mostly 4-flowered. Corolla tube to 3.5cm long with divided limb, the lower lip reflexed, intense ruby-red. Where winters are mild, flowering begins in midsummer; where tops freeze back new growth, to 1m high by midsummer, begins to flower in late summer, continuing until killing frost or late November. Root hardy in a sheltered site, as against a hot, south-facing wall, to z6, but generally hardy z8(7). A highly desirable, late-flowering perennial beloved for its fragrant foliage and spec-tacular year end floral display; a good tub plant. Easy from cuttings or from seed which is seldom offered. The precise classification of this species is in question; many botanists retain it in *S. rutilans*.

S. flava G. Forst. China. Stems mostly unbranched, 40–90cm high. Leaves mostly basal, ovate-triangular to ovate, cordate, rugose, bright green, glossy, to 12.5cm long. Flowers yellow with a violet-blue lip; July. Requires light semi-shade. The precise classification of this little-known species is not established.

Salvia sclarea

Europeans generally refer it to *S. bulleyana;* apparently it is not yet grown in North America. z6

S. glutinosa L. Jupiter's Distaff. Europe to SW. Asia; in open mountain forests. Upright stems 0.8–1.2m high, hairy below, glandular-sticky above, 4-angled, leafy to the inflorescence. Leaves cordate-hastate to ovate, coarsely toothed, dull green, to 20cm long. Flowers pale sulphur yellow, red-brown striped, in clustered false racemes; July to September; the calyx is especially glandular-pubescent. Especially well suited for woodland margins in large gardens and parks; very long-lived and persistent. z5

S. greggii A. Gray. Autumn Sage. Texas and Mexico. Sub-shrubby to perennial, to 90cm tall. Stems with recurved hairs or glaucous. Leaves small, to 2.5cm long, oblong to spatulate, round-tipped or mucronate, entire, more or less glaucous. Inflorescence racemose. Flowers about 2.5cm long with large lower lip, rosy-red; very showy. September to November. And cultivars 'Alba', with white flowers and 'Rosea', pinkish-rose flowers. z8(7) Valuable for late flowers.

S. grandiflora Etling. (*S. officinalis* L. ssp. *major* Gams). Especially similar to *S. officinalis*, also a woody shrub, but with large and wide leaves with cordate base. Flowers large; June to August. Less winter-hardy. z7

S. haematodes see **S. pratensis** var. **haematodes**

S. hians Royle. Kashmir. Stems 60–90cm high, erect, sticky-pubescent. Leaves long-petioled, cordate to sagittate, gray tomentose. Inflorescence much branched; flowers large, pale blue, in loose, 6-flowered whorls; June to July. z6

S. jurisicii Kos. Macedonia. Stems 25–30cm high, procumbent-ascending, branched. Leaves pinnate with 4–6 pairs of narrow-linear leaflets, gray-green. Inflorescence open, much branched. Flowers light violet-blue, pubescent, usually twisted, so that the small, 3-cleft lip points upward; June to September. The white-flowering form 'Alba' is also attractive. Charming, undemanding, small, bushy, long-flowering species for the rock garden. z6

S. lavandulifolia Vahl. Spanish Sage. (*S. officinalis* L. ssp. *lavandulifolia* Gams). S. Central and E. Spain, S. France, NW. Africa. Stems woody to herbaceous, 20–30cm high. Closely related to *S. officinalis*, with a more compact, denser habit and smaller, narrower leaves. Flowers in small spikes, 6–8 in each umbel; calyx usualy bright red-purple, corolla to 2.5cm long, blue or violet-blue. Reasonably winter-hardy; also for dry stone walls. z5

S. nemorosa L. Central, SE. and E. Europe, SW. Asia. Rootstock short and

Very attractive, broad, bushy perennials, particularly for warm, sunny sites next to yellow achilleas, such as the low-growing *Achillea clypeolata* and taller *A. filipendulina* 'Coronation Gold', potentillas and *Papaver orientale*. The densely bushy form 'East Friesland' (Ostfriesland) (Pagels 1955) is highly regarded, 40cm high, violet; and the mid-May flowering 'May Night' (Mainacht) (Foerster 1956), 50cm high, with somewhat larger, black-blue flowers. Some of the better, recent hybrids by E. Pagels include: 'Blue Mound' (Blauhügel), 50cm high, pure

effective. More unique than attractive, it is easily recognized by its limp-nodding racemes. z5

S. officinalis L., Garden Salvia. S. Europe. 30–60cm high; bushy, evergreen, aromatic subshrub. Leaves elliptic to oblong, 2.5–7cm long, petioled, rugose, gray-green, woolly on both sides, tough. Stems ascending, woody and 4-angled or round below, nearly round above. False spikes slender; flowers lilac-blue; June to August. Well-known, historically cultivated culinary and medicinal plant. Also ornamental,

Salvia officinalis 'Tricolor'

Sanguinaria canadensis 'Multiplex'

firm, without leaf rosettes. Stems ascending, to 80cm high, usually red-violet, often more branched toward the apex. Leaves short-petioled, ovate-lanceolate, rugose, dull green. Flowers small, violet, in at first dense, later loose, false spikes; June to July. Rare in cultivation in Europe, not grown in North America. Quite a variable wildling of little garden merit; its reputed hybrids are incomparably better. According to recent, perhaps dubious, information, the cultivars are offspring of the pure species, but the more acceptable theory assigns them hybrid origin. The hybrids generally go by the collective name of S. × *superba* Stapf (*S. nemorosa* × *S. villicaulis*). The false spikes are slender and floriferous, the flowers short-pediceled, small, and dark to light blue-violet; calyx and bracts reddish brown; May to August. Untiring violet-blue bloomers, from summer to fall. Good bee-attracting plants. Plants bloomed out in July or August may be cut back to encourage a new flush of flowering growth.

blue; 'Negrito', 40cm high, blue; and 'Rügen', 40cm high, blue. An earlier form of 'May Night' is 'Viola Klose' (Klose), 40cm, dark blue. 'Blue Queen' (Blaukönigin) (Benary), 40cm, blue-violet, is a seed-propagated, compact-growing form. These are superb perennials for the sunny border in regions with cool or moderate summers; where summers are hot they bloom early and fairly briefly, then tend to go leggy with dead foliage at the base. *Salvia patens* is a reasonable substitute. z5

S. nutans L. SE. Europe to Central Russia. Stem 0.3–1m high, coarsely branched, from a rosette of large, rugose leaves, erect, 4-angled, strigose-hairy, almost leafless. Leaves elongated-cordate, acuminate, mostly entire, occasionally somewhat lobed, mostly basal. Bracts small, nearly orbicular. Inflorescences densely flowered, nodding before anthesis; with a 3-lobed lip, dark violet-blue; June to August. The large-flowered cultivar 'Grandiflora' is more

not only for its lilac-blue flowers, but also for the more or less evergreen foliage. Numerous cultivars are listed, primarily distinguished by their foliage, such as: 'Aurea', with golden-yellow leaves; 'Purpurascens' with dull violet leaves; 'Variegata', yellow and green dappled; 'Tricolor', leaves tricolored gray-green, violet and purple-pink, and cream-colored. The variegated forms are considerably more tender than the species. Requires a protected, warm, sunny site and light winter protection. z5

S. officinalis ssp. **lavandulifolia** see **S. lavandulifolia**

S. officinalis ssp. **major** see **S. grandiflora**

S. patens Cav. Gentian Salvia. Mexico. Rootstock of fleshy roots in a tuft. Stems 40–75cm high, short and softly pubescent. Leaves glaucous green, petioled, ovate-deltoid to hastate. Flowers 6cm long, bright ultramarine blue. The cultivar 'Cambridge Blue' is sky blue, flowers closely paired, opposite, in loose, erect racemes; also 'Alba', with white flowers. June to fall. A wonderful species for the summer border with only one drawback, that the individual flowers abscise too quickly in cool climates. Best for the gardens of warmer climates, otherwise must be overwintered frost-free and dry in the greenhouse. Plants from seed sown in early spring will flower in summer. z8(7 to 6)

S. pitcheri see **S. azurea** var. **grandiflora**

S. pratensis L. Meadow Clary. S. and Central Europe to Central Russia. Rootstock woody. Stems .3–1m high, pubescent, sticky above. Basal leaves ovate-lanceolate to oblong, 7.5–15cm

Sambucus ebulus

long, rugose, dark green, in a loose rosette. Inflorescence spike-like, scarcely branched. Flowers vary in size and shape, commonly violet-blue; but also bluish-white, pure white and pink. June to August. Quite tolerant of alkaline soils, for naturalizing in meadows. May be sown with seed of *Chrysanthemum leucanthemum*. Several cultivars are named for flower colors: 'Alba', 'Rosea', 'Atroviolacea', and more. z5

S. pratensis var. **haematodes** (L.) Briq. (*S. haematodes* L.) is more valuable with showy, dense whorls of bright blue

flowers, contrasting well with the reddish brown stems. Particularly effective in the naturalized garden in warm, sunny sites or for the herbaceous border. z5

S. recognita Fisch. et Mey. Asia Minor. Stems to 1.2m high. Basal leaves pinnately lobed with conspicuously large, oval, terminal segments, gray-green, sticky-glandular. Stems ascending, 4-angled, blue-pruinose, silky-pubescent toward the top (also the calyx). Flowers large, white with a soft pink, reddish-marked lip, 4 in whorls, in false racemes; July to August. An almost unknown species. z6

S. ringens Sibth. et Sm. S. and E. Balkan states to SE. Romania; on sunny, rocky slopes in the Thessalian Olympus Mts. Stems 30–80cm high, woody at the base, glabrous, or with few hairs below. Leaves mostly basal, pinnatisect or pinnate, terminal lobe ovate-elliptic. Flowers 4cm wide, strong blue-lilac or blue, in somewhat nodding, loose racemes; June to July. Very attractive; however, the true species is rarely found in culture. A heat-loving species for a calcareous soil,

particularly at the base of a sunny wall. The var. **romanica** Prodan., is taller, sturdier, more floriferous. z7

S. rutilans see **S. elegans**

S. scabiosifolia Lam. NE. Bulgaria, S. Russia, Crimea. Stems woody, often reddish at the base, 30cm high, procumbent-ascending in a loose clump, well-branched, softly white hairy to woolly, as are the close-spaced leaves. Leaves pinnate, with 3–8 pairs of linear leaflets, or deeply pinnate-lobed, lobes linear-oblong. Inflorescences racemose

Sanguisorba tenuifolia 'Alba' behind *Gentiana asclepiadea*

with 4–6 flowered whorls; flowers large, white, pink-blushed, upper lip pubescent, lower lip 4-lobed sinuate. Attractive, bushy growing species for the large rock or natural garden. z6(5)

S. sclarea L., Clary, Muscatel Salvia. S. Europe, Mediterranean region, W. Asia. Stems to 1m high, sticky-glandular above; biennial to weak perennial. Leaves in a basal rosette, large, rounded, petioled; the second year the plant produces a vigorous, branched, panicle with showy pink, lilac or white bracts and small, pale lilac flowers. A decorative species, which self-seeds on a sunny, gravelly site. Used in S. France for the bouquet in muscatel wines. The var. **turkestaniana** Mottet bears very large, paler bracts and whitish flowers; modern seed strains are very colorful. z5

S. × superba Stapf see **S. nemorosa**

S. verticillata L. Lilac Salvia. Central Europe to the Caucasus region. Stems erect, pubescent, 40–60cm high. Leaves cordate-ovate, especially the lower leaves, petioled, irregularly coarse-crenate, rugose. Stems leafy, lilac to lilac-blue inflorescence; flowers small, whorls to 40-flowered. July to September. Of only moderate value in the garden, occasionally troublesome from self-seeding.

S. ebulus L., Dwarf Elder. Europe, Madagascar, N. Africa, W. Asia. Usually colonizes in sunny, woodland clearings and banks, along logging roads and in meadows on moist, fertile, usually calcareous, clay loam soil. Stems stout, herbaceous, usually unbranched, 0.5–1.5m high, grooved. Leaves with 19–13 oblong-lanceolate, serrate leaflets. Suckering canes creep deeply in the soil. Flowers small, white, occasionally turning pink, sweetish-scented, in 5–16cm, 3-branched cymes; anthers dark red at first. Fruits globose, shiny black. Blooms from June to August. The entire

venation. Flowers with 2 quickly falling sepals, 8–12 petals more or less in 1 whorl, anemone-like, pure white, appearing with the leaves. Leaves envelop the flowers at first, later are outspread; April to May. 'Major' is a large-flowered form. 'Multiplex', with double, long-persistent flowers, is particularly valuable, but sterile. This early spring woodland flower thrives in full to semi-shade, in moist, high humus soil. In cool summer climates succeeds in full sun given a sufficiently moist soil during the growing season. The bare spot left by the summer dormancy

Sanicula europaea

Santolina chamaecyparissus

Santolina rosmarinifolia

For naturalizing on a sunny woodland margin; will suppress weed growth. z6(5) (Sch.& M.)

Sambucus L.
Caprifoliaceae
Elder

Forty species in the temperate and sub-tropical zones of both hemispheres. Trees, shrubs, rarely perennials with opposite, odd-pinnate leaves. Flowers in broad corymbs or panicles. Fruit a berrylike drupe with 3–5 seeds.

Only the following species should be considered for a large landscape or park situation. Despite its decorative appearance, it is not recommended for general garden use because of its invasive habit. Thrives in any moist, loamy soil in sun or semi-shade. Propagate by division of the root-crown or suckers and seed.

plant (except the flowers) is unpleasantly scented when bruised. Cultivated in Europe for medicinal purposes since the 14th century. z5 (E.)

Sanguinaria L
Papaveraceae
Bloodroot

A monospecific genus. Herbaceous perennial colonizing in North American woodlands in fertile, moist bottomlands.

S. canadensis L., Bloodroot. E. North America. 15–25cm high. Rootstock a branching rhizome, knobby, reddish-brown, brittle, with orange-red juice. Leaves basal, long-petioled, cordate to reniform, sinuately lobed or rarely entire, blue-green above, pale gray-green beneath with distinctly raised

period can be filled with small ferns and other summer-green, shade-loving perennials. Transplant and divide while plants are dormant in August or in very early spring; sow seeds immediately upon ripening, seedlings bloom after 2–3 years. z4 (Sch.)

Sanguisorba L.
Rosaceae
Burnet

More than 12 species of perennials from the temperate and cooler regions of the Northern Hemisphere, with pinnate leaves, the leaflets paired, often suborbicular toothed. Hermaphroditic or polygamous, white, greenish, or red flowers in dense, terminal heads or club-like spikes. Flowers bracted, small; sepals 4, white or colored; petals none; stamens 4; pistils simple, 1–3 with simple stigma. Some confusion exists with closely related species of *Poterium*.

S. minor, also known as *Poterium sanguisorba*, is a long-cultivated herb for the kitchen garden. To encourage leaf production, remove all flowering stems as they appear. All the other species are attractive damp meadow plants for similar uses in the naturalized garden. The most conspicuous of these are *S. obtusa* and *S. tenuifolia*, which are also suitable for cut flowers. *S. minor*, and especially *S. officinalis* can become persistent weeds because of their deep root

Georgia and Indiana; in bogs, moist lowlands and moist meadows. Similar to *S. officinalis*, but with elongated, cylindrical, erect spikes with cream-white flowers on stems to 1.5m high. Blooms from August to September. z4

S. minor Scop., Lesser Burnet. Often listed as *Poterium sanguisorba* L. Europe, temperate Asia. Grows on semidry and dry grasslands, usually on alkaline, often gravelly loam and loess. Stems 20–60cm high, with cylindrical, condensed greenish flower heads. Flowers monoecious or polygamous; male flowers with

species with erect or only slightly nodding, white inflorescences. z5

S. officinalis L., Great Burnet. Temperate Eurasia, in moist meadows, on moist to wet, fertile, often peaty, loam or sometimes clay soils. Plant with creeping rhizomes. Stems 0.3–1m high, branched toward the apex. Leaves odd-pinnate, with 5–11 leaflets. Flowers in dense, ovoid to oblong head-like spikes, blood red. Flowers from June to August. z4

S. tenuifolia Fisch. ex Link. Japan, E. Siberia, Kamchatka, Kuril Islands,

Saponaria × olivana

systems, particularly among less vigorous plants. All species perform well in average, loamy garden soil. The moisture requirements differ among the various species as evidenced in their native habitats. Propagate by seed and division.

S. albiflora see **S. obtusa**

S. canadensis L., Canada Burnet. N. America: Labrador to Michigan, south to

many exerted stamens; stigma of female flowers feathery. Blooms from May to July. z5

S. obtusa Maxim. Japan, on alpine meadows. Stems 30–60cm high. Leaves odd-pinnate, to 40cm long, with 13–17 leaflets. Spikes 4–7cm long, nodding, light pink. Flowers from August to September. The most attractive species, also suitable as a cut flower. **S. albiflora** (Mak.) Mak. is a similar Japanese alpine

Sachalin, Korea, Manchuria; on wet meadows and along rivers and streams in the lowlands and the mountains. Stems branched toward the top, 0.8–1.3m high. Leaves large, mostly basal, with 11–15 leaflets. Spikes cylindrical, erect, the longer ones nodding, 2–7cm long. Flowers reddish. 'Alba' (var. *alba* Trautv. et C.A. Mey.) is more attractive than the species, with greenish white or white flowers in frequently nodding spikes. 'Rosea' bears pinkish spikes.

Blooms from August to September. Older plants, with their decorative foliage and abundant flowers, make attractive specimens along stream banks. z4 (E.)

Sanicula L.
Umbelliferae
Snakeroot, Black Snakeroot, Sanicle

Thirty-seven nearly cosmopolitan species (except New Guinea and

Saponaria ocymoides 'Rubra Compacta'

Australia); perennial herbs with small, simple, cymose or paniculate umbels. Some are invasive weeds. The only species recommended here is the low, attractive shade plant *S. europaea*. Best suited for a shaded site in the small garden where it thrives in a moderately moist, humus-rich soil. The attractive foliage appears fresh green the entire summer. Self-seeds under favorable conditions without becoming a nuisance. Propagation is by seed and division. Very effective in combination with *Anemone nemorosa*, *Convallaria*, *Galeobdolon luteum*, *Galium odoratum*, *Luzula* species, *Maianthemum*, *Melica uniflora*, *Thelypteris phegopteris*.

S. europaea L. Europe, Africa, Central and E. Asia; in deciduous and mixed woodlands, ravines and thickets, on shaded humus-rich soils, from the plains to the subalpine elevations. Stems 20–30cm high, with erect umbels. Basal leaves long-petioled, cordate-rounded, palmate, 3–5 parted, with more or less deeply 3-lobed segments, stem leaves small and usually less divided. Inflorescences terminal, with 3–7 radiating branchlets. Flowers white or pale pink, in terminal umbels. Fruits, of the clinging

type known as "beggar's ticks", nearly globose, covered with hooklike bristles. Blooms from May to June. z5 (E.)

Sansevieria

S. carnea see **Reineckia carnea**

S. sessiflora see **Reinecknia carnea**

Saponaria pumila

Santolina L.
Compositae
Lavender-cotton

Eight or ten species of small, dense, cushion-shaped aromatic shrubs or subshrubs in the W. Mediterranean region. Leaves alternate, pinnate or pinnatisect, entire or dentate. Flower heads small- to medium-sized, solitary, on long peduncles. All disc flowers, no rays, usually fertile, yellow to whitish. Fruits without a pappus. Considerable confusion exists regarding classification, as noted in the descriptions of the following species. No santolinas are reliably winter-hardy in temperate zone gardens with −8 degrees C. (20 degrees F.) or colder weather. A pot-grown stock of *S. chamaecyparissus* and *S. rosmarinifolia* especially should be kept in a frost-free frame or cool house over winter. *S.*

elegans goes into an alpine house, where it must be protected from excess moisture. Plant this species in a mostly gravel soil with only a little humus. All species require full sun. Attractive planted singly or in small groups in the rock garden, on a south-facing wall, on a terrace, or at the foot of a dry stone wall where in a few years a plant will develop into a large, bushy plant. Since plants are evergreen and take shearing well, they make excellent low hedges for edging beds of summer flowers or herb beds. Move young plants with a root ball and plant 10–15 per running meter for

hedging purposes. Cut back with hedge shears several times through the summer to maintain a dense, low barrier. Allow plants to grow naturally, well spaced, to produce their abundant summer flowers. Propagation is easy by cuttings, *S. elegans* also by careful division. Good companion species are the same as those listed for *Lavandula*.

S. chamaecyparissus L. Pyrenees to NW. Italy and N. Africa, an escape locally in the USA; on dry slopes, gravelly soils and among rocks. Densely branched, evergreen, 10–50cm high, a spicy-scented shrub. Leaves silver-gray tomentose, 1–4cm long, pinnate, the leaflets almost thread-like, short, curving. Flower heads solitary, long-peduncled, 6–10mm wide. Flowers yellow. Blooms from July to August. In the USA at least two cultivars are offered; 'Nana', a very compact, dwarf plant, and 'Plumosus', with lacy, silvery-gray foliage. This species, its cultivars, and other santolinas are much planted in the hot, arid southwest and other mild climate regions. z7

S. chamaecyparissus ssp. **chamaecyparissus**. Quite variable in growth habit. Leaves gray- to white-tomentose. Leaflets not exceeding 2mm long. Flower peduncles not thickened toward the top. Involucral bracts usually tomentose. Flowers deep yellow. z6

S. chamaecyparissus 'Lindavica' Sün-

the rock or trough garden. Must be protected from excessive moisture the entire year, but especially in winter. Easier to maintain in the alpine house. z7

S. pinnata see **S. chamaecyparissus** ssp. **tomentosa**

S. rosmarinifolia L. (*S. viridis* Willd.). Iberian Peninsula, S. France, NW. Africa; on dry, gravelly soil, between rocks. Plants 30–60cm high, dark green, glabrous, very aromatic, with sometimes erect, but often more or less procumbent-ascending stems. Leaves

5 toothed, not scarious, not winged (as in *Vaccaria*); petals 5, clawed, with coronal scales at the juncture of claw and blade (scales lacking in *Vaccaria*), entire or emarginate; stamens 10; ovary 1-celled, styles 2, rarely 3. Flowers from May to August. Easily cultivated in any well-drained garden soil in full sun. All perennial species, except *S. officinalis* and its varieties, are suitable for the rock garden or dry stone wall. Propagate the species by seed. Hybrids and cultivars of *S. officinalis* are increased by division; the dense cushion-form hybrids are easily propagated by cuttings of the sterile

Sarracenia purpurea

Sasa kurilensis

Sasaella ramosa

derm. (*S. chamaecyparissus* ssp. *chamaecyparissus* × *S. chamaecyparissus* ssp. *tomentosa*). Gray-green; very floriferous; 20–40cm high; dense, bushy habit. Flowers yellowish. Blooms from July to August. Hybridized by Sündermann, around 1913. See classification note with the following plant. z6

S. chamaecyparissus ssp. **tomentosa** (Pers.) Arcang. (*S. tomentosa* Pers., *S. pinnata* Viv.). Pyrenees to Central Italy. A gray-white bushy plant; leaves usually glabrous, or dying to glabrous. Leaflets 2.5–7mm long. Involucral bracts usually glabrous. Flowers whitish or rarely pale yellow; from July to August. Botanists now tend to return this plant to species status, *S. pinnata*, which would make Sünderman's hybrid a cross between 2 species, identified as *S. × lindavica*. z6

S. elegans Boiss. ex DC. Spain: Sierra Nevada; at 2200m elevation in dry screes. Plant a dense, silver-white, 5–10cm high cushion. Nonflowering shoots short, densely leafy. Basal leaves incised-crenate to pinnatisect, folded, short-petioled, uppermost leaves entire, flat and sessile. Flower heads on very short peduncles. Flowers yellowish white; in summer. Usually long-lived in

quite variable in form. Lobes of the leaflets only 1mm long and distinctly spaced. Peduncles not thickened toward the top. Flower heads 7–12mm wide. Flowers yellow. Blooms from July to August. American taxonomists tend to maintain *S. rosmarinifolia* and *S. virens* as separate species, the difference involving foliage and flower head characteristics. More study is needed here. z7 (E.)

S. tomentosa see **S. chamaecyparissus** ssp. **tomentosa**

S. viridis see **S. rosmarinifolia**

Saponaria L.
Caryophyllaceae
Soapwort

About 30 Eurasian species, mostly from the Mediterranean region. Medium-sized or low, cushion-form perennials, occasionally biennials or annuals, with opposite leaves. Flowers usually pink, occasionally yellow or white, solitary, cymose, capitate or paniculate. Flowers without bracts subtending the calyx (as in *Dianthus*), calyx cylindrical or oblong,

shoots which arise after the flowers.

S. bellidifolia Sm. Balkan region. Caespitose perennial, flowering stems unbranched, with 1 pair of leaves, 20–40cm high. Basal leaves oblong-spatulate, petiolate. Inflorescence capitate, flowers almost sessile, yellow, small with yellow stamens. May to June. z7(6)

S. × boissieri see **S. caespitosa**

S. caespitosa DC. Central Pyrenees. Caespitose; stems to 15cm-high, unbranched, glabrous or hairy above. Leaves densely crowded, linear, grassy, glabrous-green. Flowers rosy-purplish in capitate cymes; calyx purplish, hairy; petals notched, narrow. May to June. A particularly vigorous form is the so-called *S. × boissieri* hort. non Sünderm. z7. The true *S. × boissieri* was hybridized by Sündermann from *S. caespitosa* × *S. ocymoides*, with large, clear pink flowers on spreading stems above a foliage mat; apparently is lost from cultivation.

S. cypria Boiss. From the mountains of Cyprus. Rootstock slender, somewhat rhizomatous. Stems 6–10cm high, in a loose tuft. Leaves oblong-spatulate, about 22mm long, gray-green, glandular pubescent, as is the calyx. Stems 1–3 flowered. Flowers 2.5cm large, carmine-pink. August to September. Very attractive, sun- and heat-loving species, but sensitive to winter wetness; better suited for the alpine house. Rarely true in culture, garden forms are usually one of various *S. cypria* hybrids. z8(7)

S. haussknechtii Simml. Macedonia, Albania. Rootstock woody. Stems procumbent to ascending, 30–40cm high, branched. Leaves lanceolate, glaucous gray-green, glabrous. Flowers to 2.5cm wide, bright pink, with deeply incised petals, in loose, axillary cymes. Calyx brownish-red, finely hairy. August to September. Forms a broad, spreading bushy plant, notable for its late flowers. Suitable for the large rock garden, effective near *Satureja montana*. z7(6)

S. × lempergii hort. (*S. cypria × S. haussknechtii*). Originated by Dr. Fritz Lemperg in Styria, Austria. Stems procumbent-ascending, 30–40cm, well-branched. Leaves lanceolate, 1cm wide, dark green, short-pubescent. Flowers axillary, bright carmine-pink, calyx teeth long, reddish. August to September. Includes the somewhat earlier flowering and paler pink 'Max Frei'. An exceptionally valuable rock garden plant for its late, colorful flowers; particularly effective when combined with the small blue-flowered shrub, *Caryopteris × clandonensis*. Propagated only by cuttings. z6

S. lutea L. S. and W. Alps. 10cm high. Caespitose perennial with woody rootstock. Basal leaves pale green, linear, acuminate, smooth; stem leaves somewhat pubescent. Inflorescence densely clustered, nearly capitate. Flowers sulfur yellow with violet stamens. June to July. Very attractive and persistent species, stronger yellow than *S. bellidifolia*. z6

S. ocymoides L., Rose Soapwort. Mountains of Spain, S. France, Italy, Alps; a lime-loving mountain species. Plant sprawling, 10–20cm high, to 60cm wide. Stems slender, procumbent-ascending, much-branched. Lower leaves obovate to ovate-lanceolate, short petioled, upper leaves oblong-lanceolate, sessile. Flowers in an umbel-like cyme, corolla to 15mm wide, rose-pink, pink or white. June to July. A well-known and popular, easily-grown rock garden plant. Also ideal for weed-free slopes and dry stone walls. Combines well with *Cerastium tomentosum*. May become troublesome by self-seeding. Cultivar 'Rubra Compacta' is small and dark red; 'Splendens'

is a bright rose-red. Both have, in recent years, been propagated by seed and therefore are rarely true in culture. Other rarer cultivars include 'Albiflora', white-flowered; 'Carnea', flowers flesh-pink; 'Rosea', flowers bright rose; and 'Versicolor', flowers open white, then turn rose. Should be propagated only by cuttings taken while in flower. z4

S. officinalis L. Bouncing Bet, Soapwort. Central and S. Europe, W. Siberia, W. Asia; widely naturalized in N. Europe and North America. Stems to 80cm high, but usually much less. Rootstock stoloniferous, wide-creeping and too invasive for most gardens. Stems stout, erect or ascending, with swollen nodes, somewhat rough. Leaves elliptic to oblong-lanceolate. Flowers pale pink or white, single or double, on short peduncles in axillary and terminal clusters. June to September. Attractive plants, the double forms with long-lasting, softly scented flowers sometimes used for cut flowers. Roots of the species have been used medicinally (hence, *officinalis*), and when crushed in water saponify, forming a detergent lather; susceptible individuals develop dermatitis from the sap. Old garden cultivars include 'Alba-plena', double white flowers; 'Roseo-plena', double pale pink flowers; and 'Rudro-plena', double rose to almost reddish flowers. z4

S. × olivana Wocke. A hybrid, *S. pumila × S. caespitosa*, bred in 1927 by E. Wocke in Oliva, near Gdansk, Poland. Plant 5cm-high, tight green cushion. Leaves small, lanceolate. Flowers 2cm wide, nearly sessile, rose-red. June to July. One of the most attractive, floriferous and undemanding cushion-form plants for the rock garden, with a spring flower display rivaling *Phlox* and *Iberis*; unfortunately, too little utilized. 'Bressingham' (*S. × olivana × S. ocymoides* 'Rubra Compacta') is a similar hybrid, flowers mallow-pink with a white eye, calyx reddish brown, softly pubescent, June to July; very long-lasting flowers and noninvasive. The latter is propagated by cuttings, *S. × olivana* by division. z6

S. pulvinaris Boiss. Lebanon, Anatolia. Plant a 3cm-high, dense, flat, small-leaved cushion resembling *Silene acaulis*. Flowers carmine-pink, in cymes. June to July. Botanists list this as *S. pumilo* Boiss, not (L.) Fenzl ex Braun (*S. pulvineris* Boiss.).

S. pumila (St.-Lager) Janch. Dwarf Soapwort. E. Central Alps, Dolomites, SE. Carpathians. Dense, cushion-form plant

3–5cm high. Leaves linear, to 2.5cm long, obtuse, somewhat fleshy. Flowers solitary, very large, to 2.5cm across, rose-pink, rarely white, short-peduncled. June. Often referred to as demanding, but actually easy to grow and free flowering in a peat-sand-gravel mix in full sun. The plants flower in an interesting way around the perimeter. z5

S. pumilo see **S. pulvinaris**

S. × wiemannii Fritsch (*S. caespitosa × S. lutea*), a hybrid developed by Sündermann. Plant a flat cushion with decumbent stems; flower stems 15–20cm high with many-flowered heads of pale salmon-rose flowers. Habit somewhat like that of *S. caespitosa*. May to June. Interesting for collectors. Unfortunately, the other hybrids from Sündermann have been lost but should be recreated: i.e. *S. ocymoides × S. pulvinaris* and *S. × boissieri* Sünd. (*S. caespitosa × S. ocymoides*). z6 (K.)

Sarcocapnos DC.
Papaveraceae

S. enneaphylla (L.) DC. E. Pyrenees to S. Central Spain. Of the few species in the genus, only this, resembling *Corydalis*, is occasionally found in alpine collections. It is a well-branched and clump-forming perennial, woody at the base; leaves 2- to 3-pinnately compound, fleshy, blue-green; flowers white, yellow or purplish; sepals 2, falling early; petals 4, erect-connivent, lower petal with basal spur, the other without, flat, inner petals narrow, coherent terminally, stamens 6. Stems with terminal, few-flowered raceme. In its natural habitat plants are usually found in shaded limestone crevices. z6 (S.)

Sarracenia L.
Sarraceniaceae
Pitcher Plant

Eight or nine species of insectivorous plants in E. North America. The leaves are modified into pitcher-shaped structures borne in rosettes. The conspicuously colored "pitchers" contain enzyme-laden water in which trapped insects are digested. The flowers are nodding on a leafless scape.

Only one species is reliably hardy; for the bog garden in soggy sphagnum and peat, together with *Drosera* species, small *Carex*, mosses and other bog plants. Best success is achieved when planted in a sunken tub or moderate-sized, water-tight container. Also suitable for a small bog section of an alpine house. These grow only in lime-free soil and nonalkaline water; rainwater is better than treated city water. A suitable substrate is a well-composted peat humus mixed with some sphagnum moss. The plants require protection from sun and wind. Propagate by careful division or seed. The flowers must be hand-pollinated for viable seed. The seeds should not be covered with soil, but pushed halfway into the substrate. Set pots with the sown seeds, after germination, the young plants, into a shallow tray of water held at 12–16 degrees C. (53–60 degrees F.). It usually takes 3–4 years from sown seeds to blooming plants.

S. purpurea L. E. North America, in acid peat bogs and swamps. Pitchers ascending, 6–35cm long, 2–10cm wide in the middle, in rosettes, rarely green to dark brown-red in full sun. A peculiarity of the flowers is the 5 locular ovary with a short style which is expanded into a 5-lobed, outspread umbrella-like cap with a stigma at each of the 5 points. Petals purple-red. Blooms from May to June. z3 (E.)

At least 7 additional species, as well as naturally-occurring and man-made hybrids, grow in the SE. USA. Gardeners with acid bogs from North Carolina south and westward (z7–9) should look into the possibility of growing some of these more tender, generally quite showy, Pitcher Plants.

Sasa Mak. et Shib.
Gramineae
Dwarf Bamboo

The genus *Sasa* is included in a subdivision group distinguished from the other bamboo subdivisions by its persistent stem sheaths. This group has only one branch per node (see *Pleioblastus*). Of the four genera of this group, only *Sasa* and *Sasaella* usually have stem sheaths shorter than the internodes, and the ciliate hairs at the base of the leaf blade are usually well developed. Stem nodes are conspicuously thickened above the stem sheath scar. Both the other genera, *Sasamorpha* and *Peudosasa*, have slender nodes, and the stem sheaths are longer than the internodes, at nodes on the basal portion of the stalk. The ciliate hairs at the leaf base are only slightly developed or totally lacking. *Sasa* differs from *Sasaella* in the ascending, not strictly erect stems and the ciliate hairs at right angles to the stem on the blade base. The

leaves are rough along their entire length.

Of the four genera, several of the 150 species of *Sasa* are cultivated, but generally only one each from *Sasaella*, *Sasamorpha* and *Pseudosasa*. The species of *Sasa* are understory plants from deciduous forests, well suited for low-maintenance ground covers and erosion control.

S. kurilensis (Rupr.) Mak. et Shib. Kuril to Honshu. A woodland plant of snowy slopes. Available in several taller clones and seedling selections. An attractive

Sasa palmata

foliage species, showing good winter hardiness. z7(6)

S. palmata (Marliac) Nakai. From the Kuril Islands and Sachalin throughout Japan to the islands south of Korea. The form 'Nebulosa' has brown spots on the older stems. Grows to 2m high with 30cm-long, very wide leaves when grown in warm, moist, not too sunny sites. Leaves cluster at the branch tips. Its lush appearance combines well with other large-leaved woody plants and perennials. z7(6)

S. tesselata see **Indocalamus tesselatus**

S. tsuboiana Mak. S. Honshu. A seldom grown species with glossy and persistent leaves, to 50cm high, loose clump-forming. z6

S. veitchii (Carr.) Rehd., Silver Edged Sasa, Kuma Bamboo-grass. Honshu. A very widely grown species. The tendency of the leaf tips of many *Sasa* species to dry and brown toward autumn is conspicuous with this species. The 20cm-long, to 5cm-wide leaves develop a straw-colored, dry margin in winter that is somewhat reminiscent of white-edged *Hosta* leaves in summer. This species is a weed-choking, persistent understory plant 1m high (or often shorter) for difficult site conditions. z8(7) (S.)

S. vagans see **Sasaella ramosa**

Sasaella Mak.
Gramineae

S. pygmaea see **S. ramosa**

S. ramosa Mak. Honshu and Kiushu. Sometimes listed as *Sasa vagans* and *S. pygmaea* and also *Arundinaria pygmaea*. This dwarf bamboo is seldom over 1m high in cultivation, vigorously stoloniferous. An unusually hardy dwarf bamboo, unsurpassed for greening an extensive understory area or shaded slope. z5 (S.)

Sasamorpha Nakai.
Gramineae

S. borealis (Hackel) Nakai: Japan; Hokkaido through Honshu to Korea. Little-grown, erect, large-leaved bamboo, over 1m high, for a woodland understory. z7(6) (S.)

weeks and swarm with honey bees, butterflies and bumblebees. These grow best on gravelly slopes with dry, infertile, calcareous soil, mostly in full sun; they tolerate low lime soil in cultivation. Plants combine well with most rock garden plants and provide late summer color in an otherwise color-poor season. Cut old shoots to the ground in late March. Some species may spread by self-seeding. Propagate by seed, cuttings and separation of the stolons and rooted shoots.

S. alpina see **Acinos alpinus**

S. croatica see **Micromeria croatica**

S. glabrella (Michx) Briq. A wild species indigenous to the USA; Kentucky and E. Arkansas. See **S. arkansana** which is very similar. z6(5)

S. grandiflora see **Calamintha grandiflora**

S. montana L. ssp. **illyrica** (Host) Nym. (*S. subspicata* Bartl. ex Vis., *S. pygmaea* Sieb. ex Vis., *Micromeria pygmaea* (Sieb. ex Vis.) Rchb.). Yugoslavia, Albania; on rocks and gravelly sites. Usually only 10–

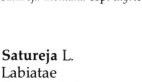

Satureja montana ssp. *illyrica*

Saururus cernuus

Saussurea pygmaea

Satureja L.
Labiatae
Savory, Calamint

See also *Micromeria*. About 30 species of small, aromatic annual or perennial herbs or subshrubs with mostly 4-angled stems and opposite leaves. Flowers in false whorls or loose cymes. Calyx tubular or campanulate, usually 10-, occasionally 13-veined, calyx tube straight, more or less pubescent. Corolla also with a straight tube, limb bilabiate, the upper lip erect, the lower lip 3-lobed, spreading. Stamens diadelphous, shorter than the tube, arched. Styles nearly even, awl-shaped. Valuable small perennial for the alpine and rock garden, and dry walls or the trough garden, for the abundant, late flowers which last for

S. arkansana (Nutt.) Briq. E. North America; Ontario and Minnesota south to Ohio, Arkansas and Texas; on limestone glades and balds, limestone ledges, and gravel bars in creeks. Winter stems prostrate, creeping and rooting, with close-set suborbicular to elliptic leaves 5–8cm across, dark green above, rose-purple below. Summer stems erect and much branched, 20–40cm high, light green. Summer leaves narrow-elliptic to needle-like with tufts of basal hairs, and pubescent above and below, light green. Tiny lavender-blue flowers over the entire plant, May-October. Entire plant pungent when crushed. Very like *S. glabrella* which is glabrous except for hairs at the nodes and has somewhat wider summer leaves at the base of the main stem. z4

15cm high, occasionally taller, with branched, more or less erect, nearly glabrous stems and smaller leaves than the ssp. *montana*. False whorls only 2–5 flowered. Corolla bright violet. Blooms from September to October. z6

S. montana L. ssp. **montana**. From Spain to S. Albania and NW. Yugoslavia; on limestone; dry slopes and screes. Subshrub with slightly floccose stems to 40cm-high, woody at the base, densely bushy, aromatic. Leaves 5–30mm long and 1–5mm wide, linear to oblanceolate, with ciliate margins. Flowers in dense, false whorls, white or pink. Blooms from August to October. z6

S. pygmaea see **S. montana** ssp. **illyrica**

S. rumelica Velen. S. Central Bulgaria; on rocks and gravelly slopes. Slightly floccose perennial 10–20cm high, with a stout, woody rootstock and nearly spatulate, rough floccose leaves 15mm long and 5mm wide. False whorls 6–10 flowered, compressed into short racemes. Corolla whitish. Flowers from August to October. z6

S. subspicata see **S. montana** ssp. **illyrica**

S. thymifolia see **Micromeria thymifolia** (E.)

Saururopsis

S. chinensis see **Saururus chinensis**

Saururus L.
Saururaceae
Lizard's-tail

Two E. North America and E. Asian species of medium-sized to tall, rhizomatous, bog plants with slender, erect stems. Leaves alternate, large, broad-cordate, entire, stipules membranous, adnate to the petioles. Flowers in slender terminal racemes, later racemes opposite the leaves. Flowers small, numerous, with no perianth but each with a bract, imbricate at first later spreading, subtending the 6–8 stamens and 3–4 basally united carpels, white, June to July. Both species are excellent collectors' plants for swampy sites or in shallow water. Require a mulch of leafmold for winter protection. Propagate by seed and division.

S. cernuus L. (*S. lucidus* Donn). Water-dragon, Swamp-lily. E. North America: Canada to Florida and Louisiana along the coast. Perennial bog plants, to 1.2m high, with widely creeping rhizomes. Leaves cordate, long-acuminate, to 15cm. Tips of the spike-like fragrant white flower racemes are nodding, June to July. z5

S. chinensis (Lour.) Baill. (*S. loureirii* Decne., *S. cernuus* Thunb. non L., *Saururopsis chinensis* (Lour.) Turcz.). China, Japan. Very similar to the above species, but much smaller, only 30–40cm high. Stems stout, ridged, leaves cordate, 6–8cm long, usually cordate at the base, light green. Flower raceme cylindrical, borne in the upper leaf axils., yellowish white, June to July. z6 (D.)

S. laureirii see **S. chinensis**

S. lucidus see **S. cernuus**

Saussurea DC.
Compositae

About 130–200 species, mostly in the mountains of Asia and North America; some are among the highest-growing flowering plants. Low- to medium-sized, variable perennials, occasionally annuals. Deep rooted. Sometimes with leafy rosettes. Stems erect, stiff, with alternate leaves. Leaves entire, toothed or pinnately divided. Flower heads solitary or corymbose, purple-red or violet, resembling *Centaurea* but the involucral bracts lack scarious or spiny appendaged; and similar to *Serratula* but the anthers are long-appendaged and the pepus plumose. Most are scarcely ornamental, resembling cones or mounds of wool, but some intrigue alpine plant enthusiasts. Grows in loamy, humus-rich, well-drained soil. These fail with competition from more vigorous companion plants. Many species are best grown in an alpine house, all are demanding. Useful collectors' plants for larger alpine plantings. Propagate by seed, division, or root cuttings.

S. alpina (L.) DC. England, Central Europe, Alps, Carpathians, NW. Russia, arctic Asia and N. America. Rhizomatous. Stems 4–10cm (rarely to 45cm) high. Leaves glabrate dark green above, gray-green, white-cottony below, basal leaves ovate to lanceolate, to 16cm long, petiolate; stem leaves shorter, narrower, sessile. Flower heads few in a dense corymb, ovoid to cylindrical, to 2cm long, violet. June to July. z1–4

S. discolor (Willd.) DC. Alps, Carpathian Mts., Apennine Mts., Ural Mts., Altai Mts., Himalaya Mts. Stems 4–30cm high. Leaves glabrous above, dark green, densely snow white tomentose. Flower heads 3–8 in a dense corymb, pale violet to rose red. June to July. Requires a lime free soil. z4

S. gnaphaloides (Royle) Sch.-Bip. Tibet, Sinkiang and Soviet Central Asia. One of the few easily cultivated Asiatic species. Stoloniferous, 1.5–6cm high. Flowers pale red. z4

S. nuda Ledeb. var. **densa** (Hook.) Hult. N. America, E. Asia. Similar to *S. alpina*. Seed is regularly offered. z4

S. pygmaea (Jacq.) Spreng. E. Alps, W. Carpathians; on limestone. Stems 3–20cm high. Leaves densely hairy, linear-lanceolate, leathery, dark green, forming basal rosettes. Stem usually 1, bearing a solitary head about 35mm long and 30mm wide; flowers blue-violet. June to July. Unfortunately, difficult to cultivate. A very beautiful species. z5

S. stella Max. Himalayas and NW. China. Stemless, the rosette 3cm high. Leaves narrowly lanceolate, with a distinct midvein, margin completely smooth, to 2cm long and 8mm wide, forming a stellate rosette appressed to the ground; midvein of the cordate leaves pink at anthesis, few to many flower heads, entirely sessile, violet-blue. July to August. Attractive, difficult to grow, rare. Fruits ripen soon after flower drop. Often propagated by root cuttings. z5 (K.)

Numerous additional *Saussurea* are listed by Western botanical gardens, including: *S. albescens* .5–3m high, Nepal; *S. elegans*, 60cm high, Caucasus Mts.; *S. gossipiphora*, 15–30cm high, (one of the woolliest), Himalaya Mts.; *S. japonica*, 60cm high, Siberia to Japan; *S. triptera*, 60cm high, Japan, with alpine var.; *S. usitchiana*, to 45cm high, Central China; *S. wernerioides*, stemless, Sikkim; *S. yakla*, stemless, Himalaya Mts.

Saxifraga L.
Saxifragaceae
Saxifrage, Rockfoil

An attractive, extensive genus of 300–370 species. Included are many natural hybrids and geographic varieties. The species are substantially different morphologically, requiring a division into Sections. Saxifrages are perennial, or rarely annual or biennial, dwarf to medium-sized plants. Usually the garden sorts are small-leaved, hard and crusty, sometimes moss-like, soft-cushion and rosette-forming, also herbaceous-leaved, small perennials. The flowers are solitary, clustered, or in floriferous panicles, racemes or cymes. The majority are white-flowered, a few are yellow, pink, salmon or rose, some also are red to purple. Flowers usually are pentamerous, rarely more; the calyx is either free or adhering to the base of the ovary (perigynous), lobes 5, erect or spreading, overlapping, imbricate in the bud; petals 5, usually entire, rarely unequal; rarely fringed, deciduous; stamens usually 10, inserted with the petals, filaments threadlike, clavate or awl-shaped, anthers 2-lobed; ovary 2-celled, perigynous, or superior or inferior, styles 2, spreading. The saxifrages produce numerous, very fine seeds.

The flowering time varies widely; some species begin to flower as the snow melts, others do not bloom until October. Most bloom from March to June. The widely variable and extensive genus *Saxifraga* is primarily composed of mountain plants, most very tolerant of harsh winter conditions. The arctic species survive nearly to the permanent snow fields, others also thrive under high alpine conditions. The genus is well distributed throughout the cool temperate Northern Hemisphere. Only a few species of the Section Dactyloides occur in the South American Andes.

Saxifrages are some of the most valuable rock garden plants, decorative not only for their flowers but for the wonderful rosetted cushions, even in a winter frost. Some few species are suitable for flatland gardens and edging. The genus is also variable regarding cultural requirements, which are described for the various species; there are species for full sun and for shaded sites, some belong in dry stone walls.

With a stoloniferous cushiony growth habit, most species are easily propagated vegetatively by division and cuttings. Seed propagation is also possible, particularly for the monocarpic species of the Section Euaizoonia. These silvery rosetted saxifrages are self-seeding under favorable conditions, such as in tufa rock. Some species of the Section Dactyloides are also propagated by seed, with hybrids offered in the trade.

Saxifrages are not generally troubled by pests and disease though alpine species often deteriorate quickly in unsuitable enviornments. Species in the Section Euaizoonia are sometimes affected by a rosette rot or various leaf-spotting fungi. Slugs and snails may be a problem for any saxifrage. A division of the various Sections is adapted here from Engler and Irmscher to outline this large genus. Only species commonly grown in gardens are included.

Other literature: Gornall, R. J. An outline of a revised classification of *Saxifraga* L. Bot. J. Linn. Soc. 95(4): 273–292 (1987) revises classification into 15 sections, 19 subsections and 34 series.

Section Euaizoonia
(Silver Rosetted-, Encrusted Saxifrages)

Characteristics: rhizomes above ground, secondary shoots usually from a primary stem rather than from the rhizome. Rosettes tough; leaves broadly ligulate or spatulate, alternate, entire or toothed, pitted along the margins, more or less encrusted with a chalky exudate. Flower stems more or less tall, with loose or dense panicles. Petals usually white, rarely rose or yellow, sometimes purple-spotted. Older rosettes usually die after flowering; the slender rhizomes pro-

Saxifraga hybrid 'Tumbling Waters' (*S. longifolia* × *S. callosa*)

duce new rosettes at their tips, so plants usually are clumped. The monocarpic species, however, are an exception. If they are indeed true to name, which they are often not in culture, they have only one rosette, and the entire plant dies after flowering. All are attractive and valuable rock garden plants. The vigorous, persistent cushions and the stiff rosettes are very decorative the year around. The flowers, in elegant panicles, are also suitable for cut flowers. The smallest, very lime-encrusted species grow best in a limestone scree or tufa rock, most tolerating full sun. The exceptions are *S. cotyledon* and *S. florulenta*, which inhabit granite or basaltic substrates. *S. cotyledon* and *S. mutata* are better suited to a somewhat shaded site. *S. longifolia* grows best in a steep, east-facing rock crevice. Among the various species of this Section are a number of very attractive and valuable garden hybrids. All species and cultivars of this Section may be propagated by division and cuttings as well as by seed.

S. aizoon see **S. paniculata**

S. altissima see **S. hostii** ssp. **hostii**

S. callosa Sm. (*S. lingulata* Bell.). Maritime Alps, Apennine Mts., Sardinia, Sicily, NE. Spain, SE. France. Quite a variable species. Rosettes tufted with a central inflorescence. Leaves channeled, blue-gray, reddish at the base, linear-spatulate (to 12cm long, 4mm wide), with lime-encrusted marginal pits. Stems to 35cm-high, rarely more, leafy. Inflorescence a many branched panicle, nodding; petals oblong, white with red spots at the base; June. Conspicuous for the narrow-leaved, irregular rosettes. Botanists distinguish 2 subspecies, ssp. *callosa* (which see) and ssp. *catalaunica*. z7

S. callosa ssp. **callosa**. Maritime Alps and mountains of S. Italy; *S. callosa* ssp. **catalaunica** is indigenous to SE. France and NE. Spain. The latter is also known as *S. catalaunica* Boiss. and *S. lingulata* var. *catalaunica*. Plants with especially decorative rosettes 7–8cm across, leaves shorter, tips dilated, flat, very firm and stiff, with conspicuous chalky exudate. z7

'Albertii' (*S. callosa* var. *albertii*) is widely grown. It has large rosettes with broader, grayer leaves and broad-spread panicles of white flowers. The cultivar from a Queenstown garden might be a hybrid of *S. callosa* × *S. cochlearis* or *S. longifolia*.

S. callosa var. **albertii** see **S. callosa** ssp. **callosa**

S. callosa var. **australis** Central and S. Italy. Rosettes larger. Leaves greener, linear, acuminate (about 4cm long, 5mm wide), stems to 25cm long. Best in partial shade in warm regions. z7

S. callosa var. **bellardii** (*S. lingulata* var. *bellardii*). Apennine Mts., SW. Alps. Rosettes irregular. Leaves thinner, linear-spatulate, vary in length, averaging 10cm long, acuminate and 2mm wide. Panicles large, on arching stems; flowers white. Best in partial shade in warm climates. z7

S. **carinthiaca** see **S. paniculata** var. **carinthiaca**

S. **cartilaginea** see **S. paniculata** ssp. **cartilaginea**

S. **catalaunica** see **S. callosa** ssp. **callosa**, ssp. **catalaunica**

S. **cochlearis** Rchb. Maritime Alps, Ligurian Alps. Established plant a high-mounded clump of rosettes. Rosettes heavily lime-encrusted, hemispherical. Basal leaves numerous, 13–25mm long,

Numerous varieties and cultivars are listed for *S. cotyledon*, including the following, more common sorts:

Var. **pyramidalis** Central Alps and Savoy Alps. Conspicuously large pyramidal inflorescences, usually branched from the base up. One of the most decorative saxifrages, not only for the garden in a somewhat shady, moderately moist site, but also for cut flowers and pot culture. Thrives in lime-free soil. Also found in the trade is var. **caterhamensis**, with distinctly red spotted flowers, from the northern portions of its range.

Saxifraga caesia

Saxifraga cochlearis 'Minor'

S. callosa var. **lantoscana**. Maritime Alps. Rosettes more uniform, more formal than the species; leaves crowded, shorter (3cm long, 5mm wide), dark green, spatulate, obtuse tips noticeably dilated, distinctly recurved; stems 20cm long, very densely flowered and attractive. Best in shade, in limestone soil. The cultivar 'Superba', with large, cream-white flowers in large, arching, plume-like panicles, belongs here. z7

S. callosa var. **latonica**. Rosette more compact than the type, with smaller leaves. Long flowering period. Flowers white, spotted red.

'Winterfeuer' (Winter Fire) (H.W.) rosettes conspicuously vermilion-red in winter.

All forms of *S. callosa* grow well in a bright, dry site, but will also thrive in shade. All are valuable and interesting rock plants. z7

spatulate, tips thickened, reflexed; upper leaves nearly round. Stems 20cm high, paniculate-branched, with pearl-like buds and pure white flowers; June. An attractive, satisfactory plant for the rockery and trough garden. 'Major', a large-rosette cultivar with larger flowers is available in the trade. 'Minor' (*S. probynii* Correv.), a dwarf cultivar with minute, crowded, silvery rosettes, stems only 10cm-high. *S. cochlearis* 'Pseudo-valdensis', is exceptionally dwarf, inflorescence only 8cm high. z7

S. **cotyledon** L. S. and Central Alps, Central Pyrenees, Norway, Iceland; only found in lime-free regions. Rosettes flat, in flat clusters, to 12cm wide, leaves tongue-shaped, fleshy, glabrous, finely toothed. Stems leafy, to 60cm high, branching almost from the base; in compound, many-flowered, arched panicles with fragrant white flowers; June. z5

'Montavonensis' a small-leaved form with smaller inflorescences. 'Norvegica', with acute-tipped leaves, from the Central Alps, a natural selection; inflorescence branching 8cm above the base, occurs toward the north of the species' range.

'Somerset Seedling' with petals distinctly red-spotted at the base, inflorescence 50–60cm high; very attractive. z4

S. **crustata** Vest (*S. incrustata* Vest). E. Alps to Central Yugoslavia. Many rosettes in a dense cushion; rosettes firm and flat. Leaves narrowly linear, to 7.5cm long, tips recurved, blue-green to glossy green with marginal chalky exudate resembling silver beads. Stems 15–(rarely) 40cm high. Inflorescences racemose-paniculate, similar to those of *S. aizoon*, but more slender; flowers cream-white. Grows in full sun in infertile, limestone gravelly soil. Vigorous in garden culture. Flowers from May to June. And var. **vochinensis**, Julian Alps. Rosettes 5–7.5cm across; leaves of very unequal lengths, stems to 30cm high, arching, with almost white flowers. Free flowering. Out of flower, rosettes resemble those of *S. callosa* var. *bellardii*. z5

S. engleri see Hybrid **S. × paradoxa**

S. hostii Tausch. S. and E. Dolomite Alps. Rosettes to 15cm wide, starry-spreading.

when the radiating rosettes turn red. z6 The botanists distinguish:

S. hostii ssp. **hostii** (*S. altissima* Kerner, var. *altissima* (Kerner) Engl.). Often grown in the trade as *S. hostii* var. *altissima*, from Styria Provence (Austria) with larger, more recurved leaves and stout, much branched, over 60cm-high inflorescences. More demanding and rarely true in culture. z6

S. hostii ssp. **rhaetica** (Kerner) Braun-Blanq. Rhaetian Alps. Distinguished by

S. lingulata see **S. callosa**

S. lingulata var. **bellardii** see **S. callosa** var. **bellardii**

S. lingulata var. **catalaunica** see **S. callosa** ssp. **callosa**

S. longifolia Lapeyr. E. Spain, Pyrenees Mts.; on limestone outcrops to 2400m. Rosettes very leafy and symmetrical, to 15cm wide with age. Leaves stiff, linear-spatulate, acuminate, entire or slightly crenate, silvery gray-green, 3.5–10cm

Saxifraga longifolia

Saxifraga paniculata

Leaves tongue-shaped (1cm wide, 10cm long), margins slightly crenate and beaded with lime, hard and brittle, dark green. Stems stiff, 30–60cm high, quite leafy. Inflorescence a flat-clustered corymbose panicle; flowers milky white, sometimes purple-spotted; May to June. An attractive, somewhat stiff (in flower) species, vigorous, stoloniferous, mat-forming, quickly covering a large area. Conspicuous all year, especially in fall,

its narrower (3–5mm wide, 4–6cm long) leaves, wine red at the base. Considered by experts to be less ornamental than the species. z6

S. hostii var. **altissima** see **S. hostii** ssp. **hostii**

S. incrustata see **S. crustata**

S. kolenatiana see **S. paniculata** ssp. **kolenatiana**

long. Stems to 70cm long and floriferous to the base (unlike other species in this section), stiff, glandular-pubescent. Inflorescence conical-cylindrical with up to 1000 white flowers to 13mm across; July. This beautiful alpine perennial, the "King of the Rockfoils" thrives in the garden, especially in a vertical, east-facing rock crevice or in a dry stone wall. Unfortunately, plants often die after flowering without forming secondary rosettes. Since *S. longifolia* crosses readily with related species, flowers must be isolated and pollinated by hand for pure seed, or remove the flowers of all neighboring Euaizoonia Saxifrages. The seedlings grow vegetatively for several years before blooming. 'Tumbling Waters' is a beautiful, rare and valuable hybrid (*S. longifolia* × *S. callosa*). The rosettes resemble those of *S. longifolia*, but have many secondary rosettes and are very floriferous, with 60cm-high inflorescences. Other hybrids with this species are listed elsewhere. z6

S. mutata L. Alps, S. Carpathian Mts.; on moist, rocky (usually limestone) and gravelly sites. Rosettes resemble *S. cotyledon*, but without stolons, and are regular, with ascending leaves. The rootstock is a thick rhizome. Leaves linear-spatulate, olive green without chalky exudate but margins cartilaginous. Stems 22–30cm high, with white glandular hairs. Flower panicles loosely pyramidal; flowers yellow to orange. Lives only 2–3 years; rosettes die after flowering, often without offset rosettes and can only be maintained by regularly sowing seed. Interesting collector's plant. June to July. And var. **demisa**. Carpathian Mts., smaller, stems 10–12cm high. Grows in bright shade on limestone in nature. z5

S. paniculata Mill. (*S. aizoon* Jacq.). Found in many catalogs and books under the synonym. Arctic and alpine species from Spain to the Caucasus Mts. and arctic Europe and N. America. Leaves narrow-spatulate, fleshy, incurved, toothed, light gray-green, 3–5cm long. Stems erect, with scattered leaves, umbellate panicles branching near the top, flowers usually white; May to June. Due to its wide range, this species includes many forms; generally easy to cultivate, at least where summers are cool; quickly forms a sizable carpet of crowded rosettes. The best of the dwarf forms are:

'Balcana' (*S. aizoon* 'Balcana'), rather small, with flat rosettes; stout, to 20cm high, erect stems; panicles with showy, bright rose-spotted (punctate). A selection with more spots goes by the name of 'Multipunctata'.

'Baldensis' (*S. aizoon* var. *baldensis*), small-rosetted form, distinguished from *S. paniculata* var. *minutifolia* by its reddish stems. z1

S. paniculata ssp. **brevifolia** (*S. aizoon* var. *minor*, *S. aizoon* 'Minor'). Rosettes with short leaves (1cm long, 5mm wide); stems to 15cm high; flowers white; sparse bloomer, but attractive mat forming plant for the trough garden. z3

S. paniculata ssp. **cartilaginea** (Willd.) D.A. Webb (*S. cartilaginea* Willd., *S. aizoon* var. *cartilaginea*). Caucasus Mts. Distin-

guished by the rosetted leaves with acuminate tips, 25mm long and 6mm wide, margins crenate, cartilaginous. Floriferous, white. z3

S. paniculata ssp. **kolenatiana** (Regel) D.A. Webb (*S. kolenatiana* Regel). Caucasus Mts. Distinguished from the above variety by its pink flowers and long, narrow leaves. Prefers a somewhat more shaded site. 'Labradorica' is a compact cushion of rosettes; inflorescences only about 8cm high.

'Lutea' (*S. aizoon* 'Lutea'), with sulfur yellow flowers. z3

S. paniculata var. **carinthiaca** (*S. aizoon* var. *carinthiaca*, *S. carinthiaca*). Carinthia (Austria/Yugoslavia). Rosettes with a few loose, linear-spatulate leaves (1.5cm long, 4mm wide), dark green, very lime-crusted, very rigid; stems 15–20cm high, glabrous; flowers cream-white. z5

S. paniculata var. **major** (*S. aizoon* 'Malbyi'). Commonly found in Dalmatia (Yugoslavia), occasionally in the Alps. A larger type with exceptionally attractive fall and winter color. z4

S. paniculata var. **minutifolia**. Forms dense cushiony mats of tiny rosettes. Sparse flowering. Not very different from *S. paniculata* 'Baldensis'.

'Orientalis'. Medium-sized rosettes; cream-white, red-spotted flowers.

'Rex'. Attractive silver-gray cushions of rosettes with mahogany red flower stems, 25cm high.

'Rosea' (*S. aizoon* 'Rosea'). Bulgaria. An attractive, soft pink-flowered variant, from which many additional selections are made. z4

S. paniculata var. **sturmiana** (*S. aizoon* var. *sturmiana*). Central Alps. Rosettes small, loose, with incurved leaves; leaves cuneate (14mm long, 4mm wide), serrate with ciliate tips; stems brown, 5–15cm high; flowers cream-white. z5

Specialized rock garden publications and encyclopedic works list numerous additional varieties and cultivars of *S. paniculata*.

S. pectinata see Hybrid **S. × fritschiana**

S. peltata see **Peltiphyllum peltatum**

S. probynii see **S. cochlearis**

S. squarrosa Sieber. Very similar to *S. caesia*, but smaller. Occurs in the SE. Alps. Rosette cluster 4–7cm in diameter. Plants not the easiest to cultivate. Once

erroneously listed as *S. caesia* in the Section Kabschia. z5

S. valdensis DC. SW. Alps. Rosettes hemispherical, dense, only 1–2cm high. Leaves linear-spatulate, 4–6mm long, very recurved, densely crusted with chalky exudate. Stems 4–15cm high, with few (5–10) white florets, June. Charming, dwarf species, especially attractive for the miniature rockery or trough garden. z6

Hybrids of the Section Euaizoonia
From this Section come a large number of attractive garden hybrids.

S. × andrewsii Harvey (*S. hirsuta* × *S. paniculata*). An interesting hybrid with parent species from Sections Euaizoonia and Robertsonia. Loose rosettes of green, fleshy, narrow, denticulate leaves; stems 20cm high, a vigorous, satisfactory garden plant. z6

S. × bellunensis see **S. × churchillii**

S. × burnatii (*S. aizoon* × *S. cochlearis*). A natural hybrid from the Maritime Alps. Small, cushiony form, intermediate between the parents in habit. z5

S. × churchillii (*S. hostii* × *S. paniculata*). A natural hybrid, larger than *S. paniculata*, with distinctly toothed leaf margins. Also distributed under the name *S. × bellunensis*. z5

S. × farreri (*S. cochlearis* × *S. callosa*). Small, clustered rosettes; reddish stems 20cm high, white flowers. z5

S. × fritschiana (*S. pectinata*; *S. paniculata* × *S. crustata*). Elegant rosettes with narrow leaves, with pronounced chalky exudate. A reliable garden plant.

'Kathleen Pinsent' a very attractive hybrid (*S. aizoon* ssp. *kolenatiana* × *S. lingulata*) with 20cm-long, pink inflorescences above attractive, symmetrical, lime-crusted rosettes; flowers in early summer.

'Kathrin' has a small cushion, red flowers.

'Lindau', round-rosettes in a globose cushion, white flowers. z5

S. × paradoxa (*S. engleri*; *S. hostii* × *S. crustata*). Natural hybrid from the E. Alps. Very silvery cushions, cream-white flowers, dark brown flower stems.

'Southside Seedling' (hybrid with *S. cotyledon*). Rosettes 12-15cm wide. Large, dense inflorescences about 40cm high. The white flowers are intensely red-spotted. Very ornamental.

'Vreny'. Attractive, flat rosettes, 2.5–3cm across, leaf margins strongly toothed, distinctly lime-crusted. Pure white flowers, inflorescences 15cm high, good for trough gardens.

'Whitehill' (*S. paniculata* × *S. cochlearis?*). Blue-green rosetted leaves, slightly reddish-toned at the base. Inflorescences 12–15cm high. z5

Section Porophyllum
(Kabschia and Engleria Saxifrages)
Early Spring Rockfoils

Botanists do not separate the Kabschia and Engleria species, as the characteristics are not sufficiently distinct and significant; horticulturists, however, sometimes separate them based on differences here listed.

Kabschia characteristics: cushions dense and firm, evergreen; rosettes do not die after flowering, and secondary rosettes remain attached to the parent rhizome. Leaves small and stiff, usually awl-shaped, needle-sharp or rounded, more or less with a chalky exudate. Flowers white, yellow, lilac, pink, or soft red, never spotted, solitary or few on a short, branched peduncle; flower very early in the spring. Nearly all are lime-loving, only a few centimeters high and prized collectors' plants for rock gardens, dry stone walls and the alpine house. Also attractive for trough gardens, planters or container growing. Flowering plants in pots are delightful.

All the Kabschia Saxifrages grow best with a shaded east or north exposure in the rock garden since they burn easily in full sun. Plants thrive in a deep, narrow hole in tufa rock. The more vigorous sorts will succeed in the crevices of rock walls. The preferred medium is humus, well mixed with sand and fine limestone gravel. When planting, it is important the root ball be moist and pressed firmly into place. Firmly set plants will resist heaving and moving out of their crevices. On vertical faces plants are sometimes wedged in with sphagnum moss or even partially plugged in with concrete. Plants require good drainage, being sensitive to wetness, particularly in winter. Propagation of all these species is easiest by cuttings, either May or late fall. These are stuck in sand-filled containers under glass in October; plants will root by the following spring. The true species, especially *S. grisebachii*, are primarily grown from seed; seedlings flower the third year.

Engleria characteristics: leaves broader, more spreading, and longer, usually gray-green, silver-gray margined due to the chalky crust, rosettes usually flat. Inflorescences many-flowered, racemose, nearly spicate with colorful, usually red, stem leaves and calyces; flowers small; more decorative in the bud stage than when open.

In the following descriptions, the Engleria species are specifically noted as such, all others are Kabschia forms.

S. aretioides Lapeyr. Pyrenees Mts.; on limestone outcroppings. Cushions very small and dense. Leaves to 6mm long, linear-ligulate, leathery, margins cartilaginous. Stems to 5cm high, 3–5 flowered; flowers 13mm across, golden-yellow. April. z6

S. aretioides var. **primula** see **S. diaphensioides** var. **lutea**

S. boryi see **S. marginata** var. **marginata**

S. burseriana L. E. Alps; in shelving ledges and crevices in shaded dolomite and limestone. Cushions gray-green, rosettes dense-prickly-leaved. Leaves linear-subulate, to 12mm long, margins cartilaginous. Flowers pure white, 2.5cm across, solitary, on 5–10cm high, reddish brown stems. One of the earliest and most attractive spring bloomers, with flowers appearing in early March. A very variable species in its natural habitat. Small- or large-flowered forms with entire or crenate petals may be found on the same site. The following forms are found in culture:

S. burseriana var. **burseriana** (*S. burseriana* 'Minor', *S. burseriana* var. *minor*). Karawanken Mts. Dwarf and compact; stems shorter than 4cm, flowers round.

S. burseriana var. **minor** see **S. burseriana** var. **burseriana**

S. burseriana var. **tridentata** Lancetino, Italy. Rosettes and inflorescences more robust; flowers large. A superior variety, parent of numerous large-flowered cultivars including: *S.b.* var. *major*, *S.b.* 'Major', 'Brookside', 'Crenata', with crenate petals, 'Seissera' and several more. Cultivars with pink or pale yellow flowers listed under *S. burseriana* probably are hybrids.

S. caesia L. Pyrenees Mts., Alps, Apennine Mts., Carpathian Mts. Dense, hemispherical, gray-green cushions of small rosettes with recurved leaves. Leaves linear-oblong, about 4–7mm long. Stems slender with 1–2(–5) white flowers together, about 13mm across. Requires a somewhat moist, very gravelly soil. May to July. z5

S. calyciflora see **S. media**

S. caucasica Somm. et Lv. Caucasus. Several varieties may be distinguished. The one of greatest garden importance is *S. caucasica* var. **desoulavayi** (Oett.) Engl. et Irmsch. A somewhat decorative plant. Small, clustered, loose rosettes. Basal leaves lanceolate, spiny, to 3m long, dark green. Stems with few leaves, to 7.5cm high, with terminal corymbs; flowers deep yellow, to 6mm across. Requires ample moisture during periods of vegetative growth. Blooms in March. z5

S. corymbosa see **S. luteoviridis**

S. diapensioides Bell. SW. Alps. Dwarf, rigid, gray-green, dense mats. Leaves stiff, blunt, to 6.5mm long, linear, very crowded. Flowering stems 2–4.5cm high, rarely more, with 2–9 flowers. Flowers rounded, to 1cm across, milk-white. April. The var. **lutea** (= *S. aretioides* var. *primulina*) may belong here. z6

S. ferdinandi-coburgii Kellerer et Sünderm. Bulgaria (Rhodope, Pirin Mts.). Cushions of silver-grey, firm rosettes. Leaves narrow-oblong, spiny-tipped, ciliate, about 12mm long. Stems leafy, 7–10cm high, 2–12 flowered. Flowers roundish, to 8mm across, yellow. Much like *S. aretioides*, but indigenous to E. Europe. z6

S. ferdinandi-coburgii var. **pravislavii** see **S. ferdinandi-coburgii** var. **radoslavovii**

S. ferdinandi-coburgii var. **radoslavovii** Stoj. (known also as var. *pravislavii*) from the Ali Botusch Mts., Macedonia. This variety is superior: substantially more vigorous, more floriferous, with larger, rich yellow flowers, sepals and stems red-brown. April to May. z6

S. frederici-augustii see **S. sempervivum**

S. grisebachii Degen et Dörfl. (*S. porophylla* var. *montenegrina* (Hal. et Bald.) Engl. et Irmsch.) Macedonia. Engleria Type. Rosettes to 8cm across, eventually developing a high humped colony. Leaves to 4cm long, spatulate-ligulate, gray-green with cartilaginous margins. Stems to 15cm high, erect silky-pubescent. Stem leaves spatulate, reddish with green tips. Inflorescence almost spike-like, nodding at first, then erect. Flowers 5mm across, bluish-pink. Calyx glowing carmine red. A beautiful, highly prized rock garden plant. The selection 'Wisley Variety' is especially colorful and with vigorous red flowers. Following the introduction of 'Wisley Variety' the same plant was discovered growing wild in a gorge on Mt. Tsukala, Albania. April. z6

S. juniperifolia Adams. Caucasus Mts. Vigorous, dark green, mosslike, prickly-leaved mats. Rosettes firm. Leaves stiff, narrow-lanceolate, to 2cm long, ciliate, juniper-scented. Flowering stems to 7.5cm high, leafy. Inflorescence nearly globose, with 4–8 flowered racemes of

Saxifraga Kabschia Hybrid

yellow flowers to 5mm across. A rather poor bloomer, but attractive cushion plant. Variable, with several varieties, including var. **brachyphylla**, columner "rosette" with small, overlapping leaves, stem leaves tiny; var. **brotheri**, rosette and stem leaves upright, stem leaves to 2cm long; var. **cineria**, rosettes gray-green, stem leaves reflexed; var. **kasnezowiana**, leaves oblong-lanceolate in tufted, gray-green rosettes, petals 5-nerved; var. **macedonica**, leaves very short, lanceolate, ciliate, flower stems slightly higher than the species; var. **pseudosanota**, leaves needle-like, to 12mm long, flowers large, on 5cm stems; var. **stevensii**, like var. *brotheri* but stem leaves 2× longer. April to May. z5

S. kotschyi Boiss. Asia Minor. Rosettes multiply to make a mounded, dense cushion. Leaves blunt, spatulate-ligulate, gray-green. Stems leafy, glandular-pubescent, 5–7.5cm high with loose corymbs of 7–13 very small yellow, upright flowers with exserted anthers. April. z6

S. laevis M.B. Caucasus Mts. Small, loose rosettes or mats of overlapping, short, dark green ciliate leaves; with small, soft yellow flowers in clusters, 3–5cm high. Requires lime-free soil. Somewhat difficult; not very ornamental. April to May. z6

S. lilacina Duthie. W. Himalaya Mts. Flat, grasslike cushions of tiny, gray-green rosettes. Leaves oblong, to 4.5mm long, margins cartilaginous. Stems 2.5–5cm high. Flowers solitary, amethyst. Grows best in moist, sandy, peaty, lime-free gravel in light shade. April. This species

Saxifraga × *salmonica* 'Assimilis'

is one parent of most pink, reddish and purple hybrids in Section Porophyllum. z5

S. luteoviridis Schott et Kotschy (*S. corymbosa* Boiss. non Luce). Balkan Region, Carpathian Mts. Rosettes to 5cm wide, flat-spreading. Leaves spatulate to 2.5cm long, entire, glaucous, sometimes purplish beneath. Inflorescence a false umbel or panicle, to 15cm high and to 15-flowered; flowers 6mm across, greenish-yellow to yellow. Only of interest to collectors; a demanding species. April. z6

S. marginata Sternb. Balkan Region, S. Carpathian Mts., Central and S. Italy. Variable species with a wide natural range. z6 Some ornamental varieties are:

S. marginata var. **coriophylla** (Griseb.) Engl.; Balkans. Dense mats or cushions of very leafy rosettes; leaves small, 4–6mm long, 0.8–1.6mm wide, gray-green, covered with chalky scales. Stems 2–5cm high, densely corymbose, with many

small white flowers. z6

S. marginata var. **eumarginata** see **S. marginata** var. **marginata**

S. marginata var. **marginata** (*S. marginata* var. *eumarginata* Engl. et Irmsch., *S. boryi* Boiss. et Heldr.). Greece. Flat cushions, mats, or hummocks of attractive, rounded rosettes; leaves variable, gray-green, linear-oblong to obovate spatulate, to 12cm long, with translucent margins. Stems 1–7cm high, inflorescence corymbose, flowers white, rarely pale pink. A poor bloomer, but a very

Saxifraga grisebachii 'Wisley Variety'

attractive, vigorous-growing cushion plant. z6

S. marginata var. **rocheliana** (Sternb.) Engl. et Irmsch. Balkans. Vigorous, bluish gray-green cushions, to 50cm across in its native habitat; leaves and rosettes twice as large as those of the type species; leaves spatulate to obtuse, with conspicuous chalk-encrusted margins. Stems to 10cm high, with dense corymbs of small white flowers.

There are a number of other cultivars with more or less insignificant differences. All *marginata* forms flower in May. At least two natural varieties with pale pink flowers and a pale yellow-flowered variety are listed by specialists but are not generally available. z6

S. media Gouan (*S. calyciflora* Lap.) Pyrenees Mts. Engleria Type. Rosettes flat-spreading, to 3.5cm wide. Leaves to 2.5cm long, oblong to linear-spatulate, leathery, gray, margins cartilaginous, with lime pits. Stems 7.5–12.5cm high. Inflorescence glandular-pubescent; calyx very large red-hairy; flowers pale pink. Grows on limestone gravel. Parent of numerous hybrids. z6

S. porophylla Bertol. (Not identical to *S.*

S. porophylla var. **sibthorpiana** see **S. sempervivum**

S. sancta Griseb. Greece, Athos, on marble, W. Asia Minor. Flat, clustered, dark green, mosslike, stiff cushions. Leaves very acute and short. Stems to 5cm high or less. Inflorescence an umbellate panicle, strictly erect. Flowers small, petals yellow, stamen filaments widely exserted, stigmas with reddish tips; March to April. This species may appear as a variety or subspecies of *S. juniperifolia*, but proably is distinct. z7

flowers; March to April. z9(8 or 7)

S. sempervivum K. Koch (*S. porophylla* Bertol. var. *sibthorpiana* (Griseb.) Engl. et Irmsch., *S. frederici-augustii* Bias.) Engleria Type. An attractive, variable species from the Balkan region on limestone screes and outcroppings. Often classified as *S. porophylla* var. *sibthorpiana*. Rosette leaves spatulate, acute-tipped, more or less glaucous, spreading, not erect, to 12cm long, rarely longer. Stems 15–22.5cm high. Inflorescence a shallow panicle. Flowers pale purple with darker purple calyx. Some varieties are found in

Saxifraga Arendsii Hybrid

Saxifraga × *apiculata* 'Gregor Mendel'

thessalica or *S. porophylla* var. *thessalica*. *S. porophylla* var. *montenegrina* is *S. grisebachii* and *S. porophylla* var. *sibthorpiana* is *S. sempervivum*) Apennine Mts., Abruzzi, Balkan Region. Engleria Type. Quite a variable species with dense, leafy rosettes. Leaves to 12mm long, oblong-spatulate to linear, acuminate, glaucous, margins hard, with lime pits. Stems 10–15cm high. Inflorescence nodding, racemose; flowers 4mm across, sessile, calyx inflated, reddish, petals pink to purple. As indicated above, the definition of this species is not exact. Probably the Montenegro varieties *thessalica* and *thessalica* f. *alba* are valid. z6

S. sartorii see **S. scardica**

S. scardica Griseb. (*S. sartorii* Heldr.). Greece. Cushions of crowded rosettes mounded, hard, gray-green. Rosettes almost columnar. Leaves stiff, to 12mm long, oblong to lanceolate, keeled beneath, chalk-encrusted, acuminate. Stems 10cm high. Inflorescence an umbellate panicles of up to 15 flowers, flowers 8cm across, white to pale pink. Several tender varieties from Greece are listed; the horticultural 'Rosea' is typical *S. scardica* with pink flowers. z7

S. scardica var. **erythrantha** Hal. from Peloponnesus has rich pink-colored

the trade. April to May. z7(6)

S. spruneri Boiss. Mountains of N. Albania to Central Greece. Very similar to *S. marginata* but smaller overall. A small cushiony cluster. Rosettes hemispherical. Leaves gray-green, glandular-hairy beneath. Flowers in a close corymb, small, creamy-white to white; May. Valued only by collectors. Best cultivated in the alpine house. z8

S. stribrnyi (Velen.) Podp. N. Greece, Bulgaria. Engleria Type. The coarsely branched inflorescence is characteristic. Rosette leaves oblong-spatulate, to 2.5cm long, all lying flat, rounded at the tips, silvery-gray with marginal lime glands. Stems 7.5–10cm high, branching, the secondary branches and inflated calyx closely hairy. Panicle with 10–30 flowers. Flowers are purplish-pink. Var. **zollikoferi** (Bulgaria) with paler, salmon-pink flowers. Some cultivars in the trade are: 'Tristan' and 'Isolde'. z6

S. tombeanensis Boiss. ex Engl. (*S. diapensioides* Neilr., not to be confused with *S. diapensioides* Bell) Italian Alps; Monte Baldo region. Hard, domed cushions of crowded rosettes to 10cm wide or wider. Rosettes very small. Leaves ovate to linear-lanceolate, only 3.5mm long, reflexed, thick, keeled beneath, silvery-gray sometimes tinged reddish. Stems about 5cm high with 2–3 relatively large, white flowers. Grows especially well on tufa rock. z7

Hybrids of the Section Porophyllum

Sündermann, Kellerer and Heinrich in W. Germany, and several English breeders have developed a host of cultivars by repeated crossings of the Kabschia and Engleria Saxifrages. Some are truly delightful plants with brightly colored flowers or buds and particularly attractive rosettes. However, there are also a number of superfluous cultivars, especially the poor-flowering forms which should be removed from cultivation. The following descriptions provide an overview of the most popular hybrids. The Czechoslovakian botanists, Dr. Horny, Dr. Sojak and Dr. Webr, have classified the hybrids according to parentage. This has made necessary a renaming of many cultivars.

S. × anglica 'Cranbourne' ('Cranbourne' *S. lilacina × S. luteopurpurea*). Rosettes dark colored, leaves blue-green, flowers strong rose-red. z6

S. × anglica 'Myra' ('Myra', *S. lilacina × S. luteopurpurea*). Gray-green cushions of silver-gray rosettes; bright salmon red flowers which fade to light or cherry red. z6

S. × anglica 'Winifred' ('Winifred' *S. lilacina × S. luteopurpurea*). Small cushion of tiny rosettes, flowers dark carmine-pink, very attractive, but not easy to grow. z7

S. × apiculata 'Gregor Mendel' (*S. × apiculata*, from *S. marginata × S. sancta*). Pale yellow, floriferous, strong-growing and undemanding. The white-flowering

form is superfluous. z6

S. × arco-valleyi 'Arco' (*S. × arco-valleyi*, from *S. lilacina × S. marginata*). Grassy, rosettes small, to 1cm across. Silvery-gray. Stems to 2.5m high. Flowers rosy-red; free-flowering. z6

S. × bertolonii 'Antonio' (*S. bertolonii, S. porophylla × S. sempervivum*). A nearly exact intermediate form of both parents. Flowers carmine purple, calyx glandular-pubescent. z6

S. × biasolettii 'Phoenix' (*S. biasolettii*, from *S. grisebachii × S. sempervivum*). Rosette leaves long and acute. Especially attractive in bud, carmine-red, free-flowering. z6

S. × boeckeleri 'Armida' (*S. boeckeleri, S. ferdinandi-coburgii × S. stribrnyi*). Rosettes flat, silver-gray. Inflorescence branched, flowers bright orange-yellow. z6

S. × borisii 'Sofia' (*S. × borisii, S. ferdinandi-coburgii × S. marginata*). Blue-gray cushions; flowers lemon yellow. z6

S. × boydii 'Faldonside' (*S. × faldonside, S. aretioides × S burseriana*). Plants form attractive, dense mats. Flowers grouped 1–3, large, light yellow. Poor bloomer. 'Delia' (*S. lilacina × S. × godroniana*). Sea green, small-leaved rosettes in hummocks. Flowers lilac tinged white on 2.5cm high stems. z6

S. × doerfleri 'Ignatz Doerfler' (*S. × doerfleri, S. grisebachii × S. stribrnyi*). Gray-green rosettes. Inflorescence well branched, densely gray-glandular-pubescent. Flowers red-purple with inflated calyx. z6

S. × edithae 'Edith' (*S. × edithae, S. marginata × S. stribrnyi*). Compact, sea green, tight rosettes. Flowers light pink on 5cm high stems. Late and free-flowering. z6

S. × elisabethae 'Carmen' (*S. × elisabethae, S. burseriana × S. sancta*). Dense mats of small rosettes, poor flowering, flowers light yellow. z6

S. × eudoxiana 'Haagii' (*S. × haagii, S. ferdinandi-coburgii × S. sancta*). Very vigorous green mats of hard rosettes. Floriferous, yellow-flowered, undemanding and attractive. z6

S. × geuderii 'Eulenspiegel' (*S. × geuderii, S. × boydii × S. ferdinandi-coburgii*). Dense cushions, flowers rich yellow. z6

S. × hoerhammeri 'Lohengrin' (*S. × hoerhammeri, S. grisebachii × S. marginata*). Tough, hard rosettes; small, stems 7.5cm high, with pink flowers charming, especially in the bud stage. z6

S. × hornibrookii 'Riverslea' ('Riverslea', *S. lilacina × S. porophylla*). Compact cushions of silver-gray rosettes, slow-growing. Relatively large, almost campanulate flowers, carmine-wine red. z6

S. × irvingii 'Jenkinsae' (*S. × jenkinsae, S. burseriana × S. lilacina*). Vigorous, spiny gray-green rosettes in close tufts, undemanding, flowers lilac-pink with a darker eye. One of the first to flower, often beginning in February. z6

S. × irvingii 'Mother of Pearl' ('Mother of Pearl', *S. burseriana × S. lilacina*). Rosettes silver-gray, flowers soft pink, very early. z6

S. × irvingii 'Rubella' (*S. × rubella, S. burseriana × S. lilacina*). Gray-green, grasslike leaves, flowers lilac-white, on 5cm-long stems. z6

S. × irvingii 'Walter Irving' (*S. × irvingii, S. burseriana × S. lilacina*). Cushions smaller, rosettes blue-gray, flowers pink, nearly sessile. z6

S. × kellereri 'Johann Kellerer' (*S. × kellereri, S. burseriana × S. stribrnyi*). Gray rosettes, flowers soft peach-pink, on long-stemmed, well-branched racemes, vigorous. Earliest form, often flowers as early as January. z6

S. × kellereri 'Landaueri' (*S. × landaueri*, from *S. × kellereri × S. marginata* var. *rocheliana*). Stout, hard rosettes; flowers soft pink, to 8, stems branched, stems 10cm high. z6

S. × kellereri 'Sündermannii' (*S. × sündermannii* 'Purpurea', *S. burseriana × S. stribrnyi*). Dense, hard, gray-green cushions; flowers bright pink, nearly sessile at first, later stems elongate to 10cm high, very floriferous. z6

S. × mariae-theresiae 'Theresia' (*S. maria-theresiae, S. burseriana × S. grisebachii*). Vigorous, gray-green rosettes, fiery red buds and small pink flowers. z6

S. × megaseaeflora 'Robin Hood' (*S. × megaseaeflora, S. burseriana × S. anglica*). Dwarf, hard, gray cushions. Flowers usually solitary, occasionally in 2's or 3's, on 3–5cm high stems, bright rose. z6

S. × **paulinae** 'Paula' (S. × *paulinae*, S. *burseriana* 'Minor' × S. *ferdinandi-coburgii*). Dense, gray cushions; very floriferous, light yellow. z6

S. × **paulinae** 'Franzii' (S. × *franzii*, S. *burseriana* × S. *ferdinandi-coburgii*). Rosetted cushions similar to S. *burserana*, but leaves flatter, very floriferous, light yellow, to 6 flowers on a stem. z6

S. × **paulinae** 'Kolbiana' (S. × *kolbiana*, from S. *burseriana* × S. *ferdinandi-coburgii*). Attractive cushions with flatter leaves than those of S. *burseriana*, light yellow flowers, floriferous. z6

S. × **petraschii** 'Kaspar Maria Sternberg' (S. × *petraschii*, S. *burseriana* × S. *tombeanensis*). Small, gray-green rosettes; 1–3 flowered, flowers large, white with wavy petals. z6

S. × **pragensis** 'Golden Prague' ('Zlata Praha', S. × *edithae* × S. *ferdinandi-coburgii*). Attractive blue-green cushions, rather large rosettes; flowers orange-yellow. z6

S. × **prossenii** 'Regina' (S. × *prossenii*, S. *sancta* × S. *stribrnyi*). Green, gray-encrusted rosettes in hummocky cushions; inflorescences bunched, floriferous, calyx copper-colored, petals small, ocher yellow. z6

S. × **salmonica** 'Marie Louise' ('Marie Louise', S. *burseriana* × S. *marginata*). Dense, short-leaved mats; buds reddish, flowers white, large, with rust-colored stems, very floriferous. z6

S. × **salmonica** 'Obristii' (S. × *obristii*, S. *burseriana* × S. *marginata*). Dense, short-leaved mats; buds reddish, flowers large, white. z6

S. × **schottii** 'Perstribrnyi' (S. × *schottii*, S. *luteoviridis* × S. *stribrnyi*). Short-leaved, vigorous cushions, flower stems branched, calyx copper-pink, petals light ocher yellow. z6

S. × **smithii** 'Vahlii' (S. × *vahlii*, from S. *marginata* × S. *tombeanensis*). Small-leaved, dense cushions with up to 5 flowers on a stem, white, very abundant and late-flowering. z6

S. × **steinii** 'Agnes' (S. *steinii*, from S. *aretioides* × S. *tombeanensis*). Very small-rosette in gray cushions, to 6 flowers on a stem, floriferous and late, light yellow. z6

The plants listed here are only a limited selection of the many hybrids of this Section. Much more extensive information on the cultivars may be found in the book *Saxifrages* by Fritz Köhlein.

Section Dactyloides
Mossy Saxifrages, Moss Rockfoils

Characteristics: green, soft-leaved rosettes, which persist after flowering; the mat increases by above ground stolons and offshoots; forms a low, dense mat; leaves usually 3-lobed (or more), rarely linear, toothed. Leaves never lime-encrusted. The mossy saxifrages, especially the S. Arendsii Hybrids, are commonly grown rock garden plants. Very effective on shady terrace walls and in crevices and shaded beds with primulas, *Helleborus, Viola, Muscara* and other small perennials. These are attractive, not only in flower, but also in late summer and especially in fall and winter with frost on the margins of the evergreen leaves. Mossy Saxifrages thrive in loose, gritty to gravelly soil with ample humus. The soil needs to be constantly damp through the growing season and somewhat drier but never arid in winter. Propagation is best done in late fall by cuttings stuck in a loose, sandy soil and covered with glass over winter. Vigorous plants will result during the course of the following year. The mats are also easily divided. Old mats tend to brown off in the middle; lift these, divide, and replant the vigorous outer pieces in renewed soil.

S. **Arendsii Hybrids**, Arends. This is a collective name for all the garden hybrids of mixed parentage of species within this Section, especially S. *decipiens* and S. *hypnoides*; crossed first by G. Arends and later other breeders. Plants produce more or less vigorous, mossy mats with multiple-flowered stems of small, airy, pastel flowers in May. Some especially attractive selections are:
'Biedermeier' ('Bride's Maid'), flowers white, petals crisply wavy, 15cm; 'Blütenteppich' ('Flower Carpet'), rose-pink, 15cm; 'Carnival', bright rose-red, not fading, 15cm; 'Dornröschen' ('Sleeping Beauty') (Benary), bright red, flowers 2cm wide; 'Dubarry', red, large- and late-flowering, 20cm; 'Feuerwerk' ('Fireworks'), carmine-pink, early blooming, 20cm; 'Grandiflora Alba', white, 20cm; 'Ingeborg' (Marx), dark red flowers above dense foliage; 'Juwel' ('Jewel'), also short-stemmed, red flowers; 'Leuchtkäfer' ('Lightning Bug') (Benary), (introduced by Klose), slow-growing, dense cushion; 'Luschtinez' ('Harder Zwerg'), stems only 8cm high, blood red flowers, vigorous mat, tolerates full sun; 'Purpurteppich' ('Purple Carpet'), light carmine-red, vigorous, 15cm; 'Riedel's Farbenkissen' ('Riedel's Bright Cushion'), deep fiery red, fading to pink, 20cm; 'Rosenschaum' ('Rose Foam'), pink, 15–20cm; 'Schneeteppich' ('Snow Carpet'), white, 20cm; 'Schwefelblüte' ('Sulfur Flower'), sulfur yellow, 15cm; 'Triumph', dark red, 10–15cm.

S. **cebennensis** Rouy et E.G. Camus. France, Cevennes Mts. Cushions the size of a man's fist, hemispherical, compact, gray-green. Leaves 1cm long, cuneate, shallow-trilobed, finely pubescent. Stems 3–5cm high, 3–6 flowered. Flowers white; May. A beautiful species for shaded rock gardens and trough gardens. z7

S. **cespitosa** L. Arctic to Subarctic Europe, Asia and N. America. A very variable species. Tufted, slowly forms loose mats. Leaves 3-lobed, to 5mm long. Flowers on slender, branching stems to 15cm high. Flowers white, to 12cm across. Botanists describe several varieties. Plants by this name in the trade are usually not the true species. It is best to substitute one of the hybrids for garden use. May. z1–7

S. **conifera** Coss. et Durieu. N. Spain, Algeria. Leaves entire, linear-lanceolate, awn-tipped. The rosettes close up in summer, forming ovate, acuminate, gray-green "buds" which resemble *Sedum tenuifolium*. Interesting collectors' plants for the alpine house. Drought tolerant in summer. z6

S. **corbariensis** Timb.-Lagr. E. Pyrenees and E. Spain; on limestone screes and outcroppings. About 25cm high with attractive, white flowers and broad stiff mats. A plant for a sunny site. z6

S. **cuneata** Willd. W. Pyrenees, N. Spain. Cushions large, hemispherical, loose, or sometimes densely grasslike. Shoots with rosetted leaves at the tips; leaves tough, leathery, glossy dark green or chalky gray, especially in the fall. Inflorescence an umbellate-raceme; flowers white; June. A valuable garden species, tolerates a sunny site; a very attractive cushion plant. z6

S. **decipiens** see S. **rosacea**

S. **gemmifera** see S. **hypnoides** var. **egemmulosa**

S. **geranoides** L. E. Pyrenees, NE. Spain. Thrives on limestone. Petioled leaves variously dissected, the segments leathery, hairy, fragrant when bruised. Stem 20cm high, with a compact cluster of 6–9 pure white, campanulate flowers. Grows best in light semi-shade in the garden. June. z6

S. globulifera Desf. S. Spain, NW. Africa. Cushions small; foliage loose, grasslike. Stems usually only 1cm long. Leaves oval to reniform, 3–5 lobed. Leaves often with axillary bulbils. Quite variable. Rarely encountered but desirable for the alpine house are var. *erioblasta* (see next entry), var. *gibraltarica*, var. *granatensis*, var. *ornanensis* and var. *spathulata*, similar

southeastward to the Vosges Mts. Mats loose to densely grasslike. Leaves long-petioled, pale green, finely 3–5 incised, with axillary bulbils. Stems slender, sparingly leafy, few-flowered. Flowers white. May to June. Varieties occasionally encountered include: *cantabrica*, *condensata*, 'Kingsii' (see *S. hyp.* var. *egemmulosa*, below), 'Lutescens', *purpuea*, 'Whitlavei', and 'Variegata'. All are attractive in the garden. z6

S. hypnoides var. **egemmulosa** Engl. et Irmsch. (*S. gemmifera* hort., *S. kingii* hort.). Particularly attractive, with dense, bright

trough garden. Several varieties and cultivars are more worth growing than the species: var. **acaulis**, dense and short stemmed; var. **atropurpurea**, flowers purple to orangish; 'Cloth of Gold', with yellowish-bronze foliage; 'Compacta', plant very dense, dwarf; var. **crocea**, like the species but flowers yellow; 'Florepleno', flowers semi-double, cream-colored; var. **laxa**, small, large mat; var. **lineata**, loose mat, short-stemmed, flowers white to pale yellow. May to June. z5

Saxifraga stolonifera 'Cuscutiformis'

Saxifraga oppositifolia

Saxifraga stellaris

S. muscoides All. Alps, high alpine, lime-intolerant species found on moraine and in deep crevices, with firm, flat, resinous fragrant cushions and small, pale yellow flowers. Very difficult to maintain and not worth the effort on deep garden soils. Nearly all plants cultivated under this name are actually progeny of a cross with *S. cespitosa*. The cultivar 'Findling' has dense, dark green cushions and abundant white flowers in May. z5

S. pedemontana All. W. and Central Alps, Carpathians, Balkan Peninsula; over an igneous rock substrate. Loose, pale green, carpeting habit. Stems procumbent-ascending, very leafy. Leaves cuneate, long-petioled; 3–7 parted, glandular, soft, nearly fleshy. Inflorescence a paniculate false umbel, 3–10 flowered, flowers white; June. z6

S. pedemontana var. **cervicornis** (Viv.) Engl. Corsica. Has wide, hemispherical leaves and narrow lobes. A collector's plant for a shaded, humus-rich site in the alpine garden. Other somewhat hardier

in flower but varying in foliage and bulbil characteristics. z7

S. globulifera var. **erioblasta** Engl. et Irmsch. Spain: Sierra Nevada Mts., on limestone screes. Particularly attractive, dense cushions, with 5–7mm long, cuneate, very short, 3-lobed leaves; the rosettes shrivel into tight gray-brown, densely white shaggy balls during the summer, resembling a dwarf *Sempervivum arachnoideum*; flowers small, pink, on slender stems. June.

S. hypnoides L., Dovedale Moss, Eve's Cushion, Moss Rockfoil. NW. Europe,

green mats which color an attractive bronze-red in fall. A valuable ornamental plant. z6

S. kingii see **S. hypnoides** var. **egemmulosa**

S. moschata Wulf. Mountains of Central and S. Europe, W. Asia, Siberia. Forms a dense cushion; stems without gemmaceous bulbils. Inflorescence usually with only 2–3 flowers. Flowers cream-colored to a soft, deep yellow, sometimes purple, purplish or white. The plants require a carefully chosen, sheltered site in semi-shade; or grow in a varieties include **baldaccii**, more woody-stemmed, and **cymosa**, with small leaves and large, white flowers. z7

S. rosacea Moench. (*S. decipiens* Erh., a name still in common botanical and horticultural usage). Various local varieties occur in NW. and Central Europe. Grows just as well on limestone as on a limestone-free soil. Some varieties produce dense, compact cushions, others a loose carpet. An exceptionally variable species. Leaves broad with blunt divisions or narrow, with acute-tipped segments. The slender flower stems are leaf-

Saxifraga × irvingii 'Jenkinsae'

less and bear 2–5 pure white or pale pink flowers. The species in its several varieties is important to the rock garden, and is a parent to many hybrids. Tolerates a rather dry site. z6

S. tenella Wulf. SE. Alps; on moist, mossy, shaded rocks. Cushion yellowish-green, loose carpet-forming, with many, densely spreading, creeping leafy shoots. Leaves linear-lanceolate, entire, with awl-shaped tips. Inflorescence a loose panicle, 2–9 flowered; flowers small, cream-yellow; June. For shaded sites, also useful as a ground cover. Vigorous-growing species. z6

S. trifurcata Schrad. N. Spain. Cushions matte green, loosely hemispherical, to 20cm high and very wide. Shoots slender, brittle, woody. Leaves long-petioled, reniform in outline, 3-lobed, the lobes much divided. Stems 15cm long. Inflorescence an umbellate panicle, many-flowered, flowers white; May to June. Very valuable, late flowering; thrives on sunny sites, a good edging plant for a low border. z6

Section Porphyrion

Characteristics: stems with crosswise opposite leaves, slender, lying on the ground and rooting, or more or less upright in a dense evergreen cushion. Leaves small, leathery, evergreen. Flowers short-peduncled, purple.

S. oppositifolia L. A variety-rich species with a circumpolar range. Outside the Arctic region, populations may be found and distinguished geographically in the Pyrenees, Alps, Apennines, Sudetes, Carpathians and Rhodope Mts. of

Saxifraga rotundifolia

Bulgaria, as well as in Great Britain and North America. Ascending into the high mountains to 3500m. Tolerates a lime-rich or acidic substrate, on rocky ridges and cliffs, moraines and loamy, sparsely grassy slopes. Stems many, creeping, slender; with various-sized, small, elliptic, obtuse, ciliate-margined leaves, forming flat cushion-mats. Flowers wine red, solitary, nearly sessile, appearing immediately after the snow melt. The deep purplish-red flowering 'Splendens'; the selection 'Wetterhorn', strong rose-red; and the var. *latina*, are more valuable than the species. Many more varieties and cultivars are offered in the trade. z1–7

S. oppositifolia var. **latina** Terr. from the Apennines, has larger, close-crowded leaves distinguishable by 3 little indentations. This is the most easily cultivated of the many varieties. It is very dense and compact in habit, large-flowered and floriferous, less sensitive to dryness and sun scald than the type species. An attractive, but still relatively demanding collector's plant; cultivate in a shaded site of the alpine garden in a humus-rich, gravelly soil with ample moisture. z6

Section Robertsoniana

Characteristics: evergreen plants with aboveground stolons. All or nearly all leaves basal in rosettes, leaves leathery, rounded or cuneate, often spoon-shaped, variously toothed but not lobed; flowers with equally long petals. All are valuable, shade-loving plants of easy cultivation, with many garden uses, especially as a ground cover.

S. cuneifolia L., N. Spain, Pyrenees Mts., European Alps, N. Apennines, E. Carpathian Mts., NW. Yugoslavia; generally on a substrate of igneous rock, growing in coniferous forests. Rosettes dense, in grass-like mats. Leaves cuneate, thick and leathery, glabrous, dull-glazed, with a cartilaginous margin, only slightly toothed, undersides violet-red, especially in winter. Stems to 20cm high, paniculate. Flowers small, starry, white, with one yellow spot at the base of each petal; June to July. Useful for a shady rock slope or dry stone wall. The low, small, dense mat-forming hybrid, S. × tazetta (S. taygetea × S. cuneifolia), is especially recommended for collectors. Several varieties and one cultivar are listed. z5

S. geum see **S. × geum, S. hirsuta**

S. hirsuta L., Rough-leaved Rockfoil. N. Spain, Pyrenees Mts., SW. Ireland. Rosettes with long-stalked basal leaves; the petiole is narrowly channeled, twice to many times as long as the blade; both pubescent on both sides. The glandular pubescent flower stems are 12–30cm high, with white flowers in many-flowered panicles. Forms persistent rosette cushions. Grows best in high humus soil with somewhat more moisture than the other species. Garden worthy. S. geum L. sometimes is listed under this name but is a hybrid; S. hirsuta × S. umbrosa = S. × geum. z6

S. spathularis Brot. N. Portugal and NW. Spain. Rosettes in cushions with above-ground secondary shoots. This species is rarely found in cultivation. Leaves long-petioled, spatulate, obtuse to 3-lobed; flower stems with scattered, short-petioled leaves, to 20cm high; inflorescence wide-branched, starry. Significant as a parent of S. × urbium (S. umbrosa 'London Pride' of garden culture). This is not the S. spathulata of older British literature which today is S. globulifera var. spathulata. See below. z6

S. umbrosa L., Porcelain Flower, Jehovah's Flower. W. and Central Pyrenees. Plants distributed under this name are nearly always S. × urbium. The true species forms dense carpets of flat rosettes with leathery, obovate to oblong-oval leaves with broad-crenate margins. The white petals of the flowers have many red spots. May to June. z6

Hybrids of the Section Robertsoniana

S. × geum (S. geum L.). This hybrid has long been considered a species, but this is clearly a hybrid of S. hirsuta × S. umbrosa. Rosettes very open, soon forming a dense, dark green leafy carpet. Leaves long-petioled, pubescent, leaf blade rounded to oval, leaf margin crenate or denticulate. Flower stems to 40cm high, brittle, reddish, glandular-pubescent above. Inflorescence sparsely branched, flowers small, white with yellow or reddish spots, stamen filaments and petals of equal length; June to July. z6

S. × urbium = S. spathularis × S. umbrosa = S. umbrosa (of garden culture) = Porcelain Flower = 'London Pride'.

Loose rosettes, forming a dense, dark green, leafy carpet. Leaves with winged petioles; leaf blades obovate to spatulate, tapered to a short petiole, reddish on the underside. Flower stems to 30cm high, sticky-glandular, loose-panicled. Flowers small, starry, white, reddish in the center, stamen filaments longer than the petals; May to June.

'Aureopunctata' with yellow-speckled leaves; 'Elliott's Variety' is compact growing, very floriferous and effective with the reddish stalks and pink flowers, 20cm high; excellent for edging in semi-shade. S. × urbium var. primuloides 'Ingwersen's Variety' is also very attractive, yet smaller with pretty, bronze-toned leaf rosettes. Flower stems reddish. Flower color deep pink. Often listed in the trade as S. serratifolia, with distinctly toothed leaves. Its origin is not fully clear, but the plant is best listed as S. × urbium var. serratifolia since this refers to the plant as a hybrid.

Section Diptera (Ligularia)

Characteristics: plants perennial, generally hairy with runners. Leaves rounded. Flowers strongly irregular, with petals of unequal length; summer and fall bloomer. All thrive, like most forest plants of E. Asia, in high humus soil in a semi-shaded site.

S. cortusifolia Sieb. et Zucc., Fall Rockfoil. Japan, S. Sachalin, S. Kuril, Korea, Manchuria, Ussuri, China. Plants without stolons, deciduous. Leaves long-petioled, rounded to reniform, cordate at the base, 5–11 lobed, fleshy, green. Flower stems 30–45cm high with umbellate or pyramidal panicles. Flowers white, to 20cm long; September to October. And 'Rosea', dwarfer plants with pink flowers. z5

S. cortusifolia var. **fortunei** (Hook.f.) Maxim. Japan; leaves reniform, to 10cm wide, 7-lobed, brownish green, undersides reddish; flowers later than the species. The cultivar 'Rubrifolium' is more effective with glossy red flower stems and the reddish brown leaves contrasting with the snow white flowers; blooms in early September and therefore is not susceptible to frost damage. The species is one of the latest flowering rock garden plants and is subject to frost damage; winter protection is advisable. Very effective companions for the Autumn Gentians. z6

S. sarmentosa see **S. stolonifera**

S. stolonifera Meerb. (S. sarmentosa L.f.), Mother-of-Thousands, Strawberry-Geranium. China, Japan. Rosettes loose with long, thread-like stolons. Leaves slightly vaulted, rounded to reniform, undulate-lobed, olive green above with silver-gray venation, undersides reddish, bristly-pubescent, especially the petioles. Flower stems to 30cm high, pubescent, paniculate. Flowers zygomorphic, white with red spots. Very popular as a house plant and reasonably hardy (z6). A hardier form, 'Cuscutiformis' which some authors list as a separate species (S. cuscutiformis) and others as var. minor of S. stolinifera, is recommended as a ground cover; leaf rosettes are loose, with thread-like, red stolons; leaves rounded-reniform, 5–9cm wide, 7–10 sinuately lobed, somewhat vaulted, dull-glazed, brown-green with fine, light gray venation and long shaggy pubescence, undersides glabrous, glossy, reddish; flower stems 20cm high, paniculate; flowers large, white, the lower two petals are much longer than the others; July to August. Very attractive and sufficiently hardy for a protected, semi-shaded rock garden site. Also 'Tricolor', (z7), with leaves variegated dark green, gray-green, and ivory-white, with pink to rose tinges over all. Blooms poorly. z5–6

S. veitchiana Balf. W. Hopeh. Rosettes loose, with long, reddish stolons or with runners. Leaves long-petioled, rounded, shallowly crenate, uniquely dark matte green above; undersides glossy, brown-red and bristly pubescent as are the petioles; rarely marble-variegated. Inflorescence racemose-panicled, flowers small, white-, yellow- or pink-spotted above; poor bloomer. Especially useful for greening up a shaded stone wall. May to June. z7

Section Nephrophyllum (Saxifraga)

Characteristics: plants biennial, rarely perennial or annual, secondary shoots often with basal bulblets, rarely with bulbils in the leaf axils and even on the flower stem. Leaves reniform to ovate, toothed to divided, never with lime pits or secretions.

S. granulata L. Fair Maids of France, Meadow Saxifrage. Europe, NW. Africa; in moderately moist and dry meadows. Bulbils clustered at stem base. Rosettes loose; long-petioled leaves with thick, deeply crenate, reniform blades. Flower stems 30–50cm high, loosely paniculate above, sticky-glandular. Flowers milk white; May to June. Cultivar 'Plena', Pretty Maids, is attractive, with double flowers resembling small stocks, also used for cut flowers. Plants die back right after flowering. Easily propagated by the seedlike bulbils; especially vigorous in a sandy soil. z7

S. irrigua M.B. Crimea. Rosettes pale green, loose. Leaves long-petioled, blades reniform, 3-parted to the base, lobes toothed. Flower stems to 30cm high, with branched, umbellate panicles. Flowers loose, white, June; entire plant softly pubescent. Very attractive and effective, thrives in a sunny site in the rock garden in a humus-rich soil. Plants monocarpic, usually dying after seed-set; easily propagated by seed. z6

S. sibirica L. E. Russia, W. Himalayas. Rosettes with small basal plantlets rather than bulbils. Leaves basal, ivy-shaped; 15cm-long, stout flower stems; relatively large, white flowers. Dies back after flowering, but still recommended for rock and trough gardens. z6

Section Trachyphyllum

Characteristics: evergreen, grasslike cushion plants. Leaves simple, entire, linear-lanceolate and awned or apically 3-toothed.

S. aspera L. emend. DC. Europe, Alps, N. Apennine Mts., E. and Central Pyrenees Mts.; over igneous rock. Cushions bright green, flat, expanding to dense carpets. Vegetative shoots creeping, very leafy. Leaves linear-lanceolate, prickly-ciliate, glossy. Flower stems 5–15cm high, 1–10 flowered. Flowers cream-yellow with orange spots. Only for collectors. Requires lime-free, gravelly humus in a moderately dry and shaded site. July to August. Var. **bryoides**, considered by some authors to be a separate species (*S. bryoides*), grows in small rounded hummocks; dwarfer; flower stems un-branched, 1-flowered, yellow flowers often red-spotted; and var. **hugueninii**, flowers solitary, sessile or nearly so, larger than the species. z6

S. bronchialis L. N. Ural Mts., N. Asia, Alaska. Cushions densely carpet-forming, dark green. Shoots short, branched, very leafy. Leaves tough, glossy, awl-shaped, with terminal awns. Stems sparsely leafy, with 2–5, soft yellow, orange-spotted flowers. June to July. Sometimes a poor bloomer; only for collectors; grows as well in full sun as in shady sites. And var. **funstonii** (Small) Hult., Alaska, petals clawed, pale yellowish-white with darker yellow spots. z4

S. bryoides L. see **S. aspera** var. **bryoides**

Ornamental Saxifrages from Other Sections

S. aizoides L. Section Xanthizoon. Yellow Mountain Saxifrage. Mountains of Europe, arctic Asia and N. America. A loose, carpet-forming, evergreen mat of procumbent, creeping shoots with uncrowded foliage. Leaves fleshy, thick, linear (resembling *Sedum album*). Flower stems 3–10cm high or higher, ascending, branched. Flowers yellow to deep orange, often red-spotted, in cymes; June to August. A charming alpine plant from moist spring sites, but somewhat difficult to grow in cultivation. Only for experienced collectors. The blood-red flowering cultivar, 'Atrorubens', is the easiest to grow, requiring a moist, well-drained, gravelly soil. Other cultivars include 'Aurantia', with orange flowers, and 'Autumnalis', plant compact, flowers large, orange. A closely related hybrid is *S. × primulaize*, a hybrid with a small form of *S. × urbium*, and its selection 'Salmon' with salmon-colored flowers over rich green mats; July to September; requires a humus-rich soil and semi-shade. z1–5

S. brunoniana Wall. Section Hirculus. Sikkim, Himalaya Mts. Acute-leaved, bristly ciliate rosettes, with many thread-like, bright red stolons to 20cm long, with large terminal buds. Flowers 3–4 (often rare in cultivation), on 8–12cm long sparsely leafy stems, bright yellow. Occasionally with bulbils in stem leaf axil. An interesting collector's plant for a moist, humus soil. Winter protection with conifer branches is advisable, as well as potting and keeping reserve rosettes frost-free over winter. z7

S. cymbalaria L. ssp. **huetiana** Engl. et Irmsch. Section Cymbalaria. E. Carpathian Mts., SW. Asia, N. Africa. Annual to rarely biennial. Leaves in basal rosettes and on branching stems. Leaves reniform to round, 3-lobed, bright green, glossy. Flower stems 3–10cm high. Flowers starry, yellow; May to September. A low-growing plant for a shady rock crevice or dry stone wall. Once established, plants will persist by self-seeding. The species is more tender and demanding than this subspecies. z6

S. diversifolia Wall. Section Hirculus. Yunnan, Himalaya Mts. Deciduous, clump-forming small perennial with habit of *Parnassia*. Basal leaves long-petioled, cordate-ovate, entire. Flower stems erect with scattered, smaller sessile leaves. Inflorescences racemose, flowers few, rich yellow; August to September. Very attractive collector's plant for moist, humus, shaded sites. z6

S. manschuriensis Kom. Section Boraphila. Manchuria, Korea. Relatively large, fleshy, reniform leaves, all basal; margins lightly crenate, long-petioled. To 40cm high flower stems, pubescent with a compact, white, flower umbel; June. Covered with small red fruits in fall. Requires a moist site with acidic soil, in shade. Reasonably hardy. z5

S. pensylvanica L. Section Boraphila. Swamp Saxifrage. E. and Central N. America. A stately plant, 0.6–1m high. Stout plant with a thick rootstock. Leathery leaves all basal, 30cm-long, large. The inflorescence is pyramidal with many small, yellowish-white to greenish flowers. May to June. Not an outstanding plant, but interesting for a shady, moist, woodland garden or large rock garden. Only for collectors and naturalists. z5

S. petraea L. Section Tridactylites. Lake Como, Italy to the SE. Dolomite Mts.; on moist limestone outcroppings. Not reliably perennial, usually only a biennial, but occasionally persisting longer. Leaves palmately 3-lobed, angular to roundish in outline, the lobes divided almost to the base into many toothed segments, glandular-pubescent, basal and cauline. The soft flower stems are weak, sometimes decumbent, 10–12cm long, with inflorescence a loose panicle. Flowers white. Despite its short flowering period, this species is recommended for its abundance of flower. Easily grown from seed. z7(6)

S. rotundifolia L. Section Miscopetalum. Mountains of Europe, Caucasus. A small, bushy perennial with short, above-ground knobby rootstock. Leaves long-petioled, rounded to mostly reniform, margin toothed, light green. Stems leafy, 30–60cm high. Flowers in a loose, floriferous panicle, white to rarely yellow, mostly rose-spotted; June to July. Very useful, vigorous garden plant for a more or less shaded site, especially at the edge of a small pool with ferns; very effective for its veil of small white flowers; persists by self-seeding in favorable sites. Numerous varieties are listed, including: var. **heucherifolia**, smaller overall, less hairy, flowers less spotted, inflorescence wider-spreading; var. **heucherifolia** f. **geoides**, stem to 20cm high or less, leafless, very hairy, flowers heavily purple-spotted; var. **rapanda**, generally taller than the species, stems glandular-hairy. z6

S. stellaris L. Section Boraphila. Mountains of Europe, Arctic. Rhizomes mostly below-ground. Leaf rosettes loose. Leaves obovate, toothed toward the apex, smooth, leathery, dark green, stem leaves smaller, often sessile. Flower stems 5–15cm high with well-branched cymes. Flowers small, starry, white with yellow spots; June. Grows in the mountains near springs; demanding in culture; requires gritty, well drained, constantly moist soil; and recommended only for dedicated alpine collectors; requires a cool, moist site. z1–6

S. taygetea Boiss. et Heldr. Section Miscopetalum. Greece, Albania and small areas in S. Italy. Resembles *S. rotundifolia*, but plants substantially smaller. Leaves all basal, reniform, with crenulate margins. Leafless stems 10–20cm high. The loose panicle bears white, red- or purple-spotted flowers in early summer. This species thrives in a less moist site than other species of Section Miscopetalum. z7

Lit.: Engler and Irmscher: *Das Pflanzenreich*, pp.67–69: *Saxifraga*. Köhlein, F.: Saxifrages. Verlag Eugen Ulmer, Stuttgart (1980)); Timber Press, Portland, Oregon. (Sch. & Kö.)

Scabiosa L.
Dipsacaceae
Pincushion-flower

A genus of 60–80 species. Annual to biennial or perennial herbs which may be woody at the base if persistent. Leaves simple, lobed or pinnately divided. Flowers small, 5-lobed in shallow-rounded to hemispherical involucrate heads on dichotomous or simple stems. Most are indigenous to the Mediterranean region. The most important garden species, aside from the annual *S. atropurpurea*, is *S. caucasica*; the other species are well suited for rock or naturalized gardens. All require full sun. Alkaline soils are preferable but plants will thrive in any good garden soil. These

are very sensitive, however, to excess winter wetness. Propagate by seed, division and cuttings.

S. alpina see **Cephalaria alpina**

S. caucasica M.B. Caucasus Region. Flowering stems 30–60cm high. Leaves smooth, gray-green, basal leaves usually simple, lanceolate, stem leaves pinnatisect. Stems simple or sparsely branched. Flower heads flat with large marginal florets, lilac-blue; June to September. Valued as a beautiful cut flower and border perennial, especially on warm,

Scaevola hookeri

sunny sites and on dry to moderately moist soil. Good companion plants include *Achnatherum calamagrostis* and *Melica transsilvanica*, *Scabiosa ochroleuca* and all sun- and heat-loving lilies, including the Asiatic Hybrids. Remove the spent blossoms to encourage flowering. Also, top dress with fertilizer frequently in spring and summer; plants should be divided and transplanted every 2–4 years. Plants may be successfully propagated by division in spring with the emergence of new growth. Plants may also be divided from August to September.

Despite its popularity as a cut flower, the blooms last only 3–5 days in water. The flowers should be cut just as the marginal florets are developing and before the central flowers open. The cultivar with the longest-lasting flowers is the dark violet 'Nachtfalter'. Some other cultivars include: 'Blauer Atlas' (Blue Atlas), deep blue, stiff-stemmed; 'Clive Greaves', pale lobelia blue, large-flowered; 'Miss Willmott', cream-white; and 'Prachtkerl' (Great Guy), bright blue. Caucasian Scabiosa is short-lived, unfortunately, where summers are hot and arid. Older cultivars include 'Alba',

white flowers; 'Goldingensis', flowers deep lavender; and 'Perfecta', flowers lavender. z4

S. graminifolia L. Pyrenees Mts., S. Alps, Dalmatia. Stems 20 to rarely 40cm high; subshrub or with a woody rootstock, a hemispherical bushy habit. Leaves entire, narrow-lanceolate, grasslike, silver-silky-pubescent on both sides (especially beneath). Flower heads pale lilac to rose on slender, firm stalks; June to September. Attractive and valuable, particularly for sunny stone walls. z6

S. japonica Miq. Japan. Stems 30cm high, rarely higher. Leaves glossy green, pinnatisect with narrow-lanceolate lobes. Stems forked. Flower heads violet-blue on long stems; August to October. A biennial, but may self-sow. z7

S. japonica var. **alpina** Takeda. Low and bushy, only 10–20cm high, especially valuable for the rock garden because of its late, persistent flowers. Colonizes well; quite winter hardy, unlike the species. z5

S. lucida Vill. Pyrenees Mts., Alps,

Vosges Mts., Jura Mts., Carpathian Mts. Stems 15–30cm high. Rootstock cylindrical; with rosetted vegetative shoots and flowering stems. Leaves glabrous, glossy, the basal leaves coarsely toothed to almost lyrate, the stem leaves simple to bipinnatisect. Flowers rose-lilac with purple-black, glossy, bristly involucral bracts; June to September. A collector's plant for the rock and naturalized garden. z5

S. ochroleuca L. Central Europe to Siberia, in high meadows. Stems 60–80cm high. Rootstock spindle shaped.

Leaves densely soft-short-haired, often nearly gray, the lower leaves petioled, entire to crenate, stem leaves deeply pinnate-lobed. Stems erect, abundantly branched with long-stalked, solitary flower heads. Flowers light yellow; June to October. An attractive, undemanding, persistent, flowering perennial for the wild and rock gardens; spreads by self-seeding. The var. **webbiana** (D. Don.) Boiss., from SE. Europe and Asia Minor, is a mountain plant growing only to 15cm high; leaves crinkled, flower heads creamy white; a rock garden plant. Tender. z7–6

Schivereckia podolica

S. perennis ssp. **parnassii** see **Pterocephalus parnassii**

S. silenifolia Waldst. et Kit. W. Balkan Peninsula. Stems 15–25cm high. Rootstock woody, with sessile leaf rosettes and sparsely branched, erect stems with few leaves. Basal leaves narrow-spatulate, entire; stem leaves lanceolate with a few lanceolate-pinnate lobes. Flower heads blue-violet, involucral bract bristles yellowish; July to August. Useful for dryish rock garden sites. z6

S. succisa see **Succisa pratensis**

S. vestita Facch. ex W.D.J. Koch. Trentino Alps, Italy. Stems 15–25cm high. Similar to *S. silenifolia*, but with better branched and leafier stems, with lilac flower heads; June to August. A collector's plant. z7 (M.)

Scabiosa caucasica 'Blauer Atlas'

Scaevola L.
Goodeniaceae

More than 80 pantropical species, primarily from Australia and the Pacific Islands. Shrubs or herbs with normally large leaves and small flowers. Some are utilized in their native regions as a form of paper. Flowers in May. Grow in high humus soil in full sun or light shade. Useful as an evergreen, dark-leaved ground cover. Propagate by removal of rooted shoots. Most are too tender for Temperate Region gardens.

closely related to *Draba*. Small, grassy, shaggy-pubescent perennials with gray-green leaves and dense, white, flower racemes. Differs from *Draba* in the winged anthers on the innermost stamens.

Undemanding, early-flowering, low carpet perennials for the rock garden, rock bed or trough. Plants thrive in any well-drained soil in rock crevices or among rocks together with *Draba* and other slow-growing cushion plants. Both listed species are lime-loving. Propagate by seed, division and cuttings.

flowered. A more vigorous plant than the previous species. Blooms from April to May. z6 (E.)

Schizocodon

S. soldanelloides see **Shortia soldanelloides**

Schoenoplectus see Scirpus

Scilla hispanica

Scilla sibirica

S. hookeri F. Muell. ex Hook.f. Victoria, New South Wales and Tasmania; scattered in coastal regions at subalpine and alpine elevations. Stems with alternate leaves, creeping and rooting along the ground. Leaves oval-oblong, irregularly toothed, 8–15mm long. Flowers fan-shaped, with the 5 lobes all directed to one side, 10mm wide, white or pale violet, sessile in the leaf axils. Interesting; hardiest species of the Goodeniaceae, hardier than *Selliera radicans*. Has withstood −24 degrees C. (−11 degrees F.) without snow cover. z6 (K.)

Schivereckia Andrz. ex DC.
Cruciferae

Two to five species of perennial herbs from Russia, Asia Minor and SE. Europe,

S. bornmuelleri see **doerfleri**

S. doerfleri (Wettst.) Bornm. (*S. bornmuelleri* Prantl, *Draba doerfleri* Wettst.). SW. Yugoslavia; Sar Planina, Asia Minor; on rocky, grassy sites. Plants caespitose, of loose carpet habit. Flower stems simple or branched, 5–15cm high. Basal leaves more or less rosetted, oblanceolate, entire, densely stellate-pubescent, gray. Stem leaves also usually entire. Racemes to 15-flowered. Blooms in April and May. z6

S. podolica (Bess.) Andrz. W. Ukraine, Moldavia, NW. Rumania. Dense, caespitose carpet habit with flower stems to 25cm. Basal leaves rosetted, oblanceolate to oblong-spatulate, with 2–5 teeth on either side. Stem leaves sessile with 1–4 teeth on either side. Racemes to 30-

Scilla L.
Liliaceae
Squill, Spanish Bluebell

Mostly spring-flowering bulbous plants with basal, linear leaves, few to many-flowered, racemose, scapose inflorescence, flattened, and campanulate or spreading; normally blue flowers with petals distinct or slightly connate at the base. Petals 1-nerved; stamens 6. Scillas are among the most satisfactory and popular of spring flowers. *Scilla hispanica*, *S. nonscripta* and *S. sibirica* are excellent for massing in gardens and parks. These grow best in open woodlands and thickets, with semi-shade and a moderately moist soil; quickly spreading by self-seeding once established. Combine well with *Galanthus*, *Eranthis* and the spring primulas. *S sibirica* is especially effective when naturalized under *Forsythia*. *S. hispanica* clumps in various colors are also very attractive in the spring border with *Iberis, Epimedium, Doronicum, Dicentra,* etc. The tall scapes are also suitable for cutting. Propagate by bulblets and division of the bulb clumps in summer. In addition to the following described *Scilla* species, several rarely cultivated and frost sensitive South African species with decoratively colored leaves are listed. These have been recently placed into the genus *Ledebouria* Roth. and are only suitable for the temperate greenhouse.

winter, and expand to 15cm long in early spring, dying away in early summer. August to September. Only for collectors. z6

S. bifolia L. Spain to Asia Minor, and in Central Europe in woodland clearings and along rivers, ascending to subalpine zones, usually in a calcareous, humus, moist loamy soil. Scape 8–12cm high. Leaves usually only 2, channeled with closed tips, linear, to 10–20cm long. Flowers starry, in loose, to 10-flowered racemes, blue, in March. The blue is not as attractive and conspicuous as that of *S.*

racemes; April. Best in boggy soil, moist in spring. Commonly found together with *Leucojum aestivum* in nature. Closely related to the later flowering *S. amoena* L. z6

S. campanulata see **S. hispanica**

S. chinensis see **S. scilloides**

S. diziensis see **S. mischtschenkoana**

S. hispanica Mill. (*S. campanulata* Ait., *Endymion hispanicus* (Mill.) Chouard, *Hyacinthoides hispanica* (Mill.) Rothm.).

Scilla mischtschenkoana

Scilla non-scripta

Currently, the genus *Scilla* has undergone several revisions with various species removed to *Endymion* or other genera; gardeners will find it convenient to retain these in *Scilla*, as presented here, while keeping up with the various reassignments of species in the technical literature.

S. amethystina Vis. (*S. litardierei* Braistr., the current designation.) Dalmatia. Scape 20cm high. Attractive, conspicuous species, valuable for its late flowers. Closely related to *S. pratensis*, with 3–6 linear leaves and with racemes twice as large of 12–35 clear blue campanulate flowers; late May to June. z6

S. autumnalis L. Autumn Scilla. Scattered from S. England to SE. Europe. Scape 10–15cm high. Flowers small, pale purplish-blue in rather inconspicuous, 6–20 flowered, short racemes; the 5–10 channeled, linear dark green leaves begin to emerge during anthesis, over-

sibirica, which blooms earlier. The species is quite variable. Sets abundant seed; easily naturalizes beneath shrubs; 'Rosea' (= forma *rosea*) is common in the trade, with pinkish-white flowers; also spreads by seed. Other cultivars are found in the trade, such as 'Alba', with white flowers, and 'Praecox', light blue, earlier and more vigorous than the species. *S. bifolia* occasionally hybridizes with *Chionodoxa luciliae* Boiss.: × *Chionoscilla allenii* J. Allen ex Nichols. z6

S. bifolia and its cultivars may be effectively combined with: *Helleborus, Primula vulgaris, Hacquetia, Hepatica, Cyclamen coum, Daphne mezereum, Abeliophyllum distichum, Prunus tomentosa.*

S. bithynica Boiss. E. Bulgaria, Asia Minor. Scapes 15cm high. Usually with three lanceolate leaves, strap-shaped but tapered toward the base, not clasping the scapes. Flowers bluish-lilac, starry, nearly 2cm wide, in 7–15 flowered, erect

Spain, Portugal. Scape 20–40cm high. Bulbs large and fleshy; leaves thin, channeled, strap-shaped to broadly lanceolate, glossy, in dense, rosetted clumps; flowers pendulous, campanulate with recurved lobes in pyramidal racemes, resembling a hyacinth, blue, pink or white. May. Self-seeds to the point of being troublesome under favorable conditions. Bulbs are not eaten by rodents. Vigorous, thrives even in competition with tree roots. Some good cultivars of this easily grown, decorative bulbous plant are: 'Excelsior', deep lavender-blue bells in broad, stout inflorescences; 'Myosotis', pure blue; 'Queen of the Pinks', deep pink; 'Rosabella', pink; 'Skyblue', dark blue, late; 'White Triumphator', white. z5(4)

S. japonica see **S. scilloides**

S. lilio-hyacinthus L. Pyrenees, Central and S. France; in woodlands and moist meadows. Bulbs with imbricate scales, similar to a lily bulb; leaves glossy bright green, linear. 15–25cm long, 1–2.5cm wide, abruptly tapered at the tip, leaf cluster funnelform, ascending. Flowers light blue, 1.5cm wide in 5–15 flowered, crowded, 15–25cm high, racemes in May to June. A collector's plant. z6

S. litardierei see **S. amethystina**

S. mischtschenkoana Grossh. (*S. tubergeniana* J.M.C. Hoog, *S. diziensis* Grossh.). N. Persia, in the vicinity of Tabriz; collected in 1928 by Georg Egger. Scape to 20cm high, inflores-

One of the loveliest of spring-flowering bulbous plants. Plants thrive in many soil types, flowers effective even from a distance, lasting several weeks in sometimes foul, early spring weather. The bulbs are not damaged by rodents; never weedy from overseeding. Persists in meadows mown 2–3 times a year. It is presumed that the adopted name of naturalized plants, *S. tubergeniana*, is seldom used in the trade. The selection 'Zwanenburg' has more colorful flowers and is an improvement, but is rarely offered today. z6

yet to develop when *S. non-scripta* is in bloom. Desirable for naturalizing. Often planted in England as a blue ground cover under rhododendrons and azaleas. z6

S. nutans see **S. non-scripta**

S. sicula see **Puschkinia scilloides** var. **libanotica**

S. peruviana L. Not from Peru (erroneously referred to in England as Cuban Lily), but from Portugal, Spain, Italy, where it is found in moist meadows

Scilla sibirica var. *taurica* 'Spring Beauty'

Scirpus lacustris

cence 3–6 flowered. Flowers broadly campanulate, 2cm wide, the lightest blue to blue-white with darker midveins (resembling *Puschkinia*, but earlier, with larger flowers); flowers appear toward the base in February and open gradually as scape lengthens, to 20cm over the next 4–5 weeks. Self-seeds much less than *S. sibirica* or *Puschkinia*; perpetuates by bulblets. Very attractive with *Narcissus cyclamineus*, *Eranthis × tubergenii* 'Guinea Gold', *Primula vulgaris* ssp. *sibthorpii*, *Cyclamen coum*, *Adonis amurensis*, *Helleborus* hybrids, *Pulmonaria rubra*, *Daphne mezereum*, *Hamamelis japonica* 'Zuccariniana', *Rhododendron mucronulatum*, *R. dauricum*.

S. non-scripta (L.) Hoffmgg. et Link (*S. nutans* Sm. *Endymion nutans* (Sm.) Dumort., *E. non-scriptus* (L.) Garcke, *Hyacinthoides non-scripta* (L.) Chouard). W. Europe, Great Britain, W. Germany, naturalized in E. Friesland. Scape 20–30cm high; similar to *S. hispanica*, but flowers longer and narrower, often fewer, on one-sided, nodding, dark blue, or rarely white and pink racemes, May. The flowers are sweetly scented. Flowers more tubeform than those of *S. hispanica*, anthers cream-colored (bluish on *S. hispanica*). Easily crosses with *S. hispanica*. Known as Blue Bells in England; commonly planted with Bracken Ferns (*Pteridium*) which have

and low sites. Leaves in a funnel-like rosette, about 3cm wide. Numerous, to 100, starry flowers in broadly conical racemes, about 25cm high; the lower flower pedicels are longer, making the racemes about 15cm across at the base; dark blue in May and June, also white. The large bulbs are planted only slightly below the surface of the ground in a warm, protected site, best near a south-facing wall. z8

S. pratensis Waldst. et Kit. Dalmatia. Scape 20–25cm high. Flowers starry, outward-facing, pale violet-blue in broadly pyramidal racemes of up to 50 flowers; May. Undemanding and attractive, clump-forming rock garden plant. Suitable companions include *Anemone sylvestris*, *Narcissus × gracilis*, *Tulipa patens*, *T. didieri*, *T. mauritiana*.

S. scilloides (Lindl.) Druce (*S. chinensis* Benth., *S. japonica* Bak.). China, Korea,

Japan, Ryukyu Islands, Taiwan, Manchuria, Ussuri; on sandy dunes and gravelly slopes. Scape 15–20cm high. Plants with 2–3 channeled, lanceolate, glossy green leaves, visible for most of the year. Bears dense racemes of green, globose buds and smaller, starry, pink flowers; August to September. A charming plant, recommended for collectors, better than *S. autumnalis*, notable for its late flowering period. Combines well with *Satureja*, *Leucojum autumnale* and *Crocus kotschyanus*. z5

S. sibirica Haw. Bosnia, Asia Minor, S. Russia; to 2500m. Scape 10–15cm high; 2–4 broadly linear leaves with hoodlike tips, 1–5 broadly campanulate, nodding, deep, intense blue flowers; 'Alba' has pure white flowers, March. One of the best of blue spring flowers. Among the most persistent bulbous plants, forms colonies in nature and tolerates heavy soils. Self-seeds under favorable conditions, covering large areas. Thrives also in open grassy sites. Attractive in combination with *Forsythia* cultivars or *Corylopsis* species. z5

S. sibirica var. **taurica** Arn. Asia Minor. Flowers earlier, often in early February, a bright, intense blue with a darker midstripe; not so abundantly self-seeding, recommended for the rock garden. The form 'Spring Beauty' (*atrocoerulea* Harshb.) is particularly vigorous and attractive, darker blue; grows substantially taller than *S. sibirica*, sterile. Effective with narcissus. z5

S. tubergeniana see **S. mischtschenkoana**

Many other scillas are grown by rock garden and small bulb enthusiasts but these seldom appear on the market, rather, gardeners grow them from seed from plant society seed exchanges. (Sch. & Mü)

Schoenoplectus
S. lacustria see **Scirpus lacustria**

S. tabernaemontani see **Scirpus tabernaemontani**

Scirpus L.
Cyperaceae
Bullrush

About 200 species of perennial or annual grassy herbs, usually with a widely-creeping rhizome. Flowers in cone-like umbellate spikelets, axillary or usually

terminal, with a leaf-like, subtending bract. Distributed throughout the world; typical plants of shallow water and swampy sites. Only three species need be considered for the garden; these spread rapidly in a large pond with a loamy bed. Propagation is by division in spring.

S. caespitosus see **Eleocharis caespitosa**

S. lacustris L. (*Schoenoplectus lacustris* (L.) Palla). Bullrush. Cosmopolitan, at the edge of standing or slowly flowing water, occasionally in water to 1m deep. Stems round, dark green, 1–3m long, drooping, whiplike. The lower leaf sheaths are brown. Flowers terminal, laterally compressed by the subtending bract. Spikelets capitate, 1cm long, on 7cm-long branches, brown, June to October.

A decorative, but vigorously spreading plant, often referred to as a reed. For large ponds in parks and spacious gardens. Plants should be confined to tubs in small gardens. Suitable for breaking up large expanses of water-lilies. Utilized in recent years for cleaning up polluted water. Also harvested for caning chair bottoms. The best garden variety is the pale, yellowish-green-striped form 'Albescens', the White Bullrush. Grows to 2m high and combines well, with its bright whiplike stems, against a dark background. z4

S. maritimus L., Beach Bullrush. A cosmopolitan species, found especially near the coast. Stems to 1.2m high, sharply 3-sided, rough above, leafy. Rhizomes globose-thickened at the tips. Flowers terminal with 3 bracts, long-stalked, in 1–2cm long spikelets, brown, June to August. Resembles *Cyperus*. For water 10–30cm deep and shallow bank plantings. Also grows in a normal garden soil, if not allowed to dry out. Vigorous, should be contained in tubs. Thrives in brackish water. Young shoots are edible. The variety **variegatus**, also world-wide in distribution, is showier, with yellow banding on the green foliage and stems; shorter, usually 45–90cm high. z5

S. tabernaemontani C. C. Gmel. (*Schoenoplectus tabernaemontani* (C. C. Gmel.) Palla), Rock Bullrush. Indigenous to Europe and elsewhere. Similar to the previous species, only to 1.2m high, stems gray-green. Spikelets clustered, June to July.

A very interesting, decorative Japanese cultivar is 'Zebrinus' (*Juncus zebrinus* hort.), the Zebra Bullrush. Stays somewhat lower. The round stems are green and creamy white-ringed, espe-

cially when young, resembling the spines of a porcupine in habit. Because of its conspicuous color, companion plants should be unpretentious, such as *Alisma*, *Calla* and the green-leaved water-lilies. The stems will green up somewhat in summer. Thrives in constantly moist soil with water from 0–20cm deep. z5 (D.)

Scleranthus L.
Caryophyllaceae
Kmawe

Scleranthus biflorus

About 10 species from Europe, Asia, Africa, S. America, Australia, New Guinea and New Zealand. Annuals or perennials, normally dense-branched or cushion habit. Leaves small, hard-textured, awlshaped, opposite, connate, without stipules. Flowers small, without petals and inconspicuous, solitary or clustered. Flowers in June. Grow in well-drained soil in full sun and protect from excessive winter wetness. The species discussed here will partially die out after a rough winter. Attractive cushion plants for the collector's garden. Propagate by seed and cuttings.

S. biflorus (J.R. et G. Forst.) Hook.f. New Zealand. Mat to 10cm high. Densely branched habit, similar to *Herniaria*. Leaves yellowish-green, subulate, to 9mm long, submucronate. Flowers in sessile pairs; sepals 4, stamen 1. Not very ornamental, but easy to cultivate. z7

S. siguliflorus (F. Muell.) Mattf. Australia. Similar to *S. uniflorus*, but with a 5-part calyx. Perhaps identical to *S. uniflorus.* z7

S. uniflorus P.A. Williamson. New Zealand: S. Island. Shoots well-branched, mat dense, compact, rarely over 5cm high, a brownish yellow cushion resembling thick moss, spreading to 20cm wide. Leaves 2–4mm long and 0.5mm wide, with colorless tips. Flowers solitary on lateral pedicels, with 2 membranous bracts; sepals 4, only 1 stamen. Fruits 3mm long and 1mm thick. The most compact cushion plant introduced in recent years. z7 (K.)

Scopolia carniolica

Scoliopus Torr.
Liliaceae

Two species in W. North America. Low, glabrous perennials with short, slender rhizomes. Leaves usually radical, paired, wide, with purple spots. Flowers terminal, greenish purple, unpleasantly scented, in a sessile umbel, with 6 deciduous perianth segments, and 3 stamens. Flowers from May to June. Grow in a well-drained, humus-rich, moist soil in the shade, together with *Trillium* and other shade-loving plants. Propagation is by seed or division.

S. bigelovii Torr. California, Oregon, in the cool, moist, dense shade of *Sequoia sempervirens.* Leaves paired, occasionally in threes, elliptic to oblong, acuminate, normally speckled, 10–17.5cm long. Flowers greenish purple, resembling those of *Tricyrtis,* 2.5cm wide, flower stalks about as long as the leaves. z7 (K.)

Scolopendrium see **Phyllitis**

Scopolia Jacq. corr. Link
Solanaceae

Six species of poisonous herbs from Central and S. Europe to Himalayas and Japan; rarely found in gardens. Perennials with a creeping, fleshy rhizome, simple, alternate leaves and usually pendulous flowers borne singly in the leaf axils. Flowers with a campanulate, persistent calyx and a cylindrical to campanulate corolla with 5 short lobes.

Scorzonera austriaca

Shade-loving plants recommended for botanic gardens and collectors for their early flowers; plants die back in early summer. These thrive in a loamy humus, spreading in the open shade of trees and taller shrubs. Propagation is by seed and division of the fleshy rhizomes. Good companions include *Luzula nemorosa* and *L. sylvatica, Astrantia major, Dentaria bulbifera, Galeobdolon, Galium odoratum, Lamium orvala, Pulmonaria, Sanicula europaea.*

S. carniolica Jacq. Central and SE. Europe to Italy, Central Ukraine and Lithuania; usually in beech forests of rocky, wooded mountain slopes, gorges and ravines. Stems 20–60cm high, erect, simple or dichotomously branched, fleshy. Leaves 20 × 8cm, entire, petioled. Flowers on long, wiry, drooping pedicels. Corolla dark brown-violet outside, interior yellowish-green. Blooms from April to May. Probably cultivated as a medicinal plant for centuries in the E. Carpathian countries. Poisonous. z6 (E.)

Scorzonera L.
Compositae

About 90–150 species in Europe, especially in the Mediterranean region. Biennial or perennial with a carrotlike taproot and milky sap. Similar to *Tragopogon.* Leaves simple, entire, linear to oval-lanceolate, rarely lobed or dissected. Flower heads yellow or purple-pink. Blooms in early summer. Grow in well-drained, rocky soil (in well-drained sandy loam for culinary roots), in full sun. Undemanding collector's plants for the wild or rock garden. Propagate by seed; older plants may also be divided.

S. austriaca Willd. Central Europe to Siberia; on sunny, rocky sites and bright, gravelly, pine-covered slopes. Stems 5–40cm. Leaves broadly linear-lanceolate, bluish green, as long as the flowering stems. Roots with a conspicuous fibrous crest at the crown. Flower heads large, yellow. April to May. Very attractive, early-flowering species. z4

S. purpurea L. ssp. **purpurea.** Central Germany and Lithuania, S. to Central Italy, Central Greece, SE. Russia, S. Central France; scattered on the grassy steppes or open coniferous forests. Stems to 50cm high. Leaves basal, narrowly lanceolate, nearly grasslike, to 30cm long. Stems branched and sparsely leafy. Flower heads to 5cm, purple-pink. May to June. z6

S. purpurea L. ssp. **rosea** (Waldst. et Kit.) Nym. E. Central Europe, Balkan region,

N. and Central Italy. Like ssp. *purpurea*, but only 30cm high, stems unbranched. The most attractive species. Both subspecies have an interesting scent; the flowers smell like warm chocolate. z6 (K.)

The culinary species, *S. hispanica* L., Black-salsify, with yellow flower heads on 60–90cm high leafy stems and hose-like black roots also may be naturalized in full to partial sun.

Scrophularia L.
Scrophulariaceae
Figwort

About 200 species in temperate Eurasia, 12 species in N. and tropical America. Coarse, strong-scented perennial herbs or small shrubs with 4-angled stems and usually opposite, simple or bipinnatisect leaves. The inconspicuous flowers are grouped in terminal racemose or paniculate cymes. The calyx is 5-parted; corolla tubular, zygomorphic, 5-lobed, stamens 4 functional and 1 rudimentary. From this large genus, only *S. nodosa* 'Variegata', with yellowish white-checkered leaves is, albeit slightly, garden worthy. Remove flowering shoots immediately, to encourage development of the attractive foliage. Recommended only for collectors of variegated plants. Thrives in any good, but not too dry garden soil. Easily propagated by division. z5

S. canina L. ssp. **hoppii** (W.D.J. Koch) P. Fourn. Jura Mts., S. Alps, Apennines. Plants bushy when pruned, 80–100cm high. Blackish-red flowers, corolla 6–8mm long, with white, lateral lobes. Upper lip of the more than half as long as the corolla tube. Sepals white-membranous-bordered. Pedicels as long as the calyx, with long-stalked glandular hairs. Blooms from June to August. Leaves once or twice pinnately divided. For large rock gardens. An attractive plant resembling a "landscape Boronia" with its double, blackish-brown flowers. z6

S. nodosa L. Europe, N. America, N., W. and E. Asia; on moist to moderately wet sites in deciduous or mixed forests and moist clearings. Rhizome thickened, tuberlike. Stems erect, 4-angled, 60–80cm high. Leaves ovate, glabrous, dark green, usually biserrate. Flowers inconspicuous, rich brown-red. Flowers from June to August. Cultivar 'Variegata', leaves yellowish-green white-checked. An old medicinal plant, cultivated since the 17th century and probably earlier. z4 (E.)

Scutellaria L.
Labiatae
Skullcap

About 300 species of perennial herbs and subshrubs, distributed throughout the world (except South Africa). Stems usually 4-angled in cross-section. Leaves opposite, usually simple. Flowers in pairs, sparsely arranged or in crowded, oblong, occasionally paniculate racemes. Calyx campanulate, bilabiate. Upper lip with a hollow, round crest, abscising, lower lip without a crest and persistent;

Scrophularia nodosa

corolla tube long-exserted, limb bilabiate; upper lip erect, hoodlike, lower lip pendulous, drooping; stamens 4, anthers hairy. Fruit a cluster of 4 nutlets.

The species of the first group are fairly useful summer bloomers for the rock garden. They require full sun and a drier site in a well-drained, gravelly, calcareous loam. The species of the second group, especially *S. incana*, are suitable for the herbaceous border, while *S. altissima* is better for naturalizing in open deciduous woodlands and thickets. Both species thrive in any average soil in full sun or light semi-shade and are easily propagated by seed or division. *S. altissima* self-seeds under favorable conditions.

Species under 30cm high

S. alpina L. S. and E. Spain, in the Pyrenees Mts., the Alps and Apennine Mts. to the N. Balkan region, S. and Central Russia, S. Siberia from the Ural

Mts. to Turkestan and Altai Mts., on limestone to 2500m, or in the plains. Spreading plant 15–30cm high, somewhat woody at the base with prostrate to ascending, simple or branched, glabrous to pubescent, floccose stems which root down. Leaves 1.5–3cm long, mostly ovate, crenate-serrate, occasionally nearly entire, glabrous to pubescent, the lower leaves petioled, the upper leaves nearly sessile. Inflorescence a crowded, terminal, 4-angled raceme; bracts 8–15mm long, longer than the calyx, imbricate, sessile, entire, violet, occasionally green. Corolla tube glandular-floccose

Scutellaria alpine ssp. *alpina* 'Rosea'

inside, 20–25cm long, purple or with yellow lower lip. z4

S. alpina ssp. **alpina**. From Spain to Greece and Rumania; on limestone and dolomitic loess from 750–2500m. Leaves and bracts more or less pubescent. Corolla blue-violet, lower lip often whitish. 'Alba' with white, 'Rosea' with pink flowers. Blooms from June to July. z5

S. alpina ssp. **supina** (L.) I.B.K. Richards. (*S. lupulina* L., *S. alpina* var. *lupulina* (L.) Boiss.). Russia to the Altai Plains. Erect habit, flowers light yellow, blooms 2–3 weeks earlier than ssp. *alpina*; May to June. Lime-loving. z5

S. alpina var. **lupulina** see **S. alpina** ssp. **supina**

S. baicalensis Georgi (*S. macrantha* Fisch.). E. Siberia. Plant 20–30cm high, rarely to 60cm. Bushy habit. Stems basally decumbent, then ascending, tinged purple, with pubescent stripes only on the angular ridges. Leaves subsessile, lanceolate, obtuse, entire, ciliate. Bracts longer than the calyx. Flowers in dense, one-sided racemes. Upper lip dark blue or violet, lower lip sky blue. Corolla tube much widened. Blooms from June to September. Lime-loving. Attractive for the rock or wild garden, on dry stone walls and low borders. Suitable companions are *Cypsophila paniculata* and *Zauschneria californica*. Cultivar 'Coelestina' with bright blue flowers in spike-like racemes, and var.

greatly in dissection of leaves and in size and shape of bracts. z5

S. orientalis var. **pinnatifida** Boiss., Greece to Iran. Lower leaves deeply pinnatifid, upper leaves less so, mats flatter. Lime-loving. z6

S. scordiifolia Fisch. ex Schrank. Siberia, Korea. Annual to perennial, 20cm high, creeping underground, forming a dense bush with erect stems. Leaves oblong, dark green, usually to 2.5cm long, crenate-serrate. Flowers in the axils of the uppermost leaves. Calyx purple.

S. incana Spreng. (*S. canescens* Nutt.). Central and SE. USA, in moist woodlands and thickets. Stems 0.6–1.2m high; short-hairy perennial with erect stems, usually much branched above. Leaves petioled, ovate, oval or oblong, firm, crenate, cuneate at the base. Flowers 1.5–2cm long, in terminal, many-flowered, showy, more or less corymbose panicles. Corolla light blue, exterior gray-haired. Blooms from August to September. A valuable late bloomer for the border. Also its ash gray seed structures are decorative after flowering. Effective with the lower-growing *Rudbeckia* and

Scutellaria orientalis **var.** *pinnatifida*

Sedum acre **(to the left) and** *Sagina subulata*

amoena, from China, with oblong leaves and bright blue flowers. z4

S. lupulina see **S. alpina** ssp. **supina**

S. macrantha see **S. baicalensis**

S. orientalis L. SE. Europe from Albania to Crimea, the mountains of S. Spain, Asia Minor and Iran, on dry, usually alkaline, gravelly sites. Forming mats 20–30cm high. Stems procumbent, rooting, sparsely tomentose. Leaves ovate, 1–1.5cm long and 0.5–2cm wide, lower leaves deeply crenate to almost pinnatisect, upper leaves entire, leaves dark green above and floccose, gray-tomentose below, petioled. Inflorescence a crowded, oblong, usually 4-angled spike. Bracts purple or yellowish green, glabrous to pubescent. Corolla 15–30mm long, yellow, occasionally pink. Lower lip often reddish. Blooms from July to September. The plants vary

Corolla 1–2cm long, violet-blue. Blooms from June to August. A valuable, lasting bloomer for the rock garden. z4

Species over 30cm high

S. altissima L. E., Central and SE. Europe, Central and S. Italy, Caucasus; in open deciduous woodlands and infertile meadows or warm slopes. Stems 0.4–1m high, erect, simple or branched. Leaves ovate to ovate-lanceolate, broadly cordate, 5–15cm long and 2–5cm wide. Flowers paired in 30cm-long false spikes. Calyx with or without a few long, white, glandless hairs. Corolla 12–16mm long, creamy-yellow to bluish, lower lip whitish. Blooms from June to July. Some attractive companions are *Buglossoides purpurocaeruleum*, *Nepeta* × *faassenii* and *Phlomis tuberosa*. z6

S. canescens see **S. incana**

Helenium forms. z5

Several other Eurasian and American Skullcaps are listed; some are not hardy, some annual, others more or less aquatic or coarse, suitable only for the naturalized area.

Sedum L.
Crassulaceae
Stonecrop, Orpine

An extensive genus with 500–600 species, many of which are well worth growing. Most are perennial and subshrubby succulents, but some are annual or biennial. Some are evergreen, others deciduous, a few die back to the ground in winter. The flowers are usually 5-merous, in more or less abundant cymes. Sepals 5, separate or nearly so, equal or not so, with or without spurs, petals 5, separate or basally connate, spreading, stamens 10 or rarely 5, distinct, carpels usually separate or nearly so. The flower color may be white, yellow, or pink to carmine. The nomenclature is often confused by the many synonyms. The genus *Rhodiola* has been split from the genus *Sedum*.

The natural range includes much of the Northern Hemisphere, and some species reach far to the south (Mexico, Central Africa). Some of the latter are quite tender. Nearly all the winter-hardy *Sedum* species are easy to cultivate. Best suited for the rock garden or similar sunny, dry sites. The small species are ideal for trough gardens and pot culture, especially in combination with sempervivums. Some low species make good ground covers and edging plants (*Sedum hybridum*, *Sedum spurium*). The taller species, such as the hybrids of *Sedum telephium* and *Sedum spectabile*, are appropriate for the perennial border, together with other fall bloomers, as *Aster amellus* and *Aster dumosus* cultivars. Sedums are also attractive combined with dwarf conifers and grasses with fall color.

Sedums are impartial to soil, but need good drainage to prevent rot and subsequent disease. Some dwarf North American species require a slightly acidic soil reaction. Fertilizer is only necessary for the tall species. Propagation is relatively easy by seed for the pure species, otherwise increase by division and leaf cuttings.

Sedums may be grouped taxonomically into 8 reasonably well defined groups. The technical literature dealing with the vast number of species utilizes this system. The present treatment, however, is based on garden usage.

1. Low spreading species forming carpets and cushions.

S. acre L., Golden-carpet, Wallpepper. Europe, W. and N. Asia, N. Africa; common on sunny slopes of sandy ridges, walls and rocks. Plant 5–10cm high, carpetforming. Stems very leafy. Leaves alternate, in 4–6 rows along the stem, ovate, fleshy, green, with a sharply bitter taste. Flowers starry, in leafy, cymose inflorescences, bright yellow; June to July. Weedy and invasive in a rock garden; suitable as a substitute for turf on dry sandy sites. Available in varieties. z4

S. acre var. krajinae see **S. krajinae**

S. acre var. majus pale green, substantially taller cushions (10cm), from Morocco. Often grown in England under the name 'Maweanum'; 'Minor' (*S. acre* var. *microphyllum* Stef.) lower, 2.5cm-high mats; 'Aureum' pale green leaf color, the shoot tips yellow in spring. z4

S. aizoon ssp. middendorffianum see **S. kamtschaticum ssp. middendorffianum**

S. album L. Europe, W. and N. Asia, N. Africa, often found with *S. acre* among rocks, and on walls. Plants 10–15cm high, loose carpet habit. Stems very leafy. Leaves brittle-succulent, cylindrical to almost globose, obtuse, dark green or reddish. Flowers white in umbellate panicles; June to August. Some superior cultivars are: 'Micranthum Chloroticum', 5cm high, small-leaved, densely carpet habit, pale green, white-flowering; 'Murale', 10cm high, leaves brown-red, flowers pale pink; 'Coral Carpet', green in summer, bronze red in winter, is very valuable as a dense ground cover; 'Laconicum' is a vigorous, dark green, cultivar. Specialists grow several other cultivars. z4

S. album ssp. gypsicolum see **S. gypsicolum**

S. altissimum see **S. sediforme**

S. amplexicaule see **S. tenuifolium**

S. anacampseros L. Evergreen Orpine. Pyrenees, SW. Alps, Apennines. Stems 10–15cm high, very leafy, procumbent, rooting. Leaves sessile, obtuse to nearly round or broadly cordate. Inflorescence very crowded, hemispherical, dull bluish-purple; July to August. More attractive in the vegetative state than in bloom with its dull, dark flowers. z5

S. anglicum Huds. W. Europe, SW. Sweden. Flowering stems 3–5cm high, similar to *S. acre* when not in flower, leaves, however, are widest in the middle rather than at the base. Flowers starry, soft pink or white; June to July; attractive with its reddish fruits. Somewhat demanding in a moist climate. And cultivar 'Minus', smaller, flowers deeper pink. z4

S. anopetalum see **S. ochroleucum**

S. bithynicum see **S. hispanicum** var. **minus**

S. boloniense see **S. sexangulare**

S. cauticola Praeg. Japan, among rocks on the south coast of Yezo (Hokkaido). Very like *S. sieboldii* but leaves opposite on short petioles, stems laxer, 10–12cm high, bushy habit. Stems to 30cm long, procumbent, red-brown. Leaves rounded to spatulate, slightly crenate, strongly blue-gray pruinose, reddish purple-margined. Flowers pinkish-magenta at first, later carmine-rose, in crowded, leafy cymes; August to September. Flowers 3 weeks before *S. sieboldii*. A very valuable species, also widely distributed as a container plant. 'Robustum', 20 to 25cm high, is a noteworthy hybrid cultivar, substantially larger in all respects, carmine red inflorescences in September; originated by G. Arends from a cross with *S. telephium*. The cultivar *S. cauticola* f. *lidakense* is not substantially different from the species. z4

S. cyaneum Rud. (*S. pluricaule* Kudo). Japan, Amur, Sachalin. Plant 7–10cm high, small bushy habit. Shoots procumbent, branched. Leaves alternate, rounded to oval, gray-green, bluish-pruinose. Flowers carmine pink in floriferous corymbs. Older plants become somewhat woody at the base; July to August; 'Rosenteppich' (Rose Carpet) is more richly colored. Very attractive, satisfactory rock garden plant, especially when spilling over the edges of a trough garden or wall. z4

S. elegans see **S. forsterianum** ssp. **elegans**

S. ellacombianum see **S. kamtschaticum** ssp. **ellacombianum**

S. ewersii Ledeb. W. Himalayas to Mongolia. Flowering stems 10cm high. Stems procumbent-ascending, unbranched, red-brown, very leafy. Leaves opposite, sessile, somewhat stem-clasping, broadly cordate, glaucous blue-gray, with a narrow red-brown margin especially in dry sites. Inflorescence dense, hemispherical. Flowers pink; July to August. Plants are not evergreen, usually lose at least some leaves as early as August, then are unattractive. *S. ewer-sii* var. *homophyllum* Praeg. is smaller in all respects and more glaucous; 'Nanum' is even smaller. These are further described in Group 2, which see. The cultivar 'Turkestanicum' is not substantially different from the species type. z4

S. floriferum Praeg. NE. China. Plant 10cm high. Rootstock knobby, woody; roots thickened. Crown many-stemmed, stems reddish, 20–25cm long, procumbent, very leafy, branched above the middle. Leaves sessile, spatulate to lanceolate, crenate, dark green. Flowers greenish yellow in well-branched, flat cymes, forming very floriferous, hemispherical clumps; July (after *S. kamtschaticum* and before *S. hybridum*). The gold-yellow flowering cultivar 'Weihenstephaner Gold', an ideal groundcover, is particularly attractive. z4

S. forsterianum Sm. ssp. **elegans** (Lej.) E.F. Warb. (*S. rupestre* L.p.p., *S. elegans* Lej.). Morocco. Plant 20cm high, open carpet habit, rootstock thin, spindleform, stems procumbent-ascending, rooting, branched. Leaves substantially thinner than those of *S. reflexum* and more crowded. The leaves are small, acute, linear; tips curved, and glaucous bluish-green, often with a reddish cast. Inflorescence pendulous in bud, flowers yellow in loose cymes. This often is considered to be a cultivar of *Sedum rupestre*. z4

S. forsterianum Sm. ssp. **forsterianum**. Europe, Asia Minor. Not bluish-green, rather pure green. z4

S. glaucum see **S. hispanicum**

S. gracile C.A. Mey. N. Iran, Caucasus. Stems 5cm high. Brownish green mats,

Sedum dasyphyllum

resembling *S. sexangulare*, but has narrow-linear leaves and horizontal, 2–3 branched cymes with white flowers; June to July. A collector's plant. z4

S. gypsicolum Boiss. et Reut. Spain and Portugal. Often listed as a subspecies of *S. album* (*S. album* ssp. *gypsicolum*). With gray-green leaves at the branch tips, sessile and conelike in arrangement. Stems root upon contact with the ground. The inflorescences are much-branched, flowers white; June to July. z6

S. hispanicum L. (*S. glaucum* Waldst. et

Sedum kamtschaticum var. *middenorffianum* f. *diffusum*

Kit. non Poir., *S. lydium* 'Glaucum' hort. non Boiss.). Very rapid-growing, gray-green cushion plant. Leaves alternate, linear to oblong-lanceolate, cylindrical or nearly so, acute tipped, glaucous. Not long-lived, usually biennial or annual. Very loose, 6-rayed, whitish inflorescences. 'Aureum' is lower, with yellowish-green leaves. *S. hispanicum* var. **minus** Praeg., now usually listed as *S. bithynicum*, is longer lived but more closely aligned with Group 2. z6

S. hybridum L. Not a hybrid, but a species from Siberia and Mongolia.

Stems 10cm high, in an open, more or less evergreen mat. Stems procumbent-ascending, reddish. Leaves alternate, bright green in summer, reddish in winter, spathulate, cartilaginous-toothed on the upper half. Flowers starry, in branched cymes, yellow. Blooms sparsely in May, more floriferous in July and August. An excellent bee-attracting plant; valued for edging and groundcover use, especially the cultivar 'Immergrünchen' (Little Evergreen). z4

S. kamtschaticum Fisch. et Mey. Japan,

Sachalin, Kuril Islands, Kamchatka, Ussuri. Plant 15–20cm high. Rootstock thick, branched, woody. Stems erect, more or less deciduous. Leaves sessile, oblong to spatulate, toothed on the upper third, dark green, glossy; short, very leafy young shoots appear in late summer, overwinter and bloom the following year. Inflorescences open, leafy, calyx lobes short, flowers orange-yellow; also attractive after blooming with colorful, starry orange follicles; August to September. Cultivar 'Variegatum', with irregular, yellowish-white leaf margins is among the most attrac-

tive of small variegated perennials. Good companions include *Dianthus* and *Festuca* species. z4

S. kamtschaticum Fisch. et Mey. ssp. **ellacombianum** (Praeg.) R.T. Clausen (*S. ellacombianum* Praeg.). Japan. Often listed as a separate species in trade catalogs. Always with unbranched stems. Leaves abscise in late fall, light green, unlike the darker-leaved *S. hybridum*, and broadly crenate. Crowded inflorescences, 15cm wide, yellowish. z4

S. kamtschaticum ssp. **middendorf-**

Sedum floriferum 'Weihenstephaner Gold'

fianum (Maxim.) R. T. Clausen (*S. middendorffianum* Maxim., *S. aizoon* ssp. *middendorffianum* (Maxim.) R.T. Clausen). E. Siberia, Manchuria. Plant 20cm high. Rootstock thick, much-branched. Stems unbranched, erect, very leafy. Leaves bright green, narrowly lanceolate, deeply toothed near the apex, inflorescences leafy, dichotomous-branched. Calyx lobes long, flowers yellow; July to August. z4

S. kamtschaticum ssp. **middendorffianum** f. **diffusum** Praeg. (*S. middendorffianum* var. *diffusum*). Distinguished from the subspecies in the narrower, longer, greenish leaves. Blooms several weeks before the type; 15–20cm high, a yellow flowery cushion. z4

S. krajinae Domin (*S. ukrainae* hort., *S. acre* var. *krajinae*). S. Slovakia. Often included with *S. acre*. Mats dense, remaining bright green in winter; leaves rounded-ovate, very blunt; cymes with two erect, usually 4-flowered, straight pedicels with yellow flowers. z4

S. lydium 'Glaucum' see **S. hispanicum**

S. **middendorffianum** see **S. kamt-schaticum** ssp. **middendorffianum**

S. **middendorfianum** var. **diffusum** see S. **kamtschaticum** ssp. **middendorf-fianum** f. **diffusum**

S. **mite** see **S. sexangulare**

S. **nicaeense** see **S. sediforme**

S. **ochroleucum** Chaix (*S. anopetalum* DC.). S. Europe, north to SW. Rumania, S. Sweden, Central France and W. Asia. Two forms are cultivated, one with bright

Sedum cyaneum

green leaves, the other with olive green, often reddish, linear leaves. Evergreen plants with creeping stems in mats. Leaves crowded, alternate, linear to linear-lanceolate, almost cylindrical, acute- to spine-tipped. Similar to *S. reflexum* in many respects, but slower-growing and small. Erect, white to pale yellow flowers, not reflexed like those of *S. reflexum*. The subsp. **montanum** is yellow-flowered, the petals more spreading. z4

S. **oreganum** Nutt. N. California to W. Alaska. Loose evergreen cushion 5–7cm high. Stems creeping with ascending branches. Leaves nearly rosetted at branch ends, broadly spatulate, very fleshy, glossy dark green, strongly red-brown tinged on very sunny sites. Inflorescence 2–3 branched; flowers yellow, with acute-tipped petals, funnel-form; July to August. An attractive cushion plant. 'Metallicum' is a cultivar with coppery-bronze leaves. z5

S. **pluricaule** see **S. cyaneum**

S. **populifolium** Pall. Siberia. Sub-

shrubby, bushy habit, 20–40cm high, roots woody. Cordate, toothed leaves. White pale pink, hawthorne scented flowers in much branched corymbose cymes in late summer. A slow grower. z4

S. **pulchellum** Michx. USA: Virginia to Georgia, Indiana, Missouri, Texas. Stems 10–15cm high, erect, very leafy. Leaves narrow-linear, obtuse, glaucous light green. Inflorescence 3–5 branched, branches horizontally spreading, recurved clawlike at the tips; starry flowers many-rayed, pink; spring to summer. A very attractive species, forming dense,

Sedum spectabile 'Brillant'

evergreen tufts, thrives in moist, sunny to semi-shady sites. Tends to be biennial. z4

S. **reflexum** L. (*S. rupestre* ssp. *reflexum* (L.) Hegi et Schmid, *S. rupestre* L.p.p.). Stone Orpine. Central Europe, Norway, Finland, W. Ukraine, Mt. Athos (Greece), Sicily, W. France. Evergreen perennial 15–30cm high, with creeping to ascending, slightly woody stems, branched and rooting, in open mats. Leaves imbricate, linear, blue-green, acute. Flowers with golden yellow, involuted tips; July. Some variegated cultivars are 'Chameleon' and 'Sandy's Silver Crest'. *S. reflexum* f. **cristatum** is a fasciating, bizarre form, known as Cockscomb Sedum. Forma *cristatum* is grown as a medicinal plant

and the spring leaves have been used in soups and salads in Europe. z4

S. **rupestre** see **S. forsterianum** ssp. **elegans**

S. **rupestre** ssp. **reflexum** see **S. reflexum**

S. **sarmentosum** Bunge. China, Japan. Stems pale pink to reddish-brown, prostrate, vigorously creeping, rooting at the tips. Leaves sessile, broad-lanceolate, flat, acuminate, usually in whorls of three, light green. Flowers yellow, in flat, sparsely branched cymes;

Sedum spathulifolium 'Purpureum'

July. Easily distinguished from all the other species. z5

S. **sediforme** (Jacq.) Pau (*S. altissimum* Poir., *S. nicaeense* All.). Mediterranean region to Asia Minor. Stems 15–40cm high, procumbent-ascending, evergreen. Flowering stems unbranched. Leaves alternate, elliptic lanceolate, cuspidate, and flattened toward stem tips. Resembles *S. reflexum*, but distinguished by the tougher, flattened, lanceolate, gray-blue leaves; the erect, not-nodding, budded flowering stems and the whitish or rarely pale yellowish flowers. Growers list two cultivars 'Latifolium' and 'Latifrons' with leaves flatter and more spreading than those of the species. z6

S. **sexangulare** L. (*S. mite* Gilib., *S. boloniense* Loisel.). Finland, Lithuania, Moldau (Vltava) River region, Central Greece, Central France. Evergreen, glabrous. Resembles *Sedum acre*, but the leaves are very crowded, arranged in 6 rows and without a bitter taste. Flowers smaller, lemon yellow. The type 'Weisse Tatra' (White Tatra) is a particularly good cushion cultivar. Requires better soil than *S. acre.* z4

S. sieboldii Sweet. Japan. October Plant, October-daphne. Rootstock carrot-like. Stems herbaceous, clustered, 15–20cm high, low-arching, unbranched, green in summer, purple in cool weather. Leaves usually in threes, sessile, rounded to spatulate, glaucous blue-gray, wavy margins rose-tinged on choice plants. Flowers pink, in globose cymes; October. Attractive species, but may require winter protection. Often grown in hanging baskets. Cultivars 'Medio-variegatum' with leaves yellowish-white in the center, and 'Variegatum', leaves marbled cream and glaucous blue. z6

S. spurium M.B. N. Iran, Caucasus, Armenia, Kurdistan. A well-known, widely grown, small, evergreen sedum. Flowering stems 10–15cm high. Non-flowering stems creeping, rooting. Leaves opposite, short-petioled, obovate, leaf margin crenate and very finely pubescent. Flowers funnelform, 5-rayed, pink to purple, in flat cymes; July to August. Some valuable cultivars are: 'Album Superbum', white, rarely flowers, the best, rich, green ground cover selection; 'Roseum Superbum', pink; 'Purpurteppich' (Purple Carpet), leaves and flowers dark purple-red; 'Schorbuser Blut', dark leaves, rich, carmine red flowers; 'Erdblut' (Earth's Blood), dark red flowers, leaves green-red; 'Fuldaglut' (Fulda Embers), dark red leaves, carmine red flowers; 'Tricolor' with variegated leaves, pink-white-green. All are easily grown, persistent, evergreen sedums, tolerant of semi-shade. Useful both for edging and for ground cover plantings. z4

S. tatarinowii Maxim. N. China, Mongolia. Glabrous, herbaceous plants with erect-arching, simple stems, 10–15cm high. Rootstock thickened, roots carrot-like. Leaves linear-lanceolate to oblanceolate, short-petioled, upper margin coarsely toothed. Crowded, pinkish-white inflorescence; July to August. Recommended for garden cultivation. z4

S. tenuifolium (Sibth. et Sm.) Strobl (*S. amplexicaule* DC.). Indigenous to the Mediterranean region from Portugal to Asia Minor. More interesting than attractive. In summer, the sterile stems shrink up to spindle shaped, brownish knots, roughened by leaf base racemes, making the plants appear dead. At the same time, the rich yellow, 6–10-merous radiating flowers on 2-branched cymes are

unfolding on slender, 10cm-long stems. In the fall, the dormant vegetative stems revive again with new, cylindrical, narrow, glaucous gray-green leaves, which persist through the winter. Only for collectors. z6

S. ternatum Michx. USA: the eastern states. Flowering stems 10cm high, ever-green, sterile stems creeping and rooting to form attractive cushions. Leaves in whorls of 3, roundish to obovate, rounded at the apex, narrowing at the base. Flowers in June, white with purple-red stamens. Not vigorous, thrives in a

Sedum sempervivoides

moist, open woodland site. z5

S. tsugaruense Hara. Japan. A recent introduction, similar to *S. sieboldii*, but substantially more vigorous, stems 20cm long, in tufts, erect-arching. Pink fall bloomer. z5

S. ukrainae see **S. krajinae**

2. Dwarf species for troughs, containers and other small garden areas.

S. beyrichainum see **S. nevii**

S. dasyphyllum L. Europe, N. Africa; on rocks and walls, especially on gravelly sites. Evergreen stems tufted, 2–5cm high, much branched and wiry, blue-green. Flowering shoots thicker, upright to 10cm, leaves less crowded. Leaves 3–7mm long, sessile, nearly globose, glaucous gray-green. Flowering shoots brownish, buds soft pink. Flowers starry;

white, pink on the back, with reddish brown stigmas; June to July. Also var. **glanduliferum** (Guss.) Moris., plant densely glandular-pubescent, and var. **macrophyllum** Rouy & E. Camus, larger over all, leaves notably larger. z5

S. dasyphyllum var. **suendermannii** Praeg. Spain. Closely overlapping leaves, larger flowers later than the type. Plant generally pubescent-hairy, but hairiness varies greatly within the variety. A charming plant; increases by fallen, rooting leaves and stems without becoming invasive. Suitable for open sites in the rock garden. z5

S. divergens S. Wats. (*S. globosum* hort.). N. America: British Columbia to Oregon. Slender, prostrate, rooting vegetative stems and erect flowering stems (leaves sometimes alternate on these). Glabrous, evergreen, ovate to obovate, nearly globose, opposite leaves, 6mm long, green or with deep reddish-copper tones in the summer months. Bright yellow flowers on an open, flattish inflorescence. Slow growing. For troughs, but not always completely winter hardy. The cultivar 'Atropurpureum' is even more colorful. z6

S. ewersii var. **homophyllum** Praeg. Twiggy, much branched rootstock. Stems more or less herbaceous, mostly trailing, round, unbranched, to rarely 10cm long. Leaves mostly opposite, ovate-cordate, mostly entire, glaucous. Flowers pink or pale violet in crowded convex cymes in late summer. Very decorative, small, rare form, particularly well suited for trough planting. Plants should be transplanted occasionally to enhance vigor. z5

S. globosum see **S. divergens**

S. laxum Brg. (*Gromania laxum* Br.) USA: Oregon. Blue-green rosettes to 5cm across; leaves fleshy, spatulate, 1.2–5cm long, .6–2.5cm wide, alternate on stems, opposite on offset rosettes. Inflorescence paniculate, 10–40cm high, flowers whitish, petals whited below. Flowers fade to wine red. A variable species, small to large, and including 5 distinct but related subspecies; also intergrades with the yellow-flowered *S. obtusatum*. z6

S. laxum var. **obtusatum** see **S. obtusatum**

S. nevii A. Gray (*S. beyrichianum* Mast.). E. USA: from the mountains of Virginia to Alabama. Flowering stems 3–5cm high, above a flat, loose carpet of sterile rosetted stems. Stems prostrate to procumbent-ascending, with rosetted leaves at the tips. Leaves alternate, short-spatulate, entire, glaucous green. Inflorescence with 3 or more unbranched rays. Flowers 4-merous, white; June. Attractive, very small species. Requires a moderately moist, bright shady site. z5

S. obtusatum A. Gray (*S. laxum* var. *obtusatum, S. rubroglaucum* Praeg.). NW. USA: Klamath Mountains, Sierra Nevada. Evergreen; stems prostrate, forms large blue-green rosettes; leaves spatulate, entire, 12–25mm long, pink-margined and entire leaf turning orange-red with age. Cymes umbellate, 10–20cm high; flowers lemon yellow. Somewhat similar to *S. laxum*. z5

S. oregonense (S. Wats.) M. E. Pech (*S. watsonii* (Britt.) Tidestrom.). Not to be confused with *S. oreganum* Nutt. USA: Oregon. Glabrous; offset rosette leaves opposite, on stems, alternate; leaves usually yellowish-green, spatulate, about 2.5cm long. Flower stems to 28cm high. Inflorescence a paniculate cyme, flowers cream-colored to white, crowded. Plants in the trade often are hybrids or subspecies of this or other related sedums; see also *S. laxum* and *S. obtusatum*. z6

S. pilosum M.B. Asia Minor, Iran, Caucasus. Biennial 5–10cm high. The first year a dense rosette of narrow-spatulate, dark green hairy leaves in 3–4cm wide, hemispherical. The second year, very leafy stems to 10cm high bear convex, much branched panicled cymes of crowded rose-colored flowers; May to July. Dies out after flowering, sets abundant seed; easily grown under glass. Collector's plant. z5

S. rubroglaucum see **S. obtusatum**

S. sempervivoides Fisch ex M.B. (*S. sempervivum* Ledeb.). Caucasus. Biennial; conspicuous and unmistakable for the *Sempervivum*-like fleshy, spatulate-acute, gray-purple, soft-haired, first year rosettes. Plants die late the following summer following the appearance of the beautiful red flowers in paniculate inflorescences on 15–20cm high stems with scattered leaves. New plants are easily grown from seed. z4

S. sempervivum see **S. sempervivoides**

S. spathulifolium Hook. W. North America. Evergreen, glabrous, flat rosettes 2–3cm wide, with secondary stems 5–7cm high. Leaves broadly spatulate, short-acuminate, fleshy, smooth, gray-green. Flowers yellow, in flat, often 3 dichotomous-branched cymes. May to July. Some attractive cultivars include: 'Purpureum' with deep purple-colored, white-glaucous leaves and strong inflorescences, as well as the cultivar 'Capa Blanco' with thick silver-white glaucous, decorative leaf rosettes. In recent years, some other cultivars have been introduced, such as: 'William Pascade' with bluish-green, rose-tinged leaves; 'Aureum', a compact cultivar with yellowish leaves; 'Roseum' with primarily reddish tones on the leaves. All are beautiful plants of cushion habit, but require somewhat more attention than most other species. These are intolerant of too moist soil, they thrive in a lime-free, coarse sandy soil. z5

S. watsonii see **S. oregonense**

3. Medium and tall species

S. aizoon L. (*S. maximowiczii* Regel). Siberia, China, Japan. Rootstock thick, knobby. Stems herbaceous, unbranched, stiffly erect, 40–80cm high, green. Leaves distant, alternate, sessile, broadly oval to oblong-lanceolate, coarsely and irregularly toothed. Flowers yellow to orange, in crowded to open, leafy corymbose cymes. July. An old, well-distributed garden plant, known by various names; somewhat stiff, but recommended for large rock gardens. Cultivars include 'Atrosanguineum', foliage reddish;

'Floribundum', tall, narrow-leaved; and 'Major', larger overall with wider flower panicles. z4

S. alboroseum Bak. E. Asia. 40–50cm high. Rootstock with thickened, carrot-like roots. Herbaceous stems round and smooth, unbranched, erect. Leaves opposite, ascending, ovate to obovate-cuneate, obtuse-toothed, concave, glaucous gray-green. Flowers in irregularly high, dense cymes, greenish white with pink carpels; September. Cultivar 'Mediovariegatum' with leaves with a broad, green margin and central cream-white blotch; colors best in a shaded site. A highly recommended cultivar for collectors of variegated plants. Currently, in America there is some confusion about the taxonomic status of this commonly grown species due to the apparently unreferenced entry in *Hortus Third*. z4

S. maximowiczii see **S. aizoon**

S. spectabile Bor. Korea, Manchuria. Roots fleshy, spindle-shaped. Stems deciduous, erect, 30–55cm high, smooth, light gray-green. Leaves glaucous, opposite or whorled in 3's or 4's, broadly obovate to about 7.5cm long, slightly toothed, fleshy. Flowers in flat to convex, broad clusters, pale pink; August to September. Some desirable forms are: 'Album', flowers white, 'Brilliant', carmine pink, and 'Carmen', dark carmine-pink; 'Septemberglut' (September Glow), 50cm high, dark red; 'Meteor', 40cm high, flowers carmine; 'Rosenteller', (Pink Plate) low-growing, deep pink flowers; 'Humile', 15–20cm high, but more delicate. Some older, still good cultivars are: 'Atropurpureum', and 'Rubrum', flowers rose to purplish pink, 'Variegatum', with cream variegated leaves, also 'Purpureum', foliage purple-tinged. Perhaps the best of all the tall *Sedum* species, with many uses, including pot culture, attractive in troughs and planters; likes a fertile soil. z4

S. telephium L. Orpine, Live-forever. Europe to Siberia. Herbaceous species with numerous subspecies and varieties intergrading with *S. maximum* but distinguished by alternate leaves and purplish flowers. *S. telephium* ssp. *telephium*, 30–40cm high, is exceptionally attractive. Rhizomes with thickened roots. Stems erect, very leafy. Leaves alternate, oblong to oblong-ovate, irregularly toothed, glaucous bluish-gray. Flowers purple-red in crowded, axillary and terminal cymes; August to September.

Cultivar 'Munstead Dark Red' red-bronze leaves and reddish bronze flowers. The hybrid 'Herbstfreude' (Autumn Joy) (*S. telephium* × *S. spectabile*, 40–50cm high, strongly upright, bushy, is more attractive and highly prized. Inflorescences are large, flat to convex, bronze-red; September to October; also effective in leaf after flowering and throughout the winter, therefore should not be cut back until spring. A valuable plant for borders and natural gardens. z4

Plant breeders continue to introduce more cultivars and hybrids of these upright-growing, large-leaved border sedums; beautiful in themselves, they are not too easily blended into a temperate, moist climate planting, but combine well with some hot climate grasses, the yuccas and other dry climate plants.

The taxonomist's list of *Sedum* species is very extensive; the horticulture list, based on species available in the trade, is much shorter, omitting numerous beautiful but relatively unknown species. Watch for these strangers in botanical gardens and specialists' collections.

Lit.: Clausen, Robt.T.: *Sedum of North America North of the Mexican Plateau.* Cornell University Press, 1975. Praeger, R.L.: *An account of the Genus Sedum as found in cultivation.* Royal Hort. Soc., London 1921. Frödenström, H.: *The Genus Sedum. Acta Horti Gotoburgensis,* 1930–1935, Gothemburg, Sweden. Köhlein, F.: *Freilandsukkulenten.* Verlag Eugen Ulmer, Stuttgart, W. Germany 1977. (Sch. & Kö.)

Selaginella P. Beauv.
Selaginellaceae
Little Club Moss,
Spike Club Moss

About 700 species of moss-like plants intermediate between mosses and ferns; mostly tropical and sub-tropical, a few temperate zone species which grow in moist, humid, shady sites. The hardy species make excellent ground cover plants in a damp, high humus, woodsy place. Many are favored greenhouse and hanging basket specimens.

S. apoda (L.) Spring. Meadow Spice Moss, Basket Spike Moss, E. North America. Mats of prostrate, delicate stems to 40cm wide; leaves of 2 shapes, 4-ranked, tiny, pale green. z3

S. caulescens see **S. involvens**

S. douglasii (Hook. et Grev.) Spring. Douglas's Spike Moss. W. North America. Stems 10cm high, with scale-like leaves in 4 rows, forming dark green tufts, evergreen; attractive when covered in a hoar frost. z6

S. helvetica (L.) Link. Mountains of Europe to E. Asia. Stems matted, dense, a pale, creeping species with remotely pinnate-branched stems and acute, oblong-oval, flat leaves; moss green; reddish brown in dry conditions, and in

Selaginella involvens

fall. Thrives in moist, shaded, rock garden sites and damp, dry stone walls; densely covers stones and the ground. z5

S. involvens (Sw.) Spring emend. Hieron. (*S. caulescens* (Wall.) Spring). India to Japan. Stems 15–30cm high, rootstock with underground runners. Stems erect, much branched only on the upper half, broadly triangular in outline, with flat, fanlike, outspread pinnae, bright green. Very attractive, winter hardy when given a thick mulch of conifer needles. Recommended as a ground cover for the bog garden between low-growing rhododendrons and azaleas. Growth is in late spring, so be cautious when working the ground. z6 (D.)

Club mosses are scarcely known in home gardens but deserve far greater use where soil, climatic and general environmental conditions are conducive to their vigorous development. Local botanical gardens and native plant specialists are good sources of information about species suitable for a specific locality.

Selliera Cav.
Goodeniaceae

Only 2 species of perennial herbs from Australia, Tasmania, New Zealand, Chile. Glabrous, fleshy, procumbent, stem-rooting herbs with creeping root-

Semiaquilegia ecalcarata

stocks or with compressed stems and creeping runners. Flowers usually solitary in the leaf axils. Calyx 5-lobed, Corolla 5-lobed, oblique, outspread. Stamens 5, ovary 2-celled, fruits fleshy, indehiscent.

S. radicans Cav. E. Australia, Tasmania, New Zealand, Chile; on coastal mud flats, on sandy and gravelly sites in salty coastal air, but also found along inland lakes and rivers; to 1000m in the mountains of New Zealand. A widely variable species. Low, spreading mat, with long stems rooting at the nodes. Leaves obtuse-spatulate, 2–4cm long and 0.8–1.6cm wide, somewhat fleshy, glossy green, with small to large leaves on the same plant. Flowers very small, usually solitary, occasionally paired, in the leaf axils. Corolla white to bluish. Blooms in July and August. z7

S. radicans is an interesting, green, mat perennial for the collector and botanic garden. Unfortunately, it is not entirely winter hardy and should be over-wintered in a frost-free alpine house or temperate greenhouse. Best kept in pots in a loamy bog soil. Plants may be set into a very moist rock garden site in late spring where they will form attractive green mats with charming white flowers by fall. Propagation is by separation of the rooted stem segments or division. z8 (E.)

Semiaquilegia Mak.
Ranunculaceae

A genus very closely related to *Aquilegia* and previously included in it. Contains about 7 species. Distinguishing characteristics include petals gibbous at the base rather than with spurs and stamens including a whorl of membranous stamenoids; unlike *Isopyrum*, but like *Aquilegia*, the innermost anthers are modified into staminodes. Only one species is of garden merit.

S. adoxoides see **S. ecalcarata**

S. ecalcarata (Maxim.) Sprague et Hutchins. (*Aquilegia ecalcarata* Maxim.). W. China. Plant 15–20cm high. Spurs entirely lacking. A soft, fine-textured plant with delicate, pubescent, ternate, gray-green leaves. Flowers small, cup-shaped, violet-purple to reddish. For the rock garden and similar natural sites in semi-shade. A charming plant for a somewhat cool, moist soil. In horticulture, confusion exists regarding the proper classification of garden species. Some experts feel that plants in cultivation are *S. adoxoides* (DC.) Mak., others assign them to *S. ecalcarata*, as above. But, as flower descriptions are equally divergent, more study is needed. z6 (Sch. & S.)

Semiarundinaria Mak. ex Nakai
Gramineae
Bamboo

Three species of running, rhizomatous bamboos from E. Asia, including Japan. Stems erect, woody, branches 2 to several at each node. One species generally cultivated.

S. fastuosa (Mitf.) Mak. Narihira Bamboo. Honshu. Grows strictly upright to 8m high, with short lateral branchlets and is therefore columnar in appearance, runners short and usually formed only on older plants. Stems round below, but like *Phyllostachys*, flattened on the branched side on the upper third. Leaf blades broad, to 18cm long and 2.5cm wide, long-pointed, clustered at the branch tips. Of the hardy species, in moderately warm climates, *S. fastuosa* is the tallest-growing. Requires relatively little space with its strongly columnar habit; hence suitable and attractive in small gardens. 4–8m high. z7

S. yashadake (Mak.) Mak. Japan. Only known in cultivation. Botanically distinguished from the previous species by the

Sempervivella sedoides

hairy stem sheaths; horticulturally distinguished by its stoloniferous habit. The species requires more room because of its large-leaved, broad-bushy, spreading habit. Slightly less hardy, especially the foliage, which is easily frost-burned. 3–7m high. z8 (S.)

Sempervivella Stapf
Crassulaceae

Four species of succulent Himalayan plants, recently including the genus *Rosularia*. Small, stoloniferous carpets of rosetted plants with white, 6–8 petaled, short-pediceled flowers. Not absolutely winter hardy and require protection from winter wetness, therefore best grown in the alpine house in a well-drained soil. Most quickly forms dense carpets and is easily propagated by division.

S. alba (Edgew.) Stapf. Himalaya Mts. from 1500–3000m elevation. Loose rosettes to 3cm wide of fleshy, oval-oblong, obtuse, finely glandular-pubescent, pale green leaves, which are tinged rose or red. Flower stems axillary, procumbent-ascending, 2–3cm long. Cymes few to 8-flowered, terminal. Flowers white, to 1.5cm; July to August. z5

S. sedoides (Decne.) Stapf (*Sempervivum sedoides* Decne.). Kashmir. Differs little from the previous species, but smaller and less pubescent. Linear-oblong leaves, outer leaves often reddish on exposed sites; starry flowers with 6–8 petals, larger than those of the previous species. z5 (Sch. & Kö.)

Sempervivum arachnoideum

Sempervivum L.
Crassulaceae
Houseleek, Hens and Chickens

About 30–40 species, plus many natural hybrids, geographic varieties, garden hybrids and cultivars. This genus is unfortunately confused since every natural hybrid and regional form seems to have been given species status. Plants are thick-leaved rosetted perennials, spreading by axillary offsets, occasionally by offsets on short, axillary stolons, forming large, tight mats in time. Leafy, stout, upright stems bear dichotomous branched cymes in summer, with 6–18 petaled, usually red, pink, purple, yellow or white, flowers. The genus ranges from the Pyrenees Mts. to the Alps, Balkans, Asia Minor and Caucasus Mts. to Iran. *Sempervivum* is a first-rate performer in dry, infertile sites. Plants require a sunny, dry site nesting tightly in narrow rock crevices or covering small rock garden slopes; *S. tectorum* cultivars are popular edging plants for small gardens. Most species are easily propagated by division; seed propagation is needless.

However, species cross so readily that seed propagation often gives rise to interesting hybrids.

S. allionii see **Jovibarba allionii.** This plant is retained in *Sempervivum* by American and British authors.

S. altum Turrill. Caucasus. A little known and relatively demanding species. Protect from rain. Pale green, rather loose rosettes, 2.5–4cm wide. Leaves with scarlet red tips, when grown on exposed sites. June. z5

variable species. Rosettes small to medium sized, 12–20cm across, globose, flat-topped, brownish green to reddish, densely covered with cobweblike white hairs. Offsets sessile, crowded. Leaves about 50, cuspidate. Flower stems 7–12.5cm high. Flowers 9–12 petaled, bright rosy red, summer. Numerous cultivars are listed in addition to the two varieties described below. z5

S. arachnoideum ssp. **glabrescens** Willk. (*S. doellianum* C.B. Lehm., *S. arachnoideum* ssp. *doellianum* (C.B. Lehm.)

garden hybrids are: 'Alpha', 'Beta', 'Gamma' and others. z5

S. arenarium see **Jovibarba arenaria**

S. assimile see **S. marmoreum**

S. atlanticum Ball. Morocco; Grand Atlas Mts. Generally similar to *S. tectorum*. Rosettes not widely opened, 3.5–6.5cm across. Leaves .9–3.25cm long, 1cm wide, fine-hairy on both sides. Flower stem to 30cm high, leaves small, red-purple, flowers 12-merous, 3cm wide, white

Sempervivum calcareum
'Sir William Lawrence'

with a broad rose-purple band. Poor bloomer in cool, moist regions. Often not winter hardy. June. z7

S. ballsii Wall. Bulgaria, Greece, Albania. Rosette to 3cm across, interior leaves tighter, outer leaves more spreading to erect. Rosettes olive green to yellow-green. Produces relatively few offset rosettes. Flowers soft pink. Various geographic forms are known. z7

S. blandum see **S. marmoreum**

S. borisii see **S. ciliosum**

S. borisovae Wale. Caucasus. Rosettes 3cm wide, rather open and flat. Leaves smooth and glabrous. Forms large, dense clumps of rosettes, which are green below, reddish-brown above where light is stronger. Easily cultivated. z6

S. calcareum Jordan. French Alps (*S. tectorum* ssp. *calcareum* (Jord.) Cariot et St. Lager). Closely related to *S. tectorum*, or a subspecies of it. Rosette leaves gray-

Rock garden with *Saxifrages* and *Sempervivums*

S. andreanum Wale. N. Spain. Green rosettes, 3–4cm wide. Characteristic are the short, stout, distinctly curved marginal hairs on the rosettes and sub-tending leaves. Forms broad mats, not particularly colorful. June. z7

S. arachnoideum L., Cobweb Houseleek. Pyrenees, Carpathians. Attractive, quite

Schinz et Keller). Rosettes ovate, leaves less cobwebby. z5

S. arachnoideum ssp. **tomentosum** (C.B. Lehm. et Schnittsp.) Schinz et Thell. (*S. laggeri* Schott); rosettes globose, densely silver-white webbed, conspicuously attractive and showy with decorative red flowers; July to August. Some good

green with very prominent brown tips. Several cultivars are listed: 'Mrs. Giuseppi', more compact, with deep red-tipped leaves; 'Sir William Lawrence' somewhat larger with globose rosettes and distinctly red-tipped leaves; 'Greenii' small and compact. z5

S. cantabricum J.A. Huber. N. Spain. Somewhat open rosettes, 4–5cm wide. Offset rosettes develop on long stolons. Rosetted leaves equally glandular-pubescent above and beneath. Flowers dark pink to dark carmine. Easily cultivated. z7

S. caucasicum Rupr. Caucasus. Several different species and hybrids are sometimes listed under this name. Rosettes 3.5–5cm wide, rather open, leaves glabrous but ciliate with stout hairs, green with small, dark brown tips. Offsets on short stolons. Flower stems 12–20cm high; corymbs few-flowered, flowers starry; petals 14, rose-red with median stripe. z6

S. ciliosum Craib. Bulgaria, Yugoslavia, NW. Greece. Rosettes medium-sized, 2.5–5cm across, globose, tight or somewhat open, gray-green. Leaves many, imbricate, incurved, to 2.5cm long, gray-pubescent with outspread, ciliate marginal hairs. A particularly long-haired form with short stolons is cultivated as *S. borisii* Deg. et Urum. Flowers starry, 10–12 petaled, yellow. June to July. z6

S. dolomiticum Facch. E. Alps. With half open rosettes, 2–4cm wide. Bright green with purple-red tips. Older rosette leaves reddish on the outside, glandular-hairy, tipped with longer white hairs. Slender stolons with tightly rosetted offsets. Stem about 10cm high, shaggy white-haired, leaves purple tipped. Flowers rose-red with darker median stripe and white marginal flecks, 10–14 petaled. Slow-growing, poor-flowering in overcast regions. Often confused with *S. montanum*. June to July. z5

S. erythraeum Velen. Bulgaria. Rosettes to 6.5cm wide, many-leaved, flat and open. Leaves broad and short, gray-purple, densely covered with white, glandular hairs. Flowering stems to 20cm high, very hairy; flowers 2cm wide, starry, 11–12 petaled, purplish-red, finely white-haired on the dorsal side. A rarely cultivated, dense cushion plant. July to August. z6

S. giuseppii Wale. N. Spain. Crowded clumps of rosettes at least 2cm-wide,

pubescent. Green with no other foliage color, but recommended for its dense cushion habit. Flowers are showy rose-red, petals with narrow, white margins. z7

S. globiferum see **S. wulfenii**

S. grandiflorum Haw. S. Switzerland, N. Italy. Relatively large, open rosettes, 5–10cm wide, rarely to 22cm wide, leaves dark green, clammy pubescent with dark brown tips. Long, slender, leafy stolons, sub-globose offsets. Plants have a characteristic scent. Flower color whitish to yellow to greenish yellow, with purple stains at base of petals. z6

S. grandiflorum f. **fasciatum** is a compact, banded form.

S. heuffelii see **Jovibarba heuffelii**

S. hirtum see **Jovibarba hirta**

S. ingwersenii Wale. Caucasus. Rosettes 2cm-wide, bright green, finely pubescent, with small red-brown tips. Offset rosettes on long, brownish-red stolons. Petals red with narrow white margins. Easily cultivated. z6

S. kindingeri Adamov. Macedonia. Rosettes 4–6.5cm wide, flat and open, leaves pale yellow-green to bright green, with purple tips, and with long hairs on both sides of upper portion. Stolons medium long, flower color pale yellow. Will not tolerate winter wetness. Flower stems very leafy, to 25cm high, flowers 12–14-merous, ivory with red center. Flowers poorly and develops few offset rosettes. July. z7

S. kosaninii Praeg. Yugoslavia. Open, flat rosettes, 6–8cm wide. Glandular-pubescent above and beneath. Ciliate marginal hairs twice as long as the leaf surface hairs. Rosettes dark green with purple tips. Flowers reddish purple. Easily grown. July. z6

S. laggeri see **S. arachnoideum** ssp. **tomentosum**

S. leucanthum Panc. Bulgaria: Rila Mts. Broad, flat rosettes, 4–7cm wide, with 70–80 rosette leaves, leaves glandular-pubescent above and below, with unequally ciliate margins, green with dark red-purple tips. Flower stems 10–20cm high. Flowers 11–13-merous, pale greenish-yellow. July. z6

S. macedonicum Praeg. SW. Yugoslavia. Rosettes small, 3–5cm across. Leaves

matte green, somewhat reddish at the tips in exposed sites, densely fine glandular-pubescent, with marginal cilia. Flowers soft red-purple. The rosettes are deeper and more open than those of *S. montanum*. Easily grown, but a poor bloomer. Grows as a loose mat due to the long, leafy stolons. June. z7

S. marmoreum Griseb. (*S. schlehanii* Schott, *S. assimile* Schott, *S. blandum* Schott). Balkan region, E. Europe. Rosettes flat, open, to 10cm wide; leaves 60–80, 2.5–5cm long, red-brown on the base, green at the tips. Pubescent when young, later glabrous and glossy. Flower stems 10–15cm high; flowers 2.5cm wide, starry, 12–13-merous, purple-pink with conspicuous white margins. Many cultivars are grown which exhibit better color: 'Bruneifolium', 'Rubicundum' ('Rubrifolium'), 'Rubicundum Ornatum'. August. z5

S. minus Turill. N. Turkey. Rosettes 1–2cm across; leaves fine glandular-pubescent above and beneath, soft olive green, purple at the base. Offset rosettes on short stolons, nearly stemless. Flowers starry, pale yellow. An attractive, small species, forming dense clumps. Green rosettes, bronze-toned in exposed sites. z5

S. montanum L. Pyrenees Mts., Corsica, Alps, Carpathian Mts. Rosettes 3–4cm wide, many-leaved, open. Carpet habit with numerous, 1–3cm long stolons. Leaves matte green, densely covered with glandular pubescence. Flower stems 5–8cm high, with a few starry, 10–15-merous, soft violet-purple flowers. Several varieties are listed; this intermediate species hybridizes readily with several other European species to yield attractive hybrids and cultivars. z5

S. montanum ssp. **burnatii** Wettst.; rosettes to 15cm wide. z5

S. montanum ssp. **stiriacum** Wettst.; rosettes 4–5cm wide, open, leaves with conspicuous, red-brown tips; flowers to 5cm wide. June to August. z5

S. nevadense Wale. S. Spain. Rosettes 2.5–3cm; leaves strongly incurved, fine, soft, glandular-pubescent. With short, slender stolons. Flowers reddish-carmine. Very easily cultivated, forms dense mats. This relatively unknown species is a delightful ornamental where hardy; suitable for the alpine house. z7

S. octopodes Turill. S. Yugoslavia. The species is not very widely distributed, but the var. *apetalum* is. Rosettes 2cm wide; rosette leaves incurved, finely soft-pubescent. Flowers yellow, petals with pale red base. Petals absent on *S. octopodes* var. *apetalum*. Requires lime-free soil. z6

S. ossetiense Wale. Caucasus Mts. Few-leaved, very succulent rosettes, 3cm wide. Floccose-pubescent, marginal stiff hairs, green with a small brown tip. Flowers with a purple middle band and white margins. Sensitive to wetness, often poor bloomer. The best distin-

green; outer leaves red. Some cultivars have purple-colored leaves. Offset rosettes borne on short, stout stolons. Flowers 10–12-merous, carmine-red with white borders. Slow-growing, producing few offsets. Not to be confused with *Jovibarba heuffelii* varieties of the same name. June to July. z7(6)

S. ruthenicum Schnittsp. et Lehm. SE. Europe. Included with *S. zeleborii* by many authors. Species status is, however, justified. Dense rosettes 3–5.5cm wide but contracting in winter; leaves

parted, 2.5cm wide, soft purple-red. Quite variable, common species with numerous varieties and still more cultivars. Flowers appear from June to August. Probably most of the garden-grown sempervivums are cultivars or hybrids of *S. tectorum*. This is certainly the most vigorous and easily cultivated species. Planted at one time on the slate or sod roofs of European country houses where they were thought to ward off lightning. Some popular cultivars of *S. tectorum* include: 'Atropurpureum', rosettes with large, dark gray-purple

Sempervivum hybrids

Sempervivum ruthenicum

Sempervivum tectorum ssp. *tectorum* 'Atropurpureum'

guishing characteristic is the fleshy foliage. z5

S. pittonii Schott, Nyman et Kotschy. E. Alps. Flat, many-leaved rosettes, 2.5–5cm across; leaves incurved, glandular-pubescent above and beneath, with glandular ciliate margins. Leaf tips distinctly dark purple. Offset rosettes on short stolons (2–3cm long). Stem 5cm high with many, erect, purple-tipped leaves. Flowers 9–12-merous pale greenish-yellow. Forms small clumps. z5

S. pumilum M.B. Caucasus Mts. Small rosettes of 1–2cm wide, green, short, finely pubescent on the upper and lower surface, glandular ciliate margins. Flowers pink-purple with a pale white margin. Secondary rosettes grow quickly to full size. There are 4 geographic forms. July. z5

S. reginae-amaliae Heldr. et Guicc. ex Hal. S. Albania to Greece. Rosettes 2.5–3cm across, open; leaves 1cm long, .3cm wide, flattish above, convex below, softly pubescent, with marginal cilia, soft

somewhat inarched, to 3cm long, densely pubescent above and below, rarely with purplish tips. Offset rosettes produced on short, stout stolons. Stems 10–15cm high; flowers 11–12-merous, petals pale green or greenish-yellow, with purple centers. Distinguished from *S. zeleborii* Schott by the large rosettes, taller flower stalks and the light yellow flowers. z6

S. schlehanii see **S. marmoreum**

S. sedoides see **Sempervivella sedoides**

S. soboliferum see **Jovibarba sobolifera**

S. tectorum L. Houseleek, Hen-and-Chickens, St. Patrick's Cabbage. From the Pyrenees Mts. through Central Europe to the Balkans. Rosettes to 20cm wide, flat and open, with stout, usually reddish stolons. Leaves to 5cm long, very fleshy, glabrous, dull-glazed, green, usually with purple-reddish tips. Flower stems 20–30cm high with lanceolate, hairy leaves, stem also white-hairy; flowers starry, 12–16-merous usually 13-

leaves; 'Atroviolaceum' with dark violet foliage; 'Robustum' with very large, blue-green rosettes; and 'Triste' with dark gray rosettes; 'Royanum' with yellowish-green rosettes and reddish leaf tips; 'Nigrum' is apple green with dark purple-red leaf tips. z5

S. tectorum ssp. **calcareum** see **S. calcareum**

S. thompsonianum Wale. S. Yugoslavia. Flat, globose, somewhat open rosettes; leaves yellowish green, finely soft-pubescent, with long marginal cilia. Foliage reddish-tinged on the outside in exposed sites. Offset rosettes on 8cm-long stolons. Petals have purple-red centers, yellow tips and white margins. z6

S. transcaucasicum Muirh. Caucasus Mts. Rather open rosettes 5–7cm across, leaves finely soft-pubescent, yellowish green, with pink-tinged tips. Offset rosettes on short, stout stolons. Poor bloomer in some climates, requires protection from winter wetness. June. z5

S. wulfenii Hoppe ex Mert. (*S. globiferum* Wulf.). Austrian and Swiss Alps; on igneous rocks. Rosettes 5–9cm across, open, but young leaves closely imbricate. Leaves 2–4cm long, smooth, light gray-green, usually rosy-purple at the base. Easily recognizable for the budlike cone formed by the inner leaves. With only a few stout stolons. Flower stems 20cm high; flowers 2.5cm wide, funnel-shaped to starry, 12–15 petalled, yellow with purple centers. Slow-growing in cultivation, somewhat demanding, recommended only for collectors. July to August. z5

S. zeleborii see **S. ruthenicum**

S. Hybrids. In addition to the species, innumerable worthwhile hybrids are listed, with many new cultivars developed each year. Descriptions are not possible within the scope of this book, but some recommended cultivars are: 'Adlerhorst' (Eagle's Nest), 'Commander Hay', 'Gamma', 'Jubilee', 'Metallicum Giganteum', 'Othello', 'Pilatus', 'Pseudo-ornatum', 'Rauhreif' (Hoarfrost), 'Rheinkiesel', 'Rotsandsteinriese', 'Rubin' (Ruby), 'Säntis', 'Skovtrold's Triumph', 'Spinell', 'Topas' (Topaz), 'Wunderhold', 'Zackenkrone' (Jagged Crown).

Lit.: Praeger, R.L.: *An Account of the Sempervivum Group.* Royal Hort. Soc., London 1932. Köhlein, F.: Freilandsukkulenten. Verlag Eugen Ulmer, Stuttgart, W. Germany 1977. (Sch. & Kö.)

Senecio L.
Compositae
Groundsel, Ragwort

A genus including 2000–3000, quite variable species of annuals, biennials, and perennials, shrubs (some tree-like), vines, and succulents distributed throughout the world. Leaves alternate, occasionally all basal. Flower heads usually radiate, occasionally without ray flowers, corymbose, sometimes solitary. Involucral bracts in a single row, with or sometimes without small bracts at the base. Receptacle flat or slightly convex, usually naked. Flowers usually yellow, rarely orange, red, blue or purple. Achenes usually cylindrical, ribbed. Pappus with soft, whitish, often numerous bristles. All species described here are primarily collectors' plants for the alpine garden, rock garden or wild garden, a few small enough for trough gardens. Some of the low-growing species are short-lived. Propagate by seed, division, or occasionally, by cuttings.

A few *Senecio* species are hardy in temperate regions and no few of these are weedy or noxious weeds; few are truly first class ornamental perennial. These include the following species described in this work:

abrotanifolius p. 615
adonidifolius p. 615
alpinus see *cordatus* pp. 614–615
aurantiacus see *integrifolius* ssp. *aurantiacus* pp. 615–616
aureus p. 614
capitatus see *integrifolius* ssp. *capitatus* p. 616
—ssp. *capitatus* p. 616

carniolicus see *incanus* ssp. *carniolicus* p. 616
cordatus pp. 614–615
doronicum p. 615
— var. *hosmeriensis* p. 615
flettii p. 615
fuschii see *nemorensis* ssp. *fuschii* p. 615
halleri p. 616
incanus p. 616
— ssp. *carniolicus* p. 616
— ssp. *incanus* p. 616
integrifolia p. 615
— ssp. *aurantiacus* pp. 615–616
— ssp. *capitatus* p. 616
kämpferi see *Ligularia tussilaginea* pp. 358–359
ledebourii see *Ligularia macrophylla* p. 358
leucophyllus pp. 616–617
nemorensis ssp. *fuschii* p. 615
palmatifidus see *Ligularia japonica* pp. 357–358
przewalskii see *Ligularia przewalskii* p. 358
tanguticus see *Ligularia tangutica* p. 358
uniflorus see *halleri* p. 616
veitchianus see *Ligularia veitchiana* p. 359
wilsonianus see *Ligularia wilsoniana* p. 359

Also see *Ligularia* for *Senecio ledebourii, S. palmatifidus, S. przewalskii, S. tanguticus, S. veitchianus, S. wilsonianus.*

1. Species over 40cm

S. alpinus see **S. cordatus**

S. aureus L. Golden Ragwort. N. America; Labrador to Georgia, westward to North Dakota south to Texas; in swales, damp thickets and prairies. Stems 20–90cm high, sparsely tomentose in spring, later glabrous. Roots very aromatic. Basal leaves long-petioled,

Senecio cordatus

cordate-ovate, to 15cm long, toothed, often purple on the underside. Basal offset plants often present. Stem leaves pinnatisect. Flower heads in loose cymes, 18mm wide, with 8–12 ray flowers, golden yellow. Blooms from March to July, depending on latitude. A good species for naturalizing in damp to wet wild-garden site. Plants will stay smaller under drier conditions, but are still attractive. Apt to become an invasive weed in its habitat. Propagate by seed and division. z2

S. cordatus Koch. (*S. alpinus* auct. non Scop.). Alps, N. and Central Apennine Mts.; on alpine meadows and tall grass clearings with moist to wet, fertile, usually alkaline loam or clay soil, to 1860m elevation. Erect stems 0.3–1m high, ribbed, branched only within the corymbs. Leaves to 15 × 10cm, ovate, cordate or rounded at the base, petioled, dark green above, with cobweb-like indusium beneath. Flower heads long-peduncled, 30–40mm wide, few, in corymbs. Flowers golden yellow. Pappus three times longer than the fruits. Blooms from July to August. Only for large alpine gardens or botanic gardens, where it requires a moist soil in semi-shade. Unfortunately quite susceptible to powdery mildew. Effective combined with *Aconitum napellus* and *Ranunculus aconitifolius.* z5

S. fuchsii see **S. nemorensis** ssp. **fuchsii**

S. nemorensis L. ssp. **fuchsii** (C.C. Gmel.) Celak. (*S. fuchsii* C.C. Gmel.). Central and S. Europe; in beech forests, balds and mountain clearings on moist, fertile humus; to 2000m in the Alps. Stems 0.5–1.5m high, often with short basal stolons, brownish-red, usually glabrous, very leafy, branched only toward the top. Leaves lanceolate or elliptic-lanceolate, 5–7 times as long as wide, tapered toward the base, glabrous on both sides or finely downy beneath or between the teeth. Flower heads with 8 glabrous involucral bracts, 20–35mm wide, in more or less compound corymbs. Flowers yellow, fragrant. Blooms from July to September.

An attractive naturalizing plant valuable for its late flowers. Thrives as an understory planting with a humus-rich, moderately moist loam soil. Mostly for for large parks, but also for small gardens in suitable sites. A good specimen or massing plant. Propagate by seed and division, self-seeds under favorable conditions. Effective when combined with other plants of open beech woodlands, i.e. *Digitalis purpurea, Galium odoratum, Luzula* species, *Melica nutans, Mercurialis.* z6

2. Species under 40 cm

S. abrotanifolius L. Central and E. Alps, N. Yugoslavia, mountains of the Balkan Peninsula; among Mugo Pines and dwarf alpine shrubs or on open rocky slopes of the subalpine elevations on limestone and lime-free substrata, in shallow, gravelly soil. Subshrub, 15–45cm high, with slender, branched, creeping rhizomes. Stems glabrous to downy, sprawling to upright, with few flower heads. Leaves more or less glabrous, lowest leaves twice 2- to 3-pinnatisect, upper leaves 1-pinnate, sessile, with a translucent margin, rich glossy green. Flower heads orange-yellow, with brownish stripes, solitary or few in corymbs, to 40mm wide. Ray flowers 10–13. Blooms from July to September. In the rock garden, plant in well-drained, stony, peaty soil. z6

S. adonidifolius Loisel. Pyrenees. S. France; on gravelly soil in the mountains, lime-intolerant. Glabrous herb 30–40(70)cm high, with procumbent-ascending, rooting stems. Leaves 1-pinnate with very slender segments. Inflorescence branched at the top with numerous, small, fairly crowded flower heads. Flower heads with 4–5 golden yellow ray flowers. Blooms from July to August. This species requires full sun and moderately moist, humus-rich loam with gravel. Tolerates neutral to slightly alkaline soil; this species closely resembles *S. abrotanifolius* with which it is

Senecio abrotanifolius

often confused. *S. abrotanifolius* var. *tirolensis* is the most attractive of this group. It is intolerant of alkaline soils. Propagate by seed and division. The best site for both plants is the alpine garden or the rock garden, best combined with *Pinus mugo, Juniperus communis* ssp. *alpina* (*J. nana*), *Rhododendron ferrugineum* and *R. hirsutum, Erica herbacea.* z6

S. aurantiacus see **S. integrifolius** ssp. **aurantiacus**

S. capitatus see **S. integrifolius** ssp. **capitatus**

S. doronicum (L.) L. Leopard's-bane Ragwort. Mountains of Central and S. Europe; above 1500m elevation in moist to dry, calcareous, loose, humus-rich soil. Quite a variable species. Stems 15–40cm high, very erect, cobweb-woolly, or rarely nearly glabrous, usually with few leaves and solitary flower heads. Basal leaves tough and leathery, ovate, oblong-ovate to lanceolate or oblanceolate, undivided, dentate, usually woolly-

cobwebby below, dark green above. Flower heads large, 3–6cm wide, solitary or 4–7 in a loose corymb. Ray flowers 12–16, orange-yellow, often pubescent beneath. Blooms from June to July. Includes the cultivar 'Sunburst', 40cm high and deep orange-yellow, and var. **hosmariensis**, dwarf, 7.5–15cm high, leaves ovate-cordate, flower heads 3.75cm across. More tender than the species. For the alpine garden or rockery, in full sun on a scree with only a little humus rich soil mixed through. Propagate by seed. Good companions include the grasses, such as *Carex ornithophora, C. sempervirens, Festuca pumila, Sesleria caerulea* as well as *Alchemilla alpina, Dryas octopetala, Erica herbacea* and *Rhododendron hirsutum.* z5

S. flettii Wieg. NW. USA: Washington; in the mountains on open gravelly sites, especially on screes. Stems glabrous or nearly so, 10–30cm high. Basal leaves ovate to obovate in outline, pinnately deep lobed to lyrate pinnatifid, lobes toothed. Petioles often as long as the blade. Stem leaves few, becoming gradually smaller toward the top. Flower heads 2–10 in a terminal, corymbose cluster with 5–10 ligulate flowers, yellow. Blooms from June to July. Uses, cultivation and propagation as for *S. abrotanifolius.* z6

S. integrifolius (L.) Clairv. Widely distributed throughout Europe in isolated locations. A variable species with only the following two subspecies commonly cultivated. Stems branched only in the inflorescence, 10–70cm high. Basal leaves in a rosette, to 10 × 5cm, ovate to oblong-elliptic, entire or toothed, narrowing to a winged petiole as long as or shorter than the blade. Lower stem leaves are oval-lanceolate to lanceolate, sessile or tapered to a short, winged petiole; the middle and upper stem leaves much reduced, lanceolate to linear, sessile. Flower heads 15–25mm wide, solitary or to 15 in a corymb with 12–15 ray flowers, yellow to golden yellow. z5

S. integrifolius ssp. **aurantiacus** (Hoppe ex Willd.) Briq. et Cavillier (*S. aurantiacus* (Willd.) Briq. et Cavillier (*S. aurantiacus* (Willd.) Less.). Mountains of E. Central Europe: E. Alps, Istria, Bohemia, Moravia, Carpathians; in mountain meadows or ravines, in dry, open woodlands, on limestone. Perennial, but often biennial in culture. Stems 20–50cm high, glabrous or sparsely pubescent except in the juvenile stage of growth, otherwise like the species. Flower heads

2–6. Involucral bracts purple-brown. Ray flowers orange-yellow, orange-red or brown-red, occasionally lacking. Flowers from June to August. Garden uses and culture like that of *S. abrotanifolius*. Propagate by seed. z5

S. integrifolius ssp. **capitatus** (Wahlenb.) Cuf. (*S. capitatus* (Wahlenb.) Steud.). Alps, Carpathians, Albania; in alpine meadows. Like the species, but 15–30cm high, usually densely gray-white woolly or tomentose. Basal leaves ovate-oblong or elliptic, stem leaves numerous. Usually with only one stiff, erect stem

3. Species under 15cm

S. carniolicus see **S. incanus** ssp. **carniolicus**

S. halleri Dandy (*S. uniflorus* (All.) All. non Retz.). SW. and S. Central Alps; on short-grass meadows, as a pioneer plant near rocks and in rock crevices. Lime-intolerant, 5–15cm high, white-tomentose perennial with short, branched, woody rootstocks and erect, unbranched stalks with solitary flower heads, therefore easily distinguished from corymbose *S. incanus* and *S. leuco-*

gray tomentose-green above, undersides white-tomentose. Stem leaves pinnatisect, the uppermost reduced, simple. Flower heads several in a dense corymb. Ray flowers 4–6, egg-yolk yellow. Disc flowers yellow. Blooms from June to August. z5

S. incanus ssp. **carniolicus** (Willd.) Braun-Blanq. (*S. carniolicus* Willd.). Central and E. Alps, Carpathian Mts.; on limestone and neutral soil. Differs in the oblanceolate or narrowly obovate in outline blades of the basal leaves, silky-gray-haired at first, later glabrous. Nutlets

Senecio doronicum

Serratula seoanei

and a few clustered flower heads. Involucral bracts usually purple. Ray flowers opening brown-red, later orange-yellow, but often lacking. Blooms from June to July. z5

Attractive, but somewhat difficult species for the alpine garden or rock gardens of experienced collectors of alpine plants. Plants are lime-intolerant but thrive in a neutral soil in a somewhat moist north- or northeast-facing rock crevice or on a scree. The species is unfortunately short-lived; therefore propagate regularly from seed. Overwinter the seedlings in an alpine case or cold frame. Suitable companions include *Callianthemum coriandrifolium*, *Homogyne alpina*, *Plantago nivalis* and *Sibbaldia procumbens*.

phyllus. Basal leaves tapered to a long petiole, undivided, coarsely toothed or incised, oblong-obovate, white to gray-tomentose, appressed-pubescent. Flower heads solitary, 20–25mm wide, erect. Ray flowers about 20, golden yellow, disc flowers yellow. Blooms from June to August. Uses, cultivation and propagation like that of *S. incanus*. z6

S. incanus L. Alps, N. Apennines, Carpathian Mts.; usually on dry, gravelly sites with pioneer vegetation and dwarf shrubs, especially over igneous substrata at alpine elevations. Plants reach 5–15cm high, more or less entirely dense gray to white tomentose, with a short, woody, branched rootstock. Stems erect, branched only within the corymb, sparsely leafy. Basal leaves 3–10cm long, usually lobed or pinnately cleft, petioled,

glabrous. Lime tolerant. z5

S. incanus ssp. **incanus**. SW. and S. Central Alps, N. Apennine Mts. Blades of the basal leaves more or less broadly ovate in outline. Nutlets pubescent. Lime intolerant. z5

S. leucophyllus DC. On screes in the E. Pyrenees Mts. and S. Central France. Plants to 20cm high. Basal leaves thick and, like the stem leaves, always pinnately cleft. Flower heads larger. Nutlets always pubescent. Similar to the closely related *S. incanus*, but more vigorous. z6

Landscape uses, cultivation and propagation of the species of Group 3 are similar to those of *S. integrifolius*, but these require somewhat drier soil and protection from winter wetness. Demanding, and extremely sensitive to lime. Young replacement plants grown from seed should always be available. Best cultivated in the alpine house. z6 (E.)

S. uniflorus see **S. halleri**

Serratula L.
Compositae

Seventy species of perennial herbs from Europe and the Mediterranean region to E. Asia. Leaves alternate, toothed or pinnate lobed, usually not prickly. Flower heads large and solitary or small and in corymbs. Flowers all tubular and usually perfect, purple, pink or violet, occasionally white. Pappus bristles in multiple rows, finely serrate, uneven. Fruits glabrous, nearly cylindrical or obtuse angular. Only the following species is very ornamental. It belongs in the rock garden and has attractive foliage, and its chief merit is its late flowering time. Requires a sunny site and a loamy soil, best planted between rocks. Plants improve in appearance with age when left undisturbed. Propagate by seed and division. Some good companions include *Artemisia* (the low species), *Micromeria thymifolia*, *Nepeta* × *faassenii*, *Satureja montana* and *S. rumelica*.

S. depressa see **Jurinea depressa**

S. seoanei Willk. (*S. shawii* hort.). N. Portugal, NW. Spain, SW. France. Stems 20–30cm high, a dense, bushy perennial with dark green, finely divided, pinnately deep-cut leaves and branched stems. Flower heads in loose corymbs. Flowers purple-pink. Blooms from September to October. z7 (E.)

S. shawii see **S. seoanei**

A few additional species, all more or less thistle-like in appearance, sometimes appear in wildflower or naturalized gardens. These include *S. atriplicifolia*, 1.6m; *S. centauroides*, 30–45cm; *S. coronata*, 1.5m; *S. gmelinii*, 60–90cm; *S. marginata*, 75cm; *S. nudicaulis*, 20–37.5cm; *S. pinnatifida*, 7.5–25cm and *S. tinctoria*, Sawwort, 90cm.

Seseli L.
Umbelliferae

Eighty species of perennial, occasionally biennial herbs from Europe to Central Asia, of which only *S. caespitosum* has much garden merit, though a few

other species are grown in wild or medicinal gardens. This is an elegant, small, blue-green, fully winter-hardy perennial for the alpine garden, rockery and trough. It thrives in a sunny, dry, rocky site in well-drained, loamy soil. The loose, 10–20cm high plants with finely divided, blue-green leaves are effective in combination with many low, white and green variegated ground cover plants or among large rocks. Propagate by seed or careful division in late summer. Grow young plants in containers in an alpine case.

Sesleria autumnalis

S. caespitosum Sibth. et Sm. NW. Asia Minor. Flowering stems 10–20cm high above blue-green foliage clumps. The root crown is fibrous. Leaves 2- to 3-pinnatisect with small, oblong, acutely incised segments, blue-green on both sides. Flowering stems round, slender, leafless. Umbels usually 3–5 parted. Flowers small, white. Blooms from July to August. z6 (E.)

S. montanum L. S. Europe, is grown occasionally in British gardens. Similar to *S. caespitosum* but flowering stems taller, 40–60cm. Numerous pinkish white umbels from July to September. z5

Sesleria Scop.
Gramineae
Moor Grass

A genus of mostly clump grasses with panicled, but dense, spicate, globose to cylindrical, bluish, gray or white inflorescences. The flowering time of most species, either quite early (March) or very late, makes them conspicuous, this alone being sufficient reason for inclusion in garden culture. Species of *Sesleria* are suitable for many garden situations, as indicated in the individual species descriptions. Choose selected clones for garden plantings; they are easily propagated by division. Despite the many desirable qualities of *Sesleria* species, few are found in cultivation. There are a number of clones of unclear parentage.

S. albicans Kit. ex Schult. (*S. caerulea* (L.) Ard. ssp. *varia* (Jacq.) Hayek, *S. caerulea* ssp. *calcarea* (Celak.) Hege, *S. varia* (Jacq.) Wettst.). Central and W. Europe, to the Apennines and Montenegro. A vigorous, deep-rooting clump grass with 2–5mm wide, flat or channeled leaves with disinct midvein. The uppermost subtending leaves are about 1cm long. Inflorescences appear in early March, 10–40cm high, with oblong-oval, to 30mm-long, 7mm-wide, violet to steel-blue spicate panicles just above or well above the foliage. An effective spring bloomer and typical plant of steeply sloping limestone meadows. While plants are usually found in the mountains, they are also found in the lowlands on similar soil and exposure. z5

S. argentea Savi (*S. cylindrica* DC.), Italy, through France to N. Spain. A loose clump grass; leaves to 5mm wide, flowering culms 50cm high, leafy to half that height, the uppermost subtending leaves 3cm or longer. Inflorescences 3.5–10cm long, about 8mm wide, silvery-white. A variable species for warm, calcareous sites. Many cultivars or varie-

flowering culms, and the uppermost stem leaves are bluish-pruinose, margins often involuted. The inflorescences appear in late March and are 10–14mm long, 7–9mm wide. The plants grow naturally in boggy, calcareous soils but adapt to garden conditions. Often confused with *S. albicans* in the trade. z5

S. caerulea ssp. **calcarea** see **S. albicans**

S. cacrula ssp. **uliginosa** see **S. caerulea**

S. caerula ssp. **varia** see **S. albicans**

80cm, distinctly higher than the foliage clump. The panicled spikes are dense, to 30mm long and half as wide. Corresponding to its native habitat, this species thrives in well-drained, humus-rich limestone soil. It combines well with other heat-loving plants. z6

S. rigida Heuff. ex Reichenb. Mountains of the Balkan Peninsula. A clump grass with 2mm-wide, channeled or creased leaves in 15cm-high clumps. The silver-gray to purple-colored inflorescences are usually no longer than the leaves.

Shibataea kumasaca

Shortia soldanelloides

ties from Italy strongly resemble *S. autumnalis.* z6

S. autumnalis (Scop.) F.W. Schultz, Autumn Moor Grass. From N. and E. Italy to Albania. A strong, 30cm-high clump grass with 4mm-wide, rough-margined leaves and 40cm-high flowering culms, with 4–8cm long leaves to more than halfway up the stem. The inflorescences are 4.5–10cm long, to 7mm wide, loose and silvery white at first, appearing after September. Very effective when planted with other fall bloomers. Thrives in alkaline soils and tolerates root competition from woody companion plants. z6

S. caerulea (L.) Scop. (*S. uliginosa* Opiz, *S. caerulea* ssp. *uliginosa* (Opiz) Hayek), Blue Moor Grass. From NW. Russia and Sweden to Bulgaria and Montenegro. Very similar to *S. albicans*, but with stiffer

S. cylindrica see **S. argentea**

S. heuffleriana Schur, Green Moor Grass. SE. Europe. A loose (denser in its ssp. *ungarica* (Ujhelyi) Deyl.), 50cm-high clump grass. Leaves about 5mm wide, very glaucous above when young, stems to 70cm high, flowers appear in April in 30mm-long, 10mm-wide, black, paniculate spikes with yellow-green anthers. This grass thrives on limy soils. Plants in nature occur in shaded sites and open woodlands, therefore are best suited for a woodland margin planting. With sufficient moisture, clumps become very wide and remain green long into winter. z5

S. nitida Ten., Nest Moor Grass. Central and S. Italy. A clump grass with flat, to 6mm-wide, bluish, rough-margined leaves. The flowering culms appear in April, leafy to above the middle, stiff, to

This species grows best on a rocky slope and, with its short stature, needs low companion plants. z5 (S.)

S. ulignosa see **S. caerulea**

S. varia see **S. albicans**

Setaria P. Beauv.
Gramineae
Foxtail

S. plicatilis E. Africa. Most species of this genus are nearly cosmopolitan annuals, many are serious weeds. This is the only commonly grown perennial species. It grows to about 1m high, with stiff stems and leaves to 2.5cm wide and 45cm long. The inflorescences are cattail-like, spicate, dense panicles, 30cm long and 7cm thick, erect at first, later nodding, with long awns, silky pink to glossy green. Requires a warm, moist site and winter protection. Plants may be divided; propagation by seed must be under glass in cool summer regions. z6 (S.)

Shibataea Mak. ex Nakai
Gramineae
Bamboo

Two species of bamboos, one in China, one in Japan. Both species quite dwarf. Rhizomes elongated. Stems nearly solid,

dentate leaves. Flowers white, pink or blue, nodding, on slender scapes. Calyx deeply 5-lobed; corolla campanulate, 5-lobed; stamens 5 fertile, alternating with 5 staminodes.

A charming, small, but not easily grown evergreen perennial for the experienced plantsman. Plants will thrive only where soil and water are nonalkaline. Probably the best of the 3 rarely offered species is *S. galacifolia*. Plants are suitable for the rockery or bog garden in a shaded or semi-shaded, evenly moist site given a mixture of peat

S. galacifolia Torr. et A. Gray. Oconee-bells. USA: S. Appalachian Mts. About 15cm high, with long-petioled, rounded to ovate, glossy, crenate-dentate leaves, blades to 7.5cm across, which turn crimson bronze in winter. Flowers solitary, 2.5cm across, on a scape about 12cm long, white, pink or blue. Blooms from May to June. The hardiest species. z5

S. soldanelloides (Sieb. et Zucc.) Mak. (*Schizocodon soldanelloides* Sieb. et Zucc.), Fringed Galax. Japan; in mountain forests and thickets, or on more open,

Shortia uniflora 'Grandiflora

Sibbaldia procumbens

Sibthorpia europaea

zig-zag. Flattened and grooved on one side. Branches very short, 3–5 at a node; leaf blades short petioled, broad.

S. kumasaca (Zoll.) Mak. ex Nakai. Japan. Wild stands eradicated; today only found in cultivation. The species is easily recognized for its much flattened, slender stems to 2m, rarely higher. The leaves are short and wide, often drying at the tips, especially in soils lacking in acidity. Otherwise, like most bamboo species, *Shibataea* tolerates wet sites, but not standing water. Also suitable for tub planting. Damage to the 0.5–1.5m high stems can occur at −12 degrees C. (10 degrees F.). z8(7) (S.)

Shortia Torr. et A. Gray
Diapensiaceae

About 8 species of small, evergreen, stemless perennials with creeping rootstocks from temperate E. North America and Asia. Plants with basal, simple, long-petioled, rounded to cordate, crenate-

and leafmold. Combines well with *Kalmia latifolia* or small, acid-loving rhododendron species. In favorable sites plants may be left undisturbed for many years. In general, out of habitat, plants are most successfully cultivated in containers in an alpine house in a shady site. *S. soldanelloides* and *S. uniflora* are exceptionally difficult to maintain in the landscape.

Propagation is by division, but to avoid disturbing the mother plant, remove and pot up the rooted plantlets on runners. Seeds are seldom set on plants in cultivation, and seed propagation is difficult and tedious, following a technique used for rhodendrons. *Shortia* combines well in the garden with *Cypripedium* and *Epigaea*, since these also require a lime-free humus soil in shady sites. All species should be covered loosely in winter with a dry pine needle mulch or conifer boughs. Remove this cover in mid- to late March, depending upon the region and winter conditions, then apply a deep summer mulch of leafmold and peat.

sunny sites in the alpine regions. Perennial 10–15cm high with creeping, sparsely branched rhizomes and few, long-petioled, leathery, to 6 × 5cm, coarse-toothed leaves, which turn reddish bronze in winter. Flowers 3–10, on 10–30cm long, reddish scapes. Flowers funnelshaped or campanulate, pink, similar to *Soldanella*, petals fringed or cut. Blooms from March to April. The most attractive, but unfortunately, most difficult to grow species, hardly recommended for the landscape. Plants are best cultivated in an alpine house or frost-free cold frame. Several varieties are listed, differing in height, leaf size, number and color of the flowers, but these are rarely offered in the trade. z7

S. uniflora (Maxim.) Maxim. Nippon-bells. Japan; in mountain forests. Similar to *S. galacifolia*, but generally smaller and more widely creeping. Leaves reniform to rounded, 2.5–7cm long and nearly as wide, cordate or rounded at the base, sinuate-toothed. Flowers solitary on 15cm-long scapes, pale pink, 2.5–3cm wide, thick-papery, with deep, obtuse-toothed lobes. Blooms from April to May. Cultivar 'Grandiflora' with 4cm-wide flowers, opening pink, fading white. More floriferous than the species. z6 (E.)

Sibbaldia L.
Rosaceae

Eight to ten species, circumpolar in the Northern Hemisphere. Similar to *Potentilla*, distinguished by fewer carpels

Sidalcea 'Elsie Heugh'

(5–12) and only 5 (rarely 4–10) stamens. The petals are small, 1–2mm long, shorter than the calyx, leaves alternate, ternate, gray-green.

S. procumbens L. Arctic-alpine, circumpolar; in snowy valleys and snow-laden depressions at alpine elevations. Plant 5–10cm high, with limited carpet habit. Stems procumbent, 10–30cm long. Leaves petioled, ternate, gray-green. Flowers in small terminal cymes, orange-yellow to greenish yellow, or petals absent, inconspicuous. Blooms in June. Grow on lime-free soil in a cool, shaded moist site; not easy to maintain through summer heat and humidity or snowless winters. A collector's plant. Propagate by seed and division. z1 (K.)

Sibthorpia L.
Scrophulariaceae

A genus of 6 species of prostrate, perennial, hairy herbs which root at the nodes to form carpets, found in Europe, Africa, S. Asia (Nepal), and South Africa. Leaves alternate or whorled, petioled, blade

orbicular to kidney-shaped, deep-toothed. Flowers in leaf axils, small, yellow or reddish.

S. europaea L. Cornish Moneywort. W. Europe, north to 52 degrees North latitude in England, south to Greece and Crete. A small, creeping, collector's plant with tiny, rounded toothed, green leaves. The form 'Variegata' has golden-green leaves splotched silver-white. Blooms from May to August, but inconspicuous. A groundcover for a cool, moist site. Requires winter protection. Best cul-

Silene acaulis 'Plena'

tivated in an alpine house. Propagate by division. z8 (Kö.)

Sidalcea A. Gray
Malvaceae
False Mallow

A genus of about 22 annual and perennial species. These are erect, often bushy, somewhat stiff herbs with a fibrous or rhizomatous rootstock; leaves usually orbicular, palmately lobed or divided, glossy; and stiffly upright, crowded terminal racemes, to 1m-high, with small white, pink or purple, sessile or short-pediceled, mallow flowers in summer. Calyx 5-cleft, usually without bracteoles, petals 5, spreading, stamens many, united by the filaments in 2 whorls (1 whorl in *Malva*), anthers free, styles with branching, thread-like stigmas (capitate in stipe in *Sphaeralcea*) which protrude

through the hollow column of stamens; fruit a schizocarp. Indigenous to W. North America, on well-drained, lime-free, sandy humus loam in the grassland regions. False Mallow thrives in a loose, humus rich, sandy garden soil in full sun or brief, bright shade. Plants are damaged by standing water and sometimes fail to overwinter in heavy soils. Decorative plants for open perennial beds if given the proper conditions. In bloom from July to September. Cut back immediately after flowering. The species are easily grown from seed; cultivars are propagated by division.

S. candida A. Gray. W. USA: Wyoming, Colorado, New Mexico, Utah. Glaucous, glabrate plant 60–90cm high. Stems well-branched, bushy. Basal leaves nearly orbicular, 5–7 lobed or deeply crenate; stem leaves 5–7 parted. Racemes 5–13cm long. Flowers 2.5cm wide, white with bluish anthers. Flowers after June, the earliest-blooming species. A parent, with *S. malviflora*, of most modern cultivars and strains. z5

S. hendersonii S. Wats. W. North America: British Columbia south to Oregon. Plants glabrous to glabrate, with several erect stems 60–180cm high. Rootstock a massive taproot (older plants) or a deep rooted rhizome. Lower leaves to 15cm across, orbicular, with 5 shallow lobes; upper leaves nearly palmate-dissected, the 3–5 divisions laciniate. Racemes spicate, many-flowered, crowded. Flowers 2–3.2cm across, pinkish-lavender to deep rose, in early summer.

S. malviflora (DC.) A. Gray, Checkerbloom, Prairie Mallow. W. North America: Oregon, California, N. Baja California, to 1m high. Stems sparsely-pubescent. Basal leaves unlobed to shallow-lobed, incised-crenate; stem leaves 5-parted, segments laciniate high on the stem. Flowers 5cm across, pinkish-rose to watermelon-pink, in single or compound racemes. Several subspecies are listed, also cultivar 'Listeri' with satiny pink flowers. Most cultivars stem from this species directly or as hybrids. z7(6)

S. neomexicana A. Gray. W. North America: Oregon to Wyoming, south to Mexico. Roots fleshy, taprooted or several stout roots. Stems branched, 1m high, softly hirsute. Basal leaves 7.5cm across, round, 5–9 shallow-lobed; stem leaves mostly with 5 segments. Flowers in simple or branched, many flowered racemes, white to pink, about 2cm across. z5

S. oregana (Nutt. ex Torr. et A. Gray) A. Gray. W. North America: Washington to California and Nevada. Stems 60–120cm high, plant glabrous to sparsely pubescent, with massive taproot, branching root crown, often with rhizomes. Basal leaves to 15cm across, 5–7 shallow-lobed, glossy green; stem leaves 5–7 parted. Flowers many, small, in spicate racemes, pinkish to deep pink. The cultivar 'Brilliant' with flowers carmine red, 60cm high. z6

While the described species are interesting to botanists and plant breeders, gardeners find cultivars showier and somewhat easier to grow. Garden hybrids which are especially noteworthy include:

'Croftway Red', nearest to pure red, 100cm.
'Elsie Heugh', clear satiny-pink, large, fringed, 90cm.
'Mrs. Alderson', clear pink, large, late-flowering, 120cm.
'Mrs. Galloway', deep rose-red, 120cm.
'Loveliness', shell-pink, fragile looking, 75cm.
* 'Oberon', soft rose-pink, very tidy plant, 75cm.
* 'Puck', clear pink, midseason, 60cm.
'Rev. Page Roberts', pale pink, 135cm.
'Rose Queen', rose-pink, 10cm.
'Sussex Beauty', glowing satiny pink, 120cm.
* 'Titania', satiny-pink, very sturdy, 75cm.
'Wensleydale', rose-red, erect, 120cm.
'William Smith', salmon-rose, many-flowered spike, 105cm.

*The notable Bressingham Gardens introductions of lower habit; beautiful but somewhat temperamental.

In addition to asexually propagated cultivars, plant breeders have produced meritorious Sidalcea Hybrid strains to be grown from seed. The Stark Hybrids are an example. The early-flowering, red-flowered 'Mr. Lindbergh' is reputed to be a cultivar which comes true from seed.

Sideritis L.
Labiatae

About 100 species of annual and perennial herbs and small shrubs, from N. temperate and subtropical Eurasia. Stems mostly square in cross section; leaves opposite, entire or toothed. Flowers in 2– many flowered false whorls in spikes or racemes. Prophylla lacking. Calyx campanulate, 10 nerved and 5 toothed. Corolla zygomorphic, usually yellow, tube no longer than the calyx, limb 2-lipped, upper lip almost concave, lower lip 3-lobed; stamens diadelphous, included.

Only a few species are grown today by collectors and botanic gardens, but probably other more or less ornamental species await introduction into cultivation. Very heat-tolerant plants, well-suited to hot, sunny rock gardens and dry stone walls, but seldom showy, and short-lived. Plants are easily killed by winter wetness, requiring well-drained, limy, humus loam mixed with gravel. All species thrive in a warm, dry location in full sun. Propagate by seed and late summer cuttings.

S. glacialis Boiss. Mountains of S. Spain, among rocks and on screes. Bushy, more or less tomentose perennial 15–20cm high; cushion habit. Leaves 10 × 2mm, lanceolate to obovate-spatulate, entire or with a few teeth at the base. Flowers in 1–3 false whorls. Corolla yellow, interior with dark brown or purple markings. Blooms from June to July. z7

S. scardica Griseb. Central Balkan region, in the mountains among rocks. Dense white woolly plant 20–30cm high, with oblong-lanceolate leaves; larger than the previous species. False whorls compressed into a dense spike. Flowers yellow. Blooms from June to July. z6 (E.)

Sieversia

S. ciliata see **Geum triflorum**

S. reptans see **Geum reptans**

Silene L.
Caryophyllaceae
Campion, Catchfly, Cushion Pink

A genus of about 500, quite variable, annual to perennial species, distributed throughout the world. Several cushion- or clump type perennial plants are primarily used for sunny rock and wild garden sites where they will thrive. Generally impartial to soil though good drainage is essential and a few are better on acidic soil. Two easily grown, low, spreading European species are S. schafta and S. vulgaris. Low-growing E. North American Catchflies of landscape value include S. caroliniana and S. caroliniana ssp. wherryi, S. virginiana, and somewhat tender, S. baldwynii. Several more or less prostrate species with large to very large flowers grow in the far W. USA, mostly from California northward to Washington but these are very difficult to maintain out of their habitat. They include: S. californica E. Durand, S. douglasii Hook., and S. hookeri Nutt. ex Torr & A. Gray. Several other silenes, growing from 30–100cm high, are fine naturalizing ornamentals for the shady to sunny wild garden and some are finding their way into herbaceous borders. Propagation is easy from seed, division and cuttings.

S. acaulis (L.) Jacq. Moss Campion, Cushion Pink. Alps, Mts. of Arctic Asia and America. A dense, flat cushion 2cm high. Leaves linear-subulate, 6–12mm long. Flowers borne above the foliage, 12mm across, solitary, petals 5, 2-lobed, pink to purplish; May to June. Usually free-flowering in its mountain habitat, but may flower poorly and be short-lived in lowland gardens; plants should be divided and moved every 2 years. Requires gravelly, but not too dry soil; only for collectors. S. acaulis ssp. **exscapa** (All.) Braun-Blanq. is a particularly good, low form. A more floriferous cultivar is 'Floribunda'; 'Alba' flowers white. A cultivar listed as 'Plena' or 'Cenisia' has double flowers. These are more reliable bloomers. z2

S. alba see **S. pratensis**

S. alpestris see **S. quadrifida**

S. baldwynii Nutt. SE. USA: Georgia to Florida. Evergreen to deciduous perennial. Stems 30–40cm long, prostrate, in a loose mat, flowering tips ascending. Leaves spatulate to obovate, 2.5–7cm long, grayish-green. Inflorescence a few-flowered terminal raceme. Flowers 3.5–5cm across, petals 5, deeply lacerate, clear pink or rarely white. Grows in average garden loam which is neutral to acidic, moist during the growing season. Thrives in partial shade, tolerates full sun in a cool, moist climate. A beautiful rock garden plant. This has been hybridized recently with *S. virginica* to yield an out-

Silene schafta

standing progeny of intermediate cultivars. z6

S. californica E. Durand. California Indian Pink. W. USA: Oregon to California. Sturdy perennial with stems 60–120cm high, hairy; leaves ovate to ovate-elongate, 7–10cm wide, to 3.7cm wide, margins crenate, both sides pubescent. Inflorescence a few to many flowered panicle, pedicels and calyx glandular-pubescent to hairy; flowers to 4.5cm across, petals with two dissected lobes, crimson; very showy. z7

S. caroliniana Walt. Wild Pink. E. USA: New Hampshire south to Florida, west to Missouri. Herbaceous perennial to 20cm high, branching freely from the base. Stems glabrous to pubescent. Basal leaves spatulate to ovate-oblanceolate, 7–12cm long, 2.5cm wide, glabrous to pilose. Stem leaves smaller. Inflorescence a loose panicle. Flowers about 1.5cm across, showy, petals lacerate, white to deep pink. And ssp. **pensylvanica** (Michx.) R. T. Clausen. Calyx narrow, glandular; and ssp. **wherryi** R. T. Clausen. Calyx broad,

without glands; occurs on dry, acidic sandy soil or among chirt rocks. These are beautiful but challenging rock garden ornamentals. z5

S. caryophylloides (Poir.) Otth. ex DC. Asia Minor, on stony hillsides. Caespitose perennial, stems ascending to 40cm, glandular-pilose; basal leaves almost deltoid, to 2cm long, acute, stem leaves linear to lanceolate, pubescent, often glandular-sticky. Inflorescence 1–2 flowered. Calyx long, narrow, hairy; corolla *Dianthus*-like, white to pink. Ssp. **echinus** (Boiss. & Heldr.) Coode &

Silphium laciniatum

Cullen. Turkey. Basal rosette leaves bristly-ciliate, calyx without glands, petals bright rose pink. A better ornamental. z8(7 or 6)

S. cucubalis see **S. vulgaris**

S. dioica (L. emend. Mill.) Clairv. (*Lychnis dioica* L. emend. Mill., *L. diurna* Sibth., *Melandrium dioicum* (L.emend. Mill.) Coss. et Germ., *M. rubrum* (Weigel) Garcke). Europe. 0.8–1m high. Flowers light purple-red; May to September. 'Roseum Plenum' ('Rubra Plena') is an old garden plant, valued for its long-lasting, *Matthiola*-like flowers, carmine pink. Propagation is by division. z6

S. douglasii Hook. (*S. lyallii* Wats.) W. USA: Mts. of British Columbia south to California and Nevada. A variable species. Stems 10–90cm high, pubescent, with many more or less basal or low leaves. Leaves narrow-oblanceolate, 2.5–

7cm long and to 12mm wide, long petioled, the opposite petioles united at the node. Stem leaves nearly sessile. Inflorescence pubescent, few-flowered. Flowers to 1.5cm across, creamy-white, often tinged pink, purple, brown or green. z6

S. elisabethae Jan (*Melandrium elisabethae* (Jan) Rohrb.) S. Alps. Basal rosettes of glabrous, lanceolate leaves, stems 10–20cm high, simple, with 1–3 pink-red, 2–3cm wide flowers from July to August. A beautiful rock plant, lime-loving; unfortunately somewhat fastidious in culture.

Requires a scree bed or sunny rock crevice. Only for experienced collectors. z6

S. glauca see **S. vulgaris**

S. hookeri Nutt. ex Torr. & A. Gray (*S. ingramii* Tidestr. & Dayt.). NW. USA: SW. Oregon to NW. California. Stems prostrate to prostrate-ascending, many, gray-hairy. Leaves opposite, oblanceolate, 5–10cm long, gray-green, pubescent. Inflorescence a few-flowered cyme; flowers large, 4–5cm wide, petals deeply cleft to usually 4 segments, white to pink, occasionally violet to purple. Very choice but demanding rock garden plant. z7

S. inflata see **S. vulgaris**

S. ingramii see **S. hookeri**

S. keiskei Miq. (*S. keiskei* var. *major* Hort.) Japan. Plants caespitose with glabrous to puberulent stems. Leaves sessile, opposite, linear-lanceolate, to 5cm long. Inflorescence a few-flowered cyme; flowers purple, petals only notched. Mat plant for the rock garden. Var. **minor**, smaller in all parts, red-stemmed mat with flowers to 5cm high, leaves, pedicels and calyx soft-hairy. z6

S. keiskei var. **major** see **S. keiskei**

S. laciniata Cav. Fringed Indian Pink, Mexican Campion. North America: Mts. California, New Mexico and Mexico. Stems 1–few, erect, pubescent to glandular, to 90cm high. Leaves opposite, sessile, narrow-lanceolate to obovate, to 5cm long, closer together low on the stem. Inflorescence terminal, 1–few-flowered. Flowers to 2.5cm across; petals 4-cleft, bright red. Showy. z7(6)

S. lyallii see **S. douglasii**

S. maritima see **S. vulgaris** ssp. **maritima**

S. pratensis (Rafn.) Godr. et Gren. (*S. alba* (Mill.) E.H.L. Krause, *Melandrium album* (Mill.) Garcke, *Lychnis alba* Mill., *L. vespertina* Sibth.). Europe, N. Africa, W. Asia, Siberia. The double-flowered cultivar 'Multiplex' is occasionally found in cultivation. Stems 40–50cm high. Leaves lanceolate-acute, flowers white, double, carnation-like, in cymes; May to October. Often only biennial. z4

S. pygmaea Adams (*S. spathulata* Bieb.) S. Europe; Alps, Caucasus Mts. Loose cushion habit; stems to 20cm high, densely pubescent; basal leaves in a rosette, long-petioled, round, pubescent with longer hairs; stem leaves opposite, subsessile to sessile above, spatulate. Inflorescence a loose cyme. Flowers to nearly 2cm across; petals white, rarely pink or lavender. A rock garden plant. z7(6)

S. quadrifida (L.) L. (*S. alpestris* Jacq., (*Heliosperma alpestre* (Jacq., Rchb.). Found in the higher mountains from the Pyrenees to the Carpathians and Balkans. Plant a loose, subglabrous to hairy cushion, 15–30cm high, stems ascending, forked, leathery, green. Leaves obovate-lanceolate to linear-lanceolate. Inflorescence corymbose-paniculate, viscid. Flowers long-pediceled, 4–6 petaled, very decorative, white or rarely rose-tinged. Cultivar 'Pleniflorum' with double white flowers from June to August. Attractive for the rock garden or dry stone wall. Valued for its late flowering period. Soil should be a well-drained, loose humus, not too dry. Grows in full sun and semi-shade. Easily grown from seed and division. z5

S. regia Sims. Royal Catchfly. E. USA, Ohio to Missouri south to Georgia and N. Arkansas, on prairies and forest margins, usually in moister areas. Stems strongly erect, mostly unbranched, 45–150cm high, glandular-pubescent to rarely glabrescent; leaves elongate lanceolate, 5–12cm long, puberulent to subglabrous. Inflorescence a terminal panicle 12–30cm long with numerous flowers open simultaneously; flowers to 2.5cm wide, rarely wider, brilliant red, very showy, petals notched; early summer to midsummer. z6(5)

S. sachalinensis Fr. Schmidt. Siberia, Sachalin, Japan. Plants grow as small mats, flower stems to 10cm high. Basal leaves petioled, spatulate, to 5cm long, 1cm wide, middle stem leaves sessile, ovate-lanceolate, upper stem leaves small, acute, pubescent. Stems 1-flowered, flowers white, in May. z4

S. saxifraga L. S. Europe, north to Sweden and the S. Carpathian Mts. A dense, hemispherical, cushion. Stems 15–20cm high, slender, sparsely leafy. Leaves linear-spatulate, sessile. Flowers on slender pedicels, white, sometimes greenish, sometimes reddish beneath; June to August. An attractive, lime-loving rock plant for sun and semi-shade. A nocturnal bloomer; the twice cleft petals roll inward in the morning hours, showing the reddish undersides. Spreads by self-seeding. z6

S. schafta S.G. Gmel. ex Hohen. Caucasus Mts. Flower stems to 10cm high, loose carpet habit. Stem tips ascending. Leaves ovate to rarely lanceolate, basal, rosette leaves 12mm long, 5–6mm wide, acuminate, sessile, green. Flowers with twice-cleft petals, pink to purplish, bright, deep pink on the cultivar 'Splendens'; August to September. One of the most valuable and undemanding rock garden plants for its late flowers. Quite susceptible to the rust fungi. z5

S. schmuckeri Wettst. Found in the mountains of Macedonia. Develops compact mats, flower stems 10–15cm high. Leaves 1cm long, linear-lanceolate. Inflorescence with 1–6 (occasionally to 8) flowers, pinkish-white, occasionally also pale purple-red; June. z7

S. spathulata see **S. pygmaea**

S. vallesia L. W. Alps, Apennine Mts., Balkan Region Mts. Forms a low cushion. Leaves lanceolate to linear, pubescent. Flower stems to 15cm high, with 1–3 flowers. Petals pale pink above, reddish beneath. Blooms from July to August. A night bloomer. Charming in a rock crevice. z6

S. virginica L. Fire Pink. E. USA: New Jersey to Minnesota, south to Georgia and Oklahoma; usually at the forest edge on gravelly or stony, acid soil. Stems several, outward growing from a central crown, glandular-puberulent, rarely nearly glabrous below, 30 to very rarely 90cm long. Leaves oblanceolate, 5–10cm long, 1–2cm wide, pubescent to rarely almost glabrous; stem leaves subsessile, smaller. Inflorescence a loose terminal panicle; flowers to 3cm across, very showy, intense red, petals 2-lobed. Late spring to early summer. See also *S. baldwynii* entry. Choice rock garden plant. z5(4)

S. vulgaris (Moench) Bladder Campion, Maiden's Tears. (*S. cucubalis* Wibel; *S. glauca* Sm. ex Steud., not Salisb.; *S. inflata* (Salisb.)) Sm. Europe, temperate Asia, NW. Africa. Clump with several stems, erect or spreading-ascending, 30–40cm high, glabrous to pubescent, rarely glaucous. Leaves strap-like to ovate, 4–8cm long, mostly glabrous to pubescent. Flowers solitary or in a few-flowered cyme; calyx large, inflated; petals large, 2-lobed, white, rarely rose or red. Subspecies **maritima** (With.) A. et D. Löve (*S. maritima* With.). Coasts of W. Europe. Stems 10–20cm, diffuse, nearly caespitose. Leaves linear-lanceolate to spatulate to broadly spatulate at the base, glaucous. Flowers white. Cultivar 'Weisskehlchen', calyx light green rather than brownish as in the subspecies; 'Plena', double-flowered, resembling a small carnation; 'Rosea', about 10cm high, flowers bright pink. Ssp. *maritima* and its cultivars are somewhat less hardy than the species. Rock garden and edging plants. z6

S. zawadzkii Herbich (*Melandrium zawadzkii* (Herbich) A. Br.). E. Carpathian Mts. Stems 20cm high, in a tuft. Basal leaves rosetted, lanceolate; stem leaves sessile, smaller. Flowers white, in paniculate racemes, calyx pale green, inflated; July to August. Requires a semi-shaded, not too dry site; quite vigorous. z5 (Sch. & Kö.)

Siler

S. montanum see **Laserpitium siler**

Silphium L.
Compositae
Rosinweed, Compass Plant

Twenty species of tall, perennial herbs in the E. and Central USA, with sparsely branched stems and glabrous to usually stiff-haired leaves. Many species have opposite leaves toward the base of the stem and alternate leaves toward the top of the stem. Flower heads starry, sunflower-like, in corymbs or umbellate panicles; involucre broad, almost flat, several rows of coarse, awned scales.

Rarely found outside of botanic gardens. Mostly tall perennials which thrive in any well-drained, deep, fertile soil; easily propagated by seed and division. All grow best in full sun and (except *S. perfoliatum*) normal soil moisture. *S. laciniatum* and (less so) *S. terebinthinaceum* are botanically interesting, since their leaves, especially on young plants, are erect and oriented so that the edges point north/south and the flat surfaces face east/west (hence, Compass Plant). The midday sun therefore strikes the narrow edge of the leaves. *S. perfoliatum* collects water in the cuplike, perfoliate leaves. The sap of many species contains resin.

S. integrifolium Michx. USA: Ohio, Minnesota and Nebraska, south to Mississippi and Oklahoma; in fields and roadsides. To 1.5m high, with a woody rootstock, occasionally creeping. Stems rough-haired, roundish-4-angled to round, umbellate-branched near the top. Leaves all opposite, rarely sub-opposite below the inflorescence, simple, sessile to sub-perfoliate, ovate-acute, more or less scabrous, to 15cm long. Flower heads yellow, in broad corymbs. Blooms from August to September. z5

S. laciniatum L., Compass Plant. USA: Ohio to Minnesota and South Dakota, south to Alabama and Texas. Stems to 2m high, stiff-haired. Leaves alternate, deep pinnate-cleft to 2-pinnate-cleft, lobes more or less rounded, rough-haired, basal leaves to 50cm long; stem leaves becoming smaller toward the inflorescence. Flower heads to 12cm wide. Ray flowers butter yellow, disc flowers darker yellow to orange. Blooms from July to September. z4

S. perfoliatum L., Cupplant. N. America:

Ontario to South Dakota, south to Georgia, Mississippi and Oklahoma; in moist to damp soil in open woodlands or prairies. Stems several, erect, in a massive clump from a woody rootstock, to 2.5m high, glabrous, sharply 4-angled, branched only toward the top. Leaves opposite, simple, connate-perfoliate, triangular to ovate-acute, to 35cm long, rough on both sides, irregularly scabrous-toothed. Inflorescence dichotomous, long-petioled, with many yellow, to 8cm-wide, flower heads. Blooms from July to September. z3

S. terebinthinaceum Jacq., Prairie Dock, Rosinweed. N. America: S. Ontario and Ohio to Minnesota, south to Georgia and Oklahoma; on the prairies and very open woodlands. To 3m high, with a woody taproot. Stems slender, round, mostly leafless, bright green, glabrous or mostly so. Leaves nearly all basal, long-petioled, simple, stiff leathery, rough, ovate to oblong or elliptic, cordate, scabrous-toothed, to 60cm long. Flower heads in loose-branched, corymbose panicles, to 8cm wide, yellow. Blooms from July to September. z3 (E.)

Sinarundinaria nitida

Sinarundinaria Nakai
Gramineae
Umbrella Bamboo

A genus of much debated validity; this treatment follows recent, keyed nomenclature; species previously included in *Arundinaria*. Both of the following species thrive in mild, cool climates. Few other species are so versatile. These are more or less clump habit with many short stolons making the clumps very dense. The foliage is very decorative and usually winter hardy. Shoot elongation

of variants is to be expected from which better garden selections may be made. The plants develop dense clumps. The young canes are strictly erect at first, typically nodding over the years with the increasing foliage weight. The canes reach to 3m high or more under favorable conditions and are very leafy. The leaves are abruptly acuminate past the midpoint and pea green, to 10cm long and 15mm wide. Descriptions of heretofore vegetatively grown material must be updated with the increasing occurence of seedling-grown plants. z5

leaves are usually somewhat smaller and narrower than those of *S. murielae*. They are short acuminate and have parallel leaf margins. The strictly upright selections normally found in culture are good screening plants and windbreaks as are all the hardy bamboo. The flexible stems and leaves help calm the wind, actually providing a better windbreak than a solid obstacle. The refined, uniformly leafy clump habit plants make a suitable specimen in the middle of, or as background for perennial beds. The leaf color and shape makes an especially nice contrast with dark evergreens. Unlike many

Sisyrinchium angustifolium

Smilacina racemosa

and stem branching do not take place in the same year, thereby providing well-developed, stately plants even in climates with cool, short summers. Future selections should be made to further enhance the garden merit of this genus.

Propagation is by division in early spring; grow young plants in containers for at least the first year. Division is most successful from small, many-stemmed plants. Avoid planting Umbrella Bamboo in sites with standing moisture or in excessively hot, dry sites. Both species listed here are found naturally on north-facing mountain slopes. Both are suitable for specimen use, screen planting or for the woodland margin.

S. murielae (Gamble) Nakai, Pale Green Umbrella Bamboo. West Hupeh. Plants of this species were once vegetatively propagated and became known as *Thamnocalamus spathaceus* (Franch.) Soderstrom. With the introduction of seed-grown plants, a larger assortment

S. nitida (Mitf.) Nakai, Dark Green Umbrella Bamboo. S. Kansu. Plants in western cultivation are from collected seed. It is regrettable that only a few, not exceptionally attractive, clones are grown in the trade, while many cultivars, sizes and colors which would be quite suitable for many garden uses may be found in older collections. Examples of choice cultivars are: 'Eisenach', with dense foliage and over-arching canes, and 'Nymphenburg' with narrow, lacy leaves and nodding, less crowded canes. These thrive best in cool semi-shade.

The normally purple-tinged stems have 2 leaves at the tip during the first winter. In the following year plants will develop up to 5 branches per node, or even more in the third year. Canes ultimately reach to more than 4m high. The

bamboos, sinarundinarias may be maintained by thinning out the old shoots or sheared back to any size. z5 (S.)

Sisyrinchium L.
Iridaceae
Blue-eyed Grass

About 75 species. Mostly low, tufted, evergreen to herbaceous perennials with fibrous roots, and basal, iris-like leaves. Flowers regular, several, from terminal or axillary sheaths. A Western Hemisphere genus; only a few species are winter hardy. These plants are mostly recommended for collectors and may be found in flat rock garden sites, some in prairie or steppe gardens. Propagation is by division and seed. Often self-seeding.

S. albidum Raf. Eastern Blue-eyed Grass. E. North America; S. Ontario to the Gulf of Mexico, excluding the North Atlantic States, west to Wisconsin and Missouri; on prairies, swales, meadows and railroad right-of-ways. Tufted clump with several to many unbranched stems, pale green or glaucous, 1–3mm wide. Leaves narrow-linear, to 25cm high, rarely higher. Flowers white to pale violet in mid-spring. z4

S. anceps see **S. angustifolium**

S. angustifolium Mill (*S. gramineum* Lam., *S. anceps* Cav.). N. America: Newfoundland, British Columbia, south to Virginia, Michigan, Rocky Mts. Erroneously distributed as *S. bermudianum*. *S. bermudiana* is, however, a somewhat taller, much more tender species. *S. angustifolium* grows to 15–20cm high, and is densely tufted. Leaves are narrow, dark green. Stems are compressed, broadly winged, branched. Flowers are in small clusters, bright violet-blue, yellow at the throat; May to June. The hardiest species; persists by self-seeding. z3

S. brachypus see **S. californicum**

S. californicum (Ker-Gawl.) Dryand. (*S. brachypus* hort.). Golden-eyed Grass. USA: Oregon to California. A low clump, leaves swordlike; flowering stems unbranched, broad-winged, with golden yellow flowers, about 10cm high. Blooms from May to July. Requires a somewhat moist site in full sun. Relatively persistent plants, also suitable for trough gardens. Often self-seeding, but non-invasive. z8

S. campestre Bickn. Praire Blue-eyed Grass. Central North America: Wisconsin and Manitoba south to Illinois, Louisiana and Texas; in prairies, rocky open woods, rocky glades, drier sites than *S. albidum*. Tufted glaucous-bluish clump with several to very many stems; an established plant many show 100 or more flowers at one time. Stems unbranched, lateral wings much reduced. Flowers emerge from a single papery spathe at the base of the terminal bract. Botanists define several forms: forma *flaviforum*, flowers yellow; forma *kansanum*, flowers white; and *S. campestre* forma *campestre*, flowers powder-blue. This is the earliest to bloom North American species. z4

S. douglasii A. Dietr. (*S. grandiflorum* Dougl. non Cav.). Grass Widow, Purple-eyed Grass. N. America: British Columbia to N. California. A variable plant. Produces tufts of narrow leaves and 15–25cm high flower stems, covered in spring with reddish-purple, nodding, campanulate flowers; May to June. An attractive white variety is reminiscent of *Paradisea*. Plants die back quickly after flowering. Makes a better plant for the temperate greenhouse. z7

S. gramineum see **S. angustifolium**

S. graminifolium Lindl. (*S. majale* Link et Klotzsch). Chile. 20–25cm high. Leaves linear to swordlike, narrow and erect. Flower stems erect, 18–22cm high, branched. Flowers yellow; May to June. Better as a cool greenhouse plant. z8

S. grandiflorum see **S. douglasii**

S. macrocarpon E.P. Bickn. N. America. Stems 25cm, leaves bluish green, to 5mm wide. Flowers ocher-yellow, 25mm wide. Fruits 10mm, triangular. Very attractive species, worthy of further trial use. z6

S. majale see **S. graminifolium**

S. montanum Greene (*S. angustifolium* auct.p.p. non Mill.). N. America: Quebec, Michigan, Minnesota, Rocky Mts. Stems unbranched, conspicuously tall, 12–50cm high, depending upon location. Nodding leaves yellowish-green. Flowers violet-blue from June to July. Winter protection is advised. z7

S. striatum Sm. Argentina, Chile. Stiff, Large, iris-like, glaucous basal leaves 20–35cm long, to 2cm wide. Erect, 60–80cm high flower stems with 1–2 much smaller leaves; inflorescence spicate, flowers along most of the length of the stem, cream yellow or pale yellow. June to July. A cultivar is listed with variegated leaves. A large rock garden or wild garden plant for full sun in well-drained soil. z8

'Mrs. Spinvey' is a hybrid, 20cm high, flowers white, yellow at the base; from June to August. (Sch. & Kö.)

Smilacina Desf.
Liliaceae
False Soloman's Seal

Woodland plant developing dense colonies; rhizomatous, closely related to the true Soloman's Seal. Stems erect to nodding, unbranched, leaves alternate, sessile. Flowers in white or pink to purple, in terminal racemes; decorative red berries. About 25 species in N. America and Asia. *S. racemosa* is a particularly choice shade plant for loamy, high humus-rich, not too dry soil. Easily grown and effective with ferns. Propagate by division and seed.

S. racemosa Desf. False Spikenard. N. America. Stems 80–90cm high, arching to ascending, green, turning brownish, slightly nodding in fruit. Leaves short-petioled to 15cm long, 7cm wide, broadly lanceolate, acuminate, light green above, dull, underside glossy-pubescent with distinctly raised venation. Terminal panicles to 15cm long, many-flowered; white to creamy-white; May. Berries cream-colored at first, eventually bright red, sometimes purple spotted; plants sometimes lack fruit, self-sterile. z4

S. stellata Desf. Starflower. NW. North America. Stems erect, 80cm high, green, usually somewhat flexuose. Leaves lanceolate to oblanceolate, usually folded lengthwise, light green above, dull-glaucous, undersides finely gray-pubescent. Inflorescence erect, short, to 20-flowered racemes; flowers small, short-pediceled, creamy-white. Berries dark red. (Sch. & M.)

Soldanella L.
Primulaceae
Blue Moonwort

Ten species in Europe. Small alpine perennials or woodland plants with leathery, evergreen, rounded, entire or crenate leaves and fimbriate flower "bells" in early spring. Two Sections are distinguished by the flower development: either tubular, short-fimbriate and solitary or funnelform, long-fimbriate, borne in few flowered umbels. The Sections are the Tubiflores (**T**) and Soldanella (Crateriflores, **S**).

The species from Section Tubiflores are seldom easy to grow, especially in lowland gardens, often not very floriferous. Plants do best in full sun, but require moist and cool sites. Flowers are less abundant in shade. The species of Section Soldanella are nearly all woodland plants, easily cultivated in a semi-shaded peaty substrate, except for *S. alpina* and *S. hungarica* ssp. *hungarica*. Useful as charming collectors' plants for the rock, bog or shade garden. The soldanellas are susceptible to several leaf-blighting fungi which may be controlled with a timely preventive spray. Slugs may also be a problem since they will eat the flower buds in the fall. All species are susceptible to later frost damage to the flowers and flower buds. Propagation is by division after flowering, or seed, the latter especially for species of the Section Soldanella.

S. alpina L. **(S)**. Europe, from the Central Pyrenees Mts. to Montenegro, north to the Black Forest, south to Calabria (Italy); on moist slopes and cliffs, 450–3000m. Leaves all basal, to 4cm wide, 15cm high, rounded to reniform with a wide basal sinus. Scape to 15cm, 1–3, rarely to 4-flowered. Petals deeply

Leaves orbicular-reniform, cordate, entire. Similar to *S. hungarica*, but leaves bluish-pruinose beneath. Scape 2–3 flowered, flowers violet. April to May. z6

S. hungarica Simonkai **(S)**. Mts. of E. Central Europe, the Balkan Peninsula, 2 sites in Calabria (Italy). Leaves 4–6cm high; petioles densely covered with short, persistent glands; blades rounded reniform, to 2.5cm across. Scape to 10cm high, 1–3 flowered. Includes 2 subspecies: ssp. **hungarica**. E. and S. Carpathian Mts., Balkan Peninsula, mountain meadows. Scape to 10cm high,

wide. Scape to 15cm high at flowering time, 3–10 flowered. Flowers violet, to 18-lobed. Very undemanding and ideal for the bog garden. May to June. z6

S. pindicola Hausskn. **(S)**. NW. Greece, near Metsovon. Similar to *S. carpatica*, but leaves ashy, azure blue below, petioles pruinose without glands. Flowers with broadly funnel-shaped corolla, deeply lobed, rose-lilac. z6

S. pusilla Baumg. **(T)**. Central and E. Alps, S. Carpathian Mts.; occurs locally in the N. Apennine Mts. and SW.

Soldanella alpina

Soldanella alpina f. *alba*

lobed, with more than 30 segments. Flowers usually lilac blue, occasionally light blue or white. April to May. For a sunny, moist site. z5

S. austriaca Vierh. **(T)** Austria: especially the N. Dolomites. Leaves orbicular, subcordate, .5–1cm across. Scape 1-flowered, 4–9cm high. Corolla tubular-campanulate, cut to about ¼ of the depth, bluish-violet, lined inside, rarely pink or white. Similar to *S. minima*, but hairs short-glandular. April to May. z5

S. carpatica Vierh. **(S)**. W. Carpathians. Leaves usually violet beneath, hairs short-glandular. Scape to 20cm long, to -flowered. Flowers violet, occasionally white, with about 15 lobes. April to May. Attractive and easily cultivated. z5

S. cyanaster see **S. montana**

S. dimoniei Vierh. **(S)**. Mountains of Macedonia, E. Albania and Bulgaria.

1–3, rarely to 4 flowers, leaves to 2cm wide; and ssp. **major** (Neilr.) S. Pawl, throughout the range of the species, except Macedonia, in woodlands. Scape to 25cm, to 10-flowered. Leaves to 6cm wide. Blooms in May. The latter is easy to grow and suitable for the bog garden. z6

S. minima Hoppe **(T)**. E. Alps, Central Apennine Mts.; always on limestone. Leaves to 5cm high or shorter; petioles densely covered with long glands; blade to 1cm wide, rounded to oblong, not cordate, thick, fleshy. Scape 2.5–7cm high, 1-flowered. Flowers pale violet, pink-violet or white. April to May. Very attractive, but not always easy to grow. For a sunny, but cool, moist site. z6

S. montana Willd. **(S)**. (*S. cyanaster* Schwarz). Central Europe, Italian Alps, Mts. of Bulgaria; in forests and meadows, between 700 and 1600m elevation. Leaf petioles densely covered with persistent, 1mm-long glands; blades to 7cm

Bulgaria; on moist, alpine sites, from 1800–3100m, lime-intolerant. Characteristic are the leathery-rugose, cordate to suborbicular, entire leaves and the single-flowered scape, 5–10cm high. Corolla narrowly campanulate, to 12mm long, dissected to about ¼ the petal depth, blue to pale violet. April. The species most difficult to grow, recommended only for the most dedicated collector. z5

S. villosa Darracq **(SW)**. W. Pyrenees Mts.; on moist, shaded sites. Similar to *S. montana*, but sometimes stoloniferous, villous and smaller in stature. Leaves more or less orbicular, petioles persistently villous. Scapes with 1–4 blue flowers. Blooms in May. Frequently cited as the easiest *Soldanella* for lowland gardens. z6

Natural hybrids occur frequently, some of these should be tested for their ornamental value. (K).

Soleirolia Gaudich.
Urticaceae
Baby's Tears

One species in Italy and the W. Mediterranean islands. Low, monoecious, herbaceous perennial, with slender, creeping stems capable of quickly covering large areas. Suitable for a dense carpet between stepping stones, among boulders or as a substitute for turf. Grows best in semi-shaded to shady sites in any moderately moist garden soil. Unfortunately, plants are not reliably winter hardy, but some stems usually resprout in spring, particularly those protected between rocks, or, where summers are long and hot, seedlings appear. Propagation is easy by division, stem cuttings bedded in the soil will quickly take root.

S. soleirolii (Req.) Dandy (*Helxine soleirolii* Req.). Italy, Corsica, Sardinia, Elba and other islands in the W. Mediterranean Sea, naturalized in W. and SW. Europe and easily becomes weedy. Small plants with thread-like stems closely covered with glossy green, nearly orbicular leaves, 2–6mm wide; plants cover the ground densely. The inconspicuous flowers are monoecious, the lower ones pistillate, the upper ones staminate. Blooms in summer. z9(8–7) (E.)

Solenanthus Ledeb.
Boraginaceae

About 12 species of biennial and short-lived perennial herbs from south and W. Europe, and W. Asia. Closely related to *Cynoglossum* in which it is often included, but differs in the calyx which is 5-lobed to the base, the prominent style, exerted stamens and occasionally, winged nutlets. *S. apenninus* sometimes is found in botanic gardens. Plants are effective (used like *Anchusa*) as a background for larger perennials. Requires well-drained soil and protection from winter wetness. Plants are biennial, with seeds sown in spring or summer. Grow seedlings in deep pots the first season, overwinter in a frost-free cold frame, and set into the display bed the following spring. Propagate by seed.

S. apenninus (L.) Fisch. et Mey. Central and S. Italy, Sicily; in mountain forests and on meadows. Biennial, 0.6–1.2m high, pubescent plant. Stem thick, hollow, hairy. Basal leaves 30–50cm long and 5–10cm wide, elliptic to broadly lanceolate with 3–6 lateral veins, petioled. Stem leaves smaller, sessile. Flowers in axillary, paniculate cymes. Corolla 7–9mm wide, with obovate, obtuse lobes, blue to purplish. Blooms from May to July. z7 (E.)

Other species sometimes appear in Botanic Gardens, especially *S. circinatus*, with the habit of the above species but flowers ashy-blue, racemose in a terminal thyrse.

Solidago L.
Compositae
Goldenrod

About 130 species, most medium-height to tall, bushy perennials with thick rootstocks, erect, alternate-leaved stems and small yellow flowers in floriferous, racemose panicles in summer and fall. Nearly all are indigenous to North America where most are pernicious weeds. Some, especially *S. canadensis* and *S. gigantea*, are naturalized in Europe. Commonly found on prairies, roadsides, and riverbanks where they dominate the neighboring herbaceous vegetation and are very conspicuous with a yellow, late summer floral display. The true species are seldom found in cultivation, having been replaced by the many superior cultivars. The following species, however, may be considered for bed plantings, particularly in rock and natural gardens. All species are easily propagated by division and cuttings. Plants sometimes are damaged by powdery mildew during dry periods.

S. bicolor L. Silver Rod, White Golden Rod. North America: Nova Scotia to Wisconsin, south to North Carolina and Arkansas. Fibrous-rooted. Stems 60–120cm high, gray-green, soft-hairy. Leaves oblanceolate to elliptic, 5–15cm long, serrate to crenate, decreasing in size up the stem. Heads in a spike-like panicle; ray flowers white, rarely creamy, disc flowers pale yellow. Included for its atypical color.

S. brachystachys see **S. cutleri**

S. caesia L. Wreath Goldenrod, Bluestem Goldenrod. E. North America: Nova Scotia to Wisconsin, south to Florida and Texas. Stems slender, 30–90cm high, wiry, glabrous and glaucous, usually sparsely branched at the inflorescence, slightly nodding, leafy to the tips. Leaves sessile, lanceolate, willow-leaf-like, toothed, light green. Flower heads in decorative, sessile clusters in the leaf axils; late September. Very attractive in a loose planting of *Ceanothus* and *Caryopteris* as well as *Liatris* and *Echinacea purpurea*. Besides the attractive, loose and outspread-branched type, a dense, bushy, sparsely branched form with nonglaucous stems is occasionally found. This is often erroneously listed in Europe as *S. graminifolia*, and is of little garden worth. z4

S. canadensis L. North America: Newfoundland to Manitoba, south to Virginia, Missouri and Colorado. Rhizomatous; running in warm climates. Stems to 1.5m high, often shorter, hairy above the middle. Basal and lowest stem leaves narrow-elliptic, falling early; upper stem leaves many, linear-lanceolate or wider, to 15cm long, long-alternate with 3 prominent veins, glabrous to scarious above, pubescent below, sharply serrate, uppermost leaves only slightly reduced. Flower heads in large to very large panicles with 1-sided, recurving branches, bright golden-yellow. This species and *S. virgaurea* are parents of the tall-growing cultivars. Several subspecies and varieties are listed. z4(3)

S. cutleri Fern. (*S. brachystachys* hort., *S. virgaurea* L. var. *alpina* Bigel.). E. North America, high mountain regions from Maine to New York. A dense tuft of leafy, glabrous stems 10– to rarely 35cm high. Basal leaves spatulate-ovate, to 15cm long, glabrous, serrate to crenate; stem leaves few, smaller. Inflorescence very short, floriferous, with golden-yellow corymbs or racemes, in September. The cultivar 'Robusta' is 30cm high, 'Pyramidalis', 50cm. All are valuable late bloomers for the rock garden. This is one parent of the dwarf cultivars. z4

S. lateriflora see **Aster lateriflorus**

S. missouriensis ssp. **shortii** see **S. shortii**

S. odora Ait. Sweet Goldenrod. E. North America. Rootstock a woody crown. Stems unbranched to the inflorescence, 50–60cm high. Leaves linear-lanceolate, pinnately veined, anise-scented, the basal and lower stem leaves often falling early; upper stem leaves sessile, linear-lanceolate to lanceolate. Flower heads in large, one-sided pyramidal panicles; July. Notable for its long-persisting flowers and tolerance of dryish, sandy soil. z4

S. riddellii Frank. Central North America: S. Ontario to Ohio, west to

Minnesota, Missouri; on wet meadows. Stems 0.6–1m high. Leaves glabrous, stem-clasping, linear, entire, 20cm-long, light green. Inflorescences terminal, erect, panicled-corymbose, flower heads large, golden yellow, very showy; August to September. A rare, almost aquatic species now nearly eradicated. z4

S. rigida L. N. America: Massachussetts to Saskatchewan, southward to Georgia, Lousiana and Texas; on dry, sandy or stony soils. Rhizomatous. Stems coarse, to 1.6m high. Basal leaves to 30cm long,

Solidago caesia

lanceolate to ovate, early-deciduous; stem leaves oval, sessile, serrate, gray-tomentose on both sides. Flowers in umbrellalike corymb; flower heads large, golden-yellow. August to September. z3–8

S. shortii Torr. et A. Gray. N. America: near Blue Licksand and Rock Island, Kentucky. Rootstock stoloniferous. Stems to more than 1.6m high, stiffly erect, pubescent-hairy. Leaves oblong-lanceolate, serrate. Inflorescence an attractive, broadly pyramidal, umbellate panicle with recurved branches; September to October. Some late-flowering cultivars have come from this species. Certainly a valid species, this is listed as *S. missouriensis* ssp. *shortii* in some older literature. z5

S. virgaurea L. Europe, N. and W. Asia, N. Africa. Stems 60–90cm high, glabrous beneath, sparsely pubescent toward the apex. Leaves broadly lanceolate with winged petioles, coarsely serrate; becoming progressively smaller, sub-sessile and finally sessile up the stem. Flowers in terminal, globose or cylin-

drical thyrse, yellow; July to September. The form 'Nana' is only 40–50cm high; 'Praecox' flowers in July. z5

S. virgaurea ssp. **alpestris** see **S. virgaurea** ssp. **minuta**

S. virgaurea ssp. **minuta** (L.) Arcang. (ssp. *alpestris* (Waldst. et Kit. ex Willd.) Hayek). Stems very short, to 20–30cm; in the high mountains and subalpine regions. Interesting only for collectors of rock garden plants, except for the cultivar 'Goldzwerg' (Golden Dwarf). The 5cm-high form 'Minutissima' (often

Solidago hybrid 'Strahlenkrone'

erroneously listed as *S. minutissima*), also belongs here if not to *S. cutleri*. z4

S. virgaurea var. **alpina** see **S. cutleri**

The garden hybrids are more important in gardens than the species. The taller cultivars of stiff habit may be traced back to *S. canadensis, S. vigaurea*, and rarely to *S. shortii*. Despite a robust habit, the cultivars are not quite as invasive as some of the seedling-grown species. Plants are undemanding, effective bedding perennials for late summer color and excellent cut flowers. Some especially good, time-tested forms include:

'Ballardii', 1.5–1.8m high; branching sprays of bright, golden yellow. August to September.
'Cloth of Gold', 45cm high; dwarf, strong-growing, heads deep yellow. August to September.
'Crown of Rays' (= 'Strahlenkrone', 'Radiant Crown'), 60cm high; stiff, columnar clump with large, flat golden-yellow inflorescences. July to August.
'Golden Falls', 60–75cm high; upright, compact habit, strong buttercup yellow heads. August to September.
'Golden Gates' (?= 'Goldwedel'), 45–60cm high; bushy, compact habit, heads loose, spreading, bright lemon-yellow. Blooms early, sometimes in June, reblooms later if cut back.
'Goldenmosa', 75cm high; bushy,

compact habit; heads very large, mimosa-yellow. Mid- to late summer.
'Golden Plume', 75–90cm high; fairly columnar, compact habit; heads spreading horizontally, lemon-yellow tinged buttercup-yellow. Mid- to late summer.
'Golden Shower', 80cm high; stems erect, with nodding, horizontal heads, bright, clear yellow. August to September.
'Golden Thumb', 30cm high; dwarf, bushy plant with yellow-green to gold-colored foliage; heads fluffy, clear yellow. August to September.
'Goldwedel' see 'Golden Gates'

Sparaxis hybrid 'Fire King'

'Golden Wings', 1.5–1.8m high; inflorescences much branched, golden-yellow. August to September.
'Goldstrahl' (= 'Peter Pan'), 75–90cm high; erect habit, sprays dense, symmetrical, bright canary-yellow. September.
'Laurin', 30cm high; upward-slanting, triangular heads, deep yellow. August to September.
'Lemore', 75cm high; dense, erect habit, heads wide-branching, soft primrose-yellow to lemon-yellow. September.
'Lena', 75cm high; bushy, spreading habit, heads pale golden-yellow. August to September.
'Leraft', 75cm high; close, columnar habit, heads arching, bright golden-yellow. August to September.
'Mimosa', 1.5m high; stems erect, inflorescences much branched, golden-yellow. August to September.
'Peter Pan' see 'Goldstrahl'
'Radiant Crown' see 'Crown of Rays'
'Strahlenkrone' see 'Crown of Rays'

× **Solidaster** Wehrh.
Compositae

A bigeneric hybrid (sometimes listed as × *Astarago* T.H. Everett) between *Aster ptarmicoides* and an unidentified *Solidago*, found as a natural hybrid in the Leonard Lille Nurseries, near Lyon, France about 1910.

× **S. luteus** M.L. Green ex Dress. Stems scabrous, to 75cm high. Leaves to 15cm long, narrowly lanceolate to almost linear up the stem, remotely serrate. Ray flowers pale yellow, disc flowers golden-yellow, in much-branched corymbose panicle; July to September. Lacks vigor, not suitable for bed planting, valued rather as a cut flower. Propagation is by division and cuttings. z6 (Sch. & M.)

Sonchus L.
Compositae

About 60 species of latex-producing herbs (many invasive weeds), sub-shrubs or shrubs with basal rosettes or sessile stem leaves; resembling dandelion leaves. Flower heads solitary, in racemes or panicles, yellow. Distributed throughout Europe, Asia and Africa, 10 species also on the Canary Islands. The Canary species are especially interesting for pot culture. Only one species is suitable for the temperate landscape.

S. palustris L. Europe, S. Russia; along river banks and in moist meadows. Rootstock cylindrical, tuberous, not stoloniferous, with a 4-angled central cavity. Stems erect, 2–3m high, 4-angled, hollow. Leaves lanceolate in outline, deeply pinnate-cleft, the upper leaves sagittate at the base with acute, outspread auricles, bluish green. Flowers in open, many-headed panicles, yellow, July to September. Especially conspicuous in spring with its erect shoots and pointed, decorative leaves. For pond banks in large gardens. Care should be taken to prevent established plants from becoming invasive weeds. Propagate by division and seed. z6 (D.)

Sorghastrum Nash
Gramineae

About 15 species of perennial grasses, most tufted, large, in the Americas and Africa. Culms erect; leaf sheaf with auricled ligules; blades narrow to 1cm wide, flat. Panicles terminal, more or less cylindrical but loose and lax prior to

pollination. Spikelet with one perfect, terminal floret above a sterile floret.

Combines well with other heat-loving perennials such as *Kniphofia*, *Salvia azurea*, *Galtonia* and *Aster amellus*. Avoid overwatering or fertilizing this grass as the culms will become brittle, breaking over in the wind or weight of rain water. When seeds are available, sow under glass, or outside in warm climates. Pot up divisions in a well-aerated medium and set in full sun. The flower panicles are attractive for cutting, used fresh or dried. z6 (S.)

Sorghastrum nutans

S. nutans (L.) Nash. (*Chrysopogon nutans* (L.) Benth.), Indian Grass. E. and Central North America. Rhizomes short, branched and scaly. Leaves mostly basal, bright green, flat, elongate, high arching or ascending, to 50cm long, 1cm wide, becoming bright rust in late fall, fading to beige. Flower stems (culms) to 1.5m high, sparsely leafy (leaves smaller) terminating in a narrow panicle to 22cm long in August to September. The panicle is lax, graceful, brilliant pale rust-colored with conspicuous yellow anthers; following pollination the panicle contracts, becoming narrower, darker. As the flowers ripen, the entire plant turns reddish. A showy grass for naturalized prairie gardens; full sun and heavy, calcareous loam give best results. z5(4)

Sorghum Moench
Gramineae

S. halepense (L.) Pers. Johnson Grass. E. Mediterranean region. A pioneer grass species, found especially in warm climates on cropped fields as an indicator of moist sites. z5(4) (S.)

Listed here only to note its vigorous rhizomatous spreading habit which has led to its being declared a noxious weed in most southern states in the USA.

Other sorghums, largely annual, are important grain crops, world-wide, in temperate regions.

Sparaxis Ker-Gawl.
Iridaceae
Wandflower, Harlequin Flower

A genus of 6 species from S. Africa forming small clusters. The flowers are usually variable in color. Closely related to the genera *Ixia* and *Freesia*. Rootstock a tunicate corm (as crocus). Leaves mostly basal, 2-ranked, strap-shaped, linear or sword-shaped. Spathe valves membranous. Flowers more or less trumpet-shaped, perianth segments 6, stamens 3, style branched. Cannot be considered a landscape plant in north temperate gardens as plants will overwinter only in the most protected sites. Often used as a cool greenhouse plant. Where winters are sufficiently mild so soil does not freeze, *Sparaxis* provides weeks of unbelievably brilliant colors.

S. grandiflora (F. Delar.) Ker-Gawl. (*Ixia grandiflora* F. Delar.). SW. Cape Province. Flowering scapes to about 45cm high, bearing several trumpet flowers, purple or yellow, with darker centers, 3–5cm wide. Flowers from August to October in its native habitat, from April to May in the Northern Hemisphere. Numerous varieties are listed. z6

Sparganium L.
Sparganiaceae
Bur-reed

Nineteen or twenty species are listed. Few have ornamental value. Rhizomatous perennial, grass-like bog and aquatic plants which develop dense colonies. Stems erect, leaves erect-arching, floating or emerging above the water, then substantially longer than the flower stems. Leaves clasping the base of the flower stems, narrow-linear, 3-

Europe, Mediterranean, W. and Central Asia. Vigorous species, leaves exceeding 1m high, flower stems lower, thick, usually with several side branches. Flowers in spikes 6–12cm across, densely globose, unisexual, greenish white, June to July. Quite vigorous, therefore only suited to large ponds, best naturalized in 0–30cm deep water. Excellent for tub planting in smaller gardens. z6

S. minimum Fr. Europe. Leaves floating, thread-like, 3mm wide, flat, thin, to

Sparganium erectum

Speirantha convallarioides

S. pillansii L. S. Africa. Scapes to 60cm high. Flowers rose-colored with deep yellow throat; stamen filaments white; anthers purple.

S. tricolor (Curt.) Ker-Gawl. (*Ixia tricolor* Curt.). SW. Cape Province. Scapes to 45cm high with several flowers opening at once. Flower colors pink, red, orange and purple with yellow throats, often with darker shades in the center. A white-flowering cultivar is also listed. Plants bloom in S. Africa from August to October, April to May in the Northern Hemisphere. Most plants in the trade are *Sparaxis tricolor* hybrids, which produce larger, more brightly colored flowers. Mixed colors are commonly offered. z6 (Kö.)

angled at the base.

   Flowers in axillary spikes, lower flowers pistillate, upper ones staminate, greenish white. Fruits clustered in a burr which breaks up into separate nutlets, bristly, green. Habitat primarily in the temperate and arctic Northern Hemisphere, but also in Australia and New Zealand. Suitable for pond banks and shallow streams with *Typha*, *Scirpus* and *Iris pseudacorus*, *Gunnera* and various *Lobelia* species. Not very conspicuous, but interesting, undemanding and vigorous. Propagate by division and seed.

S. emersum Rehm. (*S. simplex* auct. non Huds.). Europe, W. and Central Asia, N. America. Leafy stems to 60cm high. Flowers with short peduncles, apical ones sessile. For boggy sites in 0–20cm deep water. z5

S. erectum L. (*S. ramosum* Huds.).

60cm long. Stems mostly floating, flowering tips ascending. Inflorescence exserted above the foliage, 30–40cm high in shallow water; will grow on wet land but makes a poor specimen. z5 (D.)

S. ramosum see **S. erectum**

S. simplex see **S. emersum**

Spartina Schreb.
Gramineae

Sixteen species of mostly coastal grasses in North and South America, Europe and N. Africa. Herbaceous. Leaf blades long, tough. Culms with 2–many spikes, appressed racemose. Spikelets 1-flowered, laterally compressed, sessile, imbricate on one side of an elongated rachis. Most are weedy.

S. michauxiana see **S. pectinata**

S. pectinata Link (*S. michauxiana* Hitchc.), Prairie Cord Grass (so named for the coarse stems and leaves). North America, cool regions. A species found in the inland regions along riverbanks as opposed to the more maritime, brackish water habitat of the rest of the genus. The stout, well-branched rhizomes terminate in large tufts of arching, 1m-long, 1.5cm-wide leaves and an erect, leafy, stiff, 1.5m-high flowering culm. The inflorescence has several one sided spikes. The species is almost exclusively represented in horticulture by the cultivar 'Aureomarginata'. This Variegated Cord Grass features a broad yellow leaf margin. An important use for this grass is in cut-flower arranging. Propagate by division. z5 (S.)

Speirantha Bak.
Liliaceae

Monotypic Chinese genus. Rootstock a thick, oblique stoloniferous rhizome. Leaves basal, evergreen. Almost unknown in horticulture and barely frost hardy.

S. convallarioides Bak. (*S. gardenii*). China. Stoloniferous, clump-form, evergreen perennial. Leaves basal, oblanceolate to broadly lanceolate, sub-erect, 12–15cm high, dark green. Scape 20–30cm high. Flowers white, fragrant, starry, 20–30 in a loose raceme; May to June. Rare, but attractive, shade plant for moist, humus-rich soil; very useful for underplanting rhododendrons. Propagate by division in spring. z8(7)

S. gardenii see **S. convallaroides** (Sch.)

Spartina pectinata 'Aureomarginata'

Spenceria Trim.
Rosaceae

Two species of herbaceous perennials from W. China, related to *Agrimonia* but differing with 30–40 stamens, spineless but pilose calyx tube, an infundibular involucre of two connate bracts, and thread-like, not capitate, stigmas. Rare, low summer bloomer for collectors. Suitable for planting in rock garden crevices and troughs in full sun. Impartial to soil type, requires only good drainage. A light winter protection with

Spigelia marilandica

conifer branches is advisable. Other low, silver-haired alpine plants provide good companions. Propagate by seed and careful division in spring.

S. ramulana Trim. W. China, in dry mountain meadows between 3000 and 5000m. Rhizomes short-branched. Entire plant silver-white pubescent. Basal leaves pinnate, with leaflets in 6 pairs, leaflets broadly elliptic, 1.5cm long, with 2 large, lobe-like apical teeth. Stem leaves with 2–4 leaflets or simple. Stems many, upright, to 30cm high; inflorescence a stiff raceme. Flowers gold or brownish-yellow, about 2.5cm wide, on 3–4cm long pedicels. Flowers from June to July. z5 (E.)

Sphaeralcea St.-Hil.
Malvaceae

About 50 species in the warmer regions of North America, a few in South America. Perennial herbs, subshrubs or small shrubs, usually stellate-pubescent. Leaves rather thick, linear-lanceolate to orbicular, shallowly toothed or palmately divided or compound, the segments serrate. Inflorescences racemose, thyrsoid or paniculate. Involucral bracts 3 or rarely 0, falling early. Corolla cuplike, petals 5, some species pink or lavender, rarely white, yellow, orange or red. Stamens united into a hollow tubular column. Styles 10–20, branched, stigmas capitate to barely decurrent. Blooms from June to September. Grow in sunny, dryish beds in well-drained, gravelly soil. Very attractive with

Spodiopogon sibiricus

Opuntia, Yucca, Zauschneria, and other dry region ornamentals. A collector's plant. Propagate by seed.

S. angustifolia (Cav.) G. Don. S. North America: Texas and Mexico. Rootstock a woody crown. Stems solitary or few, to 1.8m high, gray-pubescent. Leaves lanceolate to oblanceolate, to 12cm long, unlobed or scarcely lobed, serrate. Inflorescence a narrow, interrupted thyrse, terminal. Flowers solitary or paired. Flowers 2.5cm across, mauve to lavender. z8(7)

    More important in gardens is var. **cuspidata** (Britt.) A. Gray. Kansas to Colorado south to Texas, California and Mexico. Leaves linear-lanceolate, flowers orange. z6(5)

S. coccinea (Nutt.) Rydb. (*Malvastrum coccineum* (Nutt.) Gray). Prairie Mallow. W. North America. Plants to 35cm high. Leaves 3–5 parted to the base, to 4cm long, the lobes further divided. Flowers in short racemes. Involucre absent.

Sepals 5–8mm long, petals 5, salmon orange to red, 1–2cm. z5(4)

S. munroana (Dougl. ex Lindl.) Spach ex Gray. W. North America. Plant several stemmed, to 80cm high; from a woody crown. Leaves mostly ovate to subrhombic, cuneate to cordate, to 4cm long, 3–5 shallow lobes or crenate, flowers 2.5cm across, close in terminal and axillary panicles. Calyx 3–8mm, petals salmon to reddish, 8–15mm long. z6(5) (K.)

Stachys lavandulifolia

Spigelia L.
Loganiaceae
Pinkroot

About 30 species of herbs to subshrubs from the SE. USA to tropical South America. Stems and leaves mostly glabrous, leaves opposite, entire. Cymes 1-sided. Flowers 5-merous, corolla tubular.

S. marilandica L., Pinkroot. SE. North America: Maryland, S. Ohio, S. Illinois, S. Missouri, to Florida and Oklahoma. Stems stiff, erect, slender, 30–60cm high. Leaves opposite, lanceolate, acute, sessile, thin. Cymes terminal, one-sided; flowers upright, corolla tubular, with 5 acute tips, exterior carmine red, interior yellow; July to September. Very charming, elegant, but poisonous plant, for specialty collectors; introduced into European gardens from N. America in 1754, but still rare in culture. Native to shaded woodland sites, but also thrives in full sun given sufficient moisture and a deep humus soil. Propagated by division and seed. z5 (Sch.)

Spiraea

S. aruncus see **Aruncus dioicus**

S. astilboides see **Astilbe astilboides**

S. caespitosa see **Petrophyton caespitosa**

S. filipendula see **Filipendula vulgaris**

S. hendersonii see **Petrophyton hendersonii**

S. kamtschatka see **Filipendula kamtschatka**

S. lobata see **Filipendula rubra**

S. palmata see **Filipendula palmata, F. purpurea**

S. ulmaria see **F. ulmaria**

Spodiopogon Trin.
Gramineae

S. sibiricus Trin. Frost Grass, Graybeard Grass. (*Andropogon sibiricus* Steud., erroneously listed also as *Muehlenbergia alpestris* and *Lasiagrostis splendens* in the trade). Siberia, to N. China and Japan. Sturdy, erect, clump grass; culms to 1.5m high, with 25mm-wide and 25cm-long leaves, which turn increasingly russet in the fall. Inflorescences an ovate panicle of glossy, purple-tinged spikelets; the panicles contract, becoming narrower, after flowering in July. Opening again when ripe. Habit and size make this reliable grass an ideal companion for daylilies. Also suitable for woodland margins. Tolerant of drought, but develops better with sufficient moisture. Propagated commonly by division; thrives in most garden soils. z3 (S.)

Stachys L.
Labiatae
Betony, Woundwort

A genus of 200–300 species depending on authority. Mostly bushy, erect, partly stoloniferous perennials and subshrubs with opposite leaves and flower whorls in erect, terminal spikes or subglobose heads. Flowers small; calyx tubular-campanulate, 5-lobed, corolla zygomorphic, the tube with a ring of leaves inside, often curved, upper lip erect or spreading, lower lip 3-lobed; stamens diadelphous, epipetalous; ovary matures into 4 close nutlets. Found in temperate and subtropical regions. Only a few are acceptably ornamental. The species described here are all easily cultivated and propagated by division. Some have yet to be introduced into North American gardens.

S. byzantina K. Koch (*S. lanata* Jacq. non Crantz, *S. olympica* auct. vix Poir.), Lamb's Ears. Crimea, Caucasus to N. Iran. An important foliage species for the temperate zone garden. Sometimes naturalizes from culture. Leaves thick, petioled, oblong-elliptic, densely white-tomentose, to 10cm long, lying flat in dense mats. Stems stout, white-woolly, 30–50cm high with few small leaves and whorled flowers. Flowers small, pink to purple, not very effective. A well-known, pleasing, creeping plant, suitable for edging or ground cover plantings in dry, sunny sites. 'Silver Carpet' is a scarcely blooming form, ideal for covering large areas with a silvery-white carpet in full sun. Also a good edging for a rose bed. July to September. z5

S. densiflora see **S. monnieri**

S. grandiflora (Stev. ex Willd.) Benth. (*Betonica grandiflora* Stev. ex Willd., *B. macrantha* K. Koch). Caucasus, Iran. Stems 30–50cm high, dense-bushy, above a basal rosette. Leaves to 7cm long, long-petioled, blades ovate to elongated, cordate, crenate-serrate, rugose; basal leaves much larger than stem leaves which decrease in size up the stem. Flowers in dense whorls (verticillasters), large, corolla to 4cm long, violet; July to August. The large-flowered selection 'Superba', with showy-purple-violet flowers, is an excellent garden perennial, thriving in sun and semi-shade, quickly forming a dense clump. Also suitable as cut flowers. Other cultivars include 'Alba', white-flowered; 'Robusta', sturdy, earlier-flowering, plant larger overall; and 'Violacea', flowers lilac-lavender. z6

S. lanata see **S. byzantina**

S. lavandulifolia Vahl. Asia Minor, Caucasus Mts., Iran. Stoloniferous shrub, stems 10–15cm high. Leaves narrowly elliptic-lanceolate, to 5cm long, entire, pale gray-green, silky-pubescent. Inflorescence cylindrical, whorled; flowers rose-purple, calyx long-lobed, glossy, silky-haired; June to July. Very attractive rock garden plant requiring ample space to spread in a dry, gravelly sunny site. z6

S. monnieri (Gouan) P.W. Ball (*S. densiflora* Benth.). S. Europe: Alps, Pyrenees Mts. Basal rosette leaves often overwinter; stems 45–50cm high, unbranched, with scattered small leaves and a long interrupted spike of verticillasters. Leaves rugose, glossy, dark green, 5–7cm long, ovate-oblong, cordate-based, petioled. Deep pink, flesh-colored or white flowers in whorls or terminal spikes. June to August. z5

This durable and attractive but little grown border perennial appears in horticulture under several names, including *S. densiflora* and *S. spicata densiflora*.

S. nivea Labill. (*Betonica nivea* Stev.). Caucasus Mts. Densely pubescent subshrub, stems 20–30cm high. Leaves obovate to oblanceolate, 2.5–3cm long, obtuse, coarsely crenate, rugose, green, sessile to petioled. Flowers small, in loose whorls, white; June to July. z5

S. officinalis (L.) Trev. Betony. (*Betonica officinalis* L.). Europe, N. Africa, Asia Minor. The basal leaves form a dense mat, similar to *S. grandiflora*, with many stiff, erect stems to 90cm high, terminating in a false spike with 2–3 verticillasters. Flowers small, purplish-red, clear pink, or white. Includes the cultivars 'Rosea' and 'Alba'. July to August. Collector's plant for the naturalized garden. z6 (Sch. & Kö.)

S. olympica see **S. byzantina**

Statice

S. tatarica see **Goniolimon tataricum**

S. speciosum see **Goniolimon speciosum**

Steironema

S. ciliatum see **Lysimachia ciliate**

S. lanceolatum see **Lysimachia lanceolata**

Stellaria L.
Caryophyllaceae
Starwort, Chickweed

One hundred twenty or fewer species of annual and perennial herbs distributed throughout the world. Stems erect or procumbent; leaves opposite. Flowers solitary or in a branched cyme. Sepals 4–5; petals 4–5 (or 0), deeply 2-lobed, white; stamens 8–10 (rarely fewer); ovary 1-celled, styles 3(4). The common Chickweed, *S. media*, belongs to this genus.

flowers. Propagation is easy by division and seed. A pretty combination is achieved with *Anemone nemorosa, Arum maculatum, Brachypodium sylvaticum, Carex sylvatica, Convallaria, Galeobdolon, Glechoma, Luzula pilosa, Maianthemum, Oxalis acetosella,* and various woodland ferns. z5 (E.)

Stenanthium Wats.
Liliaceae
Featherbells, Featherfleece

cence a panicle to 60cm long with 10–16 decurrent-nodding branches and a vertical terminal branch. Flowers small, to 12mm across, mostly whitish, perianth segments 6, stamens 6, styles 3, mid-June to September, depending on exposure. Occurs naturally in moist, rocky woods, at the moist base of wooded bluffs, occasionally on open banks or open thickets. Suitable for naturalizing and cutting. z4 And var. **robustum** (S. Wats) Fern, similar to the species but leaves longer and wide, stems to 1.5m high, thick, fruits erect (usually reflexed on the species). More limited distribution,

Stellaria holostea

Stenanthium robustum

Sternbergia clusiana

S. holostea L. Greater Stitchwort. Europe, N. Africa, W. Asia; in open woodlands, hedges or fence rows, or under thickets. Requires a cool, moderately dry site in a lime-free, neutral to moderately acidic, sandy or loam soil. A rhizomatous perennial with 20–60cm long, more or less procumbent-ascending stems, lanceolate, long-acuminate, sessile leaves and large, white flowers. Blooms from April to June.

The European *S. holostea*, because of its excessive vigor, has no place in the small to average-sized garden. It may be used, rather, in the large, naturalized garden, park or woodland margin. Suitable for naturalizing beneath open-growing shrubs where it will dominate the existing herbaceous vegetation. Plants thrive in any good garden soil in light shade and are attractive for many weeks with large, abundant, white

Grass-like, perennial herbs in North America and E. Asia; 4–5 species, depending on classification. Leaves linear, in a basal tuft from a somewhat bulbous rootstock. Stems stout, erect, 30–150cm high, usually with a few scattered, linear leaves. Inflorescence racemose or paniculate, the branches often nodding. Flowers small, whitish, greenish or dark purple; perianth segments connate below, separate and wide-spread above. Fruit an ovoid capsule.

S. gramineum (Ker.-Gawl.) Morong. Featherbells. USA: Mid-Atlantic States westward to Indiana and Missouri, south to the Gulf of Mexico. Rootstock bulbous, increasing by short, bulbous-tipped stolons. Leaves deciduous, a dense tuft, strap-shaped to linear, to 30cm long, 15mm wide. Stem to 1.2m, solid, stiff, with few leaves; inflores-

Pennsylvania and Maryland westward to Indiana. z6(5)

Stenotus

S. acaulis see **Haplopappus acaulis**

S. lyallii see **Haplopappus lyallii**

Sternbergia Waldst. et Kit.
Amaryllidaceae
Winter-daffodil

Five or more species in the Mediterranean region and Asia Minor, mostly in rocks on banks. Bulbs tunicate, with basal, narrow, straplike, glossy green to glaucous leaves which appear with or after the flowers. Flowers solitary, erect, on a short scape, apparently occasionally sessile, yellow or white, similar to *Crocus* but larger, with 6 corolla lobes and anthers. Blooms appear in fall or spring, depending on species. Cultivated in a lime-rich, gravelly soil in warm, sunny sites. Suitable for a collector's rock garden in a dry stone wall, a bulb case or pots in the alpine house. The fall blooming sternbergies are an exciting addition to the garden. Plant the bulbs 15cm deep in gravelly soil in full sun where they will bake during summer; sizable, free-flowering clumps develop very quickly. Propagate by removing offset bulblets around the parent bulb, by seed and by bulb scale cuttings.

S. candida B. Matthew et T. Baytop. S. Turkey: Fethiye, Mugla vilayet. The only white-flowered *Sternbergia*, discovered in 1978 and now in the trade, but rare. Similar to *S. fischeriana*, but white, with broad perianth segments, fragrant. February to April. Best kept in the alpine house. z7(6)

S. clusiana Ker-Gawl. ex Schult. S. Turkey to Israel, eastward to Iran. Flowers to 7cm long (possibly the largest of the genus), usually golden-yellow. Leafless during anthesis, September to October. Leaves develop during winter, glaucous-green, to 2cm wide. Reasonably hardy and worth planting. z6(5)

S. colchiciflora Waldst. et Kit. From Yugoslavia to Crimea, Caucasus and Iran. Flowers very small, scarcely 3cm wide, pale yellow, sessile, opening on the ground, ovary is in the soil. Leafless at anthesis, August to September; leaves develop later, narrow, dark green. Often fails to bloom or blooms underground and only produces seed. z5

S. fischeriana (Herb.) Rupr. Caucasus, Iran, Uzbekistan. Flowers to 4cm long, bright yellow, appearing simultaneously with the glaucous-green leaves. March to April. Similar to *S. lutea*, but spring-flowering. Easy to cultivate, but sometimes sparsely flowering; where summers are hot and dry, this species flowers profusely. z6(5)

S. lutea Ker-Gawl. ex Spreng. Spain and Algeria to Iran and Central Russia. Flowers 5cm long, bright yellow, appearing with the partially emerged glossy green leaves in September to October. The easiest species to grow. It is important for the leaves to come through winter without frost damage; therefore a thick, but well-ventilated cover (pine boughs) is advised on exposed sites. Similar to *S. sicula* Tin. and *S. sicula* var.

graeca Hal. from Sicily and Greece respectively, with equally large flowers, although smaller in habit. z6(5) (K.)

Stipa L.
Gramineae
Feather Grass, Needle Grass

About 150 species of tufted herbaceous perennial grasses with channeled or convoluted leaves, especially during dry periods. The inflorescence usually is narrow-paniculate, with 1-flowered

Stipa pulcherrima f. *nudicostata*

spikelets. All species occur in open, dry sites. Some species are quite ornamental in the garden. The major attraction is the long, feathery awned plumes which wave in the slightest breeze. Plants are most effective in well-spaced groups. It is important to note that, unlike many ornamental grasses, most *Stipa* species are decorative for only a short time. A mass planting should therefore include other plant species for lasting effect. Propagation is best by seed; divisions often lack vigor. Sow

seeds on end right after harvest to germinate the following spring. Self-seeding in cultivation is not unusual. Grow young plants in containers. The exact species classification of many plants in cultivation is unclear. Classification of the wide-ranging and correspondingly variable native species is also difficult.

S. barbata see **S. pulcherrima** f. **nudicostata**

S. calamagrostis see **Achnatherum calamagrostis**

S. capillata L. Mediterranean region and S. Central Europe to Siberia. A tufted, deciduous grass with stiffly erect, involuted, glaucous leaves; culms to 1m high with scarcely spreading panicles. Distinguished from the following species, such as *S. pulcherrima* f. *nudicostata*, by flower panicles borne much above the foliage and by the glabrous, shorter, 20cm-long, white to pale brown awns. This species is effective after flowering and fruiting in July and August with its dense, gray-green foliage clump. Unlike the silvery

Feather Grasses, this species is better used as a specimen or in small groups. Flowered culms are suitable for dry arrangements when cut before ripening. z6

S. gigantea Lag. (*Macrochloa arenaria* (Brot.) Kunth), Giant Feather Grass. Central and south Spain, Portugal. Leaves many, in large, dense clumps, to 50cm high. Panicles to 50cm long, very loose, on 2.5m high, stiffly erect culms. Awns glabrous, golden, to 12cm long, flexuous. July to August. This large grass requires a warm, protected site, and

grass with 1mm-wide leaves; leaf undersides scarious. Flowering stems to 1m high, with panicles 10–15cm long. The awns on the ripe seeds may become 50cm long. z6

S. pulcherrima K. Koch f. **nudicostata** Matinovsky (also distributed under the name *S. barbata* Desf.). E. Central Europe. A clump grass with long, narrow, gray-green leaves, margins often involuted. Panicle with feathery, silvery-silky awns to 40cm long. Culms usually reach 80cm high at flowering time, July to August. For best development and persistence,

slender. Leaves always over-arching. Culms less rigidly erect than other species. A valuable addition to a Feather Grass planting because its earlier flowering prolongs the decorative season. z6

S. zalesskii Wilensky (*S. rubens* Smirnov) Noteworthy among the many other species for the bright rust-brown fall color of a very fine-leaved clump. This species remains very small and is suitable for planting in large troughs.

Many other *Stipa* are garden worthy for

Stipa capillata

Stipa pennata

winter protection may be necessary. For improved hardiness, plant seed obtained from higher mountain elevations. This species may also be propagated by division with young plants grown in containers. z7(6)

S. pennata L., European Feather Grass. S. and Central Europe. A narrow-leaved clump grass with 40cm-high stems with 10cm-long, narrow panicles. The leaves are smooth and glabrous beneath, unlike the following species. The awns are up to 20cm long. z7

S. pennata ssp. **mediterranea** see **S. pulcherrima**

S. pulcherrima K. Koch (*S. pennata* ssp. *mediterranea* Trin. et Rupr., Aschers. et Graebn.). S. Europe, Outer Iberian Peninsula, to Central France, N. Germany and Central Russia. A clump

plant in calcareous soil in a warm, protected site. z7

S. rubens see **S. zalesskii**

S. stenophylla see **S. tirsa**

S. tirsa Stev. (*S. stenophylla* (Czern. ex Lindem.) Trautv.). Central, S. and E. Europe. A loose clump to stoloniferous grass. Leaves are involuted, 0.5cm wide and to 1m long, often turned to one side by the wind. The 60cm-high culms bear a solitary, constricted panicle. The awns grow to 40cm long. This species requires much heat to bloom. In its natural habitat, the species grows on gravelly, alkaline, but lime-free loam soil. z7

S. ucrainica Smirnov, Ukrainian Feather Grass. Ukraine and Rumania. Another clump Feather Grass with leaves always involuted, therefore appear to be

their seed-bearing panicles alone. z6 (S.)

Stokesia L'Hérit.
Compositae
Stokes' Aster

The genus is represented by a single species:

S. laevis (Hill) Greene (*S. cyanea* L'Hérit.), Stokes' Aster. SE. USA: South Carolina to Florida and Louisiana. Flowering stems 30–40cm long, erect, ascending to almost prostrate. Rootstock fleshy, sparsely branched; bears loose, leafy rosettes. Lower leaves to 20cm long, petioled, lanceolate, entire or somewhat spring-ciliate toward the base, smooth. Stem leaves sessile, clasping. Stems erect to decumbent, coarsely branched. Flower heads to 10cm wide, aster-like, with fimbriate ray flowers, lilac-blue, disc lighter; June to September. Some good cultivars include: 'Blue Moon', hyacinth blue, and 'Blue Star', light blue flowers on sturdy stems, late-flowering. Additional older cultivars include 'Alba', flowers white; 'Caerulea', flowers light blue; 'Lilacina', flowers lilac; 'Purpurea', flowers tinged purple, foliage darker green; 'Rosea', flowers pinkish, and 'Superba', flowers larger, bright lavender-blue; 'Praecox' is said to bloom earlier than the species. Plants are also interesting after flowering, with their rosettes of leafy

Stokesia laevis

green involucral bracts and lettuce green foliage.

Stokes' Aster requires a sunny bed and thrives in a well-drained sandy-loam. Poor drainage resulting in water logged soil is conducive to root rot or crown rot and some winter protection may be advisable. Propagate the species by seed; divide cultivars and established plants in spring. Some good companions include *Liatris*, *Sidalcea*, *Oenothera* and *Solidago caesia*, in loose arrangement on a sunny, warm slope in a moist soil. Also suitable for cut flowers if grown in good garden soil with ample moisture. z5 (Sch. & M.)

Stratiotes L.
Hydrocharitaceae
Water Soldier, Water Aloe

A single species known, although 8 fossil species have been described.

S. aloides L. Central Europe to the Caucasus and W. Siberia. An aquatic, stoloniferous perennial for standing or slow flowing water; adapts to terrestrial situations, contributing to erosion control and covering entire meadows.

Stratiotes aloides

Leaves 15–45cm long, linear-lanceolate, margins spiny-toothed, stiff, spirally arranged in brownish green rosettes, submerged in winter, somewhat exposed in summer. Plants are dioecious. The pistillate flowers are short-pediceled, solitary or paired in a flower sheath, staminate flowers paired or several on an elongated stem. Flowers to 5cm across. Petals 3, white, June to July. An interesting collector's plant for a neutral to acidic bog. Also for small streams. Spreads rapidly by vigorous stolons but is sparsely rooted and therefore easy to keep under control. Propagation is normally by stolon cuttings or the budlike overwintering shoots, or occasionally from seed. Unisexual stands are often found. z5 (D.)

Streptopus Michx.
Liliaceae
Twisted-stalk

Seven to ten species of perennials in N. temperate Eurasia and America with fleshy, slow-creeping rhizomes. Stems erect, simple or somewhat branched,

alternate-leaved. Leaves sessile or clasping. Flowers solitary or paired in the leaf axils. Fruit a many-seeded berry.

Shade-loving collectors' plants similar to *Polygonatum* but with the perianth segments distinct or nearly so, and almost equal. Grow in light shade in a evenly moist, woodland soil with additional peat. Suitable for large or small gardens and parks. Attractive in combination with *Actaea*, various anemones, *Boykinia*, *Cornus canadensis*, *Polygonatum*, *Smilacina*, *Tellima Uvularia*, *Waldsteinia*, various shady grasses, and ferns. Propa-

Streptopus amplexifolius

gate by division, or seed sown quickly after ripening.

S. amplexifolius (L.) DC. White Mandarin. Distributed throughout the N. Temperate Zone; in moist, cool mountain forests. Stems 0.5–1m high, smooth, branched below the middle. Leaves ovate-lanceolate to lanceolate, cordate at the base, undersides blue-green, stem-clasping. Flowers usually paired, inconspicuous, small, greenish white. The pendulous red berries on the yellowing plants are conspicuous in fall. Blooms from May to July. Var. *americanus* Schult., Liverberry, in the Adirondacks to 1300m, includes much of the North American material, but other American varieties are *denticulatus* Fassett, and *oreopolus* (Fern.) Fassett, both very local in distribution, distinguished by relatively obscure botanical characteristics. z5

S. roseus Michx. North America: New-foundland and Labrador, west to Michigan and Alaska to N. Oregon and British Columbia; on river banks and in moist mountain forests. Similar to the above species, but stems only 30–40cm (rarely 45cm) high, with sessile, non-clasping leaves, margins ciliate, and green on both sides. Flowers usually solitary, rose to purple. Blooms from May to July. Also with geographic distinctions. z2–7 (E.)

S. diphyllum (Michx.) Nutt. USA: Pennsylvania to Tennessee, Wisconsin, and Missouri; in moist woodlands. Ever-green perennial about 40cm high with a stout rootstock with yellow-orange sap, and mostly basal, long petioled, pinnately lobed and divided, light green leaves, roughly pubescent beneath. Stems several, erect, with a few divided and lobed stem leaves toward the top. Flowers occasionally solitary, usually in few flowered, terminal umbels, borne just above the uppermost leaves, 5cm wide, gold-yellow. Blooms in late spring to midsummer. z4 (E.)

S. pratensis Moench. Devil's Bit. (*Scabiosa succisa* L.). Europe to W. Siberia, N. Africa, naturalized in E. North America; in boggy meadows, moors, moist, somewhat infertile fields. Grows best on seasonally moist, somewhat acidic, peaty, sandy or loamy humus soil. Herbaceous perennial 15–60cm high with short rhizomes. Leaves narrowly elliptic to obovate-lanceolate, to 30cm long, entire, upper stem leaves nar-rower, lanceolate, entire or coarsely ser-rate, dark green. Stems erect, branched. Flower heads 2–3cm wide, hemi-spherical, later globose. Flowers usually

Stylophorum diphyllum

Succisa pratensis

Struthiopteris see **Matteuccia**

Stylophorum Nutt.
Papaveraceae

Three to six species, most in E. Asia, one in the USA. Similar to *Chelidonium*, sap yellow or reddish; perennial with mostly pinnately lobed basal leaves and a few pinnately lobed stem leaves, blades greenish above, pale bluish beneath. Flowers with 2 sepals and 4 petals, yellow or reddish. Seldom found outside of botanic gardens. Bushy perennials for evenly moist, shady sites in gardens or parks where they grow best in a moist woodland soil Propagate by division and seed, sown directly in the garden. Combines well with other shade-loving perennials such as those listed under *Streptopus*.

S. japonicum see **Hylomecon japonica**

Succisa Haller
Dipsacaceae

One species in Europe, W. Siberia, NW. Africa, one species in NW. Spain, one species in equatorial Africa (Cameroon region). Similar to *Scabiosa*, but the cup-shaped, 4–5 toothed calyx is enclosed in a 4-angled, 4-toothed involucel. Petals 4, stamens 4. Outer flowers of the flower heads are only slightly different from the center flowers. Chaffy hairs on the receptacle are nearly of equal length. For moist, somewhat boggy meadows in natural garden sections of the botanic garden where *Succisa* is valuable for its late and long-lasting flowers. Best com-bined with other plants of its native habitat. Propagate by division and seed.

violet-blue, rarely pink or white; from July to October. Once used as a folk medicine. z5 (E.)

Swertia L.
Gentianaceae

Fifty to about 200 species, depending on taxonomic system; glabrous, erect, perennial or annual herbs. Leaves mostly opposite, entire, mostly basal. Flowers 5-merous, rarely 4-merous, corolla rotate with a short tube, the stamens attached to its base; each corolla lobe with 2 basal nectaries; style short or lacking, stigma 2-lobed; in cymes or panicles, often dense, spike-like, blue, purplish, white, occasionally yellow. Found in the mountains of Europe, Asia and Africa. Only one species commonly available for gardens.

S. perennis L. Europe, Asia, W. North America, Alaska to California eastward to the Rocky Mts. A desirable bog or swamp plant. The basal leaves ovate to ovate-elliptic, stem leaves opposite, broadly ovate to ovate, narrowing above. Stems erect, 4-angled, scarcely branched, often turning violet. Flowers in racemose cymes, 5-parted, steel blue to sordid violet, July to September. A collector's plant for moist, boggy sites, often difficult to grow to perfection. Propagation is easy by seed and division. z5 (D.)

Swertia perennis

Symphyandra A.DC.
Campanulaceae
Bellflower

About 7 or 8 (–14) species; most in Asia Minor, the Balkan region, and Crete, one Korean species, *S. asiatica*. Attractive, biennial or perennial in its native habitat, often dies after flowering in cultivation. Rockery plants with fleshy roots, rosetted leaves and nodding, white or blue bell flowers in pyramidal, branched inflorescences. Differs from *Campanula* by the connate anthers. Flowers from May to September. Grow in fertile, sandy, well-drained loam in full sun or light shade. Suitable for rock and trough gardens. Propagation is easy from seed, commonly self-seeds.

S. armena (Stev.) A.DC. Georgian Republic, USSR; in rock crevices. Leaves ovate, cordate to cuneate, coarsely scabrous-toothed, with long petioles. Flower stems to 30cm, branched, flowers terminal, upright-facing, blue or white, 2cm long, calyx lobes narrow-triangular, with a reflexed appendage at each sinus. Always biennial. z7

S. hofmannii Pant. Yugoslavia: Bosnia. Stems 30–60cm high. Rootstocks very fleshy. Leaves obovate to lanceolate, acute toothed, with winged petioles, in large rosettes. Terminal panicles or racemes. Flowers nodding, to 3cm long, cylindrical-campanulate, white to cream-colored. July to September. Monocarpic. Once planted perpetuates by self-seeding. z7

S. pendula (M.B.) A.DC. Caucasus. Stems 45–60cm high, hairy. Leaves light green, to 15cm-long, broadly oval-cordate, biserrate, petioles not winged. Inflorescence a panicle. Flowers nodding, to 5cm long, campanulate, creamy-white. June to July. z6

S. wanneri (Roch.) Heuff. Mountains of Bulgaria, Rumania, E. Yugoslavia. Plants sparsely pilose; stems 15–25cm high. Leaves lanceolate to oblanceolate, acute, long cuneate to a winged petiole, or sessile on stems, toothed, dark green, glossy. Flowers nodding, infundibular-campanulate, lilac-blue, calyx without appendages, lobes reddish brown. Plant in semi-shade. May to June. z6

Lit.: Crook, H.C.: *The Genus Symphyandra*. Bull. A.G.S. 45, 246–254, 1977. (K.)

Symphytum L.
Boraginaceae
Comfrey

A genus of about 25 species, few with real ornamental value but several are grown for historic interest or as pseudo-medicinal herbs. Erect or spreading herbs, usually with bristly-pubescent, yellowish, blue or purple, tubular, nodding flowers and fleshy, sometimes tuberous roots. The range of the genus reaches throughout Europe, N. Africa and W. Asia. *S. asperum* and *S. officinale* may be grown in a large natural garden, and are attractive in association with water; the variegated forms are best planted as specimens in formal plantings; propagate only by division or root cuttings. The species are easily grown from seed. Perennial species with fleshy to tuberous roots. Leaves mostly basal, coarse and hispid, simple; stem leaves smaller, alternate to subopposite below the inflorescence, sometimes decurrent. Inflorescence a scorpioid, racemose cyme. Flowers 5-merous but with 1–4 nutlets from the deeply cleft ovary.

S. asperum Lepech. (*S. asperrimum* Donn

little-known cultivars are: 'Goldsmith', with yellow-leaves, and 'Hidcote Blue', with soft blue flowers, later fading. 'Langthorn's Pick' with pale pink flowers; 'Hidcote Variegated', like 'Hidcote Blue' but with broad splashes of creamish-white on the leaves, is quite widely grown. z5

S. officinale L. Common Comfrey. Europe to W. Siberia. Stems 30–80cm high. Differs from *S. asperum* in the long-decurrent and less rough-pubescent, broadly lanceolate leaves and longer calyx. Flowers dull violet, purple, rose or

tube-form flowers; May to August. 'Variegatum' is a conspicuous variegated cultivar with wide, gray-green, broadly cream-margined leaves. The flowers are lilac-pink. Interestingly, it loses its variegated foliage on infertile sites and reverts to dark green. z6 (Sch. & M.)

Symplocarpus Salisb. ex Nutt.
Araceae
Skunk Cabbage

A monotypic genus. Rhizome large to

Symphytum grandiflorum

Symphytum peregrinum

Symplocarpus foetidus

ex Sims), Prickly Comfrey. Caucasus, Armenia and W. Iran, naturalized in North America. Stems to 1.5m high. Leaves dark green, prickly-bristly-pubescent. Flowers reddish at first, fading to blue; June to August. The gold-variegated cultivar, 'Aureo-variegatum', is recommended for collectors. z5

S. asperrimum see **S. asperum**

S. caucasicum M.B. Caucasus. Stems 60cm high; forms an attractive, soft-hairy foliage clump. The azure blue flowers, nodding in clusters on the leafy stems, are particularly appealing; June to August. One of the more ornamental species; suitable for the sunny rock garden. z5

S. grandiflorum DC. Caucasus. Stems to 30cm, sometimes decumbent. Rootstock rhizomatous, spreading. Leaves ovate, acute-tipped. Flowers cream-yellow, buds tipped red; May. Suitable as a groundcover between shrubs and under trees; dense-growing, constantly spreading, sometimes invasive. *Brunnera* makes a good companion plant. Some

creamy-white; May to July. The cultivar 'Argenteum' is conspicuous for its white-variegated leaves. z5

S. peregrinum Ledeb. E. Caucasus. Stems 0.8–1.2m high, roots thick, spindle-shaped. Bushy and vigorous, rough-leaved. Flowers bright blue; June to July. Very floriferous and shade-tolerant species. The red-flowered cultivar 'Alexandrit' originates from a cross between *S. peregrinum* × *S. officinale*.

S. rubrum hort. Only known in cultivation. Possibly a hybrid between *S. officinale* 'Coccineum' and *S. grandiflorum*. Stems about 50cm high, only moderately spreading. A very attractive ground cover for a cool site. The dark red flowers are pendulous in small helicoid cymes above the pubescent foliage; June to July. z5

S. × uplandicum Nym. (*S. asperum* × *S. officinale*). Occasionally naturalized in Europe. Stems 1.2m tall. Often labeled as *S. peregrinum* or *S. asperrimum*. Good foliage plant with well-branched stems terminating in drooping clusters of blue

very large, vertical. The characteristic spate enclosing the spadix emerges in early spring, followed by the very large leaves. Flowers perfect, perianth 4-parted, stamens 4, ovary 1-celled, with one ovule. Fruit berry-like.

S. foetidus (L.) Nutt. Temperate E. Asia: Amur, Japan; E. North America. Leaves to 50cm high; a swamp and bog plant with a deeply anchored rootstock. Leaves short-petioled, ovate-cordate, to 75cm long and 25cm wide, appearing after the flowers. Spathe leathery, globose-hoodlike, curved at the acute tip, dark, yellowish, purple and red-brown mottled, about 10cm high enclosing the globular, short-stalked, violet spadix which is entirely covered with small, crowded, all fertile flowers. Generally the first spring perennial flower in nature, often peeking from the ground as early as January. Very interesting collector's plant for swampy, deep topsoil along streams and ponds in sun and semi-shade. The unappealing name "Skunk Cabbage" is actually unfounded since the plant has no scent except for a slight fetid or garlic scent when crushed.

Best propagated by seed sown as soon as it ripens in late summer. The pea-sized, hard seeds are found in a red to brownish-black, fleshy fruit. Division of older plants is possible, but difficult. z4 (Sch.)

Syndesmon

S. thalictroides see **Anemonella thalictroides**

Synthyris Benth.
Scrophulariaceae

North American genus, closely related to *Wulfenia*, with 14–15 species. Fairly decorative woodland plants, attractive both in flower, and in early winter with bright green leafy tufts. Mostly rhizomatous. Leaves basal, cordate, reniform or deeply cleft, serrate, long petioled. Inflorescence a scapose raceme. Flowers blue to violet-blue or white; calyx 4-parted, corolla campanulate or rotate, 4-lobed, barely 2-lipped; stamens 2. Grow in a semi-shady to shady site in a humus-rich, cool and moist soil which never dries, even briefly, in summer. Suitable for the shady border. Attractive companions include *Corylopsis pauciflora* and trilliums. Propagate by seed and division after blooming. However, plants suffer with frequent transplanting and are most effective if left undisturbed for several years in a suitable location.

S. missurica Pursh ex Raf. USA: NE. Washington and N. Idaho to N. California and S. Central Idaho. Not found in Missouri, as may be inferred from the name. Glabrous plant to 40cm high but rachis and pedicels sometimes with rufous hairs. Leaves orbicular-cordate to reniform, shallowly lobed or toothed. Flowers bright bluish-purple, about 6cm long, in an erect, many-flowered raceme. Var. **major** (Hook.) Penn. Plants taller; flowers in denser racemes, rachis and pedicels white-haired. Unlike the more common *S. stellata* this species has shallowly lobed leaves with obtuse dentation. z6

S. reniformis Benth. (*S. rotundifolia* A. Gray). USA; California to Washington. Stems 5–22cm high. Leaves orbicular-cordate to reniform, 1.75–2.5cm across, doubly crenate, pilose above or rarely glabrous. Racemes short. Flowers 6mm long, blue or purple, corolla bell-shaped. Var. **cordata** A. Gray. Leaves ovate-cordate, deeper cut; flowers darker blue. Cultivar 'Alba', flowers white. z7

S. rotundifolia see **S. reniformis**

Synthyris rubra see **Besseya rubra**

S. stellata Pennell (*S. reniformis* hort.). USA: Oregon. Stems 20cm-high, often less; a dense, bushy perennial. Leaves basal, orbicular-cordate, doubly serrate, to 8cm across, long-petioled, rounded to reniform, scabrous-toothed, glossy. Flowers appear with the unfolding spring leaves, small, campanulate, violet-blue in densely compact, to 40-flowered, pyramidal racemes; March to April. The most common species in cultivation. z6 (Sch. & S.)

American gardeners in the Pacific Northwest, especially, grow additional species (sometimes available through plant society seed exchange programs) including:

S. cymopteroides Penn. USA: SW. Montana to Central Idaho. Stems upright to 15cm, white tomentose becoming glabrate. Leaves 2-pinnatisect, segments very narrow, to 5cm long. Flowers in close racemes, 6mm long, violet-blue, spring or summer. z5

S. hendersonii Penn. USA: Idaho. Stems to 7.5cm high, white tomentose becoming glabrescent, as the above species. Leaves to 5cm long, coarsely 2-pinnatifid, segments ovate, acuminate, tips calloused. Flowers sky-blue. Summer-flowering. z5

S. paysonii Penn & L.O. Williams. USA: W. Wyoming and adjacent Idaho. Rosettes single or in clusters. Stems to 20cm high, white tomentose becoming glabrescent. Leaves 2-pinnatifid, to 14cm long, segments linear-attenuate. Flowers small, violet-blue, in crowded racemes. Summer-flowering. z5

S. pinnatifida S. Wats. USA: Mts. N. Utah. Stems erect, to 15cm high. Leaves to 10cm long, 2–3 pinnate, leaflets linear, pubescent. Racemes slender, elongate. Flowers to 14mm long, violet-blue, in summer. z5 Var. **lanuginosa** (Piper) Cronq. Washington. Leaves and stems white-tomentose all season.

Talinum Adans.
Portulacaceae
Fameflower

More than 50 species in tropical and subtropical, rarely temperate regions of both hemispheres, especially in Mexico. Closely related to *Calandrinia*, but often with cylindrical leaves. Glabrous, succulent herbs or subshrubs, stems simple or branched. Leaves alternate to subopposite, without stipules. Flowers solitary or in a simple racemose panicle, white, pink, rose red or violet; sepals 2, deciduous, petals 5 (or more), stamens 5 to many. Flowers are short-lived, but open sequentially for extended season. Flowers from June to July. Grow in well-drained sandy or rocky soil in full sun. Needs some protection from excessive winter wetness. Attractive collectors' plants for pots and trough gardens. The following species are quite hardy. Propagate by seed or cuttings.

T. calycinum Engelma. North America: Missouri to Mexico. Rootstock thick, deep. Stem simple, leaves mostly basal, cylindrical or nearly so, 2–5cm long, glaucous. Scape thread-like, wiry, to 20cm high; flowers rose-pink, 2.5cm across or more. On stony ground the blossoms seem to float in the air. z6

T. okanoganense English. NW. USA: Washington. Low, scarcely 2cm-high, succulent cushion. Leaves to 5mm long, tear-drop-shaped, gray-green, red in fall, on creeping branchlets. Flowers solitary, 2cm wide, flat-funnelform, white, on 3cm long peduncles. June to August. z6

T. parviflorum Nutt. USA: Minnesota southward to Texas and Arizona. Root almost carrot-like. Vegetative stem short, mostly branching, to 4cm high. Leaves nearly cylindrical, glaucous, 2–4cm long. Scape threadlike, wiry to 20cm high, flowers soft pink, to 2cm across. Similar to *T. calycinum* but this species branches freely, flowers are smaller, paler, and with only 4–8 stamens (*T. calycinum* with 45–50). z4

T. spinescens Torr. W. USA: Washington Mts. Stems thorny below, dense cushion 5cm high and 15cm wide. Leaves to 15mm long, cylindrical or nearly so. Flowers 2cm wide, rose to carmine-violet, in branched racemes, 15cm high. June to September. Very attractive and quite hardy. z6

T. 'Zoe'. This is a hybrid of *T. okanoganense* × *T. spinescens*. Resembles a vigorous *T. okanoganense*, inflorescence flat, on the foliage cushion. Flowers are 15mm wide and pink. Lovely, with long-lasting flowers. Only propagated by cuttings. z6 (K.)

Tamus L.
Dioscoreaceae

Four Old World, herbaceous, twining, creepers, with large tuberous roots, annual stems 1.5–4m high, with alter-

Synthyris reniformis

nate, shining, cordate or 3-lobed leaves. Summer flowers in axillary racemes, small, yellowish-green sepals, 3, petals 3 (all similar), male flowers with 6 stamens, filaments slender, and an aborted pistil, female flowers with perianth of 6 segments, vestigial stamens, and an inferior ovary.

T. communis L. Black Byrony. Europe, W. Asia, N. Africa, Canary Islands. A dioecious, twining perennial, to 2m high. Fleshy, tuberous rootstock, leaves cordate. The small, greenish flowers in axillary racemes appear from May to June. Male flowers with 6 perianth segments and 6 stamens, female flowers with similar perianth but stamens 0, and an inferior ovary. Female plants later develop red berries. Not difficult to cultivate in a deep topsoil and warm site. However, winter protection is advisable. Attractive vine for large gardens and parks. This is a very poisonous plant in all its parts; livestock have died from eating the vegetation, children from eating the attractive fruits. Propagate by division and seed. z7 (Kö.)

Tanacetum L.
Compositae
Tansy

Aromatic, mostly ferny-leaved perennials in about 50 annual and perennial species in the Northern Hemisphere, most Old World, but some widely naturalized. Leaves simple (mostly annuals) to 1–3 pinnately compound, much divided, especially basal foliage. Flower heads commonly in corymbs, rarely solitary, mostly yellow discoid, rarely with yellow ray flowers. Some

Tamus communis

species grown in rock gardens, and one in herb gardens as a medicinal and moth-repellent perennial; moderately ornamental, most easily grown in any well drained garden soil in full sun. Propagate by division, also seed.

T. argenteum see **Chrysanthemum argentum**

T. compactum H. M. Hall. S. Nevada. Caespitose perennial, rarely to 45 cm high, silvery-silky-tomentose over all. Leaves to 2cm long, pinnate-compound. Flower heads solitary, to 2cm across. For a warm, sunny rock garden site; useful for attractive foliage color. z7

T. haradjanii see **Chrysanthemum haradjanii**

T. herderi Regal & Schmall. Turkestan. Caespitose perennial to 30cm, all parts gray-hairy. Leaves 2–3 pinnately compound. Stems with few leaves, several discoid flower heads in corymbs, bright yellow. Attractive rock garden or dry wash ornamental plant. z6–7

T. macrophyllum see **Chrysanthemum macrophyllum**

T. millefolium see **Chrysanthemum millefoliatum**

T. vulgare L. (*Chrysanthemum vulgare* (L.) Bernh.). Tansy, Golden Button. Europe to Caucasus, Armenia, Siberia. To over 1m high, stiff-growing perennial. Leaves twice pinnately cleft, dark green. Yellow flower heads without ray florets in dense corymbs; July to September. The entire plant is strongly aromatic; an old medicinal plant. Commonly grows along

Tanakaea radicans

Tanacetum vulgare

railroad tracks, roadsides, riverbanks and similar sties. While a common European native, this species has hardly any garden significance; sometimes used as a bank cover in the landscape. Var. *crispum* DC. with more finely cut, larger, luxuriant foliage and lacking flowers in cool-summer areas, is a good herb plant. z4 (Sch. & M.)

Taraxacum Wiggers
Compositae
Dandelion

Many species, varying according to the interpretation of the genus, from temperate and arctic regions, especially in the Northern Hemisphere. Stemless perennials, with a fleshy taproot, leaves rosetted, basal, simple or pinnate. Flower heads on hollow leafless scapes, flowers yellow, pinkish-orange or white. Flowers from February to November. Cultivation of the arctic and Japanese

morning hours. z3 (K.)

T. officinalis var. **albiflorum** see **T. albidum**

Telekia Baumg.
Compositae

Two species of perennials, closely related to *Buphthalmum* and *Inula*. Erect herbaceous perennials with coarse foliage and radiate, solitary flower heads on leafy stems. Involucral bracts in 3–4 rows, imbricate; ray flowers with long,

Telekia speciosa

Tellima grandiflora

Tanakaea Franch. et Sav.
Saxifragaceae

A single species. A woodland perennial from Japan.

T. radicans Franch. et Sav. China and Japan. Small evergreen perennial with a slender rhizome and with slender, above-ground runners terminating in offset plantlets. Leaves in a basal rosette, long-petioled, ovate-lanceolate, acuminate, serrate, leathery. Scape to 20cm high, usually leafless; inflorescence paniculate. Flowers very small, greenish-white, calyx tube short, perigynous, calyx lobes 5; petals 0; stamens 10; ovary nearly superior, styles short, fruit a capsule. June to July. Resembles a miniature *Astilbe*. A collector's plant for a semi-shaded site, requires sandy, high humus, somewhat acidic soil, and an annual topdressing of mulch (composted bark). Winter protection is necessary where weather is harsh. z7 (Sch. & Kö.)

species can be difficult. These require well-drained, gravelly, not too humus-rich soil in full sun or light shade. Useful as collectors' plants in the rock garden. Propagate by seed and root cuttings.

Two of the many species of garden interest are:

T. albidum Dahlst. (*T. officinalis* var. *albiflorum* Makino). Japan: Honshu, Shikoku, Kyushu. Similar to *T. officinale*, but the leaves narrower, more ascending, the scape to 20cm high. Flower heads smaller, 4–5cm wide, creamy-white, closing up in the early afternoon. z6

T. carneocoloratum Nels. Alaska: Kuskokwim Mts.; in high alpine screes, extremely rare. Rosettes lying completely flat, to 8cm wide. Scape procumbent-ascending, to 5cm long. Flower heads 3cm wide, orange-pink to purple. Very attractive. Unfortunately, flower heads open for only a few

slender ligule, pistillate, disc flowers perfect, anthers tailed, ovary 3-angled; receptacle flat or nearly so, scaly.

T. speciosa (Schreb.) Baumg. (*Buphthalmum speciosum* Schreb.). SE. Alps, and W. Carpathian Mts., Balkan region, Caucasus Mts. Transcaucasus, Asia Minor. Stems to 2m high. Rootstock cylindrical, knobby. Leaves alternate, very large, glabrous above, hairy below, especially on the veins, basal leaves long-petioled, coarsely serrate, broadly triangular to cordate, acuminate, the upper stem leaves sessile, broadly ovate. Stems strongly erect, often brownish-red, racemose-branched at the top, flower heads 5–6cm wide, rays many, slender, yellow; June to August. Very decorative wildflower for a semi-shaded location and not too dry soil. Particularly well suited for naturalizing in parks or large wild gardens, for example, for underplanting along riverside thickets. Propagate by division and seed. z5

T. speciosissima (L.) Less. (*Buphthalmum speciosissimum* L.). S. Alps. Stem 20–30cm tall, always with a solitary flower head, stiffly erect, brownish and very finely pubescent. Lower leaves oblong-ovate, stiff, stem-clasping, slightly toothed. Flower heads 7cm-wide, yellow, slender involucral bracts imbricate. Flowers from July to September. Recommended for the large rock garden. Likes a deep, rock crevice in full sun. Attractive in combination with *Aster alpinus*. Propagate by seed; division is difficult. z6 (Me. & Kö.)

Telesonix jamesii see **Boykinia jamesii**

Tellima R. Br.
Saxifragaceae
False Alumroot

One species in W. North America. A rhizomatous, low plant with hairy, more or less glandular, rounded to cordate, lobed or distinctly toothed leaves. Flowers in terminal racemes on few-leaved stems to 60cm high. Flowers greenish-white; calyx campanulate-tubular, 5-lobed; petals 5, reflexed, lacerate; stamens 10, included; ovary perigynous, carpels separate above, beak-like, styles short. Suitable for understory planting in semi-shade. Vigorous and naturalizes, but not very showy. Propagate by division and seed. Several species once classified as *Tellima* have been transferred to *Lithophragma*. *Tellima* is an anagram from the closely related *Mitella*.

T. grandiflora (Pursh) Dougl. ex Lindl. Fringecups. W. North America: Alaska to California. Flower stem erect, glandular-hairy, to 60cm high. Basal leaves rounded-cordate, long-petioled, in a rosette. Flowers in terminal racemes, small; petals whitish to greenish, lacerate. Fruit a 2-beaked, many-seeded capsule. May to June. Cultivar 'Rubra', compact habit, leaves reddish, flowers yellowish or light green. z6 (Me. & Kö.)

T. parviflora see **Lithophragma parviflora**

Tephrosia Pers.
Leguminosae
Hoary Pea

Perhaps 200–300 species of herbs or shrubs, most from warmer climates. Roots extremely long, wiry, crown hard, woody, with several to many, ascending to erect stems. Plant a flattened bush. Leaves alternate, odd-pinnate, mostly ashy-pilose. Flowers papilionaceous, standard silky-hairy outside; stamens connate except the upper stamen free to the middle or entirely so. Of only marginal ornamental value. Used like *Galega*, prefers a dry, sandy or stony soil. Needs winter protection in wet climates.

T. virginiana (L.) Pers. Devil's Guts, Goat's Rye. E. and Central North America; on dry, stony or sandy soils. A loose cushion or dense bush to 50cm

Tetragonolobus maritimus

high. Stems much branched, silky-pubescent, ashy. Leaves odd-pinnate, leaflets 8–14 pairs, linear-oblong. Racemes terminal, a dense to loose cluster. Flowers to 2cm across, standard chartreuse-yellowish, keel deep rose; June to July. Very hardy, to at least −26 degrees C. (−15 degrees F.) when growing in a well-drained, dry site. z6 (Mü.)

Tetragonolobus Scop.
Leguminosae

Four or more species in Europe. *Lotus*-like plants, but with ternate leaves, herbaceous stipules. Flowers solitary or paired. Calyx teeth regular. Pods 4-angled, edges winged or keeled. Flowers from June to September. Easy to grow in any garden soil in full sun. Suitable for the natural garden. Propagate by seed.

T. maritimus (L.) Roth (*Lotus siliquosus* L.). Central, E. and S. Europe, Asia Minor, Caucasus, N. Africa. Perennial, stems trailing, hairy to rarely glabrescent, often somewhat ascending, to 40cm high. Leaves oblanceolate to obovate to 30 × 15mm, stipules short-adnate. Flowers papilionaceous, 25–30mm, pale yellow. July to September. Very attractive combined with small blue, naturalizing perennials, such as *Campanula carpatica*. z6 (K.)

Teucrium L.
Labiatae
Germander

About 300 species in the warmer regions and temperate zones throughout the world; deciduous to evergreen perennials, subshrubs and shrubs. Flower in 2- to many-flowered verticillasters, axillary, spicate, racemose or in heads. Summer-blooming. Propagation and garden uses differ among the species.

T. canadense L. American Wood Sage. E. North America. Herbaceous perennial with short rhizomatous rootstock. Stems glabrescent, 60–90cm high, 4-angled. Leaves opposite, ovate-lanceolate, 3–7.5cm long, acute-tipped, serrate, pilose beneath. Inflorescence a spicate raceme

10–20cm long, sometimes interrupted; bracts lanceolate, verticillasters mostly 6-flowered. Corolla to 2cm long, pale pinkish-purple to almost creamy-colored. Found in open forests and at forest margins in humus-rich soil. Attractive in the shady wildflower garden or border. z4

T. chamaedrys L. Wall Germander. Europe, S. Central Russia, N. Africa, Asia Minor; on dry rocky slopes, usually over limestone. Subshrub 25cm-high, root-stock sometimes creeping. Leaves oblong to ovate, 12–18mm long, deeply

pink, in spicate racemes, from May to October. Otherwise very similar to *T. chamaedrys*. Very serviceable evergreen plant. Often used like dwarf Boxwood, for small hedges and edgings. Takes shearing well. Not reliably winter hardy. Propagate by seed, division and cuttings. z6

T. musimonum Humbert ex Maire. 3–5cm high, forming flat mats. Entire plant gray-tomentose. Leaves petioled, small, ovate-crenate. Flowers pink, in dense, hemispherical heads; June to September. For sunny, dry sites in the rock

carpet. Leaves green, orbicular, 12–18mm across, irregularly crenate, short-petioled. Flowers large, white, light yellow or purplish, in loose heads; June to July. Attractive, reasonably hardy species for the dry stone wall or rock garden. z7(6)

T. scorodonia L. European Wood Sage. W. Europe and W. Central Europe to S. Scandinavia, also the S. Balkan region and N. Africa; in oak and pine forests or on moors. Shrubby, rhizomatous. Stems erect, 30–60cm high, usually branched toward the tip, shaggy-pubescent.

Teucrium chamaedrys

Teucrium scorodonia

Thalictrum aquilegifolium

serrate to crenate, more or less ever-green, opposite, softly glabrescent-hispid. Bracts as long as the flowers; flowers to 6 in a whorl, mostly rose to purplish, occasionally white, long-stalked, usually in a loose to dense spicate raceme; June to August. The cultivar 'Nanum' or 'Prostratum' is exceptionally bushy, spreading, to only 10cm high; tolerates a dry, infertile site and is an attractive, persistent, carpetforming plant. Plants found in cultivation as *T. chamaedrys* hort. generally are *T. massiliense* or hybrids with *T. lucidum* (*Teucrium × lucidrys*). These are completely evergreen, to 40cm high but often lower and with non-creeping root-stocks. z5

T. massiliense L. (*T. chamaedrys* hort.). W. Mediterranean region, Crete. Stems erect, to 40cm high, pubescent. Leaves evergreen, petioled, oblong-ovate (uppermost leaves lanceolate), crenate, to 2cm long, pubescent. Flowers rose-

garden. z6

T. polium L. (*T. tomentosum* Vill.). S., N. and E. Spain, S. France, N. Africa. Frosty-looking evergreen; more or less woody; stems procumbent or ascending, to 15cm high, entire plant gray tomentose. Leaves deltoid to linear, sessile, crenate, rugose, 12–25mm long. Flowers very small, few, white, yellowish to purple, fairly insignificant. z7

T. polium ssp. **aureum** (Schreb.) Arcang. Golden-yellow leaves, broadly linear. Flowers in oblong heads, yellow or white; July to August. Suitable for the alpine house or rock garden in loose, gravelly, humus-rich soil. Requires a sunny, dry, protected site. Not reliably winter hardy. Propagation is by division and cuttings. z7

T. pyrenaicum L. N. Spain, SW. France. Stems villous, slender, creeping, to 20cm long, 3–5cm high, branched, in a dense

Leaves cordate-ovate to oblong, fine crenate, somewhat rugose, petioles 1–2cm long. Flowers pale greenish-yellow, reddish at the base, in nearly one-sided, loose, long, false racemes; July to September. Attractive in the heather garden on lime-free, sandy soil, among pines, junipers and brooms (*Genista*). Cultivar 'Crispum' 20–30cm high, with distinctly crispate leaf margins. z6 (Sch. & M.)

T. tomentosum see **T. polium**

Thalia L.
Marantaceae

About 7 species native to warm and tropical America; tall, aquatic or marsh herbaceous perennials with clumpy, rhizomatous rootstock. Leaves all basal, large, more or less *Canna*-like. Flowers small, in a lax terminal, panicle on a tall, leafless scape. Flowers very irregular;

sepals 3, small, corolla 3-lobed, the segments unequal; and roacium of 5 stamens, partially fused basally, 1 anther and ½ of another anther with fertile pollen, leaving 3–½ staminoidea; ovary inferior, 1–3 celled, style partially joined to the base of the stamens, stigma usually 2-lobed, with appendage.

T. dealbata J. Fraser. USA; S. Carolina to Florida westward to S. Missouri and E. Texas. Plants white-powdery overall. Leaves to 1m, strongly erect, petiole round or somewhat grooved, blade to 50cm or longer, oblong-ovate to

colored and showy, pistils several; in panicles, racemes or corymbs. Plants may produce all staminate or all pistillate flowers, or bear 1-sexed flowers mixed with perfect flowers, or produce all perfect flowers; in spring and late summer. Most species are indigenous to the North Temperate Zones. The species from the mountains of S. America and tropical and S. Africa, as well as the S. Pacific Islands are less important in horticulture. The large species are charming flowering plants for open woodland plantings, or in sunny or semi-shaded beds together with other meadow-type

T. aquilegifolium L. E. and Central Europe, mountains of S. Europe, Siberia, Japan. Plants form stately clumps, 1m high and more, depending on location. The foliage is very similar to the common *Aquilegia*. The large inflorescences have a tufted, feathery appearance, lacking a corolla but with large, brightly colored stamens. Flowers purple-lilac to lilac-pink. May to July. Grows best in moderately acidic soil, in full sun or semi-shade. Plants are more susceptible to insect damage in shady or dry sites. Flowers of garden plants vary substantially in colors. Cultivars include:

Thalictrum dipterocarpum

Thalictrum flavum ssp. *glaucum*

lanceolate-elliptic, slightly asymmetric. Scape slender, wand-like, with a terminal inflorescence which is narrow, lax. Flowers small, pale blue to purplish-blue. Very handsome plant for the sunny marsh planting or for shallow quiet water. z6

Thalictrum L.
Ranunculaceae
Meadow Rue

This genus includes about 130 species. All are perennial herbs and most are winter hardy, except those of tropical and subtropical origin. Some are tall, elegant plants with ternate or decompound (many times compound) foliage. The leaflets usually are lobed or dentate. The flowers are usually small, greenish, yellow, pink, rose-lilac, violet or white, mostly with a reduced perianth, sepals 4–5, petals 0, stamens many, sometimes

plants. The smaller species are suitable for the alpine garden. Propagation is by seed and division. Very few of the considerable number of species and cultivars once grown in Victorian gardens remain in the trade today.

T. alpinum L. Alpine Meadow Rue. Circumpolar extending southward in Mts. of N. Asia, Europe, including Great Britain, and North America south to Rocky Mts. and California Sierras. Caespitose, 7–15cm high, somewhat stoloniferous. Leaves basal, ternate, with 3 pinnate or ternate leaflets, the segments 3–5 lobed or deep-toothed, thickened, glaucous beneath. Flowers in a few-flowered raceme, perfect, erect, then nodding, stamens purple, anthers yellow. A tidy little lacy cushion for the cool, sunny rock garden. z3

T. anemonoides see **Anemonella thalictroides**

'Album', white; 'Atropurpureum' with violet stamens, stems glaucous-violet; 'Aurantiacum', flowers orangeish; 'Roseum', lilac-rose; 'Thundercloud' and 'Purple Cloud' dark purple flowers. z5

T. chelidonii DC. E. Himalayas. Flower stems 50–90cm (–3m) high. Leaves ternate, recompounded; leaflets usually ovate to narrowly obovate, 7–13 lobed or toothed, glabrous, 0.5–3cm wide. Flowers large, about 2cm in diameter, few to many, in panicles. Sepals petaloid, mauve; August to September. Very attractive plants, similar to *T. delavayi* and often also confused with *T. reniforme*. Another similar species, *T. rochebrunnianum*, is somewhat more difficult to cultivate. z5

T. coreanum Lév. N. Asia. Stems to 20cm high. Leaves ternate, recompounded, leaflets broadly ovate, coarsely crenate, metallic green above, margins brownish, gray-green beneath. Flowers on wiry stems in few-flowered umbellate panicles, pale pink, sepals quickly abscising; May. For humus-rich soil pockets in the rock garden. z4

T. dasycarpum Fisch & Lall. Purple Meadow Rue. North America: S. Central Canada southward to Louisiana and Arizona. Plants usually dioecious, with a short, thick crown. Stems erect, to 2m tall, usually purple. Leaves decompound, lower petioled, upper sessile, leaflets firm, oblong, entire, fine-pubescent beneath. Inflorescence corymbose-paniculate, large and showy. Sepals 2.5mm long, equalling the stamens; flowers nodding, whitish tinged purple. Grows naturally in low, open woodlands in moist humusy soil, often below limestone cliffs; foliage remains green through dry weather long into fall. Regional varieties are described. z3

T. delavayi Franch. W. China. Stems slender, to 1.2m high. Leaves long-petioled, 2–3 ternate or pinnately decompound. Leaflets long-stalked, as long or longer than wide, usually 3-lobed. Inflorescence a loose, many-flowered panicle. Flowers perfect, mauve, lilac, or rarely white, 1.5–2.5cm across; July to August. The species is similar in appearance to *T. dipterocarpum,* but the flowers are larger, the fruits narrower and longer. Often erroneously listed as *T. dipterocarpum.*

Suitable for planting among well-spaced shrubs which provide protection for the stems carrying flowers high above the foliage. Includes cultivars 'Album' (1920) which requires more shelter, high shade, and water during dry periods and 'Hewitt's Double' with double flowers, lacking anthers; both usually listed under the following species. z5

T. dioicum L. Early Meadow Rue. North America: Quebec to North Dakota southward to Georgia and Missouri; in open woodlands, especially on north slopes. Stems to 90cm high. Leaves mostly basal, decompound, petioled; leaflets reniform to obovate, blunt or crenate-toothed. Flowers in early spring, insignificant. This rarely, easily grown herb is grown in shady wildflower gardens for its beautiful, pale foliage which holds up long into the fall. z4

T. dipterocarpum Franch. W. China. Stems slender, 60–150cm high. Similar to *T. delavayi* in appearance, and often confused with it in horticulture. Leaves 3-recompound, light green above, bluish beneath; leaflets nearly orbicular, 3-lobed or notched at the end. Panicles narrowly pyramidal; flowers about 12mm wide, rose-violet; July to August. Garden use as for the previous species, grows best in moist, slightly acid soil. Cultivars include 'Album', white flowered; 'Magnificum', panicle large, more open, flowers larger; 'Minus', plant semi-dwarf. z5

T. flavum L. Europe to Central Siberia and the Caucasus region. Rhizomes creeping. Stems to 1.2m high, usually unbranched, ridged. Leaves 2–3 pinnate; leaflets obovate-cuneate, 3–4 lobed.

Thelypteris decursivepinnata

Flowers in oblong panicles, sepals white, stamens yellow, fragrant; June to July. Plant in fairly moist soil in sunny site; any average garden soil is suitable. z5

T. flavum ssp. **glaucum** (Desf.) Batt. (*T. speciosissimum* L., *T. glaucum* Desf.). Spain, Portugal, NW. Africa. Stems to 1.5m high, striped, glaucous, orangeish, as are the leaves. Leaves 5-pinnate compound or 2-pinnate, blue-green. Flowers in large terminal panicles, sulfur yellow; July to August. Cultivar 'Illumination' is only 1.2m high with spheroid, lemon yellow panicles. z6

T. foetidum L. Europe. Somewhat creeping rootstock. Stems erect, to 50cm high, lightly glandular-pubescent, branched. Leaves 3–4 pinnate, scented glandular pubescent on both sides. Flowers in loose, branched panicles, yellow; June to August. Thrives in a drier, light soil in a sunny site. z6

T. glaucum see **T. flavum** ssp. **glaucum**

T. kiusianum Nakai. Japan. Roots stoloniferous, sometimes tuberous. Stems 10–15cm high. Leaves dark green, 1–2 ternate, leaflets small, toothed, purplish. Flowers lilac to purple, the species is like *T. aquilegifolium;* June to August. Charming miniature for loose humus soil in a shaded rock garden or trough garden. z6

T. minus L. Europe, N. and E. Asia, W. Asia, NW. Africa, Abyssinia, S. Africa. Caespitose to stoloniferous. Stems .3– 1.2m high, leafy, or leafless at the base, commonly flexuose. Leaves 3–4 pinnate, leaflets fern-like, rounded or cuneate to obovate, 3-toothed or 3-cleft, lobes with 1–3 segments. The very open panicles bear inconspicuous greenish-yellow flowers. Insignificant for cultivation in the garden. The form 'Adiantifolium' is more useful, to only 40cm high. The foliage resembles *Adiantum* fronds and is used for cutting. z6

T. orientale Boiss. S. Greece, S. Anatolia, N. Syria. Stems 10–20cm high, flexuous, often decumbent. Leaves 2-ternate, spaced on the stem, alternate; leaflets rounded or broadly ovate, 3-lobed, crenate. Flowers large, 7–26mm across, sepals petal-like, white, stamens erect. May to June. Dense-clump-forming species for a shady, humus rich site. z7

T. rochebrunianum Franch. & Sav. Japan. Plant glabrous overall. Leaves decompound, upper leaves 2-pinnate, leathery, leaflets obtuse, entire or terminal leaflets 3-lobed. Inflorescence an open panicle with scattered flowers. Flowers white to pink, to 12mm across, stamens very long. Often not true in cultivation. Plant in semi-shade to shade in cool, damp, humus rich soil. z6

T. speciosissimum see **T. flaxum** ssp. **glaucum** (Sch. & M.)

pinnatifid, fronds which often narrow toward the base. The sori are small, round, scattered or in close rows on the margins of the pinnae.

T. decursive-pinnata (van Hall) Ching (*Dryopteris d.-p.* Kunze, *Lastrea d.-p.* J. Sm., *Phegopteris d.-p.* (van Hall) Fee). Japan, Korea, China, Vietnam, Taiwan; on rocky slopes in mountain forests. Rhizomes short, slightly creeping, forming a multiple-stemmed plant. Fronds 1-pinnate to 2 pinnatifid, clustered, variable in height, stiffly erect, tips elegantly drooping, 20–60cm long, 6–

T. limbosperma (All.) H.P. Fuchs (*Dryopteris oreopteris* Maxon, *Oreopteris limbosperma* (All.) Holub, *T. oreopteris* Slosson). Europe; on moist to wet midrange mountain slopes, also at higher elevations in alpine forests, in clearings, on gravelly slopes and grassy sites, often together with *Blechnum spicant*. Rhizomes not creeping, fronds developing a funnelform clump, to 1m long, 20cm wide, narrowly lanceolate, with pinnae nearly to the base. Pinnae short, broadly triangular at the base, horizontal, upper pinnae elongate-triangular. Rachis yellowish-green,

Thelypteris limbosperma

Themeda triandra

Thamnocalamus Munro
Gramineae

A genus established by Munro in 1866 in a revision of the flowering *Sinarundinaria murielae*. Includes *T. spathiflorus T. falconeri* and more recently *T. aristatus*, all from Himalaya. Other species from S. China, such as *T. cuspidatus*, appear to be geographical variants of the species *T. spathaceus*. These species often are listed under *Arundinaria*. (S.)

T. spathaceus see **Sinarundinaria murielae**

Thelypteris Schmidel
Polypodiaceae
Beech Fern

Perhaps 500–800 species from all zones of the world with a few suitable for temperate zone gardens. Medium-sized ferns, quite variable in form, often with creeping rhizomes and 1–2 pinnate-

12cm wide, narrowly lanceolate, long-acuminate. Rachis winged, the wings continuing between the pinnae as triangular lobes, short, brown toward the base, yellow-green above, loosely covered with pointed, brown, chaffy scales. Pinnae elongate-deltoid, alternate, loosely arranged along the midrib. Fronds softly herbaceous, light green. An interesting fern for a somewhat protected site in combination with rhododendrons and large rocks or stumps. Propagate by division or spores. Spores ripen from July to September. z6

T. hexagonoptera (Michx.) Weatherby (*Dryopteris h.* C. Chr., *Phegopteris h.* Fee), American Beech Fern. E. USA in moist, humus-rich woodlands or dry high-humus soil. Rhizomes vigorously creeping, rachis slender, fronds to 40cm high and wide, irregularly triangular, bipinnate, with 6-sided wings on the rachis. Pinnae pale green, fragrant, fading creamy-white in fall. Garden use and propagation as for *T. phegopteris*, the European Beech Fern. z5

loosely covered with light brown, chaffy scales. Fronds pale green, apple-scented, turning pale yellow in fall. Sori in dense rows on the margin of the pinnae. Suitable for a moderately dry, acidic site with *Blechnum spicant*, *Calluna vulgaris*, *Erica tetralix*, *Andromeda polyfolia* and *Gentiana pneumonanthe*. Propagate by spores, ripening from August to September. z5

T. nevadensis (Bak.) C.V. Mort. (*Dryopteris nevadensis* (Bak.) Underw.; *D. oregana* C. Chv.) W. North America: British Columbia to Nevada and California. Sierra Water Fern. Fronds lanceolate, 45–90cm high; 10–15cm wide; 1-pinnate, pinnae wide below, narrowing abruptly to linear-lanceolate, deeply pinnatifid; lower pinnae wide-spaced, much smaller than those in the center of the frond.

T. noveboracensis (L.) Nieuwl. (*Dryopteris noveboracensis* (L.) A. Gray), New

York Fern. North America. In moist woodlands and swampy sites of Canada and the USA. Fronds to 60cm long, 18cm wide, pale green, 1-pinnate, pinnae deeply cleft. Similar to *T. palustris* in site preference and appearance. Also propagated like *T. palustris*. z4

T. oreopteris see **T. limbosperma**

T. palustris Schott (*Dryopteris thelypteris* (L.) A. Gray), Marsh Fern. Throughout the North Temperate Zone in peat bogs, open forests and maritime regions, often in 10–30cm deep water, but also on

(Michx.) Watt), Narrow Beech Fern. Deciduous woodlands, especially beech forests of the Northern Temperate Zone and is indigenous to the mountains of S. Europe. Rhizome slender, creeping, branched. Fronds 20–40cm long, nearly as wide, triangular, lanceolate in outline, becoming shorter from the base to the tip. 1-pinnate, pinnae deeply pinnatifid, terminal segment entire. Pinnules rounded, glandular-pubescent, dull green. Sori marginal, with no indusium. Requires lime-free soil. Both Beech Ferns (see also *T. hexagonoptera*) are suitable for underplanting Trhodo-

warm climate to produce flowers. Selections should be made from cooler climates for earlier-flowering specimens. Will not suffer winter damage if given sufficient moisture. This uncommon grass is a good choice for sunny terrace beds in combination with *Salvia azurea* or *Phygelius capensis*. Propagate by division in spring; pot up the divisions in a well-drained soil and keep warm. z6 (S.)

Thermopsis montana

Thlaspi rotundifolium

moist banks. Rhizome black, slender, creeping. Fronds alternate, erect, 0.3–1m high and 15cm wide, 1-pinnate, the pinnae deeply pinnatifid, oblong-lanceolate, conspicuously soft-herbaceous. Rachis green, glabrous, often the lower half without pinnae. Pinnae with small basal lobes; pinnae furl on the fertile fronds in summer thereby appearing much narrower. Like *T. palustris* and *T. noveboracensis*, suitable for shallow water and waterside plantings. Very attractive in combination with *Iris kaempferi*. Vigorous. Propagate by division and spores. Var. **pubescens** (G. Laws.) Nakai. Snuffbox Fern, Meadow Fern, N. North America. Plant more hairy, indusia without glandular hairs. z4

T. phegopteris (L.) Slosson (*Dryopteris ph.* C. Chr., *Gymnocarpium ph.* Newm., *Phegopteris vulgaris* Mett., *P. connectilis*

dendrons and other acid soil woody plants in semi-shade to deep full shade. May be overly vigorous and invasive. Propagate by division and spores. Spores ripen from July to August. z5 (D.)

Themeda Forssk.
Gramineae

T. triandra Forssk. var. **japonica** (Willd.) Makino. China, Japan. A charming, very leafy clump grass. Stems, 1m high, erect, inflorescence often branched, with several racemes. Leaves are densely hirsute, especially the leaf sheath and basal part of the leaf blade. Gradually turns red in summer, beginning at the base. Dried foliage retains the coppery-red color deep into winter. Outward-nodding panicles with many brightly colored bracts. This species needs a very

Thermopsis R. Br.
Leguminosae
False Lupine, Aaron's Rod, Bush Pea

About 20–30 species in N. America and NE. Asia with alternate, usually petioled, palmately compound, ternate leaves with leafy stipules. Inflorescence erect, terminal or axillary, loose racemes. Flowers papilionaceous with a rounded banner petal, equal in length to the wings and keel; stamens 10, separate. Fruit sessile, a slender flat, legume. Lupinelike perennials occasionally troublesome in the garden due to their spreading habit. Suitable for borders, but best naturalized in park settings with deep topsoil. Impartial to soil, but best in light, fertile loam. Propagation is best by seed under glass in moderately warm soil. Many species, such as the somewhat rhizomatous *T. fabacea*, are also increased by division, but seedlings develop better. Seedlings should be transplanted to the garden as soon as possible with a soil ball intact.

T. caroliniana Curt. Carolina Lupine. USA: North Carolina to Georgia; in the low mountains. Scarcely branched stems 0.8–1.5m high. Leaves petioled; leaflets ovate to blue-green, silky-pubescent beneath, 5–9cm long and 2.5cm wide. Racemes terminal, dense, to 25cm long, with yellow flowers. Pods straight, erect,

T. lupinoides Link. (*T. lanceolata* R. Br. ex Ait.f.) SE. Russia, temperate Asia, Alaska. Stems to 30cm high, with dense spikes of yellow flowers. Leaves nearly sessile, the lowermost and uppermost often simple; leaflets ovate-lanceolate, 3–4cm long, silvery-pubescent. Fruits recurved, to 5cm long. Flowers in June and July. z6

T. montana Nutt. USA: Washington to Montana, southward to Nevada and Colorado. Stems 30–90cm high, silky pubescent, with terminal spikes to 20cm long with yellow flowers. Leaves long-petioled, leaflets 4–9cm long, linear to

T. dubia Bunge. N. China, Amur region, locally naturalized in parts of Central and SE. Europe. Entire plant softly pubescent, with 1.5–3m long stems and 5–10cm long, broadly cordate-ovate, toothed leaves. Pistillate flowers solitary, staminate flowers in short racemes, golden-yellow. Fruits 4–5cm long and 2.5cm wide, oblong-rounded, with 10 shallow, longitudinal ribs, blackish green at first, later dark red. Blooms from June to July.

T. dubia is a reasonably winter hardy, climbing herb, which may become inva-

Thlaspi stylosum

Thymus × citriodorus

to 5cm long, densely villous. Flowers from late spring to summer. z6

T. fabacea (Pall.) DC. Kamchatka, Kurile. Stems to 1m high, similar to the above species, but with axillary flower spikes and 10–12cm long, straight pods. Leaves long-petioled. Leaflets to 7cm long, broadly elliptic to obovate. Flowers yellow. Blooms in June and July. z5

T. gracilis T.J. Howell. W. North America: British Columbia and Montana to California. Stems to 75cm high, glabrescent, purplish-green, more or less glaucous. Leaflets obovate to oblanceolate, to 5cm long. Inflorescence a 15cm long, loose, terminal raceme. Flowers yellow, pealike. Fruits villous, to 7cm long, spreading. z5

T. lanceolata see **T. lupinoides**

linear-lanceolate. Pods linear, straight, erect, 5cm and longer, pubescent. Blooms in May. z4 (E.)

Thladiantha Bunge
Cucurbitaceae

Seven to fifteen species of dioecious, tendril-climbing, yellow-flowered perennial herbs with tuberous roots; from E. Asia to Malaysia. Calyx campanulate, 5-lobed. Calyx tube covered at the base with a single, horizontal scale. Corolla deeply 5-parted, with a reflexed limb. Staminate flowers with 5 separate stamens. Pistillate flowers with 5 linear staminodes, pistil with oblong ovary, style deeply 3-cleft, stigmas reniform. Fruits fleshy, green or red, many-seeded.

sive. Used for covering south-facing walls, pergolas and all forms of lattice work, but also an impenetrable ground-cover. Male and female plants should be planted together to produce the decorative red fruits. Propagate by seed and tubers. A similar species, *T. oliveri*, is even more vigorous, stems longer, leaves larger, glabrous overall, but somewhat more tender; rarely in the trade. z5 (E.)

Thlaspi L.
Cruciferae
Penny Cress

About 60 species of annual or perennial herbs, most in N. temperate Eurasia, a few in N. and possibly S. America. Often with sessile stem leaves. A few are rosetted alpine plants with racemose inflorescences lacking bracts. Flowers white, pink or violet. Stamens distinct, without an appendage. Fruit a short silicle, laterally compressed, round or cordate, usually winged, many-seeded. The genus includes, in addition to common Field Pennycress (*T. arvense*), a number of low, carpet forming rosetted alpine plants for the rock garden, trough and alpine house. They are not easily cultivated and therefore are only recommended for experienced collectors. Plants require a loamy humus soil incorporating abundant gravel. Suitable for scree beds and rock crevices with even moisture in full sun. Need some protection from the midday sun by a nearby rock or dwarf shrub. Propagate by seed, which sets abundantly even in cultivation. Many species may be increased by careful division or cuttings, such as *T. alpinum*, *T. montanum* and *T. rotundifolium*. Grow seedling plants in containers. *T. stylosum* is certainly one of the most attractive species, suitable also for the alpine house. This species deteriorates after about two years, so young progeny should be kept in reserve. Good companions include many other small, lime-loving species such as *Arabis pumila*, *Cerastium alpinum* ssp. *lanatum*, *Linaria alpina*, *Papaver kerneri*, *Scutellaria alpina*, *Silene alpestris* and *Veronica fruticulosa*. Rock gardeners grow numerous species of *Thlaspi*; among the most familiar are the following:

T. alpinum Crantz. E. and Central Alps; on rocky slopes, on moist sites among Mugo Pines at alpine elevations to more than 3000m. Grows only on limestone, sometimes in wet screes. Small mats 5–10cm high, with stolon-like rhizomes. Basal leaves in a rosette, obovate to elliptic, long-petioled. Stem leaves oblong-lanceolate, stem-clasping, glabrous, somewhat leathery. Inflorescence hemispherical, later elongating. Flowers white, anthers yellow. Blooms in May and June. z5

T. bellidifolium Griseb. N. and E. Albania, and neighboring regions of Yugoslavia; on alpine balds. Dense, low mats; long-lived. Basal leaves in rosettes, oblong-spatulate, sparsely dentate. Petals dark purple to lilac; anthers yellow. Blooms in May. z6

T. montanum L. Mountains of Central Europe to France, N. Italy and S. Yugoslavia; on rock outcrops and screes, on shaded rocky slopes and open pine and oak forests on shallow, gravelly loam, humus-rich soils, especially over limestone. Dense to loose carpets, 10–15cm high, with runner-like, elongated branches from the main stem. Basal leaves in rosettes, rounded-ovate to spatulate, turning somewhat blue-green; stem leaves ovate, clasping, with rounded lobes. Inflorescences hemispherical at first, later elongated, with large, white flowers. Anthers pale yellow. Blooms from April to May. The most vigorous species for sun and semi-shade. z5

T. rotundifolium (L.) Gaud. European Alps; in moist screes of fine limestone at alpine elevations 1400–3400m. Stoloniferous. 5–10cm high with the main stem branched at ground level. Leaves in rosettes, thickish, bluish-green, somewhat crenate or dentate, basal leaves suborbicular to ovate, stem leaves elliptic. Flowers in floriferous, hemispherical, corymbose inflorescences, not elongating, or only slightly so, pale violet with darker venation. Blooms in May and June. Only for very experienced rock gardeners. Short-lived in lowland gardens, best grown in the alpine house or frame in pots with limestone gravel and very little soil. z5

T. stylosum (Ten.) Mutel. Central and S. Apennines; on moist screes and in rock crevices. Stems 2–3cm high, small carpet perennial. Rosettes with entire, spatulate leaves tapered to the petiole. Stem leaves 2–4, sessile. Petals rose to lilac, darker-veined. Anthers violet. Flowers very fragrant. Blooms in April and May. One of the most attractive species. z6 (E.)

Thymus L.
Labiatae
Thyme

Three hundred to 400 species of aromatic, perennial herbs or small subshrubs and shrubs from temperate Europe and Asia. Stems 4-angled, erect, flat-spreading or creeping, woody, at least at the base. Leaves opposite, small, entire. False whorls 1- to many-flowered, usually clustered into terminal heads or in spicate racemes. Calyx cylindrical or campanulate, usually 2-labiate. Upper lip 3-dentate, lower lip of 2 narrow teeth. Calyx tube straight; after flowering, throat becomes very hairy. Corolla 2-labiate, with a straight tube, the upper lip notched, lower lip 3-lobed, the middle lobe larger. Stamens 4, mostly exserted, straight, somewhat divaricate or the 2 inner ones paired.

A genus of many small species, cultivars and hybrids, difficult to distinguish. The nomenclature of many species in the trade is unreliable. *Flora Europaea* is an excellent work dealing with the technical classification of *Thymus* in more detail.

The mat, carpet, and cushion *Thymus* species are important garden plants suitable for the rock garden, heath planting, and wild gardens, where they bring color to the summer landscape, even on very dry sites. Good ground covers for small spring-flowering bulbs. *T. pseudolanuginosus* is recommended for dry stone walls. *T. vulgaris* is an old medicinal and culinary herb, attractive as a low edging hedge, especially in the herb or vegetable garden. As in nature, thymes thrive in full sun, in infertile, dry soil. Good companions include *Antennaria*, various *Campanula* species. *T. serpyllum* spreads easily by self-seeding. Propagation varies with species, from seed to division and cuttings.

1. Species with erect or ascending stems

T. × citriodorus (Pers.) Schreb. (*T. pulegioides × T. vulgaris*). A natural hybrid from S. France. Commonly planted in southern gardens. Lemon-scented shrublet 10–30cm high, erect, with glabrous or slightly pubescent, small, rhombic-ovate to lanceolate leaves, usually with revolute margins. Flowers in oblong heads, pale pink to lilac. Flowers in summer. 'Argenteus' and 'Silver Queen' with white-variegated leaves, 'Aureus' and 'Golden Dwarf' yellow-variegated. Suitable for edging, but unfortunately not reliably winter hardy in colder climates. Young plants should be maintained frost free for replacements. Propagate by cuttings or layering. z5

T. marschallianus see **T. pannonicus**

T. membranaceus Boiss. SE. Spain. Globose shrublet 10–20cm high, with very many outspread or ascending hairy stems; leaves linear to rhombic-lanceolate, to 2cm-long, ciliate on the base. Inflorescence nearly globose, with conspicuous, thin-membranous, whitish, 3 × 8mm bracts. Corolla about 15mm wide, white. Blooms in summer. Not winter hardy, but attractive for the alpine house. z7

T. montanus see **T. pulegioides**

T. pannonicus All. (*T. marschallianus* Willd.). E. Central and E. Europe, north to about 57 degrees latitude in Central Russia; in dry meadows, on sunny, dry hills and steppes. Stems 10–30cm high, erect or ascending, often branched, woody at the base. Leaves sessile, herbaceous, with indistinct veins. Inflorescence a short woolly-pubescent raceme. Calyx campanulate, with a ring of erect hairs, upper lip longer than the tube. Corolla pale pink to rose. Blooms in mid-to late summer. z4

T. pulegioides L. (*T. montanus* Waldst. et Kit.). Europe to the Caucasus Mts.; on dry, sterile sites along roads and woodland margins, around rocks on more or less neutral, sandy loam or gravelly soil, from the plains to the alpine

toward the apex. Calyx 4–6mm, corolla 6–10mm long, deep pink. Blooms in midsummer. Only marginally winter hardy, therefore cover with evergreen branches in an open garden; best cultivated in the alpine house or coldframe. z7

T. vulgaris L., Garden Thyme. W. Mediterranean region to S. Italy; among other herbaceous species on rocky slopes and meadows. A large, grayish-green subshrub or shrub, well-branched, 10–37cm high, very aromatic, with a stout taproot. Branches erect or

Flowering shoots 1–8cm high, erect. Leaves to 10 × 1mm, linear to linear-lanceolate, sessile, glabrous to velvety-pubescent, usually herbaceous. Margins more or less revolute, ciliate, at least on the basal half. Bracts occasionally purple. Corolla 5–7mm long, pink. July to August. A rare, attractive species for the rock garden. z6

T. doerfleri Ronn. NE. Albania. A dubious species, probably a form of *T. praecox* Opiz, but differing in the completely pubescent stems and leaves, densely covered with long and short

Thymus vulgaris

Thymus serpyllum

valleys. Quite a variable species. Loose to densely bushy, shrub or woody at the base. Flowering shoots 5–35cm, occasionally taller, sometimes branched, 4-angled, pubescent only on the ridges. Leaves 18 × 10mm, ovate or oblong-lanceolate, ciliate at the base, petioled, thin. Inflorescence an interrupted false spike, oblong. Corolla mauve-colored. Cultivars include 'Alba', white-flowered'; 'Coccineus' and 'Kermesianus', both rosy red-flowered. See also the groundcover species *T. serpyllum*. z5

T. villosus L. SW. Spain, S. Portugal. A variable species. Rounded bush 10–20cm tall, with ascending to erect branches, leaves clustered at the nodes. Stem leaves to 10 × 1mm, linear, sessile, margins reflexed, covered with long, white hairs. Inflorescence to 4cm long, subglobose to oblong-conical; bracts 20 × 10mm, greenish at the base, purplish

ascending, upper portion softly tomentose overall. Leaves to 8 × 2.5mm, linear to elliptic, short-petioled, undersides densely tomentose, the margins revolute. Flowers in crowded axillary cymes, in a spicate inflorescence. Corolla pale lilac to pink, occasionally nearly white. Blooms from May to October. Cultivated down through the ages, but first brought into N. Europe after 1100. A culinary and medicinal plant for the herb garden. Sow seed in early April under glass; plant into the garden in mid-May. z4

2. Creeping, ground cover species

T. alsinoides see **T. cherlerioides**

T. cherlerioides Vis. (*T. alsinoides* Form.). Mountains of the Central Balkan Peninsula, Crimea. A variable, carpeting species with long, creeping branches and leaves clustered at the nodes.

hairs. Blooms from May to June. Includes the form 'Bressingham Seedling' with pure pink flowers. Especially vigorous and persistent. z6

T. lanuginosus see **T. pseudolanuginosus**

T. praecox Opiz. Europe. Carpeting or tufted perennial, stems somewhat woody, creeping, slender, to 10cm high; leaves often clustered, especially below, nearly leathery, suborbicular to obovate. Bracts similar to the foliage, calyx campanulate, corolla purplish. See also *T. serpyllum*. z5

The species is seldom grown but is represented in gardens by two subspecies with a plethora of synonyms: Ssp. **arctus** (E. Durand) Jalas. Stems hairy on 2 sides only, leaves mostly obovate, to 6mm long, glandular-dotted; inflorescence subglobose, flowers rose-purple;

and ssp. **skorpilii** (Velen.) Jalas. Stems densely hairy on 4 sides, basal leaves on flowering stems sessile, corolla purplish. Cultivars with white and red flowers are listed for both of these.

T. pseudolanuginosus Ronn. (*T. lanuginosus* hort. non Mill.). Probably simply a form of another species, possibly *T. praecox* Opiz. Native habitat unknown. Dense, spreading carpet with long, creeping, procumbent stems. Leaves broadly elliptic, about 3mm long, both sides dense-gray-hairy. Flowers pale pink, but only rarely appearing, sporadical through the season, from May to July. The large, attractive gray mats are useful for the large rock garden or dry stone wall where plants will completely cover large stones. This evergreen species will freeze out, unfortunately, in cold, wet winters. Propagate by division. A good ground cover for small bulbs. The dwarf campanulas are attractive companions, especially *Campanula cochleariifolia*. z6(7)

T. serpyllum L. Europe, north from NE. France, N. Austria and N. Ukraine; in sandy, pine woodlands, on dry, usually lime-free soil. Quite a variable species. Plants have long, slender, creeping, sterile shoots, woody at the base, rooting at the nodes. Flowering shoots seldom over 10cm high, uniformly pubescent. Leaves nearly sessile, small, linear to linear-elliptic, ciliate at the base. Flowers mostly in head-like false spikes. Calyx 3–5mm long, campanulate, upper teeth as long as wide, usually ciliate. Corolla purple-red. 'Albus' is white, 'Coccineus' is crimson. Flowers from May to October. Probabaly cultivated before 1500 as a medicinal plant. Propagate desirable selections by division. Plants listed in the trade under this name often are other species, such as the lime-loving *T. praecox* or *T. pulegioides* L. z5 (E.)

Tiarella L.
Saxifragaceae
Foamflower, False Mitewort

About 7 species in E. Asia and N. America. Rhizomatous herbs. Leaves with scattered bristly hairs, usually basal, more or less ovate-cordate, rarely ovate, palmately lobed or parted, long-petioled. Flowers small, white or reddish, in simple racemes or branched racemes, with few-flowered clusters. Calyx 5-lobed, more or less petaloid, calyx tube very short, petals 5, entire, wide at the base. Stamens 10, ovary with 2 unequal beak-like projections. An excellent, floriferous small perennial for the shade; mostly in a loose humus soil. Propagate by division and seed.

T. californica Rydb. California. Similar to *T. unifoliata*, 30cm high, white. Outside its native range, almost unknown in horticulture. z7

T. cordifolia L. Foam Flower. N. America; Nova Scotia, Ontario, south through the Appalachian Mts. to Georgia and Alabama. Stem rhizomatous, more or less stoloniferous; glowing stem to 30cm high, with racemes of

Tiarella cordifolia

white, rarely reddish, flowers above the foliage. Leaves bright green, glossy, broadly ovate-cordate, 5-lobed, margin serrate, April to May. Plant in a shaded site in moist, humus-rich soil. The most common species in gardens. Cultivars include 'Lilacina', flowers pale lilac; 'Major', flowers salmon-rose to wine-red; 'Marmorata', leaves bronze-gold turning very dark green, purple-mottled, flowers reddish; 'Purpurea', foliage purple-tinged, petioles maroon, flowers purple-red. z4

T. laciniata Hook. N. America: S. Alaska to Oregon. A rare species. Rhizomes slender, creeping. Leaves completely divided; 3 leaflets deeply cleft into irregularly toothed segments. Inflorescence a slender, loose panicle with white flowers. z6

T. parviflora see **Lithopragma parviflora**

T. polyphylla D. Don. E. Asia, China, Himalaya Mts. Plants freely stoloniferous. Leaves suborbicular-cordate, 3-lobed, toothed; petiole hairy. Flowering stem 30–45cm high with a simple raceme of small white or reddish flowers. Petals thread-like, sometimes lacking. z5

T. trifoliata L. W. North America: Alaska to Oregon, eastward in mountains to Rocky Mts. Leaves divided into 3 leaflets, the middle segment is 3-lobed, both the outer segments 2-lobed, all coarsely toothed. Flowering stems 15 to rarely 40cm high; inflorescence narrow, loose, with minute white flowers. Petals white, thread-like; stamens of differing length. May. z6

Tofieldia calyculata

T. unifoliata Hook. Sugar-scoop. S. Alaska southward to W. Montana and Central California. Flowering stems 20–30cm high, similar to *T. laciniata*, but not stoloniferous. Leaves cordate to subdeltoid, palmately 3–5 shallow-lobed, with scattered hairs, crenate, dentate. New foliage brownish, later olive-green. Panicles loose, flowers white; May. z5

T. wherryi Lakela. USA: Virginia and Tennessee, to Georgia, Alabama, and Mississippi. To 35cm high, without stolons. Leaves ovate-cordate, 3 to rarely 9 shallow-lobed, emerald green, sometimes brown-spotted at the base, reddish in fall. Stem 15–35cm high, inflorescence a simple, dense raceme. Flowers white, pink-blushed, fragrant; May to June. Very showy in flower, moderately so in autumn when the foliage colors. z5 (Me. & Kö.)

Tithymalopsis

T. corollata see **Euphorbia corollata**

Tofieldia Huds.
Liliaceae
False Asphodel

Twenty or fewer species of herbaceous perennials from North America, South America, Europe and Asia, in wet, acidic soil, with tufted grassy foliage from a knotted, rhizomatous rootstock. Leaves sessile, basal, narrowly linear, 2-ranked. Flowers in terminal racemes, small, greenish-white, yellowish or brown. Perianth of 6 separate segments in 2 whorls, 6 stamens, anthers attached

perianth dark brown.

T. glutinosa (Michx.) Pers. North America: Newfoundland to Minnesota, Maine, Ohio, Michigan and S. Alleghany Mts. Basal leaves tufted, erect, to 20cm high; stem leaves to 5cm long, few. Stems to 50cm high with many blackish-brown glands; inflorescence a slender raceme, flowers short-pediceled, usually in 3's, rarely 1–4, white. And var. **montana** (C. L. Hitchk.) R. S. Davis. Mts. Idaho, Montana, Wyoming and adjacent Canada, scapes with short, sticky hairs, pedicels shorter, seeds lighter in color.

superior. Grow like *Tiarella*. Also suitable as a houseplant for a cool room. Propagate by gemmaceous plantlets, which root easily. Well-established mother plants usually produce many young. A collector's plant for botanical collections.

T. menziesii (Pursh) Torr. et A. Gray. Pickaback Plant, Piggyback Plant. N. America: British Columbia to N. California. Flower stems to 30–60cm high; rootstock creeping. Leaves long-petioled, rounded to cordate, with irregularly biserrate lobes, hairy. Often with

Tolmiea menziesii

Townsendia grandiflora

basally, ovary 3-angled, styles 3. For the alpine garden; relatively easy to cultivate in a peaty bog soil with constant moisture. Propagate by division and seed.

T. alpina see **T. pusilla**

T. borealis see **T. pusilla**

T. calyculata (L.) Wahlenb. Pyrenees Mts., Alps, Carpathian Mts. in peaty meadows. Flowering stem 10–25cm high with 2–3 small leaves. Basal leaves 5–15cm high, 3–7mm wide, several-nerved. Stems erect, usually somewhat flexuose; flowers crowded in a terminal raceme, greenish-yellow, large. June to August. z5

T. coccinea Richardson. Japan. Basal leaves tufted, to 5cm long, margins scarious; stem leaves 1–2, to 3cm long. Scapose stem to 14cm high; flowers several, white to brownish, nodding. And var. **fusca** (Miyale & Kudo) Hara.,

T. palustris see **T. pusilla**

T. pusilla (Michx.) Pers. (*T. borealis* (Wahlenb.) Wahlenb., *T. alpina* Hoppe et Sternb., *T. palustris* Huds.p.p.). Europe: Alps and Arctic, usually in high-alpine sites over an igneous substrate. Stems 5–10cm high, leaves 3-nerved. Flowers without a subtending bract, whitish. July to August. z1 (D.)

Tolmiea Torr. et A. Gray
Saxifragaceae

A single species in the moist coastal forests of Pacific Northwest. Rhizome well developed; leaves long-petioled with large stipules, blades cordate, shallow-lobed, palmate-veined. Closely related to *Heuchera*, differing in the leafier stems, looser, one-sided racemes with slender, reflexed petals. Calyx tube cylindrical, free from the ovary, deep cleft on one side, with 3 large and 2 small lobes. Petals usually 4; stamens 3; ovary

adventitious buds and well-developed plantlets on the basal leaves. Inflorescence a 15–25cm long raceme; flowers small, purplish to greenish. Not especially ornamental; more of a curiosity. May to June. z6 (Me.)

Tommasinia

T. altissima see **Peucedanum verticillare**

Tonestus

T. lyallii see **Haplopappus lyallii**

Tormentilla

T. erecta see **Potentilla erecta**

Townsendia Hook.
Compositae

About 20 annual, biennial or perennial herbaceous species from Canada to Mexico. Longer-lived species have thickened, deep-growing taproots. Low plants with rosetted, alternate, linear or spathulate, entire, glabrous to long-haired leaves and large, radiate, daisy-like flower heads, pediceled or sessile, white, rose to violet. Flowers from late spring to early summer. Grow in very well-drained, gravelly soil in full sun, in

Townsendia rothrockii

rock crevices or screes. Foliage must be kept dry in winter. Suitable for the rock garden, troughs or the alpine house. Usually not long-lived in cultivation. Propagate by seed, often self-seeds under favorable conditions.

T. exscapa (Richards.) Porter. Easter Daisy. (*T. sericea* Hook., *T. wilcoxiana* A. Wood non hort.). Canada to Mexico. Leaves linear-spatulate, 2.5–7cm long, gray, with distinctly appressed pubescence. Buds form early, noticeable even in fall. Flower heads sessile or nearly so, to 5cm across, white to pinkish. A most attractive species. z4

T. florifera (Hook.) A. Gray. USA: Washington to Utah. Winter annual or biennial. Leaves spatulate, pubescent. Flowering stems to 10cm high. Flower heads to 4cm wide, lavender-blue to pink. z4

T. grandiflora Nutt. W. USA: South

Dakota to New Mexico. Mostly biennial. Leaves spatulate to oblanceolate, to 5cm long, grayish-appressed, stiff hairs. Flowering stems 5–7.5cm high, few, slender, branched, spreading. Flower heads subtended by leaves, to 6cm wide, white, rays often rose-striped below. z4

T. hookeri Beaman. Easter Daisy. W. North America: Alberta and Sasketchewan southward to Utah and Arizona. Compact, caespitose perennial. Leaves linear to narrow oblanceolate, to 5cm long, silky-strigose. Stems 5–7.5cm high, branched, thick, woody. Flower heads sessile or short-pediceled, about 2.5cm across, white, pinkish beneath. z4(3)

T. parryi D.C. Eaton. W. North America: Alberta south to Idaho and Wyoming. Biennial or rarely perennial if dry in summer. Basal leaves in rosettes, spatulate, 4–10cm long, glabrous to strigose. Stems 1 or few, to 30cm high, rarely higher, scapose, upright. Flower heads sessile or short-pediceled, to 6.5cm across, rays violet-blue.

T. rothrockii A. Gray ex Rothrock (*T. wilcoxiana* hort.). USA: Colorado. Leaves in rosettes, narrowly spatulate to oblanceolate, to 4cm long, thick, glabrous. Flowering stems 5–7.5cm high, becoming woody. Flower heads short-pediceled or sessile, to 4cm across, disc yellow, violet ray flowers violet-blue. Involucre ciliate, red-tipped. Attractive, well-known species. z4

T. sericea see **T. exscapa**

T. wilcoxiana see **T. exscapa**, **T. rothrockii** (K.)

Trachelium L.
Campanulaceae
Throatwort

Seven to 10 species of perennials or subshrubs in the Mediterranean region including the Balkan Peninsula. Flowers in corymbose clusters, occasionally solitary and axillary. Calyx with 5 lobes. Corolla narrowly tubular, limb salverform with 5 short lobes, small. Stamens separate, slender, glabrous. Styles glabrous or nearly so, exserted from the corolla, thickened just below the stigma. Capsule opening with 2 or 3 pores at the base. The Greek species, *T. asperuloides* Boiss, is only 2–3cm high, a small, tender cushion plant suitable primarily for the alpine house, quite rare. *T. caeruleum* L. is a tender greenhouse plant often grown as an annual.

T. jacquinii (Sieber) Boiss. ssp. **rumelianum** (Hampe) Tutin (*T. rumelianum* Hampe, *Diosphaera rumeliana* Hampe) Bornm.). SE. Europe: Mts. of Bulgaria and Greece; in rock crevices. Stems sprawling 15–30cm high, glabrous or short-haired. Leaves oblong to ovate, to 2.5cm long, acute, somewhat serrate, the basal leaves short-petioled, the others sessile. Flowers in dense, terminal corymbs. Corolla violet or pale blue; tube about 5mm long. Flowers from July to September.

A valuable, late-flowering, small peren-

Trachelium jacquinii ssp. *rumelianum*

nial for the rock or trough garden, but thrives only in calcareous soils. Suitable for a sunny or semi-shaded site, or narrow rock crevice from which the slender shoots can hang, similarly suited for the edge of trough plantings. Propagate by seed and cuttings in May and June. Cuttings root well with botton heat. Good companion plants include *Achillea umbellata*, *Artemisia nitida*, *A. schmidtiana* 'Nana', small *Campanula* species, *Chrysanthemum haradjanii*. z6 (E.)

T. rumelianum see **T. jacquinii** ssp. **rumelianum**

Trachomitum Woods.
Apocynaceae

T. venetum (L.) Woods. (*Apocynum venetum* L.). Europe to China. Stems branched, to 1m high. Rootstock a creeping, underground rhizome. Leaves broadly lanceolate, short-petioled, somewhat cartilaginous on the margin. Flowers pale purple, small, fine-tomentose, pleasantly scented; July to August. May occasionally become invasive. A poisonous plant. z5 (C.J.)

Trachystemon D. Don
Boraginaceae

Two species from Asia Minor are known, only one in cultivation. Erect, medium-high, rough-hairy plants. Flowers in loose cymes, peduncled; calyx 5-cleft, corolla tube short, with 5 scales in the throat. Lobes spreading, linear, much longer than the tube, stamens 5, long-exserted. Nutlets hollowed at the base and encircled by a ring. Suitable for shady, not too dry woodland sites. Propagate by seed and division.

T. orientalis (L.) G. Don (*Psilostemon orientalis* DC.). Rhizome fleshy, cylindrical, with stolons. Stems rough-hairy, 0.4–1.2m high. Lower leaves 30cm long, 20cm wide, strigose-hairy, long-petioled, cordate, acuminate; upper leaves ovate-lanceolate, narrow at the base. Flowers on long peduncles in many-flowered cymes, purple-violet to sky blue; May to June. z6 (Sch.)

Tradescantia L.
Commelinaceae
Spiderwort

Between 30 and 100 species from North and South America, depending on the interpretation. Erect or procumbent perennials. Inflorescence terminal or terminal and axillary, often with paired leaflike or spathlike (single, below axillary flowers) bracts. Flowers with separate sepals and petals, and 6 fertile stamens with sterile hairs on the filaments, ovary 3-celled. The individual flowers are usually open only through the morning. Blooms late spring through summer. Some of the tender species are cultivated under glass. Trouble-free and long-flowering perennials for bed planting, in combination with reedlike grasses and other perennials with grasslike leaves, such as *Iris siberica* and *Hemerocallis*. Also useful for elevated waterside sites where plants will naturalize by seed. Propagate by division and cuttings. Seedlings often bear flowers of variable color.

T. × andersoniana Garden Spiderwort. The floriferous cultivars nearly always fall into the hybrid complex: *T. ohiensis* × *T. subaspera* × *T. virginiana*. Progeny carry many of the traits of the parents. Plants tufted, stems upright, mostly 40–60cm high. Inflorescences terminal, flowers to 2.5cm across, brightly colored cyanic hues, pink, rose, lavender, blue and purple, also white. Very conspicuous for the long flowering period, spring to fall, and the green foliage, lasting late into fall, unlike typical *T. virginiana*. The plants should be cut back, or at least the inflorescences removed after the first flush of bloom, both to discourage unwanted seedling production and to

Tradescantia × *andersoniana* hybrid 'I.C. Weguelin'

encourage reblooming. The newer cultivars are much more floriferous than their predecessors. The following standard cultivars are only a moderate list of the many available:

'Alba Major', 50cm, white, early; 'Gisela', 50cm, white; midseason; 'I.C. Wegülin', 50cm, sky blue, late; 'Innocence', 30–60cm, pure white, midseason; 'Isis', 50cm, large white, mid- to late flowering; 'Karminglut' ('Carmine Embers'), 40cm, carmine-red, middle-late; 'Osprey', 50cm, white with blue stamen filaments, early; 'Purewell Giant', 30–45cm, purplish-rose, midseason; 'Purple Dome', 45cm, large, rosy-purple, midseason; 'Zwanenburg Blue', 50cm, large-flowered, dark blue. Some noteworthy new forms are: 'Eva', white; 'Karin', red; 'Marianne', violet. z5

T. bracteata Small. Central USA: Michigan to Montana southward to Indiana and Kansas; on prairies and open meadows. Small, clump-forming

perennial, stems rarely exceeding 30cm, mostly about 12cm high. Leaves (and stem) glabrous to sparsely hairy, leaves slender, channeled, grass-like. Flowers mostly bright rose to purple, less frequently blue, lavender, violet or white. Blooms May to July, and plants go completely dormant once seeds mature. z4

T. canaliculata see **T. ohiensis**

T. ernestiana Anderson & Woodson. Central USA: SW. Missouri, NW. Arkansas, NE. Oklahoma; in open

Tradescantia × *andersoniana* hybrid 'Karminglut'

woodlands in fertile, damp soil. Stems 10–45cm high; blades of upper leaves much broader than their sheaths; sepals and pedicels without glandular hairs; stems and foliage glossy, bright green. Flowers very large, to 3.3cm across, petal margins somewhat to very ruffled. Flowers dark blue, purple shades, or rose-red. See also *T. ozarkana*. z6

T. longipes Anderson & Woodson. Wild Crocus. S. Central USA: S. Missouri; on acid, stony (sandstone, chert, granitic) soil, limited to the Ozarks uplands. Plant a tuft with lax, decumbent foliage, hairy overall except the petals. Leaves to 15cm long, very slender, apparently all basal. Stems several, very short, less than 1cm high at flowering, with several to many flowers at once, giving the effect of a Victorian nosegay, flat on the ground. Flower colors very deep purple, deep rose, rarely pink or pinkish, April-May. See also *T. tharpii*. z6(5)

T. ohiensis Raf. (*T. canaliculata* Raf., *T. reflexa* Raf.). USA: Massachusetts to Minnesota and Nebraska, southward to Florida and Texas. Stems to 65cm high, glabrous, very glaucous, blue-green. Leaf blade linear to elongate-lanceolate. Sepals glabrous or pubescent only at the tips; flowers blue to rarely pink or white; April to June. z5(4)

T. ozarkana Anderson & Woodson. Central USA: SW. Missouri, NW. Arkansas, NE. Oklahoma; in low, open woodlands with fertile, moist soil. Stems 10–45cm high with terminal flower

elliptic to elongate lanceolate, tapered to the sheathing base. Flowers pale to dark blue, occasionally white; June to July. Hybridizes readily in nature and in the garden. z5

T. tharpii Anderson & Woodson. S. Central USA: SW. Missouri and S. Kansas to Oklahoma and Texas; on rocky prairies and along railroads in fertile soil. Plant very hairy throughout except petals. Leaves narrowly elliptic-lanceolate; basal leaves more grass-like. Stems at flowering time very short, 1–2cm high, with terminal clusters of very many

progeny of shade garden hybrids with very large flowers with ruffled petals; and the flat-growing species *T. longipes* and *T. tharpii* should be used much more widely.

Trapa L.
Trapaceae (formerly Onagraceae)
Water Chestnut

Three or 4 species of floating, annual aquatic plants with nearly rhombic

Trapa natans, Eichornia crassipes, Myriophyllum aquaticum

Trichosanthes japonica

clusters. Leaves basal and cauline; leaf blades glabrous, glaucous, silvery or gray-green, 1.5–5cm wide, broadest high on the stem. Flowers very large, to 3.3cm across, petals with ruffled margins. Flowers in light shadow, pink, lavender blue or white, often beautifully tinged. Scarcely in cultivation; most native colonies destroyed by White River impoundments. Hybridizes with *T. ernestiana* which shares its habitat, and other nearby species. z6(5)

T. pilosa see **T. subaspera**

T. reflexa see **T. ohiensis**

T. subaspera Ker-Gawl. (*T. pilosa* Lehm.). E. USA, in open woodlands on limestone soils. Stems to 80cm high, not glaucous, somewhat hairy, zig-zag and flexuose toward the apex. Leaf blade

flowers. Flowers to 1.7cm across, deep rose to purple and purplish-blue. Much like *T. longipes* at flowering time (habitat differs, leaves somewhat wider, more erect), but as flowers fade stems elongate to 10–15cm high. April-May. z6(5)

T. virginiana L. (*T. virginica* L.). E. North America. Stems to 90cm high. Leaf blade linear to lanceolate, to 30cm long, 2.5cm wide. Stems and leaves very glaucous. Sepals more or less inflated, uniformly pubescent, never glandular. Flowers bright blue to violet-blue, rarely rose or white; April to May. Plant turns yellow and dies back after blooming. A shorter cultivar is 'Brevicaulis'. z6 (Sch. & M.)

T. virginica see **T. virginiana**

Plant breeders would do well to use *T. ernestiana* and *T. ozarkana* to achieve a

surface leaves forming dense rosettes, coarsely sinuate-serrate at the outer edge; submerged leaves opposite, pinnate-compound, the segments thread-like, resembling roots. Petioles long, somewhat inflated, with air-filled spongy tissue serving to keep the rosettes afloat. Flowers solitary, axillary, peduncled, small and inconspicuous, white, June to August. Fruits single-seeded, bilocular, but one of the seeds is aborted. The fruit is nut-like, with 2–4 horns. Fruits are edible and taste somewhat like Sweet Chestnuts. Commonly eaten in E. Asia. Plants die in fall. The fruits anchor themselves in the muddy bottom of standing water, then give rise to a thread-like stem in spring, eventually with 4 feather-like underwater leaves resembling roots. The first floating leaves are formed when the stems reach the water's surface. Europe, India,

E. Asia. For sunny pools and small streams with 30–60cm deep water. Particularly attractive for its intense red fall color. Propagate by seed, self-seeds under favorable conditions. Seeds will not germinate if allowed to dry out even briefly. One species is in Western cultivation:

T. natans L., Water Chestnut. Warmer parts of Central Europe to the Orient. Evidence of plants has been dated back to the Tertiary Period, which spread northward to Sweden in the Ice Age. Indigenous stands are found locally

Tricyrtis hirta

throughout its wide range. Cultivated in warm sites. Very attractive in water gardens with yellow and coppery water lilies, *Sagittaria* and *Butomus*. Fruits brown with 4 small horns. The 2-horned species from India (*T. bispinosa* Roxb.) and China (*T. bicornis* L.) are unsuitable for cool climates. z7 (D.)

Trichophorum

T. caespitosum see **Eleocharis caespitosa**

Trichosanthes L.
Cucurbitaceae

Forty or more species of tendriled, climbing, annual and perennial herbs in SE. Asia, Polynesia and N. Australia. Flowers axillary, white, corolla deeply 5-cleft, rotate, the lobes long-fringed; staminate flowers racemose with 3 stamens; pistillate flowers solitary with an inferior ovary, the stigma 3–6 lobed. Fruit a large, elliptical to elongate or globose, pepo, gourd-like, often bright-colored and ornamental. None are truly frost hardy.

T. japonica see **T. kirilowii** var. **japonica**

T. kirilowii Maxim. Indigenous to the warmer regions of E. Asia.

T. kirilowii var. *japonica* (Miq.) Kitamura (*T. japonica* Regel). Japan, Riukiu Island. Roots thickened, tuberlike. Herbaceous tendriled stems to 5m long, brown-pubescent when young, dying back in winter. Leaves suborbicular, 3–5 lobed, lobes shallow, short, soft-haired above, crenate-toothed. Staminate flowers in few-flowered racemes, pistillate flowers

solitary. Corolla white, lobes deeply incised and fimbriate. Fruits ovate-rounded, somewhat attenuate at both ends, smooth, yellow, 8–10cm long and nearly as wide. Blooms from July to August. The flowers open in the evening and remain open until about midday in overcast weather.

T. kirilowii var. *japonica* is a climbing plant for covering a warm, sunny wall or lattice, but requires a deep winter mulch of dry leafmold. Plants are, however, rarely offered in the trade and are recommended only for collectors and botanic

Tricyrtis macrantha

gardens, particularly for their attractive flowers. Often freezes out despite winter protection in snowless winters; therefore replacement plants are advisable, grown from cuttings taken in late summer. Overwinter these in a bright, cool greenhouse and plant them out in early May. The mother plant may be lifted in fall, keeping the soil ball intact, to overwinter dry and frost free. Grows best in a rich, fertile, loamy soil. z8(7) (E.)

Tricyrtis Wall.
Liliaceae
Toad-lily

Eighteen species from the Himalaya Mtn. region to Japan, Korea, Taiwan. Rhizomes slender, short, creeping. Stems 0.2–1m, erect or nodding. Leaves alternate, distichous, usually stem-clasping. The species can be arranged into 3 groups according to flower form: **(C)** flowers radiate, starry, in terminal corymbs and in the apical leaf axils; **(F)** flowers radiate, starry, in fascicles of 2–3 in the leaf axils and **(G)** flowers campanulate, 1–2 in the leaf axils.

Various species bloom from June to October, each for 2–4 weeks. Most grow best in acidic, peaty, shaded woodland soil with a topdressing of leafmold or pine needle mulch. Transplant in spring. Generally hardy, but will benefit from a dry leafy mulch where winters are cold and snowless, especially *T. stolonifera*. Interesting collectors' plants, but also grown for cut flowers. Some prized for their late flowering period. Propagate by seed or division. These plants just now are coming onto the Western market; considerable confusion exits regarding species identification and nomenclature.

T. affinis Makino **(F)**. Japan. Stems 30–60cm, flexuous. Leaves oblong-ovate to oblanceolate, 14cm long, 2cm wide, pubescent or glabrous. Flowers axillary, white with lilac spots, petals radiate. Probably the very beautiful cultivar. 'Miyazaki' belongs here. September. z6

T. bakeri see **T. latifolia**

T. flava Maxim. **(F)**. (*T. formosana* var. *stolonifera* (Matsum.) Masam.; *T. stolonifera* Matsam.) Japan. 30–50cm. Leaves oblanceolate to broadly elliptic, 7–15cm long, lowermost leaves longer. Flowers yellow with purple or brownish spots. September to October. Sometimes leaves conspicuously brown-spotted. z6

T. formosana Bak. **(C)**. Taiwan. Stems 30–60cm high, flexuous. Leaves oblanceolate, glossy, base unevenly clasping, to 12cm long. Inflorescence a loose terminal cyme; flowers many, white to pinkish spotted and blotched purple, to 2.5cm across. Sepals short-spurred. This species apparently is variable and plants are marketed under several names, including *T. stolonifera*; none are reliably hardy north of z7, requiring deep winter mulch. *T. f.* 'Amethystina', erect, 60–90cm high stems; flowers terminal, petals white, blue, red-tinged at the tips, and red-spotted; July-October; var. **glandulosa** (Simizu) Lin et Ying, shorter than 30cm.

T. formosana var. **stolonifera** see **T. flava**

T. hirta (Thunb.) Hook. **(F)**. Japanese Toad-Lily. Japan. 40–80cm. Leaves glabrous, very white-hairy, oblong to ovate, to 15cm long, clasping. Flowers axillary and terminal, solitary or clustered; petals radiate, white spotted purple, with very distinct markings, or pure white in cultivation 'Alba'. September to October. z5

T. ishiana see **T. macranthopsis**

T. latifolia Maxim. (*T. bakeri* Koidz., *T. macropoda* Bak. non Miq.) **(C)**. China and Japan. Stems stiffly erect, 40–80cm. Leaves oblong below, most broadly ovate, abruptly acuminate, glabrous, light green. Flowers few in branching terminal cymes, yellow with brown spots. June. The earliest species to flower. z5

T. macropoda see **T. latifolia**

T. macrantha Maxim. **(G)**. Japan: Shikoku. Stems 40–80cm long, with coarse brown hairs. Leaves ovate-oblong to ovate-lanceolate, to 10cm long, not stem-clasping, both basal lobes on the upper side of the stem. Flowers distinctly pendulous, long-peduncled, campanulate, 3–4cm long, deep primrose yellow, red-brown spotted inside. September to October. z6

T. macranthopsis Masum. (including *T. ishiana* (Kitag. et T. Koyama) Ohwi et Okuyama) **(G)**. Japan: Honshu. Similar to *T. macrantha*, but the leaves are stem-clasping. z6

T. macropoda Miq. **(C)**. Japan and China. Stems 40–70cm. Leaves oblong to ovate, to 12cm long, not stem-clasping. Flowers axillary and terminal, white, spotted purple, petals drooping downward. See also *T. latifolia*. September. z5

T. maculata (D. Don) J.F. McBride (*T. pilosa* Wall.) **(C)**. Himalaya Mtn. region to N. China. Stems hairy, 50–75cm. Leaves oblong, stem-clasping. Flowers in a loose, terminal corymb, greenish-white, yellowish-white or yellow with red-brown spots. Was much cultivated in the 19th century. Plants grown today as *T. pilosa* (note synonymy above) are almost certainly hybrids of *T. hirta* × *T. formosana*. Flowers violet with purple spots. Plants conspicuous for their pollenless anthers and empty fruit capsules. z5

T. nana Yatabe **(F)**. Japan. Similar to *T. flava*, but only 5–15cm high. z6

T. ohsumiensis Masam. **(F)**. Japan. Similar to *T. flava*, but the flowers are larger and pale yellow. August to September. z6

T. perfoliata Masam. **(F)**. Japan: Kiushu. Similar to *T. macrantha*. Leaves thickened, hard. Flowers pendulous, yellow with light purple spots. October. z6

T. pilosa see **T. maculata**

T. puberula Nakai et Kitagawa **(C)**. N. China. Similar to *T. latifolia*, but with more pubescent leaves. June. Early-flowering, floriferous. z5

T. stolonifera see **T. formosana**

Trientalis L., Primulaceae Starflower

Four species of small perennials in the North Temperate Zone. Rhizomes creeping, with erect stems; few small to scale-like, alternate stem leaves and 5–7 larger, terminal, whorled leaves, obovate-elliptic to lanceolate, entire. Flowers solitary or 2–3, subterminal; long, slender peduncled, calyx 5–9 parted, persistent; corolla rotate with short tube and 5–9 elliptic lanceolate lobes, stamens 5–9. These charming small plants will cover large areas under open conifer stands where summers are not hot and dry. Plants require an acidic, sandy, humus-rich soil, conditioned with conifer needles, in semi-shade. Star-flowers will not tolerate an alkaline soil. Propagation is difficult, best done by division, but also possible by seed in a very acidic medium. Seeds require light for germination and therefore should be only lightly covered with soil, if at all. It takes several years from seed to flowering plants.

T. americana see **T. borealis**

T. arctica Fisch. & Hook. E. Siberia and North America, Aleutian Isls. to Oregon. Stems to 20cm high. Leaves mostly in terminal whorl but also cauline, oblanceolate to ovate, obtuse, to 3.75cm long. Flowers white, rarely pink, to 2cm across. A cold rainforest plant. z5(7), cool, wet summers only.

T. borealis Raf. (*T. americana* Pursh.) Starflower. North America: Labrador to Virginia and Illinois. Stems to 23cm high. Terminal whorl of 5–10 leaves, lanceolate, to 10cm long, acuminate; stem leaves scale-like or absent. Flowers white, 12cm across, on thread-like peduncles to 5cm long. z4

T. europaea L. N. and Central Europe, very common in the Scandinavian countries, N. Asia; in birch, fir and pine forests on hummocks in a moist, acidic, fertile, sandy loam or bog soil. Stems 5–25cm high, with white, underground, very slender rhizomes with swollen ends. Stems usually unbranched. Uppermost leaves whorled, larger than the lower leaves, obovate to lanceolate, tapered to a long petiole. Flowers long-peduncled, solitary or paired in the axils of the whorled leaves. Corolla white, flat-outspread, 1–2cm wide, usually 7-lobed. Blooms from June to July. z4 (E.)

T. europaea var. **latiolia** see **T. latifolia**

T. latifolia Hook. (*T. europaea* var. *latiolia* (Hook.)Torr.) W. North America: S. Alberta and British Columbia to Central California. Stems 10–20cm high. Leaves in a terminal whorl of 4–8, ovate or more

turf. Only *T. repens* 'Purpureum' (see note below) is generally used as an ornamental or for erosion control. Plants, however, can easily become troublesome weeds. The other species described here may be included in the larger alpine areas of botanic gardens; short-lived, generally, in lowland gardens, especially *T. alpinum*. Plants require a sunny, somewhat moist scree habitat with a mix of ⅓ loam and ⅔ gravel. *T. alpinum* and *T. pallescens* are lime-intolerant, *T. badium* and *T. thalii*, on the other hand, need some alkalinity. Propagation is easy by seed.

and rocky slopes, from 1600–2600m, over limestone. Carpet-forming perennials with 8–20cm long, densely pubescent stems. Flower heads rounded, often nodding. Corolla about 15mm wide, creamy-white. Blooms from June to July. z4

T. pallescens Schreb. Mountains of Central and S. Europe; on moist screes and among alpine mats above 1800m, lime-intolerant. Glabrous, carpet-forming perennial, usually with a very stout tap root and 5–10cm long, procumbent or ascending, nonrooting stems. Flowers

Trientalis europaea

Trifolium alpinum

Trifolium badium

or less obovate, to 7.5cm long, acute or acuminate. Flowers rose-pink or white, to 2cm across.

Trifolium L.
Leguminosae
Clover

About 300 species of annual, biennial and perennial herbs, most in the temperate and subtropical zones of the Northern Hemisphere; a few also occur in the mountains of tropical Africa and America, as well as subtropical S. America. Leaves alternate, nearly always trifoliate, occasionally 5-part palmate. Flowers papilionaceous, in dense heads or short spikes. Calyx 5-part, corolla 5-part, standard oblong or ovate, wings narrow, keel shorter, obtuse; stamens 9 with connate filaments plus 1 (upper) free, ovary simple. Many clover species are important for livestock fodder, others are mixed into park and pasture

T. alpinum L., Alpine Clover. Europe: Alps, N. and Central Apennine and Pyrenees Mts., in alpine meadows, usually between 1700 and 2500m. Lime-intolerant. Dense, carpet-forming, glabrous perennial with stout taproots. Corolla 18–25mm wide, rose-red, occasionally purple or yellowish, very fragrant. Blooms from June to August. z3

T. badium Schreb. Pyrenees Mts., Alps, Balkan Region, Apennine Mts.; mostly in meadows at subalpine levels from about 1200-2200m, on limestone. Stems ascending, 6–15cm high. Upper leaves nearly opposite, leaflets ovate to oblong, minutely toothed. Flower heads large, globose, compact. Corolla golden-yellow at first, later becoming leathery brown. Blooms from June to August. z4

T. noricum Wulf. Alps, Apennine Mts., mountains of the W. Balkan Peninsula; among alpine cushion plants, on screes

sweetly scented. Corolla 5–10mm wide, pale yellow to pink, later becoming dark brown. Blooms from June to August. z5

T. repens L., White Clover. Europe, N. and W. Asia, N. Africa. A meadow plant for heavy, loamy soil. Well suited for planting between stepping stones if it can be contained. Stems procumbent, rooting, 20–50cm long. Flowers fragrant. Corolla 8–13mm wide, white or tinged reddish. Blooms from spring to fall. 'Purpureum', (in England, 'Purpurascens', in America 'Atropurpureum') leaves bronze-colored to brown-red with a greenish margin. This species is not recommended for general garden use since it can easily become a noxious weed. z4

T. thalii Vill. Spanish mountains, Alps, Apennine Mts.; in meadows, mostly from subalpine elevations, on a lime-rich, rocky soil; in the Alps from 1400–2400m. Very similar to *T. pallescens*, but with shorter stems and white, later reddish, flowers. Blooms from July to August. z5 (E.)

Trillium L.
Liliaceae
Wake-robin

The following information is based on a series of articles by Paul Christian in the *Bulletin of the Alpine Garden Society*. Vol. 48, 1980. The name *Trillium* refers to the 3-part nature of the plant, with its terminal whorl of three leaves, three sepals and three petals, six stamens and a three-celled ovary. The genus includes 30–50 species, some very similar and difficult to distinguish. These range from the Himalaya Mts. through Japan and Kamchatka to North America. Species in the USA are most abundant in the Appalachian Mts. Many of the most attractive species also come from this region. The American species are generally more easily cultivated than the Asiatic species. Commonly found in cultivation, but usually collected from the wild; therefore, plants are quite variable with many species being confused. For example, *T. luteum* of the horticulture trade often is a mixture of collected, yellow-flowering plants of typically purplish-red or brownish-flowering species, not the botanist's *T. lutem*, which may be a natural variety of *T. viride*.

The trilliums are mostly spring blooming and, with few exceptions, deciduous woodland wildflowers. They have underground rhizomes, and some species will develop a many-stemmed clump, others a dense colony.

The unbranched herbaceous stems arise from the ends of the rhizomes at a scale-like bract. The stem terminates in a whorl of 3 simple, entire, leaves and a solitary, peduncled or sessile, flower. The sepals are usually green, the petals white, yellow, green, brown, rose or purple, or occasionally bicolored. After flowering, a fleshy berry is formed, with large brown or black seeds which are very slow to germinate.

Most species are long-lived ornamental plants if given the required conditions. Being generally from wetter climates, trilliums need abundant moisture during the vegetative period, and bright, half, or fully shaded location. They tolerate more shade later in the season as woodland foliage develops. Trillium foliage dies back with the advent of drier summer conditions. Suitable for underplanting deciduous, deep-rooted trees or shrubs which are late coming into leaf, for example, the dogwoods and magnolias. Deep soil is best; the rhizome roots of some species reach to 25cm deep. From a decorative standpoint, flowers and foliage, often beautifully marbled, are of primary consideration. Flowers are available in many colors and sizes; some species have yielded double-flowering cultivars more interesting than handsome. Foliage often lasts longer in cultivation.

Trilliums need highly organic soil, some more acidic, some more alkaline. Generally speaking, the species from the NE. USA and the Appalachian Mts. grow best in a cool, shady site in acidic soil, while the species from the midwest thrive in a neutral, more mineral-rich soil in full to semi-shade. Some few species occur in open meadows, and some in alpine, gravelly-humus-rich soil. The vegetative period is usually short. Plants grown from seed will not bloom for about 5 years. Seeds are seldom produced, and they must be sown immediately after harvest. Seeds often require a warm-cold-warm-cold stratification followed by warm germination. Tests have proven that the time between seed ripening and the following spring is sometimes sufficient for germination. The yield of vegetative propagation may be increased by severing the terminal bud from the rhizome at the beginning of the summer dormancy period. The surface where the bud was removed is then hollowed out, cup-like; eventually a ring of several new buds form around the cup rim. After one season's growth on the parent rhizome, the young plants are able to stand on their own. Young plants should be container-grown in a medium similar to that of the species' native habitat. The difficult nature of propagation and tedious cultural requirements keep trilliums somewhat rare in culture. But their beauty and long-lived nature are well worth the effort. The species descriptions are classified by geographical region.

The following species are described:

Asiatic Species

The following Asiatic species are less important in ornamental plantings.

T. × amabile Miyabe et Tatow. Japan. Genetically consistent hybrid with often incompletely developed flowers, hardly decorative. z6

T. apetalon see **T. smallii**

T. govanianum Wall. Kashmir to China. Somewhat resembles *Paris* species. Sepals and petals are very similar, green with purple markings. z5

T. kamtschaticum Pall. (*T. pallasii* Hult.). Kamchatka to NE. China and Hokkaido. Leaves to 15cm, sepals to 5cm long, green, petals white. Long lasting, but flowers poorly in cultivation. z5

T. pallasii see **T. kamtschaticum**

T. smallii Maxim. (*T. apetalon* Makino). Japan. Stems to 40cm-tall. Leaves rhombic-orbicular, to 15cm long, abruptly acuminate. Flowers twisted laterally, turning upright when spent, on peduncles to 4cm long. Sepals to 2cm long, petals short (or absent), thick, purple-brown and often stunted, occasionally replaced by modified anthers. Fruits fleshy, occasionally red-speckled. A questionable species; possibly a hybrid. z6

T. tschonoskii Maxim. Japan, Himalaya Mtn. Region. A widely variable species, corresponding with its wide range. Stem about 15cm high. Leaves sessile, rhombic-orbicular to suborbicular, to 16.5cm long. Flowers on peduncles to

Trillium chloropetalum

4cm long, petals white or pinkish, to 2.5cm long. z5

Trillium Species from Western North America

The species in W. North America are completely separated geographically from those of the E. USA. Despite many listings of west coast forms of *T. sessile*, this species is only found in the E. USA. The following four species have often mistakenly been classified as *T. sessile*.

T. albidum J.D. Freeman. California; occurs over a sizable range; this recently defined species is often cultivated as *T. chloropetalum, T. sessile* or *T. californicum*.

The only Pacific Coast white-flowering species with sessile flowers, green ovaries and anther appendages. Plant in well-drained, humus-rich soil. Blooms from April to May. z6

T. angustipetalum (Torr.) J.D. Freeman. Sierra Nevada Mts. and the San Francisco area. Until recently, considered a variety of *T. sessile* or *T. chloropetalum* and often often so listed in the trade. The species is easily recognized by its 4–5cm long and only 1cm-wide, deep red-brown petals and similarly colored ovaries. z6

T. californicum see **T. albidum, T. ovatum**

T. chloropetalum (Torr.) Howell. Washington to Central California. Stems to 75cm high, very sturdy; leaves rhombic-ovate, to 15cm long, sessile, usually brown-mottled. Flowers sessile, dark maroon or brown to greenish-yellow or white (light flowered forms with no leaf mottling), to 7.5cm long, often fetid. The species name refers to plants with yellow or greenish petals from the region around San Francisco and Monterey. See also *T. albidum*. Two forms are distinguished.

T. chloropetalum var. **angustipetalum** see **T. angustipetalum**

T. chloropetalum var. **chloropetalum** (Torr.) Howell. Petals always somewhat purple-tinged, even the yellow ones, never white; the ovary is also purplish-red. z6

T. chloropetalum var. **giganteum** (Hook. et Arn.) Munz. The petals are white to purple-red, never yellow or yellowish. Pure white-flowering plants may be confused with *T. albidum*, but these have reddish anther appendages, unlike the green appendages on *T. albidum*. z6

Both forms are attractive garden plants. The flowers are more attractive than those of many other species with sessile flowers. They thrive in high humus-rich, somewhat gravelly soil.

T. hibbersonii Wiley. Vancouver Island and the neighboring mainland. A charming species with extensively branched rhizomes, leaves sessile, flowers pink-tinged, similar to *T. nivale*. Thrives under conditions similar to those for *T. rivale*. z6

T. kurabayashii J.D. Freeman. The species is easily recognized by the spotted involucral leaf at the stem base and the bright maroon petals. These are twice as long as wide. The luxuriant leaves are broadly cordate. z6

T. ovatum Pursh. Coast Trillium. (*T. californicum* Kellogg.) Ranges from British Columbia to Central California and possibly east to Wyoming and Colorado, though authorities disagree on species assignment of the intermountain trilliums. Leaves subsessile, rhombic-ovate, abruptly acuminate, to 15cm long, with 5 distinct veins, usually mottled; stems 10–50cm high. Flowers with spreading perianth, petals white, fading to rose, petals to 5cm long; peduncle to 7.5cm long. The species somewhat resembles *T. grandiflorum*, but usually flowers earlier, from March to April depending on the climate. This species has reddish stems turning more reddish after blooming, those of *T. grandiflora* are reddish only after flower drop and then rarely. The species responds well to organic fertilizers. z5

T. petiolatum Pursh. Washington and Idaho. The only species with long-petioled leaves. Flowers are green and purple-brown. Rarely cultivated species from wetland meadows. z5

T. rivale Wats. NW. California and SW. Oregon. Leaves with petioles to 2.5cm long, ovate-lanceolate, to 5cm long; plants 10–25cm high. Flowers on slender peduncles to 8cm long, borne above the foliage, usually erect but eventually nodding. Petals white, marked irregularly rose-carmine, especially in the throat, to 5cm long. The flower colors are most effective in semi-shade. Plants thrive in less humus than the other species and tolerate summer dryness in their native open coniferous woodlands. z6

T. sessile see **T. albidum**

T. sessile var. **angustipetalum** see **T. angustipetalum**

Trillium Species from Eastern North America which are Important in Gardens.

These *Trillium* species come from North America east of the Great Plains. The following list includes the most commonly cultivated species, both currently available and recommended.

T. album see **T. erectum** f. **album**

T. catesbaei L. Rosy Wake-robin. North Carolina to Georgia and Alabama. Leaves large, elliptic to ovate; stems 30–45cm high. Flowers on nodding peduncles to 32mm long, often downward-facing, petals 2cm long, pink to rose, sometimes white, anthers purple-red. This species is easily cultivated in moist, acidic, high-humus soil. A particularly good garden form is var. **macranthum**, from the Appalachian Mts. z4

T. cernuum L. Nodding Trillium. Newfoundland to Georgia. Stems 30–45cm high, smooth. Leaves sessile or rarely with petiole to 1cm long, broadly rhombic-ovate, abruptly acuminate, narrowing at the base, to 10cm long. Peduncle to 32mm long, flexuous. Flowers white or pinkish, nodding, often below the foliage; petals wide-spaced, margins wavy, equalling or exceeding the sepals; anthers often purplish, ovary whitish. Thrives in moist, acidic, humus-rich loam in bright shade. Var. **macranthum** from the S. Appalachian Mts. is showier. z6(5)

T. cuneatum Raf. Whippoorwill Flower. SE. North America. Stems thickened, to 25cm high. Leaves suborbicular to ovate, to 15cm long, unmarked or faintly mottled. Flowers sessile, to 11.5cm long, dark maroon or brown, fetid-scented, stamens short, to one-third the petal

length. Pollen is released to the outside, that of *T. sessile* is released inward. This coarse but vigorous species grows in limy soils. z7(6)

T. decumbens Harbison. Georgia and Alabama; on acidic soil over a limestone substrate. The mottled leaves lie outspread over the soil on stems 1–10cm high; colonizes from the branching rhizomes. Flowers dark maroon, 5cm-long; sessile. Petals strongly erect, sepals shorter, green. Very promising species for garden culture. z6

Trillium erectum

T. erectum L. Purple Trillium, Stinking Benjamin Squawroot, Brown Beth, Wet Dog (s.s. only). E. North America: Ontario and Quebec southward to NE. Illinois, to Georgia and North Carolina. A variable species. Stems 15–60cm high, including the 10cm peduncle. Leaves broadly rhombic-ovate, to 17.5cm long, sessile. Flowers nearly erect, peduncled, brownish-purple to purple, rarely white, yellow or green, to 5cm long, petals flaired outward from the base. Anthers purple-red, like the stigmas, but with white pollen. z4

T. erectum f. **albiflorum** R. Hoffm. Flowers white, greenish-tinged; handsome garden plant.

T. erectum f. **album** (*T. album* Small). Now included in the above forma. Wax Trillium. Quite common in some southern mountain regions and previously listed as a species. Flowers white or pink-tinged, anthers yellow, otherwise like forma *erectum*.

T. erectum f. **luteum**, petals yellow to chartreuse-yellow, often finely deep red veined, and with a red ovary. The plant is elegent in all respects, about 10cm high and very attractive. See also *T. viride* var. *luteum*.

Other varieties are listed for *T. erectum*, some with dwarf habit. All are satisfactory and valuable garden plants for bright woodland sites with humus-rich soil.

T. erythrocarpum see **T. undulatum**

Trillium grandiflorum

T. flexipes Raf. New York to Minnesota south to Missouri. Very often confused with *T. cernuum*, but distinguished by the erect to declined peduncle with flowers always above the leaves, petal margins smooth, recurved but not undulate, and white or pink ovary. Stems to 40cm high. Leaves to 15cm long, sessile, broadly rhombic, abruptly acuminate. Peduncles to 12cm long, declined, spreading, or rarely erect. Flowers mostly white, to 5cm long, petals wide-spread. Stamens with filaments half the length of the anthers. Pink and brown-red forms are known also. z4

T. grandiflorum (Michx.) Salisb. White Wake-robin. E. North America: Quebec to Minnesota south to South Carolina, Georgia and Missouri. Stems stout, to 45cm high. Leaves rhombic to suborbicular, acuminate, base cuneate, sessile or rarely short-petioled, to 13cm long, deep green. Peduncle to 7.5cm long. Flowers to 7.5cm long; sepals short, broad, green; petals gleaming white, wide, margins undulate, and anthers yellow on green filaments; blooms from April to June. Flowers often fade to pink.

Easily grown species, requiring semi-shade and ample spring moisture. A number of varieties and cultivars are listed. z3–9

T. grandiflorum f. **parvum** Gates. New Hampshire, Vermont and Illinois. Smaller than forma *grandiflora* flowers quickly turn pink, then become increasingly darker. z4

T. grandiflorum f. **flore pleno** hort. Several more or less double-flowered clones are listed. The best is 'Snow Bunting', which is usually the one offered as a double *T. grandiflorum*, but all lose the simple beauty of the single-flowered parent, more resembling a white paper wad. z5

T. grandiflorum f. **roseum** hort. The true forma turns pink within a few hours of anthesis and proceeds to nearly rose. Foliage of such plants also may be reddish. z4

T. grandiflorum f. **variegatum** Sm. Applies to plants with inconsistent, but more or less conspicuous, greenish-striped petals. These plants are very often sterile. Plants described as *T. chandleri* Farwell have fully green petals and many lack leaves. z4

T. lancifolium Raf. Alabama, N. Florida, Georgia and SE. Tennessee. Leaves lanceolate, to 9cm long, on 10–35cm high stems. Flowers sessile; petals narrower than the leaves, 4.5cm long and greenish to purple. The species is related to *T. recurvatum*, and probably is a variety of it. z6

Trillium sessile

T. luteum see **T. viride**

T. nivale Ridd., Dwarf White Trillium, Snow Trillium. W. Pennsylvania to Minnesota southward to Nebraska and Missouri. Stems 5–12cm high. Leaves appear early, elliptic to ovate, to 5cm long, obtuse, petioled, bright green. Peduncles to 2.5cm long. Flowers 2.5–4cm long (relatively large for such small plants), erect, white marked purple or rarely pure white. This species flowers in very early spring and also dies back early, about June. Found on well-

Carolina, North Carolina and Kentucky, in moist woodlands. Stems 10–20cm high. Leaves sessile, oblong to lanceolate-ovate, 3-nerved, 2–6cm long, bronze-green. Peduncle to 32mm long. Flowers small, only 1–3cm long, petals inclined strongly upward, white, fading cherry red. A challenging, beautiful dwarf trillium. z6

T. pusillum var. **ozarkanum** see **T. ozarkanum**

T. recurvatum Beck. Purple Trillium,

purple, with 6 ridges. z5

T. sessile f. **viridiflorum** hort. Flower with no red pigment, but yellowish-green. z5 This is not the *T. viride* or *T. viride* var. *luteum*.

T. sessile var. **luteum** see **T. viride**

T. undulatum Willd. Painted Trillium. (*T. erythrocarpum* Michx.). E. North America: Quebec and E. Manitoba southward to Georgia and Tennessee. An under-appreciated species. Stems

Trillium undulatum

Triosteum pinnatifidum

drained, gravelly limestone or chert soil and is the only lime-tolerant *Trillium*. The soil should have good moisture retention. This is one of the few species with seed which germinates after only one cold period. Plants will self-seed under favorable conditions. z4

T. ozarkanum Palmer & Steyermand. Ozark Trillium. SW. Missouri, NW. and N. Central Arkansas; very restricted in range, never common, on upland acid chert soil in oak forests. Stems 15–25cm high, rarely higher, dark red. Leaves sessile, elongate-oblong to elliptic, 5–10cm long, 5-nerved, bronze to olive green. Pedicels upright, 3–4cm long. Flowers opening almost flat, 3–4cm across, white, then turning cerise from the petal tips downward. Long included as a western variety of *T. pusillum*, botanists recently have reassigned this plant full species status. z6

T. pusillum Michx. SE. Virginia, South

Purple Wake-robin, Bloody Butcher. Michigan to Iowa southward to Alabama and Mississippi. Stems to 45cm high. Leaves bluish-green, mottled brown, to 12cm long, elliptic to obovate. Petiole to 2.5cm long. Flowers brown-purple, to 4.5cm long, sessile. Sepals green, recurved to between the leaf petioles, petals erect, clawed. The species grows in heavy soil of acid to neutral pH. z5

T. sessile L. Toad-shade, Wake-robin. E. North America. The name is often used for many other similar species in culture, even some from W. North America. Stems stout, often red or reddish, to 30cm high. Leaves ovate to suborbicular, sessile, to 10cm long, often mottled. Flowers sessile, erect, fragrant, sepals green, brown-red at the base, 1–4cm long and, like the petals, conspicuously narrow, petals regular, erect, purplish-brown, maroon, or yellow-green, anthers blackish-violet with purple pollen; ovaries and ripe berries are also

slender, to 50cm long. Leaves bluish-green, petioled, ovate, to 18cm long, sharply acuminate, margins undulate. Peduncles to 6.5cm long, slender. Flowers erect or somewhat nodding; sepals 1cm-long, green, red-veined petals to 3cm-long, white or pale pink, with purplish markings near the base. Plants bear decorative red fruits well above the foliage. This attractive species comes from moist, often mountain, woodlands with acidic, fertile, leafmold soil which remains cool in the summer. This species is intolerant of summer heat, drought, or of limy soils. z3–8

T. vaseyi Harbison. E. North America: Alleghany Mts. Similar to and requiring the same culture as *T. erectum*, but larger in all respects, flowers to 10cm wide with brown-red petals and yellow stigmas (reddish on *T. erectum*). z5 (S.)

T. viride L. Beck. Wood Trillium. SW. Illinois to SE. Kansas southward to N.

Arkansas and E. Oklahoma; mostly in sparse, dry upland oak forests with neutral to acidic chert soils. Stems stout, to 50cm high, mostly pubescent toward the top, reddish below. Leaves sessile, lanceolate to suborbicular, to 10cm long, often mottled, veins finely pubescent below. Flowers sessile, to 5cm long, greenish, stamens very short, one-fourth to one-third the petal length. And var. **luteum** (Muhlenb.)Gleason (*T. luteum* (Muhlenb.)Herb.; *T. sessile* var. *luteum* Muhlenb.) Mts. Kentucky to Georgia, lowlands, South Carolina to Florida. Stems and leaves glabrous; flowers yellow. z7(6)

Triosteum L.
Caprifoliaceae
Horse Gentian, Feverwort, Wild Coffee

A small genus of 5–6 species, from the Himalaya Mtn. region, China, and to North America. Medium-high perennials with opposite, sessile, obovate to lyrate, entire, leaves and inconspicuous, axillary, sessile or rarely spicate, solitary or clustered, flowers. Calyx lobes leafy, corolla slightly zygomorphic, tubular, 5-lobed, the lobes scarcely open, sordid white, yellowish or purplish, stamens 5, epipetalous, ovary 3-celled, style long, unbranched, stigma capitate. More valuable in autumn for the leathery fruits (berry-like drupes). Propagate by division and seed. Seedlings often volunteer. These are coarse, somewhat weedy, scarcely ornamental perennials suitable only for naturalizing in dry woods.

T. perfoliatum L. USA: Midwest. Stems solitary, or few, unbranched, 90–125cm high, softly pubescent. Leaves to 23cm long, ovate to elliptical, acuminate, abruptly narrowed at the base and mostly basally united. Flowers sordid purplish, to 2cm long, not showy. Fruits orange or reddish in sessile clusters; flowers in midsummer, fruits color up in the fall. Similar to the somewhat hardier *T. aurantiacum* Bickn. with leaves not united basally, dull reddish flowers, and orange-red fruits. z6

T. pinnatifidum Maxim. NW. China. Stems 1 or few, unbranched, soft, glandular-hairy, to 60cm high. Leaves deeply pinnately lobed, flowers yellowish or greenish, brownish-purple inside, in short, terminal spikes; August. Fruits attractive, white, berry-like, persisting into late fall. For fertile garden soil in full sun to semi-shade. z4 (Sch. & M.)

Tripleurospermum see Matricaria

Tripsacum L.
Gramineae
Gamma Grass

T. dactyloides (L.) L. North America: Massachusetts to Michigan and Nebraska; south to the W. Indies and S. America. This grass has been long cultivated for livestock fodder, but little

Tritelia laxa 'Queen Fabiola'

used as an ornamental. Clustered culms grow to 3m high from the thick, rhizomatous rootstock. Leaf sheath tightly appressed to the stem, leaf blades to 60cm long and 2.5cm wide. The white midrib contrasts well with the bright, olive-green leaves. Leaves gradually turn reddish, then light brown in the fall. Inflorescences of a one-sided panicle with a few, to 25cm-long, compound spikes. The individual spikelets are staminate on the apical portion and pistillate toward the base. Plants thrive in heavy, damp soil, in full sun, best in regions with warm summers. Suitable only for re-creating a North American prairie, or similar naturalized planting. Propagate by division in spring, or by seed. z5 (S.)

Tripterocalyx

T. cyclopterus see **Abronia cycloptera**

Trisetum Pers.
Gramineae
False Oats

T. flavescens (L.) P. Beauv. Yellow Oats. Europe and E. Asia, naturalized in E. USA; grows in fertile meadows. An open ground cover grass with short rhizomes. Panicled, yellow-green inflorescence. Leaves tufted, sheath shorter than the internode, more or less pubescent, ligule about 0.5mm long, blade 4–13cm long, 2–5mm wide, scabrous, sparingly hairy.

Triteleia × *tubergenii*

Culms 45–75cm high, tall, erect, unbranched, smooth and glabrous. Panicle open, 5–12cm long, spikelets 3–4 flowered, yellow turning dull brown. Suitable for mixed meadow plantings in fertile soil. Naturalizes freely from seed. Not a very ornamental plant. z5 (S.)

Triteleia Dougl. ex Lindl.
Amaryllidacea (previously Liliaceae)

A genus of about 14 species from W. North America, once included with *Brodiaea* and including species now transferred to other genera. Cormaceous plants, flowering in summer and remotely resembling some *Allium* species, but not scented. Mostly with blue, purple-violet and white flowers.

Space-saving, easily cultivated ornamentals, species of this genus should be planted more often, especially in warmer climates. They require well-drained, average garden loam; but many species grow poorly outside a California-type environment. The leaves are so narrow and transitory that these plants combine well even with small ground cover perennials. Winter protection is necessary, however, in cooler climates. Suitable for cut-flower cultivation in the cold frame. Propagation is by cormlets and seed of the species.

Corms with a pale, fibrous-netted tunic; leaves 1–2, narrowly-linear and elongate, more or less flat but the midrib prominent below, slightly channeled above. Scape scabrous or hairy below, slender; umbel terminal, subtended by 2 spathe valves, green or rarely purplish. Flowers jointed at the pedicel, perianth tube long or short, segments spreading, usually colorful, stamens 6, ovary superior, stigmas 3-lobed. *Dichelostemma* leaves are also keeled, but with 3 fertile and 3 sterile anthers, stigma entire; *Brodiaea* leaves are rounded beneath, and with 3 fertile anthers, and 3 sterile, and 3-lobed stigmas.

T. laxa Benth. Grass Nut, Triplet Lily. (*Brodiaea laxa* (Benth.) S. Wats.). USA: California to Oregon. Scapes to 75cm high, grassy foliage to about 50cm high. Many-flowered umbels with 3–4cm long pedicels; flowers about 3cm across, mostly deep violet-blue or blue, or rarely white. Late spring or early summer.

'Queen Fabiola' (*Brodiaea hybrida* 'Fabiola'). About 50cm-high, deep violet-blue starry flowers on long pedicels, for a loose-flowered effect. Probably the most common *Triteleia* marketed, with *T.* × *tubergenii* sharing top billing in Europe. z7(6)

T. peduncularis Lindl. (*Brodiaea peduncularis* (Lindl.) S. Wats.). USA: coastal ranges of California; in wet ground. Leaves in a lax tuft, 90–100cm long, 1cm wide. Scape flexuous, to 90cm high. Umbel 3–15 flowered, pedicels 2–5 times as long as flowers. Flowers white, blue- or lavender-blushed, perianth to 2.5cm long, narrow-campanulate, lobes half as deep as the tube, stamens inserted at two levels. Width of the loose umbel is about 25cm, about 50cm high, beginning in July. An incomparable species for the collector. z6

T. × **tubergenii** (*Brodiaea* × *tubergenii*) (*T. peduncularis* × *T. laxa*). The first hybrid to be developed, and equally indispensible as *T. laxa* 'Queen Fabiola'. Intermediate between the parents, flowering after July, soft blue, exterior somewhat darker. Attractive in the rock garden or

prairie garden together with *Cistus*, *Liatris*, *Anaphalis triplinervis*, *Anthemis marschalliana*, *Inula ensifolia*, *Hieracium waldsteinii*, *Geranium* 'Ballerina', *G. subcaulescens* 'Splendens', *G. sanguineum* var. *prostratum*, *Sedum*, *Sempervivum*, *Yucca*, *Opuntia*. z5 (Mü.)

T. uniflora see **Ipheion uniflorum**

While the above-listed triteleias are generally available in the trade, many more are planted locally in W. and SW. USA and Mexico, elsewhere around the world where climatic conditions are comparable. These include: *T. bridgesii* (S. Wat.) Green, to 45cm high, flowers lilac or blue; *T. crocea* (A. Wood) Greene, to 30cm high, flowers bright yellow; *T. grandiflora* Lindl., scape to 60cm high, flowers bright blue, rarely white; *T. hendersonii* Greene, scape to 30cm high, flowers yellow with deep purple stripes, and var. *leachiae* (Peck) Hoover, flowers white, usually blue-tinged; *T. hyacinthina* (Lindl.) Greene, scape to 75cm high, flowers blue to lilac, more bowl-shaped than tubular; *T. ixioides*, scape to 60cm high, flowers golden-yellow with darker stripes, var. *scabra* (Green) Hoover cream-colored to deep yellow, flowers narrower; *T. lugens* Greene, scape to 45cm high, flowers sordid yellow to brownish-purple.

Tritoma see Kniphofia

Tritonia Ker-Gawl.
Iridaceae
Montbretia (in part)

Perhaps 50 species of cormaceous perennials from South Africa. Leaves basal, sword-shaped to linear. Inflorescence a spike, simple or branched; flowers sessile, spathe valves emarginate, brown; perianth tube usually shorter than the lobes, tapering basally but dilated to a wide throat, lobes 6, not quite equal; stamens 3, stigmas 3-lobed. These bloom in early to midsummer, with numerous flowers open at one time but the spike elongating with many buds so the flowering period is prolonged. Plant in well-drained, very deep, humus-enriched sandy loam which is never droughty through the growing period; set large, tunic-covered corms about 10cm deep. Full sun is essential for best development. Corms send out long stolons terminating in additional corms; spring growth begins very early, necessitating a deep cover of pine

boughs to hold in the cold and slow a too early emergence. These respond well to liquid fertilizing from early spring through completion of flowering. A single species sometimes is encountered in the trade, though several others ought to be made available; for closely related species see also *Crocosmia*.

T. aurantiaca see **T. crocata**

T. crocata (L.) Ker-Gawl. (*T. aurantiaca* Eckl.: *Montbretia crocata* (L.) Voigt). Montbretia. South Africa. Leaves 4–10, 12–25cm high, broadly linear–sword-shaped, curved, striate, acute, shorter than the flowering spike. Spike 30–60cm high, seldom branched, loose-flowered, with 7–9 flowers in 2 ranks, about 32mm long, segments flaired, about twice as long as the tube. In the wild, mostly tawny-yellow to orangeish, but numerous cultivars are listed including: 'Aurantiaca', orange-red; 'Coccinea', scarlet; 'Purpurea', purplish-red; and 'Sanguinea', bright, blood-red. The cultivar (or sometimes listed as a variety) *miniata* is smaller, with bright red flowers and dark green leaves; it may turn out to be a separate species; more tender than *T. crocata* and its cultivars. z7(6)

Trollius L.
Ranunculaceae
Globeflower

This genus with 20 or more species from the cooler and temperate zones of the Northern Hemisphere, is closely related to *Caltha*. The genus is generally distinguished from *Caltha* by the colorful, petaloid sepals, no petals, of *Caltha*; and the petaloid sepals narrow, reduced or strap-shaped petals of *Trollius* which sometimes resemble nectaries. Petals inserted interior to the colorful sepals, and are exserted past the outspread anthers. The open flowers of *Trollius* more or less resemble yellow ranunculus or yellow anemones. *Trollius* differs from these in the fruits.

Ranunculus bear a single-seeded achene, whereas the *Trollius* bears a many-seeded follicle. The nectaries of *Trollius europaeus* are very narrow and no longer than the stamens; on most other species they are somewhat longer, wider and deeper orange.

Globeflowers are moist to wet meadow plants. Plants perform poorly on light, dry soil, dying back prematurely and dying out altogether in dry years. After the first flush of flowers fade, cut back stems and fertilize plants to encourage reblooming. Propagate the cultivars only by division, the species by seed. Seedlings vary slightly in color and are desirable for cut-flower beds. Globeflowers can be forced with moderate warmth after early March. The earliest-flowering forms are best for forcing.

T. acaulis Lindl. Asia; Himalaya Mts. Plants tufted; stems several, 7.5–25cm high. Leaves 5–7 part palmate, divisions 3-lobed or much cut, serrate. Flowers solitary, about 5cm across, golden yellow, spreading, overtopped by the leaves; sepals 9, lanceolate; petals linear-

12; nectary-petals 20, darker orange, twice as long as the stamens; July to August, the latest-flowering species. Usually found in cultivation as the cultivar 'Golden Queen' with exceptionally large flowers on stiffly upright stems. Comes true from seed and is usually so propagated. Plants cultivated as *T. ledebourii*, very rarely seen, usually are *T. chinensis*. z5

T. europaeus L., Common Globeflower. Europe, especially in the Central mountains; in moist meadows. Stems rarely branched, 30–60cm high. Basal leaves

parted, segments wedge-shaped, much cleft, and toothed. Flowers solitary, to 5cm across, greenish-yellow; inflated sepals flat-spreading, petals many, shorter than stamens. z4 And var. **albiflorus** A. Gray. NW. North America, British Columbia to Washington and Colorado, high mountain meadows. Stems 15–30cm high. Leaf segments 5. Flowers shallow cup-shaped, white or pale yellow; sepals spreading, 5–7; nectary-petals 10–15, about equalling the stamens in length; both spring-flowering. z4

Trollius chinensis

Trollius europaeus

Trollius yunnanensis

cuneate, rounded at the tips, shorter than the many stamens; follicles 15. Ideal by the rock garden pool or stream. z6

T. americanus see **T. laxus**

T. asiaticus L. NE. Russia, Siberia, Turkestan. Stems to 60cm high, with bronze-green foliage. Sepals usually 10, usually orange, globose; nectary-petals usually 10, longer than the stamens; May to June. Rarely true in cultivation. Cultivar 'Bryne's Giant', 90cm, bright yellow, large. 'Fortunei', sepals many = double-flowered; and 'Giganteus', larger, sturdier overall. z4

T. chinensis Bunge (*T. ledebourii* hort.). NE. China. Stem stout, grooved, to 90cm high. Leaves palmate 5-part, segments broad-lanceolate, lobed, toothed. Lower leaves reniform, upper leaves round. Peduncles to 30cm long. Flowers shallow bowl-shaped, orange-yellow; sepals 10–

petioled. Leaves dark green above, paler below, palmate usually 5–7 parted; segments rhombic, 3-lobed. Stems with a solitary flower. Petaloid sepals 10–15, pale yellow, in a tight globe; nectary-petals 5–10, about as long as the egg yolk yellow stamens; May to June. The cultivar 'Superbus' is especially desirable, to 60cm high, pale lemon yellow, late. Other good cultivars include; 'Giganteus', plant very sturdy; 'Grandiflorus', flowers larger and brighter than the species; and 'Loddigesii', flowers deep, butter yellow; additional cultivars are listed in Europe but are not available in America. z5

T. laxus Salisb. Spreading Globe-flower. (*T. americanus* Mühlenb. ex DC.). NE. USA: New England States southward to Pennsylvania, in wet meadows and bogs. Stems several, ascending to spreading, 45–60cm high. Lower leaves petioled, stem leaves sessile; leaves palmate 5–7

T. ledebourii Rchb.f. E. Siberia. Stems several, to 90cm high. Leaf blades completely cleft, segments lobed and toothed. Flowers cup-shaped, to 6.5cm across; petaloid sepals 5, spreading, nectary-petals 10–12, narrow-linear, longer than the stamens; stamens dark orange. Plants offered under this name in the trade usually are *T. chinensis*.

T. patulus see **T. ranunculinus**

T. pumilus D. Don. Himalaya Mtn. Region. Stems glabrous, to 25cm high, unbranched. Leaves mostly basal, small, 0.12–5cm across, ovate to suborbicular, deeply 5-cleft, segments laciniate, short petioled. Flowers cup-shaped, golden-yellow, long-peduncled; nectaried petals as long as the stamens; June to July. For the alpine garden or rock garden. z5

T. pumilus var. **yunnanensis** see **T. yunnanensis**

T. ranunculinus (Sm.) Stearn (*T. patulus* Salisb.). Caucasus Mtn. Region, Asia Minor to Iran. Stem scape-like, to 40cm high. Leaves palmately cleft, segments lobed, margins sinuate or toothed. Flowers cup-shaped, golden-yellow; sepals 5–10, spreading, petals 1–10, narrow-lanceolate, as long as the stamens; styles the same color, less than half as long as the ovaries; May to June. z6

T. yunnanensis (Franch.) Ulbr. (*T. pumilus* D. Don var. *yunnanensis* Franch.). W. China. Stems glabrous, 50–65cm

orange-yellow, large-flowered, early; 'Golden Monarch', 90cm, canary yellow; 'Goldquelle' ('Golden Fountain'), 70cm, yellow, late; 'Hohes Licht' (Highlight), 80cm, yellow, large-flowered, mid-season; 'Lemon Queen' (Shoot), 60cm, light yellow, large-flowered, midseason; 'Maigold' ('May Gold') 50cm, golden-yellow, early; 'Orange Globe', 60cm, orange-yellow, midseason. 'Orange Princess', 75–90cm, orange-yellow, mid-season; 'Prichard's Giant', 90cm, golden-orange, globe-shaped; 'Salamander', 50–75cm, very deep orange. z5 (Me. & M.)

warms up in spring may take 4 months or more to germinate.

T. pentaphyllum Lam. South America: Argentina to Bolivia. Rootstock with long, knobby tubers. Stems to 4m, climbing, glabrous, purple. Leaves peltate, 5-lobed, the elliptical usually obtuse. Flowers tubular, 2.5–3cm long, with a long, conical spur, light red and green. This species initiates vegetative growth in fall. The shoots will tolerate temperatures somewhat below freezing, but they are difficult to protect from lower temperatures. Therefore they are

Trollius hybrid 'Goldquelle'

Tropaeolum tricolor

high, 1–3 flowered; stems with 1–2 leaves. Most leaves basal, long-petioled, 5-angled, deeply 3–5 cleft, the segments broadly ovate to obovate, coarse toothed and prickly tipped. Flowers golden-yellow, 4–5cm across, sepals 5, spreading; nectary-like petals 12, shorter than the stamens. Otherwise resembles *T. pumilus*; June to July. z5

T. Hybrids (*T.* × *cultorum* Bergm.). Included here are all the cultivars. Most have originated from *T. asiaticus*, *T. chinensis* and *T. europaeus*. The flower colors range from light lemon yellow to deep orange. Among the best known cultivar is *T. chinensis* 'Golden Queen'; others include 'Canary Bird', 75cm, pale yellow; 'Earliest of All', 50cm, golden-yellow, early; 'Empire Day', 60cm, orange-yellow, large, early; 'Fire Globe', 50–65cm, dark orange; 'First Lancers', 60–70cm, fiery orange, large; 'Frühlings-bote' ('Spring Messenger'), 60cm, light

Tropaeolum L.
Tropaeolaceae
Nasturtium

South American genus, with 50–60 species from Mexico to Central Argentina and Chile, most in the mountains. In addition to the familiar annual species, just a few tender species and fewer somewhat hardy (z8(7)) species are of interest to gardeners. These have a tuberous rootstock, sometimes rhizoma-tous, which may be dug and stored frost-free during the dormant period. Some, however, are very sensitive to disturbance and cannot be moved. The tubers are sensitive to excess moisture, requiring fast drainage, but they need even moisture during the growing season. All species grow best in acidic soil with a good humus content. Seed propagation is often difficult for some species; seeds sown as soon as the soil

best cultivated only in very mild climates and near a building. z8

T. polyphyllum Cav. Chile. South America; rootstock a crown with one or several simple or branched tubers. Stems prostrate to procumbent, very leafy, to 1.2m long. Leaves glabrous, rounded, peltate, deeply 7–9 lobed; lobes obovate, often variably cut, silvery blue-green. Flowers axillary, pale golden yellow, orange, or ochre, long-spurred, borne on stiff petioles above the foliage. This species is rarely offered in the trade. The tubers are very difficult to transplant and once established, difficult to transplant. Plants are slow to establish themselves. Annual growth increases gradually from year to year. In its habitat, the species grows in gravelly meadows with little rain but high humidity. Plants in cultivation require soil with good water retention and a warm site. Plant tubers at least 20cm deep; they require winter protection. In addition to division and seed, propagation is possible by stem cuttings. z8

T. speciosum Poepp. et Endl. Flame Nasturtium. South America: Chile. Rootstock a more or less fleshy rhizome. Stems high climbing, to more than 3m long. Leaves peltate, 6-lobed, soft-hairy beneath like the 3-part stipules. Flowers spurred, petals very long-stalked, widespread, vermilion-red, appear in summer over several weeks, borne on flexuous peduncles, followed by fleshy, blue-black fruits.

This species is an herbaceous climber from a moderate climate with relatively cool summer temperatures and quite mild winters. Plants, therefore, thrive in summer-cool locations such as a north exposure, but also require ample winter protection. Companion plants which help form a winter mulch, such as ferns, grasses, and similar dense herbage, are advantageous. Plant the rhizome horizontally about 10cm deep in an evenly moist, fertile, high humus soil. Propagation is possible by division of the tubers, seed or cuttings from the long stems. z8

T. tricolor Sw. South America: Peru. Rootstock with small tubers. Stems slender, to 1m long or more. Leaves small, peltate, 6–7 segmented, with linear to obovate lobes. Flowers more or less cone-shaped with a massive spur and small petals, variously colored; calyx orange-scarlet, lobes tipped black, petals orange to yellow. The prominent spur varies from red to yellow with blue to green tip, the calyx may be blue, violet, red or yellow. The species is suitable as a winter bloomer for the greenhouse, or frost-free alpine house where it will bloom in spring. Requires plenty of water and fertilizer during the vegetative period. z8

T. azureum Miers. is similar in cultural requirements but tender, and perhaps somewhat more demanding, with lilac-blue flowers; and *T. brachyceras* Hook. et Arn. with small green-yellow flowers.

T. tuberosum Ruiz. et Pav. South America: Peru and Bolivia. Tubers large, marbled yellow and maroon. Stem climbing to 3m or more, glabrous; stem, petioles and peduncles usually reddish, purplish or bluish. Leaves peltate, deeply 5–6 lobed, the lobes mucronate; petioles mostly long. Flowers on long peduncles, sepals red, petals slightly exceeding the sepals, upper rounded, lower narrower, orange or scarlet, spur straight, usually scarlet; flowers in late summer or early fall. Requires a warm,

sunny location with good drainage and humus-rich, never arid soil. Mulch deeply in winter. z8 (S.)

Tulipa L.
Liliaceae
Tulip

The genus includes about 100–110 species distributed from SE. Europe to Asia but centering in Central Asia. It is here that many of the most attractive species are found. Tulips are very familiar, sometimes stolon-forming bulbous plants. Bulb sizes vary corresponding to the ultimate plant size, from hazelnut-sized for charming little species to the hen's egg size of *T. hoogiana*. Bulbs are covered with a light to black-brown tunic which may be papery, leathery, even almost hard and horn-like. On some species the inside of the tunic is covered with a woolly tomentum, and with a few hairs at the tip of the bulb. Tulips differ from most of the other bulbous plants, such as *Hyacinthus* and *Lilium*, in that in cultivation they may be relatively short-lived. In cultivation, tulip bulbs, especially the bred-up garden cultivars, may die out during late spring while new bulbs are being formed at the base of the mother bulb, though in nature the bulbs are truly persistent. Most species bear a single flower atop an alternate-leaved, erect stem. A few species have branched stems with multiple flowers. A tulip flower has 6 separate perianth segments (3 petal-like sepals outside, 3 similar but slightly broader petals inside), no nectaries, 6 stamens, the anther attached basally to the filament, and 2–3-angled superior ovary with a sessile 3-lobed stigma. Flowers are usually erect, campanulate to slender bulb-urn shaped. Blossoms open only on sunny days and often spread flat outward. The fruit is a 3-locular capsule with overlapping, flat, winged seeds.

Tulips are among the the best known and most popular spring garden and forcing flowers. Almost every garden has tulips of some kind. The cultivars of the various classes of garden tulips are especially desirable; however, species (wild) tulips are also highly prized and cultivated by avid gardeners and collectors.

It is not possible within the scope of this work to go deeply into the history of the origins and introduction of the garden tulips. By way of introduction, it is supposed that the first tulips were planted in gardens of Persia about the

year 1000. Plants were brought to Central Europe in the mid-16th century from Constantinople by the Flemish nobleman and envoy of Emperor Ferdinand I, Ghiselain de Busbeque. Soon thereafter, a passionate enthusiasm for this plant arose in Holland. Among the wealthy class, enormous sums (to 11,500 guilders or $5,750 in today's currency) were paid for a single bulb of a new, colorfully striped form. The years 1636–37 were the boom years for "Tulipomania" in the Dutch bulb market. At the end of this period the tulip had found its master and a new garden home. Innumerable cultivars have been developed over the centuries with new cultivars constantly replacing older ones. To assist in organizing the vast array of tulip species and cultivars, a system of classification was devised by the British Royal Horticultural Society (R.H.S.) and the Dutch Koninklijke Allgemeene Vereeniging Voor Bloemoollencultur. The first "Classified List and International Register of Names" appeared in 1917; the most recent, in 1981, includes the following 15 classes:

Early-Blooming

1. Single Early Tulips
2. Double Early Tulips

Midseason-Blooming

3. Triumph Tulips
   Hybrids between Single Early × Late Flowering Tulips
4. Darwin Hybrid Tulips
   Primarily, crosses of the Darwin Tulips with *Tulipa fosteriana*.

Late Flowering (May-Flowering)

5. Single Late Tulips
   This class includes the Darwin and Cottage Tulips, among others; the hybrids lack the distinguishing characteristics of the earlier classes.
6. Lily-Flowered Tulips
   Flowers with pointed, reflexed perianth segments.
7. Fringed Tulips
   Tulips with finely fimbriate perianth segment margins
8. Viridiflora Tulips
   Tulips with partly greenish-toned flowers
9. Rembrandt Tulips
   So-called "Broken Tulips", brown, bronze, purple, pink-, red-striped or flamelike red, white or yellow base.
10. Parrot Tulips
    Fringed, undulate petals, usually late-blooming
11. Double Late Tulips (peony-flowered)

Wild Tulips

12. Kaufmanniana, varieties and hybrids
    Very early-flowering, leaves occasionally mottled or striped.
13. Fosteriana, varieties and hybrids
    Sturdy, usually short plants, very early-flowering, some cultivars with mottled or striped leaves.
14. Greigii, varieties and hybrids
    Flowers later than *T. kaufmanniana*, leaves brownish-red spotted or striped.
15. Wild Tulips (*Tulipa* species)

This latest Dutch classification reflects not so much popular tastes in tulips (amateur gardeners tend to plant advertised varieties) as the economics of commercial bulb production. Certain of the newest classes of tulips are easily propagated and brought to flowering size quickly; fair enough, but while capitalizing on these, superb old strains, such as the Duc van Tol and Mendel Tulips, among others, are excluded from the classification system. This means that they will be lost to cultivation, an inditement of over-commercialization of tulip growing.

A listing of the cultivars of garden tulips has been intentionally omitted. Such a list would be superfluous in this general text, and is best obtained from current trade literature.   Garden tulips thrive in any average, well-drained garden soil, failing only on an exceptionally acidic or poorly drained, heavy, wet soil. The recommended planting time is October to early November; the planting depth ranges from 10–20cm depending on soil, summer weather, and bulb size; some tulip species bulbs require shallower planting. Plants will persist for a few years in the same site if fertilized

Tulipa hybrids 'Bestseller' and 'Hibernia'

when or just before shoots appear in the spring. Garden tulips in beds should be dug and reset in a new or reworked bed every 3–4 years. Species tulips in the rock garden should be planted deeper (some shallower) and will persist longer without transplanting. Botanists collecting tulips from their native habitat are often astonished at the depth wild bulbs are found in gravelly soil.

Many of the choice wild tulips in cultivation were collected at about the turn of the century by employees of the C.G. Van Tubergen Nursery, Haarlem (The Netherlands) from Central Asia and

with purple blotch at the base of the petals, sepals carmine-red on the reverse, 1–2 flowered. Bulbs small, rounded. z5

T. aitchisonii ssp. **cashmeriana** A.D. Hall. Leaves more erect, glossy, 2–3 flowered, yellow, without red exterior. z5

T. aitchisonii var. **clusianoides** Wendelbo. E. Afghanistan, Chitral, Kashmir. Flowers large, white with a purple basal spot, sepal margins striped carmine-red. z5

linear, to 17.5cm long, glaucous. Flowers to 5cm long, segments broad, buff-yellow with olive-tinged basal spot, stamens yellow. Attractive cultivars are: 'Bright Gem', sulfer yellow, orange-tinged; 'Bronze Charm', apricot and bronze-colored. April to May. This is one of the best rock garden tulips. z5

T. biflora Pall. Caspian region, Caucasus Mts. Stem 5–15cm high, with 1–5 flowers; miniature tulip. Leaves more or less glaucous, linear, to 13cm long, 2cm wide. Flowers white with yellow center; sepals tinged or streaked greenish or

Tulipa hybrid 'Couleur Cardinal'

Tulipa hybrid 'Peach Blossom'

Tulipa hybrid 'Delmonte'

named by E.A. Regel. More recently, Russian botanists have described several additional species which have been introduced through botanic gardens, but these are only slowly becoming available on the market. British collectors, too, are contributing to the list of new *Tulipa* introduction.

Among the most important garden species are:

T. acuminata Vahl ex Hornem. Origin unknown, possibly an old Persian garden tulip, a variant of *T. gesneriana*. Stem 45cm high; usually 3 leaves,with an undulate margin. Flowers pale yellow, occasionally pink, often with red stripes. Perianth segments uniform, lanceolate, very long-acuminate with involuted, sometimes undulate margins. April. z5

T. agenensis see **T. oculus-solis**

T. aitchisonii A.D. Hall. Central Asia; Chitral, Kashmir. Flowering stem 10–12cm high. Leaves 2–4, glabrous, spreading, 8–10cm long, 0.5cm wide. Flowers starry, about 3.5cm across, white

T. aitchisonii ssp. **ladakh**, M.H. Hoog. Kashmir, near the border of Tibet. Flowers yellow, exterior pale orange-tinged. z5

T. aucheriana Bak. Iran, Syria. Flowering stems 5–8cm high, leaves 2–5, about 12cm long, to 0.5cm wide, lanceolate, glossy dark green, often lying flat; flowers starry when widely open, segments soft pink with a brownish-yellow basal spot; one of the smallest tulips. April to May. z5

T. australis Link. W. Mediterranean region, France, Italy. Stem to 20cm high. Closely related to *T. sylvestris* but smaller. Leaves narrow, to 20cm long, creased buds nodding, urn-shaped; flowers bright yellow, exterior reddish-tinged, especially near the tips, fragrant. April. z7

T. bakeri see **T. saxatilis**

T. batalinii Regel. Central Asia, Pamir Mts. Possibly a yellow form of *T. linifolia*. Flowering stem to 15cm high. Leaves

reddish outside. April. Var. *major*, larger overall. This tulip is easily confused with *T. turkestanica*. z5

T. celsiana see **T. patens**

T. clusiana DC. Kashmir, Iran, Afghanistan, naturalized in the Mediterranean region. Stems 20–30cm high, leaves linear, creased, not undulate, gray-green, to 26cm long. Flowers narrowly urn-shaped, opening out flat, starry, milk-white with a violet blotch inside, sepals red with white margins outside. *T. clusiana* is known in England as "Lady Tulip" and, with its varieties and cultivars, is one of the most beautiful of all the tulips. The bulbs are very small and should be planted in a well-protected, warm site in a sandy soil. Cultivar 'Cynthia', flowers yellow with a purple blotch inside; outside yellow, margined carmine red. z6

T. clusiana DC. var. **chrysantha** (A.D. Hall) Sealy. N. Afghanistan, Chitral. Stems 15–20cm high, slender, narrow-leaved. Flowers golden-yellow inside, sepals crimson-red, yellow margined outside. The selection 'Tubergen's Gem' has larger flowers. April. z5

T. clusiana DC. var. **stellata** Regel. NW. India. Flowers very similar to *T. clusiana*, but with a yellow basal blotch. z7

T. dasystemon (Regel) Regel. This rare Central Asian tulip is not in cultivation. Bulbs sold under this name probably are *T. tarda* which is very similar but leafier and with hairless tunic.

T. didieri Jord. Mediterranean region,

recurved tips, light golden yellow, exterior tinged orange-red. Bulb tunic hard-leathery. May. Stems occasionally with 2 flowers. z5

T. fosteriana Th. Hoog ex W. Irv. Central Asia, Pamir Mts., Samarkand Mts.; at about 2000m elevation. Stems 20cm high, more or less pubescent, stout. Leaves 3–4, to 20cm long, broadly ovate, glaucous. Flowers fiery red, segments to 10cm long, opening flat, with black, yellow-bordered basal blotch inside, lighter red outside, stamens black. Numerous cultivars are listed, including:

purple. z5

The status of this species is much debated; horticulturists tend to aggregate all the ancient garden tulips as well as their more or less reverted offspring, now naturalized, especially in SE. Europe and Italy, and call them *T. gesneriana* and the term becomes a *Nomen nudum*. Botanists use the name for certain wild tulips in the geographic range described above. With expert collectors now moving more freely in the region, possibly the original species will be re-identified.

Tulipa Darwin Hybrid 'Golden Appledoorn'   *Tulipa* Cottage Hybrid 'San Marino'   *Tulipa* hybrid 'Queen of Sheba'

Savoy Alps. Stem 30 to rarely 40cm high. Leaves 4, to 20cm long, more or less undulate, ciliate. Flowers large. Perianth segments with somewhat recurved tips, bright scarlet-red, basal blotch blackish-purple to dark olive with an irregular yellow margin; filaments black, anthers yellow; late-flowering. May. z7(6)

T. eichleri Regel. Transcaucasus Region, NW. Iran. Stems slightly pubescent, 20 to rarely 30cm high. Leaves to 20cm long, broadly strap-shaped, glaucous, undulate. Flowers large, to 12cm, segments bright, glossy, scarlet, basal blotch black with a yellow margin inside, outer segments (sepals) pale buff, sometimes reddish tinged, acuminate. One of the most beautiful, persistent wild tulips. Cultivars include: 'Excelsa', flowers larger, brilliant scarlet; and 'Maxima', later-blooming, flowers larger. April to May. z5

T. ferganica Vved. Central Asia; Fergana Mts. Stems 25–35cm high. Leaves 2, glaucous, folded, very undulate, acute. Flowers large; segments with somewhat

'Burpeeana', to 40cm high, flowers vermilion flushed fiery orange, yellow base; 'Defiance', flowers with yellow blotch and stamens; 'Mme Lefebre' (= 'Red Emperor'), to 60cm high, flowers very large; 'Princeps', flowers orange-red with yellow blotch; 'Purissima', flowers large, milk-white. Recently a group of cultivars have appeared named by color, as 'Yellow Emperor', 'Pink Emperor', and so on. *T. fosteriana* is often used in hybridizing, giving rise to many colorful cultivars in red, yellow and orange hues, and even white. All are notable for their enormous flowers, many have brown-striped leaves. April. z5

T. fulgens see **T. gesneriana**

T. gesneriana L. (*T. fulgens* hort ex Bak.) S. Russia; Armenia. Stems to 60cm high, usually less. Leaves glaucous, mostly basal, ovate-lanceolate, to 15cm long. Flowers cup-shaped opening to saucer-shape; segments soft crimson to scarlet, basal blotch, inside only, olive or blackish, yellow-margined; stamens

T. greigii Regel. Central Asia, Tien Shan Mts. Stems sturdy, 15–25cm high, downy to pubescent; leaves glaucous, maroon-brown striped and spotted. Flowers open-cup-shaped, fiery scarlet-red with a black, yellow-bordered basal blotch. April to May. 'Aurea' is a selection from a wild population from western Tien Shan with glossy golden yellow flowers and red basal blotch. *T. greigii* is often appropriately referred to as the "King of the Tulips." During the past few decades a number of colorful *Tulipa greigii* hybrids have come onto the market, all recognizable by more or less brown-striped leaves. A colorful mix is offered as "Peacock Tulips." The flowering period is late April to May. z5

T. hageri see **T. orphanidea**

T. hoogiana B. Fedtsch. Central Asia, mountains of Turkestan, NE. Iran. Stems glabrous, 30–40cm high. Leaves 4–8, glabrous, to 20cm long, lanceolate-acuminate, creased. Flowers pale scarlet-red with a black, yellow-bordered basal blotch, outer segments longer and wider than the inner. Bulbs large, ovate with a woolly tomentum inside the tunic. A beautiful, heat-loving species; bulbs need well-drained, sandy soil and should be planted at least 30cm deep. Late-flowering, May. z5

T. humilis see **T. pulchella**

T. ingens J.M.C. Hoog. Central Asia, Pamir Mts. Stems reddish, more or less pubescent, 20–25cm high. Leaves 3–5, glaucous, to 25cm long, lanceolate. Flowers large, to 11.5cm long, glossy vermilion-red with a black basal blotch

leaves. In addition to the many named cultivars, with numbers increasing yearly, a mix is offered as the "Rainbow Tulips." *T. kaufmanniana* and its hybrids are very long-lived garden plants. The leaves, however, may be eaten by slugs. All are primarily suited for the rock garden and perennial border where they are most effective planted with *Chionodoxa, Muscari* and *Scilla*. z5

T. kolpakowskiana Regel. Central Asia, N. Tien Shan, S. Ala Tau Mts. Stems 10–20cm high, curved-ascending to erect. Leaves 2–4, glaucous, narrow-lanceo-

"Sun's Eye Tulip" group (*T. oculus-solis*). Requires a very protected site in full sun since the foliage emerges very early; flowers in April. z7

T. linifolia Regel. Central Asia, Pamir Mts. Stems 10–15cm high. Leaves all basal, linear to narrowly lanceolate, glaucous with reddish-tinge, usually prostrate. Flowers bright, glossy red, segments with a wide black basal blotch inside, opening widely in the sun, to 8cm wide. Bulbs small with a leathery, light brown tunic, yellowish brown, woolly-haired inside and toward the apex. A

Tulipa hybrid 'Saint Patrick's Day'

Tulipa hybrid 'White Favorite'

Tulipa fosteriana hybrid 'Orange Emperor'

without the yellow border, loose cup-shaped, open to 20cm wide. A beautiful, not too cold-hardy, rare species. April to May. z6

T. kaufmanniana Regel. Water-lily Tulip. Central Asia, Tien Shan. Stems pubescent to hairy, 10–20cm high. Leaves 3–5, to 25cm long, broadly oblong, somewhat glaucous. Flowers shallowly cup-shaped, opening almost flat, starry, mostly cream-white with a wide, rich yellow, basal blotch, exterior red-tinged. Apparently, considerable color variation, white to deep yellow, occurs in the wild. Selections from wild plants include 'Aurea', golden-yellow with broad red stripes on the outside, and 'Coccinea', red with a green base. The flowers open to 12cm wide with recurved tips during sunny weather, hence the name "Water Lily Tulips." These bloom with the earliest tulips, late March to April. A important significant garden species with hybrids and cultivars in white, light to dark yellow, and pink to red hues. Hybrids with *T. greigii* are recognized by the brown-striped

late, creased, margins somewhat to very undulate, cartilaginous, nearly prone. Flowers deep cup-shaped, segments narrowly acuminate. Only the yellow-flowering form with broad, faded carmine-red stripes outside, opening 6–8cm wide, is found in culture. This species is quite variable in nature, ranging from reddish to orange (possibly hybrids) to pure yellow. March to April. This beautiful tulip grows wild on rocky bluffs in gravel; a rock garden species. z6

T. lanata Regel. Central Asia, Pamir Mts., E. Afghanistan, NE. Iran, Kashmir. Stems soft-pubescent, 40–50cm high. Leaves 4–5, somewhat glaucous, lanceolate, the basal leaves to 25cm long, very wide; crowded stem leaves narrowly lanceolate. Flowers cup-shaped, both sides of the segments bright orange-scarlet, not glossy, with a blackish-green, yellow-bordered basal blotch. Bulbs large, stoloniferous; the parchment-like, brown tunic with dense, woolly tomentum inside. A beautiful, but unfortunately temperamental species of the

charming rock garden tulip, similar in habit to the yellow- flowering *T. batalinii*. April to May. z5

T. marjolettii Perr. et Song. SE. France, Savoy Alps. Stems 40–50cm high. Leaves 3–5, narrow-lanceolate, margin undulate. Perianth segments yellow, pink-tinged on the reverse. May be a naturalized reversion from ancient gardens, as the horticulturist's *T. gesneriana*. Blooms in mid-May. z6

T. mauritiana Jord. SE. France, Savoy. Stems 30–40cm high. Leaves usually 4, broadly lanceolate to linear-lanceolate, margins undulate and somewhat ciliate. Flowers broadly bell-shaped, to 7.5cm wide, perianth segments brick red with a black, yellow-bordered basal blotch inside; reverse yellowish-tinged at the base. Status of this species questionable; see above species, final remark. May. z6

T. maximowiczii Regel. Central Asia: Pamir Mts. Similar to *T. linifolia*. Stem flexuous, 10–15cm high. Distinguishing characteristics: leaves very narrow, not undulate, more or less erect; stems green, not turning red; flowers somewhat smaller, red, basal blotch small bluish-black, or lacking. Flowers 10 days before *T. linifolia*. April. For rock gardens and troughs. z5

T. montana see **T. wilsoniana**

T. oculus-solis St. Amans (*T. agenensis* DC.), Sun's Eye Tulip. S. France: Languedoc, Tarn, Garonne; Italy: Bologna, Florence. Stems glaucous, to 20cm high. Leaves usually 4, glabrous green, lanceolate, the lowest to 25cm

Tulipa acuminata

long, 5cm wide, erect. Flowers to 7.5cm long, segments bright lacquer red with yellow-edged, blackish basal patch inside, reverse dull green and brown-tinged. April to May. More interesting than eye-catching, suitable for naturalizing and rock garden plantings. z6

T. orphanidea Boiss. ex Heldr. (*T. hageri* Heldr.). Balkan Peninsula; Bulgaria, Greece, Turkey. Stems 10–20cm high, often reddish above. Leaves 3–4, clustered low on the stem, linear to linear-lanceolate, lowest to 20cm long, creased, glossy. Flowers borne below foliage tips, to 5cm wide, opening flat; segments variable in color, inside from orange to orange-brown and brownish-red with darker basal patch, reverse orangeish, green-ish or dull purple-tinged. 'Flava', pale yellow, open flowers starry, tips somewhat recurved. Some botanists list *T. hageri* Heldr. as a distinct, but similar and closely related species with overlapping range. April. z5

T. ostrowskiana Regel. Central Asia: Tien Shan. Stem 15–20cm high. Leaves 2–4, narrowly lanceolate, distinctly

undulate, to 30cm long, erect. Flowers to 6cm long, widely cup-shaped; perianth segments acuminate and recurved, bright scarlet-red, with interior greenish-black to olive, yellow-bordered basal blotch. April to May. Hybridizes in nature with *T. kolpakowskiana* where their ranges overlap. z5

T. patens Agardh. ex Schult. Schult.f. (*T. celsiana* DC.; *T. persica* Willd. ex Kunth.) W. Siberia, Altai Mts. Stems 15–25cm high. Leaves 2–3, to 14cm long, narrowly lanceolate, folded, mostly on the stem. Flowers 1–3 on short peduncles, to

Tulipa batalinii 'Bronze Charm'

4.5cm long; segments creamy white to yellowish, with yellow basal blotch, reverse greenish or tinged pale red. This very rare species is stoloniferous and naturalized well. May. z5

T. persica see **T. patens**

T. praecox Ten. N. Italy; commonly found in country gardens on the Balkan Peninsula. Stems stout, more or less puberulent, 40–50cm high. Leaves oblong-ovate to oblong-lanceolate, margin undulate or flat, glaucous, glossy. Flowers to 7cm long, conical, but opening widely; perianth segments soft scarlet with a yellow-bordered, black-green basal spot inside, petals shorter and narrower than the reflexed sepals; sepals dull orange or greenish outside; stamens black or dark olive. Tunic papery with a dense, woolly tomentum. Stoloniferous, spreading widely. March to April. z5

T. praestans Th. Hoog. Central Asia: Pamir Mts. Stem somewhat pubescent, 30–40cm high, with leaves along its length. Basal leaf to 20cm long, 10cm

wide, broadly lanceolate, stem leaves (4–5) much narrower, folded, green. Flowers 1–4, cup-shaped, monochrome, pale scarlet (pale brick red); perianth segments more or less similar with no blotch. Bulb ovoid-acute, with a leathery, bronze-brown tunic with a few silky hairs inside. The cultivar 'Füsilier' has light scarlet-red flowers; 'Tubergens Variety' is shorter, flowers orange-scarlet. All are useful, persistent garden plants for the rock garden but the monochrome flowers on leafy stems are less eye-catching than some other species. April. z5

Tulipa clusiana

T. pulchella (Regel) Fenzl ex Bak. Asia Minor, Cilician Taurus. Stem 7 to very rarely 12cm high. Leaves 2–3, narrowly linear, more or less flat, to 15cm long, olive-green, clustered at the stem base, often prone. Flowers ovate, about 3cm long, nodding at first, then upward-facing, opening wide; segments pinkish to pale purple turning to lilac, with a white-margined, dark bluish basal blotch; quite variable, including 'Alba Coerulea Oculata' (= 'Pallida'), white with steel blue blotch; 'Humilis', flowers violet-pink; 'Violacea', purple-violet with a greenish-black basal blotch. One of the earliest tulips, and so needs protection from late frosts; early March. Rix and Phillips indicate that the three often listed species, *T. humilis* Herb., *T. pulchella* Fenzl. and *T. violacea* Boiss et. Buhse (see cvs. above) are variants of the same species, which they list as *T. humilis*. z5

T. saxatilis Sieb. Crete. Stems 15–25cm high, 1–3 flowered. Basal leaf 1, sometimes 2, narrow to broadly lanceolate, to 20cm long, stem leaf 1–2, low, narrow, shining green. Flowers shallow cup-shaped, opening almost flat, to 6 cm long, pale pinkish-lilac with yellow base. Fragrant. Bulb globose with pale brown, pink-tinged tunic, pubescent inside. Stoloniferous, multiplying freely. Requires a sunny, very warm site and infertile soil, best situated among rocks, otherwise does not flower freely. *T. bakeri* is almost identical but with darker violet flowers. April. z6

T. sprengeri Bak. NW. Turkey. Stems 30–45 cm high with 2–3 narrowly linear, flat leaves. Basal leaves usually 2, to 22.5 cm long, linear-lanceolate, glossy green.

Tulipa greigii 'Engadin'

Flowers to 6.5 cm long, outer segments (sepals) narrowly ovate, tips recurved, inner segments (petals) ovate; segments uniformly brownish-crimson inside, with no basal blotch, outer segment pale orange outside; stamens yellow. A valuable, persistent garden plant; the only tulip which commonly self-seeds. Bulbs medium-sized, tunic dark brown, papery, with a few silky hairs inside. Plant deeply whenever possible. This adaptable species grows in sun, in semi-shade, or in bright shade. The latest tulip to flower; first of May to early June. A recent report suggests that *T. sprengeri* is now extinct in the wild. z5

T. sylvestris L. North Africa, Iran, the Caucasus Region and S. Europe; naturalized in Europe and E. USA. Stems 20–40 cm high, flexuous. Leaves 2–5, the lower one broader, leaves linear-lanceolate, to 22.5 cm long, somewhat channeled, glaucous. Flowers 1–3, nodding at first, later erect, to 5 cm long;

segments narrow with reflexed, reddish tips, yellow with a green- or greenish-tinged exterior, fragrant. Bulbs ovoid, tunic bright yellow tinged red; stoloniferous, usually very vigorous and where summers are cool and moist may be poor-flowering. Subspecies *australis* reputedly is diploid, ssp. *sylvestris* is reported to be triploid or tetraploid; cultivar 'Major', freer-flowering, flowers golden-yellow, 2–3 per stem; 'Tabriz', taller, flowers larger, more free-flowering. April to May. z5

T. tarda Stapf (*T. dasystemon* hort. non

T. kaufmanniana 'Gaiety', 'Fritz Kreisler'

Regel). Central Asia: Tien Shan Mts. Stem about 7.5 cm high, with 1–7 flowers. Leaves 4–7, linear to narrowly lanceolate, to 22 cm long, 2 cm wide, slightly channeled, glaucous, in a loose rosette. Flowers erect, opening to a flat stem; segments creamy white, the lower 1/2–3/4 orange-yellow inside, the outer segments mostly glaucous green, creamy margined outside, inner segments with a green outside streak, all may show some hairline red striping outside. Bulbs ovoid, tunic yellowish-brown, stoloniferous. Excellent rock garden plant. z5

T. tubergeniana Th. Hoog. Central Asia, Pamir Mts. Stems somewhat pubescent, 40–50 cm high. Leaves 4–5, wide, glaucous, hairy, long-acuminate to 30 cm long, erect. Flowers 9–10 cm long, large, opening to a flat cup; segments bright, glossy vermilion with a small, yellow-margined dark olive blotch, filaments black, anthers deep purple. Bulbs large with a papery, red-brown tunic. A beautiful, heat-loving species. April to May. z5

T. turkestanica Regel. Central Asia, Tien

Shan and Pamir Mts., NW. China. Stems pubescent, 15–20 cm high, 1–7 flowered. Leaves 2–3, linear-acute, channeled, glaucous. Flowers about 4 cm high, deep-centered starry, segments ivory-white with an orange-yellow blotch inside, outer segments reddish without. Bulbs stoloniferous, small, ovate, with a glossy, red-brown tunic. A collector's plant for the rock garden. Several species are very similar, differing in stem pubescence, the presence, density, and position of hairs within the tunic, and anther color; including *T. biflora* and *T. bifloriformis*. April. z5

Tulipa praestans 'Füsilier'

T. urumiensis Stapf. NW. Iran, E. Turkey. Stems 8–12 cm high, with 1–4(5) flowers. Leaves narrowly linear-lanceolate, to 13 cm long, channeled, glabrous, dull green, mostly basal. Flowers to 4 cm long, urn-shaped, opening widely in sunlight, segments rich golden yellow, outer segments green, olive and red-tinged without. Bulb stoloniferous, small, nearly round, tunic orange-brown. Valuable for the rock garden or trough garden. Perhaps extinct in the wild. April. z5

T. vvedenskyi Z. Botsch. Central Asia: Tien Shan Mts. Stem hairy, 20, rarely to 35 cm high. Leaves 4–5, to 23 cm long, lanceolate to narrowly lanceolate, glaucous, channeled, margins not undulate. Flowers cup-shaped, to 9 cm long; segments scarlet, sometimes orange, or straw-buff, inside shading yellowish at the base, rarely shading olive just at the pistil, outside self-colored; in sunlight, perianth segments spread widely, tips reflexed. A beautiful, but rare species. April to May. z5

T. violacea see **T. pulchella**

T. whittallii (Dykes) A. D. Hall. W. Turkey. Stem 25–35cm high. Leaves 3–4, to 20cm long, less than 2cm wide, narrowly lanceolate, glabrous green, somewhat channeled. Flowers inverse bell-shaped; segments acuminate, interior bright orange with rounded, dark olive-colored basal blotch, exterior buff and green. Closely related to *T. orphanidea*, but more brightly colored, more vigorous, and flowers somewhat earlier. April. z5

T. wilsoniana J. M. C. Hoog. Turkestan (Kopet Dagh Mts.). Stem 12–20cm high.

Tulipa sylvestris

Leaves 3–5, to 12cm long, 2cm wide, narrowly lanceolate, flat, margins undulate, glaucous. Flowers to 5cm high, segments spreading flat in sunlight, acuminate, glossy, blood red with small, blue-black basal patch. Closely related to *T. montana* Lindl., and occasionally listed under this name. The single distinction is apparently the rounded perianth segments of the latter. Very attractive for the rock garden. April. z5

The Most Common Diseases of Tulips

Botrytis Blight (*Botrytis tulipae*) or Tulip Fire is evidenced by sunken, brown, decayed patches on otherwise white bulb scales, beneath the brown papery tunic. Later, botrytis may be detected as shoots emerge; these are crippled and distorted, with soggy, blackened tissue. Later, watery or sunken gray-brown spots on the leaves and paler, brownish, translucent spots on the flowers causing stunting are typical symptoms. A weekly fungicide application beginning at or just before shoot emergence is recommended as a preventive. Another preventive measure is to remove spent

blossoms to keep them from falling on the leaves and soil, thereby serving as a source of inoculum. Also, tulips should not be replanted in the same beds, especially if disease has already been a problem. Other tulip diseases include gray bulb rot, crown rot, basal and stem rot. Prevention, as always, is the best policy. Infected bulbs should normally be discarded, in addition, treat bulbs and soil with appropriate fungicides. Tulips may also be damaged by various virus diseases such as Breaking, Mosaic and Necrosis. Insects such as bulb flies, mites and aphids not only parasitize tulip

Typha latifolia

bulbs, stems and leaves, they also transmit diseases, especially viruses. Consult the current literature for further descriptions and control measures. (Sch.)

Tunica

T. saxifraga see **Petrorhagia saxifraga**

Tussilago

T. anandria, **T. lyrata** see **Leibnitzia anandria**

Typha L.
Typhaceae
Cattail, Reed-mace, Bulrush

About 15 species, almost world wide, in tropical and temperate regions. Winter-hardy marsh and aquatic plants with a thick, creeping, rhizomatous rootstock. Leaves erect, linear, flat, parallel-veined, sheathed at the base. Stem unbranched. Flowers in a long, spadix-like terminal spike, staminate flowers above, pistillate flowers below. Flowers greatly reduced, perianth a few short hairs in male

Typha gracilis

flowers, more, longer hairs in female flowers; male flowers with 2–5 (rarely 1) stamens with united filaments, female flowers with 1 pistil, simple stigma, elongated style, simple, superior ovary with 1 ovule, and, often, vestigial, non-functional stamens. Fruit small, an achene (nutlet) with long perianth hairs in a thick, velvety brown spike. All species are suitable only for marshy sites in the garden. The broad-leaved *Typha latifolia* is a typical plant of moors and marshlands in acidic to neutral, clay loam. Other species grow in less acidic soils. Propagation is by division in spring, and seed from April to June in pots or flats, kept moist to wet. Seed also may be sown in shaded beds if the soil is moisture-retentive, fertile loam. The mature spikes often are used in cut-flower arrangements. Spray with hair spray or a similar sealing material to prevent shattering of cut cattails.

T. angustifolia L., Narrow-leaved Cattail. Europe, N. America; commonly found in shallow water, 20–80cm deep. Plants grow to 2m high. Leaves to 8 or 10mm wide, dull green. Pistillate spike 10–

20cm long, 8–34mm thick, chestnut brown, separated from the staminate spike by 2–5cm. Flowers from July to August. z3

T. gracilis Europe. To 75cm high, similar to *T. minima*, but with leafy flower stems, leaves reach beyond the spike. Male and female portions of the spike distinctly separated, August to September. For small streams and tubs with 10cm-deep water. z5

T. latifolia L., Common Cattail, Broadleaved Cattail, Cossack Asparagus.

Typha minima

Europe, Africa, Asia, N. America; in standing water. Foliage to 3m high. Leaves flat, swordlike, 2.5 to rarely 4cm wide, to 1–2m long, grayish-green. The staminate flower portion continuous with pistillate portion abscising after flowering. Fruiting spike 10–30cm long, 3–4cm thick, eventually blackish-brown. Blooms from July to August. Vigorous grower. The rhizome is invasive, sufficiently sturdy to penetrate asphalt paving. Planting in tubs is advisable. Naturalize in large garden and park situations together with *Iris pseudacorus*, *Phragmites* and *Sparganium*; a good background for water-lilies. Requires constantly moist soil with 10–20cm deep water. z3

T. latifolia ssp. **shuttleworthii** see **T. shutterworthii**

T. laxmannii Lepech. E. Europe, Asia. Foliage 0.75–1.5m high. Leaves conspicuously narrow, usually only 2–5mm wide, half-rounded, overtopping the spikes. Pistillate spike brown, scarcely 5cm long, staminate portion distinctly separate, to 3 times as long. July to August. Vigorous. Requires constantly moist soil with a 0–20cm depth of water. z4

T. minima Funck ex Hoppe. Europe, Asia. Stems 50–75cm high. Leaves on sterile stems very narrow, less than 2mm wide, rounded, on fertile stems leaves are reduced to enlarged basal sheaths or nearly so. Flowering stem 30–75cm high, leafless, always above the foliage. Pistillate portion of the spike ovate to short-cylindrical, contiguous to the staminate portion or rarely separate, appearing in May, disentegrating in July. Suitable for the smallest streamsides, tubs or troughs together with *Nymphaea tetragona*, *Caltha*, *Nymphoides*. Grows best in somewhat gravelly soil with water to 10cm deep. z6(5)

T. shuttleworthii W.D.J. Koch et Sond. (*T. latifolia* ssp. *shuttleworthii* (W. D. J. Koch et Sond.) Stoj et Stef.). Europe. Similar to *T. angustifolia*, but only to 1.5m high, leaves 1cm wide, reaching beyond the spike. Male and female portions contiguous, the female portion longer. Fruiting spikes quickly disintegrate as with all the *Typha* species. July to August. Used like *T. angustifolia*. z5

T. stenophylla Fisch. et Mey. Italy. Very narrow-leaved species, leaves 1.2–1.5m high, 5–6mm wide, partially rounded. Flowering stems leafy, shorter than the leaves. Staminate portion of the spike twice as long as the pistillate, distinctly separated. Mature spike 5–8cm long, 2cm thick, rounded at the tip, brown. Flowers in July to August. An elegant, graceful species for small garden sites. Possibly only a variety of *T. laxmannii*. z6 (D.)

Ulmaria see Filipendula

Umbilicus DC.
Crassulaceae

Six to 15 species of more or less tender, succulent perennial herbs from S. Europe, N. and Central Africa and W. Asia. Rootstock mostly rhizomatous. Stems and leaves glabrous, fleshy. Leaves alternate, petioled below, reduced above, peltate, or blades cordate. Inflorescence terminal, racemose. Flowers small, 5-merous, sepals separate, corolla tubular, short-lobed, stamens 10 or 5, ovary with 5 more or less free carpels.

The currently included species, *U.*

erectus, U. horizontalis and *U. rupestris* are not generally winter hardy in the open landscape beyond zone 7.

U. aizoon see **Rosularia aizoon**

U. chrysantha see **Rosularia pallida**

U. chrysanthus see **Rosularia pallida**

U. rupestris (Salisb.) Dandy (*Cotyledon umbelicus* L.) Navelwort, Pennywort. Asia Minor, S. Europe and Great Britain, Canary Isles. Flowering stems 15–25cm high. Basal leaves peltate, blades orbicu-

Uniola latifolia

lar, 2.5–7.5cm across, sinuate crenate. Inflorescence terminal, a nearly flat raceme. Flowers nodding, on long peduncles, corolla to 1cm long, lobes mucronate, dull-colored. More weedy than ornamental. z8(7) (Kö.)

U. spinosus see **Orostachys spinosa**

Unifolium

U. canadense see **Maianthemum canadense**

Uniola L.
Gramineae
Sea Oats, Spike Grass

U. latifolia Michx., Spike Grass. Central and SE. North America. Loose clump grass with short rhizomes found in species-rich woodlands on fertile soil, especially in summer-warm sites. Culms very leafy; leaf blades to 20cm long and 2cm wide. Culms 60–120cm high; terminal panicles loose, somewhat nodding, with many flat-compressed

spikelets, often blue-violet marked; after midsummer. Good companions include *Actaea, Cimicifuga, Anemone, Kirengeshoma* or *Polygonum filiforme*. Valuable for its shade tolerance. The dried or fresh panicles are desirable for cut-flower arranging. Propagate by division or seed. One recent reclassification refers to this species as *Chasmanthium latifolium* (Michx.) Yates. z4 (S.)

Uropetalum see Dipcadi

Uvularia grandiflora

Uvularia L.
Liliaceae
Bellort, Merry Bells

Five species of E. North American perennials with thick, creeping rhizomes. Stems erect, 40–75cm-high, simple or branched, leafless below, alternate-leaved above. Leaves sessile or perfoliate, ovate to lanceolate. Flowers terminal, usually solitary or rarely paired, campanulate, pendulous on long, slender peduncles, yellow. Perianth segments 6, separate, pistil with 3-angled, superior ovary and 3-parted style. *U. grandiflora* is the most attractive and only species generally found in the trade. An elegant spring-flowering herb for

collectors and botanic gardens. Grows in shaded to semi-shaded locations in an open, deciduous woodland, in parks or large rock gardens. Plants thrive in any humus-rich garden soil; environmental requisites similar to that of *Polygonatum* and *Streptopus*, which also make good companion plants. Propagation is tedious by seed; rhizome division gives better results.

U. grandiflora Sm. N. America: SW. Quebec to Minnesota, south to Tennessee, Arkansas and Oklahoma; in fertile, mixed deciduous woodland.

Valeriana officinalis

Stems sometimes 2-branched, 30–75cm high. Leaves to 12cm long, stem-clasping, oblong to lanceolate-ovate, acuminate, pubescent beneath. Flowers to 5cm long, pendulous, slender, segments slightly twisted, lemon-yellow. Stamens longer than the pistil. Blooms in April and May. z4

U. caroliniana (J.F. Gmel.) Wilb., *U. perfoliata* L. and *U. sessilifolia* L. are also attractive, but smaller in all respects, including the flowers, which are pale yellow or greenish-tinged yellow. Not generally found outside of botanic gardens, but seed sometimes is available. Not as easily grown as *U. grandiflora*. z4 (E.)

Valeriana L.
Valerianaceae
Valerian, Garden Heliotrope

More than 200 species of annual or perennial herbs, subshrubs and shrubs on all continents except Australia. The thickened tap roots and rhizomes, and often the entire plant, are strongly scented. Leaves opposite. Basal leaves often rosetted, usually simple, stem leaves pinnatifid to pinnately compound. Inflorescence terminal, in clustered or panicled cymes. Flowers small, perfect, staminate or pistillate. Calyx limb inrolled through anthesis, becoming stiff, bristle-like, with 5–15 feathery segments in fruit. Corolla usually white or pink, rose, or yellowish, rotate, infundibular or campanulate, often pouchlike at the base. Stamens usually 3. Ovary inferior, partially 3-celled, stigmas more or less 3-cleft. Fruit a nutlet, single-seeded, usually compressed, crowned by the feathery calyx. Valerians are seldom recommended for general garden use. Plants are pleasant in appearance but not outstanding; more suitable for specialists. The tall species thrive in semi-shaded woodlands, spreading by self-seeding under favorable conditions. These require somewhat damp soil, but will tolerate a moderately dry site in any average garden soil. The low-growing species belong in the alpine garden or rock garden. Except for the lime-intolerant *V. celtica* and *V. dioica*, species mentioned here are lime-intolerant and grow best in limestone or dolomite screes and rock crevices. *V. dioica* grows in moist, peaty soil; *V. celtica* is a typical inhabitant of a coarse, high humus soil. Propagate by seed (requires light for germination), division or cuttings.

Tall, erect species over 30cm

V. alliariifolia Adams. E. Greece, Caucasus Region, Asia Minor; in woodlands and along streams of subalpine elevations over 1000m. Rootstock a thick, branching rhizome. Stem glabrous, grooved, 50–90cm high. All leaves simple, 5–20cm wide, cordate, crenate or shallowly toothed, lower leaves long-petioled, large, upper stem leaves smaller, sessile, lanceolate or ovate. Flowers pink, perfect, in a terminal compound, widely spreading cyme. Blooms from June to July. z5

V. coccinea var. **rubra** see **Centranthus ruber**

V. officinalis L., Common Valerian, Garden Heliotrope. Europe and Asia, widely naturalized elsewhere, including Canada and the USA, along streams and other wet areas including open woodlands and willow thickets, on fertile, often soggy loam soil. Tolerates drier, more calcareous fields. A variable species. Rhizomes little branched, occasionally with short stolons. 0.3–1.5m high, more or less grooved. All leaves odd-pinnate with 15–21 segments, segments entire or serrate. Inflorescence a corymb. Flowers very fragrant, light pink, lavender or white, in bloom from

Valeriana montana

June to August. Cultivars include 'Alba', flowers white; 'Coccinea', flowers dark red; and 'Rubra', flowers brighter red. The powdered, dried rhizome used as a medicinal plant before 1500. Plants attract cats. Grows in full sun and semi-shade, moist to dry. Propagate by seed sown as soon as ripe in August, or from March to April. Fruits should be uncovered or only lightly covered with soil since light is required for germination. Division is also possible. z4

V. phu L. Origin uncertain, probably indigenous to Anatolia, naturalized locally in Europe and Asia Minor. Similar to *V. officinalis*, but usually with simple basal leaves and lobed stem leaves, smooth, ungrooved stems, and rhizomes never stoloniferous. Inflorescence a paniculate corymb of white flowers. Blooms from June to August. Used as a medicinal plant as early as the 16th century. Young growths of cultivar 'Aurea' is yellow-leaved. The existence

of the true species in cultivation is questionable. z6

Low species, under 30cm

V. dioica L., Swamp Valerian. W. and Central Europe to SE. Norway, Macedonia, W. Russia, S. Italy; in swampy lowlands, on stream banks, and other wet, calcareous or lime-free soil. Rhizomes stoloniferous. Stems 15–30cm high. Basal leaves broadly ovate, long-petioled on sterile stems; middle leaves lyre shaped. Inflorescence a compound corymb. Flowers of one sex pink, occasionally white. Staminate flowers 3mm long, pistillate flowers 1mm long. Blooms in May, June. Cultivated in Switzerland as early as 1561. A good plant for a moist, high humus location along watercourses or on a pond bank with *Caltha palustris, Calla palustris, Carex fusca, Molina caerulea, Myosotis palustris* and *Tofieldia*. z4

V. montana L., Mountain Valerian. Pyrenees Mts., Alps, Carpathian Mts., Italian Mts. and the Balkan Mts.; a pioneer plant in gravelly limestone meadows and rock crevices, from about 600–2800m; primarily on a lime-rich, usually loamy, moist, loess soil. Creeping perennial, rhizome with many stems, without stolons. Stems 10–40cm high, glabrous or nearly pubescent. Leaves simple (long-petioled, ovate on sterile stems) lower leaves oblong or obovate, 40cm long, obtuse, slightly toothed, upper leaves lanceolate, acute, sessile. Flowers perfect, staminate and pistillate, white to light pink or lilac, in a long-pediceled, loose cyme. Blooms from May to June. Typical companion species are *Pinus mugo* and *Rhododendron hirsutum, Adenostyles, Petasites paradoxus, Sesleria*. z5

V. tripteris L. SW. European Mts. to the Carpathian Mts., Sudeten Mts., and N. Greece; in gravelly mountain forests, on rocks, brushy slopes, screes and rock crevices at the subalpine elevations, to 2700m in the Alps. Rhizomes branched, with several to many stems, without stolons. Flower stems 10–40cm high, nodes pubescent. Leaves of sterile stems and all basal leaves long-petioled, cordate, coarsely dentate. Stem leaves pinnate decompound. Segments toothed. Flowers white or pale pink, in a loose, repeatedly 3-part corymb. Blooms from May to June. Grows mostly on lime soils, but also grows on neutral, high-humus soil. Like *V. montana*, for a shady or semi-shaded site in the alpine garden, with *Pinus mugo*, and *Rhododendron* *hirsutum, Asplenium* species and *Sesleria.* z5

Low species, under 30cm, creeping or procumbent

V. celtica L. W. and E. Alps; from 1800–2800m, in mixed herbaceous stands in deep topsoil, or in colonies on shallow alpine soils, among rocks on acidic, lime-free soil, usually on snow-covered north and northwest slopes. Rhizomes creeping, sparsely branched, obliquely ascending, or exposed on the surface. Stems 5–15cm high, glabrous. Leaves to 4cm long, simple, entire, obovate, oblanceolate or linear; stem leaves 1 or 2 pairs. Inflorescence a loose panicle. Flowers yellowish to buff. Blooms from July to August. Entire plant is fragrant. Used for medicinal purposes for more than 2000 years. Difficult to grow, recommended only for experienced gardeners. Needs sun to bright semi-shade and a lime-free, cool, moist, coarse humus soil. Propagate by division or seed. z5

V. globulariifolia Ram. ex DC. Europe: Pyrenees Mts., Cantabrian Mts.; among rocks in the high mountains. Rhizome branched, woody, creeping, with stolons. Stems grooved, 6–10cm high. Basal leaves small, oval, entire, occasionally ternate. Lower stem leaves pinnately cleft, upper ones pinnatisect with 1–2 pairs of more or less linear segments, uppermost leaves simple. Flowers pink, in large corymbs. Entire plant scented. Blooms from May to June. Garden uses and cultivation as for *V. montana.* z5

V. saliunca All. W. and S. Alps, Central Apennine Mts.; from 1800–2700m on rocky alpine meadows, in rock crevices and screes. Stems woody at the base, with several foliage rosettes, not creeping. Flowering stems erect, 5–10cm high. Leaves crowded, simple, entire, dark green; stem leaves rarely deeply lobed. Inflorescence a dense corymb. Flowers deep pink, fragrant. Blooms from June to July. Best on calcareous soils. One of the most attractive species, but difficult to grow, often short-lived in the garden. Only for the experienced alpine gardener. z5

V. × suendermannii Melchior (*V. montana × V. supina*). N. Italy; Dolomite Mts. Stems 5–10cm high, forming dense mats. Leaves simple, orbicular to spatulate. Flowering stems usually with 3or 4 leaf pairs. Flowers white, in an open corymb. Stems, leaves, roots and flowers very fragrant. Blooms from May to June. Discovered and introduced about 1900

by Sündermann. Easier to grow than either parents, in gravelly limestone soil. Propagation is only by division since plants set no seed. z5

V. supina Ard., Dwarf Valerian. Central European Mts.; at 1800-2900m; on rock outcrops and in snow pockets, especially on fine to coarse, limy scree or loose, loess soil. Rhizomes creeping, much branched. Stems in dense mats, erect or ascending, 5–10cm high, short appressed-pubescent, leaves thickish, spatulate or more or less rounded, entire, occasionally crenate, dark shining

Vancouveria hexandra

green. Flowers in dense corymbs enveloped in linear bracts, dark pink, fragrant. Blooms from June to July. One of the most attractive low species for limy, infertile, gravelly soil in a sunny to partially shaded bed in the alpine garden. z5 (E.)

Unifolium

U. **canadense** see **Maianthemum canadense**

Vancouveria C. Morr. et Decne. Berberidaceae

Three species in W. North America. The genus is closely related to *Epimedium* (distinguished by 6, instead of 4, inner sepals, petals and stamens). Rhizomatous rootstock slender; leaves mostly or all basal, biternate, the leaflets cordate, more or less 3-lobed; flowers white or

yellow reflexed bracts and nectaries, in a nodding panicle on a leafless stem; sepals 6–9, the 6 inner petaloid, petals 6, narrow with apical nectaries, stamens 6, ovary 2-celled. A woodland plant, conspicuous, with open, attractive foliage. Garden uses, cultivation and propagation as for *Epimedium.* Requires winter protection, particularly in the first year, occasionally freezes out in snowless winters.

V. chrysantha Greene. Stems to 30cm high, foliage more or less evergreen. Leaves 2- or 3-ternate or with 5 leaflets,

Veratrum nigrum

leaflets to 4cm long, firm to leathery, margins cartilaginous and somewhat undulate, pubescent beneath. Flowers 12cm long, golden-yellow.

V. hexandra (Hook.) C. Morr. et Decne. (*Epimedium hexandrum* Hook.). USA: N. Washington to N. California. Stems to 45cm high, often shorter. Leaves 2- to 3-ternate, deciduous, leaflets to 4cm long, thin, nearly glabrous beneath; flowers to 12mm long, white, nodding; late spring. Very vigorous, spreading species; forms an attractive summer-foliage carpet. z7

V. planipetala Calloni. Oregon and California. Stems 30–45cm high, foliage evergreen. Leaves 2- or 3-ternate or rarely with 5 leaflets, leaflets to 4cm long, firm, margins more or less undulate, cartilaginous-thickened, nearly glabrous beneath. Flowers 8cm long, white or tinged lavender. Slower-growing than the previous species. z7 (Me. & M.)

Veratrum L.
Liliaceae
False Hellebore

Twenty to 45 species, depending on botanical interpretation of the genus, in Europe, Siberia and N. America. Mostly a tall-growing, stately perennial with thick, very poisonous rhizomatous rootstock. Leaves alternate, often broad, pleated, tapering to a large sheath. Inflorescence a terminal panicle. Flowers white, green, brown, maroon or purple on short peduncles, perfect or unisexual; perianth segments of perfect flowers somewhat connate at the base, forming a short tube, the flowers bell-shaped, segments of staminate or pistillate flowers separate, spreading, starry; segments 6, nearly equal, stamens 6, pistil superior with 3-angled ovary and 3 styles. Fruits many-seeded, septicidal capsule; seeds flat, winged. Not too ornamental, but bold, suitable for park plantings, also large gardens and alpine rock gardens as specimens or in colonies. Requires moist, fertile deep loam. Propagate by division; seed propagation is tedious.

V. album L. European White Hellebore. Northern mountains of Europe to E. Asia, Alaska. Stems to 1.5m high, downy. Leaves oblong to elliptic, finely tomentose beneath. Panicle to 60cm long. Flowers 15mm or more across, greenish outside, whitish inside, segments; July to August. Chiefly of interest to specialists. Poisonous, with medicinal properties; the powdered rhizome useful in destroying caterpillars. z5

V. californicum E. Durand. Corn Lily, Skunk Cabbage (both names very misleading). W. USA: Washington to California, east to the Rocky Mts. Stems to 2m high. Leaves broadly elliptic to ovate, lanceolate above, to 40cm long and 20cm wide near the base. Inflorescence to 45cm long, lower branches erect; flowers bell-shaped, 2cm across, sordid white, petals glabrous; July to August. The showiest and most interesting species. z5

V. nigrum L. South Central and S. Europe, Asia. Stems 60–120cm high, base somewhat enlarged, many-leaved. Leaves glabrous, broadly elliptic to oblong below, 30cm long, 20cm wide, to linear-lanceolate above. Panicle slender, 30–90cm long. Flowers 2–4mm across, black-purple, sour-fetid scented; July to August. An interesting, vigorous-growing species. z6 (Me. & M.)

Verbascum L.
Scrophulariaceae
Mullein

More than 300 species, of mostly biennial herbs, rarely subshrubs or perennials. Indigenous to Europe, N. Africa, W. and Central Asia, some widely naturalized, even weedy, in North America and elsewhere. Most species are tall, 1–2m high, more or less hairy or woolly. Leaves form a basal rosette; stems more or less foliate, leaves alternate, becoming smaller toward the top. Flowers are in spikes, racemes, or panicles, often clustered, on short peduncles. Calyx deeply 5 parted; corolla nearly rotate, deeply 5-lobed, tube short, limb nearly flat; stamens 5, epipetalous; fruit a capsule. Flowers usually yellow, occasionally red, purple, brownish, coppery, cream-colored, or rarely white. Individual flowers are proportionally small but the inflorescence often is large, showy, and new flowers open over a very long time, so the effective flowering period lasts from early to late summer.

Suitable for naturalized or wild garden plantings and park landscapes; plant in a sunny, dry location on banks and slopes, cultivars in beds. It is difficult to completely separate the biennial and perennial species because environment affects longevity. No species is persistent on a moist fertile soil. Under favorable conditions, a few species are perennial. Nearly all species grow best on sandy or rocky, very well-drained soil or on screes with some limestone; some will tolerate rather acidic sandy soil. Biennial species generally are planted in spring or early summer. Plants will increase by self-seeding in favorable sites, thereby making even the biennial species persistent. Propagate by seed, root cuttings or secondary rosettes. The number of hybrids is unusually large since the species hybridize readily.

V. bombyciferum Boiss. (*V. lagurus* hort. non Fisch. et Mey.). W. Asia Minor; Bithynian Olympus Mts. Biennial. To 1.8m high, entire plant densely felted, white-tomentose, especially the flowering spike. Basal leaves ovate-oblong, to 35cm long, in a very effective, full rosette. Inflorescence a spike with densely clustered flowers. Flowers to 4cm across, sulfur-yellow, 3–7 in each cluster. Very decorative species; also in the trade as 'Broussa' or *V. lagurus*. (The true *V. lagurus* Fisch. et Mey. is much less densely tomentose, flower stems distinctly visible.). Plants should be iso-

lated whenever possible to prevent cross-pollination as hybrids are usually less attractive than the species. The pure species is available in the seed trade as 'Polarsommer' ('Polar Summer'). A choice cultivar of the Brusa Strain is 'Silver Spires'. This species deteriorates very quickly on poorly drained or damp soil. z6

V. bugalifolium see **Celsia bugalifolia**

V. chaixii Vill. Nettle-leaved Mullein. S., Central and E. Europe. Perennial. Stems to 1m high, erect, branched toward the apex, slightly angular and white tomentose. Lower leaves wedge-shaped at the base, tapering to the long petiole, deeply incised-crenate; middle stem leaves short-petioled, upper leaves with broadly rounded to cordate bases, sessile. Flowers pale yellow, filaments purple-hairy in clusters of 2–5, short-peduncled in a panicle, usually well-branched below; July to August. 'Album' is a very appealing, white-flowering cultivar. This species is a parent of many garden hybrids. z5

V. dumulosum Davis et Hub.-Mor. SW. Asia Minor; Antalya. Stems 30–40cm high, plant suffruticose, densely bushy, white-tomentose overall. Leaves elliptic, to 6cm long and 3.5cm wide. Inflorescence a spike, flowers lemon yellow, 3cm across, very many, close-set on short peduncles. May to June. A beautiful species, especially for the alpine house or very dry sunny sites in the rockery or stone wall. Protection from prolonged periods of wetness is essential. Propagate by cuttings in August, and seed. z8(7)

V. lagurus see **V. bombyciferum**

V. leianthum Benth. Asia Minor. Biennial. One of the tallest, most stately species, stems erect, to 4m high in its native habitat, plant densely white tomentose. Basal leaves to 1.2m long and to 60cm wide; stem leaves oblong, crenate, rugose, with a decurrent base, both sides covered with white hairs. Flowers 1.8cm across, bright yellow, in a large, much branched, open panicle, to 2m-long and 75cm-wide many-flowered; July to August. z8(7)

V. longifolium Ten. Italy, Serbia, Macedonia. Stems to 1.2m high, very leafy, with a dense yellowish or whitish woolly tomentum. Leaves undulate, the basal leaves to 60cm long, narrowly ovate or oblong-lanceolate, short-petioled; the upper leaves sessile, stem-clasping. Flowers peduncled, to 2.5cm across, golden-yellow, in a dense spike, to 30cm-long, 9cm-wide. Stamen filaments with light violet hairs. The stamen filaments of the Bulgarian *V. longifolium* var. *pannosum* (Vis.) Murb. have whitish or yellowish hairs. Blooms from June to August. Its densely tomentose leaves and the ornamental leaf rosettes are always decorative in any garden. z7(6)

V. nigrum L. Central Scandinavia to NE. Spain, N. Italy, N. Balkans, Siberia, Alai Mts. A persistent perennial, stems to 1m high, ridged, with long hairs; leaves

naturalized garden and similar locations where it can be left undisturbed. A parent of some vigorous hybrids, which are propagated by root division. z5

V. olympicum Boiss. Greece; Bithynian Mts. Long-lived perennial, where hardy. Stems to 2m high, branching from near the base for a candelebra effect, with a dense gray-white tomentum. Leaves mostly or all basal, to 15cm long, in a large rosette, broadly lanceolate, acuminate, gray-white tomentose. Flowering stem appears in the 2nd or 3rd year. Flowers clustered on the racemes, to

borne just above the leaf rosette. Flowers 2.5cm across, rich golden-yellow; May to June. Very attractive, especially in the alpine house. Propagate by cuttings and seed. z7

V. phoeniceum L. Purple Mullein. SE. and E. Central Europe, Asia. Perennial. Stems 40–60cm high, to 1.5m in fertile soil. Basal leaves ovate, coarsely crenate, dark green, glabrous above, pubescent beneath, in a flat rosette, stem leaves few, small. Flower stems usually red-violet to the base. Inflorescence a simple, slender, glandular raceme; flowers dark purple-

Verbascum bombyciferum 'Polarsommer'

glabrous above, gray-tomentose beneath, the basal leaves to 30cm long, long-petioled with cordate base. Flowers 12–18mm across, dark yellow, sometimes red-dotted, with violet anthers; borne in leaf axils and terminal spike, in erect, slightly branched racemes. A reliable species, renewing itself from a fleshy rootstock. Only for the large

3cm wide, bright, golden-yellow, filament hairs whitish or yellowish. Plants often die after blooming; June to August. z8(7 or 6)

V. pestalozzae Boiss. W. Asia Minor; Lycian Taurus Mts. Subshrubby, to 25cm high, entire plant gray-tomentose; similar to *V. dumulosum*, but flowers

violet, red, or sometimes shades of pink, rose, lavender, purple, or very rarely white, solitary, very long-peduncled; May to June. A parent of some colorful cultivars. Often seeds freely in the garden and may become weedy. z5

V. spinosum L. Crete. Low, wide-branching subshrub to 30cm high with gnarled, woody, gray stems which end in spines. Leaves to 5cm long, .6cm wide, narrow oblanceolate, coarse-toothed, rarely entire, white-tomentose, mostly clustered on stubby twigs along the stems. Flowers yellow in a small, twiggy panicle. For very dry, warm sites in the rock garden. Scarcely winter hardy, even under favorable conditions. z8

V. wiedemannianum Fisch. et Mey. Asia Minor. Evergreen biennial. Stems to 1m high, stems and leaves densely gray-white cobwebby-hairy. Basal rosette leaves 7.5–13cm long, elliptic, tapered to

Verbascum hybrid 'Densiflorum'

the petiole, stem leaves smaller, sessile. Flowers 3.2cm across, solitary, indigo blue fading to violet, in a very long, simple, open-branched raceme; stamen filaments with purple hairs; June to August. z6

V. Hybrids. In addition to the species, many cultivars with origins difficult to establish are available. These often are notable not only for their ornamental habit and conspicuous flowers, but also because they live longer in cultivation than the species. Only a few are propagated by seed.

'Densiflorum' (*V. vernale* hort., *V. densiflorum* × *V. nigrum*). Stem to 1.8m high, a stately and strong-growing cultivar; dark green-leaved, with erect, many-panicled inflorescence. Flowers yellow with lilac anthers; July to August. Not to be confused with the biennial *V. densiflorum* Bertol. (*V. thapsiforme* Schrad.). Propagates easily by root cuttings.

'Silberkandelaber' ('Silver Candelabra') (*V. bombyciferum* × *V. olympicum*?). Stem 1.5m high. Conspicuous, attractive, silver-white, pubescent rosette. Inflorescence tall and wide, well-branched, candelabra-fashion. July to August. Unlike *V. bombyciferum*, not especially sensitive to damp soil. (This is true of many spontaneous hybrids and is consistent in their progeny). Sets seed only moderately, but generally produces true progeny.

Lower, densely bushy cultivars, some woody:

'Golden Bush'. A chance seedling of

Verbascum hybrid 'Letitia'

V. nigrum × *V. spinosum*, Hillier 1963. Subshrub 60cm-high; dense, ascending panicles of pure yellow flowers. June to August. Only propagated by root cuttings.

'Letitia' (*V. dumulosum* × *V. spinosum*). Subshrubby, 30cm high, densely branched, globose bush habit. Flowers uncommonly abundant and long-lasting; May to July. Propagated by rosette cuttings in late summer. Requires a very dry site with a cover in periods of wetness.

Some similar, but rarely found collector's cultivars include (*V. pestalozzae* × *V. spinosum*) 'Golden Dawn' and (*V. pestalozzae* × *V. dumulosum* × *V. spinosum*) 'Sunrise'. All are very attractive plants for the alpine house.

Cotswold Hybrids; a strain developed by Cotswold in 1935 from crosses of *V. phoeniceum* with various other species. Notable for their showy flower colors. More vigorous and persistent than *V. phoeniceum*, but propagated only by root cuttings or separation of secondary rosettes. A few additional modern cultivars include:

'Boadicea', 1.8m high, with copper-colored flowers with violet centers; 'Cotswold Queen', 1.5m high, vigorous, flowers amber-colored to bronze-salmon, anthers pale lilac, a unique color combination; 'Gainsborough', pyramidal panicles, light yellow; 'Pink Domino', 1m high, with pink flowers. (Me. & M.)

Verbena peruviana

Verbena L.
Verbenaceae

Two hundred to 250 species of mostly hairy, erect to prostrate, herbaceous plants, shrubs and subshrubs from tropical and temperate North and South America. Stems often 4-angled. Leaves opposite or rarely in whorls of 3 or alternate, toothed, lobed, or dissected, rarely entire. Flowers small, mostly in compact, terminal spikes which elongate during fruiting, or in corymbs, or broad panicles, or rarely solitary. Calyx 5-toothed, 5-ribbed, sometimes oblique; corolla more or less zygomorphic, salverform or funnelform, 5-lobed, usually somewhat 2-lipped; stamens epipetalous, 4, didynamous, or rarely 2, anthers often appendaged at the connective; ovary globose, not 4-angled, style terminal, stigmas 2-lobed. Some herbaceous species and many hybrids are cultivated as attractive, ornamental annuals. Only *V. bonariensis* L., among the South American Verbenas, is winter hardy in the milder climates, but freezes out in cold or snowless winters; often seedlings will appear the following spring. It is, however, usually handled as an annual. Numerous North American species, such as *V. hastata*, are more or less hardy, some growing in zone 4 regions. Most thrive in average garden soil which never is droughty, in a sunny location. The three, low, spreading, North American species, *V. bipinnatifida*, *V. bractata* (not showy), and *V. canadensis* (very showy) grow best on very well drained, fairly infertile, neutral to somewhat alkaline soils. North American species may be planted with other open-growing wildflowers, preferably in the foreground of a woodland margin. Some self-seed, only a few become weedy. Propagation is best by seed. Verbenas are sun plants; where skies are often overcast, as in the USA Pacific and much of Western Europe, plants flower poorly and normally winter hardy species tend to become frost sensitive.

V. bipinnatifida Nutt. Dakota Verbena. North America: South Dakota to Alabama westward to Arizona and in adjacent Mexico, on dry prairies and plains. More or less prostrate, hispid-hairy herbaceous perennial with ascending flowering stems to 42.5cm high, leafy. Leaves to 5cm long, deltoid in outline, usually 2-pinnate or 3-part, the segments bipinnate. Inflorescence a dense, hairy spike, mostly terminal. Flowers lilac-purple (rarely pink or lavender), to 12mm across; summer. For strong, stony, hot, sunny banks or the dry wall. z4

V. bonariensis L. Brazil to Argentina, naturalized in SW. USA and West Indies. Marginally hardy, coarse, erect, herbaceous perennial; stems 90–120cm high, 4-angled, scarcely branched. Leaves 4.5–10cm long, sessile, oblong-lanceolate, base cordate, clasping, margin serrate below the middle, entire beyond. Inforescence a spike, dense, to 4cm long, spikes mostly clustered in panicles. Flowers lilac in the wild, but commercial seed often yields flowers lilac, bluish-violet and purple. Summer-flowering. z8(7)

V. bractata Laq. & Kodr. (*V. bracteosa* Jacq.) Prostrate Verbena (or Vervain). Central North America: Ontario and British Columbia southward to Florida and Mexico. Stems several, prostrate-ascending, usually much branched, to 15cm high, often less. Leaves 3.5–5.5cm long, usually 3-lobed or sometimes pinnately lobed, narrowing below to a short petiole, lateral lobes narrow, spreading widely, terminal lobe cuneate-

obovate, toothed or shallow-lobed. Inflorescence a thickish terminal spike. Flowers small, almost obscured by the more or less leafy bracts, purplish, rarely other cyanic colors in cultivation. More curious than showy; suitable summer ground cover for a hot, sunny, sandy bank or slope, or among paving stones bedded in sand. Summer-flowering. z4

V. bracteosa see **V. bractata**

V. canadensis (L.) Britt. Rose Verbena, Rose Vervain. North America: Virginia, Iowa and Colorado southward to Florida and Mexico; in full sun, on banks, rocky outcrops, prairie stem glades; fails on fertile soils. Stems branching, creeping and rooting to form mats 0.5–1m across, and 15 to rarely 40cm high. Leaves papery, 2.5–5cm long, ovate or ovate oblong, sometimes 3-cleft, truncate or base cuneate, toothed irregularly, tending to be evergreen south. Inflorescence a dense corymbose panicle in flower, elongating into a crowded spike in fruit, terminal on all stems and branches so the entire mat often is covered with showy flowers. Flowers 1–1.5cm across in heads to 6cm across, bright rose, but often variable, lavender-pink, rosy-purple or other bluish shades of pink or rose. Also, forma **candidissima**, flowers white, appearing variously in the trade with names indicating white, and numerous cultivars for flowers variously colored, and 'Compacta', plants dense, lower-growing. For the sunny wild-flower garden on a sunny bank, or in the dry wall or rock garden. z4

V. hastata L. Blue Vervain. North America: Nova Scotia to British Columbia southward to Florida and Arizona; often in damp meadows, prairies, and wasteland, and open woodlands. Upright perennial, unbranched or somewhat branched above, the branches short, erect. 0.5–2m high, appearing stiff. Leaves 7–15cm long, lanceolate to oblanceolate, regularly serrate except for the entire base. Inflorescence a panicle of spikes originating from the uppermost nodes. Flowers small, about 0.5cm across, lavender-blue (rarely white or rose-pink in the wild); midsummer blooming. z4

V. rigida K. Spreng (*V. venosa* Gillies & Hook.) Vervain. South America: Brazil and Argentina; naturalized in SE. USA and elsewhere. Rootstock tuberous, with long stolons. Stems 30 to rarely 60cm high, ascending or erect, little branching (branches freely if clipped back in bedding), leafy, 4-angled. Leaves 4–7cm

long, sessile, clasping, oblong, acute, irregularly toothed, very stiff (rigid) and harsh. Spikes terminal in 3's to form a broad-pyramidal inflorescence. Flowers about 5mm across, usually pinkish-purple, but also 'Alba', white-flowered, and 'Lilacena', bluish-lilac. Roots may be lifted in autumn and stored as are dahlia tubers. This is the species, planted by the hundreds of thousands, as the background in the carpet beds at Versailles, Malmaison, and to a lesser extent, at Fontainbleu. z7

V. simplex Vent. (Lehm.) North America: Quebec to Ontario, Minnesota and Nebraska southward to Florida, Mississippi and Kansas; on stony, gravelly or sandy soil, often acidic, in prairies or on roadsides. Stems 12–60cm high, stout below, erect and simple or branched above the middle, glabrous or nearly so. Leaves very narrowly lanceolate to oblanceolate, 3–10cm long, thickish, sharply serrate or biserrate. Spikes solitary or few in an open panicle, pencil-like; flowers lavender-blue (heliotrope), to 6mm across, borne well above the foliage. This is perhaps the showiest of the erect North American Verbenas. z4

V. stricta Vent. Hoary Vervain. North America: Ontario to Montana southward to Tennessee, Oklahoma and New Mexico, naturalized widely elsewhere; in prairies, glades, and along roadsides. Stems densely hairy, stout, erect, slightly 4-angled, mostly simple, rarely branched above, 30–90cm high. Leaves oblong to broadly obovate, or rounded elliptic, 6–10cm long, 3–6cm wide, pilose beneath, irregularly coarse toothed. Spikes terminal or few in an open, terminal panicle. Flowers 4–5mm across, deep blue or purplish-blue, or very rarely rose, pink, or white; midsummer-blooming. z4

V. venosa see **V. rigida**

Verbesina L.
Compositae
Crown-beard

About 200 species of annual and perennial herbs, subshrubs and occasionally shrubs. Most are from the warmer Americas, only a few from temperate North America. Leaves simple, alternate or opposite. Flower heads radiate or discoid, often asymmetric or appearing so, large or small, solitary or in terminal corymbs or or corymbose panicles. Ray flowers yellow or white, ligulate, mostly spreading, entire or 2–3 toothed, pistillate, occasionally sterile or lacking; disc flowers perfect, fertile, yellow; receptacle convex or conical, scaly. Nutlets compressed, 2-winged. Pappus usually with 2 distinct awns. Coarse, late-flowering plants occasionally grown in ecological plantings in the botanic garden, but none are very ornamental, though excellent bee plants. Tall or medium-sized perennials, which grow best in fertile, loamy, humus-rich soil in semi-shade to full sun. Not suitable for small gardens. Propagate by seed and

Verbesina helianthoides

division. *V. purpusii* T.S. Brandeg., introduced from the mountains of Mexico around 1920 by A. Purpus, is no longer in cultivation. Plants form an attractive, 20–30cm high bush in the alpine house.

V. alternifolia (L.) Britt. (*Actinomeris alternifolia* (L.) DC.). North America: New York and S. Ontario to Iowa, south to Florida, Louisiana and Oklahoma; in moist, fertile, woodland clearings and along streams. Stems 1–3m high, somewhat hairy, winged or at least strongly ridged, branching only near the top. Leaves 10–20cm long, narrowly lanceolate to elliptic, alternate or the lower opposite (or all opposite or in 3's). Flower heads numerous, 2.5–5cm across, in a more or less flattened panicle. Ray flowers 2–8, irregular, yellow, usually drooping, pistillate. Disc flowers yellow. When mature, achenes spread in all directions in a loose globe. Blooms from August to October. z5–8

V. helianthoides Michx. (*Actinomeris helianthoides* (Michx.) Nutt.). USA: Ohio south to Iowa, south to Georgia and Texas; on prairies and dry thickets. Stems 60–110cm high, hairy, usually unbranched, widely 4-winged by the decurrence of the sessile, ovate to ovate-

lanceolate, alternate leaves which are scabrous above, soft hairy beneath, 5–15cm long. Flower heads 4cm across, solitary or few in a compact cyme. Ray flowers yellow, 8–15, outspread, not drooping, to 3cm long. Disc flowers yellow. Blooms from May to October. z5–8 (E.)

The most common SE. USA white-flowering *Verbesina*, *V. virginica* L., is similar to these, but rays are white. Of interest in habitat because when a sudden overnight freeze late in the season follows a long, damp, mild autumn, sap at the base of the stem ruptures the stem angles in short slits and oozes out, freezing as it emerges, to make large basal rosettes of paper-thin, 2–4cm wide ice ribbons resembling wood curls from a carpenter's plane. These melt soon after dawn. Locally this species is known as Frostweed.

Vernonia Schreb.
Compositae
Ironweed

Large genus, 500–1000 species, perennials, subshrubs, shrubs, trees, and woody climbers, most in South America, some in North America, Asia, Africa, and Australia. The North American species are perennials, the tropical species are usually woody. The perennial species grow as an erect, columnar clump, 2–3m high if the soil is sufficiently moist and fertile. Plants somewhat resemble *Eupatorium*, but have alternate, rarely opposite, sessile leaves, inflorescence a more or less flat corymbose cyme. Flower heads discoid, 15–many-flowered, flowers very small, tubular, perfect, involucre shorter than the flowers, of many imbricated phyllaries, mostly purple, rarely white. Vernonias are vigorous and sturdy late summer and fall bloomers which combine well with *Aconitum, Chelone, Aster divaricatus* and other fine-textured perennials. Propagation of the species is by seed. Selections of the seedling population should be made which may be propagated by cuttings or division in early summer. At best, vernonias are barely acceptable in the garden, the plants having rough, dull foliage and dark purple, mostly sordid flower heads which fade to rust-color and so remain for weeks.

V. altissima Nutt. E. North America. Tall-growing perennial, stems 1.5–3m high, glabrous, leafy. Leaves 30cm-long, lanceolate or lanceolate oblong, entire or irregularly serrate, thin, glabrous above,

sparsely hairy below, netted veins raised, petiole short. Inflorescence a flattened, loose, corymbose cyme. Flower heads to 12mm across, flowers purple. After August. Little used in modern garden plantings. z5

V. arkansana see **V. crinita**

V. crinita Raf. (*V. arkansana*). Central USA: Illinois to E. Kansas southward to Arkansas and Oklahoma. Rarely over 2m high in cultivation, to 3m high in its native habitat. Stems glabrous, more or less glaucous, leafy. Leaves linear or

Vernonia crinita

linear-lanceolate, 10–17.5cm long, 0.5–2cm wide, usually glabrous, entire to denticulate. Flower heads to 2.5cm across, many-flowered, in large, terminal, flattened corymbose cymes, bright purple-violet, followed in the fall by purple-tinged, rusty seed clusters. The best vernonia for the garden, often with vegetatively propagated selections. Quite effective, particularly for warmer climates and protected sites in full sun. In its habitat, this species hybridizes freely with several species which share its range; some of the hybrids are showier than either parent. z4

V. noveboracensis (L.) Willd. New York Ironweed. E. North America. Stems 90–180cm high, glabrous or slightly hairy, never glaucous. Leaves long lanceolate to lanceolate-oblong, to 20cm long, 1.5–4.7cm wide, gradually tapering to the base, somewhat scabrous above, glabrous or slightly pubescent below. Cymes open, heads about 12mm across. Flowers dull purple, or in forma *albiflora*, white. z4 (Me. & S.)

The best landscape use for vernonias is in sunny to partially shaded prairie restoration wildflower gardens. The name Ironweed reflects the rust color of the spent flower heads, a liability in the garden but appropriate in the naturalized planting.

Veronica L.
Scrophulariaceae
Speedwell

About 250–300 species of annual and perennial herbs, most from the North Temperate Zone, many high-alpine plants. Leaves usually opposite, occasionally whorled, frequently alternate in the inflorescence, entire or often dentate. Flowers usually in terminal or sometimes axillary racemes or solitary in leaf axils, small, blue, white, pink or purple. Calyx deeply 4-lobed, occasionally 3- or 5-lobed, lobes often uneven; corolla tube usually short, limb rotate to bell-shaped, 4-lobed, rarely 3-, 5- or 6-lobed, lobes often unequal, stamens 2, epipetalous, pistil with inferior, 2-carpeled ovary, style and stigma simple, undivided. Fruit usually an obtuse or scalloped, flat, many-seeded, loculicidal capsule. The tall and medium-sized species are suitable for the perennial border and informal woodland settings. Some are valuable for their late flowering period and most for their blue flower color. Plants thrive in any fertile, not too light, loamy soil in full sun and semi-shade. The low, often cushion or mat habit species belong in the alpine garden or large rock garden. The most compact, low growers are good for smaller rock gardens and trough gardens; they are sensitive to cold and poor drainage, better suited for the alpine house or covered alpine case. All are such attractive alpine plants that no collector of alpines should be without them. Propagation is by seed, division or cuttings. The taller species look well in perennial borders and some are especially suitable for wildflower gardens. The list of species in this genus declines steadily as woody species are transferred to the genus *Hebe*. *Veronicastrum* species superficially resemble the veronicas and sometimes are included in *Veronica* by horticulturists, but the distinctions are obvious: leaves always whorled; the corolla tube long, the limb short, the corolla nearly funnelform or even tubular; the capsule opens by 4 slits

rather than locucidally. For further details, refer to the respective species descriptions.

The species *Veronica* selected for this work:

Veronica spicata

Veronica bombycina

1. Tall and medium-sized, erect species

V. austriaca L. A species with several subspecies, some with cultivars.

V. austriaca ssp. **austriaca**. E., E. Central and SE. Europe, Asia Minor, Caucasus Region; in dry grasslands, on slopes, woodland margins and clearings, on dry, sunny, warm, usually calcareous gravel-loam. Stems 20–50cm high, erect or ascending. Leaves linear-lanceolate to nearly round or deltoid in outline, entire or bipinnatisect with linear lobes, the uppermost leaves and basal leaves toothed to pinnately cleft. Inflorescence near the top of the stem, terminal and 2–4 axillary, elongate racemes. Flowers close-clustered. Corolla to 12cm across, deep azure blue. Calyx and capsule more or less emarginate, usually pubescent. Blooms from May to July. z6

V. austriaca ssp. **teucrium** (L.) D.A. Webb (*V. teucrium* L.). E. Europe, Asia Minor, W. and E. Siberia, Altai Mts.; in thickets, woodland margins, open beech and oak forests, moderately dry grasslands, on more or less dry, usually calcareous loam, loess, or gravelly soil. Stems 0.3–

1m high, erect, ascending or decumbent. Leaves 20–70mm long, 6–45mm wide, ovate to oblong, sessile, truncate at the base or nearly cordate, crenate or incised-serrate. Racemes long, terminal and upper axillary. Calyx and capsules pubescent or glabrous. Corolla sky blue to azure blue, mostly with dark venation. Blooms from May to July. The classification of this well-known plant is in dispute tracing back to *Linnaeus* and *Jacquin*, where species' descriptions and herbarium sheet specimens did not agree. Later authors furthered the confusion. Sometimes this plant today is listed under *V. austrica*, as have (rarely), or a *V. latifolia*, or, especially in horticulture, as *V. teucrium*.

Includes some more or less similar cultivars such as 'Crater Lake Blue', 30cm high, bright blue, in short racemes; 'Royal Blue' ('Königsblau'), to 45cm, deep blue, a dense bushlet; 'Shirley Blue', 20–25cm, bright blue; 'Kapitän', gentian blue; 'Blue Fountain', 60cm, with dense racemes of bright blue flowers; 'Knallblau' ('Blue Explosion'), 25cm, deep gentian blue. Attractive border perennial for a sunny to semi-shaded site, also for naturalizing in the wild garden among open-canopied trees. Grows best on calcareous soils. z4

V. gentianoides Vahl. Asia Minor, Crimea, Caucasus Region, and Central Russia; in mountain meadows. Stems erect in a dense tuft, 15–80cm, but usually 20–50cm high. Leaf size quite variable, basal leaves usually to 60mm long × 15mm wide, entire or indistinctly crenate, usually glabrous. Basal leaves in a rosette, linear to broadly lanceolate, short-petioled, thickish, glossy. Stem leaves ovate to oblong-lanceolate, sessile, alternate or opposite. Flowers on 8–25cm long racemes. Calyx with 4 somewhat unequal lobes. Corolla 10–12mm wide, light blue with dark blue veins (occasionally white). Blooms from May to June. Includes the cultivar 'Variegata' with white-variegated leaves and blue flowers. For the perennial border and large rock garden in a sunny to semi-shaded site with somewhat damp soil. z5

V. incana see **V. spicata** ssp. **incana**

V. latifolia see **V. urticifolia**

V. longifolia L. (*Pseudolysimachion longifolium* (L.) Opiz). N., E. and Central Europe, Siberia and E. Asia, naturalized in E. North America; along riverbanks, ditches, in swampy meadows and the margin of moors; usually on wet to moist, more or less peaty or clay, lime-free to calcareous, but neutral soil. Stems 0.4–1.2m high, stout, erect, usually unbranched. Leaves opposite or in whorls of 3, petioled, to 12cm long × 2cm wide, lanceolate to linear-lanceolate, very long-acuminate, margins toothed or 2-serrate. Inflorescence a dense terminal raceme to 25cm long, usually with one or several short axillary branchlets. Bracts slender. Corolla lilac. Capsule glabrous, distinctly emarginate. Quite variable in height, leaf size and habit. With several cultivars, including 'Blauriesin' (Blue Giantess), vigorous, 80cm

Veronica longifolia

high, bright blue; 'Förster's Blue', 75cm, bushy, deep blue; 'Romilley Purple', 60cm, deep violet-blue; 'Schneeriesin' (Snow Giantess), 80cm, white. z4

V. longifolia var. **subsessilis** see **V. subsessilis**

V. spicata L. (*Pseudolysimachion spicatum* (L.) Opiz). N. Europe, Asia Minor, Central and E. Asia; on the steppes and in dry grasslands, on gravelly sites and stable dunes; in full sun, summer-warm and dry, lime-poor, more or less neutral, gravel or sandy soil from the plains to mountains, 2100m in the Alps. Stems 15–45cm high, erect or ascending from a mat of rooting, decumbent leafy stems, usually with plain and glandular hairs. Leaves 2.5–4cm long, mostly short-petioled, oblong to ovate-lanceolate, tapered below, toothed or crenate except at base and tip. Flowers in a dense spike, to 30cm-long; the pedicels normally less than 1mm, shorter than the bracts. Corolla 4–10mm wide, blue. Capsule slightly emarginate, obtuse. Blooms from July to August. Numerous cultivars are listed: 'Alba', flowers white; 'Alpina', plants lower, dense; 'Caerulea', flowers sky-blue; 'Corymbosa', with axillary spikelets; 'Rosea', flowers pink; 'Rubra', flowers rose-red; and more, in horticulture. This species name often is incorrectly assigned to other similar species. z5

V. spicata ssp. **incana** (L.) Walters (*V. incana* L.). Russia, on the steppes, in infertile to fertile, dry, neutral soils in full sun. Distinguished from ssp. *spicata* by the dense, silver-white to gray pubescence of stems and foliage, and by subtle differences in foliage, inflorescence, and flower structure. This plant almost always is listed as the species *V. incana* L., probably valid, in view of its unique habit, a mat of prostrate stems with almost evergreen, silvery-hairy leaves, and other features referred to above. Includes 'Candidissima' and 'Saraband', both exceptionally dense silver-gray pubescent, with deep violet-blue flowers, and 'Wendy', gray foliage, loose habit. z5

V. spicata ssp. **spicata**. Range and habitat of the species. Stems densely pubescent below, calyx more or less densely pubescent and usually glandular. Includes some beautiful cultivars: 'Alba', white; 'Baccarole', 50cm, dark pink; 'Erika', 30cm, dark pink; 'Heidekind', only 20cm, bright wine red; 'Minuett'

Veronica filiformis

('Minuet'), 40cm, pure pink; 'Rotfuchs' (Red Fox), 30cm, bright pink-red. One of the most attractive, but unfortunately, rarely used species. The species, subspecies, and their cultivars thrive in dryish, well-drained, sandy, humus-rich soil, in full sun, but do poorly on heavy or poorly drained soils. Recommended for dwarf shrub beds, heather gardens and large rock gardens. Propagate by division or seed, the cultivars by division or stem cuttings. z5

V. subsessilis (Miq.) Carr. (*V. longifolia* var. *subsessilis* Miq., 'Subsessilis', 'Hendersonii'). Japan. Similar to *V. longifolia*, but more compact in all respects, and less hardy. Leaves downy beneath, finely dentate, sessile or short-petioled. Inflorescence longer than those of *V. longifolia*, very dense, corolla larger, darker violet-blue. Blooms from July to August. For the perennial border, but best on stream and pond margins. De-

velops to its fullest only in amply and uniformly moist soil. Some good companion plants include *Achillea ptarmica*, *Filipendula palmata*, *F. rubra*, *F. ulmaria*, *Lysimachia thyrsiflora* and *L. vulgare*, *Lythrum salicaria*, *Carex grayi* and *C. pendula*. z6

V. teucrium see **V. austriaca** ssp. **teucrium**

V. urticifolia Jacq. (*V. latifolia* auct. non L.). S. and Central Europe; from the Jura and Carpathian Mts. to NE. Spain, Central Italy and S. Greece; Central and S. Ural Mts.; usually grows to 2000m, in mixed herbaceous stands, mixed, open woodlands, on moist, usually calcareous, neutral, humus-rich, gravelly or mineral loam. Rootstock stoloniferous. Stems 20–50cm high, erect, sparsely pubescent. Leaves to 8cm long, 4cm wide, sessile, ovate with a broadly rounded base, upper leaves long-acuminate, with scattered hairs, margins incised-serrate. Racemes loose, spreading, opposite, in the leaf axils, 10–25 flowered. Corolla small, light blue to lilac. Pedicels curved upward below the calyx, causing the fruits to be borne vertically. Blooms from May to July. Grow in light shade; naturalize in an open woodland with loose, high-humus soil. Not especially ornamental but a useful, reliable filler plant for massing. z5

V. virginica see **Veronicastrum virginianum**

2. Low, usually cushion-forming or matted species

V. allionii Vill. Europe: SW. Alps; on dry alpine sites, lime-intolerant, matted perennial. Stems decumbent, rooting, to 30cm long, ascending branches to only 5cm high; woody at the base. Leaves evergreen, leathery, ovate, to 2cm long, 1.3cm wide, entire or finely toothed, soft green. Racemes axillary, spicate, dense, many-flowered. Corolla deep violet. Blooms from June to July. An evergreen ground cover for covering large rock garden ledges in a short time. Plants do well in full sun and semi-shade, in warm sites and somewhat damp, loamy, lime-free humus soil. Propagation is easiest by division of the rooted shoots, but also by seed. z6

V. aphylla L. Mountains of Central and S. Europe, from the Jura and Carpathian Mts., south to the Pyrenees Mts., S. Italy and Central Greece; in exposed, gravelly, barren sites or in shaded rock crevices especially between 1500–2500m, occasionally to 3000m; grows well above a calcareous rock substrate, in cool, moist, moderately humus-rich, loose soil. Stems procumbent, 1–4cm high, with short sterile runners. Leaves to 1.5cm long, 1cm wide, elliptic-oblong to broadly obovate or spathulate, tapered to a short petiole, clustered near the shoot tips in loose clusters. Inflorescence a short, corymbose raceme with 2–8 flowers. Corolla deep blue, occasionally pink. Throat and corolla tube white. Blooms from June to August, but only briefly. For the experienced collector of alpine garden plants for the alpinum or trough. This lime-loving dwarf tolerates full sun and semi-shade. Performs best in a narrow crevice or on a scree in loamy humus mixed with crushed stone grit and kept evenly moist. Propagate by division and cuttings, or by seed. z5

V. armena Boiss. et Huet. Asia Minor, Armenia; on alpine screes. A tufted, many-stemmed cushion, woody below, 5–10 cm high. Leaves small, green, opposite, deeply pinnatisect, to 6mm long, glabrous to pubescent. Flowers in short, loose, floriferous, axillary racemes. Corolla bright blue or violet-blue, more or less dark-veined. Blooms from May to June. Attractive but wet-sensitive species for the rock garden or trough. Thrives in an infertile, well-drained soil in full sun. A cover to protect from moisture in winter is recommended. Propagation is best by division and cuttings. z6

V. bandaiana see **V. schmidtiana** var. **bandaiana**

V. beccabunga L. European Brooklime. Europe, Asia Minor, W. Asia to Iran, Himalaya Mts., N. Africa; grows among reeds near flowing watercourses, ditches, springs, on wet or flooded sites in a mild to moderately acidic, humus-rich soil. Found from the plains to nearly 1900m in the Alps. Entire plant glabrous. Stems 30–60cm long, creeping, rooting at the nodes; flowering branches usually ascending. Leaves to 4cm long, 2cm wide, broadly elliptic to nearly orbicular, entire or more or less toothed, short-petioled, fleshy, entire. Axillary racemes usually with 10–30 flowers. Corolla light to dark blue. Blooms from May to August.

Attractive plants for planting along streams and ponds. Plants thrive in a swampy or periodically flooded soil in full sun or semi-shade. Also, an excellent underwater plant for the cold-water aquarium. Some suitable companions include *Caltha palustris*, *Cardamine amara* and *C. pratensis*, *Hippuris*, *Lysimachia nummularia*, *Myosotis palustris* and *Ranunculus flammula*. z5

V. bombycina Boiss. et Kotschy. Asia Minor; Syria, Lebanon; on rocky outcroppings in the higher mountains. Tufted or matted plant, densely silky white-hirsute, only a few centimeters in height with very small, occasionally to 6mm-long, sessile, ovate to oblong-spatulate leaves. Inflorescence a terminal raceme, 1–5 flowered; corolla pale milky blue, twice as wide as the calyx. Fruits small, round, tomentose. Flowers from June to July, but sometimes flowers sparsely. An attractive, but unfortunately wet-sensitive species. Recommended only for experienced alpine gardeners with troughs and pots in a frame or alpine house. Plants in the rock garden must be covered to protect the foliage from winter wetness. Also requires good subsurface drainage. Provide a substrate composed of two parts limestone gravel and one part loamy humus; then water infrequently, never wetting the foliage. Propagate by division, cuttings or seed. z6

V. bonarota see **Paederota bonarota**

V. caespitosa Boiss. Asia Minor, Greece. Dwarf, cushion habit, gray-hirsute, thick-leaved, 2–5cm high alpine plants. Leaves to 10cm long, linear-spatulate, opposite, with reflexed margins. Inflorescence few-flowered, racemes short, or flowers occasionally solitary, scarcely reaching beyond the leaves. Corolla almost 1cm across, pink. Blooms in May. Garden use, cultivation and propagation like that of *V. bombycina*, but short-lived in the rock garden unless situated in a narrow rock crevice in limestone soil and protected from moisture. In habitat, often a limestone moraine plant. z4

V. cinerea Boiss. et Bal. Asia Minor. Velvety gray, cushion habit perennial. Stems woody at the base, 10–15cm long, ascending, rooting on contact with the soil. Leaves small, lanceolate to linear, sessile or tapered to a short petiole,

Veronica beccabunga

crenate, with involuted margins, gray-velvety. Racemes axillary, loose, 10–20 flowered. Corolla light blue or pink. Blooms from June to July. Attractive but somewhat demanding species for the rock garden or trough garden. Plant in infertile, gravelly, well-drained soil in full sun and protect the foliage from water, especially in winter. z5

V. cuneifolia D. Don. Asia Minor. Mat or tuft habit 5–7.5cm high, stems slender, procumbent or ascending, rooting. Leaves 5–7mm long, cuneate-obovate, softly pubescent. Flowers in solitary, not paired, axillary racemes. Corolla blue, white-bordered. 'Villosa' (*V. dichrus* Schott et Kotschy), strongly pubescent beneath. Flowers from June to July. For the trough or rock garden in well-drained, gravelly loam with added peat, and with small and large stones mixed through and on the surface; in sun. z5

V. dichrus see **V. cuneifolia**

V. filiformis Sm. N. Asia Minor, naturalized in parts of Europe and much of North America, where it has become a pernicious weed in lawns and flowerbeds. Plants with diffuse mat habit or merely sprawling, 2–10cm high, with slender, rooting stems to 50cm-long. Leaves 5–10mm across, petioled, more or less orbicular to reniform, crenate, usually opposite on sterile stems, alternate on flowering stems. Flowers solitary, axillary, commonly reflexed after opening, sky blue, darker-veined. The lower corolla segments usually white. Blooms from March to May. Possibly

Veronica saturejoides

suitable as a ground cover where the growing season is sufficiently cool, cloudy, and damp to limit its vigor, in semi-shaded sites with a loamy humus soil. Quickly forms a bright green carpet, combining well with small bulbous plants. May become invasive in the rock garden. Propagation is by division. z5

V. fruticans Jacq. Rock Speedwell. (*V. saxatilis* Scop.). Europe, in rock crevices, on gravelly, infertile slopes at alpine and subalpine elevations, to 3100m in the Alps, over a lime-free substrate. Suffruticose, tufted perennial, stems 5–15cm high, branches erect. Leaves 7–12mm long, thickish, obovate to oblong, entire or slightly crenate, short-petioled or sessile, uppermost leaves sessile. Flowers in short-pediceled, loose, 4–10 flowered, erect, terminal racemes. Corolla to 12mm across, deep blue, with a dark red eye. Capsule glandless. Blooms from May to June. A collector's plant for the alpine garden, rock garden and trough in full sun or semi-shade.

Grows best in a rock crevice or in a rocky bed in loamy-humus-rich soil. Often weak in cultivation. Propagate by seed, division and cuttings. z4–8

V. fruticulosa L. W. and S. Central Europe, from the Vosges Mts. and Sierra Nevada to NW. Yugoslavia; on sunny, south-facing sites in rock crevices, on screes and rocky outcrops of subalpine to alpine elevations on moderately moist, always calcareous gravelly soil; to 2750m high in the Alps. Resembles the closely related *V. fruticans*, but leaves larger, always petioled, the flowers somewhat larger, pedicels with glandular hairs. Corolla pink, with darker venation, or white, early abscising. Capsule and calyx glandular-pubescent. Blooms from June to July. Attractive and, unlike *V. fruticans*, an easily grown evergreen species for the alpine garden, rock garden or trough in sun or semi-shade, in loamy, humus-rich soil. Grows best in a rock crevice or scree. Propagate by seed, division and cuttings. Good companions for both species include *Arabis pumila*, *Androsace* species, *Carex curvula*, *C. firma*, *Draba aizoides*, *Globularia cordifolia*, *Nardus stricta*, *Potentilla caulescens*, *Primula auricula*, *P. marginata*, *Saxifraga paniculata*, *Thlaspi rotundifolia*. z5

V. lutea see **Paederota lutea**

V. orientalis Mill. Asia Minor, S. Russia, E. Mediterranean Region; on dry, rocky slopes. Cushion habit, woody at the base, stems prostrate, procumbent or ascending, 10–25cm long, more or less softly pubescent. Leaves 20mm long, 4mm wide, linear, linear-oblong to oblanceolate, entire to irregularly deeply lobed, toothed, but the uppermost usually entire. Racemes axillary, 2–4 (–8)cm long, loose. Calyx with irregularly long lobes. Corolla 10–12mm across, pale blue, occasionally pink. Blooms from June to August. A rarely offered species for the collector. Best planted in the rock garden in dry, sandy loam in full sun. Relatively easy to grow, somewhat drought-tolerant. Propagate by seed, division and cuttings. z5

V. petraea Stev. Caucasus Region. Caespitose perennial, stems outspread or ascending, downy, red-brown, about 10cm high. Leaves sessile or shortly petioled, oblong, lanceolate or elliptic, 12–20mm long, cuneate and slightly toothed at the base, often entire toward the apex. Racemes solitary, axillary, long-petioled, 10–20 flowered. Corolla lilac-blue to blue, rarely pink. Blooms from May to June. The dark foliage of this species makes it conspicuous in the rock garden. z5

V. prostrata L. (*V. rupestris* hort.). From Holland and N. Central Russia, south to N. Spain, Central Italy and Macedonia; Caucasus, Siberia; on sunny, grassy slopes and woodland clearings. Loose carpet habit. Sterile stems prostrate, flowering stems ascending, to 10–25cm. Leaves to 2.5cm long, 1.2cm wide, linear-oblong to ovate, base wedge-shaped with very short petiole, crenate to nearly entire, margin often reflexed. Racemes terminal, sometimes axillary, compact, many-flowered. Flowers long-pediceled, calyx glabrous, usually with 5 uneven lobes. Corolla 6–12mm across, light blue. Blooms in May and June. Included among the many cultivars: 'Alba', white; 'Mrs. Holt', pale pink; 'Rosea', pink; 'Royal Blue', dark blue; 'Spode Blue', rich royal blue; 'Silver Queen', silvery blue; 'Trahanii', racemes to 25cm high, flowers large, china blue. Attractive species with carpet habit for the heather or rock garden. Quickly covers the ground on dryish, somewhat infertile, sandy loam slope in full sun. Propagate by division and cuttings, or seed. Effective when combined with other groundcovers, especially the gray- and silvery-leaved perennials. A good ground cover for small bulbous plants. z3

V. repens Clarion ex DC. Mountains of Corsica and S. Spain; in alpine meadows and moist sites. A dense, creeping, rooting mat; flowering stems to 5cm high. Leaves glabrous, 4–12mm long, ovate, short petioled, entire or with a few rounded teeth, glossy, glabrous, bright green. Flowers in short, axillary, 3–6 flowered racemes. Calyx with 4 uneven lobes. Corolla 10mm in diameter, pale, whitish-blue, pink on var. *macrocarpa* from Spain. Blooms mid- to late spring. Attractive, very low carpet-forming perennial for the rock garden, trough or as a ground cover among stepping stones or small bulbs. Thrives in a sunny site with damp, not- too-dry soil. Protection from winter wetness is advisable, however. Plants will easily freeze out in cold or snowless winters; it is best overwintered in a pot in an alpine case. Propagate by seed and division. z8

V. rupestris see **V. prostrata**

V. saturejoides Vis. Balkan States: N. Albania to SW. Bulgaria; grows over and among rocks and on screes. Stems tufted from a woody base 10–30cm long, loosely outspread or decumbent,

flowering tips seldom higher than 7cm. Leaves glossy evergreen, opposite, 6–9mm long, oblong or obovate, entire or slightly toothed, rather thick, margin more or less pubescent, densely imbricate, as are most of the shoot tips. Racemes terminal, subglobose, with 6–12 flowers. Corolla about 7mm in diameter, bright blue, almost without venation. Blooms in April and May. The closely related *V. kellereri* Deg. et Urum., is more vigorous and floriferous. Introduced in 1910 by Sündermann at Pirin, Belgium. A rare alpine plant, only for the experienced collector. Cultural requirements similar to those of *V. fruticans*, but best grown in the alpine house. Propagate by seed, division and cuttings. z7

V. saxatilis see **V. fruticans**

V. schmidtiana Regel. Japan, Sachalin and S. Kuril Islands; on alpine slopes. Rootstock rhizomatous, short. Stems spreading to prostrate, 10–25cm long, unbranched or with few branches, leafy, soft-puberulent. Lower leaves in clusters, somewhat thick, long petioled, broadly lanceolate to ovate, to 4cm long, 2cm wide, obtuse, base truncate to broadly cuneate, glabrous or sparsely soft-pubescent, feathery -incised or -parted. Racemes loose, 10–30 flowered, 5–10cm long. Calyx 4-lobed; corolla pale purple, dark-veined, or 'Alba', white-flowered. Blooms from June to August. z5

V. schmidtiana var. **bandaiana** Mak. (*V. bandaiana* (Mak.) Takeda). Japan: Honshu, at alpine elevations. Very similar to the species, but with shallow, nearly acute leaf lobes. Attractive, small, carpet plant for the rock garden or trough garden. z5

V. selleri see **V. stelleri**

V. stelleri Pall. (*V. selleri* hort.). Japan, Sachalin, S. Kuril Islands, N. Korea; on alpine slopes. Stems in loose clusters, erect, 7–15cm high, softly white-pubescent, with 5–8 pairs of leaves. Leaves to 2.5cm long, 1.5cm wide, ovate, with a few teeth, sparsely soft-haired, sessile. Racemes loose, few-flowered. Corolla pale bluish-purple, 7–8mm across. Blooms from July to August. Rare, small species for the rock garden or trough. z5

V. surculosa Boiss. et Bal. Asia Minor, in alpine meadows. Plant a small mat 5–8mm high, stems creeping, rooting; entire plant densely whitish gray-pubescent. Leaves 5–15mm long, rounded-elliptic, deeply coarse-crenate, with involuted margins when young, bristly whitish gray-pubescent, tapered to a very short petiole. Flowers in 5–7cm long racemes. Corolla pale blue, with a large, dark red eye. Blooms from May to June.

A charming, small, mat-forming species, covered with flowers in spring; also effective later for its grayish-white, hairy foliage. A collector's plant for the rock garden or trough garden, for full sun, in dry, rocky, loam. Plant among large and small stones which it will soon cover. Spreads by self-seeding in suitable sites. Propagate by seed, division and cuttings. Attractive in combination with other carpet-forming alpine plants or the small bulbs. z6

V. turrilliana Stoj. et Stef. SE. Bulgaria: Strandzha Mts.; on limestone in nature. Stems to 40cm long, woody at the base, prostrate procumbent, or ascending, softly hirsute, hairs usually in 2 opposing rows. Leaves to 12mm long, 8mm wide, elliptic-oblong to ovate, otbuse, very short-petioled, crenate, leathery, glabrous. Racemes axillary and terminal, 2–8, opposite, 4–8cm long, rather loose. Corolla 8–10mm across, blue. Capsule nearly round, glabrous. Blooms from May to June. Attractive, evergreen species for the rock garden or large trough. z6 (E.)

Veronicastrum Fabr.
Scrophulariaceae
Culver's Physic

Two species, one Siberian, the other North American, superficially resembling a tall-growing *Veronica* but differing as indicated below:

Veronicastrum Characteristics
  Corolla salverform, tube long, lobes short
  Stamens 2, inserted near base of the tube, much exerted
  Capsule ovoid, swollen, blunt, rupturing along 4 apical sectures
  Seeds terete, surface reticulated
  Leaves whorled, in 3's (to 9's)
  Plant, especially root, cathertic-cmetic (containing leptandrin)

Veronica Characteristics
  Corolla rotate, tube short, lobes long
  Stamens 2, inserted one on each side of the upper corolla lobe, exerted
  Capsule compressed, cordate, or emarginate, loculicidal
  Seeds more or less compressed, or

convex on one side, surface smooth or minutely pebbled
  Leaves opposite, or upper leaves alternate
  Plants often bitter-unpalatable, but seldom toxic

Veronicastrum virginicum (L.) Farw. Culver's Physic. (*Leptandra virginica* (L.) Nutt. *Veronica virginica* L.) North America: Vermont to Ontario and Manitoba, south to Florida and Texas; in prairies, open woodlands, meadows, road and railroad right-of-ways. Stems 0.6–2m high, erect, glabrous or nearly so (stems hairy, leaf blades densely hairy beneath in *V. villosum*). Leaves in whorls of 6 (or 3–9), to 15cm long, lanceolate to lanceolate-ovate, sharply toothed, acuminate, usually glabrous on both sides, short-petioled. Flowers panicled in many terminal and upper axillary spicate racemes, with the terminal spike flowering first. Pedicels as long as the calices. Corolla salverform, the tube much longer than the 5 scarcely flaired lobes, white or pale pinkish to purplish. Blooms from late spring to early fall. Includes the cultivars 'Alba', flowers white; and 'Rosea' flowers soft pink.

A stately, garden-worthy perennial for its late flowering period; for the large perennial garden, also for small, isolated groups and for planting in light shade in the woodland garden. Requires a moist, loamy humus-rich soil. Some good companion plants include the various woodland grasses, *Aconitum napellus*, *Actaea*, *Cimicifuga*, *Campanula lactiflora*, *C. trachelium*, *Euphatorium purpureum* and *Monarda*. z3

Vicia L.
Leguminosae
Vetch, Tore

About 150 species of annual and perennial climbing herbs. The genus includes many fodder plants and weeds from the North Temperate Zone and S. America. Leaves ending in tendrils (except in erect subsp.), even-pinnate, usually with several pairs of leaflets and with nearly sagittate stipules. Flowers papilionaceous, stamens 10, 9 with connate filaments and 1 free, variously colored, solitary, clustered or racemose. Differs from *Lathyrus* by wing petals connate with the keel, the style thread-like with a tuft or ring of hairs below the stigma. Of this large genus, only a few species are grown as ornamentals and they are rarely offered in the trade.

V. oroboides Wulf., S. Europe and N.

Africa; in meadows in open mountain woodlands. Suitable only for semi-shaded sites in a large alpine or woodland garden. Lime-tolerant, of marginal garden value. Stems 30–60cm high. Leaflets ovate, mucronate, grayish-hairy to almost smooth. Racemes axillary, 3–4 or sometimes fewer, many-flowered. Flowers blue; late spring to early summer. z5

V. pyrenaica Pourr. Mountains of Spain and S. France; in alpine meadows and gravelly slopes. Plants somewhat stoloniferous. Stems 10–30cm high, semiprocumbent. Leaves tendriled, tendrils usually unbranched; more or less with 3–6 pairs of leaflets, leaflets oblong-cordate to nearly rounded, mucronate. Flowers solitary, axillary, violet-purple. Blooms from June to July. An attractive, tidy species for the small alpine garden or large rock garden. Requires a sunny or semi-shaded site in well-drained, gravelly, humus-rich loamy soil. Attractive as a specimen between large rocks; occasionally freezes out despite winter protection. Propagate by seed and division. Gardeners in both Europe and the New World who are interested in naturalized plantings are reappraising *Vicia* species indigenous to their regions as these help fill out the picture of a native reconstruction. z8 (E.)

Vinca L.
Apocynaceae
Periwinkle, Creeping Myrtle

About 12 species in Europe, the Mediterranean region, E. Asia and the tropics. Trailing or rarely erect, evergreen perennials or subshrubs. Leaves opposite, entire. Flowers axillary, solitary, calyx deeply 5-lobed, corolla salver-shaped, tube short, 5-lobed, lobes large, showy, stamens 5, epipetalous, inserted about the middle of the tube, anthers included, appendaged, pistil 2-carpels, styles united; fruit a pair of terete follicles; rather large, blue, red or white. Flat-growing ground cover for semi-shade to shady understory beddings. *V. minor* is a commonly used evergreen species where winters are cold; *V. major* replaces it in mild winter regions. These thrive in loose, woodland humus soil or fertile, compost enriched, loam. Propagation is by division of clumps, rooted stems, or cuttings.

V. herbacea Waldst. et Kit. E. Central and SE. Europe, north to S. Central Russia. Herbaceous creeper. Stems glabrous, simple, decumbent, rarely prostrate, not rooting. Leaves finely ciliate, basal leaves elliptic to ovate, upper leaves lanceolate, short- petioled. Flowers blue-violet with obliquely oblong lobes; May to June. For full sun or semi-shade. z5

V. major L. Greater Periwinkle, Blue Buttons. West. S. Central and SE. Europe; widely naturalized in temperate regions world wide. Subshrubby, stems erect, decumbent and prostrate, rooting, to 30cm high. Lower leaves ovate-cordate, wide, upper leaves ovate-lanceolate, leathery, to 5cm long and 2cm

Vinca minor

wide, evergreen. Flowers periwinkle-blue with a funnelform tube; April to May. 'Acutiloba', large-leaved, later-flowering; 'Reticulata', leaves yellow-veined; 'Variegata', leaves creamy-white margined and blotched. Grows well in a warm, semi-shaded, well-drained, rather dry site. Plants do poorly in cool, damp situations and are less winter hardy under such conditions. A light winter cover is advisable. z7

V. minor L. Common Periwinkle. Europe, east to Lithuania and the Caucasus region, Asia Minor. Flowering stems to 15cm high; non-flowering stems long, procumbent or prostrate, rooting at the nodes, somewhat woody at the base. Leaves leathery, glossy, oblong to elliptic-ovate. Flowers solitary, blue-violet or pale blue with a funnelform tube; April to May. The species has yielded numerous cultivars, including: 'Alba', flowers white; 'Alboplena', flowers white, double; 'Argenteo-variegata', flowers lilac-blue, leaves silver-white variegated; 'Azurea', flowers sky-blue; 'Azureaplena' (= 'Caeruleoplena'), flowers sky-blue, double; 'Bowles Variety', flowers very large, deep lilac-blue; 'Cuprea', flowers

reddish-copper; 'Gertrude Jekyll', very free-flowering, white, growth dense, slow; 'Grüner Teppich', (= 'Green Carpet'), flowers few, pale lavender-blue, leaves large, growth very dense; 'LaGrave', flowers lavender, very large; 'Multiplex', flowers purple-red, double; 'Rubra' (= 'Punicea') flowers reddish-purple; 'Roseoplena', flowers reddish, double; and 'Variegata', flowers lilac-blue, leaves variegated butter-yellow. All cultivars are attractive spring bloomers and excellent ground covers for a shady understory site. z5 (Me. & M.)

Viola L.
Violaceae
Violets, Pansy, Viola, Violetta

About 500 species and numerous subspecies of perennial or biennial herbs, occasionally subshrubs or annuals, distributed throughout the world. Plants stemmed, leaves alternate, or plants stemless, leaves basal, long-petioled, ovate or cordate, often with large and variable stipules. Flowers solitary, rarely paired, in the leaf axils. Plants often produce 2 types of flowers; the showy, but sometimes seedless spring flowers, referred to as chasmogamous flowers, and the later cleistogamous flowers, often consisting solely of a pistil which matures into a swollen capsule, often underground, which sets seed abundantly. This characteristic is virtually unique with *Viola* species. The seeds have sugar and oil containing appendages (elaiosoma). *Viola* flowers are somewhat irregular; sepals 5, unequal, petals 5, unequal, the lower petal with a slight pouch, or a short or long spur, stamens 5, the lower 2 with nectary appendages which fit into the petal pouch or spur, pistil various, ovary superior, carpels 3, glabrous or hairy, style slender or massive, bent, crooked, or straight, stigma concave, convex or plane, often to one side of the style axis. Fruit a 3-valved capsule. Several system grouping *Viola* species systematically are published, dividing the genus into numerous sections; a convenient, simplified system, used here, includes:

Section Dischidium Ging. (D) Perennial herbs. Stipules not leaflike. Plants with cleistogamous flowers. Style with a dichotomous stigma. Includes only *V. biflora*.

Section Melanium Ging. (M) Herbaceous. Stipules normally large, leaflike, often parted. The lateral flower petals are directed upward. The open flowers are blue or yellow, occasionally white. Plants without cleistogamous flowers. Styles

bent at the base, with a wide, capitate stigma. Ripe capsules erect, glabrous. Includes the Pansies.

Section Viola (Nomimium Ging.) (V) Herbaceous. Stipules not leaflike. Open flowers blue, violet or white. Plants occasionally with cleistogamous flowers. Style straight or variously crooked, stigmas irregular, concave, fringed, or tilted, European species often beaked. Includes all the Violets.

Section Xylinosium W. Bekker (X) Perennial, subshrubby. Open flowers lilac or yellow, occasionally with cleistogamous flowers. Styles curved from the base, club-shaped, neither capitate nor beaked. Includes *V. delphinantha* and related species.

Violas are quite variable in cultural requirements, ranging from easy to difficult. Gardeners tend to use a more practical classification, referring to Pansies, the large-flowered, non-rhizomatous ornamentals usually grown as winter annuals or biennials with *V. tricolor*, *V. altaka*, *V. lutea*, and other important parents; Violas, more or less resembling smaller-flowered pansies but somewhat more heat tolerant, also often grown as biennials, with *V. gracilis* as a major parent; Violettas, or Crested Violas, with narrower petals (flowers less "round"), and perennial, at least in moderate climates, with *V. cornuta* as one parent; and Violets. The latter category is endlessly divided, usage depending largely on geography. Europeans use their mostly stemless, often sweetly scented plants and refer to Sweet Violets, those with large, long-peduncled, sweetly-scented flowers, for cutting, beds and borders; and alpine violets, the smaller-growing sorts are grown in the rock garden. Americans enviously speak of Sweet Violets, meaning the European *Vioderubs* and its cultivars (American *Viola* species are almost all odorless) and rhizomatous violets, the species with no upright stem but a vigorous, creeping rhizome; and the stemmed violets, those with an upright leafy stem with axillary flowers and short or almost no rhizome. Some species, such as *V. pedata* fit neither category, having a small, hard rootstock with many fibrous roots below and a tuft of all basal leaves and flowers aboveground. Many species are easily grown rock garden plants, others are ideal for the woodland understory. Some species are grown for their cut flowers. Propagation is by seed, division or cuttings.

The most commonly encountered species include:

V. adunca Sm. Western Dog Violet, Hook-spur Violet. **(V)**. W. North America, spread increasingly sparsely to the Atlantic Coast, mostly in meadows. Stem short, to 10cm high, stem and leaves puberulent. Leaves rounded-ovate to elliptic-ovate, finely crenulate, petioles to 6.5cm long, basal leaves often more rounded. Flowers bluish to violet. Several geographical varieties are listed. May to June. z5

V. alba Bess. **(V).** Central and S. Europe, Algeria, Asia Minor; on limestone. Rhizomes creeping, often with long stolons. Leaves basal, evergreen, cordate, acuminate, 5–10cm high. Flowers white, with dark eye and veins to violet, to 2.3cm across, erect, fragrant. April to May. Numerous varieties and cultivars are listed. Used like *V. odorata.* z7

V. alpina Jacq. **(M).** Alpine Pansy. NE. Alps, Carpathian Mts.; on limestone. Leaves basal, long-petioled, somewhat cordate, broadly ovate to oblong-ovate, acuminate, shallowly crenate, stipules lanceolate. Flowers large, to 2.2cm across, violet, sometimes with darker spots or stripes, occasionally white. Spur short, arched upward. April to May. Generally very difficult to grow, best for a cool, high humus soil mixed with limestone gravel. A gravel mulch around the crown of the plant is beneficial. Quite susceptible to slugs and root nematodes. Only for the experienced collector. z5

V. altaica Ker-Gawl. **(M).** Altai Mts., Siberia. A loose mat-habit plant with slender, creeping rhizomes. Stems to 12cm high, leafy. Leaves to 2cm, broad, elliptic to broadly ovate, crenate, tapered to the long petiole. Stipules pinnatisect. Flowers large, 2–4cm across, sometimes yellow, violet, bicolored or white. May to July. Probably a parent (with *V. tricolor* and *V. lutea*) of the common garden pansy. Rarely found in cultivation today. z7(6)

V. beckwithii T. et G. **(V).** Great Basin Violet. W. USA: E. Oregon southward to NE. California and Nevada; in gravelly soil which is damp through early summer, later quite arid. Rhizome stout, with many fibrous roots. Stem leafy, 5–10cm high. Leaves palmately 3 times 3-parted into linear lobes. Flowers large, to 2cm across, 2 upper petals deep purple, 3 lower petals pale violet, sometimes white. April to May. Grows well with *Lewisia rediviva.* z4

V. bertolonii Pio **(M).** Maritime Alps, N. Apennine Mts., S. Italy, NE. Sicily. More or less taprooted. Stems leafy, glabrous, to 30cm high. Leaves variable in form, the basal leaves more or less orbicular,

differing from the upper leaves which are narrower. Flowers large, violet or yellow, squarish in outline, the lowermost petal truncate, notched, with a long spur. May to June. Several geographic races are defined as varieties or subspecies; closely allied to *V. gracilis.* z7(6)

V. betonicifolia F. Muell. **(V).** Australia. Short-stemmed, leafy. Leaves oblong, lanceolate or sagittate, occasionally cordate at the base. Flowers white with violet eye and veins or entirely violet. May to June. Surprisingly hardy.

Viola biflora

Apparently not now in European-American cultivation. z6

V. biflora L. **(D).** Mountains of the North Temperate Zone. Rhizome short, creeping. Leafy stems weak. Leaves glabrous, broadly reniform-rounded to 4.5cm across, long-petioled below, upper leaves short-petioled; stipules ovate to lanceolate. Flowers small, bright yellow, somewhat brown-streaked, very short spurred. May to July. Grows in loose, never acidic, humus-rich soil in semi-shade. A charming, easily grown, often abundantly seeding collector's

plant for the alpine garden. Not showy. z4

V. bosniaca see **V. elegantula**

V. calcarata L. **(M).** Alps, S. Jura Mts., W. Balkan Mts. Rootstock a slender rhizome with stolons. Plant 7.5–10cm high in flower. Stems usually short, internodes congested. Leaves very small, broadly ovate to lanceolate, tapered to the petiole, margins crenate, stipules pinnately cleft. Flowers large, to 3cm across, solitary, occasionally paired, on arched peduncles. Quite variable in color; violet, yellow, bicolor or rarely white. Spur straight or slightly curved upward. May to July. Very difficult to grow and often shy blooming in the garden, only for the collector. Often attacked by root nematodes. Propagate from freshly gathered seed. z5

V. calcarata ssp. **zoysii** see **V. zoysii**

V. canadensis L. Tall White Violet, Canada Violet. North America; New Brunswick to Alabama; Rocky Mts., Pacific Northwest. Rhizome stout, without stolons (except in var. *rugulosa*

(Greene) C.L. Hitchc.). Stems erect, to 30cm (rarely to 45cm) high, leafy. Leaves to 6.5cm across, broadly ovate, cordate, acute, serrate, nearly glabrous beneath. Flowers axillary, to 2.5cm across, white, tinged purplish outside, yellow throat inside, lower petal often veined purplish; spring to midsummer. Several geographic varieties are listed, and 'Alba', flowers pure white. z4

V. canina L. **(V)**. Dog Violet. Greenland, Europe, Asia to Japan, south to Kashmir. Rhizome short, creeping. Stem at flowering about 7.5cm high. Leaves all cauline, 2cm wide or less, broadly ovate, subcordate or truncate, with long petioles, stipules narrowly lanceolate. Flowers not fragrant, light to dark violet, with white or yellowish white spurs. April to June. A variable species with several cultivars; for naturalizing. z3

V. cazorlensis Gand. **(X)**. SE. Spain: Sierra de Cazorla; on limestone. Rootstock woody. Stems erect, 10–15cm high, twiggy, dense. Leaves narrow-elliptic to narrow-lanceolate, to 1cm long, 2cm wide, stipules free to the base, very narrow undivided or divided to the base so leaf appears to have 3 or 5 linear segments. Flowers small, petals narrow. Similar to *V. delphinantha*, but with intensely reddish-purple coloration, the lower petal notched, with a long spur. Flowers in early summer. z7

V. cenisia L. **(M)**. SW. Alps, occasionally in the Central Alps; over limestone. Taprooted, crown with slender, barely subterranean, stolons to 22cm long, turning upward, with stems 3–5cm high, numerous, procumbent. Leaves about 1cm long, basal leaves ovate, apical leaves oblong. Stipules resemble small leaves. Flowers 2.5cm-across, bright violet. May to June. An attractive species, cultivated like *V. alpina*. z5

V. cornuta L. **(M)**. Horned Violet, Viola. Pyrenees Mts.; also locally in W. Central and S. Europe. To 25cm high. Rootstock short, creeping. Stems 10–30cm long, prostrate, then ascending, leafy, more or less 3-angled. Leaves to 2.5cm wide, ovate or oblong-ovate, shallow-crenate, glabrous above, somewhat hairy below, tapering to the petiole, stipules leafy, deeply cut, triangular, sessile. Flowers with curved peduncles, violet. Includes many cultivars; hybridized with the garden pansy (*V.* × *wittrockiana*) to yield the tufted pansies, Violas and Violettas (*V.* × *williamsii*), and with *V. gracilis* to yield the hardy *V. visseriana* cultivars such as 'Lord Nelson' and 'Jersey Gem'.

Some cultivars come true from seed and are particularly valuable, such as 'Blaue Schönheit' (Blue Beauty'), pure violet-blue, or the attractive 'Jesse East', pinkish-violet, marked yellow. z5

Some important cultivars are: 'Altona', cream-yellow; 'Angerland', soft lilac-blue; 'Blaue Schönheit' (Blue Beauty'), bright blue; 'Blauwunder' ('Blue Wonder'), bright violet-blue; 'Blue Carpet', pure blue; 'Boullion', dark lemon yellow; 'Buttercup', bright yellow; 'Famös' ('Famous'), wine red; 'Germania', dark

Viola calcarata

purple-violet; 'Gretchen Hein', light blue with a silvery cast; 'Gustav Wermig', violet-blue; 'Hansa', dark blue (although also found in a light blue form by the same name); 'John Wallmark', light violet; 'Jutta', marine blue, late-flowering; 'Landgren's Yellow', pale primrose yellow; 'Martin', dark velvety purple; 'Moonlight', light yellow; 'Nora Leigh', lavender-blue, long-lived; 'Northfield Gem', violet-purple; 'Primrose Dame', light yellow, large-flowered; 'Ruhm von Eisenach', dark violet; 'White Perfection' pure white; 'White Superior', pure white. Many others are listed, some needing further trial in cultivation. The cultivars are primarily propagated by cuttings.

V. cucullata Ait. Marsh Blue Violet (*V. obliqua* Hill.). North America: New-foundland to Georgia (Mts.), westward locally to Missouri. Rhizome thick, scaly; plant stemless. Leaves all basal, glabrous, long-petioled, cordate-ovate, crenate, 8–9cm wide. Flowers on long peduncles overtopping the foliage, blue-violet, usually darker in the center. In forma *thurstonii* flowers irregularly blue and

white; forma *albiflora*, flowers pure white, very attractive. Spring to early summer. For moist or wet, shady to sunny locations. At least 11 hybrids of this with other violets sharing its habitat have been identified.

V. cyanea see **V. suavis**

V. delphinantha Boiss. **(X)**. SE. Europe; mountains of N. Greece, Bulgaria and one area of S. Greece; in crevices on a southeast-facing limestone cliff. Rootstock woody. Stems 5–10cm, twiggy,

Viola dubyana

erect or ascending in a dense bushlet. Leaves 0.75–1cm long, less than 2mm wide, linear to very narrow-lanceolate, acuminate, entirely sessile, stipules undivided or divided to the base, somewhat shorter than the leaves. Flowers rosy-lilac to reddish-violet, on long peduncles, with long spurs. May to June. Best grown in tufa or limestone; recommended for the alpine house. Propagation is by seed or very early cuttings, which must set winter buds. See also *V. cazorlensis*. z7

V. dissecta Ledeb. **(V)**. E. Asia. Only cultivated as var. *chaerophylloides* (Regel) Makino f. *eizanensis* (Makino) E. Ito (*V. eizanensis* (Mak.) Mak.). Plant stemless, in flower to about 10cm high. Rhizome short, without stolons. Leaves divided into 3 (or 4) short petioluled segments, each segment deeply 2- or 3-lobed, toothed (later leaves may be undivided, ovate-lanceolate), glabrous or sparsely hairy, long petioled; stipules attached half their length, upper part lanceolate. Flowers all rose, pale purplish or whitish, 1.5cm across, fragrant. April to May. Attractive and interesting species, but only flowers well in acidic soil in semi-shade. Sometimes with only cleistogamous flowers, abundantly seeding. z6

V. douglasii Steud. **(V)**. W. North America: Oregon, California. Rhizome deep-growing, short, stout. Stems several, 5–12cm high. Leaves 2-pinnate, segments linear or oblong; stipules lanceolate, entire or incised. Flowers to 3cm across, golden-yellow or orange-yellow, the two upper petals brownish-purple outside (the insides also sometimes tinged). April to May. Not easy to grow; plant in a stone crevice with gravel and humus, as *Lewisia*. z7(6)

V. dubyana Burnat ex Gremli **(M)**.

stripes. June to July. Grows in well-drained soil; usually short-lived. Several cultivars, describing flower color, are listed. z7(6)

V. eugeniae Parl. **(M)**. Italy; Apennine Mts.; on limestone, but also on granite. Similar to *V. calcarata*, but smaller overall, stipules smaller, less dissected to almost entire. Flowers yellow or violet. May to June. Very attractive. Probably the same as *V. zoyzii*. z6

V. × florariensis Correv. **(M)**. (*V. cornuta*

V. grisebachiana Vis. **(M)**. Central Balkan Peninsula, in alpine meadows. Rhizome subterranean, slender, branching. Short-stemmed (3.5–7.5cm high in flower) or stemless, similar to *V. alpina*. Leaves crowded, 1.5–3cm, ovate-rounded to spatulate, entire or slightly crenate, stipules resemble the leaves, but smaller. Flowers 2cm across, round, violet or blue, May to June. Very attractive alpine pansy, but difficult to grow in gardens; best managed as suggested for *V. alpina*. z6

Viola odorata

Viola sororia 'Albiflora'

Italian Alps, on limestone screes. Rhizome short, deep rooted. Stems leafy, 10–30cm long. Lower leaves orbicular, to 4cm across, upper leaves narrowly lanceolate to linear; stipules pinnately divided. Flowers to 2.5cm across, violet, basal petals with yellow blotch; spur curved to 6mm long. May to June. Unfortunately often suffers from crown-rot. z7

V. eizanensis see **V. dissecta**

V. elegantula Schott **(M)**. (*V. bosniaca* Form.). W. Yugoslavia and Albania; subalpine and alpine meadows. Taprooted. Stems prostrate then ascending, weak, leafy, to 10cm high. Lower leaves orbicular, upper leaves oval-lanceolate, crenate; stipules large, palmately divided into irregular segments. Flowers of cultivated selections mostly pale rose-violet, wild plants violet or yellow or bicolor, occasionally white or pink, the lower petals with yellow blotch and

× *V. rothomagensis*). Originated in "Floraire," Henry Correvon's alpine garden near Geneva, Switzerland. A very attractive pansy, petals light and dark violet-blue, lower petal with yellow basal blotch; short spurred. Self-seeds in the garden without becoming a nuisance. June to August. z5(6)

V. gracilis Sibth. et Sm. **(M)**. Balkan States to Asia Minor. Plants with a loose carpet habit, stems 10–15cm long, prostrate then ascending, more or less hairy. Lower leaves to 1cm wide, broadly ovate, upper leaves elliptic, cuneate; stipules leafy, pinnately divided, the end segment large. Flowers large, to 4cm across, deep violet. June to August. Closely related to *V. cornuta* with which it has been hybridized, producing some beautiful hybrids, such as 'Lord Nelson'. Numerous cultivars, names descriptive of color or plant size, are listed. z7(6)

V. hallii Gray **(V)**. W. USA: Oregon and California. Similar to *V. beckwithii*, but stems taller, to 15cm high, leaves oval to oblong, in outline palmately 2–3 parted into narrow segments. Flowers somewhat smaller, distinctly bicolored, the upper 2 petals deep violet or blue, the lower 3 yellow or white. May. z5

V. hirta L. **(V)**. Europe, W. Asia, eastward to the Altai Mts. Similar to *V. odorata*, but without stolons. Plants 6–10cm high when in flower. Leaves all basal, broadly ovate, crenate, hairy at first, later more or less glabrous, long petioled; stipules lanceolate with ciliate margins. Flowers odorless, to 2cm across, pale blue-violet, white or pink at the base, sometimes white; spurs straight, tip hooklike. March to May. z5

V. jooi Janka **(V)**. SE. Europe. Rhizome stout, creeping, without stolons. Leaves tufted, 2cm across, thin, glabrous, cordate, crenulate, long-petioled; stipules lanceolate, acuminate or 3-cleft at the tip. Flowers small, pinkish-violet, mildly fragrant. April to May. An easily grown species. z6

V. labradorica Schrank (**V**). N. America: Newfoundland to Alaska, southward to New Hampshire and Minnesota; Greenland. Very small plant; stem to 1cm high or almost lacking. Leaves essentially glabrous, dark green, tinged purple-violet, nearly orbicular, stipules linear, entire above. Flowers small, to 2cm across, not fragrant, porcelain blue to lavender. April to May. The leaves of 'Viride' are light green. Attractive, self-seeding species for semi-shade. Very closely allied to *V. adunca*. z3

V. lutea Huds. (**M**). W. and Central Europe, southward to the Pyrenees Mts. Rhizome subterranean, slender, branching. Stems ascending or erect, slender, 7.5–15cm high in flower, triangular. Lower leaves orbicular to ovate, upper leaves narrow-lanceolate, cuneate; all crenate, long-petioled, nearly glabrous. Flowers to 3cm across, bright yellow with black-purple nectary stripes on the lower petal, or 2 upper petals violet to purple, or entire flower violet or purple. June to August. A collector's plant for the alpine garden in a semishady to sunny site. Probably a parent species of the modern garden pansy. z5

V. mirabilis L. (**V**). Eurasia. Rhizome branched, thick, horizontal, creeping. Plants stemless, about 10cm high through anthesis; later stem develops 12–45cm high, with cleistogamous flowers. Leaves broadly ovate, to 7.5cm across, shallow-cordate, crenate, long-petioles; stipules lanceolate, entire. Flowers large, fragrant, light lilac to pale rose-lavender. April to May. Suitable for planting in a woodland understory. z5

V. missouriensis Greene. Missouri Violet. Central USA: Indiana to Nebraska southward to Kentucky and Texas; in low, damp, woodlands. Rhizome fleshy, thickened, without stolons. Plants stemless. Leaves ovate-cordate, toothed, long-petioled. Peduncles long; flowers pale violet to violet, marked with purple around a white eye; mid-spring to early summer. In the trade sometimes confused with *V. jooi*. z5

V. nuttallii Pursh. Prairie Yellow Violet, Western Yellow Violet. North America: British Columbia and California east-ward to Central USA; among grasses, in open sites. Rootstock a small crown with deep, fibrous roots. Stem at anthesis 5–12cm long, leafy, but most leaves basal. Leaves lanceolate to narrowly elliptic, mostly entire. Flowers to 12cm across, yellow, 3 lower petals brown-veined; spur very short. Several geographic western varieties are less hardy. z4

V. obliqua Hill. (**V**). (*V. cucullata*) E. North America. Rhizome short and thick, lacking stolons. Leaves cordate, acuminate. Flowers very long-stalked, blue-violet with a light eye, usually rising above the foliage. April to June. The form 'Albiflora' is particularly conspicuous and attractive. For moist or wet, sunny and shady sites. z5

V. odorata L. (**V**). Sweet Violet. W. Europe, Mediterranean region to Caucasus and Kurdistan. Rootstock a short, more or less vertical rhizome with stolons, with plantlets which bloom in the second year, often in the fall of the first year; plants stemless. Leaves broadly ovate to reniform, to 7cm across, deeply cordate at the base, toothed, long-petioled, tending to be evergreen. Peduncles with 2 prophylla in the center. Flowers deep purple-violet, very fragrant. February to April. The species is reasonably hardy (z6 or 7); the florist-type cultivars are intolerant of winter cold or summer heat; garden cultivars vary. z7 (midsummer) to z5.
Includes various cultivars; many come true from seed, others are propagated only by cuttings: 'Albiflora', pure white, small-flowered; 'Bechtel's Ideal', blue-violet; 'Heidi', blue, double; 'Irish Elegance', orange-yellow; 'Königin Charlotte" ('Queen Charlotte'), pale violet-blue, comes true from seed; 'Red Charm', red-purple, moderate bloomer; 'Rubra', red-purple, small flowers; 'Sulphurea', apricot yellow; 'Triumph', violet-blue, large-flowered, similar to 'Donau' ('Blue Danube'), but more vigorous.   Many other cultivars are found in England in nurseries which specialize in violets. Sweet Violets are among the most popular flowering plants where they can be grown. Propagation is by seed or division after flowering. Many cultivars also are propagated by stolon cuttings. Suitable for many garden uses, including planting beneath woody plants, for example, Foerster's *Viola odorata* under *Paeonia suffruticosa*. The cultivars are especially valuable as cut flowers.

V. palmata L. (**V**). Early Blue Violet. E. North America: Massachusetts to Minnesota southward to N. Georgia. To 20cm high. Rhizome thick, short, somewhat branched. Plant stemless. Leaves palmately 5–11 parted, or lobed almost to the middle of the leaf blade, variably toothed. Flowers to 2cm across, long-peduncled, violet-purple, sometimes with white eyed, dark purple-lined lower petals. April to May. Suitable for understory planting in moist, high humus soil. Seeds abundantly under favorable conditions, sometimes becoming weedy. z5

V. papilionacea see **V. sororia**

V. pedata L. (**V**). Bird's Foot Violet. E. and Central USA; in prairies and open, dry woodlands on well-drained, stony or sandy, acidic soils. A short, thick, hard rootstock. Plant stemless, with a tuft of completely glabrous foliage. Leaves short at anthesis, later to 15cm high, blade broad-deltoid in outline, palmately 3–5 divided, segments 2–4 cleft, lobed, or toothed near the apex. Flowers on long peduncles, petals all in one plane, appearing pansy-like, to 2.5cm across. Variable in color; pure lavender (var. *concolor* or *lineariloba*) or bicolor with both upper petals velvety purple and the lower petals lavender-colored (var. *bicolor* or *pedata*). Occasionally white, white with violet, pink or reddish-violet tinged. March to June, occasionally September to October. Very difficult to grow. Intolerant of lime; grows best in very gravelly, humus-rich soil. Protect from excessive winter wetness. Propagate by seed or root cuttings. z5

V. pedunculata T. et G. (**V**). California Golden Violet. W. USA: California. Rhizome stout, deep in the soil. Plants to 4–25cm high or higher, leafy-stemmed. Leaves rounded-ovate, to 5cm wide, coarsely crenate, base truncate or subcordate, blunt, long-petioled. Flowers 3cm across, golden-yellow, lower petals veined purple or brownish, upper petals occasionally with brownish reverse. April to May. Cultivated like *V. beckwithii*. z8(7)

V. pinnata L. (**V**). Central Europe and N. Asia; a mountain habitat. Rhizome short, horizontal, shallow-growing. Leaves all basal, more or less broad-ovate in outline, palmately divided into many narrow segments (unique among European Violets); stipules adnate to the petiole, tips lanceolate. Flowers to 12mm across, pale violet, fragrant. May to June. A demanding collector's plant for the alpine garden, grows in full sun and, unfortunately, often produces only cleistogamous flowers. z5

V. pontica see **V. suavis**

V. priceana see **V. sororia** var. **priceana**

V. reichenbachiana Jord. ex Bor. **(V)**. Woods Violet. (*V. sylvestris* Lam. emend. Rchb., *V. silvatica* Fries). Europe, north to Sweden, eastward to Estonia and Central Ukraine, Canary Islands, NW. Africa, Asia. Rhizome short, erect or rarely somewhat creeping. Leaves basal on long petioles, broadly ovate, acuminate, crenate, long-hairy; stipules narrowly lanceolate. Flowers pale violet, white toward the center, sometimes dark violet-striped, the spur slender, dark purple. April to June. Useful for the shade garden. z4

V. rhodopaea see **V. stojanowii**

V. rhodopeia see **V. stojanowii**

V. riviniana Rchb. **(V)**. Dog Violet, Wood-violet. Europe, Mediterranean region, Asia Minor, Caucasus Region, Iran. Similar to *V. reichenbachiana*, but with larger leaves and larger flowers, rosetted, but often with leafy, ascending axillary stems. Spur yellowish white, thick. April to June. Very common locally in Great Britain, sometimes carpeting the forest floor. z5

V. sepincola see **V. suavis**

V. silvatica see **V. reichenbachiana**

V. sororia Willd. (*V. papilionacea* Pursh) **(V)**. Woolly Blue Violet. E. North America, widely naturalized elsewhere. Rhizome shallow, stout, fleshy, well-branched. Plants stemless, 10–15cm high, larger south, smaller north, densely pubescent to almost glabrous. Leaves long-petioled, reniform to ovate, with a shallowly cordate base. Flowers flattish but not pansy-like, to 2cm across, deep lavender-blue, deep violet, but also reddish, pale violet, white or gray-white, often with white center. April to May. The pure white var. *beckwithas*, in horticulture cultivars 'Albiflora' and 'Immaculata', is especially attractive. Var. **priceana** Poll., Confederate Violet, is gray-white with lavender-blue veins. The very glabrous form of this species sometimes is called *V. papilionacea* Pursh. Within habit regions, this violet, and especially var. *priceana*, often become pernicious weeds, though handsome in flower. z5

V. stojanowii Becker (*V. rhodopaea* hort., non *V. rhodopeia* Becker) **(M)**. S. Bulgaria, NE. Greece. Biennial to perennial. Rootstock a slender, erect rhizome.

Plant about 10cm high, fine pubescent overall, densely bushy; stems leafy; leaves narrow oblanceolate to narrow-elliptic, crenate. Flowers long-peduncled, 2cm across, yellow, occasionally with both upper petals violet-blushed. May to July. Attractive, satisfying species, widely self-seeding in well-drained soil without becoming troublesome. z7

V. suavis M.B. (*V. sepincola* Jord., *V. pontica* Becker, *V. cyanea* Beck), Parma Violet. **(V)**. S., Central and E. Europe. Rhizome short, thickened, often with subterranean stolons. Foliage rosetted in spring, 3–8cm high, later to 20cm high. Leaves glabrous or short hairy, ovate-oblong to broadly ovate, leaf petioles normally very long. Prophylla in the peduncle lower than the middle. Flowers fairly large to large, the "wild" form blue or bluish with a white center, very fragrant. April to May. Variable species. The cultivars listed especially attractive: 'Marie Louise', light violet, distinctly double, 1.5cm across; and 'Princesse de Galles' ('Princess of Wales'), dark violet, to 2.5cm wide. Much more susceptible to spider mites than the closely related *V. odorata*. Botanists debate endlessly about the proper classification of this species. The cultivars were developed long ago for greenhouse production of cut flowers and most do poorly in the garden; all require chilly, frost-free winter and cool, damp summer conditions. z7

V. sylvestris see **V. reichenbachiana**

V. uliginosa Bess., Moor Violet **(V)**. E. Europe, north to Denmark and Finland, west to E. Germany and NW. Yugoslavia. Rhizome short, somewhat slender, with underground stolons, tips emerging with leafy rosettes. Leaves cordate-ovate, densely brown-glandular, petiole margins slightly winged, stipules oval-lanceolate, entire, adnate. Flowers not fragrant, rather large, bright violet. April to May. For a sunny site in marshy soil. z4

V. variegata Fisch. **(V)**. Korea, Manchuria, Siberia. Only var. *nipponica* Makino is found in cultivation. Plant to 5cm high. Leaves in flattened rosettes, cordate, about 2cm wide, dark reddish green with silver markings, purplish beneath. Flowers small, light purple. Many cleistogamous flowers in summer. April to May. Self-seeding in sunny to semishady sites. Particularly showy, grown mostly for its leaf markings, worthy of more use, but intolerant of snowless, cold winters or hot, dry summers.

V. verecunda A. Gray var. **yakusimana** (Nakai) Ohwi (*V. yakusimana* Nakai) **(V)**. Japan; Yakushima Island. The smallest violet, leafy stems 1–3cm high. Leaves pale green, 3–7mm, reniform-cordate, shallowly toothed, glabrous. Flowers white with violet lines, 3–4mm across. April to May. An excellent collector's plant for pot culture or trough gardens. Easily grown from seed. z7

V. yakusimana see **V. verecunda**

V. zoysii Wulfen (*V. calcarata* ssp. *zoysii* (Wulfen) Merxm.) **(M)**. SE. Europe; W. Balkans, E. Alps; on limestone. Similar to *V. calcarata*, but the stems shorter. Leaves broadly ovate to suborbicular; stipules shallowly cut or lobed. Flowers roundish, 2–3cm across, usually yellow, rarely lilac. May to July. Very attractive species, sought after by collectors. z6 (K.)

Numerous additional *Viola* species are cultivated locally from indigenous species, and by specialists. One caveat applies when introducing wild violets into the garden; some may become difficult to eradicate weeds.

Viorna

V. viorna see **Clematis viorna**

V. scottii see **C. scottii**

Viscaria see Lychnis

Vitaliana Sesler
Primulaceae
Golden-primula

A single diverse species. Attractive, low alpine plant for the alpine garden, rock garden or trough. For experienced gardeners and botanic gardens. Not always easy to grow and sometimes shy-blooming, especially ssp. *primuliflora*; ssp. *praetutiana* is more floriferous. Plants thrive in full sun or light semi-shade, best planted on an east-facing gravelly slope or in a rock crevice. Requires abundant moisture in spring. Well-drained, sandy, humus-rich loam of neutral pH is best; tolerates some limestone. Topdress periodically with fresh soil. Sets seed only sparsely in cultivation, therefore best increased by division and fall cuttings. Seed germination requires a long, cold stratification period and a thin soil covering. Sow seed right after ripening;

if this is not possible, keep seed moist. Some good companion species include *Androsace carnea, Dianthus glacialis, Draba aizoides, Erigeron uniflorus, Minuartia recurva, M. verna, Primula minima, Sempervivum montanum, Senecio incanus, S. halleri.*

V. primuliflora Bertol. (*Douglasia vitaliana* (L.) Hook.f. ex Pax), Goldenprimula. Mountains of S. and W. Central Europe, eastward to the SE. Alps and Central Spain; in low mats at alpine elevations, usually over 2000m, on gravelly slopes, occasionally on rocks. In

Vitaliana primuliflora

the garden plant in gravelly, lime-free soil with ample moisture through the blooming period. Stems more or less creeping, mat- or cushion-forming. Leaves 2–12mm long, 1–2mm wide, linear to oblong-lanceolate, acute, acuminate or rounded. Flowers solitary or clustered to 5 from the center of the foliage rosette. Solitary flowers are borne in the axils of the uppermost leaves, with a 2–4mm long peduncle. Calyx tubular-campanulate, 4–10mm long, glabrous or pubescent. Corolla yellow, 6–22mm long. Corolla tube 1.5–2.5 times as long as the calyx. Flowers from April to May. z4

V. primuliflora ssp. **cinerea** (Sünderm.) I.K. Fergus. Central and SW. Alps, E. Pyrenees. Stems creeping or densely carpet-forming. Leaves acuminate, densely pubescent to gray-tomentose. Calyx pubescent. Corolla 12–22mm long. z5

V. primuliflora ssp. **praetutiana** (Buser ex Sünderm.) J.K. Fergus. Central Apennines. Stems creeping, loose carpet-forming. Leaves obtuse or rounded at the apex, densely gray-tomentose above and beneath. Calyx pubescent. Corolla 8–12mm long. More floriferous than both the other subspecies. z5

V. primuliflora ssp. **primuliflora**. SE. Alps. Stems creeping, loose carpet-forming. Leaves acuminate, glabrous or occasionally ciliate. Calyx glabrous or ciliate. Corolla 10–16mm long. Often flowers poorly. z5 (E.)

Wahlenbergia Schrad. ex Roth
Campanulaceae
Rockbell

About 120 species of widely disseminated plants, especially in the Southern Hemisphere. Annuals or perennials, often creeping herbs with usually solitary flowers. Calyx 3–4, rarely 5–10 lobed; corolla 3–4, rarely 5–10 lobed, mostly campanulate or rotate, regular; stamens usually 5, separate; ovary united to the perianth (perigynous). Capsules open by valve slits at the tips. Flowers blue, violet, white or red. Blooms from May to July. Only short-lived species from New Zealand are commonly cultivated. They grow best in moist, well-drained soil in full sun, where they may self-seed abundantly. *W. hederacea* is a peat bog plant for collectors. Propagation is by seed or division.

W. albomarginata Hook. New Zealand: South Island, Stewart Island. Rootstock of slender, branching rhizomes, tips producing leafy rosettes 1.5–4cm across. Leaves small, lanceolate to spatulate, leathery, margins white, denticulate. Flowers 2–3cm across, campanulate, solitary on very slender, 20cm-high peduncles, to 5 from a rosette, light blue or white, often with darker venation. June to July. z7

W. hederacea (L.) Rchb. (*Campanula hederacea* L.). W. Europe, from Scotland to Portugal and Spain in shallow springs, peat bogs and similarly moist, lime-free sites. Stems creeping, filamentous, rooting, leaves petioled, suborbicular, more or less angled or 5-lobed. Flowers nodding, campanulate, to 8mm long, pale blue on 2–5cm high peduncles. May to September. Attractive, but generally not very persistent. z7 (K.)

W. kitaibelii see **Edraianthus graminifolius**

W. serpyllifolius see **Edraianthus serpyllifolius**

Most other wahlenbergias can be grown in an alpine house if it can be kept cool in summer, and if lime-free water is available. A plant of distinction; wahlenbergias dehisce through apical slits or pores at the apex of the capsule; campanulas dehisce through valve apertures at the side, mostly covered by the calyx; edrainthuses dehisce irregularly; the capsule more or less crumbles.

Waldsteinia Willd.
Rosaceae
Barren Strawberry, Golden Strawberry

Five species of small, creeping herbs in Central Europe, N. Asia and N. America. Rootstock creeping, spreading underground, rhizome tips emerging with virtually stemless tufts of foliage. Leaves alternate, mostly basal, petioled with 3–5 cleft, or parted, leaflets, entire or lobed. Flowers yellow, in 2–5 flowered corymbs

Bulgaria and W. Ukraine. To 25cm high. Rhizome short, horizontal, slow-creeping, without stolons or runners. Plants 5–22cm high. Leaves cordate-reniform in outline, 3 to usually 5 deep lobed, lobes coarsely toothed. Flowers about 2cm across, 5–9 on a scape, yellow, borne slightly above the foliage. April to June. z5

W. sibirica see **W. ternata**

W. ternata (Steph.) Fritsch (*W. sibirica* Tratt., *W. trifolia* Roch. ex W.D.J. Koch). Central Europe to Siberia and Japan.

simple or sometimes branched. Flowers sessile, in spikes. Perianth tube covered, with 6 segments more or less similar, usually spreading; stamens 3, epipetalous, styles 3, stigmas bifid or sometimes 12. Where hardy, these develop sizeable clumps which bloom freely. For garden use, experts at Kew Gardens propose two categories, those which flower in spring and early summer, including *W. aletroides*, *W. coccinea*, *W. fulgens*, *W. marginata*, *W. meriana*, *W. pyramidata* and *W. versfeldii*, and those which flower from midsummer onwards, including *W. ardernei*, *W.*

Waldsteinia geoides

Weldenia candida

on scapose stems. Calyx tube conical, limb 5-cleft with 5 bractlets alternating with the lobes; petals 5, obovate; stamens many, inserted on the throat of the calyx; pistils 2–6 with terminal styles deciduous from a basal joint. Fruit of several (2–6) achenes. Suitable as an evergreen ground cover (especially *W. ternata*) in shade and semi-shade. Attractive, relatively trouble-free plants which tolerate rather dry soil. Propagate by division in spring and fall.

W. fragarioides (Michx.) Tratt. North America: New Brunswick to Minnesota, south to Georgia, Tennessee and Missouri. Rhizome creeping, without stolons. Plants 12–20cm high. Leaves pubescent or nearly glabrous, leaflets 3 or rarely 5, broadly cuneate, toothed. Flowers to 20mm across, yellow; May to June. Not too common in cultivation. z3

W. geoides Willd. E. Central Europe to S.

Rootstock of short rhizomes with many fibrous roots. Plants with pilose, creeping stems, with terminal foliage rosettes. Leaves long-petioled, evergreen, to 10cm high, ternate, leaflets with short petiolules, leathery, glossy, rather densely pubescent. Flowers to 15mm in diameter, yellow, to 7 in a loosely clustered raceme; April to May. z3

W. trifolia see **W. ternata**

(Me. & M.)

Watsonia Mill.
Iridaceae
Bugle-lily

About 60 species of cormaceous, gladiolus-like perennials, most from South Africa, one from Madagascar. Corms solid, fibrous-tunicate; leaves sword-shaped, stiff; spikes leafless,

beatricis, *W. densiflora*, *W. galpinii*, *W. longiflora* and *W. wordsworthiana*. Corms of the first group may be lifted and stored, gladiolus-fashion; the second group, tending to be evergreen, does not survive long desiccation and is better left in the garden. These grow in well-drained sandy loam enriched with peat or compost which never dries excessively; full sun is necessary for good results. Very few watsonias are hardy enough to warrant inclusion in this text, but a single species and several cultivars must be mentioned.

W. beatricis Mathews & L. Bolus. Bugle-lily. South Africa: Cape Province. Leaves 3–4, basal, to 90cm high, 32mm wide, subglaucous, margins thickened, yellowish. Flowering stems 90–120cm high; inflorescence a congested spike with many flowers, most open at one time, large, about 7.5cm long, segments wide-flaired, stamens and stigmas extruded; orange-red, but seedlings vary in color intensity. Blooms in late summer. z7

Several cultivars appear in current trade lists, often cited as cultivars of *W. beatricis*; variation in color and form suggests the possibility of their being hybrids of this and another species; in most cases, they are as hardy or slightly more so than *W. beatricis*. These include: 'Malvern', clear orchid-pink; 'Mrs. Bullard's White', pure white; and 'Rubra', deep wide-crimson. Other colors, usually obtained in commercial

W. candida Schult. f. Mexico, Guatemala; in well-drained mountain meadows, first discovered in a volcano crater. Root-stock fleshy, more or less tuberous, branched. Stem a short axis, partly to mostly underground; internodes un-elongated. Leaves 2–6, linear-lanceo-late, to 20cm long, margins undulate with tufts of white hair. Inflorescence of 2 flowers in a scorpioid cyme, or solitary, on erect scapes, 10–40, axillary, from the leafy rosette. Flowers pure white, 3–4cm wide; calyx membranous, tube oblique, 3 lobed or split, spathe-like, corolla tube

beneath, indusia star-shaped or with lobes, curving around the sori, with hairlike cilia.

W. alpina (Bolt.) S.F. Gray. Northern Woodsia. Arctic regions southward to cold temperate Europe, Great Britain, Asia and North America, southward to New York, Ontario, Minnesota, etc., often in mountains or on damp to dry slate or calcareous rock. Fronds 1-pinnate, 5–15cm high, lanceolate, yellowish-green, underside chaffy-scaly with segmented hairs at first, later

Woodsia polystichoides

Yucca glauca

mixtures, includes shades of pink, rose, apricot and various reds.

Weingaertneria

W. canescens see **Corynephorus canescens**

Weldenia Schult. f.
Commelinaceae

A monotypic genus. Flowers from May to September. Cultivated in a fertile, but well-drained soil in full sun. After dying back in fall plants should be removed and kept dry and frost-free during the winter. An attractive collector's plant for the alpine house, trough and similar situations. Propagation is by seed (seeds are situated deeply in the rosette) or root cuttings.

5cm-long, lobes ovate, spreading. Vigorous plants will produce up to 50 flowers in the summer. A charming, showy, obviously tropical plant, beauti-ful in itself but appears out of place in a temperate zone planting. z8 or 9 (K.)

Woodsia R. Br.
Polypodiacea

Sixteen to 40 species, depending on interpretation of the genus; small, tufted ferns growing on rocks and mountain screes in temperate and cool temperate regions of both Hemispheres. A few species are suitable for garden plantings. These are mostly delicate ferns; some are difficult to grow and maintain in cultiva-tion, but *W. obtusa* can be grown almost everywhere. Rhizomes erect, fronds more or less upright, tufted, deciduous, 1- or 2-pinnate, often with chaffy hairs

glabrous. Stipe blackish at the base, pinnae ovate, obtuse, pinnately lobed, with a few sinuses. Suitable for a shady site in the alpine garden. Propagation is by spores. z5

W. glabella R. Br. Smooth Woodsia. Circumpolar in northern regions, south-ward to cold summer areas, usually in thin moss or humus on calcareous rock, in shade, and in the European Alps on limestone. Stipe glabrous, mostly straw-colored, with old, chaffy stipe bases among green fronds. Fronds to 15cm long, linear or linear-lanceolate, 1-pinnate, pinnae triangular-acuminate or ovate, crenate-lobed. Difficult to grow, possibly more suited to cold maritime regions south of habitat. Propagation is by spores and division. z1

W. ilvensis (L.) R. Br. Fragrant, or Rusty Woodsia. Mountains of the North

Temperate Zone and cooler regions of N. America and Greenland; in dry, calcareous rock crevices and on screes. Rhizomes often with several crowns. Stipe with rusty chaff beneath, fronds 1-pinnate, lanceolate, often brownish green, scaly-pubescent, to 25cm long, 4mm wide, with 8–20cm ovate-oblong pinnae, pinnules oblong, wavy-toothed. Suitable for shady to partly sunny rock gardens, troughs and slopes. Propagation is by spores and division. The species epithet, *ilvensis*, means of the Island of Elba, suggesting that the species range extends far southward in mountainous terrain. z1

W. obtusa (Spreng.) Torr. Common Woodsia, Blunt-lobed Woodsia. Grows in the lowlands (to the Gulf of Mexico States), hills, and mountains of North America; in sun or bright shade among non-calciferous rocks. Rhizomes sometimes with several clustered crowns, fronds numerous, erect, to 40cm high, 10cm wide, pinnate-pinnatifid to 2-pinnate, elliptic lanceolate to broadly lanceolate, light green, pinnules mostly oblong, blunt, crenulate. Indusia broad-lobed. Stipe straw-colored, reddish toward the base, loosely scaly. An elegant, medium-sized fern for planting in semi-shade with low-growing perennials. Propagation is by division and spores. Spores ripen from August to October. Within its natural range this fern invariably appears as a volunteer from wind-blown spores in rock gardens and on dry walls. z4

W. polystichoides Eaton. Japan, Korea, Manchuria and the bordering mountainous regions. Differs considerably from the other *Woodsia* species, more resembling a 1-pinnate *Polystichum*. Fronds clustered, tips somewhat nodding, 12–20cm long, 2–4cm (sometimes much more) wide, 1-pinnate, narrow- to broadly-lanceolate, soft green. Pinnae short-stalked, some with auricles. Sori in a row along the margin, light brown, indusium of 4–5 incurved hairs. Suitable for planting between large rocks in semi-shade, very attractive in the trough garden and among stepping stones. Needs a cool, moist site. Seems to be quite hardy. Propagation is by spores which ripen from August to October. z4

W. pulchella Bertol. European Alps, in limestone crevices. Quite rare. Fronds 3–12cm high, lanceolate, translucent-yellowish green. Pinnae pinnately lobed, tips rounded. For the collector. Propagation is by spores. z5 (D.)

Several other woodsias are grown by specialists, mostly local species, especially in the United States. Some of these North American species are *W. appalachiana, W. cathcartiana, W. mexicana, W. oregana,* and *W. scopulina.* These are all smaller, upright-growing ferns with lacy, graceful fronds; attractive among rocks.

Woodwardia Sm.
Polypodiaceae (Blechnaceae)
Chain Fern

Ten or more species of ferns, cosmopolitan in the Warm Temperate and Subtropical Zones, many in Central America. Only two species, one in Europe, are generally grown in gardens. The name Chain Fern refers to the oblong sori borne in chain-like rows paralleling the pinnae midribs.

W. virginica (L.) Sm., Virginian Chain-fern. E. and Central North America in moist to wet woodlands. Rhizomes stout, long-creeping. Fronds 70cm long, 15–20cm wide, oblong-lanceolate, 1-pinnate, deeply pinnatifid, leathery, firm, reddish brown at first, later dark green; pinnae linear-lanceolate with linear-oblong lobes, stipe ⅓ of the frond length, dark brown at the base, green toward the tip. Sori oblong, in short chains along the lateral veins of the pinnae. Grows in acid to neutral soil in wet sites near or in shallow water. Propagation is by division and from spores. z4 (D.)

In North American, East Coast gardeners sometimes cultivate wild-collected *W. areolata*, with dimorphic fronds to 40cm high, an acid bog plant hardy to z5; on the West Coast, British Columbia southward, *W. fimbriata*, found locally in wet ground in the rain forest, is stunning in the garden, with fronds to 2.7m high, 45cm wide. z8(7)

Wulfenia Jacq.
Scrophulariaceae

Five species of almost glabrous, rosetted perennial plants with thick rhizomes, from the mountains of SE. Europe, W. Asia and the Himalaya Mts. Leaves simple, mostly basal, petioled, crenate to almost lobed, almost succulent-looking. Flowers terminal in spicate racemes on simple, leafless or slightly bracted scapes, somewhat nodding, blue. Calyx deeply 5-parted, the segments linear; corolla tube greatly exceeding the calyx, limb 4-lobed, lobes lateral and central, broadly ovate, somewhat reflexed,

stamens 2, exerted. The wulfenias are attractive, if not very conspicuous, plants for large and small alpine gardens, rock gardens, and troughs. Recommended for collectors and botanical gardens. All species, except *W. baldaccii,* do not tolerate lime, but grow best in a mixture of leafmold and half-composted conifer needles with about 25% incorporated loamy soil. Plants require a semi-shaded site, best with a northeast, northwest or east exposure. The site should remain moist from spring to late summer, but the species are sensitive to excessive winter wetness. *W. amherstiana* and *W. baldaccii* grow best in rock crevices, on a shady, somewhat sloping site. Plants should be covered in winter with a layer of conifer branches. Propagation is by seed and division. Some good companions for *W. carinthiaca* are *Rhododendron ferrugineum, Campanula barbata, Soldanella montana, Viola lutea,* as well as the ferns, *Blechnum spicant, Cryptogramma crispa* and *Polypodium vulgare.*

W. amherstiana Benth. W. Himalayas and adjacent Afghanistan mountains. Leaves in a rosette, to 15cm long, oblong-ovate to broadly lanceolate, rugose, coarsely crenate to sinuate. Scape leafless, to 20cm high with a loose, one-sided raceme. Flowers blue, 7mm long. Blooms from June to July. z5

W. baldaccii Degen. N. Albania, on screes, in rock crevices and on shaded limestone boulders. Leaves long-petioled, oblong to broadly elliptic, to 10cm long, deeply crenate and toothed. Scape to 15cm long, flowers few, in a loose raceme to 6cm long. Flowers about 1cm long, violet-blue. Blooms from May to June. z7

W. carinthiaca Jacq. SE. Europe: N. Albanian Alps (Prokletije Mts.), Carinthia at 1400–1800m elevations; in mats on north-sloping, wind-protected balds and meadows in moist, fertile, lime-free, rather shallow, sandy loam. Leaves 7–25cm long, oblong to oblanceolate, shallowly or deeply coarsely crenate, glossy green, in rosettes. Stem 12–30cm high, with scattered small leaves and bracts. Flowers usually in a one-sided, dense, blue-violet raceme. Blooms from July to August. z5

W. orientalis Boiss. Asia Minor, Taurus Mts.; grows at lower elevations than the other species. To 25cm high. Leaves 10–30cm long, oblong to oblanceolate, obtuse, undulate, crenate or toothed, glossy, leathery. Flower stem steel blue, 15–40cm high, inflorescence many-flowered, 12–20cm long, loose. Flowers about 2.5cm long, heliotrope blue. Blooms from June to August. Unfortunately not reliably winter hardy, even with good winter cover; best kept in the alpine house or in an alpine case in a wide pot. z8

W. × suendermannii hort. (*W. baldaccii* × *W. carinthiaca*). Originated by Sündermann, Lindau. Quite a vigorous, freeflowering hybrid, more or less intermediate between the parents. Blooms from June to July. z6 (E.)

W. helianthoides Nutt., Mule's Ears. W. America, on spring-moist meadows and slopes. Stems to 40cm, few leaved. Basal leaves short petioled, to 30 × 9cm, lanceolate to elliptic ovate, entire or shallow-toothed. Stem leaves smaller. Plants develop 1–4 crowns, the basal foliage 6–9cm high, white tomentose early, becoming nearly glabrous. Flower heads to 13cm across, usually solitary; ligulate flowers sulfur yellow, 2.5–4cm long. Disc flowers yellow. z5 (K.)

Other species, more or less similar to W.

habitat. Requires lime-free, humus-rich soil, moist in summer, dry in winter. Suitable as a specimen perennial, given proper conditions on the edge of a shallow bog in full sun. Propagate by seed. Young plants will not bloom for 5–7 years.

X. asphodeloides (L.) Nutt. Turkeybeard, Mountain Asphodel. E. USA: New Jersey to Tennessee and Georgia; in open, dry to somewhat moist pine forests. Flowering stems to 1.5m high. Leaves very narrow, to 2mm wide, basal

Wulfenia × suendermannii

Xerophyllum tenax

Wyethia Nutt.
Compositae

About 14 species in the W. USA and British Columbia. Balsam-scented, coarse herbs. Root thick, fleshy. Stems mostly unbranched, with few alternate leaves or leafless, 30–120cm high. Leaves mostly basal, or alternate, linear to ovate, entire or serrate, pubescent or glandular-hairy, especially when young, sometimes shining-glabrous. Flower heads usually solitary or few, ray flowers pistillate, ligules spreading, yellow or white, disc flowers perfect, yellow. Spring to summer blooming. Grow in humus-rich, gravelly soil in full sun; intolerant of drought, excess heat, or poor drainage. Suitable for the reconstituted alpine meadow or large rock garden. Plants from seed require several years to bloom; crowns can be divided.

helianthoides, sometimes available in the trade include: *W. amplexicaulis, W. angustifolia,* and *W. mollis.*

Xerophyllum Michx.
Liliaceae
Turkey Beard, Elk Grass, Fire Lily

Two species in North America. Leaves grasslike, usually in a dense tuft, arising from a short, hard, woody crown. Stem stiffly erect yet somewhat flexuous, with scattered leaves, smaller toward the top. Inflorescence terminal, a many-flowered, dense, pyramidal or cylindrical raceme. Flowers white, long peduncled. Perianth segments 6, very similar, separate, stamens 6, pistil 3-carpeled, ovary superior, styles 3. Flowers from May to July. Very difficult to cultivate out of

leaves to 45cm long, stem leaves progressively shorter. Racemes to 30cm long. Flowers creamy white, 8mm across, fragrant. z6

X. tenax (Pursh) Nutt. Bear Grass, Elk Grass, Basket Grass, Fire Lily. W. North America: British Columbia southward to Wyoming and Central California. Very similar to *X. asphodeloides,* but requires a somewhat moister situation. Larger overall; basal leaves to 90cm long, 6mm wide, stem leaves progressively shorter and narrower; stem to 2m high with terminal racemes to 60cm long; flowers to 12cm across, fragrant. z6 (K.)

Yucca L.
Agavaceae
Adam's-needle, Spanish-bayonet, Spanish Dagger

About 40 species in North and Central America; a few are winter hardy. Stemless or short or tall-trunked plants with numerous, more or less leathery, tough, or hard-textured, sword-shaped leaves in tufts. Inflorescence terminal; flowers cream-colored or white, sometimes tinged pinkish, rose, or lavender, attractive, in large panicles, occasionally in racemes. Perianth cup- or saucer-shaped, the calyx and corolla very similar, segments 6, separate or barely united basally, somewhat fleshy, stamens 6, pistil superior with 3 carpels, style short, stigmas 3. Flowers 3.5–7cm long, usually nodding. Suitable primarily for the natural garden, with other xerophytes, succulents and grasses, or as a specimen plant in a sunny site. Grows best in shady, well-drained, calcareous soil. Propagation is by division and seeds (often requires hand pollination); pollinated in its native habitat by the Yucca Moth, *Pronuba yuccasella*. Dry winters are necessary in cool climates.

Y. angustifolia see **Y. filamentosa**

Y. filamentosa L. Adam's-needle, Needle-palm. (*Y. angustifolia* hort., *Y. smalliana* Fern.). SE. USA: North Carolina to Mississippi and Florida, but hardy. Nearly stemless, with a short, woody, more or less underground stem. Leaves tufted, 30–50, to 75cm long, 2.5cm wide, gray-green with a bluish cast, spatulate, narrowing abruptly to a hard terminal spine, margins with long, curly threads. Flowering stem straight or sometimes flexuose, 2–4.5m high (often short in cool climates); inflorescence paniculate, involving much of the stem. Flowers nearly white, to 5cm long, nodding. In the trade *Y. flaccida* and *Y. smalliana* often are offered under this name; midsummer to fall. 'Elegantissima' is distinguished from the species by its stiffer symmetry, larger inflorescence and vigorous habit. Cultivar 'Variegata', with leaves margined and striped clear, pale yellow; valuable as a specimen in a xerophyte planting. Karl Foerster selected, especially for winter hardiness, a few superior forms from thousands of plants, but these have been little disseminated, and closer examination into their parentage is needed because the pink coloration suggests the introduction of *Y. glauca* or other hardy species known to

carry genes for colored flowers. They are also greatly superior for their stately candelabrum-like inflorescences. More recently, some smaller, extremely hardy forms have been named. Unfortunately, the soft pink cultivar 'Rosenglocke' (Pink Bells), has proven somewhat less vigorous. The following cultivars have been introduced in Europe since 1950:

'Eisbär' ('Polar Bear'), with a uniformly branched inflorescence, to 1.5m high. Flowers nearly pure white, medium-sized. Flowering begins in early July. Young plants flower in the

Yucca recurvifolia

third year, which is 1–3 years earlier than the other cultivars. More decorative in all respects.

'Fontäne' ('Fountain'), only 1.2m high. Like *Y. glauca*, but with wider leaves. Inflorescence with short branchlets to low on the stem. Flowers large, creamy-white. Blooms middle-late.

'Glockenriese' ('Giant Bell'), more than 2m tall, with very many creamy-white flowers. Flowers rounded campanulate, brownish-tinged outside. Most of the stem is a rather tight candelabrum; a good substitute for *Yucca recurvifolia* in colder climates. Stiff leaves.

'Schellenbaum' ('Bell Tree'), nearly as tall as the above cultivar, with a huge candelabrum, loosely branched, dark reddish-brown stem. Flowers light

brownish-tinged outside.

'Schneefichte' ('Snow Spruce'), 2m high, perianth segments narrower, more starry, therefore, more elegant; an indispensable cultivar; the tuft of foliage is, however, somewhat irregular.

'Schneetanne' ('Snow Fir'), 2m high, flowers white with a yellow-green blush, beginning somewhat later; stiff foliage tuft. These Foerster cultivars flower reliably every year even in climates with cooler summers where the species rarely blooms. z5

Y. flaccida Haw. (*Y. puberula* Haw.). SE. USA: North Carolina to Alabama, often cultivated as *Y. filamentosa*. Leaves softer, tips more distinctly reflexed. Leaf margin filaments long, fine, but straight, not curling. Leaves 30–60cm long, 2.5–3.75cm wide, tips pointed, not hard. Inflorescence 1.75cm high or higher. Flowers 5–6.5cm long, nodding, creamy-white, in downy panicles. z6

Y. glauca Nutt. ex Fras. (*Y. angustifolia* Pursh). Central USA: South Dakota to New Mexico, Missouri to Colorado. Stem woody, short or somewhat elongated, but prostrate. Leaves in a rosette, erect and slightly reflexed, 30–70cm long, 1.2–1.75cm wide, linear to 12mm wide, gray-green, white-margined with few white filaments. Inflorescence to 1m, very rarely to 2m high, a simple or short-branched columnar raceme, extending nearly to the base. Flowers nodding, greenish-white, often tinged brownish-red outside, globose-campanulate or somewhat elongated; midsummer to fall. 'Rosea', flowers strongly rose-tinged outside. z4

Y. glauca var. **stricta** Trel. (*Y. angustifolia stricta* Bak.) Kansas. Stem erect, woody; leaves longer, stiffer, glabrous blue-gray at first, marginal threads develop early; inflorescence somewhat taller, with slightly longer branches at the base, lowest flowers in the rosette; flowers greenish white, often somewhat rose-tinged, globose to oblong-campanulate, with obtuse-rounded petals. z4

Tolerates a heavy frost and generally better for cooler climates. *Yucca glauca* is a handsome, if somewhat incompatible, foliage plant even in climates not conducive to flowering. Vegetatively propagated or easily grown from seed.

Y. gloriosa L. SE. USA. Requires winter protection in cooler climates. Very stiff, dangerously sharp-tipped leaves. Inflorescence candelabrum-like about 2m high, dense, in early fall. Develops a short, massive, woody stem. z7(6)

Y. × karlsruhensis Graebn. (*Y. glauca* × *filamentosa* or *flaccida*). Leaves stiff, about 45cm long, 1.5cm wide, glaucous blue-green. Inflorescence to 1.5m high; flowers soft lilac-tinged outside. Very attractive and hardy garden hybrid, unfortunately difficult to propagate by division and therefore little disseminated. Blooms more readily in cooler climates than *Y. glauca*. Perhaps several clones exist? z5

Y. puberula see **Y. flaccida**

leaves to 55cm long, 2cm wide, with terminal spine, margins yellowish or brownish, finely toothed. Flowers cream-colored, sometimes purple-tinged outside, fragrant. Inflorescence to 4m high, a columnar panicle. Only for the warmest sites with good winter protection, intolerant of winter wetness. Several botanical varieties are listed; while the type species, *Y. whipplei* var. *whipplei* usually dies after flowering, the other varieties persist. z8 (Me. & Mü.)

Z. californica (K. Presl.) (*Z. californica* ssp. *angustifolia* (Keck). SW. USA: coastal California, and perhaps Mexico. Stems 30–60cm high, woody at the base and somewhat pubescent. Leaves linear, to linear-lanceolate, densely white woolly, velvety to the touch. Flowers to 4cm long, bright red; floriferous in warm summers from August to frost. Long-lived given good drainage. Stoloniferous. Not very winter hardy. z8

Z. california ssp. **angustifolia** see **Z. californica**

Zauschneria californica

Zauschneria cana

Y. recurvifolia Salisb. SE. USA. Stem short, woody, often branched. Leaves, unlike *Y. gloriosa*, strongly recurved, longer. Inflorescence huge, nearly columnar candelabrum of white, rounded-campanulate flowers in midsummer. An imposing, very exotic species, more common in warmer climates and occasionally mistaken for *Y. gloriosa* from which it is easily distinguished by the reflexed leaves. Hardier than *Y. gloriosa*, but a warm, protected site is advisable in cool climates. Rarely flowers in cool climates but worthwhile for its foliage effect. Var. **variegata** (Carriére) Tral. Leaves with a central yellow stripe, showy. z7

Y. smalliana see **Y. filamentosa**

Y. whipplei Torr. Our-Lord's-Candle. W. USA: California. Stemless or nearly so. Silvery-gray rosette of narrow, stiff

Zauschneria K.B. Presl.
Onagraceae (Oenotheraceae)
California-Fuchsia

Perennials, some woody at the base, in the W. USA and NW. Mexico; the taxonomy of this genus changes frequently, species being reduced to subspecies and varieties. Mostly well-branched, densely leafy, with a bushy habit. Flowers red, in leafy spikes at the stem tips, fuchsia-like. Stems with shredding epidermis when mature. Leaves alternate, or opposite toward the base of the plant. Flowers borne horizontally; calyx tube 4-lobed, inflated above the ovary, funnel-shaped below; petals 4; stamens 8; exerted, pistil 4-carpeled, ovary inferior. Seeds with a tuft of hairs.

Z. arizonica see **Z. california** ssp. **latifolia**

Z. californica ssp. **latifolia** (Hook.) Keck (*Z. arizonica* A. Davids., *Z. latifolia* (Hook.) Greene var. *arizonica* (A. Davids.) hort.). USA: mountainous regions of Oregon, California, Arizona, Nevada, New Mexico. Stems 20–40cm high, erect or procumbent, branched, herbaceous, not woody at the base. Leaves green, ovate to lanceolate-ovate, often glandular, not pubescent. Flowers small, to 3cm long, scarlet-red, not as showy as those of *Z. californica*, but the plant is hardier. Blooms from late July to October.

A charming plant for the collector or botanic garden. Subshrubby plant for the rock garden, flowering continuously from summer to fall. Somewhat winter hardy if grown in sandy loam overlaying a well-drained gravel substrate. A protective mulch of conifer needles is advised. Root summer cuttings in colder regions and overwinter them in a cool greenhouse for planting out after the last spring frost. Cut back early in the spring, old plants especially, for best flower production. Grow in a sunny south exposure. Some strains flower freely, others only sparsely; cultivars which flower well are generally available. If not obtainable, select the most floriferous plants at the nursery. Propagation is by seed, separation of rooted runners and summer cuttings, kept frost free and light over winter. An attractive companion for *Zauschneria* is the blue-flowering *Ceratostigma plumba-*

Z. californica var. **villosa** see **Z. californica** ssp. **mexicana**

Z. cana (Greene.) (*Z. californica* var. *microphylla* A. Grey, *Z. microphylla* (A. Grey) Moxl.). SW. USA; California; only in coastal regions. Stems to 20cm high. Leaves narrow, less than 3mm wide, gray-glabrous, fascicled. Flowers smaller, orange-red. z8 (E.)

Z. latifolia var. **arizonica** see **Z. californica** ssp. **latifolia**

cence. Flowers solitary or few, sessile or short-petioled. Perianth of 6 more or less similar segments, more or less united at the base, the outer segments (calyx) often slightly narrower, trumpet-shaped, white, pink, red, copper-colored or yellow; stamens 6 in 2 series, the 3 inner stamens shorter, alternating with the longer outer 3; pistil elongate, ovary more or less inferior, stigma 3-lobed. Bulbs more or less tulip-like with a shining brown or tan papery tunic, mostly ovate, (*Cooperia* bulbs globose to

Zigadenus nuttallii

Zizania aquatica

ginoides, or in milder areas, the pretty, but tender *C. willmottianum*. Both flower with *Zauschneria*. z7

Z. californica ssp. **mexicana** (K. Presl.) Raven (*Z. californica* var. *villosa* (Greene) Jeps., *Z. mexicana* (K. Presl.)). California. Sprawling, decumbent, or mat habit (perhaps due to vegetative propagation, from decumbent stems), sometimes only 5cm high, but taller in habitat. Quickly covers a large area under favorable conditions. Leaves lanceolate, very densely gray-pubescent. Blooms from July through August. Free-flowering; flowers orange-red, relatively large, about 2.5cm long. An attractive species, best for the rock garden or dry stone wall. z7(6)

Z. californica var. **microphylla** see **Z. cana**

Z. mexicana see **Z. californica** ssp. **mexicana**

Z. microphylla see **Z. cana**

Zephyranthes Herb.
Amaryllidaceae
Atamasco-lily, Zephyr-lily,
Rain-lily

Thirty-five to 40 species (depending on the indusiin of about 5 species of the closely related genus *Cooperia*), small, herbaceous bulbous plants from the warm regions of the Western Hemisphere (at least 1 *Cooperia* genus as far north as the plains of S. Central Kansas). Leaves all basal, tufted, narrowly strap-shaped to almost thread-like. Scape leafless, terminating in 2 spathe valves which enclose the developing inflores-

flattened-globose), usually deep-growing in native habitat. Only two species are sufficiently hardy to include here. Plant these in half-sun to bright shade in fertile loam along streams or pond margins. The lily-like flowers are a nice addition to a bottomland wild garden.

Z. atamasco (L.) Herb. (*Amaryllis atamasco* L.). Atamasco-lily. SE. USA: Virginia to Florida but hardy farther north. Leaves several, to 30cm long, 3–5mm wide, strap-shaped with abruptly rounded to acute tips, over-arching by midsummer, bright green. Scapes to 30cm high; spathe 2-valved, more or less 3cm long, 1-flowered, pedicel very short. Perianth trumpet-shaped, facing upward and outward, 7–10cm long, to 6cm across, pure white or white flushed pink. Spring flowering. In the proper environment these develop large, many-flowered clumps, especially suitable for edging walks in low-lying spring-flowering woodland gardens with *Mertensia*, *Rhodendron viscosum* and various ferns.

Z. candida (Lindl.) Herb. White Rain-lily. South america, along the LaPlata River. Often confused with *Z. atamasco* in the trade. Leaves several, 20–30cm long, 2–4cm wide, erect, rush-like, evergreen, thick. Scape erect, 10–25cm high, spathe to 3cm long, valves saceate above. Flower solitary, usually solitary, more or less upright-facing, perianth to 5cm long, wide-based trumpet-shaped, segment tips somewhat flaired, green toward the base, pure white, sometimes faintly flushed rose-pink. Summer and fall-blooming; in warm, dryish regions reblooms with each rain or deep watering. 'Major' is larger in all parts. If the foliage is protected with evergreen boughs in winter, reasonably hardy. Use as described for *Z. atamasco*. z6

Zigadenus Michx.
Liliaceae
Death Camas

About 15 species in N. America and Asia, poisonous herbs with a rhizomatous rootstock or a bulb. Leaves to 50cm long, linear, acuminate, channeled, gray-green, nearly all basal, few on the stems. Flowers in simple or paniculate racemes. Perianth segments connate at the base, flat-spreading, oblong to ovate, with 1 or 2 glands at the base, peristent; stamens 6; ovary partially or entirely inferior. Suitable for the natural garden, or pond and stream banks. A collector's plant. Propagate by seed or division.

Z. elegans Pursh. White Camas. N. America: Manitoba to Alaska, south to Missouri, New Mexico and Arizona; on moist sites. Bulb with a membranous tunic. Leaves keeled, to 30cm long, 4–12mm wide, glaucous, acute. Stem to 90cm high, with few reduced leaves. Raceme loose, simple or rarely branched at the base; bracts ovate to lanceolate, reddish; perianth segments adnate to the ovaries, greenish-white, 15mm in diameter; the 3 petals narrowed sharply at the base to a broad claw; glands 2-lobed; style about 5mm long; June to August. For a sunny to semi-shaded wild or rock garden. Very long lived under favorable conditions. z3

Z. fremontii (Torr.) Torr. ex S. Wats. Starlily. USA: Oregon to S. California. Leaves to 40cm long, 2.5cm wide, several to many in a basal tuft. Stem to 90cm high, few-leaved. green, bracts not red. Flowers large, soft yellow; perianth segments clawed glandular, distinct from the ovary; June to August. z8(7)

Z. nuttallii A. Gray. Death Camas. USA: Tennessee to Kansas, south to Texas. Bulb deep-growing. Leaves light green, to 45cm long, to 20mm wide, leathery, sickle-shaped. Stem stout, to 75cm high with few small leaves. Raceme simple, occasionally somewhat branched, many-flowered, bracts scaly; flowers about 12mm across, yellowish-white; petals not clawed but with a single basal gland. Perianth segments distinct from the ovary. May to June. For dryish, stony sites. Combines well with grasses such as *Deschampsia*, *Molinia caerulea* 'Variegata', *Milium effusum* 'Aureum'. z6 (Me. & Kö.)

Zizania L.
Gramineae
Wild Rice

Two or 3 species of annual or perennial aquatic grasses in North America and S. Asia. Rhizomes stout, with runners. Culms erect, 2–3m high. Leaves flat, narrowly linear, acute, to 2.5cm wide. Flowers in large, loose, narrow panicles, 30–50cm long, lower flowers staminate, pendulous, upper flowers pistillate, erect when ripe. Suitable for large, cold water ponds and lakes in large gardens and parks. Propagate by division or seed.

Z. aquatica L. Central and E. North America; in marshes, lakes, ponds, and streams, usually in shallow water. Indians protect wild stands and harvest the for grain along the US-Canadian border, west of the Great Lakes. This is a self-seeding annual plant. Very similar to the following species:

Z. caduciflora (Turcz.) Hand.-Mazz. (*Z. latifolia* (Griseb.) Turcz. ex Stapf). Japan, S. Russia, NE. India and Burma. Grows under conditions similar to those for *Z. aquatica*. A large, imposing grass with large, conspicuous panicles of nutritious grain. Requires moist to constantly wet soil with a water depth of 0–20cm. z8(7) (D.)

z. latifolia see **Z. caduciflora**

Zwackhia

Z. aurea see **Halacsya sendtneri**

List of Common Names

Aaron's Beard: *Hypericum calycinum*
Aaron's Beard: *Hypericum*
Aaron's Rod: *Thermopsis*
Absinth: *Artemisia absinthium*
Acanthus-leaved Thistle: *Carlina acanthifolia*
Aconite: *Aconitum*
Adam's-needle: *Yucca filamentosa*
Adam's-needle: *Yucca*
Adam-and-Eve: *Arum maculatum*
Adder's-tongue: *Erythronium*
Adobe-lily: *Fritillaria pluriflora*
African Lily: *Agapanthus*
Alabama Lip Fern: *Cheilanthes alabamensis*
Algerian Iris: *Iris unguicularis*
Allegheny Monkey Flower: *Mimulus ringens*
Allegheny Spurge: *Pachysandra procumbens*
Alp Lily: *Llogdia*
Alpine Aster: *Aster alpinus*
Alpine Balsam: *Erinus alpinus*
Alpine Bistort: *Polygonum viviparum*
Alpine Chrysanthemum: *Chrysanthemum alpinum*
Alpine Clover: *Trifolium alpinum*
Alpine Coltsfoot: *Homogyne alpina*
Alpine Edelweiss: *Leontopodium alpinum*
Alpine Fern: *Cryptogramma*
Alpine Fescue: *Festuca alpina*
Alpine Forget-me-not: *Eritrichium*
Alpine Forget-me-not: *Myosotis alpestris*
Alpine Lady Fern: *Athyrium distentifolium*
Alpine Lady's Mantle: *Alchemilla alpina*
Alpine Lily: *Lilium parvum*
Alpine Meadow Rue: *Thalictrum alpinum*
Alpine Pansy: *Viola alpina*
Alpine Poppy: *Papaver burseri*
Alpine Shooting-Star: *Dodecatheon alpinum*
Alpine Wormwood: *Artemisia umbelliformis*
Alpine-violet: *Cyclamen*
Alumroot: *Heuchera*
Amaryllis: *Amaryllis*
American Beech Fern: *Thelypteris hexagonoptera*
American Cowslip: *Dodecatheon*
American Ipecac: *Gillenia stipulata*

American Lotus: *Nelumbo lutea*
American Mountain Mint: *Pycnanthemum*
American Ostrich Fern: *Matteuccia pensylvanica*
American Spatterdock: *Nuphar advena*
American Wall Fern: *Polypodium virginianum*
American Wood Sage: *Teucrium canadense*
Amur Silver Grass: *Miscanthus sacchariflorus*
Anemone: *Anemone*
Angel's Fishing-rods: *Dierama pendulum*
Angel's Tears: *Narcissus triandrus*
Anise: *Pimpinella*
Ankara Crocus ('Golden Bunch'): *Crocus ancyrensis*
Antelope Horn: *Asclepias viridis*
Apple Mint: *Mentha suaveolens*
Arctic Bramble: *Rubus arcticus*
Arctic Daisy: *Chrysanthemum articum*
Arrow Arum: *Peltandra*
Arrowhead: *Sagittaria sagittifolia*
Arrowhead: *Sagittaria*
Arrowleaf: *Peltandra virginica*
Artichoke: *Cynara scolymus*
Artichoke: *Cynara*
Ashy Sunflower: *Helianthus mollis*
Asiatic Poppy: *Meconopsis*
Asphodel: *Asphodeline lutea*
Atamasco-lily: *Zephyranthes atamasco*
Atamasco-lily: *Zephyranthes*
Atlas Daisy: *Anacyclus depressus*
Atlas Fescue: *Festuca mairei*
Autumn Moor Grass: *Sesleria autumnalis*
Autumn Sage: *Salvia greggii*
Autumn Scilla: *Scilla autumnalis*
Autumn-crocus: *Colchicum autumnale*
Autumn-crocus: *Colchicum*
Avalanch-lily: *Erythronium grandiflorum*
Avens: *Geum*
Baby's Breath: *Gypsophila paniculata*
Baby's Breath: *Gypsophila*
Baby's Tears: *Soleirolia*
Bald-money: *Meum*
Balloon Flower: *Platycodon*
Balm: *Melissa officinalis*
Balm: *Melissa*
Balsam Root: *Balsamorhiza*

Bamboo Cane: *Arundinaria*
Bamboo: *Semiarundinaria*
Bamboo: *Shibataea*
Baneberry: *Actaea*
Barren Strawberry: *Duchesnea*
Barren Strawberry: *Waldsteinia*
Barrenwort: *Epimedium*
Basket Grass: *Xerophyllum tenax*
Basket of Gold: *Aurinia saxatilis*
Basket of Gold: *Aurinia*
Bayonet-plant: *Aciphylla*
Beach Bullrush: *Scirpus maritimus*
Beach Rush: *Juncus maritimus*
Beach Sand-verbena: *Abronia umbellata*
Beach Wormwood: *Artemisia stelleriana*
Bear Grass: *Xerophyllum tenax*
Bearded Bellflower: *Campanula barbata*
Beard-tongue: *Penstemon*
Bear's Breech: *Acanthus*
Bear's Paw: *Polystichum polyblepharum*
Bedstraw: *Galium*
Beech Fern: *Thelypteris*
Beetleweed: *Galax*
Beggar Ticks: *Desmodium*
Begonia: *Begonia*
Bell Flower: *Campanula*
Belladonna-lily: *Amaryllis belladonna*
Belle Isle Cress: *Barbarea verna*
Bellflower: *Symphyandra*
Bellort: *Uvularia*
Bergamot: *Monarda*
Berry Bladder Fern: *Cystopteris bulbifera*
Betony: *Stachys officinalis*
Betony: *Stachys*
Bibleaf Costmary: *Chrysanthemum balsamita*
Big Blue Stem: *Andropogon gerardii*
Big Quaking Grass: *Briza media*
Bindweed: *Calystegia*
Bindweed: *Convolvulus*
Birds-foot Trefoil: *Lotus corniculatus*
Bird's Foot Sedge: *Carex ornithopoda*
Bird's Foot Violet: *Viola pedata*
Bird's Nest Fern: *Asplenium*
Bird's-eye Primrose: *Primula farinosa*
Bird's-eye Primrose: *Primula laurentiana*
Bird's-eye Primrose: *Primula mistassinica*
Bird-on-the-Wing: *Polygala pauciflora*
Bishop's Cap: *Mitella*
Bishop's Weed: *Aegopodium podograria*

Bishop's Weed: *Aegopodium*
Bistort: *Polygonum bistorta*
Bitter Root: *Lewisia rediviva*
Bitter Root: *Lewisia*
Bittercress: *Cardamine*
Black Bamboo: *Phyllostachys nigra*
Black Byrony: *Tamus communis*
Black Calla: *Arum*
Black Knapweed: *Centaurea nigra*
Black Snakeroot: *Sanicula*
Black Spleenwort: *Asplenium adiantum-nigrum*
Blackberry-lily: *Belamcanda*
Blackberry: *Rubus*
Black-eyed Susan: *Rudbeckia hirta*
Black-striped Fern: *Asplenium adiantum-nigrum*
Bladder Campion: *Silene vulgaris*
Bladder Fern: *Cystopteris*
Blanket Flower: *Gaillardia*
Blazing-star: *Liatris*
Bleeding Heart: *Dicentra*
Blister Cress: *Erysimum*
Bloodroot: *Sanguinaria canadensis*
Bloody Butcher: *Trillium recurvatum*
Bloody Cranesbill: *Geranium sanguineum*
Blue Buttons: *Vinca major*
Blue Cardinal Flower: *Lobelia siphilitica*
Blue Catmint: *Nepeta* × *faassenii*
Blue Cohoch: *Caulophyllum*
Blue False Indigo: *Baptisia australis*
Blue Fescue: *Festuca cinerea*
Blue Grama: *Bouteloua gracilis*
Blue Moonwort: *Soldanella*
Blue Moor Grass: *Sesleria caerulea*
Blue Oat Grass: *Helictotrichon sempervirens*
Blue Passion-flower: *Passiflora caerulea*
Blue Poppy: *Meconopsis betonicifolia*
Blue Poppy: *Meconopsis*
Blue Sage: *Salvia azurea*
Blue Star: *Amsonia*
Blue Succory: *Catananche*
Blue Vervain: *Verbena hastata*
Blue Wild Rye: *Elymus glaucus*
Blue Wood Aster: *Aster cordifolius*
Bluebead-lily: *Clintonia borealis*
Bluebells: *Mertensia virginica*
Bluebells: *Mertensia*
Bluebell: *Campanula rotundifolia*
Bluegrass: *Poa*
Bluestem Beard Grass: *Andropogon*
Bluets: *Houstonia*
Blue-eyed Grass: *Sisyrinchium*
Blue-green Rush: *Juncus inflexus*
Blue-green Sedge: *Carex flacca*
Blue-jasmine: *Clematis crispa*
Blue-oxalis: *Parochetus*
Blue-stem Goldenrod: *Solidago caesia*
Blunt-lobed Woodsia: *Woodsia obtusa*
Bog Asphodel: *Narthecium*
Bog Rush: *Juncus*
Bogbean: *Menyanthes*
Bog-violet: *Pinguicula*
Boltonia: *Boltonia*
Boneset: *Eupatorium*
Bonnet Bellflower: *Codonopsis*

Borage: *Borago*
Bottle Gentian: *Gentiana andrewsii*
Bottle Gentian: *Gentiana clausa*
Bottlebrush Grass: *Hystrix*
Bottlebrush: *Hystrix patula*
Boulder Fern: *Dennstaedtia punctilobula*
Bouncing Bet: *Saponaria officinalis*
Bowman's Root: *Gillenia trifoliata*
Bowman's Root: *Gillenia*
Bracken Fern: *Pteridium*
Brake: *Pteridium*
Braun's Holly Fern: *Polystichum braunii*
Bride's-bonnet: *Clintonia uniflora*
Brittle Fern: *Cystopteris fragilis*
Britton's Phlox: *Phlox subulata* ssp. *brittonii*
Broadleaf Bird's-foot Trefoil: *Lotus corniculatus* var. *arvensis*
Broadleaved Arrowhead: *Sagittaria latifolia*
Broadleaved Cattail: *Typha latifolia*
Brome Grass: *Bromus*
Bronze Fennel: *Foeniculum vulgare* var. *consanguineum*
Brown Beth: *Trillium erectum*
Brown Sedge: *Carex petriei*
Bryony: *Bryonia*
Buckbean: *Menyanthes*
Buckler Ferns: *Dryopteris*
Buffalo-pea: *Baptisia leucophaea*
Bugle-lily: *Watsonia beatricis*
Bugle-lily: *Watsonia*
Bugle: *Ajuga*
Bulblet Bladder Fern: *Cystopteris bulbifera*
Bullrush: *Scirpus lacustris*
Bullrush: *Scirpus*
Bulrush: *Typha*
Bunchberry: *Cornus canadensis*
Bunchberry: *Cornus*
Bunchflower: *Melanthium hybridum*
Burnet: *Sanguisorba*
Burning Bush: *Dictamnus*
Bur-reed: *Sparganium*
Bush Bamboo: *Pleioblastus*
Bush Monkey Flower: *Mimulus aurantiacus*
Bush Pea: *Thermopsis*
Butterbur: *Petasites*
Buttercup: *Ranunculus*
Butterfly Weed: *Asclepias tuberosa*
Butterfly Weed: *Asclepias*
Butterwort: *Pinguicula*
Butter-and-eggs: *Linaria vulgaris*
Button Snake-root: *Eryngium yuccifolium*
Button-snakeroot: *Liatris*
Calamint: *Calamintha*
Calamint: *Satureja*
California Bluebell: *Phacelia*
California Buckwheat: *Eriogonum fasciculatum*
California Coneflower: *Rudbeckia californica*
California Indian Pink: *Silene californica*
California Tree Poppy: *Romneya*
California-Fuchsia: *Zauschneria*
Camass: *Camassia*

Cames: *Camassia*
Campion: *Lychnis*
Campion: *Silene*
Canada Burnet: *Sanguisorba canadensis*
Canada Violet: *Viola canadensis*
Canadian Lily: *Lilium canadense*
Canary Grass: *Phalaris*
Candlestick Lily: *Lilium pensylvanicum*
Candy Carrot: *Athamanta*
Candytuft: *Iberis*
Canebreak Bamboo: *Arundinaria gigantea*
Cane: *Pleioblastus*
Canker-root: *Coptis groenlandica*
Cape Cod Pink Water Lily: *Nymphaea odorata* var. *rosea*
Cape Fuschia: *Phygelius*
Cape Pondweed: *Aponogeton*
Capweed: *Lippia nodiflora*
Cardinal Flower: *Lobelia cardinalis*
Cardinal Flower: *Lobelia*
Cardoon: *Cynara cardunculus*
Cardoon: *Cynara*
Carnation: *Dianthus*
Carolina Larkspur: *Delphinium carolinianum*
Carolina Lupine: *Thermopsis caroliniana*
Carolina Phlox: *Phlox carolina*
Carpathian Bellflower: *Campanula carpatica*
Carpathian Harebell: *Campanula carpatica*
Carpathian Thistle: *Carduus kerneri*
Catchfly: *Lychnis*
Catchfly: *Silene*
Catesby's Gentian: *Gentiana catesbaei*
Catmint: *Nepeta*
Catnip: *Nepeta cataria*
Catnip: *Nepeta*
Cattail: *Typha*
Cat's Breeches: *Hydrophyllum capitatum*
Cat's ear: *Hypochaeris*
Caucasian Lily: *Lilium monadelphum*
Caucasian Scabiosa: *Scabiosa caucasica*
Celandine Crocus: *Crocus korolkowii*
Centaury: *Centaurium*
Century Plant: *Agave*
Chain Fern: *Woodwardia*
Chamomile: *Anthemis*
Chaparrel Lily: *Lilium rubescens*
Chatterbox: *Epipactis gigantea*
Checkerbloom: *Sidalcea malviflora*
Checkered Lily: *Fritillaria meleagris*
Checkered Lily: *Fritillaria*
Cheddar Pink: *Dianthus gratianopolitanus*
Chickweed: *Stellaria*
Chimney Bellflower: *Campanula pyramidalis*
Chincherinchee: *Ornithogalum thyrsoides*
Chinese Lantern: *Physalis*
Chinese Pennisetum: *Pennisetum alopecuroides*
Chinese Peony: *Paeonia lactiflora*
Chinese Rhubarb: *Rheum palmatum*
Chinese Shady Bamboo: *Indocalamus latifolius*
Chinese Silver Grass: *Miscanthus sinensis*
Chinese Water Chestnut: *Eleocharis*

Chinese White Lily: *Lilium leucanthum*
Chinese Yam: *Dioscorea batatas*
Chinese-lantern Plant: *Physalis alkekengi*
Chives: *Allium schoenoprasum*
Chocolate Root: *Geum rivale*
Cholla: *Opuntia*
Christmas Fern: *Polystichum acrostichoides*
Christmas Fern: *Polystichum*
Christmas Rose: *Helleborus niger*
Christmas Rose: *Helleborus*
Cinnamon Fern: *Osmunda cinnamomea*
Cinnamon Fern: *Osmunda*
Cinnamon Vine: *Dioscorea*
Cinnamon-vine: *Dioscorea batatas*
Cinquefoil: *Potentilla*
Clary: *Salvia sclarea*
Cleavers: *Galium*
Clematis: *Clematis*
Cleveland Lip Fern: *Cheilanthes clevelandii*
Cliff Brake: *Pellaea atropurpurea*
Cliff Brake: *Pellaea*
Cliff-green: *Paxistima canbyi*
Climbing Fern: *Lygodium palmatum*
Climbing Fern: *Lygodium*
Closed Gentian: *Gentiana clausa*
Closed Gentian: *Gentiana rubricaulis*
Cloth-of-gold Crocus: *Crocus angustifolius*
Cloudberry: *Rubus chamaemorus*
Clover: *Trifolium*
Clump Sedge: *Carex sempervirens*
Clustered Bellflower: *Campanula glomerata*
Clustered Poppy Mallow: *Callirhoe triangulata*
Cluster-head Pink: *Dianthus carthusianorum*
Coast Lily: *Lilium maritimum*
Coast Trillium: *Trillium ovatum*
Coat Flower: *Petrorhagia saxifraga*
Cobweb Houseleek: *Sempervivum arachnoideum*
Cohosh Bugbane: *Cimicifuga*
Colewort: *Crambe cordifolia*
Colewort: *Crambe*
Coltsfoot: *Galax*
Columbia Lily: *Lilium columbianum*
Columbine: *Aquilegia vulgaris*
Columbine: *Aquilegia*
Comfrey: *Symphytum*
Common Asparagus: *Asparagus officinalis*
Common Bladder Fern: *Cystopteris fragilis*
Common Bleeding Heart: *Dicentra spectabilis*
Common Boneset: *Eupatorium perfoliatum*
Common Buttercup: *Ranunculus acris*
Common Butterwort: *Pinguicula vulgaris*
Common Cattail: *Typha latifolia*
Common Comfrey: *Symphytum officinale*
Common Dogbane: *Apocynum androsaemifolium*
Common Foxglove: *Digitalis purpurea*

Common Globeflower: *Trollius europaeus*
Common Hops: *Humulus lupulus*
Common Horehound: *Marrubium vulgare*
Common Lungwort: *Pulmonaria officinalis*
Common Maidenhair Fern: *Adiantum capillus-veneris*
Common Monkey Flower: *Mimulus guttatus*
Common Periwinkle: *Vinca minor*
Common Rue: *Ruta graveolens*
Common Snowdrops: *Galanthus nivalis*
Common Sundrops: *Oenothera tetragona*
Common Toadflax: *Linaria vulgaris*
Common Valerian: *Valeriana officinalis*
Common Water Plantain: *Alisma plantago-aquatica*
Common Woodsia: *Woodsia obtusa*
Common Yarrow: *Achillea millefolium*
Compass Plant: *Silphium laciniatum*
Compass Plant: *Silphium*
Coneflower: *Echinacea*
Coneflower: *Rudbeckia*
Cook's Foot: *Dactylis*
Copper Shield Fern: *Dryopteris erythrosora*
Coppertips: *Crocosmia*
Coral Bells: *Heuchera sanguinea*
Coral Bells: *Heuchera*
Coral Lily: *Lilium pumilum*
Coral-drops: *Bessera elegans*
Corn Flag: *Gladiolus*
Corn Lily: *Veratrum californicum*
Cornflower: *Centaurea*
Cornish Moneywort: *Sibthorpia europaea*
Corn-lily: *Clintonia borealis*
Corn-lily: *Ixia*
Corsican Mint: *Mentha requienii*
Corsican Sandwort: *Arenaria balearica*
Cossack Asparagus: *Typha latifolia*
Cottage Pink: *Dianthus plumarius*
Cotton Grass: *Eriophorum*
Cotton Thistle: *Onopordum*
Cow Lily: *Nuphar*
Cowslip Lungwort: *Pulmonaria angustifolia*
Cowslip: *Caltha*
Cowslip: *Primula veris*
Cow-parsnip: *Heracleum*
Crackerberry: *Cornus canadensis*
Cranesbill: *Geranium*
Creeping Baby's Breath: *Gypsophila repens*
Creeping Bellflower: *Campanula rapunculoides*
Creeping Charlie: *Lysimachia nummularia*
Creeping Forget-me-not: *Omphalodes verna*
Creeping Jenny: *Lysimachia nummularia*
Creeping Liriope: *Liriope spicata*
Creeping Mint: *Meehania cordata*
Creeping Myrtle: *Vinca*
Creeping Phlox: *Phlox subulata*
Crested Gentian: *Gentiana septemfida*
Crested Wood Fern: *Dryopteris cristata*

Crimson Bramble: *Rubus arcticus*
Crinum-lily: *Crinum*
Crocus: *Crocus*
Cross Fern: *Polystichum tripteron*
Cross Gentian: *Gentiana cruciata*
Crowfoot: *Ranunculus*
Crown Imperial: *Fritillaria imperialis*
Crown Imperial: *Fritillaria*
Crown-beard: *Verbesina*
Crown-vetch: *Coronilla*
Cuckoo Flower: *Cardamine pratensis*
Cuckoo Flower: *Lychnis flos-cuculi*
Cuckoopint: *Arum maculatum*
Cudweed: *Artemisia ludoviciana*
Culver's Physic: *Veronicastrum virginicum*
Culver's Physic: *Veronicastrum*
Cup Fern: *Dennstaedtia*
Cupid's Dart: *Catananche*
Cupplant: *Silphium perfoliatum*
Curly-leaf Spearmint: *Mentha spicata* 'Crispa', 'Crispata' or 'Crispii'
Cushion Pink: *Silene*
Cyclamen Narcissus: *Narcissus cyclamineus*
Cyperus Sedge: *Carex pseudocyperus*
Cypress Spurge: *Euphorbia cyparissias*
Daffodil: *Narcissus pseudonarcissus*
Daffodil: *Narcissus*
Daisy Fleabane: *Erigeron*
Dakota Verbena: *Verbena bipinnatifida*
Dalmatian Insect Flower: *Chrysanthemum cinerariifolium*
Dalmatian Pyrethrum: *Chrysanthemum cinerariifolium*
Damewort: *Hesperis*
Dame's Rocket: *Hesperis matronalis*
Dandelion: *Taraxacum*
Danesblood Bellflower: *Campanula glomerata*
Dark Green Umbrella Bamboo: *Sinarundinaria nitida*
Dark-eye Sunflower: *Helianthus atrorubens*
Dayflower: *Commelina*
Daylily: *Hemerocallis*
Dead Nettle: *Lamium*
Death Camas: *Zigadenus nuttallii*
Death Camas: *Zigadenus*
Deciduous Broad-leaved Sedge: *Carex siderosticha*
Deer Fern: *Blechnum*
Deer Grass: *Rhexia*
Deer Tongue Grass: *Panicum clandestinum*
Deer-tongue Fern: *Phyllitis*
Desert Candle: *Eremurus*
Devil's Bit: *Succisa pratensis*
Devil's Claw: *Physoplexis comosa*
Devil's Guts: *Tephrosia virginiana*
Dittany of Crete: *Origanum dictamnus*
Dock: *Rumex*
Dog Fennel: *Anthemis*
Dog Violet: *Viola canina*
Dogbane: *Apocynum*
Dogtooth violet: *Erythronium dens-canis*
Dogtooth-violet: *Erythronium*
Dolomite Cinquefoil: *Potentilla nitida*

Douglas's Spike Moss: *Selaginella douglasii*
Dovedale Moss: *Saxifraga hypnoides*
Downy Gentian: *Gentiana puberula*
Dragon Mouth: *Horminum pyrenaicum*
Dragonhead: *Dracocephalum*
Drooping Coneflower: *Ratibida pinnata*
Dropwort: *Filipendula vulgaris*
Dropwort: *Filipendula*
Duck Potato: *Sagittaria latifolia*
Dune Grass: *Elymus*
Dusty Miller: *Artemisia stelleriana*
Dusty Miller: *Centaurea ragusina*
Dusty-miller: *Centaurea*
Dutchman's Breeches: *Dicentra cucullaria*
Dutchman's Pipe: *Aristolochia*
Dutchman's Pipe: *Clematis*
Dwarf Bamboo: *Sasa*
Dwarf Bearded Iris: *Iris pumila*
Dwarf Bellflower: *Campanula cochleariifolia*
Dwarf Cornel: *Cornus canadensis*
Dwarf Cress: *Lepidium nanum*
Dwarf Crested Iris: *Iris cristata*
Dwarf Elder: *Sambucus ebulus*
Dwarf Elecampane: *Inula acaulis*
Dwarf Hawk's Beard: *Crepis pygmaea*
Dwarf Larkspur: *Delphinium tricorne*
Dwarf Lilyturf: *Ophiopogon japonicus*
Dwarf Morning Glory: *Convolvulus*
Dwarf Pillow Sedge: *Carex firma*
Dwarf Rush: *Juncus ensifolius*
Dwarf Soapwort: *Saponaria pumila*
Dwarf Sweetflag: *Acorus gramineus*
Dwarf Valerian: *Valeriana supina*
Dwarf Water Lily: *Nymphaea tetragona*
Dwarf White Trillium: *Trillium nivale*
Dwarf-snapdragon: *Chaenarrhinum*
Dyer's Woad: *Isatis*
Early Blue Violet: *Viola palmata*
Easter Daisy: *Townsendia exscapa*
Easter Daisy: *Townsendia hookeri*
Easter-lily: *Erythronium albidum*
Ebony Spleenwort: *Asplenium platyneuron*
Edelweiss: *Leontopodium*
Edging Candytuft: *Iberis sempervirens*
Elderberry Iris: *Iris sambucina*
Elder: *Sambucus*
Elecampane: *Inula helenium*
Elecampane: *Inula*
Elk Grass: *Xerophyllum tenax*
Elk Grass: *Xerophyllum*
Enchanter's Nightshade: *Circaea*
English Daisy: *Bellis perennis*
English Daisy: *Bellis*
English Hedge Fern: *Polystichum setiferum*
English Primrose: *Primula vulgaris*
Eryngo: *Eryngium*
Eulalia-grass: *Miscanthus sinensis*
Eulalia: *Miscanthus*
Eurasian Mountain Plant: *Delphinium elatum*
Eureka Lily: *Lilium occidentale*
European Brooklime: *Veronica beccabunga*

European Dune Grass: *Elymus arenarius*
European Feather Grass: *Stipa pennata*
European Ostrich Fern: *Matteuccia struthiopteris*
European Parsley Fern: *Cryptogramma crispa*
European Polypody: *Polypodium interjectum*
European White Hellebore: *Veratrum album*
European Wood Sage: *Teucrium scorodonia*
Evans' Begonia: *Begonia grandis*
Evening Primrose: *Oenothera*
Evergreen Broad-leaved Sedge: *Carex plantaginea*
Evergreen Orpine: *Sedum anacampseros*
Everlasting: *Helichrysum*
Eve's Cushion: *Saxifraga hypnoides*
Fair Maids of France: *Ranunculus aconiti-folius* 'Flore-pleno'
Fair Maids of France: *Saxifraga granulata*
Fairy Hyacinth: *Hyacinthus orientalis* 'Borah'
Fairy Moss: *Azolla*
Fairy Water Lily: *Nymphoides aquatica*
Falkland Island Holly Fern: *Polystichum mohrioides*
Fall Gentian: *Gentiana sino-ornata*
Fall Rockfoil: *Saxifraga cortusifolia*
False Asphodel: *Tofieldia*
False Camomile: *Matricaria*
False Dragonhead: *Physostegia*
False Garlic: *Nothoscordum inodorum*
False Garlic: *Nothoscordum*
False Hellebore: *Veratrum*
False Hemp: *Datisca cannabina*
False Hemp: *Datisca*
False Indigo: *Baptisia*
False Lily-of-the-Valley: *Maianthemum*
False Lupine: *Thermopsis*
False Mallow: *Sidalcea*
False Mitewort: *Tiarella*
False Oats: *Trisetum*
False Rue Anemone: *Isopyrum biternatum*
False Rue Anemone: *Isopyrum*
False Soloman's Seal: *Smilacina*
False Spikenard: *Smilacina racemosa*
False Starwort: *Boltonia*
Fameflower: *Talinum*
Feather Grass: *Stipa*
Featherbells: *Stenanthium gramineum*
Featherbells: *Stenanthium*
Featherfleece: *Stenanthium*
Fee's Lip Fern: *Cheilanthes feei*
Fennel: *Foeniculum vulgare*
Fennel: *Foeniculum*
Fescue: *Festuca*
Feverwort: *Triosteum*
Fiddleneck: *Phacelia*
Field Daisy: *Chrysanthemum leucanthemum*
Figwort: *Ranunculus ficaria*
Figwort: *Scrophularia*
Finger Sedge: *Carex digitata*
Fire Lily: *Lilium bulbiferum*
Fire Lily: *Xerophyllum tenax*

Fire Lily: *Xerophyllum*
Fire Pink: *Silene virginica*
Firecracker Flower: *Brevoortia*
Fireweed: *Epilobium angustifolium*
Fireweed: *Epilobium*
Flame Nasturtium: *Tropaeolum speciosum*
Flax-leaf Wallflower: *Erysimum linifolium*
Flax: *Linum perenne*
Flax: *Linum usitatissimum*
Flax: *Linum*
Fleabane: *Erigeron*
Fleece Vine: *Polygonum*
Floating-heart: *Nymphoides*
Flowering Rush: *Butomus umbellatus*
Flowering Spurge: *Euphorbia corollata*
Foam Flower: *Tiarella cordifolia*
Foamflower: *Tiarella*
Forest Sedge: *Carex sylvatica*
Forget-me-not: *Myosotis*
Fountain Grass: *Pennisetum setaceum*
Fountain Grass: *Pennisetum*
Foxglove: *Digitalis*
Foxtail Lily: *Eremurus*
Foxtail: *Setaria*
Fox-Red Sedge: *Carex buchananii*
Fragile Fern: *Cystopteris fragilis*
Fragrant Lip Fern: *Cheilanthes fragrans*
Fragrant Water Lily: *Nymphaea odorata*
Fragrant Woodsia: *Woodsia ilvensis*
Fraser's Sedge: *Carex fraseri*
Fremont's Crowfoot: *Clematis fremontii*
French Honeysuckle: *Hedysarum*
Fringed Galax: *Shortia soldanelloides*
Fringed Indian Pink: *Silene laciniata*
Fringed Orchid: *Platanthera*
Fringed Polygala: *Polygala pauciflora*
Fringed Poppy Mallow: *Callirhoe digitata*
Fritillary: *Fritillaria*
Frogbit: *Hydrocharis morsus-ranae*
Frogbit: *Hydrocharis*
Frostweed: *Verbesina helianthoides*
Frost Grass: *Spodiopogon sibiricus*
Galingale: *Cyperus*
Gamma Grass: *Tripsacum*
Garden Chervil: *Chaerophyllum aureum*
Garden Heliotrope: *Valeriana officinalis*
Garden Heliotrope: *Valeriana*
Garden Lysimachia: *Lysimachia punctata*
Garden Peony: *Paeonia lactiflora*
Garden Phlox: *Phlox paniculata*
Garden Salvia: *Salvia officinalis*
Garden Spiderwort: *Tradescantia* × *andersoniana*
Garden Thyme: *Thymus vulgaris*
Gas Plant: *Dictamnus*
Gaura: *Gaura*
Gay Feather: *Liatris*
Gentian Salvia: *Salvia patens*
Gentian: *Gentiana*
Germander: *Teucrium*
Giant Allium: *Allium giganteum*
Giant Bellflower: *Ostrowskia magnifica*
Giant Bellflower: *Ostrowskia*
Giant Chinese Silver Grass: *Miscanthus floridulus*
Giant Daisy: *Chrysanthemum serotinum*
Giant Dune Grass: *Elymus racemosus*

Giant Feather Grass: *Stipa gigantea*
Giant Fennel: *Ferula*
Giant Fescue: *Festuca gigantea*
Giant Helleborine: *Epipactis gigantea*
Giant Hogweed: *Heracleum mantegazzianum*
Giant Holly Fern: *Polystichum munitum*
Giant Horsetail: *Equisetum telmateia*
Giant Lily: *Cardiocrinum giganteum*
Giant Meadow Grass: *Glyceria maxima*
Giant Reed: *Arundo donax*
Giant Sedge: *Carex pendula*
Giant Snowdrops: *Galanthus*
Giant Sunflower: *Helianthus giganteus*
Giant Water Dock: *Rumex hydrolapathum*
Giant-groundsel: *Ligularia wilsoniana*
Gibraltar Candytuft: *Iberis gibraltarica*
Gibralter Mint: *Mentha pulegium* var. *gibraltarica*
Gill-over-the-ground: *Glechoma hederaceae*
Gladwyn: *Iris foetidissima*
Globe Daisy: *Globularia*
Globe Thistle: *Echinops*
Globe Tulip: *Calochortus*
Globeflower: *Trollius*
Glory-of-the-Snow: *Chionodoxa*
Goatsbeard: *Aruncus dioicus*
Goatsbeard: *Aruncus*
Goat's Rue: *Galega*
Goat's Rye: *Tephrosia virginiana*
Gold Crocus: *Crocus flavus*
Gold Turk's Cap Lily: *Lilium hansonii*
Golden Aster: *Chrysopsis*
Golden Bamboo: *Phyllostachys aurea*
Golden Bamboo: *Phyllostachys*
Golden Beard Grass: *Chrysopogon gryllus*
Golden Button: *Tanacetum vulgare*
Golden Club: *Orontium aquaticum*
Golden Eardrops: *Dicentra chrysantha*
Golden Flax: *Linum flavum*
Golden Foxtail: *Alopecurus pratensis*
Golden Nettle: *Lamiastrum galeobdolon*
Golden Ragwort: *Senecio aureus*
Golden Ray: *Ligularia*
Golden Saxifrage: *Chrysosplenium*
Golden Shield Fern: *Dryopteris affinis*
Golden Star: *Chrysogonum virginianum*
Golden Strawberry: *Waldsteinia*
Golden Violet: *Viola pedunculata*
Goldenrod: *Solidago*
Goldenseal: *Hydrastis*
Golden-carpet: *Sedum acre*
Golden-drop: *Onosma*
Golden-eyed Grass: *Sisyrinchium californicum*
Golden-primula: *Vitaliana primuliflora*
Golden-primula: *Vitaliana*
Goldie's Shield Fern: *Dryopteris goldiana*
Goldie's Wood Fern: *Dryopteris goldiana*
Goldilocks: *Aster linosyris*
Goldthread: *Coptis trifolia*
Goldthread: *Coptis*
Gold-banded Lily: *Lilium auratum*
Gold-thistle: *Carlina acanthifolia*
Gooseneck Loosestrife: *Lysimachia clethroides*

Gout Weed: *Aegopodium*
Grama Grass: *Bouteloua*
Grape Hyacinth: *Muscari*
Grass Nut: *Triteleia laxa*
Grass Pink: *Dianthus plumarius*
Grass Sweetflag: *Acorus gramineus*
Grass Widow: *Sisyrinchium douglasii*
Grassleaved Arrowhead: *Sagittaria graminea*
Grassy-bells: *Dierama pendulum*
Grassy-bells: *Edraianthus*
Grass-Leaved Water Plantain: *Alisma gramineum*
Grass-of-Parnassus: *Parnassia*
Graybeard Grass: *Spodiopogon sibiricus*
Gray-head Coneflower: *Ratibida pinnata*
Great Bellflower: *Campanula latifolia*
Great Burnet: *Sanguisorba officinalis*
Great Globe Thistle: *Echinops sphaerocephalus*
Great Lobelia: *Lobelia siphilitica*
Great Solomon's-seal: *Polygonatum commutatum*
Greater Algae Fern: *Azolla filiculoides*
Greater Periwinkle: *Vinca major*
Greater Polypody: *Polypodium interjectum*
Greater Spearwort: *Ranunculus lingua*
Greater Stitchwort: *Stellaria holostea*
Grecian Foxglove: *Digitalis lanata*
Greek Valerian: *Polemonium caeruleum*
Green Coneflower: *Ratibida pinnata*
Green Coneflower: *Ratibida*
Green Dragon: *Arisaema dracontium*
Green Milkweed: *Asclepias viridis*
Green Moor Grass: *Sesleria heuffleriana*
Green-stem Joe-Pye Weed: *Eupatorium purpureum*
Grizzly Bear Cactus: *Opuntia erinacea* var. *ursina*
Gromwell: *Lithospermum*
Ground Cherry: *Physalis*
Ground Elder: *Aegopodium podograria*
Ground Elder: *Aegopodium*
Groundnut: *Apios americana*
Groundnut: *Apios*
Groundsel: *Senecio*
Ground-ivy: *Glechoma hederaceae*
Guernsey Lily: *Nerine sarniensis*
Guinea Grass: *Panicum maximum*
Guinea-hen Tulip: *Fritillaria meleagris*
Gum Plant: *Grindelia*
Gumweed: *Grindelia lanceolata*
Hair Grass: *Deschampsia*
Hairy Lip Fern: *Cheilanthes lanosa*
Hairy Lip Fern: *Cheilanthes vestita*
Harbinger-of-spring: *Erigenia bulbosa*
Hardhead: *Centaurea nigra*
Hardy Bamboo: *Pseudosasa*
Hardy Begonia: *Begonia grandis*
Hardy Geranium: *Geranium*
Hardy Gloxinia: *Incarvillea*
Hardy Shield Fern: *Polystichum aculeatum*
Hardy-ageratum: *Eupatorium coelestinum*
Harebell: *Campanula rotundifolia*
Hare's Ear: *Bupleurum*

Hare's-foot Fern: *Davallia*
Harlequin Flower: *Sparaxis*
Hartford Fern: *Lygodium palmatum*
Hart's-tongue Fern: *Phyllitis*
Harvest Brodiaea: *Brodiaea coronaria*
Hawkweed: *Hieracium*
Hawk's Beard: *Crepis*
Hay-scented Fern: *Dennstaedtia punctilobula*
Heal-all: *Prunella*
Heath Aster: *Aster ericoides*
Hedge Bindweed: *Calystegia sepium*
Hedge Fern: *Polystichum aculeatum*
Hedge Fern: *Polystichum setiferum*
Helensflower: *Helenium*
Hellebore: *Helleborus*
Helleborine: *Epipactis*
Hemp-agrimony: *Eupatorium cannabinum*
Hens and Chickens: *Sempervivum*
Hen-and-Chickens: *Sempervivum tectorum*
Herb-of-Grace: *Ruta graveolens*
Herniaria: *Herniaria*
Heron's-bill: *Erodium*
High Daisy: *Chrysanthemum serotinum*
Himalayan Poppy: *Meconopsis*
Hime-Kana-Warabi: *Polystichum tsussimense*
Hoary Cinquefoil: *Potentilla argentea*
Hoary Pea: *Tephrosia*
Hoary Vervain: *Verbena stricta*
Holly Fern: *Cyrtomium fortunei*
Holly Fern: *Cyrtomium*
Holly Fern: *Polystichum*
Hollyhock Mallow: *Malva alcea*
Hollyhock: *Alcea ficifolia*
Hollyhock: *Alcea*
Honesty Plant: *Lunaria*
Honeywort: *Cerinthe*
Hook-spur Violet: *Viola adunca*
Hoop Petticoat Daffodil: *Narcissus bulbocodium*
Hops: *Humulus*
Horehound: *Marrubium*
Horned Poppy: *Glaucium*
Horned Rampion: *Phyteuma*
Horned Violet: *Viola cornuta*
Horse Gentian: *Triosteum*
Horseshoe Vetch: *Hippocrepis*
Horsetail: *Equisetum*
Hound's Tongue: *Cynoglossum*
Houseleek: *Sempervivum tectorum*
Houseleek: *Sempervivum*
Humboldt Lily: *Lilium humboldtii*
Hunangamoho Grass: *Chionochloa conspicua*
Hyacinth: *Hyacinthus orientalis*
Hyacinth: *Hyacinthus*
Indian Grass: *Sorghastrum nutans*
Indian Hemp: *Apocynum cannabinum*
Indian Lotus: *Nelumbo nucifera*
Indian Paintbrush: *Castilleja*
Indian Physic: *Gillenia trifoliata*
Indian Plantain: *Cacalia*
Indian Strawberry: *Duchesnea indica*

Indian's Dream Fern: *Cheilanthes siliquosa*
Indigo: *Indigofera*
Interrrupted Fern: *Osmunda claytoniana*
Interrupted Fern: *Osmunda*
Iris: *Iris*
Ironweed: *Vernonia*
Italian Arum: *Arum italicum*
Italian Aster: *Aster amellus*
Italian Bellflower: *Campanula isophylla*
Ivory-thistle: *Ptilostemon afer*
Ivory-thistle: *Ptilostemon*
Jaburan Lilyturf: *Ophiopogon jaburan*
Jack-in-the-Pulpit: *Arisaema triphyllum*
Jack-in-the-Pulpit: *Arisaema*
Jacob's Ladder: *Polemonium caeruleum*
Jacob's Ladder: *Polemonium*
Jacob's Rod: *Asphodeline*
Japanese Bindweed: *Calystegia hederacea*
Japanese Cow Lily: *Nuphar japonicum*
Japanese Dead Nettle: *Meehania*
Japanese Holly Fern: *Dryopteris varia*
Japanese Holly Fern: *Polystichum polyblepharum*
Japanese Hops: *Humulus japonicus*
Japanese Lily: *Lilium speciosum*
Japanese Mat Rush: *Juncus effusus*
Japanese Ostrich Fern: *Matteuccia orientalis*
Japanese Painted Fern: *Anthyrium nipponicum*
Japanesc Sedge: *Carex morrowii*
Japanese Shield Fern: *Dryopteris erythrosora*
Japanese Spurge: *Pachysandra terminalis*
Japanese Thistle: *Cirsium japonicum*
Japanese Toad-Lily: *Tricyrtis hirta*
Japanese Turk's Cap Lily: *Lilium hansonii*
Jehovah's Flower: *Saxifraga umbrosa*
Jerusalem Sage: *Phlomis fruticosa*
Jerusalem Sage: *Phlomis*
Jerusalem-Cowslip: *Pulmonaria officinalis*
Joe's Flower: *Lychnis flos-jovis*
Joe-Pye Weed: *Eupatorium maculatum*
Johnson Grass: *Sorghum halepense*
John's Cabbage: *Hydrophyllum virginianum*
Jonquil: *Narcissus jonquilla*
Jumonji-Shida: *Polystichum tripteron*
June Grass: *Koeleria glauca*
Jupiter's Beard: *Centranthus*
Jupiter's Distaff: *Salvia glutinosa*
Kamchatka-lily: *Fritillaria camtschatcensis*
Kenilworth Ivy: *Cymbalaria muralis*
Kenilworth Ivy: *Cymbalaria*
Kidney Vetch: *Anthyllis vulneraria*
Kingcup: *Caltha palustris*
Kingcup: *Caltha*
King's Lily: *Lilium regale*
King's Spear: *Asphodeline lutea*
Kmawe: *Scleranthus*
Knapweed: *Centaurea*
Knotweed: *Polygonum*
Kuhn Bracken: *Pteridium aquilinum*
Kuma Bamboo-grass: *Sasa veitchii*
Lady Fern: *Anthyrium filix-femina*
Lady Fern: *Athyrium*

Lady in Mourning: *Iris susiana*
Ladybells: *Adenophora*
Lady's Mantle: *Alchemilla*
Lady's Slipper: *Cypripedium arietinum*
Lady's Slipper: *Cypripedium*
Lady's Smock: *Cardamine pratensis*
Lady's Smock: *Cardamine*
Lady's-fingers: *Anthyllis vulneraria*
Lamb's Ears: *Stachys byzantina*
Large Yellow Lady's Slipper: *Cypripedium calceolus* var. *pubescens*
Large-leaved Chinese Shady Bamboo: *Indocalamus tesselatus*
Larkspur: *Delphinium*
Lavender Harvest Brodiaea: *Brodiaea elegans*
Lavender-cotton: *Santolina*
Lavender: *Lavandula angustifolia*
Lavender: *Lavandula*
Leadwort: *Ceratostigma plumbaginoides*
Leadwort: *Ceratostigma*
Leather Flower: *Clematis versicolor*
Leather Flower: *Clematis viorna*
Leather Flower: *Clematis*
Leather Wood Fern: *Dryopteris marginalis*
Lebanon Cress: *Aethionema coridifolium*
Lemon Balm: *Melissa officinalis*
Lemon Balm: *Melissa*
Lemon Lily: *Lilium parryi*
Lemon Verbena: *Lippia*
Lemon-lily: *Hemerocallis liliousphodelus*
Lenten Rose: *Helleborus*
Leopard Flower: *Belamcanda*
Leopard Lily: *Lilium catesbaei*
Leopard Lily: *Lilium pardalinum*
Leopard Plant: *Ligularia tussilaginea* 'Aureo-maculata'
Leopard Plant: *Ligularia*
Leopard's-bane Ragwort: *Senecio doronicum*
Leopard's-bane: *Doronicum*
Lesser Algae Fern: *Azolla caroliniana*
Lesser Burnet: *Sanguisorba minor*
Lesser Butterfly Orchid: *Platanthera bifolia*
Lesser Celandine: *Ranunculus ficaria*
Lesser Spatterdock: *Nuphar pumila*
Lesser Spearwort: *Ranunculus flammula*
Lesser Turk's Cap Lily: *Lilium pomponium*
Lesser Water Plantain: *Baldellia ranunculoides*
Licorice Fern: *Polypodium glycerrhiza*
Life-of-man: *Aralia racemosa*
Lilac Salvia: *Salvia verticillata*
Lilyturf: *Liriope*
Lilyturf: *Ophiopogon*
Lily-of-the-Altai: *Ixiolirion tataricum*
Lily-of the-Valley: *Convallaria*
Lily: *Lilium*
Lime Oak Fern: *Gymnocarpium robertianum*
Lindheimer's Gaura: *Gaura lindheimeri*
Lip Fern: *Cheilanthes marantae*
Lip Fern: *Cheilanthes*
Little Club Moss: *Selaginella*
Liver Balsam: *Erinus*
Liverberry: *Streptopus amplexifolius*

Liverleaf: *Hepatica*
Live-forever: *Sedum telephium*
Lizard's-tail: *Saururus*
Locoweed: *Oxytropis besseyi*
Locoweed: *Oxytropis*
Longroot: *Arenaria caroliniana*
Long-head Coneflower: *Ratibida columnifera*
Loosestrife: *Lysimachia*
Loosestrife: *Lythrum*
Lords and Ladies: *Arum maculatum*
Lotus: *Nelumbo*
Lovage: *Levisticum officinale*
Lovage: *Levisticum*
Love Grass: *Eragrostis*
Low Sedge: *Carex humilis*
Lowsewort: *Pedicularis*
Lungwort: *Pulmonaria*
Lupine: *Lupinus*
Madder: *Rubia tinctorum*
Madonna Lily: *Lilium candidum*
Madwort: *Aurinia*
Magellan Bluegrass: *Agropyron*
Magic Lily: *Lycoris squamigera*
Maiden Pink: *Dianthus deltoides*
Maidenhair Fern: *Adiantum*
Maidenhair Spleenwort: *Asplenium trichomanes*
Maiden's Tears: *Silene vulgaris*
Male Fern: *Dryopteris filix-mas*
Mallow: *Althaea*
Mallow: *Hibiscus*
Mallow: *Malva*
Maltese Cross: *Lychnis chalcedonica*
Mapleleaf: *Aceriphyllum*
Mare's Tail: *Hippuris vulgaris*
Marginal Shield Fern: *Dryopteris marginalis*
Marguerite: *Chrysanthemum leucanthemum*
Mariposa Lily: *Calochortus*
Marsh Blue Violet: *Viola cucullata*
Marsh Clematis: *Clematis crispa*
Marsh Fern: *Thelypteris palustris*
Marsh Mallow: *Althaea officinalis*
Marsh Mallow: *Hibiscus moscheutos*
Marsh Mallow: *Hibiscus*
Marsh Marigold: *Caltha palustris*
Marsh Marigold: *Caltha*
Marsh Trefoil: *Menyanthes*
Marsh-rosemary: *Limonium*
Martagon Lily: *Lilium martagon*
Masterwort: *Astrantia*
Matgrass: *Lippia nodiflora*
Matilija Poppy: *Romneya*
Mauve Catmint: *Nepeta mussinii*
Maximilian Sunflower: *Helianthus maximilian*
May Apple: *Podophyllum peltatum*
May Apple: *Podophyllum*
Maypop: *Passiflora incarnata*
Meadow Beauty: *Rhexia virginica*
Meadow Beauty: *Rhexia*
Meadow Clary: *Salvia pratensis*
Meadow Cranesbill: *Geranium pratense*
Meadow Fern: *Thelypteris palustris* var. *pubescens*

Meadow Foxtail: *Alopecurus*
Meadow Grass: *Glyceria*
Meadow Grass: *Poa*
Meadow Lily: *Lilium canadense*
Meadow Phlox: *Phlox maculata*
Meadow Rue: *Thalictrum*
Meadow Saxifrage: *Saxifraga granulata*
Meadow Sweet: *Filipendula*
Meadowsweet: *Filipendula palmata*
Meehan's Mint: *Meehania cordata*
Meehan's Mint: *Meehania*
Melic Grass: *Melica nutans*
Melic Grass: *Melica*
Melic: *Melica*
Menthella: *Mentha requienii*
Merry Bells: *Uvularia*
Metake: *Pseudosasa*
Mexican Campion: *Silene laciniata*
Mexican Hat: *Ratibida columnifera*
Mexican Hat: *Ratibida*
Milk Vetch: *Astralgalus*
Milkmaids: *Dentaria californica*
Milkwort: *Polygala*
Milky Bellflower: *Campanula lactiflora*
Millet Grass: *Milium*
Miner's Lettuce: *Montia*
Mint: *Mentha*
Missouri Primrose: *Oenothera missouriensis*
Mistflower: *Eupatorium coelestinum*
Mistflower: *Eupatorium*
Miterwort: *Mitella*
Moccasin Flower: *Cypripedium acaule*
Mondo Grass: *Ophiopogon japonicus*
Mondo Grass: *Ophiopogon*
Money Plant: *Lunaria*
Money Plant: *Lysimachia nummularia*
Monkey Flower: *Mimulus*
Monkshood: *Aconitum*
Monk's Rhubarb: *Rumex alpinus*
Montbretia: *Crocosmia*
Montbretia: *Tritonia crocata*
Montbretia: *Tritonia*
Monte Baldo Sedge: *Carex baldensis*
Moonwort: *Lunaria*
Moor Grass: *Molinia*
Moor Grass: *Sesleria*
Moor Violet: *Viola uliginosa*
Morning Star Sedge: *Carex grayi*
Mosquito Fern: *Azolla caroliniana*
Moss Phlox: *Phlox subulata*
Moss Pine: *Phlox subulata*
Moss Rockfoil: *Saxifraga hypnoides*
Mother-of-Thousands: *Saxifraga stolonifera*
Mount Atlas Daisy: *Anacyclus*
Mountain Asphodel: *Xerophyllum asphodeloides*
Mountain Avens: *Dryas octopetala*
Mountain Avens: *Dryas*
Mountain Bluet: *Centaurea montana*
Mountain Fleece: *Polygonum amplexicaule*
Mountain Geum: *Geum montanum*
Mountain Lady's Slipper: *Cypripedium montanum*
Mountain Phlox: *Phlox ovata*
Mountain Pride: *Penstemon newberryi*

Mountain Rhubarb: *Rumex alpinus*
Mountain Rice: *Oryzopsis*
Mountain Rock Cress: *Arabis alpina*
Mountain Sedge: *Carex montana*
Mountain Sorrel: *Oxyria*
Mountain Sow Thistle: *Lactuca alpina*
Mountain Thistle: *Carduus defloratus*
Mountain Valerian: *Valeriana montana*
Mountain-lover: *Paxistima canbyi*
Mouse Plant: *Arisarum proboscideum*
Mouse-ear Chickweed: *Cerastium*
Mouse-ear Hawkweed: *Hieracium pilosella*
Mule's Ears: *Wyethia helianthoides*
Mullein Pink: *Lychnis coronaria*
Mullein: *Verbascum*
Muscatel Salvia: *Salvia sclarea*
Musk Flower: *Mimulus moschatus*
Musk Hyacinth: *Muscari racemosum*
Musk Mallow: *Malva moschata*
Musk Plant: *Mimulus moschatus*
Myriad Leaf: *Myriophyllum verticillatum*
Myrrh: *Myrrhis*
Myrtle Euphorbia: *Euphorbia myrsinites*
Naked Lady: *Lycoris squamigera*
Narihira Bamboo: *Semiarundinaria fastuosa*
Narrow Beech Fern: *Thelypteris phegopteris*
Narrow Bird's-foot Trefoil: *Lotus corniculatus* var. *tenuifolium*
Narrow Holly Fern: *Polystichum tsussimense*
Narrow-leaved Cattail: *Typha angustifolia*
Narrow-leaved Cotton Grass: *Eriophorum angustifolium*
Nasturtium: *Tropaeolum*
Navelwort: *Omphalodes cappadocica*
Navelwort: *Omphalodes*
Navelwort: *Umbilicus rupestris*
Needle Grass: *Stipa*
Needle-palm: *Yucca filamentosa*
Nerve Root: *Cypripedium acaule*
Nest Moor Grass: *Sesleria nitida*
Nettle-leaved Bellflower: *Campanula trachelium*
Nettle-leaved Mullein: *Verbascum chaixii*
New England Aster: *Aster novae-angliae*
New York Ironweed: *Vernonia noveboracensis*
New Zealand Bur: *Acaena*
Nippon Daisy: *Chrysanthemum nipponicum*
Nippon-bells: *Shortia uniflora*
Nishiki Shida: *Anthyrium nipponicum*
Nodding Pearl: *Melica nutans*
Nodding Trillium: *Trillium cernuum*
Northern Maidenhair: *Adiantum pedatum*
Northern Oak Fern: *Gymnocarpium robertianum*
Northern Small White Lady's Slipper: *Cypripedium passerinum*
Northern Woodsia: *Woodsia alpina*
Nutmeg Hyacinth: *Muscari racemosum*
Oak Fern: *Gymnocarpium dryopteris*
Oats Grass: *Arrhenatherum*
Oats: *Avena*

Obedient Plant: *Physostegia*
Oconee-bells: *Shortia galacifolia*
October Plant: *Sedum sieboldii*
October-daphne: *Sedum sieboldii*
Old Man: *Artemisia abrotanum*
Old Woman: *Artemisia stelleriana*
One-flowered Pyrola: *Moneses uniflora*
One-flowered Shineleaf: *Moneses uniflora*
Orange Lily: *Lilium bulbiferum*
Orange-bell Lily: *Lilium grayi*
Orange-cup Lily: *Lilium philadelphicum*
Orchard Grass: *Dactylis*
Orchis: *Orchis*
Oregano: *Origanum*
Oregon Lily: *Lilium columbianum*
Orpine: *Sedum telephium*
Orpine: *Sedum*
Ostrich Fern: *Matteuccia*
Our-Lord's-Candle: *Yucca whipplei*
Oxeye Daisy: *Chrysanthemum leucanthemum*
Oxeye: *Buphthalmum*
Oxeye: *Heliopsis*
Oxlip: *Primula elatior*
Ozark Sundrops: *Oenothera missouriensis*
Ozark Trillium: *Trillium ozarkanum*
Painted Daisy: *Chrysanthemum coccineum*
Painted Trillium: *Trillium undulatum*
Painted-cup: *Castilleja*
Pale Green Umbrella Bamboo: *Sinarundinaria murielae*
Palm Leaf Sedge: *Carex muskingumensis*
Pampas Grass: *Cortaderia*
Panic Grass: *Panicum*
Pansy: *Viola*
Panther Lily: *Lilium pardalinum*
Paradise Lily: *Paradisea*
Parrot's Feather: *Myriophyllum aquaticum*
Parsley Ligularia: *Ligularia tussilaginea* 'Crispata'
Partridge Berry: *Mitchella*
Pasque Flower: *Pulsatilla*
Passion-flower: *Passiflora*
Peach-leaved Bellflower: *Campanula persicifolia*
Peanut: *Apios*
Pearl Fern: *Onoclea*
Pearlwort: *Sagina*
Pearly Everlasting: *Anaphalis*
Penny Cress: *Thlaspi*
Pennyroyal: *Mentha pulegium*
Pennywort: *Umbilicus rupestris*
Peony: *Paeonia*
Pepper Grass: *Lepidium*
Pepperwort: *Marsilea quadrifolia*
Pepperwort: *Marsilea*
Perennial Flax: *Linum perenne*
Perennial Phlox: *Phlox paniculata*
Perfumed fairy-lily: *Chlidanthus fragrans*
Perfumed fairy-lily: *Chlidanthus*
Periwinkle: *Vinca*
Persian Buttercup: *Ranunculus asiaticus*
Persian Stonecress: *Aethionema grandiflorum*
Persian-violet: *Cyclamen*
Peruvian Lily: *Alstroemeria*

Pheasant's Eye: *Adonis*
Pickaback Plant: *Tolmiea menziesii*
Pickerelweed: *Pontederia*
Piggyback Plant: *Tolmiea menziesii*
Pilewort: *Ranunculus ficaria*
Pimpernel: *Anagallis*
Pincushion-flower: *Scabiosa*
Pine Barrens Sandwort: *Arenaria caroliniana*
Pine Lily: *Lilium catesbaei*
Pineapple Mint: *Mentha suaveolens* 'Variegata'
Pineapple Sage: *Salvia elegans*
Pine-barrens Gentian: *Gentiana porphyrio*
Pink Coneflower: *Echinacea pallida*
Pink Fogfruit: *Lippia nodiflora*
Pink Fritillary: *Fritillaria pluriflora*
Pink Sandwort: *Arenaria purpurascens*
Pink Tickseed: *Coreopsis rosea*
Pink Wintergreen: *Pyrola asarifolia*
Pinkroot: *Spigelia marilandica*
Pinkroot: *Spigelia*
Pink: *Dianthus*
Pipsissewa: *Chimaphila*
Pitcher Plant: *Sarracenia*
Plantain Lily: *Hosta*
Plantain: *Plantago*
Pleasing Root: *Asclepias tuberosa*
Plumbago: *Ceratostigma plumbaginoides*
Plumbago: *Ceratostigma*
Plume Grass: *Eriunthus*
Plume Poppy: *Macleaya cordata*
Plume Poppy: *Macleaya*
Plume Thistle: *Cirsium*
Poet's Narcissus: *Narcissus poeticus*
Pokeberry: *Phytolacca*
Pokeweed: *Phytolacca americana*
Pokeweed: *Phytolacca*
Polypody: *Polypodium*
Pondweed: *Potamogeton*
Poppy Mallow: *Callirhoe papaver*
Poppy Mallow: *Callirhoe*
Poppy: *Papaver*
Porcelain Flower: *Saxifraga umbrosa*
Porcupine Cactus: *Opuntia erinacea* var. *hystricina*
Pot Marjoram: *Origanum vulgare*
Potato Bean: *Apios americana*
Pot-of-Gold Lily: *Lilium iridollae*
Prairie Allium: *Allium mutabile*
Prairie Blue-eyed Grass: *Sisyrinchium campestre*
Prairie Coneflower: *Ratibida columnifera*
Prairie Coneflower: *Ratibida*
Prairie Cord Grass: *Spartina pectinata*
Prairie Dock: *Silphium terebinthinaceum*
Prairie Dogtooth Violet: *Erythronium mesochoreum*
Prairie Indian Plantain: *Cacalia tuberosa*
Prairie Mallow: *Sidalcea malviflora*
Prairie Mallow: *Sphaeralcea coccinea*
Prairie Phlox: *Phlox pilosa*
Prairie Poppy Mallow: *Callirhoe involucrata*
Prairie Rocket: *Erysimum asperum*
Prairie Tea: *Potentilla rupestris*

Prairie Yellow Violet: *Viola nuttallii*
Prickly Pear: *Opuntia*
Prickly-thrift: *Acantholimon*
Primrose: *Primula*
Prince's-pine: *Chimaphila*
Prophet Flower: *Arnebia pulchra*
Prostrate Verbena: *Verbena bractata*
Puccoon: *Lithospermum*
Purple Avens: *Geum rivale*
Purple Foxglove: *Digitalis purpurea*
Purple Locoweed: *Oxytropis lambertii*
Purple Loosestrife: *Lythrum salicaria*
Purple Meadow Rue: *Thalictrum dasycarpum*
Purple Milkweed: *Asclepias purpurascens*
Purple Moor Grass: *Molinia caerulea*
Purple Mullein: *Verbascum phoeniceum*
Purple Prairie Clover: *Petalostemon purpureum*
Purple Rock Cress: *Aubrieta deltoidea*
Purple Trillium: *Trillium erectum*
Purple Trillium: *Trillium recurvatum*
Purple Wake-robin: *Trillium recurvatum*
Purple-eyed Grass: *Sisyrinchium douglasii*
Pussytoes: *Antennaria*
Pyrethrum: *Chrysanthemum coccineum*
Quaking Grass: *Briza*
Quamash: *Camassia quamash*
Quamash: *Camassia*
Queen of the Meadow: *Filipendula ulmaria*
Queen of the Prairie: *Filipendula rubra*
Ragged-robin: *Lychnis flos-cuculi*
Ragwort: *Senecio*
Rain-lily: *Zephyranthes*
Ram's-head: *Cypripedium arietinum*
Raspberry: *Rubus*
Rattlesnake Master: *Eryngium yuccifolium*
Rattlesnake Root: *Prenanthes*
Ravenna Grass: *Erianthus ravennae*
Ravenna Grass: *Erianthus*
Red Hot Poker: *Kniphofia uvaria*
Red Hot Poker: *Kniphofia*
Red Spider-lily: *Lycoris radiata*
Red Switch Grass: *Panicum virgatum*
Red Valerian: *Centranthus*
Red Water Milfoil: *Myriophyllum hippuroides*
Redwood Lily: *Lilium rubescens*
Red-yucca: *Beschorneria yuccoides*
Reed Canary Grass: *Phalaris arundinacea*
Reed Cosmopolitan Grass: *Phragmites autralis*
Reed-mace: *Typha*
Reed: *Phragmites*
Regal Lily: *Lilium regale*
Rein Orchid: *Platanthera*
Rest-harrow: *Ononis*
Resurrection Fern: *Polypodium polypodioides*
Resurrection-Lily: *Lycoris squamigera*
Rhubarb: *Rheum*
Ribbon Grass: *Phalaris*
Rice Grass: *Oryzopsis*
Roan Lily: *Lilium grayi*
Rock Brake: *Cryptogramma*

Rock Bullrush: *Scirpus tabernaemontani*
Rock Cinquefoil: *Potentilla rupestris*
Rock Cress: *Arabis*
Rock Cress: *Aubrieta*
Rock Jasmine: *Androsace*
Rock Polypody: *Polypodium virginianum*
Rock Purslane: *Calandrinia*
Rock Rose: *Helianthemum*
Rock Speedwell: *Veronica fruticans*
Rockbell: *Wahlenbergia*
Rocket: *Hesperis*
Rockfoil: *Saxifraga*
Rock-geranium: *Heuchera americana*
Rock-spiraea: *Petrophyton*
Rock-thyme: *Acinos*
Roger's Flower: *Astilboides*
Roman Wormwood: *Artemisia pontica*
Roof Iris: *Iris tectorum*
Rose Campion: *Lychnis coronaria*
Rose Mallow: *Hibiscus moscheutos*
Rose Mallow: *Hibiscus*
Rose Soapwort: *Saponaria ocymoides*
Rose Verbena: *Verbena canadensis*
Rose Vervain: *Verbena canadensis*
Rosette-mullein: *Ramonda*
Rose-of-Sharon: *Hypericum calycinum*
Rose-of-Sharon: *Hypericum*
Rosinweed: *Grindelia*
Rosinweed: *Silphium terebinthinaceum*
Rosinweed: *Silphium*
Rosy Wake-robin: *Trillium catesbaei*
Rough-leaved Rockfoil: *Saxifraga hirsuta*
Round-leaved Bellflower: *Campanula rotundifolia*
Rover Bellflower: *Campanula rapunculoides*
Royal Fern: *Osmunda regalis*
Royal Fern: *Osmunda*
Royal Lily: *Lilium regale*
Rue Anemone: *Anemonella*
Rue: *Ruta*
Rupturewort: *Herniaria glabra*
Rupturewort: *Herniaria*
Rush: *Juncus*
Rusty Woodsia: *Woodsia ilvensis*
Rusty-back Fern: *Ceterach officinarum*
Rutland Beauty: *Calystegia sepium*
Saffron: *Crocus sativus*
Sage: *Salvia*
Salmonberry: *Rubus chamaemorus*
Salt and Pepper: *Erigenia bulbosa*
Salt Rush: *Juncus lesueurii*
Sampson's Snakeroot: *Gentiana catesbaei*
Sand Phlox: *Phlox bifida*
Sand Strawflower: *Helichrysum arenarium*
Sandwort: *Arenaria*
Sandwort: *Minuartia*
Sand-lily: *Leucorinum*
Sand-verbena: *Abronia*
Sanicle: *Sanicula*
Savory: *Satureja*
Saw Fern: *Blechnum spicant*
Saw Fern: *Blechnum*
Saxifrage: *Saxifraga*
Scale Fern: *Ceterach officinarum*
Scarlet Gaura: *Gaura coccinea*

Scarlet Monkey Flower: *Mimulus cardinalis*
Scarlet Turk's Cap Lily: *Lilium chalcedonicum*
Scented Oak Fern: *Gymnocarpium robertianum*
Scorpion Weed: *Phacelia*
Scotch Crocus: *Crocus biflorus*
Scotch Thistle: *Onopordum*
Scouring Rush: *Equisetum hyemale*
Scurvy Grass: *Barbarea verna*
Sea Bindweed: *Calystegia soldanella*
Sea Daffodil: *Pancratium*
Sea Holly: *Eryngium maritimum*
Sea Holly: *Eryngium*
Sea Kale: *Crambe maritima*
Sea Kale: *Crambe*
Sea Lavender: *Limonium latifolium*
Sea Lavender: *Limonium*
Sea Lyme Grass: *Elymus arenarius*
Sea Lyme Grass: *Elymus*
Sea Oats: *Uniola*
Sea Pink: *Armeria*
Sea Poppy: *Glaucium*
Sea-heath: *Frankenia*
Sedge: *Carex*
Self-heal: *Prunella*
Senna: *Cassia*
Sensitive Fern: *Onoclea*
Serpentine Spleenwort: *Asplenium cuneifolium*
Serpentine-striped Fern: *Asplenium adulterinum*
Serpent-grass: *Polygonum viviparum*
Shade Sedge: *Carex umbrosa*
Shaggy Foxtail: *Alopecurus lanatus*
Shamrock-pea: *Parochetus*
Sheep Fescue: *Festuca ovina*
Sheep's-bit: *Jasione laevis*
Sheep's-bit: *Jasione*
Shepherd's-scabious: *Jasione laevis*
Shield Ferns: *Dryopteris*
Shield Fern: *Polystichum braunii*
Shield Fern: *Polystichum*
Shield-leaf Roger's Flower: *Astilboides tabularis*
Shin Plasters: *Orchis*
Shineleaf: *Pyrola*
Shooting Star: *Dodecatheon*
Showy Lady's Slipper: *Cypripedium reginae*
Showy Lily: *Lilium speciosum*
Showy Sunflower: *Helianthus × laetiflorus*
Siberian Bugloss: *Brunnera*
Siberian Melic: *Melica altissima*
Siberian Purslane: *Montia sibirica*
Siberian Tea: *Bergenia crassifolia*
Sideoats Grama: *Bouteloua curtipendula*
Sierra Lily: *Lilium parvum*
Sierra Shooting-Star: *Dodecatheon jeffreyi*
Sierra Water Fern: *Thelypteris nevadensis*
Sikkim Rhubarb: *Rheum acuminatum*
Silky Prairie Clover: *Petalostemon villosum*
Silky-spike Melic: *Melica ciliata*
Silver Banner Grass: *Miscanthus sacchariflorus*

Silver Cinquefoil: *Potentilla argentea*
Silver Edged Sasa: *Sasa veitchii*
Silver Rod: *Solidago bicolor*
Silver Sage: *Salvia argentea*
Silver Spike Grass: *Achlys calamagrostis*
Silver Thistle: *Carlina acaulis*
Silvermound Mugwort: *Artemisia schmidtiana*
Silver-leaf Geranium: *Geranium argenteum*
Skullcap: *Scutellaria*
Skunk Cabbage: *Symplocarpus foetidus*
Skunk Cabbage: *Veratrum californicum*
Skunk-cabbage: *Lysichiton*
Slender Lip Fern: *Cheilanthes feei*
Small Solomon's-seal: *Polygonatum biflorum*
Small White Aster: *Aster vimineus*
Small White Lady's Slipper: *Cypripedium candidum*
Small Yellow Lady's Slipper: *Cypripedium calceolus* var. *parviflorum*
Smartweed: *Polygonum*
Smelly Pig-salad: *Aposeris foetida*
Smilo Grass: *Oryzopsis miliacea*
Smokeweed: *Eupatorium maculatum*
Smooth Aster: *Aster laevis*
Smooth Woodsia: *Woodsia glabella*
Snake Head: *Chelone*
Snakehead: *Chelone glabra*
Snakeroot: *Asarum canadense*
Snakeroot: *Cimicifuga*
Snakeroot: *Sanicula*
Snakeweed: *Polygonum bistorta*
Snapdragon: *Antirrhinum*
Sneezeweed: *Helenium*
Sneezewort: *Achillea ptarmica*
Snow Edelweiss: *Leontopodium alpinum* ssp. *nivale*
Snow Poppy: *Eomecon chionantha*
Snow Sedge: *Carex baldensis*
Snow Trillium: *Trillium nivale*
Snowdrops: *Galanthus*
Snowflake: *Leucojum*
Snow-in-Summer: *Cerastium tomentosum*
Snow-in-Summer: *Cerastium*
Snow-lover: *Chionophila*
Snuffbox Fern: *Thelypteris palustris* var. *pubescens*
Soapwort Gentian: *Gentiana saponaria*
Soapwort: *Saponaria officinalis*
Soapwort: *Saponaria*
Soft Rush: *Juncus effusus*
Solomon's Seal: *Polygonatum odoratum*
Solomon's-seal: *Polygonatum*
Sorrel: *Rumex*
Southern Cane: *Arundinaria gigantea*
Southernwood: *Artemisia abrotanum*
Sowbread: *Cyclamen*
Sow-teat Strawberry: *Fragaria vesca*
Spanish Bluebell: *Scilla*
Spanish Buttons: *Centaurea nigra*
Spanish Dagger: *Yucca*
Spanish Iris: *Iris xiphium*
Spanish Sage: *Salvia lavandulifolia*
Spanish-bayonet: *Yucca*
Spatterdock: *Nuphar*

Spear Grass: *Achnatherum*
Speargrass: *Aciphylla*
Spearmint: *Mentha spicata*
Speckled Wood-lily: *Clintonia umbellulata*
Speedwell: *Veronica*
Spiderwort: *Tradescantia*
Spider-lily: *Crinum*
Spider-lily: *Hymenocallis occidentalis*
Spider-lily: *Hymenocallis*
Spike Club Moss: *Selaginella*
Spike Grass: *Uniola latifolia*
Spike Grass: *Uniola*
Spike Rush: *Eleocharis*
Spiked Milfoil: *Myriophyllum spicatum*
Spiked Rampion: *Phyteuma spicatum*
Spikenard: *Aralia racemosa*
Spleenwort: *Asplenium*
Spotted Cranesbill: *Geranium maculatum*
Spotted Dead Nettle: *Lamium maculatum*
Spotted Wintergreen: *Chimaphila maculata*
Spreading Dogbane: *Apocynum androsaemifolium*
Spreading Globeflower: *Trollius laxus*
Spring Adonis: *Adonis vernalis*
Spring Gentian: *Gentiana verna*
Spring Meadow Saffron: *Bulbocodium*
Spring Snow Sedge: *Carex fraseri*
Spring Snowflake: *Leucojum vernum*
Spring-beauty: *Claytonia virginica*
Spurge: *Euphorbia*
Spurge: *Pachysandra*
Squawroot: *Trillium erectum*
Squill: *Scilla*
Squirrel Corn: *Dicentra canadensis*
Staggerweed: *Dicentra eximia*
Stake Bamboo: *Phyllostachys aureosulcata*
Star of Persia: *Allium christophii*
Star Tickseed: *Coreopsis pubescens*
Star Violet: *Houstonia*
Starflower: *Smilacina stellata*
Starflower: *Trientalis borealis*
Starflower: *Trientalis*
Starry Grasswort: *Cerastium arvense*
Starwort: *Stellaria*
Star-lily: *Leucorinum montanum*
Star-lily: *Leucorinum*
Star-of-Bethlehem: *Campanula isophylla*
Star-of-Bethlehem: *Ornithogalum pyrenaicum*
Star-of-Bethlehem: *Ornithogalum umbellatum*
Star-of-Bethlehem: *Ornithogalum*
Statice: *Limonium latifolium*
Statice: *Limonium*
Stiff Bear's Paw Fern: *Polystichum rigens*
Stiff Sedge: *Carex elata*
Stiff Sunflower: *Helianthus rigidus*
Stinking Benjamin: *Trillium erectum*
Stinking Gladwyn: *Iris foetidissima*
Stinking Hellebore: *Helleborus foetidus*
Stocks: *Matthiola*
Stokes' Aster: *Stokesia laevis*
Stonecress: *Aethionema*
Stonecrop: *Sedum*
Storksbill: *Erodium*

Strawberry-Geranium: *Saxifraga stolonifera*
Strawberry-raspberry: *Rubus ilecebrosus*
Strawberry: *Fragaria*
Strawflower: *Helichrysum*
Striped Squill: *Puschkinia*
St. Andrew's-cross: *Hypericum*
St. Bernard's Lily: *Anthericum*
St. Bruno's Lily: *Paradisea*
St. Johnswort: *Hypericum*
St. Patrick's Cabbage: *Sempervivum tectorum*
Sugar-scoop: *Tiarella unifoliata*
Sulfur Flower: *Eriogonum umbellatum*
Sulphur Flower: *Eriogonum*
Summer Gentian: *Gentiana septemfida*
Summer Phlox: *Phlox paniculata*
Summer-hyacinth: *Galtonia*
Sun Rose: *Helianthemum*
Sundew: *Drosera*
Sundrops: *Oenothera fruticosa*
Sundrops: *Oenothera perennis*
Sundrops: *Oenothera*
Sunflower: *Helianthus*
Sunset Lily: *Lilium pardalinum* 'Giganteum'
Sun's Eye Tulip: *Tulipa oculus-solis*
Swamp Forget-me-not: *Myosotis scorpioides*
Swamp Loosestrife: *Decodon*
Swamp Pink: *Helonias*
Swamp Potato: *Sagittaria sagittifolia*
Swamp Saxifrage: *Saxifraga pensylvanica*
Swamp Sedge: *Carex acutiformis*
Swamp Valerian: *Valeriana dioica*
Swamp-lily: *Saururus cernuus*
Swan Potato: *Sagittaria sagittifolia*
Sweet Coltisfoot: *Petasites*
Sweet Goldenrod: *Solidago odora*
Sweet Joe-Pye Weed: *Eupatorium purpureum*
Sweet Vetch: *Hedysarum*
Sweet Violet: *Viola odorata*
Sweet William: *Dianthus barbatus*
Sweet William: *Phlox maculata*
Sweet Woodruff: *Galium odoratum*
Sweetflag: *Acorus calamus*
Sweetflag: *Acorus*
Switch Grass: *Panicum*
Sword-leaved Iris: *Iris ensata*
Sword-lily: *Gladiolus*
Tall Bellflower: *Campanula americana*
Tall Larkspur: *Delphinium exaltatum*
Tall Purple Moor Grass: *Molinia caerulea* ssp. *arundinacea*
Tall Tickseed: *Coreopsis tripteris*
Tall White Violet: *Viola canadensis*
Tansy Daisy: *Chrysanthemum macrophyllum*
Tansy: *Tanacetum vulgare*
Tansy: *Tanacetum*
Tarragon: *Artemisia dracunculus*
Tarweed: *Grindelia*
Tatarian Statice: *Goniolimon tataricum*
Teaberry: *Mitchella*
Tenby Daffodil: *Narcissus pseudonarcissus* ssp. *obvallaris*

The Easter Lily: *Lilium longiflorum*
The Mourning Iris: *Iris susiana*
Thick-leaf Phlox: *Phlox carolina*
Thimble Lily: *Lilium bolanderi*
Thin-leaf Sunflower: *Helianthus decapetalus*
Thistle: *Carduus*
Thistle: *Cirsium*
Thoroughwax: *Bupleurum*
Thoroughwort: *Eupatorium perfoliatum*
Thoroughwort: *Eupatorium*
Three Birds Flying: *Linaria triornithophora*
Thrift: *Armeria*
Throatwort: *Campanula trachelium*
Throatwort: *Trachelium*
Thyme: *Thymus*
Tibetan Orchid: *Pleione*
Tick Clover: *Desmodium*
Tickseed: *Coreopsis*
Tiger Lily: *Lilium lancifolium*
Toadflax: *Linaria*
Toad-lily: *Tricyrtis*
Toad-shade: *Trillium sessile*
Toothwort: *Dentaria diphylla*
Toothwort: *Dentaria*
Torch Flower: *Kniphofia uvaria*
Tore: *Vicia*
Trailing Bellflower: *Cyananthus*
Trailing Phlox: *Phlox nivalis*
Treacle Mustard: *Erysimum*
Tree Celandine: *Macleaya cordata*
Tree Mallow: *Lavatera*
Trelease's Larkspur: *Delphinium treleasei*
Trieste Pink: *Dianthus sylvestris* ssp. *tergestinus*
Triplet Lily: *Triteleia laxa*
Tritoma: *Kniphofia*
Trout-Lily: *Erythronium*
Trout-lily: *Erythronium americanum*
Trumpet Narcissus: *Narcissus pseudonarcissus*
Tuckahoe: *Peltandra virginica*
Tufted Lysimachia: *Lysimachia thyrsiflora*
Tulip: *Tulipa*
Tunic Flower: *Petrorhagia saxifraga*
Turban Lily: *Lilium pomponium*
Turkey Beard: *Xerophyllum*
Turkey Corn: *Dicentra eximia*
Turkey-beard: *Xerophyllum asphodeloides*
Turkish Poppy: *Papaver orientale*
Turk's Cap Lily: *Lilium duchartrei*
Turk's Cap Lily: *Lilium martagon*
Turtle Head: *Chelone*
Turtlehead: *Chelone glabra*
Tussock Bellflower: *Campanula carpatica*
Tussock Grass: *Chionochloa*
Twinflower: *Linnaea borealis*
Twinleaf: *Jeffersonia*
Twinspur: *Diascia*
Twisted-stalk: *Streptopus*
Two-leaved Solomon's Seal: *Maianthemum canadense*
Ukrainian Feather Grass: *Stipa ucrainica*
Umbrella Bamboo: *Sinarundinaria*
Umbrella Leaf: *Diphylleia*
Umbrella Plant: *Eriogonum allenii*

Umbrella Plant: *Eriogonum*
Umbrella Plant: *Peltiphyllum peltatum*
Umbrella Sedge: *Cyperus*
Upland Cress: *Barbarea*
Upland Cress: *Lepidium*
Uruguay Pennisetum: *Pennisetum latifolium*
Valerian: *Valeriana*
Vanilla Leaf: *Achlys*
Vanilla Onion: *Nothoscordum inodorum*
Vase Vine: *Clematis viorna*
Velvet Grass: *Holcus*
Venus' Hair Fern: *Adiantum venustum*
Venus-hair Fern: *Adiantum capillus-veneris*
Vernal Grass: *Anthoxanthum*
Vervain: *Verbena bractata*
Vervain: *Verbena rigida*
Vetchling: *Lathyrus*
Vetch: *Vicia*
Viola: *Viola cornuta*
Viola: *Viola*
Violet Wood Sorrel: *Oxalis violacea*
Violets: *Viola*
Violetta: *Viola*
Violet-Iris: *Iris verna*
Virginia Bluebells: *Mertensia virginica*
Virginia Cowslip: *Mertensia virginica*
Virginia Waterleaf: *Hydrophyllum virginianum*
Virginian Chain-fern: *Woodwardia virginica*
Virgin's Bower: *Clematis virginiana*
Volga Wild Rye: *Elymus racemosus*
Wake-robin: *Trillium sessile*
Wake-robin: *Trillium*
Walking Fern: *Camptosorus*
Wall Germander: *Teucrium chamaedrys*
Wall Iris: *Iris tectorum*
Wall Polypody: *Polypodium interjectum*
Wall Rock Cress: *Arabis caucasica*
Wall Rue Fern: *Asplenium ruta-muraria*
Wallflower: *Erysimum*
Wallpepper: *Sedum acre*
Wand Flower: *Galax*
Wandflower: *Sparaxis*
Wapato: *Sagittaria latifolia*
Washington Lily: *Lilium washingtonianum*
Water Aloe: *Stratiotes*
Water Arum: *Calla palustris*
Water Arum: *Calla*
Water Avens: *Geum rivale*
Water Buttercup: *Ranunculus aquatilis*
Water Chestnut: *Trapa natans*
Water Chestnut: *Trapa*
Water Clover: *Marsilea*
Water Dock: *Orontium aquaticum*
Water Fern: *Azolla*
Water Lily: *Nymphaea*
Water Milfoil: *Myriophyllum*
Water Soldier: *Stratiotes*
Waterfowl Iris: *Iris milesii*
Waterfringe: *Nymphoides peltata*
Waterleaf: *Hydrophyllum*
Water-dragon: *Saururus cernuus*
Water-lily Tulip: *Tulipa kaufmanniana*
Water-mat: *Chrysosplenium americanum*

Water-plantain: *Alisma*
Water-shield: *Brasenia schreberi*
Water-shield: *Brasenia*
Water-willow: *Decodon*
Wavy Hair Grass: *Avenella flexuosa*
Wax Trillium: *Trillium erectum* f. *album*
Weather-Thistle: *Carlina acaulis*
Weather-thistle: *Carlina*
Welsh Poppy: *Meconopsis*
Western Bleeding-heart: *Dicentra formosa*
Western Blue Flag: *Iris missouriensis*
Western Dog Violet: *Viola adunca*
Western Lily: *Lilium occidentale*
Western Milfoil: *Myriophyllum hippuroides*
Western Mugwort: *Artemisia ludoviciana*
Western Orange-cup Lily: *Lilium philadelphicum* var. *andinum*
Western Polypody: *Polypodium hesperium*
Western Sword Fern: *Polystichum munitum*
Western Wallflower: *Erysimum asperum*
Western Yellow Violet: *Viola nuttallii*
Wheel Lily: *Lilium medioloides*
Whippoorwill Flower: *Trillium cuneatum*
Whippoorwill Shoe: *Cypripedium calceolus* var. *parviflorum*
White Arrow Arum: *Peltandra sagittifolia*
White Bachelor's Buttons: *Ranunculus aconitifolius*
White Bedstraw: *Galium mollugo*
White Bryony: *Bryonia alba*
White Butterbur: *Petasites albus*
White Camas: *Zigadenus elegans*
White Cinquefoil: *Potentilla alba*
White Clover: *Trifolium repens*
White Dead Nettle: *Lamium album*
White Dogtooth Violet: *Erythronium albidum*
White Evening Primrose: *Oenothera speciosa*
White Fritillary: *Fritillaria liliacea*
White Golden Rod: *Solidago bicolor*
White Lilyturf: *Ophiopogon jaburan*
White Mandarin: *Streptopus amplexifolius*
White Mugwort: *Artemisia lactiflora*
White Pond Lily: *Nymphaea odorata*
White Prairie Clover: *Petalostemon candidum*
White Rain-lily: *Zephyranthes candida*
White Sanicle: *Eupatorium rugosum*
White Snakeroot: *Eupatorium rugosum*
White Toothwort: *Dentaria enneaphyllos*
White Trumpet Lily: *Lilium longiflorum*
White Upland Aster: *Aster ptarmicoides*
White Wake-robin: *Trillium grandiflorum*
White Water Lily: *Nymphaea alba*
White Wood Aster: *Aster divaricatus*
White Woodland Aster: *Aster lateriflorus*
White Woolly Mint: *Mentha pulegium* var. *gibraltaria*
Whitecup Cupflower: *Nierembergia repens*
Whitlow Grass: *Draba*
Whitlow-wort: *Paronychia*
Wild Bleeding-heart: *Dicentra eximia*

Wild Buckwheat: *Eriogonum*
Wild Calla: *Calla palustris*
Wild Camomile: *Matricaria*
Wild Coffee: *Triosteum*
Wild Crocus: *Tradescantia longipes*
Wild Geranium: *Geranium maculatum*
Wild Ginger: *Asarum canadense*
Wild Ginger: *Asarum*
Wild Lily-of-the-Valley: *Maianthemum canadense*
Wild Lily-of-the-Valley: *Pyrola rotundifolia*
Wild Marjoram: *Origanum*
Wild Morning-glory: *Calystegia sepium*
Wild Morning-glory: *Calystegia*
Wild Passion-flower: *Passiflora incarnata*
Wild Pea: *Lathyrus*
Wild Pink: *Silene caroliniana*
Wild Rice: *Zizania*
Wild Rye: *Elymus*
Wild Sarsaparilla: *Aralia nudicaulis*
Wild Senna: *Cassia hebecarpa*
Wild Senna: *Cassia marilandica*
Wild Sweet William: *Phlox divaricata*
Wild White Indigo: *Baptisia leucantha*
Wild Yellow Lily: *Lilium canadense*
Wild-hyacinth: *Camassia*
Wild-snapdragon: *Linaria vulgaris*
Willow Gentian: *Gentiana asclepiadea*
Willow Herb: *Epilobium*
Willow-grass: *Polygonum amphibium*
Willow-leaved Sunflower: *Helianthus salicifolius*
Windflower: *Anemone*
Wine Cups: *Callirhoe involucrata*
Wine Cups: *Callirhoe*
Winter Aconite: *Eranthis*
Winter Cress: *Barbarea*
Winter Heliotrope: *Petasites fragrans*
Winter Sweet: *Origanum*
Wintergreen: *Chimaphila*
Wintergreen: *Pyrola*
Winter-Begonia: *Bergenia ciliata*
Winter-daffodil: *Sternbergia*
Wire Plant: *Muehlenbeckia axillaris*
Witch's Weed: *Circaea*
Woad: *Isatis*
Wood Betony: *Pedicularis*
Wood Lily: *Lilium philadelphicum*
Wood Rush: *Luzula*
Wood Sorrel: *Oxalis acetosella*
Wood Sorrel: *Oxalis*
Wood Spurge: *Euphorbia amygdaloides*
Wood Trillium: *Trillium viride*
Woodbine: *Clematis virginiana*
Woodland Forget-me-not: *Myosotis sylvatica*
Woodland Star: *Lithophragma*
Woodland Strawberry: *Fragaria vesca*
Woodruff: *Asperula*
Woodruff: *Galium*
Woods Violet: *Viola reichenbachiana*
Wood-violet: *Viola riviniana*
Woolly Blue Violet: *Viola sororia*
Woolly Lip Fern: *Cheilanthes lanosa*
Woolly Sunflower: *Eriophyllum*
Woolly Thistle: *Cirsium scopulorum*

Wormwood: *Artemisia absinthium*
Woundwort: *Stachys*
Wreath Goldenrod: *Solidago caesia*
Yam: *Dioscorea*
Yanquapin: *Nelumbo lutea*
Yarrow: *Achillea*
Yellow Adder's-tongue: *Erythronium americanum*
Yellow Allium: *Allium flavum*
Yellow Archangel: *Lamiastrum galeobdolon*
Yellow Asphodel: *Narthecium americanum*
Yellow Bedstraw: *Galium verum*
Yellow Coneflower: *Echinacea paradoxa*
Yellow Cow Lily: *Nuphar luteum*
Yellow Everlasting: *Helichrysum arenarium*
Yellow False Indigo: *Baptisia tinctoria*
Yellow Floating Heart: *Nymphoides peltata*
Yellow Foxglove: *Digitalis grandiflora*
Yellow Foxglove: *Digitalis lutea*
Yellow Gentian: *Gentiana lutea*
Yellow Grass: *Narthecium*
Yellow Mountain Saxifrage: *Saxifraga aizoides*
Yellow Oats: *Trisetum flavescens*
Yellow Passion-flower: *Passiflora lutea*
Yellow Pond Lily: *Nuphar*
Yellow Puccoon: *Lithospermum incisum*
Yellow Rocket: *Barbarea verna*
Yellow Sand-verbena: *Abronia latifolia*
Yellow Sedge: *Carex flava*
Yellow Skunk-cabbage: *Lysichiton americanus*
Yellow Star Grass: *Hypoxis hirsuta*
Yellow Turk's Cap Lily: *Lilium pyrenaicum*
Yellow Water Buttercup: *Ranunculus flabellaris*
Yellow Water Lily: *Nymphaea mexicana*
Yellow-green Bamboo: *Phyllostachys aureosulcata*
Yellow-tuft: *Alyssum murale*
Zephyr-lily: *Zephyranthes*
Zig-Zag Bamboo: *Phyllostachys flexuosa*

Photo Credits

Abbreviations: t. top; b. bottom; l. left; r. right; m. middle.

Apel, Johannes, Baden-Baden: pages 63 r., 65 r., 114 r., 117 l., 125 r., 126, 133 m., 184, 218 l., 220, 243 r., 268 l., 352 r., 367, 384 l., 398 l., 402 r., 410, 422 r., 428 l., 430 r., 434 l., 448, 467 l., 470 t.l., 479 r., 488 l., 489 r., 493 r., 508 r., 540 m.–r., 545 l., 552 r., 554 l., 555, 563, 564 (2), 624, 632, 638 m., 643 m., 644 r., 646 l., 680 r., 691 l.

Bärtels, Andreas, Waake: page 571 l.

Bechtel, Helmut, Düsseldorf: pages 105 t.l., 136 r., 148 r., 388 l., 445 l.

Benary, Ernst, Hannoversch-Münden: page 87.

Botti, Stephen J., Yosemite-National Park, California (USA): page 470 r.

Brünner, Gerhard, Hamburg: page 51 r.

Cuveland, Helga and Justus de, Norderstedt: pages 31 l., 420, 429, 565 r., 572 l., 635 l.

Denkewitz, Lothar, Hamburg: pages 73 r., 122 l., 183 l., 192, 213, 215, 508 l., 509, 609 l., 648, 702 l.

Dittrich, Werner, Tübingen: pages 14 r., 19 l., 105 b., 135, 146, 181 r., 194 l., 195 l., 223, 242, 251 m., 259, 277 l., 306 r., 311 r., 348 l., 382 m., 399 r., 443 m., 503 r., 506 r., 578 r., 601 r., 627 l., 631 l., 637 r., 655 r., 678 l.

Ehsen, Horst, Osnabrück: pages 54, 190 l., 358 m., 415 r., 450 l., 484 l., 512 l., 559, 629 l., 633 m., 687 r.

Erhardt, Walter, Neudrossenfeld: page 460 l.

Ewald, Gudrun, Leiferde: pages 362 m., 363 m., 366 l.

Felbinger, Alois, Leinfelden-Echterdingen: dust cover front, frontispiece, and pages 162 m., 189 r., 208 l., 300, 389 l.

Feldmaier, Carl, Pfarrkirchen: pages 362 r., 366 r., 377 m.–r., 378 l.

Fessler, Alfred, Tübingen: pages 149, 157 l., 190 r., 391, 418 l., 462 (2), 655 l.

Fuchs, Hermann, Hof: pages 404 r., 417, 571 r., 616 r., 656 l., 685 r., 700.

Goersch, Hans, Stuttgart: page 461 r.

Grandhomme, Wilhelm, Schotten: page 465 l.

Haase, Magda, Munich: pages 13 r., 56, 88 l., 268 r., 274 r., 314 l., 348 m., 484 r.

Haberer, Martin, Raidwangen: pages 80 m., 88 r., 148 m., 225 r., 241 r., 307 r., 403 l., 415 l., 453, 515 t.r., 543 l., 587 (2), 613 r., 614, 625 l., 629 m., 641 m., 676 l., 707 l.

Hahn, Eugen, Kirchheimbolanden: pages 28 r., 62, 67, 97, 104 r., 115 (2), 118 r., 124, 127 l., 136 l., 180, 221, 237 l., 298 l., 385, 461 l., 515 l., 573, 596 l., 664 r., 679, 689.

Hase, Elisabeth, Frankfurt am Main: page 638 l.

Hay/Synge/Herklotz/Menzel, Das grosse Blumenbuch: pages 106 r., 110 r., 129 l.

Heimhuber, Christian, Sonthofen: page 247.

Jaekel, Erhard, Obernholz: pages 20 r., 107 r.

Jantzen, Friedrich, Arolsen: pages 232 l., 290 r.

Josifko, Jiri, Prague: pages 187 r., 449 l., 545 r.

Kaule, Giselher, Stuttgart: page 431 (2).

Kerspe, Heiner, Hohenlimburg: page 497.

Koch, Ursula, Kürten-Oberbörsch: pages 50 l., 70, 100 r., 224 l., 251 l., 496 r., 577, 578 m., 619 r.

Köhlein, Fritz, Bindlach: pages 22 r., 28 l., 48 r., 63 l., 78 m., 86 r., 92 r., 100 l., 114 l., 117 r., 118 l., 130 l., 131, 144, 147 l., 154, 155, 178 l., 182 l., 186 l., 194 r., 227, 241 l., 244, 246, 248 r., 270, 288 (2), 295 l., 298 l., 313 r., 320 (3), 321 (2), 323, 324 m.–r., 330, 331, 332, 333, 334 l.–m., 339 r., 354, 400 l., 406 r., 424 b., 427 r., 442, 443 r., 444, 454 r., 455, 457, 464 l., 478 l., 498, 519

(2), 520 (2), 522, 523, 524 (2), 525, 526, 532, 533, 536 l., 537 (2), 546 l., 562 r., 581, 582 r., 583 r., 586 (3), 590 (3), 591 (2), 596 r., 607, 610 (2), 611 (2), 613 (3), 616 l., 620 r., 622 l., 635 r., 643 l., 651 (2).

Kummert, Fritz, Wohngraben (Austria): pages 37, 39 (2), 96 l., 128, 166 l., 206 l., 318, 353 l., 387 l., 450 r., 463 l., 481, 482 (2), 483, 503 l.–m., 541 l., 565 l., 574 (2), 594, 622 r., 639 l., 659 r.

Kurzmann, Franz, Baden bei Wien: page 323.

McRae, Edward, Boring, Oregon (USA): page 378 m.

Marx, Karl-Heinz, Plettstadt: page 414 r.

Möller, Friedrich, Uelzen 3: pages 130 r., 266 l., 512 m.

Morell, Eberhard, Dreieich: pages 163 m., 310 r., 348 r.

Müller, Bruno, Frankfurt am Main: pages 22 l., 36, 43, 46 l., 98 r., 129 r., 236, 266 r., 289 m.–r., 290 (3), 295 r., 316 r., 342 (2), 393, 403 r., 412 l., 416 l., 418 r., 423 (3), 426 l., 431 l., 432 l., 449 r., 554 r., 560 r., 597 l., 618 l., 666 r., 667 (2), 687 l., 702 r., 705.

Müssel, Hermann, Freising-Weihenstephan: pages 240, 262 r., 358 r., 649 r.

Oberbeck, Helmut, Backnang: pages 33 r., 546 r., 627 r.

Partsch, Karl, Ofterschwang: pages 12 l., 23 l., 214, 440 m., 649 l.

Pasche, Erich jun., Velbert: pages 33 m./t., 172 m.–r., 173 l., 205 l., 269 l., 656 r.

Pfennig, Horst, Herford-Stedefreund: page 500.

Raalte, Dick van, Frederiksoord (Holland): page 29.

Reinhard, Hans, Heiligkreuzsteinach-Eiterbach: pages 11 (2), 23 m., 26 r., 27 l., 72 (2), 91 r., 102 l., 103 r., 157 l., 163 l., 193 l., 196 r., 229 l., 234 l., 299 r., 307 l., 308 m., 345, 396 r., 399 l., 404 m., 406 l., 427 m., 451 r., 465 r., 476, 494, 515 b., 540 l., 544, 561 r., 615, 640, 661 l.–m., 669 m.

Reiser, Ernst, Wetzlar: pages 12 r., 231 l., 600 r., 646 r.

Reisigl, Herbert, Innsbruck: pages 454 l., 458 r., 696 r.

Richter, Wolfram, Göttingen: page 400 r.

Riedmiller, Andreas, Martinszell: pages 237 r., 265 l., 536 r., 556.

Rücker, Karlheinz, Stuttgart: pages 10, 27 r., 55 r., 65 l., 69 l., 137 m., 159, 263 r., 282, 356, 411, 446 l., 449 m., 490 (2), 492, 510, 570 l., 575 m., 582 l., 650 l., 657 r., 684.

Schacht, Dieter, Munich: pages 18, 50 r., 90, 99, 101 b./r., 110 l., 137 l., 156, 166 r., 186 b./r., 196 l., 255, 287, 294 l., 299 l., 308 l., 338 l., 387 r., 404 l., 409 l., 470 b., 477 l., 517, 529, 538 (2), 539, 551 r., 557, 558, 653 r., 661 r., 685 m., 688 r., 691 r., 701 r., 706 r.

Schacht, Wilhelm, Frasdorf: pages 7, 8 (2), 15, 17 r., 21, 24, 25, 33 l., 35, 38, 45, 46 r., 47, 48 l., 53, 57, 59, 64, 65 l., 66, 68 r., 69 r., 71, 83, 86 l., 92 l., 93, 101 t./r., 104 l., 105 r., 108, 109, 110 b., 116, 119 (2), 121, 122 m.-r., 123, 127 r., 133 r., 141, 148 l., 150, 151, 152 r., 153 l., 158 l., 160, 163 r., 165, 171, 173 r., 175, 177, 179, 182 l., 183 r., 186 t./r., 187 l., 188, 198, 199, 201 r., 202, 204 r., 205 r., 208 r., 209, 217 (2), 229 r., 231 r., 239 l., 263 l., 264, 265 r., 267 l., 275 l.-m., 283 r., 285 r., 292 (2), 296 (2), 297, 303, 306 l., 310 l., 312, 313 l., 314 r., 339 l., 340 r., 346, 347 r., 350, 352 l., 381, 396 l., 397 (2), 398 r., 401 (2), 402 l., 407, 409 r., 412 r., 413 l., 414 l., 416 m.-r., 428 r., 432 l., 435 l., 436, 439 r., 440 r., 445 r., 456, 460 r., 463 r., 466 (2), 469 (2), 473, 475 (2), 477 r., 479 l., 489 l., 495, 496 l., 499, 504, 506 l.-m., 541 l., 548 r., 549 r., 551 l., 552 l., 560 l., 569, 570 r., 583 l., 599, 602 l., 618 r., 619 l., 625 r., 629 r., 631 r., 635 m., 636, 638 r., 641 r., 643 b.-r., 644 l., 647 l., 650 r., 658 r., 666 l., 670 r., 678 r., 680 l.-m., 681 l., 682 l., 695, 696 l., 701 l., 704 r.

Schmidt, Erwin, Wetzlar: pages 84, 92 m., 132, 137 r., 152 l., 181 l., 248 l., 338 r., 496 m., 645, 669 l., 706 l. Scholz, Johannes, Bielefeld: page 13 l.

Schrempp, Heinz, Breisach-Oberrimsingen: pages 23 r., 30 l., 51 l., 58, 101 l., 103 l., 139 l., 161 l., 161 r., 195 r., 230 l., 243 l., 273 r., 275 r., 293 l., 353 r., 390 l., 439 l., 440 l., 447 l., 452, 467 r., 478 r., 548 l., 550, 566 l., 572 m., 597 r., 598 r., 602 l., 619 m., 639 r., 646 m., 653 l., 654 r., 678 m., 688 l., 704 l.

Siebold, Hans, Hannover: pages 16, 17 l., 20 l., 30 r., 33 b., 55 l., 61, 68 l., 74, 78 r., 79 r., 81, 91 l., 125 l., 145, 164, 167 l.-r., 169, 174 (2), 193 r., 201 l., 206 r., 230 r., 239 r., 256 r., 273 l., 278 (2), 294 r., 308 r., 311 l., 340 l., 380, 382 l., 390 r., 392 (2), 405, 419, 441, 443 l., 541 m., 568 l., 575 r., 578 l., 595 (2), 605 r., 606 (3), 609 r., 641 l., 654 l., 673 (3), 674 (3), 675 (3), 677 r.

Seidl, Sebastian, Munich: pages 6, 27 m., 31 r., 32, 49 (2), 73 l., 82 l., 94 l., 96 r., 98 l., 102 r., 107 l., 134, 139 r., 153 r., 167 m., 170 (2), 172 l., 178 r., 189 l., 204 l., 210, 218 r., 219 r., 222 (2), 225 l., 228 r., 235, 250 (2), 251 r., 256 l., 257 (2), 262 l., 271, 274 l., 285 l., 301, 304, 309, 324 l., 329, 334 r., 335, 336, 347 l., 351 r., 355, 362 l., 363 l.-r., 366 m., 378 r., 384 r., 388 r., 394 m.-r., 398 m., 413 r., 418 m., 422 l., 424 t., 426 r., 427 l., 434 r., 435 r., 439 m., 447 r., 451 l., 485 r., 488 r., 493 l., 549 l., 561 l., 562 l., 566 r., 575 l., 630, 633 l., 637 l., 647 r., 658 l., 659 l., 663, 664 l., 665, 672, 676 m.-r., 677 l.-m., 685 l., 694, 707 r.

Sorger, Friederike, Vienna: page 406 m.

Stehling, Wolfram, Hamburg: pages 52, 110 m., 142 r., 314 m., 337, 682 r., 697 r., and dust cover back.

Stein-Zeppelin, Helene von, Sulzburg-Laufen: page 94 r.

Stölzle, Gretl, Kempten: pages 5, 42 l., 78 l., 82 r., 85, 89, 142 l., 200, 201 m., 224 r., 281 l., 289 l., 351 l., 382 r., 394 l., 430 l., 464 r., 480, 486, 521, 543 r., 620 l.

Ulmer, Günter A., Schönaich: pages 234 r., 280, 327, 458 l., 502, 697 l.

Volk, Steffen, Schorndorf: pages 219 l., 283 l.

Wagner, Konrad, Hannover-Münden: page 389 r.

Walden, Georg A., Slöinge (Sweden): page 377 l.

Walke, Michael, Karben: page 267 r.

Walser, Urs, Weinheim: pages 79 l., 252, 277 r., 511 r., 633 r.

Weigel, Bernd, Baden-Baden, pages 42 r., 598 l.

Wilhelm, Gisela, Berlin: pages 19 r., 60, 158 r., 485 l., 572 r., 604, 670 l., 690.

Wohlschlager, Josef, Sindelfingen: page 602 r.

Woog, Dieter, Stuttgart: pages 9, 14 l., 26 l., 106 l., 133 l., 143, 212, 228 l., 233, 269 r., 281 r., 316 l., 358 l., 438, 512 r., 567, 568 r., 605 l., 617, 657 l., 669 r.